BRITISH AND IRISH INVENTORIES

For Martin
who has toiled in neighbouring
vineyards
from
The author/compiler
Simon
16 . xi . 2010

THE FURNITURE HISTORY SOCIETY
GRATEFULLY ACKNOWLEDGES
CONTRIBUTIONS FROM THE FOLLOWING
TOWARDS THE COST OF THIS VOLUME:

THE MERCERS' COMPANY

THE IDLEWILD TRUST

THE MARC FITCH FUND

British and Irish Inventories

A List and Bibliography of Published Transcriptions
of Secular Inventories

SIMON SWYNFEN JERVIS

'…in this undertaking, the *Reader* may see what Furniture (though it
lye disperst) our *Publick Records* will afford for *History*…'

Elias Ashmole, *Order of the Garter*, 1672

FURNITURE HISTORY SOCIETY
2010

The full reference for the quotation on the title page is Elias Ashmole, *The Institution Laws & Ceremonies of the most Noble Order of the Garter*, London, 1672, p. 643 (Chapter XXVI, Of the Founder, The First Knights-Companions and their Successors, Sect. I, Of what Number the Institution consisted)

ISBN: 978 0 903335 15 7

PRODUCED BY OUTSET SERVICES LTD
BOSTON SPA

CONTENTS

FOREWORD

In late 1967, a mere twenty-four, and less than a year after joining the Department of Furniture at the Victoria & Albert Museum, I was approached by the late Thelma E. Vernon of the Wiltshire Record Society with a query about the meanings of some words in the 1575 inventory of Lacock Abbey, which she was to publish in the following year. In our correspondence she referred at one point to 'Mr F. W. Steer of Inventory fame', and later explained that his *Farm and Cottage Inventories of Mid Essex 1635 to 1749* (1950), along with his editions of certain inventories of great houses, had made him a leader in this field. Accordingly, in January 1968, I wrote to Francis W. Steer explaining that our Departmental Archive at the V & A had for the past two years been trying to build up information of all kinds on furniture and decoration and asking for his help 'in assembling at least a list of where such inventories are printed in the various local learned journals all over this country.' He replied at length with a list of his own publications, a reference to M. A. Havinden's *Household and Farm Inventories in Oxfordshire, 1550-1590* (1965), and other good advice. This episode may be said to constitute the prehistory of the present volume. Its prototype was Fernand De Mély and Edmund Bishop's great but still too little known *Bibliographie Générale des Inventaires Imprimés* (1892-1895), although this was international and incorporated a vast number of ecclesiastical inventories. I came across it in about 1970 and obtained a photocopy for the V & A Department.

The next episode in a long saga was in the mid-1980s when, after the completion of the monumental *Dictionary of English Furniture Makers 1660-1840* (1984), with which I had been involved as London co-ordinator, I proposed that the Furniture History Society should publish 'A List and Bibliography of English Secular Inventories' and in 1987 I sent out a letter and schema to 'test the water'. Among those consulted were, in no particular order, the late Tom Ingram, the Furniture History Society's then President, Geoffrey Beard, its Chairman, Philippa Glanville in the V & A's Metalwork Department, Frances Collard in the Furniture Department, Peter Earle at the London School of Economics, Alison Kelly, Pauline Agius, and, last but not least, Dr Mark Overton, then of the Department of Geography, Newcastle University, whose willingness, in 1986, that the project might make use of his pioneering *A Bibliography of British Probate Inventories* (1983), had provided crucial underpinning. However positive reactions and good intentions came to nothing: there were various changes at the V & A and in 1990 I moved firstly to become Director and Marlay Curator of the Fitzwilliam Museum in Cambridge and then, in 1995, Historic Buildings Secretary (later Director of Historic Buildings) of the National Trust. Inevitably the project went into abeyance.

As it turned out abeyance was not oblivion. In 2004, by then retired from the National Trust, I re-presented the scheme to the Council of the Furniture History

Society, who were supportive as were, again, Geoffrey Beard, Dr Mark Overton and Nicholas Goodison, who included some approving words in his *Furniture History: Forty Years On* (2004). At this time the concept comprised, as in the 1980s, a large-scale volunteer effort with multiple contributors, and a small Steering Group was formed to guide its progress, consisting of Elizabeth White, then the Society's Secretary, Clarissa Ward, the Activities Secretary who also acted as the Group's secretary, James Yorke, in charge of the V & A Department's Information Section, and Jane Wainwright, who supplied the necessary, and otherwise lacking, skill and experience in information technology. Meetings were held, minutes written, ever more elaborate guidance notes were drafted, forms, a scheme for inputting by email and a database were devised, Jane Wainwright and Clarissa Ward making crucial contributions. As chairman of the Steering Group it was my responsibility to drive matters forward, but in late 2005, *mea culpa*, progress faltered to a halt. Much useful thought and discussion had nonetheless taken place and Clarissa Ward had heroically assembled a bibliography, heavily indebted to Overton's and to that made available on-line by the Royal Historical Society, with over nine hundred entries.

In September 2008 I decided that the nettle must be grasped and took with me on a French holiday Michael Reed's Buckinghamshire Record Society volume (1988), J. A. Johnston's for the Lincoln Record Society (1991), Malcolm Wanklyn's for the Worcestershire Historical Society (1998), and the first of Edwin and Stella George's Bristol Record Society series (2002). Thenceforward a substantial pile of notes of published inventory transcriptions accumulated, which were transferred as a work in progress to the *List* published here, the references being recorded at the same time in the *Bibliography*. My explorations, founded on Clarissa Ward's combined bibliography, have ranged from the systematic, including such sources as Joseph P. Byrne's *Online Bibliography of Medieval and Early Modern Wills and Inventories* and Maurice Howard's checklist of inventories and surveys published in *Architectural History* (1998), to the serendipitous or aleatory, the only certainty being that I am bound to have missed many published transcriptions scattered elsewhere, particularly in genealogical and topographical publications. The library of the Society of Antiquaries of London, the Guildhall Library, those of the Institute of Historical Research and of the Society of Genealogists, the London Library and the British Library proved fertile sources. Nonetheless several obscure or ephemeral publications remained difficult to pin down, and I had made it a rule to look at every book or article to which reference was made. I should be grateful for a note of any consequent omissions, and of other errors, inevitable in a work on this scale.

What has now emerged is at once more and less than what was originally envisaged in 1986. More, because the *List* incorporates Scotland, Wales and Ireland, the Isle of Man and the Channel Islands, and less, because the *Bibliography* is limited to those sources which include full transcriptions. Originally it was intended that this should also cover works which discussed inventories or made substantial use thereof. Useful as this undoubtedly would have been it would have made the book, already substantial, much longer and more open-ended, especially in view of the explosion of studies of 'material culture', 'consumption', *et hoc genus omne* over the last few decades.

The Furniture History Society hopes in due course to make this text available on the Internet, and there are those who will maintain that this should have been its natural home *ab initio*. Its compiler understands this point of view, but is unrepentant, believing that books still possess their own distinctive versatility and virtues, and that this one, for all its imperfections, will constitute an historiographical base-line, if nothing more.

To conclude this long apologia for what amounts to a quite simple, though I hope useful, tool I wish to record my thanks to the donors listed on an earlier page, to all those mentioned above, to the many others who have helped along the way, within and without the Furniture History Society, not least the few who responded to an appeal for extra references in its *Newsletter* of May 2009, David Adshead, James Rothwell, Susan Bracken and Elizabeth Jamieson, and, in particular, to Graham Maney, who has supervised every aspect of design and publication with his customary skill and efficiency. My final thanks are to Fionnuala Jervis, who has had to put up with too extended a passage of what Samuel Johnson might have called harmless drudgery.

SIMON SWYNFEN JERVIS

INTRODUCTORY ESSAY

In Rudyard Kipling's chilling short story, 'Mary Postgate', published in 1915, shortly before his son, John, was killed at Loos, there is an evocative description of the possessions of a youthful pilot, killed in an accident:

> ... thumbed and used Hentys, Marryats, Levers, Stephensons, Baroness Orczys, Garvices, school books, and atlases, unrelated piles of the *Motor Cyclist*, the *Light Car*, and catalogues of Olympia Exhibitions; the remnants of a fleet of sailing-ships from nine-penny cutters to a three-guinea yacht; a prep.-school dressing-gown; bats from three-and-sixpence to twenty-four shillings; cricket and tennis balls; disintegrated steam and clockwork locomotives with their twisted rails; a grey and red tin model of a submarine; a dumb gramophone and cracked records; golf-clubs ... walking sticks, and an assegai; photographs of private and public school cricket and football elevens and his O.T.C. on the line of march; kodaks, and film-rolls; some pewters, and one real silver cup, for boxing competitions and Junior Hurdles; sheaves of school photographs; Miss Fowler's photograph ...; a play box with a secret drawer; a load of flannels, belts and jerseys, and a pair of spiked shoes; ... letters ...; a five-day attempt at a diary; framed pictures of racing motors in full Brooklands career, and load upon load of undistinguishable wreckage of tool-boxes, rabbit-hutches, electric batteries, tin soldiers, fret-saw outfits, and jig-saw puzzles.[1]

An earlier instance of the inventory as a literary device is the poem, 'A True and Faithful Inventory of the Goods belonging to Dr. SWIFT, Vicar of *Lara Cor*; upon lending his House to the Bishop of *Meath*, until his own was built', written by Thomas Sheridan and first published in the *London Journal* in 1726:[2]

> An Oaken, broken, Elbow-Chair;
> A Cawdle-Cup, without an Ear;
> A batter'd, shatter'd Ash Bedstead;
> A Box of Deal, without a Lid;
> A Pair of Tongs, but out of Joint;
> A Back-Sword Poker, without Point;
> A Pot that's crack'd a-cross, around,
> With an old knotted Garter bound;
> An Iron Lock, without a Key;
> A Wig, with hanging, quite grown grey;

---

1 Rudyard Kipling, *A Diversity of Creatures*, (London, 1917), p. 431.
2 *Swift, Poetical Works*, ed. by Herbert Davis (Oxford, 1967), p. 259. In 1726 Maurice Johnson attributed the verses to Dr John Arbuthnot, see 'The Correspondence of the Spalding Gentlemen's Society 1710-1761', ed. by Diana and Michael Honeybone, *Lincoln Record Society*, 99 (2010), 33.

A Curtain worn to Half a Stripe;
A Pair of Bellows, without Pipe;
A Dish, which might good Meat afford once;
An *Ovid*, and an old *Concordance*;
A Bottle Bottom, Wooden Platter,
One is for Meal, and one for Water:
There likewise is a Copper Skillet,
Which runs as fast out as you fill it;
A Candlestick, Snuff dish, and Save-all
And thus his Houshold Goods you have all.
These, to your Lordship, as a Friend,
Till you have built, I freely lend:
They'll save your Lordship for a shift;
Why not, as well as Doctor *Swift*?

These verses evidently formed the model for 'An INVENTORY *of the* FURNITURE *of a* COLLEGIAN's *Chamber*' published by John Winstanley in 1742[3]:

IMPRIMIS, there's a *Table* blotted;
A tatter'd *Hanging* all besnotted;
A *Bed* of Flocks, as one may rank it,
Reduc'd to *Rug*, and half a *Blanket*;
A *Tinder-box*, as People tell us;
A broken-winded pair of *Bellows*.
A pair of *Tongs*, bought from a Broker,
A *Fender*, and a rusty *Poker*,
A *Penny-pot*, and *Basan*, this
Design'd for Water, that for Piss.
A *Trencher*, and a *College-bottle*
Riding on *Locke*, or *Aristotle*;
A smutty *Ballad*, musty *Libel*,
A *Burgersdiscius*, and a *Bible*;
A *Prayer-book*, he seldom handles;
Item, a Pound of *Farthing-candles*.
A rusty *Fork*, a blunted *Whittle*,
To cut his *Table*, and his *Vittle*.
There is likewise a pair of *Breeches*,
But patch'd, and fallen in the Stitches.
Item, a *Surplice*, not unmeeting
Either for *Chappel*, or for *Sheeting*,
Hung up in Study very little,
Plaister'd with Cobwebs, Ink and Spittle,

---

3   John Winstanley, *Poems Written Occasionally* (Dublin, 1742), pp. 86-87. A later variation on the same theme is 'An Inventory of the Furniture of Dr Priestley's Study', probably written in about 1770 but first published in 1825, see *Anna Letitia Barbauld, Selected Poetry and Prose*, ed. by William McCarthy and Elizabeth Kraft (Peterborough, Ontario, 2002), pp. 77-75.

With lofty *Prospect*, all so pleasing,
And *Sky-light windows* without Glazing.
Item, if I am not mistaken,
A *Mouse-trap*, with a Bit of *Bacon*,
A *Candlestick*, without a *Snuffer*,
Whereon his Fingers often suffer:
And *Chairs* a couple, (I forgot 'em)
But each of them without a *Bottom*.
A *Bottle-Standish*, *Pen* unmended,
His INVENTORY thus is ended.

Of course the poetic canon, however strict or liberal its definition, incorporates many more generalised, and often romantic or sentimental, approaches to old furniture and domestic possessions. Albeit the Chartist poet Eliza Cook's 'The Old Arm-Chair' of 1838:

I love it, I love it; and who shall dare
To chide me for loving that old Arm-chair,

is notorious, its essential sentiment is not far removed from the '...meubles luisants, Polis par les ans' of Baudelaire's 'Invitation au Voyage' (1855), or the '...hands of the generations That owned each shiny familiar thing' in Thomas Hardy's 'Old Furniture' (1917). Sheridan and Winstanley's *Inventories* jest or moralise in detail, implicitly and explicitly, but is there an English equivalent to an eighteenth century *Stammbuch* leaf in Bamberg which pictorially inventorises, in four contiguous rectangles, Necessary (clothing, money, a spittoon), Useful (books, a desk, a spinet), Pleasurable (tobacco pipes, wine, a recorder and a faithful dog) and Dangerous (duelling pistols and swords, cards, dice and a seductive female) possessions?[4] Perhaps, by contrast, the catalogue of ships which occupies approaching three hundred lines in the second book of Homer's *Iliad* and may stand as an early (in this case about 800 B.C., although quite possibly much earlier in origin) instance of the incantatory rather than moralising force of cumulation, another quality inherent in many a substantial inventory.

Setting aside the poetic and moral resonances of inventories, be they factual or fictional, there can be no doubt as to their antiquity – and quite possibly their precedence – in the written record. The Pylos tablets, whose discovery in 1939 in a Mycenaean palace of about 1300 BC led to Michael Ventris's decipherment of Linear B as Greek, were 'almost without exception ... lists, inventories or catalogues'[5]. One record, for instance, lists '3 ewers, 6 tripod cauldrons ... 3 boiling pans ... 2 fire tongs, 1 fire-rake, 11 tables, 5 chairs, 15 footstools', and several of the pieces of furniture are described in some detail, as 'footstool, ebony, inlaid with ivory figures of men and lions'[6]. Among the tablets discovered at Vindolanda in Northumberland, probably

---

4 Werner Taegert, *Edler Schatz holden Erinnerns, Bilder in Stammbüchern aus vier Jahrhunderten* (Bamberg, 1995), p. 132.
5 John Chadwick, *The Decipherment of Linear B* (Cambridge, 1970), p. 46.
6 Chadwick, ibid., pp. 118-119 and Hollis S. Baker, *Furniture in the Ancient World* (London, 1966), pp. 248-249.

dating from about AD 100, is a fragmentary inventory of household objects, including shallow dishes, a bronze lamp and bread baskets, which has been compared to another fragmentary inventory, in this case of silver, on an Egyptian papyrus of about the same date, now in Berlin.[7] The point hardly needs labouring that inventories are ubiquitous, perennial and essential for a variety of purposes.

Given the ubiquity and variety of inventories their usefulness as historical evidence was bound, sooner or later, to be recognised and exploited. Narrowing the focus to Great Britain and Ireland it is a curiosity that the first series of English secular inventories to be printed in full, those of the directors of the South Sea Company, were contemporary, not historical, documents, and indeed parliamentary records. Much later in the eighteenth century a trickle of inventory transcriptions began to be published for their historical interest, including that of Henry V (1424) in Rev. John Strachey FSA's *Rotuli Parliamentorum* and one of Sherburn Hospital, near Durham (1724) in the book on that ancient institution published in 1771 by George Allan FSA, a prolific and generous antiquary. In the 1790s the pace began to quicken. In 1792 William Boys, surgeon and topographer, published the 1640 inventory of James Smyth, master of the Free Grammar School, in his history of Sandwich, and in 1794 Robert Smith FSA published in *Archaeologia, or Miscellaneous Tracts relating to Antiquity*, the irregular periodical of the Society of Antiquaries of London, the 1539 inventory of Sir Thomas Clifford of Berwick Castle. The connection with the Society of Antiquaries and its Fellows is no coincidence. In 1787 for instance John Topham FSA became Treasurer of the Society and in 1790 he bought at the sale of his deceased friend, Gustavus Brander FSA, the manuscript inventory of Henry VIII with a view to publication, an ambition finally achieved in 1998[8]. And in November 1796 John Croft FSA dedicated his *Excerpta Antiqua* (1797) to the Society of Antiquaries: it includes a transcription of the 1558 inventory of Sir William Fairfax of Steeton and Denton. But the real breakthrough came in another 1797 book, *Illustrations of the Manners and Expences of Antient Times in England*, by John Nichols FSA, one of the most industrious and productive antiquaries of his day: *Illustrations* transcribed no fewer than seven inventories dating from 1485 (Marino Contarini, merchant of Venice, in Botolph Lane) to 1612 (George Hitchcock, landlord of the Mouth Tavern, Bishopsgate). A further precedent was set in Edinburgh in 1815 in *A Collection of Inventories and Other Records of the Royal Wardrobe and Jewelhouse; and of the Artillery and Munitioun in some of the Royal Castles* compiled by Thomas Thomson, another prolific antiquary, and an intimate friend of Sir Walter Scott; his *Collection* is dominated by royal inventories of James V and VI of Scotland and of Mary, Queen of Scots, from 1539 to 1580.

In 1841 John Gough Nichols FSA, grandson of the John Nichols mentioned above[9], issued an appeal in the *Gentleman's Magazine*:

---

7 http://vindolanda.csad.ox.ac.uk/TVII 194 (*Tab. Vindol.* II 194); *Aegyptische Urkunden aus den Königlichen Museen zu Berlin, Griechische Urkunden*, [BGU] (Berlin, III, 1903), No. 781.

8 David Starkey, 'The Manuscripts and Their History' in *The Inventory of Henry VIII, The Transcript*, ed. by Starkey (London, 1998), pp. xxi-xxii.

9 His father, John Bowyer Nichols FSA was also a published antiquary.

Mr J. G. Nichols requests to be favoured with references to any topographical or other works into which inventories of household furniture and other property, particularly of the time of Elizabeth and James I, have been introduced.[10]

Nichols was then engaged in preparing his *The Unton Inventories*, published that very year. In its preface he observed that 'Documents of this kind, when they have been published, have generally been considered as replete with curious illustrations of the domestic lives of our forefathers; but it is remarkable that very few have appeared in print…', and went on to characterise the 1835 volume of Northern wills and inventories edited by James Raine FSA for the Surtees Society as the first systematic collection of such documents. Nichols then presented a list of some fifteen published inventories, dating from 1459 to 1650, presumably in part at least the harvest of his *Gentleman's Magazine* appeal, half of which are full transcriptions eligible for inclusion here,[11] the remainder being extracts only, some in the third volume of Joseph Strutt's *Manners, Customs, Arms, Habits, &c., of the People of England* (London, 1776). Surprisingly Nichols does not refer to the seven transcriptions in his grandfather's 1797 *Illustrations*, and makes no mention of Thomson. However Raine, whose son, another James Raine FSA, was to publish further transcriptions after his father's death in 1858, certainly deserves credit. A classic clergyman antiquary who was appointed cathedral librarian of Durham in 1816 and was in 1819 encouraged by Sir Walter Scott to study 'the treasure of ancient papers' preserved there, Raine was in 1834 instrumental in founding the Surtees Society, named for his friend and patron, Robert Surtees FSA, the remarkable gentleman antiquary of Mainforth Hall. Raine himself acknowledged inspiration from observations made by Joseph Hunter FSA, another energetic clergyman antiquary, in this case Unitarian, in the preface to the second volume of his *History and Topography of the Deanery of Doncaster* (London, 1831). Hunter underlined the importance of the wills and, by implication, the inventories 'lurking, unseen by every eye, in the dispersed, the dark and dusty depositories of the testamentary evidence of England'[12]: 'a better acquaintance with these evidences would be', he proclaimed, in a delicious phrase, 'the creation of a new world in our gentilitial Antiquities'.

In 1854 the Shakespearian antiquary James Orchard Halliwell FSA (later Halliwell-Phillipps) published his *Ancient Inventories*, containing transcriptions of four grand inventories.[13] He mentions Nichols's bibliography of a decade earlier, and

---

10 *Gentleman's Magazine*, 15 (1841), p. 2; reprinted in *Furniture History Society Newsletter*, 174 (2009), p. 7, in soliciting contributions to the present work.

11 Nos *193, 312, 1574, 2136, 3767, 3845, 4862* and *6649* in the *List* below.

12 Raine (p. viii) recounts that: 'A Registrar of the Consistory Court of Durham, during the first half of the last [18th] century, was in the habit of lighting his pipe with one of the Wills under his charge, and of glorying in his deed. "Here goes the testator" was his usual exclamation when he was so employed. Things are not so now.'

13 One of these, of Cockesden in 1611 (pp. 59-86), has not hitherto been pinned down. Peter Thornton in *Seventeenth-Century Interior Decoration in England, France and Holland* (London, 1978), p. 330 suggested: 'The property concerned was probably one belonging to the Earls of Leicester'. In fact Cockesden, Coaxdon or Coxden, a sub-manor of Chardstock, then in Dorset, now in Devon, was the house of Richard Symonds [or Simonds], a rich Middle Temple lawyer, who died in 1611. He was

the Bury wills and inventories collected by Samuel Tymms FSA, the Suffolk
antiquary, who acknowledged his personal debt to Nichols, for the Camden Society
in 1850, but concludes that: 'a large collection is still a desideratum', adding: 'It is
almost impossible to overrate the importance of this class of documents, in
investigating the habits of our ancestors, and the character of their domestic life'.[14]
By this time the publication of transcriptions of inventories was becoming
increasingly frequent – and it should not be forgotten that ecclesiastical inventories
were a particular focus of study, with Mackenzie Walcott FSA (1821-1880) among its
protagonists. Such progress had been made internationally on all fronts that in the
mid-1880s two then relatively young scholars, Edmund Bishop (1846-1917) and
Fernand Dusaussay de Mély (1852-1935) independently conceived the idea of
publishing a bibliography of printed inventories.

Bishop, the son of a Devon innkeeper, worked as a clerk in the Education Office
from 1864 to 1885. The hours, from eleven to five, and the generous holidays allowed
him to spend his own time in intensive self-education, at home and abroad.
Converted to Catholicism in 1867 and a regular guest at Downside Abbey from 1883,
the multi-lingual Bishop's principal interest was the history of the liturgy, and his
deep knowledge and intuitive brilliance, combined with scrupulous accuracy, won
him an international reputation, such that in 1886 Comte Paul Riant, the rich and
influential French scholar of the Crusades, hailed him as 'un savant de premier ordre'
and pronounced that: 'Il y a, en lui, l'étoffe d'un Montfaucon ou d'un Mabillon'.[15] It
was probably Riant who in 1887 advised the younger scholar, Fernand de Mély, to
write to Bishop, whose established contacts already included Mgr. Xavier Barbier de
Montault (1830-1901), the great French authority on, *inter alia*, ecclesiastical
inventories. De Mély, a *protégé* of Riant, was a wealthy landowner, with a château in
Normandy (converted by him into a field hospital during the Great War), a
prodigious output of scholarly articles and books, and a European correspondence.
By June 1887 Bishop and de Mély, who became firm friends, exchanging some three
hundred letters over thirty years, had agreed to turn their independently conceived
inventory bibliographies into a collaboration. The *Revue de l'Art Chrétien* decided
not to pursue the project, but in 1888 the Ministère de l'Instruction Publique et des
Beaux-Arts adopted it as an official publication. The two set to work and, despite
Bishop's loss of over a thousand *fiches* at Paddington Station in 1888 and his illness in
1891, the work rapidly moved to completion. It was published as two volumes in
three parts from 1892 to 1895 as the *Bibliographie Générale des Inventaires
Imprimés*. Now a very rare book the *Bibliographie Générale* was an heroic feat of
organisation and compilation, wholly international and covering both ecclesiastical
and secular inventories.[16] A charming contrast to this monument of assiduity is

   grandfather to Sir Simonds D'Ewes (1602-1650), whose autobiography and correspondence Halliwell
   had published in two volumes in 1845. A section of the house survives.
14 Halliwell, p. 160.
15 Quoted by Nigel Abercrombie, *The Life and Work of Edmund Bishop* (London, 1959), p. 101.
16 Some statistics are worth noting: Volume I (1892), ix + 335 pp., contains the French 1 (831) to 1331
   (1790) and English 1332 (c. 930) to 4231 (1794) entries; Volume II, part 1 (1894), 370 pp., contains
   Germany 4232 (c. 810) to 4703 (1794); Denmark 4704 (1213) to 4751 (1743?); Scotland 4752 (1291) to

supplied by an article by Edmund Bishop, 'Character Sketches from Mediæval Inventories', published in the *Downside Review* of 1894.[17] Three of Bishop's subjects are Italian (the account of one, Oliviero Forzetta of Treviso, is based not on an inventory but on his celebrated 1335 'shopping list' for purchases in Venice), another three French, and two English, Thomas Keble, esquire, serjeant at law of Humberstone, Leicestershire, whose 1500 inventory appeared in John Nichols, *Illustrations* (1797), and John Underwood, a York advocate, whose 1515 inventory had been published quite recently, in James Raine (junior), *Eboracensia* (1884).[18] The characterisations, Underwood as an old bachelor who made his money and then lived in 'meanness, discomfort and dowdiness', and Mr Serjeant Keble as a 'wealthy, prosperous and a generous liver', are perhaps no more than plausible, but the whole article evinces Bishop's relish for such documents and his imagination in interpreting them as 'revelations of individual character, with their unexpected turns of nature'.

In the hundred and twenty years, or thereabouts, since de Mély and Bishop published their *Bibliographie Générale* many more transcriptions of inventories have been published, as well as many partial transcriptions or selected extracts. Evidence from inventories has been applied to an ever-widening range of historical purposes. Landscape history and agricultural history may stand as an example, with W. G. Hoskins among its great protagonists from the 1930s to the 1970s. Earlier foundations include a 1909 article on agriculture in Cumberland by Francis Grainger, descended from Cumberland yeomen and active not only as an antiquary and farmer, but also in almost every aspect of local affairs in his remote native area (and later as a collaborator with Ruskin's great disciple, the artist and antiquary W. G. Collingwood).[19] 'Local worthy' has a condescending ring, but the availability of inventory transcriptions owes much to the Stakhanovite industry of provincial scholars, many of them amateurs. Dr G. H. Fowler (1861-1940), the marine biologist who founded the Bedfordshire Historical Record Society in 1912, may be seen as the founder of a highly productive dynasty. He was responsible for the appointment of F. G. Emmison FSA (1907-1995) as the first Bedfordshire Clerk of the Records, in 1925. In 1938, the year he moved to Essex to serve as its first County Archivist, Emmison published the first substantial mid-twentieth century collection, *Jacobean Household*

4840 (1716); Spain 4841 (780) to 4999 (1754); Holland 5000 (1174) to 5108 (18th century); Hungary 5109 (11th-12th century) to 5263 (1707-10); Iceland 5264 (1179) to 5475 (1343); Italy 5476 (471) to 6084 (18th century); the Orient 6085 (1150) to 6088 (1201); Poland 6089 (1101) to 6181 (1750); Sweden and Norway 6182 (1311) to 6205 (1652); Switzerland 6206 (9th century) to 6251 (1799); France 6252 (603-21) to 7115 (18th century); and England and Scotland 7116 (c. 930) to 7451 (1791); Volume II, part 2 (1895), 258 pp., contains the indices.

17   13, (1894), pp. 17-29. The *Review* was a mixture of serious theology, Benedictine history, and variegated scholarship, and of school news and reminiscences, these latter often facetious in tone; it included in 1894 advertisements for J. W. Singer & Sons, Art Metal Works, Frome, Somerset, and John Hardman & Co., Artists in Stained Glass, Birmingham, and the Bristol Steam Cabinet Works, whose products were available from Laverton & Co., Upholsterers, Bristol. The 1894 volume contains a second article by Bishop (pp. 192-206), 'An Antiquary of the Ninth Century', on Andreas Agnellus, the author of the *Liber Pontificalis Ecclesiæ Ravennatis*.

18   These inventories are nos *272* and *303* in the present work.

19   W. G. Collingwood in Grainger and Collingwood, 1929 (see Short Title Index and Bibliography below).

Inventories. In 1950 one of Emmison's disciples, Francis Steer FSA (1912-1978), published the next, *Farmhouse and Cottage Inventories of Mid-Essex*, an out-of-hours production. Fowler had been an Assistant Professor of Zoology at University College, London, but neither Emmison nor Steer went to university.

In recent decades inventories have been much used as the basis for ever more sophisticated and professional analyses, often with a cliometric bias towards statistics, and sometimes involving the application of complex algorithms, whether in the field of agriculture, or of particular trades or industries, or in tackling such broader themes as prices, wealth and class, and production and consumption.[20] But, lest it be thought that the dismal science has become wholly predominant, there are plentiful examples of the application of evidence drawn from inventories to the study of almost every branch of the arts, both fine and decorative or applied, and of architecture and interior decoration. Two notable and monumental instances are *Jewels and Plate of Queen Elizabeth I* (British Museum, 1955) by Arthur Jefferies Collins FSA (1893-1976) and *Queen Elizabeth's Wardrobe Unlock't* (Leeds, 1988) by Janet Arnold FSA (1932-1998).[21] Many publications present information distilled from unpublished inventories.[22] As the *List* which follows this essay demonstrates, the distribution of published transcriptions is remarkably uneven, being weighted towards the rural and the provincial, London, in particular, being markedly under-represented. It is to be hoped that in the future new collections will redress the balance, that more full transcriptions will appear of inventories previously printed in part only, and that more inventories made for purposes other than probate will be published.[23]

One expression of the growth in popularity of probate inventories as a source for history was the production in 2000 of an excellent guide to their study and interpretation, *When Death Do Us Part*.[24] Inventories do need to be treated critically and the several references in this work to Margaret Spufford's 1990 article, 'The

---

20 Mark Overton, Jane Whittle, Darron Dean, and Andrew Hann, *Production and Consumption in English Households, 1600-1750*, Abingdon, 2004, is a notable example.

21 Both are based on specialised inventories which are on that account not eligible for inclusion in the *List* below.

22 Two examples must suffice: Pauline Agius, 'Late Sixteenth- and Seventeenth-Century Furniture in Oxford, A survey of that listed in the probate inventories of members of the University 1568-1699', *Furniture History*, 7 (1971), pp. 72-86; and David M. Mitchell, 'Fashions in Bed and Room Hangings in London, 1660-1735', *Riggisberger Berichte*, 17 (2009), pp. 21-34, 223-236, mainly based on the Court of Orphans inventories in the London Metropolitan Archive.

23 See no. 6137: this transcription is complete, by contrast with Randall Davies, 'An inventory of the Duke of Buckingham's pictures &c. at York House in 1635', *Burlington Magazine*, 10 (1907), pp. 376-82. It is invidious to single out candidates for full transcription but extracts published in 1910 from the Ormonde inventories of Dublin Castle, Chapelizod, Phoenix, Islandridge, Kilkenny, Dunmore and Clonmel (Royal Commission on Historical Manuscripts, *Calendar of the Manuscripts of the Marquess of Ormonde, K. P.* [formerly] *Preserved at Kilkenny Castle*, New series, 7, London, 1912) certainly whet the appetite.

24 See Arkell, Evans, Goose, 2000, below.

25 See pp. 35, 72, 92, 95, 116, 222, 229, 300 and 303. The Spufford article appeared in *English rural society, 1500-1800: essays in honour of Joan Thirsk*, ed. by J. Chartres and D. Hey (Cambridge, 1990), pp. 139-174.

limitations of the probate inventory', echo her cautions.[25] Reinforcement is to be found in a 2002 article by Lena Cowen Orlin, which tabulates no fewer than twelve different ways in which the goods in an inventory might not tally with those the owner would have known.[26] She concludes: '...inventories can most legitimately be read anecdotally and with scepticism rather than systematically and with faith'. A memorandum attached to the inventory of Mary, Queen of Scots's possessions, taken after her execution at Fotheringay in 1587 is a rare explicit mention of excluded goods: 'there remayneth in the sayd late Quenes cabinet and other places, a greate number of books, drinking glasses, and other small things not mentioned in this Inventarye, which are also claymed by the severall servaunts as geven to them by their mistris'[27] The Queen's concern for the fate of her servants after her death is reflected in another clause: 'All which parcelles ... were apoynted by the sayd late Quene to be sold by the sayd Melvin [her steward] and the Physician [Bourgoing], and the money thereof to be imployed towards the expences of the whole companye in their journey homewardes'.

Perhaps the greatest recent achievement in the publication of English inventories was the appearance in 1998, under the aegis of the Society of Antiquaries of London, of the transcript of that of Henry VIII, edited by David Starkey FSA, with 17,810 entries, many covering a multitude of objects.[28] Not on that scale, but still worthy of note is the recent publication of a new edition of the unique illustrated Lumley Inventory of 1590, with eleven supporting essays and three appendices.[29] Inventories doubtless have their limitations, but they are nonetheless irreplaceable and their uses are protean. Let the last word be with the great Victorian scholar of ecclesiastical inventories, Mackenzie Walcott, FSA: 'Inventories are the primer, grammar and glossary of the archaeologist'.[30]

---

26 'Fictions of the Early Modern English Probate Inventory', in *The Culture of Capital, Property, Cities and Knowledge in Early Modern England* ed. by Henry S. Turner (New York, 2002), pp. 51-83.

27 See no. 2498 in the *List* below (Labanoff, 1844), p. 274.

28 See no. 582 below reinforced, remarkably, by no. 457.

29 *Art Collecting and Lineage, The Lumley Inventory and Pedigree, Facsimile and Commentary on the Manuscript in the Possession of The Earls of Scarbrough*, ed. by Mark Evans (The Roxburghe Club, 2010). See no. 2805 below. This new edition appeared too late for inclusion in the *List*.

30 In his introduction to a paper on 'The Inventories and Valuations of Religious Houses at the Time of the Dissolution', *Archaeologia*, 43 (1871), p. 202.

LIST OF PUBLISHED TRANSCRIPTIONS
OF SECULAR INVENTORIES

SCOPE

The List attempts to assemble all published transcriptions of secular inventories from Great Britain and Ireland (including the Isle of Man and also incorporating the Channel Islands) of whatever date. The vast majority are domestic probate inventories. Only full transcriptions of full inventories are included (a few early published inventories may be translations from the Latin), specialised inventories or selective transcriptions of, say, paintings, jewellery, plate, dress or linen being excluded.

DATES

Dates are given in the New Style, with the year beginning on 1 January following the reform ordered by Pope Gregory XIII on 24 February 1582, first adopted in England, Wales and Ireland on the day after 31st December 1751 (Scotland had already adopted the New Style on the day after 31st December 1599).

Some dates may have been wrongly adjusted or left unadjusted through inadvertence, error, or doubt as to the practice of the editor of the inventory in question, but the margin should not exceed a year.

Undated inventories are sometimes grouped by approximate quarter century, in which cases **1575-1600**, for example, will be found to precede the year **1575**. Similarly other groupings, for instance **1285-1290 (undated)**, are inserted before the first year, in this case **1285**. By contrast approximately or uncertainly dated inventories, as **1430 (c.)**, follow the year in question.

LOCATIONS

The inventories are organised under each date first by county and then by location, in descending order. The counties are those which existed at the time when the inventory was taken. Exceptionally London, treated as a county, is allowed to subsume some locations formerly in Middlesex, Surrey and Kent. When in doubt both London and the former county should be checked.

Another inconsistency is that Scotland, Ireland, Wales, the Isle of Man, Jersey and Guernsey are treated as counties. Relatively few inventories have so far been published from these locations, so they should be not too difficult to pinpoint, while there is practical advantage in grouping them together.

Where no location is known the inventory is listed under '**Unlocated**' when the county is unknown, or 'Unlocated' when the location within a county is unknown.

When an inventory covers more than one location the main entry is placed under the principal location with a note of others as 'also listed …', while the other locations are cross-referenced back to the principal location as 'see …'.

Modern spelling has been adopted for all locations.

NAMES, TITLES, PROFESSIONS, TRADES

Earlier editors have sometimes silently modernised names. Where the original spelling has been transcribed this has been retained, sometimes with variations in square brackets. Under each main location within a county names are in alphabetical order of surname: thus in Barchester, John Brown, living at The Rectory, will precede John Smith, living at The Brewery.

Titles are given, with the exception of 'Sir' as the early, but confusing, honorific for a priest. Baronets are usually specified as such, to distinguish them from knights.

Where the original inventory includes a profession or a trade this is noted, but where the authority is the will rather than the inventory itself, or the profession or trade can be extrapolated by other means, this is also noted, but placed in square brackets. These bracketed categories may in general be relied upon. One idiosyncrasy is that almost all members of the clergy are noted as 'clergyman'.

REFERENCES

A pragmatic system of brief references is used within this List; all these brief references are listed in the Short Title Index (p. 333) before the main *Bibliography* (p. 347). There should be little difficulty in tracing the fuller entries there.

Care has been taken to insert the page numbers of the transcribed inventory in almost every case. Many inventories on a single page may prove to be brief, even minimal, and the same may often apply to those which span two pages. But three pages or more are usually an indication of some degree of wealth and, possibly, variety.

DATING KEY

The following Key will help to pin down the rough date of each transcription by its reference number.

1 to 118	:	1278 to 1400
119 to 276	:	1401 to 1500
277 to 659	:	1501 to 1550
660 to 1761	:	1551 to 1575
1762 to 3595	:	1576 to 1600
3596 to 5507	:	1601 to 1625
5508 to 7051	:	1626 to 1650
7052 to 8492	:	1651 to 1675
8493 to 10329	:	1676 to 1700
10330 to 11390	:	1701 to 1725
11391 to 11975	:	1726 to 1750
11976 to 12257	:	1750 to 1800
12258 to 12316	:	1801 to 1864

LIST OF PUBLISHED TRANSCRIPTIONS
OF SECULAR INVENTORIES

1278
Kent
Romney
  1 Robert le Pere
    Woodruff, 1934, pp. 30-31

1280 (c.)
Essex
Warley
  2 Reginald de Ginges
    Turner, 1848, pp. 152-153

1283
Lincolnshire
Long Bennington
  3 Christiana, widow of John, son of William de
Bennington
    Foster, *Lincoln*, 1912, pp. 3-4

1285-1290 (undated)
Norfolk
King's Lynn
  4 Iohannes de Bauseie
    Owen, *King's Lynn*, 1984, p. 244
  5 Philippus de Bekx
    Owen, *King's Lynn*, 1984, pp. 247-248
  6 Petrus de Birche
    Owen, *King's Lynn*, 1984, pp. 240-241
  7 Walterus de Bradefeld
    Owen, *King's Lynn*, 1984, p. 243
  8 Radulphus de Bretham
    Owen, *King's Lynn*, 1984, pp. 248-249
  9 Emma, widow of Willelmus Burel
    Owen, *King's Lynn*, 1984, pp. 245-246
  10 Walterus de Bury
    Owen, *King's Lynn*, 1984, pp. 244-245
  11 Robertus Coleville
    Owen, *King's Lynn*, 1984, p. 247
  12 Willelmus de Cranewyz
    Dashwood, 1847, pp. 338-340
    Owen, *King's Lynn*, 1984, p. 235
  13 Petrus Dice
    Owen, *King's Lynn*, 1984, p. 237
  14 Henricus de Gernemuta [Yarmouth]
    Owen, *King's Lynn*, 1984, p. 249
  15 Thomas de Holebech
    Owen, *King's Lynn*, 1984, p. 242
  16 Petrus Le Ankersmit
    Owen, *King's Lynn*, 1984, pp. 242-243
  17 Ricardus Le Barbur
    Owen, *King's Lynn*, 1984, pp. 246-247

  18 Robertus Le Barbur
    Owen, *King's Lynn*, 1984, p. 239
  19 Iohannes Le Coupere de Walton
    Owen, *King's Lynn*, 1984, p. 246
  20 Godefridus called Le Franceys
    Owen, *King's Lynn*, 1984, p. 238
  21 Henricus Le Iremonger
    Owen, *King's Lynn*, 1984, p. 245
  22 Hugo Le Moygne
    Owen, *King's Lynn*, 1984, pp. 243-244
  23 Willelmus Le Peter
    Owen, *King's Lynn*, 1984, p. 240
  24 Robertus Le Poleter
    Owen, *King's Lynn*, 1984, p. 249
  25 Symon de Leverington
    Owen, *King's Lynn*, 1984, pp. 235-236
  26 Robertus de Londonia, mayor of King's Lynn,
1271-1272
    Dashwood, 1847, pp. 342-343
    Owen, *King's Lynn*, 1984, pp. 238-239
  27 Reginaldus Molendarius
    Owen, *King's Lynn*, 1984, p. 244
  28 Thomas de Newerk
    Owen, *King's Lynn*, 1984, p. 241
  29 Walterus de Nichole
    Owen, *King's Lynn*, 1984, p. 240
  30 Iohannes Quitloc
    Owen, *King's Lynn*, 1984, pp. 241-242
  31 Radulphus de Rudham
    Owen, *King's Lynn*, 1984, p. 243
  32 Iohannes de Schuldham
    Owen, *King's Lynn*, 1984, p. 240
  33 Iohannes Sterion
    Owen, *King's Lynn*, 1984, pp. 237-238
  34 Margaret, widow of Ranulphus de Suthmer
    Owen, *King's Lynn*, 1984, p. 240
  35 Agnes de Swafham
    Owen, *King's Lynn*, 1984, p. 242
  36 Reginaldus Tabernarius
    Owen, *King's Lynn*, 1984, pp. 236-237
  37 Thomas de Weynflet, mayor of King's Lynn, 1293-
1294
    Dashwood, 1847, pp. 344-345
    Owen, *King's Lynn*, 1984, pp. 239-240

1291-1300 (undated)
Norfolk
King's Lynn
  38 Ricardus Crispyn, felon
    Owen, *King's Lynn*, 1984, p. 424
  39 Walterus de Seleby, clergyman, chaplain, suicide
    Owen, *King's Lynn*, 1984, p. 424

1292
Northumberland
Berwick-on-Tweed, Castle
  40 Sir John Pottow
    Stevenson, 1870, I, 341-344

1293
Hampshire
Newton Valence (?)
  Reginald Labbe (see Oakwood, Surrey)
Surrey
Oakwood
  41 Reginald Labbe (also listed Newton Valence (?),
Hampshire)
    Walford, 1846, p. 66
    Sheehan, 1963, pp. 321-322
Wales
Breconshire, Llanddewi Skirrid (?)
  42 Thomas Beck, bishop of St David's
    Jones, 1964, pp. 16-20

1298
Northumberland
Berwick-on-Tweed, Castle
  43 Sir Hugh de Audley
    Stevenson, 1870, pp. 322-325

1304
London
Fulham Palace
  44 Richard de Gravesend, bishop of London
    Hale and Ellacombe, 1874, pp. 47-60

1308
Sussex
Saddlescombe
  45 Templars
    Blaauw, 1857, pp. 240-241
Shipley
  46 Templars
    Blaauw, 1857, pp. 253-254

1308 (c.)
Unlocated
Unlocated
  47 Queen Isabella
    Rhodes, 1897, pp. 518-521

1310
Devonshire
Exeter
  48 Thomas de Button, bishop of Exeter
    Hale and Ellacombe, 1874, pp. 1-12

1314
Co. Durham
Ravensworth Castle
  49 Sir John Marmaduk
    Hardy, 1873, 2, pp. 673-680
Northumberland
Norham Castle
  50 William Rydd
    Hardy, 1873, 1, pp. 598-599

1316
Yorkshire
Richmond
  51 Juliana Fitz-Eyas de Richmund
    Lawson, 1857, p. 196

1317
London
Unlocated
  52 Richard de Blountesham
    Riley, *Memorials*, 1868, pp. 123-125

1322
Herefordshire
Wigmore Castle and Abbey
  53 Roger de Mortimer
    Larking, *Mortimer*, 1858, pp. 359-362

1323
Wales
Glamorgan, Llandaff, Manor of Tregof
  54 Richard de Haltone, clergyman, canon of Llandaff
    Royal Commission, 1879, p. 690

1324
Berkshire
Steventon
  55 Priory
    Morgan, 1939, pp. 145-149
Somersetshire
Stogursey, Priory
  56 [Peter de Grana, prior ?]
    Tremlett and Blakiston, 1949, pp. xxi-xxxi
Wiltshire
Ogbourne
  57 Priory
    Morgan, 1939, p. 145

1326
Co. Durham
Gateshead
  58 Hospitalis Sancti Edmundi [Hospital of St
Edmund]
    Raine, *Wills and Inventories*, 1835, I, pp. 22-23
Lincolnshire
Wilsford
  59 Priory
    Morgan, 1939, pp. 143-144

1328
Devonshire
Exeter
  60 Walter de Stapeldon, bishop
    Hingeston-Randolph, 1892, pp. 562-575

1331
Kent
Canterbury, Christchurch
  61 Henry [of Eastry], prior
    Hope, 1896, pp. 262-270

1334
Kent
 Canterbury, Christchurch
  62 Richard [of Oxenden], prior
   Hope, 1896, pp. 270-282

1337
London
 Unlocated
  63 Hugh le Bevere, felon
   Riley, *Memorials*, 1868, pp. 199-200

1339
Kent
 Canterbury, Christchurch
  64 Robert [Hathbrand], prior
   Hope, 1896, p. 283

1341
Middlesex
 Harefield
  65 Thomas de Luda [Louth] and Margaret, his wife
   Le Hardy, 1951, pp. 249-251

1343
Cornwall
 Philleigh, Tolverne
  66 Rose Le Soor
   Orme, 2007, p. 26
Kent
 Dover Castle
  67 William de Clinton, Earl of Huntingdon, former constable
   Way, 1854, pp. 381-383

1347
Co. Durham
 Ravensholme
  68 Johannis Marmaduk [John Fitz Marmaduke, Lord of Horden] (also listed Silksworth)
   Raine, *Wills and Inventories*, 1835, I, pp. 16-20
 Silksworth
  Johannis Marmaduk (see Ravensholme)

1349
Oxfordshire
 Cuxham
  69 Thomas ate Grene
   Harvey, 1976, pp. 151-152
  70 Robert Oldman
   Harvey, 1976, p. 153
   Dyer, 1989, p. 170

1350
Yorkshire
 Scarborough
  71 John Horne
   Stell, *York*, 2006, p. 493

1352
Norfolk
 Great Plumstead
  72 Laurence de Leek, Prior of Norwich
   Yaxley, 1988, pp. 6-7

 Hemsby
  73 Laurence de Leek, Prior of Norwich
   Yaxley, 1988, pp. 14-15
 Hindolveston
  74 Laurence de Leek, Prior of Norwich
   Yaxley, 1988, pp. 39-40
 Hindringham
  75 Laurence de Leek, Prior of Norwich
   Yaxley, 1988, pp. 35-36
 Newton
  76 Laurence de Leek, Prior of Norwich
   Yaxley, 1988, pp. 17-18
 North Elmham
  77 Laurence de Leek, Prior of Norwich
   Yaxley, 1988, p. 9
 Norwich, Eaton
  78 Laurence de Leek, Prior of Norwich
   Yaxley, 1988, p. 11
 Sedgeford
  79 Laurence de Leek, Prior of Norwich
   Yaxley, 1988, pp. 23-24
 Sedgeford, Gnatingdon,
  80 Laurence de Leek, Prior of Norwich
   Yaxley, 1988, p. 27
 Taverham
  81 Laurence de Leek, Prior of Norwich
   Yaxley, 1988, pp. 42-43
 Thornham
  82 Laurence de Leek, Prior of Norwich
   Yaxley, 1988, p. 29

1355
Staffordshire (?)
 Tamworth Castle (?)
  83 Monsieur [Sir] Baudewyn de Fryvill [Baldwin de Freville]
   Stevenson, 1911, p. 465

1356
London
 St Michael, Cornhill
  84 Stephen le Northerne
   Riley, *Memorials*, 1868, pp. 282-284

1361
Kent
 Dover Castle
  85 Johan de Beauchampe de Warwick, former constable
   Way, 1854, pp. 383-385

1362
Wales
 Caernavonshire, Aberaeron
  86 Ievan ap Kenric Vaghan
   Wynne, 1865, pp. 270-271

1367
Kent
 Preston, Wingham
  87 Lady Juliana de Leyborne, Countess of Huntingdon
   Larking, 1858, pp. 3-6

1370
Suffolk
Stanton
88 Adam de Stanton, clergyman, chaplain
Tymms, 1850, p. 1

1374
Leicestershire
Appleby Magna
89 Sir Edmund Appleby
Astill, 1974, pp. 279-283

1376
London
Lombard Street, tavern 'Chichestre Seler'
Richard Lyons [Lyouns], merchant (see Unlocated)
Lombard Street, tavern 'La Galeye'
Richard Lyons [Lyouns], merchant (see Unlocated)
Unlocated
90 Richard Lyons [Lyouns], merchant (also listed Lombard Street)
Myers, *Lyons*, pp. 317-329

1377
Wiltshire
Salisbury, St Edmunds
91 Richard Gilbert, gentleman
Benson, Hatcher, Hoare, 1843, pp. 101-102

1378
Co. Durham
Harton
92 Thomas Page
Booth, 1886, p. 151
Moorsley
93 Rob. De Suthwyk
Booth, 1886, p. 151
London
St Ewen's Parish
94 Thomas Trewe, haberdasher
Riley, *Memorials*, 1868, pp. 422-423
Archer, 1991, pp. 1-2
Unlocated
Unlocated
95 Alicia Perrers
Rymer, 4, 1869, p. 28

1381
Co. Durham
Hesledon
96 Joh. De Raynton
Booth, 1886, p. 168
London
St Martin, Ludgate
97 Adam Ledyard, [jeweller]
Riley, *Memorials*, 1868, p. 455

1383
Nottinghamshire
Wollaton
98 Sir William Furnyvall
Stell, *York*, 2006, p. 493

1384
Lancashire
Liverpool
99 William, son of Adam
Radcliffe, 1892, p. 284

1386
Essex
Mountnessing
100 Arnald Monteny
Steer, 1958, pp. 152-156
London
Unlocated
101 Richard de Ravenser, clergyman, Archdeacon of Lincoln (also listed Stretton, Rutlandshire)
Pretyman, 1850, pp. 317-327
Rutlandshire
Stretton
Richard de Ravenser, clergyman, Archdeacon of Lincoln (see London)

1387
Cornwall
St Ive
102 John Keych
Orme, 2007, p. 41

1388
Worcestershire
Holt
103 Sir John Beauchamp
Saul, 2005, pp. 11-16
Yorkshire
Kingston upon Hull
104 Michael de la Pole, Earl of Suffolk
Calendar, Chancery, 1962, pp. 68-95

1389 (c.)
Berkshire
Abingdon Abbey
105 Brother John Eynsham, gardener
Kirk, 1892, pp. 57-58

1391
London
Unlocated
106 Richard Toky, grocer
Thomas, *Calendar*, 1932, pp. 209-215

1393
Devonshire
Aveton Gifford
Sir John Damarle [Daumarle] (see Lustleigh)
Flete
Sir John Damarle [Daumarle] (see Lustleigh)
Lustleigh
107 Sir John Damarle [Daumarle] (also listed Aveton Gifford and Flete)
Peskett, 1971, pp. 80-82

1395
Rutlandshire
Empingham
108 John Meton
Gibbons, 1888, p. 59

Yorkshire
York
109 Robert de Crakall, mason
Stell, *York*, 2006, pp. 493-496
110 John de Scardeburgh, clergyman, notary, rector of
Titchmarsh, Northamptonshire
Raine, *Eboracensia*, 1865, pp. 2-8

1396
Oxfordshire
Oxford, New College
111 Thomas Cranleghe, warden
Riley, 1871, pp. 232-234

1397
Essex
Pleshey Castle
112 Thomas, Duke of Gloucester
Dillon, 1897, pp. 287-308

1398
Leicestershire
Barrow-on-Soar
113 John Wadyngham, clergyman, vicar of Barrow-
on-Soar
Farnham, *Quorndon*, 1912, p. 117
London
The Treasury
114 Richard, Earl of Arundel
Palgrave, 1836, III, pp. 303-307

1399
Yorkshire
Unlocated
115 Symon Lastyngham, clergyman
Stell, *York*, 2006, pp. 496-497

1400-1425 (undated)
Yorkshire
York, Monkgate
116 Rich[ard] Marshall
Arnold, 2008, p. 21

1400
Yorkshire
York
117 Thomas de Dalby, clergyman, Archdeacon of
Richmond, canon residentiary at York
Raine, *Eboracensia*, 1865, pp. 9-17
Stell, *York*, 2006, pp. 496-507

1400 (c.)
Wales
Pembrokeshire, Haverfordwest Castle
118 King Richard II
Palgrave, 1866, III, pp. 358-361

1402
Yorkshire
York
119 Geoffrey and Idonea Couper
Stell, *York*, 2006, pp. 507-508
120 John de Scardeburgh, clergyman, prebendary
Stell, *York*, 2006, pp. 508-514

1403
Cheshire
Baguley
121 William Legh
Beamont, 1885, p. 351
Kinderton
122 Sir Richard Vernon
Beamont, 1885, p. 351
Westbury, Caus Castle
123 Griffith ap Madoc
Beamont, 1885, p. 351
Yorkshire
Market Weighton
124 John de Scarle, clergyman, formerly Lord
Chancellor of England
Raine, *Eboracensia*, 1865, pp. 24-25
Stell, *York*, 2006, p. 514

1406
Co. Durham
Durham
125 Walter Skirlaw, Bishop of Durham
Raine, *Eboracensia*, 1836, pp. 317-325
London
Unlocated
126 John Olyver, draper
Thomas, *Calendar*, 1943, pp. 2-5

1409
Yorkshire
Scarborough
127 Robert Schylbotyll
Stell, *York*, 2006, pp. 525-527

1410
Yorkshire
York
128 Hugh Grantham, mason
Raine, *Eboracensia*, 1865, pp. 47-53
Stell, *York*, 2006, pp. 517-521
129 William de Kexby, clergyman, precentor of York
Raine, *Eboracensia*, 1865, pp. 44-47
Stell, *York*, 2006, pp. 514-517

1412
Co. Durham
Gainford
130 Rogerus [Roger] de Kyrkby, clergyman
Raine, *Wills and Inventories*, 1835, I, p. 56
Storey, 1957, pp. 20-21

1413
Yorkshire
York
131 Thomas Catton, weaver
Stell, *York*, 2006, pp. 521-523

1415
London
Thames Street, Scrope's Inn
132 Henry le Scrope, Lord Scrope of Masham (also
listed South Cave, Faxfleet, and Pontefract Castle, both
Yorkshire)
Kingsford, 1920, pp. 87-99

Unlocated
  133   Richard Gurmyn, baker
    Kingsford, 1920, pp. 99-100
  134   John Hexham, apothecary
    Trease and Hodson, 1965, p. 79

Yorkshire
Pontefract Castle
  Henry le Scrope, Baron Scrope of Masham (see Thames Street, London)
South Cave, Faxfleet
  Henry le Scrope, Baron Scrope of Masham (see Thames Street, London)
York
  135   Robert Talkan, girdler
    Stell, *York*, 2006, pp. 523-525

1417
Yorkshire
Wilton
  136   William Litster
    Stell, *York*, 2006, pp. 527-529

1418
Wiltshire
Lacock, Bewley Court
  137   Thomas Calston, [High Sheriff of Wiltshire]
    Harvey and Slocombe, 1987, pp. 65-67

1421
Yorkshire
York
  138   Thomas Greenwood, clergyman, canon of York
    Raine, *Eboracensia*, 1865, pp. 64-65
    Stell, *York*, 2006, pp. 529-534

1422
Yorkshire
York
  139   William Plovell, merchant
    Stell, *York*, 2006, pp. 534-535

1423
Yorkshire
York
  140   Henry Bowet, Archbishop of York
    Raine, *Eboracensia*, 1865, pp. 69-85
    Stell, *York*, 2006, pp. 535-545

1424
Berkshire
Windsor Castle
  King Henry V (see Westminster)
London
Tower of London
  King Henry V (see Westminster)
Westminster
  141   King Henry V (also listed Tower of London and Windsor, Berkshire)
    Strachey, 1767, pp. 213-242
Nottinghamshire
Misson
  142   Beatrice Clerk
    Stell, *York*, 2006, p. 552

Yorkshire
Skipton Castle (?)
  143   Elizabeth, Lady Clifford, widow
    Raine, *Eboracensia*, 1865, pp. 85-87
    Stell, *York*, 2006, pp. 545-546

1425
Norfolk
Paston
  144   William Paston and William Joye
    Gairdner, *Paston*, III, 1875, pp. 418-420

1426
Yorkshire
York
  145   John Cotom, mason
    Stell, *York*, 2006, pp. 549-550
  146   Henry Thorlthorpe, clergyman, vicar choral
    Stell, *York*, 2006, pp. 546-549

1427
Yorkshire
York
  147   William Selby
    Stell, *York*, 2006, p. 550

1428
Yorkshire
York
  148   Roger de Burton, skinner
    Stell, *York*, 2006, pp. 550-552

1429
Lancashire
Altcar
  149   John Ruggeley, abbot of Merivale, Warwickshire
    France, 1944, pp. 126-127

1430 (c.)
Yorkshire
York
  150   John Talkan, [taverner and vintner]
    Raine, *Eboracensia*, 1865, pp. 87-89

1436
Yorkshire
York
  151   Thomas Baker, stringer
    Stell, *York*, 2006, pp. 552-554

1438
Oxfordshire
Oxford, Brasenose
  152   Thomas Cooper
    Anstey, *Munimenta*, 1868, pp. 515-516
Yorkshire
Helperby
  153   Robert Conyng
    Stell, *York*, 2006, pp. 555-556
York
  154   John Bradford, mason
    Raine, *Eboracensia*, 1865, pp. 95-96
    Stell, *York*, 2006, pp. 554-555
  155   William Ledale, clergyman, chaplain
    Stell, *York*, 2006, p. 556

1439
Yorkshire
York
156 Robert Tankard, girdler
Stell, *York*, 2006, pp. 557-558

1439 (c.)
Yorkshire
Beverley
157 John Cadeby, mason
Raine, *Eboracensia*, 1865, pp. 97-101
Stell, *York*, 2006, pp. 558-560
York (?)
158 William Garton
Stell, *York*, 2006, pp. 562-563

1440
Wiltshire
Salisbury, The Old Deanery
159 The Dean of Salisbury
Drinkwater, 1964, pp. 56-58

1441
Oxfordshire
Oxford
160 Harry Keys
Anstey, *Munimenta*, 1868, p. 525

1443
Oxfordshire
Oxford
161 John Brett and Nicolas Belyane
Anstey, *Munimenta*, 1868, p. 532
Oxford, Canterbury College
162 Canterbury College
Pantin, *Canterbury College*, 1947, pp. 1-9

1444
Yorkshire
Northallerton
163 Johannes [John] Danby
Raine, *Wills and Inventories*, 1835, I, p. 90
Stell, *York*, 2006, pp. 563-565
York
164 Thomas Overdo, baker
Stell, *York*, 2006, pp. 565-567

1445
Oxfordshire
Oxford, Eagle Hall
165 James Hedyan, principal
Anstey, *Munimenta*, 1868, pp. 544-546

1446
Co. Durham
Durham
166 Prioratus Dunelm [Durham Priory]
Raine, *Wills and Inventories*, 1835, I, pp. 90-96
Yorkshire
Kirkby Sigston
167 Thomas Birdale
Stell, *York*, 2006, pp. 568-569
York
168 Thomas Gryssop, chapman
Raine, *Eboracensia*, 1865, pp. 101-105
Stell, *York*, 2006, pp. 569-573

1447
Oxfordshire
Oxford
169 Harry Layton, clergyman, chaplain
Anstey, *Munimenta*, 1868, pp. 565-566
170 John Moris, clergyman, chaplain
Anstey, *Munimenta*, 1868, pp. 566-567

1448
Hampshire
Southampton
171 Richard Thomas, merchant
Roberts and Parker, *Southampton*, I, 1992, pp. 2-10
Oxfordshire
Oxford, Broadgate's Hall
172 Ralph Dreff
Anstey, *Munimenta*, 1868, pp. 282-284
Oxford, Colsell Hall
173 Simon Beryngton
Anstey, *Munimenta*, 1868, p. 579

1449
Yorkshire
York
174 Thomas Morton, clergyman, canon residentiary
Raine, *Eboracensia*, 1865, pp. 107-111
Stell, *York*, 2006, pp. 573-579

1449 (c.)
London
Blackfriars
John, Duke of Bedford (see Walbrook)
Walbrook
175 John, Duke of Bedford (also listed Blackfriars)
Stratford, 1993, pp. 165-244

1450-1475 (undated)
Yorkshire
York
176 John Newark, [apothecary]
Arnold, 2008, p20
177 John Newark (?), [apothecary]
Arnold, 2008, p. 21

1451
Oxfordshire
Oxford
178 Henry Caldey, clergyman, vicar of Cuckfield, Sussex
Anstey, *Munimenta*, 1868, pp. 609-613
Hughes, *Sussex*, 2007, pp. 247-248
Yorkshire
Strenshall
179 Thomas Vicars, [farmer]
Raine, *Eboracensia*, 1865, pp. 118-124
Stell, *York*, 2006, pp. 583-589
York
180 John Stubbes, barber
Stell, *York*, 2006, pp. 579-583

1452

Cambridgeshire
Cambridge, Kings College
181 Robert Wodelarke, provost
Clark, 1881, pp. 289-290
Willis and Clark, 1886, pp. 350-351
Oxfordshire
Oxford, Canterbury College
182 John Style, [secular scholar?]
Pantin, *Canterbury College*, 1947, p. 80
Yorkshire
York
183 John Kexby, chancellor
Stell, *York*, 2006, pp. 589-591

1453

Oxfordshire
Oxford
184 William Mylle
Anstey, *Munimenta*, 1868, p. 658
Yorkshire
Beverley
Mr William Duffield, clergyman, canon residentiary of
York, Southwell and Beverley (see York)
Cawood
Mr William Duffield, clergyman, canon residentiary of
York, Southwell and Beverley (see York)
York
185 Mr William Duffield, clergyman, canon
residentiary of York, Southwell and Beverley (also
listed Beverley and Cawood)
Raine, *Eboracensia*, 1865, pp. 129-152
Stell, *York*, 2006, pp. 591-608

1454

Yorkshire
York
186 Thomas Peerson, toller
Stell, *York*, 2006, p. 610
187 William Welwyk, clergyman, vicar choral
Stell, *York*, 2006, p. 609

1455

Oxfordshire
Oxford, 'Vinea' Hall
188 John Lassehowe
Anstey, *Munimenta*, 1868, pp. 663-664

1456

Yorkshire
Acomb
189 John Scott
Stell, *York*, 2006, pp. 612-613
Helperby
190 William Atkynson, husbandman
Stell, *York*, 2006, pp. 610-612

1457

Worcestershire
Elmley Castle
191 Richard Sclatter
Dyer, 1989, p. 170

1458

Yorkshire
Tollerton
192 John Crosby
Stell, *York*, 2006, p. 613

1459

Norfolk
Caister
193 Sir John Fastolf
Amyot, 1827, pp. 252-279
Oxfordshire
Oxford, Canterbury College
194 William Thornden, warden
Pantin, *Canterbury College*, 1947, pp. 9-17

1460

Northamptonshire
Peterborough
195 Richard Ashton, clergyman, abbot
Myers, 1969, pp. 1146-1150
Yorkshire
Ripon
196 John Monkton
Fowler, 1874, pp. 364-365
Stell, *York*, 2006, pp. 615-616
York
197 Robert Fawcette, pewterer
Stell, *York*, 2006, pp. 613-615

1460 (c.)

Oxfordshire
Oxford, St Mary Magdalen College
198 [Richard] Bernys
Macray, 1882, p. 19

1461

Yorkshire
Dunnington
199 Emmota Cowper
Stell, *York*, 2006, p. 616
York (?)
200 Katherine North
Stell, *York*, 2006, pp. 617-618

1462 (c.)

Oxfordshire
Oxford
201 W. Lydbery, clergyman
Anstey, *Munimenta*, 1868, p. 698

1463

Oxfordshire
Oxford
202 John Hosear
Anstey, *Munimenta*, 1868, pp. 704-705
Unlocated
'litill Barw'[?]
203 No name
Anon., *Household Inventory*, 1853, pp. 101-102
Yorkshire
Huby
204 John Faysby
Stell, *York*, 2006, pp. 618-619

1464
Nottinghamshire
Southwell
William Bothe, Archbishop (see York)
Yorkshire
York
205 William Bothe, Archbishop (also listed Southwell, Nottinghamshire)
Stell, *York*, 2006, pp. 619-620

1465
Norfolk
Hellesdon
206 Sir John Paston
Gairdner, *Paston*, III, 1875, pp. 434-437

1466
Oxfordshire
Ewelme Manor
207 Alice de la Pole
Goodall, 2001, pp. 282-291
Yorkshire
York
208 Richard Hawkesworth, clergyman, vicar
Stell, *York*, 2006, pp. 622-624

1468
Yorkshire
Sewerby
209 Elizabeth Sywardby, widow
Raine, *Eboracensia*, 1865, pp. 161-168
Stell, *York*, 2006, pp. 625-630
York, Holgate
210 John Hall, husbandman
Stell, *York*, 2006, pp. 624-625

1471
Herefordshire
Unlocated
211 Dame Cecile Whityngton [Whittington]
Anon., *Whittington*, 1960, p. 251

1472
Yorkshire
York
212 William Gale
Stell, *York*, 2006, pp. 630-634
213 Johannes Pykeryng [John Pykering], clergyman
Raine, *Wills and Inventories*, 1835, I, pp. 96-97
Stell, *York*, 2006, p. 634

1473
Norfolk
Billingford
214 John Dowes [yeoman]
Calendar, Chancery, 2003, pp. 241-243

1474
Norfolk
Stokesby (?)
215 James Gloys, clergyman
Gairdner, *Paston*, III, 1875, pp. 406-411

1475
Yorkshire
York
216 John Brown
Stell, *York*, 2006, pp. 634-636

1475-1500 (undated)
Yorkshire
Ripon (?)
217 Elsabethe Lofthus and Margere Smyrthwete
Fowler, 1874, pp. 376-377

1476
Wiltshire
Salisbury
218 Richard Gilbert, gentleman
Myers, 1969, pp. 1152-1153

1477
Cheshire (?)
Chester (?)
219 Alexander Staney
Earwaker, *Lancashire and Cheshire*, 1884, pp. 1-4

1479
Essex
Marks, Dagenham
220 Sir Thomas Urswick
Steer, 1954, pp. 8-18
Nottinghamshire
Lowdham
221 William Haley
Stell, *York*, 2006, p. 460
Saundby
222 Thomas Ealmesley, clergyman, rector
Stell, *York*, 2006, p. 639
Wollaton
223 Sir Peter Legh
Stell, *York*, 2006, pp. 636-639
Yorkshire
York
224 Brian Sampall, mariner
Stell, *York*, 2006, p. 641
Swyston
225 Thomas Smyth
Stell, *York*, 2006, p. 641

1480
Nottinghamshire (?)
West Retford (?)
226 Roger Coke
Stell, *York*, 2006, p. 642
Yorkshire
York
227 Robert Danby, clergyman, vicar
Stell, *York*, 2006, pp. 642-644

1481
Yorkshire
Wharral-le-Street
228 William Acklum
Stell, *York*, 2006, pp. 644-645

York
229   William Coltman, brewer
Raine, *Eboracensia*, 1865, p. 261
Stell, *York*, 2006, pp. 645-646

1482
Yorkshire
Unlocated
230   Thomas Kirkeby
Stell, *York*, 2006, pp. 647-648

1484
Shropshire
Shrewsbury
231   The Mercers', Ironmongers' and Goldsmiths'
Company
Leighton, 1885, p. 395

1485
London
Botolph Lane
232   Marynn Conteryn [Contarini], merchant of
Venice
Nichols, *Illustrations*, 1797, pp. 118-119
Littlehales, 1905, pp. 28-29
Yorkshire
Ripon
233   Margaret Pigott
Fowler, 1874, pp. 365-376
Stell, *York*, 2006, pp. 652-657
York
234   John Carter, tailor
Raine, *Eboracensia*, 1865, pp. 300-304
Stell, *York*, 2006, pp. 648-652

1486
Yorkshire
Brompton
235   Emmota Beveryngham, widow
Stell, *York*, 2006, p. 657
236   William Fox, husbandman
Stell, *York*, 2006, p. 660
Northallerton
237   William Eryame, husbandman
Stell, *York*, 2006, pp. 659-660
238   Jacobus Lune
Stell, *York*, 2006, p. 658
York
239   William Coltman, shoemaker
Stell, *York*, 2006, pp. 658-659

1487
London
Unlocated
240   Dame Elizabeth Browne
Gairdner, *Paston*, III, 1875, pp. 463-466

1488
Hertfordshire
Standon
Robert Morton, gentleman (see London)
London
Leathersellers' Hall
241   Company of Leathersellers
Black, 1871, pp. 98-99

Unlocated
242   Robert Morton, gentleman (also listed Standon,
Hertfordshire)
Thompson, 1877, pp. 315-329
Yorkshire
Beverley
243   Thomas Creyke [Crake], gentleman (also listed
Kilham)
Raine, *Eboracensia*, 1869, pp. 34-38
Stell, *York*, 2006, pp. 660-664
Kilham
244   Thomas Creyke [Crake], gentleman (see Beverley)

1490
London
Pewterers' Hall
245   Pewterers' Company
Welch, 1902, 1, pp. 68-77
Yorkshire
Brompton
246   John Robynson
Stell, *York*, 2006, pp. 667-668
York
247   John Colan, goldsmith
Raine, *Eboracensia*, 1869, pp. 56-60
Stell, *York*, 2006, pp. 664-667
248   Thomas Symson, clergyman, parson
Stell, *York*, 2006, pp. 668-671

1491
Cambridgeshire
Cambridge
249   Thomas Nandyk, clergyman [necromancer]
Rawcliffe, 2003, pp. 392-397

1493
Northamptonshire
Great Addington
250   Henry Vere [de Vere], esquire
Kennedy, 1954, pp. 22-26

1494
Yorkshire
Bishop Burton
251   Richard Symson
Stell, *York*, 2006, pp. 673-675
York
252   John Gaythird, husbandman
Stell, *York*, 2006, pp. 671-673

1495
Hampshire
Southampton
253   Matthew Salman
Roberts and Parker, *Southampton*, I, 1992, pp. 10-11

1496
Nottinghamshire
Nottingham
254   Nicholas Atkynson
Stevenson, *Nottingham*, 1885, p. 297
Oxfordshire
Oxford, Canterbury College
255   Robert Eastry, warden
Pantin, *Canterbury College*, 1947, pp. 82-83

1497

London
Founders' Hall
  256 Company of Founders
  Williams, 1867, pp. 43-45
  Stahlschmidt, 1886, pp. 165-167
Yorkshire
Kirby Sigston
  257 John Scroby
  Stell, *York*, 2006, p. 677
Northallerton
  258 William Caype, clergyman, parson
  Stell, *York*, 2006, pp. 675-676
Unlocated
  259 Richard Barber
  Stell, *York*, 2006, pp. 677-678
West Rownton
  260 Thomas Smyth
  Stell, *York*, 2006, pp. 676-677

1498

Co. Durham
Bishop Auckland
  261 Collegii de Auckland Episcopi [Bishop Auckland College]
  Raine, *Wills and Inventories*, 1835, I, pp. 101-103
Nottinghamshire
Nottingham
  262 Thomas Balle, tailor
  Stevenson, *Nottingham*, 1885, pp. 298-299
Oxfordshire
Oxford, Beef Hall
  263 Master Richard Denbi
  Mitchell, *Registrum*, 1980, p. 201
Oxford, London College
  264 Master Newton
  Mitchell, *Registrum*, 1980, p. 201
Yorkshire
Brompton
  265 William Ryman
  Stell, *York*, 2006, p. 678
Northallerton
  266 John Stevynson, smith
  Stell, *York*, 2006, pp. 678-679

1499

Yorkshire
Bubwith
  267 William Leeke, clergyman, vicar
  Stell, *York*, 2006, p. 680
Northallerton
  268 Thomas Arkyndall
  Raine, *Wills and Inventories*, 1835, I, p. 104
  Stell, *York*, 2006, p. 679
  269 John Smyth
  Stell, *York*, 2006, p. 681
Unlocated
  270 John Artayse
  Stell, *York*, 2006, p. 682
  271 Johanna Yolson
  Stell, *York*, 2006, pp. 681-682

1500

Leicestershire
Humberstone
  272 Thomas Keble, esquire, serjeant at law
  Nichols, *Illustrations*, 1797, pp. 239-242
Oxfordshire
Oxford
  273 William Collys
  Mitchell, *Registrum*, 1980, p. 212
Oxford, Broadgates Hall
  274 Thomas Fordergill, scholar
  Mitchell, *Registrum*, 1980, pp. 212-213
Oxford
  275 Pelle, scholar
  Mitchell, *Registrum*, 1980, pp. 209-210

1500 (c.)

Yorkshire
York
  276 Rychard Bysshope [Richard Bishop]
  Raine, *Eboracensia*, 1869, pp. 191-193

1501

Oxfordshire
Oxford, Canterbury College
  277 Thomas Chaundler, warden
  Pantin, *Canterbury College*, 1947, pp. 18-33
  278 Robert Holynbourne, warden
  Pantin, *Canterbury College*, 1947, pp. 34-44
Oxford
  279 Christopher Coke, stationer
  Mitchell, *Registrum*, 1980, pp. 254-255

1502

Oxfordshire
Oxford
  280 John Fosbroke [Fossebroke]
  Mitchell, *Registrum*, 1980, pp. 283-284
  281 Peter Fourbour
  Mitchell, *Registrum*, 1980, p. 280

1503

Oxfordshire
Oxford, Broadgates Hall
  282 Otwell Erlskole
  Mitchell, *Registrum*, 1980, pp. 225-226
Oxford
  283 Thomas Pety
  Mitchell, *Registrum*, 1980, p. 225

1504

Oxfordshire
Oxford, Broadgates Hall
  284 Roger Grene, scholar
  Mitchell, *Registrum*, 1980, pp. 232-233
Oxford
  285 Richard Tomblynson, hosier
  Mitchell, *Registrum*, 1980, p. 234

1505

Oxfordshire
Oxford
  286 John Gylle
  Mitchell, *Registrum*, 1980, p. 308

1506
Oxfordshire
Oxford
  287 Robert Andrewson
    Mitchell, *Registrum*, 1980, p. 312

1507
Northamptonshire
Boddington
  288 Rychard Blande, clergyman, parson
    Peacock, 1881, p. 243

1508
London
Mercers' Hall
  289 Mercers' Company
    Lyell, 1936, p. 315
Yorkshire
York
  290 Dan Thomas Cuthbert, clergyman, fellow of St William's College
    Raine, *Eboracensia*, 1869, pp. 267-268

1509
Leicestershire
Market Harborough
  291 Agnes Smyth, widow
    Stocks and Bragg, 1890, pp. 230-234
London
Cannon Street
  292 Edmund Dudley
    Kingsford, 1921, pp. 39-42
Yorkshire
Alne
  Mr Martin Collins, clergyman, Treasurer of York (see York)
Bishop Wilton
  Mr Martin Collins, clergyman, Treasurer of York (see York)
York and York, Horsefair
  293 Mr Martin Collins, clergyman, Treasurer of York (also listed Alne and Bishop Wilton)
    Raine, *Eboracensia*, 1869, pp. 279-300

1509 (c.)
Oxfordshire
Oxford, Canterbury College
  294 Richard Stone
    Pantin, *Canterbury College*, 1947, pp. 88-90

1510
Oxfordshire
Oxford, Canterbury College
  295 Edward Bocking, warden
    Pantin, *Canterbury College*, 1947, pp. 45-55

1512
London
Merchant Taylors' Hall
  296 Merchant Taylors' Company
    Clode, 1875, pp. 84-92
Nottinghamshire
Rampton
  297 Thomas Robynete
    Kennedy, *Nottinghamshire*, 1963, pp. 6-7

Yorkshire
York
  298 William Thwaites, founder
    Raine, *Eboracensia*, 1884, pp. 35-36

1513
Essex
Castle Hedingham
  299 John de Veer, Earl of Oxford (also listed Earls Colne, and Sudbury, Suffolk)
    Hope, 1915, pp. 320-348
Earls Colne, Colne Priory
  John de Veer, Earl of Oxford (see Castle Hedingham)
Norfolk
Unlocated
  300 John West
    Bolingbroke, 1904, p. 92
Suffolk
Sudbury, Sudbury College
  John de Veer, Earl of Oxford (see Castle Hedingham, Essex)

1514
Middlesex
Hampton Court Palace
  301 Cardinal Thomas Wolsey
    Anon., *Wolsey*, 1834, p. 47
    Law, 1890, p. 343

1515
Nottinghamshire
Cropwell Bishop
  302 William Howtchenson [Huchenson]
    Kennedy, *Nottinghamshire*, 1963, pp. 7-8
Yorkshire
York
  303 Mr John Underwood, advocate
    Raine, *Eboracensia*, 1884, pp. 68-70

1516
Cheshire
Lea, Bunbury (?)
  304 Dame Christiana Calveley, widow of Sir Hugh
    Piccope, *Lancashire and Cheshire*, 1860, p. 134
Hampshire
Southampton
  305 John Davey
    Roberts and Parker, *Southampton*, I, 1992, pp. 11-13
Scotland
Invernesshire, Castle of Halhill
  306 Sir William Ogilvy of Stratherne
    Anon. *Rose*, 1848, pp. 187-191
Yorkshire
York
  307 John Tennand, founder
    Raine, *Eboracensia*, 1884, pp. 79-80

1517
London
Unlocated
  308 Pouchmakers' Company
    Black, 1871, p. 48

Scotland
Glasgow
309 John Mure of Caldwell
Dillon and Fullarton, 1831, pp. 194-196
MacGregor, 1890, pp. 233-235

1518

Derbyshire
Norbury
310 John Fitzherbert
Cox, 1885, pp. 236-239

Gloucestershire
Buckland Manor
311 James Aspery [Apperry]
Hart, 1867, pp. 302-304
Bazeley, 1884-1885, pp. 118-119

Leicestershire
Staunton Harold
312 Sir Rauff [Ralph] Shirley
Shirley, *Shirleiana*, 1873, pp. 417-426

1519

Lincolnshire
Kirton-in-Lindsey
313 Robt. Abrahm.
Peacock, 1864, pp. 501-502

Scotland
Aberdeen
314 Alexander Gordon, clergyman, bishop of
Aberdeen
Anon., *Registrum*, 1845, pp. 174-178

1520

Lancashire
Scarisbrick
315 Thomas Scharesbreke, esquire
Piccope, *Lancashire and Cheshire*, 1857, p. 187

London
Unlocated
316 Dan Thomas Goldwynne, monk
Brewer, *Letters and Papers*, 1867, pt.1, pp. 204-205
(No. 606)

1521

Buckinghamshire
Whitchurch
317 Antony Carswalle, clergyman, vicar
Woodman, 1947, pp. 311-313

Cambridgeshire
Cambridge, King's College
318 Bryan Rowe, Vice-Provost
Norton, 1954-1958, pp. 341-351

Derbyshire
Chesterfield
319 Raufe Asche
Bestall and Fowkes, *Chesterfield*, 1977, pp. 1-2

Oxfordshire
Oxford, Canterbury College
320 William Hadley, warden
Pantin, *Canterbury College*, 1947, pp. 55-65

Scotland
Stirling
321 Johen Elphinstoun
Renwick, 1887, p. 13

Suffolk
Hundon
322 Margarete Baxster
Tymms, 1850, pp. 119-121

1522

Cambridgeshire
Kirtling
323 Rici [Richard] Pythchye
Tymms, 1850, pp. 121-124

1523

Lancashire
Hornby Castle
324 Lord Mounteagle
Brewer, *Letters and Papers*, 1867, pt. 2, pp. 1253-1556
(No. 2968)

London
Unlocated
325 Robert Collyns, citizen and haberdasher
Brewer, *Letters and Papers*, 1867, pt. 2, pp. 1325-1326
(No. 3175)
Anon., *Collyns*, 1893, pp. 107-109

Somersetshire
Farleigh Hungerford Castle
Dame Agnes Hungerford, widow (see Heytesbury,
Wiltshire)

Wiltshire
Heytesbury (?)
326 Dame Agnes Hungerford, widow (also listed
Farleigh Hungerford, Somerset)
Nichols and Jackson, 1860, pp. 353-372

Yorkshire
York
327 Thomas Barton, clergyman, vicar of st Lawrence
Cross, *York*, II, 1989, pp. 6-7

1524

Oxfordshire
Oxford, Canterbury College
328 Richard Thornden, warden
Pantin, *Canterbury College*, 1947, pp. 65-72

Shropshire
Shrewsbury
329 The Mercers', Ironmongers' and Goldsmiths'
Company
Leighton, 1885, pp. 395-396

Suffolk
Framlingham Castle
330 Thomas Howard, Duke of Norfolk
Ridgard, 1985, pp. 131-158

Surrey
Lingfield
331 Lingfield College
Anon., *Lingfield*, 1843, pp. 39-42
Leveson-Gower, 1880, pp. 230-235

1525
Yorkshire
 York
 332 York
   John Grene [Greyn], glover
   Raine, *Eboracensia*, 1884, pp. 195-196
 333 York Minster
   Richard Plummar, clergyman, Master of the Choristers
   Cross, *York*, I, 1984, pp. 4-6

1525 (c.)
London
 Billingsgate (?)
 334 John Port [Porth], late the king's servant
   Nichols, *Illustrations*, 1797, pp. 119-127

1526
Gloucestershire
 Clifford Chambers
 335 William Raynesford
   Hart, 1867, pp. 310-311
   Maclean, 1889-1890, p. 62
London
 Bridewell Palace (?)
 336 Henry Fitzroy, Duke of Richmond and Somerset
   Nichols, 1855, pp. 1-21

1527
Lincolnshire
 Bilsby
 337 John Asserby, [gentleman]
   Foster, *Lincoln*, 1914, pp. 65-66

1528
Essex
 Pleshey
 338 College
   Hope and Atchley, 1920, pp. 163-172
Lincolnshire
 Conisholme
 339 John Langholm [Langham], esquire
   Foster, *Lincoln*, 1914, pp. 65-66
   Cornwall, 1974, pp. 36-38, 40
 Leverton
 340 Thomas Kecher
   Foster, *Lincoln*, 1914, pp. 85-86
London
 Clothworkers' Hall
 341 Company of Shearmen
   Wickham, 2005, pp. 19-21
Yorkshire
 Acklam
   William Melton, clergyman, Chancellor of York
   Minster (see York Minster)
 York Minster
 342 William Melton, clergyman, Chancellor of York
   Minster (also listed Acklam)
   Raine, *Eboracensia*, 1884, pp. 253-263
   Cross, *York*, I, 1984, pp. 11-25

1529
Kent
 Lewisham
 343 Dioness Gryme, widow
   Duncan, 1907, pp. 61-63

Nottinghamshire
 Beckingham
 344 Robert Hall
   Leach, 1891, pp. 135-136
 Dunham-on-Trent
 345 William Rennar [Rayner]
   Kennedy, *Nottinghamshire*, 1963, pp. 8-9
Oxfordshire
 Oxford, Canterbury College
 346 John Coles M.A., [secular sojourner]
   Pantin, *Canterbury College*, 1947, pp. 93-95

1530
Lincolnshire
 Stainfield
 347 Robert Covell
   Foster, *Lincoln*, 1927, p. 74

1530 (c.)
Lancashire (?)
 Unlocated
 348 Edward Lord
   Raine, *Richmond*, 1853, p. 10
Nottinghamshire
 Unlocated
 349 John Leeke
   Kennedy, *Nottinghamshire*, 1963, pp. 10-12
Worcestershire
 Evesham, Hampton
 350 William Patewyn, clergyman, vicar of Hampton
   Knapp, 1914, pp. 195-199

1531
Devonshire
 Unlocated
 351 [Richard] Poke
   Cash, *Devon*, 1966, p. 1
Lincolnshire
 Quadring
 352 John Goodall
   Foster, *Lincoln*, 1927, pp. 98-99
Oxfordshire
 Oxford
 353 Robert Carow, carpenter
   Harvey, *Mediaeval Craftsmen*, 1975, pp. 200-202
Yorkshire
 Worsall
 354 Johannes [John] Sayer, esquire
   Raine, *Wills and Inventories*, 1835, I, pp. 109-110
 York, St Michael-le-Belfry
 355 Robert Locksmith, vestment maker
   Raine, *Eboracensia*, 1884, p. 324

1531 (?)
London
 Unlocated
 356 John Porth, King's Servant
   Littlehales, 1905, pp. 36-50

1532
Kent
 Leeds Castle
 357 Sir Henry Guldeforde [Guildford], Controller of
   the Kings Household
   Robertson, 1883, pp. 382-385

Lincolnshire
Fosdyke
358 Jacobus [James] Hartley
Foster, *Lincoln*, 1927, pp. 227-228
Market Rasen
359 Richard Vassell
Neave, *Market Rasen*, 1985, p. 42
Pinchbeck
360 Jane Hunte
Foster, *Lincoln*, 1927, p. 105
Nottinghamshire
Southwell (?)
361 John Saunsum
Kennedy, *Nottinghamshire*, 1963, pp. 12-13
Worcestershire
Crowle
362 Wm More, [clergyman, Prior of Worcester]
Noake, 1866, pp. 156-157

1533

Cumberland
Muncaster Castle
363 Sir William Pennington
Raine, *Richmond*, 1853, pp. 10-11
Derbyshire
Chesterfield
364 Elsabeth Laurens, widow
Bestall and Fowkes, *Chesterfield*, 1977, p. 3
Leicestershire
Braunstone
365 Elizabeth Walinggar, widow
Wilshere, *Braunstone*, 1983, p. 1
Shropshire
Hodnet
366 Raphe Bostocke
Phillips, 1900, p. 195

1534

Derbyshire
Walton
367 Thomas Ellyott
Bestall and Fowkes, *Chesterfield*, 1977, pp. 4-5
Kent
Canterbury, St Saviour's
368 Elysabeth Barton, nun
Wright, 1843, p. 26
Halling, Manor
Cardinal John Fisher, Bishop of Rochester (see Rochester)
Rochester, Bishop's Palace
369 Cardinal John Fisher, Bishop of Rochester (also listed Halling)
Peacock, 1870-1873, pp. 296-299
Gairdner, *Letters and Papers*, 1883, pp. 221-222, No. 557
London
Brooke House, Hackney
370 Henry VIII
Draper, *Brooke House*, 1960, pp. 76-78
Oxfordshire
Oxford, Canterbury College
371 William Sandwich, warden
Pantin, *Canterbury College*, 1947, pp. 72-76

1535

Derbyshire
Chesterfield
372 Agnes Holme
Bestall and Fowkes, *Chesterfield*, 1977, pp. 6-7
373 John Poynton
Bestall and Fowkes, *Chesterfield*, 1977, p. 6
London
Brooke House, Hackney
374 Henry VIII
Draper, *Brooke House*, 1960, pp. 78-79
Yorkshire
Mappleton
375 John Baron
Raine, *Richmond*, 1853, p. 12
York
376 Richard Oliver, clergyman, vicar of All Saints, North Street
Cross, *York*, II, 1989, pp. 14-16

1536

Derbyshire
Calow
377 Richard Watson
Bestall and Fowkes, *Chesterfield*, 1977, pp. 9-10
Chesterfield
378 John Crosland
Bestall and Fowkes, *Chesterfield*, 1977, pp. 8-9
379 Richard Wedoson
Bestall and Fowkes, *Chesterfield*, 1977, pp. 12-14
Dunston
380 Thomas Legge
Bestall and Fowkes, *Chesterfield*, 1977, p. 11
Newbold
381 Thomas Foxe
Bestall and Fowkes, *Chesterfield*, 1977, p. 12
Leicestershire
Leicester
382 William Wigston, merchant
Thompson, 1933, pp. 39-46
Wales
Lamphey, Pembrokeshire
383 Richard Rawlins, bishop of St David's
Gairdner, *Letters and Papers*, 1887, pp. 173-176 (No. 431)
Warwickshire
Coventry
384 John Dudley, [draper]
Hulton and Castle, *Tudor*, 1987, pp. 4-6
Foleshill
385 Thomas Cartwryghte
Upton, *Foleshill*, 1993, pp. 5-6
386 Willm Whittmay
Upton, *Foleshill*, 1993, pp. 3-4
Worcestershire
Huddington
387 Roger Wynter [Wintour], esquire
Wanklyn, *Worcestershire*, 1998, pp. 1-6

1536 (c.)
Lincolnshire
Legbourne
  388 Nunnery (also listed Somercotes)
    Whitworth, 1958, pp. 32-38
Somercotes
  Legbourne Nunnery (see Legbourne)

1537
Derbyshire
Brimington
  389 Olyver Wostenem
    Bestall and Fowkes, *Chesterfield*, 1977, pp. 14-15
Chesterfield
  390 John Modson [Mordson]
    Bestall and Fowkes, *Chesterfield*, 1977, p. 16
  391 Henry Rensha'
    Bestall and Fowkes, *Chesterfield*, 1977, p. 17
Walton
  392 Katheryn Elyote, widow
    Bestall and Fowkes, *Chesterfield*, 1977, pp. 15-16
Lancashire
Whalley Abbey
  393 Abbot's House
    Whitaker, 1874, pp. 185-188
Lincolnshire
Clee
  394 Wylyam [William] Stapylls
    Ambler, Watkinson, *Clee*, 1987, p. 42
Market Rasen
  395 Johne Watson
    Neave, *Market Rasen*, 1985, p. 43
London
Baynard's Castle
  396 Katharine of Aragon, Princess Dowager
    Nichols, 1855, pp. 23-41
Warwickshire
Stoneleigh
  397 John Allyt, weaver
    Alcock, *Warwickshire*, 1993, pp. 31-32
Worcestershire
Hartlebury
  398 John Hornyholde [Horniold], gentleman
    Wanklyn, *Worcestershire*, 1998, pp. 6-10

1538
Derbyshire
Chesterfield
  399 Rychard Alwodd, butcher
    Bestall and Fowkes, *Chesterfield*, 1977, pp. 19-21
  400 Nicholas Helle
    Bestall and Fowkes, *Chesterfield*, 1977, p. 19
  401 Richard Shemeld
    Bestall and Fowkes, *Chesterfield*, 1977, p. 18
Leicestershire
Braunstone
  402 Wyllym Halyday
    Wilshere, *Braunstone*, 1983, p. 1
Lincolnshire
Clee
  403 John Masson
    Ambler, Watkinson, *Clee*, 1987, pp. 42-43

London
Unlocated
  404 John Rastell, citizen and stationer
    Roberts, 1979, pp. 35-36
Nottinghamshire
North Leverton
  405 Henrie Doggson
    Kennedy, *Nottinghamshire*, 1963, p. 29
Warwickshire
Shottery
  406 Richard Burman
    Jones, *Stratford*, I, 2002, p. 4
Stratford-on-Avon
  407 Isabell Androws [Isabel Andrew]
    Jones, *Stratford*, I, 2002, p. 8
  408 John a Charley
    Jones, *Stratford*, I, 2002, p. 7
  409 William Feysye
    Jones, *Stratford*, I, 2002, pp. 5-6
  410 Robart Myddelltonne [Robert Middleton], clergyman, chanter of the College of Stratford
    Jones, *Stratford*, I, 2002, p. 3
Yorkshire
Grinton
  411 Raulfe Pacoke [Paycok]
    Raine, *Richmond*, 1853, p. 15
York Minster
  412 Henry Gelsthrop, clergyman, chantry priest in York Minster
    Cross, *York*, I, 1984, pp. 34-35

1539
Derbyshire
Chesterfield
  413 Roger Bakeley
    Bestall and Fowkes, *Chesterfield*, 1977, p. 21
Gloucestershire
Frampton Cotterell
  414 Henry Dagge, [husbandman]
    Moore, *Frampton Cotterell*, 1976, p. 39
Stoke Gifford
  415 William Merycke, weaver
    Moore, *Frampton Cotterell*, 1976, p. 39
Northumberland
Berwick-on-Tweed, Berwick Castle
  416 Sir Thomas Clifford
    Smith, 1794, pp. 435-440
Nottinghamshire
Rampton
  417 Robert Whitmore, gentleman
    Kennedy, *Nottinghamshire*, 1963, pp. 27-28
Scotland
Edinburgh (?)
  418 James V of Scotland
    Thomson, *Edinburgh*, 1815, pp. 31-54
Yorkshire
Dewsbury
  Edward Kellett [Calet], clergyman, Precentor of York Minster (see York Minster)
Grinton
  419 Ralph Pacoke
    Berry, *Swaledale*, 1998, p. 52

York Minster
420 Edward Kellett [Calet], clergyman, Precentor of York Minster (also listed Dewsbury)
Cross, *York*, I, 1984, pp. 38-45

1540

Derbyshire
Glossop
421 Raffe Andrew
Bryant, Lee, Miller, *New Mills*, I, 1995, p. 4

France
Calais
422 Arthur Plantagenet, Viscount Lisle
Byrne, 1981, pp. 189-210

Ireland
Dublin, St Mary's Abbey
423 Lord Leonard Grey, late Lord Deputy (also listed Maynooth)
Pinkerton, 1859, pp. 202-211
Co. Kildare, Maynooth
Lord Leonard Grey, late Lord Deputy (see Dublin)

Leicestershire
Quorndon
424 Joan Wamysley
Farnham, *Quorndon*, 1912, p. 196

Lincolnshire
Clee
425 Christopher Johnson
Ambler, Watkinson, *Clee*, 1987, pp. 43-44
426 Henry Mason
Ambler, Watkinson, *Clee*, 1987, p. 43

London
Blackfriars
Sir Adrian Fortescue (see Shirburn Castle, Oxfordshire)

Nottinghamshire
Darlton
427 Robert Cosen
Kennedy, *Nottinghamshire*, 1963, pp. 31-32
North Leverton
428 Agnes Mowre
Kennedy, *Nottinghamshire*, 1963, pp. 30-31
Unlocated
429 John Barnebie
Kennedy, *Nottinghamshire*, 1963, p. 30

Oxfordshire
Shirburn Castle
430 Sir Adrian Fortescue (also listed Blackfriars, London)
Clermont, 1869, pp. 216-233

Worcestershire
Belbroughton, Forfield
431 Johannes Wheler
Roper, *Belbroughton*, 1967-1968, p. 1

Yorkshire
York Minster
432 William Crosby, clergyman, vicar choral
Cross, *York*, I, 1984, pp. 46-47

1540 (c.)

Nottinghamshire
Beckingham
433 William Hall
Kennedy, *Nottinghamshire*, 1963, pp. 28-29

434 Gilbert Walshame
Kennedy, *Nottinghamshire*, 1963, pp. 32-33

1541

Cambridgeshire
Cambridge, St John's College
435 Leonard Metcalfe
Cooper, 1842, pp. 398-399

Cheshire
Bramhall
436 William Davenport, esquire
Piccope, *Lancashire and Cheshire*, 1857, pp. 19-81
Chester
437 Thomas Clarke, clergyman, dean of Chester
Piccope, *Lancashire and Cheshire*, 1857, pp. 126-130

Derbyshire
Brimington
438 William Bradbere
Bestall and Fowkes, *Chesterfield*, 1977, pp. 21-22
439 John Spitillous
Bestall and Fowkes, *Chesterfield*, 1977, pp. 22-23
Chesterfield
440 Robert Eyre, clergyman
Bestall and Fowkes, *Chesterfield*, 1977, p. 23

Hampshire
The Vyne
441 Sir William Sandys, Baron Sandys
Howard and Wilson, *Vyne*, 2003, pp. 142-155

Lancashire
Dalton in Furness
442 Roger Peles, clergyman, parson of Dalton in Furness
Raine, *Richmond*, 1853, pp. 21-23

Leicestershire
Great Stretton
443 John Marsthall
Wilshere, *Great Stretton*, 1984, p. 15

Lincolnshire
Clee
444 Wylm [William] Colbes
Ambler, Watkinson, *Clee*, 1987, p. 44

Norfolk
Kenninghall
445 Robt. Seffrey
Rye, 1889-1890, p. 378

Nottinghamshire
Unlocated
446 Thomas Goodhyne, [wheelwright]
Kennedy, *Nottinghamshire*, 1963, p. 36

Worcestershire
Belbroughton
447 John Waldern, [scythesmith]
Roper, *Scythesmiths*, 1967, p. 8
Roper, *Belbroughton*, 1967-1968, p. 2
Cotheridge
448 John Ketelby, esquire
Wanklyn, *Worcestershire*, 1998, pp. 10-13
Kidderminster
449 Nicholas Wright, clergyman, chaplain of St Mary's Chantry
Roper, *Worcestershire*, 1972, p. 1

Yorkshire
Grinton, Oxnop
450 Thomas Parkk
Berry, *Swaledale*, 1998, pp. 54-55

1542
Bristol
Bristol, St Mark
451 John Gorwey
George, *Bristol*, 1, 2002, pp. 1-2
Cumberland
Carlisle, Stanwix
452 Izabel Lynschall
Raine, *Richmond*, 1853, p. 27
Derbyshire
Findern
453 Humfry Howdyn
Holden, 1930, pp. 10-11
Leicestershire
Braunstone
454 Wyllyam Gregore
Wilshere, *Braunstone*, 1983, p. 2
Glenfield
455 Roger Gaylard
Wilshere, *Glenfield*, 1983, p. 1.
Quorndon
456 William Hebbe
Farnham, *Quorndon*, 1912, p. 200
London
Whitehall Palace
457 Henry VIII
Hayward, *Whitehall*, 2004, II, pp. 15-270
Nottinghamshire
Darlton
458 John Tailyor
Kennedy, *Nottinghamshire*, 1963, pp. 33-34
Dunham-on-Trent
459 Robert Wode
Kennedy, *Nottinghamshire*, 1963, p. 35
Upton
460 Richard Smythe
Kennedy, *Nottinghamshire*, 1963, p. 13
Scotland
Edinburgh
461 James V of Scotland
Thomson, *Edinburgh*, 1815, pp. 57-106
Surrey
Sutton Place
462 Sir Richard Weston (also listed West Clandon)
Harrison, 1893, pp. 206-213
West Clandon
Sir Richard Weston (see Sutton Place)
Westmorland
Witherslack
463 Edmunde Peresone, tanner
Raine, *Richmond*, 1853, pp. 28-29
Yorkshire
Barton, Bretaneby
464 Wyllyam Witheman, gentleman (also listed Thicket)
Raine, *Richmond*, 1853, pp. 41-42

Bretton Hall
465 Sir Thomas Wentworth
Brears, *Yorkshire*, 1972, pp. 2-3
Marske
466 Phyllis Bukden
Berry, *Swaledale*, 1998, p. 58
Thicket
Wylliam Witheman, gentleman (see Barton, Bretaneby)

1542 (c.)
Derbyshire
Chesterfield
467 Jamys Durrant, gentleman
Bestall and Fowkes, *Chesterfield*, 1977, pp. 24-25

1543
Cheshire
Wrenbury
468 John Starkie, esquire
Pixton, *Wrenbury*, 2009, pp. 3-5
Derbyshire
Chesterfield
469 Henry Tryge, clergyman
Bestall and Fowkes, *Chesterfield*, 1977, pp. 25-26
470 Francis Wright
Bestall and Fowkes, *Chesterfield*, 1977, p. 27
Essex
Blackmore [Smyth's Hall]
471 John Smyth, esquire
King, 1865, pp. 60-62
Leicestershire
Houghton on the Hill
472 Jhon Hereke [Herrick]
Fletcher, 1888, pp. 128-129
Lincolnshire
Market Rasen
473 Hugt [Hugh] Saynton
Neave, *Market Rasen*, 1985, p. 44
London
Unlocated
474 Elizabeth Barton, widow
Darlington, *London*, 1967, pp. 99-100
475 Katheryne Brase, widow
Darlington, *London*, 1967, pp. 102-107
476 Robert Fosster, tailor
Darlington, *London*, 1967, pp. 86-87
477 Phillip Hampton
Darlington, *London*, 1967, pp. 113-114
478 Johanne Hawdy, widow
Darlington, *London*, 1967, pp. 97-98
479 Wylyam Massyngere
Darlington, *London*, 1967, pp. 88-89
480 Bartellmu Mere, woolpacker
Darlington, *London*, 1967, pp. 114-116
481 Jhon Pattryck, [porter of the King's Wardrobe]
Darlington, *London*, 1967, pp. 117-119
482 Rychard Pendryth
Darlington, *London*, 1967, p. 90
483 Cescle [Cecylye] Whaplyt
Darlington, *London*, 1967, p. 95
484 Joone Wharnby
Darlington, *London*, 1967, pp. 123-124

Wood Street
485 Ame Ryan, widow
Darlington, *London*, 1967, p. 121

Nottinghamshire
Cropwell Bishop
486 William Fox
Kennedy, *Nottinghamshire*, 1963, pp. 36-37
Ragnall
487 Richard Hawkesmore
Kennedy, *Nottinghamshire*, 1963, p. 37
Southwell
488 Gilbert Byrkhed
Kennedy, *Nottinghamshire*, 1963, p. 14

Westmorland
Bradleyfield
489 James Layburne
Raine, *Richmond*, 1853, p. 39
Kirkby Lonsdale
490 Edward Mansarghe [Mansergh]
Raine, *Richmond*, 1853, p. 38
Skelsmergh
491 Edward Pykerynge
Raine, *Richmond*, 1853, p. 35

Yorkshire
Bedale
492 Thomas Walker
Raine, *Richmond*, 1853, pp. 30-31
Marrick
493 John Tiplady
Berry, *Swaledale*, 1998, p. 60
Ripley
494 Alysander Atkinson
Raine, *Richmond*, 1853, pp. 43-44
York Minster
495 John Chambre, clergyman, succentor of the vicars choral
Cross, *York*, I, 1984, pp. 55-56

1543 (c.)

Nottinghamshire
Beckingham
496 Robert Hayles
Kennedy, *Nottinghamshire*, 1963, pp. 38-39
Dunham-on-Trent
497 Alice Wode
Kennedy, *Nottinghamshire*, 1963, p. 38
South Muskham
498 Master Guye Fairfax, esquire
Kennedy, *Nottinghamshire*, 1963, pp. 40-42

1544

Co. Durham
Egglescliffe
499 Barthe Paige [Bartholomew Page]
Hodgson, *Wills and Inventories*, 1906, III, p. 3

Co. Durham (?)
Unlocated
500 Annes Horsley
Raine, *Wills and Inventories*, 1835, I, pp. 121-122

Hampshire
Southampton
501 Richard Smith
Roberts and Parker, *Southampton*, I, 1992, pp. 13-15

Lancashire
Osbaldeston
502 Sir Alexander Osbaldeston
Piccope, *Lancashire and Cheshire*, 1860, pp. 52-55

Lincolnshire
Clee
503 Harry Barthylimew
Ambler, Watkinson, *Clee*, 1987, pp. 44-45
Clee, Itterby
504 Harry Humfre
Ambler, Watkinson, *Clee*, 1987, p. 45

London
Unlocated
505 Anys Borde
Darlington, *London*, 1967, pp. 125-126
506 Jasper Hylltreman, Dutchman, shoemaker
Darlington, *London*, 1967, pp. 130-131
507 Rychard Wycherley
Darlington, *London*, 1967, p. 140

Nottinghamshire
North Leverton, Coates
508 Alexander Garthe
Kennedy, *Nottinghamshire*, 1963, pp. 42-43
Rampton
509 Thomas Couper
Kennedy, *Nottinghamshire*, 1963, pp. 44-45

Staffordshire
Dudley
510 John Sowthall
Roper, *Dudley*, 1965, p. 1

Surrey
Lingfield
511 Lingfield College
Leveson-Gower, 1880, pp. 236-245

Warwickshire
Foleshill
512 Willya[m] Amorson, clergyman, curate of Foleshill
Upton, *Foleshill*, 1993, pp. 7-8
513 John Hatton
Upton, *Foleshill*, 1993, p. 12

Worcestershire
Belbroughton
514 Raffe Coll
Roper, *Belbroughton*, 1967-1968, pp. 5-6
Bredicot
515 Henry More, clergyman, rector of Bredicot
Roper, *Worcestershire*, 1972, p. 2
Cropthorne
516 William Cowghton, clergyman
Roper, *Worcestershire*, 1972, p. 3
Dodderhill, Wych, The Hill
517 Thomas Langthorne, clergyman, vicar
Roper, *Worcestershire*, 1972, pp. 3-4
Stourbridge, Old Swinford
518 Thomas Grene
Hatcher and Barker, *Pewter*, 1974, p. 98
Worcester, St Peter's
519 Thomas Strobyge, clergyman
Roper, *Worcestershire*, 1972, pp. 4-5

Yorkshire
Grinton
520   William Blaydes
Berry, *Swaledale*, 1998, p. 82
York Minster
521   Richard Layton, clergyman, dean of York
Cross, *York*, I, 1984, pp. 57-64

1544 (c.)

Nottinghamshire
North Leverton
522   John Boythbie
Kennedy, *Nottinghamshire*, 1963, pp. 43-44

1545

Derbyshire
Markeaton Hall
523   Vincent Mundy, esquire
Clark-Maxwell, 1930, pp. 124-134
Hampshire
Winchester
524   Arthur Robys, alderman
Walcott, 1871-2, pp. 86-87
Hertfordshire
St Albans, Burston
525   William Cockes
Munby, *Worldly Goods*, 1991, p. 16
St Albans, St Stephens
526   Marg[er]y Wylcokkes, widow
Parker, *Worldly Goods*, 2004, pp. 29-30
London
Unlocated
527   Elizabeth Foxe, [widow]
Darlington, *London*, 1967, p. 144
Northumberland
Holy Island
528   John Hymers
Raine, *Wills and Inventories*, 1835, I, p. 114
Nottinghamshire
Farnsfield
529   Richard Bary [Barrye]
Kennedy, *Nottinghamshire*, 1963, pp. 16-18
Halam
530   John Atkynson
Kennedy, *Nottinghamshire*, 1963, pp. 14-16
531   Henry Waryn
Kennedy, *Nottinghamshire*, 1963, pp. 19-20
North Leverton
532   James Nightgale
Kennedy, *Nottinghamshire*, 1963, pp. 45-46
Rampton
533   Richard Sobie
Kennedy, *Nottinghamshire*, 1963, pp. 46-47
Southwell
534   Henry Luddelam
Kennedy, *Nottinghamshire*, 1963, p. 19
Worcestershire
Hadzor
535   Thomas Mountford [Mumford] (?), clergyman
Roper, *Worcestershire*, 1972, pp. 7-8
Halesowen
536   William Taylor, clergyman, [last abbot]
Roper, *Worcestershire*, 1972, pp. 5-6

Upton Snodsbury
537   Raffe Myston, clergyman, vicar of Upton
Snodsbury
Roper, *Worcestershire*, 1972, p. 9
Worcester, St Peter's
538   Humfry Fawnes, clergyman
Roper, *Worcestershire*, 1972, p. 11
Worcester, St Helen's
539   Hugh Whytbroke, [saddler]
Dyer, *Worcestershire*, 1967, pp. 32-37
Yorkshire
Barton, Bretaneby
540   Mathew Witham
Raine, *Richmond*, 1853, p. 57
Brignall
541   Christofer Thomsonn, clergyman, vicar of
Brignall
Raine, *Richmond*, 1853, pp. 52-53
Cundall
542   William Clowdesleye, clergyman
Raine, *Richmond*, 1853, pp. 54-55
Grinton, Muker
543   Edmond Mylner [Milner]
Berry, *Swaledale*, 1998, pp. 62-63
Marrick
544   William Metcalf
Berry, *Swaledale*, 1998, p. 61
Westerdale
545   Thomas Yoward
Crossley, *Yorkshire*, 1929, p. 55
York
546   William Vavisoure [Vavasour], clergyman, St
Mary Bishophill
Cross, *York*, II, 1989, pp. 35-36

1545 (c.)

Nottinghamshire
South Muskham
547   William Aston
Kennedy, *Nottinghamshire*, 1963, pp. 47-48
Unlocated
548   Gregory Barton
Kennedy, *Nottinghamshire*, 1963, p. 18
549   Thomas Clarke (?)
Kennedy, *Nottinghamshire*, 1963, pp. 20-22

1546

Cambridgeshire
Cambridge, St Sepulchre's
550   Peter Bright, [stationer]
Gray and Palmer, *Cambridge*, 1915, pp. 6-10
Cambridge, Great St Mary's
551   Nicholas Pilgrim, [stationer and binder]
Gray and Palmer, *Cambridge*, 1915, pp. 11-29
Derbyshire
Chesterfield
552   James Boler
Bestall and Fowkes, *Chesterfield*, 1977, pp. 28-30
553   John Lyndoppe
Bestall and Fowkes, *Chesterfield*, 1977, pp. 27-28
Hertfordshire
St Albans, St Stephens
554   Wyllyam Wyls[here]
Parker, *Worldly Goods*, 2004, p. 32

Lincolnshire
Bicker
   555 Robert Todd [Toode], [yeoman]
   Peacock, 1871-2, pp. 150-151
Clee
   556 Wyllm [William] Coke, husbandman
   Ambler, Watkinson, *Clee*, 1987, p. 46
Clee, Oole
   557 Jhon Frele
   Ambler, Watkinson, *Clee*, 1987, pp. 45-46
Clee
   558 William Homptone
   Ambler, Watkinson, *Clee*, 1987, pp. 47-48
   559 Jenott Ranneor, widow
   Ambler, Watkinson, *Clee*, 1987, p. 47
Clee, Oole
   560 Anne Swadall
   Ambler, Watkinson, *Clee*, 1987, p. 47
London
Near the Tower
   561 Hospital of St Katherine
   Hope, 1890, pp. 151-157
Nottinghamshire
Edingley, Greaves Lane
   562 Margerie Cowper
   Kennedy, *Nottinghamshire*, 1963, p. 22
Halam
   563 John Wattes
   Kennedy, *Nottinghamshire*, 1963, p. 24
North Leverton
   564 William Calton
   Kennedy, *Nottinghamshire*, 1963, pp. 48-49
Rampton (?)
   565 John Cotham
   Kennedy, *Nottinghamshire*, 1963, pp. 49-50
Warwickshire
Coventry
   566 Joan Dudley, [widow]
   Hulton and Castle, *Tudor*, 1987, pp. 11-15
Warwick, St Nicholas
   567 John Eberall
   Sheasby, 1994, pp. 44-45
Worcestershire
Evesham St Lawrence
   568 Edmonde Feelde, clergyman, vicar of St Lawrence
   Roper, *Worcestershire*, 1972, p. 13
Huddington (?)
   569 William Blackemore, clergyman
   Roper, *Worcestershire*, 1972, pp. 9-10
Unlocated
   570 John Athorne, clergyman
   Roper, *Worcestershire*, 1972, pp. 11-12
Yorkshire
York
   571 George Bellerbie, clergyman, rector of St Wilfrid's
   Cross, *York*, II, 1989, pp. 39-40

1546 (c.)
Nottinghamshire
Ragnall
   572 Richard Fox
   Kennedy, *Nottinghamshire*, 1963, p. 25
South Wheatley
   573 Richard Bowthe
   Kennedy, *Nottinghamshire*, 1963, pp. 50-51

1547
Berkshire
Windsor Castle
   Henry VIII (see Whitehall, London)
Cambridgeshire
Cambridge, St John's College
   574 Master's Lodge
   Willis and Clark, 1886, pp. 351-352
Derbyshire
Chesterfield
   575 Thomas Boithies
   Bestall and Fowkes, *Chesterfield*, 1977, pp. 30-31
Co. Durham
Stanhope, Weardale
   576 Lionell [Lionel] Wall, smith
   Raine, *Wills and Inventories*, 1835, I, p. 128
Essex
New Hall (Beaulieu)
   Henry VIII (see Whitehall, London)
Hertfordshire
The More
   Henry VIII (see Whitehall, London)
Kent
Greenwich
   Henry VIII (see Whitehall, London)
Leicestershire
Braunstone
   577 Thomas Yng
   Wilshere, *Braunstone*, 1983, p. 2
Great Stretton
   578 Thoms. Eiton
   Wilshere, *Great Stretton*, 1984, p. 15
Kirby Muxloe
   579 Annys King
   Wilshere, *Kirby Muxloe*, 1983, p. 1
Lincolnshire
Market Rasen
   580 Robt. Mosy
   Neave, *Market Rasen*, 1985, p. 45
   581 Wyllm Neyffe
   Neave, *Market Rasen*, 1985, p. 45
London
Durham Place
   Henry VIII (see Whitehall)
St James's Palace
   Henry VIII (see Whitehall)
St John's Clerkenwell
   Henry VIII (see Whitehall)
Tower of London
   Henry VIII (see Whitehall)
Whitehall (Westminster) Palace
   582 Henry VIII (also listed Durham Place, St James's
   Palace, St John's Clerkenwell,
   Tower of London, and Windsor Castle, Berkshire, New
   Hall (Beaulieu), Essex, The
   More, Hertfordshire, Greenwich, Kent, Hampton
   Court, Middlesex, Nottingham
   Castle, Nottingham, Woodstock, Oxfordshire, and
   Beddington, Nonsuch, Oatlands
   and Richmond, all Surrey)
   Starkey, *Henry VIII*, 1998

Lincolnshire
Clee
583 Thomas Ramsay
Ambler, Watkinson, *Clee*, 1987, pp. 48-49
Middlesex
Hampton Court
Henry VIII (see Whitehall, London)
Nottinghamshire
Cropwell Bishop
584 Richard and Alice Huchenson
Kennedy, *Nottinghamshire*, 1963, pp. 51-52
Nottingham Castle
Henry VIII (see Whitehall, London)
Southwell
585 Richard Dykson
Kennedy, *Nottinghamshire*, 1963, p. 23
586 John Payne
Kennedy, *Nottinghamshire*, 1963, pp. 23-24
Oxfordshire
Woodstock
Henry VIII (see Whitehall, London)
Surrey
Beddington
Henry VIII (see Whitehall, London)
Nonsuch
Henry VIII (see Whitehall, London)
Oatlands
Henry VIII (see Whitehall, London)
Richmond
Henry VIII (see Whitehall, London)
Warwickshire
Foleshill
587 Nycholas Pawfreyma[n]
Upton, *Foleshill*, 1993, pp. 9-10
Yorkshire
East Cowton
588 Wylliam Wylde
Raine, *Richmond*, 1853, p. 66
Escrick
Thomas Marser, clergyman, Prebendary of Langtoft
(see York Minster)
Grinton, Low Whitaside
589 George Carter
Berry, *Swaledale*, 1998, p. 65
Westerdale
590 Isabell Wylson
Crossley, *Yorkshire*, 1929, p. 51
York Minster
591 John Hixon, clergyman, chantry priest in York
Minster
Cross, *York*, I, 1984, pp. 78-79
592 Thomas Marser, clergyman, Prebendary of
Langtoft (also listed Escrick)
Cross, *York*, I, 1984, pp. 70-76
York
593 John Watson, clergyman, chantry priest of St
Saviour's
Cross, *York*, II, 1989, pp. 42-43

1548
Derbyshire
Brimington
594 Phelep Madyn
Bestall and Fowkes, *Chesterfield*, 1977, p. 31

Hampshire
Southampton
595 Walter Forward, tallow chandler
Roberts and Parker, *Southampton*, I, 1992, pp. 15-18
596 Nicholas Garnesay
Roberts and Parker, *Southampton*, I, 1992, pp. 18-19
597 William Pecock, yeoman
Roberts and Parker, *Southampton*, I, 1992, p. 20
Hertfordshire
St Albans, St Stephens
598 Thomas Heywarde, labourer
Parker, *Worldly Goods*, 2004, p. 33
St Albans, St Stephens, Park Street
599 Thomas Nuttkyn
Parker, *Worldly Goods*, 2004, pp. 34-36
Ireland
Cork
600 [William Fitz Edmund] Roche, [merchant]
Caulfield, *Cork*, 1861-1862, p. 166 (1862)
Lancashire
Rossendale
601 George Gregore [Gregory], clergyman
Piccope, *Lancashire and Cheshire*, 1860, pp. 200-201
Northumberland
Morpeth
602 Thomas Schaffto
Raine, *Wills and Inventories*, 1835, I, p. 129-130
Newcastle
603 Thomas Stantone
Hodgson, *Wills and Inventories*, 1906, III, pp. 5-6
Suffolk
Mendham Hall
604 Princess Mary Tudor
Fitch, 1859, pp. 243-247
Wales
Presteigne, Powys (formerly Radnorshire)
605 John ap Jevan a Meyryck
Cole, 1956, p. 29
Worcestershire
Cotheridge
606 Margery Ketylby [Ketelby], gentlewoman
Wanklyn, *Worcestershire*, 1998, pp. 13-18
Grafton
607 Sir John Talbott [Talbot]
Wanklyn, *Worcestershire*, 1998, pp. 19-20
Peopleton
608 John Yate, clergyman, curate of Peopleton
Roper, *Worcestershire*, 1972, p. 12

1549
Derbyshire
Brimington
609 Robert Brook
Bestall and Fowkes, *Chesterfield*, 1977, p. 32
Chesterfield
610 Alese Rotheram
Bestall and Fowkes, *Chesterfield*, 1977, pp. 32-33
Hampshire
Southampton
611 Henry Clark, mariner
Roberts and Parker, *Southampton*, I, 1992, pp. 20-22
612 John Newton, clergyman, parson of St John's
Roberts and Parker, *Southampton*, I, 1992, pp. 22-23

613 Richard Stockdale
  Roberts and Parker, *Southampton*, I, 1992, pp. 23-28
Lancashire
Smithills Hall, Bolton
  614 Andrew Barton, esquire
  Piccope, *Lancashire and Cheshire*, 1860, pp. 102-103
  Bolton, *Bolton*, 1987, pp. 23-24
Lincolnshire
Clee, Itterby
  615 Dorythe Colman
  Ambler, Watkinson, *Clee*, 1987, p. 49
Market Rasen
  616 Margret Byllyngay
  Neave, *Market Rasen*, 1985, p. 47
  617 Thomas Lamkyn
  Neave, *Market Rasen*, 1985, p. 46
Norfolk
Norwich
  618 Sir Robert Townsend
  Moreton, 1993, pp. 393-398
Sussex
Chesworth Manor
  619 Thomas, Lord Seymour, Lord High Admiral (also
  listed Sheffield Manor and Worth Forest)
  Ellis, 1861, pp. 120-131
Sheffield Manor
  Thomas, Lord Seymour, Lord High Admiral (see
  Chesworth Manor)
Worth Forest
  Thomas, Lord Seymour, Lord High Admiral (see
  Chesworth Manor)
Yorkshire
Grinton, [Whitaside]
  620 Anthony Bradryke
  Berry, *Swaledale*, 1998, pp. 68-69
Grinton, Calvert Houses
  621 William Mylner
  Berry, *Swaledale*, 1998, pp. 72-73
Marrick
  622 Robert Loufhous
  Berry, *Swaledale*, 1998, pp. 74-76
  623 James Spenslay
  Berry, *Swaledale*, 1998, pp. 70-71
Norton Conyers
  624 James Duffield
  Raine, *Richmond*, 1853, p. 61
Westerdale
  625 George Cowtus
  Crossley, *Yorkshire*, 1929, p. 49
  626 Edward Fletcher
  Crossley, *Yorkshire*, 1929, p. 50

1549 (c.)
Yorkshire
Westerdale
  627 John Johnson
  Crossley, *Yorkshire*, 1929, p. 50

1550-1575 (undated)
Nottinghamshire
Wollaton Hall
  628 Sir Henry Willoughby
  Stevenson, 1887, pp. 76-87

Oxfordshire
Arncott
  629 William Hewes
  Havinden, *Oxfordshire*, 1965, p. 315
Burford
  630 William Beachampe
  Havinden, *Oxfordshire*, 1965, p. 315
Swyncombe, Cotes
  631 John Barnade
  Havinden, *Oxfordshire*, 1965, p. 314
Unlocated
  632 Richard Symmons
  Havinden, *Oxfordshire*, 1965, p. 316

1550
Derbyshire
Brimington
  633 Jhorn Broke [Brooke]
  Bestall and Fowkes, *Chesterfield*, 1977, pp. 35-36
  634 Lauranse Smythe
  Bestall and Fowkes, *Chesterfield*, 1977, p. 35
Chesterfield
  635 John Alwood
  Bestall and Fowkes, *Chesterfield*, 1977, pp. 33-34
  636 Richard Mouldyng
  Bestall and Fowkes, *Chesterfield*, 1977, pp. 36-37
  637 William Shacklocke
  Bestall and Fowkes, *Chesterfield*, 1977, pp. 34-35
Ockbrook
  638 Jhon Adam
  Johnson, 1994, p. 21
Walton
  639 Johan Bruke, widow
  Bestall and Fowkes, *Chesterfield*, 1977, pp. 37-38
Co. Durham
Durham Cathedral
  640 Raff [Ralph] Blaxton, clergyman
  Raine, *Wills and Inventories*, 1835, I, p. 131
Hampshire
Selborne
  641 Christopher Baker
  Yates, 2009, p. 152
Southampton
  642 Robert Apryce, [merchant]
  Roberts and Parker, *Southampton*, I, 1992, pp. 28-29
  643 Elizabeth Forward, widow
  Roberts and Parker, *Southampton*, I, 1992, pp. 30-34
  644 John Rocheford
  Roberts and Parker, *Southampton*, I, 1992, pp. 34-36
  645 Sampson Thomas, esquire [merchant]
  Roberts and Parker, *Southampton*, I, 1992, pp. 36-39
Wyke
  646 Doctor [Nicholas] Harpsfelde, clergyman
  Baigent, 1863, pp. 197-198
Lancashire
Hall i' th' Wood, Tonge, Bolton
  647 Lawrence Brownlow, gentleman
  Irvine, 1903, pp. 25-27
Prestwich, Tonge
  648 Lawrence Brownelowe, gentleman
  Bolton, *Bolton*, 1994, pp. 10-11

London
Pewterers' Hall
  649 Pewterers' Company
  Welch, 1902, I, pp. 164-169
Oxfordshire
Dorchester (?)
  650 Richard Mathewe
  Havinden, *Oxfordshire*, 1965, p. 41
Stadhampton
  651 Thomas Coner
  Havinden, *Oxfordshire*, 1965, p. 42
Warwickshire
Middleton
  652 Sir Henry Willoughby
  Stevenson, 1911, pp. 474-485
Yorkshire
Grinton, Calvert Houses
  653 John Qworton
  Berry, *Swaledale*, 1998, pp. 79-80
Richmond
  654 Dame Joan Harkay, last prioress of Ellerton
Priory
  Berry, *Swaledale*, 1998, p. 78
Westerdale
  655 Robert Gyll
  Crossley, *Yorkshire*, 1929, p. 50
York
  656 Richard Rundall, clergyman, rector of St
Saviour's
  Cross, *York*, II, 1989, pp. 50-53
  657 Thomas Worrall, clergyman, St Michael's
Spurriersgate
  Cross, *York*, II, 1989, pp. 53-55

1550 (c.)
Nottinghamshire
South Wheatley
  658 Gefrey Spenser
  Kennedy, *Nottinghamshire*, 1963, pp. 25-26
Yorkshire
Richmond
  659 Dame Joan Harkay, formerly a nun
  Raine, *Richmond*, 1853, p. 70

1551
Cumberland
Rockcliffe
  660 Ralf Guy
  Raine, *Richmond*, 1853, pp. 70-71
Derbyshire
Chesterfield
  661 Henry Baldwen
  Bestall and Fowkes, *Chesterfield*, 1977, p. 39
  662 Joan Poynton, widow
  Bestall and Fowkes, *Chesterfield*, 1977, pp. 38-39
  663 Robarte Wilson
  Bestall and Fowkes, *Chesterfield*, 1977, pp. 40-41
Glossop, Roworth
  664 Edward Robothum, [husbandman]
  Bryant, Lee, Miller, *New Mills I*, 1995, pp. 4-5
Newbold
  665 James Rotheram, husbandman
  Bestall and Fowkes, *Chesterfield*, 1977, p. 41

Hampshire
Southampton
  666 Patrick Cavell, mariner
  Roberts and Parker, *Southampton*, I, 1992, pp. 39-41
  667 William Joysse, cooper
  Roberts and Parker, *Southampton*, I, 1992, pp. 41-42
  668 Thomas Weeks, butcher
  Roberts and Parker, *Southampton*, I, 1992, pp. 43-47
Lancashire
Ordsall
  669 Dame Anne Radcliffe, widow
  Earwaker, *Lancashire and Cheshire*, 1884, pp. 17-18
Whittington
  670 Richard Newton, gentleman
  Earwaker, *Lancashire and Cheshire*, 1893, pp. 128-129
Lincolnshire
Clee
  671 Emett Lusbye
  Ambler, Watkinson, *Clee*, 1987, p. 50
Market Rasen
  672 Jhon Howlt, mercer
  Neave, *Market Rasen*, 1985, pp. 48-49
London
Hackney, Sir William Sharington's House
  673 Sir Walter Bonham
  Kidston, 1938, pp. 286-291
Northumberland
Newcastle-upon-Tyne
  674 Will'm [William] Bee, clergyman
  Raine, *Wills and Inventories*, 1835, I, p. 136
  675 William Lawson
  Raine, *Wills and Inventories*, 1835, I, pp. 133-134
Staffordshire
Dudley
  676 Thomas Wall, clergyman, vicar of Dudley
  Roper, *Dudley*, 1965, pp. 2-3
Warwickshire
Birmingham
  677 Robert Elsmore, [tanner]
  Holt, Ingram, Jarman, *Birmingham*, 1985, pp. 4-7
Worcestershire
Dudley
  678 Thomas Wall, clergyman, vicar of Dudley
  Roper, *Worcestershire*, 1972, pp. 14-15
Yorkshire
Marske
  679 William Lawekland
  Berry, *Swaledale*, 1998, p. 81
York
  680 Robert Agregge, clergyman, curate of St Helen on
the Walls
  Cross, *York*, II, 1989, p. 59
Warwickshire
Birmingham
  681 James Byrch, blacksmith
  Holt, 1985, pp. 27-28
Stoneleigh
  682 Thomas Roweley, yeoman
  Alcock, *Warwickshire*, 1993, pp. 68-69

1552

Derbyshire
Walton
683 John Elyot [Elyatt]
    Bestall and Fowkes, *Chesterfield*, 1977, p. 42
Hampshire
Southampton
684 Thomas Hutton, clergyman
    Roberts and Parker, *Southampton*, I, 1992, pp. 47-48
Hertfordshire
St Albans, St Stephens
685 Wather Rowysse [Royce], yeoman
    Parker, *Worldly Goods*, 2004, pp. 37-39
Lincolnshire
Clee, Oole
686 Johne Awdman
    Ambler, Watkinson, *Clee*, 1987, pp. 50-51
Lancashire
Deane
687 John Carlill
    Bolton, *Bolton*, 1987, p. 48
Warwickshire
Coventry
688 Alice Fan
    Hulton and Castle, *Tudor*, 1987, pp. 24-26
Stoneleigh
689 Robert Dene
    Alcock, *Warwickshire*, 1993, pp. 46-47
Worcestershire
Old Swinford, Wollescote
690 Rychard Cole, [scythesmith]
    Roper, *Scythesmiths*, 1967, pp. 9-10
Pershore, Pendesson
691 John Mosse, clergyman, curate of Pendesson
    Roper, *Worcestershire*, 1972, p. 18
Worcester
692 Edward Brat, mercer
    Dyer, *Worcestershire*, 1967, pp. 8-10
Yorkshire
Aysgarth, Skellgill
693 Edmunde Coot [Coates]
    Thwaite, *Abbotside*, 1967, p. 2
Grinton [Whitaside]
694 Ralph Spenslay
    Berry, *Swaledale*, 1998, p. 83
Lunds
695 John Parkyn [Parkin]
    Thwaite, *Abbotside*, 1967, pp. 1-2
South Cave
696 Margerett Byrde
    Kaner, *South Cave*, 1994, p. 47
Westerdale
697 John Dayll
    Crossley, *Yorkshire*, 1929, p. 51
York Minster
698 John Coltman, clergyman, Prebendary of Apethorpe
    Cross, *York*, I, 1984, pp. 90-92

1553

Cambridgeshire
Cambridge, Great St Mary's
699 John Sowght [South], [stationer and binder]
    Gray and Palmer, *Cambridge*, 1915, p. 34

Derbyshire
Calow
700 Jamys Rigatt
    Bestall and Fowkes, *Chesterfield*, 1977, pp. 43-44
Chesterfield
701 Hughe Cluworth
    Bestall and Fowkes, *Chesterfield*, 1977, pp. 49-50
702 Robert Homysfeld
    Bestall and Fowkes, *Chesterfield*, 1977, pp. 45-46
703 John Woodward
    Bestall and Fowkes, *Chesterfield*, 1977, pp. 46-48
Temple Normanton
704 William Alwood
    Bestall and Fowkes, *Chesterfield*, 1977, pp. 42-43
Hampshire
Selborne
705 John Fisher
    Yates, 2009, p. 148
Southampton
706 Edward Markant, merchant
    Roberts and Parker, *Southampton*, I, 1992, pp. 48-51
Hertfordshire
St Albans, St Stephens
707 Thomas Atkynes
    Parker, *Worldly Goods*, 2004, pp. 40-42
708 John Heywarde, labourer
    Parker, *Worldly Goods*, 2004, p. 33
St Albans, St Stephens, Bone Hill
709 Andrew Woodwarde
    Munby, *Worldly Goods*, 1991, p. 20
Lincolnshire
Faldingworth
710 John Nevell [Neville], gentleman
    Peacock, 1855, pp. 231-234
London
Battersea
711 Robert Holgate, Archbishop of York (also listed Yorkshire, Cawood)
    Anon., *Holgate*, 1825, pp. 596-597
Paget Place, St Clement Danes
712 Sir William Paget, Lord Paget of Beaudesert
    Wolsey and Luff, 1968
Oxfordshire
Dorchester
713 John Sims
    Havinden, *Oxfordshire*, 1965, pp. 43-44
Oxford, St Nicholas in Oxford Castle
714 William Thomas, alias Plumber, [plumber]
    Havinden, *Oxfordshire*, 1965, pp. 42-43
Warwickshire
Birmingham
715 William More
    Holt, Ingram, Jarman, *Birmingham*, 1985, pp. 8-10
Coventry
716 John Castell, [butcher and grazier]
    Hulton and Castle, *Tudor*, 1987, pp. 29-31
717 Thomasine Castell, [widow]
    Hulton and Castle, *Tudor*, 1987, pp. 33-35
Worcestershire
Belbroughton
718 John Broke [Brooke]
    Roper, *Belbroughton*, 1967-1968, p. 7

Upton Warren
719 Walter Bradeley, clergyman, parson of Upton
Warren
Roper, *Worcestershire*, 1972, pp. 16-17
Yorkshire
Barforth
720 Margarett Pudsey, widow
Raine, *Pudseys*, 1858, pp. 179-183
Cawood
Robert Holgate, Archbishop of York (see London,
Battersea)
Grinton, Feetham
721 Margaret Natbe
Berry, *Swaledale*, 1998, pp. 86-87
Westerdale
722 John Brotton, clergyman, curate of Westerdale
Crossley, *Yorkshire*, 1929, pp. 52-53
York
723 Thomas Nelson, clergyman
Cross, *York*, II, 1989, pp. 63-64

1554
Cheshire
Christleton
724 Raff Egerton, gentleman
Bland, *Christleton*, 2002, pp. 2-3
Derbyshire
Chesterfield
725 John Hadfield
Bestall and Fowkes, *Chesterfield*, 1977, pp. 55-56
726 John Ward
Bestall and Fowkes, *Chesterfield*, 1977, pp. 51-54
727 James Waterhosse
Bestall and Fowkes, *Chesterfield*, 1977, pp. 54-55
Glossop, Mousley Bottom
728 John Haghe
Bryant, Lee, Miller, *New Mills I*, 1995, p. 7
Hasland
729 Roger Fletcher
Bestall and Fowkes, *Chesterfield*, 1977, p. 57
Hampshire
Southampton
730 Edmund Bishop, alderman
Roberts and Parker, *Southampton*, I, 1992, pp. 51-53
731 Thomas Harrison, girdler
Roberts and Parker, *Southampton*, I, 1992, pp. 53-61
732 Thomas Huttoft
Roberts and Parker, *Southampton*, I, 1992, pp. 61-65
Hertfordshire
St Albans, St Stephens
733 Thomas Prate [Pratt]
Parker, *Worldly Goods*, 2004, pp. 44-45
Lancashire
Deane
734 John Crompton
Bolton, *Bolton*, 1987, p. 67
Myerscough
Thurstan Tyldesley, esquire (see Wardley Hall)
Wardley Hall
735 Thurstan Tyldesley, esquire (also listed
Myerscough)
Piccope, *Lancashire and Cheshire*, 1857, pp. 105-114
Lincolnshire
Pinchbeck
736 Richard Cust, yeoman
Cust, 1898, pp. 56-58

Staffordshire
Hales
737 John Sclader
Twemlow, *Tyrley*, 1948, p. 278
Warwickshire
Coventry
738 Henry Goodall
Hulton and Castle, *Tudor*, 1987, p. 37
Worcestershire
Worcester
739 William Ryse, clergyman
Roper, *Worcestershire*, 1972, p. 19
Yorkshire
Brantingham
740 Richard Smetheley [Smethley], esquire
Kaner, *South Cave*, 1994, pp. 48-51
South Cave
741 Thomas Tavell
Kaner, *South Cave*, 1994, pp. 47-48

1555
Derbyshire
Calow
742 Wyllyam Chapman
Bestall and Fowkes, *Chesterfield*, 1977, p. 58
Chesterfield
743 Jhon Ashe
Bestall and Fowkes, *Chesterfield*, 1977, pp. 62-64
744 Thomas Hadfield
Bestall and Fowkes, *Chesterfield*, 1977, pp. 55-56
745 Hanry Watson, saddler
Bestall and Fowkes, *Chesterfield*, 1977, pp. 59-61
Glossop, Whittle
746 Thomas Bower
Bryant, Lee, Miller, *New Mills I*, 1995, p. 9
Devonshire
Dunkeswell
747 Margery Butte, widow
Cash, *Devon*, 1966, pp. 1-2
Hampshire
Southampton
748 Thomas Goddard, merchant
Roberts and Parker, *Southampton*, I, 1992, pp. 65-72
749 Denis Hore, shipmaster
Roberts and Parker, *Southampton*, I, 1992, pp. 72-73
750 George Morell [weaver]
Roberts and Parker, *Southampton*, I, 1992, pp. 73-75
Hertfordshire
St Albans, St Stephens
751 William Morrys
Munby, *Worldly Goods*, 1991, p p. 23-25
Unlocated
752 Jone Wynsor
Munby, *Worldly Goods*, 1991, pp. 21-23
Lincolnshire
Clee
753 George Comons
Ambler, Watkinson, *Clee*, 1987, p. 51
London
Clothworkers' Hall
754 Clothworkers' Company
Wickham, 2005, pp. 23-31

Northumberland
Berwick-on-Tweed
755 Sir Robert Bowes
Raine, *Wills and Inventories*, 1835, I, p. 145
Elsdon
756 Clemet Red [Clement Reed]
Raine, *Wills and Inventories*, 1835, I, p. 147
Newcastle
757 Rauffe Hardynge [Ralph Harding], mariner
Hodgson, *Wills and Inventories*, 1906, III, p. 12

Warwickshire
Birmingham
758 Rychard Wyre [Wyar]
Holt, Ingram, Jarman, *Birmingham*, 1985, p. 12
Coventry
759 Robert Clawghton, [tanner]
Hulton and Castle, *Tudor*, 1987, pp. 42-43

Worcestershire
Unlocated
760 William Walter, clergyman
Roper, *Worcestershire*, 1972, p. 21

Yorkshire
Aysgarth, Sedbusk
761 Kataryn Thwait [Thwaite], widow
Downholme, Ellerton
Thwaite, *Abbotside*, 1967, p. 4
762 John Cleyssbe
Berry, *Swaledale*, 1998, pp. 93-94
Grinton
763 John Hucheson
Berry, *Swaledale*, 1998, pp. 97-98
Grinton, Calvert Houses
764 James Mylner
Berry, *Swaledale*, 1998, pp. 95-96
Westerdale
765 Edmund Strynger
Crossley, *Yorkshire*, 1929, p. 55
York
766 Christopher Ashton, clergyman, rector of All
Saints, North Street
Cross, *York*, II, 1989, pp. 67-69

1555 (c.)
Yorkshire
Grinton, High Whitaside
767 Simon Spenselay
Berry, *Swaledale*, 1998, pp. 91-92

1556
Derbyshire
Chesterfield
768 John Aulte, husbandman
Bestall and Fowkes, *Chesterfield*, 1977, pp. 65-66
769 Richard Blakelowe
Bestall and Fowkes, *Chesterfield*, 1977, pp. 68-69
770 Thomas Vicars
Bestall and Fowkes, *Chesterfield*, 1977, pp. 67-68
Glossop, Bank Head
771 Thomas Garrat, [yeoman]
Bryant, Lee, Miller, *New Mills I*, 1995, p. 15
Newbold
772 John Newbold
Bestall and Fowkes, *Chesterfield*, 1977, pp. 66-67

Co. Durham
Old Park, Spennymoor
773 Rauf [Ralph] Claxton, esquire (also listed St
Helen Auckland)
Raine, *Wills and Inventories*, 1835, I, pp. 151-154
St Helen Auckland
Ralph Claxton (see Old Park)

Hertfordshire
St Albans, St Stephens
774 Robard Thewer
Munby, *Worldly Goods*, 1991, pp. 26-27

Lancashire
Manchester
775 Robert Bryddocke, clergyman
Piccope, *Lancashire and Cheshire*, 1860, p. 143
Worsley, Wardley
776 Thomas Tyldesley, esquire
Earwaker, *Lancashire and Cheshire*, 1884, pp. 13-15

Oxfordshire
Nether Worton
777 James Boulster (Bulstred), gentleman
Havinden, *Oxfordshire*, 1965, pp. 44-45

Surrey
Loseley House
778 William More, esquire
Evans, 1855, pp. 288-293
Kew
779 Sir Edward Courtenay, Earl of Devon
Couch, 1867, pp. 226-233

Sussex
Firle
780 Sir John Gage
Rice, 1902, pp. 119-127

Warwickshire
Ashow
781 William Powres
Alcock, *Warwickshire*, 1993, p. 106
Stoneleigh, South Hurst Farm
782 Humphrey Hylles, [husbandman]
Alcock, *Warwickshire*, 1993, pp. 23-24
Stoneleigh, Finham
783 William Nycolles
Alcock, *Warwickshire*, 1993, pp. 50-51
Stratford-on-Avon
784 Hewghe Raynoldes [Hugh Reynolds], [yeoman
and alderman]
Tomes, 1860, 334-339
Jones, *Stratford*, I, 2002, pp. 9-11

Westmorland
Kendal
785 Richard Gurnell, clothier
Raine, *Richmond*, 1853, p. 86

Worcestershire
Belbroughton
786 Roger Wackeman
Roper, *Belbroughton*, 1967-1968, p. 17
Birtsmorton
787 John Nanfan, esquire
Wanklyn, *Worcestershire*, 1998, pp. 24-25
Halesowen
788 John Huntebach, clergyman
Roper, *Worcestershire*, 1972, pp. 27-28

Kempsey, The Holdings
  789 Richard Mucklowe [Mucklow], esquire
  Wanklyn, *Worcestershire*, 1998, pp. 21-24
Madresfield
  790 Sir Richard Ligen [Lygon]
  Wanklyn, *Worcestershire*, 1998, p. 21
Shrawley
  791 John Butler, clergyman
  Roper, *Worcestershire*, 1972, pp. 26-27
Worcester
  792 Bartram Coxe, dyer
  Dyer, *Worcestershire*, 1967, pp. 18-19
Worcester, St Peter's
  793 Rychard Davyes, clergyman, vicar of St Peter's
  Roper, *Worcestershire*, 1972, pp. 29-30
Yorkshire
Lunds [?]
  794 Frances Parkyn
  Thwaite, *Abbotside*, 1967, pp. 4-5
York
  795 Lawrence Harryson, clergyman, vicar of St
  George's Fishergate
  Cross, *York*, II, 1989, pp. 71-72

1557

Derbyshire
Brimington
  796 Ellen Casken, widow
  Bestall and Fowkes, *Chesterfield*, 1977, p. 71
  797 Henry Hurste
  Bestall and Fowkes, *Chesterfield*, 1977, p. 79
Chesterfield
  798 George Ashe
  Bestall and Fowkes, *Chesterfield*, 1977, pp. 80-81
Chesterfield, Grassmoor
  799 John Cooke
  Bestall and Fowkes, *Chesterfield*, 1977, p. 72
Chesterfield
  800 Elizabeth Fletcher, widow
  Bestall and Fowkes, *Chesterfield*, 1977, pp. 69-70
  801 Richard Newbold, clergyman, priest of the
  dissolved guild
  Bestall and Fowkes, *Chesterfield*, 1977, pp. 72-73
Hasland
  802 William Webster, husbandman
  Bestall and Fowkes, *Chesterfield*, 1977, p. 70
Co. Durham
Neasham
  803 Jane Lawson, last Prioress of the monastery of
  Neasham
  Raine, *Wills and Inventories*, 1835, I, pp. 158-159
Hampshire
Southampton
  804 Thomas Boke
  Roberts and Parker, *Southampton*, I, 1992, pp. 75-76
  805 George Leche, [armourer?]
  Roberts and Parker, *Southampton*, I, 1992, pp. 76-77
  806 Simon Note
  Roberts and Parker, *Southampton*, I, 1992, pp. 77-78
  807 Robert Sparkes, [cooper]
  Roberts and Parker, *Southampton*, I, 1992, pp. 78-79
  808 Lawrence Sutton, clergyman
  Roberts and Parker, *Southampton*, I, 1992, pp. 79-80

  809 John Swalo
  Roberts and Parker, *Southampton*, I, 1992, p. 80
Lancashire
Kirkham, Mowbreck
  810 William Westby, esquire
  Raine, *Richmond*, 1853, pp. 91-93
Leicestershire
Braunstone
  811 Thomas Neale
  Wilshere, *Braunstone*, 1983, p. 3
Evington
  812 Hugh Lewyne, clergyman, curate of Evington
  Wilshere, *Evington*, 1985, p. 1
Quorndon
  813 Francis Farnham, esquire
  Farnham, *Quorndon*, 1912, p. 219
Lincolnshire
Clee, Oole
  814 William Awdmane, husbandman
  Ambler, Watkinson, *Clee*, 1987, pp. 52-53
Clee, Weelsby
  815 Herry Beryes
  Ambler, Watkinson, *Clee*, 1987, p. 52
Clee
  816 Robart Curteis
  Ambler, Watkinson, *Clee*, 1987, p. 53
Northumberland
Newcastle-upon-Tyne
  817 Rob'te Goodchylde [Robert Goodchild], parish
  clerk of St Andrew's
  Raine, *Wills and Inventories*, 1835, p. 154
Oxfordshire
Great Milton
  818 Andrew Smythe, alias Cocke
  Havinden, *Oxfordshire*, 1965, pp. 45-46
Staffordshire
Dudley
  819 Adam Persehouse alias Parke
  Roper, *Dudley*, 1965, p. 4
  Roper, *Sixteenth Century*, 1968, pp. 31-32
Surrey
Leatherhead
  820 Robert Russell, clergymen, vicar of Leatherhead
  Blair, 1974, pp. 244-245
Newdigate
  821 John Lewer, husbandman
  Herridge, *Surrey*, 2005, p. 4
Warwickshire
Alcester
  822 Adrian Norton, [tailor]
  Ory, 1992/1993, pp. 202-203
Coventry
  823 Richard Goldryng, [dyer]
  Hulton and Castle, *Tudor*, 1987, pp. 50-51
Foleshill
  824 Henry Bartton
  Upton, *Foleshill*, 1993, pp. 18-19
  825 John Wolfe
  Upton, *Foleshill*, 1993, pp. 25-26
Stoneleigh
  826 William Pyppe, [fuller]
  Alcock, *Warwickshire*, 1993, pp. 27-28

Worcestershire
Alderminster
827 Jone Stanley, widow
Arkell, Evans, Goose, 2000, p. 372
Belbroughton
828 John Hertyll
Roper, *Belbroughton*, 1967-1968, p. 9
Bishampton
829 Edmunde Blemeley, clergyman [vicar of
Bishampton]
Roper, *Worcestershire*, 1972, p. 31
Bromsgrove
830 Thomas Jamys, clergyman
Roper, *Worcestershire*, 1972, p. 24
831 John Tybson, clergyman
Roper, *Worcestershire*, 1972, pp. 37-38
Claines
832 Wyllyam Paytewyne, clergyman
Roper, *Worcestershire*, 1972, pp. 34-35
Droitwich, St Peter's
833 John Wythe
Wanklyn, *Worcestershire*, 1998, pp. 25-27
Elmley Lovett
834 Mr Philip Balarde alias Haford, clergyman, Dean
of Worcester (also listed Worcester)
Barnard, 1929, pp. 58-69
Fladbury
835 Thomas Stanson, clergyman, curate of Fladbury
Roper, *Worcestershire*, 1972, p. 32
Pershore
836 Thomas Quarell, clergyman
Roper, *Worcestershire*, 1972, p. 34
Worcester
Mr Philip Balarde alias Haford, clergyman, Dean of
Worcester (see Elmley Lovett)
Yorkshire
Aysgarth, Skellgill [?]
837 Elezabeith Twait [Elizabeth Twaite]
Thwaite, *Abbotside*, 1967, p. 5
Hutton, West Layton
838 Roger Laiton
Raine, *Richmond*, 1853, p. 88
Marske
839 William Conyers, esquire
Raine, *Richmond*, 1853, p. 94
Berry, *Swaledale*, 1998, pp. 101-103
840 John Grene
Berry, *Swaledale*, 1998, p. 104
Thornton Bridge
841 Wyllyam Knyvett, gentleman
Raine, *Richmond*, 1853, pp. 98-102

1557 (c.)
Yorkshire
South Cave
842 William Rymer, husbandman
Kaner, *South Cave*, 1994, p. 52

1558
Cheshire
Chester, St John's Churchyard
Richard Brereton, esquire (see Middlewich, The Ley)
Middlewich, The Ley
843 Richard Brereton, esquire (also listed Chester)
Piccope, *Lancashire and Cheshire*, 1857, pp. 169-183

Derbyshire
Chesterfield
844 Hare Calver
Bestall and Fowkes, *Chesterfield*, 1977, p. 84
845 Thomas Fletcher, farmer
Bestall and Fowkes, *Chesterfield*, 1977, pp. 76-77
846 Thomas Hethcote
Bestall and Fowkes, *Chesterfield*, 1977, pp. 84-86
Chesterfield, Holme
847 Thomas Holmes
Bestall and Fowkes, *Chesterfield*, 1977, p. 86
Chesterfield
848 William Lee, shoemaker
Bestall and Fowkes, *Chesterfield*, 1977, pp. 73-74
849 Johan Wudwarde, widow
Bestall and Fowkes, *Chesterfield*, 1977, pp. 78-79
Glossop, Broadhurst
850 Thomas Arnefield
Bryant, Lee, Miller, *New Mills I*, 1995, pp. 11-12
Hasland
851 Richard Alwood
Bestall and Fowkes, *Chesterfield*, 1977, pp. 74-75
852 Robert Wedoson, farmer
Bestall and Fowkes, *Chesterfield*, 1977, pp. 76-77
Temple Normanton
853 Robert Watkenson, yeoman
Bestall and Fowkes, *Chesterfield*, 1977, p. 83
Devonshire
Totnes
854 Nicholas Smith, gentleman
Cash, *Devon*, 1966, p. 2
Co. Durham
Sedgefield
855 Robert Hyndmer, clergyman
Raine, *Wills and Inventories*, 1835, I, pp. 161-164
Hampshire
Southampton
856 Raffe [Ralph] Alporte, merchant
Roberts and Parker, *Southampton*, I, 1992, pp. 81-85
857 Richard Ameshin, clergyman, parson of
Allhallows
Roberts and Parker, *Southampton*, I, 1992, p. 86
858 John Bys
Roberts and Parker, *Southampton*, I, 1992, p. 87
859 William Byston, shearman
Roberts and Parker, *Southampton*, I, 1992, pp. 88-90
860 Thomas Challys, [fishmonger]
Roberts and Parker, *Southampton*, I, 1992, p. 90
861 Arthur Cook
Roberts and Parker, *Southampton*, I, 1992, pp. 91-95
862 Alice Cox, widow
Roberts and Parker, *Southampton*, I, 1992, pp. 95-99
863 John Elyn
Roberts and Parker, *Southampton*, I, 1992, pp. 99-102
864 Robert Erryngton [Arrington], mercer
Roberts and Parker, *Southampton*, I, 1992, pp. 102-105
865 Robert Evans [Evyns, Evons, Yevan]
Roberts and Parker, *Southampton*, I, 1992, pp. 105-109
866 Thomas Flemyng, mariner
Roberts and Parker, *Southampton*, I, 1992, pp. 109-111
867 Rowland Gavin, blacksmith
Roberts and Parker, *Southampton*, I, 1992, pp. 111-112
868 Henry Gold
Roberts and Parker, *Southampton*, I, 1992, pp. 112-116

869 Nicholas Grant, beer brewer
Roberts and Parker, *Southampton*, I, 1992, pp. 116-119
870 Richard Hawkins, woollen draper
Roberts and Parker, *Southampton*, I, 1992, pp. 119-122
871 Jasper Keire [Kayer]
Roberts and Parker, *Southampton*, I, 1992, pp. 122-124
872 Richard Mershe, cloth merchant
Roberts and Parker, *Southampton*, I, 1992, pp. 124-127
873 Nicholas Myssick [Musyke], shearman
Roberts and Parker, *Southampton*, I, 1992, pp. 127-129
874 Alice Note, widow
Roberts and Parker, *Southampton*, I, 1992, pp. 129-131
875 Robert Parret [Parratt], parish clerk
Roberts and Parker, *Southampton*, I, 1992, pp. 131-132
876 Thomas Prince, shoemaker
Roberts and Parker, *Southampton*, I, 1992, pp. 133-134
877 John Vouerte, draper
Roberts and Parker, *Southampton*, I, 1992, pp. 134-136
878 John Vybard [Viberd], shoemaker
Roberts and Parker, *Southampton*, I, 1992, pp. 137-139

Hertfordshire
St Albans, St Stephens
879 [...] Trotte
Parker, *Worldly Goods*, 2004, pp. 47-48
880 Thomas Woodward
Munby, *Worldly Goods*, 1991, pp. 27-28
881 Andro Wynsor
Munby, *Worldly Goods*, 1991, pp. 31-32
Sarratt
882 Jeames Baldwyn, husbandman
Bullen, *Sarratt*, [1982], pp. 36-37
Watford, Waterdell
883 Edmond Woodward
Munby, *Worldly Goods*, 1991, p. 29

Ireland
Cork
884 [Patrick] Ponche
Caulfield, *Cork*, 1861-1862, p. 166 (1862)

Lancashire
Manchester
885 George Collier, clergyman, warden of Manchester Collegiate Church
Earwaker, *Lancashire and Cheshire*, 1884, pp. 18-22

Leicestershire
Braunstone
886 Alys Neale
Wilshere, *Braunstone*, 1983, p. 3

Lincolnshire
Allington
887 Rychard Maysson
Pask, *Allington*, 1989, p. 22
Clee, Oole
888 Katharine Awdman, widow
Ambler, Watkinson, *Clee*, 1987, pp. 54-55
Clee
889 Robert Burstoy, husbandman
Ambler, Watkinson, *Clee*, 1987, p. 54
Clee, Oole
890 Elysabethe Stables, widow
Ambler, Watkinson, *Clee*, 1987, pp. 55-56
Market Rasen
891 Jhon Burnesley, mercer
Neave, *Market Rasen*, 1985, pp. 57-58

892 Rychard Clerke, yeoman
Neave, *Market Rasen*, 1985, pp. 50-51
893 Agnes Farthyngton, widow
Neave, *Market Rasen*, 1985, p. 56
894 Jhon Farthynton, glover
Neave, *Market Rasen*, 1985, p. 54
895 Agnes Lamkynge, widow
Neave, *Market Rasen*, 1985, p. 56
896 Thoms Sowden
Neave, *Market Rasen*, 1985, p. 55
897 Isabell Thymblebye
Neave, *Market Rasen*, 1985, p. 49
Saxby
898 William Smith, gentleman
Smith, 1883-1885, pp. 203-205

London
Ave Maria Lane, Stationers' Hall
899 The Sationers' Company
Nichols, *Illustrations*, 1797, pp. 226-228
Arber, 1875, pp. 87-90
St Michael Paternoster
900 Gregorye Isham, mercer of London (also listed Braunston, Northamptonshire)
Ramsay, 1962, pp. 155-165

Northamptonshire
Braunston
Gregorye Isham, mercer of London (see St Michael Paternoster, London)

Nottinghamshire
Cropwell Bishop
901 William Richardes
Kennedy, *Nottinghamshire*, 1963, pp. 57-58
Eaton
902 William Butler
Kennedy, *Nottinghamshire*, 1963, pp. 26-27
Kirklington
903 Thomas More
Kennedy, *Nottinghamshire*, 1963, p. 56
Normanton, Southwell
904 Joan Willoughbie, widow
Kennedy, *Nottinghamshire*, 1963, pp. 60-62
Rampton
905 John Money [Monye], clergyman, vicar of Rampton
Kennedy, *Nottinghamshire*, 1963, pp. 55-56
Southwell
906 Raufe Langley
Kennedy, *Nottinghamshire*, 1963, pp. 54-55

Oxfordshire
Brize Norton
907 Harry Ballowe
Havinden, *Oxfordshire*, 1965, pp. 46-47

Surrey
Charlwood
908 Tolley
Herridge, *Surrey*, 2005, pp. 4-5
Cranleigh
909 Sir Edward Braye
Herridge, *Surrey*, 2005, p. 6
Kingston-upon-Thames
910 Jone Burgies, widow
Herridge, *Surrey*, 2005, pp. 1-2

Limpsfield
911 John Cole [Cooll], husbandman
Herridge, *Surrey*, 2005, p. 2
Lingfield
912 Christian Botley, widow
Herridge, *Surrey*, 2005, p. 1
Morden
913 John Frysbee, husbandman
Herridge, *Surrey*, 2005, p. 9
Weybridge
914 Myles Codde, clergyman, parson of St Nicholas, Weybridge
Herridge, *Surrey*, 2005, pp. 8-9

Wales
Flintshire, Iscoed
915 Robert Lloide, gentleman
Pearson, *Malpas*, [2005], pp. 19-20

Warwickshire
Coventry
916 Margaret Clawghton, [widow]
Hulton and Castle, *Tudor*, 1987, pp. 44-47
917 William Dale, weaver
Hulton, 1987, p. 19
Hulton and Castle, *Tudor*, 1987, pp. 63-64
Foleshill
918 Thomas Bacon the elder and Thomas Bacon his sonne
Upton, *Foleshill*, 1993, pp. 21-24
919 Morgan James
Upton, *Foleshill*, 1993, pp. 27-28
920 Henry Randull, clergyman, vicar of Coleshill
Upton, *Foleshill*, 1993, pp. 33-34
921 Jhon Wylkynson
Upton, *Foleshill*, 1993, p. 32
Stratford-on-Avon
922 Thomas Phyllypes [Phillips], [mercer and alderman]
Jones, *Stratford*, I, 2002, pp. 12-13
Stratford-on-Avon, Old Stratford
923 Richard Smyth [Smith]
Jones, *Stratford*, I, 2002, pp. 14-15

Worcestershire
Arley
924 William Eleson, clergyman, parson of Arley
Roper, *Worcestershire*, 1972, pp. 44-45
Belbroughton
925 Rafe Lassheforde
Roper, *Belbroughton*, 1967-1968, p. 10
926 Rych[ard Smythe], [scythesmith]
Roper, *Belbroughton*, 1967-1968, p. 14
927 Wyllyam Smythe
Roper, *Belbroughton*, 1967-1968, p. 12
Bretforton
928 John Robyns, clergyman, vicar of Bretforton
Roper, *Worcestershire*, 1972, pp. 40-41
Cropthorne
929 John Hyggins, clergyman
Knapp, 1911, pp. 166-167
Roper, *Worcestershire*, 1972, pp. 39-40
Defford
930 Raffe Holland, clergyman, curate of Defford
Roper, *Worcestershire*, 1972, p. 43
Doverdale
931 Hugh Briskow, clergyman, parson of Doverdale
Roper, *Worcestershire*, 1972, p. 47

Elmbridge
932 Thomas Hyll, clergyman, curate of Elmbridge
Roper, *Worcestershire*, 1972, pp. 42-43
Peopleton
933 Gylbart Gybbyns, clergyman
Roper, *Worcestershire*, 1972, p. 42
Pershore, Holy Cross
934 Rycharde Pullen, clergyman, curate of Holy Cross
Roper, *Worcestershire*, 1972, p. 33
Powick
935 Edmund Kenyon, clergyman, vicar of Powick
Roper, *Worcestershire*, 1972, p. 46
White Ladies Aston
936 William Balle, clergyman, vicar of White Ladies Aston
Roper, *Worcestershire*, 1972, p. 38

Yorkshire
Denton
Sir William Fairfax (see Steeton)
Grinton, Crackpot
937 Alexander Proctor
Berry, *Swaledale*, 1998, pp. 105-106
Knaresborough
938 James Willinson, merchant
Raine, *Richmond*, 1853, pp. 126-127
Lunds [?]
939 Wyllm Parkyn [William Parkin]
Thwaite, *Abbotside*, 1967, p. 6
South Cave
940 Bartholomew Byrde [Birde], labourer
Kaner, *South Cave*, 1994, p. 53
941 William Clark
Kaner, *South Cave*, 1994, p. 59
942 Janett Dunslaye [Jennett Dunsley], widow
Kaner, *South Cave*, 1994, pp. 54-55
943 Thomas Hodgeson, [husbandman]
Kaner, *South Cave*, 1994, pp. 55-56
944 Lettes Lyghtfouth
Kaner, *South Cave*, 1994, pp. 58-59
945 Elisabeth Simson, grasswoman
Kaner, *South Cave*, 1994, p. 58
Steeton
946 Sir William Fairfax (also listed Denton)
Croft, 1797, pp. 22-30
Westerdale
947 Richard Coyltes
Crossley, *Yorkshire*, 1929, p. 58
York Minster
948 William Bait, clergyman, vicar choral
Cross, *York*, I, 1984, pp. 94-95

Westmorland
Kendal
949 Ane Nychollson [Nycolson] de Cruke, widow
Raine, *Richmond*, 1853, p. 107

Worcestershire
Elmley Castle
950 Edmond Rayneford
Ransford, 1930, pp. 311-312

1558 (c.)
Lincolnshire
Clee
951 Richard Beetnyffe
Ambler, Watkinson, *Clee*, 1987, p. 54

Nottinghamshire
Holme
  952 William Ellott
    Kennedy, *Nottinghamshire*, 1963, pp. 52-53
Surrey
Lingfield
  953 Henry Copsell, fletcher
    Herridge, *Surrey*, 2005, p. 3
Worcestershire
Worcester
  954 Thomas Border
    Noake, 1877, pp. 9-11
Yorkshire
Well, Snape Low Park
  955 John Laton
    Raine, *Richmond*, 1853, p. 109

1559

Derbyshire
Brimington
  956 John Cowper alias Byngham, scythesmith
    Bestall and Fowkes, *Chesterfield*, 1977, pp. 86-87
Chesterfield
  957 Thomas Hethcote, butcher
    Bestall and Fowkes, *Chesterfield*, 1977, pp. 91-93
  958 Rychard Johnson alias Edmondson
    Bestall and Fowkes, *Chesterfield*, 1977, pp. 94-96
  959 Wylliam Ragge, clergyman
    Bestall and Fowkes, *Chesterfield*, 1977, p. 97
  960 Robert Rolenson
    Bestall and Fowkes, *Chesterfield*, 1977, pp. 89-90
  961 Richarde Whitworthe, clergyman
    Bestall and Fowkes, *Chesterfield*, 1977, pp. 90-91
Dunston
  962 Richard Rygott
    Bestall and Fowkes, *Chesterfield*, 1977, p. 87
Staveley
  963 Sir Peter Frethevile [Frecheville]
    Nichols, *Illustrations*, 1797, pp. 233-234
Walton
  964 Thomas Bramell alias Swyndell
    Bestall and Fowkes, *Chesterfield*, 1977, pp. 96-97
Co. Durham
Greatham
  965 John Emson, clergyman
    Raine, *Wills and Inventories*, 1835, I, pp. 170-171
Hilton, Hilton Castle
  966 Sir Thomas Hilton, Governor of Tynemouth
Castle (also listed Tynemouth Castle,
Northumberland)
    Raine, *Wills and Inventories*, 1835, I, pp. 181-184
Hampshire
Southampton
  967 John Anderson, blacksmith
    Roberts and Parker, *Southampton*, I, 1992, pp. 139-140
  968 James Cornish, shoemaker
    Roberts and Parker, *Southampton*, I, 1992, pp. 141-144
  969 Charles Harrison, physician
    Roberts and Parker, *Southampton*, I, 1992, pp. 144-148
  970 Nicholas Le Neve, [blacksmith and mercer]
    Roberts and Parker, *Southampton*, I, 1992, pp. 148-150
  971 Margaret Pyd, widow
    Roberts and Parker, *Southampton*, I, 1992, pp. 150-154

  972 Jane Rigges, widow
    Roberts and Parker, *Southampton*, I, 1992, pp. 154-159
  973 John Smith
    Roberts and Parker, *Southampton*, I, 1992, pp. 159-164
  974 John Staveley, grocer
    Roberts and Parker, *Southampton*, I, 1992, pp. 164-175
Hertfordshire
St Albans, St Stephens
  975 William Lane
    Parker, *Worldly Goods*, 2004, pp. 51-52
  976 Robert Russell
    Parker, *Worldly Goods*, 2004, pp. 52-53
  977 Harry Stokes
    Parker, *Worldly Goods*, 2004, pp. 55-56
Sarratt
  978 Jhon Salter
    Bullen, *Sarratt*, [1982], p. 41
Unlocated
  979 Thomas Marson
    Parker, *Worldly Goods*, 2004, pp. 58-59
Lancashire
Westby, Kirkham
  980 Thomas Clifton, esquire
    Piccope, *Lancashire and Cheshire*, 1860, pp. 73-80
Leicestershire
Braunstone
  981 Henry Lytherland, clergyman
    Wilshere, *Braunstone*, 1983, p. 4
Kirby Muxloe
  982 William Flecher, [husbandman?]
    Wilshere, *Kirby Muxloe*, 1983, p. 1
Lincolnshire
Clee
  983 Thomas Yngylbye
    Ambler, Watkinson, *Clee*, 1987, p. 56
Market Rasen
  984 Legard Howghtby, [tanner]
    Neave, *Market Rasen*, 1985, p. 63
  985 Robt. Inberye
    Neave, *Market Rasen*, 1985, p. 64
  986 Wyllm Lemyn
    Neave, *Market Rasen*, 1985, p. 61
  987 Laurans Rawlet
    Neave, *Market Rasen*, 1985, p. 62
  988 James Wryght
    Neave, *Market Rasen*, 1985, pp. 59-60
Northumberland
Newcastle-upon-Tyne
  989 Henry Anderson, alderman and merchant
    Raine, *Wills and Inventories*, 1835, I, pp. 166-168
Tynemouth, Tynemouth Castle
Sir Thomas Hilton (see Hilton, Co. Durham)
Nottinghamshire
Beckingham
  990 William Snell
    Kennedy, *Nottinghamshire*, 1963, pp. 58-60
Bleasby
  991 Brian Bagulay, yeoman
    Kennedy, *Nottinghamshire*, 1963, pp. 62-63
Blidworth
  992 John Froste
    Kennedy, *Nottinghamshire*, 1963, pp. 53-54

Eaton
  993 Thomas Blacknall
    Kennedy, *Nottinghamshire*, 1963, pp. 63-65
Southwell
  994 Amies Pechey [Agnes Peachie]
    Kennedy, *Nottinghamshire*, 1963, p. 57
Upton
  995 Henry Smethe [Smythe], husbandman
    Kennedy, *Nottinghamshire*, 1963, pp. 65-66
Oxfordshire
Filkins
  996 Thomas Toornor
    Havinden, *Oxfordshire*, 1965, pp. 47-48
Staffordshire
Dudley
  997 William Feredie, [tanner]
    Roper, *Dudley*, 1965, p. 5
    Roper, *Sixteenth Century*, 1968, pp. 33-34
  998 Roger Whyt
    Roper, *Dudley*, 1965, p. 7
    Roper, *Sixteenth Century*, 1968, pp. 29-30
Netherton
  999 Olyver Shawe
    Roper, *Dudley*, 1965, p. 8
Surrey
Eashing
  1000 William Chitty, husbandman
    Herridge, *Surrey*, 2005, pp. 7-8
Farnham
  1001 John Bekeham, clergyman, vicar of Farnham
    Herridge, *Surrey*, 2005, pp. 5-6
Frensham, Pitfold
  1002 Richard Peerson
    Herridge, *Surrey*, 2005, p. 10
Ham
  1003 Johan Tornor, widow
    Herridge, *Surrey*, 2005, p. 11
Morden
  1004 Nycholas Goryng, labourer
    Herridge, *Surrey*, 2005, p. 10
Warwickshire
Birmingham
  1005 Elizabethe Willes
    Holt, Ingram, Jarman, *Birmingham*, 1985, pp. 14-15
Coventry
  1006 Christopher Dale, weaver
    Hulton, 1987, pp. 22-23
    Hulton and Castle, *Tudor*, 1987, pp. 69-70
Foleshill
  1007 Kyrstoyver [Christopher] Dure
    Upton, *Foleshill*, 1993, pp. 35-36
  1008 Nicholas Elsse
    Upton, *Foleshill*, 1993, pp. 37-38
Stoneleigh
  1009 Godfrey Parton
    Alcock, *Warwickshire*, 1993, p. 45
Stratford-on-Avon
  1010 Richard Machyn [Machin]
    Jones, *Stratford*, I, 2002, p. 15
Worcestershire
Eastington, Longdon
  1011 Gyles Brudges [Brydges], esquire
    Wanklyn, *Worcestershire*, 1998, pp. 27-30

Yorkshire
Grinton, Thorns
  1012 Richard Alderson
    Berry, *Swaledale*, 1998, p. 110
Hipswell
  1013 Francys Wandysforde [Wandisford], esquire
    (also listed Kirklington)
    Raine, *Richmond*, 1853, pp. 132-138
    McCall, 1904, pp. 152-154
Kirklington
  Francys Wandysforde [Wandisford], esquire (see
    Hipswell)
Marske
  1014 Cuthbert Clarkson
    Berry, *Swaledale*, 1998, pp. 107-108
Marske, Skelton
  1015 John Symson
    Berry, *Swaledale*, 1998, p. 109
Middleham
  1016 Willyam Wylle, clergyman, dean and parson of
    Middleham
    Raine, *Richmond*, 1853, p. 129
Richmond
  1017 Alice Conyers, widow
    Raine, *Richmond*, 1853, p. 128
  1018 Richard Crosby, auditor
    Raine, *Richmond*, 1853, p. 141
Ripon Park
  1019 Nynian Staveley, esquire
    Brears, *Yorkshire*, 1972, pp. 3-8
South Cave
  1020 William Donwell, labourer
    Kaner, *South Cave*, 1994, p. 61
  1021 Christofer Pepper, labourer
    Kaner, *South Cave*, 1994, p. 62
  1022 Thomas Tawell [Tavell]
    Kaner, *South Cave*, 1994, p. 62
Westerdale
  1023 Thomas Dayll
    Crossley, *Yorkshire*, 1929, p. 56
  1024 Robert Roger
    Crossley, *Yorkshire*, 1929, pp. 56-57
York
  1025 Robert Morres, clergyman, rector of St Mary's
    Bishophill Senior
    Cross, *York*, II, 1989, pp. 87-89

1559 (c.)
Derbyshire
Chesterfield
  1026 William Heathcott, clergyman
    Bestall and Fowkes, *Chesterfield*, 1977, p. 88
Surrey
Wotton
  1027 Thomas Chesman
    Herridge, *Surrey*, 2005, p. 7

1560
Cheshire
Tarvin
  1028 Ann Reade
    Bland, *Christleton*, 2002, p. 6

Derbyshire
 Brimington
  1029 Thomas Croft
  Bestall and Fowkes, *Chesterfield*, 1977, pp. 98-99
 Calow
  1030 Thomas Bakester
  Bestall and Fowkes, *Chesterfield*, 1977, p. 98
 Chesterfield
  1031 Henry Cluworthe, glover
  Bestall and Fowkes, *Chesterfield*, 1977, pp. 100-101
Co. Durham
 Stillington, near Redmarshall
  1032 John Hartborne [Hartburne]
  Raine, *Wills and Inventories*, 1835, I, p. 187
Essex
 Tendring
  1033 George Gibbon
  Emmison, *Essex*, 1, 1982, p. 248
Hertfordshire
 St Albans, St Stephens
  1034 Hellen Laine, widow
  Parker, *Worldly Goods*, 2004, pp. 64-65
  1035 Rychard Mann
  Parker, *Worldly Goods*, 2004, pp. 61-62
  1036 Alice Skeylle
  Munby, *Worldly Goods*, 1991, p. 35
 Sarratt
  1037 Jhon Swetynge
  Bullen, *Sarratt*, [1982], pp. 43-44
Leicestershire
 Braunstone
  1038 John Giliv[er]
  Wilshere, *Braunstone*, 1983, p. 5
Lincolnshire
 Allington
  1039 Thomas Wynter
  Pask, *Allington*, 1989, pp. 23-24
 Clee, Oole
  1040 Thomas Burde, husbandman
  Ambler, Watkinson, *Clee*, 1987, pp. 56-57
London
 Ave Maria Lane, Stationers' Hall
  1041 Stationers' Company
  Arber, 1875, pp. 139-143
Norfolk
 Norwich
  1042 Sir Henrye Parker
  Hall, 1887, pp. 149-153 (also 1888, pp. 149-152)
Nottinghamshire
 Cropwell Bishop
  1043 Wylliam Mabbott, husbandman
  Kennedy, *Nottinghamshire*, 1963, pp. 68-69
 Southwell
  1044 James Ynkersell, mercer
  Kennedy, *Nottinghamshire*, 1963, pp. 66-68
Oxfordshire
 Great Bourton
  1045 Edward Kempsale
  Havinden, *Oxfordshire*, 1965, pp. 48-49
Scotland
 Stirling
  1046 Duncan Kar
  Renwick, 1887, pp. 74-75

1047 James Reddocht
 Renwick, 1887, pp. 73-74
1048 Johne Smart
 Renwick, 1887, p. 72
Surrey
 Dorking
  1049 William Whyte
  Herridge, *Surrey*, 2005, pp. 35-36
 Nutfield
  1050 John Clemente
  Herridge, *Surrey*, 2005, pp. 11-12
 Wotton
  1051 Robert Lylley, yeoman
  Herridge, *Surrey*, 2005, pp. 12-13
Warwickshire
 Luddington
  1052 Jhon Elyatte [John Elliott]
  Jones, *Stratford*, I, 2002, pp. 16-17
 Stratford-on-Avon
  1053 Roberte Balamy
  Jones, *Stratford*, I, 2002, pp. 17-19
  1054 Elyzabeth Byddell [Elizabeth Biddle]
  Jones, *Stratford*, I, 2002, p. 19
Westmorland
 Kendal
  1055 Allis Pearsone
  Raine, *Richmond*, 1853, pp. 146-147
Worcestershire
 Birtsmorton
  1056 Maud Nanferne [Nanfan], widow
  Wanklyn, *Worcestershire*, 1998, p. 31
 Little Malvern
  1057 Henry Russell
  Wanklyn, *Worcestershire*, 1998, pp. 31-34
Yorkshire
 Downholme
  1058 Leonard Loftus, yeoman
  Raine, *Richmond*, 1853, p. 145
  Berry, *Swaledale*, 1998, pp. 114-115
 Huttons Ambo, Gaterly
  1059 Anne Lademan
  Raine, *Richmond*, 1853, pp. 133-134
 Marske
  1060 William Bene
  Berry, *Swaledale*, 1998, p. 112
 Richmond
  1061 Charles Johnson
  Fieldhouse, 1974, pp. 15-16
 South Cave
  1062 Wylliam Spofardes [Spofard], grassman
  Kaner, *South Cave*, 1994, p. 63

1560 (c.)
Hampshire
 Southampton, Kingsbury
  1063 J. Holloway
  Hall, 1887, p. 157 (also 1888, p. 157)

Worcestershire
Worcester
1064 Thomas Border
Noake, 1877, pp. 9-11

1561
Derbyshire
Chesterfield
1065 Richard Stevenson, nailer
Bestall and Fowkes, *Chesterfield*, 1977, p. 102
Dorset
Bingham's Melcombe
1066 Robarte Bingham, esquire
Bingham, 1860, pp. 153-156
Lancashire
Stubley Hall, Littleborough
1067 Robert Holt [Holte], esquire
Piccope, *Lancashire and Cheshire*, 1860, pp. 173-174
Leicestershire
Cossington
1068 Matthew Knyghtley, clergyman, parson of
Cossington
Hoskins, 1940, pp. 99-100
Hoskins, *Parson*, 1950, pp. 9-10
Lincolnshire
Clee, Thrunscoe
1069 Mathew Tuplyne, husbandman
Ambler, Watkinson, *Clee*, 1987, pp. 57-58
Scotland
Edinburgh (?)
1070 Mary, Queen of Scots
Thomson, *Edinburgh*, 1815, pp. 123-161
Staffordshire
Hales
1071 Thomas Grococke
Twemlow, *Tyrley*, 1948, pp. 279-280
Surrey
Alfold
1072 Thomas Moyr
Herridge, *Surrey*, 2005, pp. 27-28
Chertsey
1073 Jhone Mychell, widow
Herridge, *Surrey*, 2005, pp. 28-29
East Betchworth
1074 John Saker, husbandman
Herridge, *Surrey*, 2005, p. 31
Ewell
1075 Christopher Thorne, husbandman
Herridge, *Surrey*, 2005, pp. 34-35
Farnham, Runfold
1076 Thomas Haywarde
Herridge, *Surrey*, 2005, pp. 23-24
Frensham
1077 Oliver Fanner, tile maker
Herridge, *Surrey*, 2005, pp. 18-19
1078 Bartyllmew Steyll
Herridge, *Surrey*, 2005, pp. 33-34
Guildford
1079 Richard Forde, shoemaker
Herridge, *Surrey*, 2005, pp. 19-20
Guildford, St Mary's
1080 George Glover, clothier
Herridge, *Surrey*, 2005, pp. 20-23

Guildford, Holy Trinity
1081 Henry Selwode, painter
Herridge, *Surrey*, 2005, pp. 32-33
Hambledon
1082 Water Mabancke, mason
Herridge, *Surrey*, 2005, pp. 25-26
Horley
1083 Richard Lucas, clergyman, vicar of Horley
Herridge, *Surrey*, 2005, p. 25
Ockham
1084 Crystofer Lamboll, yeoman
Herridge, *Surrey*, 2005, pp. 24-25
Puttenham
1085 John Byckenall
Herridge, *Surrey*, 2005, p. 15
Send
1086 Petter Davy, weaver
Herridge, *Surrey*, 2005, p. 18
Shere
1087 John Shudde
Herridge, *Surrey*, 2005, pp. 32-33
Tandridge
1088 Robert Mowse
Herridge, *Surrey*, 2005, pp. 26-27
Thursley
1089 Harry Hedger
Herridge, *Surrey*, 2005, p. 24
Wonersh
1090 William Chanell
Herridge, *Surrey*, 2005, pp. 16-17
Worcestershire
Astley
1091 Walter Blount, esquire
Wanklyn, *Worcestershire*, 1998, pp. 34-37
Worcester
1092 Roger Yelfe, capper
Dyer, *Worcestershire*, 1967, pp. 19-21
Yorkshire
Grinton, West Stonesdale
1093 Ralph Alderson
Berry, *Swaledale*, 1998, p. 117
Grinton, Smarber
1094 Edmond Typladye
Berry, *Swaledale*, 1998, p. 116
Richmond
1095 Thomas Aykrigge, clergyman
Raine, *Richmond*, 1853, p. 149
Spaldington
1096 George Vavasor, gentleman
Brears, *Yorkshire*, 1972, pp. 9-13
Westerdale
1097 Alice Johnson
Crossley, *Yorkshire*, 1929, p. 56

1561 (c.)
Hertfordshire
St Albans, St Stephens
1098 John Turner
Parker, *Worldly Goods*, 2004, p. 63
Surrey
Bletchingley
1099 John Cacot
Herridge, *Surrey*, 2005, pp. 15-16

Chertsey
1100　John Banester
　Herridge, *Surrey*, 2005, p. 14
Fetcham
1101　William Roger
　Herridge, *Surrey*, 2005, pp. 29-30
Shere
1102　Thomas Wyght
　Herridge, *Surrey*, 2005, p. 36
Thursley
1103　Willyam Collen, yeoman
　Herridge, *Surrey*, 2005, p. 17

1562

Cheshire
Wrenbury
1104　Thomas Pexton, [husbandman]
　Pixton, *Wrenbury*, 2009, pp. 11-12
Wybunbury, Weston
1105　Dame Cicele Delves, widow of Sir Henry Delves
　Piccope, *Lancashire and Cheshire*, 1860, pp. 29-35
Derbyshire
Brimington
1106　Thomas Maryote
　Bestall and Fowkes, *Chesterfield*, 1977, pp. 102-103
Temple Normanton
1107　John Cleye, husbandman
　Bestall and Fowkes, *Chesterfield*, 1977, pp. 103-104
Walton
1108　Alen Lyngard, husbandman
　Bestall and Fowkes, *Chesterfield*, 1977, pp. 99-100
Co. Durham
Biddick
1109　Will'm Hilton, esquire
　Raine, *Wills and Inventories*, 1835, I, p. 203
Norton
1110　Nycholas Blaxton
　Raine, *Wills and Inventories*, 1835, I, p. 206
Shildon
1111　Bartholomewe Lylbourne [Bartholomew Lilburne]
　Raine, *Wills and Inventories*, 1835, I, pp. 193-194
Stockton
1112　Alleson Fleta' [Fletame]
　Raine, *Wills and Inventories*, 1835, I, p. 199
Essex
Boreham
1113　Richard Malte
　Emmison, *Essex*, 1, 1982, pp. 53-54
Hampshire
Southampton
1114　Thomas Etuer
　Roberts and Parker, *Southampton*, I, 1992, pp. 175-179
1115　John Fletcher, grocer
　Roberts and Parker, *Southampton*, I, 1992, pp. 179-184
Lancashire
Burscough
1116　William Asspinwall, clergyman, canon of the dissolved monastery of Burscough
　Piccope, *Lancashire and Cheshire*, 1860, p. 55
Ribchester
1117　John Townelay of Dutton
　Raine, *Richmond*, 1853, p. 152

Lincolnshire
Clee, Oole
1118　Thomas Dune
　Ambler, Watkinson, *Clee*, 1987, pp. 58-59
Norfolk
Bacton
1119　Thomas, William and Henry Calke
　Hall, 1887, p. 158
Northumberland
Bothal Castle
1120　Robert, Lord Ogle
　Raine, *Richmond*, 1853, pp. 154-155
Nottinghamshire
Eaton
1121　Thomas Wotton
　Kennedy, *Nottinghamshire*, 1963, pp. 77-79
Oxfordshire
Great Milton
1122　John Ives, husbandman
　Havinden, *Oxfordshire*, 1965, pp. 49-51
Scotland
Edinburgh, Holyrood Palace
1123　Mary Queen of Scots
　Robertson, *Royne Descosse*, 1863, pp. 28-48
Forfarshire, Balmady
　Agnes Betoune (also listed Kelly)
Forfarshire, Kelly
1124　Agnes Betoune (also listed Balmady)
　Hutcheson, 1916-1917, pp. 233-236
Staffordshire
Hales, Almington
1125　Richard Allen
　Twemlow, *Tyrley*, 1948, pp. 283-284
Hales, Bloore-in-Tyrley
1126　Humfrey Bate
　Twemlow, *Tyrley*, 1948, p. 293
Hales, Almington
1127　Richard Wade
　Twemlow, *Tyrley*, 1948, p. 281
Hales, Bloore-in-Tyrley
1128　Robert Wade
　Twemlow, *Tyrley*, 1948, p. 285
Suffolk
Chevington Hall
1129　Margaret, Countess of Bath
　Gage, 1838, pp. 326-327
Surrey
Capel
1130　John Peter
　Herridge, *Surrey*, 2005, p. 37
1131　Thomas Stere
　Herridge, *Surrey*, 2005, pp. 37-38
Warwickshire
Birmingham
1132　John Flavelle, [weaver]
　Holt, Ingram, Jarman, *Birmingham*, 1985, p. 17
Foleshill
1133　John Bakhowsse
　Upton, *Foleshill*, 1993, p. 40
Shottery
1134　Phylipe Welles [Philip Wells]
　Jones, *Stratford*, I, 2002, pp. 20-21

Westmorland
Kendal, Stramongate
  1135 Robert Doddinge
    Raine, *Richmond*, 1853, p. 156
Kendal
  1136 Robert Storreye
    Raine, *Richmond*, 1853, pp. 152-153
Yorkshire
Cleasby
  Rauf Cleysbie (see Scruton, Thrintoft)
Grinton, Satron
  1137 John Kereton
    Berry, *Swaledale*, 1998, p. 118
Knayton
  1138 Robert Prat, [farmer and blacksmith]
    Raine, *Wills and Inventories*, 1835, I, pp. 206-208
Richmond, St Nicholas
  1139 Johanna Wykeclyf, widow
    Raine, *Richmond*, 1853, pp. 161-164
Scruton, Thrintoft
  1140 Rauf Cleysbie (also listed Cleasby)
    Raine, *Richmond*, 1853, pp. 166-167
South Cave
  1141 Ellyng Wryght [Wright], grasswoman
    Kaner, *South Cave*, 1994, p. 64

1562 (c.)

Bedfordshire
Old Warden
  1142 Robert Gostwick
    Freeman, *Bedfordshire*, 1952, p. 102

1563

Derbyshire
Newbold
  1143 William Newbold alias Parkynson, husbandman
    Bestall and Fowkes, *Chesterfield*, 1977, pp. 104-105
Temple Normanton
  1144 Nicholas Bacon
    Bestall and Fowkes, *Chesterfield*, 1977, pp. 105-106
Co. Durham
Walworth
  1145 Ralfe [Ralf] Huton
    Raine, *Wills and Inventories*, 1835, I, pp. 209-210
Hertfordshire
St Albans, St Stephens
  1146 Robarde Cullys
    Parker, *Worldly Goods*, 2004, pp. 68-70
  1147 Robart Kentyshe
    Munby, *Worldly Goods*, 1991, pp. 38-40
Northumberland
Newcastle (?)
  1148 Robert Lynton, pedlar
    Raine, *Wills and Inventories*, 1835, I, p. 199
Nottinghamshire
Bleasby
  1149 John Bagaley
    Kennedy, *Nottinghamshire*, 1963, pp. 69-71
  1150 Nycholas Chapman
    Kennedy, *Nottinghamshire*, 1963, p. 72
  1151 Mytchell Horsepull
    Kennedy, *Nottinghamshire*, 1963, p. 74

Goverton
  1152 John Crane
    Kennedy, *Nottinghamshire*, 1963, pp. 73-74
Norwell Woodhouse
  1153 Thomas Sturtyvant, husbandman
    Kennedy, *Nottinghamshire*, 1963, p. 77
Southwell
  1154 Thomas Collye, husbandman
    Kennedy, *Nottinghamshire*, 1963, pp. 72-73
  1155 Richer Martine [Rycharde Martyne]
    Kennedy, *Nottinghamshire*, 1963, p. 75
  1156 John Michelle [Mytchell], husbandman
    Kennedy, *Nottinghamshire*, 1963, pp. 76-77
Upton
  1157 Thomas Calverton
    Kennedy, *Nottinghamshire*, 1963, pp. 71-72
Scotland
Edinburgh
  1158 Hugh, Earl of Eglinton
    Fraser, 1859, II, pp. 197-198
Staffordshire
Hales, Bloore-in-Tyrley
  1159 Agnes Gervis, widow
    Twemlow, *Tyrley*, 1948, p. 287
Hales Almington
  1160 Robert Hurlebutte
    Twemlow, *Tyrley*, 1948, p. 286
Surrey
Farnham, Runfold
  1161 Harry and Alice Juer
    Herridge, *Surrey*, 2005, p. 46
Farnham
  1162 Jone Hawle, widow, innholder
    Herridge, *Surrey*, 2005, pp. 38-40
Farnham, Runfold
  1163 Peter Mantte [Mawnte], weaver
    Herridge, *Surrey*, 2005, pp. 46-47
Hambledon
  1164 John Hull, gentleman
    Herridge, *Surrey*, 2005, pp. 40-45
Unlocated
  1165 Robert Conyers
    Raine, *Wills and Inventories*, 1835, I, p. 209
Warwickshire
Coventry
  1166 Robert Dudley, [draper]
    Hulton and Castle, *Tudor*, 1987, pp. 18-21
Foleshill
  1167 Hwghe Hurden
    Upton, *Foleshill*, 1993, pp. 41-42
Hatton
  1168 Lawrence Ebrall
    Sheasby, 1994, p. 47
Westmorland
Brantfell, Windermere
  1169 Mathew Dixon
    Raine, *Richmond*, 1853, p. 169
Morland, Thrimby
  1170 John Salkeld, [gentleman]
    Moore, *Salkelds*, 1988, p. 182
Yorkshire
Grinton, Raw
  1171 Richard Allderson
    Berry, *Swaledale*, 1998, p. 119

Grinton, Storthwaite Hall
1172 Matthew Hall
Berry, *Swaledale*, 1998, pp. 121-122
Grinton, Oxnop
1173 Robert Johnson
Berry, *Swaledale*, 1998, pp. 123-125
Westerdale
1174 John Fayrewedder
Crossley, *Yorkshire*, 1929, p. 58
1175 John Kyldale
Crossley, *Yorkshire*, 1929, pp. 57-58

1563 (c.)

Yorkshire
Westerdale
1176 [Leonard] Watson
Crossley, *Yorkshire*, 1929, p. 57

1564

Cheshire
Tarvin
1177 Wyllyam Thorneton
Bland, *Christleton*, 2002, pp. 6-9
Cumberland
Burgh by Sands
1178 William Threlkeld, bailiff of Burgh
Jackson, 1889, p. 39
Derbyshire
Chesterfield
1179 William Braylisforthe
Bestall and Fowkes, *Chesterfield*, 1977, pp. 106-107
1180 John Mychell, butcher
Bestall and Fowkes, *Chesterfield*, 1977, pp. 107-108
Ockbrook
1181 Thomas Adam
Johnson, 1994, p. 23
Devonshire
Exeter
1182 Robarte Mathewe, baker
Portman, *Exeter*, 1966, pp. 94-96
Co. Durham
Durham Cathedral
1183 John Bynley, minor canon
Raine, *Wills and Inventories*, 1835, I, pp. 220-221
Gateshead
1184 Margaret Cottom, widow
Raine, *Wills and Inventories*, 1835, I, pp. 223-224
Hunter Banks
1185 Lionell Emerson
Raine, *Wills and Inventories*, 1835, I, p. 226
Stainton-le-Street
1186 Robert Lambton
Raine, *Wills and Inventories*, 1835, I, pp. 212-213
Hampshire
Southampton
1187 William Christmas, brewer [and innholder]
Roberts and Parker, *Southampton*, I, 1992, pp. 184-193
1188 John Johnson, merchant
Roberts and Parker, *Southampton*, I, 1992, pp. 193-201
1189 John Lughting, merchant
Roberts and Parker, *Southampton*, I, 1992, pp. 201-223

1190 William Morrell, clergyman, parson of St Lawrence
Roberts and Parker, *Southampton*, I, 1992, pp. 223-225
Hertfordshire
Sarratt
1191 Jhon Okeley
Bullen, *Sarratt*, [1982], pp. 45-46
Lancashire
Astley, Morleys
1192 Thome Leylonde [Thomas Leyland], esquire
Piccope, *Lancashire and Cheshire*, 1857, pp. 166-167
Lytham (?)
1193 Thomas Premytt, clergyman
Raine, *Richmond*, 1853, p. 172
Lincolnshire
Clee, Itterby
1194 William Clarkson
Ambler, Watkinson, *Clee*, 1987, pp. 59-60
Oxfordshire
Somerton
1195 Joyce Bullen
Havinden, *Oxfordshire*, 1965, pp. 51-52
Staffordshire
Dudley
1196 Phylyppe Cartwright
Roper, *Dudley*, 1965, p. 9
Warwickshire
Birmingham
1197 Edward Carter, tanner
Holt, Ingram, Jarman, *Birmingham*, 1985, p. 18
Foleshill
1198 Bartylmoe Royle
Upton, *Foleshill*, 1993, pp. 43-45
Stratford-on-Avon
1199 Agnes Eliette [Eliott], widow
Jones, *Stratford*, I, 2002, pp. 23-24
1200 Robert Mylles [Mills], [brewer]
Jones, *Stratford*, I, 2002, p. 22
Worcestershire
Belbroughton
1201 John a Pen
Roper, *Belbroughton*, 1967-1968, p. 19
Besford
1202 Thomas Harrwell [Harwell], esquire
Wanklyn, *Worcestershire*, 1998, p. 412
Worcester, All Saints
1203 Willm. Heynes
Noake, 1877, pp. 11-13
Yorkshire
Birstwith
1204 Miles Stubbe
Collins, *Stubbs*, 1915, pp. 92-93
Easby
1205 Mychaell Clerkson, clergyman (also listed Richmond)
Raine, *Richmond*, 1853, pp. 173-174
Grinton, Satron
1206 George Braedreg
Berry, *Swaledale*, 1998, p. 133

Marske, West Applegarth
  1207 Thomas Myddelton, gentleman
    Raine, *Richmond*, 1853, pp. 171-172
    Berry, *Swaledale*, 1998, pp. 127-131
Richmond
  Mychaell Clerkson, clergyman (see Easby)

1565

Cheshire
Cholmondeley
  1208 John Dod
    Pearson, *Malpas*, [2005], p. 34

Cumberland
Melmerby
  1209 Roland Threlkeld, clergyman, parson of
  Melmerby
    Jackson, 1889, pp. 29-32

Derbyshire
Walton
  1210 Godfrey Elyot
    Bestall and Fowkes, *Chesterfield*, 1977, p. 109

Co. Durham
Gateshead
  1211 Richard Bayne, tanner
    Hodgson, *Wills and Inventories*, 1906, III, pp. 30-31
Ryton, Thornley
  1212 Robert Tempest, gentleman
    Raine, *Wills and Inventories*, 1835, I, pp. 242-243
St Andrew Auckland
  1213 Thomas Wrangh'm [Wrangham], clergyman
    Raine, *Wills and Inventories*, 1835, I, pp. 245-246
South Shields
  1214 Richard Atkinson, fisherman
    Raine, *Wills and Inventories*, 1835, I, p. 247
Washington
  1215 Roland Pratt, parson
    Raine, *Wills and Inventories*, 1835, I, pp. 226-227
Witton Gilbert
  1216 Jhone Coplant [John Coplane]
    Raine, *Wills and Inventories*, 1835, I, p. 225
  1217 Cuthberte Richardson, yeoman
    Raine, *Wills and Inventories*, 1835, I, pp. 243-244

Hampshire
Longparish, Gavelacre
  1218 Thomas Yngpen, esquire
    Ingpen, 1916, pp. 186-189
Southampton
  1219 Alice Aberie
    Roberts and Parker, *Southampton*, I, 1992, pp. 225-231
  1220 Stephen Cockerell, merchant
    Roberts and Parker, *Southampton*, I, 1992, pp. 231-233
  1221 John Cotton, mariner
    Roberts and Parker, *Southampton*, I, 1992, pp. 233-237

Hertfordshire
St Albans, St Stephens
  1222 William Collyns
    Parker, *Worldly Goods*, 2004, p. 71
  1223 Jhon Hills
    Munby, *Worldly Goods*, 1991, p. 44
Sarratt
  1224 John Reynolde
    Bullen, *Sarratt*, [1982], p. 47

Lincolnshire
Clee, Oole
  1225 Rychard Betneyff
    Ambler, Watkinson, *Clee*, 1987, pp. 60-61
Clee
  1226 Bartylmewe Colbye
    Ambler, Watkinson, *Clee*, 1987, p. 61
Clee, Itterby
  1227 Robert Pell
    Ambler, Watkinson, *Clee*, 1987, p. 60

Nottinghamshire
Halam
  1228 Jone Wattes, widow
    Kennedy, *Nottinghamshire*, 1963, pp. 93-94
Hexgreave Park, Kirklington
  1229 Henrye Fornys [Furnes]
    Kennedy, *Nottinghamshire*, 1963, pp. 84-85
North Leverton, Coates
  1230 William Cook
    Kennedy, *Nottinghamshire*, 1963, pp. 83-84
Southwell, Westhorpe
  1231 William Brythley
    Kennedy, *Nottinghamshire*, 1963, pp. 81-82
Southwell, Easthorpe
  1232 William Towers, husbandman
    Kennedy, *Nottinghamshire*, 1963, pp. 92-93

Oxfordshire
Kidlington
  1233 William Haworthe, baker
    Havinden, *Oxfordshire*, 1965, pp. 52-54

Surrey
Chobham
  1234 John Bonyon, yeoman [chandler]
    Herridge, *Surrey*, 2005, pp. 48-49
  1235 Rycharde Marlyn
    Herridge, *Surrey*, 2005, p. 49
Cranleigh
  1236 Margaret Amy, widow
    Herridge, *Surrey*, 2005, pp. 47-48
Godalming
  1237 Richard Oliver, innholder
    Herridge, *Surrey*, 2005, pp. 50-51
Horley
  1238 Nicholas Alyngham, husbandman
    Herridge, *Surrey*, 2005, p. 47
Horsell
  1239 Anthony Worthyngton, husbandman
    Herridge, *Surrey*, 2005, p. 52
Merton
  1240 Thomas Morrell, tailor
    Herridge, *Surrey*, 2005, pp. 49-50

Warwickshire
Stratford-on-Avon
  1241 John Bretchegyrdle, clergyman, vicar of
  Stratford
    Jones, *Stratford*, I, 2002, p. 28
  1242 William Perotte [Perrot], [innkeeper]
    Jones, *Stratford*, I, 2002, pp. 25-27

Yorkshire
East Grinton
  1243 Robert Wardall
    Berry, *Swaledale*, 1998, p. 136

Knaresborough
1244 John Birnand, esquire
Raine, *Richmond*, 1853, pp. 178-180
Richmond
1245 Peter Wryght
Fieldhouse, 1974, pp. 16-17
Templehirst
Matthew Stuart, Earl of Lennox (see Temple Newsam)
Temple Newsam
1246 Matthew Stuart, Earl of Lennox (also listed
Templehirst)
Crossley, 1920, pp. 94-100
Westerdale
1247 John Whyte
Crossley, *Yorkshire*, 1929, p. 59

1565 (c.)
Lancashire
St Helens, Windle
1248 Elsabeth Wynstanley, widow
St Helens, *Angells*, 1999, pp. 3-4
Surrey
Horsell
1249 Robert Taylor, husbandman
Herridge, *Surrey*, 2005, pp. 51-52

1566
Derbyshire
Calow
1250 John Stubbinge, husbandman
Bestall and Fowkes, *Chesterfield*, 1977, pp. 110-111
Co. Durham
Aycliffe
1251 Edward Strangwishe
Raine, *Wills and Inventories*, 1835, I, p. 263
Barnard Castle
1252 Radulphus [Ralph] Bayles, clergyman
Raine, *Wills and Inventories*, 1835, I, p. 260
Burn Hall
1253 Will'm [William] Claxton, esquire
Raine, *Wills and Inventories*, 1835, I, pp. 252-253
Durham
1254 Will'm [William] Watton, draper
Raine, *Wills and Inventories*, 1835, I, pp. 256-259
Elton
1255 Margaret Burdon, widow
Raine, *Wills and Inventories*, 1835, I, p. 240
Hampshire
Appuldurcombe, Isle of Wight
1256 Sir Richard Worsley
Whitehead, 1904-1906, pp. 279-295
Nursling
1257 Thomas Mill, gentleman (see Southampton)
Southampton
1258 Annes James, widow
Roberts and Parker, *Southampton*, I, 1992, pp. 237-239
1259 Nowell Messervye, merchant
Roberts and Parker, *Southampton*, I, 1992, pp. 240-243
1260 Thomas Mill, gentleman (also listed Nursling)
Roberts and Parker, *Southampton*, II, 1992, pp. 244-258
Hertfordshire
St Albans, St Stephens
1261 Jone Collyn, widow
Parker, *Worldly Goods*, 2004, p. 72

Ireland
Kinsale
1262 Andrew Browne
Caulfield, 1862, p. 301
Kent
Ashford
1263 John Bullen alias Gilham, [joiner]
Melling, 1965, pp. 20-21
Northumberland
Berwick
1264 John Selbye, gentleman
Raine, *Wills and Inventories*, 1835, I, p. 236
Haughton
1265 Thomas Swynburne [Swinburne]
Raine, *Wills and Inventories*, 1835, I, pp. 237-238
Unlocated
1266 Edward Athey, clergyman
Raine, *Wills and Inventories*, 1835, I, p. 241
Nottinghamshire
Beckingham
1267 John Hall
Kennedy, *Nottinghamshire*, 1963, pp. 114-116
Simpson, 1985, pp. 294-297
Bleasby
1268 William Buller, clergyman
Kennedy, *Nottinghamshire*, 1963, pp. 82-83
Calverton
1269 Margarette Olyver, widow
Kennedy, *Nottinghamshire*, 1963, p. 85
Dunham-on-Trent
1270 George Cartwright
Kennedy, *Nottinghamshire*, 1963, pp. 99-100
Farnsfield
1271 Tomesine Whyteheade
Kennedy, *Nottinghamshire*, 1963, p. 108
Halam
1272 Robert Albyn, husbandman
Kennedy, *Nottinghamshire*, 1963, p. 81
Halloughton
1273 Elizabethe Marcrofte, widow
Kennedy, *Nottinghamshire*, 1963, pp. 104-105
Kirklington
1274 John Walker, husbandman
Kennedy, *Nottinghamshire*, 1963, p. 107
Normanton, Southwell
1275 Wylliam Sonsum
Kennedy, *Nottinghamshire*, 1963, p. 80
Norwell
1276 Barth[olomew] Broune
Kennedy, *Nottinghamshire*, 1963, pp. 95-96
1277 William Farneton, husbandman
Kennedy, *Nottinghamshire*, 1963, pp. 100-101
Norwell Woodhouse
1278 John Lee, labourer
Kennedy, *Nottinghamshire*, 1963, p. 104
Oxton
1279 Ezabell Knowlles, widow
Kennedy, *Nottinghamshire*, 1963, p. 103
1280 Elizabethe Markham, widow
Kennedy, *Nottinghamshire*, 1963, pp. 105-106
South Muskham
1281 Thomas Smyth [Smythe]
Kennedy, *Nottinghamshire*, 1963, pp. 106-107

1282 Thomas Sudbury, yeoman
Kennedy, *Nottinghamshire*, 1963, pp. 85-92
Southwell
1283 William Bulbie, tanner
Kennedy, *Nottinghamshire*, 1963, pp. 96-97
1284 Wyllyam Calverton, husbandman
Kennedy, *Nottinghamshire*, 1963, pp. 97-99
1285 Roberte Franke
Kennedy, *Nottinghamshire*, 1963, pp. 101-102
Southwell, Easthorpe
1286 Christofer Yarworthe
Kennedy, *Nottinghamshire*, 1963, p. 108
Upton
1287 Robert Huddlestone
Kennedy, *Nottinghamshire*, 1963, pp. 102-103
Scotland
Edinburgh Castle
1288 Mary, Queen of Scots
Thomson, *Edinburgh*, 1815, pp. 165-177
Surrey
Horne
1289 William Elvyn
Herridge, *Surrey*, 2005, pp. 54-55
Kingston-upon-Thames
1290 Nicholas Walker, yeoman and smith
Herridge, *Surrey*, 2005, pp. 55-56
Reigate
1291 William Amias, husbandman
Herridge, *Surrey*, 2005, p. 53
Warwickshire
Birmingham
1292 William Askereicke
Holt, Ingram, Jarman, *Birmingham*, 1985, pp. 19-21
Foleshill
1293 Wllm Smyth, [husbandman]
Upton, *Foleshill*, 1993, pp. 46-47
Stratford-on-Avon
1294 John Lews [Lewis] alias [Atkins], baker
Jones, *Stratford*, I, 2002, pp. 29-30
Westmorland
Crook
1295 Christofer Phillipson
Raine, *Richmond*, 1853, p. 189
Worcestershire
Halesowen
1296 William Grove
Davenport, 1912, pp. 4-5
Norton-juxta-Kempsey, Wood Hall
1297 William Gower, esquire
Wanklyn, *Worcestershire*, 1998, pp. 37-41
Yorkshire
Downholme, Stainton
1298 John Lawkeland
Berry, *Swaledale*, 1998, pp. 145-146
East Grinton
1299 William Dawson
Berry, *Swaledale*, 1998, pp. 140-145
Hipswell
1300 Jane Fulthrop, widow
Raine, *Richmond*, 1853, pp. 183-184
Hudswell
1301 James Rayne, yeoman
Berry, *Swaledale*, 1998, p. 138

Richmond
1302 Christine Burgle, gentlewoman, late prioress of Nunkeeling, Yorkshire
Raine, *Richmond*, 1853, p. 193
South Cave
1303 Richard Cave
Kaner, *South Cave*, 1994, pp. 65-66
Westerdale
1304 Katheren Whyte
Crossley, *Yorkshire*, 1929, pp. 59-60

1567
Derbyshire
Chesterfield
1305 Henry Fletcher
Bestall and Fowkes, *Chesterfield*, 1977, pp. 111-112
1306 Henry Ludlam
Bestall and Fowkes, *Chesterfield*, 1977, p. 110
Glossop, Thornsett
1307 Nycholas Garleke, [gentleman]
Bryant, Lee, Miller, *New Mills I*, 1995, pp. 23-24
Glossop, Ladshayebothum
1308 Robert Nedam, [husbandman]
Bryant, Lee, Miller, *New Mills I*, 1995, p. 26
Co. Durham
Beaumont Hill
1309 Edwarde P'kinson [Edward Parkinson]
Raine, *Wills and Inventories*, 1835, I, pp. 271-272
Durham, South Bailey
1310 Jane Haule, widow
Raine, *Wills and Inventories*, 1835, I, pp. 278-279
Durham
1311 John Welles, clergyman
Raine, *Wills and Inventories*, 1835, I, p. 274
Harperley
1312 Sir George Conyers
Raine, *Wills and Inventories*, 1835, I, pp. 266-268
Hunwick
1313 Elizabeth Hootton [Hutton], widow
Raine, *Wills and Inventories*, 1835, I, pp. 249-251
Staindrop [?]
1314 Xp'ofor [Christofor] Todd
Raine, *Wills and Inventories*, 1835, I, p. 271
Stanhope in Weardale
1315 Anthony Trollope
Hodgson, *Wills and Inventories*, 1906, III, p. 37
Hampshire
Southampton
1316 John Raynoldes, fishmonger
Roberts and Parker, *Southampton*, II, 1992, pp. 258-260
Hertfordshire
St Albans, St Stephens
1317 Robert Marston
Parker, *Worldly Goods*, 2004, p. 73
Ireland
Cork
1318 William Verdon
Caulfield, 1862, pp. 299-300
Kent
Canterbury, St George's
1319 Harman Vearson, [glazier]
Melling, 1965, pp. 21-22

Lincolnshire
 Allington
  1320 Thomas Graunte
   Pask, *Allington*, 1989, pp. 28-29
 Clee
  1321 William Neave
   Ambler, Watkinson, *Clee*, 1987, pp. 61-62
 Market Rasen
  1322 John Elstones
   Neave, *Market Rasen*, 1985, p. 65
Nottinghamshire
 Edingley, Greaves Lane
  1323 Elizabeth Leeke
   Kennedy, *Nottinghamshire*, 1963, pp. 118-119
 Farnsfield
  1324 John Atkyne
   Kennedy, *Nottinghamshire*, 1963, p. 94
  1325 Richard Barrie, gentleman
   Kennedy, *Nottinghamshire*, 1963, pp. 110-111
  1326 Thomas Dawson, husbandman
   Kennedy, *Nottinghamshire*, 1963, p. 100
  1327 John Rodes
   Kennedy, *Nottinghamshire*, 1963, p. 106
 Norwell
  1328 Adam Fenwick, clergyman, vicar of Norwell
   Kennedy, *Nottinghamshire*, 1963, p. 113
 Ragnall
  1329 Wylliam Pyckhaver
   Kennedy, *Nottinghamshire*, 1963, pp. 120-121
 Southwell
  1330 William Bee
   Kennedy, *Nottinghamshire*, 1963, p. 95
  1331 Margarett Bulbie, widow
   Kennedy, *Nottinghamshire*, 1963, pp. 111-112
  1332 Christofer Pennell, clergyman, vicar choral of
   Southwell
   Kennedy, *Nottinghamshire*, 1963, pp. 128-131
 Woodborough
  1333 William Alvye, husbandman
   Kennedy, *Nottinghamshire*, 1963, p. 109
Staffordshire
 Dudley
  1334 Henry Tomens
   Roper, *Dudley*, 1965, p. 10
Surrey
 Ewhurst
  1335 Nycholas Hyll, husbandman
   Herridge, *Surrey*, 2005, p. 61
 Farnham
  1336 Thomas Webb
   Herridge, *Surrey*, 2005, pp. 64-65
 Fetcham
  1337 John Bet
   Herridge, *Surrey*, 2005, pp. 57-58
 Frensham, West End
  1338 Bartholemew Hardynge, husbandman
   Herridge, *Surrey*, 2005, pp. 58-59
 Hascombe
  1339 William Birle
   Herridge, *Surrey*, 2005, p. 59
 Kingston-upon-Thames
  1340 John Rawstricke, saddler
   Herridge, *Surrey*, 2005, pp. 61-62

 Wonersh, Blundells
  1341 John Harper alias Harfell, yeoman
   Herridge, *Surrey*, 2005, pp. 59-60
 Wrecclesham
  1342 Steven Sherube [Sherubbe]
   Herridge, *Surrey*, 2005, pp. 62-64
Warwickshire
 Stratford-on-Avon
  1343 Harry Sydnolle [Henry Sydnall]
   Jones, *Stratford*, I, 2002, pp. 30-31
Westmorland
 Morland, Thrimby
  1344 [An]ne Salkeld, widow
   Moore, *Salkelds*, 1988, p. 183
Worcestershire
 Worcester, St Peter's
  1345 Thomas Yeatt, smith
   Dyer, *Worcestershire*, 1967, pp. 21-25
Yorkshire
 Downholme
  1346 Christopher Lofthouse
   Berry, *Swaledale*, 1998, pp. 148-150
 Fixby
  1347 John Thornhill, esquire
   Brears, *Yorkshire*, 1972, pp. 14-19
 Grinton, Calvert Houses
  1348 John Melner
   Berry, *Swaledale*, 1998, p. 147
 Hudswell
  1349 John Rawe, husbandman
   Berry, *Swaledale*, 1998, pp. 150-151
  1350 William Scrafton, husbandman
   Berry, *Swaledale*, 1998, p. 139
 Mortham
  1351 Thomas Rokebie, esquire
   Raine, *Richmond*, 1853, pp. 200-204
 Richmond
  1352 Rauf Gower, esquire
   Raine, *Richmond*, 1853, pp. 196-198
 Spofford
  George Nevill, clergyman, late master of Well hospital
  (see Well)
 Toothill
  1353 Mrs Elizabeth Thornehill, widow
   Brears, *Yorkshire*, 1972, pp. 19-20
 Well
  1354 George Nevill, clergyman, late master of Well
  hospital (also listed Spofford)
   Raine, *Richmond*, 1853, pp. 209-212

1568
Buckinghamshire
 Sydenham
  1355 Thomas Kempet
   Hall, 1887, p. 157
Derbyshire
 Chesterfield
  1356 Lawrence Boller
   Bestall and Fowkes, *Chesterfield*, 1977, pp. 116-117
  1357 Elizabeth Johnson alias Edmondson, widow
   Bestall and Fowkes, *Chesterfield*, 1977, pp. 112-113

Hasland
  1358 Thomas Shaw, husbandman
    Bestall and Fowkes, *Chesterfield*, 1977, p. 114
Newbold
  1359 Robert Baggeleye, husbandman
    Bestall and Fowkes, *Chesterfield*, 1977, pp. 114-115
Tapton
  1360 Rolande Durraunt, gentleman
    Bestall and Fowkes, *Chesterfield*, 1977, pp. 115-116
Dorsetshire
Wimborne Minster
  1361 John Ace, clergyman
    Hutchins, 1868, p. 261
Co. Durham
Bishop [North] Auckland
  1362 Jhone [John] Bayles, [shopkeeper]
    Raine, *Wills and Inventories*, 1835, I, pp. 293-294
Darlington
  1363 Margaret Gascoigne
    Raine, *Wills and Inventories*, 1835, I, p. 273
Durham, St Margarets
  1364 Alexander Woodmons, clergyman
    Raine, *Wills and Inventories*, 1835, I, p. 284
Hartlepool
  1365 John Fetherstone
    Raine, *Wills and Inventories*, 1835, I, pp. 274-275
Herrington
  1366 Katherine Lady Hedworth, widow
    Raine, *Wills and Inventories*, 1835, I, pp. 281-283
Shotton
  1367 Anne Hebborne [Hebburn], widow
    Hodgson, *Wills and Inventories*, 1906, III, pp. 44-45
Walworth, Heighington
  1368 Sampson Wyvell [Wyvill]
    Hodgson, *Wills and Inventories*, 1906, III, pp. 43-44
Hampshire
Southampton
  1369 John Norton
    Roberts and Parker, *Southampton*, II, 1992, pp. 260-261
Leicestershire
Braunstone
  1370 George Cater, yeoman
    Wilshere, *Braunstone*, 1983, pp. 6-7
Lincolnshire
Clee
  1371 Crystofer Homptone
    Ambler, Watkinson, *Clee*, 1987, pp. 62-63
  1372 William Tuplyne
    Ambler, Watkinson, *Clee*, 1987, p. 63
Nottinghamshire
Bathley
  1373 John Nyckson
    Kennedy, *Nottinghamshire*, 1963, pp. 126-128
Bleasby
  1374 George Charleton, clergyman
    Kennedy, *Nottinghamshire*, 1963, pp. 122-123
Blidworth
  1375 William Emley, clergyman, vicar of Blidworth
    Kennedy, *Nottinghamshire*, 1963, p. 112
  1376 Thomas Heylow
    Kennedy, *Nottinghamshire*, 1963, pp. 125-126

Edingley
  1377 John Bulbye
    Kennedy, *Nottinghamshire*, 1963, p. 122
North Leverton
  1378 William Lawrance
    Kennedy, *Nottinghamshire*, 1963, pp. 117-118
  1379 Henrie Peace, clergyman, vicar of Norwell
    Kennedy, *Nottinghamshire*, 1963, pp. 119-120
Norwell
  1380 John Johnson, husbandman
    Kennedy, *Nottinghamshire*, 1963, pp. 116-117
Southwell, Westhorpe
  1381 Robert Ambre
    Kennedy, *Nottinghamshire*, 1963, p. 110
Oxfordshire
Hampton Poyle
  1382 Robert Holland, day labourer
    Havinden, *Oxfordshire*, 1965, p. 54
Sydenham (?)
  1383 Thomas Kempet
    Hall, 1887, p. 157
Unlocated
  1384 William Bowden
    Havinden, *Oxfordshire*, 1965, pp. 55-56
Staffordshire
Dudley
  1385 William Goslinge
    Roper, *Dudley*, 1965, p. 11
  1386 Clare Jones, [widow]
    Roper, *Dudley*, 1965, p. 13
  1387 Robert Wheler
    Roper, *Dudley*, 1965, p. 12
Surrey
Ashstead
  1388 Thomas Otwey
    Herridge, *Surrey*, 2005, p. 67
Warwickshire
Luddington
  1389 Rychard Hunt, husbandman
    Jones, *Stratford*, I, 2002, p. 34
Stratford-on-Avon
  1390 Rychard Samyell [Richard Samuel]
    Jones, *Stratford*, I, 2002, p. 33
Westmorland
Troutbeck
  1391 John Rolandson
    Raine, *Richmond*, 1853, pp. 225-226
Yorkshire
Grinton, Harkerside
  1392 John Paikcoke
    Berry, *Swaledale*, 1998, pp. 152-153
Healaugh
  1393 Sir Thomas Wharton, Lord Wharton
    Evans, 1945, pp. 140-150
    Brears, *Yorkshire*, 1972, pp. 23-36
York Minster
  1394 William Rokebie, clergyman, Archdeacon of the East Riding
    Cross, *York*, I, 1984, pp. 106-107

1568 (c.)

Buckinghamshire
Dorney, Sypenham
1395 Thomas Kempe
Hall, 1888, p. 157
Staffordshire
Wall
1396 Charles Nedham
Vaisey, *Lichfield*, 1969, p. 41
Surrey
Gatton
1397 Jone Beste, widow
Herridge, *Surrey*, 2005, p. 66
Kingston-upon-Thames
1398 Robert Andrew
Herridge, *Surrey*, 2005, p. 65
Worplesdon
1399 Thomas Meede, tile maker
Herridge, *Surrey*, 2005, p. 66

1569

Cumberland
Melmerby
1400 Christopher Threlkeld, esquire
Jackson, 1889, pp. 33-34
Derbyshire
Glossop, Holehouse
1401 Wylliam Andrew, [husbandman]
Bryant, Lee, Miller, *New Mills I*, 1995, p. 29
Glossop, Thornsett Fields
1402 Wylliam Bramall, husbandman
Bryant, Lee, Miller, *New Mills I*, 1995, p. 31
Hasland
1403 William Lane
Bestall and Fowkes, *Chesterfield*, 1977, pp. 117-118
Devonshire
Kenn
1404 [name lost]
Cash, *Devon*, 1966, pp. 2-3
Rewe
1405 Robert Catlake
Cash, *Devon*, 1966, p. 3
Co. Durham
Coniscliffe
1406 Henry Plomber, clergyman, vicar of Coniscliffe
Raine, *Barnes*, 1850, pp. cvii-cviii
Durham
1407 Bartram Robson
Raine, *Wills and Inventories*, 1835, I, p. 308
Gateshead
1408 John Tedcastle, cutler
Raine, *Wills and Inventories*, 1835, I, p. 302
Stanley
1409 Thomas Tempest, gentleman
Hodgson, *Wills and Inventories*, 1906, III, p. 48
Hampshire
Southampton
1410 Andrew Boke, [shoemaker]
Roberts and Parker, *Southampton*, II, 1992, pp. 262-263
Hertfordshire
St Albans, St Stephens, Cuckmans
1411 Crystover Marson
Parker, *Worldly Goods*, 2004, pp. 73-75

Kent
Boughton under Blean
1412 Thomas Wyhall
Barley, *Farmhouse and Cottage*, 1961, p. 277
Lancashire
Reddish
1413 John Reddish, esquire
Earwaker, *Lancashire and Cheshire*, 1884, pp. 35-38
Leicestershire
Braunstone
1414 Wylliam Clarke, husbandman
Wilshere, *Braunstone*, 1983, p. 8
Lincolnshire
Clee, Itterby
1415 Roberte Masone
Ambler, Watkinson, *Clee*, 1987, pp. 63-64
London
Camberwell
1416 Richard Basyngton, yeoman
Herridge, *Surrey*, 2005, pp. 67-68
Nottinghamshire
Haughton
1417 John Derrye, husbandman
Kennedy, *Nottinghamshire*, 1963, pp. 124-125
Surrey
Dunsfold
1418 William Baker
Herridge, *Surrey*, 2005, p. 71
Witley
1419 George Byrche, clergyman, vicar of Witley
Herridge, *Surrey*, 2005, pp. 68-69
Wales
Montgomeryshire, Moughtrey
1420 Lewys ap Edward
Morris, 1893, p. 250
Warwickshire
Birmingham
1421 Rychard Hammond, [draper]
Holt, Ingram, Jarman, *Birmingham*, 1985, p. 24
Stoneleigh, Hurst
1422 Humphrey Partrige alias Dowland
Alcock, *Warwickshire*, 1993, pp. 76-77
Stratford-upon-Avon
1423 Jhon Freman [John Freeman]
Jones, *Stratford*, I, 2002, pp. 35-36
Westmorland
Kendal
1424 William Benson
Raine, *Richmond*, 1853, p. 224
Sizergh Castle
1425 Walter Strikland, esquire (also listed Halnaby, Yorkshire)
Raine, *Richmond*, 1853, pp. 218-224
Hornyold, 1928, pp. 94-98
Worcestershire
Belbroughton
1426 Humfreye Siche
Roper, *Belbroughton*, 1967-1968, p. 22
Worcester, St Nicholas
1427 Henry Grene, [pewterer and bell founder]
Dyer, *Worcestershire*, 1967, pp. 25-28

Yorkshire
Downholme Park
  1428 William Harlande
    Berry, *Swaledale*, 1998, p155-156
Grinton, The Castell
  1429 James Bynkes
    Berry, *Swaledale*, 1998, pp. 159-162
Grinton, High Smarber
  1430 Margaret Parke
    Berry, *Swaledale*, 1998, pp. 163-164
Halnaby
  Walter Strikland, esquire (see Sizergh Castle, Westmorland)
Marske, Skelton
  1431 Isabel Hutchinsonn, widow
    Berry, *Swaledale*, 1998, pp. 157-158

1569 (c.)
Lincolnshire
Market Rasen
  1432 Elyn Clarke, widow
    Neave, *Market Rasen*, 1985, p. 65

1570
Derbyshire
Calow
  1433 Rauffe Watson, husbandman
    Bestall and Fowkes, *Chesterfield*, 1977, pp. 119-120
  1434 Richard Watson, husbandman
    Bestall and Fowkes, *Chesterfield*, 1977, pp. 118-119
Co. Durham
Darlington
  1435 Cristopher Dayll [Christopher Dale], innholder
    Hodgson, *Wills and Inventories*, 1906, III, pp. 52-53
Denton
  1436 Robert Estby [Estbye], clergyman
    Raine, *Wills and Inventories*, 1835, I, pp. 342-343
Durham, Sidegate
  1437 Marione Randall
    Raine, *Wills and Inventories*, 1835, I, pp. 343-344
Edmondbyers
  1438 John Foster, clergyman
    Raine, *Wills and Inventories*, 1835, I, p. 313
Gateshead
  1439 Will'm [William] Dagg, spurrier
    Raine, *Wills and Inventories*, 1835, I, pp. 333-334
Gibside
  1440 Roger Blaixton [Blakiston], gentleman
    Hodgson, *Wills and Inventories*, 1906, III, p. 49
Hart
  1441 Rychard [Richard] Gregge, clergyman
    Hodgson, *Wills and Inventories*, 1906, III, p. 55
Thornley
  1442 M'gerye Trolope [Margerye Trollope], [widow]
    Raine, *Wills and Inventories*, 1835, I, pp. 303-304
Unlocated
  1443 William Wren
    Hodgson, *Wills and Inventories*, 1906, III, pp. 51-52
Weardale
  1444 Alexander Fetherston [Featherston]
    Hodgson, *Wills and Inventories*, 1906, III, p. 55
Winston
  1445 Richard Farroo [Farrow], clergyman
    Raine, *Barnes*, 1850, pp. cix-cx
    Hodgson, *Wills and Inventories*, 1906, III, p. 54

Hampshire
Southampton
  1446 Thomas Edmondes [Edmunds], [cloth merchant]
    Roberts and Parker, *Southampton*, II, 1992, pp. 264-270
  1447 Eustace Hammon
    Roberts and Parker, *Southampton*, II, 1992, p. 270
  1448 John Lumberte, tailor
    Roberts and Parker, *Southampton*, II, 1992, pp. 270-275
  1449 John Morley
    Roberts and Parker, *Southampton*, II, 1992, pp. 275-276
  1450 Elizabeth Morley, widow
    Roberts and Parker, *Southampton*, II, 1992, pp. 276-277
  1451 Elizabeth Pace, widow
    Roberts and Parker, *Southampton*, II, 1992, pp. 277-280
  1452 Edward Willmott, merchant and innkeeper
    Roberts and Parker, *Southampton*, II, 1992, pp. 280-289
Hertfordshire
St Albans, St Stephens
  1453 William Royse
    Parker, *Worldly Goods*, 2004, pp. 75-77
Unlocated
  1454 Christoffar Roys
    Parker, *Worldly Goods*, 2004, p. 77
Lancashire
Manchester
  1455 John Nabbs, [cloth maker, woollen weaver]
    Lowe, 1972, pp. 102-103
Preston, Ashton Bank
  1456 Christopher Hodgkinsonn, labourer
    Raine, *Richmond*, 1853, pp. 228-229
Lincolnshire
Market Rasen
  1457 Robert Feyldinge
    Neave, *Market Rasen*, 1985, pp. 68-69
London
Basinghall Street, Coopers Hall
  1458 Coopers Company
    Firth, 1848, p. 124
Tooting Bec
  1459 Robert Altham, yeoman
    Herridge, *Surrey*, 2005, pp. 69-71
Northamptonshire
Stonyard
  1460 Thomas Bellamy
    Cowper, 1890, p. 60
Northumberland
Rock
  1461 Jhone Swynnow [John Swinhoe]
    Raine, *Wills and Inventories*, 1835, I, p. 344
Staffordshire
Dudley
  1462 Arthure Dixon
    Roper, *Dudley*, 1965, p. 15
Lichfield
  1463 Thomas Whitmore, baker
    Vaisey, *Lichfield*, 1969, pp. 41-43
Surrey
Compton
  1464 James Westbroke
    Herridge, *Surrey*, 2005, pp. 75-76
Guildford
  1465 John Northall, saddler
    Herridge, *Surrey*, 2005, pp. 74-75

Ockley
  1466 Thomas Chittey
    Herridge, *Surrey*, 2005, p. 71
  1467 John Constable
    Herridge, *Surrey*, 2005, p. 72
Wrecclesham
  1468 Robert Marshar
    Herridge, *Surrey*, 2005, pp. 80-81
  1469 John Winne, labourer
    Herridge, *Surrey*, 2005, p. 77
Warwickshire
Foleshill
  1470 Richard Grene, yeoman
    Upton, *Foleshill*, 1993, pp. 49-50
Stratford-on-Avon
  1471 Edman Calle [Edmund Cale], [shepherd]
    Jones, *Stratford*, I, 2002, pp. 36-37
Westmorland
Grasmere
  1472 William Jackson, clergyman, curate of Grasmere
    Raine, *Richmond*, 1853, p. 227
Worcestershire
Earls Croome
  1473 William Jeffrey [Jefferies], gentleman
    Wanklyn, *Worcestershire*, 1998, pp. 41-43
Yorkshire
Hutton Conyers
  1474 Richard Cook, [yeoman]
    Raine, *Richmond*, 1853, pp. 229-231
Ingleton
  1475 John Harling, innholder
    Bentley, 1990, p. 43
South Cave
  1476 Ellin Atkinsone [Atkinson]
    Kaner, *South Cave*, 1994, pp. 73-74
  1477 John Johnson
    Kaner, *South Cave*, 1994, p. 70
  1478 Robert Spofforthe
    Kaner, *South Cave*, 1994, pp. 70-74
Westerdale
  1479 William Lukes, husbandman
    Crossley, *Yorkshire*, 1929, p. 60

1570 (c.)
Oxfordshire
Hornton
  1480 John Eburne
    Havinden, *Oxfordshire*, 1965, p. 56
Surrey
Chiddingfold
  1481 John Hoke
    Herridge, *Surrey*, 2005, pp. 72-73

1571
Cheshire
Malpas, Oldcastle Mill
  1482 Thomas Rome, miller
    Pearson, *Malpas*, [2005], p. 36
Derbyshire
Glossop, Beard
  1483 Edwarde Downes, [husbandman]
    Bryant, Lee, Miller, *New Mills II*, 1995, p. 4

Glossop, Roworth
  1484 Thomas Goddard
    Bryant, Lee, Miller, *New Mills I*, 1995, p. 33
Co. Durham
Croxdale
  1485 Gerrerd Salveyn [Salvin], esquire
    Raine, *Wills and Inventories*, 1835, I, pp. 347-351
Dalton on Tees
  Anthony Place, gentleman (see Low Dinsdale)
Gateshead
  1486 John Heworth, quarryman
    Raine, *Wills and Inventories*, 1835, I, p. 354
Low Dinsdale
  1487 Anthony Place, gentleman (also listed Dalton on Tees)
    Raine, *Wills and Inventories*, 1835, I, pp. 317-320
Newcastle
  1488 Bartrami [Bertram] Anderson, merchant and alderman (also listed Pittington)
    Raine, *Wills and Inventories*, 1835, I, pp. 335-342
Pittington, Haswell
  Bartrami [Bertram] Anderson, merchant and alderman (see Newcastle)
Raby
  1489 Thomas Newell, gentleman
    Raine, *Wills and Inventories*, 1835, I, pp. 331-332
Hampshire
Southampton
  1490 John Brodocke, apothecary
    Roberts and Parker, *Southampton*, II, 1992, pp. 290-306
  1491 John Cooper, merchant
    Roberts and Parker, *Southampton*, II, 1992, pp. 306-307
  1492 William Demes, shearman
    Roberts and Parker, *Southampton*, II, 1992, pp. 307-309
  1493 Robert Foster, mariner
    Roberts and Parker, *Southampton*, II, 1992, pp. 309-310
  1494 James Fuller
    Roberts and Parker, *Southampton*, II, 1992, pp. 310-312
  1495 Andrew Kyche
    Roberts and Parker, *Southampton*, II, 1992, p. 312
  1496 John Peerson, brother of God's House
    Roberts and Parker, *Southampton*, II, 1992, p. 313
  1497 Richard Record, porter
    Roberts and Parker, *Southampton*, II, 1992, pp. 313-317
  1498 John Reneger, gentleman
    Roberts and Parker, *Southampton*, II, 1992, pp. 317-322
  1499 William Vallet, gardener
    Roberts and Parker, *Southampton*, II, 1992, pp. 322-325
  1500 John Weaste, shipwright
    Roberts and Parker, *Southampton*, II, 1992, pp. 326-327
Hertfordshire
St Albans, St Stephens
  1501 George Hill
    Munby, *Worldly Goods*, 1991, p. 45
Ireland
Cork
  1502 David Tyrry Fitz Edmonde
    Caulfield, *Cork*, 1861-1862, p. 444 (1862)
Lancashire
Bolton, Halliwell
  1503 Roger Tayer [Taylier]
    Bolton, *Bolton*, 1994, p. 110

Leicestershire
Kirby Muxloe
1504 Robarte Martyne, [husbandman]
 Wilshere, *Kirby Muxloe*, 1983, p. 2
Lincolnshire
Boston
1505 Thomas Boothe, shoemaker
 Barley, *Lincolnshire*, 1951, pp. 261-263
Market Rasen
1506 Antony Harwick, husbandman
 Neave, *Market Rasen*, 1985, pp. 66-67
1507 John Kent
 Neave, *Market Rasen*, 1985, p. 70
1508 Francs Tibils, [shoemaker]
 Neave, *Market Rasen*, 1985, p. 69
Northumberland
Crawley
1509 Will'm [William] Heron, gentleman
 Raine, *Wills and Inventories*, 1835, I, p. 335
Elwick
1510 Thomas Gray
 Raine, *Wills and Inventories*, 1835, I, p. 366
[Temple] Healey
1511 John Widdrington
 Raine, *Wills and Inventories*, 1835, I, p. 322
Newcastle
1512 Mr John Wilkinsone [Wilkinson], [merchant]
 Raine, *Wills and Inventories*, 1835, I, pp. 359-365
Seaton Delaval
1513 Sir John Dallaval
 Raine, *Wills and Inventories*, 1835, I, p. 377
Oxfordshire
Marsh Baldon
1514 John Battene, husbandman
 Havinden, *Oxfordshire*, 1965, pp. 56-57
Staffordshire
Cannock Chase
1515 Cannock Furnace and Forge
 Morton, 1964-1965, p. 36
Dudley
1516 Richard Harrison
 Roper, *Dudley*, 1965, p. 16
Surrey
Bletchingley
1517 Richard Gylman, gentleman
 Herridge, *Surrey*, 2005, pp. 80-81
Capel
1518 Robert Wysdome
 Herridge, *Surrey*, 2005, p. 90
East Betchworth
1519 Nicholas Parker, husbandman
 Herridge, *Surrey*, 2005, pp. 84-85
Farnham
1520 Hugh Tew, shoemaker
 Herridge, *Surrey*, 2005, pp. 85-87
1521 Thomas Warner, [clothier]
 Herridge, *Surrey*, 2005, pp. 87-89
Godalming, Catteshall
1522 Julyan Elyot, widow
 Herridge, *Surrey*, 2005, pp. 79-80
Haslemere
1523 Richard Osborne
 Herridge, *Surrey*, 2005, p. 84

1524 Francis West
 Herridge, *Surrey*, 2005, pp. 89-90
Horne
1525 John Monnyarde
 Herridge, *Surrey*, 2005, p. 83
Thames Ditton
1526 Robert Bundell
 Herridge, *Surrey*, 2005, p. 78
Thursley
1527 Richard Hedger, husbandman
 Herridge, *Surrey*, 2005, p. 82
Wrecclesham
1528 William Channell, husbandman
 Herridge, *Surrey*, 2005, pp. 90-91
Warwickshire
Luddington
1529 Rychard Smartt [Richard Smart], [husbandman]
 Jones, *Stratford*, I, 2002, pp. 37-38
Worcestershire
Belbroughton
1530 John Colle
 Roper, *Belbroughton*, 1967-1968, p. 22
Dudley
1531 Jefferey [Jeffrey] Dudley, esquire
 Wanklyn, *Worcestershire*, 1998, pp. 43-47
Worcester
1532 Thomas Porter, butcher
 Dyer, *Worcestershire*, 1967, pp. 50-52
Yorkshire
Aysgarth, New Houses
1533 John Whalley
 Thwaite, *Abbotside*, 1967, pp. 7-8
Bainbridge, Brockhill Cote
1534 James Braidrig [Broderick?]
 Thwaite, *Abbotside*, 1967, pp. 8-9
Downholme
1535 John Cagyll
 Berry, *Swaledale*, 1998, p. 166
Felliscliffe
1536 William Bilton
 Collins, *Stubbs*, 1915, p. 172
Grinton, Crackpot
1537 Richard Clarkson
 Berry, *Swaledale*, 1998, p. 165
Grinton, Calvert Houses
1538 Edward Milner
 Berry, *Swaledale*, 1998, pp. 170-171
South Cave
1539 John Howden
 Kaner, *South Cave*, 1994, pp. 74-75
Spaldington
1540 Anne Vavasor, widow
 Brears, *Yorkshire*, 1972, pp. 37-41
York Minster
1541 Thomas Atkinson, clergyman, Prebendary of
Stillington
 Cross, *York*, I, 1984, pp. 114-119

1571 (c.)
Northumberland
Netherwitton, Colt Park
1542 Lionell Snawdon, labourer
 Raine, *Wills and Inventories*, 1835, I, pp. 330-331

1572

Buckinghamshire
Maids Moreton
  1543 Thomas Lee
    Lee, 1856, pp. 170-174
Cheshire
Malpas
  1544 Wyllyam Tewe
    Pearson, *Malpas*, [2005], pp. 38-39
Derbyshire
Chesterfield
  1545 John Brocke
    Bestall and Fowkes, *Chesterfield*, 1977, pp. 120-122
Glossop, Shydearde
  1546 Edwarde Swyndelles, husbandman
    Bryant, Lee, Miller, *New Mills II*, 1995, p. 9
Glossop, Thornsett
  1547 Anthonye Wendysley, gentleman
    Bryant, Lee, Miller, *New Mills II*, 1995, pp. 5-6
Co. Durham
Unlocated, (Ffaernton Hall)
  1548 George Blaixton
    Raine, *Wills and Inventories*, 1835, I, p. 359
Hampshire
Southampton
  1549 Peter Breame, glazier
    Roberts and Parker, *Southampton*, II, 1992, pp. 327-331
  1550 Margery Hancock, widow
    Roberts and Parker, *Southampton*, II, 1992, pp. 331-333
Lancashire
Tatham
  1551 Nicholas Clifton, clergyman, parson of Tatham
    Earwaker, *Lancashire and Cheshire*, 1893, pp. 138-139
Lincolnshire
Clee, Thrunscoe
  1552 John Covell
    Ambler, Watkinson, *Clee*, 1987, p. 65
  1553 John Tuplyn
    Ambler, Watkinson, *Clee*, 1987, p. 64
Northamptonshire
Canons Ashby
  1554 George Cope, esquire (also listed Knowle, Warwickshire)
    Anon., *Ancient Inventory*, 1856, pp. 323-332, 362-366
Northumberland
Edlingham
  1555 Thom's Swinburn [Thomas Swinburne], esquire
    Raine, *Wills and Inventories*, 1835, I, pp. 372-373
Great Whittington
  1556 Ranold Carnabye [Carnaby]
    Raine, *Wills and Inventories*, 1835, I, pp. 367-368
Staffordshire
Dudley, Russells Hall
  1557 Jeffery Dudley, esquire
    Roper, *Dudley*, 1965, p. 19
Dudley
  1558 William Smalmon [Smallman]
    Roper, *Dudley*, 1965, p. 18
    Hatcher and Barker, *Pewter*, 1974, p. 98
Surrey
Abinger
  1559 John Lypscombe
    Herridge, *Surrey*, 2005, p. 93

Alfold
  1560 John Holt
    Herridge, *Surrey*, 2005, pp. 91-92
East Betchworth
  1561 Alice White, widow
    Herridge, *Surrey*, 2005, p. 95
Elstead
  1562 Henry Boxsold, husbandman
    Herridge, *Surrey*, 2005, p. 96
Guildford, St Mary
  1563 Dorothy Snellinge, widow
    Herridge, *Surrey*, 2005, pp. 113-114
Thursley
  1564 Robert Machyke, yeoman
    Herridge, *Surrey*, 2005, pp. 93-94
Tolworth
  1565 Sence Starr, widow
    Herridge, *Surrey*, 2005, p. 94
Warwickshire
Knowle
  George Cope, esquire (see Canons Ashby, Northamptonshire)
Shottery
  1566 Clement Swallowe, gentleman
    Jones, *Stratford*, I, 2002, pp. 39-41
Stratford-on-Avon
  1567 Thomas Burman
    Jones, *Stratford*, I, 2002, p. 41
Stratford-on-Avon, Bridgetown
  1568 Nicholas Checket
    Jones, *Stratford*, I, 2002, p. 42
Stratford-on-Avon
  1569 Raff [Ralph] Chester
    Jones, *Stratford*, I, 2002, pp. 38-39
Yorkshire
Grinton, Angram
  1570 Thomas Bainbrige
    Berry, *Swaledale*, 1998, pp. 167-168
Grinton, Muker
  1571 Anthony Metcalf
    Berry, *Swaledale*, 1998, pp. 173-174
Marrick
  1572 Adam Nyccolson
    Berry, *Swaledale*, 1998, p. 172
Marske, Hyngynge Houses
  1573 William Been
    Berry, *Swaledale*, 1998, p. 169
Skipton Castle
  1574 Henry Clifford, Earl of Cumberland
    Whitaker, 1805, pp. 285-296
South Cave
  1575 Edmond Foster
    Kaner, *South Cave*, 1994, pp. 76-77

1572 (c.)

Surrey
Horley
  1576 Peter Bonwick
    Herridge, *Surrey*, 2005, p. 95

1573

Bristol
Bristol
  1577 Harry Mayo [alias Henry Patch], sailor
    George, *Bristol*, I, 2002, pp. 3-4

Cheshire
Tattenhall
  1578 Peter Astell, yeoman
    Bland, *Christleton*, 2002, pp. 9-10
Derbyshire
Brimington
  1579 John Turner
    Bestall and Fowkes, *Chesterfield*, 1977, pp. 125-126
Chesterfield
  1580 Martin Lane, clergyman, vicar of Chesterfield
    Bestall and Fowkes, *Chesterfield*, 1977, pp. 123-124
  1581 Robert Newbold
    Bestall and Fowkes, *Chesterfield*, 1977, pp. 126-127
Temple Normanton
  1582 John Braylisforthe
    Bestall and Fowkes, *Chesterfield*, 1977, p. 123
Co. Durham
Croxdale (?)
  1583 Richard Salvine [Salvin]
    Raine, *Wills and Inventories*, 1835, I, p. 393
Essex
Hornchurch
  1584 Edmund Leyam [Heyam]
    Emmison, *Essex*, 3, 1986, p. 78
Hampshire
Breamore
  1585 Harry Jacob
    Jacob, 1889, pp. 19-20
Southampton
  1586 John Clark, mason
    Roberts and Parker, *Southampton*, II, 1992, p. 334
  1587 Richard Coode, baker
    Roberts and Parker, *Southampton*, II, 1992, pp. 334-338
  1588 Nicholas Corle, carpenter
    Roberts and Parker, *Southampton*, II, 1992, pp. 338-341
  1589 Branken de Marin [Brancino de Marini ?]
    Roberts and Parker, *Southampton*, II, 1992, pp. 341-343
  1590 Gregory Gobbs, merchant
    Roberts and Parker, *Southampton*, II, 1992, pp. 343-345
  1591 Richard Goddard, merchant
    Roberts and Parker, *Southampton*, II, 1992, pp. 346-371
  1592 Reynold Howse [Reginald House], merchant
    Roberts and Parker, *Southampton*, II, 1992, pp. 371-383
  1593 Annes Huttoft, widow
    Roberts and Parker, *Southampton*, II, 1992, pp. 383-384
  1594 Thomas Morley, husbandman
    Roberts and Parker, *Southampton*, II, 1992, pp. 384-385
  1595 Robert Sende, gentleman
    Roberts and Parker, *Southampton*, II, 1992, pp. 386-390
  1596 Christopher Stevens, ship's carpenter
    Roberts and Parker, *Southampton*, II, 1992, pp. 390-391
  1597 Richard Stryde
    Roberts and Parker, *Southampton*, II, 1992, pp. 391-392
  1598 Robert Votier [Vautier]
    Roberts and Parker, *Southampton*, II, 1992, pp. 393-396
Hertfordshire
St Albans, St Stephens
  1599 John Wythe, [yeoman]
    Parker, *Worldly Goods*, 2004, pp. 78-79
Lancashire
Newton-le-Willows
  1600 Dame Anne Langton, widow of Sir Thomas
  Langton
    Piccope, *Lancashire and Cheshire*, 1860, pp. 59-62

Nuthurst
  1601 John Chetham, gentleman
    Earwaker, *Lancashire and Cheshire*, 1884, pp. 60-65
Westhoughton
  1602 Adame Rigbie
    Bolton, *Bolton*, 1994, p. 59
Lincolnshire
Clee
  1603 Steven Bynge
    Ambler, Watkinson, *Clee*, 1987, p. 65
Market Rasen
  1604 Adam Harryson
    Neave, *Market Rasen*, 1985, pp. 71-72
London
Carpenters Hall
  1605 Carpenters Company
    Jupp, 1887, pp. 641-642
Rotherhithe
  1606 John Waters, shipwright
    Herridge, *Surrey*, 2005, p. 115
Southwark, St Saviour
  1607 Robert Fylden
    Herridge, *Surrey*, 2005, p. 101
Southwark
  1608 Robert Woodward, barber
    Herridge, *Surrey*, 2005, pp. 116-117
Northamptonshire
Overthorpe, parish of Banbury, Oxfordshire
  1609 John Magodd
    Havinden, *Oxfordshire*, 1965, p. 61
Northumberland
Elwick
  1610 Thomas Dawson, clergyman
    Raine, *Wills and Inventories*, 1835, I, pp. 378-379
Oxfordshire
Banbury
  1611 John Allen, [barber]
    Havinden, *Oxfordshire*, 1965, pp. 57-58
  1612 William Dudley, smith
    Havinden, *Oxfordshire*, 1965, p. 62
Banbury, Overthorpe
  1613 John Magodd
    Havinden, *Oxfordshire*, 1965, p. 61
  1614 Henry Shuttelworthe, shoemaker
    Havinden, *Oxfordshire*, 1965, pp. 58-60
Bodicote
  1615 Matthew Tusten
    Havinden, *Oxfordshire*, 1965, p. 61
Staffordshire
Dudley
  1616 Thomas Bekensall, clergyman, vicar of Dudley
    Roper, *Dudley*, 1965, p. 20
  1617 Thomas Cartwright
    Roper, *Dudley*, 1965, p. 22
  1618 Henrie Finche
    Roper, *Dudley*, 1965, p. 25
  1619 Ric: Jones
    Roper, *Dudley*, 1965, p. 21
    Roper, *Sixteenth Century*, 1968, pp. 34-35
Surrey
Abinger
  1620 Christopher Lyllye, husbandman
    Herridge, *Surrey*, 2005, pp. 105-106

Byfleet
  1621   Robert Hardewyn, yeoman
    Herridge, *Surrey*, 2005, pp. 102-104
Compton
  1622   Thomas Martyn
    Herridge, *Surrey*, 2005, pp. 107-108
Egham, Stroude
  1623   Thomas Reynolde, husbandman
    Herridge, *Surrey*, 2005, pp. 112-113
Frensham
  1624   Thomas Fulston
    Herridge, *Surrey*, 2005, pp. 100-101
  1625   Agnes Reves, widow
    Herridge, *Surrey*, 2005, pp. 111-112
Godalming
  1626   Edward West, dyer
    Herridge, *Surrey*, 2005, p. 116
Horley
  1627   George Payne
    Herridge, *Surrey*, 2005, pp. 109-110
Horsell
  1628   John Isam, yeoman
    Herridge, *Surrey*, 2005, p. 104
Ockham
  1629   Robert Clebroke, clergyman, parson of Ockham
    Herridge, *Surrey*, 2005, p. 97
Pirbright
  1630   Richard Fagatere
    Herridge, *Surrey*, 2005, pp. 98-99
Puttenham
  1631   George Marlyn, husbandman
    Herridge, *Surrey*, 2005, pp. 106-107
Send
  1632   Henry Punter
    Herridge, *Surrey*, 2005, pp. 110-111
Tandridge
  1633   Gyles Fynnes, carpenter
    Herridge, *Surrey*, 2005, p. 102
Woking
  1634   Edward Matthewe
    Herridge, *Surrey*, 2005, pp. 108-109
Wonersh
  1635   Thomas Warner
    Herridge, *Surrey*, 2005, p. 114-115
Wrecclesham
  1636   William Ede
    Herridge, *Surrey*, 2005, pp. 97-98

Warwickshire
Birmingham
  1637   Henry Byrch
    Holt, Ingram, Jarman, *Birmingham*, 1985, p. 25
Foleshill
  1638   Thoms Wolfe
    Upton, *Foleshill*, 1993, pp. 52-53

Worcestershire
Belbroughton, Morehall Mill
  1639   Antony Colle, [miller]
    Roper, *Belbroughton*, 1967-1968, p. 24
Cotheridge
  1640   John Ketelby, esquire
    Wanklyn, *Worcestershire*, 1998, pp. 47-49

Yorkshire
Gilling
  1641   Cutberde Thomson, clergyman, vicar of Gilling
    Raine, *Richmond*, 1853, pp. 241-242
Grinton, Thwaite
  1642   John Cote
    Berry, *Swaledale*, 1998, pp. 175-176
Grinton, Harkerside
  1643   Christopher Payckocke
    Berry, *Swaledale*, 1998, pp. 182-183
Grinton, Crackpot
  1644   Lawrence Wray
    Berry, *Swaledale*, 1998, pp. 184-185
Hudswell
  1645   William Lillfourthe, yeoman
    Berry, *Swaledale*, 1998, p. 187
Marske, Skelton
  1646   Christopher Mylner
    Berry, *Swaledale*, 1998, pp. 176-177
South Cave
  1647   Jane Howden
    Kaner, *South Cave*, 1994, pp. 80-81
South Cave, Faxfleet
  1648   Gorg Medellwode [George Meddelwood]
    Kaner, *South Cave*, 1994, pp. 81-82
South Cave
  1649   John Syther
    Kaner, *South Cave*, 1994, pp. 79-80
  1650   Robert Wetheral [Wetherall]
    Kaner, *South Cave*, 1994, p. 78
Thirsk
  1651   Leonard Pykeney [Pinkney]
    Brears, *Yorkshire*, 1972, pp. 42-45
York Minster
  1652   Robert Mell, clergyman, vicar choral
    Cross, *York*, I, 1984, pp. 120-124
  1653   John Steell, clergyman, vicar choral
    Cross, *York*, I, 1984, pp. 127-132

1573 (c.)
Oxfordshire
Banbury
  1654   Anne Dartes
    Havinden, *Oxfordshire*, 1965, pp. 62-64

1574
Cheshire
Tarvin, Burton
  1655   Henrye Balle
    Bland, *Christleton*, 2002, p. 13
Tarvin, Clotton
  1656   Thomas Bratherton
    Bland, *Christleton*, 2002, p. 15
Tarvin
  1657   Catheren Chetam, widow
    Bland, *Christleton*, 2002, pp. 11-12
Tarvin, Ashton
  1658   William Cocker
    Bland, *Christleton*, 2002, p. 16

Cumberland
Burgh-by-Sands
  1659   Roger Burghe, esquire
    Raine, *Richmond*, 1853, pp. 245-248
Little Salkeld
  1660   Lancelott Salkeld
    Moore, *Salkelds*, 1988, p. 54

Derbyshire
Brimington
1661 Elizabeth Turner, widow
Bestall and Fowkes, *Chesterfield*, 1977, pp. 128-129
Chesterfield
1662 Rychard Foxe, shoemaker
Bestall and Fowkes, *Chesterfield*, 1977, pp. 127-128
Co. Durham
St Andrew Auckland
1663 Margerye Brantingham
Raine, *Wills and Inventories*, 1835, I, p. 395
Hampshire
Southampton
1664 John Hodgson
Roberts and Parker, *Southampton*, II, 1992, pp. 396-397
1665 John Hurlock, [clergyman and schoolmaster]
Roberts and Parker, *Southampton*, II, 1992, pp. 397-400
1666 Christopher Nutley, joiner
Roberts and Parker, *Southampton*, II, 1992, pp. 400-401
1667 Edmund Prowting, husbandman
Roberts and Parker, *Southampton*, II, 1992, pp. 401-402
1668 John Quick, merchant
Roberts and Parker, *Southampton*, II, 1992, pp. 402-404
1669 Lawrence Williams
Roberts and Parker, *Southampton*, II, 1992, pp. 405-414
Hertfordshire
St Albans, St Stephens
1670 Nicholas Stretle
Parker, *Worldly Goods*, 2004, pp. 79-80
1671 George Wetherall, clergyman, vicar of St
Stephens
Parker, *Worldly Goods*, 2004, pp. 83-85
Kent
Maidstone
1672 William Lynford
Melling, 1965, p. 16
Lancashire
Ainsworth
1673 Robart Grenehalgh
Bolton, *Bolton*, 1987, pp. 106-107
Bolton, Quarlton
1674 Thurstan Grinehalghe, husbandman
Bolton, *Bolton*, 1987, p. 109
Bolton (?)
1675 Harrye A Knowe
Bolton, *Bolton*, 1994, p. 19
Northumberland
Belford
1676 Maister Frances Armorar [Armorer], gentleman
Raine, *Wills and Inventories*, 1835, I, pp. 404-405
Bolam
1677 David Tailor, clergyman, vicar of Bolam
Raine, *Wills and Inventories*, 1835, I, p. 394
Willimoteswick
1678 Nicholas Ridley, esquire
Raine, *Wills and Inventories*, 1835, I, p. 399
Oxfordshire
Banbury
1679 John Mason, alias Lawrance, [labourer]
Havinden, *Oxfordshire*, 1965, p. 65
1680 John Wyllyby, alias Wright, [surgeon]
Havinden, *Oxfordshire*, 1965, p. 64

Scotland
Glasgow
1681 Robert Baxter
Smith, 1832, pp. 33-35
Staffordshire
Lichfield
1682 Ricard Harpar
Vaisey, *Lichfield*, 1969, pp. 43-44
Surrey
Alfold
1683 John Browne
Herridge, *Surrey*, 2005, pp. 120-121
Chiddingfold
1684 Thomas Penvey, miller
Herridge, *Surrey*, 2005, pp. 118-119
Seale
1685 Thomas Dakin, clergyman, curate
Herridge, *Surrey*, 2005, p. 117
Wrecclesham
1686 Thomas Hayward, weaver
Herridge, *Surrey*, 2005, p. 118
Wales
Montgomeryshire, Kerry
1687 John ap David Lloyd
Morris, 1893, p. 253
Warwickshire
Stratford-on-Avon, Drayton
1688 John Edwards
Jones, *Stratford*, I, 2002, pp. 43-44
Westmorland
Kentmere, Hartrigg (?)
1689 John Wilkinson
Raine, *Richmond*, 1853, p. 242
Worcestershire
Chaddesley Corbett
1690 John Walderne
West, *Village Records*, 1962, p. 94
Yorkshire
Grinton, Ivelet
1691 Edward Clarson
Berry, *Swaledale*, 1998, p. 188
Richmond
1692 John Cornefurth, butcher
Raine, *Richmond*, 1853, pp. 248-249
South Cave
1693 John Chaice
Kaner, *South Cave*, 1994, pp. 85-88
1694 Leonarde Tompson
Kaner, *South Cave*, 1994, p. 82
1695 William Wilkynson [Wilkinson], miller
Kaner, *South Cave*, 1994, pp. 83-84
Westerdale
1696 William Peirson
Crossley, *Yorkshire*, 1929, p. 62

1575-1600 (undated)
Ireland
Dublin
1697 Robert FitzSymons, merchant
Fenlon, *Ireland*, 2003, pp. 13-14

1575

Bedfordshire
Biggleswade
 1698 John Rachford, husbandman
  Freeman, *Bedfordshire*, 1952, pp. 102-103

Cheshire
Bickerton
 1699 Hary Walle, husbandman
  Pearson, *Malpas*, [2005], p. 44
Bickley
 1700 Thomas Webster
  Pearson, *Malpas*, [2005], p. 46
Nantwich
 1701 Amy Bromhall, widow
  Cockcroft, *Nantwich*, 1999, pp. 45.3-4

Cumberland
Carlisle, White Hall
 1702 Lady Jane Dacre
  Jones, 1988, pp. 142-148
Corby
 Richard Salkeld (see Rosgill, Shap, Westmorland)
Highhead Castle
 1703 John Richemond, esquire
  Jackson, *Richmonds*, 1876, pp. 124-125
Holm Cultram, Souterfeld
 1704 John Borrowdale
  Grainger, 1909, pp. 129-130
  Grainger and Collingwood, 1929, p. 241

Derbyshire
Chesterfield
 1705 Wylliam Hethe
  Bestall and Fowkes, *Chesterfield*, 1977, pp. 129-131
Glossop, Holehouse
 1706 Angneys [Agnes] Andrewe
  Bryant, Lee, Miller, *New Mills II*, 1995, p. 11
Glossop, Ollersett
 1707 Nycholas Bradburye, gentleman
  Bryant, Lee, Miller, *New Mills II*, 1995, p. 16
Glossop, Whittle, Abothry
 1708 Raphe Bredbury
  Bryant, Lee, Miller, *New Mills II*, 1995, p. 13
Hasland
 1709 Raphe Leeke, esquire
  Bestall and Fowkes, *Chesterfield*, 1977, pp. 131-135

Hampshire
Southampton
 1710 Thomas Austen [Austell], merchant
  Roberts and Parker, *Southampton*, II, 1992, pp. 414-416
 1711 William Barat, mariner
  Roberts and Parker, *Southampton*, II, 1992, pp. 417-418
 1712 John Davison
  Roberts and Parker, *Southampton*, II, 1992, pp. 418-420
 1713 William Follyatt, tailor
  Roberts and Parker, *Southampton*, II, 1992, pp. 421-422
 1714 Lowes Mariner, [carpenter?]
  Roberts and Parker, *Southampton*, II, 1992, p. 422
 1715 Richard Nutley, weaver
  Roberts and Parker, *Southampton*, II, 1992, pp. 423-424
 1716 Richard Rastryck, porter
  Roberts and Parker, *Southampton*, II, 1992, pp. 424-428
 1717 John Seare
  Roberts and Parker, *Southampton*, II, 1992, pp. 428-429

Hertfordshire
St Albans, St Stephens
 1718 Alexander Kentishe
  Munby, *Worldly Goods*, 1991, p. 46

Ireland
Maynooth Castle, co. Kildare
 1719 Gerald FitzGerald, Earl of Kildare
  Fenlon, *Ireland*, 2003, pp. 10-11

Lancashire
Bolton, Great Levr
 1720 Even Grundye, husbandman
  Bolton, *Bolton*, 1987, p. 122
Deane, Over Hulton
 1721 Elyzabeth Gregorye
  Bolton, *Bolton*, 1987, p. 116
Westhoughton, Chequerbent
 1722 William Cheetame
  Bolton, *Bolton*, 1987, p. 56

Lincolnshire
Market Rasen
 1723 Joys Cockerell
  Neave, *Market Rasen*, 1985, p. 75
 1724 Richard Cowp [Cowper]
  Neave, *Market Rasen*, 1985, p. 73
 1725 Willm Lightfote
  Neave, *Market Rasen*, 1985, p. 74
 1726 Richard Rawlinson
  Neave, *Market Rasen*, 1985, p. 75
 1727 Thomas Wright
  Neave, *Market Rasen*, 1985, pp. 76-77

London
Lambeth Palace
 1728 Matthew Parker, Archbishop of Canterbury
  (also listed Croydon, Surrey)
  Sandys, 1844, pp. 7-30
South Lambeth
 1729 Rocko Bonetto [Rocco Bonetti]
  Robertson, 1989, pp. 40-41
Southwark, St George the Martyr
 1730 John Mantill, joiner
  Herridge, *Surrey*, 2005, pp. 125-126

Northumberland
Mitford (?)
 1731 Wyllm' Fynveck' [William Fenwick]
  Raine, *Wills and Inventories*, 1835, I, pp. 405-406
Mitford, Thorphill
 1732 John Mytfurth [Mitford]
  Raine, *Wills and Inventories*, 1835, I, p. 400

Oxfordshire
Banbury
 1733 Anne Compton, widow
  Havinden, *Oxfordshire*, 1965, p. 66
 1734 Alyce Gate
  Havinden, *Oxfordshire*, 1965, pp. 66-67
 1735 Thomas Mayho, [shoemaker]
  Havinden, *Oxfordshire*, 1965, pp. 67-69
 1736 Elizabeth Sly
  Havinden, *Oxfordshire*, 1965, pp. 65-66
  Hatcher and Barker, *Pewter*, 1974, p. 97

Surrey
Bramley
 1737 Steven Petoe, yeoman
  Herridge, *Surrey*, 2005, pp. 126-127

Byfleet
1738 Robert Geale, day labourer
Herridge, *Surrey*, 2005, pp. 121-122
Compton
1739 Thomas Turner
Herridge, *Surrey*, 2005, p. 127
Croydon Palace
Matthew Parker, Archbishop of Canterbury (see
Lambeth Palace, London)
Frensham, Pitfold
1740 Thomas Allen
Herridge, *Surrey*, 2005, pp. 119-120
Haslemere
1741 Agnes Chaundler
Herridge, *Surrey*, 2005, p. 121
Shalford
1742 John Waterer, tailor
Herridge, *Surrey*, 2005, pp. 128-129
Tilford
1743 William Brodebridge
Herridge, *Surrey*, 2005, pp. 130-131
Wonersh
1744 John Gosden, yeoman
Herridge, *Surrey*, 2005, pp. 122-123
Warwickshire
Stoneleigh, Stareton
1745 Simon Tyler
Alcock, *Warwickshire*, 1993, p. 36
Westmorland
Shap, Rosgill
1746 Richard Salkeld (also listed Corby, Cumberland)
Moore, *Salkelds*, 1988, pp. 57-58
Wiltshire
Lacock Abbey
1747 Sir Henry Sharington
Vernon, 1968, pp. 74-82
Worcestershire
Little Malvern
1748 Milborowe Russelles [Milburgha Russell],
widow
Wanklyn, *Worcestershire*, 1998, pp. 50-51
Yorkshire
Bishopdale
1749 Galfryde Calvert
Raine, *Richmond*, 1853, pp. 254-256
Downholme Park
1750 William Bradrige
Berry, *Swaledale*, 1998, pp. 190-191
Downholme, Ellerton
1751 Isabel Wylson, widow
Berry, *Swaledale*, 1998, pp. 192-193
Eryholme
1752 Edmund Smythson, clergyman, curate of
Eryholme
Raine, *Richmond*, 1853, pp. 259-260
Grinton, Whitaside
1753 Ralph Braydredg
Berry, *Swaledale*, 1998, pp. 195-196
Grinton, Healaugh
1754 John Close
Berry, *Swaledale*, 1998, p. 197
Hudswell, Thorpe
1755 William Kiplinge, yeoman
Berry, *Swaledale*, 1998, p. 194

Richmond
1756 Richard Thompson, [hosier]
Raine, *Richmond*, 1853, p. 233
South Cave
1757 Henrye Arkell
Kaner, *South Cave*, 1994, pp. 88-89
1758 Dunstone Bellard, husbandman
Kaner, *South Cave*, 1994, pp. 92-94
1759 Robarte Hunt
Kaner, *South Cave*, 1994, pp. 90-92
Wensley
1760 Reginald Hyndmer, clergyman, parson of
Wensley
Raine, *Richmond*, 1853, pp. 252-254

1575 (c.)
Surrey
West Molesey
1761 Robert Lake, husbandman
Herridge, *Surrey*, 2005, p. 124

1576
Cheshire
Malpas, Oldcastle, Newton
1762 William Probyn, husbandman
Pearson, *Malpas*, [2005], p. 49
Derbyshire
Hasland
1763 Rycharde Heath, husbandman
Bestall and Fowkes, *Chesterfield*, 1977, p. 136
Devonshire
Landkey
1764 John Whytfield, weaver
Cash, *Devon*, 1966, p. 3
Uffculme
1765 Ellin Dowdeny [Helen Dowdney], widow
Wyatt, *Uffculme*, 1997, p. 1
1766 Florence Pearsie [Persye], widow
Wyatt, *Uffculme*, 1997, pp. 1-3
1767 William Read [of Ashell]
Wyatt, *Uffculme*, 1997, p. 4
1768 William Read [of Gaddon]
Wyatt, *Uffculme*, 1997, pp. 3-4
Dorsetshire
Yetminster [?]
1769 Thomas Sheryes
Machin, *Yetminster*, 1976, No.1, (2 pp.)
Hertfordshire
St Albans, St Stephens
1770 William Francys, husbandman
Parker, *Worldly Goods*, 2004, pp. 87-88
Sarratt
1771 Richard Kytson
Bullen, *Sarratt*, [1982], pp. 49-51
Lancashire
Bolton, Darcy Lever
1772 John Bradshaye
Bolton, *Bolton*, 1987, p. 35
Leicestershire
Braunstone
1773 George Gregorie, husbandman
Wilshere, *Braunstone*, 1983, p. 9

Glenfield
1774 Unknown
Wilshere, *Glenfield*, 1983, p. 1
Lincolnshire
Clee
1775 Raph Charlesworth
Ambler, Watkinson, *Clee*, 1987, pp. 65-66
1776 Thomas Grymilbie, husbandman
Ambler, Watkinson, *Clee*, 1987, pp. 66-67
Market Rasen
1777 Robert Wykam
Neave, *Market Rasen*, 1985, p. 78
Northumberland
Stamfordham
1778 Gawyn Swinburne, gentleman
Raine, *Wills and Inventories*, 1835, I, pp. 410-411
Oxfordshire
Banbury (?)
1779 William Brasbrigges
Havinden, *Oxfordshire*, 1965, pp. 70-71
Banbury, Huscote
1780 Thomas Palmer, husbandman
Havinden, *Oxfordshire*, 1965, pp. 69-70
Staffordshire
Dudley
1781 William Harryson
Roper, *Dudley*, 1965, p. 23
1782 John Southall
Roper, *Dudley*, 1965, p. 24
Suffolk
Bildeston
1783 Andrew Myles, tanner
Emmison, 1966, pp. 91-92
Surrey
Chertsey
1784 William Newman, clergyman, vicar of Chertsey
Herridge, *Surrey*, 2005, pp. 135-137
Chiddingfold
1785 Thomas Peytowe, yeoman
Herridge, *Surrey*, 2005, p. 138
Egham
1786 John Mabancke, yeoman
Herridge, *Surrey*, 2005, pp. 134-135
Farnham, Runfold
1787 John Astlett, husbandman
Herridge, *Surrey*, 2005, pp. 129-130
1788 John Jewer, husbandman
Herridge, *Surrey*, 2005, pp. 133-134
Frensham
1789 Eden Field
Herridge, *Surrey*, 2005, p. 131
Great Bookham, Eastwick
1790 Henrie Wilkyns, husbandman
Harvey, 1974, pp. 56-57
Herridge, *Surrey*, 2005, p. 144
Guildford
1791 Thomas Northall, saddler
Herridge, *Surrey*, 2005, pp. 137-138
Horne
1792 William Todham
Herridge, *Surrey*, 2005, pp. 141-142

Pirbright
1793 Bartholemew Smethurst, yeoman
Herridge, *Surrey*, 2005, p. 139
West Molesey
1794 Robert Wicker
Herridge, *Surrey*, 2005, pp. 142-143
Witley
1795 Robert Holt, tailor
Herridge, *Surrey*, 2005, pp. 132-133
1796 John Stynt
Herridge, *Surrey*, 2005, pp. 140-141
Unlocated
1797 Rechartt Swinborne
Raine, *Wills and Inventories*, 1835, I, p. 409
Worcestershire
Belbroughton
1798 Richard Wytton
Roper, *Belbroughton*, 1967-1968, p. 26
Yorkshire
Aysgarth, Shaw Cote
1799 Radilphe Prate [Ralph Pratt], [yeoman]
Thwaite, *Abbotside*, 1967, p. 10
Birstwith
1800 William Stubb, yeoman
Collins, *Stubbs*, 1915, pp. 97-98
Downholme, Stainton
1801 Lancelot Turner
Berry, *Swaledale*, 1998, pp. 200-201
Grinton, Angram
1802 Brian Kypling
Berry, *Swaledale*, 1998, p. 203
Grinton, Low Whitaside
1803 Janet Metcalf, widow
Berry, *Swaledale*, 1998, p. 199
Grinton, High Smarber
1804 Simon Parke
Berry, *Swaledale*, 1998, pp. 204-205
Hudswell
1805 William Raine, yeoman
Berry, *Swaledale*, 1998, p. 202
Knaresborough, Scriven
1806 John Casse
Raine, *Richmond*, 1853, p. 260
Ripon
1807 Marmaduk Elderkar
Fowler, 1874, pp. 377-379
South Cave
1808 John Brown
Kaner, *South Cave*, 1994, pp. 94-95
1809 Thomas Marshall
Kaner, *South Cave*, 1994, pp. 96-98

1576 (c.)
Northumberland
Harbottle Castle
1810 Sir George Heron
Raine, *Wills and Inventories*, 1835, I, pp. 411-412

1577
Berkshire
Padworth
1811 Robert Littlefield alias Turner
Sharp, 1901, p. 131

Cheshire
Malpas, Edge
1812 Ranulph Dodde, esquire
Pearson, *Malpas*, [2005], p. 51
Malpas, Ebnal
1813 Thomas Torporley
Pearson, *Malpas*, [2005], pp. 42-43
Derbyshire
Chesterfield
1814 Raphe Clarke, yeoman
Bestall and Fowkes, *Chesterfield*, 1977, pp. 143-148
1815 Raphe Hethcote, brasier
Bestall and Fowkes, *Chesterfield*, 1977, pp. 137-143
Dunston
1816 Nycolesse Chatterton
Bestall and Fowkes, *Chesterfield*, 1977, p. 135
Glossop, The Hollens
1817 Edward Robothum
Bryant, Lee, Miller, *New Mills II*, 1995, p. 18
Hasland
1818 Rychard Hardweke, clergyman
Bestall and Fowkes, *Chesterfield*, 1977, pp. 136-137
Hertfordshire
St Albans, St Stephens
1819 Margaret Fisher, [servant]
Parker, *Worldly Goods*, 2004, p. 86
1820 Henry Kentisshe, yeoman
Munby, *Worldly Goods*, 1991, pp. 51-56
1821 Robert Skeale
Munby, *Worldly Goods*, 1991, pp. 48-49
Sarratt
1822 Will[ia]m Rowe
Bullen, *Sarratt*, [1982], pp. 51-52
Ireland
Cork
1823 John Teige McCartie, merchant
Caulfield, *Cork*, 1861-1862, pp. 504-505 (1861)
Lancashire
Hall i' th' Wood, Tonge, Bolton
1824 Roger Brownlawe [Brownlow], gentleman
Irvine, 1903, pp. 27-29
Bolton, *Bolton*, 1994, pp. 12-13
Turton
1825 Roger Wrygley, clergyman
Bolton, *Bolton*, 1994, p. 155
Lincolnshire
Bassingthorpe
1826 Thomas Cony, esquire
Peacock, 1888-1889, pp. 132-133, 164-166, 198-199, 230-233
Clee
1827 George Townend
Ambler, Watkinson, *Clee*, 1987, p. 67
Market Rasen
1828 John Sowith
Neave, *Market Rasen*, 1985, p. 79
Northumberland
Alnwick, Calleche Park
1829 George Harbottell, gentleman
Raine, *Wills and Inventories*, 1835, I, p. 408
Newcastle
1830 Thomas Leddell [Liddell], merchant and alderman
Raine, *Wills and Inventories*, 1835, I, pp. 413-416

Oxfordshire
Banbury
1831 Thomas Flemynge, shoemaker
Havinden, *Oxfordshire*, 1965, p. 74
Banbury, Nethercote
1832 John Teye, husbandman
Havinden, *Oxfordshire*, 1965, pp. 79-80
Banbury
1833 Richard West, [shoemaker]
Havinden, *Oxfordshire*, 1965, pp. 80-81
Cropredy
1834 Elizabeth Gibbs, widow
Havinden, *Oxfordshire*, 1965, pp. 71-73
1835 Elizabeth Howes, widow
Havinden, *Oxfordshire*, 1965, pp. 74-75
Great Milton
1836 John Colles
Havinden, *Oxfordshire*, 1965, pp. 75-77
Lower Heyford
1837 William Bruce
Havinden, *Oxfordshire*, 1965, pp. 77-79
Wardington
1838 Agnes Kinton, [widow]
Havinden, *Oxfordshire*, 1965, pp. 73-74
Staffordshire
Dudley
1839 Jhon Worsley
Roper, *Dudley*, 1965, p. 26
Surrey
Frensham
1840 Thomas Bicknell
Herridge, *Surrey*, 2005, pp. 147-148
Shalford
1841 John Sherwood, carpenter
Herridge, *Surrey*, 2005, p. 145
Warwickshire
Foleshill
1842 William Hart
Upton, *Foleshill*, 1993, pp. 54-55
Worcestershire
Chaddesley Corbett
1843 Henry Sitch, [scythesmith]
Roper, *Scythesmiths*, 1967, p. 11
Worcester
1844 William Uncles, cooper
Dyer, *Worcestershire*, 1967, pp. 38-39
Worcester, St Martin's
1845 William Wilkox, walker
Dyer, *Worcestershire*, 1967, pp. 15-19
Yorkshire
Aysgarth, Fossdale
1846 Thomas Metcalf, yeoman
Thwaite, *Abbotside*, 1967, pp. 11-12
Grinton, Keld
1847 Simon Alderson
Berry, *Swaledale*, 1998, p. 214
Grinton, Crackpot
1848 Thomas Metcalf, yeoman
Berry, *Swaledale*, 1998, pp. 208-209
Grinton, Healaugh
1849 John Sympson
Berry, *Swaledale*, 1998, p. 207

Grinton, [Low Whitaside]
  1850 Abraham Waine
    Berry, *Swaledale*, 1998, p. 211
Hudswell
  1851 Ralph Place, yeoman
    Berry, *Swaledale*, 1998, pp. 205-206
Leeds, Kirkgate
  1852 John Pawsone [Pawson]
    Norcliffe, 1895, pp. 163-166
West Layton
  1853 John Laton
    Raine, *Richmond*, 1853, pp. 263-265

1578

Cambridgeshire
Cambridge
  1854 John Denys, [bookbinder and stationer]
    Gray and Palmer, *Cambridge*, 1915, pp. 35-59

Cheshire
Broxton
  1855 Thomas Oreton
    Pearson, *Malpas*, [2005], pp. 54-55
Malpas, Aston Heath
  1856 Thomas Brette, husbandman
    Pearson, *Malpas*, [2005], p. 53
Stockport
  1857 [Richard] Nabbs
    Phillips and Smith, *Stockport*, 1985, pp. 3-4
Stockport, The Bothams
  1858 Robert Ryle, yeoman
    Phillips and Smith, *Stockport*, 1985, p. 2

Derbyshire
Chesterfield, Holme
  1859 George Bennet, carpenter
    Bestall and Fowkes, *Chesterfield*, 1977, pp. 148-149
Chesterfield
  1860 Edward Hadshead
    Bestall and Fowkes, *Chesterfield*, 1977, pp. 150-151
  1861 John Wythede alias Bundell
    Bestall and Fowkes, *Chesterfield*, 1977, pp. 151-154
Walton
  1862 Roland Nell, yeoman
    Bestall and Fowkes, *Chesterfield*, 1977, pp. 149-150

Co. Durham
Durham, Crook Hall
  1863 John Billingh'm [Billingham]
    Raine, *Wills and Inventories*, 1835, I, pp. 417-420
Witton Gilbert, Saggerston Heugh
  1864 Mr Leonerde Temperleyes, gentleman
    Raine, *Wills and Inventories*, 1835, I, pp. 420-423

Hertfordshire
St Albans, St Stephens
  1865 George Atkyns, labourer
    Parker, *Worldly Goods*, 2004, pp. 93-94
  1866 John Latheburye
    Parker, *Worldly Goods*, 2004, pp. 92-93
Sarratt
  1867 Mawde Rowe
    Bullen, *Sarratt*, [1982], pp. 55-56
  1868 John Sweetinge, [husbandman]
    Bullen, *Sarratt*, [1982], pp. 54-55

Ireland
Cork
  1869 William Skiddie
    Caulfield, *Cork*, 1861-1862, p. 443 (1862)

Lancashire
Blackrod
  1870 Edwarde Norres, gentleman
    Bolton, *Bolton*, 1994, p. 29
Bolton
  1871 Richarde Sharples alias Warde
    Bolton, *Bolton*, 1994, p. 82
Deane, Over Hulton
  1872 Margaret Astley
    Bolton, *Bolton*, 1987, p. 14
Deane, Rumworth
  1873 Raffe Crompton
    Bolton, *Bolton*, 1987, pp. 69-70

Oxfordshire
Banbury
  1874 Thomas Allins, [shoemaker]
    Havinden, *Oxfordshire*, 1965, pp. 86-87
  1875 William Moseley, carpenter
    Havinden, *Oxfordshire*, 1965, pp. 81-83
Banbury, Neithrop
  1876 George Robins
    Havinden, *Oxfordshire*, 1965, pp. 98-99
Banbury
  1877 Robert Turner
    Havinden, *Oxfordshire*, 1965, p. 84
  1878 William Wyese, yeoman
    Havinden, *Oxfordshire*, 1965, pp. 84-86
Banbury (?)
  1879 Thomas Byssope
    Havinden, *Oxfordshire*, 1965, pp. 100-101
  1880 William Man
    Havinden, *Oxfordshire*, 1965, pp. 94-95
Bourton
  1881 Joan Claredges, widow
    Havinden, *Oxfordshire*, 1965, p. 96
Cropredy
  1882 Emma Bryans, widow
    Havinden, *Oxfordshire*, 1965, p. 88
  1883 William Gullyvor, [day labourer]
    Havinden, *Oxfordshire*, 1965, p. 88
  1884 Ralph Newbery [Nubery], husbandman
    Havinden, *Oxfordshire*, 1965, pp. 91-94
  1885 Richard Rede, [husbandman]
    Havinden, *Oxfordshire*, 1965, pp. 83-84
Great Milton
  1886 Mrs Cowles, widow
    Havinden, *Oxfordshire*, 1965, pp. 89-90
Mollington
  1887 Thomas Garner, [husbandman]
    Havinden, *Oxfordshire*, 1965, pp. 96-97
  1888 Thomas Meekes
    Havinden, *Oxfordshire*, 1965, pp. 88-89
  1889 Richard Sparkes
    Havinden, *Oxfordshire*, 1965, pp. 97-98

Northamptonshire
Warkworth
  1890 Thomas Butler
    Havinden, *Oxfordshire*, 1965, p. 100

Scotland
Edinburgh Castle
1891 James VI of Scotland
Thomson, *Edinburgh*, 1815, pp. 203-273
Surrey
Chertsey
1892 William Wapshote
Herridge, *Surrey*, 2005, p. 153
Chobham
1893 Annys Channell, widow
Herridge, *Surrey*, 2005, p. 148
Guildford, St Mary
1894 Thomas Barne, smith
Herridge, *Surrey*, 2005, p. 146
Headley
1895 John Hays
Herridge, *Surrey*, 2005, pp. 149-150
Ockley
1896 Richard Tydey
Herridge, *Surrey*, 2005, pp. 151-152
Wanborough
1897 William Foster
Herridge, *Surrey*, 2005, pp. 148-149
Worplesdon
1898 William Bearde
Herridge, *Surrey*, 2005, p. 147
Wales
Montgomeryshire, Kerry
1899 Thomas Danylley
. Morris, 1893, p. 255
Warwickshire
Birmingham
1900 James Grundy
Holt, Ingram, Jarman, *Birmingham*, 1985, pp. 26-27
Shottery
1901 Richard Pace, husbandman
Jones, *Stratford*, I, 2002, pp. 47-48
Stratford-on-Avon, Drayton
1902 Richard Barbur, yeoman
Jones, *Stratford*, I, 2002, pp. 44-46
Westmorland
Kendal
1903 Henri Fissher
Raine, *Richmond*, 1853, pp. 281-282
1904 Edward Kyrkelands
Raine, *Richmond*, 1853, p. 274
Kirkby Lonsdale
1905 James Backhouse
Raine, *Richmond*, 1853, pp. 275-281
Worcestershire
Belbroughton
1906 Gilbert Colle
Roper, *Belbroughton*, 1967-1968, p. 30
1907 Oswald Penn, [farmer, scythesmith]
Roper, *Belbroughton*, 1967-1968, p. 28
Yorkshire
Grinton, Healaugh
1908 Anthony Arundell, gentleman
Berry, *Swaledale*, 1998, pp. 222-223
Grinton
1909 Leonard Arundell
Berry, *Swaledale*, 1998, p. 221
1910 Thomas Mylner
Berry, *Swaledale*, 1998, pp. 215-216

Grinton, Healaugh
1911 Simon Robinson
Berry, *Swaledale*, 1998, pp. 217-219
Marske
1912 John Lauckland, yeoman
Berry, *Swaledale*, 1998, pp. 219-220
Richmond
1913 Thomas Pasmore
Raine, *Richmond*, 1853, pp. 268-270
South Cave
1914 Cristofer Clarkes [Christofer Clark], [yeoman]
Kaner, *South Cave*, 1994, pp. 101-104
1915 John Jacson
Kaner, *South Cave*, 1994, pp. 104-105
South Cave, Faxfleet
1916 Lawrence Stamper
Kaner, *South Cave*, 1994, pp. 98-99
Stockeld Park
1917 William Myddilton, esquire
Brears, *Yorkshire*, 1972, pp. 45-54
York
1918 Alexander Adam, clergyman, vicar of St Maurice's
Cross, *York*, II, 1989, p. 99

1578 (c.)
Surrey
Woking
1919 Margaret Stansted, widow
Herridge, *Surrey*, 2005, pp. 150-151
Wales
Montgomeryshire, Kerry
1920 Griffith ap John ap Morys
Morris, 1893, pp. 256-257
Warwickshire
Kenilworth Castle
1921 Robert Dudley, Earl of Leicester
Goldring, 2007

1579
Cheshire
Broxton
1922 Humfrey Gregorie
Pearson, *Malpas*, [2005], pp. 57-58
Wythenshawe
1923 Robert Tatton, esquire
Piccope, *Lancashire and Cheshire*, 1860, pp. 100-102
Derbyshire
Brimington
1924 Thomas Shaye
Bestall and Fowkes, *Chesterfield*, 1977, pp. 158-160
Chesterfield
1925 George Assh, tanner
Bestall and Fowkes, *Chesterfield*, 1977, pp. 154-155
1926 Agnes Atkynson, widow
Bestall and Fowkes, *Chesterfield*, 1977, pp. 155-156
1927 Edmond Renshaw
Bestall and Fowkes, *Chesterfield*, 1977, pp. 157-158
Co. Durham
Sockburn
1928 Francis Trolloppe [Trollope], clergyman
Raine, *Wills and Inventories*, 1835, I, p. 427
Ireland
Cork
1929 Nicholas Faggan, merchant
Caulfield, *Cork*, 1861-1862, p. 36 (1861)

Lancashire
Bewsey Hall, Warrington
  1930   Sir Thomas Butler
    Piccope, *Lancashire and Cheshire*, 1860, pp. 120-126
Deane, Rumworth
  1931   James Grundye
    Bolton, *Bolton*, 1987, p. 124
Horwich
  1932   Alyxander Stones
    Bolton, *Bolton*, 1994, p. 105
Lincolnshire
Clee, Oole
  1933   Thomas Yates
    Ambler, Watkinson, *Clee*, 1987, pp. 68-69
London
Southwark, St Saviour's
  1934   William Beston, gentleman
    Herridge, *Surrey*, 2005, pp. 159-160
Oxfordshire
Banbury
  1935   Thomas Elson
    Havinden, *Oxfordshire*, 1965, p. 106
Banbury, Overthorpe
  1936   Richard Chelley [Shelley]
    Havinden, *Oxfordshire*, 1965, p. 114
Banbury, Grimsbury
  1937   John Jervice, [husbandman]
    Havinden, *Oxfordshire*, 1965, pp. 107-108
Banbury
  1938   Joan Shiltylworth [Shuttleworth], [widow]
    Havinden, *Oxfordshire*, 1965, pp. 111-114
Banbury (?)
  1939   Peter Gylld
    Havinden, *Oxfordshire*, 1965, p. 111
  1940   Thomas Newayll
    Havinden, *Oxfordshire*, 1965, pp. 114-115
Cassington
  1941   Richard Chirrie [Cherry], [husbandman]
    Havinden, *Oxfordshire*, 1965, pp. 102-104
Cropredy
  1942   Joanna Robbins, widow
    Havinden, *Oxfordshire*, 1965, pp. 104-106
Mollington
  1943   John Galliovere, [husbandman]
    Havinden, *Oxfordshire*, 1965, p. 109
  1944   Mathew Greene
    Havinden, *Oxfordshire*, 1965, p. 107
Wardington
  1945   John Eydon
    Havinden, *Oxfordshire*, 1965, p. 110
  1946   Roger Frenche, [husbandman]
    Havinden, *Oxfordshire*, 1965, pp. 101-102
Scotland
Edinburgh
  1947   Thomas Bassinden, printer
    Anon., *Bassandyne*, 1836, pp. 191-203
Staffordshire
Dudley
  1948   Richard Mason alias Robenson
    Roper, *Dudley*, 1965, p. 28

  1949   Jone Veridee, widow
    Roper, *Dudley*, 1965, p. 27
Surrey
Dunsfold
  1950   John Manfilde, husbandman
    Herridge, *Surrey*, 2005, pp. 156-157
Pirbright
  1951   John Rempnant, weaver
    Herridge, *Surrey*, 2005, p. 158
Worplesdon
  1952   George Collier, yeoman
    Herridge, *Surrey*, 2005, pp. 154-155
Westmorland
Helsington
  Alan Bellingham, esquire (see Levens)
Kendal
  1953   William Braythewaite, [vintner]
    Raine, *Richmond*, 1853, pp. 286-287
Levens (?)
  1954   Alan Bellingham, esquire (also listed Helsington)
    Raine, *Richmond*, 1853, pp. 284-286
Worcestershire
Bushley
  1955   George Carre [Carr], gentleman
    Wanklyn, *Worcestershire*, 1998, pp. 51-54
Harvington Hall
  1956   John Pakyngton [Pakington], esquire
    Hodgetts, 1962, pp. 10-11
Yorkshire
Downholme, Stainton
  1957   Richard Blaydes
    Berry, *Swaledale*, 1998, pp. 232-233
Downholme
  1958   Robert Kagill
    Berry, *Swaledale*, 1998, pp. 228-229
Grinton
  1959   Richard Blaides
    Berry, *Swaledale*, 1998, pp. 230-231
Grinton, Whitaside
  1960   John Spenselay
    Berry, *Swaledale*, 1998, pp. 225-227
Grinton
  1961   Christopher Swaill
    Berry, *Swaledale*, 1998, p. 234
Marske, Skelton
  1962   Ciciley Bynkes, widow
    Berry, *Swaledale*, 1998, pp. 212-213
South Cave
  1963   William Colyer
    Kaner, *South Cave*, 1994, pp. 107-108
  1964   John Wright
    Kaner, *South Cave*, 1994, pp. 108-110
York Minster
  1965   James Crosthwaite, clergyman, Prebendary of
  Tockerington
    Cross, *York*, I, 1984, pp. 101-106

1579 (c.)
Surrey
Frensham
  1966   Jonne Fulstone, widow
    Herridge, *Surrey*, 2005, pp. 155-156

1580

Cheshire
Malpas, Oldcastle
1967 John Griffith
Pearson, *Malpas*, [2005], pp. 59-60

Derbyshire
Chesterfield
1968 William Boler
Bestall and Fowkes, *Chesterfield*, 1977, pp. 162-163
1969 Raffe Claye, smith
Bestall and Fowkes, *Chesterfield*, 1977, pp. 156-157
1970 John Cottrell
Bestall and Fowkes, *Chesterfield*, 1977, pp. 161-162
1971 Raph Holden
Bestall and Fowkes, *Chesterfield*, 1977, pp. 160-161
Glossop, Broadhurst
1972 Robert Arnefeld, yeoman
Bryant, Lee, Miller, *New Mills II*, 1995, pp. 20-22
Glossop, Beard
1973 William Bearde, [gentleman]
Bryant, Lee, Miller, *New Mills II*, 1995, pp. 31-32
Glossop, Roworth
1974 Robert Goddart, [husbandman]
Bryant, Lee, Miller, *New Mills II*, 1995, p. 25

Dorsetshire
Chetnole
1975 John Oldish
Machin, *Yetminster*, 1976, No.2, (3 pp.)

Co. Durham
Chester-le-Street
1976 John Lawson
Greenwell, *Wills and Inventories*, 1860, II, pp. 20-21
Long Newton
1977 Edward Conyers
Raine, *Wills and Inventories*, 1835, I, p. 428

Hertfordshire
St Albans, St Stephens
1978 Elizabeth Felde, widow
Munby, *Worldly Goods*, 1991, p. 57
St Albans, St Stephens, Park Street
1979 George Francis, [smith]
Parker, *Worldly Goods*, 2004, pp. 89-91
St Albans, St Stephens
1980 Jhon Skelle
Munby, *Worldly Goods*, 1991, pp. 58-59

Kent
Harrietsham
1981 Thomas Steade
Goodsall, 1949, pp.20-22

Lancashire
Westhoughton
1982 Robart Jamesson
Bolton, *Bolton*, 1987, p. 158

Leicestershire
Great Stretton
1983 Tho. Cowper
Wilshere, *Great Stretton*, 1984, p. 16
Quorndon
1984 Thomas Barton, husbandman
Farnham, *Quorndon*, 1912, pp. 274-275

Lincolnshire
Clee, Oole
1985 Rychard Dodson
Ambler, Watkinson, *Clee*, 1987, pp. 69-70

Clee
1986 Thomas Marshall
Ambler, Watkinson, *Clee*, 1987, p. 70
Market Rasen
1987 Edward Moysie
Neave, *Market Rasen*, 1985, pp. 81-82

London
Unlocated
1988 Unknown
Freshfield, 1889, pp. 378-380

Northumberland
Longbenton, Walker
1989 John Fenwik
Greenwell, *Wills and Inventories*, 1860, II, p. 35

Oxfordshire
Banbury
1990 David Evans, chapman
Havinden, *Oxfordshire*, 1965, pp. 121-122
1991 Thomas Hadley, tailor
Havinden, *Oxfordshire*, 1965, pp. 120-121
1992 William Wheatlie
Havinden, *Oxfordshire*, 1965, pp. 117-118
Banbury (?)
1993 William Golde
Havinden, *Oxfordshire*, 1965, p. 119
Chadlington
1994 Thomas Drake, [husbandman]
Havinden, *Oxfordshire*, 1965, pp. 122-123
Claydon
1995 Thomas Borman
Havinden, *Oxfordshire*, 1965, pp. 115-116
Cropredy
1996 Thomas Browne, whittawer
Havinden, *Oxfordshire*, 1965, pp. 116-117
1997 John French, husbandman
Havinden, *Oxfordshire*, 1965, p. 121
1998 Avis Gardner
Havinden, *Oxfordshire*, 1965, p. 120
Deddington
1999 Anthony Cowper, husbandman
Havinden, *Oxfordshire*, 1965, pp. 118-119

Scotland
Dumbarton Castle
2000 James VI of Scotland
Thomson, *Edinburgh*, 1815, pp. 299-302
Edinburgh
2001 Johne Ross, printer
Anon., *Bassandyne*, 1836, pp. 204-206

Staffordshire
Dudley
2002 Thomas Bate
Roper, *Dudley*, 1965, p. 31
2003 Jhon Robinson
Roper, *Dudley*, 1965, p. 30
2004 Joyes Wheller, widow
Roper, *Dudley*, 1965, p. 29

Warwickshire
Ashow
2005 Thomas Cox
Alcock, *Warwickshire*, 1993, pp. 55-57
Birmingham
2006 John Smyth
Holt, Ingram, Jarman, *Birmingham*, 1985, pp. 28-29

Coventry
2007 Richard Fitzherbert, [haberdasher]
  Hulton and Castle, *Tudor*, 1987, pp. 55-60
Stratford-on-Avon
2008 Rycharde Balamy, [smith]
  Jones, *Stratford*, I, 2002, pp. 49-50
Yorkshire
Downholme
2009 Edmond Jeffrason, yeoman
  Berry, *Swaledale*, 1998, pp. 243-248
2010 William Milner
  Berry, *Swaledale*, 1998, pp. 237-238
Grinton, West Stonesdale
2011 Agnes Alderson
  Berry, *Swaledale*, 1998, pp. 235-236
Grinton, Whitaside
2012 Lawrence Close
  Berry, *Swaledale*, 1998, pp. 240-241

1580 (c.)
Oxfordshire
Great Milton
2013 Edward Colles
  Havinden, *Oxfordshire*, 1965, pp. 123-126

1581
Cambridgeshire
Cambridge
2014 John Sheres, [stationer and binder]
  Gray and Palmer, *Cambridge*, 1915, p. 62
Cheshire
Bickley
2015 Thomas Golborne, husbandman
  Pearson, *Malpas*, [2005], p. 65
Malpas, Carden
2016 John Tayler
  Pearson, *Malpas*, [2005], pp. 63-64
Shocklach
2017 Richard Pova
  Pearson, *Malpas*, [2005], p. 67
Tarvin, Ashton
2018 Margery Whitbie, [widow]
  Bland, *Christleton*, 2002, p. 17
Cumberland
Holme Cultram
2019 William Threlkeld
  Jackson, 1889, pp. 39-40
Derbyshire
Chesterfield
2020 Isabell Johnson
  Bestall and Fowkes, *Chesterfield*, 1977, p. 164
Ockbrook
2021 Rychard James
  Johnson, 1994, pp. 29-31
Devonshire
Uffculme
2022 Bennett [Bennet] Fryer, miller
  Wyatt, *Uffculme*, 1997, pp. 4-5
Co. Durham
Darlington
2023 Jacobi [James] Forrest, [parish clerk of
  Darlington]
  Greenwell, *Wills and Inventories*, 1860, II, pp. 28-29

2024 Christofer Foster [Christopher Forster]
  Hodgson, *Wills and Inventories*, 1906, III, pp. 85-86
Houghton-le-Spring
2025 John Ironside
  Raine, *Wills and Inventories*, 1835, I, p. 438
Long Newton
2026 Rauphe Conyers, gentleman
  Raine, *Wills and Inventories*, 1835, I, p. 430
Stranton
2027 Phillip Hatherley, clergyman, vicar of Stranton
  Raine, *Barnes*, 1850, pp. cxiv-cxv
Hampshire
Newport, Isle of Wight
2028 Thomas Bracklie, draper
  Carter, 1971, pp. 107-119
Hertfordshire
St Albans, St Stephens
2029 Thomas Dyche
  Parker, *Worldly Goods*, 2004, pp. 95-96
Ireland
Cork
2030 Edmonde Fitz Nicholas alias Frankaghe
  Caulfield, *Cork*, 1861-1862, p. 37 (1861)
2031 Andrewe Galwey, alderman
  Caulfield, *Cork*, 1861-1862, p. 260 (1861)
Lancashire
Bolton
2032 William Tylson, clergyman
  Bolton, *Bolton*, 1994, pp. 113-114
Clayton (?)
2033 Elizabeth, Lady Byron, [widow]
  Piccope, *Lancashire and Cheshire*, 1860, p. 162
Turton
2034 John Orrell, gentleman
  Bolton, *Bolton*, 1994, pp. 41-42
Westhoughton
2035 Thomas Cowpere, husbandman
  Bolton, *Bolton*, 1987, p. 60
Leicestershire
Braunstone
2036 Margret Bente, widow
  Wilshere, *Braunstone*, 1983, p. 10
Evington
2037 Henrie Noone, husbandman
  Wilshere, *Evington*, 1985, p. 2
Lincolnshire
Clee
2038 Richard Marshall
  Ambler, Watkinson, *Clee*, 1987, p. 71
Market Rasen
2039 Isabell Johnson
  Neave, *Market Rasen*, 1985, p. 80
Northumberland
Blenkinsopp Castle
2040 Wylliam Blenkinsopp
  Greenwell, *Wills and Inventories*, 1860, II, pp. 29-30
Newcastle
2041 Gyles Andersone [Anderson], tailor
  Hodgson, *Wills and Inventories*, 1906, III, p. 88
2042 Robert Rookebye [Rokeby], merchant
  Raine, *Wills and Inventories*, 1835, I, pp. 429-430

Ogle Castle
2043 Dame Isabell Gray, widow
Greenwell, *Wills and Inventories*, 1860, II, pp. 51-52
Tweedmouth
2044 William Preston, pensioner
Greenwell, *Wills and Inventories*, 1860, II, p. 61

Oxfordshire
Chipping Norton
2045 Richard Dannyell
Havinden, *Oxfordshire*, 1965, pp. 130-131
Deddington
2046 Richard Holland, blacksmith
Havinden, *Oxfordshire*, 1965, p. 132
Idbury
2047 Joan Heyeres, widow
Havinden, *Oxfordshire*, 1965, p. 131
Kidlington
2048 Robert Bridges, [mercer]
Havinden, *Oxfordshire*, 1965, p. 125
Shirburn
2049 William Horskins, [husbandman]
Havinden, *Oxfordshire*, 1965, pp. 125-126
Witney
2050 Leonard Dalton
Havinden, *Oxfordshire*, 1965, pp. 128-130
Wolvercote
2051 Henry Hitches, husbandman
Havinden, *Oxfordshire*, 1965, pp. 127-128
Wroxton
2052 Thomas Homan, [husbandman]
Havinden, *Oxfordshire*, 1965, p. 127

Staffordshire
Dudley
2053 Elezabethe Batte, [widow]
Roper, *Dudley*, 1965, p. 32
2054 Elezabethe Mason
Roper, *Dudley*, 1965, p. 34
2055 William Wheler
Roper, *Dudley*, 1965, p. 33

Surrey
Elstead
2056 Annys Dayer, widow
Herridge, *Surrey*, 2005, pp. 161-162
Godalming
2057 William Chytte
Herridge, *Surrey*, 2005, p. 160
Ockley
2058 Katherine Brand
Herridge, *Surrey*, 2005, pp. 165-166
Stockwell
2059 Robert Rundell, yeoman
Herridge, *Surrey*, 2005, pp. 162-164
Woking
2060 John Shaddatt alias Sherratt
Herridge, *Surrey*, 2005, pp. 177-178

Wales
Montgomeryshire
2061 Edward ap Hoell
Morris, 1893, p. 249

Worcestershire
Hindlip
2062 John Abyngton [Habington], esquire, cofferer to the Queen
Wanklyn, *Worcestershire*, 1998, pp. 60-78

Yorkshire
Grinton, Low Whitaside
2063 James Carter
Berry, *Swaledale*, 1998, pp. 250-251
Lunds
2064 John Parkinges [Parking, Parkin]
Thwaite, *Abbotside*, 1967, p. 13
North Cave
2065 Rychard Barsayes [Richard Barsay]
Kaner, *South Cave*, 1994, pp. 112-114
South Cave
2066 Rychard Coulsonne [Richard Coulson]
Kaner, *South Cave*, 1994, pp. 115-116
South Cave, Oxmardyke
2067 Thomas Iyon, labourer
Kaner, *South Cave*, 1994, p. 115
South Cave
2068 John Robyngson [Robison]
Kaner, *South Cave*, 1994, pp. 111-112

1581 (c.)
Surrey
Frensham
2069 William Fulston
Herridge, *Surrey*, 2005, p. 162
West Horsley
2070 John Cresey, husbandman
Herridge, *Surrey*, 2005, p. 161

1582
Bedfordshire
Podington
2071 Richard Childe
Orlebar, 1930, pp. 11-13
Derbyshire
Brimington
2072 Peter Fletcher, husbandman
Bestall and Fowkes, *Chesterfield*, 1977, pp. 166-167
Chesterfield
2073 Phillipp Yeates, scythesmith
Bestall and Fowkes, *Chesterfield*, 1977, pp. 165-166
Staveley
2074 Peter Fretevile [Frecheville], esquire
Nichols, *Illustrations*, 1797, pp. 235-238
Devonshire
Uffculme
2075 John Myll [Mill]
Wyatt, *Uffculme*, 1997, p. 6
2076 John Sander [Saunder]
Wyatt, *Uffculme*, 1997, p. 6
2077 Wyllyam [William] Toser
Wyatt, *Uffculme*, 1997, p. 5
Co. Durham
Durham, Kingsgate
2078 Richard Marshall, public notary
Greenwell, *Wills and Inventories*, 1860, II, pp. 26-28
Durham
2079 Isable Rood, widow
Greenwell, *Wills and Inventories*, 1860, II, pp. 65-66

2080 John Stout
Greenwell, *Wills and Inventories*, 1860, II, p. 55
East Brandon
2081 Willyam Lee
Greenwell, *Wills and Inventories*, 1860, II, pp. 43-48
East Murton
2082 Anthony Preston, gentleman
Hodgson, *Wills and Inventories*, 1906, III, p. 90

Hertfordshire
St Albans, St Stephens, Parkbury
2083 Edward Cocke
Parker, *Worldly Goods*, 2004, pp. 97-98
St Albans, St Stephens
2084 Robert Marshall, [smith]
Parker, *Worldly Goods*, 2004, p. 100
2085 John Skeale, [yeoman]
Munby, *Worldly Goods*, 1991, pp. 60-61

Ireland
Cork
2086 Christopher Galwey, alderman
Caulfield, *Cork*, 1861-1862, p. 262 (1861)
2087 Richard Tyrry Fitz Adame
Caulfield, *Cork*, 1861-1862, pp. 710-711 (1862)

Lancashire
Bolton, Entwistle
2088 [Gyles] Entwisill
Bolton, *Bolton*, 1987, p. 94
Bolton, Edgworth
2089 John Knowell, husbandman
Bolton, *Bolton*, 1994, p. 22
Deane
2090 William Richardson
Bolton, *Bolton*, 1994, pp. 56-57
Farnworth
2091 William Tonge, husbandman
Bolton, *Bolton*, 1994, p. 116

Leicestershire
Braunstone
2092 Richarde Hackett, husbandman
Wilshere, *Braunstone*, 1983, pp. 11-12
2093 Xtopher Wirrall, [yeoman?]
Wilshere, *Braunstone*, 1983, p. 47

Lincolnshire
Allington
2094 Rawfe Giles
Pask, *Allington*, 1989, p. 35
Clee, Oole
2095 Thomas Johnson, fisherman
Ambler, Watkinson, *Clee*, 1987, p. 76
2096 George Marshall, fisherman
Ambler, Watkinson, *Clee*, 1987, p. 75
2097 John Mason, fisherman
Ambler, Watkinson, *Clee*, 1987, pp. 75-76
2098 Robt Preston
Ambler, Watkinson, *Clee*, 1987, pp. 74-75
2099 Thomas Preston
Ambler, Watkinson, *Clee*, 1987, pp. 71-72
Clee
2100 Bryane West
Ambler, Watkinson, *Clee*, 1987, pp. 72-73
2101 Thomas West
Ambler, Watkinson, *Clee*, 1987, p. 72

2102 Richard Wright
Ambler, Watkinson, *Clee*, 1987, pp. 73-74
Northumberland
Berwick
2103 Thomas Morton, alderman
Greenwell, *Wills and Inventories*, 1860, II, pp. 71-72
2104 Harrie Strowther [Strother]
Greenwell, *Wills and Inventories*, 1860, II, p. 73
Callaly
2105 Roberte Clavering
Greenwell, *Wills and Inventories*, 1860, II, pp. 58-60
Newcastle
2106 Cuthberte Ellysone, merchant
Raine, *Wills and Inventories*, 1835, I, pp. 434-437
2107 John Sotheren [Sotheran], merchant
Greenwell, *Wills and Inventories*, 1860, II, pp. 68-70
2108 Mathewe Welkensonne [Mathew Wilkinson], blacksmith
Hodgson, *Wills and Inventories*, 1906, III, p. 93
Stamfordham
2109 Arthure Shaftoe, clergyman, vicar of Stamfordham
Raine, *Barnes*, 1850, pp. cxvi-cxvii

Oxfordshire
Aston Rowant
2110 William Cosynne
Havinden, *Oxfordshire*, 1965, p. 141
Banbury (?)
2111 Thomas Pitman
Havinden, *Oxfordshire*, 1965, p. 143
Bloxham
2112 John Turbett
Havinden, *Oxfordshire*, 1965, pp. 139-140
Chadlington
2113 Edmund Crosse
Havinden, *Oxfordshire*, 1965, p. 140
Chipping Norton
2114 Thomas Tynson, butcher
Havinden, *Oxfordshire*, 1965, p. 136
Combe
2115 John Twynches
Havinden, *Oxfordshire*, 1965, p. 135
Drayton
2116 Thomas Darlowe, husbandman
Havinden, *Oxfordshire*, 1965, pp. 132-133
2117 Roger Dyxon
Havinden, *Oxfordshire*, 1965, pp. 137-138
Hook Norton
2118 Richard Tasker, [husbandman]
Havinden, *Oxfordshire*, 1965, pp. 136-137
Oxford, St Giles
2119 John Trendar
Havinden, *Oxfordshire*, 1965, pp. 133-134
Steeple Aston
2120 Margery Carter
Havinden, *Oxfordshire*, 1965, pp. 134-135
Wardington
2121 Christopher Helye
Havinden, *Oxfordshire*, 1965, pp. 138-139
Suffolk
Dennington
2122 Beatrice Girling, widow
Anon., *Mid-Elizabethan*, 1940, pp. 32-33

Laxfield
2123 Agnes Alymere, widow
Anon., *Mid-Elizabethan*, 1940, pp. 18-19

Surrey
Albury
2124 Bartholemew Bowdoxe, clergyman, parson
Herridge, *Surrey*, 2005, pp. 164-165
Bramley
2125 Christopher Mellershe, yeoman
Herridge, *Surrey*, 2005, pp. 173-175
Frimley
2126 Richard Exold, husbandman
Herridge, *Surrey*, 2005, p. 170
Kingston-upon-Thames
2127 Peter Buckland, waterman
Herridge, *Surrey*, 2005, pp. 166-167
Seale
2128 William Hampton
Herridge, *Surrey*, 2005, p. 171
Thorpe
2129 William Becham
Herridge, *Surrey*, 2005, p. 164
West Clandon
2130 Lawrence Elliott, husbandman
Herridge, *Surrey*, 2005, pp. 169-170
Worplesdon
2131 George Burt alias Loveland, husbandman
Herridge, *Surrey*, 2005, pp. 166-167
2132 Richard and Margaret Clifton
Herridge, *Surrey*, 2005, pp. 168-169
2133 John Russell, yeoman
Herridge, *Surrey*, 2005, pp. 175-177

Sussex
Aldingbourne
Richard Curteys, bishop of Chichester (see Horsham, Chesworth)
2134 Horsham, Chesworth
Richard Curteys, bishop of Chichester (also listed Aldingbourne)
Ellis, 1858, pp. 56-58

Warwickshire
Birmingham
2135 Maurice Harwell
Holt, Ingram, Jarman, *Birmingham*, 1985, pp. 30-31

Westmorland
Sizergh Castle
Sir Thomas Boynton (see Barmston, Yorkshire)

Yorkshire
Barmston
2136 Sir Thomas Boynton (also listed Sizergh, Westmorland)
Poulson, *Holderness*, 1840, pp. 215-224
Grinton, Healaugh
2137 Ralph Gallaway
Berry, *Swaledale*, 1998, p. 253
Grinton
2138 Richard Wenselay
Berry, *Swaledale*, 1998, p. 254
Sheffield, Castle and Lodge
2139 George Talbot, Earl of Shrewsbury
Tucker, 1874, pp. 251-263

South Cave, Faxfleet
2140 Miles Atkinson
Kaner, *South Cave*, 1994, pp. 121-123
South Cave
2141 Roger Hilton
Kaner, *South Cave*, 1994, pp. 117-120
2142 William Norman
Kaner, *South Cave*, 1994, pp. 123-124
South Cave, Faxfleet
2143 Richard Seresmith [Shearsmith]
Kaner, *South Cave*, 1994, p. 117
Wath, Middleton Quernhow
2144 Richard Best
Robinson, 1857, pp. 171-173

1582 (c.)
Surrey
Frensham
2145 William Luffe, yeoman
Herridge, *Surrey*, 2005, pp. 172-173
Walton-on-the-Hill
2146 Charles Holman, weaver
Herridge, *Surrey*, 2005, p. 172
West Horsley
2147 William Stint
Herridge, *Surrey*, 2005, pp. 178-179

1583
Cheshire
Malpas, Carden
2148 George Huxley
Pearson, *Malpas*, [2005], pp. 83-84
Malpas, Bradley
2149 John Macefene, husbandman
Pearson, *Malpas*, [2005], pp. 72-73
Malpas, Bobberhill
2150 Rychard Stocketon
Pearson, *Malpas*, [2005], p. 82
Malpas, Carden
2151 William Tailior, husbandman
Pearson, *Malpas*, [2005], p. 85
Malpas
2152 Edmund Wyndell
Pearson, *Malpas*, [2005], pp. 80-81
Tarvin, Stapleford
2153 Jone Fylken
Bland, *Christleton*, 2002, p. 21
Tarvin, Ashton
2154 Margarett Thomason, widow
Bland, *Christleton*, 2002, p. 20
Tarvin, Duddon
2155 Richard Wean [Wayne], [husbandman]
Bland, *Christleton*, 2002, p. 23

Derbyshire
Chesterfield
2156 Raphe Blackwall
Bestall and Fowkes, *Chesterfield*, 1977, pp. 167-170
2157 William Mylner alias Holmes
Bestall and Fowkes, *Chesterfield*, 1977, pp. 170-171
Glossop, Broadhurst
2158 Margery Armfeld
Bryant, Lee, Miller, *New Mills II*, 1995, p. 33
Glossop, Breregreave

2159 Thomas Shuttleworthe
Bryant, Lee, Miller, *New Mills II*, 1995, p. 35

Devonshire
Exeter
2160 John Dynham, weaver
Portman, *Exeter*, 1966, pp. 96-98

Co. Durham
Gateshead
2161 James Coll, blacksmith
Greenwell, *Wills and Inventories*, 1860, II, p. 67
Lambton
2162 Robert Lambton, esquire
Greenwell, *Wills and Inventories*, 1860, II, pp. 63-64
Long Newton
2163 John Tonnstall [Tunstall]
Greenwell, *Wills and Inventories*, 1860, II, pp. 80-81
Morpeth
2164 Philloppe Grene
Greenwell, *Wills and Inventories*, 1860, II, pp. 82-83
Newton Bewley
2165 John Thompsone, husbandman
Greenwell, *Wills and Inventories*, 1860, II, pp. 77-79
Sherburn, Pittington
2166 John Smith
Hodgson, *Wills and Inventories*, 1906, III, p. 100

Essex
Stanford-le Hope
2167 John Knight
Emmison, *Essex*, 4, 1987, p. 225

Hertfordshire
St Albans, St Stephens
2168 Robert Lane, [yeoman]
Parker, *Worldly Goods*, 2004, p. 102

Jersey
St Helier, Presbytery
2169 Pierre Dangey, minister
Anon., *St Hélier*, 1885-1889, pp. 364-365

Lancashire
Haydock
2170 Dowce Kenyan, widow
St Helens, *Angells*, 1999, pp. 5-6
Manchester
2171 Robert Berche [Birch], linen draper
Lowe, 1972, pp. 103-105
Rainhill
2172 Elizabeth Ackers
St Helens, *Angells*, 1999, p. 6

Leicestershire
Glenfield
2173 Robart Atkings
Wilshere, *Glenfield*, 1983, p. 2

Lincolnshire
Allington
2174 Rycharde Rycheman, husbandman
Pask, *Allington*, 1989, pp. 32-33
Market Rasen
2175 George Feyldhouse
Neave, *Market Rasen*, 1985, p. 82
2176 Thomas Rawlinson
Neave, *Market Rasen*, 1985, pp. 83-84

Norfolk
Old Buckenham
John Wilkinson, gentleman (see Ipswich, Suffolk)

Northumberland
Lowick, Bowsden
2177 Katherine Muschance, widow
Greenwell, *Wills and Inventories*, 1860, II, p. 305
Morpeth
2178 Thomas Craw, merchant
Greenwell, *Wills and Inventories*, 1860, II, pp. 67-68
Newcastle
2179 Marione Chapman, widow
Greenwell, *Wills and Inventories*, 1860, II, pp. 73-75
2180 John Shafto, merchant
Hodgson, *Wills and Inventories*, 1906, III, p. 103
Thirlwall
2181 Lancelot Thirlwall
Greenwell, *Wills and Inventories*, 1860, II, pp. 76-77
Trewhitt
2182 Anthony Fenwik [Fenwick], gentleman
Hodgson, *Wills and Inventories*, 1906, III, p. 105

Oxfordshire
Bladon
2183 Alice Cock [Cook]
Havinden, *Oxfordshire*, 1965, pp. 161-163
Bodicote
2184 Richard Cowles
Havinden, *Oxfordshire*, 1965, pp. 149-150
Chadlington
2185 Gregory Hoskins
Havinden, *Oxfordshire*, 1965, p. 166
Checkendon
2186 John Bodie
Havinden, *Oxfordshire*, 1965, pp. 144-145
Cropredy
2187 Henry Walsall
Havinden, *Oxfordshire*, 1965, pp. 164-165
Headington (?)
2188 Nicholas Tripllatt
Havinden, *Oxfordshire*, 1965, pp. 148-149
Henley-on-Thames
2189 Thomas Barretes
Havinden, *Oxfordshire*, 1965, pp. 146-148
2190 Anthony Dee
Havinden, *Oxfordshire*, 1965, pp. 141-142
Hook Norton
2191 John Clyfton
Havinden, *Oxfordshire*, 1965, pp. 165-166
Newton Purcell
2192 Mary Tayler, widow
Havinden, *Oxfordshire*, 1965, p. 167
Oxford, St Michaels
2193 Elinor Pare
Havinden, *Oxfordshire*, 1965, pp. 143-144
Spelsbury, Taston
2194 Ann Elkes
Havinden, *Oxfordshire*, 1965, p. 150
Swerford
2195 Henry Edes
Havinden, *Oxfordshire*, 1965, pp. 145-146
Witney
2196 Thomas Taylor, yeoman
Havinden, *Oxfordshire*, 1965, pp. 150-151
Wootton
2197 Thomas Hutchynnes, [labourer]
Havinden, *Oxfordshire*, 1965, pp. 163-164

Staffordshire

Dudley, Russells Hall
2198 Elynor Duddeley, widow
Roper, *Dudley*, 1965, pp. 37-38
Dudley
2199 John Homewood, [butcher]
Roper, *Dudley*, 1965, p. 39
2200 Thomas Shawe
Roper, *Dudley*, 1965, p. 35

Suffolk

Aldeburgh
2201 Thomas Baokies
Anon., *Mid-Elizabethan*, 1940, p. 3
2202 Robart Bingis, mariner
Anon., *Mid-Elizabethan*, 1940, pp. 20, 22, 24
Dunwich
2203 Willians Sargentes, merchant
Anon., *Mid-Elizabethan*, 1940, pp. 5-6. 8,10,12,14-15, 17
Ipswich
2204 Thomas Bonner, blacksmith
Reed, *Ipswich*, 1981, pp. 18-19
2205 John Kenynggale
Reed, *Ipswich*, 1981, pp. 9-11
2206 Margaret Lowe, widow
Reed, *Ipswich*, 1981, pp. 11-13
2207 Jacob Person, sailor
Reed, *Ipswich*, 1981, p. 20
2208 John Wilkinson, gentleman (also listed Old
Buckenham, Norfolk)
Reed, *Ipswich*, 1981, pp. 13-18
Lowestoft
2209 Willyam Brews
Anon., *Mid-Elizabethan*, 1940, pp. 24,27-28, 30
Shotley
2210 John Alderton, sailor
Anon., *Mid-Elizabethan*, 1940, pp. 37,39
Ufford
2211 Thomas Smallheds
Anon., *Mid-Elizabethan*, 1940, p. 40

Surrey

Albury
2212 Richard Hiller, husbandman
Herridge, *Surrey*, 2005, p. 181
Buckland
2213 Thomas Ladd
Herridge, *Surrey*, 2005, pp. 181-182
Chertsey
2214 Thomas Drewe
Herridge, *Surrey*, 2005, p. 180
Leigh
2215 Mathewe Byshopp
Herridge, *Surrey*, 2005, pp. 179-180
Newdigate
2216 Agnes Newdegate, widow
Herridge, *Surrey*, 2005, pp. 182-183
West Horsley
2217 William Giles
Herridge, *Surrey*, 2005, p. 231

Warwickshire

Stratford-on-Avon
2218 John Asshwell [Aswell], wheelwright
Jones, *Stratford*, I, 2002, pp. 54-55

2219 Thomas Robartes [Roberts], [shoemaker]
Jones, *Stratford*, I, 2002, pp. 55-57
2220 John Sadler, yeoman [and miller]
Jones, *Stratford*, I, 2002, pp. 51-53

Worcestershire

Dudley
2221 Elynor Duddeley [Eleanor Dudley]
Wanklyn, *Worcestershire*, 1998, pp. 78-80

Yorkshire

Grinton, Fremington
2222 William Place
Berry, *Swaledale*, 1998, p. 259
Marrick
2223 Spenselaye
Berry, *Swaledale*, 1998, pp. 256-257
Marske
2224 William Clerkson
Berry, *Swaledale*, 1998, pp. 257-258
Ripon
2225 Rauf Ripley
Fowler, 1874, pp. 379-382
South Cave
2226 Roberte Barker
Kaner, *South Cave*, 1994, pp. 126-127
2227 John Spofforth, grassman
Kaner, *South Cave*, 1994, p. 125

1583 (c.)

Suffolk

Bruisyard
2228 Arthur Rous, gentleman
Anon., *Mid-Elizabethan*, 1940, p. 35

1584

Cheshire

Tarvin, Ashton
2229 Robert Hignete, husbandman
Bland, *Christleton*, 2002, pp. 25-26
Wrenbury, Newhall
2230 Thomas Massye
Pixton, *Wrenbury*, 2009, p. 16

Derbyshire

Brimington
2231 Margery Boller
Bestall and Fowkes, *Chesterfield*, 1977, pp. 174-175
2232 James Kenryck
Bestall and Fowkes, *Chesterfield*, 1977, pp. 171-172
Chesterfield
2233 John Asshe
Bestall and Fowkes, *Chesterfield*, 1977, pp. 177-180
Newbold
2234 Edward Foxe
Bestall and Fowkes, *Chesterfield*, 1977, pp. 180-182

Devonshire

Buckland in the Moor
2235 Richard [...]decomb
Cash, *Devon*, 1966, p. 4

Co. Durham

Aycliffe
2236 Dr William Bennett, clergyman, vicar of Aycliffe
Raine, *Barnes*, 1850, pp. cxix-cxxii
Bishop Middleham
2237 Thomas Myddeltonn, clergyman, vicar of
Bishop Middleton
Raine, *Barnes*, 1850, p. cxxvii

Heighington
2238 William Hardinge, clergyman, vicar of
Heighington
Raine, *Barnes*, 1850, pp. cxxiv-cxxv
Horsley
2239 Robert Lyghtton, clergyman, vicar of Horsley
Raine, *Barnes*, 1850, pp. cxxviii-cxxix
Houghton-le-Side
2240 Ralph Willey, gentleman
Greenwell, *Wills and Inventories*, 1860, II, p. 98
Kirk Merrington
2241 William Melmerbey, clergyman, vicar of
Merrington
Raine, *Barnes*, 1850, p. cxviii
Stanhope
2242 William Emerson, yeoman
Greenwell, *Wills and Inventories*, 1860, II, p. 99
[Stockton-on-Tees]
2243 Robert Tonstall
Greenwell, *Wills and Inventories*, 1860, II, pp. 104-105

Hertfordshire
Sarratt
2244 Katheren Lovett, [widow]
Bullen, *Sarratt*, [1982], pp. 57-58

Kent
Halling
2245 William Dallison, esquire
Robertson, *Dalison*, 1883, pp. 391-393

Lancashire
Billinge
2246 Anne Lathome, widow
St Helens, *Angells*, 1999, pp. 8-9
Blackrod
2247 George Holme, yeoman
Bolton, *Bolton*, 1987, pp. 148-149
Bolton
2248 Katherin Sanderson, widow
Bolton, *Bolton*, 1994, pp. 71-72
Deane, Rumworth
2249 William Horrocks
Bolton, *Bolton*, 1987, pp. 151-152
Deane, Little Hulton
2250 Arthure Smithe
Bolton, *Bolton*, 1994, p. 101

Lincolnshire
Allington
2251 Thomas Gibson, husbandman
Pask, *Allington*, 1989, pp. 41-42
2252 Agnis Warde, widow
Pask, *Allington*, 1989, pp. 38-39
Clee, Oole
2253 Rycharde Twivell
Ambler, Watkinson, *Clee*, 1987, pp. 76-77
Clee, Itterby
2254 Thomas Willson
Ambler, Watkinson, *Clee*, 1987, p. 77
Market Rasen
2255 Isabell Burnslay
Neave, *Market Rasen*, 1985, pp. 85-86
2256 John Rawlinson, glover
Neave, *Market Rasen*, 1985, pp. 88-89
2257 Richard Seele
Neave, *Market Rasen*, 1985, p. 90

2258 John Tomson
Neave, *Market Rasen*, 1985, p. 87
2259 Raulfe Wodcocke
Neave, *Market Rasen*, 1985, pp. 91-92

Northumberland
Newcastle
2260 Trestram Hearone [Tristram Heron], musician
Greenwell, *Wills and Inventories*, 1860, II, pp. 94-95
2261 John Hudsson [Hudson], merchant
Greenwell, *Wills and Inventories*, 1860, II, pp. 102-103
Stannington
2262 Thomas Bell, gentleman
Hodgson, *Wills and Inventories*, 1906, III, p. 106

Oxfordshire
Barford St John
2263 Alice Clarke, widow
Havinden, *Oxfordshire*, 1965, pp. 176-177
Burford
2264 Thomas Plome, butcher
Havinden, *Oxfordshire*, 1965, pp. 178-180
Checkendon
2265 William Boddy, [husbandman]
Havinden, *Oxfordshire*, 1965, pp. 180-181
Clanfield
2266 Richard Tayler
Havinden, *Oxfordshire*, 1965, pp. 168-169
Culham
2267 Margery Carpinter, widow
Havinden, *Oxfordshire*, 1965, pp. 170-171
Deddington
2268 John Coxe, husbandman
Havinden, *Oxfordshire*, 1965, pp. 169-170
Dorchester
2269 William Cobb
Havinden, *Oxfordshire*, 1965, pp. 173-176
Duns Tew
2270 Richard Baker, [servant]
Havinden, *Oxfordshire*, 1965, p. 176
Great Tew
2271 Margery Carter, widow
Havinden, *Oxfordshire*, 1965, p. 171
Holton
2272 Richard Bendforde
Havinden, *Oxfordshire*, 1965, pp. 172-173
South Newington
2273 Richard Clyfton, husbandman
Havinden, *Oxfordshire*, 1965, p. 181
Standlake, Brighthampton
2274 Joyce Hossier
Havinden, *Oxfordshire*, 1965, pp. 114-115
Swalcliffe
2275 Luke Baggat
Havinden, *Oxfordshire*, 1965, p. 169
Whitchurch
2276 John Blakalle
Havinden, *Oxfordshire*, 1965, pp. 177-178

Staffordshire
Dudley
2277 George Atwood, cordwainer
Roper, *Dudley*, 1965, pp. 40-41
2278 William Wiat
Roper, *Dudley*, 1965, p. 42

Suffolk

Aldeburgh
  2279 George Malins, sailor
    Anon., *Mid-Elizabethan*, 1940, p. 4
Ipswich
  2280 John Marrns alias Golames
    Reed, *Ipswich*, 1981, p. 21
  2281 John Seely
    Reed, *Ipswich*, 1981, pp. 22-23

Surrey

Abinger
  2282 William Netelfould
    Herridge, *Surrey*, 2005, pp. 186-187
Carshalton
  2283 Robert Fraye
    Herridge, *Surrey*, 2005, p. 185
Godalming
  2284 Joane Hamptonne
    Herridge, *Surrey*, 2005, p. 186
Godstone
  2285 Edward Scrafton, weaver
    Herridge, *Surrey*, 2005, pp. 187-188
Horsell
  2286 William Potter, yeoman
    Herridge, *Surrey*, 2005, pp. 274-275
Puttenham
  2287 John Clifton
    Herridge, *Surrey*, 2005, pp. 184-185
Wonersh
  2288 Richard Babbe, weaver
    Herridge, *Surrey*, 2005, pp. 183-184

Wales

Montgomeryshire, Llanbrynmair
  2289 John Stepleton
    Williams, 1889, p. 187

Warwickshire

Birmingham
  2290 John Baylie
    Holt, 1985, pp. 36-38
    Holt, Ingram, Jarman, *Birmingham*, 1985, pp. 32-34
  2291 James Byrch, blacksmith
    Holt, 1985, pp. 27-28
    Holt, Ingram, Jarman, *Birmingham*, 1985, p. 36
  2292 Christopher Elsmore, shoemaker
    Holt, Ingram, Jarman, *Birmingham*, 1985, p. 35
Stratford-on-Avon
  2293 Thomas Asteley, [butcher]
    Jones, *Stratford*, I, 2002, p. 58

Worcestershire

Worcester
  2294 Frances Pereson, barber
    Dyer, *Worcestershire*, 1967, pp. 53-55

Yorkshire

Grinton, Crackpot
  2295 John alias Jenkin Blaydes
    Berry, *Swaledale*, 1998, pp. 262-264

1585

Cheshire

Harthill
  2296 Herry Barowe
    Pearson, *Malpas*, [2005], p. 86

Malpas, Hampton
  2297 William Stocketon
    Pearson, *Malpas*, [2005], p. 87
Tarvin
  2298 John Forbour, parish clerk
    Bland, *Christleton*, 2002, p. 28

Derbyshire

Chellaston
  2299 Thomas Whynyates, gentleman
    Whinyates, 1894, pp. 31-35
Chesterfield
  2300 John Stansall, blacksmith
    Bestall and Fowkes, *Chesterfield*, 1977, pp. 175-176
  2301 Richard Whitworthe alias Ramsden
    Bestall and Fowkes, *Chesterfield*, 1977, p. 183
Glossop, Roworth
  2302 William Dewsnap
    Lee and Miller, *New Mills*, 1999, p. 9
Hasland
  2303 Robert Alwoode, husbandman
    Bestall and Fowkes, *Chesterfield*, 1977, p. 182
  2304 Agnes Layne
    Bestall and Fowkes, *Chesterfield*, 1977, pp. 176-177
Newbold
  2305 William Moore, yeoman
    Bestall and Fowkes, *Chesterfield*, 1977, pp. 173-174

Devonshire

Uffculme
  2306 Phillipp Havell
    Wyatt, *Uffculme*, 1997, pp. 6-7

Co. Durham

Brancepeth
  2307 Rawfe Richerson [Richeson]
    Greenwell, *Wills and Inventories*, 1860, II, pp. 109-110

Hertfordshire

St Albans, St Stephens, Great Hansteads
  2308 John Harris, [husbandman]
    Munby, *Worldly Goods*, 1991, pp. 62-63

Lancashire

Deane, Rumworth
  2309 Richard Lye, husbandman
    Bolton, *Bolton*, 1987, pp. 174-176
Turton
  2310 Alexander Orrell, gentleman
    Bolton, *Bolton*, 1994, p. 36

Lincolnshire

Clee, Itterby
  2311 Thomas Beale
    Ambler, Watkinson, *Clee*, 1987, p. 78
  2312 Christopher Makens
    Ambler, Watkinson, *Clee*, 1987, pp. 78-79

London

Southwark, St Saviour's
  2313 Geffrey Warde, waterman
    Herridge, *Surrey*, 2005, pp. 209-210
Wandsworth
  2314 John Edwin
    Herridge, *Surrey*, 2005, pp. 193-194

Northamptonshire

Edgecote House
  2315 William Chauncy [Chauncey], esquire
    Beeson, 1965, pp. 19-22

Northumberland
Duddo, Gatherick
  2316 Robert Muschampe, gentleman
    Greenwell, *Wills and Inventories*, 1860, II, p. 305
Newcastle
  2317 Ralph Cole, [merchant]
    Greenwell, *Wills and Inventories*, 1860, II, pp. 134-135
  2318 William Grey, miller
    Greenwell, *Wills and Inventories*, 1860, II, pp. 113-115
Ponteland
  2319 James Shaftow
    Greenwell, *Wills and Inventories*, 1860, II, p. 112
Oxfordshire
Aston
  2320 Margery Harris
    Havinden, *Oxfordshire*, 1965, pp. 181-182
Bloxham
  2321 John Edwardes
    Havinden, *Oxfordshire*, 1965, p. 189
Chadlington
  2322 Nicholas Coates, husbandman
    Havinden, *Oxfordshire*, 1965, pp. 182-183
Garsington
  2323 John Tapsell
    Havinden, *Oxfordshire*, 1965, pp. 185-186
Great Rollright
  2324 George Hylton, alias Luddington
    Havinden, *Oxfordshire*, 1965, p. 182
Great Tew
  2325 Joan Hyarne, widow
    Havinden, *Oxfordshire*, 1965, pp. 184-185
Launton
  2326 Thomas Cottesforde
    Havinden, *Oxfordshire*, 1965, pp. 191-192
Little Tew
  2327 Agnes Bull, [widow]
    Havinden, *Oxfordshire*, 1965, p. 183
Lower Heyford
  2328 Thomas Bruce, husbandman
    Havinden, *Oxfordshire*, 1965, pp. 198-199
Merton
  2329 Mrs Katherine Doyle, [widow]
    Havinden, *Oxfordshire*, 1965, pp. 192-198
Nuneham Courtenay
  2330 William Chamleye
    Havinden, *Oxfordshire*, 1965, pp. 187-188
Sandford St Martin, Ledwell
  2331 John Busbye
    Havinden, *Oxfordshire*, 1965, p. 186
Somerton
  2332 Henry Tredwell, husbandman
    Havinden, *Oxfordshire*, 1965, pp. 186-187
Standlake
  2333 Robert Haynes, [husbandman]
    Havinden, *Oxfordshire*, 1965, p. 185
Steeple Aston
  2334 William Baker
    Havinden, *Oxfordshire*, 1965, p. 191
Stratton Audley
  2335 Henry Basson, [ropemaker]
    Havinden, *Oxfordshire*, 1965, pp. 201-202
Warborough
  2336 Ralph Arnet
    Havinden, *Oxfordshire*, 1965, p. 201

Watlington
  2337 Simon Bartlett, husbandman
    Havinden, *Oxfordshire*, 1965, pp. 199-200
Wheatley
  2338 Richard Day
    Havinden, *Oxfordshire*, 1965, pp. 189-190
Suffolk
Ipswich
  2339 John Smith
    Reed, *Ipswich*, 1981, pp. 23-24
Surrey
Abinger
  2340 Thomas Songhurst
    Herridge, *Surrey*, 2005, p. 205
Bisley
  2341 Thomas Underwood
    Herridge, *Surrey*, 2005, p. 207
Carshalton
  2342 Richard Bottomley, yeoman
    Herridge, *Surrey*, 2005, p. 189
Cobham
  2343 John Colton, husbandman
    Herridge, *Surrey*, 2005, pp. 191-192
Cranleigh
  2344 Thomas Sayer, yeoman
    Herridge, *Surrey*, 2005, pp. 202-203
Eashing
  2345 Henry Chytty, yeoman
    Herridge, *Surrey*, 2005, pp. 190-191
Ewhurst
  2346 Elizabeth Cowicke, widow
    Herridge, *Surrey*, 2005, p. 192
Godalming
  2347 William Chittie, clothier
    Herridge, *Surrey*, 2005, pp. 228-229
Guildford, Stoke
  2348 Elizabeth Fuller, maidservant
    Herridge, *Surrey*, 2005, p. 198
Guildford
  2349 John Procker, cardmaker
    Herridge, *Surrey*, 2005, pp. 201-202
Leigh
  2350 William White, yeoman
    Herridge, *Surrey*, 2005, pp. 211-213
Mickleham
  2351 Raff Mose, husbandman
    Herridge, *Surrey*, 2005, pp. 200-201
Mitcham
  2352 William Walter, yeoman
    Herridge, *Surrey*, 2005, pp. 213-214
Ockham
  2353 Robart Freelande, husbandman and sawyer
    Herridge, *Surrey*, 2005, pp. 196-197
Tatsfield
  2354 Denise Towler, widow
    Herridge, *Surrey*, 2005, p. 206
West Horsley
  2355 Harry Skete
    Herridge, *Surrey*, 2005, p. 204
Woking, Sutton
  2356 Henry Lee, husbandman
    Herridge, *Surrey*, 2005, pp. 199-200

Wonersh
2357 Thomas Astrete, husbandman
Herridge, *Surrey*, 2005, pp. 188-189
Worplesdon
2358 Agnes Underwode, widow
Herridge, *Surrey*, 2005, pp. 206-207
Wotton
2359 William Worsfold, yeoman
Herridge, *Surrey*, 2005, pp. 213-214
Sussex
Michelgrove
2360 William Shelley, esquire
Whitley, 1912, pp. 286-298
Warwickshire
Birmingham
2361 John Parr
Holt, Ingram, Jarman, *Birmingham*, 1985, p. 37
Bishopton
2362 Elizbeth Smart, widow
Jones, *Stratford*, I, 2002, pp. 59-60
Worcestershire
Belbroughton, Hortle
2363 Thomas Griffin
Roper, *Belbroughton*, 1967-1968, p. 31
Worcester
2364 Michael Grene, [weaver]
Dyer, *Worcestershire*, 1967, pp. 12-14
2365 Thomas Pattrick, clothier
Dyer, *Worcestershire*, 1967, pp. 14-15
Yorkshire
Grinton, Thwaite
2366 Richard Harcay
Berry, *Swaledale*, 1998, p. 266
Hudswell
2367 Thomas Tailor
Berry, *Swaledale*, 1998, pp. 268-269
Lunds
2368 Jainne Parkyn [Jane Parkin]
Thwaite, *Abbotside*, 1967, p. 14
Marrick
2369 Francis Sayer
Berry, *Swaledale*, 1998, p. 265
South Cave
2370 Isabell Meason
Kaner, *South Cave*, 1994, p. 133
2371 Agnes Teavill
Kaner, *South Cave*, 1994, pp. 129-132

1585 (c.)
Surrey
Bisley
2372 John Farnham
Herridge, *Surrey*, 2005, pp. 194-195
Pyrford
2373 Robarte Fenne, yeoman
Herridge, *Surrey*, 2005, pp. 195-196
Windlesham
2374 Thomas Freland, husbandman
Herridge, *Surrey*, 2005, p. 197

1586
Cheshire
Malpas, Carden, Howsband
2375 John Teleyor
Pearson, *Malpas*, [2005], pp. 88-89

Tattenhall
2376 Thomas Broster, [yeoman]
Bland, *Christleton*, 2002, p. 28
Cornwall
Lanherne
Edwarde Arundell , esquire (see St Columb Major)
St Columb Major, Treveliew
2377 Edwarde Arundell, esquire (also listed Lanherne)
North, 2001, pp. 46-56
Derbyshire
Chesterfield
2378 Renoulde Bretland
Bestall and Fowkes, *Chesterfield*, 1977, pp. 184-185
Chesterfield, Spital
2379 Robert Harrys, husbandman
Bestall and Fowkes, *Chesterfield*, 1977, pp. 185-186
Glossop, Ringstones
2380 Edward Robothum
Lee and Miller, *New Mills*, 1999, p. 3
Devonshire
Exeter
2381 Leonard Yeo
Cash, *Devon*, 1966, pp. 4-5
Co. Durham
Durham
2382 Thomas Hall, draper
Greenwell, *Wills and Inventories*, 1860, II, pp. 162-164
Gateshead, Redheugh
2383 Mathewe White, gentleman
Greenwell, *Wills and Inventories*, 1860, II, pp. 138-140
Redmarshall
2384 Robert Richardson, clergyman, vicar of Redmarshall
Raine, *Barnes*, 1850, pp. cxxix-cxxx
Wolsingham
2385 Richarde Brischo [Brisco]
Greenwell, *Wills and Inventories*, 1860, II, p. 125
Hertfordshire
St Albans, St Stephens
2386 John Skeyle, [yeoman]
Munby, *Worldly Goods*, 1991, p. 65
Lancashire
Bolton, Halliwell
2387 Custance Woodes
Bolton, *Bolton*, 1994, pp. 148
Leicestershire
Evington
2388 Edmund Presgrave, clergyman, vicar of Evington
Wilshere, *Evington*, 1985, p. 3
Lincolnshire
Clee
2389 Stephen Bartlemew
Ambler, Watkinson, *Clee*, 1987, p. 79
London
Cutlers' Hall
2390 Cutlers' Company
Welch, 1923, pp. 326-334
Northumberland
Alnwick, Hulme Park
2391 Odnell [Odonel] Selbey
Greenwell, *Wills and Inventories*, 1860, II, p. 137

Berwick
 2392 Stephani [Stephen] Ayre
 Hodgson, *Wills and Inventories*, 1906, III, p. 118
 2393 Thomas Brickwell, esquire
 Greenwell, *Wills and Inventories*, 1860, II, pp. 128-129
Kirkhaugh
 2394 Richerd Wallas [Wallis]
 Greenwell, *Wills and Inventories*, 1860, II, p. 126
Newcastle
 2395 Robert Lambe, merchant
 Greenwell, *Wills and Inventories*, 1860, II, pp. 119-121
 2396 William Reade [Read], merchant
 Hodgson, *Wills and Inventories*, 1906, III, pp. 118-119
 2397 Mary Thornell
 Greenwell, *Wills and Inventories*, 1860, II, pp. 137-138
 2398 Christofer Wilson, Sergeant at Mace
 Greenwell, *Wills and Inventories*, 1860, II, p. 123
Newsham
 2399 John Ogle, gentleman
 Greenwell, *Wills and Inventories*, 1860, II, pp. 131-133
Willimoteswick
 2400 Nicholas Ridleye, esquire
 Greenwell, *Wills and Inventories*, 1860, II, pp. 121-122

Oxfordshire
Bladon
 2401 Thomas Clarke, [husbandman]
 Havinden, *Oxfordshire*, 1965, p. 203
Cropredy
 2402 Thomas Lighe
 Havinden, *Oxfordshire*, 1965, pp. 206-208
Garsington
 2403 James Carves [Carvell]
 Havinden, *Oxfordshire*, 1965, pp. 205-206
Mollington
 2404 William Hall, husbandman
 Havinden, *Oxfordshire*, 1965, pp. 203-204
 2405 John White, husbandman
 Havinden, *Oxfordshire*, 1965, p. 206
Waterstock
 2406 William Baker, [day labourer]
 Havinden, *Oxfordshire*, 1965, p. 202
Wheatley
 2407 William Carpenter
 Havinden, *Oxfordshire*, 1965, p. 204

Scotland
Edinburgh
 2408 Alexander Arbuthnet, burgess
 Anon., *Bassandyne*, 1836, p. 208
 2409 Robert Gourlaw, bookbinder
 Anon., *Bassandyne*, 1836, pp. 209-216

Staffordshire
Chartley Holme, Chartley Castle
 2410 Mary, Queen of Scots
 Labanoff, 1844, pp. 231-249
Dudley
 2411 Thomas Lowe
 Roper, *Dudley*, 1965, p. 43
Unlocated
 2412 Lewis Pryse
 Roper, *Dudley*, 1965, p. 44

Surrey
Effingham
 2413 William Kythchiner, yeoman
 Herridge, *Surrey*, 2005, pp. 217-219

Frensham
 2414 Thomas Filpe, yeoman
 Herridge, *Surrey*, 2005, pp. 216-217
Horsell
 2415 John Walden
 Herridge, *Surrey*, 2005, pp. 220-221
Nutfield
 2416 Richard Alyngham, yeoman
 Herridge, *Surrey*, 2005, pp. 214-215
Ockley
 2417 Walter Songhurst
 Herridge, *Surrey*, 2005, pp. 219-220
Reigate
 2418 Henry Bray, tanner
 Herridge, *Surrey*, 2005, pp. 215-216

Unlocated
Unlocated
 2419 Sir Edward Littleton
 West, *Village Records*, 1962, pp. 109-115

Wales
Montgomeryshire, Kerry
 2420 Phillip Jones
 Morris, 1893, p. 260

Warwickshire
Birmingham
 2421 Thomas Swyfte
 Holt, Ingram, Jarman, *Birmingham*, 1985, pp. 38-39
Foleshill
 2422 Robert Jenner
 Upton, *Foleshill*, 1993, p. 56
Stratford-on-Avon
 2423 William Badger, glover
 Jones, *Stratford*, I, 2002, pp. 60-62
 2424 Raph [Ralph] Boote, button maker
 Jones, *Stratford*, I, 2002, pp. 62-64
 2425 John Browne, woollen draper
 Jones, *Stratford*, I, 2002, pp. 64-74
 2426 William Deye
 Jones, *Stratford*, I, 2002, p. 62
 2427 Christopher Smyth [Smith] alias Court, yeoman
 Jones, *Stratford*, I, 2002, pp. 76-77
Stratford-on-Avon, Shottery (?)
 2428 William Such
 Jones, *Stratford*, I, 2002, pp. 74-75

Wiltshire
Salisbury, The Old Deanery
 2429 The Dean of Salisbury
 Drinkwater, 1964, p. 58

Worcestershire
Belbroughton
 2430 Henry James, gentleman
 Wanklyn, *Worcestershire*, 1998, pp. 81-85
Broadway
 2431 Raphe [Ralph] Sheldon, gentleman
 Wanklyn, *Worcestershire*, 1998, pp. 80-81
Worcester, St Andrew's
 2432 Samuel Blackenegge, waterman
 Dyer, *Worcestershire*, 1967, pp. 55-59

Yorkshire
Aysgarth, Sedbusk
 2433 Mathew Twhait [Thwaite], yeoman
 Thwaite, *Abbotside*, 1967, p. 15

Grinton, Angram
  2434 Matthew Alderson
    Berry, *Swaledale*, 1998, pp. 270-271
Grinton, Gunnerside
  2435 Wilfred Hougholter
    Berry, *Swaledale*, 1998, pp. 269-270
Lunds
  2436 James Parkine [Perking, Parkin]
    Thwaite, *Abbotside*, 1967, p. 16
South Cave
  2437 Grace Marshall
    Kaner, *South Cave*, 1994, pp. 134-135
Toothill
  2438 Elizabeth Thornhill, widow
    Brears, *Yorkshire*, 1972, pp. 55-57

1587

Bedfordshire
Blunham
  2439 Matthew Gardner, husbandman
    Freeman, *Bedfordshire*, 1952, pp. 104-105
Campton (?)
  2440 Fulke Paternoster
    Freeman, *Bedfordshire*, 1952, p. 103
Cockayne Hatley
  2441 Nicholas Write
    Freeman, *Bedfordshire*, 1952, p. 105
Eaton Socon, Begwary
  2442 William Jarvis
    Freeman, *Bedfordshire*, 1952, p. 104
Little Staughton
  2443 Robert Dave [Daue]
    Freeman, *Bedfordshire*, 1952, p. 104
Marston Moretaine
  2444 Robert Franklin
    Freeman, *Bedfordshire*, 1952, pp. 103-104

Buckinghamshire
Ibstone
  2445 Robert Cory, clergyman, parson of Ibstone
    Havinden, *Oxfordshire*, 1965, pp. 226-227

Cheshire
Malpas, Calcott
  2446 Ranulph Calcott, gentleman
    Pearson, *Malpas*, [2005], pp. 92-93
Malpas, Edge
  2447 William Candland, husbandman
    Pearson, *Malpas*, [2005], pp. 97-98
Tarvin, Stapleford
  2448 Robert Bruen, esquire
    Bland, *Christleton*, 2002, pp. 33-34
  2449 Beatriche Hatton
    Bland, *Christleton*, 2002, p. 30
Tarvin, Ashton
  2450 Hugh Kaye, yeoman
    Bland, *Christleton*, 2002, p. 32

Derbyshire
Chesterfield
  2451 Thomas Flecher
    Bestall and Fowkes, *Chesterfield*, 1977, pp. 188-191
  2452 William Holland
    Bestall and Fowkes, *Chesterfield*, 1977, pp. 198-199
  2453 Thomas Robynson, chapman
    Bestall and Fowkes, *Chesterfield*, 1977, pp. 191-193

  2454 Agnes Tattersall, widow
    Bestall and Fowkes, *Chesterfield*, 1977, pp. 195-197
Glossop, Ollersett, Gibhay
  2455 Ottiwell Anderewe, [husbandman]
    Lee and Miller, *New Mills*, 1999, pp. 5-6
Hasland
  2456 William Callowe
    Bestall and Fowkes, *Chesterfield*, 1977, pp. 186-188
Devonshire
Bishopsteignton
  2457 Hugh Tapley
    Cash, *Devon*, 1966, p. 5
Co. Durham
Barnard Castle
  2458 John Dobson
    Hodgson, *Wills and Inventories*, 1906, III, pp. 132-133
  2459 John Parkinn [Parkin]
    Hodgson, *Wills and Inventories*, 1906, III, p. 143
Beechburn
  2460 Henry Jackson (see Ferryhill)
Coniscliffe
  2461 Margaret Myddelton [Middleton], widow
    Hodgson, *Wills and Inventories*, 1906, III, p. 122
Darlington, Blackwell
  2462 Stephen Chamber, yeoman
    Hodgson, *Wills and Inventories*, 1906, III, p. 131
Darlington
  2463 Ralff Ewrie [Ewrey], esquire (see Edgnoll)
Denton
  2464 Roger Sympson [Simpson]
    Hodgson, *Wills and Inventories*, 1906, III, pp. 137-138
Durham
  2465 Anthony Cooke [Cook], tanner
    Hodgson, *Wills and Inventories*, 1906, III, p. 135
  2466 Cuthbert Rackett
    Hodgson, *Wills and Inventories*, 1906, III, p. 141
  2467 William Raw, yeoman
    Hodgson, *Wills and Inventories*, 1906, III, p. 124
Easington, Eden Dene
  2468 Leonarde Throulloppe [Trollop]
    Greenwell, *Wills and Inventories*, 1860, II, pp. 148-149
Edgnoll
  2469 Ralff Ewrie [Ewrey], esquire (also listed
  Darlington)
    Greenwell, *Wills and Inventories*, 1860, II, pp. 149-151
Ferryhill
  2470 John Ferrye [Ferry]
    Hodgson, *Wills and Inventories*, 1906, III, p. 129
  2471 Henry Jackson (also listed Beechburn)
    Hodgson, *Wills and Inventories*, 1906, III, pp. 133-134
Gainford
  2472 Peter Maddeson [Maddison]
    Hodgson, *Wills and Inventories*, 1906, III, p. 123
Gainford, Langton
  2473 Rauff [Ralph] Singleton
    Hodgson, *Wills and Inventories*, 1906, III, p. 127
Hart
  2474 James Brimley
    Hodgson, *Wills and Inventories*, 1906, III, p. 131
Kirk Merrington
  2475 Elizabeth Kirkhouse, widow
    Greenwell, *Wills and Inventories*, 1860, II, pp. 308-310

Murton
  2476 Margarie Belassis [Belasyse]
    Greenwell, *Wills and Inventories*, 1860, II, pp. 316-318
Ovingham
  2477 Radulfe Suyrteis [Surtees]
    Greenwell, *Wills and Inventories*, 1860, II, p. 161
Pockerley
  2478 Raiphe Hedworthe [Hedworth], gentleman
    Greenwell, *Wills and Inventories*, 1860, II, p. 311
Walworth
  2479 John Sigswick [Sedgwick]
    Hodgson, *Wills and Inventories*, 1906, III, pp. 142-143

Essex
Rayleigh
  2480 Joan Ireland, widow
    Emmison, *Essex*, 5, 1989, p. 74

Gloucestershire
Frampton Cotterell
  2481 Thomas Tiler, husbandman
    Moore, *Frampton Cotterell*, 1976, p. 39
Iron Acton
  2482 Thomas Atwood, tailor
    Moore, *Frampton Cotterell*, 1976, p. 40

Hertfordshire
St Albans, St Stephens, Netherwild
  2483 Thomas Byrchmore, [yeoman]
    Munby, *Worldly Goods*, 1991, pp. 68-70
St Albans, St Stephens, Park Street
  2484 Robert Nutkyn, [yeoman]
    Parker, *Worldly Goods*, 2004, pp. 104-105
St Albans, St Stephens
  2485 Thomas Sibley, [labourer]
    Parker, *Worldly Goods*, 2004, p. 108

Lancashire
Bolton
  2486 William Chisnall, carpenter
    Bolton, *Bolton*, 1987, p. 58
  2487 James Forde
    Bolton, *Bolton*, 1987, p. 100
Deane, Over Hulton
  2488 Rodger Turner
    Bolton, *Bolton*, 1994, p. 118
Hurstwood
  2489 Edmund Spenser, yeoman
    Earwaker, *Lancashire and Cheshire*, 1893, p. 7
Leigh, Morleys Hall
  2490 Edward Tildesley, esquire
    Earwaker, *Lancashire and Cheshire*, 1884, pp. p. 151-153
Rochdale, Newbold
  2491 John Cledge [Clegg]
    Lowe, 1972, p. 105
Turton
  2492 Nycholas Kyrshawe, husbandman
    Bolton, *Bolton*, 1987, p. 164

Lincolnshire
Clee, Itterby
  2493 Richard Gleadston
    Ambler, Watkinson, *Clee*, 1987, pp. 80-81
  2494 Genit Gowland, widow
    Ambler, Watkinson, *Clee*, 1987, pp. 81-82
Clee, Oole
  2495 John West
    Ambler, Watkinson, *Clee*, 1987, pp. 79-80

London
Bermondsey
  2496 Henry Graye, loriner
    Herridge, *Surrey*, 2005, pp. 231-232
Rotherhithe
  2497 Joan Kidwelle, widow
    Herridge, *Surrey*, 2005, pp. 249-252

Northamptonshire
Fotheringay Castle
  2498 Mary, Queen of Scots
    Labanoff, 1844, pp. 254-274

Northumberland
Adderstone
  2499 Thomas Forster (also listed Lucker)
    Greenwell, *Wills and Inventories*, 1860, II, pp. 303-304
Chatton
  2500 Thomas Wetwoode, gentleman
    Greenwell, *Wills and Inventories*, 1860, II, p. 160
Duddo
  2501 William Claveringe [Clavering], gentleman
    Greenwell, *Wills and Inventories*, 1860, II, p. 152
Lucker
  Thomas Forster (see Adderstone)
Newcastle
  2502 Edward Bewicke [Bewick], baker
    Hodgson, *Wills and Inventories*, 1906, III, p. 126
  2503 William Jeneson [Jenison], merchant and alderman
    Greenwell, *Wills and Inventories*, 1860, II, pp. 153-159
  2504 Thomas Smythe [Smith], shipwright
    Hodgson, *Wills and Inventories*, 1906, III, pp. 120-121
North Shields
  2505 Robert Brown
    Hodgson, *Wills and Inventories*, 1906, III, p. 122
Ponteland
  2506 Julian Mitford, widow
    Greenwell, *Wills and Inventories*, 1860, II, pp. 299-300

Oxfordshire
Bampton, Brighthampton
  2507 John Benatt
    Havinden, *Oxfordshire*, 1965, pp. 228-229
Bampton
  2508 John Cooper, [husbandman]
    Havinden, *Oxfordshire*, 1965, pp. 233-234
Bampton, West Weald
  2509 Edmond Cripps, husbandman
    Havinden, *Oxfordshire*, 1965, pp. 208-209
Banbury
  2510 Robert Symons, baker
    Havinden, *Oxfordshire*, 1965, pp. 213-215
Banbury, Nethercote
  2511 Henry Tey, [husbandman]
    Havinden, *Oxfordshire*, 1965, pp. 218-219
Barford St Michael
  2512 John Cooke
    Havinden, *Oxfordshire*, 1965, pp. 231-232
Blackthorn
  2513 Richard Hartes
    Havinden, *Oxfordshire*, 1965, pp. 217-218
Bicester
  2514 Richard Hossell
    Havinden, *Oxfordshire*, 1965, pp. 249-250

Cassington
2515 Thomas Boselie
Havinden, *Oxfordshire*, 1965, pp. 222-223
Chadlington
2516 Thomas Carter, husbandman
Havinden, *Oxfordshire*, 1965, pp. 210-211
Charlbury
2517 Louise Brieris
Havinden, *Oxfordshire*, 1965, p. 229
Charlton-on-Otmoor
2518 John Bassett, husbandman
Havinden, *Oxfordshire*, 1965, pp. 216-217
Chastleton, Bookend
2519 Robert Durrande
Havinden, *Oxfordshire*, 1965, p. 218
Chipping Norton
2520 Walter Edkins, alias Boucher, tanner
Havinden, *Oxfordshire*, 1965, pp. 237-238
2521 William Troute, [shoemaker]
Havinden, *Oxfordshire*, 1965, pp. 221-222
Cropredy
2522 Joanna French, widow
Havinden, *Oxfordshire*, 1965, p. 220
2523 John Hunte, husbandman
Havinden, *Oxfordshire*, 1965, pp. 239-241
Fifield
2524 Alice Brackley, widow
Havinden, *Oxfordshire*, 1965, p. 210
Harwick, Tusmore
2525 David Cadwalder, [husbandman]
Havinden, *Oxfordshire*, 1965, p. 221
Henley-on-Thames
2526 John Culles
Havinden, *Oxfordshire*, 1965, pp. 234-237
Lewknor, Postcombe
2527 William Brooke
Havinden, *Oxfordshire*, 1965, pp. 242-243
Little Tew
2528 Thomas Hanwell
Havinden, *Oxfordshire*, 1965, pp. 215-216
Mollington
2529 Thomas Claridge, husbandman
Havinden, *Oxfordshire*, 1965, pp. 232-233
2530 George Wodhall [Odhull], gentleman
Havinden, *Oxfordshire*, 1965, p. 220
Nuffield
2531 John Haley, labourer
Havinden, *Oxfordshire*, 1965, p. 251
Oxford, St Thomas
2532 John Dysell, [weaver]
Havinden, *Oxfordshire*, 1965, p. 250
Oxford, St Michaels
2533 Thomas Heath, blacksmith
Havinden, *Oxfordshire*, 1965, pp. 243-247
Piddington
2534 Alice Abraham
Havinden, *Oxfordshire*, 1965, pp. 241-242
Shiplake
2535 John Thorne, [husbandman]
Havinden, *Oxfordshire*, 1965, pp. 238-239
Shutford
2536 William Cooke
Havinden, *Oxfordshire*, 1965, pp. 212-213

South Weston
2537 Walter Barnes
Havinden, *Oxfordshire*, 1965, p. 248
Stanton Harcourt
2538 John Butler
Havinden, *Oxfordshire*, 1965, p. 232
Stonesfield
2539 Thomas Hakins [Hawkins], [labourer]
Havinden, *Oxfordshire*, 1965, pp. 211-212
Stratton Audley
2540 John Bearnsley
Havinden, *Oxfordshire*, 1965, pp. 227-228
Wardington
2541 Henry Allibon, husbandman
Havinden, *Oxfordshire*, 1965, p. 241
Wardington, Williamscote
2542 Thomas Gyll
Havinden, *Oxfordshire*, 1965, pp. 248-249
Wardington
2543 William Hunscott, husbandman
Havinden, *Oxfordshire*, 1965, pp. 251-252
2544 John Ryton, husbandman
Havinden, *Oxfordshire*, 1965, pp. 229-230
Wendlebury
2545 Edmund Brotherton
Havinden, *Oxfordshire*, 1965, pp. 230-231
Whitchurch
2546 Thomas Higges
Havinden, *Oxfordshire*, 1965, p. 209
Wolvercote
2547 Richard Collins, husbandman
Havinden, *Oxfordshire*, 1965, pp. 223-226
Staffordshire
Dudley
2548 John Mondaie, mercer
Roper, *Dudley*, 1965, p. 45
2549 Elizabeth Robynes
Roper, *Dudley*, 1965, p. 46
Surrey
Abinger
2550 Thomas Morer, husbandman
Herridge, *Surrey*, 2005, pp. 252-253
Betchworth
2551 Henrye Charlewood, tanner
Herridge, *Surrey*, 2005, p. 228
Cobham
2552 Richard Taylier, husbandman
Herridge, *Surrey*, 2005, pp. 243-244
Coulsdon
2553 Thomas Blake
Herridge, *Surrey*, 2005, pp. 225-226
Cranleigh
2554 Thomas Lipscomb, husbandman
Herridge, *Surrey*, 2005, p. 233
Dorking
2555 John Barnard, [weaver]
Herridge, *Surrey*, 2005, pp. 223-224
2556 Robert Sheffeilde, yeoman
Herridge, *Surrey*, 2005, pp. 240-241
East Molesey
2557 John Parson, husbandman
Herridge, *Surrey*, 2005, pp. 234-235

Elstead
  2558 Mawdlyn Boxold, widow
    Herridge, *Surrey*, 2005, pp. 226-227
Farncombe
  2559 John Peeter
    Herridge, *Surrey*, 2005, pp. 235-236
Fetcham
  2560 John Atwell, husbandman
    Herridge, *Surrey*, 2005, pp. 222-223
Godalming
  2561 Margaret Parkehurst, widow
    Herridge, *Surrey*, 2005, pp. 233-234
Kingston-upon-Thames
  2562 William Whitfeilde, yeoman
    Herridge, *Surrey*, 2005, pp. 244-245
Newdigate
  2563 William Dibble, yeoman
    Herridge, *Surrey*, 2005, pp. 246-247
Ockley
  2564 Agnes Songhurst, widow
    Herridge, *Surrey*, 2005, p. 242
Pirbright
  2565 John Russell
    Herridge, *Surrey*, 2005, pp. 238-239
Send
  2566 Johane Shurloke, widow
    Herridge, *Surrey*, 2005, p. 241
Wanborough
  2567 Obarte Seagare, husbandman
    Herridge, *Surrey*, 2005, pp. 239-240
Wotton
  2568 John Bristowe, husbandman
    Herridge, *Surrey*, 2005, p. 227
Warwickshire
Birmingham
  2569 Hugh Hammond
    Holt, 1985, pp. 29-30
    Holt, Ingram, Jarman, *Birmingham*, 1985, pp. 43-44
  2570 William Severne
    Holt, Ingram, Jarman, *Birmingham*, 1985, pp. 41-42
Bishopton
  2571 Simon Beard
    Jones, *Stratford*, I, 2002, pp. 80-81
King's Coughton
  2572 William Boovye
    Saville, *King's Coughton*, 1973, pp. 40-42
Stratford-on-Avon
  2573 John Pattreket, [shearman]
    Jones, *Stratford*, I, 2002, pp. 82-83
  2574 Thomas Tayler [Taylor], fuller
    Jones, *Stratford*, I, 2002, pp. 78-79
Worcestershire
Belbroughton, Madeley
  2575 John Broke
    Roper, *Belbroughton*, 1967-1968, p. 33
Belbroughton
  2576 William Smithe
    Roper, *Belbroughton*, 1967-1968, p. 35
Yorkshire
Grinton, Whitaside
  2577 Emote Close, widow
    Berry, *Swaledale*, 1998, p. 274

Grinton, Healaugh
  2578 Simon Tayler
    Berry, *Swaledale*, 1998, pp. 271-272
South Cave
  2579 Myles Atkinson
    Kaner, *South Cave*, 1994, pp. 141-142
  2580 Agnes Barker
    Kaner, *South Cave*, 1994, p. 143
  2581 Edward Barker
    Kaner, *South Cave*, 1994, pp. 136-137
  2582 Isable [Isabell] Barker
    Kaner, *South Cave*, 1994, pp. 145-148
  2583 John Barker
    Kaner, *South Cave*, 1994, p. 144
  2584 Alison Mowbeyrie
    Kaner, *South Cave*, 1994, p. 142
  2585 Robert Todd
    Kaner, *South Cave*, 1994, pp. 138-140
Hutton Bonville
  2586 Elizabeth Newton, widow
    Hodgson, *Wills and Inventories*, 1906, III, p. 136

1587 (c.)
London
Southwark, St Olave's
  2587 John Atkynsonne, cooper
    Herridge, *Surrey*, 2005, p. 222
Surrey
Ashstead
  2588 Thomas Richbeale, husbandman
    Herridge, *Surrey*, 2005, pp. 237-238
Chiddingfold
  2589 Richard Benet
    Herridge, *Surrey*, 2005, pp. 224-225
  2590 Alice Furlonger, widow
    Herridge, *Surrey*, 2005, pp. 230-231
Coulsdon
  2591 Richard Pyggen [Piggen]
    Herridge, *Surrey*, 2005, pp. 236-237
Ewhurst
  2592 Joane Hill, servant
    Herridge, *Surrey*, 2005, p. 232
Stoke D'Abernon
  2593 Robert Crosse
    Herridge, *Surrey*, 2005, pp. 229-230

1588
Bedfordshire
Bedford
  2594 Thomas Edwards
    Freeman, *Bedfordshire*, 1952, p. 105
Edworth
  2595 Richard Hart
    Freeman, *Bedfordshire*, 1952, p. 105
Flitwick (?)
  2596 Robert Leay, servant
    Freeman, *Bedfordshire*, 1952, p. 106
Kempston
  2597 Robert Goddye
    Freeman, *Bedfordshire*, 1952, p. 106
Turvey
  2598 Robert Whytehed
    Freeman, *Bedfordshire*, 1952, p. 106

Buckinghamshire
Winslow
2599 William Davis, [chapman]
  Spufford, *Reclothing*, 1984, pp. 172-177
Cambridgeshire
Cambridge
2600 Thomas Thomas, [University printer and binder]
  Gray and Palmer, *Cambridge*, 1915, pp. 65-70
Cheshire
Christleton
2601 Raff Cotgrave
  Bland, *Christleton*, 2002, p. 46
Shocklach
2602 Ann Broughton, widow
  Pearson, *Malpas*, [2005], pp. 75-76
Shocklach Oviatt
2603 John Pova, husbandman
  Pearson, *Malpas*, [2005], pp. 100-101
Tarvin, Ashton
2604 John Bolland, husbandman
  Bland, *Christleton*, 2002, pp. 46-48
Tarvin, Kelsall
2605 Richard Leightfoote, tanner
  Bland, *Christleton*, 2002, pp. 39-41
Tarvin
2606 Raphe Pickrine, [husbandman]
  Bland, *Christleton*, 2002, p. 36
Tushingham, Barrel
2607 William Brereton
  Pearson, *Malpas*, [2005], p. 103
Waverton,Hatton
2608 James Monkes
  Bland, *Christleton*, 2002, pp. 34-35
Wrenbury
2609 John Woodfaine
  Pixton, *Wrenbury*, 2009, p. 18
Derbyshire
Chesterfield
2610 Margaret Capper alias Shearshawe
  Bestall and Fowkes, *Chesterfield*, 1977, pp. 214-215
2611 Thomas Denyson, draper
  Bestall and Fowkes, *Chesterfield*, 1977, pp. 201-205
2612 John Holis
  Bestall and Fowkes, *Chesterfield*, 1977, pp. 199-200
2613 William Memott, yeoman
  Bestall and Fowkes, *Chesterfield*, 1977, pp. 205-206
2614 John Wilson
  Bestall and Fowkes, *Chesterfield*, 1977, pp. 200-201
2615 William Whythead, blacksmith
  Bestall and Fowkes, *Chesterfield*, 1977, pp. 206-207
2616 Thomas Woodhouse
  Bestall and Fowkes, *Chesterfield*, 1977, pp. 193-194
Glossop, Broadhurst
2617 John Armfeyld, [yeoman]
  Lee and Miller, *New Mills*, 1999, p. 11
Glossop, Bearhaught
2618 Randle Stafford
  Lee and Miller, *New Mills*, 1999, pp. 13-14
Devonshire
Bishops Nympton
2619 John Sealake, husbandman
  Cash, *Devon*, 1966, pp. 5-6

Stoke Gabriel
2620 Robert Kinge
  Cash, *Devon*, 1966, p. 5
Uffculme
2621 John Hodge
  Wyatt, *Uffculme*, 1997, pp. 7-8
Co. Durham
Darlington
2622 Richard Glover, yeoman
  Hodgson, *Wills and Inventories*, 1906, III, p. 139
2623 Jane Nicholson, widow
  Hodgson, *Wills and Inventories*, 1906, III, p. 140
Hartlepool, Stranton
2624 Wyllyam Massie, clergyman, vicar of Stranton
  Greenwell, *Wills and Inventories*, 1860, II, pp. 311-312
Stainton
2625 Rychard Marshall, clergyman
  Greenwell, *Wills and Inventories*, 1860, II, pp. 321-322
Windlestone
2626 John Edon [Eden], gentleman
  Greenwell, *Wills and Inventories*, 1860, II, pp. 328-331
  Eden, 1907, pp. 13-15
Essex
Saffron Walden, Brook Walden (Audley End)
2627 John Webbe
  Emmison, *Essex*, 5, 1989, p. 205
Stanford Rivers
2628 Geoffrey Gladwine, labourer
  Emmison, *Essex*, 5, 1989, p. 115
Hertfordshire
St Albans, St Stephens, Park Street
2629 Richard Royse, [husbandman]
  Parker, *Worldly Goods*, 2004, pp. 106-107
Lancashire
Bolton, Great Lever
2630 James Hardman
  Bolton, *Bolton*, 1987, pp. 135-136
Bolton
2631 John Ouldham
  Bolton, *Bolton*, 1994, pp. 33-34
Bolton, Anglezarke
2632 James Pilkington
  Bolton, *Bolton*, 1994, p. 49
Bolton, Haulgh
2633 Adam Sharples, clothier
  Bolton, *Bolton*, 1994, pp. 78-79
Bolton, Sharples
2634 Francis Walkden, [husbandman]
  Bolton, *Bolton*, 1994, p. 129
Bradshaw
2635 Alexander Bradshawe
  Bolton, *Bolton*, 1987, p. 32
Caton
2636 Christopher Bateson, yeoman
  Earwaker, *Lancashire and Cheshire*, 1893, pp. 149-150
Graythwaite
2637 Mr Christopher Sandys
  Earwaker, *Lancashire and Cheshire*, 1893, pp. 151-152
Manchester
2638 Thomas Becke [Beck], gentleman
  Earwaker, *Lancashire and Cheshire*, 1893, pp. 8-9

Rivington
  2639 Mr Robert Dewhurst, gentleman
    Bolton, *Bolton*, 1987, pp. 78-79
Unlocated
  2640 Lawrance Sharples
    Bolton, *Bolton*, 1994, p. 90
Leicestershire
Braunstone
  2641 Robete Pultney
    Wilshere, *Braunstone*, 1983, p. 13
Lincolnshire
Clee, Oole
  2642 John Petche, husbandman
    Ambler, Watkinson, *Clee*, 1987, pp. 83-84
Clee, Thrunscoe
  2643 Christofer Stones
    Ambler, Watkinson, *Clee*, 1987, p. 85
Clee
  2644 Rycharde Walles
    Ambler, Watkinson, *Clee*, 1987, p. 83
Cleethorpes
  2645 Anne West
    Ambler, Watkinson, *Clee*, 1987, pp. 82-83
Market Rasen
  2646 Thomas Marshall, clergyman, vicar of East
  Rasen
    Neave, *Market Rasen*, 1985, pp. 93-94
London
Leicester House
  2647 Robert Dudley, Earl of Leicester
    Kingsford, 1923, pp. 28-46
Paternoster Row
  2648 Nicholas Willmer, citizen of London [silkman]
    Foster, Green, 1888, pp. 285-287
Southwark, St Olave's
  2649 Cornelius Eggen, cooper
    Herridge, *Surrey*, 2005, p. 248
Woolstaple, Westminster
  2650 Sir John Trevor
    Schofield, 1987, p. 148
Norfolk
Kimberley
  2651 Sir Roger Woodhouse
    Bolingbroke, 1904, pp. 94-108
Northumberland
Berwick
  2652 Raphe Selbye [Ralph Selby], gentleman
    Greenwell, *Wills and Inventories*, 1860, II, p. 256
Dilston
  2653 Georgii Ratcliffe [Sir George Radclyffe]
    Greenwell, *Wills and Inventories*, 1860, II, pp. 325-326
Newcastle
  2654 James Dodds, tanner
    Hodgson, *Wills and Inventories*, 1906, III, pp. 146-147
Woodhorn
  2655 Thomas Hondley, clergyman
    Hodgson, *Wills and Inventories*, 1906, III, pp. 145-146
Oxfordshire
Banbury
  2656 John Addams, miller
    Havinden, *Oxfordshire*, 1965, pp. 271-273
  2657 Deans Anstie
    Havinden, *Oxfordshire*, 1965, p. 258
    Hatcher and Barker, *Pewter*, 1974, pp. 97-98

  2658 Nicholas Bancrafte
    Havinden, *Oxfordshire*, 1965, pp. 254-256
  2659 John Cotes
    Havinden, *Oxfordshire*, 1965, pp. 268-269
  2660 Joyce Edgellffyld
    Havinden, *Oxfordshire*, 1965, pp. 252-253
  2661 John Hasker
    Havinden, *Oxfordshire*, 1965, p. 257
  2662 Ranige Mason
    Havinden, *Oxfordshire*, 1965, p. 258
  2663 Richard Perrin
    Havinden, *Oxfordshire*, 1965, p. 264
  2664 Henry Pilkington, alderman
    Havinden, *Oxfordshire*, 1965, pp. 265-268
  2665 [Alice] Whetley [Wheateley], widow
    Brinkworth and Gibson, *Banbury*, I, 1975, p. 111
Benson
  2666 Margaret Penny, widow
    Havinden, *Oxfordshire*, 1965, pp. 274-276
Berrick Salome (or Prior)
  2667 John Taubit [Talbot], [husbandman]
    Havinden, *Oxfordshire*, 1965, pp. 269-270
Chipping Norton
  2668 Henry Backer
    Havinden, *Oxfordshire*, 1965, pp. 259-260
Deddington
  2669 Alice Cox, widow
    Havinden, *Oxfordshire*, 1965, pp. 276-277
Great Milton
  2670 Richard Coxe, [husbandman]
    Havinden, *Oxfordshire*, 1965, pp. 253-254
Idbury
  2671 Richard Heyres
    Havinden, *Oxfordshire*, 1965, pp. 260-261
Launton
  2672 John Brandsby, [weaver]
    Havinden, *Oxfordshire*, 1965, p. 270
Mollington
  2673 Ann Write, widow
    Havinden, *Oxfordshire*, 1965, pp. 256-257
North Newington
  2674 Thomas Skilman
    Havinden, *Oxfordshire*, 1965, pp. 273-274
Oxford, St Mary Magdalen
  2675 Giles Haell
    Havinden, *Oxfordshire*, 1965, pp. 261-262
South Newington
  2676 Anthony Hall, gentleman
    Havinden, *Oxfordshire*, 1965, pp. 262-264
Unlocated
  2677 Margery Buston
    Havinden, *Oxfordshire*, 1965, p. 254
Wardington
  2678 Thomas Hill, mason
    Havinden, *Oxfordshire*, 1965, pp. 258-259
Witney
  2679 Edward Dodswell
    Havinden, *Oxfordshire*, 1965, p. 271
Staffordshire
Dudley
  2680 Elizabeth Bailies alias Thatcher
    Roper, *Dudley*, 1965, p. 48
    Hatcher and Barker, *Pewter*, 1974, p. 99

2681 William Downing
  Roper, *Dudley*, 1965, p. 47
  Hatcher and Barker, *Pewter*, 1974, p. 99
2682 Humfrey Jukes, blacksmith
  Roper, *Dudley*, 1965, p. 49

Suffolk
Ipswich
2683 William Miles
  Reed, *Ipswich*, 1981, p. 25

Surrey
Elstead
2684 Thomas Howyke
  Herridge, *Surrey*, 2005, p. 249
Esher
2685 Richard Fellowe
  Herridge, *Surrey*, 2005, pp. 248-249
Guildford
2686 Symon Tally, vintner
  Herridge, *Surrey*, 2005, pp. 253-255
West Molesey
2687 Francis Lake
  Herridge, *Surrey*, 2005, p. 261
2688 Richard Wicker, yeoman
  Herridge, *Surrey*, 2005, pp. 256-257
Worplesdon
2689 Henry Atfeld alias Ripley, husbandman
  Herridge, *Surrey*, 2005, pp. 245-246

Sussex
Wiston
2690 Sir Thomas Shirley
  Shirley, *Shirleiana*, 1873, p. 252

Warwickshire
Birmingham
2691 John Ryckarte alias Wylson
  Holt, Ingram, Jarman, *Birmingham*, 1985, pp. 45-47
2692 Jone Smythe, widow
  Holt, Ingram, Jarman, *Birmingham*, 1985, pp. 48-49
Foleshill
2693 John Carter, [husbandman]
  Upton, *Foleshill*, 1993, p. 58
Kenilworth Castle
2694 Robert Dudley, Earl of Leicester
  Halliwell, *Inventories*, 1854, pp. 115-154
Stratford-on-Avon
2695 Alice Bell, widow
  Jones, *Stratford*, I, 2002, p. 95
2696 Rychard Cowper, shepherd
  Jones, *Stratford*, I, 2002, pp. 85-86
2697 John [George] Granams [Grannams], weaver
  Jones, *Stratford*, I, 2002, pp. 83-84
2698 Thomas Pyrry [Perry], butcher
  Jones, *Stratford*, I, 2002, pp. 86-87
2699 John Robins, [wool driver]
  Jones, *Stratford*, I, 2002, pp. 92-94
2700 Peter Smart [Smarte], [husbandman]
  Jones, *Stratford*, I, 2002, pp. 90-92
Stratford-on-Avon, Old Stratford
2701 Willyam Tayler [Taylor], day labourer
  Jones, *Stratford*, I, 2002, pp. 89-90
Stratford-on-Avon
2702 John Tonge, [tailor]
  Jones, *Stratford*, I, 2002, pp. 87-88

Worcestershire
Belbroughton
2703 Richard Lashford, scythesmith
  Roper, *Belbroughton*, 1967-1968, p. 37
2704 John Waldren, scythesmith
  Roper, *Scythesmiths*, 1967, p. 12
  Roper, *Belbroughton*, 1967-1968, p. 39
Worcester
2705 Humfrey Smith, baker
  Dyer, *Worcestershire*, 1967, pp. 48-50

Yorkshire
Downholme
2706 Ciciley Jeffrason, widow
  Berry, *Swaledale*, 1998, p. 276
Downholme, Stainton
2707 Thomas Pearson
  Berry, *Swaledale*, 1998, pp. 280-281
Grinton, Smarber
2708 Elizabeth Clarkeson
  Berry, *Swaledale*, 1998, p. 277
Hudswell
2709 Agnes Brunskell, widow
  Berry, *Swaledale*, 1998, pp. 278-279
Ingleton
2710 Rychard Coop, miller
  Bentley, 1990, p. 61
Nostell
2711 Sir Cotton Gargrave (also listed Upton)
  Cartwright, 1891, pp. 280-286
South Cave
2712 John Johnson
  Kaner, *South Cave*, 1994, pp. 152-153
2713 Thomas Punsworth
  Kaner, *South Cave*, 1994, pp. 151-152
2714 George Wallis
  Kaner, *South Cave*, 1994, pp. 149-150
Upton
Sir Cotton Gargrave (see Nostell)

1589
Bedfordshire
Stevington
2715 Ralph Cucheth, clergyman
  Freeman, *Bedfordshire*, 1952, pp. 106-107
Bristol
Bristol
2716 Roberte [Robert] Clement, haberdasher
  George, *Bristol*, 1, 2002, pp. 4-7
Cheshire
Chester, St John's
2717 William Glaseor, esquire, vice chamberlain and
  alderman of Chester (also listed Lea Newbold)
  Piccope, *Lancashire and Cheshire*, 1860, pp. 132-142
Lea Newbold, Chester (?)
  William Glaseor, esquire, vice chamberlain and
  alderman of Chester (see Chester)
Derbyshire
Brimington
2718 Myles Fidelere
  Bestall and Fowkes, *Chesterfield*, 1977, pp. 207-208
Chesterfield
2719 Andrew Coplaye alias Willye
  Bestall and Fowkes, *Chesterfield*, 1977, pp. 211-213

2720 Richard Foxe
    Bestall and Fowkes, *Chesterfield*, 1977, pp. 208-209
Newbold
    2721 Elizabeth Newbold alias Parkynson, widow
    Bestall and Fowkes, *Chesterfield*, 1977, pp. 209-210
Co. Durham
Archdeacon Newton
    2722 Thomas Frankland, alias Frankleine [Francklin],
    gentleman
    Greenwell, *Wills and Inventories*, 1860, II, p. 144
Essex
Heydon
    2723 Roger Ryckerd
    Emmison, *Essex*, 5, 1989, p. 212
Lancashire
Ainsworth
    2724 William Allens, husbandman
    Bolton, *Bolton*, 1987, pp. 4-6
    2725 William Widdowsone, husbandman
    Bolton, *Bolton*, 1994, p. 144
Bolton, Little Lever
    2726 [R]ichard Lever, gentleman
    Bolton, *Bolton*, 1987, pp. 178-180
Farnworth
    2727 John Seddon, husbandman
    Bolton, *Bolton*, 1994, p. 76
Kearsley
    2728 Margerie Bothomley, widow
    Bolton, *Bolton*, 1987, p. 30
Middleton
    2729 Robert Nicholson, [schoolmaster]
    Earwaker, *Lancashire and Cheshire*, 1893, pp. 156-157
Turton
    2730 Margret Taylier
    Bolton, *Bolton*, 1994, p. 108
Leicestershire
Evington
    2731 Peter Plumer, husbandman
    Wilshere, *Evington*, 1985, p. 4
Glenfield
    2732 John Browne, [yeoman]
    Wilshere, *Glenfield*, 1983, p. 3
Leicester
    2733 Phyllppe ffreake [Philip Freake], butcher
    Hoskins, *Butcher*, 1950, pp. 117-122
Lincolnshire
Clee, Itterby
    2734 John Thompsonne
    Ambler, Watkinson, *Clee*, 1987, pp. 85-86
Market Rasen
    2735 Mr Jhon Moygne
    Neave, *Market Rasen*, 1985, p. 95
Norfolk
Norwich
    2736 Mr Robert Sucklinge, alderman
    Beecheno, 1921, pp. 166-177
Oxfordshire
Banbury
    2737 Richard Baggett, butcher
    Havinden, *Oxfordshire*, 1965, pp. 286-287
    2738 Christopher Gold, glazier
    Havinden, *Oxfordshire*, 1965, p. 282

Bloxham (?)
    2739 Edmund Colesborne
    Havinden, *Oxfordshire*, 1965, pp. 279-280
Cassington
    2740 Robert Browne
    Havinden, *Oxfordshire*, 1965, p. 291
Charlbury
    2741 William Brierhurst, [husbandman]
    Havinden, *Oxfordshire*, 1965, p. 299
Churchill
    2742 William Beard
    Havinden, *Oxfordshire*, 1965, p. 289
Drayton St Leonard
    2743 Edmund Hall
    Havinden, *Oxfordshire*, 1965, p. 281
Elsfield
    2744 John Day, [husbandman]
    Havinden, *Oxfordshire*, 1965, p. 297
    2745 Richard Day, [husbandman]
    Havinden, *Oxfordshire*, 1965, p. 298
Great Bourton
    2746 William Hall, husbandman
    Havinden, *Oxfordshire*, 1965, pp. 277-279
Idbury
    2747 Thomas Mowlinge
    Havinden, *Oxfordshire*, 1965, p. 298
Islip
    2748 John Wriglesworth
    Havinden, *Oxfordshire*, 1965, pp. 289-290
Lower Heyford
    2749 William Mine, [husbandman]
    Havinden, *Oxfordshire*, 1965, pp. 292-293
Mollington
    2750 John Ennock, [husbandman]
    Havinden, *Oxfordshire*, 1965, pp. 282-283
North Leigh
    2751 John Lowgrove [Lovegrove]
    Havinden, *Oxfordshire*, 1965, pp. 287-288
Oxford, St Ebbes
    2752 Margaret Bower
    Havinden, *Oxfordshire*, 1965, pp. 283-284
Salford
    2753 John Rossell [Russell], [husbandman]
    Havinden, *Oxfordshire*, 1965, pp. 291-292
South Stoke, Exlade
    2754 Walter Etheridge, husbandman
    Havinden, *Oxfordshire*, 1965, pp. 292-294
Stoke Lyne, Fewcott
    2755 John Berdys [Burge]
    Havinden, *Oxfordshire*, 1965, pp. 284-285
Unlocated
    2756 Mary Sylle
    Havinden, *Oxfordshire*, 1965, pp. 285-286
Watlington, Christmas House
    2757 Alice Bremar
    Havinden, *Oxfordshire*, 1965, p. 285
Wigginton
    2758 Humphrey Wylkes
    Havinden, *Oxfordshire*, 1965, pp. 296-297
Woodstock
    2759 John Reyley, [chandler]
    Havinden, *Oxfordshire*, 1965, pp. 294-296

Staffordshire
Dudley
  2760 William Goslinge
    Roper, *Dudley*, 1965, p. 50
Suffolk
Ipswich
  2761 Matilda Fowles, widow
    Reed, *Ipswich*, 1981, pp. 29-30
  2762 Elizabeth Smithe
    Reed, *Ipswich*, 1981, pp. 28-29
  2763 Henry Wiseman, brickstriker
    Reed, *Ipswich*, 1981, pp. 25-27
Surrey
Albury
  2764 William Mathewe, labourer
    Herridge, *Surrey*, 2005, p. 261
Alfold
  2765 Thomas Stroydwick, husbandman
    Herridge, *Surrey*, 2005, p. 268
Carshalton
  2766 William Downing, shepherd
    Herridge, *Surrey*, 2005, pp. 258-259
Chertsey
  2767 William Thatcher
    Herridge, *Surrey*, 2005, pp. 268-269
Chiddingfold
  2768 John Rapley by West [of West End]
    Herridge, *Surrey*, 2005, pp. 264-265
Elstead
  2769 Steven Penycod
    Herridge, *Surrey*, 2005, p. 264
Farnham
  2770 Henry Parker, yeoman
    Herridge, *Surrey*, 2005, pp. 263-264
Guildford
  2771 Margaret Smallpece, widow
    Herridge, *Surrey*, 2005, p. 266
Ham
  2772 Richard Smythe, weaver
    Herridge, *Surrey*, 2005, p. 267
Hambledon
  2773 John Molynge, clergyman, parson of Ham
    Herridge, *Surrey*, 2005, pp. 262-263
Haslemere
  2774 Robert Chaundler, husbandman
    Herridge, *Surrey*, 2005, p. 271
Horsell
  2775 Richard Pagge, husbandman
    Herridge, *Surrey*, 2005, p. 263
Mickleham
  2776 William Arnolde, yeoman
    Herridge, *Surrey*, 2005, pp. 257-258
Warwickshire
Birmingham
  2777 Roger Davys
    Holt, 1985, pp. 34-36
    Holt, Ingram, Jarman, *Birmingham*, 1985, pp. 50-51
Shottery
  2778 Elizabeth Pace, widow
    Jones, *Stratford*, I, 2002, pp. 96-97
Stratford-on-Avon
  2779 Robert Hynd, [chapman or haberdasher]
    Jones, *Stratford*, I, 2002, pp. 97-98

Yorkshire
Askrigg, Helm
  2780 Edmund Blyeth [Blyth]
    Thwaite, *Abbotside*, 1967, p. 17
Downholme, Stainton
  2781 John Hagstaine
    Berry, *Swaledale*, 1998, pp. 284-285
Grinton, Kearton
  2782 Thomas Kiplinge
    Berry, *Swaledale*, 1998, pp. 287-288
Grinton, [Ivelet]
  2783 John Whorton
    Berry, *Swaledale*, 1998, p. 286
South Cave
  2784 Peter Benesonn
    Kaner, *South Cave*, 1994, p. 154
  2785 George Emerson, [husbandman]
    Kaner, *South Cave*, 1994, pp. 155-158

1589 (c.)
Surrey
Kingston-upon-Thames
  2786 Richard Jennings, fisherman
    Herridge, *Surrey*, 2005, pp. 259-260

1590
Cheshire
Cholmondeley
  2787 Thomas Boothe, gentleman
    Pearson, *Malpas*, [2005], pp. 111-112
Christleton, Littleton
  2788 Roberte Bonelle
    Bland, *Christleton*, 2003, pp. 194-195
Church Shocklach
  2789 Richard Benian, husbandman
    Pearson, *Malpas*, [2005], pp. 78-79
Stretton
  2790 Robert Good, husbandman
    Pearson, *Malpas*, [2005], pp. 108-109
Waverton
  2791 Peter Katherall, husbandman
    Bland, *Christleton*, 2002, pp. 51-52
Derbyshire
Chesterfield
  2792 Richard Hardman
    Bestall and Fowkes, *Chesterfield*, 1977, pp. 216-218
  2793 Steven Rogers
    Bestall and Fowkes, *Chesterfield*, 1977, pp. 219-222
Dunston
  2794 Richarde Riggotte, husbandman
    Bestall and Fowkes, *Chesterfield*, 1977, pp. 222-223
  2795 Anthonye Smythe
    Bestall and Fowkes, *Chesterfield*, 1977, pp. 218-219
Devonshire
Ashburton
  2796 Richard Oack
    Cash, *Devon*, 1966, p. 8
Ashburton [?]
  2797 Lawrence Wyndeat, cordwainer
    Cash, *Devon*, 1966, p. 7
Ashburton
  2798 William Wyndeate
    Cash, *Devon*, 1966, p. 6

Ashton
2799 Margery Bullocke, widow
Cash, *Devon*, 1966, p. 6
Dawlish
2800 Joan Brownscombe
Cash, *Devon*, 1966, p. 7
Staverton
2801 Richard Emmet
Cash, *Devon*, 1966, p. 8
Co. Durham
Darlington
2802 Henrie Brickwell, gentleman
Greenwell, *Wills and Inventories*, 1860, II, pp. 168-170
Dinsdale
2803 Thomas Blakeston [Blakiston], parson of
Dinsdale
Greenwell, *Wills and Inventories*, 1860, II, pp. 202-203
Hart, Thorp Bulmer
2804 John Lawson, gentleman
Greenwell, *Wills and Inventories*, 1860, II, pp. 184-186
Lumley Castle
2805 John, Lord Lumley (also listed Nonsuch, Surrey
and Tower Hill, London)
Cust, 1918, pp. 21-29
Ireland
Co. Kerry, Castleisland
2806 Sir William Herbert
O'Shea, 1982-1983, pp. 37-46
Lancashire
Bolton, Halliwell
2807 Elen Wodworth
Bolton, *Bolton*, 1994, pp. 151-152
Deane
2808 Margrett Almon
Bolton, *Bolton*, 1987, p. 8
Deane, Middle Hulton
2809 Thomas Grunedy
Bolton, *Bolton*, 1987, p. 128
Hawkshead Hall (now Cumbria)
2810 Rowland Nicholson
Cowper, 1891, pp. 32-33
Ordsall
2811 Sir John Radcliffe
Piccope, *Lancashire and Cheshire*, 1860, pp. 71-72
Trafford
2812 Sir Edmund Trafford
Piccope, *Lancashire and Cheshire*, 1860, pp. 72-74
Westhoughton
2813 Richard Rogerson, gentleman
Bolton, *Bolton*, 1994, p. 66
Lincolnshire
Clee, Thrunscoe
2814 Agnes Shorte, widow
Ambler, Watkinson, *Clee*, 1987, pp. 86-87
2815 George Shorte
Ambler, Watkinson, *Clee*, 1987, p. 86
Faldingworth
2816 John Nevill
Peacock, 1856, pp. 29-32
London
Lombard Street
2817 Sir Thomas Ramsey, Lord Mayor of London
Fairholt, 1866, pp. 323-341

Tower Hill
John, Lord Lumley (see Lumley Castle, Co. Durham)
Norfolk
Kings Lynn
2818 Robert Ladiman, shipmaster
Parker, *Kings Lynn*, 1971, pp. 180-182
Terrington St John
2819 Richard Kynne, yeoman
Overton, 1995, p. 139
Northumberland
Alnwick
2820 William Gray
Emmison, 1966, pp. 92-93
Newcastle
2821 Roberte Barker, merchant and alderman
Greenwell, *Wills and Inventories*, 1860, II, pp. 178-183
Oxfordshire
Banbury
2822 George Colchester, yeoman
Brinkworth and Gibson, *Banbury*, I, 1975, p. 115
2823 Robert Poope [Pope], skinner
Brinkworth and Gibson, *Banbury*, I, 1975, p. 114
2824 Arthur Salle [Sale]
Brinkworth and Gibson, *Banbury*, I, 1975, p. 116
2825 John Smarte
Brinkworth and Gibson, *Banbury*, I, 1975, pp. 114-115
Chipping Norton
2826 Elinor Simkins, widow
Havinden, *Oxfordshire*, 1965, pp. 301-303
2827 Richard Youne, [butcher]
Havinden, *Oxfordshire*, 1965, pp. 308-309
Mollington
2828 Joan Kylby, widow
Havinden, *Oxfordshire*, 1965, pp. 299-300
Noke
2829 Robert Dyckenson, goodman
Havinden, *Oxfordshire*, 1965, pp. 309-310
Over Norton
2830 John Tytmarche
Havinden, *Oxfordshire*, 1965, p. 300
Radford
2831 Richard Busbye
Havinden, *Oxfordshire*, 1965, pp. 310-312
Sarsden
2832 Thomas Bennett
Havinden, *Oxfordshire*, 1965, p. 313
Wardington
2833 John Allibond, husbandman
Havinden, *Oxfordshire*, 1965, pp. 307-308
Waterperry
2834 Thomas Hickes
Havinden, *Oxfordshire*, 1965, pp. 312-313
Witney
2835 Nicholas Hill, baker
Havinden, *Oxfordshire*, 1965, pp. 303-307
Staffordshire
Dudley
2836 Elizabeth Atwoode, widow
Roper, *Dudley*, 1965, p. 51
2837 Thomas Bradley
Roper, *Dudley*, 1965, p. 52

Suffolk
Ipswich
2838 Edward Barnes, sailor
Reed, *Ipswich*, 1981, pp. 30-31
2839 Richard Barnes, husbandman
Reed, *Ipswich*, 1981, pp. 40-41
2840 Thomas Bowles, butcher
Reed, *Ipswich*, 1981, pp. 41-43
2841 Richard Boyes
Reed, *Ipswich*, 1981, p. 37
2842 John Cumberland
Reed, *Ipswich*, 1981, pp. 38-40
2843 John Denie, butcher
Reed, *Ipswich*, 1981, pp. 35-36
2844 Stephen Grosse
Reed, *Ipswich*, 1981, pp. 32-33
2845 John Hard, blacksmith
Reed, *Ipswich*, 1981, pp. 33-34
2846 John Payne, yeoman
Reed, *Ipswich*, 1981, pp. 37-38
2847 Ede Riffam, maidservant
Reed, *Ipswich*, 1981, p. 34
Surrey
Alfold
2848 Thomas Constable, husbandman
Herridge, *Surrey*, 2005, pp. 272-273
Ash
2849 John Boylett
Herridge, *Surrey*, 2005, pp. 269-271
Chobham
2850 Walter Grene, labourer
Herridge, *Surrey*, 2005, p. 273
East Clandon
2851 George Hannaway, husbandman
Herridge, *Surrey*, 2005, p. 274
Hersham
2852 John Woodclerk, yeoman
Herridge, *Surrey*, 2005, pp. 278-280
Long Ditton
2853 James White, labourer
Herridge, *Surrey*, 2005, p. 278
Mickleham
2854 John Tooth, husbandman
Herridge, *Surrey*, 2005, p. 277
Nonsuch
John, Lord Lumley (see Lumley Castle, Co. Durham)
Wrecclesham
2855 John Pratt
Herridge, *Surrey*, 2005, p. 276
Warwickshire
Birmingham
2856 Thomas Bache, scythesmith
Holt, 1985, pp. 31-34
Holt, Ingram, Jarman, *Birmingham*, 1985, pp. 53-57
2857 John Baker, tanner
Holt, 1985, pp. 28-29
Holt, Ingram, Jarman, *Birmingham*, 1985, p. 52
Stratford-on-Avon
2858 Mr Robert Coxe
Jones, *Stratford*, I, 2002, pp. 101-102
2859 Robert Grafton, husbandman
Jones, *Stratford*, I, 2002, pp. 103-104
2860 Wyllyam Homes, weaver
Jones, *Stratford*, I, 2002, pp. 99-101

2861 Wyllyam Jones, husbandman
Jones, *Stratford*, I, 2002, pp. 98-99
Worcestershire
Feckenham, Beanhall
2862 Walter Hanbury, gentleman
Wanklyn, *Worcestershire*, 1998, pp. 85-88
Yorkshire
Grinton, Harkerside
2863 Mark Close
Berry, *Swaledale*, 1998, pp. 292-293
Grinton
2864 Ralph Scotson
Berry, *Swaledale*, 1998, pp. 291-292
Marske, Applegarth
2865 John Wood
Berry, *Swaledale*, 1998, pp. 289-290
South Cave
2866 Isabell Browne
Kaner, *South Cave*, 1994, p. 160
South Cave, Faxfleet
2867 Elizabeth Thruske, widow
Kaner, *South Cave*, 1994, p. 160

1590 (c.)
Surrey
Guildford, St Nicholas
2868 Mawdlen Bromefeld
Herridge, *Surrey*, 2005, p. 271

1591
Bedfordshire
Barton
2869 Mathew Woodward
Freeman, *Bedfordshire*, 1952, p. 107
Cheshire
Church Shocklach
2870 John Povay, husbandman
Pearson, *Malpas*, [2005], pp. 120-121
Malpas
2871 Rychard Byckerstaffe, husbandman
Pearson, *Malpas*, [2005], p. 117
Stockport
2872 John Burges
Phillips and Smith, *Stockport*, 1985, p. 5
Stockport, Hillgate
2873 Alexander Daniell, weaver
Phillips and Smith, *Stockport*, 1985, pp. 6-7
Stockport
2874 Thomas Diconson, linen draper
Phillips and Smith, *Stockport*, 1985, pp. 10-14
2875 John Jackson
Phillips and Smith, *Stockport*, 1985, pp. 5-6
Wrenbury, Chorley
2876 Ellen Bebbington, [widow]
Pixton, *Wrenbury*, 2009, pp. 19-20
Derbyshire
Glossop, Gibhey
2877 Agnes Andrew
Lee and Miller, *New Mills*, 1999, pp. 35-36
Temple Normanton
2878 Nicholas Ludloum, husbandman
Bestall and Fowkes, *Chesterfield*, 1977, p. 224
2879 Thomas Wylede
Bestall and Fowkes, *Chesterfield*, 1977, pp. 224-225

Devonshire
Heavitree, Wonford
  2880 John Leighe
    Cash, *Devon*, 1966, p. 9
Kingskerswell
  2881 William Crockwill, servant
    Cash, *Devon*, 1966, p. 8
Sheldon
  2882 Richard Hake
    Cash, *Devon*, 1966, pp. 9-10
Uffculme
  2883 Richard Mander
    Wyatt, *Uffculme*, 1997, p. 8
Co. Durham
Low Dinsdale
  2884 Thomas Blackson, clergyman, parson of
  Dinsdale
    Raine, *Barnes*, 1850, pp. cxxx-cxxxi
Redworth
  2885 John March, [merchant adventurer] (also listed
  Newcastle, Northumberland)
    Greenwell, *Wills and Inventories*, 1860, II, pp. 193-196
Hampshire
Ashley
  2885a William Hewett, clergyman, rector of Ashley
    Hewett, 2004, pp. 71-76
Lancashire
Blackrod
  2886 Anne Norres, widow
    Bolton, *Bolton*, 1994, pp. 24-26
Farnworth
  2887 John Dicksone, husbandman
    Bolton, *Bolton*, 1987, p. 81
Lostock
  2888 Bryan Ligh, husbandman
    Bolton, *Bolton*, 1987, p. 169
Leicestershire
Evington
  2889 Thomas Jacam, [husbandman?]
    Wilshere, *Evington*, 1985, p. 5
Lincolnshire
Clee
  2890 Robert Howldsworth, yeoman
    Ambler, Watkinson, *Clee*, 1987, pp. 87-90
  2891 William Richardson, husbandsman
    Ambler, Watkinson, *Clee*, 1987, pp. 90-91
Clee, Itterby
  2892 William Stallinborow
    Ambler, Watkinson, *Clee*, 1987, p. 92
Market Rasen
  2893 Richard Chapman, [tanner]
    Neave, *Market Rasen*, 1985, pp. 98-99
  2894 Emett Merrie
    Neave, *Market Rasen*, 1985, p. 97
  2895 Willm Pattricke
    Neave, *Market Rasen*, 1985, p. 99
  2896 Jannett Sowden
    Neave, *Market Rasen*, 1985, pp. 96-97
  2897 Willm Wilkinson alias Butcher
    Neave, *Market Rasen*, 1985, p. 101
London
Bermondsey, St Mary Magdalen
  2898 Richard Harrison
    Herridge, *Surrey*, 2005, pp. 287-288

Southwark, St Olave's
  2899 Margarett Brigmann, widow
    Herridge, *Surrey*, 2005, pp. 283-285
Norfolk
Attleborough
  2900 Roberte Chamberlyne [Robert Chamberlin],
  gentleman
    Wilson, *Wymondham*, 1983, p. 5
Kings Lynn
  2901 Thomas Purdy
    Parker, *Kings Lynn*, 1971, pp. 182-183
Wymondham
  2902 Thomas Jacksonn [Jackson], gentleman
    Wilson, *Wymondham*, 1983, pp. 5-7
  2903 John Woodfall, clergymen
    Wilson, *Wymondham*, 1983, pp. 34-35
Northumberland
Newcastle
  John March, [merchant adventurer] (see Redworth,
  Co. Durham)
Oxfordshire
Ramsden
  2904 William Thackborowe
    Havinden, *Oxfordshire*, 1965, pp. 313-314
Suffolk
Ipswich
  2905 Robert Jower, turner
    Reed, *Ipswich*, 1981, pp. 43-45
  2906 Richard Kinge
    Reed, *Ipswich*, 1981, p. 47
  2907 Leonard Marshall
    Reed, *Ipswich*, 1981, pp. 45-47
Surrey
Albury
  2908 John Astone
    Herridge, *Surrey*, 2005, pp. 282-283
  2909 William Tickmore, yeoman
    Herridge, *Surrey*, 2005, pp. 294-295
Bramley
  2910 John Stedman, husbandman
    Herridge, *Surrey*, 2005, p. 291
Chertsey
  2911 William Slatt, husbandman
    Herridge, *Surrey*, 2005, pp. 290-291
Cranleigh
  2912 Henry Kempe, tailor
    Herridge, *Surrey*, 2005, pp. 288-289
Epsom
  2913 Elizabeth Michell, widow
    Herridge, *Surrey*, 2005, p. 290
Great Bookham
  2914 Margaret Charlewodd, widow
    Herridge, *Surrey*, 2005, pp. 284-285
  2915 John Hibbard, yeoman
    Harvey, 1974, p. 55
    Herridge, *Surrey*, 2005, p. 288
Malden
  2916 Richard Alden, yeoman
    Herridge, *Surrey*, 2005, pp. 280-282
Peper Harow
  2917 Robert Stoner, husbandman
    Herridge, *Surrey*, 2005, p. 292

West Humble
2918 John Lucas
Herridge, *Surrey*, 2005, p. 289
Windlesham
2919 Thomas Crue, labourer
Herridge, *Surrey*, 2005, p. 285
Wonersh
2920 Agnes Streete, widow
Herridge, *Surrey*, 2005, pp. 292-294
Worplesdon
2921 John Goringe, yeoman
Herridge, *Surrey*, 2005, pp. 286-287
Warwickshire
Birmingham
2922 John Bollevaunt, smith
Holt, Ingram, Jarman, *Birmingham*, 1985, pp. 61-62
2923 Thomas Rastell, [draper]
Holt, Ingram, Jarman, *Birmingham*, 1985, pp. 59-61
Foleshill
2924 John Sheppard, [labourer]
Upton, *Foleshill*, 1993, pp. 59-60
Shottery
2925 John Debdale [Dibdale], husbandman
Jones, *Stratford*, I, 2002, pp. 104-106
Stratford-on-Avon
2926 Mrs Katerine Salisberie [Katherine Salisbury], [widow]
Jones, *Stratford*, I, 2002, pp. 106-109
Wiltshire
Marlborough
2927 Thomas Dippen, baker
Williams and Thomson, *Marlborough*, 2007, p. 1
2928 William Frybens
Williams and Thomson, *Marlborough*, 2007, pp. 1-2
Yorkshire
Aysgarth, Skellgill
2929 Luke Twaytes
Thwaite, *Abbotside*, 1967, p. 19
Browsholme Hall (now Lancashire)
2930 [Robert Parker, gentleman]
Jervis, *Browsholme*, 1986, pp. 8-12
Grinton, Fremington
2931 William Collyer
Berry, *Swaledale*, 1998, p. 297
2932 Richard Hamond
Berry, *Swaledale*, 1998, p. 303
Grinton, Thwaite
2933 Edmond Harcaye
Berry, *Swaledale*, 1998, pp. 304-305
Grinton, Muker
2934 George Melner
Berry, *Swaledale*, 1998, pp. 300-301
Grinton, Rash
2935 Edward Milner
Berry, *Swaledale*, 1998, pp. 294-295
Hudswell
2936 Richard Rayne, yeoman
Berry, *Swaledale*, 1998, pp. 298-299
Lunds
2937 Rainolde Parkyn [Reginald Parkin]
Thwaite, *Abbotside*, 1967, pp. 17-18

Marske
2938 John Mason, yeoman
Berry, *Swaledale*, 1998, p. 306
South Cave
2939 Charytye [Charitie] Norman
Kaner, *South Cave*, 1994, p. 165
2940 Christopher Sharpe, yeoman
Kaner, *South Cave*, 1994, pp. 163-164
2941 Alyson Todd
Kaner, *South Cave*, 1994, pp. 166-168
2942 Alizon Wetherall
Kaner, *South Cave*, 1994, pp. 161-162
Wighill
2943 Nicholas Houghton, clergyman, Prebendary of Bilton
Cross, *York*, I, 1984, pp. 145-146

1591 (c.)
Yorkshire
Browsholme Hall (now Lancashire)
2944 Robt. Parker, gentleman
Jervis, *Browsholme*, 1986, pp. 5-7

1592
Cheshire
Broxton
2945 Ales Dod, widow
Pearson, *Malpas*, [2005], p. 130
Church Shocklach
2946 Morgan Dye, husbandman
Pearson, *Malpas*, [2005], pp. 123-124
Malpas
2947 Hugh Catherall
Pearson, *Malpas*, [2005], p. 127
Malpas, Edge
2948 John Game
Pearson, *Malpas*, [2005], pp. 131-132
Shocklach
2949 John Massye, husbandman
Pearson, *Malpas*, [2005], p. 126
2950 Randulphe Overton, husbandman
Pearson, *Malpas*, [2005], pp. 128-129
Stockport, Hillgate
2951 George Daniell, yeoman
Phillips and Smith, *Stockport*, 1985, pp. 16-17
Tarvin, Stapleford
2952 Raffe Towres
Bland, *Christleton*, 2002, pp. 54-55
Waverton
2953 Thomas Dutton, webster
Bland, *Christleton*, 2002, pp. 55-56
Derbyshire
Calow
2954 John Rowbothom
Bestall and Fowkes, *Chesterfield*, 1977, pp. 225-226
Chesterfield
2955 Robert Shakerlye
Bestall and Fowkes, *Chesterfield*, 1977, pp. 228-229
Dunston
2956 John Pointon
Bestall and Fowkes, *Chesterfield*, 1977, p. 227
Glossop, Hollins
2957 Jhon Rowbotum, [husbandman]
Lee and Miller, *New Mills*, 1999, pp. 15-16

Hasland
 2958 Thomas Stanley, yeoman
  Bestall and Fowkes, *Chesterfield*, 1977, pp. 229-230
Devonshire
 Culmstock
 2959 Edward Chamber
  Cash, *Devon*, 1966, pp. 10-11
 Culmstock, Prescott
 2960 Salomon Westbeare, weaver
  Cash, *Devon*, 1966, pp. 11-12
 East Teignmouth
 2961 Edward and Joan Packe
  Cash, *Devon*, 1966, p. 10
 Littleham
 2962 Robert Rondell
  Cash, *Devon*, 1966, pp. 12-13
 Teignmouth
 2963 George Grosse
  Cash, *Devon*, 1966, p. 10
 Uffculme
 2964 John Dowdney
  Wyatt, *Uffculme*, 1997, pp. 8-9
 2965 Richarde Marshall, husbandman
  Wyatt, *Uffculme*, 1997, pp. 9-10
Dorsetshire
 Leigh
 2966 Henry Rowswell
  Machin, *Yetminster*, 1976, No.3, (2 pp.)
 2967 Phillip Royde, husbandman
  Machin, *Yetminster*, 1976, No.4, (2 pp.)
 Yetminster
 2968 William Comber, [carpenter]
  Machin, *Yetminster*, 1976, No.7, (1 p.)
 2969 John Evered, [blacksmith]
  Machin, *Yetminster*, 1976, No.5, (2 pp.)
  Machin, 1978, pp. 165-166
 2970 John Sherry
  Machin, *Yetminster*, 1976, No.6, (1 p.)
Co. Durham
 Barnard Castle, The Castle
 2971 Mr Henrie Bowes
  Surtees, 1840, pp. 87-88
 Darlington
 2972 John Johnson
  Greenwell, *Wills and Inventories*, 1860, II, pp. 210-213
 Hebburn
 2973 Thomas Fisher
  Hodgson, *Wills and Inventories*, 1906, III, p. 153
 Old Durham
 2974 Robert Booth, gentleman
  Greenwell, *Wills and Inventories*, 1860, II, pp. 208-209
 Willington
 2975 Humfrey Bracke
  Greenwell, *Wills and Inventories*, 1860, II, p. 214
Lancashire
 Bolton
 2976 Ales Brucke, widow
  Bolton, *Bolton*, 1987, p. 46
 Bolton, Longworth
 2977 William Maiio [Mayo]
  Bolton, *Bolton*, 1987, pp. 191-192
 Harwood
 2978 Roger Crompton
  Bolton, *Bolton*, 1987, p. 71

 2979 John Grenhaugh
  Bolton, *Bolton*, 1987, p. 102
 St Helens, Sutton
 2980 Cyslye Dugarde, [widow]
  St Helens, *Angells*, 1999, pp. 9-10
 2981 Ellene Garnet, widow
  St Helens, *Angells*, 1999, pp. 11-12
 Westhoughton
 2982 John Smith, husbandman
  Bolton, *Bolton*, 1994, p. 103
Leicestershire
 Evington
 2983 Bryan Worthington, [husbandman]
  Wilshere, *Evington*, 1985, p. 6
Lincolnshire
 Allington
 2984 Alice Newboes
  Pask, *Allington*, 1989, pp. 43-44
 Clee, Itterby
 2985 Annesse Stones
  Ambler, Watkinson, *Clee*, 1987, p. 94
 Clee
 2986 John Thorppe, husbandman
  Ambler, Watkinson, *Clee*, 1987, pp. 92-93
 2987 Robart Yates
  Ambler, Watkinson, *Clee*, 1987, pp. 93-94
 Market Rasen
 2988 Nicolas Banks, [school usher]
  Neave, *Market Rasen*, 1985, p. 101
 2989 Richard Cater, yeoman
  Neave, *Market Rasen*, 1985, p. 102
 2990 Mrtin Clarke
  Neave, *Market Rasen*, 1985, p. 100
 2991 Edmunde Dawson
  Neave, *Market Rasen*, 1985, p. 103
London
 Southwark, St Olave's
 2992 Thomas Tomson
  Herridge, *Surrey*, 2005, p. 304
Norfolk
 Wymondham
 2993 Alyis Ludkyn [Alice Ludkin]
  Wilson, *Wymondham*, 1983, p. 35
Northumberland
 Newcastle
 2994 Roberte Mytforth [Mitford]
  Greenwell, *Wills and Inventories*, 1860, II, pp. 214-218
 2995 Henrie Robinsone, keelman
  Greenwell, *Wills and Inventories*, 1860, II, pp. 252-253
 2996 James Tenand, blacksmith
  Greenwell, *Wills and Inventories*, 1860, II, p. 210
Oxfordshire
 Water Eaton
 2997 William Meare
  Offord, *Water Eaton*, 1986, pp. 4-5
Staffordshire
 Dudley
 2998 Richard Barrett
  Roper, *Dudley*, 1965, p. 53
Surrey
 Bisley
 2999 John Cobbat
  Herridge, *Surrey*, 2005, p. 296

Guildford, Stoke
  3000 Thomas Aneve, yeoman
    Herridge, *Surrey*, 2005, p. 295
Hersham
  3001 John Feelder, yeoman
    Herridge, *Surrey*, 2005, p. 297
Leatherhead
  3002 Walter Steven, labourer
    Herridge, *Surrey*, 2005, p. 303-304
Mitcham
  3003 Robert Seith, yeoman
    Herridge, *Surrey*, 2005, pp. 300-302
Shere
  3004 John Slarkes, yeoman
    Herridge, *Surrey*, 2005, pp. 302-303
Walton-on-Thames
  3005 John Hellons, yeoman
    Herridge, *Surrey*, 2005, pp. 298-299
  3006 Katheryn Lydgold, widow
    Herridge, *Surrey*, 2005, pp. 299-300
Wales
Pembrokeshire, Carew Castle
  3007 Sir John Perrot
    Barnwell, 1866, pp. 339-358
Warwickshire
Shottery
  3008 Roger Burman, husbandman
    Jones, *Stratford*, I, 2002, pp. 110-111
Stratford-on-Avon
  3009 Wyllyam Beddell [William Biddle], butcher
    Jones, *Stratford*, I, 2002, pp. 119-121
  3010 Henry Field, tanner
    Jones, *Stratford*, I, 2002, pp. 116-118
Stratford-on-Avon, Drayton
  3011 Jhon Pearke
    Jones, *Stratford*, I, 2002, pp. 122-123
Stratford-on-Avon
  3012 Raph [Ralph] Shawe, wool driver
    Jones, *Stratford*, I, 2002, pp. 114-115
  3013 Thomas Wotton, weaver
    Jones, *Stratford*, I, 2002, pp. 112-113
Warwick
  3014 Nicholas Eyffeler, glazier
    Farr, 1977, pp. 48-57
Wiltshire
Marlborough
  3015 Thomas Burgies, yeoman
    Williams and Thomson, *Marlborough*, 2007, pp. 2-3
  3016 Thomas Cockye, tailor
    Williams and Thomson, *Marlborough*, 2007, p. 3
  3017 Jhon Merchant
    Williams and Thomson, *Marlborough*, 2007, pp. 3-5
  3018 William Symmes, shoemaker
    Williams and Thomson, *Marlborough*, 2007, pp. 6-7
  3019 Thomas Typper, tanner
    Williams and Thomson, *Marlborough*, 2007, pp. 5-6
Worcestershire
Wolverley, Blakeshall
  3020 John Sebright, gentleman
    Wanklyn, *Worcestershire*, 1998, pp. 88-90
Yorkshire
Hudswell
  3021 Nicholas Plewes
    Berry, *Swaledale*, 1998, pp. 307-309

South Cave
  3022 Grace Barker
    Kaner, *South Cave*, 1994, p. 182
  3023 John Millington, grassman
    Kaner, *South Cave*, 1994, pp. 169-170
  3024 Thomas Newtonn [Newton]
    Kaner, *South Cave*, 1994, p. 179
  3025 Richard Sotheron, labourer
    Kaner, *South Cave*, 1994, p. 181
  3026 George Tayler
    Kaner, *South Cave*, 1994, pp. 170-174
  3027 Ambrose Tenann alias Robinson
    Kaner, *South Cave*, 1994, pp. 174-177
  3028 Agnes Tindale
    Kaner, *South Cave*, 1994, p. 178
  3029 John Wetherall, [blacksmith]
    Kaner, *South Cave*, 1994, pp. 182-184

1592 (c.)
Surrey
West Horsley
  3030 William Atlee
    Herridge, *Surrey*, 2005, p. 296

1593
Cheshire
Christleton
  3031 John Jannion
    Bland, *Christleton*, 2002, p. 64
Christleton, Cotton
  3032 Katherine Partington, widow
    Bland, *Christleton*, 2003, pp. 197-199
Christleton
  3033 John Seller, [husbandman]
    Bland, *Christleton*, 2002, pp. 68-69
Church Shocklach
  3034 David Povey, yeoman
    Pearson, *Malpas*, [2005], pp. 137-139
Malpas, Edge
  3035 Bartholomewe Candland, husbandman
    Pearson, *Malpas*, [2005], pp. 140-141
Tarvin, Oscroft
  3036 John Blease, [husbandman]
    Bland, *Christleton*, 2002, p
Tarvin, Mouldsworth
  3037 Hamnet Boulde, [husbandman]
    Bland, *Christleton*, 2002, p. 74
Tarvin, Stapleford
  3038 Allice Rogerson, widow
    Bland, *Christleton*, 2002, p. 63
Tarvin, Foulk Stapleford [Hargrave]
  3039 John Rossingreve, yeoman
    Bland, *Christleton*, 2002, pp. 69-70
Tarvin
  3040 James Tapley, victualler
    Bland, *Christleton*, 2002, pp. 77-79
Tarvin, Duddon
  3041 John Weane [Wayne], husbandman
    Bland, *Christleton*, 2002, p. 67
Tilston, Horton
  3042 John Baker, husbandman
    Pearson, *Malpas*, [2005], pp. 134-135
Waverton, Huxley
  3043 Mistress Jane Clive, [widow]
    Bland, *Christleton*, 2002, pp. 79-85

3044 Richard Johnson
Bland, *Christleton*, 2002, p. 65
Wrenbury, Chorley
3045 William Bebbington
Pixton, *Wrenbury*, 2009, pp. 22-24
Wrenbury, Newhall
3046 Robert Tench
Pixton, *Wrenbury*, 2009, p. 30

Derbyshire
Chesterfield
3047 Alice Harries, widow
Bestall and Fowkes, *Chesterfield*, 1977, pp. 231-232
Dunston
3048 Thomas Eyre, gentleman
Bestall and Fowkes, *Chesterfield*, 1977, pp. 231-238
Glossop, Broadhurst
3049 Christopher Armfeelde
Lee and Miller, *New Mills*, 1999, pp. 19-20
Glossop, Knightweeke
3050 William Greene
Lee and Miller, *New Mills*, 1999, pp. 16-17

Devonshire
Culmstock
3051 Agnes Browne
Cash, *Devon*, 1966, p. 13
Littleham
3052 Gilbert Peron
Cash, *Devon*, 1966, pp. 13-14
Sidbury
3053 John Clapp
Cash, *Devon*, 1966, p. 13
Uplyme
3054 Alice Newall
Cash, *Devon*, 1966, p. 14
Uffculme
3055 Thomas Butstone [Butston]
Wyatt, *Uffculme*, 1997, p. 10
3056 Henrye Godffraye [Godfrye]
Wyatt, *Uffculme*, 1997, p. 12
3057 John Peppreell [Peperell]
Wyatt, *Uffculme*, 1997, pp. 11-12
3058 Elizabeth Rudge, widow
Wyatt, *Uffculme*, 1997, pp. 10-11

Dorsetshire
Yetminster
3059 John Warr alias Bartlet
Machin, *Yetminster*, 1976, No.8, (1 p.)

Co. Durham
Darlington, Cockerton
3060 Thomas Radcliff [Radclyffe]
Greenwell, *Wills and Inventories*, 1860, II, pp. 239-242
Durham, Gilligate
3061 Rychard Conyers
Greenwell, *Wills and Inventories*, 1860, II, p. 222

Hertfordshire
St Albans, St Stephens
3062 Thomas Trott, [yeoman]
Parker, *Worldly Goods*, 2004, p. 116

Lancashire
Blackrod
3063 Gennet Houlden, widow
Bolton, *Bolton*, 1987, p. 144

Bolton, Longworth
3064 William Bromille [Bromily], yeoman
Bolton, *Bolton*, 1987, p. 40
Bolton, Brightmet
3065 George Crompton
Bolton, *Bolton*, 1987, pp. 62-63
Bolton
3066 John Wrighte, clothworker
Bolton, *Bolton*, 1994, pp. 154-155
Bradshaw
3067 Richard Haslome
Bolton, *Bolton*, 1987, p. 138
Deane, Middle Hulton
3068 Thomas Edge
Bolton, *Bolton*, 1987, p. 88
Deane, Little Hulton
3069 Richard Mather
Bolton, *Bolton*, 1987, p. 190
Deane, Middle Hulton
3070 Margret WilliamDaughter
Bolton, *Bolton*, 1994, p. 146
St Helens, Eccleston
3071 Alice Cowpar, widow
St Helens, *Angells*, 1999, pp. 14-15
Turton
3072 John Sharples, husbandman
Bolton, *Bolton*, 1994, pp. 87-88
Westhoughton
3073 Roger Robartson, husbandman
Bolton, *Bolton*, 1994, p. 63

Lincolnshire
Cleethorpes
3074 William Barnes
Ambler, Watkinson, *Clee*, 1987, p. 95
Market Rasen
3075 Jane Cater, widow
Neave, *Market Rasen*, 1985, p. 104
3076 Willm Sowthe
Neave, *Market Rasen*, 1985, p. 105

London
Dulwich
3077 Christopher Curson
Herridge, *Surrey*, 2005, pp. 305-306

Norfolk
Wymondham
3078 Thomas Woodcock, beer brewer
Wilson, *Wymondham*, 1983, pp. 25-26

Northumberland
Bedlington, Choppington
3079 Ellinor Woddringtone [Widdrington], widow
Greenwell, *Wills and Inventories*, 1860, II, pp. 220-221
Berwick
3080 Hector Woddrington [Widdrington], constable
of horse (also listed Chibburn)
Greenwell, *Wills and Inventories*, 1860, II, pp. 233-234
Sir Henrye Woddrington [Widdrington], marshal and
Deputy Governor (see Widdrington)
Chibburn
Hector Woddrington [Widdrington], constable of horse
(see Berwick)

Newcastle
  3081 George Bourn, cooper
  Hodgson, *Wills and Inventories*, 1906, III, p. 155
  3082 Thomas Bowes, merchant
  Greenwell, *Wills and Inventories*, 1860, II, pp. 236-237
  3083 Thomas Philipsone, cordwainer
  Greenwell, *Wills and Inventories*, 1860, II, pp. 229-231
  3084 George Rochester, saddler
  Hodgson, *Wills and Inventories*, 1906, III, p. 152
Widdrington
  3085 Sir Henrye Woddrington [Widdrington],
  marshal and Deputy Governor (also listed
  Berwick)
  Greenwell, *Wills and Inventories*, 1860, II, pp. 226-229

Oxfordshire
Banbury
  3086 Edward Bosse [Bose], barber
  Brinkworth and Gibson, *Banbury*, I, 1975, p. 118
  3087 Elizabeth Brightwell [Bryghtwell], widow
  Brinkworth and Gibson, *Banbury*, I, 1975, p. 124
Banbury, Nethercote
  3088 Robert Bull, husbandman
  Brinkworth and Gibson, *Banbury*, I, 1975, pp. 120-121
  3089 Henry Greene, husbandman
  Brinkworth and Gibson, *Banbury*, I, 1975, pp. 118-119
Banbury
  3090 John Helmdon, labourer
  Brinkworth and Gibson, *Banbury*, I, 1975, pp. 121-122
  3091 Robert Isard [Izard], tallow chandler
  Brinkworth and Gibson, *Banbury*, I, 1975, pp. 122-123
  3092 Richard Phill, bookbinder
  Brinkworth and Gibson, *Banbury*, I, 1975, p. 117
  3093 Benne[n]t Savage
  Brinkworth and Gibson, *Banbury*, I, 1975, p. 124
Marston
  3094 Nicholas Hore, [yeoman]
  Portman, 1974, pp. 154-155
Water Eaton
  3095 Richard Harper
  Offord, *Water Eaton*, 1986, p. 2

Surrey
Bagshot
  3096 John Todie alias Farrawle
  Herridge, *Surrey*, 2005, pp. 313-314
Elstead
  3097 John Williamson, wareburner
  Herridge, *Surrey*, 2005, p. 317
Fetcham
  3098 John Griffine
  Herridge, *Surrey*, 2005, pp. 307-308
  3099 Roger Marete
  Herridge, *Surrey*, 2005, p. 309
  3100 Thomas Peter, husbandman
  Herridge, *Surrey*, 2005, pp. 311-312
Great Bookham
  3101 Agnes Peeters
  Herridge, *Surrey*, 2005, pp. 310-311
Little Bookham
  3102 George Hudshon, clergyman, rector of Little
  Bookham
  Herridge, *Surrey*, 2005, p. 308
Reigate
  3103 Rowland Marden, husbandman
  Herridge, *Surrey*, 2005, p. 309

Thames Ditton
  3104 Roger Mathew, collier
  Herridge, *Surrey*, 2005, p. 310
Woking
  3105 Richard Frayle, yeoman
  Herridge, *Surrey*, 2005, pp. 306-307
Warwickshire
Lapworth
  3106 Henry Castlon
  Ball, 1973, p. 14
Stratford-on-Avon
  3107 Thomas Alegh, [shepherd]
  Jones, *Stratford*, I, 2002, p. 140
  3108 Arther Boyce
  Jones, *Stratford*, I, 2002, pp. 129-132
  3109 Richard Holands [Homes], weaver
  Jones, *Stratford*, I, 2002, pp. 138-139
  3110 Griphyn [Griffin] ap Roberts, butcher
  Jones, *Stratford*, I, 2002, pp. 136-137
  3111 William Smarte [Smart], [baker]
  Jones, *Stratford*, I, 2002, pp. 132-135
  3112 George Whateley, [draper, alderman]
  Jones, *Stratford*, I, 2002, pp. 123-128
Wiltshire
Marlborough
  3113 Jhon Clerke, carpenter
  Williams and Thomson, *Marlborough*, 2007, pp. 10-11
  3114 Roger Elson, [saddler]
  Williams and Thomson, *Marlborough*, 2007, p. 7
  3115 John Purlyn, barber
  Williams and Thomson, *Marlborough*, 2007, pp. 9-10
  3116 John Squire
  Williams and Thomson, *Marlborough*, 2007, pp. 8-9
  3117 John Stumpe, shoemaker
  Williams and Thomson, *Marlborough*, 2007, pp. 11-12
Yorkshire
Grinton, Healaugh
  3118 James Place
  Berry, *Swaledale*, 1998, pp. 312-313
Hudswell
  3119 Ciciley Thomson, widow
  Berry, *Swaledale*, 1998, pp. 310-312
South Cave, Weedley
  3120 John Wasse
  Kaner, *South Cave*, 1994, pp. 185-186
South Cave, Faxfleet
  3121 Henrye Wright
  Kaner, *South Cave*, 1994, pp. 187-188

1593 (c.)
Lancashire
Rainhill
  3122 Eline Accars, widow
  St Helens, *Angells*, 1999, p. 13
Surrey
Wotton
  3123 John Ridford, yeoman
  Herridge, *Surrey*, 2005, pp. 312-313
Wiltshire
Marlborough
  3124 Walter Harrys
  Williams and Thomson, *Marlborough*, 2007, p. 9
  3125 John Lyddorl
  Williams and Thomson, *Marlborough*, 2007, pp. 7-8

1594

Cheshire
Wrenbury cum Frith
  3126 Humphrey Bickerton, [husbandman]
  Pixton, *Wrenbury*, 2009, pp. 32-33

Derbyshire
Chesterfield
  3127 Raphe Pursglove
  Bestall and Fowkes, *Chesterfield*, 1977, pp. 240-241
  3128 Humfrey Stansall
  Bestall and Fowkes, *Chesterfield*, 1977, pp. 238-239
Glossop, Aspenshaw
  3129 John Bowdon, [yeoman]
  Lee and Miller, *New Mills*, 1999, p. 24

Devonshire
Uffculme
  3130 John Colliford, [husbandman]
  Wyatt, *Uffculme*, 1997, pp. 13-14
  3131 Thomas Cortone [Courton]
  Wyatt, *Uffculme*, 1997, p. 15
  3132 John Howe [alias Tanner]
  Wyatt, *Uffculme*, 1997, p. 13
  3133 William Norton, [weaver]
  Wyatt, *Uffculme*, 1997, pp. 15-16
  3134 Johane Osmonnde [Joan Osmonde], widow
  Wyatt, *Uffculme*, 1997, pp. 16-17
  3135 John Seagar [Segar], vicar of Uffculme
  Wyatt, *Uffculme*, 1997, pp. 14-15
  3136 Henrye Skinner
  Wyatt, *Uffculme*, 1997, p. 16

Dorsetshire
Chetnole
  3137 Henry Fooke, yeoman
  Machin, *Yetminster*, 1976, No.10, (3 pp.)
Leigh
  3138 William Downton, [husbandman]
  Machin, *Yetminster*, 1976, No.11, (2 pp.)
  3139 Henry Kibbie
  Machin, *Yetminster*, 1976, No.9, (2 pp.)

Co. Durham
Lambton
  3140 Radulphi Lampton [Lambton], gentleman
  Greenwell, *Wills and Inventories*, 1860, II, pp. 243-246

Essex
West Ham
  3141 George Wilmer
  Foster, Green, 1888, pp. 97-98

Hertfordshire
Kings Langley
  3142 Alice Field, widow
  Munby, *Kings Langley*, 1981, pp. 35-36
St Albans, St Stephens, The Holte
  3143 William Pope
  Munby, *Worldly Goods*, 1991, p. 71

Lancashire
Bolton, Longworth
  3144 William Entwisle
  Bolton, *Bolton*, 1987, p. 96
Bolton, Great Lever
  3145 Arthure Isherwood, yeoman
  Bolton, *Bolton*, 1987, pp. 154-155

Bolton, High Horrocks
  3146 Olyver Pilkington
  Bolton, *Bolton*, 1994, p. 51
Bolton
  3147 Edmond Sharples alias Ward
  Bolton, *Bolton*, 1994, p. 82
Manchester, Hanging Ditch
  3148 Unnamed
  Axon, 1915, pp. 1-3

Leicestershire
Kirby Muxloe
  3149 William Ballarde, labourer
  Wilshere, *Kirby Muxloe*, 1983, p. 3
Melton Mowbray, Eye Kettleby
  3150 Edwarde Pate, esquire
  North, 1873-1874, pp. 276-279
  North, 1878, pp. 265-268
Wigston
  3151 Robert Freer
  Hoskins, 1957, p. 297

Lincolnshire
Clee, Oole
  3152 Robert Bartle
  Ambler, Watkinson, *Clee*, 1987, p. 97
Clee, Thrunscoe
  3153 James Portesse
  Ambler, Watkinson, *Clee*, 1987, pp. 95-96
Clee
  3154 Rycherd Sutton
  Ambler, Watkinson, *Clee*, 1987, p. 95
Clee, Itterby
  3155 Henry Ulyetson
  Ambler, Watkinson, *Clee*, 1987, pp. 97-98

London
Streatham
  3156 Christopher Mathew, husbandman
  Herridge, *Surrey*, 2005, pp. 315-316

Northamptonshire
Warkworth
  3157 Alice [Ales] Butler
  Brinkworth and Gibson, *Banbury*, I, 1975, p. 129

Northumberland
Berwick (?)
  3158 William Carey, esquire
  Greenwell, *Wills and Inventories*, 1860, II, pp. 231-232
Kirkharle
  3159 Marmaduck Fenwick, gentleman
  Greenwell, *Wills and Inventories*, 1860, II, p. 248
Wallsend
  3160 Thomas Lorens, gentleman
  Hodgson, *Wills and Inventories*, 1906, III, p. 159

Oxfordshire
Banbury
  3161 Thomas Brasbridge, clergyman, vicar of Banbury
  Brinkworth, 1966, pp. 71-73
  Brinkworth and Gibson, *Banbury*, I, 1975, pp. 127-128
Banbury, Calthorpe
  3162 Thomas Harrys [Harris], husbandman
  Brinkworth and Gibson, *Banbury*, I, 1975, pp. 131-132
Banbury
  3163 William Man
  Brinkworth and Gibson, *Banbury*, I, 1975, p. 125

3164 Michael Nethercott
Brinkworth and Gibson, *Banbury*, I, 1975, p. 125
3165 John Overton [Overtoun]
Brinkworth and Gibson, *Banbury*, I, 1975, pp. 129-130
3166 William Penton, tanner
Brinkworth and Gibson, *Banbury*, I, 1975, p. 134
3167 George Pynder [Pinder], tailor
Brinkworth and Gibson, *Banbury*, I, 1975, p. 133
3168 Robert Southam [Sowthame]
Brinkworth and Gibson, *Banbury*, I, 1975, pp. 126-127
Oxford, Cross Inn
3169 William Hough, innholder
Pantin, 1955, pp. 65-70

Staffordshire
Dudley
3170 John Jewkes, stringer
Roper, *Dudley*, 1965, p. 55
3171 John Rodes
Roper, *Dudley*, 1965, p. 54

Surrey
Bisley
3172 John Hone
Herridge, *Surrey*, 2005, pp. 314-315
Dorking
3173 Marie Bishop, widow
Herridge, *Surrey*, 2005, p. 314
Seale
3174 Richard Mychinall
Herridge, *Surrey*, 2005, p. 316
Windlesham
3175 William Mylton
Herridge, *Surrey*, 2005, p. 327

Warwickshire
Shottery
3176 John Richardson, [husbandman]
Jones, *Stratford*, I, 2002, pp. 143-144
Stratford-on-Avon
3177 Humfrey Plymley, yeoman
Jones, *Stratford*, I, 2002, pp. 141-142

Wiltshire
Marlborough
3178 Ellen Andros
Williams and Thomson, *Marlborough*, 2007, pp. 12-13

Worcestershire
Bredon
3179 Richard Evans
West, *Village Records*, 1962, pp. 118-119
Little Comberton
3180 Roberte Willoughbie [Robert Willoughby], gentleman
Wanklyn, *Worcestershire*, 1998, pp. 90-94
Oldswinford, The Lye
3181 Richard Brookehowse, [scythesmith]
Roper, *Scythesmiths*, 1967, pp. 13-14
Worcester, St Michael Bedwardine
3182 Robert Payne, [shoemaker]
Dyer, *Worcestershire*, 1967, pp. 30-32
Worcester
3183 Antony Tollye, joiner
Macdonald, 1942, pp. 7-8

Yorkshire
Marske
3184 Gilbert Tompson
Berry, *Swaledale*, 1998, p. 314

South Cave
3185 Petronill Aire
Kaner, *South Cave*, 1994, pp. 189-190

1595
Cheshire
Malpas, Higher Wych
3186 John Bradchawe
Pearson, *Malpas*, [2005], p. 147
Shocklach
3187 Edward Povey, yeoman
Pearson, *Malpas*, [2005], pp. 145-146
Warmingham
3188 John Barloe, clergyman, parson of Warmingham
Pearson, *Malpas*, [2005], pp. 114-115
Waverton, Hatton
3189 Anthonie Large
Bland, *Christleton*, 2002, p. 87
Wrenbury, Newhall
3190 Raffe Barnett
Pixton, *Wrenbury*, 2009, pp. 35-36

Devonshire
Uffculme
3191 John Bussell, yeoman
Wyatt, *Uffculme*, 1997, p. 17
3192 John Colle [Cole], alias Kerswill
Wyatt, *Uffculme*, 1997, p. 18
Unlocated
3193 Katherine Monck, widow
Cash, *Devon*, 1966, p. 15

Dorsetshire
Sherborne
3194 Sherborne Almshouse
Moon, 1982, pp. 191-200
Yetminster
3195 John Hayward
Machin, *Yetminster*, 1976, No.12, (2 pp.)

Co. Durham
Durham
3196 Thomas Swinnoe [Swinhoe], musician
Greenwell, *Wills and Inventories*, 1860, II, p. 251

Hertfordshire
St Albans, St Stephens
3197 John Cowley, [chandler]
Parker, *Worldly Goods*, 2004, pp. 121-123
3198 John Prior
Parker, *Worldly Goods*, 2004, pp. 117-118
3199 Johane Trott
Parker, *Worldly Goods*, 2004, p. 117

Lancashire
Blackrod
3200 Hughe Watmoughe
Bolton, *Bolton*, 1994, p. 138
Bolton
3201 Richard Morris
Bolton, *Bolton*, 1987, pp. 195-197
Bradshaw
3202 Richarde Walche, husbandman
Bolton, *Bolton*, 1994, p. 136
Deane
3203 Margaret Astley
Bolton, *Bolton*, 1987, p. 12
Deane, Middle Hulton
3204 Adam Edge
Bolton, *Bolton*, 1987, pp. 82-83

Farnworth
  3205 James Rosco, husbandman
    Bolton, *Bolton*, 1994, p. 68
Prescot
  3206 Margaret Dycchefield, widow
    St Helens, *Angells*, 1999, pp. 16-17
Turton
  3207 Thomas Bromley
    Bolton, *Bolton*, 1987, p. 43
Westhoughton
  3208 Nicholas Balfronte
    Bolton, *Bolton*, 1987, p. 16

Leicestershire
Evington
  3209 John Fylke, [yeoman]
    Wilshere, *Evington*, 1985, p. 7

Lincolnshire
Market Rasen
  3210 Richard Anderton
    Neave, *Market Rasen*, 1985, p. 106
  3211 Heugh Stainforth
    Neave, *Market Rasen*, 1985, pp. 107-108

London
Lambeth
  3212 Roger Foster, victualler
    Herridge, *Surrey*, 2005, pp. 322-323
Lambeth Deane
  3213 Robert Wardell, blacksmith
    Herridge, *Surrey*, 2005, pp. 329-330
Southwark
  3214 Tristram Blabye, gentleman
    Herridge, *Surrey*, 2005, p. 318

Northamptonshire
Overthorpe
  3215 William Larden alias Tailor, husbandman
    Brinkworth and Gibson, *Banbury*, I, 1975, pp. 137-138

Oxfordshire
Banbury
  3216 Robert Edens [Yeedens, Edoms], alderman
    Brinkworth and Gibson, *Banbury*, I, 1975, p. 140
Banbury, Calthorpe
  3217 Hanry Hale [Hall, Hole], yeoman
    Brinkworth and Gibson, *Banbury*, I, 1975, p. 138
  3218 Margaret Harrys [Harris], widow
    Brinkworth and Gibson, *Banbury*, I, 1975, pp. 135-136

Staffordshire
Smethwick
  3219 George Byrche, yeoman
    Guest, 1997, pp. 193-195

Surrey
Chertsey
  3220 Thomas Bushe, husbandman
    Herridge, *Surrey*, 2005, pp. 318-319
Chiddingfold
  3221 Henry Rapley, servant
    Herridge, *Surrey*, 2005, pp. 328-329
Cobham
  3222 Elizabeth Goddard, widow
    Herridge, *Surrey*, 2005, p. 324
Dorking
  3223 John Fuller, carpenter
    Herridge, *Surrey*, 2005, pp. 323-324

Egham
  3224 Roger Crose, yeoman
    Herridge, *Surrey*, 2005, pp. 319-320
Milford
  3225 Robert Hooke, yeoman
    Herridge, *Surrey*, 2005, pp. 324-325
Shalford
  3226 Robert Elliot, yeoman
    Herridge, *Surrey*, 2005, pp. 321-322
Stoke D'Abernon
  3227 Michaell Winge
    Herridge, *Surrey*, 2005, pp. 330-331
West Horsley
  3228 William Marshall, labourer
    Herridge, *Surrey*, 2005, p. 326
  3229 Elizabeth Stint, widow
    Herridge, *Surrey*, 2005, p. 329
Windlesham
  3230 William Phillip
    Herridge, *Surrey*, 2005, pp. 327-328

Warwickshire
Birmingham
  3231 John Bennett
    Holt, Ingram, Jarman, *Birmingham*, 1985, pp. 63-64
Foleshill
  3232 Wyllm Ashmore, [yeoman]
    Upton, *Foleshill*, 1993, pp. 62-63
  3233 Richard Chestlen
    Upton, *Foleshill*, 1993, pp. 65-66
Stratford-on-Avon
  3234 William Bainton
    Jones, *Stratford*, I, 2002, pp. 151-152
Stratford-on-Avon, Old Stratford
  3235 Richard Baker, husbandman
    Jones, *Stratford*, I, 2002, pp. 149-150
Stratford-on-Avon
  3236 Michaell Shacleton [Shackleton], [shearman]
    Jones, *Stratford*, I, 2002, pp. 153-154
  3237 Julia Stevens, [widow]
    Jones, *Stratford*, I, 2002, p. 145
  3238 Mr Thomas Trussell, [lawyer]
    Jones, *Stratford*, I, 2002, pp. 154-155
  3239 Robert Yong [Young], dyer
    Jones, *Stratford*, I, 2002, pp. 146-148

Wiltshire
Marlborough
  3240 John Romsey, hosier
    Williams and Thomson, *Marlborough*, 2007, p. 13

Worcestershire
Belbroughton, Bromehill
  3241 John Cole
    Roper, *Belbroughton*, 1967-1968, p. 42

Yorkshire
Downholme, Walburn
  3242 John Lonsdaile
    Berry, *Swaledale*, 1998, p. 316
Fixby
  3243 Richard Thornill [Thornhill]
    Brears, *Yorkshire*, 1972, pp. 57-58
Gilling Castle
  3244 Sir William Fairfax
    Peacock, *Inventories*, 1884, pp. 123-136

Grinton, Whitaside
 3245 Anthony Spenselay
 Berry, *Swaledale*, 1998, p. 319
Grinton, Low Row
 3246 John Freer
 Berry, *Swaledale*, 1998, p. 324
South Cave
 3247 Thomas Simsonn [Simson]
 Kaner, *South Cave*, 1994, p. 191

1595 (c.)
Surrey
Cobham
 3248 Henry Feilde, yeoman
 Herridge, *Surrey*, 2005, pp. 321-322

1596
Berkshire
Faringdon
 Sir Henrie Unton (see Wadley)
Wadley
 3249 Sir Henrie Unton (also listed Faringdon)
 Nichols, *Unton*, 1841, pp. 1-14
Cheshire
Chester
 3250 Hugh Bellot, clergyman, bishop of Chester
 Piccope, *Lancashire and Cheshire*, 1860, pp. 1-8
Malpas, Charlton
 3251 Randulph Mylton, husbandman
 Pearson, *Malpas*, [2005], p. 149
Stockport
 3252 John Smyth, baker
 Phillips and Smith, *Stockport*, 1985, pp. 20-24
Tarvin, Oscroft
 3253 Roberte Blease
 Bland, *Christleton*, 2002, pp. 90-91
Tarvin, Foulk Stapleford
 3254 John Blyth, husbandman
 Bland, *Christleton*, 2002, p. 92
Tarvin, Stapleford
 3255 Raffe Bordman, smith
 Bland, *Christleton*, 2002, pp. 93-94
Tarvin, Duddon
 3256 Richard Mylner, husbandman
 Bland, *Christleton*, 2002, p. 89
Waverton
 3257 Piter Rawlinson, husbandman
 Bland, *Christleton*, 2002, pp. 96-97
Derbyshire
Glossop, Roworth
 3258 John Goddard
 Lee and Miller, *New Mills*, 1999, pp. 25-26
Glossop, Mousley Bottom
 3259 Gerveys Haigh, [husbandman]
 Lee and Miller, *New Mills*, 1999, pp. 28-29
Newbold
 3260 Homfraye Roland
 Bestall and Fowkes, *Chesterfield*, 1977, pp. 241-242
Devonshire
Uffculme
 3261 Thomas Cotterell [Cottrell]
 Wyatt, *Uffculme*, 1997, p. 21
 3262 Robert Mydelton [Middleton]
 Wyatt, *Uffculme*, 1997, pp. 18-19

 3263 Mary Saunder, widow
 Wyatt, *Uffculme*, 1997, p. 19
Dorsetshire
Yetminster
 3264 John Beard
 Machin, *Yetminster*, 1976, No.13, (2 pp.)
Yetminster [?]
 3265 Thomas Warr
 Machin, *Yetminster*, 1976, No.14, (1 p.)
Co. Durham
Barnard Castle
 3266 Ambrose Mason, dyer
 Greenwell, *Wills and Inventories*, 1860, II, pp. 258-259
Eppleton
 3267 Sir Cuthburt Collingwoode [Collingwood]
 Greenwell, *Wills and Inventories*, 1860, II, pp. 270-272
Ryton
 3268 John Nelson, clergyman
 Raine, *Barnes*, 1850, p. cxxxiv
Twissell
 3269 Sir John Selbye [Selby]
 Greenwell, *Wills and Inventories*, 1860, II, pp. 257-258
Hertfordshire
Sarratt
 3270 John Lovet
 Bullen, *Sarratt*, [1982], p. 58
Lancashire
Bolton, Halliwell
 3271 Richard Marshe
 Bolton, *Bolton*, 1987, pp. 183-184
Bolton, Anglezarke
 3272 Hughe Pylkington, husbandman
 Bolton, *Bolton*, 1994, p. 47
Leicestershire
Evington
 3273 Peter Winter, [husbandman]
 Wilshere, *Evington*, 1985, p. 8
Lincolnshire
Allington
 3274 Hughe Johnsonne, labourer
 Pask, *Allington*, 1989, p. 45
Barrow-on-Humber
 3275 John Wilkyne, [yeoman]
 Johnson and Johnson, 1934, pp. 179-180
Norfolk
Lingwood (?)
 3276 Richard Trendell, chapman
 Spufford, *Reclothing*, 1984, pp. 158-160
Northamptonshire
Warkworth
 3277 John Snason alias Tafftes [Toftes], labourer
 Brinkworth and Gibson, *Banbury*, I, 1975, p. 141
Northumberland
Newcastle
 3278 Mr Robert Atkynson, merchant and alderman
 Greenwell, *Wills and Inventories*, 1860, II, pp. 254-264
Nottinghamshire
Wollaton
 3279 Sir Francis Willoughby
 Marshall, *Wollaton*, 1996, pp. 100-102
 3280 Sir Francis Willoughby
 Marshall, *Wollaton*, 1996, pp. 103-105

Oxfordshire
Water Eaton
3281 John Bellcher, [yeoman]
Offord, *Water Eaton*, 1986, p. 6
Scotland
Clackmannanshire, Castle Campbell (Gloume), Dollar
3282 Archibald Campbell, Earl of Argyll
Campbell, 1913, pp. 301-304
Edinburgh
3283 Katherine Norvell
Anon., *Bassandyne*, 1836, pp. 208-220
Suffolk
Ipswich
3284 Thomas Evered, chandler
Reed, *Ipswich*, 1981, pp. 48-49
Surrey
Bramley
3285 William Deringe, yeoman
Herridge, *Surrey*, 2005, p. 335
Chertsey
3286 William Cutt, husbandman
Herridge, *Surrey*, 2005, pp. 332-333
Chobham
3287 John Payne, husbandman
Herridge, *Surrey*, 2005, pp. 338-339
Epsom
3288 Agnes Tegg, widow
Herridge, *Surrey*, 2005, p. 343
Fetcham
3289 John Roger
Herridge, *Surrey*, 2005, p. 340
Fetcham, Cannon Court
3290 John Steven, yeoman
Herridge, *Surrey*, 2005, pp. 340-342
Oxted
3291 Robert Fowle, husbandman
Herridge, *Surrey*, 2005, pp. 335-336
Shere
3292 Rychard Davye, sawyer
Herridge, *Surrey*, 2005, pp. 333-334
Thursley
3293 John Marner the elder
Herridge, *Surrey*, 2005, pp. 337-338
3294 John Marner the younger
Herridge, *Surrey*, 2005, p. 338
Walton-upon-Thames
3295 John Cooke, parish clerk
Herridge, *Surrey*, 2005, pp. 331-332
West Clandon
3296 Henry Ligeard
Herridge, *Surrey*, 2005, pp. 336-337
Woking
3297 John Pen
Herridge, *Surrey*, 2005, pp. 339-340
Wonersh, Northowe
3298 Richard Ticknor, yeoman
Herridge, *Surrey*, 2005, pp. 343-344
Warwickshire
Stratford-on-Avon
3299 Anne Hickoxe [Hiccox], widow
Jones, *Stratford*, I, 2002, pp. 157-160
3300 Elizabeth Nott, widow
Jones, *Stratford*, I, 2002, pp. 156-157

Westmorland
Casterton
3301 James Hardy
Hardy, 1913, p. 23
Worcestershire
Belbroughton
3302 John Wakman, scythesmith
Roper, *Belbroughton*, 1967-1968, p. 43
Worcester, St Martin
3303 Adam Wilson, draper
Dyer, *Worcestershire*, 1967, pp. 10-12
Yorkshire
Grinton, Crackpot
3304 Stephen Blaides
Berry, *Swaledale*, 1998, pp. 320-321
Grinton, Low Row
3305 John Freer
Berry, *Swaledale*, 1998, p. 324
Knaresborough, Tentergate
3306 John Nettleton
Brears, *Yorkshire*, 1972, pp. 59-61
Marske
3307 John Dowson
Berry, *Swaledale*, 1998, pp. 328-329
Marske, Skelton, Moor House
3308 John Huchingson
Berry, *Swaledale*, 1998, p. 322
South Cave
3309 John Tomlinson
Kaner, *South Cave*, 1994, pp. 192-193

1596 (c.)
Surrey
Dunsfold
3310 Thomas Woodier, labourer
Herridge, *Surrey*, 2005, p. 344

1597
Cheshire
Broxton
3311 George Dod, gentleman
Pearson, *Malpas*, [2005], p. 160
Christleton
3312 Ales Brine, widow
Bland, *Christleton*, 2002, p. 98
Malpas, Carden
3313 Jhon Clutton
Pearson, *Malpas*, [2005], pp. 152-153
Malpas, Higher Wych
3314 Richarde Estwycke, yeoman
Pearson, *Malpas*, [2005], pp. 155-156
Tarvin
3315 Margret Catherow
Bland, *Christleton*, 2002, p. 97
Tarvin, Hoofield
3316 Richarde Nielde, husbandman
Bland, *Christleton*, 2002, pp. 100-101
Wrenbury, Chorley
3317 Elizabeth Patrick alias Wilson
Pixton, *Wrenbury*, 2009, p. 40
Cumberland
Workington
3318 Sir Henry Curwen,
Jackson, *Curwens*, 1881, pp. 314-317

Derbyshire
Chesterfield
3319 John Cleworthe, glover
Bestall and Fowkes, *Chesterfield*, 1977, pp. 242-243
3320 Raphe Heathcott, tanner
Bestall and Fowkes, *Chesterfield*, 1977, pp. 245-246
3321 Jude Kayndricke, locksmith
Bestall and Fowkes, *Chesterfield*, 1977, pp. 247-249
3322 Alban Leeke
Bestall and Fowkes, *Chesterfield*, 1977, pp. 243-245
Glossop, Whittle
3323 Edward Bore [Blore]
Lee and Miller, *New Mills*, 1999, pp. 34-35
Glossop, Holecrofthouse
3324 Richard Selvester, [husbandman]
Lee and Miller, *New Mills*, 1999, pp. 33-34

Devonshire
Exeter
3325 John Fawell, yeoman
Portman, *Exeter*, 1966, pp. 99-101
3326 Richard Hedgland, joiner
Portman, *Exeter*, 1966, pp. 98-99
Uffculme
3327 Roberte Westcoumbe [Westcombe], husbandman
Wyatt, *Uffculme*, 1997, pp. 21-23
3328 Alice Woode [Wood], widow
Wyatt, *Uffculme*, 1997, pp23-24

Dorsetshire
Stratton
3329 Robert Croome
Willsher, 2002, p. 43

Co. Durham
Crook Hall
3330 Ralph Billingham, gentleman
Greenwell, *Wills and Inventories*, 1860, II, p. 279
Durham
3331 John Farbeck, [mercer and alderman]
Greenwell, *Wills and Inventories*, 1860, II, pp. 281-283
Langton
3332 John Burrell
Hodgson, *Wills and Inventories*, 1906, III, pp. 166-167
St Andrew Auckland, Old Park
3333 Robert Claxton
Greenwell, *Wills and Inventories*, 1860, II, p. 296

Hertfordshire
St Albans, St Stephens
3334 Roberte Antrobus
Parker, *Worldly Goods*, 2004, pp. 123-125
3335 Ambrose Mylforde
Parker, *Worldly Goods*, 2004, pp. 126-127

Kent
Sandwich
3336 Fraunceis Walker, widow
Shaw, 1870, p. 230

Lancashire
Belmont, Hordern
3337 Thomas Bromilaye [Bromeley], husbandman
Bolton, *Bolton*, 1987, pp. 37-38
Bolton, Edgworth
3338 Edward Hobkinson, husbandman
Bolton, *Bolton*, 1987, p. 142

Bolton, Halliwell
3339 Richard Mershe
Bolton, *Bolton*, 1987, p. 188
Bolton
3340 Roger Warmsley, yeoman
Bolton, *Bolton*, 1994, pp. 132-134
Eccles, Booths
3341 John Heye [Hey], [linen weaver]
Lowe, 1972, pp. 105-106
Horwich
3342 Nicholas Whitle, yeoman
Bolton, *Bolton*, 1994, pp. 141-142
Rivington
3343 Williame Barns
Bolton, *Bolton*, 1987, p. 18

Lincolnshire
Clee
3344 Robert Barchard, clergyman, vicar of Clee
Ambler, Watkinson, *Clee*, 1987, p. 99
3344a William Sutton, husbandman
Ambler, Watkinson, *Clee*, 1987, pp. 98-99
Clee, Oole
3345 Jhon West
Ambler, Watkinson, *Clee*, 1987, pp. 99-100

London
Peckham
3346 William Plogg
Herridge, *Surrey*, 2005, pp. 353-355
3347 Isabell Savage, widow
Herridge, *Surrey*, 2005, pp. 355-356

Northumberland
Eslington
3348 Thomas Collingoode [Collingwood], esquire
Greenwell, *Wills and Inventories*, 1860, II, p. 268
Newcastle
3349 John Carre [Carr], merchant
Greenwell, *Wills and Inventories*, 1860, II, pp. 298-299
3350 William Greenwell, merchant and alderman
Greenwell, *Wills and Inventories*, 1860, II, pp. 266-267

Oxfordshire
Banbury
3351 Anthonie Greene, carpenter
Brinkworth and Gibson, *Banbury*, I, 1975, pp. 142-143
Banbury, Neithrop
3352 Annis Robins
Brinkworth and Gibson, *Banbury*, I, 1975, pp. 141-142
3353 Richard Sowtham, yeoman
Brinkworth and Gibson, *Banbury*, I, 1975, pp. 143-144
Banbury
3354 William Tomkins, shepherd
Brinkworth and Gibson, *Banbury*, I, 1975, p. 144

Surrey
Ash
3355 Edward Crauly, husbandman
Herridge, *Surrey*, 2005, pp. 345-346
3356 Henry Eede, yeoman
Herridge, *Surrey*, 2005, pp. 347-349
Ash, Henley Park
3357 Thomas Thorp, yeoman
Herridge, *Surrey*, 2005, pp. 360-361
Chobham
3358 Richard Edmeade, husbandman
Herridge, *Surrey*, 2005, pp. 346-347

Eashing
3359 Rychard Stylwell, husbandman
Herridge, *Surrey*, 2005, pp. 359-360
Farnham
3360 Henry Martin, glover
Herridge, *Surrey*, 2005, pp. 352-353
Guildford, St Nicholas
3361 Thomas Key, clergyman, parson
Evans, 1856-1859, pp. 182-183
Herridge, *Surrey*, 2005, pp. 350-352
Seale, Hampton
3362 James Rysse
Herridge, *Surrey*, 2005, p. 355
Shackleford
3363 Katherine Vine, gentlewoman
Herridge, *Surrey*, 2005, pp. 361-363
Sutton
3364 Jefferie Smith, yeoman
Herridge, *Surrey*, 2005, pp. 356-357
Tilford
3365 Thomas Hardinge, husbandman
Herridge, *Surrey*, 2005, p. 350
Witley
3366 Henry Edwardes
Herridge, *Surrey*, 2005, p. 347
Worplesdon
3367 Henry Martin, weaver
Herridge, *Surrey*, 2005, p. 353
3368 Richard Stanbridge, beer brewer
Herridge, *Surrey*, 2005, pp. 358-359
Wrecclesham
3369 John Foster, yeoman
Herridge, *Surrey*, 2005, p. 349

Wales
Flintshire, Iscoed
3370 Richard Paynter, shoemaker
Pearson, *Malpas*, [2005], pp. 158-159

Warwickshire
Birmingham
3371 Roger Sheldon
Holt, Ingram, Jarman, *Birmingham*, 1985, p. 64
Foleshill
3372 William Hache, [labourer]
Upton, *Foleshill*, 1993, pp. 67-68
Stoneleigh
3373 Henry Waren, fuller
Alcock, *Warwickshire*, 1993, p. 32
Stratford-on-Avon
3374 Thomas Ballamy [Balamy], labourer
Jones, *Stratford*, I, 2002, pp. 168-169
3375 Robert Byddle [Biddle], shoemaker
Jones, *Stratford*, I, 2002, pp. 172-174
3376 William Cootes, skinner
Jones, *Stratford*, I, 2002, pp. 169-170
3377 Joane Patrick, almswoman
Jones, *Stratford*, I, 2002, p. 171
3378 Henry Rogers, [butcher]
Jones, *Stratford*, I, 2002, pp. 166-167
3379 Wylliam Rogers, sergeant-at-mace [mercer and victualler]
Jones, *Stratford*, I, 2002, pp. 160-165
Warwick
3380 Amilion Holbache, gentleman
Anon., *Warwickshire*, 1860, pp. 200-208

Yorkshire
Downholme
3381 William Lofthus
Berry, *Swaledale*, 1998, pp. 331-332
Downholme, Wathgill
3382 Ralph Scrafton
Berry, *Swaledale*, 1998, pp. 339-341
Grinton, Birkdale
3383 John Alderson
Berry, *Swaledale*, 1998, pp. 344-345
Grinton, Reeth
3384 John Carter
Berry, *Swaledale*, 1998, pp. 334-335
3385 Peter Cowplande
Berry, *Swaledale*, 1998, pp. 336-337
Grinton, Melbecks
3386 John Frear
Berry, *Swaledale*, 1998, pp. 341-342
Grinton, Keld
3387 Simon Harcay
Berry, *Swaledale*, 1998, p. 343
Lunds
3388 Rawlande Parkinge [Rowland Parkin]
Thwaite, *Abbotside*, 1967, p. 21
Marske, Skelton
3389 Henry Hodgeson
Berry, *Swaledale*, 1998, p. 347
South Cave
3390 Steven Cottam, [blacksmith]
Kaner, *South Cave*, 1994, pp. 194-196
3391 John Emersonn [Emerson]
Kaner, *South Cave*, 1994, pp. 196-198
3392 Robert Tenan alias Robinson
Kaner, *South Cave*, 1994, p. 194

1597 (c.)
Devonshire
Colyton
3393 John Knowles
Cash, *Devon*, 1966, p. 15

1598
Cambridgeshire
Cambridge, King's College
3394 The Colledge Chambers
Bradshaw, 1864-1876, pp. 183-194
Cheshire
Broxton
3395 Harry Smithes, husbandman
Pearson, *Malpas*, [2005], p. 165
Tarvin, Stapleford
3396 John Bostocke, husbandman
Bland, *Christleton*, 2002, pp. 102-103
Tattenhall
3397 Cisely Speede, widow
Bland, *Christleton*, 2002, p. 106
Cumberland
Burgh by Sands
3398 Thomas Threlkelde, bailiff of Burgh
Jackson, 1889, pp. 43-44
Derbyshire
Brimington
3399 Henry Parker, yeoman
Bestall and Fowkes, *Chesterfield*, 1977, p. 257

Calow
3400 Henry Stubbinge
Bestall and Fowkes, *Chesterfield*, 1977, pp. 250-251
Chesterfield
3401 Thomas Cottrell
Bestall and Fowkes, *Chesterfield*, 1977, p. 253
3402 Robert Eyre
Bestall and Fowkes, *Chesterfield*, 1977, pp. 258-259
3403 Elizabeth Humston
Bestall and Fowkes, *Chesterfield*, 1977, pp. 249-250
Glossop, Thornsett Fields
3404 Richard Bramall
Lee and Miller, *New Mills*, 1999, pp. 38-39
Glossop, Stryndes
3405 Nicholas Wombwell, gentleman
Lee and Miller, *New Mills*, 1999, pp. 41-42
Newbold
3406 Thomas Knowles
Bestall and Fowkes, *Chesterfield*, 1977, pp. 254-255
3407 Richard Newbold
Bestall and Fowkes, *Chesterfield*, 1977, p. 252
Walton
3408 James Bramhall alias Swindell
Bestall and Fowkes, *Chesterfield*, 1977, pp. 255-256

Devonshire
Alverdiscott
3409 Arthur Lippincotte, esquire
Cash, *Devon*, 1966, pp. 15-16
Uffculme
3410 John Marshall
Wyatt, *Uffculme*, 1997, p. 24

Dorsetshire
Yetminster
3411 Robert Piddle, parchment maker
Machin, *Yetminster*, 1976, No.15, (1 p.)

Co. Durham
Monkwearmouth
3412 Robert Wodrington [Widdrington], esquire
Greenwell, *Wills and Inventories*, 1860, II, pp. 286-288

Hertfordshire
St Albans, St Stephens
3413 Robert Kentishe, yeoman
Munby, *Worldly Goods*, 1991, pp. 76-78
3414 Richard Knowlton, [yeoman]
Parker, *Worldly Goods*, 2004, pp. 128-129
Sarratt
3415 Richard Renouldes
Bullen, *Sarratt*, [1982], pp. 59-60

Kent
Cranbrook
3416 John Hollands, husbandman
Melling, 1965, p. 16

Lancashire
Bolton
3417 William Halliwell, merchant
Bolton, *Bolton*, 1987, pp. 131-134
Bolton, Edgworth
3418 James Knowles, husbandman
Bolton, *Bolton*, 1987, pp. 166-167
Deane
3419 Joone Cheetam, widow
Bolton, *Bolton*, 1987, p. 50

Farnworth
3420 Henry Grunedye
Bolton, *Bolton*, 1987, p. 122
3421 Richard Scolecraft, yeoman
Bolton, *Bolton*, 1994, pp. 73-74
Horwich
3422 George Urmistone
Bolton, *Bolton*, 1994, p. 121
Little Lever
3423 Thomas Bouthe
Bolton, *Bolton*, 1987, p. 27
Parr
3424 Elizabeth Ellom
St Helens, *Angells*, 1999, pp. 20-21
Prestwich, Tonge
3425 William Greenhalhe, webster
Bolton, *Bolton*, 1987, pp. 112-113
Rochdale
3426 Edward Butterworth, [woollen weaver]
Lowe, 1972, p. 106
St Helens, Eccleston
3427 Margrete Dronninge, widow
St Helens, *Angells*, 1999, pp. 19-20
Salford
3428 George Houlte [Holt], [woollen clothier]
Lowe, 1972, pp. 106-112
Turton
3429 William Pilkyngton, tanner
Bolton, *Bolton*, 1994, pp. 53-54

Leicestershire
Evington
3430 William Burly, [husbandman]
Wilshere, *Evington*, 1985, p. 9

Lincolnshire
Clee
3431 William Neave
Ambler, Watkinson, *Clee*, 1987, p. 103
3432 Leonarde Pell, husbandman
Ambler, Watkinson, *Clee*, 1987, pp. 100-101
3433 Richard Pickering
Ambler, Watkinson, *Clee*, 1987, pp. 101-103

Northamptonshire
Nethercote
3434 John Grene, husbandman
Brinkworth and Gibson, *Banbury*, I, 1975, pp. 150-152

Northumberland
Warkworth, Togston
3435 George Horsley
Hodgson, *Wills and Inventories*, 1906, III, p. 165

Oxfordshire
Banbury
3436 Joane Greene, widow
Brinkworth and Gibson, *Banbury*, I, 1975, p. 145
3437 John Jurdaine [Jourden, Jurdenn]
Brinkworth and Gibson, *Banbury*, I, 1975, p. 146
3438 John Mayoe [Maio], miller
Brinkworth and Gibson, *Banbury*, I, 1975, p. 149
3439 George Richardes
Brinkworth and Gibson, *Banbury*, I, 1975, pp. 149-150
3440 James Sawbridge alias Richardson, alderman
Brinkworth and Gibson, *Banbury*, I, 1975, p. 147
3441 Thomas Smyth, shoemaker
Brinkworth and Gibson, *Banbury*, I, 1975, p. 145

Scotland
Perthshire, Balloch Castle
  Sir Duncan Campbell (see Finlarg Castle)
Perthshire, Finlarg Castle
  3442 Sir Duncan Campbell (also listed Balloch Castle)
    Innes, 1855, pp. 319-335
Staffordshire
Dudley
  3443 George Gresbrocke
    Roper, *Dudley*, 1965, p. 56
Suffolk
Ipswich
  3444 John Fellgate
    Reed, *Ipswich*, 1981, p. 50
Surrey
Alfold
  3445 Richard Deane, husbandman
    Herridge, *Surrey*, 2005, pp. 363-364
Frensham
  3446 Richard Pereson, tailor
    Herridge, *Surrey*, 2005, pp. 367-368
Kingston-upon-Thames
  3447 Catherine Hills, widow
    Herridge, *Surrey*, 2005, pp. 364-366
Long Ditton
  3448 Henry Pencoste, matchmaker
    Herridge, *Surrey*, 2005, pp. 366-367
Witley
  3449 Thomas Stilwell, yeoman
    Herridge, *Surrey*, 2005, pp. 368-369
Warwickshire
Shottery
  3450 John Rychardson [Richardson]
    Jones, *Stratford*, I, 2002, p. 177
Stoneleigh, Stareton
  3451 Thomas Tuter, husbandman
    Alcock, *Warwickshire*, 1993, p. 35
Stratford-on-Avon, Drayton
  3452 Richard Barbur, husbandman
    Jones, *Stratford*, I, 2002, pp. 174-176
Stratford-on-Avon
  3453 Simon Hunt, [schoolmaster]
    Jones, *Stratford*, I, 2002, pp. 176-177
Wiltshire
Marlborough
  3454 Richard Franckelyn, sawyer
    Williams and Thomson, *Marlborough*, 2007, pp. 13-14
Worcestershire
Belbroughton
  3455 William Smithe
    Roper, *Belbroughton*, 1967-1968, p. 50
  3456 Thomas Smythe
    Roper, *Belbroughton*, 1967-1968, p. 49
Yorkshire
Grinton, Fremington
  3457 Simon Hamond
    Berry, *Swaledale*, 1998, pp. 356-357
Grinton, Gunnerside
  3458 Anthony Kearton
    Berry, *Swaledale*, 1998, p. 346
Grinton, Angram
  3459 Christopher Shaw
    Berry, *Swaledale*, 1998, pp. 349-350

Knaresborough
  3460 Leonard Fawcett
    Brears, *Yorkshire*, 1972, pp. 61-62
Lunds
  3461 Elizabeth Morland
    Thwaite, *Abbotside*, 1967, p. 23
Marske
  3462 Christopher Browne
    Berry, *Swaledale*, 1998, p. 354
South Cave, Faxfleet
  3463 Agnes Atkinson
    Kaner, *South Cave*, 1994, p. 200
South Cave
  3464 Agnes Boore
    Kaner, *South Cave*, 1994, p. 202
South Cave, Oxmardyke
  3465 Thomas Gott
    Kaner, *South Cave*, 1994, pp. 203-204
  3466 Thomas Johnson
    Kaner, *South Cave*, 1994, pp. 201-202
  3467 Henrye Lamley
    Kaner, *South Cave*, 1994, p. 199

1599
Cheshire
Astbury
  3468 Dame Mary Egerton, widow of Sir Richard Egerton
    Piccope, *Lancashire and Cheshire*, 1860, pp. 275-276
Bickerton
  3469 William Collye, husbandman
    Pearson, *Malpas*, [2005], pp. 169-170
Malpas
  3470 Ales Hatton, widow
    Pearson, *Malpas*, [2005], p. 173
Stockport
  3471 Raphe Hunt, [yeoman]
    Phillips and Smith, *Stockport*, 1985, pp. 26-27
  3472 Roberte Shawe, carpenter
    Phillips and Smith, *Stockport*, 1985, p. 25
Stretton
  3473 Charles Bagot, husbandman
    Pearson, *Malpas*, [2005], pp. 168-169
Tarvin, Oscroft
  3474 Marie Mores, widow
    Bland, *Christleton*, 2002, pp. 111-112
Tattenhall
  3475 John Astbrooke, husbandman
    Bland, *Christleton*, 2002, pp. 108-109
  3476 Ellen Nicall, widow
    Bland, *Christleton*, 2002, p. 110
  3477 Ellen Tylston, widow
    Bland, *Christleton*, 2002, pp. 110-111
Cumberland
Corby
  3478 George Salkeld
    Moore, *Salkelds*, 1988, p. 179
Derbyshire
Brimington
  3479 Godfrey Bingham
    Bestall and Fowkes, *Chesterfield*, 1977, pp. 263-264
  3480 Robert Parker
    Bestall and Fowkes, *Chesterfield*, 1977, p. 262

Calow
3481 Henry Duckemanton
Bestall and Fowkes, *Chesterfield*, 1977, p. 263
3482 Henry Stubbing, scholar
Bestall and Fowkes, *Chesterfield*, 1977, p. 265
Chesterfield
3483 Rowland Bowne
Bestall and Fowkes, *Chesterfield*, 1977, pp. 264-265
3484 Henry Dyckons, glover, and Alice Dyckons
Bestall and Fowkes, *Chesterfield*, 1977, pp. 260-262
3485 John Fletcher
Bestall and Fowkes, *Chesterfield*, 1977, pp. 257-258
3486 George Shearshawe, tanner
Bestall and Fowkes, *Chesterfield*, 1977, pp. 266-267
Glossop, Haigh
3487 Elizabeth Hyde
Lee and Miller, *New Mills*, 1999, pp. 42-43
Glossop, Thornsett Bank
3488 Richarde Warrington, shearman
Lee and Miller, *New Mills*, 1999, p. 45
Walton
3489 John Eliott
Bestall and Fowkes, *Chesterfield*, 1977, p. 259
Devonshire
Uffculme
3490 William Read
Wyatt, *Uffculme*, 1997, pp. 24-26
Dorsetshire
Yetminster
3491 Roger Willmonth
Machin, *Yetminster*, 1976, No.16, (2 pp.)
Co. Durham
Sedgefield
3492 Robert Swift, attorney, of Lincoln's Inn
Hodgson, *Wills and Inventories*, 1906, III, p. 176
Stanhope
3493 Anne Navell [Neville], widow
Greenwell, *Wills and Inventories*, 1860, II, p. 337
Hertfordshire
St Albans, St Stephens
3494 Cicileye Ewer, widow
Parker, *Worldly Goods*, 2004, pp. 138-139
3495 George Ewer
Parker, *Worldly Goods*, 2004, pp. 136-137
3496 Agnes Lane, widow
Parker, *Worldly Goods*, 2004, pp. 134-135
3497 Robert Nutkyn
Parker, *Worldly Goods*, 2004, pp. 131-132
3498 Thomas Selbye
Parker, *Worldly Goods*, 2004, p. 145
Sarratt
3499 Henry Horwood, [husbandman]
Bullen, *Sarratt*, [1982], pp. 61-62
Lancashire
Blackrod
3500 John Vausse
Bolton, *Bolton*, 1994, p. 127
Bolton, Entwistle
3501 Cissolye Entwisle
Bolton, *Bolton*, 1987, p. 91
Bolton, Brightmet
3502 Lawrance Greenhalghe, husbandman
Bolton, *Bolton*, 1987, p. 104

Deane, Rumworth
3503 William Edge
Bolton, *Bolton*, 1987, p. 88
Farnworth
3504 Margret Cheetham
Bolton, *Bolton*, 1987, pp. 52-53
Lincolnshire
Allington
3505 Thomas Abels [Abell]
Pask, *Allington*, 1989, p. 47
Clee
3506 Leonard Curtes, gentleman
Ambler, Watkinson, *Clee*, 1987, pp. 104-105
Cleethorpes
3507 Bryane Yates
Ambler, Watkinson, *Clee*, 1987, pp. 103-104
Market Rasen
3508 Thomas Argrams
Neave, *Market Rasen*, 1985, p. 108
Northamptonshire
Nethercote
3509 Elizabeth Goodrytche [Goodritche, Guddriche], widow
Brinkworth and Gibson, *Banbury*, I, 1975, pp. 154-156
Northumberland
Newcastle
3510 Henrye [Henry] Mitford, merchant
Hodgson, *Wills and Inventories*, 1906, III, p. 173
Willimoteswick
3511 William Ridly [Ridley], esquire
Greenwell, *Wills and Inventories*, 1860, II, pp. 335-336
Nottinghamshire
Sneinton
3512 Hewghe Hemsley, husbandman
Stevenson, *Nottingham*, 1889, pp. 292-252
Wollaton
3513 Sir Percival Willoughby
Marshall, *Wollaton*, 1996, pp. 105-107
Oxfordshire
Banbury, Neithrop
3514 John Bushill, husbandman
Brinkworth and Gibson, *Banbury*, I, 1975, p. 153
Banbury
3515 Thomas Hadley, ironmonger
Brinkworth and Gibson, *Banbury*, I, 1975, p. 157
Banbury, Wickham
3516 John Humfrys
Brinkworth and Gibson, *Banbury*, I, 1975, p. 152
Shropshire
Condover
3517 Thomas Owen, Justice of the bench
Anon., *Condover*, 1949-1950, pp. 200-206
Shrewsbury
3518 Shrewsbury Free Grammar School
Oldham, 1933-1934, pp. 122-133
Suffolk
Ipswich
3519 Peter Inglishe
Reed, *Ipswich*, 1981, pp. 50-51
3520 Mathew Nicholas, mariner
Reed, *Ipswich*, 1981, pp. 51-52
3521 John Pye, glasier
Reed, *Ipswich*, 1981, pp. 52-53

Surrey

Albury, Weston
  3522 Edward Aburne, husbandman
    Herridge, *Surrey*, 2005, p. 369
Farnham
  3523 Margarett Bennet, widow
    Herridge, *Surrey*, 2005, pp. 370-371
  3524 Andrew Fellmore, servant
    Herridge, *Surrey*, 2005, p. 374
Long Ditton
  3525 John Brownewend, clergyman, parson
    Herridge, *Surrey*, 2005, pp. 371-374
Reigate
  3526 William Arnoulde, yeoman
    Herridge, *Surrey*, 2005, p. 270

Warwickshire

Bishopton
  3527 William Baule [Ball], [labourer]
    Jones, *Stratford*, I, 2002, p. 179
Coventry
  3528 Thomas Fynis, [mercer]
    Hulton and Castle, *Tudor*, 1987, pp. 72-80
Foleshill
  3529 John Oldernes
    Upton, *Foleshill*, 1993, pp. 69-72
Stratford-on-Avon
  3530 Jone [Joan] Griffyn, widow
    Jones, *Stratford*, I, 2002, p. 178

Worcestershire

Belbroughton
  3531 Edward Raibold
    Roper, *Belbroughton*, 1967-1968, pp. 45-46

Yorkshire

Bainbridge, Brockhill Cote
  3532 Edwarde Guye [Edward Guy]
    Thwaite, *Abbotside*, 1967, p. 24
Grinton, Birkdale
  3533 William Fawcett
    Berry, *Swaledale*, 1998, pp. 350-351
Grinton, Muker, Ravenseat
  3534 John Rawe, husbandman
    Berry, *Swaledale*, 1998, pp. 352-353
Knaresborough
  3535 Peter Hardcastell [Hardcastle]
    Brears, *Yorkshire*, 1972, pp. 62-63
South Cave
  3536 Robert Freeman, [tailor, labourer]
    Kaner, *South Cave*, 1994, pp. 204-205
  3537 Agnes Wright
    Kaner, *South Cave*, 1994, p. 206

1600

Cheshire

Malpas, Newton
  3538 Hughe Probyn, husbandman
    Pearson, *Malpas*, [2005], pp. 174-175
Malpas, Oldcastle
  3539 Elizabeth Gruffieth
    Pearson, *Malpas*, [2005], p. 185
Stockport, Brinnington
  Henrie Seele, yeoman (see Stockport)

Stockport
  3540 Henrie Seele, yeoman (also listed Stockport,
  Brinnington)
    Phillips and Smith, *Stockport*, 1985, pp. 27-28
Tattenhall
  3541 Anisse Whitfeld
    Bland, *Christleton*, 2002, pp. 115-116
Tilston
  3542 Jane Warburton
    Pearson, *Malpas*, [2005], pp. 176-177
  3543 William Yeardley, husbandman
    Pearson, *Malpas*, [2005], p. 180
Waverton
  3544 Elizabethe Rosongreave, widow
    Bland, *Christleton*, 2002, p. 117

Derbyshire

Chesterfield
  3545 Phillipp Boare
    Bestall and Fowkes, *Chesterfield*, 1977, pp. 267-268
  3546 James Inman, butcher
    Bestall and Fowkes, *Chesterfield*, 1977, pp. 274-275
  3547 Henry Norman
    Bestall and Fowkes, *Chesterfield*, 1977, pp. 269-273
Temple Normanton
  3548 Thomas Croslande, webster
    Bestall and Fowkes, *Chesterfield*, 1977, pp. 273-274

Devonshire

Huish
  3549 Henry Welsche, clergyman
    Cash, *Devon*, 1966, p. 16
Uffculme
  3550 John Davy, [husbandman]
    Wyatt, *Uffculme*, 1997, p. 26

Dorsetshire

Leigh
  3551 Edmund Crichell
    Machin, *Yetminster*, 1976, No.18, (2 pp.)

Co. Durham

Darlington
  3552 Christofer Collyn [Collin]
    Atkinson *et al.*, *Darlington*, 1993, p. 52
Hilton
  3553 Sir William Hilton (also listed Newcastle,
  Northumberland)
    Hodgson, *Wills and Inventories*, 1906, III, pp. 178-179
Langton
  3554 John Spencer
    Hodgson, *Wills and Inventories*, 1906, III, p. 177

Essex

Ingatestone Hall
  3555 Sir John Petre
    Emmison, *Ingatestone*, 1954, pp. 7-21

Hertfordshire

St Albans, St Stephens
  3556 Edward Crawley
    Parker, *Worldly Goods*, 2004, pp. 145-146
St Albans, St Stephens, Park Street
  3557 John Smyth
    Parker, *Worldly Goods*, 2004, pp. 146-147
Sarratt
  3558 Thomas Puddifat
    Bullen, *Sarratt*, [1982], pp. 63-64

Kent
Bishopsbourne
3559 Richard Hooker, clergyman, parson of
Bishopsbourne
Keen, 1956, pp. 231-236
Lancashire
Bolton, Entwistle
3560 Alexander Kay, husbandman
Bolton, *Bolton*, 1987, pp. 161-162
Leicestershire
Braunstone
3561 Thomas Parker
Wilshere, *Braunstone*, 1983, p. 13
Evington
3562 William Jacame, [husbandman]
Wilshere, *Evington*, 1985, p. 10
Kirby Muxloe
3563 Henrie Martin, [yeoman?]
Wilshere, *Kirby Muxloe*, 1983, p. 4
Lincolnshire
Clee
3564 George Holmes, clergyman
Ambler, Watkinson, *Clee*, 1987, pp. 105-106
Market Rasen
3565 Ales Harwick, [widow]
Neave, *Market Rasen*, 1985, p. 109
3566 Ralphe Pockley, tanner
Neave, *Market Rasen*, 1985, p. 110
Northumberland
Newcastle
Sir William Hilton (see Hilton, Co. Durham)
Oxfordshire
Banbury, Grimsbury
3567 John Bull
Brinkworth and Gibson, *Banbury*, I, 1975, pp. 157-158
Banbury
3568 Thomas Dixe, tanner and alderman
Brinkworth and Gibson, *Banbury*, I, 1975, p. 162
Banbury, Grimsbury
3569 Fraunces Genyver [Genever], day labourer
Brinkworth and Gibson, *Banbury*, I, 1975, p. 165
Banbury
3570 George Gubbin, labourer
Brinkworth and Gibson, *Banbury*, I, 1975, p. 161
3571 Edward Hadley, ironmonger
Brinkworth and Gibson, *Banbury*, I, 1975, pp. 163-164
3572 John Wilshere [Wilshyre], shoemaker
Brinkworth and Gibson, *Banbury*, I, 1975, pp. 159-160
Staffordshire
Dudley
3573 Richard Foley
Roper, *Dudley*, 1965, p. 59
3574 Henry Gorton
Roper, *Dudley*, 1965, p. 58
3575 Richard Parkeshowse
Roper, *Dudley*, 1965, p. 57
Lichfield, Stowe
3576 Thomas Mott, husbandman
Vaisey, *Lichfield*, 1969, pp. 44-45
Surrey
Dockenfield
3577 Richard Harding, yeoman
Herridge, *Surrey*, 2005, pp. 378-379

Elstead
3578 Henry Wheeler, husbandman
Herridge, *Surrey*, 2005, p. 387
Farnham
3579 John Kent alias Newbery, glover
Herridge, *Surrey*, 2005, pp. 379-381
Frensham
3580 William Valler, yeoman
Herridge, *Surrey*, 2005, pp. 385-386
Horsell
3581 Richard Edmed
Herridge, *Surrey*, 2005, p. 376
Kingston-upon-Thames
3582 Thomas Grace, blacksmith
Herridge, *Surrey*, 2005, pp. 377-378
Richmond (alias West Sheen)
3583 William Parkes, carpenter
Herridge, *Surrey*, 2005, pp. 382-383
Ripley
3584 John Stanton, fuller
Herridge, *Surrey*, 2005, pp. 384-385
Wotton
3585 John Boughton, husbandman
Herridge, *Surrey*, 2005, pp. 374-375
Wales
Flintshire, Iscoed
3586 William Mullock, husbandman
Pearson, *Malpas*, [2005], pp. 178-179
Warwickshire
Stratford-on-Avon
3587 [Thomas] Bailies [Baylis]
Jones, *Stratford*, I, 2002, p. 180
3588 William Smythe [Smith], mercer
Jones, *Stratford*, I, 2002, pp. 183-185
3589 Robert Stevens, labourer [shepherd]
Jones, *Stratford*, I, 2002, pp. 181-182
Yorkshire
Aysgarth, Shaw Cote
3590 Michaell Pratt, yeoman
Thwaite, *Abbotside*, 1967, p. 27
Cottingley, Bingley (now Bradford)
3591 John Hudson
Preston, *Co. York*, 1929, pp. 2-3
Grinton, Thwaite
3592 Phyllis Alldersonn
Berry, *Swaledale*, 1998, pp. 361-362
Marrick
3593 Christopher Tyrrye, husbandman
Berry, *Swaledale*, 1998, pp. 358-360

1600 (c.)
London
Southwark, St Thomas the Apostle
3594 Elizabeth Lambert, widow
Herridge, *Surrey*, 2005, pp. 381-382
Yorkshire
Aysgarth, Skellgill
3595 Abraham Pratt, yeoman
Thwaite, *Abbotside*, 1967, p. 25

1601
Cheshire
Bickerton
3596 John Boker, husbandman
Pearson, *Malpas*, [2005], p. 191

Cholmondeley
  3597 William Webster, yeoman
    Pearson, *Malpas*, [2005], pp. 191-193
Sale
  3598 James Massie, gentleman
    Groves, *Ashton-on-Mersey and Sale*, 1999, p. 24
Tarvin, Ashton
  3599 Richarde Raffeson, husbandman
    Bland, *Christleton*, 2002, pp. 123-124
Tarvin
  3600 Richard Reade, husbandman
    Bland, *Christleton*, 2002, p. 121
Tattenhall
  3601 Thomas Larden
    Bland, *Christleton*, 2002, pp. 126-128
  3602 Margerie Muchell
    Bland, *Christleton*, 2002, p. 119
  3603 Katherin Pigott
    Bland, *Christleton*, 2002, p. 118
Tilston, Horton,
  3604 Hughe Bykerton
    Pearson, *Malpas*, [2005], pp. 189-190
Tilston, Carden
  3605 Peter Hardee alias Hardinge, yeoman
    Pearson, *Malpas*, [2005], pp. 182-183
Derbyshire
Chatsworth
  3606 Elizabeth [Bess], Countess of Shrewsbury
    Levey, *Hardwick*, 2001, pp. 22-30
Chesterfield
  3607 Thomas Forth, butcher
    Bestall and Fowkes, *Chesterfield*, 1977, pp. 281-283
  3608 John Knottes, glover
    Bestall and Fowkes, *Chesterfield*, 1977, pp. 277-279
  3609 John Wilson
    Bestall and Fowkes, *Chesterfield*, pp. 275-277
Glossop, Haigh
  3610 Robert Cleaton, [husbandman]
    Lee and Miller, *New Mills*, 1999, pp. 49-50
Hardwick Hall
  3611 Elizabeth [Bess], Countess of Shrewsbury
    Boynton, 1971, pp. 23-40
Hardwick Old Hall
  3612 Elizabeth [Bess], Countess of Shrewbury
    Levey, *Hardwick*, 2001, pp. 33-40
Hasland
  3613 Allen Widoson, husbandman
    Bestall and Fowkes, *Chesterfield*, 1977, p. 280
Devonshire
Uffculme
  3614 Davye [Davyd] Tucker
    Wyatt, *Uffculme*, 1997, pp. 26-27
Essex
Navestock
  3615 Harrye Browne, husbandman
    Searle, 1969, pp. 32-33
Hertfordshire
Sarratt
  3616 Thomas Hobbes, [yeoman]
    Bullen, *Sarratt*, [1982], pp. 65-67
  3617 Christopher Winckefeilde, [yeoman]
    Bullen, *Sarratt*, [1982], pp. 69-70

Kent
Eastry
  3618 Richard Boteler, gentleman
    Shaw, 1870, pp. 224-227
Lancashire
Cuerden
  3619 John Cuerden, esquire
    France, 1940, pp. 196-204
Leicestershire
Braunstone
  3620 William Streatton, [husbandman]
    Wilshere, *Braunstone*, 1983, p. 48
Evington
  3621 James Hutchins, clergyman
    Wilshere, *Evington*, 1985, p. 11
Lincolnshire
Clee
  3622 Andrew Leeminge
    Ambler, Watkinson, *Clee*, 1987, p. 106
Market Rasen
  3623 Willm Patricke
    Neave, *Market Rasen*, 1985, pp. 111-113
  3624 Alice Pockley, widow
    Neave, *Market Rasen*, 1985, p. 113
  3625 Xpofer Sowden, glover
    Neave, *Market Rasen*, 1985, pp. 114-115
Nottinghamshire
Wollaton
  3626 Sir Percival Willoughby
    Marshall, *Wollaton*, 1996, pp. 94-99
Oxfordshire
Banbury
  3627 Elizabeth Browne
    Brinkworth and Gibson, *Banbury*, I, 1975, p. 167
Banbury, Grimsbury
  3628 Henry Bull, day labourer
    Brinkworth and Gibson, *Banbury*, I, 1975, p. 166
Banbury
  3629 Humfry Hadley, ironmonger
    Brinkworth and Gibson, *Banbury*, I, 1975, pp. 168-169
Water Eaton
  3630 John Meare, [yeoman]
    Offord, *Water Eaton*, 1986, pp. 8-9
Scotland
Edinburgh
  3631 Eduard Cathkin, bookseller
    Anon., *Bassandyne*, 1836, pp. 229-231
  3632 Johnne Gibsoun, bookbinder
    Anon., *Bassandyne*, 1836, pp. 222-223
Staffordshire
Dudley
  3633 Leonard Milton
    Roper, *Dudley*, 1965, p. 61
  3634 Thomas Shawe
    Roper, *Dudley*, 1965, p. 60
  3635 Edmond Thornes
    Roper, *Dudley*, 1968, p. 1
Surrey
Ash
  3636 Annys Stonner
    Herridge, *Surrey*, 2005, p. 398

Chobham
 3637 John Skete, husbandman
  Herridge, *Surrey*, 2005, pp. 393-394
 3638 Thomas Wye
  Herridge, *Surrey*, 2005, pp. 398-399
Dunsfold
 3639 Henry Harper, husbandman
  Herridge, *Surrey*, 2005, pp. 390-391
Godalming
 3640 William Dynes, husbandman
  Herridge, *Surrey*, 2005, pp. 389-390
Guildford
 3641 Nicholas Smalpeece, haberdasher
  Herridge, *Surrey*, 2005, pp. 394-397
Send
 3642 John Inwood, yeoman
  Herridge, *Surrey*, 2005, pp. 391-393
Windlesham
 3643 Mathewe Snelling
  Herridge, *Surrey*, 2005, pp. 397-398
Wales
Denbighshire, Bachymbyd
 3644 Sir Robert Salesburie [Salesbury] (also listed
 Pool Park, and Rug, Merionethshire)
  Smith, 1952, pp. 295-302
Denbighshire, Pool Park
 Sir Robert Salesburie [Salesbury] (see Bachymbyd)
Flintshire, Iscoed
 3645 Margret Richard
  Pearson, *Malpas*, [2005], pp. 185-186
Merionethshire, Rug
 Sir Robert Salesburie [Salesbury] (see Bachynbyd,
 Denbighshire)
Pembrokeshire, Haverfordwest, Syke
 3646 Peter Cheare
  Howells, 1956, p. 429
Warwickshire
Alcester
 3647 Richard Heminge, [weaver]
  Saville, *Alcester*, 1979, p. 5
Shottery
 3648 Thomas Wittington, [shepherd]
  Jones, *Stratford*, I, 2002, p. 186
Stratford-on-Avon
 3649 William Greeneway [Greenaway], carrier
  Jones, *Stratford*, I, 2002, pp. 189-192
 3650 Mychaell [Michael] Hare, husbandman
  Jones, *Stratford*, I, 2002, pp. 187-188
 3651 Willyam Hobday, glover
  Jones, *Stratford*, I, 2002, pp. 193-196
 3652 Thomas Sheffyld [Sheffield], husbandman
  Jones, *Stratford*, I, 2002, p. 193
Westmorland
Yanwath, Barton
 3653 John Laws
  Jackson, *Laws*, 1876, pp. 267-268
Wiltshire
Marlborough
 3654 Samuel Browne
  Williams and Thomson, *Marlborough*, 2007, p. 15
 3655 Thomas Whetebreade
  Williams and Thomson, *Marlborough*, 2007, p. 15

Worcestershire
Chaddesley Corbett
 3656 Rychard Pitt, [yeoman]
  Roper, *Chaddesley Corbett*, 1971, pp. 1-2
Frankley
 3657 John Littleton [Lyttleton], esquire
  Wanklyn, *Worcestershire*, 1998, pp. 96-102
King's Norton, Colmer
 3658 Robert Gower, esquire
  Wanklyn, *Worcestershire*, 1998, pp. 94-96
Yorkshire
Aysgarth, Simonstone
 3659 Elizabeth Metcalf
  Thwaite, *Abbotside*, 1967, p. 28
Aysgarth, Sedbusk
 3660 Thomas Twhaytes [Thwaites], yeoman
  Thwaite, *Abbotside*, 1967, p. 26

1601 (c.)
Surrey
East Molesey
 3661 Henry Cartwright
  Herridge, *Surrey*, 2005, p. 388

1602
Cheshire
Ashton-on-Mersey
 3662 Margaret Barlow, widow
  Groves, *Ashton-on-Mersey and Sale*, 1999, pp. 25-26
Broxton
 3663 Thomas Dod, gentleman
  Pearson, *Malpas*, [2005], pp. 193-199
Cholmondeley
 3664 Raffe Manninge
  Pearson, *Malpas*, [2005], p. 203
Dunham Massey, Sinderland
 3665 Thomas Clayton, [husbandman]
  Groves, *Dunham Massey*, 2008, pp. 19-20
Hale
 3666 Ralph Wright alias Vergus
  Groves, *Hale 1*, 2005, p. 18
Malpas
 3667 Raph Gitten, husbandman
  Pearson, *Malpas*, [2005], p. 201
Stockport
 3668 Hew Ridgwaye, [smith]
  Phillips and Smith, *Stockport*, 1985, pp. 30-31
 3669 Roger Woodd, yeoman
  Phillips and Smith, *Stockport*, 1985, pp. 29-30
Tarvin, Ashton
 3670 Roger Holland, yeoman
  Bland, *Christleton*, 2002, pp. 131-132
Tarvin, Duddon
 3671 [Richard] Huxley
  Bland, *Christleton*, 2002, pp. 140-141
Tilston, Grafton
 3672 John Downes, husbandman
  Pearson, *Malpas*, [2005], pp. 199-200
Wrenbury, Chorley
 3673 Humphrey Wilson
  Pixton, *Wrenbury*, 2009, pp. 42-43
Derbyshire
Chesterfield
 3674 Thomas Berisford, tanner
  Bestall and Fowkes, *Chesterfield*, 1977, p. 288

3675 Heugh Hall
    Bestall and Fowkes, *Chesterfield*, 1977, pp. 284-286
3676 Thomas Inman, alderman, weaver and cloth worker
    Bestall and Fowkes, *Chesterfield*, 1977, pp. 283-284
3677 Raph Maunsodale
    Bestall and Fowkes, *Chesterfield*, 1977, p. 287
Glossop, Thornsett Fields
3678 Ottiwell Brammall
    Lee and Miller, *New Mills*, 1999, pp. 53-54

Devonshire
Bickington
3679 William Wotton alias Gale, yeoman
    Cash, *Devon*, 1966, p. 17
Bickleigh
3680 John Hunt
    Cash, *Devon*, 1966, p. 18
Uffculme
3681 Roger Lomone [Loman], [husbandman]
    Wyatt, *Uffculme*, 1997, pp. 27-28
3682 Thomas Rudge
    Wyatt, *Uffculme*, 1997, pp. 28-29

Hertfordshire
St Albans, St Stephens, Netherwild
3683 Thomas Feilde
    Munby, *Worldly Goods*, 1991, pp. 82-84
St Albans, St Stephens
3684 Thomas Kentishe, yeoman
    Munby, *Worldly Goods*, 1991, pp. 80-81
Sarratt
3685 Henry Child, yeoman
    Bullen, *Sarratt*, [1982], pp. 73-75
3686 Will[ia]m Dell
    Bullen, *Sarratt*, [1982], pp. 71-72

Lancashire
Bank Hall, Kirkdale
3687 William Moore [More], esquire
    Trevelyan, 1865, pp. 104-106

Lincolnshire
Clee, Itterby
3688 Richard Curtis
    Ambler, Watkinson, *Clee*, 1987, pp. 106-107
3689 Henry Yeats
    Ambler, Watkinson, *Clee*, 1987, pp. 107-108
Market Rasen
3690 William Storr, clergyman
    Neave, *Market Rasen*, 1985, p. 116

London
Southwark, St George the Martyr
3691 Margerye Clarke, widow
    Herridge, *Surrey*, 2005, pp. 401-402

Norfolk
Norwich
Sir Thomas Rous (see Henham, Suffolk)

Oxfordshire
Banbury
3692 John Boomer, butcher
    Brinkworth and Gibson, *Banbury*, I, 1975, p. 173
Banbury, Grimsbury
3693 John Rylie, glover
    Brinkworth and Gibson, *Banbury*, I, 1975, pp. 173-174

Banbury
3694 William Short, shoemaker
    Brinkworth and Gibson, *Banbury*, I, 1975, p. 170
3695 Anne Thorpe, widow
    Brinkworth and Gibson, *Banbury*, I, 1975, pp. 170-171
3696 Christian [Christiann] Warner, widow
    Brinkworth and Gibson, *Banbury*, I, 1975, pp. 172-173

Rutlandshire
Stoke Dry
3697 Mrs Anne Digbie [Digby], [widow]
    Wise, 1891, pp. 197-207

Staffordshire
Dudley
3698 Robert Lane, [yeoman]
    Roper, *Dudley*, 1968, pp. 1-2

Suffolk
Henham
3699 Sir Thomas Rous (also listed Norwich, Norfolk)
    Suckling, 1848, 2, pp. 355-364
Ipswich
3700 William Becker, mariner
    Reed, *Ipswich*, 1981, pp. 53-54
3701 Stephen Grenewich, dyer
    Reed, *Ipswich*, 1981, pp. 54-56

Surrey
Bramley
3702 John Mawdesley, clergyman [curate of Bramley]
    Herridge, *Surrey*, 2005, pp. 405-406
Chertsey
3703 Richard Myllest, husbandman
    Herridge, *Surrey*, 2005, pp. 407-409
Chertsey, Woodham
3704 Robert Warner, yeoman
    Herridge, *Surrey*, 2005, p. 410
Chiddingfold
3705 Robert Ropley
    Herridge, *Surrey*, 2005, p. 409
East Clandon
3706 Jone Stynt, widow
    Herridge, *Surrey*, 2005, p. 409
3707 Bartholomewe Williamson, yeoman
    Herridge, *Surrey*, 2005, pp. 411-412
Farnham
3708 George Osborne, yeoman
    Herridge, *Surrey*, 2005, pp. 426-427
Frensham, Shottermill
3709 Alice Mychel, widow
    Herridge, *Surrey*, 2005, pp. 406-407
Puttenham
3710 Thomas Manorie, tailor
    Herridge, *Surrey*, 2005, p. 404
Sutton
3711 Harrye Charlewood, labourer
    Herridge, *Surrey*, 2005, pp. 399-400
Walton-upon-Thames
3712 Thomas Lawson, husbandman
    Herridge, *Surrey*, 2005, p. 403

Warwickshire
Coventry
3713 Thomas Downes, [innkeeper]
    Hulton and Castle, *Tudor*, 1987, pp. 86-93

Luddington
3714 John Such, butcher
Jones, *Stratford*, I, 2002, pp. 197-198
Stratford-on-Avon
3715 Joyce Hobday, widow
Jones, *Stratford*, I, 2002, pp. 198-201
Wiltshire
Marlborough
3716 John Eiors
Williams and Thomson, *Marlborough*, 2007, pp. 15-16
Worcestershire
Chaddesley Corbett
3717 Walter Brooke, yeoman
Roper, *Chaddesley Corbett*, 1971, pp. 7-8
3718 William Robins
Roper, *Chaddesley Corbett*, 1971, pp. 2-3
Chaddesley Corbet, Winterfold
3719 Agnes Taylor, widow
Roper, *Chaddesley Corbett*, 1971, p. 4
Worcester, St Clement's
3720 James Hill, tanner
Dyer, *Worcestershire*, 1967, pp. 29-30
Yorkshire
Knaresborough, Tentergate
3721 Alice Nettleton
Brears, *Yorkshire*, 1972, pp. 64-66
Knaresborough
3722 John Webster, [tailor]
Brears, *Yorkshire*, 1972, pp. 63-64
South Cave, Faxfleet
3723 Richard Myddlewood
Kaner, *South Cave*, 1994, pp. 208-209

1602 (c.)

Devonshire
Winkleigh
3724 Roger Sowden, clergyman, vicar of Winkleigh
Cash, *Devon*, 1966, p. 18
Surrey
Weybridge
3725 Adrian Chutter
Herridge, *Surrey*, 2005, p. 400
Worcestershire
Frankley
3726 John Littleton
Wanklyn, *Worcestershire*, 1998, pp. 102-108

1603

Cheshire
Nantwich
3727 Arthur Minshull
Cockcroft, *Nantwich*, 1999, pp. 218.1-3
3728 Richard Robinson, yeoman
Cockcroft, *Nantwich*, 1999, pp. 268.1-2
3729 Henry Rocket, yeoman
Cockcroft, *Nantwich*, 1999, pp. 270.1-2
3730 Laurence Wright, gentleman
Cockcroft, *Nantwich*, 1999, pp. 360.1-3
Stockport
3731 Thomas Burdsell
Phillips and Smith, *Stockport*, 1985, pp. 34-35
3732 John Kelsall, butcher
Phillips and Smith, *Stockport*, 1985, pp. 32-34

3733 Elline Mores
Phillips and Smith, *Stockport*, 1985, pp. 35-36
Tarvin, Kelsall
3734 Robert Clecroft, husbandman
Bland, *Christleton*, 2002, p. 141
Tarvin, Duddon
3735 Richard Turner, husbandman
Bland, *Christleton*, 2002, pp. 140-141
Derbyshire
Chesterfield
3736 William Blacknalle
Bestall and Fowkes, *Chesterfield*, 1977, p. 294
3737 Thomas Freake, yeoman
Bestall and Fowkes, *Chesterfield*, 1977, pp. 290-293
3738 Alice Leake, widow
Bestall and Fowkes, *Chesterfield*, 2001, pp. 3-5
3739 Ellen Neadam
Bestall and Fowkes, *Chesterfield*, 1977, p. 295
Walton
3740 John Longeley, yeoman
Bestall and Fowkes, *Chesterfield*, 1977, p. 289
Devonshire
Exeter
3741 Mr Richard Bevys, Mayor of Exeter (also listed
Heavitree, Exeter)
Donaldson, 1909, pp. 216-240
Exeter, Heavitree
Mr Richard Bevys, Mayor of Exeter (see Exeter)
Totnes [?]
3742 [George Hoc?]ken, [clergyman?]
Cash, *Devon*, 1966, pp. 18-19
Uffculme
3743 John Welshe [Welche]
Wyatt, *Uffculme*, 1997, pp. 29-30
Dorsetshire
Leigh
3744 Elizabeth Coome, widow
Machin, *Yetminster*, 1976, No.20, (1 p.)
Stratton
3745 John Willsheare, [weaver]
Willsher, 2002, p. 59
Yetminster
3746 Bettresse Thomas, widow
Machin, *Yetminster*, 1976, No.19, (2 pp.)
Co. Durham
Darlington
3747 Mathewe Lambart, cordwainer
Atkinson *et al.*, *Darlington*, 1993, pp. 53-54
3748 Thomas Pape
Atkinson *et al.*, *Darlington*, 1993, pp. 55-57
Darlington, Cockerton
3749 William Thompson
Atkinson *et al.*, *Darlington*, 1993, pp. 58-59
Durham
3750 Christopher Smythe, clergyman, canon
Raine, *Barnes*, 1850, pp. cxliii-cxlv
Hertfordshire
St Albans, St Stephens
3751 Robert Byrchmore
Munby, *Worldly Goods*, 1991, pp. 84-86
3752 William Edmundes
Munby, *Worldly Goods*, 1991, p. 89

3753   Robert Knolton
  Parker, *Worldly Goods*, 2004, pp. 151-152
St Albans, St Stephens, Park Street
3754   William Redwood
  Parker, *Worldly Goods*, 2004, pp. 149-151
Lancashire
Prescot
3755   Mr Richard Harrington, gentleman
  Bailey, 1951, p. 79
Leicestershire
Braunstone
3756   Richard Conway, yeoman
  Wilshere, *Braunstone*, 1983, p. 14
3757   Rycharde Taylor, [husbandman?]
  Wilshere, *Braunstone*, 1983, p. 48
3758   John Wellynger
  Wilshere, *Braunstone*, 1983, p. 15
Lincolnshire
Clee, Oole
3759   William Marfleet, husbandman
  Ambler, Watkinson, *Clee*, 1987, p. 108
Norfolk
Wymondham
3760   Thomas Crane, [draper]
  Wilson, *Wymondham*, 1983, pp. 21-24
Northumberland
Earsdon, Halliwell
3761   Cuthbert Baites [Bates], gentleman
  Hodgson, *Wills and Inventories*, 1906, III, pp. 182-183
Oxfordshire
Banbury
3762   John Helmedon, labourer
  Brinkworth and Gibson, *Banbury*, I, 1975, p. 175
Banbury, Neithrop
3763   Richard Smith [Smyth], labourer
  Brinkworth and Gibson, *Banbury*, I, 1975, p. 176
Banbury, Grimsbury
3764   William Wylkyns [Willkines], husbandman
  Brinkworth and Gibson, *Banbury*, I, 1975, pp. 174-175
Scotland
Edinburgh
3765   Palace of Holyroodhouse
  Bannatyne, 1827, p. 185
3766   Margaret Wallace
  Anon., *Bassandyne*, 1836, pp. 235-237
Suffolk
Hengrave
3767   Sir Thomas Kytson
  Gage, 1822, pp. 20-37
Ipswich
3768   John Ryvett, tailor
  Reed, *Ipswich*, 1981, pp. 56-57
Surrey
Abinger
3769   Richard Constable, yeoman
  Herridge, *Surrey*, 2005, pp. 413-414
3770   Henry Sponner, yeoman
  Herridge, *Surrey*, 2005, pp. 431-432
Ash
3771   Richard Southe
  Herridge, *Surrey*, 2005, pp. 429-430
Byfleet
3772   Anthony Fen, yeoman
  Herridge, *Surrey*, 2005, pp. 416-417

3773   William Richardson, yeoman
  Herridge, *Surrey*, 2005, pp. 428-429
Chobham
3774   Henry Woddes, husbandman
  Herridge, *Surrey*, 2005, pp. 440-441
Cranleigh
3775   Katherine Mower, widow
  Herridge, *Surrey*, 2005, pp. 425-426
Eashing
3776   John Flodder, yeoman
  Herridge, *Surrey*, 2005, pp. 417-419
3777   Henry Sturte, husbandman
  Herridge, *Surrey*, 2005, pp. 434-435
Farnham
3778   George Whittingham, innkeeper
  Herridge, *Surrey*, 2005, pp. 437-440
Frensham
3779   Symon Harding, yeoman
  Herridge, *Surrey*, 2005, pp. 421-422
3780   James Raunger, weaver
  Herridge, *Surrey*, 2005, pp. 427-428
3781   Robert Steele, husbandman
  Herridge, *Surrey*, 2005, pp. 432-433
Guildford
3782   George Ireland
  Herridge, *Surrey*, 2005, p. 424
3783   John Mors, musician
  Herridge, *Surrey*, 2005, p. 425
Haslemere
3784   Thomas Chittye, husbandman
  Herridge, *Surrey*, 2005, pp. 412-413
Kingston-upon-Thames
3785   Arthur Talbot, bricklayer
  Herridge, *Surrey*, 2005, pp. 435-436
Ockham
3786   William Deacon
  Herridge, *Surrey*, 2005, pp. 414-416
Windlesham
3787   Thomas Hart, yeoman and carpenter
  Herridge, *Surrey*, 2005, p. 423
Witley
3788   Henry Flutter, husbandman
  Herridge, *Surrey*, 2005, p. 419
3789   Thomas Wodier, husbandman
  Herridge, *Surrey*, 2005, p. 441
Warwickshire
Shottery
3790   Elizabeth Such
  Jones, *Stratford*, I, 2002, pp. 219-220
Stratford-on-Avon
3791   Rychard Boyce, [tailor]
  Jones, *Stratford*, I, 2002, pp. 223-227
3792   Thomas Dixon alias Waterman, innholder
  Halliwell, 1871, pp. 92-114
  Jones, *Stratford*, I, 2002, pp. 201-219
3793   William Greene [Green]
  Jones, *Stratford*, I, 2002, pp. 220-223
Wiltshire
Marlborough
3794   Robert Cole, tanner
  Williams and Thomson, *Marlborough*, 2007, p. 17

3795 William White, [husband]man
Williams and Thomson, *Marlborough*, 2007, pp. 16-17
Worcestershire
Belbroughton
3796 William Fletcher alias Shuard
Roper, *Belbroughton*, 1967-1968, p. 47
Yorkshire
Aysgarth, Cams Houses
3797 Henrye Nealson [Henry Nelson]
Thwaite, *Abbotside*, 1967, p. 29
Crayke
3798 Jacob Shawe, clergyman, rector of Crayke
Raine, *Barnes*, 1850, pp. cxl-cxli
South Cave
3799 Marmaduke Todd, [yeoman]
Kaner, *South Cave*, 1994, pp. 212-213
3800 William Tyndaile [Tyndale]
Kaner, *South Cave*, 1994, pp. 214-215
Woolley
3801 George Downes, esquire
Wentworth, 1893, pp. 4-5

1603 (c.)
Cheshire
Nantwich
3802 Richard Lant
Cockcroft, *Nantwich*, 1999, p. 181.1
Surrey
Farnham
3803 Richard Francklyn, shoemaker
Herridge, *Surrey*, 2005, pp. 420-421
Pirbright
3804 Thomas Westbrook, husbandman
Herridge, *Surrey*, 2005, p. 437
Waverley
3805 Richard Mannam
Herridge, *Surrey*, 2005, p. 424
Wiltshire
Marlborough
3806 […] Bucke, tanner
Williams and Thomson, *Marlborough*, 2007, p. 18

1604
Cheshire
Christleton
3807 Willeam Preyce
Bland, *Christleton*, 2002, p. 147
Hale, Ringway
3808 John Bradley, [husbandman]
Groves, *Hale 1*, 2005, pp. 19-20
Little Leigh
3809 Richard Whishal, [husbandman]
Whishaw, 1935, pp. 57-59
Nantwich
3810 William Bradley, labourer
Cockcroft, *Nantwich*, 1999, p. 42.1
3811 Anne Brooke, widow
Cockcroft, *Nantwich*, 1999, p. 46.1
3812 Edmund Clowes, webster
Cockcroft, *Nantwich*, 1999, p. 85.2
3813 Raphe Crockett, gentleman
Cockcroft, *Nantwich*, 1999, pp. 97.1-4
3814 William Lightfoot, husbandman
Cockcroft, *Nantwich*, 1999, p. 191.1

3815 Nicholas Low, carpenter
Cockcroft, *Nantwich*, 1999, p. 194.1
3816 Anne Minshull, widow
Cockcroft, *Nantwich*, 1999, pp. 232.1-2
3817 Margaret Wright, widow
Cockcroft, *Nantwich*, 1999, p. 363.1
3818 Roger Wright, mercer
Cockcroft, *Nantwich*, 1999, pp. 372.1-7
Stockport, Hillgate
3819 William Haryson, linen webster
Phillips and Smith, *Stockport*, 1985, p. 37
Stockport
3820 John Latham
Phillips and Smith, *Stockport*, 1985, p. 38
3821 Anne Walmeslie
Phillips and Smith, *Stockport*, 1985, pp. 37-38
3822 Nicholas Wynn, shearman
Phillips and Smith, *Stockport*, 1985, p. 39
Tarvin, Stapleford
3823 John Prescote, [labourer]
Bland, *Christleton*, 2002, p. 144
Tattenhall
3824 Richard Hallmarke, [husbandman]
Bland, *Christleton*, 2002, pp. 142-143
Waverton, Huxley
3825 Frannces Birkhened [Birkenhead], gentleman
Bland, *Christleton*, 2002, p. 145
Wrenbury
3826 Alles Blackmore
Pixton, *Wrenbury*, 2009, pp. 50-51
Wrenbury, Newhall, Aston
3827 John Cartwright
Pixton, *Wrenbury*, 2009, p. 47
Wrenbury, Chorley
3828 Ellen Flavell, [widow]
Pixton, *Wrenbury*, 2009, pp. 43-44
Derbyshire
Brimington
3829 Margerie Fletcher, widow
Bestall and Fowkes, *Chesterfield*, 2001, pp. 2-3
Chesterfield
3830 Richard Bland, blacksmith
Bestall and Fowkes, *Chesterfield*, 2001, pp. 12-13
3831 Richard Cade, tanner
Bestall and Fowkes, *Chesterfield*, 2001, pp. 1-2
3832 Thomas Heathcott, mercer and innholder
Bestall and Fowkes, *Chesterfield*, 2001, pp. 6-10
New Mills
3833 John Warington, [shearman]
Lee and Miller, *New Mills*, 1999, pp. 57-58
Devonshire
Exeter
3834 Willyam Spicer, merchant
Portman, *Exeter*, 1966, pp. 101-110
Uffculme
3835 Will[ia]m Rawlings, yeoman
Wyatt, *Uffculme*, 1997, p. 30
Dorsetshire
Leigh
3836 Thomas Hayne
Machin, *Yetminster*, 1976, No.21, (1 p.)

Co. Durham
Billingham
  3837 Marmaduke Chapman, yeoman
    Hodgson, *Wills and Inventories*, 1906, III, p. 185
Darlington, Cockerton
  3838 Tobie Collinge
    Atkinson *et al.*, *Darlington*, 1993, pp. 63-64
  3839 Leonarde Dacke, yeoman
    Atkinson *et al.*, *Darlington*, 1993, pp. 61-62
Hertfordshire
St Albans, St Stephens, Park Street
  3840 Rogere Fynch
    Parker, *Worldly Goods*, 2004, pp. 152-153
St Albans, St Stephens
  3841 Frances Trott
    Parker, *Worldly Goods*, 2004, p. 154
Sarratt
  3842 Margery Hobbs, widow
    Bullen, *Sarratt*, [1982], pp. 76-78
Leicestershire
Evington
  3843 Richarde Beebie, [husbandman]
    Wilshere, *Evington*, 1985, p. 12
Lincolnshire
Cleethorpes
  3844 Robert Tatam, labourer
    Ambler, Watkinson, *Clee*, 1987, pp. 108-109
Northumberland
Belford, Fenham
  3845 Sir William Reade
    Raine, *North Durham*, 1852, pp. 177-178
Oxfordshire
Banbury
  3846 Robert Clemson, whittawer
    Brinkworth and Gibson, *Banbury*, I, 1975, p. 177
  3847 Humphrey Devis [Devys], miller
    Brinkworth and Gibson, *Banbury*, I, 1975, p. 178
  3848 John Dombelton, wheelwright
    Brinkworth and Gibson, *Banbury*, I, 1975, p. 179
Banbury, Neithrop
  3849 Joan Sowtham
    Brinkworth and Gibson, *Banbury*, I, 1975, p. 177
Scotland
Edinburgh
  3850 Robert Smyth, librarian
    Anon., *Bassandyne*, 1836, pp. 233-235
Suffolk
Ipswich
  3851 John Wallis, gunmaker
    Reed, *Ipswich*, 1981, pp. 57-59
Warwickshire
Stoneleigh, Hurst
  3852 Anthony Spencer, gentleman
    Alcock, *Warwickshire*, 1993, pp. 77-79
Stratford-on-Avon
  3853 William Cawdrie [Cawdry], husbandman
    Jones, *Stratford*, I, 2002, pp. 227-228
  3854 Henrij Getlej [Henry Getley], [carpenter]
    Jones, *Stratford*, I, 2002, pp. 229-232
Wiltshire
Marlborough
  3855 Henry Roosell, smith
    Williams and Thomson, *Marlborough*, 2007, pp. 18-19

Worcestershire
Chaddesley Corbett, Winterfold
  3856 John Norrisse
    Roper, *Chaddesley Corbett*, 1971, pp. 8-10
  3857 John Taylor, yeoman
    Roper, *Chaddesley Corbett*, 1971, pp. 5-6
Rous Lench
  3858 John Rouse [Rous], esquire
    Wanklyn, *Worcestershire*, 1998, p. 109
Yorkshire
Aysgarth, Sedbusk
  3859 Helten [Helen] Alderson
    Thwaite, *Abbotside*, 1967, p. 29
Aysgarth, Cotterdale
  3860 George Wine [Wynne]
    Thwaite, *Abbotside*, 1967, p. 30
Hardrow
  3861 Peter Metcalf
    Thwaite, *Abbotside*, 1967, p. 31

1605

Cheshire
Dunham Massey, Sinderland
  3862 John Ashton, [husbandman]
    Groves, *Dunham Massey*, 2008, pp. 22-23
Hale
  3863 John Chapman
    Groves, *Hale 1*, 2005, p. 20
Nantwich
  3864 Roger Bannister, husbandman
    Cockcroft, *Nantwich*, 1999, p. 19.1
  3865 Richard Boyers, saddler
    Cockcroft, *Nantwich*, 1999, p. 40.1
  3866 Robert Boyers, cutler
    Cockcroft, *Nantwich*, 1999, p. 41.1
  3867 Richard Buckley, shoemaker
    Cockcroft, *Nantwich*, 1999, p. 56.1
  3868 Robert Hardinge, yeoman
    Cockcroft, *Nantwich*, 1999, pp. 147.1-2
  3869 Roger Jeffs
    Cockcroft, *Nantwich*, 1999, p. 170.1
  3870 Richard Maisterson
    Cockcroft, *Nantwich*, 1999, p. 204.1
  3871 John Parson, labourer
    Cockcroft, *Nantwich*, 1999, p. 241.2
  3872 Jasper Rutter, gentleman
    Cockcroft, *Nantwich*, 1999, pp. 272.1-3
  3873 John Rutter, gentleman
    Cockcroft, *Nantwich*, 1999, pp. 274.1-2
  3874 John Rutter, tailor
    Cockcroft, *Nantwich*, 1999, p. 275.1
  3875 John Sare, yeoman
    Cockcroft, *Nantwich*, 1999, pp. 279.1-2
  3876 Richard Scarrett, yeoman
    Cockcroft, *Nantwich*, 1999, p. 281.1
  3877 James Simcock
    Cockcroft, *Nantwich*, 1999, p. 286.1
  3878 Raphe Smith, labourer
    Cockcroft, *Nantwich*, 1999, p. 290.1
  3879 Thomas Wright, capper
    Cockcroft, *Nantwich*, 1999, p. 373.1
Stockport
  3880 Alexander Torkington, tanner
    Phillips and Smith, *Stockport*, 1985, pp. 42-43

Tarvin, Stapleford
  3881 Richard Done, husbandman
    Bland, *Christleton*, 2002, pp. 159-160
Tarvin, Ashton
  3882 Raffe Whytbie, yeoman
    Bland, *Christleton*, 2002, pp. 160-162
Waverton, Hatton
  3883 Rowland Dutton, esquire
    Bland, *Christleton*, 2002, pp. 151-159
Wrenbury cum Frith
  3884 Elizabeth Cooke
    Pixton, *Wrenbury*, 2009, pp. 48-49
Wrenbury, Smeatonwood
  3885 John Hall, [yeoman]
    Pixton, *Wrenbury*, 2009, pp. 57-58

Derbyshire
Chesterfield
  3886 Roger Bagshaw, barber
    Bestall and Fowkes, *Chesterfield*, 2001, pp. 17-18
  3887 Edward Boler
    Bestall and Fowkes, *Chesterfield*, 2001, pp. 19-22
  3888 John Geefferstone
    Bestall and Fowkes, *Chesterfield*, 2001, pp. 14-16
Chesterfield, Temple Normanton
  3889 Robert Hill, webster
    Bestall and Fowkes, *Chesterfield*, 2001, pp. 18-19
Chesterfield
  3890 Richard Woodward, butcher
    Bestall and Fowkes, *Chesterfield*, 2001, pp. 22-25
Glossop, Thornsett Fields
  3891 Ottywell Bramhall, [husbandman]
    Lee and Miller, *New Mills*, 1999, pp. 60-61

Devonshire
Heavitree
  3892 Philip Ducke
    Cash, *Devon*, 1966, pp. 20-21
Paignton
  3893 Katherine Churchwarde
    Cash, *Devon*, 1966, p. 20

Co. Durham
Barnard Castle
  3894 Francis Saire, mercer
    Wood, *Wills and Inventories*, 1929, IV, p. 13
Bedburn Park
  William Barnes, gentleman (see Darlington)
Darlington
  3895 William Barnes, gentleman (also listed Bedburn Park)
    Atkinson *et al.*, *Darlington*, 1993, pp. 67-73
Darlington, Bondgate
  3896 Ralph Hugill, labourer
    Atkinson *et al.*, *Darlington*, 1993, pp. 76-77
Darlington
  3897 Giffray [Geoffrey] Raine, glover
    Atkinson *et al.*, *Darlington*, 1993, pp. 73-75

Hertfordshire
St Albans, St Stephens
  3898 William Etheroppe
    Munby, *Worldly Goods*, 1991, p. 92
  3899 Thomas Griffen
    Parker, *Worldly Goods*, 2004, pp. 157-158
  3900 James Joyse
    Parker, *Worldly Goods*, 2004, p. 155

St Albans, St Stephens, Park Street
  3901 Brand Redwood
    Parker, *Worldly Goods*, 2004, pp. 156-157
Lancashire
Manchester
  3902 Thomas Houghtone [Haughton]
    Axon, 1915, pp. 9-10
Torver
  3903 Christofor Dawson, clergyman, curate
    Martin, 1988, pp. 122-123
Warrington
  3904 John Wakefield, schoolmaster
    Rylands, *Lancashire and Cheshire*, 1897, p. 12
Lincolnshire
Clee
  3905 Katheryne Chapman
    Ambler, Watkinson, *Clee*, 1987, p. 109
Oxfordshire
Banbury, Grimsbury
  3906 Mary Bull, widow
    Brinkworth and Gibson, *Banbury*, I, 1975, p. 184
Banbury, Neithrop
  3907 Grace Kelye [Keelinge], widow
    Brinkworth and Gibson, *Banbury*, I, 1975, p. 183
Banbury
  3908 Margarett Sawbridge
    Brinkworth and Gibson, *Banbury*, I, 1975, pp. 181-182
  3909 John Wamesley
    Brinkworth and Gibson, *Banbury*, I, 1975, pp. 179-180
Scotland
Perthshire, Balloch Castle
  3910 Sir Duncan Campbell
    Innes, 1855, pp. 342-345
Somersetshire
Cleeve Abbey
  3911 Robert Boteler, esquire
    Parker, Ives, Allan, 2007, pp. 161-166
Staffordshire
Dudley, St Edmund's
  3912 Richard Downinge, wood collier
    Roper, *Dudley*, 1966, p. 1
Lichfield, Woodhouses
  3913 Richard Stafforde
    Vaisey, *Lichfield*, 1969, pp. 45-46
Suffolk
Ipswich
  3914 William Cleveland, linen weaver
    Reed, *Ipswich*, 1981, pp. 61-62
  3915 Richard Godshall, shoemaker
    Reed, *Ipswich*, 1981, pp. 59-61
Warwickshire
Stratford-on-Avon
  3916 William Adams, tailor
    Jones, *Stratford*, I, 2002, pp. 234-235
  3917 Elizabethe Pretty, widow
    Jones, *Stratford*, I, 2002, pp. 232-233
Wiltshire
Marlborough
  3918 John Felps, tucker
    Williams and Thomson, *Marlborough*, 2007, p. 19
Worcestershire
Belbroughton
  3919 John Hemynge, [grinder]
    Roper, *Belbroughton*, 1967-1968, p. 53

3920   Richard Prynn, scythesmith
   Roper, *Belbroughton*, 1967-1968, p. 51
Chaddesley Corbett
3921   Rychard Bayles
   Roper, *Chaddesley Corbett*, 1971, p. 11
Yorkshire
Aysgarth, Sedbusk
3922   Mathew Twhaites [Thwaites]
   Thwaite, *Abbotside*, 1967, p. 33

1606
Bedfordshire
Kempston
3923   Henry Scarborrowe
   Emmison, *Bedfordshire*, 1938, p. 53
Cheshire
Christleton
3924   Katherine Carter
   Bland, *Christleton*, 2002, p. 166
3925   William Pr[i]charde, husbandman
   Bland, *Christleton*, 2002, pp. 172-173
Nantwich
3926   James Blagg
   Cockcroft, *Nantwich*, 1999, p. 36.1
Stockport
3927   James Chorlton, linen draper
   Phillips and Smith, *Stockport*, 1985, pp. 48-50
3928   Margaret Pickering, widow
   Phillips and Smith, *Stockport*, 1985, pp. 51-52
3929   James Taylor, cutler
   Phillips and Smith, *Stockport*, 1985, pp. 45-47
Tarvin, Hockenhull
3930   John Hockenhull, esquire
   Bland, *Christleton*, 2002, pp. 171-172
Tattenhall
3931   Thomas ap Rees
   Bland, *Christleton*, 2002, pp. 168-169
3932   John Tilston, yeoman
   Bland, *Christleton*, 2002, p. 164-165
Waverton
3933   Robert Dutton, husbandman
   Bland, *Christleton*, 2003, pp. 201-202
Wrenbury, Chorley
3934   Roger Broome, [yeoman]
   Pixton, *Wrenbury*, 2009, pp. 53-55
Cornwall
St Stephen in Brannel
3935   John Whetter
   Whetter, 1974, p. 12
Cumberland
Carlisle
3936   Richard Lowry, goldsmith
   Jones, 1980, pp. 39-43
Derbyshire
Chesterfield, Walton
3937   George Heywood [Heawod], yeoman
   Bestall and Fowkes, *Chesterfield*, 2001, p. 25
Chesterfield
3938   George Norton, cutler
   Bestall and Fowkes, *Chesterfield*, 2001, pp. 26-27
3939   George Willson, [tavern-keeper]
   Bestall and Fowkes, *Chesterfield*, 2001, pp. 27-28

Glossop, Thornsett Fields
3940   Ottiwell Bramall
   Lee and Miller, *New Mills*, 1999, p. 65
Glossop, Bawdon
3941   Elizabeth [Chapman alias] Newall
   Lee and Miller, *New Mills*, 1999, pp. 62-63
Devonshire
Membury
3942   Simon Foreward
   Cash, *Devon*, 1966, p. 21
Uffculme
3943   Jane Dowdney, [widow]
   Wyatt, *Uffculme*, 1997, pp. 30-32
Co. Durham
Darlington
3944   Robert Daill [Dale], tanner
   Atkinson et al., *Darlington*, 1993, pp. 78-79
3945   John Hall, cordwainer
   Atkinson et al., *Darlington*, 1993, pp. 80-82
3946   Robert Loriman [Loryman]
   Atkinson et al., *Darlington*, 1993, pp. 84-85
Hertfordshire
St Albans, St Stephens
3947   Edward and Elizabeth Crawley
   Parker, *Worldly Goods*, 2004, p. 159
3948   Lawrence Hebs, weaver
   Parker, *Worldly Goods*, 2004, p. 160
3949   George Wynzor
   Munby, *Worldly Goods*, 1991, pp. 93-94
Sarratt
3950   Alexander Cowden
   Bullen, *Sarratt*, [1982], pp. 79-80
Lincolnshire
Cleethorpes
3951   Thomas Blackherd, husbandman
   Ambler, Watkinson, *Clee*, 1987, pp. 109-110
3952   Christopher Hompton, fisherman
   Ambler, Watkinson, *Clee*, 1987, pp. 110-111
Oxfordshire
Banbury
3953   John Dryver [Dryuer]
   Brinkworth and Gibson, *Banbury*, I, 1975, p. 193
3954   Thomas Dudley, victualler
   Brinkworth and Gibson, *Banbury*, I, 1975, p. 190
3955   Allen [Alane] Hartlet
   Brinkworth and Gibson, *Banbury*, I, 1975, p. 189
3956   Franncis Hartlette [Francis Hartlet]
   Brinkworth and Gibson, *Banbury*, I, 1975, p. 191
3957   Edward Harwood alias Tomson [Tompson],
shoemaker
   Brinkworth and Gibson, *Banbury*, I, 1975, p. 188
Banbury, Neithrop
3958   Edward Keelinge [Kelinge, Keyley], husbandman
   Brinkworth and Gibson, *Banbury*, I, 1975, p. 192
Banbury, Grimsbury
3959   David [Dave] Mayowe, servant
   Brinkworth and Gibson, *Banbury*, I, 1975, p. 186
Banbury
3960   Seth Prophet [Profytte], gardener
   Brinkworth and Gibson, *Banbury*, I, 1975, pp. 188-189
Banbury, Neithrop
3961   Robert Richards, husbandman
   Brinkworth and Gibson, *Banbury*, I, 1975, p. 187

3962 Gillian Sowtham [Gyllyan Sowthams], widow
Brinkworth and Gibson, *Banbury*, I, 1975, p. 185
Banbury
3963 Mary Wisdome
Brinkworth and Gibson, *Banbury*, I, 1975, p. 186
3964 Joice Yowick [Joyce Youycke], widow
Brinkworth and Gibson, *Banbury*, I, 1975, pp. 190-191
Water Eaton
3965 John House, [husbandman]
Offord, *Water Eaton*, 1986, p. 10

Scotland
Edinburgh
3966 Jonet Michelhill
Anon., *Bassandyne*, 1836, pp. 237-241

Suffolk
Ipswich
3967 Anne Barnarde, widow
Reed, *Ipswich*, 1981, pp. 64-65
3968 Thomas Coll
Reed, *Ipswich*, 1981, pp. 62-64
3969 William Skeete, linen weaver
Reed, *Ipswich*, 1981, pp. 69-70
3970 Jane Ward, widow
Reed, *Ipswich*, 1981, pp. 65-68
3971 Robert Wardell, clergyman
Reed, *Ipswich*, 1981, pp. 68-69

Warwickshire
Stratford-on-Avon
3972 Arthur Ange [Ainge], [shoemaker]
Jones, *Stratford*, I, 2002, pp. 240-241
3973 Hewgh [Hugh] Anger, carpenter
Jones, *Stratford*, I, 2002, pp. 250-251
3974 Thomas Badzee [Badsy], miller
Jones, *Stratford*, I, 2002, pp. 249-250
3975 Rychard Balys [Richard Baylis], fuller
Jones, *Stratford*, I, 2002, pp. 236-238
3976 Edward Bromley, yeoman [carrier]
Jones, *Stratford*, I, 2002, pp. 238-239
3977 Jone Cartwryt [Joan Cartwright] alias Baker, almswoman
Jones, *Stratford*, I, 2002, p. 245
3978 Edmunde Charles alias Cowper
Jones, *Stratford*, I, 2002, pp. 242-244
3979 Rychard Hornbye [Richard Hornby], [blacksmith]
Jones, *Stratford*, I, 2002, pp. 246-247
3980 William Somner, carpenter
Jones, *Stratford*, I, 2002, pp. 247-248
3981 Katheryn Welch, widow
Jones, *Stratford*, I, 2002, pp. 235-236
Welcombe
3982 Thomas Hiccokes [Hiccox]
Jones, *Stratford*, I, 2002, pp. 251-253

Wiltshire
Marlborough
3983 John Love, innholder
Williams and Thomson, *Marlborough*, 2007, pp. 20-22

Worcestershire
Chaddesley Corbett
3984 John Kyndon
Roper, *Chaddesley Corbett*, 1971, p. 12
Chaddesley Corbett, Cakebole
3985 Stephen Pearkes, [miller]
Roper, *Chaddesley Corbett*, 1971, pp. 13-14

Halesowen, Ludley
3986 John Grove, [grinder]
Davenport, 1912, pp. 8-9

Yorkshire
Lunds
3987 Christofer Blades
Thwaite, *Abbotside*, 1967, p. 34
South Cave
3988 Edward Mounder, [yeoman]
Kaner, *South Cave*, 1994, pp. 216-218

1607

Cheshire
Huxley
3989 Raphe Stringer, husbandman
Bland, *Christleton*, 2003, pp. 203-205
3990 Philip Wilson, yeoman
Bland, *Christleton*, 2003, pp. 212-213
Kelsall
3991 Henry Broadhurst
Bland, *Christleton*, 2003, pp. 202-209
Stockport
3992 James Willyamson, [yeoman] alderman
Phillips and Smith, *Stockport*, 1985, pp. 56-58
Tarvin, Clotton
3993 Richard Vernon
Bland, *Christleton*, 2003, p. 210
Tattenhall
3994 Rycharde Marsh
Bland, *Christleton*, 2003, pp. 207-208
Wrenbury, Newhall
3995 William Fletcher
Pixton, *Wrenbury*, 2009, pp. 61-62

Derbyshire
Brimington
3996 John Bowler [Boller]
Bestall and Fowkes, *Chesterfield*, 2001, pp. 36-37
Chesterfield
3997 Elizabeth Bramhall [Bramshall] alias Swindell, widow
Bestall and Fowkes, *Chesterfield*, 2001, pp. 29-31
Chesterfield, Calow
3998 Henry Stubbinge, husbandman [yeoman]
Bestall and Fowkes, *Chesterfield*, 2001, pp. 31-32
Glossop, Holehouse
3999 Raphe Andrewe, [tanner]
Lee and Miller, *New Mills*, 1999, pp. 68-69
Newbold
4000 John Harvye, husbandman
Bestall and Fowkes, *Chesterfield*, 2001, pp. 32-35
4001 Ann Newbold, widow
Bestall and Fowkes, *Chesterfield*, 2001, pp. 35-36

Devonshire
Hatherleigh
4002 James Wonnacott
Cash, *Devon*, 1966, p. 22
4003 George Yeo, esquire
Cash, *Devon*, 1966, pp. 22-23
Uffculme
4004 Mary Gyll [Gill], widow
Wyatt, *Uffculme*, 1997, pp. 32-33

Co. Durham
Darlington
4005 Myles Guy, cordwainer
Atkinson *et al.*, *Darlington*, 1993, pp. 88-91

4006 Richard Hoodlesse [Hudless]
Atkinson *et al.*, *Darlington*, 1993, pp. 86-87
4007 Thomas Johnson, tanner
Atkinson *et al.*, *Darlington*, 1993, pp. 91-92
4008 Thomas Nawton
Atkinson *et al.*, *Darlington*, 1993, pp. 92-94
East Murton
4009 William Maddison
Wood, *Wills and Inventories*, 1929, IV, p. 15

Hertfordshire
St Albans, St Stephens, Colney Street
4010 Agnes Trot, widow
Parker, *Worldly Goods*, 2004, p. 161
Sarratt
4011 Arthur Nicolles, [yeoman]
Bullen, *Sarratt*, [1982], pp. 88-89
4012 Bray Rolfe, gentleman
Bullen, *Sarratt*, [1982], pp. 82-86

Lancashire
Manchester
4013 Willem Clloffelld [Allofield]
Axon, 1915, p. 16
4014 Anthonie Mosley, clothier
Earwaker, *Lancashire and Cheshire*, 1893, pp. 18-20
Turton Tower, Bolton
4015 Elizabeth Orrell, widow
Piccope, *Lancashire and Cheshire*, 1860, p. 144

Leicestershire
Evington
4016 Wm. Fakner, [carpenter]
Wilshere, *Evington*, 1985, p. 13
4017 Peter Hill, [labourer]
Wilshere, *Evington*, 1985, p. 12
4018 Nicholas Noone, [husbandman]
Wilshere, *Evington*, 1985, p. 14

Lincolnshire
Clee, Itterby
4019 George Dixson, labourer
Ambler, Watkinson, *Clee*, 1987, p. 111

London
Leadenhall Street
4020 Robert Lee
Schofield, *London*, 1994, pp. 233-235
Savoy Palace
4021 Sir Henry Lee
Lee, 1885, pp. 122-124

Northamptonshire
Lilford
4022 Mrs Alice Elmes, widow (also listed
Warmington, Papley)
Anon., *Lilford*, 1935, pp. 28-45
Warmington, Papley
Mrs Alice Elmes, widow (see Lilford)

Oxfordshire
Banbury, St John's
4023 James Dryver [Dryuer], millwright
Brinkworth and Gibson, *Banbury*, I, 1975, p. 195
Banbury
4024 Thomas Harris, victualler
Brinkworth and Gibson, *Banbury*, I, 1975, p. 196
4025 Simon [Symon] Hathway
Brinkworth and Gibson, *Banbury*, I, 1975, pp. 195-196

4026 Thomas Overburye [Overberye], turner
Brinkworth and Gibson, *Banbury*, I, 1975, p. 194
Water Eaton
4027 Nicholas Reeve, [yeoman]
Offord, *Water Eaton*, 1986, pp. 12-13

Staffordshire
Dudley
4028 John Bayley
Roper, *Dudley*, 1968, p. 3

Warwickshire
Bishopton
4029 William Yonge [Young], husbandman
Jones, *Stratford*, I, 2002, pp. 253-254
Luddington
4030 Robert Hadley
Jones, *Stratford*, I, 2002, p. 255
Stoneleigh
4031 Thomas Owles
Alcock, *Warwickshire*, 1993, pp. 47-48

Wiltshire
Marlborough
4032 Francis Parker
Williams and Thomson, *Marlborough*, 2007, p. 24
4033 Antony Stevens alias Hawks
Williams and Thomson, *Marlborough*, 2007, pp. 22-23
4034 Anne Weare alias Browne, widow
Williams and Thomson, *Marlborough*, 2007, pp. 23-24

Worcestershire
Chaddesley Corbett, Bluntington
4035 William Kindon, [yeoman]
Roper, *Chaddesley Corbett*, 1971, pp. 14-15
Chaddesley Corbett, Drayton
4036 William Wilks, husbandman
Roper, *Chaddesley Corbett*, 1971, p. 24

Yorkshire
South Cave
4037 Thomas Clarke
Kaner, *South Cave*, 1994, pp. 221-222
4038 John Cleaving, [yeoman]
Kaner, *South Cave*, 1994, pp. 220-221
4039 William Stather
Kaner, *South Cave*, 1994, pp. 218-219

1608
Cheshire
Ashton-on-Sale
4040 Hamnet Barlow
Groves, *Ashton-on-Mersey and Sale*, 1999, pp. 26-27
4041 Randle Jones
Groves, *Ashton-on-Mersey and Sale*, 1999, pp. 27-28
Burton
4042 William Ince, husbandman
Bland, *Christleton*, 2003, pp. 234-235
Kelsall
4043 James Hocknell [Hockenhull]
Bland, *Christleton*, 2003, p. 230
Mouldsworth
4044 John Littler, gentleman
Bland, *Christleton*, 2003, p. 225
Rowton
4045 Thomas Poulforte [Pulford], husbandman
Bland, *Christleton*, 2003, pp. 213-214

4046 Rychard Rychardson
  Bland, *Christleton*, 2003, p. 232
Tarvin, Stapleford
  4047 Raphe Darlington, husbandman
  Bland, *Christleton*, 2003, p. 229
Tarvin
  4048 Peter Philkins
  Bland, *Christleton*, 2003, p. 226
Wrenbury cum Frith
  4049 John Tenche
  Pixton, *Wrenbury*, 2009, p. 70
Wrenbury, Coole Lane
  4050 Henry Vernon
  Pixton, *Wrenbury*, 2009, pp. 67-69

Derbyshire
Chesterfield
  4051 William Ellis
  Bestall and Fowkes, *Chesterfield*, 2001, pp. 38-39
Chesterfield, Tapton
  4052 John Key [Keye], husbandman
  Bestall and Fowkes, *Chesterfield*, 2001, pp. 42-49
Chesterfield, Dunston
  4053 Nicholas Poynton
  Bestall and Fowkes, *Chesterfield*, 2001, pp. 41-42
Chesterfield, Tapton
  4054 Anthony Purslove
  Bestall and Fowkes, *Chesterfield*, 2001, pp. 37-38
Chesterfield, Upper Newbold
  4055 Robert Stanshall, husbandman
  Bestall and Fowkes, *Chesterfield*, 2001, pp. 40-41

Co. Durham
Gibside
  4056 William Blakiston, esquire
  Wood, *Wills and Inventories*, 1929, IV, pp. 29-31

Hertfordshire
St Albans, St Stephens
  4057 William Skeale, yeoman
  Munby, *Worldly Goods*, 1991, pp. 96-97
  4058 Laurence Taylor, yeoman
  Parker, *Worldly Goods*, 2004, pp. 163-164
  4059 Agnes Wynsor
  Munby, *Worldly Goods*, 1991, p. 95

Lancashire
Scarisbrick Hall
  4060 Henry Scarisbrick, esquire
  Cheetham, 1938, pp. 126-133

Leicestershire
Evington
  4061 Robert Belgrave, [yeoman]
  Wilshere, *Evington*, 1985, p. 13

Lincolnshire
Allington
  4062 Thomas Wright, yeoman
  Pask, *Allington*, 1989, pp. 50-52
Clee
  4063 Robt Lowe
  Ambler, Watkinson, *Clee*, 1987, pp. 111-112

Northamptonshire
Warkworth
  4064 John Butler
  Brinkworth and Gibson, *Banbury*, I, 1975, p. 197

Oxfordshire
Banbury
  4065 Alice Boomer
  Brinkworth and Gibson, *Banbury*, I, 1975, pp. 198-199
  4066 Richard Taylor, weaver
  Brinkworth and Gibson, *Banbury*, I, 1975, p. 198
  4067 Thomas Tomney [Tunnye]
  Brinkworth and Gibson, *Banbury*, I, 1975, pp. 197-198
Water Eaton
  4068 Alice Meare, widow
  Offord, *Water Eaton*, 1986, p. 14

Staffordshire
Dudley, St Edmund's
  4069 Henrye Bradleye
  Roper, *Dudley*, 1966, p. 2
Dudley
  4070 William Knowles, tailor
  Roper, *Dudley*, 1968, pp. 3-4
Lichfield
  4071 John Mathewe, tanner
  Vaisey, *Lichfield*, 1969, pp. 46-48

Suffolk
Ipswich
  4072 Richard Smart, gentleman (also listed Washbrook)
  Reed, *Ipswich*, 1981, pp. 70-73
Washbrook
  Richard Smart, gentleman (see Ipswich)

Warwickshire
Bishopton
  4073 John Marshall, clergyman [curate of Bishopton]
  Jones, *Stratford*, I, 2002, pp. 255-263
Shottery
  4074 Alice Burman, widow
  Jones, *Stratford*, I, 2002, pp. 267-268
Stratford-on-Avon
  4075 Alice Fletcher, widow
  Jones, *Stratford*, I, 2002, pp. 268-269
  4076 Allice Hiccocke [Alice Hiccox], [widow]
  Jones, *Stratford*, I, 2002, p. 264
  4077 John Pyrry [Perry], butcher
  Jones, *Stratford*, I, 2002, pp. 265-267

Wiltshire
Marlborough
  4078 Thomas Browne, gentleman
  Williams and Thomson, *Marlborough*, 2007, pp. 26-27
  4079 Robert Johnson, leather dresser
  Williams and Thomson, *Marlborough*, 2007, pp. 24-26

Worcestershire
Chaddesley Corbett
  4080 John Newey
  Roper, *Chaddesley Corbett*, 1971, pp. 18-19
Chaddesley Corbett, Drayton
  4081 Christian Perkes, [scythesmith]
  Roper, *Chaddesley Corbett*, 1971, pp. 20-23
  4082 George Raybould
  Roper, *Chaddesley Corbett*, 1971, pp. 16-18
  4083 Richard Smith, [scythesmith]
  West, *Village Records*, 1962, pp. 98-102
  Roper, *Scythesmiths*, 1967, pp. 15-16
  4084 William Wilkes
  West, *Village Records*, 1962, pp. 97-98

Shelsley Beauchamp
4085 Edmond Notte [Edmund Nott], gentleman
Wanklyn, *Worcestershire*, 1998, pp. 109-112
Worcester
4086 Hugh Robinson, brewer
Dyer, *Worcestershire*, 1967, pp. 41-48
Worcester, St Peter's
4087 John Warde, labourer
Dyer, *Worcestershire*, 1967, pp. 59-60
Yorkshire
South Cave
4088 Luke Norman, yeoman
Kaner, *South Cave*, 1994, pp. 222-224
4089 John Robinson [alias Tenam]
Kaner, *South Cave*, 1994, p. 222

1608 (c.)
Cheshire
Bowdon
4090 Alice Whitley
Groves, *Bowdon*, 1997, p. 13

1609
Bristol
Bristol, St Stephen
4091 John Bauge [Baughe], turner
George, *Bristol*, 1, 2002, pp. 10-11
Bristol, St Peter
4092 Richard Mascoll, butcher
George, *Bristol*, 1, 2002, pp. 8-9
Bristol, St Michael
4093 Edward Tucker, mariner
George, *Bristol*, 1, 2002, pp. 7-8
Bristol, Temple
4094 Henry Willcox [Wilcox], shearman
George, *Bristol*, 1, 2002, pp. 9-10
Clifton
4095 John Sheppard, [husbandman]
Moore, *Clifton*, 1981, pp. 1-2
Shirehampton
4096 Arthur King, vintner
Moore, *Clifton*, 1981, pp. 4-6
Stoke Bishop
4097 William Mattock, [husbandman]
Moore, *Clifton*, 1981, pp. 3-4
4098 Richard Webb, husbandman
Moore, *Clifton*, 1981, p. 7
Westbury
4099 Alice Sergeant, widow
Moore, *Clifton*, 1981, p. 8
4100 John Weare, weaver
Moore, *Clifton*, 1981, p. 8-9
4101 Katherine Webbe, widow
Moore, *Clifton*, 1981, pp. 2-3
Cheshire
Christleton, Cotton
4102 John Finchet, husbandman
Bland, *Christleton*, 2003, pp. 248-249
Christleton
4103 William Maddock
Bland, *Christleton*, 2003, pp. 247-248
Kelsall
4104 Jone Done, husbandman
Bland, *Christleton*, 2003, pp. 241-243

Sale
4105 Robert Vawdrey
Groves, *Ashton-on-Mersey and Sale*, 1999, p. 30
Stockport
4106 John Robotham, husbandman
Phillips and Smith, *Stockport*, 1985, pp. xxi, 61
Tarvin
4107 Ellen Gregorie
Bland, *Christleton*, 2003, p. 253
Tarvin, Foulk Stapleford
4108 William Martyn, husbandman
Bland, *Christleton*, 2003, pp. 240-241
Tarvin, Stapleford
4109 William North
Bland, *Christleton*, 2003, p. 254
Tattenhall
4110 Roberte Walter
Bland, *Christleton*, 2003, p. 250
Unlocated
4111 Hughe Buckleye
Bland, *Christleton*, 2003, pp. 250-251
Wrenbury, Newhall
4112 William Sevell
Pixton, *Wrenbury*, 2009, p. 72
Devonshire
Exeter
4113 Henry Gandye, brewer
Dymond, 1887, pp. 2-4
Dorsetshire
Yetminster [?]
4114 Robert Mundyn
Machin, *Yetminster*, 1976, No.22, (1 p.)
Co. Durham
Darlington
4115 Thomas Catherick, tanner
Atkinson *et al.*, *Darlington*, 1993, pp. 101-102
4116 Anthonie Claxton
Atkinson *et al.*, *Darlington*, 1993, pp. 102-103
4117 Richard Dack
Atkinson *et al.*, *Darlington*, 1993, pp. 97-99
4118 Robert Dent
Atkinson *et al.*, *Darlington*, 1993, p. 95
Darlington, Cockerton
4119 Jhon Marshall
Atkinson *et al.*, *Darlington*, 1993, pp. 96-97
Darlington
4120 Gawin Ratcliffe
Atkinson *et al.*, *Darlington*, 1993, p. 94
Lumley Castle
4121 John, Lord Lumley
Hervey, 1918, pp. 40-43
Derbyshire
Brimington
4122 Margaret Bradbury [Bradburye]
Bestall and Fowkes, *Chesterfield*, 2001, pp. 51-52
4123 Samuel Smith [Smythe], husbandman
Bestall and Fowkes, *Chesterfield*, 2001, pp. 52-53
Chesterfield
4124 John Greensmyth [Greensmythe], husbandman
Bestall and Fowkes, *Chesterfield*, 2001, pp. 52-53
4125 Cuthbert Hutcheson, clergyman
Bestall and Fowkes, *Chesterfield*, 2001, pp. 49-50

4126 Thomas Kenricke [Kendricke], locksmith
Bestall and Fowkes, *Chesterfield*, 2001, pp. 55-57
4127 Richard More [Mower]
Bestall and Fowkes, *Chesterfield*, 2001, pp. 53-54
4128 Francis Slater [Slatter], glazier
Bestall and Fowkes, *Chesterfield*, 2001, pp. 59-60

Gloucestershire
Stoke Gifford
4129 William Large, rough mason
Moore, *Frampton Cotterell*, 1976, pp. 40-41
Winterbourne
4130 Thomas Marshall alias Stevens, [yeoman]
Moore, *Frampton Cotterell*, 1976, p. 41

Hertfordshire
St Albans, St Stephens
4131 Robert Bird
Parker, *Worldly Goods*, 2004, pp. 169-170
4132 William Pope
Munby, *Worldly Goods*, 1991, pp. 98-99
4133 John Ratcliff, schoolmaster
Parker, *Worldly Goods*, 2004, pp. 167-168
4134 Thomas Rowe
Munby, *Worldly Goods*, 1991, pp. 97-98
4135 John Wilson
Parker, *Worldly Goods*, 2004, p. 167

Kent
Faversham
4136 Elisabeth Aiscoughe [Askew], widow
Hussey, 1905, pp. 232-235

Lancashire
Billinge, Birchley
4137 Dorothie Scaresbreeke
St Helens, *Angells*, 1999, pp. 24-25
Preston
4138 Edward Lemon, gentleman
Fishwick, 1876-7, pp. 170-172

Lincolnshire
Clee, Oole
4139 John Lacebie, husbandman
Ambler, Watkinson, *Clee*, 1987, pp. 114-115
Clee
4140 William Lowe, husbandman
Ambler, Watkinson, *Clee*, 1987, pp. 113-114
Clee, Thrunscoe
4141 Helene Portas, widow
Ambler, Watkinson, *Clee*, 1987, p. 113
Clee, Oole
4142 Wylliam Yeates, husbandman
Ambler, Watkinson, *Clee*, 1987, pp. 12-113

London
St Nicholas Acon
4143 Thomas Potter, salter
Anon., *Curious*, 1884, p. 280

Nottinghamshire
Wollaton Hall
4144 Sir Percival Willoughby
Stevenson, 1887, pp. 87-93
Stevenson, 1911, pp. 485-491

Oxfordshire
Banbury
4145 John Abarrow, labourer
Brinkworth and Gibson, *Banbury*, I, 1975, pp. 200-201

4146 Michael Cartwrighte [Cartrite]
Brinkworth and Gibson, *Banbury*, I, 1975, p. 200
4147 John Harvie
Brinkworth and Gibson, *Banbury*, I, 1975, p. 199
4148 John Jackson, surgeon
Brinkworth and Gibson, *Banbury*, I, 1975, pp. 201-203
4149 Valentine Moseley, bonesetter
Brinkworth and Gibson, *Banbury*, I, 1975, pp. 203-204

Staffordshire
Dudley
4150 Humfrey Bradeley
Roper, *Dudley*, 1968, p. 4
4151 Christofer Chambers alias Ireland
Roper, *Dudley*, 1966, pp. 3-5

Warwickshire
Stratford-on-Avon
4152 William Brunte
Jones, *Stratford*, I, 2002, pp. 269-270

Worcestershire
Belbroughton
4153 William Wytton, scythesmith
Roper, *Belbroughton*, 1967-1968, p. 55
Chaddesley Corbett, Drayton
4154 Richard Smith, [scythesmith]
Roper, *Chaddesley Corbett*, 1971, pp. 25-26
Harvington
4155 Richard Cowper, [scythegrinder]
Roper, *Chaddesley Corbett*, 1971, pp. 27-28

Yorkshire
South Cave, Oxmardyke
4156 Christofer Markham
Kaner, *South Cave*, 1994, pp. 224-225
4157 Stephen Mounder, [yeoman]
Kaner, *South Cave*, 1994, pp. 225-228

1609 (c.)
Devonshire
George Nympton
4158 Richard Clotworthie
Cash, *Devon*, 1966, pp. 23-24

London
Brooke House, Hackney
4159 Elizabeth, Countess of Oxford
Robinson, 1842, 1, pp. 110-114
Merchant Taylors' Hall
4160 Merchant Taylors' Company
Clode, 1875, pp. 92-96

Wiltshire
Marlborough
4161 Robert Chapman alias Hitchcock, [weaver]
Williams and Thomson, *Marlborough*, 2007, pp. 27-28

1610
Bedfordshire
Unlocated
4162 William Stevensone
Emmison, *Bedfordshire*, 1938, pp. 53-54

Bristol
Bristol, Hospital of St Philip [and St Jacob]
4163 John Warren, almsman
George, *Bristol*, 1, 2002, pp. 11-12
Stoke Bishop
4164 John Stokes, husbandman
Moore, *Clifton*, 1981, pp. 9-11

4165   Robert Willington, [yeoman]
Moore, *Clifton*, 1981, pp. 12-13

Cheshire
Bowdon
4166   Richard Massey, yeoman
Groves, *Bowdon*, 1997, pp. 15-17
Christleton, Cotton
4167   Henrie Sandilance, husbandman
Bland, *Christleton*, 2003, pp. 262-263
Hale
4168   Richard Grantham, [yeoman]
Groves, *Hale 1*, 2005, p. 22
Stockport
4169   John Benesson
Phillips and Smith, *Stockport*, 1985, p. 65
4170   Robert Fallowes
Phillips and Smith, *Stockport*, 1985, p. 67
4171   Henry Houlme, mercer
Phillips and Smith, *Stockport*, 1985, pp. 63-65
4172   Margaret Marsland, widow
Phillips and Smith, *Stockport*, 1985, pp. 67-68
4173   Ellizabeth [Isabell] Torkynton, widow
Phillips and Smith, *Stockport*, 1985, pp. 62-63
Tarvin, Clotton
4174   Oswell Mason
Bland, *Christleton*, 2003, pp. 239-240
Tattenhall
4175   Thomas Dutton
Bland, *Christleton*, 2003, pp. 264-266
4176   William Jhones, husbandman
Bland, *Christleton*, 2003, p. 268
Waverton
4177   Robert Dutton, gentleman
Bland, *Christleton*, 2003, pp. 266-267
Wrenbury, Broomhall
4178   Margret Ankers
Pixton, *Wrenbury*, 2009, pp. 74-75
Wrenbury, Newhall, Aston
4179   James Barnet
Pixton, *Wrenbury*, 2009, pp. 78-80
Wrenbury
4180   Alles Swane, [widow]
Pixton, *Wrenbury*, 2009, p. 98
Wrenbury, Newhall, Dodds Green
4181   Roger Swann, [husbandman]
Pixton, *Wrenbury*, 2009, pp. 95-97

Derbyshire
Chesterfield, Temple Normanton
4182   John Clay, husbandman
Bestall and Fowkes, *Chesterfield*, 2001, pp. 60-61
Chesterfield
4183   Thomas Dowker, shoemaker
Bestall and Fowkes, *Chesterfield*, 2001, pp. 62-64
4184   George Holland, coverlet weaver
Bestall and Fowkes, *Chesterfield*, 2001, pp. 57-59
4185   Robert Penestone [Penyston], shearman
Bestall and Fowkes, *Chesterfield*, 2001, pp. 61-62

Devonshire
Uffculme
4186   Alexander Goodridge, [yeoman]
Wyatt, *Uffculme*, 1997, pp. 33-34
4187   William Rugge [alias Cuthbert], yeoman
Wyatt, *Uffculme*, 1997, p. 36

4188   Agnes Stone, [widow]
Wyatt, *Uffculme*, 1997, pp. 35-36
4189   Humfre[y] Tawton, yeoman
Wyatt, *Uffculme*, 1997, pp. 34-35
4190   Thomas Tucker, husbandman
Wyatt, *Uffculme*, 1997, p. 35
Unlocated
4191   William Bowring
Cash, *Devon*, 1966, pp. 24-25

Dorsetshire
Sherborne
4192   Richard Revell, gentleman
Anon., *Revell*, 1942, pp. 132-134

Co. Durham
Darlington
4193   Isabell Cattricke [Catherick]
Atkinson *et al.*, *Darlington*, 1993, pp. 104-105
4194   Anthony Dennis
Atkinson *et al.*, *Darlington*, 1993, pp. 111-117
Darlington, Blackwell
4195   William Dockera
Atkinson *et al.*, *Darlington*, 1993, pp. 105-106
Darlington, Cockerton
4196   Christopher Fawell, husbandman
Atkinson *et al.*, *Darlington*, 1993, pp. 107-109
Darlington
4197   John Lomly [Lomley]
Atkinson *et al.*, *Darlington*, 1993, p. 118
Darlington, Blackwell
4198   Rayphe Wrenne [Ralph Wrenn], yeoman
Atkinson *et al.*, *Darlington*, 1993, pp. 110-111

Gloucestershire
Stoke Gifford
4199   John Atwoode, husbandman
Moore, *Frampton Cotterell*, 1976, pp. 41-42

Hertfordshire
Hemel Hempstead, Bodsend
4200   John Longe
Anon., *Lock, Stock*, 1978, pp. 51-52
Kings Langley
4201   Ellen Pearce, widow
Munby, *Kings Langley*, 1981, p. 42
St Albans, St Stephens
4202   Thomas Chadsley, [yeoman]
Parker, *Worldly Goods*, 2004, pp. 172-173
4203   William Field
Munby, *Worldly Goods*, 1991, pp. 101-102
4204   Alice Wilson, widow
Parker, *Worldly Goods*, 2004, p. 170
Sarratt
4205   Thomas Edwards, husbandman
Bullen, *Sarratt*, [1982], pp. 91-92
4206   Edward Lovett
Bullen, *Sarratt*, [1982], pp. 93-94

Lancashire
St Helens, Sutton
4207   Katherin Johnson
St Helens, *Angells*, 1999, pp. 26-27

Leicestershire
Evington
4208   Edward Chamberlyn, [yeoman]
Wilshere, *Evington*, 1985, p. 15

Lincolnshire
Clee
4209 Wm Lowe, tailor
Ambler, Watkinson, *Clee*, 1987, pp. 115-116
Gedney
4210 Isabel Wharton, widow
Crawford and Cowing, 2000, pp. 120-121
Oxfordshire
Banbury
4211 John Clearidge
Brinkworth and Gibson, *Banbury*, I, 1975, p. 206
4212 Isabel Helmedon [Helmdene], [widow]
Brinkworth and Gibson, *Banbury*, I, 1975, pp. 208-209
4213 Alice Hirons [Alis Hearon]
Brinkworth and Gibson, *Banbury*, I, 1975, pp. 206-207
4214 John Wallsall [Walsall], butcher
Brinkworth and Gibson, *Banbury*, I, 1975, p. 205
Staffordshire
Dudley
4215 Alice [Margaret?] Gorton, widow
Roper, *Dudley*, 1968, p. 5
Lichfield
4216 Thomas Burnes, upholsterer
Vaisey, *Lichfield*, 1969, pp. 48-50
Suffolk
Ipswich
4217 Richard Cornellis, joiner
Reed, *Ipswich*, 1981, pp. 75-76
4218 Philip Helwys, merchant (also listed Redgrave)
Reed, *Ipswich*, 1981, pp. 76-78
4219 Thomas Hopkins, poldavis weaver
Reed, *Ipswich*, 1981, pp. 74-75
Redgrave
4220 Philip Helwys, merchant (see Ipswich)
Warwickshire
Stoneleigh, Canley
4221 Thomas Burton
Alcock, *Warwickshire*, 1993, p. 123
Stoneleigh
4222 Roger Hudson, tanner
Alcock, *Warwickshire*, 1993, p. 108
Wiltshire
Marlborough
4223 John Sclater, tanner
Williams and Thomson, *Marlborough*, 2007, pp. 28-29
Worcestershire
Belbroughton
4224 Edward Witten, [husbandman]
Roper, *Belbroughton*, 1967-1968, p. 57
Elmbridge
4225 Gerarde Danet [Gerard Danett], esquire
Wanklyn, *Worcestershire*, 1998, pp. 115-116
Little Malvern
4226 Henry Russelles [Russell], esquire
Wanklyn, *Worcestershire*, 1998, pp. 112-115
Yorkshire
Browsholme Hall (now Lancashire)
4227 Thomas Parker
Jervis, *Browsholme*, 1986, pp. 12-14
Cottingley, Bingley (now Bradford)
4228 Richard Nicholson
Preston, *Co. York*, 1929, pp. 8-9

South Cave
4229 Agnes Annyson
Kaner, *South Cave*, 1994, pp. 230-231
South Cave, Faxfleet
4230 John Harlan
Kaner, *South Cave*, 1994, pp. 231-233
South Cave
4231 William Hodgshon, labourer
Kaner, *South Cave*, 1994, pp. 233-234
4232 John Stanfield
Kaner, *South Cave*, 1994, pp. 228-230

1611
Bristol
Bristol, St Peter
4233 John Compton, butcher
George, *Bristol*, 1, 2002, pp. 12-13
Shirehampton
4234 Christopher Willcox, [yeoman]
Moore, *Clifton*, 1981, pp. 13-14
Cheshire
Ashton-on-Mersey
4235 Randle Barlow, carrier
Groves, *Ashton-on-Mersey and Sale*, 1999, pp. 31-32
Bowdon
4236 Edmund Simpson, yeoman
Groves, *Bowdon*, 1997, pp. 17-21
Dunham Massey
4237 W[illia]m Frith, [yeoman]
Groves, *Dunham Massey*, 2008, pp. 25-28
Hale
4238 William Ashley, [husbandman]
Groves, *Hale 1*, 2005, pp. 29-30
4239 Robert Barlow, [husbandman]
Groves, *Hale 1*, 2005, pp. 30-31
Hale, Ringway
4240 Robert Pedley, [husbandman]
Groves, *Hale 1*, 2005, pp. 24-25
Hale
4241 William Warburton, [husbandman]
Groves, *Hale 1*, 2005, pp. 27-28
Hargrave
4242 Hughe Greiffith, gentleman
Bland, *Christleton*, 2003, pp. 270-271
4243 Roberte Humston, drover
Bland, *Christleton*, 2003, pp. 288-289
Nantwich
4244 Henry Wickstead, yeoman
Cockcroft, *Nantwich*, 1999, p. 339.1
4245 Thomas Wilbraham, farrier
Cockcroft, *Nantwich*, 1999, pp. 346.1-2
Stockport
4246 James Daniell, webster
Phillips and Smith, *Stockport*, 1985, pp. 69-70
4247 William Swyndells, husbandman
Phillips and Smith, *Stockport*, 1985, pp. 71-72
Tarvin, Clotton
4248 William Rathbone
Bland, *Christleton*, 2003, pp. 285-286
Tarvin
4249 Jane Verden, widow
Bland, *Christleton*, 2003, pp. 290-291
Tarvin, Clotton Hoofield
4250 John Woodhowse, husbandman
Bland, *Christleton*, 2003, p. 280

Tattenhall, Newton
  4251 Roberte Handley
  Bland, *Christleton*, 2003, pp. 275-276
  4252 Peter Price
  Bland, *Christleton*, 2003, p. 292
  4253 Peter Ryder, yeoman
  Bland, *Christleton*, 2003, p. 273
Tattenhall
  4254 Thomas Sellor, husbandman
  Bland, *Christleton*, 2003, p. 280
Waverton
  4255 William Dyason
  Bland, *Christleton*, 2003, pp. 273-274
Wrenbury
  4256 John Bickerton
  Pixton, *Wrenbury*, 2009, p. 113
  4257 William Davies
  Pixton, *Wrenbury*, 2009, pp. 108-109
Wrenbury, Newhall
  4258 Ellen Fletcher
  Pixton, *Wrenbury*, 2009, p. 110
Wrenbury, Broomhall
  4259 Thomas Lowe
  Pixton, *Wrenbury*, 2009, pp. 99-100
Wrenbury, Chorley
  4260 William Patrick
  Pixton, *Wrenbury*, 2009, pp. 101-102
Wrenbury, Newhall
  4261 Margerie Sevell, widow
  Pixton, *Wrenbury*, 2009, p. 108
Wrenbury
  4262 Lawrence Starkie, [gentleman]
  Pixton, *Wrenbury*, 2009, pp. 111-112
Wrenbury, Coole
  4263 Hugh Whitney, [gentleman]
  Pixton, *Wrenbury*, 2009, pp. 105-106
Cornwall
St Breock
  4264 Francis Pedler
  Pedler, 1984, pp. 25-26
Derbyshire
Chesterfield
  4265 John Heathcote, tanner
  Bestall and Fowkes, *Chesterfield*, 2001, pp. 67-72
  4266 Ralph Heathcote, servant to a tanner
  Bestall and Fowkes, *Chesterfield*, 2001, p. 65
  4267 Thomas Heathcott, butcher
  Bestall and Fowkes, *Chesterfield*, 2001, pp. 65-67
  4268 Richard Syndall, glazier
  Bestall and Fowkes, *Chesterfield*, 2001, pp. 72-74
Devonshire
Shebbear
  4269 Humfry Heisett
  Cash, *Devon*, 1966, p. 25
Dorsetshire
Chardstock (now Devonshire), Coxden [Cockesden]
  4270 Richard Symonds [Simonds]
  Halliwell, *Inventories*, 1854, pp. 59-86
Co. Durham
Chester-le-Street
  4271 Elizabeth Maddeson, widow
  Wood, *Wills and Inventories*, 1929, IV, pp. 46-47

Gloucestershire
Stoke Gifford, Harry Stoke
  4272 John Batten, [husbandman]
  Moore, *Frampton Cotterell*, 1976, pp. 42-43
Stoke Gifford
  4273 Thomas Hegges, [husbandman]
  Moore, *Frampton Cotterell*, 1976, pp. 43-44
Winterbourne
  4274 Edith Thorne, widow
  Moore, *Frampton Cotterell*, 1976, p. 43
Hertfordshire
Chipperfield
  4275 Mrs Elizabeth Colt, widow
  Munby, *Kings Langley*, 1981, pp. 44-46
Kings Langley
  4276 Raph [Ralph] Deacon, yeoman
  Munby, *Kings Langley*, 1981, p. 48
  4277 Leonard Dell
  Munby, *Kings Langley*, 1981, p. 47
  4278 Richard Perry
  Munby, *Kings Langley*, 1981, p. 43
St Albans, St Stephens, Park Street
  4279 Rychard Belchare
  Parker, *Worldly Goods*, 2004, p. 175
St Albans, St Stephens
  4280 Agnes Byrd, widow
  Parker, *Worldly Goods*, 2004, pp. 174-175
Lincolnshire
Allington
  4281 Francis Hides, labourer
  Pask, *Allington*, 1989, pp. 54-55
  4282 Edward Russell
  Pask, *Allington*, 1989, pp. 58-59
Clee
  4283 John Ashton, husbandman
  Ambler, Watkinson, *Clee*, 1987, p. 120
  4284 Robert Elvish, husbandman
  Ambler, Watkinson, *Clee*, 1987, pp. 117-118
  4285 Richard Johnson, husbandman
  Ambler, Watkinson, *Clee*, 1987, pp. 116-117
Clee, Itterby
  4286 John Nutsaye, kidger [dealer]
  Ambler, Watkinson, *Clee*, 1987, p. 121
Clee, Oole
  4287 Thomas Simson, husbandman
  Ambler, Watkinson, *Clee*, 1987, pp. 118-119
Clee
  4288 Thomas Sutton, husbandman
  Ambler, Watkinson, *Clee*, 1987, pp. 118-119
Norfolk
Wymondham
  4289 Loye Agas [Aggas], [yeoman]
  Wilson, *Wymondham*, 1983, pp. 14-17
Oxfordshire
Banbury, Grimsbury
  4290 Thomas Beste, day labourer
  Brinkworth and Gibson, *Banbury*, I, 1975, p. 216
Banbury, Neithrop
  4291 Margaret Churchill
  Brinkworth and Gibson, *Banbury*, I, 1975, p. 218
Banbury
  4292 William Clarke, victualler
  Brinkworth and Gibson, *Banbury*, I, 1975, p. 211

4293 Richard Crosby
Brinkworth and Gibson, *Banbury*, I, 1975, p. 210
4294 Elizabeth Garland, widow
Brinkworth and Gibson, *Banbury*, I, 1975, p. 217
4295 John Hall, tanner
Brinkworth and Gibson, *Banbury*, I, 1975, p. 220
4296 David Harrison, carver
Brinkworth and Gibson, *Banbury*, I, 1975, p. 221
Banbury, Grimsbury
4297 Richard Hues [Hewes], tailor
Brinkworth and Gibson, *Banbury*, I, 1975, pp. 215-216
Banbury
4298 Rowland Hughes [Hewes], fletcher
Brinkworth and Gibson, *Banbury*, I, 1975, p. 212
4299 Robert Newell [Newale], weaver
Brinkworth and Gibson, *Banbury*, I, 1975, p. 217
4300 Herman van Otten, surgeon
Brinkworth and Gibson, *Banbury*, I, 1975, p. 221
4301 Richard Showell [Shewell], mercer
Brinkworth and Gibson, *Banbury*, I, 1975, p. 215
4302 Joan Smythe, widow
Brinkworth and Gibson, *Banbury*, I, 1975, p. 222
Banbury, Neithrop
4303 William Stockley
Brinkworth and Gibson, *Banbury*, I, 1975, p. 223
4304 Jane Tappertow [Tappertoe]
Brinkworth and Gibson, *Banbury*, I, 1975, p. 219
Banbury
4305 Robert Vardom, glover
Brinkworth and Gibson, *Banbury*, I, 1975, p. 219
Kelmscott
4306 Thomas Turner
Cooper, 2007, pp. 129-130

Suffolk
Ipswich
4307 Johanne Blosse, widow
Reed, *Ipswich*, 1981, pp. 80-81
4308 David Musson, glover
Reed, *Ipswich*, 1981, pp. 79-80

Warwickshire
Bishopton
4309 Thomas Cale, [yeoman]
Jones, *Stratford*, I, 2002, pp. 275-277
Hatton, Shrewley
4310 Lawrence Ebroll
Sheasby, 1994, pp. 48-49
Stratford-on-Avon
4311 Robart Broake [Robert Brooke], [innkeeper and victualler]
Jones, *Stratford*, I, 2002, pp. 278-279
4312 John Harris
Jones, *Stratford*, I, 2002, pp. 270-271
4313 Thomas Hiccokes [Hiccox], [yeoman]
Jones, *Stratford*, I, 2002, pp. 271-272
4314 John Kirke, husbandman [butcher]
Jones, *Stratford*, I, 2002, pp. 277-278

Wiltshire
Marlborough
4315 Robert Lyme, tanner
Williams and Thomson, *Marlborough*, 2007, pp. 29-30

Worcestershire
Chaddesley Corbett, Yieldingtree
4316 John Smithe
Roper, *Chaddesley Corbett*, 1971, p. 29

Yorkshire
Aysgarth, Shaw Cote
4317 Ane Prat [Anne Pratt], widow
Thwaite, *Abbotside*, 1967, p. 36
Eldwick, Bingley
4318 Issabell Marshall, widow
Preston, *Co. York*, 1929, p. 11
Oakwell Hall, Birstall
4319 Robert Batt, clergyman, rector of Newton Tony, Wiltshire
Foster, 1948, pp. 114-116
South Cave
4320 Mathew Jameson
Kaner, *South Cave*, 1994, pp. 235-236
4321 John Spofford
Kaner, *South Cave*, 1994, p. 234
4322 William Sympson
Kaner, *South Cave*, 1994, pp. 236-237

1611 (c.)
Cheshire
Hale
4323 Richard Goulden, [husbandman]
Groves, *Hale 1*, 2005, pp. 23-24
4324 Thomas Timperley, [husbandman]
Groves, *Hale 1*, 2005, pp. 25-26
Surrey
Beddington
4325 Sir Francis Carew (?)
Jenkinson, 1919, pp. 158-161

1612
Bristol
Bristol
4326 Humphrey Ellis, haberdasher
George, *Bristol*, 1, 2002, pp. 14-15
Bristol, St Mary Redcliffe
4327 Teage Jones, glover
George, *Bristol*, 1, 2002, pp. 15-16
Bristol, St Thomas
4328 William Stainred, barber
George, *Bristol*, 1, 2002, pp. 13-14
Clifton
4329 William Baylie, [husbandman]
Moore, *Clifton*, 1981, pp. 14-15
Lawrence Weston
4330 William Pearce, weaver
Moore, *Clifton*, 1981, p. 17
Shirehampton
4331 Arthur Baker, [husbandman]
Moore, *Clifton*, 1981, pp. 15-16
4332 John Cheshire alias Small, [husbandman]
Moore, *Clifton*, 1981, pp. 16-17
Cheshire
Duddon
4333 John Williamson alias Willye, husbandman
Bland, *Christleton*, 2003, pp. 311-312
Dunham Massey
4334 William Tipping, [yeoman]
Groves, *Dunham Massey*, 2008, pp. 30-31
Hale
4335 John Antrobus, [husbandman]
Groves, *Hale 1*, 2005, pp. 31-32
Hale, Ringway
4336 William Newton, [husbandman]
Groves, *Hale 1*, 2005, p. 33

Kelsall
  4337 Ales Cawley, widow
    Bland, *Christleton*, 2003, pp. 310-311
  4338 John Ithell, husbandman
    Bland, *Christleton*, 2003, pp. 296-297
Nantwich
  4339 Lewis Preece, glover
    Cockcroft, *Nantwich*, 1999, pp. 260.1-2
Rowton
  4340 John Bryne
    Bland, *Christleton*, 2003, pp. 312-313
Stockport
  4341 Hugh Mottram, wheelwright
    Phillips and Smith, *Stockport*, 1985, pp. 75-76
  4342 Ellen Taylior, widow
    Phillips and Smith, *Stockport*, 1985, pp. 77-79
  4343 John Whitacher, shoemaker
    Phillips and Smith, *Stockport*, 1985, pp. 73-74
Tarvin
  4344 William Fletcher
    Bland, *Christleton*, 2003, pp. 302-303
Tarvin, Clotton
  4345 William Hickson
    Bland, *Christleton*, 2003, pp. 299-300
Tarvin, Clotton Hoofield
  4346 Richard ap Rice alias Raynaldes, cooper
    Bland, *Christleton*, 2003, pp. 294-295
  4347 Ellyn Woodhouse, widow
    Bland, *Christleton*, 2003, p. 307
Tattenhall
  4348 Jefferey Dodd
    Bland, *Christleton*, 2003, pp. 308-309
  4349 Jane Seller
    Bland, *Christleton*, 2003, pp. 301-302
Tattenhall, Golborne Bellow, Russhall
  4350 Robert Smith
    Bland, *Christleton*, 2003, pp. 304-306
Wrenbury
  4351 Randulph Cooper, [husbandman]
    Pixton, *Wrenbury*, 2009, pp. 115-116

Cumberland
Bewcastle, Baileyhead
  4352 James Rutledge
    Harrison, 1967, p. 104

Derbyshire
Barrow-upon-Trent
  4353 Robert Jackson, yeoman
    Davies, Hutton, 2001, pp. 4-5
Brimington
  4354 Thomas Marriott, husbandman
    Bestall and Fowkes, *Chesterfield*, 2001, pp. 76-77
Chesterfield
  4355 Ralph Cleyworth [Cluworth], butcher
    Bestall and Fowkes, *Chesterfield*, 2001, pp. 78-80
  4356 James Kenrick [Kendricke], locksmith
    Bestall and Fowkes, *Chesterfield*, 2001, pp. 81-84
  4357 Richard Stainrode [Steynrod]
    Bestall and Fowkes, *Chesterfield*, 2001, pp. 74-76
  4358 Peter Stansall, rope-maker
    Bestall and Fowkes, *Chesterfield*, 2001, pp. 84-87

Devonshire
Uffculme
  4359 John Horne
    Wyatt, *Uffculme*, 1997, p. 37
  4360 William Marshall, [husbandman]
    Wyatt, *Uffculme*, 1997, pp. 36-37

Co. Durham
Darlington
  4361 Michaell Jefferyson [Jeffreyson], tanner
    Atkinson *et al.*, *Darlington*, 1993, pp. 127-129
  4362 Mr Isaac Lowden, [clergyman]
    Atkinson *et al.*, *Darlington*, 1993, pp. 122-125
Darlington, Cockerton
  4363 Thomas Robinson, yeoman
    Atkinson *et al.*, *Darlington*, 1993, pp. 120-122
Darlington, Blackwell
  4364 William Robinson, weaver
    Atkinson *et al.*, *Darlington*, 1993, pp. 131-133
Gateshead
  4365 James Hutton, clergyman, parson of Gateshead
    Raine, *Marske*, 1861, pp. 52-53

Hertfordshire
Chipperfield
  4366 Parnell Carter, widow
    Munby, *Kings Langley*, 1981, pp. 52-53
  4367 Thomas Yonge, gentleman
    Munby, *Kings Langley*, 1981, pp. 50-51
Kings Langley
  4368 Robert Grove, husbandman
    Munby, *Kings Langley*, 1981, p. 49
St Albans, St Stephens
  4369 Dannell Weddon, collier
    Parker, *Worldly Goods*, 2004, p. 176
Sarratt
  4370 Thomas Nycholls, shearman
    Bullen, *Sarratt*, [1982], pp. 102-103

Lancashire
Billinge
  4371 Jenett Lathom, widow
    St Helens, *Angells*, 1999, p. 27

Lincolnshire
Clee
  4372 Thomas Kettlewell, yeoman
    Ambler, Watkinson, *Clee*, 1987, pp. 121-123

London
Bishopsgate
  4373 George Hitchecocke, [innholder of the] Mouthe
Tavern
    Nichols, *Illustrations*, 1797, pp. 229-232

Northamptonshire
Nethercote
  4374 John Taylor alias Parishe, husbandman
    Brinkworth and Gibson, *Banbury*, I, 1975, p. 225

Oxfordshire
Banbury
  4375 Katherin Baker
    Brinkworth and Gibson, *Banbury*, I, 1975, p. 224
  4376 Mr William Bille, clergyman, vicar of Easton
Neston, Warwickshire
    Brinkworth and Gibson, *Banbury*, I, 1975, p. 226
  4377 [Joyce] Hues, widow
    Brinkworth and Gibson, *Banbury*, I, 1975, p. 226

4378 Rowland Hughes [Hewes], fletcher
Brinkworth and Gibson, *Banbury*, I, 1975, pp. 212-213
4379 Timothy Kendall
Brinkworth and Gibson, *Banbury*, I, 1975, p. 227
Banbury, Neithrop
4380 John Kymbell, husbandman
Brinkworth and Gibson, *Banbury*, I, 1975, p. 224
Banbury
4381 Henry Lockwood
Brinkworth and Gibson, *Banbury*, I, 1975, p. 209

Scotland
Orkney, Egilsay, Unyebistir
4382 Merjorie Greiffe
Barclay, 1977, pp. 28-29
Orkney, Orpher, Grindwatter
4383 Nicoll Lesk
Barclay, 1977, pp. 27-28

Staffordshire
Dudley
4384 Henrie Cartwrighte, nailer
Roper, *Dudley*, 1968, p. 6
4385 Francis Hill, [tailor]
Roper, *Dudley*, 1968, p. 8
4386 John Prise, miller
Roper, *Dudley*, 1968, p. 7
4387 Richard Veredie
Roper, *Dudley*, 1968, p. 6
Dudley, St Thomas
4388 Henry Wheeler, rough mason
Roper, *Dudley*, 1968, p. 7-8

Sussex
Iford
4389 John Aridge
Cooper, 1879, pp. 132-133

Wales
Glamorganshire, Reynoldston, Stouthall
4390 Harry Lukas
Lucas, 1986, pp. 6-7

Warwickshire
Ashow
4391 John Wright, fuller
Alcock, *Warwickshire*, 1993, p. 97
Stratford-on-Avon
4392 John Page, [smith]
Jones, *Stratford*, I, 2002, pp. 279-280

Worcestershire
Bengeworth
4393 Thomas Wattson [Watson], gentleman
Wanklyn, *Worcestershire*, 1998, pp. 117-118
Chaddesley Corbett, Cakebole
4394 John Dawkes, [yeoman]
Roper, *Chaddesley Corbett*, 1971, p. 30

Yorkshire
Cottingley, Bingley (now Bradford)
4395 Thomas Slater
Preston, *Co. York*, 1929, pp. 13-15
Eccleshill, Bradford
4396 Lionel Rayner
Brears, *Yorkshire*, 1972, pp. 67-70
Eldwick, Bingley
4397 John Breare
Preston, *Co. York*, 1929, pp. 17-18

Gristhorpe
4398 George Beswick, yeoman
Brears, *Yorkshire*, 1972, pp. 71-73
South Cave
4399 Jane Byas
Kaner, *South Cave*, 1994, pp. 239-240
South Cave, Oxmardyke
4400 Jennyt Gott
Kaner, *South Cave*, 1994, p. 238
South Cave
4401 Ann Hodgesonne
Kaner, *South Cave*, 1994, pp. 246-247
4402 Jennat Jameson
Kaner, *South Cave*, 1994, p. 241
4403 Isabell Mounder, widow
Kaner, *South Cave*, 1994, pp. 242-244
4404 Thomas Pinder
Kaner, *South Cave*, 1994, pp. 245-246
4405 Ellis Richardson
Kaner, *South Cave*, 1994, pp. 240-241

1612 (c.)
Cheshire
Dunham Massey, Sinderland
4406 William Barlow
Groves, *Dunham Massey*, 2008, p. 30
Wiltshire
Marlborough
4407 John Fleming, glover
Williams and Thomson, *Marlborough*, 2007, pp. 30-31
Worcestershire
Worcester, St Peter's
4408 Humphrey Web, chandler
Dyer, *Worcestershire*, 1967, pp. 39-43

1613
Bedfordshire
Southill
4409 Henry Rogers, carpenter
Emmison, *Bedfordshire*, 1938, pp. 132-133
Bristol
Bristol
4410 George Lane, [merchant]
McGrath, 1955, pp. 71-79
Clifton
4411 William Chandler, [sailor]
Moore, *Clifton*, 1981, p. 19
Shirehampton
4412 Elizabeth Dyer, widow
Moore, *Clifton*, 1981, p. 18
4413 Thomas Smith, [yeoman]
Moore, *Clifton*, 1981, p. 20
Cheshire
Ashton-on-Mersey
4414 James Jones, yeoman
Groves, *Ashton-on-Mersey and Sale*, 1999, pp. 34-35
Bowdon
4415 Henry Starkey, clergyman, vicar of Bowdon
Groves, *Bowdon*, 1997, pp. 23-24
Christleton
4416 John Green
Bland, *Christleton*, 2003, p. 330
Christleton, Cotton
4417 William Midlehurst, tailor
Bland, *Christleton*, 2003, pp. 332-333

Christleton
  4418 John Pricharde
    Bland, *Christleton*, 2003, p. 337
  4419 Raffe Rider, yeoman
    Bland, *Christleton*, 2003, pp. 333-334
Christleton, Cotton
  4420 William Walleyes
    Bland, *Christleton*, 2003, p. 329
Nantwich
  4421 Ann Maynwaringe, widow
    Cockcroft, *Nantwich*, 1999, p. 212.1
  4422 Richard Taylor, vintner
    Cockcroft, *Nantwich*, 1999, p. 302.1
  4423 Richard Wilberham, gentleman
    Cockcroft, *Nantwich*, 1999, pp. 342.1-7
Rowton
  4424 Randulphe Richardson
    Bland, *Christleton*, 2003, pp. 330-331
Stockport
  4425 Dorithey [Dorothy] Elcocke, widow
    Phillips and Smith, *Stockport*, 1985, pp. 80-83
  4426 Margaret Hurst
    Phillips and Smith, *Stockport*, 1985, p. 79
Tarvin
  4427 Thomas Simpson, carrier
    Bland, *Christleton*, 2003, pp. 327-328
Tattenhall, Golborne Bellow
  4428 John Golburn, gentleman
    Bland, *Christleton*, 2003, pp. 318-322
Waverton
  4429 Richard Dyason, husbandman
    Bland, *Christleton*, 2003, p. 328
Wrenbury, Sound
  4430 Edward Baskerfild [Baskerville]
    Pixton, *Wrenbury*, 2009, pp. 117-118
  4431 William Cooper, [yeoman]
    Pixton, *Wrenbury*, 2009, pp. 120-121

Cumberland
Bewcastle, Todholes
  4432 William Routledge
    Harrison, 1967, p. 105

Devonshire
Uffculme
  4433 Nicholas Dowdeny
    Wyatt, *Uffculme*, 1997, pp. 38-39
  4434 Humfry Holwill
    Wyatt, *Uffculme*, 1997, p. 39
  4435 Nicholas Tooker
    Wyatt, *Uffculme*, 1997, pp. 37-38
  4436 Barnard Tucker, weaver
    Wyatt, *Uffculme*, 1997, pp. 39-40

Derbyshire
Brimington
  4437 George Marriott, husbandman
    Bestall and Fowkes, *Chesterfield*, 2001, p. 93
Chesterfield
  4438 Francis Boller, shoemaker
    Bestall and Fowkes, *Chesterfield*, 2001, pp. 104-106
  4439 Richard Boulsover
    Bestall and Fowkes, *Chesterfield*, 2001, pp. 88-91
  4440 Martin Bretland, alderman
    Bestall and Fowkes, *Chesterfield*, 2001, pp. 96-101

Chesterfield, Temple Normanton
  4441 Richard Cowpe
    Bestall and Fowkes, *Chesterfield*, 2001, p. 101
Chesterfield
  4442 Thomas Diccons, fellmonger
    Bestall and Fowkes, *Chesterfield*, 2001, pp. 101-103
Chesterfield, Temple Normanton
  4443 Robert Hasteldyne
    Bestall and Fowkes, *Chesterfield*, 2001, p. 109
Chesterfield
  4444 Elizabeth Heathcott, widow
    Bestall and Fowkes, *Chesterfield*, 2001, pp. 91-92
Chesterfield, Tapton
  4445 Martin Lawrence, husbandman
    Bestall and Fowkes, *Chesterfield*, 2001, pp. 92-93
Chesterfield
  4446 Isabella Platts, widow
    Bestall and Fowkes, *Chesterfield*, 2001, p. 104
  4447 Edmund Snydall, miller
    Bestall and Fowkes, *Chesterfield*, 2001, pp. 109-111
  4448 William Whitworth, currier
    Bestall and Fowkes, *Chesterfield*, 2001, pp. 107-108
  4449 Agnes Woodward, widow
    Bestall and Fowkes, *Chesterfield*, 2001, pp. 94-96
Newbold
  4450 Peter Dane [Dame], smelter
    Bestall and Fowkes, *Chesterfield*, 2001, p. 94

Dorsetshire
Yetminster
  4451 Robert Willmonth
    Machin, *Yetminster*, 1976, No.23, (2 pp.)

Co. Durham
Darlington
  4452 Agnes Claxton
    Atkinson *et al.*, *Darlington*, 1993, p. 130

Gloucestershire
Stoke Gifford
  4453 Agnes Palmer, widow
    Moore, *Frampton Cotterell*, 1976, p. 44
Winterbourne
  4454 Edith Coke
    Moore, *Frampton Cotterell*, 1976, p. 44

Hertfordshire
Hertford, All Saints
  4455 Joane Hopkins, widow
    Anon., *Lock, Stock*, 1978, pp. 53-54
Kings Langley
  4456 Robert Anderson, labourer
    Munby, *Kings Langley*, 1981, p. 54
Sarratt
  4457 Goorge Flye
    Bullen, *Sarratt*, [1982], pp. 105-107
Stevenage
  4458 Josype Tewene
    Anon., *Lock, Stock*, 1978, p. 52

Lincolnshire
Clee
  4459 Elizabeth Grimblbie, widow
    Ambler, Watkinson, *Clee*, 1987, p. 123
  4460 John Lacebie
    Ambler, Watkinson, *Clee*, 1987, p. 124
Clee, Oole
  4461 Henrie Tuplin, labourer
    Ambler, Watkinson, *Clee*, 1987, p. 124

Sutton St James
    4462 Thomas Cobbe, chapman
    Spufford, *Reclothing*, 1984, pp. 178-180
Norfolk
  Kings Lynn
    4463 Robert Stonar
    Parker, *Kings Lynn*, 1971, pp. 177-179
Oxfordshire
  Banbury
    4464 James Allen
    Brinkworth and Gibson, *Banbury*, I, 1975, pp. 236-237
    4465 Michael Dixe [Dyxe]
    Brinkworth and Gibson, *Banbury*, I, 1975, p. 244
    4466 Roger Eryetaydge [Heritage]
    Brinkworth and Gibson, *Banbury*, I, 1975, p. 239
    4467 John Hathaway, [baker]
    Brinkworth and Gibson, *Banbury*, I, 1975, p. 242
    4468 Henry Kimble, labourer
    Brinkworth and Gibson, *Banbury*, I, 1975, p. 239
    4469 Isabel Moseley [Issabell Mosley], widow
    Brinkworth and Gibson, *Banbury*, I, 1975, p. 238
  Banbury, Neithrop
    4470 John Robins, husbandman
    Brinkworth and Gibson, *Banbury*, I, 1975, p. 234
  Banbury
    4471 Robert Scott, tailor
    Brinkworth and Gibson, *Banbury*, I, 1975, p. 242
    4472 Robert Secoll [Seacole]
    Brinkworth and Gibson, *Banbury*, I, 1975, p. 240
    4473 William Short [Shorte] alias Tymcott, shoemaker
    Brinkworth and Gibson, *Banbury*, I, 1975, pp. 231-232
    4474 Henry Sowtham, labourer
    Brinkworth and Gibson, *Banbury*, I, 1975, p. 229
    4475 Anne Walker, widow
    Brinkworth and Gibson, *Banbury*, I, 1975, p. 240
    4476 John Walker, butcher
    Brinkworth and Gibson, *Banbury*, I, 1975, p. 241
    4477 Edward Weston, chandler
    Brinkworth and Gibson, *Banbury*, I, 1975, p. 230
    4478 Richard Wrighton [Wryton], husbandman
    Brinkworth and Gibson, *Banbury*, I, 1975, p. 228
    4479 Lawrence Yewicke
    Brinkworth and Gibson, *Banbury*, I, 1975, p. 233
  Oxford, St John's College
    4480 Mr John English, fellow
    Costin, 1946-1947, pp. 105-116
Scotland
  Orkney, South Ronaldsay, Linklater
    4481 Margaret Brek
    Barclay, 1977, pp. 32-33
  Orkney, St Ola, Fia
    4482 Richard Cursetter
    Barclay, 1977, pp. 30-31
Staffordshire
  Dudley
    4483 Henry Wood
    Roper, *Dudley*, 1966, p. 6
Sussex
  West Itchenor
    4484 Roger Smith, clergyman [rector of West Itchenor]
    Hughes, *Sussex*, 2007, pp. 123-124

Wales
  Glamorganshire, Cowbridge
    4485 James Prainche
    Wrench, *Wrenche*, 1956, p. 33
Warwickshire
  Stratford-on-Avon
    4486 Daniell Smith, yeoman [maltster, corn dealer]
    Jones, *Stratford*, I, 2002, pp. 281-283
Wiltshire
  Marlborough
    4487 Henry Tarrant, yeoman
    Williams and Thomson, *Marlborough*, 2007, p. 31
Worcestershire
  Belbroughton
    4488 John Waldrone, [yeoman]
    Roper, *Belbroughton*, 1967-1968, p. 58
  Birtsmorton
    4489 William Nanfan, esquire
    Wanklyn, *Worcestershire*, 1998, pp. 123-124
  Doverdale
    4490 Raphe Lenche [Ralph Lench], gentleman
    Wanklyn, *Worcestershire*, 1998, pp. 122-123
  Eldersfield, Hardwick
    4491 Richard Dalamare, esquire
    Wanklyn, *Worcestershire*, 1998, pp. 118-121
Yorkshire
  Bradford, Woodhall
    4492 Edmund Greenall
    Preston, *Co. York*, 1929, p. 26
  Cottingley, Bingley (now Bradford)
    4493 Margaret Butterfield
    Preston, *Co. York*, 1929, p. 7
  South Cave
    4494 Leonard Colson
    Kaner, *South Cave*, 1994, pp. 249-250
  South Cave, Weedley
    4495 Richard Smith
    Kaner, *South Cave*, 1994, p. 247
  South Cave
    4496 John Younge, blacksmith
    Kaner, *South Cave*, 1994, p. 248
  Warley, Stock Lane
    4497 Thomas Oldfield of Bowde, [yeoman]
    Brears, *Yorkshire*, 1972, pp. 74-75

1614
Bristol
  Bristol, Redcliffe Street
    4498 George Baldwyn [Baldwin], gentleman
    George, *Bristol*, 1, 2002, pp. 16-19
  Bristol
    4499 Katherine Bowcher
    George, *Bristol*, 1, 2002, pp. 19-21
  Shirehampton
    4500 Henry Durberne, [mariner]
    Moore, *Clifton*, 1981, p. 21
Cheshire
  Bowdon
    4501 William Saunders, yeoman
    Groves, *Bowdon*, 1997, pp. 24-28
  Christleton, Cotton
    4502 John Iver, husbandman
    Bland, *Christleton*, 2003, pp. 338-339

Dunham Massey, Dunham
  4503 Anne Ogden, [widow]
    Groves, *Dunham Massey*, 2008, p. 38
  4504 Matilda Tipping, [widow]
    Groves, *Dunham Massey*, 2008, pp. 31-32
Hale
  4505 Robert Ashley
    Groves, *Hale 1*, 2005, p. 37
  4506 George Bolton, [yeoman]
    Groves, *Hale 1*, 2005, pp. 35-36
  4507 James Holt, [clothier]
    Groves, *Hale 1*, 2005, pp. 37-38
  4508 Richard Johnson, [husbandman]
    Groves, *Hale 1*, 2005, pp. 33-34
Hargrave
  4509 Hugh Humstonn
    Bland, *Christleton*, 2003, pp. 342-344
Kelsall
  4510 Catheren [Calley], widow
    Bland, *Christleton*, 2003, pp. 339-340
Nantwich
  4511 John Alvaston, yeoman
    Cockcroft, *Nantwich*, 1999, pp. 12.1-2
  4512 Randal Sandford, gentleman
    Cockcroft, *Nantwich*, 1999, pp. 278.1-2
Norten Etchells, Crossacres
  4513 Rodger Worthington, schoolmaster
    Rogers, 1967, p. 6
Stockport
  4514 Mary Allen
    Phillips and Smith, *Stockport*, 1985, pp. 91-92
  4515 Raph Ashton, mason
    Phillips and Smith, *Stockport*, 1985, p. 88
  4516 Edward Bibbie [Bibbye], linen webster
    Phillips and Smith, *Stockport*, 1985, pp. 85-86
  4517 Robert Gardner, cooper
    Phillips and Smith, *Stockport*, 1985, p. 84
  4518 Christopher Piggot, [haberdasher]
    Phillips and Smith, *Stockport*, 1985, pp. 87-88
  4519 Henrie Sclater
    Phillips and Smith, *Stockport*, 1985, p. 91
  4520 Jerom Warren, tailor
    Phillips and Smith, *Stockport*, 1985, p. 93
Wrenbury, Broomhall
  4521 Roger Hockenhull, [gentleman]
    Pixton, *Wrenbury*, 2009, pp. 126-127

Cumberland
High Close, Plumbland
  4522 William Orfeure, esquire
    Jackson, *Orfeurs*, 1878, pp. 113-116

Derbyshire
Brimington
  4523 William Abney, husbandman
    Bestall and Fowkes, *Chesterfield*, 2001, pp. 120-121
  4524 Elizabeth Sheldon, widow
    Bestall and Fowkes, *Chesterfield*, 2001, pp. 116-117
Chesterfield, Walton
  4525 William Brough, husbandman
    Bestall and Fowkes, *Chesterfield*, 2001, pp. 115-116
Chesterfield
  4526 Lancelot Butler, gentleman
    Bestall and Fowkes, *Chesterfield*, 2001, pp. 117-120
  4527 John Woodward, coverlet weaver
    Bestall and Fowkes, *Chesterfield*, 2001, p. 112

  4528 Thomas Woodward, blacksmith
    Bestall and Fowkes, *Chesterfield*, 2001, pp. 113-115
Hertfordshire
Bricket Wood
  4529 Thomas Ansell
    Munby, *Worldly Goods*, 1991, p. 104
St Albans, St Stephens
  4530 Thomas Bayley, [yeoman]
    Parker, *Worldly Goods*, 2004, pp. 178-179
  4531 William Ewer
    Munby, *Worldly Goods*, 1991, p. 103
Sarratt
  4532 Robert Smyth
    Bullen, *Sarratt*, [1982], p. 109

Kent
Greenwich
  Henry Howard, Earl of Northampton (see
  Northampton House, London)

London
Northampton House
  4533 Henry Howard, Earl of Northampton (also
  listed Greenwich, Kent)
    Shirley, 1862, pp. 348-374

Northamptonshire
Warkworth
  4534 Nicholas [Neckles] Meese [Mes], labourer
    Brinkworth and Gibson, *Banbury*, I, 1975, p. 246

Oxfordshire
Banbury
  4535 Abednego Allibon
    Brinkworth and Gibson, *Banbury*, I, 1975, p. 247
  4536 Robert Hall
    Brinkworth and Gibson, *Banbury*, I, 1975, p. 246
Banbury, Calthorpe
  4537 John Heanes, shepherd
    Brinkworth and Gibson, *Banbury*, I, 1975, p. 244
Banbury
  4538 William Marchall [Marshall], labourer
    Brinkworth and Gibson, *Banbury*, I, 1975, pp. 246-247
  4539 Margaret Pope
    Brinkworth and Gibson, *Banbury*, I, 1975, p. 244
  4540 George Rickettes [Ricketts, Rickards]
    Brinkworth and Gibson, *Banbury*, I, 1975, p. 245

Staffordshire
Sedgley
  4541 Alice Astley
    Roper, *Sedgley*, 1960, p. 1
Tettenhall
  4542 Richard Cotton, husbandman
    Roper, *Sedgley*, 1960, p. 1

Suffolk
Ipswich
  4543 Thomas Cole
    Reed, *Ipswich*, 1981, p. 81
  4544 Lewes Havord, sailor
    Reed, *Ipswich*, 1981, p. 82

Sussex
Bepton
  4545 William Ruffe, clergyman, [rector of Bepton]
    Hughes, *Sussex*, 2007, pp. 17-19
Kirdford
  4546 Thomas Waddington, tailor
    Kenyon, *Kirdford*, 1955, p. 132

Midhurst
  4547 Richard Guy, clergyman
  Hughes, *Sussex*, 2007, p. 141
Selham
  4548 John Leigh, clergyman [rector of Selham]
  Hughes, *Sussex*, 2007, pp. 182-183
Westbourne
  4549 Thomas Wilsha, clergyman [rector of Westbourne]
  Hughes, *Sussex*, 2007, pp. 230-232

Warwickshire
Coughton, Sambourne
  4550 William Windle, husbandman
  Barley, *Farmhouse and Cottage*, 1961, pp. 285-286
Stratford-on-Avon
  4551 Johane [Joan] Biddle
  Jones, *Stratford*, I, 2002, pp. 285-287
  4552 Edward Ingram
  Jones, *Stratford*, I, 2002, pp. 284-285
  4553 Thomas Kirbye, [butcher, maltster, yeoman]
  Jones, *Stratford*, I, 2002, pp. 288-290

Wiltshire
Marlborough
  4554 Robert Locar, blacksmith
  Williams and Thomson, *Marlborough*, 2007, pp. 31-32

Worcestershire
Birtsmorton
  4555 Gyles [Giles] Nanfan, esquire
  Wanklyn, *Worcestershire*, 1998, pp. 124-127
Chaddesley Corbett
  4556 Symon Bennett, scythesmith
  Roper, *Chaddesley Corbett*, 1971, pp. 32-34
Chaddesley Corbett, Cakebole
  4557 Sylvester Penne
  Roper, *Chaddesley Corbett*, 1971, pp. 31-32
Worcester
  4558 Anthoney Ould, [joiner and furniture maker]
  Dyer, *Worcestershire*, 1967, pp. 43-45

Yorkshire
Greenhill, Bingley
  4559 John Rawson
  Preston, *Co. York*, 1929, p. 29
Pudsey, Calverley
  4560 John Mytchell [Mitchell], clothier
  Preston, *Co. York*, 1929, pp. 27-28
Sheffield
  4561 Roger Lee
  Jewitt, 1861-2, pp. 231-232
Sockeld
  4562 William Middleton, esquire
  Crossley, 1938, pp. 171-181
South Cave
  4563 Francis Atkinson, labourer
  Kaner, *South Cave*, 1994, pp. 254-255
  4564 Thomas Briggs
  Kaner, *South Cave*, 1994, p. 251
South Cave, Faxfleet
  4565 John Craine
  Kaner, *South Cave*, 1994, p. 254
South Cave, Oxmardyke
  4566 Robart Greisbie
  Kaner, *South Cave*, 1994, pp. 255-256

South Cave
  4567 Richard Jarman alias Wawdman
  Kaner, *South Cave*, 1994, pp. 251-252
South Cave, Faxfleet
  4568 Henry Middlewood
  Kaner, *South Cave*, 1994, p. 253
South Cave
  4569 Elizabeth Tenant, widow
  Kaner, *South Cave*, 1994, pp. 252-253

1615
Cheshire
Ashton
  4570 Richard Whittell, husbandman
  Bland, *Christleton*, 2003, pp. 353-354
Bowdon, The Street
  4571 Anne Aldcroft, widow
  Groves, *Bowdon*, 1997, pp. 29-30
Hale
  4572 William Leather, yeoman
  Groves, *Hale 1*, 2005, p. 39
Kelsall
  4573 Robert Heapie, husbandman
  Bland, *Christleton*, 2003, p. 350
Nantwich
  4574 Roger Wright, [yeoman]
  Cockcroft, *Nantwich*, 1999, p. 371.3
Tarvin, Clotton
  4575 Thomas Thomasson, yeoman
  Bland, *Christleton*, 2003, p. 352
Wrenbury, Chorley
  4576 Thomas Falkner [Faulkner], [yeoman]
  Pixton, *Wrenbury*, 2009, p. 135
Wrenbury, Newhall
  4577 Thomas Ravenscroft
  Pixton, *Wrenbury*, 2009, pp. 123-124
Wrenbury cum Frith
  4578 Robart Tench [Tenche], [yeoman]
  Pixton, *Wrenbury*, 2009, pp. 130-131
Wrenbury
  4579 John Wilkinson, [husbandman]
  Pixton, *Wrenbury*, 2009, p. 133

Derbyshire
Brimington
  4580 Thurston Morton, yeoman
  Bestall and Fowkes, *Chesterfield*, 2001, pp. 124-125
Chesterfield, Dunston
  4581 William Hall
  Bestall and Fowkes, *Chesterfield*, 2001, p. 125
Chesterfield
  4582 Roger Stubbes
  Bestall and Fowkes, *Chesterfield*, 2001, pp. 121-124

Devonshire
Blackawton, Combe
  4583 William Toker, husbandman
  Cash, *Devon*, 1966, p. 25

Co. Durham
Darlington
  4584 Ann Dent, widow
  Atkinson *et al.*, *Darlington*, 1993, pp. 134-136
Darlington, Cockerton
  4585 Edmund Fawell, yeoman
  Atkinson *et al.*, *Darlington*, 1993, pp. 137-140

Darlington
4586 John Glover, weaver
    Atkinson *et al.*, *Darlington*, 1993, pp. 143-144
Darlington, Cockerton
4587 Jene [Jane] Surteis, widow
    Atkinson *et al.*, *Darlington*, 1993, pp. 140-141
Gainford
4588 John Swaynston
    Wood, *Wills and Inventories*, 1929, IV, p. 94
Gloucestershire
Dumbleton
4589 Olyver Diston, clergyman, parson of Dumbleton
    Barnard, *Dumbleton*, 1914, pp. 217-224
    Austin, 1924, pp. 188-193
Hertfordshire
St Albans, St Stephens
4590 Elizabeth Ewer
    Munby, *Worldly Goods*, 1991, p. 105
4591 John Hawxe
    Parker, *Worldly Goods*, 2004, p. 180
4592 Alexander Hayward
    Parker, *Worldly Goods*, 2004, p. 179
Leicestershire
Braunstone
4593 Thomas Pallet
    Wilshere, *Braunstone*, 1983, p. 16
Glenfield
4594 William Thornton alias Tysall
    Wilshere, *Glenfield*, 1983, p. 4
Kirby Muxloe
4595 Willm Scriven, [husbandman]
    Wilshere, *Kirby Muxloe*, 1983, p. 5
Lincolnshire
Allington
4596 Thomas Winter, yeoman
    Pask, *Allington*, 1989, pp. 60-61
Clee, Oole
4597 Joshian Makin, widow
    Ambler, Watkinson, *Clee*, 1987, p. 124
Clee
4598 Agnes Pell, widow
    Ambler, Watkinson, *Clee*, 1987, p. 125
Oxfordshire
Banbury
4599 Maudeline [Mawde] Harwood alias Tomson, widow
    Brinkworth and Gibson, *Banbury*, I, 1975, p. 248
Scotland
East Lothian, The Byres
4600 Sir Thomas Hamilton, Lord Binning (later Earl of Haddington)
    Fraser, 1889, pp. 289-292
Orkney, Harray, Knarstane
4601 Robert Knarstane
    Barclay, 1977, p. 36
Orkney, St Androis, Stembester
4602 Patrik Sinclair
    Barclay, 1977, pp. 34-35
Shropshire
Wellington
4603 John Allen
    Trinder, 1979, pp. 240-241

Staffordshire
Dudley
4604 Jeffrey Fyinche, yeoman
    Roper, *Dudley*, 1966, pp. 7-10
Suffolk
Hawstead Place
4605 Sir Robert Drury
    Campling, 1937, pp. 67-72
Ipswich
4606 Henry Piper, poldavis weaver
    Reed, *Ipswich*, 1981, pp. 82-85
Sussex
Waldron, Tanners
4607 John Fuller
    Storey, 1939, pp. 201-204
Warwickshire
Stratford-on-Avon
4608 Thomas Mylls [Mills]
    Jones, *Stratford*, I, 2002, p. 293
4609 Richard Pinke, [maltster, husbandman]
    Jones, *Stratford*, I, 2002, pp. 291-292
Westmorland
Winster
4610 Richard Salkelde
    Moore, *Salkelds*, 1988, p. 72
Wiltshire
Marlborough
4611 William Applegate, victualler
    Williams and Thomson, *Marlborough*, 2007, pp. 32-33
Worcestershire
Chaddesley Corbett
4612 William Leyte, [husbandman]
    West, *Village Records*, 1962, p. 102
    Roper, *Chaddesley Corbett*, 1971, pp. 34-35
Chaddesley Corbett, Cakebole
4613 William Penne
    Roper, *Chaddesley Corbett*, 1971, p. 36
Dudley
4614 Thomas [Sutton, alias Dudley, esquire]
    Wanklyn, *Worcestershire*, 1998, pp. 128-131
Yorkshire
Bingley, Beckfoot
4615 Walter Morvell
    Preston, *Co. York*, 1929, pp. 24-25
Pudsey, Calverley
4616 Isabel Wilson
    Preston, *Co. York*, 1929, p. 32
South Cave
4617 Richard Mounder
    Kaner, *South Cave*, 1994, pp. 258-259
4618 John Pescod
    Kaner, *South Cave*, 1994, p. 257

1615 (c.)
Wiltshire
Marlborough
4619 Edith Brunsdon, widow
    Williams and Thomson, *Marlborough*, 2007, p. 35
4620 William Hiller, [swordsmith]
    Williams and Thomson, *Marlborough*, 2007, pp. 33-34

1616

Bristol

Bristol, Tucker Street
4621 Hugh Watkins
George, *Bristol*, 1, 2002, pp. 21-23

Cheshire

Ashton-on-Mersey
4622 Alice Hardy
Groves, *Ashton-on-Mersey and Sale*, 1999, pp. 36-37
4623 Isabel Hurrall
Groves, *Ashton-on-Mersey and Sale*, 1999, p. 37
Christleton
4624 Reecs Huse [Hughes], clergyman, parson of
Christleton
Bland, *Christleton*, 2003, p. 361
Dunham Massey, Dunham Woodhouses
4625 Hugh Massey, [yeoman]
Groves, *Dunham Massey*, 2008, p. 39
Hale
4626 Henry Goulden
Groves, *Hale 1*, 2005, pp. 40-41
Hale, Hale Low
4627 Lawrence Leicester, [gentleman]
Groves, *Hale 1*, 2005, pp. 39-40
Hale
4628 Margaret Tipping, [widow]
Groves, *Hale 1*, 2005, p. 41
Kelsall
4629 William Cawley, husbandman
Bland, *Christleton*, 2003, pp. 360-361
4630 Richard Eare, salter
Bland, *Christleton*, 2003, pp. 355-357
Little Leigh
4631 Ales Whishall, widow
Whishaw, 1935, pp. 61-63
Nantwich
4632 Joan Baker, widow
Cockcroft, *Nantwich*, 1999, p. 18.1
4633 Thomas Hunt alias Palmer
Cockcroft, *Nantwich*, 1999, p. 160.1
4634 Evan Lewis, chapman
Cockcroft, *Nantwich*, 1999, p. 188.1
4635 Roger Parsons
Cockcroft, *Nantwich*, 1999, pp. 243.1-2
Sale
4636 Alice Worthington
Groves, *Ashton-on-Mersey and Sale*, 1999, p. 36
Stockport
4637 Elis Crossley, woollen webster
Phillips and Smith, *Stockport*, 1985, p. 101
4638 Edward Doughtye, clergyman, rector of
Stockport
Phillips and Smith, *Stockport*, 1985, pp. 96-97
4639 Edward Hall
Phillips and Smith, *Stockport*, 1985, p. 95
4640 Isabell Hibbert, widow
Phillips and Smith, *Stockport*, 1985, pp. 99-100
4641 William Norton
Phillips and Smith, *Stockport*, 1985, pp. 94-95
4642 Blannch Thomston, widow
Phillips and Smith, *Stockport*, 1985, p. 96
Waverton
4643 Robert Smyth, yeoman
Bland, *Christleton*, 2003, p. 363

Wrenbury
4644 William Barnett, [yeoman]
Pixton, *Wrenbury*, 2009, pp. 151-152
Wrenbury, Broomhall
4645 Anne Bickerton, [widow]
Pixton, *Wrenbury*, 2009, pp. 140-141
Wrenbury, Newhall
4646 John Bickerton, yeoman
Pixton, *Wrenbury*, 2009, pp. 137-138
Wrenbury, Smeatonwood
4647 Thomas Gray
Pixton, *Wrenbury*, 2009, p. 154
4648 George Kemp, [yeoman]
Pixton, *Wrenbury*, 2009, p. 143
Wrenbury, Coole
4649 Mary Whitney, [widow]
Pixton, *Wrenbury*, 2009, pp. 144-145
Wrenbury, Newhall
4650 Michaell Whitney, [husbandman]
Pixton, *Wrenbury*, 2009, pp. 155-156

Derbyshire

Chesterfield
4651 Raphe Ashe, shoemaker
Bestall and Fowkes, *Chesterfield*, 2001, pp. 128-132
4652 Thomas Greene
Bestall and Fowkes, *Chesterfield*, 2001, pp. 135-139
4653 John Launder
Bestall and Fowkes, *Chesterfield*, 2001, pp. 139-142
4654 Raphe Peniston, butcher
Bestall and Fowkes, *Chesterfield*, 2001, pp. 125-128
4655 George Shepard [Sheppard]
Bestall and Fowkes, *Chesterfield*, 2001, pp. 133-134
4656 Thomas Whithead
Bestall and Fowkes, *Chesterfield*, 2001, pp. 142-144
4657 William Whitterance
Bestall and Fowkes, *Chesterfield*, 2001, pp. 134-135
Hasland
4658 Ann Maiden
Bestall and Fowkes, *Chesterfield*, 2001, p. 135

Devonshire

Uffculme
4659 John Reade [Read], [groom]
Wyatt, *Uffculme*, 1997, pp. 40-41

Co. Durham

Darlington, Blackwell
4660 Cuthbert Corneforth, yeoman
Atkinson *et al.*, *Darlington*, 1993, pp. 147-150
Darlington
4661 Margery Lasselles [Lassells], widow
Atkinson *et al.*, *Darlington*, 1993, pp. 152-154
Darlington, Cockerton
4662 Angnes Surtise [Agnes Surtis]
Atkinson *et al.*, *Darlington*, 1993, p. 142

Hertfordshire

St Albans, St Stephens, Park Street
4663 Robart Baylye
Parker, *Worldly Goods*, 2004, pp. 183-184
St Albans, St Stephens
4664 William Dolamore
Parker, *Worldly Goods*, 2004, p. 187
4665 Richard Everingham
Parker, *Worldly Goods*, 2004, pp. 189-190

4666 Anne Field, widow
  Munby, *Worldly Goods*, 1991, p. 106
4667 Richard Griffyn
  Parker, *Worldly Goods*, 2004, p. 188
4668 Thomas Mychell
  Parker, *Worldly Goods*, 2004, p. 189
4669 John Welles
  Parker, *Worldly Goods*, 2004, p. 190
Sarratt
4670 Francis Smyth
  Bullen, *Sarratt*, [1982], p. 110
4671 John Smyth
  Bullen, *Sarratt*, [1982], pp. 111-112

Lancashire
Hawkshead Hall (now Cumbria)
4672 Allan Nicholson
  Cowper, 1891, pp. 34-36
Rainford
4673 Margarett Farehurst
  St Helens, *Angells*, 1999, pp. 31-33

Leicestershire
Glenfield
4674 Richard Hasshold
  Wilshere, *Glenfield*, 1983, p. 4
Kirby Muxloe
4675 Nathaniell Knape
  Wilshere, *Kirby Muxloe*, 1983, p. 8
4676 Thomas Nours, tailor
  Wilshere, *Kirby Muxloe*, 1983, p. 6

Lincolnshire
Allington
4677 Simon Buttree, clergyman
  Pask, *Allington*, 1989, pp. 65-67
Clee
4678 Michaell Boswell, miller
  Ambler, Watkinson, *Clee*, 1987, pp. 125-126
4679 Peter Easterbie
  Ambler, Watkinson, *Clee*, 1987, pp. 126-128
Clee, Oole
4680 Beabriel Laceby
  Ambler, Watkinson, *Clee*, 1987, p. 125

Northumberland
Druridge
4681 Lancelot Ewbank, gentleman
  Wood, *Wills and Inventories*, 1929, IV, pp. 104-105

Oxfordshire
Banbury
4682 Robert Dingley, glazier
  Brinkworth and Gibson, *Banbury*, I, 1975, p. 257
4683 Richard Draper, labourer
  Brinkworth and Gibson, *Banbury*, I, 1975, p. 253
4684 Edward Eden [Eaton]
  Brinkworth and Gibson, *Banbury*, I, 1975, p. 250
4685 Anne Hadley, widow
  Brinkworth and Gibson, *Banbury*, I, 1975, p. 252
4686 Ralph Hall
  Brinkworth and Gibson, *Banbury*, I, 1975, pp. 248-249
Banbury, Easington
4687 Margaret Hawtaine, widow [gentlewoman]
  Brinkworth and Gibson, *Banbury*, I, 1975, pp. 256-257
Banbury
4688 Wolstone Walker, shepherd
  Brinkworth and Gibson, *Banbury*, I, 1975, p. 252

4689 Thomas Webb, gentleman
  Brinkworth and Gibson, *Banbury*, I, 1975, pp. 253-255
4690 Thomas Williamson, shoemaker
  Brinkworth and Gibson, *Banbury*, I, 1975, p. 250
Staffordshire
Dudley
4691 Richard Juckes
  Roper, *Dudley*, 1966, pp. 11-12
4692 Richard Shawe, yeoman
  Roper, *Dudley*, 1968, pp. 8-9
Suffolk
Ipswich
4693 William Madocke
  Reed, *Ipswich*, 1981, p. 85
4694 Henry Sherels
  Reed, *Ipswich*, 1981, pp. 85-88
Warwickshire
Stoneleigh, Stareton
4695 Humphrey Hoo, yeoman
  Alcock, *Warwickshire*, 1993, pp. 58-60
Stratford-on-Avon, Old Stratford
4696 Humfrie Allen, [shoemaker]
  Jones, *Stratford*, I, 2002, pp. 295-296
Stratford-on-Avon
4697 William Troute, butcher
  Jones, *Stratford*, I, 2002, pp. 293-295
Wiltshire
Marlborough
4698 Jone Bowlinge, widow
  Williams and Thomson, *Marlborough*, 2007, pp. 35-36
4699 Robert Lyme, tanner
  Williams and Thomson, *Marlborough*, 2007, p. 36
4700 Robert Michell, [goldsmith]
  Williams and Thomson, *Marlborough*, 2007, pp. 36-38
Worcestershire
Belbroughton
4701 Roger Wheler
  Roper, *Belbroughton*, 1967-1968, p. 59
Severn Stoke
4702 Frannces Clyfton [Francis Clifton], esquire
  Wanklyn, *Worcestershire*, 1998, pp. 131-133
Yorkshire
South Cave
4703 Robert Baddie
  Kaner, *South Cave*, 1994, p. 261
4704 Julyan Mounder, widow
  Kaner, *South Cave*, 1994, pp. 260-261
Unlocated
4705 William Mitchell
  Preston, *Co. York*, 1929, p. 35
York
4706 John Foster, [stationer]
  Davies, 1868, pp. 342-374

1616 (c.)
Wiltshire
Marlborough
4707 William North, tanner
  Williams and Thomson, *Marlborough*, 2007, p. 36

1617
Bedfordshire
Ampthill
4708 John Smyth
  Emmison, *Bedfordshire*, 1938, p. 51

Bedford
 4709 Michael Smith
   Emmison, *Bedfordshire*, 1938, p. 68
Kempston
 4710 Bartholomew Barber alias Enterdewce, butcher
   Emmison, *Bedfordshire*, 1938, p. 101
Marston Moretaine
 4711 Thomas Pearce, yeoman
   Emmison, *Bedfordshire*, 1938, p. 50
Meppershall
 4712 John Giggell
   Emmison, *Bedfordshire*, 1938, p. 134
Sandy
 4713 John Mayes
   Emmison, *Bedfordshire*, 1938, pp. 51-52
Sutton
 4714 Thomas Beard alias Farmer, gentleman
   Emmison, *Bedfordshire*, 1938, pp. 52-53
Unlocated
 4715 Sarah, wife of Lawrence Richards
   Emmison, *Bedfordshire*, 1938, pp. 121-122

Bristol
Bristol, St James
 4716 Myles [Miles] Casse, tobacco-pipe maker
   George, *Bristol*, 1, 2002, pp. 23-24
Bristol, St Michael
 4717 Edward Pickrell, blacksmith
   George, *Bristol*, 1, 2002, pp. 24-25
Bristol
 4718 Jonas Seddon, wire-drawer
   George, *Bristol*, 1, 2002, pp. 25-26
Bristol, Little St Augustine
 4719 Katherene [Katherine] Woolvin, [lacemaker]
   George, *Bristol*, 1, 2002, pp. 26-27
Shirehampton
 4720 Elizabeth Bateman, widow
   Moore, *Clifton*, 1981, pp. 22-23
 4721 Richard Highway, [husbandman]
   Moore, *Clifton*, 1981, pp. 24-26
Westbury
 4722 Elizabeth Cross, widow
   Moore, *Clifton*, 1981, pp. 23-24
 4723 Richard Sidner, [labourer]
   Moore, *Clifton*, 1981, p. 24

Cheshire
Dunham Massey, Sinderland
 4724 George Smith, [yeoman]
   Groves, *Dunham Massey*, 2008, pp. 40-41
Hale
 4725 Richard Arstall, [husbandman]
   Groves, *Hale 1*, 2005, p. 43
Hale, Ringway
 4726 William Arstall, [husbandman]
   Groves, *Hale 1*, 2005, p. 46
Hale
 4727 William Grantham, [yeoman]
   Groves, *Hale 1*, 2005, pp. 44-45
 4728 Ralph Partington
   Groves, *Hale 1*, 2005, p. 42
Nantwich
 4729 Humphrey Edgeley, glover
   Cockcroft, *Nantwich*, 1999, pp. 121.1-2
 4730 Nicholas Goldsmith, mercer
   Cockcroft, *Nantwich*, 1999, p. 137.1

 4731 John Pratchet
   Cockcroft, *Nantwich*, 1999, pp. 254.1-3
Stockport
 4732 Edward Bennison, tailor
   Phillips and Smith, *Stockport*, 1985, pp. 115-116
 4733 Sisley Huitte, widow
   Phillips and Smith, *Stockport*, 1985, p. 102
 4734 Lawrance Rigbie
   Phillips and Smith, *Stockport*, 1985, pp. 102-103
 4735 John Robinson, yeoman
   Phillips and Smith, *Stockport*, 1985, pp. 108-114
Wrenbury, Sound
 4736 Elizabeth Baskerfild [Baskerville], [widow]
   Pixton, *Wrenbury*, 2009, pp. 157-158
 4737 Edmund Bickerton, [yeoman]
   Pixton, *Wrenbury*, 2009, pp. 161-162

Cumberland
Bewcastle, The Ash
 4738 James Routledge
   Harrison, 1967, pp. 106-107

Derbyshire
Chesterfield
 4739 John Dobbe, butcher
   Bestall and Fowkes, *Chesterfield*, 2001, p. 151
 4740 John Marshall
   Bestall and Fowkes, *Chesterfield*, 2001, pp. 145-148
 4741 William Newsam, yeoman
   Bestall and Fowkes, *Chesterfield*, 2001, pp. 155-158
 4742 Henry Scott, yeoman
   Bestall and Fowkes, *Chesterfield*, 2001, p. 152
 4743 Robert Stubbinge
   Bestall and Fowkes, *Chesterfield*, 2001, pp. 148-149
Chesterfield, Calow
 4744 Thomas Watsone
   Bestall and Fowkes, *Chesterfield*, 2001, pp. 144-145
Hasland
 4745 Richard Stanley
   Bestall and Fowkes, *Chesterfield*, 2001, p. 150

Devonshire
Exeter
 4746 Jane Sture, widow
   Cash, *Devon*, 1966, pp. 25-26
Uffculme
 4747 Robert Maunder
   Wyatt, *Uffculme*, 1997, p. 41
 4748 Thomas Reade, yeoman
   Wyatt, *Uffculme*, 1997, p. 41

Dorsetshire
Halstock
 4749 Christopher Newman
   Lemmey, *Halstock*, 1997, p. 20

Co. Durham
Darlington
 4750 John Fawcet, cordwainer
   Atkinson *et al.*, *Darlington*, 1993, pp. 155-158
Darlington, Blackwell
 4751 Stephen Ward, yeoman
   Atkinson *et al.*, *Darlington*, 1993, pp. 159-161
Wolsingham
 4752 Thomas Greenwell, yeoman
   Wood, *Wills and Inventories*, 1929, IV, pp. 116-117

Essex
Unlocated
   4753 Thos. Edwards, yeoman
     Browne, 1907, pp. 205-206
Gloucestershire
Hambrook
   4754 Edward Springhall, [shearman]
     Moore, *Frampton Cotterell*, 1976, pp. 44-45
Stoke Gifford
   4755 Joan Stirges, widow
     Moore, *Frampton Cotterell*, 1976, pp. 45-46
Winterbourne
   4756 Henry Nowell, weaver
     Moore, *Frampton Cotterell*, 1976, p. 45
Hertfordshire
St Albans, St Stephens
   4757 Richard Lightfoote, clergyman, vicar of St
   Stephens
     Parker, *Worldly Goods*, 2004, pp. 191-192
St Albans, St Stephens, Park Street
   4758 Elizabeth Nutkyn, widow
     Parker, *Worldly Goods*, 2004, p. 183
St Albans, St Stephens
   4759 Hughe Rolfe, [yeoman]
     Munby, *Worldly Goods*, 1991, p. 108
Sarratt
   4760 John Cockshot, clergyman, vicar of Sarratt
     Bullen, *Sarratt*, [1982], pp. 113-115
   4761 Edward Hammond, collier
     Bullen, *Sarratt*, [1982], pp. 115-116
   4762 James Priest
     Bullen, *Sarratt*, [1982], p. 116
Lancashire
Bold
   4763 An Houghton
     St Helens, *Angells*, 1999, pp. 39-45
Rainford
   4764 Alice Lunte, [widow]
     St Helens, *Angells*, 1999, pp. 38-39
Winstanley
   4765 James Bancks, esquire
     Bankes and Kerridge, 1973, p. 43-46
Leicestershire
Evington
   4766 William Noone, husbandman
     Wilshere, *Evington*, 1985, p. 17
   4767 Agnes Plumer, widow
     Wilshere, *Evington*, 1985, p. 16
Lincolnshire
Clee
   4768 William Bartholomewe
     Ambler, Watkinson, *Clee*, 1987, pp. 128-129
Northamptonshire
Nethercote
   4769 Nicholas [Nycolos] Stokes, labourer
     Brinkworth and Gibson, *Banbury*, I, 1975, p. 260
Northumberland
Alnwick
   4770 George Alder
     Wood, *Wills and Inventories*, 1929, IV, p. 121
Oxfordshire
Banbury
   4771 Thomas Ablestone [Ablstone, Ableston], [vintner]
     Brinkworth and Gibson, *Banbury*, I, 1975, pp. 258-259

Banbury, Grimsbury
   4772 John Bull, labourer
     Brinkworth and Gibson, *Banbury*, I, 1975, p. 271
Banbury
   4773 Peter Darrell [Dorrall]
     Brinkworth and Gibson, *Banbury*, I, 1975, p. 267
   4774 William Dixon
     Brinkworth and Gibson, *Banbury*, I, 1975, p. 264
   4775 Francis Greenhill, tanner
     Brinkworth and Gibson, *Banbury*, I, 1975, pp. 267-268
   4776 Henry [Harey] Ireland [Eyerland]
     Brinkworth and Gibson, *Banbury*, I, 1975, p. 269
   4777 Thomas Kerwood, blacksmith
     Brinkworth and Gibson, *Banbury*, I, 1975, p. 270
   4778 Thomas Kinge, [carpenter]
     Brinkworth and Gibson, *Banbury*, I, 1975, p. 267
   4779 George Reanoldes, shoemaker
     Brinkworth and Gibson, *Banbury*, I, 1975, p. 261
   4780 John Righton, shoemaker
     Brinkworth and Gibson, *Banbury*, I, 1975, p. 258
   4781 William Shorte, clergyman
     Brinkworth and Gibson, *Banbury*, I, 1975, pp. 262-263
   4782 Bartholomew [Bartlemew] Strong [Stronge],
   carpenter
     Brinkworth and Gibson, *Banbury*, I, 1975, pp. 266-267
   4783 Philip [Phillipe] Warde, [husbandman?]
     Brinkworth and Gibson, *Banbury*, I, 1975, pp. 263-264
   4784 Richard White, shoemaker
     Brinkworth and Gibson, *Banbury*, I, 1975, p. 269
   4785 John Williams [Williames], shoemaker
     Brinkworth and Gibson, *Banbury*, I, 1975, p. 265
Suffolk
Ipswich
   4786 Nicholas Crane, tailor
     Reed, *Ipswich*, 1981, p. 90
   4787 Margaret Darnsell, widow
     Reed, *Ipswich*, 1981, pp. 88-89
   4788 Robert Jackson alias Jarvies
     Reed, *Ipswich*, 1981, pp. 90-91
   4789 Richard Jennings, mariner
     Reed, *Ipswich*, 1981, pp. 91-92
Sussex
Kirdford, Crouchland
   4790 Robert Strudwick, yeoman
     Kenyon, *Kirdford*, 1955, pp. 113-115
Shipley
   4791 Robert Wates, clergyman
     Hughes, *Sussex*, 2007, pp. 188-189
Slinfold
   4792 Philip Mustian, clergyman [rector of Slinfold]
     Hughes, *Sussex*, 2007, p. 194
Wales
Cardiganshire, Strata Florida
   4793 James Stedman, esquire
     Powell, 1900, pp. 73-74
Warwickshire
King's Coughton
   4794 Edmund Gower, gentleman
     Saville, *King's Coughton*, 1973, pp. 42-44
Shottery
   4795 Roberte Munmore, [husbandman]
     Jones, *Stratford*, I, 2002, pp. 309-312

Stratford-on-Avon
4796 Francis Boyce, [tailor, sergeant at mace)
Jones, *Stratford*, I, 2002, pp. 304-306
4797 Anne Lloyd, widow
Jones, *Stratford*, I, 2002, pp. 297-299
4798 Thomas Miles [Mills], [yeoman]
Jones, *Stratford*, I, 2002, pp. 301-303
4799 Adrian Quiney, gentleman
Jones, *Stratford*, I, 2002, pp. 308-309
4800 Vallintyn [Valentine] Tant, [yeoman]
Jones, *Stratford*, I, 2002, pp. 300-301

Wiltshire
Marlborough
4801 Arter Deane
Williams and Thomson, *Marlborough*, 2007, p. 40
4802 Anthoney Lynsey, goldsmith
Williams and Thomson, *Marlborough*, 2007, pp. 39-40
4803 Alce Moore, widow
Williams and Thomson, *Marlborough*, 2007, p. 38

Worcestershire
Chaddesley Corbett, Drayton
4804 Alice Wilkes, widow
Roper, *Chaddesley Corbett*, 1971, p. 37
Pirton
4805 Thomas Folyott [Folliott], esquire
Wanklyn, *Worcestershire*, 1998, pp. 133-138

Yorkshire
Allerton, Bradford
4806 Thomas Bower
Preston, *Co. York*, 1929, pp. 140-143
Askrigg, Holehouse
4807 Jeffray [Geoffrey] Pratt
Thwaite, *Abbotside*, 1967, pp. 39-40
Aysgarth, Cams Houses
4808 Jane Nealson [Nelson], widow
Thwaite, *Abbotside*, 1967, pp. 38-39
Deighton
Sir William Ingilby (see Ripley)
Eldwick, Bingley
4809 John Hogge
Preston, *Co. York*, 1929, pp. 41-42
4810 Frauncis Howgate
Preston, *Co. York*, 1929, p. 36
4811 Richard Yeadon
Preston, *Co. York*, 1929, p. 36
Harewell, Dacre
Sir William Ingilby (see Ripley)
Priesthorpe, Calverley
4812 William Birkenshawe
Preston, *Co. York*, 1929, pp. 39-40
4813 William Hare, clothier
Preston, *Co. York*, 1929, p. 37
Pudsey, Calverley
4814 Andrew Smith
Preston, *Co. York*, 1929, p. 41
Ripley
4815 Sir William Ingilby (also listed Harewell, Dacre, and Deighton)
Crossley, 1938, pp. 182-203
South Cave
4816 Margret Hodgson
Kaner, *South Cave*, 1994, pp. 265-266

4817 William Girlington, gentleman
Kaner, *South Cave*, 1994, pp. 263-265
4818 Martin Wilson, [shepherd]
Kaner, *South Cave*, 1994, pp. 261-262

1617 (c.)
Leicestershire
Kirby Muxloe
4819 Tho. Allen
Wilshere, *Kirby Muxloe*, 1983, pp. 7-8
Warwickshire
Stratford-on-Avon
4820 An [Ann] Martin
Jones, *Stratford*, I, 2002, pp. 307-308

1618
Bedfordshire
Arlesey
4821 John Sprignells, weaver
Emmison, *Bedfordshire*, 1938, p. 139
Bromham
4822 Robert Savidge, fuller or shearman
Emmison, *Bedfordshire*, 1938, p. 103
Cardington, Cotton End
4823 Nicholas Bull, husbandman
Emmison, *Bedfordshire*, 1938, p. 140
Chalton
4824 Ann Long
Emmison, *Bedfordshire*, 1938, p. 139
Clifton
4825 Joan Randall, widow
Emmison, *Bedfordshire*, 1938, p. 122
Felmersham, Radwell
4826 Richard Barker [Baker?]
Emmison, *Bedfordshire*, 1938, p. 110
Pavenham
4827 John Rud
Emmison, *Bedfordshire*, 1938, pp. 139-140
Bristol
Bristol, St Peter
4828 Thomas Clemant [Clement], saddler
George, *Bristol*, 1, 2002, pp. 27-28
4829 Ann Large, servant
George, *Bristol*, 1, 2002, pp. 28-29
Shirehampton
4830 Thomas Cobden, [husbandman]
Moore, *Clifton*, 1981, p. 26
Westbury
4831 William Lane, [husbandman]
Moore, *Clifton*, 1981, p. 27
Cheshire
Dunham Massey, Dunham
4832 Richard Wright
Groves, *Dunham Massey*, 2008, p. 42
Hale, Ringway
4833 Lawrence Hardy, [yeoman]
Groves, *Hale 1*, 2005, p. 47
Nantwich
4834 Matthew Hawkes
Cockcroft, *Nantwich*, 1999, pp. 153.1-2
4835 Edward Massey, mercer
Cockcroft, *Nantwich*, 1999, pp. 208.1-3
4836 Margaret Wright, widow
Cockcroft, *Nantwich*, 1999, pp. 362.1-3

Stockport
4837 Jane Robinson, widow
Phillips and Smith, *Stockport*, 1985, pp. 119-120

Derbyshire
Chesterfield
4838 Robert Cade
Bestall and Fowkes, *Chesterfield*, 2001, p. 160
4839 Raphe Foxe
Bestall and Fowkes, *Chesterfield*, 2001, pp. 153-154
4840 Lucy Hall, widow
Bestall and Fowkes, *Chesterfield*, 2001, pp. 158-159
4841 William Heathcott, shoemaker
Bestall and Fowkes, *Chesterfield*, 2001, pp. 154-155
4842 John Woodleaffe
Bestall and Fowkes, *Chesterfield*, 2001, pp. 160-162

Co. Durham
Croxdale, Butterby
4843 Thomas Chaitor, esquire
Wood, *Wills and Inventories*, 1929, IV, pp. 84-87
Darlington
4844 Christofer Foster, butcher
Atkinson *et al.*, *Darlington*, 1993, pp. 162-163
Whorlton
4845 John Ovington
Wood, *Wills and Inventories*, 1929, IV, p. 123

Gloucestershire
Hambrook
4846 William Baylly, [husbandman]
Moore, *Frampton Cotterell*, 1976, p. 47
4847 William Gregorie, yeoman
Moore, *Frampton Cotterell*, 1976, p. 50
Winterbourne
4848 Robert Belsher
Moore, *Frampton Cotterell*, 1976, p. 46
4849 Thomas Gyles, husbandman
Moore, *Frampton Cotterell*, 1976, pp. 48-50
4850 Agnes Nowell, widow
Moore, *Frampton Cotterell*, 1976, p. 48

Hampshire
Bishop's Waltham
James Montagu, Bishop of Winchester (see Winchester
House, London)

Hertfordshire
Sarratt
4851 Elizabeth Flye
Bullen, *Sarratt*, [1982], pp. 117-118
4852 George Hayward
Bullen, *Sarratt*, [1982], p. 119

Kent
Eastry
4853 Mtris. Katherin Buttler, gentlewoman
Shaw, 1870, pp. 227-229

Lancashire
Bold
4854 Ales Hitchmough, widow
St Helens, *Angells*, 1999, pp. 34-35
Newton-le-Willows
4855 Elizabeth Blakeborne
St Helens, *Angells*, 1999, pp. 46-48

Leicestershire
Braunstone
4856 John Newton
Wilshere, *Braunstone*, 1983, p. 17

Glenfield
4857 Nicholas Walker
Wilshere, *Glenfield*, 1983, p. 5

Lincolnshire
Clee, Thrunscoe
4858 Thomas Stonnes, husbandman
Ambler, Watkinson, *Clee*, 1987, pp. 129-130

London
Winchester House, Southwark
4859 James Montagu, Bishop of Winchester (also
listed Bishop's Waltham, Hampshire)
Shirley, 1873, pp. 400-402

Norfolk
Wymondham
4860 Willyam Algar, yeoman
Wilson, *Wymondham*, 1983, pp. 13-14
4861 Thomas Cole, linen weaver
Wilson, *Wymondham*, 1983, pp. 30-31

Northumberland
Belford, Fenham (?)
4862 Lady Margaret Read
Raine, *North Durham*, 1852, p. 179

Oxfordshire
Banbury
4863 John Bayley [Baylie], gentleman
Brinkworth and Gibson, *Banbury*, I, 1975, pp. 265-266
4864 Simon Eyles [Eales], [ostler]
Brinkworth and Gibson, *Banbury*, I, 1975, p. 275
Banbury, Neithrop
4865 Edward French, husbandman
Brinkworth and Gibson, *Banbury*, I, 1975, pp. 277-278
Banbury, Grimsbury
4866 Thomas Gibberd [Gybberd, Gibbert],
husbandman
Brinkworth and Gibson, *Banbury*, I, 1975, p. 276
Banbury
4867 Isabel Harris, widow
Brinkworth and Gibson, *Banbury*, I, 1975, p. 281
4868 Anne Jackson, widow
Brinkworth and Gibson, *Banbury*, I, 1975, pp. 284-285
4869 Edward Jackson, surgeon
Brinkworth and Gibson, *Banbury*, I, 1975, p. 282
4870 Thomas Kinton, shoemaker
Brinkworth and Gibson, *Banbury*, I, 1975, p. 283
4871 Thomas Neale, butcher
Brinkworth and Gibson, *Banbury*, I, 1975, pp. 280-281
4872 Edward Phill [Fille], blacksmith
Brinkworth and Gibson, *Banbury*, I, 1975, pp. 274-275
4873 Robert Rogers, [grazier]
Brinkworth and Gibson, *Banbury*, I, 1975, pp. 278-280
4874 John Tredwell
Brinkworth and Gibson, *Banbury*, I, 1975, p. 274
4875 Henry Wright [Write], innholder (Three Swans)
Brinkworth and Gibson, *Banbury*, I, 1975, pp. 272-273

Staffordshire
Lichfield
4876 William Lees, brickmaker
Vaisey, *Lichfield*, 1969, pp. 52-54
4877 Julian Stonynge, [widow]
Vaisey, *Lichfield*, 1969, pp. 50-52

Suffolk
Ipswich
  4878 Simon Isam, tailor
    Reed, *Ipswich*, 1981, pp. 93-97
  4879 Richard Meynynges, mariner
    Reed, *Ipswich*, 1981, pp. 92-93
  4880 Samuel Palmer
    Reed, *Ipswich*, 1981, p. 97
  4881 John Wilkinson, clothworker
    Reed, *Ipswich*, 1981, pp. 97-99

Worcestershire
Chaddesley Corbett
  4882 Bridgett Corbett, widow
    Roper, *Chaddesley Corbett*, 1971, p. 39
  4883 Jane Hall, widow
    Roper, *Chaddesley Corbett*, 1971, p. 38
Chaddesley Corbett, Hillpool
  4884 Francis Smith, gentleman
    West, *Village Records*, 1962, pp. 104-106
    Roper, *Chaddesley Corbett*, 1971, pp. 39-41
Madresfield
  4885 Sir William Ligon [Lygon]
    Wanklyn, *Worcestershire*, 1998, pp. 138-140

Yorkshire
Aygarth, Cotterdale
  4886 Thomas Sharp
    Thwaite, *Abbotside*, 1967, p. 41
  4887 John Shawe [Shaw]
    Thwaite, *Abbotside*, 1967, p. 42
Bingley
  4888 William Scott
    Preston, *Co. York*, 1929, pp. 51-52
  4889 Edmund Whytley
    Preston, *Co. York*, 1929, pp. 53-54
Cottingley, Bingley (now Bradford)
  4890 Thomas Slater
    Preston, *Co. York*, 1929, pp. 48-50
Eldwick, Bingley
  4891 Abraham Royds
    Preston, *Co. York*, 1929, pp. 143-145
South Cave
  4892 John Arkle, [yeoman]
    Kaner, *South Cave*, 1994, pp. 267-269
  4893 Nicholas Bellard, [yeoman]
    Kaner, *South Cave*, 1994, pp. 274-276
  4894 Philip Brewster, [tailor]
    Kaner, *South Cave*, 1994, pp. 271-272
  4895 William Elvishe, [tailor]
    Kaner, *South Cave*, 1994, pp. 272-274
  4896 John Marshall, [husbandman/yeoman]
    Kaner, *South Cave*, 1994, pp. 269-270

1618 (c.)

Wiltshire
Marlborough
  4897 Joane Godderd
    Williams and Thomson, *Marlborough*, 2007, p. 40

1619

Bedfordshire
Ampthill
  4898 Jeffrey Palmer, gentleman
    Emmison, *Bedfordshire*, 1938, pp. 99-100
Arlesey
  4899 George Smythe, labourer
    Emmison, *Bedfordshire*, 1938, p. 121

Astwick
  4900 William Squire
    Emmison, *Bedfordshire*, 1938, p. 107
Barford
  4901 Nicholas Canon, labourer
    Emmison, *Bedfordshire*, 1938, pp. 119-120
Barton-le-Clay
  4902 Thomas Lander, weaver
    Emmison, *Bedfordshire*, 1938, pp. 113-114
  4903 Nicholas Pryer
    Emmison, *Bedfordshire*, 1938, pp. 117-118
Bedford
  4904 John Beche, glover
    Emmison, *Bedfordshire*, 1938, pp. 136-137
  4905 John Broune
    Emmison, *Bedfordshire*, 1938, p. 112
  4906 Luke Cooke, malt miller
    Emmison, *Bedfordshire*, 1938, p. 119
  4907 Edward Crash alias Baxter, baker
    Emmison, *Bedfordshire*, 1938, p. 125
Bletsoe
  4908 Daniel Abbotts, labourer
    Emmison, *Bedfordshire*, 1938, pp. 107-108
  4909 Thomas Millward, yeoman
    Emmison, *Bedfordshire*, 1938, p. 127
Blunham
  4910 Warine Brittine, labourer
    Emmison, *Bedfordshire*, 1938, p. 86
  4911 Henry Richardson
    Emmison, *Bedfordshire*, 1938, p. 101
Bolnhurst
  4912 Richard Allcocke, husbandman
    Emmison, *Bedfordshire*, 1938, pp. 77-78
  4913 John Blyth, yeoman
    Emmison, *Bedfordshire*, 1938, p. 118
  4914 Richard Haynes, labourer
    Emmison, *Bedfordshire*, 1938, p. 133
Bromham
  4915 Henry Haster, shepherd
    Emmison, *Bedfordshire*, 1938, p. 137
  4916 Dorothy Kyng, widow
    Emmison, *Bedfordshire*, 1938, p. 95
Caldecote
  4917 John Cumberland (also listed Clifton)
    Austin, 1928, pp. 312-314
    Emmison, *Bedfordshire*, 1938, p. 96
Cardington, Fenlake
  Richard Fisher, yeoman (see Milton Ernest)
Cardington
  4918 John Jeyes, labourer
    Emmison, *Bedfordshire*, 1938, p. 128
Chalgrave
  4919 John Rogers, husbandman
    Emmison, *Bedfordshire*, 1938, pp. 110-111
Chellington
  4920 Richard Abbott
    Emmison, *Bedfordshire*, 1938, p. 126
  4921 John Dawes, labourer
    Emmison, *Bedfordshire*, 1938, p. 91
Clifton
  John Cumberland (see Caldecote)
  4922 Thomas Tyngaie
    Emmison, *Bedfordshire*, 1938, p. 142

Clophill
 4923   Robert Hill, shoemaker
 Emmison, *Bedfordshire*, 1938, p137-138
Cockayne Hatley
 4924   Thomas Stacie, gentleman
 Emmison, *Bedfordshire*, 1938, p. 104
Cranfield
 4925   Roger Cooke
 Emmison, *Bedfordshire*, 1938, pp. 90-91
 4926   William Judgge, labourer
 Emmison, *Bedfordshire*, 1938, pp. 129-130
 4927   Thomas Luns
 Emmison, *Bedfordshire*, 1938, pp. 116-117
Dunstable
 4928   Elizabeth Ordway, widow
 Emmison, *Bedfordshire*, 1938, p. 129
 4929   Henry Smithe, tailor
 Emmison, *Bedfordshire*, 1938, p. 141
Eaton Socon, Duloe
 4930   Stephen Aucoke, labourer
 Emmison, *Bedfordshire*, 1938, pp. 91-92
Eaton Socon
 4931   Elizabeth Raynolds, widow
 Emmison, *Bedfordshire*, 1938, pp. 126-127
Elstow
 4932   Mary Collin[s]
 Emmison, *Bedfordshire*, 1938, pp. 112-113
 4933   Thomas Cooke, yeoman
 Emmison, *Bedfordshire*, 1938, p. 105
 4934   Joan Harte, widow
 Emmison, *Bedfordshire*, 1938, p. 139
 4935   William Wiante
 Emmison, *Bedfordshire*, 1938, p. 101
Eversholt
 4936   Thomas Symons
 Emmison, *Bedfordshire*, 1938, pp. 108-109
Eyeworth
 4937   Richard Durdent
 Emmison, *Bedfordshire*, 1938, p. 112
Flitton, Greenfield
 4938   John Goodin, yeoman
 Emmison, *Bedfordshire*, 1938, p. 102
Flitwick
 4939   Ralph Bate, clergyman, vicar of Flitwick
 Emmison, *Bedfordshire*, 1938, p. 131
 4940   Henry Etheridge, husbandman
 Emmison, *Bedfordshire*, 1938, pp. 136-136
 4941   Anne Misseldine, widow
 Emmison, *Bedfordshire*, 1938, p. 118
Goldington
 4942   Francis Ashby
 Emmison, *Bedfordshire*, 1938, p. 85
 4943   William Clarke
 Emmison, *Bedfordshire*, 1938, p. 92
 4944   William Morgan
 Emmison, *Bedfordshire*, 1938, pp. 122-123
 4945   John Vallett, carpenter
 Emmison, *Bedfordshire*, 1938, p. 92
Great Barford
 4946   William Wilshire, yeoman
 Emmison, *Bedfordshire*, 1938, pp. 92-93
Houghton Conquest
 4947   Michael Carteir
 Emmison, *Bedfordshire*, 1938, p. 111

 4948   Thomas Stringer, labourer
 Emmison, *Bedfordshire*, 1938, pp. 141-142
Kempston
 4949   William Wakefield, labourer
 Emmison, *Bedfordshire*, 1938, p. 106
Langford
 4950   Joan Underwood, widow
 Emmison, *Bedfordshire*, 1938, pp. 123-124
Lidlington
 4951   Thomas Hill
 Emmison, *Bedfordshire*, 1938, pp. 97-98
Luton
 4952   Edward Ashby, weaver
 Emmison, *Bedfordshire*, 1938, p. 141
 4953   Joan Chalkeley, widow
 Emmison, *Bedfordshire*, 1938, p. 97
Luton, Westhide
 4954   Robert Morris, labourer
 Emmison, *Bedfordshire*, 1938, p. 73
Marston Moretaine
 4955   Elizabeth Titte
 Emmison, *Bedfordshire*, 1938, p. 125
Maulden
 4956   George Button, gentleman
 Emmison, *Bedfordshire*, 1938, p. 126
Melchbourne
 4957   William Browne
 Emmison, *Bedfordshire*, 1938, p. 143
 4958   Thomas Neguss
 Emmison, *Bedfordshire*, 1938, p. 120
Milton Bryan
 4959   Thomas Wood, labourer
 Emmison, *Bedfordshire*, 1938, p. 106
Milton Ernest
 4960   Richard Fisher, yeoman (also listed Cardington)
 Emmison, *Bedfordshire*, 1938, pp. 75-76
Moggerhanger
 4961   Henry Retchforde, labourer
 Emmison, *Bedfordshire*, 1938, pp. 95-96
Northill, Thornecote
 4962   John Stevens
 Emmison, *Bedfordshire*, 1938, p. 135
 Hatcher and Barker, *Pewter*, 1974, p. 100
Oakley
 4963   Thomas Stokes
 Emmison, *Bedfordshire*, 1938, p. 94
 4964   Lawrence Wright, tailor
 Emmison, *Bedfordshire*, 1938, p. 75
Old Warden
 4965   Anthony Pimore
 Emmison, *Bedfordshire*, 1938, p. 86
Potton
 4966   John Hall, baker
 Emmison, *Bedfordshire*, 1938, pp. 89-90
Ravensden
 4967   Edward Bulmer, husbandman
 Emmison, *Bedfordshire*, 1938, pp. 115-116
Renhold
 4968   John Smythe, yeoman
 Emmison, *Bedfordshire*, 1938, pp. 83-84
Ridgmont
 4969   Richard Jacksonne, husbandman
 Emmison, *Bedfordshire*, 1938, pp. 120-121

Riseley
  4970 Christopher Clare
    Emmison, *Bedfordshire*, 1938, p. 128
  4971 John Thompson, clergyman, vicar
    Emmison, *Bedfordshire*, 1938, pp. 87-88
Sandy
  4972 Robert Kefford
    Emmison, *Bedfordshire*, 1938, pp. 84-85
  4973 John Langley, weaver
    Emmison, *Bedfordshire*, 1938, pp. 102-103
  4974 William Shadbolt, labourer
    Emmison, *Bedfordshire*, 1938, p. 119
Sandy, Beeston
  4975 Richard Wilsher
    Emmison, *Bedfordshire*, 1938, pp. 125-126
Sharnbrook
  4976 Gerard Rogers
    Emmison, *Bedfordshire*, 1938, p. 107
Shefford
  4977 Lawrence Grymson
    Emmison, *Bedfordshire*, 1938, p. 120
Shelton
  4978 Robert Kinge, husbandman
    Emmison, *Bedfordshire*, 1938, pp. 114-115
Shillington
  4979 Robert Elmer
    Emmison, *Bedfordshire*, 1938, p. 116
  4980 Joan Wallin alias Poulter
    Emmison, *Bedfordshire*, 1938, p. 94
Silsoe
  4981 William Burden, yeoman
    Emmison, *Bedfordshire*, 1938, pp. 81-83
Southill
  4982 John Randall
    Emmison, *Bedfordshire*, 1938, p. 130
  4983 Robert Thurgood
    Emmison, *Bedfordshire*, 1938, p. 93
Sutton
  4984 'Annis' Smyth, widow
    Emmison, *Bedfordshire*, 1938, pp. 131-132
Tempsford
  4985 Thomas Rogers, butcher
    Emmison, *Bedfordshire*, 1938, pp. 62-63
  4986 Thomas Samon, weaver
    Emmison, *Bedfordshire*, 1938, p. 135
Tilbrook
  4987 Henry Allingham, husbandman
    Emmison, *Bedfordshire*, 1938, p. 134
  4988 Robert Nickolls, husbandman
    Emmison, *Bedfordshire*, 1938, pp. 124-125
Toddington, Fancott
  4989 William Purrat, labourer
    Emmison, *Bedfordshire*, 1938, p. 130
Unlocated
  4990 William Catline
    Emmison, *Bedfordshire*, 1938, p. 108
  4991 William Cripsee alias Barnerde
    Emmison, *Bedfordshire*, 1938, pp. 104-105
  4992 John Sparks
    Emmison, *Bedfordshire*, 1938, p. 128
Wilden
  4993 Robert Tettrington, labourer
    Emmison, *Bedfordshire*, 1938, p. 122

Wilshamstead, Cotton End
  4994 George Edwards, yeoman
    Emmison, *Bedfordshire*, 1938, pp. 88-89
Wilshamstead
  4995 John Fanne
    Emmison, *Bedfordshire*, 1938, p. 118
  4996 Philip Purser, husbandman
    Emmison, *Bedfordshire*, 1938, pp. 108-109
Wrestlingworth
  4997 Barnaby Clarke alias Thomasin, yeoman
    Emmison, *Bedfordshire*, 1938, p. 109
Bristol
Bristol, St John
  4998 James Watkins, [fishmonger]
    George, *Bristol*, 1, 2002, pp. 29-30
Westbury
  4999 Stephen Hyett, yeoman
    Moore, *Clifton*, 1981, pp. 27-28
Cheshire
Ashton-on-Mersey
  Robert Hickson (see Little Budworth)
Bredbury
  Mary Arderne (see Stockport)
Dunham Massey
  5000 Ralph Lingard
    Groves, *Dunham Massey*, 2008, pp. 42-43
Hale
  5001 William Booth, [yeoman]
    Groves, *Hale 1*, 2005, p. 58
  5002 Ralph Kelsall, [yeoman]
    Groves, *Hale 1*, 2005, pp. 54-56
Hale, Hale Low
  5003 Elizabeth Leicester, [widow]
    Groves, *Hale 1*, 2005, pp. 48-50
Hale
  5004 William Partington, [yeoman]
    Groves, *Hale 1*, 2005, p. 52
Little Budworth
  5005 Robert Hickson (also listed Ashton-on-Mersey)
    Groves, *Ashton-on-Mersey and Sale*, 1999, pp. 38-39
Nantwich
  5006 Edward Dyall
    Cockcroft, *Nantwich*, 1999, p. 119.1
  5007 Edward Richardson, barber
    Cockcroft, *Nantwich*, 1999, pp. 267.1-2
  5008 Arthur Wixstead, shoemaker
    Cockcroft, *Nantwich*, 1999, pp. 355.1-2
  5009 Margery Wright, widow
    Cockcroft, *Nantwich*, 1999, p. 364.2
Stockport
  5010 Mary Arderne (also listed Bredbury)
    Phillips and Smith, *Stockport*, 1985, pp. 123-129
  5011 William Dickinson, alderman
    Phillips and Smith, *Stockport*, 1985, pp. 130-138
  5012 John Robinson, yeoman
    Phillips and Smith, *Stockport*, 1985, pp. 139-141
  5013 William Hulme
    Phillips and Smith, *Stockport*, 1985, pp. 141-142
Wrenbury
  5014 Phillip Dodd
    Pixton, *Wrenbury*, 2009, p. 166
Wrenbury, Newhall
  5015 John Egerton, gentleman
    Pixton, *Wrenbury*, 2009, p. 186

5016 Anne Kemp [Kempe], widow
Pixton, *Wrenbury*, 2009, p. 163
Wrenbury, Broomhall
5017 John Millington
Pixton, *Wrenbury*, 2009, p. 165
Wrenbury, Chorley
5018 William Taylor
Pixton, *Wrenbury*, 2009, p. 174

Derbyshire
Chesterfield
5019 Ralph Brough, yeoman
Bestall and Fowkes, *Chesterfield*, 2001, pp. 183-185
5020 Robert Forthe, yeoman
Bestall and Fowkes, *Chesterfield*, 2001, pp. 175-177
5021 Francis Heathcott, yeoman
Bestall and Fowkes, *Chesterfield*, 2001, pp. 167-172
5022 Robert Mason, tanner
Bestall and Fowkes, *Chesterfield*, 2001, pp. 163-165
5023 Mary Scott, widow
Bestall and Fowkes, *Chesterfield*, 2001, pp. 178-180
5024 John Stanley
Bestall and Fowkes, *Chesterfield*, 2001, pp. 172-173
5025 Dorothy Tagge
Bestall and Fowkes, *Chesterfield*, 2001, pp. 174-175
5026 Anthony Tupman, butcher
Bestall and Fowkes, *Chesterfield*, 2001, pp. 180-183
Chesterfield, Calow
5027 Richard Watson
Bestall and Fowkes, *Chesterfield*, 2001, pp. 162-163
Chesterfield
5028 Godfrey Wheatcroft
Bestall and Fowkes, *Chesterfield*, 2001, p. 178
5029 William Woodward, blacksmith
Bestall and Fowkes, *Chesterfield*, 2001, pp. 165-167

Devonshire
Bishops Tawton
5030 Brian Leachland
Cash, *Devon*, 1966, p. 26
Tiverton, Potcote
5031 John Tucker
Worthy, *Devonshire*, 1896, p. 15

Hertfordshire
Chipperfield
5032 William Prince
Munby, *Kings Langley*, 1981, pp. 62-63
Markyate
5033 John Carter, wheelwright
Emmison, *Bedfordshire*, 1938, p. 113
5034 Thomas Carter
Emmison, *Bedfordshire*, 1938, p. 106
St Albans, St Stephens, Park Street
5035 Roger Nutkyn
Parker, *Worldly Goods*, 2004, pp. 193-194
Sarratt
5036 Will[ia]m Woolman
Bullen, *Sarratt*, [1982], pp. 119-120

Lincolnshire
Clee, Itterby
5037 Leonard Portus, labourer
Ambler, Watkinson, *Clee*, 1987, p. 130

London
Denmark (Somerset) House
5038 Queen Anne of Denmark
Payne, 2001, pp. 27-42

Northumberland
Berwick
5039 Jane Johnson, widow
Wood, *Wills and Inventories*, 1929, IV, p. 133
Morpeth
5040 Margaret Heborne [Hebburn]
Wood, *Wills and Inventories*, 1929, IV, p. 130

Oxfordshire
Banbury
5041 Ralph Dixe, tanner
Brinkworth and Gibson, *Banbury*, I, 1975, pp. 295-296
5042 Henry Dudley (Dudlie), tailor
Brinkworth and Gibson, *Banbury*, I, 1975, p. 294
5043 Thomas Evans, mason
Brinkworth and Gibson, *Banbury*, I, 1975, p. 288
Banbury, Grimsbury
5044 William French, carpenter
Brinkworth and Gibson, *Banbury*, I, 1975, p. 292
Banbury, Calthorpe
5045 John Kimbell, husbandman
Brinkworth and Gibson, *Banbury*, I, 1975, p. 297
Banbury
5046 Epiphany [Nepiphaan] Kimnell [Kymble],
labourer
Brinkworth and Gibson, *Banbury*, I, 1975, pp. 289-290
5047 Richard Newman [Neweman], shoemaker
Brinkworth and Gibson, *Banbury*, I, 1975, pp. 290-291
5048 Allse [Elizabeth] Padberye [Padburie], [widow]
Brinkworth and Gibson, *Banbury*, I, 1975, p. 285
5049 George Pedley, shoemaker
Brinkworth and Gibson, *Banbury*, I, 1975, p. 293
5050 Henry Perkins, labourer
Brinkworth and Gibson, *Banbury*, I, 1975, p. 287
5051 Robert Rose, currier
Brinkworth and Gibson, *Banbury*, I, 1975, pp. 292-293
5052 Annis Sowtham, widow
Brinkworth and Gibson, *Banbury*, I, 1975, p. 296
5053 Edward Vardin [Fardom], [glover]
Brinkworth and Gibson, *Banbury*, I, 1975, p. 291
Banbury, Neithrop
5054 Thomas Youicke [Huicke], yeoman
Brinkworth and Gibson, *Banbury*, I, 1975, pp. 286-287

Staffordshire
Dudley
5055 Richard Bassett
Roper, *Dudley*, 1968, pp. 10-11
Lichfield
5056 Raffe Hyll
Vaisey, *Lichfield*, 1969, p. 54

Suffolk
Ipswich
5057 John Herne
Reed, *Ipswich*, 1981, pp. 100-101
5058 Richard Osborne, tailor
Reed, *Ipswich*, 1981, pp. 101-103
5059 Thomasine Scrivener, widow
Reed, *Ipswich*, 1981, p. 99

Warwickshire
Stratford-on-Avon
  5060 Eadye Whitte [Eady White], widow
    Jones, *Stratford*, I, 2002, p. 313
Wiltshire
Marlborough
  5061 Baldine Lee, labourer
    Williams and Thomson, *Marlborough*, 2007, pp. 41-42
  5062 William Woods, joiner
    Williams and Thomson, *Marlborough*, 2007, pp. 40-41
Yorkshire
Aysgarth, Cams Houses
  5063 James Outhwaite
    Thwaite, *Abbotside*, 1967, pp. 42-43
Bingley, Marshe Cote
  5064 William Midgley
    Preston, *Co. York*, 1929, pp. 21-22
Bingley
  5065 William Wright, husbandman
    Preston, *Co. York*, 1929, pp. 30-31
South Cave
  5066 William Benson, [yeoman]
    Kaner, *South Cave*, 1994, pp. 283-284
  5067 Christopher Cleeving
    Kaner, *South Cave*, 1994, pp. 281-282
  5068 Edward Clark, [yeoman]
    Kaner, *South Cave*, 1994, pp. 279-281
  5069 George Colson
    Kaner, *South Cave*, 1994, p. 284
South Cave, Faxfleet
  5070 Edmonde Jacksonn, grassman
    Kaner, *South Cave*, 1994, pp. 277-278
  5071 Helin Jackson, widow
    Kaner, *South Cave*, 1994, pp. 283-284

1619 (c.)
Bedfordshire
Kempston
  5072 Joane White, widow
    Emmison, *Bedfordshire*, 1938, p. 134
Wiltshire
Marlborough
  5073 Agnes Bordman
    Williams and Thomson, *Marlborough*, 2007, p. 41
  5074 Agnes Webb, widow
    Williams and Thomson, *Marlborough*, 2007, pp. 43-44

1620
Bedfordshire
Bedford, St Paul
  5075 John Browne, mason
    Emmison, *Bedfordshire*, 1938, p. 86
Bedford, St Mary
  5076 John Dawesworth
    Emmison, *Bedfordshire*, 1938, pp. 67-68
Bedford, St Cuthbert
  5077 Edward Glover
    Emmison, *Bedfordshire*, 1938, p. 59
    Hatcher and Barker, *Pewter*, 1974, p. 100
Bedford, St Paul
  5078 Joane Jackson, widow
    Emmison, *Bedfordshire*, 1938, p. 58
Bedford, St Peter
  5079 John Lambert
    Emmison, *Bedfordshire*, 1938, p. 59

Bedford, St Paul
  5080 John Lewes
    Emmison, *Bedfordshire*, 1938, p. 67
Bedford, St John
  5081 William Mason, tailor
    Emmison, *Bedfordshire*, 1938, pp. 142-143
Bedford, St Peter
  5082 Thomas Newton
    Emmison, *Bedfordshire*, 1938, p. 66
Blunham
  5083 John Kinge, husbandman (also listed Eynesbury, Huntingdonshire)
    Emmison, *Bedfordshire*, 1938, pp. 63-64
Biddenham
  5084 Margaret Laine, widow
    Emmison, *Bedfordshire*, 1938, p. 77
Cardington, Fenlake
  5085 Thomas Burger, carpenter
    Emmison, *Bedfordshire*, 1938, p. 55
Cardington
  5086 Thomas Hammond, shepherd
    Emmison, *Bedfordshire*, 1938, p. 75
    Hatcher and Barker, *Pewter*, 1974, p. 100
  5087 James Millward alias Smyth, labourer
    Emmison, *Bedfordshire*, 1938, p. 71
Cardington, Cotton End
  5088 Thomas Robinson, labourer
    Emmison, *Bedfordshire*, 1938, pp. 61-62
Chalgrave, Wingfield
  5089 Nicholas Groome, labourer
    Emmison, *Bedfordshire*, 1938, pp. 66-67
Dean
  5090 John Curtis, husbandman
    Emmison, *Bedfordshire*, 1938, pp. 57-58
Dunton
  5091 Richard Green
    Emmison, *Bedfordshire*, 1938, p. 123
Eaton Bray
  5092 Wm Harberde, freemason
    Emmison, *Bedfordshire*, 1938, pp. 70-71
Eaton Socon, Duloe
  5093 Robert Scott, yeoman
    Emmison, *Bedfordshire*, 1938, pp. 54-55
Goldington
  5094 Ralph Fisher, yeoman
    Emmison, *Bedfordshire*, 1938, p. 65
Haynes
  5095 John Ensame alias Borrowe
    Emmison, *Bedfordshire*, 1938, pp. 69-70
Holcot
  5096 Edward Plummer, clergyman, rector of Holcot
    Emmison, *Bedfordshire*, 1938, pp. 56-57
Husborne Crawley
  5097 John Collens, yeoman
    Emmison, *Bedfordshire*, 1938, p. 80
Lidlington
  5098 William Archer, yeoman
    Emmison, *Bedfordshire*, 1938, pp. 72-73
  5099 William Lingerd, husbandman
    Emmison, *Bedfordshire*, 1938, p. 74
Luton
  5100 Ellen Field, widow
    Emmison, *Bedfordshire*, 1938, p. 74

5101 William Winch, yeoman
Emmison, *Bedfordshire*, 1938, p. 50
Marston Moretaine
5102 Peter Clarke
Emmison, *Bedfordshire*, 1938, pp. 64-65
Millbrook
5103 Andrew Lycet, labourer
Emmison, *Bedfordshire*, 1938, pp. 55-56
Oakley
5104 Robert Gale
Emmison, *Bedfordshire*, 1938, pp. 78-79
5105 Richard Stokes
Emmison, *Bedfordshire*, 1938, p. 72
Pavenham
5106 William Ardon, freemason
Emmison, *Bedfordshire*, 1938, pp. 60-61
5107 Richard Covington
Emmison, *Bedfordshire*, 1938, p. 58
Pulloxhill
5108 John Clarke
Emmison, *Bedfordshire*, 1938, pp. 79-80
Ravensden
5109 John King, carpenter
Emmison, *Bedfordshire*, 1938, p. 59
Renhold
5110 Thomas Hodle, husbandman
Emmison, *Bedfordshire*, 1938, pp. 68-69
Southill
5111 John Amias, husbandman
Emmison, *Bedfordshire*, 1938, p. 60
5112 Robert Lenton, yeoman
Emmison, *Bedfordshire*, 1938, p. 62
Streatley
5113 Thomas Pruddon, husbandman
Emmison, *Bedfordshire*, 1938, p. 66
Upper Gravenhurst
5114 Robert Baracle
Emmison, *Bedfordshire*, 1938, p. 69
5115 Henry Randall, smith
Emmison, *Bedfordshire*, 1938, pp. 73-74
Unlocated
5116 Elizabeth Smyth, widow
Emmison, *Bedfordshire*, 1938, p. 85
Willington
5117 Thomas Man, labourer
Emmison, *Bedfordshire*, 1938, pp. 58-59
5118 William Mason, husbandman
Emmison, *Bedfordshire*, 1938, pp. 86-87
5119 Francis Rossill, labourer
Emmison, *Bedfordshire*, 1938, p. 63

Berkshire
Faringdon
5120 Lady Dorothie Shirley (also listed Astwell, Northamptonshire)
Nichols, *Unton*, pp. 17-30

Bristol
Bristol, Temple
5121 Francis Baylie, clothworker (also listed Stoke Gifford, Harry Stoke, Gloucestershire)
George, *Bristol*, 1, 2002, pp. 31-33
Bristol, St Michael
5122 Bernard Oakley, locksmith
George, *Bristol*, 1, 2002, pp. 30-31

Westbury
5123 Cicely Dossett, [widow]
Moore, *Clifton*, 1981, p. 29

Cheshire
Ashton-on-Mersey
5124 George Tipping, clergyman, rector of Ashton
Groves, *Ashton-on-Mersey and Sale*, 1999, pp. 40-42
Nantwich
5125 Margaret Boughe, widow
Cockcroft, *Nantwich*, 1999, p. 39.1
5126 John Cliffe, joiner
Cockcroft, *Nantwich*, 1999, p. 76.1
5127 Elizabeth Clutton, widow
Cockcroft, *Nantwich*, 1999, p. 87.1
5128 Thomas Dewhurst, innholder
Cockcroft, *Nantwich*, 1999, pp. 116.1-4
5129 John Walthall, butcher
Cockcroft, *Nantwich*, 1999, p. 324.1
5130 Robert Wilkes, yeoman
Cockcroft, *Nantwich*, 1999, pp. 349.1-2
Wrenbury, Newhall
5131 John Backhouse
Pixton, *Wrenbury*, 2009, pp. 169-170
Wrenbury
5132 Richard Berrington
Pixton, *Wrenbury*, 2009, p. 167
Wrenbury, Broomhall
5133 William Breese [Brees], [yeoman]
Pixton, *Wrenbury*, 2009, pp. 177-178
5134 William Heighfield, [yeoman]
Pixton, *Wrenbury*, 2009, pp. 172-173

Cumberland
Orton
5135 John Lowther
Bouch, 1940, pp. 87-89

Derbyshire
Brimington
5136 Nicholas Philipott, blacksmith
Bestall and Fowkes, *Chesterfield*, 2001, pp. 187-188
5137 Margery Smith
Bestall and Fowkes, *Chesterfield*, 2001, p. 199
Chellaston
5138 Robert Whinyats, gentleman
Whinyates, 1894, pp. 52-55
Chesterfield
5139 John Cocker
Bestall and Fowkes, *Chesterfield*, 2001, p. 194
5140 Thomas Greaves, tanner
Bestall and Fowkes, *Chesterfield*, 2001, pp. 196-199
5141 Margaret Greene
Bestall and Fowkes, *Chesterfield*, 2001, pp. 194-195
5142 Thomas Heathcote, dyer
Bestall and Fowkes, *Chesterfield*, 2001, pp. 199-201
5143 Thomas Jackson, hosier
Bestall and Fowkes, *Chesterfield*, 2001, pp. 201-202
5144 John Mather alias Denby
Bestall and Fowkes, *Chesterfield*, 2001, pp. 185-186
5145 Edward Needham, yeoman and tanner
Bestall and Fowkes, *Chesterfield*, 2001, pp. 190-193
5146 William Steward, tailor
Bestall and Fowkes, *Chesterfield*, 2001, pp. 188-189

Devonshire
Cheriton Fitzpaine
 5147 Joane Snowe, widow
  Cash, *Devon*, 1966, pp. 41-42
Co. Durham
Darlington
 5148 John Corker alias Headlam, weaver
  Atkinson *et al.*, *Darlington*, 1993, pp. 165-166
 5149 William Sober, yeoman
  Atkinson *et al.*, *Darlington*, 1993, pp. 168-170
 5150 Mrs Mary Throckmorton, widow
  Atkinson *et al.*, *Darlington*, 1993, pp. 171-173
Essex
Ardleigh
 5151 William Toller
  Browne, 1907, pp. 206-207
Gloucestershire
Stoke Gifford, Harry Stoke
 5152 Francis Baylie, clothworker (see Bristol, Temple)
Stoke Gifford
 5153 Henry Clarke, M.A., clergyman, [vicar of Stoke Gifford]
  Moore, *Frampton Cotterell*, 1976, p. 52
 5154 William Hall, husbandman
  Moore, *Frampton Cotterell*, 1976, p. 51
Stoke Gifford, Harry Stoke
 5155 John Pearce, [tailor]
  Moore, *Frampton Cotterell*, 1976, p. 51
Winterbourne
 5156 Edith Stambourne, [weaver]
  Moore, *Frampton Cotterell*, 1976, pp. 51-52
Hertfordshire
Kings Langley
 5157 Bale, widow
  Munby, *Kings Langley*, 1981, p. 63
St Albans, St Stephens
 5158 Robert Byrd, labourer
  Parker, *Worldly Goods*, 2004, pp. 194-195
 5159 Henry Fen, labourer
  Parker, *Worldly Goods*, 2004, pp. 195-196
Sarratt
 5160 John Ayres
  Bullen, *Sarratt*, [1982], pp. 121-122
 5161 Edward Claydon, tailor
  Bullen, *Sarratt*, [1982], p. 121
Huntingdonshire
Eynesbury
 John Kinge, husbandman (see Blunham, Bedfordshire)
Lincolnshire
Allington
 5162 William Kitchin, blacksmith
  Pask, *Allington*, 1989, pp. 69-70
Clee, Weelsby
 5163 Mathew Pomfrett, gentleman
  Ambler, Watkinson, *Clee*, 1987, pp. 131-133
Northamptonshire
Astwell
 Lady Dorothie Shirley (see Faringdon, Berkshire)
Northumberland
Chatton, Lyham Hall
 5164 George Muschamp, gentleman
  Wood, *Wills and Inventories*, 1929, IV, pp. 140-141

Ulgham
 5165 Henry Gray
  Wood, *Wills and Inventories*, 1929, IV, p. 142
Oxfordshire
Banbury
 5166 Thomas Bornworth [Bonworth]
  Brinkworth and Gibson, *Banbury*, II, 1976, p. 2
 5167 Reman Cardin [Cardem], joiner
  Brinkworth and Gibson, *Banbury*, I, 1975, p. 303
 5168 Goune [Joan?] Dudley, widow
  Brinkworth and Gibson, *Banbury*, I, 1975, p. 302
 5169 Elizabeth Harris
  Brinkworth and Gibson, *Banbury*, I, 1975, p. 302
 5170 Ann Hatton
  Brinkworth and Gibson, *Banbury*, I, 1975, p. 298
Banbury, Neithrop
 5171 George Heines, husbandman
  Brinkworth and Gibson, *Banbury*, I, 1975, p. 299
Banbury
 5172 John Mayo, husbandman
  Brinkworth and Gibson, *Banbury*, I, 1975, p. 303
Banbury, Grimsbury
 5173 Henry Smith, labourer
  Brinkworth and Gibson, *Banbury*, I, 1975, p. 298
Banbury
 5174 Christian Walsoe, widow
  Brinkworth and Gibson, *Banbury*, I, 1975, pp. 300-301
Staffordshire
Dudley
 5175 Anne Wheeler, widow
  Roper, *Dudley*, 1968, pp. 11-12
Uttoxeter
 5176 Richard Collier, surgeon
  Vaisey, *Lichfield*, 1969, p. 55
Sussex
Arundel
 5177 William Carus, clergyman, [vicar of Arundel]
  Hughes, *Sussex*, 2007, pp. 5-7
Earnley
 5178 Henry Warner, clergyman [rector of Earnley]
  Hughes, *Sussex*, 2007, pp. 65-66
North Stoke
 5179 Thomas Heare, clergyman
  Hughes, *Sussex*, 2007, p. 197
Warwickshire
Stratford-on-Avon
 5180 Elizabeth Hancocke
  Jones, *Stratford*, I, 2002, pp. 314-315
 5181 Anne Rogers, widow
  Jones, *Stratford*, I, 2002, pp. 317-318
 5182 Humphry Whoode [Wood], maltster
  Jones, *Stratford*, I, 2002, pp. 315-317
Wiltshire
Marlborough
 5183 John Dodshon
  Williams and Thomson, *Marlborough*, 2007, pp. 42-43
 5184 William Nobell
  Williams and Thomson, *Marlborough*, 2007, p. 44
Worcestershire
Chaddesley Corbett, Milbridge
 5185 John Davis, miller
  Roper, *Chaddesley Corbett*, 1971, pp. 41-42

Chaddesley Corbett
  5186 Nicholas Hill, [husbandman]
    Roper, *Chaddesley Corbett*, 1971, p. 47
Chaddesley Corbett, Brockencote
  5187 Thomas Norris
    Roper, *Chaddesley Corbett*, 1971, p. 43
Chaddesley Corbett, Drayton
  5188 John Smithe, [yeoman]
    Roper, *Chaddesley Corbett*, 1971, pp. 43-45
Hanbury
  5189 John Berecrofte [Bearcroft], gentleman
    Wanklyn, *Worcestershire*, 1998, pp. 140-142

Yorkshire
Barforth
  5190 Elizabeth Pudsey, widow
    Raine, *Pudseys*, 1858, pp. 184-185
South Cave
  5191 William Baccuse
    Kaner, *South Cave*, 1994, p. 291
  5192 Robert Bellard
    Kaner, *South Cave*, 1994, pp. 296-297
  5193 Francis Bellgrave
    Kaner, *South Cave*, 1994, pp. 289-290
  5194 Christopher Clarke, [yeoman]
    Kaner, *South Cave*, 1994, pp. 285-289
  5195 John Eardley
    Kaner, *South Cave*, 1994, p. 288
  5196 Thomas Todde, yeoman
    Kaner, *South Cave*, 1994, pp. 292-294
  5197 John Turner
    Kaner, *South Cave*, 1994, pp. 294-295

1621

Bristol
Bristol, St Peter
  5198 William Good, pewterer
    George, *Bristol*, 1, 2002, pp. 34-35
Bristol, St John Baptist
  5199 Nathaniel Wright, haulier
    George, *Bristol*, 1, 2002, pp. 33-34

Cheshire
Dunham Massey, Dunham
  5200 William Warburton
    Groves, *Dunham Massey*, 2008, pp. 43-44
Nantwich
  5201 Robert Horton
    Cockcroft, *Nantwich*, 1999, pp. 159.1-5
  5202 Hugh Mainwaring, gentleman
    Cockcroft, *Nantwich*, 1999, pp. 197.1-7
  5203 Richard Pratchett, butcher
    Cockcroft, *Nantwich*, 1999, p. 256.1
  5204 Anne Wilkes, widow
    Cockcroft, *Nantwich*, 1999, pp. 347.1-3
  5205 Richard Wilkes, yeoman
    Cockcroft, *Nantwich*, 1999, pp. 349.1-2
Wrenbury, Chorley
  5206 Richard Rogers
    Pixton, *Wrenbury*, 2009, p. 179

Derbyshire
Chesterfield
  5207 Godfrey Boller, gentleman
    Bestall and Fowkes, *Chesterfield*, 2001, pp. 206-209
  5208 Hugh Cottrell [Cotterell], tanner
    Bestall and Fowkes, *Chesterfield*, 2001, pp. 211-214

  5209 Edward Crawshawe, gentleman
    Bestall and Fowkes, *Chesterfield*, 2001, pp. 202-205
Chesterfield, Brierley
  5210 George Ouldfield
    Bestall and Fowkes, *Chesterfield*, 2001, pp. 214-215
Chesterfield, Calow
  5211 James Watkinson
    Bestall and Fowkes, *Chesterfield*, 2001, pp. 210-211

Devonshire
Kennerleigh
  5212 John Downeman, clergyman
    Cash, *Devon*, 1966, p. 27
Sidbury
  5213 Bartholomew Powninge, yeoman
    Cash, *Devon*, 1966, pp. 26-27

Co. Durham
Binchester
  5214 Sir Charles Wren
    Wood, *Wills and Inventories*, 1929, IV, pp. 148-149

Gloucestershire
Winterbourne
  5215 Thomas Parmiter, [yeoman]
    Moore, *Frampton Cotterell*, 1976, p. 53

Lancashire
Rainford
  5216 Ellen Lyon, widow
    St Helens, *Angells*, 1999, pp. 49-50

Leicestershire
Glenfield
  5217 Thomas [Walker]
    Wilshere, *Glenfield*, 1983, p. 6
Ratby
  5218 Henry Hunte, [husbandman]
    Wilshere, *Ratby*, 1984, p. 1

Lincolnshire
Clee
  5219 Beatrice Sutton, widow
    Ambler, Watkinson, *Clee*, 1987, pp. 133-134
Clee, Oole
  5220 Katherin West, widow
    Ambler, Watkinson, *Clee*, 1987, pp. 134-135

Northamptonshire
Nethercote
  5221 William Bell, husbandman
    Brinkworth and Gibson, *Banbury*, II, 1976, pp. 5-6
  5222 Jone [Joan] Stokes, widow
    Brinkworth and Gibson, *Banbury*, II, 1976, p. 5

Oxfordshire
Banbury
  5223 Thomas Atkins, labourer
    Brinkworth and Gibson, *Banbury*, II, 1976, pp. 3-4
  5224 William Baker, labourer
    Brinkworth and Gibson, *Banbury*, II, 1976, p. 1
  5225 John Dickes [Dixe], tanner
    Brinkworth and Gibson, *Banbury*, II, 1976, pp. 10-11
  5226 Elenor [Eleanor] Ell, maidservant
    Brinkworth and Gibson, *Banbury*, II, 1976, p. 3
  5227 Thomas Foster, mercer
    Brinkworth and Gibson, *Banbury*, II, 1976, p. 8
  5228 Thomas Harres, shoemaker
    Brinkworth and Gibson, *Banbury*, II, 1976, p. 4
  5229 John Sale [Salle], glover
    Brinkworth and Gibson, *Banbury*, II, 1976, pp. 11-12

5230 Barnaby White, labourer
Brinkworth and Gibson, *Banbury*, II, 1976, p. 7

Unlocated
Unlocated
5231 Margerie Booth
West, *Village Records*, 1962, pp. 106-108

Warwickshire
Stratford-on-Avon, Old Stratford
5232 Isabell Mecocke, [widow]
Jones, *Stratford*, I, 2002, pp. 320-321
5233 William Whittorne, [carpenter]
Jones, *Stratford*, I, 2002, pp. 319-320

Wiltshire
Marlborough
5234 Thomas Sheate, mercer
Williams and Thomson, *Marlborough*, 2007, pp. 44-45
5235 Humffry Wyatt, button maker
Williams and Thomson, *Marlborough*, 2007, p. 45

Worcestershire
Belbroughton
5236 John Lashforde
Roper, *Belbroughton*, 1967-1968, p. 60
Chaddesley Corbett
5237 Margerie Boothe, [widow]
Roper, *Chaddesley Corbett*, 1971, pp. 48-49
Lenchwick
5238 Sir Thomas Bigges [Bigge]
Wanklyn, *Worcestershire*, 1998, pp. 142-147

Yorkshire
Roydfield, Bingley
5239 Christopher Hill, clothier
Preston, *Co. York*, 1929, pp. 33-34
South Cave
5240 Robert Chapman
Kaner, *South Cave*, 1994, pp. 298-299
5241 Christopher Chappelow
Kaner, *South Cave*, 1994, pp. 309-311
5242 Thomas Foddle
Kaner, *South Cave*, 1994, p. 301
5243 Peter Orrell, gentleman
Kaner, *South Cave*, 1994, pp. 303-306
5244 Robert Pinder
Kaner, *South Cave*, 1994, pp. 307-308
5245 Thomas Sharpe
Kaner, *South Cave*, 1994, p. 302
5246 John Tayler
Kaner, *South Cave*, 1994, p. 300
5247 George Willford
Kaner, *South Cave*, 1994, pp. 308-309

1622
Cheshire
Nantwich
5248 Richard Heyes, gentleman
Cockcroft, *Nantwich*, 1999, pp. 154.2-3
Wrenbury, Aston
5249 James Brooke, [yeoman]
Pixton, *Wrenbury*, 2009, pp. 181-183
Wrenbury
5250 Arthur Starkey, esquire
Pixton, *Wrenbury*, 2009, pp. 190-197
Wrenbury, Broomhall
5251 Edward Whittingham
Pixton, *Wrenbury*, 2009, p. 188

Derbyshire
Brimington
5252 Godfrey Bradbery
Bestall and Fowkes, *Chesterfield*, 2001, pp. 215-216
Chesterfield
5253 William Bloodworth, yeoman
Bestall and Fowkes, *Chesterfield*, 2001, p. 218
5254 Thomas Greaves
Bestall and Fowkes, *Chesterfield*, 2001, pp. 224-225
5255 Ralph Owen, fellmonger
Bestall and Fowkes, *Chesterfield*, 2001, pp. 217-218
5256 Jeremy Stretton, innholder
Bestall and Fowkes, *Chesterfield*, 2001, pp. 219-222
Newbold
5257 William Harrison
Bestall and Fowkes, *Chesterfield*, 2001, pp. 222-223

Devonshire
Abbotskerswell
5258 Anne Codner
Cash, *Devon*, 1966, p. 29
Morchard Bishop
5259 George Tucker
Cash, *Devon*, 1966, p. 28
Whitchurch
5260 John Elliston, clergyman, vicar of Whitchurch
Cash, *Devon*, 1966, pp. 27-28
Uffculme
5261 Walter Keeper
Wyatt, *Uffculme*, 1997, p. 42
5262 Beaten Rudg[e], widow
Wyatt, *Uffculme*, 1997, p. 42

Co. Durham
Archdeacon Newton
5263 Raphe Thursby
Atkinson *et al.*, *Darlington*, 1993, p. 190
Darlington, Oxen-le-Field
5264 William Bower, gentleman
Atkinson *et al.*, *Darlington*, 1993, pp. 183-185
Darlington, Blackwell
5265 Robert Garnett, gentleman
Atkinson *et al.*, *Darlington*, 1993, pp. 185-186
Darlington, Morton
5266 Thomas Hodgson
Atkinson *et al.*, *Darlington*, 1993, pp. 187-189
Wolsingham, Ashes House
5267 Thomas Trotter, gentleman
Wood, *Wills and Inventories*, 1929, IV, p. 158

Lancashire
Bold
5268 Elizabeth Bold
St Helens, *Angells*, 1999, pp. 52-54

Leicestershire
Braunstone
5269 Frannces Worrall, yeoman
Wilshere, *Braunstone*, 1983, p. 17

Lincolnshire
Clee
5270 Henrie Lacebie, labourer
Ambler, Watkinson, *Clee*, 1987, p. 135
Goxhill
5271 Richard Hall, [yeoman]
Johnson and Johnson, 1934, pp. 172-174

Northamptonshire
 Nethercote
  5272 Elizabeth [Elybeth] Stokes
  Brinkworth and Gibson, *Banbury*, II, 1976, p. 16
Oxfordshire
 Banbury
  5273 Elizabeth Elkenton [Elkinton], widow
  Brinkworth and Gibson, *Banbury*, II, 1976, p. 24
  5274 Thomas Jumpsone [Jemson]
  Brinkworth and Gibson, *Banbury*, II, 1976, p. 15
  5275 Alice [Alyce] Lord, widow
  Brinkworth and Gibson, *Banbury*, II, 1976, p. 25
  5276 Isaiah [Isack] Showell [Shewell], yeoman
  Brinkworth and Gibson, *Banbury*, II, 1976, pp. 19-23
  5277 Randall [Randalphe] Simes [Symes], baker
  Brinkworth and Gibson, *Banbury*, II, 1976, pp. 16-18
  5278 Frissworth [Frisworth] Tonney [Tonny], widow
  Brinkworth and Gibson, *Banbury*, II, 1976, pp. 12-13
  5279 Mary Tredwell, widow
  Brinkworth and Gibson, *Banbury*, II, 1976, p. 13
 Banbury, Neithrop
  5280 William White, smith
  Brinkworth and Gibson, *Banbury*, II, 1976, p. 9
 Water Eaton
  5281 Katherin Pike, widow
  Offord, *Water Eaton*, 1986, p. 16
Scotland
 Edinburgh
  5282 Andrew Hart, printer
  Anon., *Bassandyne*, 1836, pp. 241-245
Staffordshire
 Dudley
  5283 Richard Chessheire, [labourer]
  Roper, *Dudley*, 1968, pp. 12-13
Sussex
 Duncton
  5284 Thomas Goble
  Jerrome, 1983, pp. 33-35
 Lancing
  5285 Walter Gibbens, clergyman [vicar of Lancing]
  Hughes, *Sussex*, 2007, pp. 129-130
 Shipley
  5286 Ralph Antrobus, clergyman
  Hughes, *Sussex*, 2007, p. 190
Warwickshire
 Ashow
  5287 Thomas Powrse, husbandman
  Alcock, *Warwickshire*, 1993, pp. 106-107
 Stratford-on-Avon
  5288 Richard Baker, woollen draper
  Jones, *Stratford*, I, 2002, pp. 321-323
  5289 William Toms, tailor
  Jones, *Stratford*, I, 2002, pp. 326-327
  5290 Alice Williams, widow
  Jones, *Stratford*, I, 2002, pp. 324-326
Wiltshire
 Marlborough
  5291 Elizabeth Lane, widow
  Williams and Thomson, *Marlborough*, 2007, p. 46
Worcestershire
 Belbroughton
  5292 John Clarke, [scythegrinder]
  Roper, *Scythesmiths*, 1967, p. 17
  Roper, *Belbroughton*, 1967-1968, p. 61

 Chaddesley Corbett
  5293 William Bentley, [labourer]
  Roper, *Chaddesley Corbett*, 1971, p. 46
Yorkshire
 Cottingley, Bingley (now Bradford)
  5294 Robarte Listers [Lister], tanner
  Preston, *Co. York*, 1929, pp. 61-63
 Pudsey, Calverley
  5295 Robert Sharpe, yeoman
  Preston, *Co. York*, 1929, pp. 55-58
 South Cave
  5296 Christopher Pownsworth
  Kaner, *South Cave*, 1994, pp. 311-312

1623
Bristol
 Bristol, St Stephen
  5297 John Dunn, fishmonger
  George, *Bristol*, 1, 2002, pp. 41-43
 Bristol, St John
  5298 John Gibbons [baker]
  George, *Bristol*, 1, 2002, pp. 43-45
 Bristol, St Mary-le-Port
  5299 John Haull [Hall], shoemaker
  George, *Bristol*, 1, 2002, pp. 40-41
 Bristol, St James
  5300 Thomas Henly, scavenger
  George, *Bristol*, 1, 2002, pp. 38-39
 Bristol, St Ewen
  5301 William Stayndred [Staindred], barber
  George, *Bristol*, 1, 2002, pp. 38-39
 Bristol, All Saints
  5302 Michael Threlkelde [Threlkelle], hosier
  George, *Bristol*, 1, 2002, pp. 36-38
 Bristol, St Thomas
  5303 [Richard] Woodsonn [Woodson], surgeon
  George, *Bristol*, 1, 2002, p. 36
 Clifton
  5304 William Lovelock, [labourer]
  Moore, *Clifton*, 1981, p. 35
 Shirehampton
  5305 Thomas Whiting, [yeoman]
  Moore, *Clifton*, 1981, pp. 32-33
  5306 William Woodham, [husbandman]
  Moore, *Clifton*, 1981, p. 34
 Stoke Bishop
  5307 Richard Reynolds, husbandman
  Moore, *Clifton*, 1981, pp. 33-34
 Westbury
  5308 John Wasborough, [yeoman]
  Moore, *Clifton*, 1981, pp. 30-31
Cheshire
 Hale, Ringway
  5309 George Hardy
  Groves, *Hale 1*, 2005, pp. 59-60
 Malpas
  5310 Thomas Coller, clergyman, rector of Malpas
  Earwaker, *Lancashire and Cheshire*, 1893, pp. 32-33
 Nantwich
  5311 John Blagge, [glover]
  Cockcroft, *Nantwich*, 1999, p. 37.1
  5312 John Church, gentleman
  Cockcroft, *Nantwich*, 1999, pp. 71.1-2

5313 Katherine Hunt, widow
Cockcroft, *Nantwich*, 1999, p. 244.4
5314 Edward Tench, tanner
Cockcroft, *Nantwich*, 1999, pp. 303.2-3
5315 Richard Wickstead, gentleman
Cockcroft, *Nantwich*, 1999, p. 337.1

Derbyshire
Brimington
5316 Frances Columbell, widow
Bestall and Fowkes, *Chesterfield*, 2001, pp. 232-234
Chesterfield
5317 Edward Boulsover
Bestall and Fowkes, *Chesterfield*, 2001, p. 231
5318 Hugh Galley, baker
Bestall and Fowkes, *Chesterfield*, 2001, pp. 225-227
5319 Thomas Renshaw, alderman, butcher
Bestall and Fowkes, *Chesterfield*, 2001, pp. 241-245
5320 Ellen Stretton, innholder
Bestall and Fowkes, *Chesterfield*, 2001, pp. 228-231
Chesterfield, Calow
5321 Godfrey Stubbinge
Bestall and Fowkes, *Chesterfield*, 2001, pp. 239-240

Devonshire
Gittisham
5322 Thomas Blampin, yeoman
Cash, *Devon*, 1966, pp. 29-31
Heavitree
5323 Nicholas Spicer, yeoman
Cash, *Devon*, 1966, pp. 31-33
Hollacombe
5324 John Lovebane
Cash, *Devon*, 1966, p. 34
Tawton [?]
5325 Nicholas [Bayley]
Cash, *Devon*, 1966, p. 33
Uffculme
5326 Anthony Brooke alias Butson, [yeoman]
Wyatt, *Uffculme*, 1997, p. 44
5327 George Starke
Wyatt, *Uffculme*, 1997, pp. 42-44

Co. Durham
Bedburn Park
5328 John Lisle, gentleman (also listed Darlington)
Atkinson *et al.*, *Darlington*, 1993, pp. 192-195
Chester-le-Street, Whitehill
5329 Robert Milott, esquire
Wood, *Wills and Inventories*, 1929, IV, pp. 158-160
Darlington, Bondgate
5330 John Atkinson, gentleman
Atkinson *et al.*, *Darlington*, 1993, pp. 175-178
Darlington
5331 Lawrence Catherricke [Catherick]
Atkinson *et al.*, *Darlington*, 1993, pp. 197-200
John Lisle, gentleman (see Bedburn Park)
5332 George Marshall.yeoman
Atkinson *et al.*, *Darlington*, 1993, pp. 179-180
Darlington, Cockerton
5333 Antony Stainsby
Atkinson *et al.*, *Darlington*, 1993, pp. 201-202

Gloucestershire
Stoke Gifford
5334 Francis Wade, labourer
Moore, *Frampton Cotterell*, 1976, p. 53

Westerleigh
5335 William Pickard, yeoman
Moore, *Frampton Cotterell*, 1976, p. 53
Winterbourne
5336 Henry Atwoode, [miller]
Moore, *Frampton Cotterell*, 1976, p. 54

Hertfordshire
Kings Langley
5337 Richard Cockupp, weaver
Munby, *Kings Langley*, 1981, pp. 67-68
5338 Thomas Tomsonn [Tomson]
Munby, *Kings Langley*, 1981, p. 67
St Albans, St Stephens, Colney Street
5339 Alyce Partridge, widow
Parker, *Worldly Goods*, 2004, p. 200
St Albans, St Stephens
5340 John Wylson, husbandman
Parker, *Worldly Goods*, 2004, p. 202
Standon Lordship
5341 Sir Ralph Sadlier
Heal, 1943, pp. 112-116

Leicestershire
Kirby Muxloe
5342 Willm. Jorden, [labourer]
Wilshere, *Kirby Muxloe*, 1983, p. 9

Northumberland
Brinkburn, Brinkheugh
5343 Mary Collingwood
Wood, *Wills and Inventories*, 1929, IV, p. 158

Northamptonshire
Grimsbury
5344 Richard Wilkins, labourer
Brinkworth and Gibson, *Banbury*, II, 1976, pp. 28-29
Nethercote
5345 Mathew [Matthew] Wise [Wyse], husbandman
Brinkworth and Gibson, *Banbury*, II, 1976, pp. 30-32
Warkworth
5346 Christian Butler [Buttler], widow
Brinkworth and Gibson, *Banbury*, II, 1976, pp. 29-30

Oxfordshire
Banbury
5347 William Eaglesfeilde [Eglesfeild], butcher
Brinkworth and Gibson, *Banbury*, II, 1976, pp. 27-28
5348 Edward Warner, baker
Brinkworth and Gibson, *Banbury*, II, 1976, pp. 25-27
Oxford, Cross Inn
5349 Thomas Breese, [innholder]
Pantin, 1955, pp. 70-72
Charlbury
5350 Thomas Harris, mercer
Vaisey, 1966, pp. 109-115
Swalcliffe
5351 Solomon Crayker, clergyman, vicar of Swalcliffe
Tiller, 1979, pp. 244-245

Sussex
Chichester
5352 Thomas Weekes [Weelkes, Wilkes], [gentleman]
McCann, 1974, pp. 46-47
Stedham
5353 Joseph Chitty, clergyman
Hughes, *Sussex*, 2007, p. 195

Wiltshire
Marlborough
  5354 Phillip Ingerom, servant
    Williams and Thomson, *Marlborough*, 2007, p. 47
  5355 Ambrose Pontin, tailor
    Williams and Thomson, *Marlborough*, 2007, pp. 47-48
  5356 William Wyat, weaver
    Williams and Thomson, *Marlborough*, 2007, pp. 46-47
Worcestershire
Chaddesley Corbett
  5357 John Bennett, scythesmith
    Roper, *Chaddesley Corbett*, 1971, p. 51
  5358 Leonard Brasnell alias Baker
    Roper, *Chaddesley Corbett*, 1971, pp. 49-50
Little Malvern
  5359 Mrs Elizabeth Russell, widow
    Wanklyn, *Worcestershire*, 1998, pp. 147-148
Yorkshire
Aysgarth, Cotterdale
  5360 Christopher Moore
    Thwaite, *Abbotside*, 1967, pp. 43-44
Lunds
  5361 Thomas Barton, esquire
    Thwaite, *Abbotside*, 1967, p. 45
Pudsey, Calverley
  5362 William Sharpe
    Preston, *Co. York*, 1929, pp. 68-69
  5363 John Smith, husbandman
    Preston, *Co. York*, 1929, pp. 64-65
South Cave
  5364 Charles Chitson, [labourer]
    Kaner, *South Cave*, 1994, p. 312
  5365 Robert Ion
    Kaner, *South Cave*, 1994, p. 312
  5366 Henry and Margaret Ladler
    Kaner, *South Cave*, 1994, p. 314
  5367 Robart Smith
    Kaner, *South Cave*, 1994, p. 313
South Cave, Broomfleet
  5368 Elisabeth Sutton
    Kaner, *South Cave*, 1994, p. 315
South Cave
  5369 William Sutton
    Kaner, *South Cave*, 1994, pp. 314-315

1623 (c.)
Wiltshire
Marlborough
  5370 William Haskins, [cooper]
    Williams and Thomson, *Marlborough*, 2007, p. 49
  5371 Alice Wyatt, widow
    Williams and Thomson, *Marlborough*, 2007, pp. 48-49
Yorkshire
South Cave, Broomfleet
  5372 Dorothy Sunderland
    Kaner, *South Cave*, 1994, p. 315

1624
Bristol
Bristol, St Thomas
  5373 John Bitfil [Bittfield], soapmaker
    George, *Bristol*, 1, 2002, pp. 50-51
Bristol, St Mary Redcliffe
  5374 William Dobbes [Dobbs], chapman
    George, *Bristol*, 1, 2002, pp. 51-52

Bristol, St Peter
  5375 John Doules [Dowles], glazier
    George, *Bristol*, 1, 2002, pp. 46-50
Bristol, Temple
  5376 Richard Lloyde [Lloyd], clothworker
    George, *Bristol*, 1, 2002, pp. 45-46
Bristol, Redcliffe
  5377 Nichollas [Nicholas] Stacy, feltmaker
    George, *Bristol*, 1, 2002, pp. 54-55
Bristol, Temple
  5378 Lewis Younge [Young], [shearman]
    George, *Bristol*, 1, 2002, pp. 52-53
Clifton
  5379 Edward Hilling, [mason]
    Moore, *Clifton*, 1981, p. 37
Redland
  5380 Arthur Young, [husbandman]
    Moore, *Clifton*, 1981, pp. 38-39
Shirehampton
  5381 John Prior, yeoman
    Moore, *Clifton*, 1981, pp. 37-38
Stoke Bishop, Sneyd Park
  5382 John Cooke, gentleman
    Moore, *Clifton*, 1981, pp. 35-36
Cheshire
Dunham Massey
  5383 Henry Neild, [yeoman]
    Groves, *Dunham Massey*, 2008, pp. 45-46
Hale
  5384 Thomas Perrin
    Groves, *Hale 1*, 2005, p. 62
Nantwich
  5385 Ranulphe Kent, schoolmaster
    Cockcroft, *Nantwich*, 1999, p. 177.5
  5386 John Maisterson, gentleman
    Cockcroft, *Nantwich*, 1999, pp. 202.3-4
  5387 Tobias Tench
    Cockcroft, *Nantwich*, 1999, pp. 309.2-3
Sale
  5388 Hamnet Moores
    Groves, *Ashton-on-Mersey and Sale*, 1999, p. 43
Wrenbury, Newhall
  5389 George Cudworth, gentleman
    Pixton, *Wrenbury*, 2009, pp. 199-200
Derbyshire
Chesterfield
  5390 Thomas Heathcote
    Bestall and Fowkes, *Chesterfield*, 2001, pp. 237-238
  5391 John Holland
    Bestall and Fowkes, *Chesterfield*, 2001, p. 238
  5392 William Lister, gentleman
    Bestall and Fowkes, *Chesterfield*, 2001, pp. 251-252
Chesterfield, Watton
  5393 James Warde, webster
    Bestall and Fowkes, *Chesterfield*, 2001, pp. 236-237
Chesterfield
  5394 Parnell Whitehead, widow
    Bestall and Fowkes, *Chesterfield*, 2001, p. 246
  5395 George Woodward
    Bestall and Fowkes, *Chesterfield*, 2001, pp. 234-236
Devonshire
Down St Mary
  5396 John Fisher
    Cash, *Devon*, 1966, pp. 34-35

Uffculme

5397 John Dune [Dunne]
Wyatt, *Uffculme*, 1997, pp. 44-45
5398 Florence Holwill, [widow]
Wyatt, *Uffculme*, 1997, pp. 46-47
5399 Marye Leyman [Mary Leman]
Wyatt, *Uffculme*, 1997, pp. 45-46
5400 Francis Taylor alias Oland
Wyatt, *Uffculme*, 1997, p. 46

Gloucestershire

Hambrook

5401 Henry Williams, [labourer]
Moore, *Frampton Cotterell*, 1976, p. 54
Stoke Gifford
5402 John Beker, husbandman
Moore, *Frampton Cotterell*, 1976, p. 54
Winterbourne
5403 Thomas Gilbert, [husbandman], and Joan,
his wife
Moore, *Frampton Cotterell*, 1976, pp. 54-55

Hertfordshire

Hitchin

5404 Marrian Warner, widow
Anon., *Lock, Stock*, 1978, pp. 54-56
St Albans, St Stephens, Park Street
5405 Elline Baylley, widow
Parker, *Worldly Goods*, 2004, pp. 202-203
St Albans, St Stephens
5406 Henry Haward, labourer
Parker, *Worldly Goods*, 2004, p. 204
St Albans, St Stephens, Serge Hill
5407 John Winsor, yeoman
Munby, *Worldly Goods*, 1991, p. 113

Lancashire

Haydock

5408 Jane Gaskell
St Helens, *Angells*, 1999, pp. 55-56
St Helens, Windle
5409 Margaret Lyon
St Helens, *Angells*, 1999, p. 59
Speke Hall
5410 Sir William Norris
Saxton, 1944, pp. 118-120
Saxton, 1946, pp. 114-143

Lincolnshire

Clee, Thrunscoe

5411 Robert Hudson, yeoman
Ambler, Watkinson, *Clee*, 1987, pp. 135-136

Norfolk

Hingham

5412 Robert Constable, gentleman
Wilson, *Wymondham*, 1983, p. 9

Northumberland

Halton Tower

5413 Lancelot Carnaby
Bates, 1891, pp. 318-320
Reaveley
5414 Thomas Collingwoode, gentleman
Wood, *Wills and Inventories*, 1929, IV, p. 173

Oxfordshire

Banbury

5415 Anne Draper, widow
Brinkworth and Gibson, *Banbury*, II, 1976, p. 34

Banbury, Neithrop

5416 Richard Ditchfeild [Dychfield], tailor
Brinkworth and Gibson, *Banbury*, II, 1976, p. 35
Banbury
5417 Alse [Ann] Halhed, widow
Brinkworth and Gibson, *Banbury*, II, 1976, p. 34
Banbury, St John's
5418 John Humphries [Humfris, Humphryse],
husbandman
Brinkworth and Gibson, *Banbury*, II, 1976, pp. 35-36
Banbury, Neithrop
5419 Alse [Alice] Pratt, widow
Brinkworth and Gibson, *Banbury*, II, 1976, p. 33

Scotland

Dumfriesshire, Comlongon Castle

5420 Sir Richard Murray, baronet of Cokpule
Reid, 1955, pp. 182-185

Staffordshire

Dudley

5421 Thomas Ferryday, [nailer]
Roper, *Dudley*, 1968, pp. 13-14
5422 William Haden
Roper, *Dudley*, 1966, p. 13

Suffolk

Dunwich

5423 John Day, shepherd
Allen, 1989, p. 329

Warwickshire

Shottery

5424 Bartholmew Hathway [Bartholomew
Hathaway], [yeoman]
Jones, *Stratford*, I, 2002, pp. 332-333
5425 William Richardson, yeoman
Jones, *Stratford*, I, 2002, pp. 337-339
Stratford-on-Avon, Old Stratford
5426 Abraham Allaway, painter
Jones, *Stratford*, I, 2002, pp. 330-331
Stratford-on-Avon
5427 Aveies [Avis] Clarke, [pedlar]
Jones, *Stratford*, I, 2002, p. 329
5428 Marye Milles [Mary Mills], widow
Jones, *Stratford*, I, 2002, pp. 334-337
5429 William Roffe, carpenter
Jones, *Stratford*, I, 2002, p. 328

Wiltshire

Marlborough

5430 John Grundie, tanner
Williams and Thomson, *Marlborough*, 2007, pp. 51-52
5431 Anthonie Gunter, glover
Williams and Thomson, *Marlborough*, 2007, pp. 50-51
5432 Alice Pagett, widow
Williams and Thomson, *Marlborough*, 2007, pp. 53-54
5433 John Redford, husbandman
Williams and Thomson, *Marlborough*, 2007, pp. 52-53
5434 Gregory Tytcumb
Williams and Thomson, *Marlborough*, 2007, p. 53

Worcestershire

Chaddesley Corbett, Winterfold

5435 John Bache, husbandman
Roper, *Chaddesley Corbett*, 1971, pp. 50-51
Mathon
5436 William Moulton, esquire
Wanklyn, *Worcestershire*, 1998, pp. 149-151

Yorkshire
Gilling Castle
  5437 Sir Thomas Fairfax (also listed Walton)
  Peacock, *Inventories*, 1884, pp. 136-151
South Cave
  5438 [Henry] Hessey, labourer
  Kaner, *South Cave*, 1994, p. 316
  5439 Anne Tod [Todd], widow
  Kaner, *South Cave*, 1994, pp. 318-319
Walton
  Sir Thomas Fairfax (see Gilling)

1625

Bristol
Bristol, St Thomas
  5440 William Brookman, [skinner]
  George, *Bristol*, 1, 2002, p. 57
Bristol, Christchurch
  5441 Richard Hollyester, fletcher
  George, *Bristol*, 1, 2002, pp. 58-59
Bristol, St Mary-the-Port
  5442 Richard Maskall [Mascall], butcher
  George, *Bristol*, 1, 2002, pp. 59-60
Bristol
  5443 John Noble
  George, *Bristol*, 1, 2002, pp. 55-57
Bristol, St Ewen
  5444 Katherine Ware, single woman
  George, *Bristol*, 1, 2002, pp. 60-61
Clifton
  5445 Nicholas Barnes, [lighterman]
  Moore, *Clifton*, 1981, pp. 41-42
  5446 Katherine Bayley, widow
  Moore, *Clifton*, 1981, p. 39
  5447 Robert Browne, yeoman
  Moore, *Clifton*, 1981, pp. 39-41
Shirehampton
  5448 George Morris, [husbandman]
  Moore, *Clifton*, 1981, p. 42
Stoke Bishop
  5449 John Farrington, [carpenter]
  Moore, *Clifton*, 1981, p. 43

Cheshire
Bowdon
  5450 John Barrington
  Groves, *Bowdon*, 1997, pp. 31-32
  5451 George Bowdon, [gentleman]
  Groves, *Bowdon*, 1997, pp. 35-37
Nantwich
  5452 Thomas Leeche, innkeeper
  Cockcroft, *Nantwich*, 1999, pp. 187.1-5
  5453 George Maddock, capper
  Cockcroft, *Nantwich*, 1999, pp. 195.2-3
  5454 Edmund Myles, innkeeper
  Cockcroft, *Nantwich*, 1999, pp. 229.3-6
  5455 Roger Pemberton
  Cockcroft, *Nantwich*, 1999, p. 246.2

Derbyshire
Chesterfield
  5456 Thomasine Galley, widow
  Bestall and Fowkes, *Chesterfield*, 2001, pp. 247-249
Chesterfield, Dunston
  5457 Francis Fullwood, gentleman
  Bestall and Fowkes, *Chesterfield*, 2001, pp. 249-250

Chesterfield
  5458 William Houghton
  Bestall and Fowkes, *Chesterfield*, 2001, pp. 250-251
Chesterfield, Calow
  5459 Laurence More, husbandman
  Bestall and Fowkes, *Chesterfield*, 2001, pp. 254-256
  5460 Henry Stubbinge
  Bestall and Fowkes, *Chesterfield*, 2001, pp. 253-254

Devonshire
Chudleigh
  5461 John Bennett, gentleman
  Cash, *Devon*, 1966, pp. 36-37
South Molton
  5462 Robert Clotworthy, gentleman
  Cash, *Devon*, 1966, p. 35
Stockleigh Pomeroy
  5463 Walter Bere, husbandman
  Cash, *Devon*, 1966, pp. 35-36
Uffculme
  5464 Richard Brooke, yeoman
  Wyatt, *Uffculme*, 1997, p. 51
  5465 Nicholas Langridg [Langbridge]
  Wyatt, *Uffculme*, 1997, pp. 47-49
  5466 Xpofer [Christopher] Marshall
  Wyatt, *Uffculme*, 1997, pp. 49-50

Essex
Hatfield Peverel, Toppingho Hall
  5467 Mary Sammes, widow
  Hope, 1943, p. 121

Gloucestershire
Westerleigh
  5468 John Robbins, [collier]
  Moore, *Frampton Cotterell*, 1976, p. 55

Hampshire
Winchester
  5469 William Standly, haberdasher
  Arkell, Evans, Goose, 2000, pp. 372-373

Hertfordshire
St Albans, St Stephens
  5470 John Belton, yeoman
  Munby, *Worldly Goods*, 1991, pp. 117-119
  5471 John Cogdell, yeoman
  Parker, *Worldly Goods*, 2004, pp. 196-197
  5472 Richard Man, labourer
  Parker, *Worldly Goods*, 2004, p. 206
  5473 Mary Rogers, widow
  Parker, *Worldly Goods*, 2004, p. 205

Lancashire
Newton-le-Willows
  5474 Susan Bradley
  St Helens, *Angells*, 1999, pp. 57-58

Leicestershire
Quorndon
  5475 William Farneham, gentleman
  Farnham, *Quorndon*, 1912, p. 344

Lincolnshire
Allington
  5476 Agnis Robinsonne, widow
  Pask, *Allington*, 1989, p. 72
Clee
  5477 Richard Curteis, labourer
  Ambler, Watkinson, *Clee*, 1987, p. 137

5478 Lyon Kirke, gentleman (also listed Grimsby)
Ambler, Watkinson, *Clee*, 1987, pp. 137-139
5479 Richard Tharold, husbandman
Ambler, Watkinson, *Clee*, 1987, pp. 139-140
Clee, Itterby
5480 Margaret Tuplin, widow
Ambler, Watkinson, *Clee*, 1987, pp. 136-137
Grimsby
Lyon Kirke, gentleman (see Clee)

Northamptonshire
Northampton
5481 Mr Edward Collis, [mercer and linen draper]
Harrison, 1982-1983, pp. 313-317

Oxfordshire
Banbury
5482 Mary Keelinge, widow
Brinkworth and Gibson, *Banbury*, II, 1976, p. 40
Banbury, Neithrop
5483 Richard Kimbell [Kimble], yeoman
Brinkworth and Gibson, *Banbury*, II, 1976, pp. 39-40
5484 John Raynolles, weaver
Brinkworth and Gibson, *Banbury*, II, 1976, p. 37
Banbury
5485 George [Gorg] Robbins [Robins], shoemaker
Brinkworth and Gibson, *Banbury*, II, 1976, p. 41
5486 Alice Tayler, widow
Brinkworth and Gibson, *Banbury*, II, 1976, p. 36
Banbury, Grimsbury
5487 Robert Taylor alias Paris, husbandman
Brinkworth and Gibson, *Banbury*, II, 1976, pp. 37-38

Shropshire
Bishop's Castle, Owlbury
Edmond Waring, esquire (see Staffordshire, Wolverhampton)

Staffordshire
Cannock, Leacroft
Edmond Waring, esquire (see Wolverhampton)
Dudley, St Thomas
5488 Elizabeth Finche, [widow]
Roper, *Dudley*, 1968, pp. 14-15
Wolverhampton
5489 Edmond Waring, esquire (also listed Cannock and Bishop's Castle, Shropshire)
Darwin, 1873-1876, pp. 364-375

Sussex
North Mundham
5490 John Keay, clergyman [vicar of North Mundham]
Hughes, *Sussex*, 2007, pp. 142-145
Sidlesham
5491 William Whalley, clergyman [vicar of Sidlesham]
Hughes, *Sussex*, 2007, pp. 191-192

Warwickshire
Stratford-on-Avon
5492 Mr John Gibbes [Gibbs], gentleman
Jones, *Stratford*, I, 2002, pp. 348-351
5493 Robert Hollis, labourer [husbandman]
Jones, *Stratford*, I, 2002, pp. 346-347
5494 Leonard Kempson, gentleman
Jones, *Stratford*, I, 2002, pp. 345-346
5495 John Sadler, gentleman [alderman, bailiff]
Jones, *Stratford*, I, 2002, pp. 341-343

5496 Margarett Smyth [Margaret Smith], widow
Jones, *Stratford*, I, 2002, pp. 339-340

Wiltshire
Marlborough
5497 Richard Deance, husbandman
Williams and Thomson, *Marlborough*, 2007, pp. 54-55
5498 Phillip Sampson, labourer
Williams and Thomson, *Marlborough*, 2007, p. 54

Worcestershire
Chaddesley Corbett
5499 John Peplowe
Roper, *Chaddesley Corbett*, 1971, pp. 52-53

Yorkshire
Bingley
5500 Thomas Scott
Preston, *Co. York*, 1929, p. 72
Knaresborough
5501 George West
Brears, *Yorkshire*, 1972, pp. 76-77
North Cave, South Cliffe
5502 Anthony Dent
Kaner, *South Cave*, 1994, pp. 319-320
South Cave, Faxfleet
5503 Elizabeth Emmerson
Kaner, *South Cave*, 1994, p. 319
South Cave
5504 Ales Robingson [Robinson]
Kaner, *South Cave*, 1994, pp. 318-319
5505 John Teavill, yeoman
Kaner, *South Cave*, 1994, pp. 324-326
Pudsey, Calverley
5506 Henry Cawdrey
Preston, *Co. York*, 1929, pp. 147-150
Ripley, Birthwaite
5507 William Stubb, yeoman
Collins, *Stubbs*, 1915, pp. 110-111

1626
Bristol
Bristol, St Peter
5508 John Jorden [Jordan], [cardmaker]
George, *Bristol*, I, 2002, pp. 61-62
Westbury
5509 Christiana Ardington, [widow]
Moore, *Clifton*, 1981, p. 44

Cheshire
Hale
5510 John Hollinpriest
Groves, *Hale 1*, 2005, pp. 63-64
5511 Lawrence Royle, [husbandman]
Groves, *Hale 1*, 2005, pp. 69-70
Nantwich
5512 Matthew Currie alias Griffin, butcher
Cockcroft, *Nantwich*, 1999, pp. 99.1-2
Wrenbury, Chorley
5513 John Pattricke, [yeoman]
Pixton, *Wrenbury*, 2009, pp. 205-206
Wrenbury
5514 Randull Starkey, gentleman
Pixton, *Wrenbury*, 2009, pp. 208-210

Derbyshire
Chesterfield, Dunston
5515 Nicholas Cockayne, gentleman
Bestall and Fowkes, *Chesterfield*, 2001, pp. 256-258

Chesterfield
  5516 Robert Farrayn, [weaver]
    Bestall and Fowkes, *Chesterfield*, 2001, pp. 258-261
  5517 George Heathcote, vintner
    Bestall and Fowkes, *Chesterfield*, 2001, pp. 261-263
Chesterfield, Dunston
  5518 William Oldacres
    Bestall and Fowkes, *Chesterfield*, 2001, pp. 263-264
Devonshire
Axmouth
  5519 George Hoskenes [Hoskyns], yeoman
    Hoskins, 1941, pp. 245-246
    Hoskins and Finberg, 1952, pp. 400-402
    Hoskins, 1966, pp. 58-60
Exeter
  5520 William Knowslye, innholder
    Portman, *Exeter*, 1966, pp. 110-115
South Tawton
  5521 Thomas Batishill
    Cash, *Devon*, 1966, p. 37
Uffculme
  5522 Elizabeth Courton [Courtney], widow
    Wyatt, *Uffculme*, 1997, pp. 51-52
  5523 John Culliford
    Wyatt, *Uffculme*, 1997, p. 51
  5524 Augusten [Augustine] Tawton
    Wyatt, *Uffculme*, 1997, p. 52
  5525 Anne Welche [Welch], {widow]
    Wyatt, *Uffculme*, 1997, p. 53
Dorsetshire
Chardstock (now Devon), Coxden [Cockesden]
  5526 Unknown
    Halliwell, *Inventories*, 1854, pp. 87-114
Co. Durham
Sedgfield
  5527 Thomas Conyers, gentleman
    Wood, *Wills and Inventories*, 1929, IV, pp. 191-192
Westholme Hall
  5528 John Dowthwaite
    Wood, *Wills and Inventories*, 1929, IV, p. 176
Essex
Upminster
  5528a Elizabeth Adley, widow
    Wilson, 1906, pp. 67-68
Gloucestershire
Frampton Cotterell
  5529 Henry Bosire, [yeoman]
    Moore, *Frampton Cotterell*, 1976, pp. 55-56
Stoke Gifford, Harry Stoke
  5530 Robert Smarte, yeoman
    Moore, *Frampton Cotterell*, 1976, p. 56
Hertfordshire
Bricket Wood
  5531 William Branch
    Munby, *Worldly Goods*, 1991, pp. 119-120
Kings Langley
  5532 Thomas Pearce, victualler
    Munby, *Kings Langley*, 1981, pp. 71-72
St Albans, St Julians
  5533 Robert Gillmet, principal burgess of St Albans
    Parker, *Worldly Goods*, 2004, p. 208
Sarratt
  5534 Thomas Babb
    Bullen, *Sarratt*, [1982], pp. 123-124

5535 Richard Newton
  Bullen, *Sarratt*, [1982], pp. 125-126
Ireland
Ormond Castle, Carrick-on-Suir, co. Tipperary
  5536 Richard Preston, Earl of Desmond
    Fenlon, *Ireland*, 2003, p. 19
Leicestershire
Evington
  5537 Thomas Burley, [labourer]
    Wilshere, *Evington*, 1985, p. 18
Lincolnshire
Clee
  5538 Katherin Lowe, widow
    Ambler, Watkinson, *Clee*, 1987, pp. 140-141
  5539 Bartholomew Portas, husbandman
    Ambler, Watkinson, *Clee*, 1987, p. 140
Norfolk
Wymondham
  5540 William Blackborne [Blackbourn], [yeoman]
    Wilson, *Wymondham*, 1983, pp. 17-19
  5541 Phillippe [Philip] Cullyer, yeoman
    Wilson, *Wymondham*, 1983, pp. 9-13
Northamptonshire
Warkworth
  5542 Richard Browne
    Brinkworth and Gibson, *Banbury*, II, 1976, p. 47
Northumberland
Low Trewhitt
  5543 Henry Widdrington, gentleman
    Wood, *Wills and Inventories*, 1929, IV, pp. 196-197
Oxfordshire
Banbury
  5544 Thomas Densey [Denzey], butcher
    Brinkworth and Gibson, *Banbury*, II, 1976, pp. 45-46
  5545 Daniel Hatton
    Brinkworth and Gibson, *Banbury*, II, 1976, pp. 46-47
  5546 William Hosier, glazier
    Brinkworth and Gibson, *Banbury*, II, 1976, pp. 42-44
  5547 Edward Pilkington
    Brinkworth and Gibson, *Banbury*, II, 1976, pp. 44-45
  5548 George Piner [Pyner], tailor
    Brinkworth and Gibson, *Banbury*, II, 1976, p. 48
Staffordshire
Dudley
  5549 Henry Jackson, clergyman, vicar of Dudley
    Roper, *Dudley*, 1966, pp. 14-16
Suffolk
Ipswich
  5550 Ann Baker, widow
    Reed, *Ipswich*, 1981, pp. 105-107
  5551 Henry Blyth
    Reed, *Ipswich*, 1981, pp. 104-105
  5552 Ann Wright, widow
    Reed, *Ipswich*, 1981, pp. 103-104
Warwickshire
Stratford-on-Avon
  5553 John Harding
    Jones, *Stratford*, II, 2003, p. 3
  5554 Willyam Smythe [William Smith], [mercer]
    Jones, *Stratford*, II, 2003, pp. 4-5
Wiltshire
Marlborough
  5555 Anne Bigges, widow
    Williams and Thomson, *Marlborough*, 2007, p. 55

5556 Willyam Patchet
Williams and Thomson, *Marlborough*, 2007, pp. 56-57

Worcestershire
Chaddesley Corbett, Winterfold
5557 Jone Leyt, widow
Roper, *Chaddesley Corbett*, 1971, pp. 53-54

Yorkshire
Eldwick, Bingley
5558 Ellen Illingworth
Preston, *Co. York*, 1929, p. 81
South Cave
5559 Richard Brigham, husbandman
Kaner, *South Cave*, 1994, pp. 328-330
5560 Thomas Cleaving, yeoman
Kaner, *South Cave*, 1994, pp. 330-331
5561 Thomas Gunby
Kaner, *South Cave*, 1994, pp. 322-323
5562 John Laverocke, labourer
Kaner, *South Cave*, 1994, p. 327
South Cave, Faxfleet
5563 John Lawne
Kaner, *South Cave*, 1994, p. 321

1626 (c.)

Wiltshire
Marlborough
5564 John Cole, tanner
Williams and Thomson, *Marlborough*, 2007, p. 56

1627

Bristol
Bristol, Christchurch
5565 Humfry Clovill, goldsmith
George, *Bristol*, 1, 2002, pp. 62-64
Redland
5566 Ann Morgan alias Thomas, widow
Moore, *Clifton*, 1981, pp. 45-47
Shirehampton
5567 Anthony Matthew, [pilot]
Moore, *Clifton*, 1981, pp. 44-45

Cheshire
Crewe
5568 Rumwell Durbare
Earwaker, 1881, p. 465
Hale
5569 John Hardy, [wheelwright]
Groves, *Hale 1*, 2005, pp. 68-69
5570 Robert Johnson, [yeoman]
Groves, *Hale 1*, 2005, pp. 71-72
5571 Elizabeth Tipping
Groves, *Hale 1*, 2005, p. 70
Hale, Bank Hall
5572 John Vawdrey, esquire
Groves, *Hale 1*, 2005, pp. 64-65
Nantwich
5573 Richard Clowes
Cockcroft, *Nantwich*, 1999, p. 83.1
5574 Elizabeth Myles, widow
Cockcroft, *Nantwich*, 1999, pp. 231.2-5
5575 John Rudyerd, gentleman
Cockcroft, *Nantwich*, 1999, pp. 272.4-5
5576 Robert Wright
Cockcroft, *Nantwich*, 1999, pp. 370.3-4

Sale
5577 Richard Chorlton
Groves, *Ashton-on-Mersey and Sale*, 1999, pp. 44-45
Wrenbury, Newhall
5578 George Dickins
Pixton, *Wrenbury*, 2009, pp. 212-213
5579 Thomas Shrowbridge, [yeoman]
Pixton, *Wrenbury*, 2009, pp. 217-218

Derbyshire
Catton Hall
5580 Right Honourable Walter Horton, esquire
Ussher, 1881, pp. 240-243
Chesterfield
5581 John Butler, currier
Bestall and Fowkes, *Chesterfield*, 2001, pp. 266-267
5582 John Cleworth, cordwainer
Bestall and Fowkes, *Chesterfield*, 2001, pp. 269-272
Newbold
5583 Thomas Barker
Bestall and Fowkes, *Chesterfield*, 2001, pp. 264-265

Devonshire
Stoke Gabriel
5584 Mary Churchward, widow
Cash, *Devon*, 1966, pp. 37-38
Uffculme
5585 Mathew Cadbury
Wyatt, *Uffculme*, 1997, pp. 53-54
5586 Thomas Hurley
Wyatt, *Uffculme*, 1997, p. 55
5587 Robert Ridge and Cateren Ridge, his wife
Wyatt, *Uffculme*, 1997, pp. 56-57
5588 Simond Shilds [Simon Childs]
Wyatt, *Uffculme*, 1997, p. 56

Co. Durham
Durham
5589 Nicholas Heath, gentleman
Wood, *Wills and Inventories*, 1929, IV, p. 208

Hertfordshire
Kings Langley
5590 Gregory Grove, clergyman, vicar of Kings
Langley
Munby, *Kings Langley*, 1981, pp. 74-75
5591 Roger Halse [Halsey]
Munby, *Kings Langley*, 1981, p. 73
St Albans, St Stephens
5592 Amye Bailey, widow
Parker, *Worldly Goods*, 2004, p. 199
5593 Johan Branch
Munby, *Worldly Goods*, 1991, p. 121
5594 Roger Burre, husbandman
Parker, *Worldly Goods*, 2004, p. 209
5595 Abraham Kilbey, weaver
Parker, *Worldly Goods*, 2004, pp. 209-210
5596 Alice Scott, widow
Parker, *Worldly Goods*, 2004, p. 210

Kent
Penshurst
5597 Robert Sidney, Earl of Leicester
Owen, 1966, pp. 547-554

Lincolnshire
Clee, Oole
5598 Richard Beal, labourer
Ambler, Watkinson, *Clee*, 1987, pp. 141-142

5599   Robert Greene, blacksmith
Ambler, Watkinson, *Clee*, 1987, p. 141

Norfolk
Wymondham
5600   John Flower, [husbandman]
Wilson, *Wymondham*, 1983, pp. 19-20
5601   John Middleton, [wool draper]
Wilson, *Wymondham*, 1983, pp. 24-25

Oxfordshire
Banbury
5602   Mathew[e] Bentley [Bentlie], mercer
Brinkworth and Gibson, *Banbury*, II, 1976, pp. 60-61
5603   Joane Borrows [Barrowes, Barosse], widow
Brinkworth and Gibson, *Banbury*, II, 1976, pp. 56-58
5604   Anne Busbee [Busbie]
Brinkworth and Gibson, *Banbury*, II, 1976, p. 66
5605   Edward Coates [Coles]
Brinkworth and Gibson, *Banbury*, II, 1976, pp. 52-53
Banbury, Calthorpe
5606   Robert Craftes [alias Ambrose], shoemaker
Brinkworth and Gibson, *Banbury*, II, 1976, pp. 65-66
Banbury
5607   George Drinckwater [Drinkwatter], husbandman
Brinkworth and Gibson, *Banbury*, II, 1976, pp. 63-65
5608   William Gooddin [Gooden, Goodwin], cordwainer
Brinkworth and Gibson, *Banbury*, II, 1976, p. 55
5609   Simon Harvy [Harvie], saddler
Brinkworth and Gibson, *Banbury*, II, 1976, pp. 53-54
Banbury, Neithrop
5610   Richard Jordan, husbandman
Brinkworth and Gibson, *Banbury*, II, 1976, p. 59
5611   John Longe, husbandman
Brinkworth and Gibson, *Banbury*, II, 1976, pp. 50-51
Banbury
5612   Susan [Shewance] Maoh [Mayoe], widow
Brinkworth and Gibson, *Banbury*, II, 1976, pp. 51-52
Banbury, Neithrop
5613   Walter Walfard [Walford, Wafford], glover
Brinkworth and Gibson, *Banbury*, II, 1976, p. 60
5614   Samuel West
Brinkworth and Gibson, *Banbury*, II, 1976, pp. 48-49
5615   Samuel Wheatly [Wheatley], woollen draper, yeoman
Brinkworth and Gibson, *Banbury*, II, 1976, p. 49

Staffordshire
Dudley
5616   Edward Roods, [nailer]
Roper, *Dudley*, 1968, p. 16

Suffolk
Ipswich
5617   John Medowe, ship carpenter
Reed, *Ipswich*, 1981, p. 108

Wales
Denbighshire, Holt
5618   George Bostocke, esquire
Anon., *Bostocks*, 1926, p. 8

Warwickshire
Stratford-on-Avon
5619   Richard Douckes [Dawkes], [plumber]
Jones, *Stratford*, II, 2003, pp. 9-10
5620   Lewis Hickockes [Hiccox], yeoman [innkeeper]
Jones, *Stratford*, II, 2003, pp. 13-16

5621   Francis Hill, innholder
Jones, *Stratford*, II, 2003, pp. 5-8
5622   Robert Ingram, fisherman
Jones, *Stratford*, II, 2003, pp. 17-19
Stratford-on-Avon, Old Stratford
5623   Robert Johnson, yeoman
Jones, *Stratford*, II, 2003, pp. 11-13

Westmorland
Kendal
5624   Ralph Tyrer, clergyman, vicar of Kendal
Earwaker, *Lancashire and Cheshire*, 1893, pp. 198-199

Wiltshire
Marlborough
5625   Thomas Trebret
Williams and Thomson, *Marlborough*, 2007, p. 57

Worcestershire
Belbroughton
5626   Hugh Sych, scythegrinder
Roper, *Belbroughton*, 1967-1968, p. 63
Chaddesley Corbett, Yieldingtree
5627   John Bache
Roper, *Chaddesley Corbett*, 1971, pp. 54-55
Chaddesley Corbett
5628   Elisabeth Clent
Roper, *Chaddesley Corbett*, 1971, p. 55
5629   Ann Saunders, widow
Roper, *Chaddesley Corbett*, 1971, pp. 56-57

Yorkshire
Aysgarth, Yorescott
5630   Augustine Metcalfe
Thwaite, *Abbotside*, 1967, p. 48
Cottingley, Bingley (now Bradford)
5631   William Hill
Preston, *Co. York*, 1929, pp. 73-75
South Cave
5632   Barbara Cleaving
Kaner, *South Cave*, 1994, pp. 331-332
5633   William Spence
Kaner, *South Cave*, 1994, pp. 332-333

1627 (c.)
Cheshire
Nantwich
5634   Katherine Cheetwood
Cockcroft, *Nantwich*, 1999, p. 65.1
Yorkshire
Pudsey, Calverley
5635   Peter Mitchell
Preston, *Co. York*, 1929, pp. 101-102

1628
Bristol
Bristol [St Werburgh]
5636   Nathaniell [Nathaniel] Butcher, merchant
George, *Bristol*, 1, 2002, pp. 64-67
Bristol, St Thomas
5637   Margarett Daye [Margaret Day], widow
George, *Bristol*, 1, 2002, pp. 67-69
Cheshire
Ashton-on-Mersey
5638   Robert Alcock
Groves, *Ashton-on-Mersey and Sale*, 1999, pp. 45-46

Christleton
  5639 Richard Sheene
    Bland, *Christleton*, 2005, pp. 566-567
Hale, Ringway
  5640 Henry Arstall, [yeoman]
    Groves, *Hale 1*, 2005, pp. 73-74
Hale
  5641 John Goulden, [yeoman]
    Groves, *Hale 1*, 2005, pp. 67-68
  5642 John Grantham
    Groves, *Hale 1*, 2005, pp. 66-67
Nantwich
  5643 William Browne, gentleman
    Cockcroft, *Nantwich*, 1999, pp. 52.2-5
  5644 Thomas Clutton, gentleman
    Cockcroft, *Nantwich*, 1999, pp. 88.1-4
  5645 Richard Jackson, tanner
    Cockcroft, *Nantwich*, 1999, pp. 165.2-3
  5646 Jasper Maddocke, yeoman
    Cockcroft, *Nantwich*, 1999, pp. 196.3-4
  5647 Edward Minshull, esquire
    Cockcroft, *Nantwich*, 1999, pp. 219.3-5
  5648 Thomas Parker, cutler
    Cockcroft, *Nantwich*, 1999, p. 240.1
Tarvin, Ashton
  5649 Richard Leadbeater, husbandman
    Bland, *Christleton*, 2005, pp. 571-572
Tattenhall
  5650 Richard Bostocke, esquire
    Bland, *Christleton*, 2005, pp. 576-577
  5651 Rauffe Downes, yeoman
    Bland, *Christleton*, 2005, pp. 573-574
  5652 Raufe Marsh, [yeoman]
    Bland, *Christleton*, 2005, pp. 577-578
Wrenbury, Chorley
  5653 Randle Hare
    Pixton, *Wrenbury*, 2009, pp. 220-223

Derbyshire
Chesterfield
  5654 Margaret Allatson, alias Hodgkinson
    Bestall and Fowkes, *Chesterfield*, 2001, pp. 272-273
  5655 Henry Roper, clothworker
    Bestall and Fowkes, *Chesterfield*, 2001, pp. 268-269
Devonshire
Chudleigh
  5656 John Gibbes
    Cash, *Devon*, 1966, p. 38
Clawton
  5657 Charity Blages, widow
    Cash, *Devon*, 1966, p. 41
Staverton
  5658 Edward Gould, merchant
    Anon., *Staverton*, 1956-1958, pp. 59-64
    Cash, *Devon*, 1966, pp. 38-40
Uffculme
  5659 Joane Cheeke
    Wyatt, *Uffculme*, 1997, p. 59
  5660 Edmund Cole, [shopkeeper]
    Wyatt, *Uffculme*, 1997, p. 60
  5661 Thomas Crosse
    Wyatt, *Uffculme*, 1997, pp. 57-58
  5662 Alice Hurley, widow
    Wyatt, *Uffculme*, 1997, pp. 62-63

  5663 Thomas Hurley
    Wyatt, *Uffculme*, 1997, pp. 58-59
  5664 Humfry [Humfrey] Lutley
    Wyatt, *Uffculme*, 1997, p. 57
  5665 John Norton
    Wyatt, *Uffculme*, 1997, pp. 59-60
  5666 Phillip Parsons, [weaver]
    Wyatt, *Uffculme*, 1997, pp. 60-62
  5667 Alexsander Starke
    Wyatt, *Uffculme*, 1997, p. 62
Dorsetshire
Sixpenny Handley, Woodcott
  5668 William Edmondes alias Younge, yeoman
    Richardson, 1914, pp. 46-49
Yetminster [?]
  5669 John Bartlet
    Machin, *Yetminster*, 1976, No.24, (1 p.)
Gloucestershire
Winterbourne
  5670 Joan Stambourne, widow
    Moore, *Frampton Cotterell*, 1976, pp. 56-57
  5671 John Stinchcombe, [labourer]
    Moore, *Frampton Cotterell*, 1976, p. 57
Hertfordshire
Chipperfield
  5672 William Rogers
    Munby, *Kings Langley*, 1981, p. 78
Kings Langley
  5673 John Buckoake [Buckoke]
    Munby, *Kings Langley*, 1981, pp. 76-77
  5674 Edward Smith
    Munby, *Kings Langley*, 1981, pp. 75-76
Ireland
Geashill, Co. Offaly
  5675 Lettice Digby, Baroness Ophaly
    Fenlon, *Ireland*, 2003, pp. 20-23
Lancashire
Speke
  5676 Edward Norres [Norris]
    Saxton, 1944, p. 135
Leicestershire
Evington
  5677 Edward Presgrave, clergyman
    Wilshere, *Evington*, 1985, p. 19
Lincolnshire
Clee, Thrunscoe
  5678 Wm Alison, husbandman
    Ambler, Watkinson, *Clee*, 1987, p. 142
Norfolk
Great Yarmouth
  5679 John Uttinge, chapman
    Spufford, *Reclothing*, 1984, pp. 182-186
Northumberland
Whittingham, Eslington
  5680 Robert Collingwood
    Wood, *Wills and Inventories*, 1929, IV, pp. 218-219
Oxfordshire
Banbury
  5681 Thomas Crowder, currier
    Brinkworth and Gibson, *Banbury*, II, 1976, pp. 62-63
  5682 Thomas Helmden, butcher
    Brinkworth and Gibson, *Banbury*, II, 1976, pp. 74-75

5683 James Hull, labourer
  Brinkworth and Gibson, *Banbury*, II, 1976, p. 72
5684 Bartholomew Naylor, cutler
  Brinkworth and Gibson, *Banbury*, II, 1976, pp. 70-71
5685 John Smith, shoemaker
  Brinkworth and Gibson, *Banbury*, II, 1976, p. 62
5686 John Warde, baker
  Brinkworth and Gibson, *Banbury*, II, 1976, pp. 72-74
5687 Thomas Winge, shoemaker
  Brinkworth and Gibson, *Banbury*, II, 1976, pp. 67-70

Scotland
Forfarshire, Easter Seaton
5688 Sir Peter Young
  Young, 1888-1889, pp. 266-267

Staffordshire
Dudley
5689 William Bakes
  Roper, *Dudley*, 1966, pp. 17-18
5690 John Cartwright
  Roper, *Dudley*, 1968, p. 17
Lichfield, Cathedral Close
5691 Thomas Glasier, gentleman [chapter clerk]
  Vaisey, *Lichfield*, 1969, pp. 55-59

Suffolk
Ipswich
5692 Ann Goodeere, widow
  Reed, *Ipswich*, 1981, pp. 108-110

Warwickshire
Stoneleigh
5693 Robert Baker, husbandman
  Alcock, *Warwickshire*, 1993, p. 95
5694 George Gregory
  Alcock, *Warwickshire*, 1993, pp. 165-166
Stratford-on-Avon
5695 Grace Amsden alias Gregory, [widow]
  Jones, *Stratford*, II, 2003, pp. 19-20
5696 Averye [Avery] Edwards, yeoman
  Jones, *Stratford*, II, 2003, pp. 21-22
5697 Edward Wilks, yeoman
  Jones, *Stratford*, II, 2003, pp. 22-24

Wiltshire
Marlborough
5698 John Clare, gentleman
  Williams and Thomson, *Marlborough*, 2007, p. 58
5699 John Glide
  Williams and Thomson, *Marlborough*, 2007, pp. 57-58

Worcestershire
Stourbridge
5700 Richard Hickmans, clothworker
  Herbert, 1979, pp. 185-187

Yorkshire
Aysgarth, Sedbusk
5701 Gregorie Mallorye [Gregory Mallory],
  gentleman
  Thwaite, *Abbotside*, 1967, pp. 48-49
Pudsey, Calverley
5702 Richard Hunter, yeoman
  Preston, *Co. York*, 1929, pp. 75-78

1629
Bristol
Bristol, Redcliffe
5703 Richard Saunders, plumber
  George, *Bristol*, 1, 2002, pp. 69-71

Bristol
5704 Mr John Whittson [Whitson], alderman
  [merchant]
  McGrath, 1955, pp. 80-89
Clifton
5705 Margaret Bennett, [widow]
  Moore, *Clifton*, 1981, pp. 47-48
5706 Richard Hilling, tucker
  Moore, *Clifton*, 1981, pp. 51-52
Shirehampton
5707 Joan Cheshire alias Small
  Moore, *Clifton*, 1981, p. 50
5708 Robert George, [husbandman]
  Moore, *Clifton*, 1981, p. 48
Westbury, Cote
5709 Robert White, [husbandman]
  Moore, *Clifton*, 1981, pp. 49-50

Cheshire
Bowdon
5710 Alexander Owen, [parish clerk]
  Groves, *Bowdon*, 1997, pp. 40-42
Dunham Massey, Dunham, Street
5711 George Smith
  Groves, *Dunham Massey*, 2008, p. 48
Nantwich
5712 Hugh Buckley, husbandman
  Cockcroft, *Nantwich*, 1999, p. 57.3
5713 Richard Golborne, yeoman
  Cockcroft, *Nantwich*, 1999, pp. 140.3-4
5714 John Lawton, yeoman
  Cockcroft, *Nantwich*, 1999, pp. 183.3-4
5715 Richard Pratchet, butcher
  Cockcroft, *Nantwich*, 1999, pp. 257.3-4
5716 Margrett Wickstead, widow
  Cockcroft, *Nantwich*, 1999, pp. 335.2-3
Wrenbury
5717 Oliver Briscoe, [husbandman]
  Pixton, *Wrenbury*, 2009, pp. 233-234
Wrenbury cum Frith
5718 William Wicksteed, senior
  Pixton, *Wrenbury*, 2009, pp. 224-225
5719 William Wicksteed, junior
  Pixton, *Wrenbury*, 2009, pp. 227-229
Wrenbury, Newhall
5720 John Wright
  Pixton, *Wrenbury*, 2009, pp. 230-231

Cornwall
Gorran
5721 Alice Rundell, [widow]
  Crow, *Rundell*, 1987-1991, pp. 63-64

Derbyshire
Chesterfield, Tapton
5722 Henry Vickers, yeoman
  Bestall and Fowkes, *Chesterfield*, 2001, pp. 273-274

Devonshire
Doddiscombsleigh
5723 Andrew Shilston, yeoman
  Cash, *Devon*, 1966, pp. 42-43
South Tawton
5724 Edward Northmore, yeoman
  Cash, *Devon*, 1966, p. 42
Uffculme
5725 Jo[hn] Champneys, gentleman
  Wyatt, *Uffculme*, 1997, p. 63

5726 John Snader, [yeoman]
Wyatt, *Uffculme*, 1997, pp. 63-64

Essex
Hatfield Peverel, Hatfield Priory
5727 Sir Thomas Barrington, baronet
Lowndes, 1889, pp. 156-176
Hutton
5728 William Warner, yeoman
Clark, 1912, pp. 158-159

Gloucestershire
Stoke Gifford
5729 Ellen Blanch, widow
Moore, *Frampton Cotterell*, 1976, pp. 57-58

Herefordshire
Hereford
Thomas Thorneton, clergyman, [Master of St
Katherine's Hospital, Ledbury] (see Ledbury)
Ledbury
5730 Thomas Thorneton, clergyman, [Master of St
Katherine's Hospital, Ledbury] (also listed Hereford]
Winnington-Ingram, 1957, pp. 216-222

Hertfordshire
Hemel Hempstead
5731 Josias Martin, doctor of physic
Anon., *Lock, Stock*, 1978, pp. 57-59
Kings Langley
5732 John Fanch, blacksmith
Munby, *Kings Langley*, 1981, pp. 80-81
St Albans, St Stephens
5733 William Barber
Parker, *Worldly Goods*, 2004, p. 215
5734 Henrie Heyward
Parker, *Worldly Goods*, 2004, p. 216
5735 Leonard Hudson
Parker, *Worldly Goods*, 2004, pp. 216-217
5736 Thomas Nutkine, [yeoman]
Parker, *Worldly Goods*, 2004, p. 214
St Albans, St Stephens, Park Street
5737 Elizabeth Smyth, widow
Parker, *Worldly Goods*, 2004, pp. 211-212

Lincolnshire
Clee, Itterby
5738 Henrye Beale, labourer
Ambler, Watkinson, *Clee*, 1987, p. 145
Clee, Oole
5739 Robert Beale, labourer
Ambler, Watkinson, *Clee*, 1987, p. 146
5740 Thomas Marshall, husbandman
Ambler, Watkinson, *Clee*, 1987, p. 144
Clee, Itterby
5741 Thomas Needler, husbandman
Ambler, Watkinson, *Clee*, 1987, pp. 143-144
Clee, Oole
5742 Matthewe Tuplin, husbandman
Ambler, Watkinson, *Clee*, 1987, pp. 142-143
5743 Thomas Tuplin, husbandman
Ambler, Watkinson, *Clee*, 1987, pp. 144-145

Norfolk
Wymondham
5744 Thomas Moore, butcher
Wilson, *Wymondham*, 1983, pp. 26-28
5745 John Page, baker
Wilson, *Wymondham*, 1983, pp. 31-32

Northamptonshire
Nethercote
5746 John Hall, husbandman
Brinkworth and Gibson, *Banbury*, II, 1976, p. 77
Overthorpe
5747 Nickelles [Nicholas] Goddene [Gooden,
Goodwin], smith
Brinkworth and Gibson, *Banbury*, II, 1976, pp. 71-72

Oxfordshire
Banbury, Wickham
5748 John Mayo
Brinkworth and Gibson, *Banbury*, II, 1976, pp. 75-76
Banbury, Calthorpe
5749 John Rimel[l] [Rymill]
Brinkworth and Gibson, *Banbury*, II, 1976, p. 78
Banbury
5750 Edward Walker, labourer
Brinkworth and Gibson, *Banbury*, II, 1976, p. 76
5751 John Wamsly [Wamslie]
Brinkworth and Gibson, *Banbury*, II, 1976, p. 77

Staffordshire
Lichfield
5752 Humfrey Kinersley
Vaisey, *Lichfield*, 1969, pp. 59-60

Suffolk
Bramfield
5753 Arthure Coke, esquire
Steer, 1952, pp. 268-283

Sussex
North Chapel
5754 John Forman, clergyman [curate of North
Chapel]
Hughes, *Sussex*, 2007, pp. 149-150

Warwickshire
Luddington
5755 Elizabeth Williams
Jones, *Stratford*, II, 2003, p. 27
Stratford-on-Avon
5756 Edward Wakeland
Jones, *Stratford*, II, 2003, pp. 28-29
5757 Richard Whiting, yeoman
Jones, *Stratford*, II, 2003, pp. 25-27

Wiltshire
Marlborough
5758 John Browne
Williams and Thomson, *Marlborough*, 2007, p. 59
5759 Richard Cornwall
Williams and Thomson, *Marlborough*, 2007, pp. 59-60
5760 Ralphe Harrold
Williams and Thomson, *Marlborough*, 2007, pp. 58-59
Salisbury
5761 John Holmes, gentleman
Payne, 2003, pp. 372-376

Worcestershire
Chaddesley Corbett
5762 John Cooke, mercer
Roper, *Chaddesley Corbett*, 1971, pp. 57-58
Chaddesley Corbett, Brockencote
5763 Frauncis Halliman, [scythesmith]
Roper, *Chaddesley Corbett*, 1971, pp. 58-59
Earls Croome
5764 Leonard Jefferey [Jefferies], esquire
Wanklyn, *Worcestershire*, 1998, pp. 151-157

Halesowen, Ludley
  5765 George Grove, yeoman
  Davenport, 1912, pp. 56-57

Yorkshire
Marske
  5766 Sir Timothy Hutton
  Clarkson, 1821, pp. 264-265
  Raine, *Marske*, 1861, pp. 59-60
Richmond
  5767 Sir Timothy Hutton
  Clarkson, 1821, pp. 221-222
  Raine, 1843, pp. 253-254
South Cave
  5768 Richard Colson
  Kaner, *South Cave*, 1994, pp. 336-337
  5769 Bartholomew Rose
  Kaner, *South Cave*, 1994, pp. 334-336

1630

Cheshire
Dunham Massey
  5770 William Moore
  Groves, *Dunham Massey*, 2008, p. 50
Nantwich
  5771 Margerye Dutton, widow
  Cockcroft, *Nantwich*, 1999, p. 118.2
  5772 Randull Dutton, yeoman
  Cockcroft, *Nantwich*, 1999, pp. 117.4-5
  5773 Anne Salmon, widow
  Cockcroft, *Nantwich*, 1999, pp. 277.2-3
  5774 John Taylor, gentleman
  Cockcroft, *Nantwich*, 1999, pp. 301.1-3
Pulford
  5775 Dorothie Humpston, widow
  Bland, *Christleton*, 2005, pp. 569-570
Tattenhall
  5776 Richard Bostock, esquire
  Anon., *Bostocks*, 1934, p. 34
Wrenbury, Sound
  5777 John Bromehall [Bromhall], [yeoman]
  Pixton, *Wrenbury*, 2009, pp. 249-253
Wrenbury, Smeatonwood
  5778 Tymothy Bulckley [Buckley], gentleman
  Pixton, *Wrenbury*, 2009, pp. 260-262
Wrenbury, Aston
  5779 John Cartwrighte, gentleman
  Pixton, *Wrenbury*, 2009, pp. 243-245
Wrenbury, Smeatonwood
  5780 Richard Hall
  Pixton, *Wrenbury*, 2009, pp. 254-256

Derbyshire
Chesterfield
  5781 Richard Ashe, tailor
  Bestall and Fowkes, *Chesterfield*, 2001, p. 281
Chesterfield, Temple Normanton
  5782 Edmund Brocksopp, yeoman
  Bestall and Fowkes, *Chesterfield*, 2001, pp. 277-280
Chesterfield
  5783 Robert Holland
  Bestall and Fowkes, *Chesterfield*, 2001, p. 281
  5784 John Potter, blacksmith
  Bestall and Fowkes, *Chesterfield*, 2001, pp. 275-277
  5785 Hamlet Worsley, cutler
  Bestall and Fowkes, *Chesterfield*, 2001, pp. 281-283

Devonshire
Uffculme
  5786 Dorothy Norton, widow
  Wyatt, *Uffculme*, 1997, pp. 64-65
  5787 Robert Welch, [yeoman]
  Wyatt, *Uffculme*, 1997, p. 65

Gloucestershire
Forthampton
  Sir Edward Blount (see Kidderminster, Worcestershire)
Winterbourne
  5788 Richard Weare, [miller]
  Moore, *Frampton Cotterell*, 1976, pp. 58-59

Hertfordshire
Kings Langley
  5789 Robert Anderson, labourer
  Munby, *Kings Langley*, 1981, pp. 81-82
  5790 William Jewett, sawyer
  Munby, *Kings Langley*, 1981, p. 84
St Albans, St Stephens
  5791 Elizabeth Cogdell
  Parker, *Worldly Goods*, 2004, p. 220
St Albans, St Stephens, Frogmore
  5792 Mary Man, widow
  Parker, *Worldly Goods*, 2004, pp. 222-223
St Albans, St Stephens
  5793 John Marshall, tailor
  Parker, *Worldly Goods*, 2004, p. 219

Ireland
Kilkenny Castle
  5794 Richard Preston, Earl of Desmond
  Fenlon, *Ireland*, 2003, pp. 26-29

Lincolnshire
Clee
  5795 Thomas Helvish, labourer
  Ambler, Watkinson, *Clee*, 1987, p. 147
Clee, Thrunscoe
  5796 Edward Nutsye, husbandman
  Ambler, Watkinson, *Clee*, 1987, p. 146
Clee
  5797 Leonard Stallingbrough, labourer
  Ambler, Watkinson, *Clee*, 1987, pp. 146-147

Norfolk
Wymondham
  5798 Dorothie Corker, widow
  Wilson, *Wymondham*, 1983, pp. 32-34

Northamptonshire
Huscote
  5799 John Leeson
  Brinkworth and Gibson, *Banbury*, II, 1976, p. 82
Northampton
  5800 Thomas Cowper, [alderman, gentleman]
  Cowper, 1892, pp. 86-87

Oxfordshire
Banbury
  5801 Anne Dudley [Dudlie], widow
  Brinkworth and Gibson, *Banbury*, II, 1976, pp. 80-81
  5802 Thomas Ell, mason
  Brinkworth and Gibson, *Banbury*, II, 1976, pp. 79-80
  5803 Thomas Weston
  Brinkworth and Gibson, *Banbury*, II, 1976, pp. 78-79
  5804 Isabell [Elizabeth] Williamson, widow
  Brinkworth and Gibson, *Banbury*, II, 1976, p. 81

Water Eaton
5805 Allen Ray, [yeoman]
Offord, *Water Eaton*, 1986, p. 18

Staffordshire
Dudley
5806 Dorithie Sutton alias Duddeley [widow]
Roper, *Dudley*, 1968, p. 18

Sussex
Donnington
5807 Thomas Harryson, clergyman [vicar of Donnington]
Hughes, *Sussex*, 2007, pp. 63-64
Wiggonholt
5808 Richard Boley, clergyman [rector of Wiggonholt]
Hughes, *Sussex*, 2007, p. 239

Warwickshire
Hatton, Shrewley
5809 Henry Eberhall
Sheasby, 1994, pp. 51-52
Stoneleigh
5810 Robert Stocken, labourer
Alcock, *Warwickshire*, 1993, p. 126
Stratford-on-Avon
5811 David Ainge, butcher
Jones, *Stratford*, II, 2003, pp. 29-31
5812 Ann Shaw [Shawe], widow
Halliwell-Phillipps,1880, pp. 7-13
Jones, *Stratford*, II, 2003, pp. 31-34

Wiltshire
Marlborough
5813 John Eaton, barber
Williams and Thomson, *Marlborough*, 2007, pp. 60-62
5814 John Hitchcocke, [baker]
Williams and Thomson, *Marlborough*, 2007, p. 63
5815 William Sockwell, haberdasher
Williams and Thomson, *Marlborough*, 2007, pp. 62-63

Worcestershire
Doverdale
5816 John Brace, esquire
Wanklyn, *Worcestershire*, 1998, pp. 158-159
Hagley
5817 Meryell Littleton
Wanklyn, *Worcestershire*, 1998, pp. 164-165
Kidderminster
5818 Sir Edward Blount (also listed Forthampton, Gloucestershire)
Wanklyn, *Worcestershire*, 1998, pp. 159-164

Yorkshire
Hardrow
5819 George Cole, of the Inner Temple, esquire
Thwaite, *Abbotside*, 1967, pp. 52-53
5820 Joane Cole, widow
Thwaite, *Abbotside*, 1967, pp. 53-54
South Cave
5821 Richard Atkinson
Kaner, *South Cave*, 1994, pp. 337-338

1630 (c.)
Yorkshire
Pudsey, Calverley
5822 Alice Sharpe
Preston, *Co. York*, 1929, pp. 78-80

1631
Bristol
Bristol, St Thomas
5823 William Bysshopp [Bishop], clothworker
George, *Bristol*, 1, 2002, pp. 71-72

Cheshire
Ashton-on-Mersey
5824 Robert Smith, weaver
Groves, *Ashton-on-Mersey and Sale*, 1999, pp. 49-52
Dunham Massey
5825 Peter Parker
Groves, *Dunham Massey*, 2008, pp. 53-54
Hale
5826 Edward Tipping, [yeoman]
Groves, *Hale 1*, 2005, pp. 74-75
Nantwich
5827 John Deane, yeoman
Cockcroft, *Nantwich*, 1999, p. 113.2
Tarvin, Oscroft
5828 Richard Jackson, yeoman
Bland, *Christleton*, 2005, pp. 579-580
Wrenbury, Chorley
5829 William Babington, [gentleman]
Pixton, *Wrenbury*, 2009, pp. 260-262
Wrenbury
5830 Emma Barnett, [widow]
Pixton, *Wrenbury*, 2009, pp. 268-269
Wrenbury, Sheppenhall
5831 John Cartwright, gentleman
Pixton, *Wrenbury*, 2009, pp. 271-272
Wrenbury, Newhall
5832 Ellen Ravenscroft, widow
Pixton, *Wrenbury*, 2009, pp. 264-265

Derbyshire
Chesterfield
5833 Godfrey Alwood, tanner
Bestall and Fowkes, *Chesterfield*, 2001, pp. 287-288
5834 Henry Foljambe
Bestall and Fowkes, *Chesterfield*, 2001, pp. 286-287
5835 Edward Kertland, gentleman
Bestall and Fowkes, *Chesterfield*, 2001, pp. 284-286
5836 Elizabeth Lister, widow
Bestall and Fowkes, *Chesterfield*, 2001, pp. 283-284

Devonshire
Crediton [?]
5837 John Wheare
Cash, *Devon*, 1966, p. 44
Ilsington
5838 John Stangcombe, husbandman
Cash, *Devon*, 1966, p. 43
Talaton
5839 James Searle
Cash, *Devon*, 1966, pp. 44-45
Uffculme
5840 John Coram, husbandman
Wyatt, *Uffculme*, 1997, pp. 66-67
5841 John Rawlins, [yeoman]
Wyatt, *Uffculme*, 1997, p. 67
5842 Robert Read
Wyatt, *Uffculme*, 1997, p. 66
5843 Joane Sander, [widow]
Wyatt, *Uffculme*, 1997, p. 68

Dorsetshire
Halstock, Coringdon
  5844 Francis Pester
    Lemmey, *Halstock*, 1997, pp. 17-19
Yetminster
  5845 Robert Baylie
    Machin, *Yetminster*, 1976, No.25, (2 pp.)
Hertfordshire
Kings Langley
  5846 Ralphe Carter
    Munby, *Kings Langley*, 1981, p. 85
St Albans, St Stephens, Park Street
  5847 Anthonye Balle, victualler
    Parker, *Worldly Goods*, 2004, p. 224
St Albans, St Stephens
  5848 Thomas Bampton, husbandman
    Parker, *Worldly Goods*, 2004, p. 225
  5849 John Wilson, carpenter
    Parker, *Worldly Goods*, 2004, pp. 223-224
Stevenage, Symonds Green
  5850 Edmund Nodes, gentleman
    Anon., *Lock, Stock*, 1978, pp. 59-61
Leicestershire
Evington
  5851 Thomas Smalley, [husbandman]
    Wilshere, *Evington*, 1985, p. 20
Kirby Muxloe
  5852 Ann Somerfeild, widow
    Wilshere, *Kirby Muxloe*, 1983, p. 9
Lincolnshire
Clee
  5853 John Lowe, wright
    Ambler, Watkinson, *Clee*, 1987, pp. 147-148
Clee, Oole
  5854 Margaret Tuplin, widow
    Ambler, Watkinson, *Clee*, 1987, pp. 148-149
London
Acton
  5854a Lady Anne Southwell
    Klene, 1997, pp. 93-96
Aldermary Churchyard
  5855 Sir Thomas Middelton (also listed Chirk Castle, Wales)
    Lawes-Wittewronge, 1903, pp. 17-26
Northumberland
Biddlestone
  5856 Alexander Selby
    Wood, *Wills and Inventories*, 1929, IV, pp. 235-236
Nottinghamshire
Bleasby
  5857 George Fox
    Mercer and Summers, 1967, p. 28
Oxfordshire
Banbury, Hardwick
  5858 Richard Boner [Banor], husbandman
    Brinkworth and Gibson, *Banbury*, II, 1976, p. 83
Banbury
  5859 Richard French
    Brinkworth and Gibson, *Banbury*, II, 1976, p. 84
  5860 Mr William Halhed, clergyman
    Brinkworth and Gibson, *Banbury*, II, 1976, pp. 95-96

Banbury, Neithrop
  5861 Alice Jones, servant
    Brinkworth and Gibson, *Banbury*, II, 1976, p. 96
Banbury
  5862 Thomas Perren
    Brinkworth and Gibson, *Banbury*, II, 1976, pp. 93-95
  5863 William Resone [Reasing], shoemaker
    Brinkworth and Gibson, *Banbury*, II, 1976, pp. 84-85
Banbury, Neithrop
  5864 Christian Richards, widow
    Brinkworth and Gibson, *Banbury*, II, 1976, p. 87
Banbury
  5865 Henry Sharpe
    Brinkworth and Gibson, *Banbury*, II, 1976, pp. 82-83
  5866 Henry Sherwood, tailor
    Brinkworth and Gibson, *Banbury*, II, 1976, pp. 85-86
Banbury, Neithrop
  5867 William Tayler [Taylor], husbandman
    Brinkworth and Gibson, *Banbury*, II, 1976, p. 88
Banbury
  5868 Robert Weston
    Brinkworth and Gibson, *Banbury*, II, 1976, pp. 89-90
  5869 Nichodemus White, glover
    Brinkworth and Gibson, *Banbury*, II, 1976, pp. 9-92
  5870 Thomas White
    Brinkworth and Gibson, *Banbury*, II, 1976, pp. 92-93
  5871 Edward Williamson
    Brinkworth and Gibson, *Banbury*, II, 1976, p. 89
  5872 Anne Winge, widow
    Brinkworth and Gibson, *Banbury*, II, 1976, p. 89
Staffordshire
Dudley
  5873 John Russon, [yeoman]
    Roper, *Dudley*, 1968, p. 19
Sedgley, Moor Field
  5874 Edward Pershouse, yeoman
    Roper, *Sedgley*, 1960, p. 2
Suffolk
Chelsworth
  5875 Marye Ballye
    Evans, 1987, p. 133
Ipswich
  5876 Jude Allin, clergyman
    Reed, *Ipswich*, 1981, p. 112
  5877 Richard Rainsford, clergyman
    Reed, *Ipswich*, 1981, pp. 110-111
Wales
Chirk Castle
  Sir Thomas Middelton (see Aldermary Churchyard, London)
Warwickshire
Stoneleigh
  5878 Thomas Hill, yeoman
    Alcock, *Warwickshire*, 1993, p. 70
Stratford-on-Avon
  5879 Barbara Cotton, widow
    Jones, *Stratford*, II, 2003, pp. 38-39
  5880 Averie [Avery] Fullwood, gentleman
    Jones, *Stratford*, II, 2003, pp. 36-38
  5881 Thomas Jelf
    Jones, *Stratford*, II, 2003, p. 44
  5882 Elnor More [Eleanor Moore], widow
    Jones, *Stratford*, II, 2003, pp. 34-35

5883 Rose Palmer, widow
   Jones, *Stratford*, II, 2003, pp. 40-43
Wiltshire
Marlborough
5884 Phillipp Martyne, yeoman
   Williams and Thomson, *Marlborough*, 2007, pp. 64-65
5885 William Turly, baker
   Williams and Thomson, *Marlborough*, 2007, pp. 63-64
Worcestershire
Belbroughton
5886 John Taylor, yeoman
   Roper, *Belbroughton*, 1967-1968, p. 65
Chaddesley Corbett, Winterfold
5887 William Bach, husbandman
   Roper, *Chaddesley Corbett*, 1971, p. 60
Yorkshire
South Cave
5888 Elizabeth Atkinson, widow
   Kaner, *South Cave*, 1994, pp. 339-340
South Cave, Oxmardyke
5889 Thomas Parker
   Kaner, *South Cave*, 1994, pp. 341-343

1631 (c.)
Cheshire
Dunham Massey, Sinderland
5890 Humphrey Frith
   Groves, *Dunham Massey*, 2008, pp. 51-52

1632
Bristol
Clifton
5891 John Satchfield, yeoman
   Moore, *Clifton*, 1981, pp. 52-54
Cheshire
Hale
5892 Robert Artenstall
   Groves, *Hale 1*, 2005, pp. 76-77
Hale, Ringway
5893 Anne Hardy
   Groves, *Hale 1*, 2005, pp. 79-80
Nantwich
5894 William Bebington, gentleman
   Cockcroft, *Nantwich*, 1999, pp. 21.3-4
5895 Margaret Manwaring, widow
   Cockcroft, *Nantwich*, 1999, pp. 200.3-4
Sale
5896 James Gratracke alias Mason
   Groves, *Ashton-on-Mersey and Sale*, 1999, pp. 53-54
5897 James Moores
   Groves, *Ashton-on-Mersey and Sale*, 1999, pp. 59-60
5898 Richard Renshaw, yeoman
   Groves, *Ashton-on-Mersey and Sale*, 1999, pp. 55-56
Tattenhall, Newton
5899 William Ryder, yeoman
   Bland, *Christleton*, 2005, pp. 580-582
Tarvin, Burton
5900 John Ellames, yeoman
   Bland, *Christleton*, 2005, pp. 590-591
Tarvin, Hockenhull
5901 John Hockenhull, esquire
   Bland, *Christleton*, 2005, pp. 587-588
Tarvin, Duddon
5902 Thomas Large
   Bland, *Christleton*, 2005, pp. 588-589

Tarvin, Hockenhull
5903 John Walker, husbandman
   Bland, *Christleton*, 2005, pp. 586-587
Tarvin, Kelsall
5904 John Wayne, yeoman
   Bland, *Christleton*, 2005, pp. 584-585
Waverton
5905 Thomas Dutton, husbandman
   Bland, *Christleton*, 2005, p. 593
Wrenbury, Newhall
5906 Edmund Crewe, [yeoman]
   Pixton, *Wrenbury*, 2009, pp. 277-278
Wrenbury
5907 Margaret Graye
   Pixton, *Wrenbury*, 2009, pp. 274-275
Wrenbury, Newhall
5908 Allese Peckston [Pextonne], [widow]
   Pixton, *Wrenbury*, 2009, p. 281
5909 Robert Tudman, [yeoman]
   Pixton, *Wrenbury*, 2009, pp. 290-291
Devonshire
Uffculme
5910 John Baker, [yeoman]
   Wyatt, *Uffculme*, 1997, p. 69
5911 Henry Rugg [Rugge], yeoman
   Wyatt, *Uffculme*, 1997, pp. 68-69
Co. Durham
Haswell
5912 William Ingleby, yeoman
   Wood, *Wills and Inventories*, 1929, IV, pp. 244-245
Gloucestershire
Winterbourne
5913 John Butler, yeoman
   Moore, *Frampton Cotterell*, 1976, pp. 59-60
Hertfordshire
St Albans, St Stephens
5914 Thomas Nutkine
   Parker, *Worldly Goods*, 2004, p. 227
St Albans, St Stephens, Park Street
5915 Francis Rigly
   Parker, *Worldly Goods*, 2004, pp. 225-226
Sarratt
5916 Ellen Child, widow
   Bullen, *Sarratt*, [1982], p. 130
Kent
Lydd
5917 Robert Allison, husbandman
   Barley, *Farmhouse and Cottage*, 1961, pp. 277-278
Leicestershire
Braunstone
5918 John Hackit
   Wilshere, *Braunstone*, 1983, p. 18
Great Stretton
5919 Thomas Cowp[er]
   Wilshere, *Great Stretton*, 1984, p. 17
South Kilworth
5920 Nicholas Leigh, tinker-errant
   Smith, 1977, p. 177
Lincolnshire
Clee
5921 Margaret Needler, widow
   Ambler, Watkinson, *Clee*, 1987, p. 149

Middlesex
Syon House
  Henry Percy, Earl of Northumberland (see Petworth
  House, Sussex)
Norfolk
Wymondham
  5922 William Turner, barber
  Wilson, *Wymondham*, 1983, p. 35
Northamptonshire
Orton
  5923 William Alderman, husbandman
  Alderman, *Alderman*, 2008, p. 39
Oxfordshire
Banbury
  5924 Elizabeth Harrison [Harris], widow
  Brinkworth and Gibson, *Banbury*, II, 1976, pp. 99-100
  5925 Thomas Hyrons [Hirons, Hiern], carpenter
  Brinkworth and Gibson, *Banbury*, II, 1976, pp. 98-99
Banbury, Neithrop
  5926 Michael Johnsonn, glover
  Brinkworth and Gibson, *Banbury*, II, 1976, p. 97
Banbury
  5927 John Knibbe [Knib], yeoman
  Brinkworth and Gibson, *Banbury*, II, 1976, pp. 100-101
  5928 John Lumley, weaver
  Brinkworth and Gibson, *Banbury*, II, 1976, pp. 96-97
  5929 Elizabeth Neale, widow
  Brinkworth and Gibson, *Banbury*, II, 1976, p. 101
Water Eaton
  5930 Ann Ray, widow
  Offord, *Water Eaton*, 1986, p. 20
Scotland
Edinburgh
  5931 James Cathkin, bookseller
  Anon., *Bassandyne*, 1836, pp. 249-251
Sussex
Amberley
  5932 Henry Spencer, clergyman
  Hughes, *Sussex*, 2007, pp. 3-4
Bignor
  5933 Thomas Sephton, clergyman [rector of Bignor]
  Hughes, *Sussex*, 2007, pp. 23-25
Kirdford
  5934 Henry Scutt
  Kenyon, *Kirdford*, 1955, pp. 93-94
Petworth House
  5935 Henry Percy, Earl of Northumberland (also
  listed Syon House, Middlesex)
  Batho, 1962, pp. 112-130
Wiltshire
Marlborough
  5936 William Dawnce, tailor
  Williams and Thomson, *Marlborough*, 2007, p. 67
  5937 William Dowse, [shearman]
  Williams and Thomson, *Marlborough*, 2007, p. 65
  5938 Robert Jefferes
  Williams and Thomson, *Marlborough*, 2007, pp. 67-68
  5939 Eelisebeth Winsor, widow
  Williams and Thomson, *Marlborough*, 2007, pp. 66-67
Worcestershire
Bredon's Hardwick
  5940 Thomas Horniold, esquire
  Wanklyn, *Worcestershire*, 1998, pp. 166-167

Charlton
  5941 Elizabeth Dingley, widow
  Barnard, 1928, pp. 58-63
Yorkshire
Aysgarth, Cams Houses
  5942 Georg Thwaites
  Thwaite, *Abbotside*, 1967, p. 54
Lunds
  5943 Edward Fawcet [Fawcett]
  Thwaite, *Abbotside*, 1967, p. 55
Knaresborough, Scriven with Tentergate
  5944 Anthony Wood, feltmaker
  Brears, *Yorkshire*, 1972, pp. 78-79
Ripley
  5945 Thomas Stubb, blacksmith
  Collins, *Stubbs*, 1915, pp. 115-116

1632 (c.)
Wiltshire
Marlborough
  5946 Thomas Buckingham
  Williams and Thomson, *Marlborough*, 2007, pp. 65-66
  5947 Maud Patie, widow
  Williams and Thomson, *Marlborough*, 2007, p. 66

1633
Bristol
Bristol, St Thomas
  5948 Walter Collins, wire-drawer
  George, *Bristol*, 1, 2002, pp. 80-81
Bristol, Christchurch
  5949 Edward Hassall, goldsmith
  George, *Bristol*, 1, 2002, pp. 74-80
Bristol, St James
  5950 Thomas James, whitawer
  George, *Bristol*, 1, 2002, pp. 73-74
Bristol, All Saints
  5951 Anthonie [Anthony] Kely, [grocer]
  George, *Bristol*, 1, 2002, pp. 72-73
Bristol, St Philip and St Jacob
  5952 William Yemens, cathedral prebend and vicar of
  St Philips
  George, *Bristol*, 1, 2002, pp. 81-82
Clifton
  5953 William Stevens alias Tombs, husbandman
  Moore, *Clifton*, 1981, p. 58
Shirehampton
  5954 Thomas Sergeant, [husbandman]
  Moore, *Clifton*, 1981, p. 55
Stoke Bishop
  5955 Ann Reynolds, widow
  Moore, *Clifton*, 1981, p. 56
Westbury
  5956 Thomas Edmonds, yeoman
  Moore, *Clifton*, 1981, p. 54
  5957 John George, husbandman
  Moore, *Clifton*, 1981, p. 57
  5958 John Price, mariner
  Moore, *Clifton*, 1981, pp. 56-57
Cheshire
Ashton-on-Mersey
  5959 Ralph Hayward alias Dean, husbandman
  Groves, *Ashton-on-Mersey and Sale*, 1999, pp. 57-58
Dunham Massey, Dunham
  5960 Peter Frith
  Groves, *Dunham Massey*, 2008, pp. 54-55

Hale, Meane Wood
  5961 William Arstall, [husbandman]
    Groves, *Hale 1*, 2005, pp. 81-82
Hale
  5962 Robert Partington
    Groves, *Hale 1*, 2005, pp. 80-81
Nantwich
  5963 Richard Arcall, grocer
    Cockcroft, *Nantwich*, 1999, pp. 13.3-4
  5964 Thomas Clayton, gentleman
    Cockcroft, *Nantwich*, 1999, pp. 73.5-8
  5965 Richard Simcock, yeoman
    Cockcroft, *Nantwich*, 1999, pp. 287.2-3
Sale
  5966 Richard Renshaw
    Groves, *Ashton-on-Mersey and Sale*, 1999, pp. 60-61
Tarvin
  5967 John Eare, salter
    Bland, *Christleton*, 2005, pp. 594-595
Tarvin, Ashton
  5968 James Raphson, yeoman
    Bland, *Christleton*, 2005, p. 604
  5969 William Raphson, yeoman
    Bland, *Christleton*, 2005, pp. 603-604
Tarvin
  5970 William Neild, yeoman
    Bland, *Christleton*, 2005, pp. 598-600
Tarvin, Duddon
  5971 Thomas Willye, innkeeper
    Bland, *Christleton*, 2005, pp. 596-597
Waverton, Huxley
  5972 Edward Gwynne, husbandman
    Bland, *Christleton*, 2005, p
Wrenbury, Aston
  5973 John Barnett, [yeoman]
    Pixton, *Wrenbury*, 2009, pp. 290-291
Wrenbury cum Frith
  5974 Richard Cheswys [Cheswis], [yeoman]
    Pixton, *Wrenbury*, 2009, p   p. 287-288

Cornwall
Port Eliot
  Sir John Eliot (see St Germans, Cuddenbeak)
St Germans, Cuddenbeak
  5975 Sir John Eliot (also listed Port Eliot)
    Hulme, 1936, pp. 1-14

Derbyshire
Brimington
  5976 Thomas Gally, blacksmith
    Bestall and Fowkes, *Chesterfield*, 2001, pp. 290-292
  5977 Thomas Varnam
    Bestall and Fowkes, *Chesterfield*, 2001, pp. 288-290
Chesterfield
  5978 William Lee, coverlet weaver
    Bestall and Fowkes, *Chesterfield*, 2001, pp. 296-297
  5979 Robert Salte, blacksmith
    Bestall and Fowkes, *Chesterfield*, 2001, pp. 297-298
  5980 Robert Shawe
    Bestall and Fowkes, *Chesterfield*, 2001, pp. 292-295

Devonshire
Bishopsteignton
  5981 John Babb
    Cash, *Devon*, 1966, p. 48

Brixham
  5982 John Lake
    Cash, *Devon*, 1966, p. 47
Crediton
  5983 Thomas Wrren [Warren], tanner
    Cash, *Devon*, 1966, p. 46
Doddiscombsleigh
  5984 Christopher Luckey
    Cash, *Devon*, 1966, pp. 45-46
Dolton
  5985 Mark Hooper
    Cash, *Devon*, 1966, p. 47
Plymouth
  5986 Richard Fownes, gentleman
    Cash, *Devon*, 1966, p. 47
  5987 John Gedger, sailor
    Cash, *Devon*, 1966, p. 46

Gloucestershire
Hambrook
  5988 Anthony Boman, [carrier]
    Moore, *Frampton Cotterell*, 1976, p. 62
Stoke Gifford
  5989 Thomas Dorny, yeoman
    Moore, *Frampton Cotterell*, 1976, pp. 61-62
  5990 Margery Strange alias Pope
    Moore, *Frampton Cotterell*, 1976, p. 62
  5991 John Yonge, yeoman
    Moore, *Frampton Cotterell*, 1976, pp. 60-61

Hertfordshire
Kings Langley
  5992 John Knight, yeoman
    Munby, *Kings Langley*, 1981, p. 89
St Albans, St Stephens, Colney Street
  5993 Mrs Anne Ewer, widow
    Parker, *Worldly Goods*, 2004, p. 226

Lancashire
Culcheth
  5994 Ralph Rylands, yeoman
    Earwaker, *Lancashire and Cheshire*, 1893, pp. 46-48

Leicestershire
Evington
  5995 Thomas Mauson, [cottier]
    Wilshere, *Evington*, 1985, p. 21
  5996 Brian Taffes, [cottier]
    Wilshere, *Evington*, 1985, p. 22

Norfolk
Boughton
  5997 Edward Bell, labourer
    Barley, *Farmhouse and Cottage*, 1961, p. 281
Holt, Thornage
  5998 Richard Coliard, yeoman
    Barley, *Farmhouse and Cottage*, 1961, pp. 280-281
Kings Lynn
  5999 Thomas Revett, town clerk
    Parker, *Kings Lynn*, 1971, pp. 184-185

Oxfordshire
Banbury
  6000 Eslys [Ellis, Eustace] Boosse [Bosse], barber
    Brinkworth and Gibson, *Banbury*, II, 1976, pp. 102-103
  6001 Alice Hayyard [Haywood, Hayward], widow
    Brinkworth and Gibson, *Banbury*, II, 1976, p. 103
  6002 Mary Humphris
    Brinkworth and Gibson, *Banbury*, II, 1976, p. 103

6003   Walter Welles, husbandman
Brinkworth and Gibson, *Banbury*, II, 1976, p. 103
Chastleton
6004   Walter Jones, esquire
Marsden, 2000, pp. 37-42
Staffordshire
Dudley
6005   Andrew Jeven
Roper, *Dudley*, 1968, p. 20
Surrey
Guildford
6006   Trinity Hospital
Palmer, 1917, pp. 38-39
Sussex
Petworth
6007   William Beeding, clergyman
Hughes, *Sussex*, 2007, p. 165
Rusper
6008   Joseph Browne, clergyman [rector of Rusper]
Hughes, *Sussex*, 2007, pp. 175-176
Wisborough Green
6009   Agnis Jackman, widow
Lawson, 1999, pp. 49-52
Warwickshire
Stratford-on-Avon
6010   John Hickcox [Hiccox], blacksmith
Jones, *Stratford*, II, 2003, p. 47
6011   Rose Jevins, widow
Jones, *Stratford*, II, 2003, pp. 45-46
Wiltshire
Marlborough
6012   Richard Browne
Williams and Thomson, *Marlborough*, 2007, p. 69
6013   William [Fry], yeoman
Williams and Thomson, *Marlborough*, 2007, pp. 70-71
6014   Henry Rabbinson
Williams and Thomson, *Marlborough*, 2007, pp. 69-70
6015   Thomas Redford
Williams and Thomson, *Marlborough*, 2007, p. 68
6016   Elizabeth Reynes, widow
Williams and Thomson, *Marlborough*, 2007, p. 72
6017   Anth[hony Sclater?]
Williams and Thomson, *Marlborough*, 2007, p. 70
6018   John Williams, glazier
Williams and Thomson, *Marlborough*, 2007, pp. 68-69
Yorkshire
Pudsey, Calverley
6019   Margarett Hunter
Preston, *Co. York*, 1929, p. 89
6020   William Lumbie
Preston, *Co. York*, 1929, pp. 96-97
South Cave
6021   John Marshall
Kaner, *South Cave*, 1994, p. 344

1634
Bristol
Bristol, St James
6022   Isacke [Isaac] Dighton, brewer
George, *Bristol*, 1, 2002, pp. 86-87
Bristol
6023   Thomas Nelmes, grocer
George, *Bristol*, 1, 2002, pp. 83-86

Bristol, St Mary-le-Port
6024   John Shipway, [shoemaker]
George, *Bristol*, 1, 2002, pp. 87-89
Bristol, St Michael
6025   John Singer, surgeon
George, *Bristol*, 1, 2002, p. 83
Clifton
6026   Agnes Hilling, widow
Moore, *Clifton*, 1981, pp. 59-60
South Mead
6027   Giles Higgs, weaver
Moore, *Clifton*, 1981, pp. 58-59
Cheshire
Ashton-on-Mersey
6028   Ann Baker, widow
Groves, *Ashton-on-Mersey and Sale*, 1999, pp. 61-62
Bowdon
6029   Alexander Vawdrey, yeoman
Groves, *Bowdon*, 1997, pp. 47-48
Christleton, Cotton
6030   Robert Newton, [wheelwright]
Bland, *Christleton*, 2005, p. 613
Nantwich
6031   Thomas Alseger, mercer
Cockcroft, *Nantwich*, 1999, pp. 11.3-4
6032   Thomas Beelin, locksmith
Cockcroft, *Nantwich*, 1999, p. 26.2
6033   Thomas Merrie, yeoman
Cockcroft, *Nantwich*, 1999, pp. 214.3-4
6034   John Minshull, gentleman
Cockcroft, *Nantwich*, 1999, pp. 222.2-6
6035   Anne Wright
Cockcroft, *Nantwich*, 1999, pp. 358.5-9
Tarvin, Ashton
6036   Katheryn Raphson, widow
Bland, *Christleton*, 2005, pp. 614-615
Tattenhall
6037   John Payne, yeoman
Bland, *Christleton*, 2005, pp. 618-619
Waverton
6038   John Swindell, yeoman
Bland, *Christleton*, 2005, p. 612
Waverton, Huxley
6039   Margery Wilson, widow
Bland, *Christleton*, 2005, pp. 617-618
Wrenbury cum Frith
6040   Robert Wade, [yeoman]
Pixton, *Wrenbury*, 2009, pp. 292-293
Derbyshire
Chesterfield
6041   Thomas Andrewe, carpenter
Bestall and Fowkes, *Chesterfield*, 2001, pp. 299-300
Grassmoor
6042   John Weaver, webster
Bestall and Fowkes, *Chesterfield*, 2001, p. 299
Norton, Jordanthorpe (now Yorkshire)
6043   Henry Brownell, scythe smith
Addy, 1923, pp. 107-109
Devonshire
Chivelstone
6044   John Gullock [?], yeoman
Cash, *Devon*, 1966, p. 48

Cotleigh
  6045 John Clarke, husbandman
    Cash, *Devon*, 1966, p. 49
Plympton St Mary
  6046 John Cockson
    Cash, *Devon*, 1966, pp. 48-49
Gloucestershire
Winterbourne
  6047 Thomas Dagge, yeoman
    Moore, *Frampton Cotterell*, 1976, p. 63
Hertfordshire
St Albans, St Stephens, Hanstead
  6048 Margarett Smith, widow
    Munby, *Worldly Goods*, 1991, p. 124
Ireland
Dublin
  6049 Sir Matthew de Renzy
    Mac Cuarta, 1997, pp. 29-30
Leicestershire
Great Stretton
  6050 Thomas Cowper
    Wilshere, *Great Stretton*, 1984, p. 17
  6051 John Eaton
    Wilshere, *Great Stretton*, 1984, p. 18
London
Covent Garden Piazza
  6052 Sir Edmund Verney
    Bruce, 1853, pp. 197-201
Norfolk
Wymondham
  6053 Richard Lincoln, wool chapman
    Wilson, *Wymondham*, 1983, pp. 29-30
Northamptonshire
Aynho
  6054 Lawrence Watts, [shepherd]
    Cooper, 1984, pp. 44-45
Overthorpe
  6055 Pe[e]ter French, husbandman
    Brinkworth and Gibson, *Banbury*, II, 1976, p. 103
Northumberland
Elwick
  6056 Mr Henerye Graye
    Raine, *North Durham*, 1852, p. 193
Oxfordshire
Banbury, Wickham
  6057 John Gill [Gyll], gentleman
    Brinkworth and Gibson, *Banbury*, II, 1976, pp. 106-108
Banbury
  6058 George Helmedon [Helmden], labourer
    Brinkworth and Gibson, *Banbury*, II, 1976, p. 110
  6059 Richard Keite [Kiete, Kite, Keate], husbandman
    Brinkworth and Gibson, *Banbury*, II, 1976, pp. 110-111
Banbury, Neithrop
  6060 Clemence Robyns [Robens], widow
    Brinkworth and Gibson, *Banbury*, II, 1976, pp. 104-105
Banbury
  6061 Reginald Wallser
    Brinkworth and Gibson, *Banbury*, II, 1976, pp. 108-109
Staffordshire
Dudley
  6062 Thomas Robinson alias Masone, butcher
    Roper, *Dudley*, 1966, pp. 19-21

Sussex
Aldingbourne
  6063 Allan Thompson, clergyman [vicar of Aldingbourne]
    Hughes, *Sussex*, 2007, pp. 1-2
Binsted
  6064 Francis Heape, clergyman [vicar of Binsted]
    Hughes, *Sussex*, 2007, pp. 30-31
Graffham
  6065 William Stepneth, clergyman [rector of Graffham]
    Hughes, *Sussex*, 2007, p. 94
Kirdford, Plaistow, Quennell House
  6066 Roberte Jackman, yeoman
    Lawson, 1999, pp. 3-4
Wales
Breconshire, Brecon
  6067 Jevan Thomas, [mercer]
    Redwood, 2000, p. 77
Flintshire, St Asaph, Taylar
  6068 Thomas Bankes, Dean of St Asaph's
    Jones, 1947, pp. 158-162
Warwickshire
Stratford-on-Avon
  6069 Edward Hunte [Hunt], yeoman
    Jones, *Stratford*, II, 2003, pp. 48-49
  6070 Thomas More, turner
    Jones, *Stratford*, II, 2003, pp. 49-50
Wiltshire
Marlborough
  6071 Joane Furnell, widow
    Williams and Thomson, *Marlborough*, 2007, pp. 72-73
  6072 John Mayhew
    Williams and Thomson, *Marlborough*, 2007, pp. 74-75
  6073 John Paine, dyer
    Williams and Thomson, *Marlborough*, 2007, pp. 73-74
  6074 Joane Powell, widow
    Williams and Thomson, *Marlborough*, 2007, p. 74
Yorkshire
Allerton, Bradford
  6075 John Hollinges [Hollings], yeoman
    Preston, *Co. York*, 1929, p. 91
Eldwick, Bingley
  6076 Edmonde Tennante, yeoman
    Preston, *Co. York*, 1929, pp. 99-100
Lunds
  6077 John Parkin
    Thwaite, *Abbotside*, 1967, p. 55

1634 (c.)
Cheshire
Dunham Massey, Dunham Woodhouses
  6078 George Smith
    Groves, *Dunham Massey*, 2008, pp. 55-56
Nantwich
  6079 John Judson
    Cockcroft, *Nantwich*, 1999, pp. 174.1-5

1635
Bristol
Bristol, St James
  6080 John Clementes [Clements], [tanner]
    George, *Bristol*, 1, 2002, p. 94
Bristol, St John
  6081 John Davies, haulier
    George, *Bristol*, 1, 2002, pp. 94-96

Bristol, St Thomas
  6082 John Doewell [Dowell], grocer
    George, *Bristol*, 1, 2002, pp. 91-92
Bristol, St Peter
  6083 Edmund Oakelie, whitawer
    George, *Bristol*, 1, 2002, pp. 89-91
Bristol, Redcliffe
  6084 John Trewman [Trueman], [hatter]
    George, *Bristol*, 1, 2002, p. 93
Westbury
  6085 William James, [fisherman]
    Moore, *Clifton*, 1981, pp. 61-62
  6086 John Payton, [parish clerk]
    Moore, *Clifton*, 1981, p. 61
  6087 Roger Williams, innholder
    Moore, *Clifton*, 1981, pp. 62-63
Buckinghamshire
Denham
  6088 John Carter, yeoman
    Cornwall, 1956, pp. 84-87
Cheshire
Adlington
  6089 Luce [Lucy] Gobert, widow
    Earwaker, *Lancashire and Cheshire*, 1893, pp. 53-54
Hale, Hale Low
  6090 James Leicester, [gentleman]
    Groves, *Hale 1*, 2005, pp. 84-85
Hale
  6091 John Litherland, [husbandman]
    Groves, *Hale 1*, 2005, pp. 86-87
  6092 Thomas Warburton, [yeoman]
    Warburton, 1970, pp. 157-158
    Groves, *Hale 1*, 2005, pp. 82-83
Nantwich
  6093 Thomas Church, gentleman
    Cockcroft, *Nantwich*, 1999, pp. 68.3-4
  6094 William Elleston, glover
    Cockcroft, *Nantwich*, 1999, p. 125.2
  6095 Cicecill [Cecily] Maisterson, widow
    Cockcroft, *Nantwich*, 1999, pp. 201.4-6
Tarvin, Kelsall
  6096 John Dodd, gentleman
    Bland, *Christleton*, 2005, pp. 620-621
Tarvin
  6097 John Grantham, yeoman
    Bland, *Christleton*, 2005, pp. 622-623
  6098 Benedicte Wrighte, husbandman
    Bland, *Christleton*, 2005, pp. 625-627
Tattenhall
  6099 John Boulton, yeoman
    Bland, *Christleton*, 2005, pp. 630-631
  6100 Thomas Gatclife, husbandman
    Bland, *Christleton*, 2005, p. 622
  6101 Thomas Larden
    Bland, *Christleton*, 2005, pp. 628-629
Wrenbury, Sheppenhall
  6102 John Cartwright, gentleman
    Pixton, *Wrenbury*, 2009, pp. 295-296
Wrenbury, Smeatonwood, The Grange
  6103 Thomas Hamnett, gentleman
    Pixton, *Wrenbury*, 2009, pp. 302-303
Wrenbury
  6104 Gilbarte Woolam [Woollam], yeoman
    Pixton, *Wrenbury*, 2009, pp. 306-307

Derbyshire
Brimington
  6105 Joan Smith
    Bestall and Fowkes, *Chesterfield*, 2001, pp. 309-310
Chapel-en-le-Frith, Bradshaw Hall
  6106 Francis Bradshawe, esquire
    Bowles, 1890, pp. 98-102
Chesterfield, Calow
  6107 John Cley
    Bestall and Fowkes, *Chesterfield*, 2001, pp. 304-306
Chesterfield
  6108 Margaret Greaves, widow
    Bestall and Fowkes, *Chesterfield*, 2001, pp. 300-304
  6109 William Stubbinge, labourer
    Bestall and Fowkes, *Chesterfield*, 2001, p. 308
Chesterfield, Calow
  6110 Thomas Wattsone
    Bestall and Fowkes, *Chesterfield*, 2001, pp. 306-307
Devonshire
Petrockstow
  6111 Anne Parnacot, widow
    Cash, *Devon*, 1966, p. 50
Topsham
  6112 Elionor Havill, widow
    Cash, *Devon*, 1966, pp. 50-51
Uffculme
  6113 Richard Baker, husbandman
    Wyatt, *Uffculme*, 1997, p. 72
  6114 Elizabeth Blackmoore
    Wyatt, *Uffculme*, 1997, p. 73
  6115 Mary Champneyes, [widow]
    Wyatt, *Uffculme*, 1997, pp. 70-71
  6116 Elizabeth Crosse, widow
    Wyatt, *Uffculme*, 1997, p. 70
  6117 Dunes Dowdney, widow
    Wyatt, *Uffculme*, 1997, pp. 71-72
  6118 James Oland alias Tayler
    Wyatt, *Uffculme*, 1997, pp. 73-74
  6119 Dorothy Pearsey, [widow]
    Wyatt, *Uffculme*, 1997, pp. 72-73
Dorsetshire
Leigh
  6120 Thomas Gaste
    Machin, *Yetminster*, 1976, No.26, (1 p.)
Co. Durham
Felling
  6121 John Brandling
    Wood, *Wills and Inventories*, 1929, IV, p. 264
Monk Hesledon
  6122 Anthony Wilkinson, yeoman
    Wood, *Wills and Inventories*, 1929, IV, p. 261
Swalwell
  6123 John Shafto, miller
    Wood, *Wills and Inventories*, 1929, IV, p. 260
Essex
Writtle
  6124 William Coleman, mason
    Steer, *Mid-Essex*, 1969, p. 71
Gloucestershire
Stoke Gifford
  6125 John Attwood, husbandman
    Moore, *Frampton Cotterell*, 1976, p. 64

Winterbourne
6126 Robert Burge alias Aburge, [husbandman]
Moore, *Frampton Cotterell*, 1976, p. 63
6127 Richard Farwelle, [gentleman]
Moore, *Frampton Cotterell*, 1976, pp. 63-64

Hertfordshire
Kings Langley
6128 John Southen, clergyman
Munby, *Kings Langley*, 1981, p. 91
St Albans, St Stephens
6129 Mary Dalamore alias Barton, widow
Parker, *Worldly Goods*, 2004, p. 233
St Albans, St Stephens, Park Street
6130 Robert Knoltton, [yeoman]
Parker, *Worldly Goods*, 2004, pp. 231-232
St Albans, St Stephens
6131 Robert Marshall, [yeoman]
Parker, *Worldly Goods*, 2004, pp. 228-229
Sarratt
6132 Simon Axtill, [yeoman]
Bullen, *Sarratt*, [1982], p. 133

Kent
Faversham
6133 John Troute, jurat [ship-master]
Laithwaite, 1968, pp. 159-162

Leicestershire
Diseworth
6134 William Lillye, yeoman
Barley, *Farmhouse and Cottage*, 1961, pp. 278-279
Mennim, 2005, p. 235
Kirby Muxloe
6135 George Somfield, [gentleman]
Wilshere, *Kirby Muxloe*, 1983, p. 10

Lincolnshire
Allington
6136 Agnis Kellam, widow
Pask, *Allington*, 1989, p. 74

London
Beaufort House, Chelsea
George Villiers, Duke of Buckingham (see York House, Strand)
Essex (formerly Leicester) House, Strand
Lettice Knollys, Countess of Leicester (see Drayton Bassett, Staffordshire)
York House, Strand
6137 George Villiers, Duke of Buckingham (also listed Beaufort House, Chelsea)
Jervis, 1997, pp. 57-74

Northamptonshire
Thorpe Malsor
6138 Richard Alderman, [yeoman]
Alderman, *Alderman*, 2008, pp. 46-47

Oxfordshire
Banbury
6139 Jeremiah Abraham, [carpenter]
Brinkworth and Gibson, *Banbury*, II, 1976, p. 115
Banbury, Neithrop
6140 Henrie [Henry] Clarage [Clerrig]
Brinkworth and Gibson, *Banbury*, II, 1976, p. 114
Banbury
6141 Hamden [Hampden, Hamdinet] Nicholes, clothier
Brinkworth and Gibson, *Banbury*, II, 1976, p. 116

6142 Thomas Pedlie [Pedley], shoemaker
Brinkworth and Gibson, *Banbury*, II, 1976, pp. 111-112
6143 Giles Toms, carpenter
Brinkworth and Gibson, *Banbury*, II, 1976, p. 112
6144 James Wilkins, labourer
Brinkworth and Gibson, *Banbury*, II, 1976, pp. 113-114

Scotland
East Lothian, Tyninghame
6145 Thomas Hamilton, Earl of Haddington
Fraser, 1889, pp. 300-304

Staffordshire
Drayton Bassett
6146 Lettice Knollys, Countess of Leicester (also listed Essex House, London)
Halliwell, *Inventories*, 1854, pp. 1-50
Wrottesley
6147 Sir Hugh Wrottesley
Wrottesley, 1903, pp. 301-305

Sussex
Warningcamp
6148 George Page, clergyman [curate of Warningcamp]
Hughes, *Sussex*, 2007, pp. 227-228

Warwickshire
Rowington
6149 Thomas Ebrall
Sheasby, 1994, pp. 53-54
Stratford-on-Avon, Old Stratford
6150 Thomas Milles [Mills], weaver
Jones, *Stratford*, II, 2003, pp. 51-52
Stratford-on-Avon
6151 Thomas Saunders
Jones, *Stratford*, II, 2003, pp. 52-53

Wiltshire
Marlborough
6152 Richard Dawnce, weaver
Williams and Thomson, *Marlborough*, 2007, pp. 75-76
6153 William Gunter
Williams and Thomson, *Marlborough*, 2007, p. 78
6154 Thomas Hawkins, shoemaker
Williams and Thomson, *Marlborough*, 2007, p. 77
6155 Beniamin Lawrence, yeoman
Williams and Thomson, *Marlborough*, 2007, pp. 76-77

Worcestershire
Chaddesley Corbett, Tanwood
6156 John Bache, yeoman
Roper, *Chaddesley Corbett*, 1971, p. 60

Yorkshire
Browsholme Hall (now Lancashire)
6157 Thomas Parker, esquire
Jervis, *Browsholme*, 1986, pp. 14-18
6158 Thomas Parker, esquire
Jervis, *Browsholme*, 1986, pp. 19-22

1635 (c.)
Devonshire
Landkey
6159 Hugh Pengel[ly]
Cash, *Devon*, 1966, p. 51

1636
Bristol
Bristol, St Philip
6160 James Yevans [Evans]
George, *Bristol*, 1, 2002, pp. 98-99

Bristol, St Mark
  6161 Mrs Susan Lardge, widow
    George, *Bristol*, 1, 2002, pp. 96-97
Bristol, St Stephen
  6162 David Oldfield, parish clerk
    George, *Bristol*, 1, 2002, pp. 97-98
Clifton
  6163 John Jones, tailor
    Moore, *Clifton*, 1981, p. 65
Westbury
  6164 Christopher Trumper, curate
    Moore, *Clifton*, 1981, pp. 63-64
  6165 Katherine Trumper, widow
    Moore, *Clifton*, 1981, p. 64
Cheshire
 Chester
  6166 Robert Bostock, gentleman
    Anon., *Bostocks*, 1934, p. 33
 Christleton, Cotton
  6167 John Middlehurst
    Bland, *Christleton*, 2005, pp. 634-635
 Clifton, Rocksavage
  6168 Thomas, Viscount Savage (also listed Melford
    Hall, Long Melford, Suffolk and
    Lumley House, Tower Hill, London)
    Boothman, Hyde Parker, 2006, pp. 77-104
 Dunham Massey
  6169 William Booth, esquire
    Groves, *Dunham Massey*, 2008, pp. 57-58
 Hale
  6170 Randle Goulden, [yeoman]
    Groves, *Hale 1*, 2005, pp. 83-84
  6171 George Perrin, [yeoman]
    Groves, *Hale 1*, 2005, pp. 85-86
 Nantwich
  6172 William Edgeley
    Cockcroft, *Nantwich*, 1999, pp. 122.1-2
  6173 Elizabeth Hassall, widow
    Cockcroft, *Nantwich*, 1999, p. 152.2
  6174 Raphe Latham, innholder
    Cockcroft, *Nantwich*, 1999, pp. 182.2-6
  6175 Mathewe Massie, innholder
    Cockcroft, *Nantwich*, 1999, pp. 211.2-3
  6176 John Moulson, gentleman
    Cockcroft, *Nantwich*, 1999, pp. 227.3-4
 Sale
  6177 Thomas Chorlton, linen weaver
    Groves, *Ashton-on-Mersey and Sale*, 1999, pp. 67-69
  6178 Richard Kelsall, husbandman
    Groves, *Ashton-on-Mersey and Sale*, 1999, pp. 64-65
 Tarvin, Foulk Stapleford
  6179 Peter Cotgreave, [yeoman]
    Bland, *Christleton*, 2005, pp. 632-633
 Wrenbury, Woodcott
  6180 John Edgley [Edgeley], [yeoman]
    Pixton, *Wrenbury*, 2009, pp. 317-318
 Wrenbury, Aston, Newhall
  6181 Thomas Gray, [clergyman]
    Pixton, *Wrenbury*, 2009, pp. 308-309
 Wrenbury, Newhall
  6182 John Hall
    Pixton, *Wrenbury*, 2009, pp. 311-312

Devonshire
 Bradninch
  6183 Ursula May
    Cash, *Devon*, 1966, p. 52
 Butterleigh
  6184 Mr Richard Foster, clergyman
    Cash, *Devon*, 1966, pp. 51-52
 Chawleigh
  6185 John Edworthy
    Cash, *Devon*, 1966, p. 51
 Uffculme
  6186 John Cornish, [yeoman]
    Wyatt, *Uffculme*, 1997, pp. 74-75
  6187 Edmund Satchell
    Wyatt, *Uffculme*, 1997, p. 74
Gloucestershire
 Hambrook
  6188 Joyce Fowler, widow
    Moore, *Frampton Cotterell*, 1976, pp. 65-66
 Stoke Gifford
  6189 Christopher Dorney, yeoman
    Moore, *Frampton Cotterell*, 1976, pp. 67-68
 Winterbourne
  6190 Mr Edward Graunt, [gentleman]
    Moore, *Frampton Cotterell*, 1976, p. 66
Hertfordshire
 Chipperfield
  6191 Francis Carter, carpenter
    Munby, *Kings Langley*, 1981, pp. 93-94
 Kings Langley
  6192 Jarman Crosby, keeper
    Munby, *Kings Langley*, 1981, p. 92
 St Albans, St Stephens
  6193 Thomas Antrobus, [gentleman]
    Parker, *Worldly Goods*, 2004, p. 233
Lancashire
 Rochdale
  6194 James Whitehead, [innkeeper]
    Fishwick, 1886, pp. 24-25
Leicestershire
 Ratby, Whittington
  6195 John North, [husbandman]
    Wilshere, *Ratby*, 1984, p. 2
Lincolnshire
 Benington
  6196 John Swaine, husbandman
    Barley, *Lincolnshire*, 1951, pp. 263-264
London
 Tower Hill, Lumley House
    Thomas, Viscount Savage (see Rocksavage, Clifton,
    Cheshire)
Northumberland
 Spindlestone
  6197 Sir Arthur Gray
    Wood, *Wills and Inventories*, 1929, IV, pp. 268-269
Oxfordshire
 Banbury
  6198 Thomas Berry
    Brinkworth and Gibson, *Banbury*, II, 1976, pp. 119-120
  6199 Henry[e] Coleing [Colling], mason
    Brinkworth and Gibson, *Banbury*, II, 1976, p. 119
  6200 Edward Kendal[l], gentleman
    Brinkworth and Gibson, *Banbury*, II, 1976, p. 120

6201 Anne Lumley, widow
Brinkworth and Gibson, *Banbury*, II, 1976, pp. 117-118
Banbury, Neithrop
6202 El[l]en Stockly [Stocklie], widow
Brinkworth and Gibson, *Banbury*, II, 1976, pp. 116-117
6203 Joyce Youicke
Brinkworth and Gibson, *Banbury*, II, 1976, p. 117
Staffordshire
Dudley, St Thomas
6204 Edward Roods, grubber
Roper, *Dudley*, 1966, p. 22
Roper, *Dudley*, 1968, pp. 21
Dudley
6205 Alles Russon, widow
Roper, *Dudley*, 1968, pp. 20-21
Suffolk
Long Melford, Melford Hall
Thomas, Viscount Savage (see Rocksavage, Clifton, Cheshire)
Walsham-le-Willows
6206 Edmund Baxter
Evans, 1993, p. 36
Warwickshire
Stratford-on-Avon
6207 Richard Hathaway, gentleman [baker]
Jones, *Stratford*, II, 2003, pp. 55-58
6208 Christopher Mace, labourer
Jones, *Stratford*, II, 2003, p. 54
6209 Ane Rennolls [Anne Reynolds]
Jones, *Stratford*, II, 2003, p. 55
Wiltshire
Marlborough
6210 Roger Gybbes
Williams and Thomson, *Marlborough*, 2007, pp. 79-80
6211 Christian Hitchcoke alias Chapman
Williams and Thomson, *Marlborough*, 2007, p. 80
6212 John Sessions, carpenter
Williams and Thomson, *Marlborough*, 2007, pp. 78-79
Worcestershire
Belbroughton
6213 Thomas Walford
Roper, *Belbroughton*, 1967-1968, p. 67
Chaddesley Corbett
6214 John Heath, clergyman, vicar of Chaddesley Corbett
Roper, *Chaddesley Corbett*, 1971, pp. 62-63
Yorkshire
Greenhill, Bingley
6215 Isabell Hall
Preston, *Co. York*, 1929, pp. 102-103
Knaresborough
6216 Widdowe Cook
Brears, *Yorkshire*, 1972, p. 80

1636 (c.)
Yorkshire
Eldwick, Bingley
6217 Edmond Wood
Preston, *Co. York*, 1929, pp. 107-108

1637
Bristol
Bristol, St Peter
6218 Thomas Bibbie, [tanner]
George, *Bristol*, 1, 2002, pp. 101-102

Bristol, St Thomas
6219 Richard Shutter, haberdasher
George, *Bristol*, 1, 2002, pp. 99-101
Bristol, Redcliffe
6220 George Weston, mariner
George, *Bristol*, 1, 2002, pp. 102-104
Clifton
6221 John Watkins, [weaver]
Moore, *Clifton*, 1981, pp. 73-74
6222 Edward Watts, [sailor]
Moore, *Clifton*, 1981, pp. 72-73
Shirehampton
6223 Margaret Ricks
Moore, *Clifton*, 1981, p. 69
Westbury
6224 Charles Cox, yeoman
Moore, *Clifton*, 1981, pp. 65-66
6225 John Hort, yeoman
Moore, *Clifton*, 1981, pp. 70-72
6226 John Large, [yeoman]
Moore, *Clifton*, 1981, pp. 66-68
Cheshire
Ashton-on-Mersey
6227 Randle Jones
Groves, *Ashton-on-Mersey and Sale*, 1999, pp. 73-74
Bowdon
6228 Robert Janney, clergyman, vicar of Bowdon
Groves, *Bowdon*, 1997, pp. 49-50
Christleton
6229 John Cotgrive [Cotgrave]
Bland, *Christleton*, 2005, pp. 657-658
6230 John Johnson
Bland, *Christleton*, 2005, p. 651
Hale
6231 Henry Royle
Groves, *Hale 1*, 2005, pp. 87-88
Mottram-in-Longdendale
6232 John Hyde, clergyman, vicar of Mottram
Earwaker, 1880, p. 128
Nantwich
6233 Raphe Arrowsmithe, yeoman
Cockcroft, *Nantwich*, 1999, pp. 15.4-6
6234 Thomas Lea, mercer
Cockcroft, *Nantwich*, 1999, pp. 185.1-3
6235 William Mainwaring, gentleman
Cockcroft, *Nantwich*, 1999, pp. 199.3-5
6236 Edward Massie, skinner
Cockcroft, *Nantwich*, 1999, p. 210.2
6237 Richard Wright, buttonmaker
Cockcroft, *Nantwich*, 1999, p. 368.2
Tarvin, Burton
6238 John Ball, yeoman
Bland, *Christleton*, 2005, pp. 653-654
Tarvin, Ashton
6239 Roberte Feild, husbandman
Bland, *Christleton*, 2005, pp. 645-646
Tarvin, Hargrave
6240 Edward Humston [Humpston]
Bland, *Christleton*, 2005, pp. 636-637
Tarvin, Oscroft
6241 Thomas Milson, salter
Bland, *Christleton*, 2005, p. 635

Tarvin, Ashton
  6242 Margery Pearson
  Bland, *Christleton*, 2005, p. 655
Tarvin, Hoofield
  6243 Richard Tayler, husbandman
  Bland, *Christleton*, 2005, p. 641
Tarvin
  6244 John Torkinton, gentleman
  Bland, *Christleton*, 2005, pp. 647-649
Tattenhall
  6245 Richard Cappur, husbandman
  Bland, *Christleton*, 2005, pp. 638-640
  6246 Margaret Stranke, widow
  Bland, *Christleton*, 2005, p. 651
Waverton, Hatton
  6247 Margret Calkin
  Bland, *Christleton*, 2005, p. 643
Winnington
  6248 John Warburton, gentleman
  Warburton, 1970, p. 158
Wrenbury
  6249 Elizabeth Briscoe, [widow]
  Pixton, *Wrenbury*, 2009, pp. 319-320
Wrenbury, Smeatonwood
  6250 Richard Dodd, [yeoman]
  Pixton, *Wrenbury*, 2009, pp. 313-314
Derbyshire
Chesterfield
  6251 Nicholas Clarke, vintner
  Bestall and Fowkes, *Chesterfield*, 2001, pp. 314-319
Chesterfield, Temple Normanton
  6252 Henry Cowle, husbandman
  Bestall and Fowkes, *Chesterfield*, 2001, pp. 310-312
Chesterfield
  6253 Ann Greaves
  Bestall and Fowkes, *Chesterfield*, 2001, p. 326
  6254 Ralph Launder, surgeon
  Bestall and Fowkes, *Chesterfield*, 2001, pp. 327-330
  6255 Beatrix Purslove, widow
  Bestall and Fowkes, *Chesterfield*, 2001, pp. 324-325
  6256 Thomas Renshawe, yeoman and butcher
  Bestall and Fowkes, *Chesterfield*, 2001, pp. 333-336
  6257 William Wagstaffe, husbandman
  Bestall and Fowkes, *Chesterfield*, 2001, p. 326
  6258 George Walker .
  Bestall and Fowkes, *Chesterfield*, 2001, pp. 312-314
  6259 Nicholas Watkinson
  Bestall and Fowkes, *Chesterfield*, 2001, pp. 322-324
Monyash
  6260 William Aston, miner
  Barley, *Farmhouse and Cottage*, 1961, p. 276
Newbold
  6261 William Webster, cutler
  Bestall and Fowkes, *Chesterfield*, 2001, pp. 320-322
Devonshire
Littleham
  6262 Ellis Creese, yeoman
  Cash, *Devon*, 1966, pp. 52-53
Morchard Bishop
  6263 Robert Beare, clergyman, gentleman, rector
  Cash, *Devon*, 1966, pp. 53-54
Paignton
  6264 Richard and Elizabeth Blackaller
  Cash, *Devon*, 1966, p. 54

Uffculme
  6265 Francis Leyman
  Wyatt, *Uffculme*, 1997, pp. 75-76
Co. Durham
Lanchester
  6266 John Greenwell, yeoman
  Wood, *Wills and Inventories*, 1929, IV, p. 273
Essex
Easton Lodge
  6267 Sir William Maynard, Lord Maynard
  Steer, *Easton*, 1952, pp. 6-21
Roxwell
  6268 William Carding
  Steer, *Mid-Essex*, 1969, pp. 71-72
Gloucestershire
Winterbourne
  6269 Lawrence Whinge alias White, [husbandman]
  Moore, *Frampton Cotterell*, 1976, p. 67
Hertfordshire
Kings Langley [?]
  6270 Mathias Carter
  Munby, *Kings Langley*, 1981, p. 94
St Albans, St Stephens
  6271 John Fuller, tailor
  Parker, *Worldly Goods*, 2004, p. 235
Sarratt
  6272 Henry Dell
  Bullen, *Sarratt*, [1982], pp. 133-134
  6273 John Watts, [labourer]
  Bullen, *Sarratt*, [1982], p. 137
Stevenage
  6274 Mr Edward Dickinson, clergyman
  Anon., *Lock, Stock*, 1978, pp. 61-62
Leicestershire
Braunstone
  6275 George Bennett
  Wilshere, *Braunstone*, 1983, p. 18
Evington
  6276 Thomas Jacombe, husbandman
  Wilshere, *Evington*, 1985, p. 24
  6277 Thomas Noone, husbandman
  Wilshere, *Evington*, 1985, p. 23
Norfolk
Stiffkey
  6278 Sir Roger Townsend, baronet
  Bradfer-Lawrence, 1929, pp. 321-324
Northumberland
Denwick, Hobberlaw
  6279 Francis Alder, gentleman
  Wood, *Wills and Inventories*, 1929, IV, pp. 272-273
Oxfordshire
Banbury
  6280 Thomas Buroes [Burrowes], tailor
  Brinkworth and Gibson, *Banbury*, II, 1976, p. 128
  6281 John Fardam [Fordham, Vardom]
  Brinkworth and Gibson, *Banbury*, II, 1976, pp. 122-123
  6282 Edward Gulliver
  Brinkworth and Gibson, *Banbury*, II, 1976, p. 126
  6283 John Hathaway
  Brinkworth and Gibson, *Banbury*, II, 1976, p. 123
  6284 William Hauks [Hawkes, Hancks]
  Brinkworth and Gibson, *Banbury*, II, 1976, pp. 124-125

Banbury, Grimsbury
  6285 Mary Hawtaine [Hawten]
  Brinkworth and Gibson, *Banbury*, II, 1976, p. 127
Banbury
  6286 John Long
  Brinkworth and Gibson, *Banbury*, II, 1976, p. 126
  6287 John Newman, shoemaker
  Brinkworth and Gibson, *Banbury*, II, 1976, pp. 121-122
  6288 Roger Tatom [Tatum], glover
  Brinkworth and Gibson, *Banbury*, II, 1976, pp. 123-124
  6289 John Vivers, mercer
  Brinkworth and Gibson, *Banbury*, II, 1976, pp. 125-126
  6290 Thomas Wise [Wyse], innholder
  Brinkworth and Gibson, *Banbury*, II, 1976, p. 124

Staffordshire
Dudley
  6291 Raphell Hollingsworth, nailer
  Roper, *Dudley*, 1966, pp. 23-24

Surrey
Thorpe
  6292 John Potter
  Clinch, 1910, pp. 79-80

Sussex
Fittleworth
  6293 Ralphe Blinstone, clergyman [rector of Egdean]
  Hughes, *Sussex*, 2007, pp. 79-80
West Grinstead
  6294 James Hutchinson, clergyman [rector of West Grinstead]
  Hughes, *Sussex*, 2007, pp. 95-98

Warwickshire
Clopton
  6295 Richard Hickes
  Jones, *Stratford*, II, 2003, pp. 58-59

Wiltshire
Marlborough
  6296 Edward Carter, yeoman
  Williams and Thomson, *Marlborough*, 2007, pp. 80-81
  6297 John Heath, innholder
  Williams and Thomson, *Marlborough*, 2007, pp. 82-84
  6298 Walter Jones, glover
  Williams and Thomson, *Marlborough*, 2007, pp. 81-82
  6299 Johane Titcombe, widow
  Williams and Thomson, *Marlborough*, 2007, p. 82

Worcestershire
Belbroughton
  6300 Richard Harrold, [gunsmith]
  Roper, *Belbroughton*, 1967-1968, p. 68
Harvington
  6301 Roger Cowper, labourer
  Roper, *Chaddesley Corbett*, 1971, p. 61

Yorkshire
Allerton, Bradford
  6302 John Cosin
  Preston, *Co. York*, 1929, pp. 103-105
  6303 Roberte Deane, yeoman
  Preston, *Co. York*, 1929, pp. 84-88
Cottingley, Bingley (now Bradford)
  6304 William Midgley
  Preston, *Co. York*, 1929, pp. 105-107

1637 (c.)
Lincolnshire
Clee, Thrunscoe
  6305 Robert Nicholson, labourer
  Ambler, Watkinson, *Clee*, 1987, pp. 149-150

1638
Bristol
Bristol, St Nicholas
  6306 Challoner Claybrooke, servant
  George, *Bristol*, I, 2002, pp. 104-105
Clifton
  6307 Agnes Bayley, widow
  Moore, *Clifton*, 1981, p. 74
Shirehampton
  6308 John Pearce, [thatcher]
  Moore, *Clifton*, 1981, pp. 74-75

Cheshire
Dunham Massey, Dunham
  6309 John Beardsley
  Groves, *Dunham Massey*, 2008, pp. 59-60
  6310 George Cottrell, [husbandman]
  Groves, *Dunham Massey*, 2008, pp. 60-61
Nantwich
  6311 Jane Badcock, widow
  Cockcroft, *Nantwich*, 1999, pp. 17.1-3
  6312 Richard Badcock, shoemaker
  Cockcroft, *Nantwich*, 1999, pp. 16.1-3
  6313 Richard Brooke
  Cockcroft, *Nantwich*, 1999, p. 47.1
  6314 Richard Church, gentleman
  Cockcroft, *Nantwich*, 1999, pp. 69.3-5
  6315 Anne Cleyton, widow
  Cockcroft, *Nantwich*, 1999, pp. 74.6-9
  6316 Hugh Emerson, joiner
  Cockcroft, *Nantwich*, 1999, pp. 126.2-3
  6317 Humfrey Podmore, wheelwright
  Cockcroft, *Nantwich*, 1999, pp. 252.5-6
  6318 Anne Pratchett, widow
  Cockcroft, *Nantwich*, 1999, pp. 253.3-4
  6319 William Thompson, chandler
  Cockcroft, *Nantwich*, 1999, pp. 310.1-3
  6320 John Thrush, gentleman
  Cockcroft, *Nantwich*, 1999, pp. 311.3-5
  6321 Raphe Wicksteed, gentleman
  Cockcroft, *Nantwich*, 1999, pp. 341.1-4
Tarvin
  6322 Roberte Lawrenson, yeoman
  Bland, *Christleton*, 2005, pp. 659-660
Tattenhall
  6323 John Anderton, gentleman
  Bland, *Christleton*, 2005, p. 672
Tattenhall, Golborne Bellow
  6324 Mary Astle
  Bland, *Christleton*, 2005, p. 669
  6325 Raph Astles, yeoman
  Bland, *Christleton*, 2005, pp. 659-660
Tattenhall
  6326 Roger Dod, husbandman
  Bland, *Christleton*, 2005, pp. 61-663
Waverton, Huxley
  6327 Roberte Farrer, yeoman
  Bland, *Christleton*, 2005, pp. 674-676

Wrenbury, Chorley
　6328　Edward Bowdon
　Pixton, *Wrenbury*, 2009, pp. 326-327
Wrenbury, Smeatonwood
　6329　George Tench
　Pixton, *Wrenbury*, 2009, p. 329

Derbyshire
Brimington
　6330　Richard Carrington
　Bestall and Fowkes, *Chesterfield*, 2001, pp. 344-345
　6331　Margaret Marriott
　Bestall and Fowkes, *Chesterfield*, 2001, pp. 337-338
　6332　Thomas Marriott
　Bestall and Fowkes, *Chesterfield*, 2001, pp. 338-340
　6333　Humphrey Smith
　Bestall and Fowkes, *Chesterfield*, 2001, pp. 332-333
Chesterfield
　6334　Edward Goodwin, weaver
　Bestall and Fowkes, *Chesterfield*, 2001, pp. 340-341
　6335　Martin Heathcott, tanner
　Bestall and Fowkes, *Chesterfield*, 2001, pp. 341-344
　6336　Martin Rolinson
　Bestall and Fowkes, *Chesterfield*, 2001, pp. 330-332
Hasland
　6337　William Hardy
　Bestall and Fowkes, *Chesterfield*, 2001, p. 338

Devonshire
Totnes
　6338　Reynold Austin, merchant
　Cash, *Devon*, 1966, p. 54
Uffculme
　6339　Elizabeth Eastbrooke
　Wyatt, *Uffculme*, 1997, pp. 77-78
　6340　[Samuell James] alias Slade, [weaver]
　Wyatt, *Uffculme*, 1997, pp. 76-77
　6341　Thomas Keeper
　Wyatt, *Uffculme*, 1997, p. 78

Dorsetshire
Chetnole
　6342　John Elford, [yeoman, candlemaker]
　Machin, *Yetminster*, 1976, No.27, (2 pp.)

Co. Durham
Archdeacon Newton
　6343　John Lumley, gentleman
　Wood, *Wills and Inventories*, 1929, IV, p. 235

Essex
Roxwell
　6344　John Burrag [Burredg], husbandman
　Steer, *Mid-Essex*, 1969, p. 72
Writtle
　6345　Christopher Bellsted, husbandman
　Steer, *Mid-Essex*, 1969, p. 82
　6346　John Bur'owes
　Steer, *Mid-Essex*, 1969, p. 77
　6347　Henry Carr
　Steer, *Mid-Essex*, 1969, pp. 77-78
　6348　Abraham Chalkes, husbandman
　Steer, *Mid-Essex*, 1969, pp. 76-77
　6349　John George, yeoman
　Steer, *Mid-Essex*, 1969, pp. 82-84
　6350　Bennett Gue
　Steer, *Mid-Essex*, 1969, p. 73

　6351　Robert Jackson
　Steer, *Mid-Essex*, 1969, pp. 75-76
　6352　John Osburne, [yeoman?]
　Steer, *Mid-Essex*, 1969, pp. 73-74
　6353　Henry Sharpe, yeoman
　Steer, *Mid-Essex*, 1969, pp. 74-75
　6354　Peter Woolmer
　Steer, *Mid-Essex*, 1969, pp. 78-79
Unlocated
　6355　Joane Harris, widow
　Steer, *Mid-Essex*, 1969, p. 74

Hertfordshire
Kings Langley
　6356　Susana Dell, widow
　Munby, *Kings Langley*, 1981, p. 98
　6357　John Douse
　Munby, *Kings Langley*, 1981, p. 96
　6358　Thomas Lovet, tailor
　Munby, *Kings Langley*, 1981, p. 97
St Albans, St Stephens, Park Street
　6359　Robert Cornelius, yeoman
　Parker, *Worldly Goods*, 2004, pp. 236-237
St Albans, St Stephens
　6360　Thomas Flanders
　Parker, *Worldly Goods*, 2004, p. 237
St Albans, St Stephens, Black Green
　6361　Richard Kempe
　Munby, *Worldly Goods*, 1991, p. 129
St Albans, St Stephens
　6362　Joane Warcope, widow
　Munby, *Worldly Goods*, 1991, p. 128

Leicestershire
Glenfield
　6363　John Scriven, husbandman
　Wilshere, *Glenfield*, 1983, p. 7
Ratby
　6364　Peter Bunney, carpenter
　Wilshere, *Ratby*, 1984, p. 3
　6365　Richard Cater, tailor
　Wilshere, *Ratby*, 1984, p. 4
　6366　Daniel Kempe, husbandman
　Wilshere, *Ratby*, 1984, p. 4

Norfolk
Besthorpe
　6367　Sir Anthonie Drewrie [Anthony Drury]
　Wilson, *Wymondham*, 1983, pp. 1-5

Northamptonshire
Nethercote
　6368　Edward Mole
　Brinkworth and Gibson, *Banbury*, II, 1976, p. 130

Oxfordshire
Banbury
　6369　William Lucas, baker
　Brinkworth and Gibson, *Banbury*, II, 1976, pp. 129-130
　6370　Abel[l] Page, carpenter
　Brinkworth and Gibson, *Banbury*, II, 1976, pp. 131-132
Banbury, Grimsbury
　6371　Ralfe [Ralph] Warren, labourer, husbandman
　Brinkworth and Gibson, *Banbury*, II, 1976, pp. 130-131
Banbury, Neithrop
　6372　Robert Youick, gardener
　Brinkworth and Gibson, *Banbury*, II, 1976, pp. 132-133

Scotland
East Lothian, Elphinstone
  6373 Alexander, Lord Elphinston
  Royal Commission, 1883, p. 194

Staffordshire
Dudley
  6374 Edward Parkes, blacksmith
  Roper, *Dudley*, 1966, p. 25

Sussex
Coldwaltham
  6375 William Bowley, clergyman
  Hughes, *Sussex*, 2007, pp. 52-53
West Thorney
  6376 Godfrey Blaxton, clergyman [rector of West
  Thorney]
  Hughes, *Sussex*, 2007, pp. 216-218

Wiltshire
Marlborough
  6377 Anthony Hatt, barber
  Williams and Thomson, *Marlborough*, 2007, pp. 85-86
  6378 John Martin, clergyman [schoolmaster]
  Williams and Thomson, *Marlborough*, 2007, p. 86
  6379 Katherine Peirse alias Dastine
  Williams and Thomson, *Marlborough*, 2007, pp. 84-85

Yorkshire
Aysgarth, Sedbusk
  6380 James Blades
  Thwaite, *Abbotside*, 1967, pp. 57-58
Aysgarth, Skellgill
  6381 Edmond Coates, [yeoman]
  Thwaite, *Abbotside*, 1967, p. 59
Bainbridge, Brockhill Cote
  6382 Richard Blaides [Blaids, Blades], [yeoman]
  Thwaite, *Abbotside*, 1967, p. 57
Bretton Park
  6383 George Wentworth
  Brears, *Yorkshire*, 1972, pp. 84-86
Greenhill, Bingley
  6384 John Rawson
  Preston, *Co. York*, 1929, pp. 109-114
Knaresborough
  6385 Robert West
  Brears, *Yorkshire*, 1972, pp. 81-83
South Cave
  6386 Thomas Brabes, clergyman, [vicar of South
  Cave]
  Kaner, *South Cave*, 1994, pp. 344-346
Thwaites, Keighley
  6387 Roberte Wilkinson
  Preston, *Co. York*, 1929, pp. 114-116

1638 (c.)
Wiltshire
Marlborough
  6388 Jeaffrey Spender
  Williams and Thomson, *Marlborough*, 2007, p. 86
Yorkshire
Knaresborough
  6389 Will Plase
  Brears, *Yorkshire*, 1972, p. 86

1639
Bristol
Bristol
  6390 John Berrowe, pump-maker
  George, *Bristol*, 1, 2002, pp. 110-111
Bristol, St Thomas
  6391 Robert Burd [Birde]
  George, *Bristol*, 1, 2002, pp. 106-107
Bristol, St Philip
  6392 Phillip [Philip] Cause, tanner
  George, *Bristol*, 1, 2002, pp. 105-106
Bristol, Temple
  6393 Mr Richard Knight, vicar of Temple
  George, *Bristol*, 1, 2002, p. 110
Bristol, St Ewen
  6394 Nicholas Meredith, merchant, late city
  chamberlain (also listed Westbury,
  Gloucestershire)
  George, *Bristol*, 1, 2002, pp. 112-115
Bristol
  6395 Richard Pley, merchant
  McGrath, 1955, pp. 90-92
Bristol, St Michael
  6396 Roger Slade, cook
  George, *Bristol*, 1, 2002, pp. 108-110
Bristol, St Thomas
  6397 Beniamime [Benjamin] Tuner, physician
  George, *Bristol*, 1, 2002, pp. 107-108
Bristol, St Stephen
  6398 George Whitt [White], [shipwright]
  George, *Bristol*, 1, 2002, pp. 115-116
Shirehampton
  6399 Margaret Smith, widow
  Moore, *Clifton*, 1981, pp. 75-76
South Mead
  6400 William Cantor, [yeoman]
  Moore, *Clifton*, 1981, pp. 77-78
Stoke Bishop
  6401 William Parker, [husbandman]
  Moore, *Clifton*, 1981, p. 79
Westbury
  6402 Nicholas Harris, [labourer]
  Moore, *Clifton*, 1981, pp. 76-77
  6403 John Sansom, [sailor]
  Moore, *Clifton*, 1981, p. 78

Cheshire
Christleton
  6404 John Middlehurst, yeoman
  Bland, *Christleton*, 2005, pp. 685-686
Dunham Massey
  6405 Ellen Neild [Nield], [widow]
  Groves, *Dunham Massey*, 2008, pp. 61-62
Hale, Ringway
  6406 William Bradley
  Groves, *Hale 1*, 2005, p. 93
Hale
  6407 Ann Grantham, [widow]
  Groves, *Hale 1*, 2005, p. 96
Hale, Ringway
  6408 Robert Leatherbarrow
  Groves, *Hale 1*, 2005, p. 88
Hale, Hale Low
  6409 Lawrence Leicester, [gentleman]
  Groves, *Hale 1*, 2005, p. 92

Hale, Ringway
  6410 Edmund Newton, [yeoman]
    Groves, *Hale 1*, 2005, pp. 89-90
Hale
  6411 George Warburton, [yeoman]
    Groves, *Hale 1*, 2005, pp. 90-91
  6412 John Warburton, [husbandman]
    Groves, *Hale 1*, 2005, p. 92
Nantwich
  6413 Thomas Alcocke, yeoman
    Cockcroft, *Nantwich*, 1999, p. 7.1
  6414 Thomas Bickerton, gentleman
    Cockcroft, *Nantwich*, 1999, pp. 31.4-7
  6415 Hugh Blackburn, mercer
    Cockcroft, *Nantwich*, 1999, pp. 33.2-3
  6416 Thomas Clowes, parish clerk
    Cockcroft, *Nantwich*, 1999, p. 83.3
  6417 Laurence Clutton, gentleman
    Cockcroft, *Nantwich*, 1999, p. 89.1
  6418 John Mainwaring, gentleman
    Cockcroft, *Nantwich*, 1999, p. 198.3
  6419 Randull Minshull, gentleman
    Cockcroft, *Nantwich*, 1999, p. 223.2
Tarvin
  6420 John Hutchinson, yeoman
    Bland, *Christleton*, 2005, pp. 678-679
Tarvin, Hockenhull
  6421 John Neild, yeoman
    Bland, *Christleton*, 2005, pp. 681-682
Tarvin, Ashton
  6422 Roger Rowe, servant
    Bland, *Christleton*, 2005, p. 688
Tarvin, Duddon
  6423 Roberte Townesend, tailor
    Bland, *Christleton*, 2005, p. 677
Tarvin, Hockenhull
  6424 Edward Wright, husbandman
    Bland, *Christleton*, 2005, p
Wrenbury, Chorley
  6425 Thomas Hare
    Pixton, *Wrenbury*, 2009, pp. 330-331
  6426 Roger Jones
    Pixton, *Wrenbury*, 2009, pp. 339-340
Wrenbury cum Frith
  6427 William Wilson, gentleman
    Pixton, *Wrenbury*, 2009, pp. 334-337
Cumberland
Skirwith Hall
  6428 Mrs Issabell Fleminge [Isabel Fleming], widow
    Collingwood, 1928
Derbyshire
Chesterfield
  6429 Robert Harris, barber-surgeon
    Bestall and Fowkes, *Chesterfield*, 2001, pp. 345-346
  6430 John Harteley
    Bestall and Fowkes, *Chesterfield*, 2001, p. 349
  6431 George Mason alias Johnson
    Bestall and Fowkes, *Chesterfield*, 2001, pp. 346-347
  6432 Thomas Ouldham
    Bestall and Fowkes, *Chesterfield*, 2001, pp. 347-349
  6433 Richard White
    Bestall and Fowkes, *Chesterfield*, 2001, pp. 350-351

Devonshire
Exeter, St Mary Steps
  6434 Simon Tucker
    Worthy, *Devonshire*, 1896, p. 182
Uffculme
  6435 Edward Bryar, [weaver]
    Wyatt, *Uffculme*, 1997, p. 80
  6436 Luce Heathfield [Heithfeild], widow
    Wyatt, *Uffculme*, 1997, p. 79
  6437 Robert Mill [Mills], yeoman
    Wyatt, *Uffculme*, 1997, pp. 80-81
  6438 James Pooke, [brewer]
    Wyatt, *Uffculme*, 1997, pp. 78-79
  6439 Beaten Rudge
    Wyatt, *Uffculme*, 1997, p. 80
Dorsetshire
St Giles's House
  6440 Sir Anthony Ashley Cooper, baronet
    Cooper, 1974, pp. 6-12
Essex
Gosfield Hall
  6441 Anne, Viscountess Dorchester
    Steer, *Dorchester*, 1953-1954, pp. 95-96, 155-158, 379-381, 414-417, 469-473, 515-519
Roxwell
  6442 Francis Bancks
    Steer, *Mid-Essex*, 1969, p. 79
  6443 Henry Bright, yeoman
    Steer, *Mid-Essex*, 1969, pp. 79-80
  6444 Thomas Raynebeard, weaver
    Steer, *Mid-Essex*, 1969, p. 81
Writtle
  6445 Janne Barnard, widow
    Steer, *Mid-Essex*, 1969, p. 80
  6446 Jeffre Bradley
    Steer, *Mid-Essex*, 1969, pp. 84-85
  6447 Thomas Larkin, husbandman
    Steer, *Mid-Essex*, 1969, p. 85
  6448 John Taverner, husbandman
    Steer, *Mid-Essex*, 1969, p. 81
Gloucestershire
Hambrook
  6449 John Weblie, husbandman
    Moore, *Frampton Cotterell*, 1976, pp. 69-70
Stoke Gifford
  6450 Robert Deverill, yeoman
    Moore, *Frampton Cotterell*, 1976, p. 70
  6451 Christopher Dorney, yeoman
    Moore, *Frampton Cotterell*, 1976, pp. 67-68
  6452 John Howell, yeoman
    Moore, *Frampton Cotterell*, 1976, pp. 68-69
Westbury
  6453 Nicholas Meredith, merchant (see Bristol, St Ewen)
Winterbourne
  6454 Arthur Strang, husbandman
    Moore, *Frampton Cotterell*, 1976, p. 68
Hertfordshire
Kings Langley
  6455 John Dell, [labourer]
    Munby, *Kings Langley*, 1981, pp. 101-102
Kings Langley [?]
  6456 Joane Kinge [Joan King], widow
    Munby, *Kings Langley*, 1981, pp. 100-101

St Albans, St Stephens
 6457 Frauncis Havarde [Hawarde], husbandman
  Parker, *Worldly Goods*, 2004, p. 242
 6458 Nicholas Kilby, [yeoman]
  Munby, *Worldly Goods*, 1991, p. 127
 6459 John Rodggers, husbandman
  Parker, *Worldly Goods*, 2004, p. 241

Ireland
 Bunratty Castle, Co. Clare
 6460 Henry O'Brien, Earl of Thomond
  O Dalaigh, 1995, pp. 147-157
 Kilkenny Castle [?]
 6461 James Butler, Earl of Ormond
  Fenlon, *Ireland*, 2003, pp. 30-31

Lancashire
 Worsley
 6462 Dame Dorothie Legh, widow of Sir Peter Legh
  Piccope, *Lancashire and Cheshire*, 1860, pp. 210-212

Leicestershire
 Evington
 6463 William Welles, husbandman
  Wilshere, *Evington*, 1985, p. 25

Lincolnshire
 Pinchbeck
 6464 Thomas Rothwell, husbandman
  Spufford, *Reclothing*, 1984, pp. 127-128

Northamptonshire
 Aynho
 6465 Elizabeth Young, [widow?]
  Cooper, 1984, pp. 45-46
 Thorpe Malsor
 6466 Elenor Alderman, widow
  Alderman, *Alderman*, 2008, p. 44

Oxfordshire
 Banbury
 6467 Anthony Bradlye
  Brinkworth and Gibson, *Banbury*, II, 1976, pp. 137-138
 6468 Susannah Devel [Devell]
  Brinkworth and Gibson, *Banbury*, II, 1976, p. 137
 6469 William Dreed[e], innholder
  Brinkworth and Gibson, *Banbury*, II, 1976, pp. 136-137
 6470 Mr Thomas Halhed, woollen draper
  Brinkworth and Gibson, *Banbury*, II, 1976, pp. 134-135
 6471 Daniel Hathaway
  Brinkworth and Gibson, *Banbury*, II, 1976, pp. 139-140
 Banbury, Neithrop
 6472 Edward Kinge, husbandman
  Brinkworth and Gibson, *Banbury*, II, 1976, pp. 135-136
 Banbury
 6473 Elizabeth Knibb
  Brinkworth and Gibson, *Banbury*, II, 1976, p. 138
 6474 Nicholas Renoldes, victualler
  Brinkworth and Gibson, *Banbury*, II, 1976, pp. 140-141
 6475 William Shipton
  Brinkworth and Gibson, *Banbury*, II, 1976, p. 139

Staffordshire
 Dudley
 6476 Alles Dixon, widow
  Roper, *Dudley*, 1968, pp. 20-21

Sussex
 Lancing
 6477 Timothy Holney, clergyman [vicar of Lancing]
  Hughes, *Sussex*, 2007, pp. 131-132

Selsey
 6478 Hugh French, clergyman [vicar of Selsey]
  Hughes, *Sussex*, 2007, pp. 187-188
Sidlesham
 6479 John Taylor, clergyman [vicar of Sidlesham]
  Hughes, *Sussex*, 2007, pp. 193-194

Warwickshire
 Stratford-on-Avon
 6480 Thomas Abbotes [Abbots], maltster
  Jones, *Stratford*, II, 2003, pp. 67-70
 6481 Thomas Bragdon, butcher
  Jones, *Stratford*, II, 2003, pp. 65-66
 6482 Richard Leatherland
  Jones, *Stratford*, II, 2003, pp. 60-62
 6483 Timothy Marshall, maltster
  Jones, *Stratford*, II, 2003, pp. 62-64
 6484 Thomas Rogers, maltster
  Jones, *Stratford*, II, 2003, pp. 72-74
 6485 Thomas Seamey, saddler
  Jones, *Stratford*, II, 2003, pp. 71-72
 Warwick
 6486 Marye Edwardes [Mary Edwards], widow
  Jones, *Stratford*, II, 2003, pp. 66-67

Wiltshire
 Marlborough
 6487 John Blake, carpenter
  Williams and Thomson, *Marlborough*, 2007, p. 87
 6488 Elianor Browne, widow
  Williams and Thomson, *Marlborough*, 2007, p. 90
 6489 Thomas Chepman alias Hitchcock
  Williams and Thomson, *Marlborough*, 2007, pp. 89-90
 6490 James Gibbes, tucker
  Williams and Thomson, *Marlborough*, 2007, p. 88
 6491 John Hilliar
  Williams and Thomson, *Marlborough*, 2007, p. 85
 6492 John Rogers, shoemaker
  Williams and Thomson, *Marlborough*, 2007, p. 87
 6493 John Sinbury, heelmaker
  Williams and Thomson, *Marlborough*, 2007, pp. 88-89

Worcestershire
 Chaddesley Corbett, Drayton
 6494 Thomas Hill
  Roper, *Chaddesley Corbett*, 1971, pp. 64-65
 6495 John Penn, [yeoman]
  Roper, *Chaddesley Corbett*, 1971, pp. 63-64

Yorkshire
 Aysgarth, Skellgill
 6496 Richard Coates
  Thwaite, *Abbotside*, 1967, pp. 59-60
 Eldwick, Bingley
 6497 William Bearce
  Preston, *Co. York*, 1929, pp. 116-117
 Swinsty Hall
 6498 Henry Robinson, gentleman
  Brears, *Yorkshire*, 1972, pp. 89-92

1640

Bristol
 Bristol, St Leonard
 6499 John Guy, gentleman
  George, *Bristol*, 1, 2002, pp. 119-120
 Bristol, Redcliffe
 6500 Thomas Palmer, clerk, vicar of St Mary Redcliffe
 and St Thomas
  George, *Bristol*, 1, 2002, pp. 117-118

Bristol, St Thomas
  6501 John Pearson, [baker]
  George, *Bristol*, 1, 2002, pp. 120-121
Bristol, St John
  6502 Robert Willsheare, tailor
  George, *Bristol*, 1, 2002, pp. 118-119
Shirehampton
  6503 William Matthews, mariner
  Moore, *Clifton*, 1981, pp. 79-80
Cheshire
Christleton
  6504 Robart Cotgrave
  Bland, *Christleton*, 2005, pp. 689-691
Combermere
  6505 Andrew Cotton, gentleman
  Pixton, *Wrenbury*, 2009, p. 344
Hale
  6506 John Brundeth
  Groves, *Hale 1*, 2005, pp. 95-96
  6507 Alice Harding
  Groves, *Hale 1*, 2005, p. 97
Nantwich
  6508 Geoffrey Cragge, yeoman
  Cockcroft, *Nantwich*, 1999, p. 94.2
  6509 Edmund Myles, innholder
  Cockcroft, *Nantwich*, 1999, pp. 230.3-5
Tarvin, Foulk Stapleford alias Hargrave
  6510 Raph Buckley, [husbandman]
  Bland, *Christleton*, 2005, p. 695
Tarvin, Ashton
  6511 William Thomasson, husbandman
  Bland, *Christleton*, 2005, p. 691
Tattenhall, Holestiche
  6512 Thomas Dod
  Bland, *Christleton*, 2005, pp. 702-703
Tattenhall
  6513 John Kerfoote, webster
  Bland, *Christleton*, 2005, pp. 639-694
  6514 Randull Lowe
  Bland, *Christleton*, 2005, pp. 699-700
  6515 Luke Yonge
  Bland, *Christleton*, 2005, pp. p. 691-692
Waverton, Huxley
  6516 Richard Bruen, yeoman
  Bland, *Christleton*, 2005, pp. 698-699
  6517 George Large, yeoman
  Bland, *Christleton*, 2005, pp. 696-697
Wrenbury, Newhall
  6518 Thomas Gray, [yeoman]
  Pixton, *Wrenbury*, 2009, p. 347
Derbyshire
Chesterfield
  6519 Robert Redferne, yeoman
  Bestall and Fowkes, *Chesterfield*, 2001, pp. 352-354
  6520 Mary Whitehead, widow
  Bestall and Fowkes, *Chesterfield*, 2001, pp. 354-355
Newbold
  6521 Nicholas Chowe, yeoman
  Bestall and Fowkes, *Chesterfield*, 2001, pp. 371-372
Devonshire
Alfington
  6522 Henry Parr
  Cash, *Devon*, 1966, p. 55

Modbury
  6523 Nicholas Downey, clergyman
  Cash, *Devon*, 1966, pp. 55-56
Uffculme
  6524 Humfrey Bray, weaver
  Wyatt, *Uffculme*, 1997, pp. 81-82
Essex
Writtle
  6525 William Bearman
  Steer, *Mid-Essex*, 1969, p. 86
Gloucestershire
Hambrook
  6526 Thomas Baylie, yeoman
  Moore, *Frampton Cotterell*, 1976, pp. 70-72
Iron Acton
  6527 William Smith, [tailor]
  Moore, *Frampton Cotterell*, 1976, p. 73
Hertfordshire
Kings Langley
  6528 Elizabeth Dowse, widow
  Munby, *Kings Langley*, 1981, p. 102
St Albans, St Stephens, The Millhouse
  6529 William Ewer, yeoman
  Munby, *Worldly Goods*, 1991, pp. 134-135
St Albans, St Stephens
  6530 Thomas Mathew, tailor
  Parker, *Worldly Goods*, 2004, p. 244
  6531 Robert Skeale
  Munby, *Worldly Goods*, 1991, p. 136
Ireland
Waterford
  6532 John Skiddie senior and John Skiddie junior
  Walton, *Waterford*, 1978, pp. 100-105
Kent
Sandwich, Free Grammar School
  6533 James Smyth, schoolmaster
  Boys, 1792, pp. 238-241
Leicestershire
Evington
  6534 Richard Butler, blacksmith
  Wilshere, *Evington*, 1985, p. 26
  6535 Anthony Clarke, [labourer]
  Wilshere, *Evington*, 1985, p. 26
Lincolnshire
Allington
  6536 Thomas Milner, carpenter
  Pask, *Allington*, 1989, p. 75
Clee, Weelsby
  6537 Marie Hudson
  Ambler, Watkinson, *Clee*, 1987, p. 150
Clee, Itterby
  6538 Hugh Tompson, petty chapman
  Ambler, Watkinson, *Clee*, 1987, pp. 150-151
Norfolk
Aylsham
  6539 Edmund Wattes, baker
  Aylsham, 1988, pp. 128-130
Oxfordshire
Banbury
  6540 Barbary [Barbara] Box[e] [Bookep], widow
  Brinkworth and Gibson, *Banbury*, II, 1976, p. 143

6541 Mary Kinch [Chinch] widow and Jeremiah Kinch, [tailor]
  Brinkworth and Gibson, *Banbury*, II, 1976, pp. 142-143
6542 Abel[l] Nicholes [Niccols], innholder
  Brinkworth and Gibson, *Banbury*, II, 1976, pp. 144-145
6543 Richard Rainbow [Rainbooe]
  Brinkworth and Gibson, *Banbury*, II, 1976, p. 142
Water Eaton
  6544 Thomas Meere, [yeoman]
  Offord, *Water Eaton*, 1986, pp. 22-23

Scotland
Dumfriess, Caerlaverock Castle
  6545 Lt Col. John Home
  Fraser, 1873, pp. 503-504
  6546 Robert, Lord Maxwell, Earl of Nithsdale
  Fraser, 1873, pp. 502-503
Edinburgh
  6547 Jonat Mayne, widow
  Anon., *Bassandyne*, 1836, pp. 253-254
Perthshire, Balloch Castle
  6548 Sir Colin Campbell, baronet (also listed Finlarg Castle)
  Innes, 1855, pp. 346-351
Perthshire, Finlarg Castle
  Sir Colin Campbell (see Balloch Castle)

Staffordshire
Dudley, St Thomas
  6549 John Bache, [yeoman]
  Roper, *Dudley*, 1968, p. 23

Sussex
Coldwaltham
  6550 William Jeoffrey, clergyman
  Hughes, *Sussex*, 2007, p. 53
Nuthurst
  6551 William Andrewes, clergyman [rector of Nuthurst]
  Hughes, *Sussex*, 2007, pp. 153-154

Warwickshire
Alcester
  6552 Elinor Bowyer, [widow]
  Saville, *Alcester*, 1979, pp. 6-7
Ashow
  6553 George Hubbold, [yeoman]
  Alcock, *Warwickshire*, 1993, p. 166
Stoneleigh
  6554 Richard Hargrave, husbandman
  Alcock, *Warwickshire*, 1993, p. 143
Stratford-on-Avon
  6555 Anne Dawkes, widow
  Jones, *Stratford*, II, 2003, pp. 75-76

Wiltshire
Marlborough
  6556 William Brewtie, innholder
  Williams and Thomson, *Marlborough*, 2007, pp. 90-92
  6557 Elizabeth Newman
  Williams and Thomson, *Marlborough*, 2007, p. 92

Worcestershire
Chaddesley Corbett
  6558 Thomas Jordan
  Roper, *Chaddesley Corbett*, 1971, pp. 65-66

Yorkshire
Greenhill, Bingley
  6559 Anne Watters, widow
  Preston, *Co. York*, 1929, pp. 118-119

1641
Bristol
Bristol, St Stephen
  6560 Edward Everard, shipwright
  George, *Bristol*, 1, 2002, pp. 122-123
Bristol, Christchurch
  6561 Mary Reade, widow, soap-maker
  George, *Bristol*, 1, 2002, pp. 123-124
Clifton
  6562 Thomas Eyton, [husbandman]
  Moore, *Clifton*, 1981, pp. 80-81
Westbury
  6563 John Jennings, tailor
  Moore, *Clifton*, 1981, p. 81

Cheshire
Ashton-on-Mersey
  6564 George Renshaw, husbandman
  Groves, *Ashton-on-Mersey and Sale*, 1999, pp. 79-80
Bowdon
  6565 Edmund Simpson, gentleman
  Groves, *Bowdon*, 1997, pp. 53-54
Christleton
  6566 John Golborne, gentleman
  Bland, *Christleton*, 2005, pp. 720-724
Hale, Ringway
  6567 William Coppock
  Groves, *Hale 2*, 2005, p. 21
Nantwich
  6568 Ann Buckley, widow
  Cockcroft, *Nantwich*, 1999, p. 55.2
  6569 Richard Gouldsmith, gentleman
  Cockcroft, *Nantwich*, 1999, pp. 138.4-6
  6570 Thomas Jackson
  Cockcroft, *Nantwich*, 1999, pp. 169.1-3
  6571 William Pickering, miller
  Cockcroft, *Nantwich*, 1999, p. 250.1
Tarvin, Kelsall
  6572 Allice Worrall, widow
  Bland, *Christleton*, 2005, pp. 704-705
Tattenhall, Golborne Bellow
  6573 Dorothy Astle, widow
  Bland, *Christleton*, 2005, pp. 705-706
Tattenhall
  6574 Thomas Hall, yeoman
  Bland, *Christleton*, 2005, pp. 707-708
Waverton, Hatton
  6575 Anne Lowe
  Bland, *Christleton*, 2005, p. 709
Wrenbury, Broomhall
  6576 John Anckers, [yeoman]
  Pixton, *Wrenbury*, 2009, pp. 376-377
Wrenbury, Newhall, The Royals
  6577 Robert Shrowbridge, [yeoman]
  Pixton, *Wrenbury*, 2009, pp. 373-374

Derbyshire
Chesterfield
  6578 Raphe Ashe, gentleman
  Bestall and Fowkes, *Chesterfield*, 2001, pp. 357-361
  6579 Thomas Barlow, yeoman
  Bestall and Fowkes, *Chesterfield*, 2001, p. 355
  6580 William Goodwin, weaver
  Bestall and Fowkes, *Chesterfield*, 2001, pp. 356-357

Devonshire
Exeter, St Edmunds
  6581 Stephen Austyn, dyer
    Cash, *Devon*, 1966, p. 60
    Portman, *Exeter*, 1966, pp. 115-116
Huish
  6582 Leonard Yeo
    Cash, *Devon*, 1966, pp. 57-59
Sandford
  6583 Frances Northcott, widow
    Cash, *Devon*, 1966, p. 56
  6584 Thomas Reed, husbandman
    Cash, *Devon*, 1966, pp. 56-57
Uffculme
  6585 Edward Branch, [schoolmaster]
    Wyatt, *Uffculme*, 1997, pp. 83-84
  6586 John Osmond [Ossmond], husbandman
    Wyatt, *Uffculme*, 1997, p. 82
  6587 Bartholomew Rawlins, yeoman
    Wyatt, *Uffculme*, 1997, pp. 82-83
Dorsetshire
Leigh
  6588 Thomas Rogers, mason
    Machin, *Yetminster*, 1976, No.28, (2 pp.)
Yetminster
  6589 Agnes Greenfield, widow
    Machin, *Yetminster*, 1976, No.29, (1 p.)
Gloucestershire
Hambrook
  6590 Nicholas Haines, miller
    Moore, *Frampton Cotterell*, 1976, p. 75
  6591 Ann Weblie, widow
    Moore, *Frampton Cotterell*, 1976, p. 73
Stoke Gifford
  6592 Robert Lawford, yeoman [schoolmaster]
    Moore, *Frampton Cotterell*, 1976, pp. 74-75
Hertfordshire
Hitchin, Hitch Wood
  6593 Roberd Myles, yeoman
    Anon., *Lock, Stock*, 1978, pp. 62-64
Kings Langley
  6594 Robart Sharpe
    Munby, *Kings Langley*, 1981, p. 105
St Albans, St Stephens
  6595 William Edmonds, yeoman
    Munby, *Worldly Goods*, 1991, pp. 138-139
Watford, Waterdell
  6596 Christopher Woodward
    Munby, *Worldly Goods*, 1991, pp. 140-141
Leicestershire
Evington
  6597 William Tafts, [labourer]
    Wilshere, *Evington*, 1985, p. 27
London
Tart Hall
  6598 Alethea Talbot, Countess of Arundel
    Cust, 1911, II, pp. 98-100, III, pp. 233-236, IV, pp. 341-343
Nottinghamshire
Cropwell Butler
  6599 John Smith [Smyth], [yeoman]
    Smith, 1861, p. 15v

Scotland
Edinburgh
  6600 John Writton, printer
    Anon., *Bassandyne*, 1836, pp. 255-256
Staffordshire
Dudley
  6601 John Cookse
    Roper, *Dudley*, 1968, p. 24
  6602 Alice Parkeshowse, widow
    Roper, *Dudley*, 1968, pp. 24-25
Sussex
Selham
  6603 John Prichard, clergyman [rector of Selham]
    Hughes, *Sussex*, 2007, pp. 184-185
Warwickshire
Stoneleigh
  6604 Susanna Colman
    Alcock, *Warwickshire*, 1993, p. 165
Wiltshire
Marlborough
  6605 William Haies, baker
    Williams and Thomson, *Marlborough*, 2007, pp. 95-96
  6606 Walter Jeffrys, baker
    Williams and Thomson, *Marlborough*, 2007, pp. 93-95
  6607 Jone Jones, widow
    Williams and Thomson, *Marlborough*, 2007, p. 95
Worcestershire
Chaddesley Corbett
  6608 John Biddle, yeoman
    Roper, *Chaddesley Corbett*, 1971, p. 70
  6609 Dorothie Pursell, widow
    Roper, *Chaddesley Corbett*, 1971, p. 67
Chaddesley Corbett, Cakebole
  6610 Thomas Turnor, [husbandman]
    Roper, *Chaddesley Corbett*, 1971, pp. 67-69
Holt Castle
  6611 Sir Thomas Bromley
    Wanklyn, *Worcestershire*, 1998, pp. 167-171
Yorkshire
Allerton, Bradford, Fairweather Green
  6612 Abraham Sutcliffe, yeoman
    Preston, *Co. York*, 1929, pp. 122-124
Aysgarth, Grange
  6613 Roger Metcalf [Metcalfe]
    Thwaite, *Abbotside*, 1967, p. 60
Cottingley, Bingley (now Bradford)
  6614 William Leache
    Preston, *Co. York*, 1929, pp. 119-120
Pudsey, Calverley
  6615 William Gaunt
    Preston, *Co. York*, 1929, pp. 131-132

1641 (c.)
Wiltshire
Marlborough
  6616 Thomas Blisset
    Williams and Thomson, *Marlborough*, 2007, pp. 96-97

1642
Bristol
Bristol, St Augustine
  6617 Richard Brace, gentleman, physician
    George, *Bristol*, 1, 2002, pp. 125-129

Bristol, St Nicholas
6618 Elizabeth Burgesse [Burges], widow
George, *Bristol*, 1, 2002, p. 125
Shirehampton
6619 Joan Taylor, [widow]
Moore, *Clifton*, 1981, p. 82

Cheshire
Christleton
6620 Raphe Sellor, yeoman
Bland, *Christleton*, 2005, pp. 728-729
Hale
6621 Edward Worsley, [yeoman]
Groves, *Hale 2*, 2005, pp. 22-23
Nantwich
6622 John Elcock, yeoman
Cockcroft, *Nantwich*, 1999, pp. 124.3-4
6623 John Ravenscroft, feltmaker
Cockcroft, *Nantwich*, 1999, pp. 264.2-4
6624 Richard Sare, ostler
Cockcroft, *Nantwich*, 1999, p. 276.2
Tarvin, Foulk Stapleford
6625 Mary Bore, widow
Bland, *Christleton*, 2005, p. 730
Tattenhall, Golborne Bellow
6626 John Buckley
Bland, *Christleton*, 2005, p. 732
Wrenbuty, Coole Lane
6627 Rowland Sallmon [Salmon], [yeoman]
Pixton, *Wrenbury*, 2009, p. 381
Wrenbury
6628 Katherine Savage
Pixton, *Wrenbury*, 2009, pp. 378-379
Wrenbury, Chorley
6629 John Woodfen, [yeoman]
Pixton, *Wrenbury*, 2009, pp. 382-384

Derbyshire
Ashbourne
6630 Willm Titterton, shoemaker
Dack, 2007, pp. 27-28
Brimington
6631 John Bagshall
Bestall and Fowkes, *Chesterfield*, 2001, pp. 361-362
Chesterfield
6632 Thomas Tidman, yeoman
Bestall and Fowkes, *Chesterfield*, 2001, p. 386
6633 Robert Travis
Bestall and Fowkes, *Chesterfield*, 2001, pp. 362-366

Devonshire
Bere Ferrers
6634 Nathaniel Edgcomb, yeoman
Cash, *Devon*, 1966, pp. 62-63
Crediton
6635 Phillip Stevens, white baker
Cash, *Devon*, 1966, pp. 60-61
Uffculme
6636 Agnes Dowdney
Wyatt, *Uffculme*, 1997, p. 84
West Teignmouth
6637 Samuel Taply, mariner
Cash, *Devon*, 1966, pp. 61-62

Gloucestershire
Stoke Gifford
6638 John Vidler, husbandman
Moore, *Frampton Cotterell*, 1976, pp. 75-76

Hertfordshire
Abbots Langley
6639 John Carter, yeoman
Munby, *Kings Langley*, 1981, pp. 106-107
Chipperfield
6640 Willyam Feilde [William Field], carpenter
Munby, *Kings Langley*, 1981, pp. 108-109
Kings Langley
6641 William Nutkin, miller
Munby, *Kings Langley*, 1981, p. 119
St Albans, St Stephens
6642 Christopher Arland, yeoman
Parker, *Worldly Goods*, 2004, pp. 245-246
6643 William Stretley, parish clerk
Parker, *Worldly Goods*, 2004, p. 247

Ireland
Co. Limerick, Castletown-Waller
6644 Sir Hardress Waller
Seymour, 1909-1911, pp. 256-258

Lancashire
Flookburgh, Canon Winder Hall
6645 Mrs Ann Preston
Hudleston, 1987, pp. 163-164
Newton in Furness
6646 John Preston
Earwaker, *Lancashire and Cheshire*, 1893, pp. 223-225

Leicestershire
Evington
6647 Roger Slater, weaver
Wilshere, *Evington*, 1985, p. 27

Norfolk
Wymondham
6648 John Toole, blacksmith
Wilson, *Wymondham*, 1983, pp. 28-29

Northumberland
Harbottle
6649 Roger Widdrington, esquire
Raine, *North Durham*, 1852, pp. 222-223
Wood, *Wills and Inventories*, 1929, IV, pp. 287-290
Newcastle-on-Tyne, St John's
6650 William Mackerrell alias Macwell [?],
[chapman]
Spufford, *Reclothing*, 1984, pp. 186-190

Oxfordshire
Banbury
6651 John Bloxham, husbandman
Brinkworth and Gibson, *Banbury*, II, 1976, p. 146

Scotland
Edinburgh
6652 James Bryssone, printer
Anon., *Bassandyne*, 1836, pp. 259-262
6653 Jonet Kene, widow
Anon., *Bassandyne*, 1836, pp. 257-258

Staffordshire
Dudley, St Edmund's
6654 Richarde Hues
Roper, *Dudley*, 1968, p. 25
Dudley
6655 Anne Wiley
Roper, *Dudley*, 1968, p. 26
Lichfield
6656 Nicholas Scott, corviser
Vaisey, *Lichfield*, 1969, p. 60

Sussex
 Horsham
  6657 John Collins, clergyman [vicar of Horsham]
   Hughes, *Sussex*, 2007, pp. 107-111
Wiltshire
 Marlborough
  6658 Thomas Paty, yeoman
   Williams and Thomson, *Marlborough*, 2007, pp. 97-98
Worcestershire
 Daylesford
  6659 Mrs Susan Hastings, widow
   Wanklyn, *Worcestershire*, 1998, pp. 171-172
 South Littleton
  6660 John Keightley, esquire
   Wanklyn, *Worcestershire*, 1998, pp. 172-173
Yorkshire
 South Cave, Broomfleet
  6661 Thomas Lister
   Kaner, *South Cave*, 1994, pp. 346-347

1643
Bristol
 Bristol, St Thomas
  6662 Barnard Benson, pewterer
   George, *Bristol*, 1, 2002, pp. 141-144
 Bristol, St Stephen
  6663 Frances Bumsted, widow
   George, *Bristol*, 1, 2002, pp. 140-141
 Bristol, St Philip and St Jacob
  6664 Thomas Collins
   George, *Bristol*, 1, 2002, pp. 130-131
 Bristol, St Stephen
  6665 John Horsam [Horsham], ship carpenter
   George, *Bristol*, 1, 2002, pp. 137-139
  6666 Frauncis [Francis] Johnson, gentleman
   George, *Bristol*, 1, 2002, pp. 132-134
  6667 Henry Marston, parish clerk
   George, *Bristol*, 1, 2002, pp. 135-136
 Bristol, St Mary-le-Port
  6668 Robert Robbins, shoemaker, and Agatha Robbins
   George, *Bristol*, 1, 2002, pp. 131-132
 Bristol, Temple
  6669 Edward Tolston, [clothworker]
   George, *Bristol*, 1, 2002, pp. 129-130
 Bristol, St Werburgh
  6670 Erasmus Wright, merchant
   George, *Bristol*, 1, 2002, pp. 144-145
 Bristol, St Mary-le-Port
  6671 Thomas Yate, baker
   George, *Bristol*, 1, 2002, pp. 134-135
Cheshire
 Beeston
  6672 William Mynshull, [gentleman]
   Anon., *Minshull*, 1920, pp. 98-99
 Nantwich
  6673 Richard Harware, apothecary
   Cockcroft, *Nantwich*, 1999, pp. 150.1-2
  6674 George Smith, gentleman
   Cockcroft, *Nantwich*, 1999, pp. 288.3-4
 Tarvin, Ashton
  6675 Raphe Holland
   Bland, *Christleton*, 2005, p. 733

  6676 Petter Leadbeatter
   Bland, *Christleton*, 2005, p. 734
Derbyshire
 Chesterfield
  6677 Godfrey Heathcote, gentleman, alderman
   Bestall and Fowkes, *Chesterfield*, 2001, pp. 366-369
 Chesterfield, Dunston
  6678 Thomas Poynton, yeoman
   Bestall and Fowkes, *Chesterfield*, 2001, pp. 369-370
Devonshire
 Bishopsteignton
  6679 Gregory Babb, husbandman
   Cash, *Devon*, 1966, pp. 66-67
 Chudleigh
  6680 Elizabeth Bissett
   Cash, *Devon*, 1966, p. 67
  6681 Richard Boggan, gentleman
   Cash, *Devon*, 1966, p. 67
 Crediton
  6682 Robert Clase, yeoman
   Cash, *Devon*, 1966, pp. 63-64
  6683 Robert Dicleg, husbandman
   Cash, *Devon*, 1966, pp. 64-65
  6684 Mary Thomas, widow
   Cash, *Devon*, 1966, p. 71
 Plymtree
  6685 Henry and Joan White
   Cash, *Devon*, 1966, p. 69
 Silverton
  6686 Henry Furse
   Cash, *Devon*, 1966, p. 66
 Tavistock
  6687 William Browne, butcher
   Cash, *Devon*, 1966, p. 63
 Unlocated
  6688 Pancras Colline
   Cash, *Devon*, 1966, p. 72
  6689 Mr Thomas Hayman [?]
   Cash, *Devon*, 1966, p. 72
 Upton Hellions
  6690 Phillip Buckingham
   Cash, *Devon*, 1966, pp. 70-71
 Whimple
  6691 Faith Knight, widow
   Cash, *Devon*, 1966, pp. 68-69
 Zeal Monachorum
  6692 Humfry Harvie, yeoman
   Cash, *Devon*, 1966, pp. 65-66
Hertfordshire
 Kings Langley
  6693 Robert Cater, yeoman
   Munby, *Kings Langley*, 1981, p. 112
  6694 Simon Goulde [Gould], yeoman
   Munby, *Kings Langley*, 1981, pp. 114-115
 Kings Langley [?]
  6695 [Nathan Hill]
   Munby, *Kings Langley*, 1981, p. 113
 Kings Langley
  6696 William Weeden [Weedon], yeoman
   Munby, *Kings Langley*, 1981, pp. 110-111
 St Albans, St Stephens
  6697 Beniamyne Fuller
   Parker, *Worldly Goods*, 2004, pp. 249-250

London

Ironmongers' Hall
6698 Company of Ironmongers
Nicholl, 1851, pp. 453-457
Strand, Worcester House
6699 Henry Somerset, Earl and Marquess of Worcester
Madge, 1945, pp. 170-180

Oxfordshire

Banbury
6700 Titus Buckingham, blacksmith
Brinkworth and Gibson, *Banbury*, II, 1976, pp. 148-149
6701 Edward Edens, gentleman, Town Clerk of Banbury
Brinkworth and Gibson, *Banbury*, II, 1976, pp. 150-151
6702 John Heynes [Haines], mercer
Brinkworth and Gibson, *Banbury*, II, 1976, pp. 151-152
6703 Thomas Perkins, glover
Brinkworth and Gibson, *Banbury*, II, 1976, pp. 146-147

Staffordshire

Dudley
6704 Thomas Finch, yeoman
Roper, *Dudley*, 1968, pp. 26-27
Lichfield, St Mary
6705 Marie Lees, widow
Vaisey, *Lichfield*, 1969, pp. 60-62
Lichfield
6706 William Wensley [Wensloe], corviser
Vaisey, *Lichfield*, 1969, pp. 62-64

Sussex

Clapham
6707 Henry Nye, clergyman [rector of Clapham]
Hughes, *Sussex*, 2007, pp. 47-48
Steyning
6708 Leonard Stalman, clergyman [vicar of Steyning]
Hughes, *Sussex*, 2007, pp. 195-197

Warwickshire

Coventry
6709 Bablake Children's Hospital
Tomes, 1860, pp. 401-402
Priors Hardwick
6710 Richard Ebrall, yeoman
Sheasby, 1994, pp. 55-57

Worcestershire

Belbroughton
6711 Nicholas Bennet, scythesmith
Roper, *Scythesmiths*, 1967, p. 18
Roper, *Belbroughton*, 1967-1968, p. 71
6712 Francis Penn, [scythesmith]
Roper, *Belbroughton*, 1967-1968, p. 69
Belbroughton, The Hollies
6713 Thomas Reade, [carpenter]
Roper, *Belbroughton*, 1967-1968, p. 72-73, 74
Chaddesley Corbett, Darrall
6714 John Newey, scythesmith
Roper, *Chaddesley Corbett*, 1971, pp. 72-73
King's Norton, Hawkesley
6715 John Middlemore, esquire
Wanklyn, *Worcestershire*, 1998, pp. 173-176
Worcester
6716 Thomas Cowcher, mercer
Griffiths, 1937, pp. 48-60

Yorkshire

Cottingley, Bingley (now Bradford)
6717 Anne Kighley
Preston, *Co. York*, 1929, pp. 130-131
Pudsey, Calverley
6718 Richard Hill, yeoman
Preston, *Co. York*, 1929, pp. 127-129
Roydfield, Bingley (?)
6719 William Farah
Preston, *Co. York*, 1929, p. 134

1644

Bedfordshire

Ampthill
6720 Robert Huett
Blaydes, *Popish Recusants*, 1887-1889, p. 190
Bedford
6721 Xpofer Turner, gentleman
Blaydes, *Popish Recusants*, 1887-1889, pp. 181-182
6722 Mr William Yarwey
Blaydes, *Popish Recusants*, 1887-1889, pp. 190-191
Toddington Manor
6723 Sir Thomas Wentworth, Earl of Cleveland
Blaydes, *Popish Recusants*, 1887-1889, pp. 194-197
Blundell, 1927, pp. 130-136
Unlocated
6724 Sir Francis Crawley
Blaydes, *Popish Recusants*, 1887-1889, pp. 191-192
6725 Richard Conquest, esquire
Blaydes, *Popish Recusants*, 1887-1889, p. 189
6726 Margaret Lady Mordant
Blaydes, *Popish Recusants*, 1887-1889, pp. 184-186
6727 Sir Peter Osborne
Blaydes, *Popish Recusants*, 1887-1889, pp. 187-189
6728 Sir William Palmer
Blaydes, *Popish Recusants*, 1887-1889, pp. 182-184
6729 Mr Spencer Potts
Blaydes, *Popish Recusants*, 1887-1889, p. 186
6730 Mr Peter Richardson
Blaydes, *Popish Recusants*, 1887-1889, p. 189
6731 Mr Richard Watson
Blaydes, *Popish Recusants*, 1887-1889, pp. 192-193

Bristol

Bristol, St Nicholas
6732 Alexander Kerswell, woollen draper
George, *Bristol*, 1, 2002, pp. 145-147
Clifton
6733 Thomas Hall, [yeoman]
Moore, *Clifton*, 1981, p. 85
Shirehampton
6734 Thomas Collins, yeoman
Moore, *Clifton*, 1981, pp. 83-85
Westbury
6735 Martha Cox, widow
Moore, *Clifton*, 1981, pp. 82-83

Buckinghamshire

Bowstridge
6736 William Knight, yeoman
Munby, *Kings Langley*, 1981, p. 118

Cheshire

Hale
6737 Roger Johnson, [yeoman]
Groves, *Hale 2*, 2005, p. 25

Nantwich
  6738 John Beckett
    Cockcroft, *Nantwich*, 1999, pp. 23.1-2
  6739 Phoebe Bennett
    Cockcroft, *Nantwich*, 1999, p. 27.1
  6740 Joyce Chapman, widow
    Cockcroft, *Nantwich*, 1999, pp. 64.2-3
Tarvin, Foulk Stapleford
  6741 Gervase Percivall, schoolmaster
    Bland, *Christleton*, 2005, p. 737
Wrenbury cum Frith
  6742 Richard Culliner alias Comber, [labourer]
    Pixton, *Wrenbury*, 2009, p. 386
Cornwall
Antony
  6743 Sir Allexander Carew, baronet
    Andrew, *Carew*, 1942-1946, pp. 41-42
Derbyshire
Chesterfield
  6744 James Brough, husbandman
    Bestall and Fowkes, *Chesterfield*, 2001, p. 379
  6745 Cuthbert Petty, clothworker
    Bestall and Fowkes, *Chesterfield*, 2001, pp. 394-395
Devonshire
Coryton
  6746 Walter Hollock, yeoman
    Cash, *Devon*, 1966, p. 75
Crediton
  6747 John Cleife
    Cash, *Devon*, 1966, pp. 76-77
Dartmouth, Townstal
  6748 Walter Wotton, gentleman
    Cash, *Devon*, 1966, p. 74
Lydford
  6749 Margery Tuddy
    Cash, *Devon*, 1966, p. 74
Milton Abbot
  6750 Nicoll Tule [?]
    Cash, *Devon*, 1966, p. 73
South Sydenham [?]
  6751 Daniel Hawkins, [yeoman]
    Cash, *Devon*, 1966, p. 76
Swimbridge
  6752 Robert Rosyer, clothier
    Cash, *Devon*, 1966, p. 75
Tavistock
  6753 Stephen Dunridge, yeoman
    Cash, *Devon*, 1966, p. 73
Uffculme
  6754 William Cape
    Wyatt, *Uffculme*, 1997, pp. 84-85
  6755 Elizabeth Langbridge, [widow]
    Wyatt, *Uffculme*, 1997, p. 84
Witheridge
  6756 Hugh Upcot alias Mayre
    Cash, *Devon*, 1966, p. 77
Hertfordshire
Kings Langley
  6757 Joseph Townson, carpenter
    Munby, *Kings Langley*, 1981, p. 120
Lincolnshire
Cleethorpes
  6758 William Tuplin
    Ambler, Watkinson, *Clee*, 1987, p. 151

London
Paternoster Row
  6759 Nicholas Willmer, citizen of London [silkman]
    Foster, Green, 1888, pp. 285-287
Strand, The Mitre
  6760 Thomas Langton, [citizen and vintner]
    Shanahan, 1961, pp. 195-197
Northamptonshire
Nethercote
  6761 Thomas Slattier, yeoman
    Brinkworth and Gibson, *Banbury*, II, 1976, pp. 152-153
Oxfordshire
Banbury
  6762 Thomas Middleton, baker
    Brinkworth and Gibson, *Banbury*, II, 1976, pp. 153-154
Staffordshire
Dudley
  6763 William Hill, nailer
    Roper, *Dudley*, 1968, pp. 27-28
Suffolk
Hengrave
  6764 Mary, Countess Rivers
    Hardy, 1906, pp. 35-51\
Sussex
Ford
  6765 John Marshall, clergyman [rector of Ford]
    Hughes, *Sussex*, 2007, p. 82
Warbleton
  6766 Edward Tredcroft, clergyman [vicar of Warbleton]
    Hughes, *Sussex*, 2007, pp. 223-226
West Grinstead
  6767 Samuel Dowlin, clergyman
    Hughes, *Sussex*, 2007, p. 98
Wiltshire
Marlborough
  6768 Richard Cornwall, shoemaker
    Williams and Thomson, *Marlborough*, 2007, p. 98
  6769 Gregory Yeomans
    Williams and Thomson, *Marlborough*, 2007, pp. 98-99
Worcestershire
Chaddesley Corbett, Yieldingtree
  6770 Frauncis Barnett, yeoman
    Roper, *Chaddesley Corbett*, 1971, pp. 71-72
Yorkshire
Whitley
  6771 Major Thomas Beaumont
    Macray, 1884, pp. 93-96

1645
Bristol
Bristol, Christchurch
  6772 Elizabeth Lymell, widow
    George, *Bristol*, 1, 2002, pp. 151-153
Bristol, St Augustine
  6773 Israell [Israel] Pownell, gentleman
    George, *Bristol*, 1, 2002, pp. 148-151
Clifton
  6774 George Clarke, yeoman
    Moore, *Clifton*, 1981, p. 86
Cheshire
Nantwich
  6775 Thomas Walthall, gentleman
    Cockcroft, *Nantwich*, 1999, pp. 325.2-3

Devonshire
Crediton
  6776 Philip Elston
    Cash, *Devon*, 1966, pp. 79-80
Lynton
  6777 John Vallacott
    Cash, *Devon*, 1966, p. 79
Morchard Bishop
  6778 John Beare, gentleman
    Cash, *Devon*, 1966, pp. 77-78
Moretonhampstead
  6779 Richard Rennolls
    Cash, *Devon*, 1966, p. 78
Tavistock
  6780 Rober Chubb
    Cash, *Devon*, 1966, p. 77
Tawstock
  6781 John Marchant
    Cash, *Devon*, 1966, pp. 78-79
Uffculme
  6782 Ambrose Cottrell [Cotterell], weaver
    Wyatt, *Uffculme*, 1997, pp. 86-87
  6783 Bartholomew Dowdney
    Wyatt, *Uffculme*, 1997, pp. 87-88
  6784 Nicholas Dowdney [Dowdeney]
    Wyatt, *Uffculme*, 1997, p. 86
Unlocated
  6785 Joane Sparke, widow
    Cash, *Devon*, 1966, pp. 80-81
West Worlington
  6786 Francis Coale
    Cash, *Devon*, 1966, pp. 81-82
Guernsey
Vingtaine de Nermont, Fief Vaugrat
  6787 Estienne Laisné
    Moullin, 1946, p. 196-203
Hertfordshire
Kings Langley
  6788 William Heydon [Haydon], butcher
    Munby, *Kings Langley*, 1981, pp. 121-122
Ireland
County Antrim, Dunluce Castle
  6789 Katherine, Duchess of Buckingham
    MacDonnell, 1992, pp. 116-127
Dublin, Cork House
  6790 Richard Boyle, Earl of Cork
    Fenlon, *Ireland*, 2003, pp. 32-34
Kent
Knole
  6791 Edward Sackville, Earl of Dorset
    Phillips, 1929, pp. 353-366
Leicestershire
Kirby Muxloe
  6792 Thomas Chapman, [victualler]
    Wilshere, *Kirby Muxloe*, 1983, p. 10
Northumberland
Lilburn
  6793 Ephraim Proctor, gentleman
    Wood, *Wills and Inventories*, 1929, IV, pp. 306-307
Oxfordshire
Banbury, Neithrop
  6794 Thomas Cornack [Curnock], husbandman
    Brinkworth and Gibson, *Banbury*, II, 1976, pp. 159-160

Banbury
  6795 Robert Gascoyne [Gascaigne], fellmonger, glover
    Brinkworth and Gibson, *Banbury*, II, 1976, pp. 155-156
  6796 Margaret[t] Heynes [Haines], widow
    Brinkworth and Gibson, *Banbury*, II, 1976, p. 158
Banbury, Calthorpe
  6797 John Sheppard [Sheapard], maltster
    Brinkworth and Gibson, *Banbury*, II, 1976, p. 160
Banbury, Neithrop
  6798 Nathaniel[l] Youick[e], yeoman
    Brinkworth and Gibson, *Banbury*, II, 1976, pp. 156-157
Scotland
Edinburgh
  6799 Thomas Lawsone, bookseller
    Anon., *Bassandyne*, 1836, pp. 267-270
Staffordshire
Dudley
  6800 John Jenkins, yeoman
    Roper, *Dudley*, 1968, pp. 28-29
Sussex
Nuthurst
  6801 George Edgly, clergyman [rector of Nuthurst]
    Hughes, *Sussex*, 2007, pp. 154-156
Wiltshire
Marlborough
  6802 Ralfe Titcombe, shoemaker
    Williams and Thomson, *Marlborough*, 2007, p. 99
Worcestershire
Belbroughton
  6803 Nicholas Bennet, [scythesmith]
    Roper, *Scythesmiths*, 1967, p. 18
Chaddesley Corbett, Drayton
  6804 [Bridgett] Deanes, widow
    Roper, *Chaddesley Corbett*, 1971, p. 74
Chaddesley Corbett, Yieldingtree
  6805 Francis Smith, yeoman
    Roper, *Chaddesley Corbett*, 1971, pp. 78-79
Chaddesley Corbett, Brockencote
  6806 Alice Taylor, widow
    Roper, *Chaddesley Corbett*, 1971, p. 75

1645 (c.)
Wiltshire
Marlborough
  6807 [Izard Lawrence], widow
    Williams and Thomson, *Marlborough*, 2007, pp. 99-100

1646
Bristol
Bristol, St Thomas
  6808 Mary Benson, widow
    George, *Bristol*, 1, 2002, pp. 155-157
Bristol
  6809 Bridgett Wilkes, widow
    George, *Bristol*, 1, 2002, pp. 153-154
Westbury
  6810 Christopher Worley, yeoman
    Moore, *Clifton*, 1981, p. 86
Cheshire
Chester, Lady Grosvenor's House
  6811 Sir William Brereton, baronet
    Carr and Atherton, 2007, pp. 295-298

Hale
  6812 Henry Hard, [husbandman]
    Groves, *Hale 2*, 2005, p. 24
  6813 Alice Royle, [widow]
    Groves, *Hale 2*, 2005, p. 26
Nantwich
  6814 John Clemens, yeoman
    Cockcroft, *Nantwich*, 1999, pp. 75.2-3
  6815 Margaret Cliffe
    Cockcroft, *Nantwich*, 1999, p. 77.2
  6816 William Lea
    Cockcroft, *Nantwich*, 1999, pp. 186.1-3
Wrenbury, Newhall, Aston
  6817 Richard Barnett, [yeoman]
    Pixton, *Wrenbury*, 2009, pp. 404-405
Derbyshire
Chesterfield
  6818 Roger Breathwaite, barber-surgeon
    Bestall and Fowkes, *Chesterfield*, 2001, pp. 376-378
  6819 Roger Columbell, gentleman
    Bestall and Fowkes, *Chesterfield*, 2001, pp. 375-376
Chesterfield, Calow
  6820 William Fletcher, husbandman
    Bestall and Fowkes, *Chesterfield*, 2001, pp. 387-388
Chesterfield, Temple Normanton
  6821 William Hill
    Bestall and Fowkes, *Chesterfield*, 2001, pp. 370-371
Chesterfield
  6822 Anne Shaw, widow
    Bestall and Fowkes, *Chesterfield*, 2001, pp. 374-375
  6823 Gilbert Webster, tanner
    Bestall and Fowkes, *Chesterfield*, 2001, pp. 373-374
Devonshire
Barnstaple
  6824 Water Blackmore, blacksmith, and Margaret Blackmore
    Cash, *Devon*, 1966, p. 91
  6825 Thomas Pearse, weaver
    Cash, *Devon*, 1966, p. 88
Chudleigh, Farleigh
  6826 William Bawdon
    Cash, *Devon*, 1966, p. 86
Crediton
  6827 Katherine Lane
    Cash, *Devon*, 1966, pp. 82-83
Heavitree
  6828 Alce Lee
    Cash, *Devon*, 1966, p. 87
Mamhead
  6829 Richard Sainthill, clergyman
    Cash, *Devon*, 1966, pp. 86-87
Paignton
  6830 John Efford
    Cash, *Devon*, 1966, p. 88
Plymouth
  6831 John Dyar
    Cash, *Devon*, 1966, p. 91
Rewe
  6832 Jane Richards, widow
    Cash, *Devon*, 1966, pp. 89-90
Shaugh Prior
  6833 Edward Mountford, husbandman
    Cash, *Devon*, 1966, pp. 90-91

South Molton
  6834 Walter Kingsland, gentleman
    Cash, *Devon*, 1966, p. 83
Tamerton Foliot
  6835 Margaret Shourte, widow
    Cash, *Devon*, 1966, p. 82
Topsham
  6836 John Weslake, yeoman
    Cash, *Devon*, 1966, pp. 84-85
Winkleigh
  6837 John Letheren
    Cash, *Devon*, 1966, p. 91-92
Zeal Monachorum
  6838 Philip Pridam, husbandman
    Cash, *Devon*, 1966, p. 85
Gloucestershire
Charlton Kings
  6839 John Pates, gentleman
    Paget and Sale, *Charlton Kings*, 2003, p. 26
Iron Acton
  6840 Robert Gale, [carpenter]
    Moore, *Frampton Cotterell*, 1976, p. 77
  6841 Edward Marten, yeoman
    Moore, *Frampton Cotterell*, 1976, pp. 77-78
Hertfordshire
Kings Langley
  6842 John King, [yeoman]
    Munby, *Kings Langley*, 1981, pp. 124-125
Kent
Knole
  6843 Edward Sackville, Earl of Dorset
    Phillips, 1929, pp. 366-370
Leicestershire
Ratby
  6844 Willm Fletcher, yeoman
    Wilshere, *Ratby*, 1984, p. 5
Lincolnshire
Lincoln, Cathedral Close
  6845 John Crispe, vicar choral
    Maddison, 1904, pp. 87-88
Northamptonshire
Sywell
  6846 Sir William Willmer
    Ussher, 1880-1881, pp. 176-178
Oxfordshire
Banbury
  6847 George Hawtayne [Hawten], innholder
    Brinkworth and Gibson, *Banbury*, II, 1976, p. 161
Water Eaton
  6848 Joan Bricknell, widow
    Offord, *Water Eaton*, 1986, pp. 24-25
Scotland
Edinburgh
  6849 Robert Bryssoune, bookseller
    Anon., *Bassandyne*, 1836, pp. 263-266
Somersetshire
Milverton
  6850 John Norris, gentleman
    Monday and Siraut, *Somerset*, 2003, pp. 171-172
Staffordshire
Lichfield
  6851 William Meeson, shearman
    Vaisey, *Lichfield*, 1969, p. 68

Lichfield, St Mary
6852 John Pate, tanner
Vaisey, *Lichfield*, 1969, p. 67
Lichfield
6853 Thomas Thacker, fellmonger
Vaisey, *Lichfield*, 1969, pp. 64-67
Wiltshire
Marlborough
6854 Alice Wilkes, widow
Williams and Thomson, *Marlborough*, 2007, p. 100
Yorkshire
Cottingley, Bingley (now Bradford)
6855 William Franck, gentleman
Preston, *Co. York*, 1929, pp. 132-134
Roydefield, Bingley
6856 Roberte Hall
Preston, *Co. York*, 1929, pp. 161-162

1646 (c.)
Devonshire
Winkleigh
6857 Henry Gay
Cash, *Devon*, 1966, p. 90

1647
Bristol
Bristol, St Mary-le-Port
6858 Thomas Collier, innholder of the Swan
George, *Bristol*, 1, 2002, pp. 159-162
Bristol, St Thomas
6859 Judith Stibbens, widow
George, *Bristol*, 1, 2002, p. 158
Redland
6860 Henry King, [carpenter]
Moore, *Clifton*, 1981, pp. 87-88
Cheshire
Combermere
6861 Dorothy Cotton
Pixton, *Wrenbury*, 2009, pp. 393-394
6862 George Cotton, esquire
Pixton, *Wrenbury*, 2009, pp. 417-422
Hale
6863 Robert Hollinpriest, [yeoman]
Groves, *Hale 2*, 2005, pp. 27-28
Nantwich
6864 Henry Challoner, province marshal
Cockcroft, *Nantwich*, 1999, p. 63.2
6865 Ann Lea, widow
Cockcroft, *Nantwich*, 1999, pp. 184.2-3
6866 John Stringer, victualler
Cockcroft, *Nantwich*, 1999, p. 296.2
6867 John Weston, yeoman
Cockcroft, *Nantwich*, 1999, p. 330.3
Wrenbury
6868 Robert Savage, [yeoman]
Pixton, *Wrenbury*, 2009, pp. 399-400
Wrenbury cum Frith
6869 Valentine Woolrich, [yeoman]
Pixton, *Wrenbury*, 2009, pp. 396-397
Derbyshire
Chesterfield
6870 Anne Beastowe, widow
Bestall and Fowkes, *Chesterfield*, 2001, pp. 389-391
6871 Thomas Beresford
Bestall and Fowkes, *Chesterfield*, 2001, pp. 384-386

6872 John Chowe
Bestall and Fowkes, *Chesterfield*, 2001, pp. 379-381
6873 Richard Collis, butcher
Bestall and Fowkes, *Chesterfield*, 2001, pp. 396-397
6874 Richard Fletcher
Bestall and Fowkes, *Chesterfield*, 2001, pp. 388-389
Chesterfield, Walton
6875 Richard Flint, yeoman
Bestall and Fowkes, *Chesterfield*, 2001, p. 393
Chesterfield
6876 Gilbert Heathcote, fellmonger
Bestall and Fowkes, *Chesterfield*, 2001, p. 401
6877 Mary Pointon
Bestall and Fowkes, *Chesterfield*, 2001, p. 373
6878 Sarah Pointon, widow
Bestall and Fowkes, *Chesterfield*, 2001, pp. 372-373
6879 Abel Tilley, chapman
Bestall and Fowkes, *Chesterfield*, 2001, p. 392
6880 Francis Woodhouse, draper
Bestall and Fowkes, *Chesterfield*, 2001, pp. 383-384
Newbold
6881 Edmond Haslam, husbandman
Bestall and Fowkes, *Chesterfield*, 2001, pp. 381-382
Devonshire
Arlington
6882 Bartholomew Bugsleigh
Cash, *Devon*, 1966, p. 93
Barnstaple
6883 Gamaliel Hawkings
Cash, *Devon*, 1966, p. 97
6884 William Jewell, shoemaker, and Joana Jewell
Cash, *Devon*, 1966, p. 94
6885 Robert Joanes, merchant
Cash, *Devon*, 1966, p. 98
Cornwood
6886 George Gripe, soldier of the garrison of Plymouth
Cash, *Devon*, 1966, p. 94
Exeter
6887 John Levermore, gentleman
Cash, *Devon*, 1966, p. 95
Molland
6888 Philip Hosegood
Cash, *Devon*, 1966, p. 96
Pilton
6889 William Gribble, butcher
Cash, *Devon*, 1966, p. 96
6890 John Dyer and Mary Fairchilde
Cash, *Devon*, 1966, p. 95
Shebbear
6891 Roger Bridgman
Cash, *Devon*, 1966, p. 98-99
Uffculme
6892 Elizabeth Andrew, widow
Wyatt, *Uffculme*, 1997, p. 88
Gloucestershire
Iron Acton
6893 Edward Thomas, yeoman
Moore, *Frampton Cotterell*, 1976, p. 78
Northumberland
Newham
6894 Peter Bradforth
Wood, *Wills and Inventories*, 1929, IV, p. 315

Scotland
 Edinburgh
  6895 Robert Crombie, bookseller
   Anon., *Bassandyne*, 1836, pp. 270-272
Staffordshire
 Dudley
  6896 Mary Bassett
   Roper, *Dudley*, 1968, p. 29
  6897 Mary English, widow
   Roper, *Dudley*, 1968, p. 30
  6898 Margery Roades, [widow]
   Roper, *Dudley*, 1968, p. 30
  6899 Jeffery Robbinson
   Roper, *Dudley*, 1968, p. 31
 Lichfield
  6900 William Amerie
   Vaisey, *Lichfield*, 1969, pp. 69-70
  6901 Mary Atkins, widow
   Vaisey, *Lichfield*, 1969, pp. 74-75
  6902 Thomas Barker and Elizabeth Barker
   Vaisey, *Lichfield*, 1969, pp. 73-74
 Lichfield, St Mary
  6903 John Cooke, cooper, and Anne Cooper
   Vaisey, *Lichfield*, 1969, pp. 75-76
 Lichfield
  6904 Thomas Harve [Harvie], carpenter
   Vaisey, *Lichfield*, 1969, pp. 76-77
  6905 Richard Sherrard [Sherratt], tanner
   Vaisey, *Lichfield*, 1969, pp. 70-71
  6906 Isaac Smith, mason
   Vaisey, *Lichfield*, 1969, pp. 72-73
 Lichfield, St Chad
  6907 Anne Smythe [Smith], widow
   Vaisey, *Lichfield*, 1969, p. 75
 Smethwick
  6908 Thomas Cowley alias Glover, blacksmith
   Bodfish, *Smethwick*, 1992, p. 15
 Whittington
  6909 Richard Smyth, yeoman
   Vaisey, *Lichfield*, 1969, pp. 71-72
Sussex
 Elsted
  6910 John Knight, clergyman [rector of Elsted]
   Hughes, *Sussex*, 2007, pp. 70-71
 Kirdford
  6911 Mr Thomas Holland, clergyman, vicar of
   Kirdford
   Kenyon, *Kirdford*, 1956, pp. 145-148
   Hughes, *Sussex*, 2007, pp. 127-129
 Wisborough Green
  6912 Thomas Jackman, yeoman
   Lawson, 1999, pp. 66-68
 Woolavington
  6913 Daniel German, clergyman [rector of
   Woolavington]
   Hughes, *Sussex*, 2007, pp. 243-246
Warwickshire
 Stratford-on-Avon
  6914 Ann Hamner alias Bowles
   Jones, *Stratford*, II, 2003, p. 76
Worcestershire
 Belbroughton
  6915 Oswald Penn, [scythesmith]
   Roper, *Scythesmiths*, 1967, p. 19
   Roper, *Belbroughton*, 1967-1968, p. 75

Yorkshire
 Felliscliffe, White Wall
  6916 Thomas Stubb
   Collins, *Stubbs*, 1915, p. 114

1647 (c.)
Devonshire
 Unlocated
  6917 William Chambers
   Cash, *Devon*, 1966, p. 93

1648
Bristol
 Bristol, St Stephen
  6918 John Cook, mariner
   George, *Bristol*, 1, 2002, pp. 163-164
 Bristol, St Thomas
  6919 Anselm Smart, glazier
   George, *Bristol*, 1, 2002, pp. 162-163
 Shirehampton
  6920 John Clement, butcher
   Moore, *Clifton*, 1981, pp. 88-89
  6921 William Rome, husbandman
   Moore, *Clifton*, 1981, p. 89
Cheshire
 Bowdon
  6922 John Hardy, butcher
   Groves, *Bowdon*, 1997, pp. 55-57
 Combermere
  6923 Elizabeth Cotton, widow
   Pixton, *Wrenbury*, 2009, pp. 406-407
 Hale
  6924 Andrew Gardener, [yeoman]
   Groves, *Hale 2*, 2005, pp. 29-30
 Nantwich
  6925 Thomas Burch, glover
   Cockcroft, *Nantwich*, 1999, pp. 59.2-3
  6926 Robert Gaudie
   Cockcroft, *Nantwich*, 1999, p. 132.1
  6927 Edward Moore, yeoman
   Cockcroft, *Nantwich*, 1999, p. 225.1
  6928 Roger Vaughan
   Cockcroft, *Nantwich*, 1999, p. 318.3
 Wrenbury, Newhall
  6929 Randle Sproston, [husbandman]
   Pixton, *Wrenbury*, 2009, pp. 426-427
 Wrenbury
  6930 George Tench
   Pixton, *Wrenbury*, 2009, p. 424
Derbyshire
 Chesterfield
  6931 John Littlewood, labourer
   Bestall and Fowkes, *Chesterfield*, 2001, p. 402
  6932 William Stubbing, yeoman
   Bestall and Fowkes, *Chesterfield*, 2001, pp. 397-398
Devonshire
 Berrynarbor
  6933 Thomas Lissett
   Cash, *Devon*, 1966, p. 102
 Bideford
  6934 Henry Cadd
   Cash, *Devon*, 1966, p. 100
 Combe Martin
  6935 John Norman, carpenter
   Cash, *Devon*, 1966, pp. 101-102

Cookbury
    6936 Humphrey Jefferie, yeoman
        Cash, *Devon*, 1966, p. 100
Crediton
    6937 Joane Barrie, widow
        Cash, *Devon*, 1966, p. 101
Crediton [?]
    6938 John Kingwill
        Cash, *Devon*, 1966, p. 103
Cruwys Morchard
    6939 George Maunder
        Hoskins, 1946, pp. 163-164
Ermington
    6940 Richard Willinge
        Cash, *Devon*, 1966, p. 102
Fremington
    6941 Nicholas Marchant
        Cash, *Devon*, 1966, p. 100
Paignton
    6942 Allan Belfield, gentleman
        Cash, *Devon*, 1966, p. 99
Tawstock
    6943 Henry Bourchier, Earl of Bath
        Gray, 1996, pp. 304-305
Uffculme
    6944 Symon Davy
        Wyatt, *Uffculme*, 1997, p. 88
Wolborough
    6945 James Langdon
        Cash, *Devon*, 1966, p. 101

Hertfordshire
Hatfield
    6946 Mary Cordell
        Anon., *Lock, Stock*, 1978, pp. 64-67
Kings Langley
    6947 Mary Kinge [King], widow
        Munby, *Kings Langley*, 1981, p. 126
    6948 John Lee, yeoman
        Munby, *Kings Langley*, 1981, pp. 130-131
Sarratt
    6949 Will[ia]m Woolman, labourer
        Bullen, *Sarratt*, [1982], p. 143

Lancashire
Warrington
    6950 Robt. Booth, stationer
        Rylands, 1888, pp. 77-115

Lincolnshire
Clee, Itterby
    6951 Robert Dutchborne, wright [joiner or carpenter]
        Ambler, Watkinson, *Clee*, 1987, pp. 151-152
    6952 Thomas Sharpe, tailor
        Ambler, Watkinson, *Clee*, 1987, p. 152

Oxfordshire
Banbury
    6953 Robert Morton, yeoman
        Brinkworth and Gibson, *Banbury*, II, 1976, pp. 162-163

Staffordshire
Dudley
    6954 John Foley, driver
        Roper, *Dudley*, 1966, pp. 29-30
    6955 John Hodgetts, [nailer]
        Roper, *Dudley*, 1966, pp. 26-28
        Roper, *Dudley*, 1968, pp. 31-33

Farewell
    6956 Ursula Masters [Master], widow
        Vaisey, *Lichfield*, 1969, pp. 1-85
Lichfield
    6957 Thomas Awkins [Aukins], chandler
        Vaisey, *Lichfield*, 1969, pp. 79-81
    6958 James Barnes
        Vaisey, *Lichfield*, 1969, p. 79
    6959 Alice Beardsley, widow, saddler
        Vaisey, *Lichfield*, 1969, pp. 77-78

Sussex
Arundel
    6960 William Hill, clergyman
        Hughes, *Sussex*, 2007, p. 7
Climping
    6961 John White, clergyman [vicar of Climping]
        Hughes, *Sussex*, 2007, pp. 48-50

Warwickshire
Luddington
    6962 Michael Smart, yeoman
        Jones, *Stratford*, II, 2003, p. 77
Stratford-on-Avon
    6963 William Cawthre [Cawdry] alias Cooke
        Jones, *Stratford*, II, 2003, p. 83
    6964 Nicholas Freeman
        Jones, *Stratford*, II, 2003, pp. 78-79
    6965 John Rutter, [innholder]
        Jones, *Stratford*, II, 2003, pp. 79-82

Wiltshire
Marlborough
    6966 Toby Crocker, husbandman
        Williams and Thomson, *Marlborough*, 2007, p. 100
    6967 John Smith
        Williams and Thomson, *Marlborough*, 2007, p. 101

Worcestershire
Chaddesley Corbett
    6968 Gilbert Chaunce
        Roper, *Chaddesley Corbett*, 1971, p. 80
Chaddesley Corbett, Hillpool
    6969 Elinor Cowper, widow
        Roper, *Chaddesley Corbett*, 1971, pp. 76-77
Chaddesley Corbett
    6970 William Fletcher, husbandman
        Roper, *Chaddesley Corbett*, 1971, p. 78

Yorkshire
Denton Hall
    6971 Ferdinando, Lord Fairfax
        Brears, *Yorkshire*, 1972, pp. 94-96

1648 (c.)
Hertfordshire
Kings Langley
    6972 Richard Spratley, labourer
        Munby, *Kings Langley*, 1981, p. 127
Oxfordshire
Banbury
    6973 Robert Bendbowe, scrivener
        Brinkworth and Gibson, *Banbury*, II, 1976, p. 161

1649
Berkshire
Windsor Castle
    Charles I (see Whitehall, London)

Bristol
Westbury
6974 Edward Creed, clergyman
Moore, *Clifton*, 1981, pp. 89-90
Cheshire
Bowdon
6975 John Sorocold, yeoman
Groves, *Bowdon*, 1997, pp. 58-59
Hale
6976 Elizabeth Goulden, [widow]
Groves, *Hale 2*, 2005, pp. 30-31
Nantwich
6977 John Parker, yeoman
Cockcroft, *Nantwich*, 1999, pp. 235.2-3
6978 John Tench, dyer
Cockcroft, *Nantwich*, 1999, pp. 305.1-5
6979 Randle Walton, blacksmith
Cockcroft, *Nantwich*, 1999, pp. 326.2-3
6980 Margaret Woodnoth, widow
Cockcroft, *Nantwich*, 1999, pp. 356.1-3
Wrenbury, Newhall
6981 Ralph Lawrence, [husbandman]
Pixton, *Wrenbury*, 2009, pp. 430-431
6982 John Ravenscroft, [yeoman]
Pixton, *Wrenbury*, 2009, pp. 439-441
Wrenbury, Smeatonwood
6983 William Taylor, [husbandman]
Pixton, *Wrenbury*, 2009, pp. 433-434
Derbyshire
Chesterfield, Walton
6984 Christopher Bower, husbandman
Bestall and Fowkes, *Chesterfield*, 2001, p. 405
Chesterfield
6985 William and Dorothy Hemsley
Bestall and Fowkes, *Chesterfield*, 2001, pp. 406-408
6986 Godfrey Hill, joiner
Bestall and Fowkes, *Chesterfield*, 2001, p. 406
6987 Peter Pynder
Bestall and Fowkes, *Chesterfield*, 2001, pp. 409-410
Newbold
6988 Edward Foxe
Bestall and Fowkes, *Chesterfield*, 2001, pp. 399
6989 Richard Sharman
Bestall and Fowkes, *Chesterfield*, 2001, pp. 400-401
6990 William Webster, cutler
Bestall and Fowkes, *Chesterfield*, 2001, pp. 402-404
Devonshire
Atherington
6991 John Giffard
Cash, *Devon*, 1966, p. 106
Braunton
6992 [John Quicke]
Cash, *Devon*, 1966, p. 107
Buckfastleigh
6993 Michael Derry
Cash, *Devon*, 1966, p. 106
Buckland Monachorum
6994 Christopher Edgcomb, yeoman
Cash, *Devon*, 1966, p. 105
Hatherleigh
6995 Mellisent Medland
Cash, *Devon*, 1966, pp. 103-104

Lifton [?]
6996 Roger Austin
Cash, *Devon*, 1966, pp. 104-105
Newton St Petrock
6997 John Potter, clergyman
Cash, *Devon*, 1966, p. 103
Witheridge
6998 Amy Norton
Cash, *Devon*, 1966, pp. 105-106
Woodleigh
6999 Philip Steare, husbandman
Cash, *Devon*, 1966, p. 105
Hampshire
Carisbrooke Castle, Isle of Wight
Charles I (see Whitehall, London)
Hertfordshire
St Albans, St Stephens
7000 Josiph Tayler
Parker, *Worldly Goods*, 2004, pp. 253-254
Sarratt
7001 Raph Sawell, [husbandman]
Bullen, *Sarratt*, [1982], pp. 144-145
Theobalds
Charles I (see Whitehall, London)
Kent
Greenwich Palace
Charles I (see Whitehall, London)
Lincolnshire
Clee
7002 George Warde, labourer
Ambler, Watkinson, *Clee*, 1987, p. 153
Clee, Oole
7003 John Yates, husbandman
Ambler, Watkinson, *Clee*, 1987, p. 153
London
St James's Palace
Charles I (see Whitehall Palace)
Somerset House (Denmark House)
Charles I (see Whitehall Palace)
Tower of London
Charles I (see Whitehall Palace)
Whitehall Palace
7004 Charles I (also listed St James's Palace, Somerset
House (Denmark House), Tower of London, and
Windsor Castle, Berkshire, Carisbrooke Castle,
Hampshire, Theobalds, Hertfordshire, Greenwich
Palace, Kent, Hampton Court Palace and Richmond
Palace, Middlesex, Holdenby House, Northamptonshire,
Ludlow Castle, Shropshire, Nonsuch Palace, Oatlands
Palace and Wimbledon House, Surrey, and Bewdley
(Tickenhill) House, Worcestershire)
Millar, *King's Goods*, 1972
Middlesex
Hampton Court Palace
Charles I (see Whitehall, London)
Richmond Palace
Charles I (see Whitehall, London)
Northamptonshire
Holdenby House
Charles I (see Whitehall, London)

Scotland
Edinburgh
  7005 James Lyndsay, printer
    Anon., *Bassandyne*, 1836, pp. 274-275
Shropshire
Ludlow Castle
    Charles I (see Whitehall, London)
Staffordshire
Lichfield
  7006 William Perkins, tanner
    Vaisey, *Lichfield*, 1969, p. 85
Sedgley
  7007 Rouse Allen, locksmith
    Roper, *Sedgley*, 1960, p. 4
Unlocated
  7008 John Petton
    Roper, *Sedgley*, 1960, p. 2
Whittington
  7009 John Smith, yeoman
    Vaisey, *Lichfield*, 1969, p. 86
Sedgley, Woodsetton
  7010 Margaret Hodgetts, widow
    Roper, *Sedgley*, 1960, pp. 11-12
Surrey
Nonsuch Palace
    Charles I (see Whitehall, London)
Oatlands Palace
    Charles I (see Whitehall, London)
Wimbledon House
    Charles I (see Whitehall, London)
Warwickshire
Stratford-on-Avon, Old Stratford
  7011 Clement Slie
    Jones, *Stratford*, II, 2003, pp. 84-85
Worcestershire
Bewdley (Tickenhill) House
    Charles I (see Whitehall, London)
Wiltshire
Marlborough
  7012 William Coleman, [carpenter]
    Williams and Thomson, *Marlborough*, 2007, p. 101
Yorkshire
Lunds
  7013 Thomas Fawcett
    Thwaite, *Abbotside*, 1967, p. 88
Sharlston
  7014 Francis Clarke, yeoman
    Brears, *Yorkshire*, 1972, pp. 96-100
Sheffield, Little Sheffield
  7015 George Lee, yeoman
    Bradley, 1861-1862, pp. 161-162
York, Tailors' Hall
  7016 Company of Tailors
    Sheils, 2006, pp. 68-69

1649 (c.)
Wiltshire
Marlborough
  7017 Thomas Grinfield
    Williams and Thomson, *Marlborough*, 2007, p. 101

1650-1675 (undated)
Devonshire
Combeinteignhead
  7018 William Bowden, husbandman
    Cash, *Devon*, 1966, p. 175

South Molton
  7019 Aaron Locke, butcher
    Cash, *Devon*, 1966, p. 175

1650
Bristol
Bristol, St James
  7020 Richard Berriman, tobacco-pipe maker
    George, *Bristol*, 1, 2002, pp. 164-166
Bristol, Christchurch
  7021 George Pearce, innholder of the White Hart
    George, *Bristol*, 1, 2002, pp. 166-168
Cheshire
Bowdon
  7022 Thomas Gleave, gentleman
    Groves, *Bowdon*, 1997, pp. 61-62
Hale, Ringway
  7023 Thomas Newton, [yeoman]
    Groves, *Hale 2*, 2005, pp. 32-33
  7024 John Pedley
    Groves, *Hale 2*, 2005, pp. 33-35
Nantwich
  7025 John Davies, glover
    Cockcroft, *Nantwich*, 1999, p. 103.2
Derbyshire
Chesterfield, Dunston
  7026 John Drabble, husbandman
    Bestall and Fowkes, *Chesterfield*, 2001, pp. 413-415
Chesterfield, Calow
  7027 Ralph Hardy, husbandman
    Bestall and Fowkes, *Chesterfield*, 2001, pp. 411-412
Chesterfield
  7028 George Heathcote, butcher
    Bestall and Fowkes, *Chesterfield*, 2001, p. 413
  7029 George Lee, husbandman
    Bestall and Fowkes, *Chesterfield*, 2001, pp. 418-419
  7030 Godfrey Webster, butcher
    Bestall and Fowkes, *Chesterfield*, 2001, pp. 415-417
Devonshire
Barnstaple
  7031 Mistress Grace Beaple, widow
    Cash, *Devon*, 1966, pp. 108-109
  7032 John Thorne, cooper
    Cash, *Devon*, 1966, p. 109
Paignton
  7033 William Bennett, yeoman
    Cash, *Devon*, 1966, pp. 107-108
Sampford Courtenay
  7034 James Ellis
    Cash, *Devon*, 1966, p. 107
Hertfordshire
Kings Langley
  7035 Jerimy King, [yeoman]
    Munby, *Kings Langley*, 1981, p. 134
  7036 Edward Puddifett [Puddifatt], yeoman
    Munby, *Kings Langley*, 1981, p. 127
St Albans, St Stephens
  7037 Francis Graie, yeoman
    Parker, *Worldly Goods*, 2004, p. 253
Tring
  7038 Andrewe Knowlinge, gentleman
    Anon., *Lock, Stock*, 1978, pp. 67-69

Unlocated
  7039 Jone Nutkin
    Parker, *Worldly Goods*, 2004, p. 254
Kent
  Ash-next-Sandwich
  7040 John Bax, yeoman
    Bax, 1950, pp. 86-88
Lincolnshire
  Clee, Itterby
  7041 Jone Tuplin
    Ambler, Watkinson, *Clee*, 1987, pp. 153-154
Oxfordshire
  Glympton
  7042 Thomas Wisdom
    Barnett, 1923, p. 64
Staffordshire
  Brierley
  7043 Edward Wilkes, nailer
    Roper, *Sedgley*, 1960, p. 8
  Coseley
  7044 Ann Jeven, widow
    Roper, *Sedgley*, 1960, p. 3
  Dudley
  7045 Thomas Askew, [nailer]
    Roper, *Dudley*, 1968, p. 33
  Rugeley
  7046 Walter Lander [Launder]
    Landor, 1934, pp. 111-119
  Sedgley, Cottwall End
  7047 John Turnor, yeoman
    Roper, *Sedgley*, 1960, p. 5
Sussex
  Walberton
  7048 Thomas James, clergyman [vicar of Walberton]
    Hughes, *Sussex*, 2007, pp. 222-223
  Wisborough Green
  7049 Richard Jackman
    Lawson, 1999, pp. 57-61
Warwickshire
  Stoneleigh, Cryfield
  7050 Anne Wilson, widow
    Alcock, *Warwickshire*, 1993, pp. 194-196
Worcestershire
  Chaddesley Corbett
  7051 Robert Turner, shoemaker
    Roper, *Chaddesley Corbett*, 1971, p. 81

1651
Cumberland
  Holm Cultram
  7052 James Jackson
    Grainger and Collingwood, 1919, p. 241
Derbyshire
  Egginton
  7053 Anne, Lady Every
    Fisher, 1954, pp. 117-18
  7054 Mary Leigh
    Fisher, 1954, pp. 119-120
  Repton
  7055 Richard Mesam
    Cox, 1914, pp. 118-119
Devonshire
  Paignton
  7056 Thomas Butland, yeoman
    Cash, *Devon*, 1966, p. 110

Hertfordshire
  Kings Langley
  7057 Henery Rickett
    Munby, *Kings Langley*, 1981, pp. 134-135
Staffordshire
  Lower Gornal
  7058 Richard Whitehouse, locksmith
    Roper, *Sedgley*, 1960, pp. 5-7
  Sedgley
  7059 David Evans
    Roper, *Sedgley*, 1960, p. 11
  7060 Isabell Jeven
    Roper, *Sedgley*, 1960, pp. 12-13
  7061 Richard Sparry
    Roper, *Sedgley*, 1960, pp. 9-10
  Sedgley, Turls Hill
  7062 John Timings, locksmith
    Roper, *Sedgley*, 1960, pp. 7-8

1652
Devonshire
  Berrynarbor
  7063 Morgan Bennett
    Cash, *Devon*, 1966, p. 111
  South Molton
  7064 Thomas Tucker
    Cash, *Devon*, 1966, pp. 110-111
Hertfordshire
  Kings Langley
  7065 Elizabeth Lea
    Munby, *Kings Langley*, 1981, p. 136
Lincolnshire
  Allington
  7066 Thomas Burton
    Pask, *Allington*, 1989, pp. 76-77
  Barton-upon-Humber
  7067 Thomas Teanby, yeoman
    Peacock, 1861, pp. 505-507
Staffordshire
  Sedgley, Woodsetton
  7068 Oliver Fellow, yeoman
    Roper, *Sedgley*, 1960, pp. 13-14
Sussex
  Kirdford
  7069 Richard Mose, yeoman
    Kenyon, *Kirdford*, 1955, pp. 115-116
  Madehurst
  7070 Adam Page, clergyman
    Hughes, *Sussex*, 2007, pp. 134-135
  West Stoke
  7071 George Welborne, clergyman
    Hughes, *Sussex*, 2007, pp. 198-200
Wales
  Pembrokeshire, Haverfordwest, Slade
  7072 Henry Leach
    Howells, 1956, p. 424
Warwickshire
  Stratford-on-Avon
  7073 Margarett Hathaway, widow
    Jones, *Stratford*, II, 2003, pp. 86-87
Worcestershire
  Chaddesley Corbett
  7074 John Yarren, scythesmith
    Roper, *Chaddesley Corbett*, 1971, pp. 81-82

Yorkshire
Calverley
  7075 Henry Claverley, esquire
    Margerison, 1888, p. 172

1653
Cumberland
Sella Park, St Bridget
  7076 Thomas Curwen, esquire
    Jackson, *Curwens*, 1881, pp. 317-320
Devonshire
Bishops Tawton
  7077 Nicholas Seaward
    Cash, *Devon*, 1966, p. 112
Exbourne
  7078 William Downe, fuller
    Cash, *Devon*, 1966, p. 113
Marwood
  7079 Anthony Harryes
    Cash, *Devon*, 1966, p. 112
North Molton
  7080 John Squire, tippler
    Cash, *Devon*, 1966, p. 113
Unlocated
  7081 Lewis Laremy
    Cash, *Devon*, 1966, pp. 111-112
France
Caen
  7082 James Butler, Marquis of Ormonde
    Fenlon, *Ireland*, 2003, pp. 35-38
Lancashire
Blackburn
  7083 George Shawe, gentleman
    Earwaker, *Lancashire and Cheshire*, 1893, pp. 90-91
Turton, Turton Tower
  7084 Humphrey Chetham
    Dart and Kay, *Turton Tower*, 1961, pp. 6-8
Lincolnshire
Winteringham
  7085 Edw. Roberts, carpenter
    Neave, *Winteringham*, 1984, p. 70
  7086 Willm: Shankster, [husbandman]
    Neave, *Winteringham*, 1984, pp. 70-71
London
Clothworkers' Hall
  7087 Clothworkers' Company
    Wickham, 2005, pp. 100-126
Scotland
Orkney, House of Birsay
  William Douglas, Earl of Morton (see Orkney, Kirkwall)
Orkney, Kirkwall
  7088 William Douglas, Earl of Morton (also listed Birsay)
    Marshall, 1888-1889, pp. 300-303
Staffordshire
Coseley
  7089 John Millard
    Roper, *Sedgley*, 1960, p. 19
Lichfield
  7090 Elizabeth Baker, widow
    Vaisey, *Lichfield*, 1969, pp. 88-90

Lichfield, Edial
  7091 Hugh Dennett [Dennis], yeoman
    Vaisey, *Lichfield*, 1969, pp. 86-88
Sedgley
  7092 Richard Haughton
    Roper, *Sedgley*, 1960, p. 18
  7093 William Holland
    Roper, *Sedgley*, 1960, p. 20
  7094 Simon Pickrill
    Roper, *Sedgley*, 1960, p. 15
  7095 William Wilks, nailer
    Roper, *Sedgley*, 1960, pp. 16-17
Yorkshire
North Kilvington
  7096 Thomas Mennell, esquire
    Aveling, 1964, pp. 90-92

1654
Cambridgeshire
Cambridge, Great St Mary's
  7097 Richard Ireland, [stationer]
    Gray and Palmer, *Cambridge*, 1915, pp. 94-95
Devonshire
Bondleigh
  7098 William Heywood
    Cash, *Devon*, 1966, p. 114
Chawleigh
  7099 Grace Webber
    Cash, *Devon*, 1966, pp. 113-114
Dorsetshire
Leigh
  7100 John Long, [yeoman]
    Machin, *Yetminster*, 1976, No.30, (2 pp.)
Lincolnshire
Winteringham
  7101 Gervase Oyle, fisherman
    Neave, *Winteringham*, 1984, p. 73
  7102 Robte Thompson, yeoman
    Neave, *Winteringham*, 1984, pp. 71-72
Scotland
Edinburgh
  7103 Johne Hill, bookseller
    Anon., *Bassandyne*, 1836, pp. 275-277
  7104 Andro Wilsone, bookseller
    Anon., *Bassandyne*, 1836, pp. 277-279
Shropshire
Wrockwardine, Admaston
  7105 John Smith, weaver
    Trinder and Cox, *Telford*, 1980, p. 402
Staffordshire
Ettingshall
  7106 John Whitehous, nailer
    Roper, *Sedgley*, 1960, p. 20
Lichfield
  7107 John Millington, baker
    Vaisey, *Lichfield*, 1969, pp. 95-97
  7108 Kenelme Smith, gentleman, citizen and haberdasher of London
    Vaisey, *Lichfield*, 1969, pp. 90-92
Wall
  7109 Anthony Ellison, yeoman
    Vaisey, *Lichfield*, 1969, pp. 93-94

Wales
Glamorganshire, Peterston-super-Ely
  7110 George Prainch
    Wrench, *Wrenche*, 1956, p. 51
Warwickshire
Stratford-on-Avon
  7111 Henry Tomlins, tailor
    Jones, *Stratford*, II, 2003, pp. 87-90

1655

Devonshire
Broad Clyst
  7112 Thomas Maye
    Cash, *Devon*, 1966, pp. 117-118
East Worlington
  7113 John Downe
    Cash, *Devon*, 1966, pp. 115-116
Sandford
  7114 Roger Lane
    Cash, *Devon*, 1966, p. 116
Unlocated
  7115 Nicholas Carpenter
    Cash, *Devon*, 1966, pp. 114-115
Hertfordshire
Unlocated
  7116 Thomas Jopson
    Parker, *Worldly Goods*, 2004, p. 230
Lincolnshire
Winteringham
  7117 Tho: Jacson, [labourer]
    Neave, *Winteringham*, 1984, p. 150
  7118 Robert Saunderson, labourer
    Neave, *Winteringham*, 1984, pp. 74-75
Staffordshire
Lichfield
  7119 James Dringe, tanner
    Vaisey, *Lichfield*, 1969, pp. 98-99
  7120 John Parker, apothecary
    Vaisey, *Lichfield*, 1969, pp. 99-102
Sedgley
  7121 Anne Bradley, widow
    Roper, *Sedgley*, 1960, p. 21
Surrey
Ham House
  7122 William Murray, Earl of Dysart
    Thornton and Tomlin, *Ham*, 1980, pp. 6-33
Sussex
Up Marden and Compton
  7123 Anthony Gray, clergyman [vicar of Compton
  with Up Marden]
    Hughes, *Sussex*, 2007, pp. 135-136
Yorkshire
Aysgarth, Cotterdale
  7124 Augustine Mettcalfe [Metcalfe]
    Thwaite, *Abbotside*, 1967, p. 70
York
  7125 Richard Jaques, merchant [grocer]
    White and Swinburne, 2002, pp. 32-36

1655 (c.)

Devonshire
Tawstock
  7126 Henry Bourchier, Earl of Bath
    Gray, 1996, pp. 313-315

1656

Cheshire
Nantwich
  7127 William Thrush, gentleman [yeoman]
    Cockcroft, *Nantwich*, 1999, pp. 312.3-4
Cornwall
St Buryan
  7128 Christopher James
    Arkell, Evans, Goose, 2000, pp. 373-374
Devonshire
Exeter
  7129 John Holt, innholder
    Cash, *Devon*, 1966, p. 118
Shobrooke
  7130 Thomas Dyer, gentleman
    Cash, *Devon*, 1966, pp. 118-119
Gloucestershire
Westerleigh
  7131 Thomas Roberts, esquire
    Moore, *Frampton Cotterell*, 1976, p. 79
Ireland
Dublin
  7132 George Fitzgerald, Earl of Kildare
    Fenlon, *Ireland*, 2003, pp. 39-40
Lincolnshire
Winteringham
  7133 Tho: Codde, skinner
    Neave, *Winteringham*, 1984, pp. 76-77
  7134 Roberte Porter, labourer
    Neave, *Winteringham*, 1984, pp. 75-76
London
Blackwell Hall, Basinghall Street
  Matthew Wilson, esquire (see Eshton Hall, Yorkshire)
Coleman Street
  Matthew Wilson, esquire (see Eshton Hall, Yorkshire)
Oxfordshire
Oxford, Cross Inn
  7135 John Smith, [innholder]
    Pantin, 1955, pp. 72-74
Staffordshire
Lichfield, St Michael, Greenhill
  7136 Thomas Hall, husbandman
    Vaisey, *Lichfield*, 1969, p. 103
Lower Gornal
  7137 John Marston alias Marson, nailer
    Roper, *Sedgley*, 1960, p. 22
  7138 Jane Parkshouse, widow
    Roper, *Sedgley*, 1960, p. 32
Yorkshire
Eshton Hall
  7139 Matthew Wilson, esquire (also listed Coleman
  Street and Blackwell Hall, London)
    Brears, *Yorkshire*, 1972, pp. 106-118
North Bierley
  7140 Richard Richardson
    Brears, *Yorkshire*, 1972, pp. 101-105

1657

Bristol
Bristol
  7141 Richard Orchard, public notary
    George, *Bristol*, 2005, pp. 1-2

Westbury
7142 Agnes [Anne] White, widow
Moore, *Clifton*, 1981, pp. 90-91

Devonshire
Uffculme
7143 John Cheeke, carpenter
Wyatt, *Uffculme*, 1997, pp. 88-89
Winkleigh
7144 John Paddon
Cash, *Devon*, 1966, pp. 119-120

Lincolnshire
Winteringham
7145 William Becke, [tanner]
Neave, *Winteringham*, 1984, p. 77

Staffordshire
Coseley
7146 William Fullwood, nailer
Roper, *Sedgley*, 1960, p. 25
Hammerwich
7147 William Bull
Vaisey, *Lichfield*, 1969, pp. 104-105
Whittington
7148 Joan Deakin alias Butterfield
Vaisey, *Lichfield*, 1969, pp. 103-104

Sussex
Stoughton
7149 Matthew Maior, clergyman, vicar of Stoughton
Steer, 1958, p. 156
Hughes, *Sussex*, 2007, pp. 204-205

Warwickshire
Stratford-on-Avon
7150 William Hopkins, innholder [maltster]
Jones, *Stratford*, II, 2003, pp. 91-93

Wiltshire
Marlborough
7151 William Elton, carpenter
Williams and Thomson, *Marlborough*, 2007, pp. 101-102

1658
Bristol
Bristol
7152 John Potter, [cooper]
George, *Bristol*, 2005, pp. 2-4
7153 John Young
George, *Bristol*, 2005, pp. 4-6

Cheshire
Sale
7154 Robert Cheshire, husbandman
Groves, *Ashton-on-Mersey and Sale*, 2000, p. 25

Devonshire
Uffculme
7155 John Trickey, weaver
Wyatt, *Uffculme*, 1997, pp. 89-90

Essex
Writtle
7156 Gregory Shettlewood, yeoman
Steer, *Mid-Essex*, 1969, pp. 86-88

Hertfordshire
Aston
7157 Thomas Betts
Orlin, 1995, pp. 105-106

Watford, Waterdell
7158 Raph Kentish, yeoman
Munby, *Worldly Goods*, 1991, pp. 145-147

Gloucestershire
Hambrook
7159 Richard Attwood, yeoman
Moore, *Frampton Cotterell*, 1976, pp. 79-81

Leicestershire
Braunstone
7160 William Freeman, tailor
Wilshere, *Braunstone*, 1983, p. 19

Lincolnshire
Clee, Oole
7161 Catherine Yates
Ambler, Watkinson, *Clee*, 1987, p. 154
Winteringham
7162 Robert Blansherd, draper
Neave, *Winteringham*, 1984, pp. 77-78

London
Dulwich College
7163 Mr [John] Skingle
Young, 1889, p. 134

Northamptonshire
Stoke Bruerne, Stoke Park
7164 Sir Edward Watson
Wise, 1891, pp. 210-211

Staffordshire
Elmhurst
Michael Biddulph, esquire (see Lichfield)
Ettingshall
7165 Frances Horner, locksmith
Roper, *Sedgley*, 1960, p. 28
7166 Mary Hickmans
Roper, *Sedgley*, 1960, p. 26
Lichfield
7167 Michael Biddulph, esquire (also listed Elmhurst)
Vaisey, *Lichfield*, 1969, pp. 105-112
7168 George Cowper
Vaisey, *Lichfield*, 1969, pp. 114-115
Lower Gornal
7169 John Fereday, petty chapman
Roper, *Sedgley*, 1960, p. 23
Sedgley
7170 Phillip Cox
Roper, *Sedgley*, 1960, p. 24
Sedgley, Woodsetton
7171 Henry Hodgetts
Roper, *Sedgley*, 1960, p. 27
Sedgley, Turls Hill
7172 William Parshouse alias Pershouse
Roper, *Sedgley*, 1960, p. 35
Wall
7173 John Quinton, gentleman
Vaisey, *Lichfield*, 1969, pp. 113-114

Wales
Breconshire, Llansantffraed, Newton-by-Usk
7174 Thomas Vaughan
Hutchinson, 1947, pp. 16-17

Yorkshire
East Lunds
7175 John Blaides [Blades], yeoman
Thwaite, *Abbotside*, 1967, p. 66

1658 (c.)

Gloucestershire
Charlton Kings
  7176 Sammuell Addams, [husbandman]
    Paget and Sale, *Charlton Kings*, 2003, pp. 30-31

1659

Cheshire
Bowdon
  7177 Margery Harding, widow
    Groves, *Bowdon*, 1998, pp. 11-12
Nantwich
  7178 John Davies, blacksmith
    Cockcroft, *Nantwich*, 1999, pp. 104.2-3
  7179 William Horbyn, glover
    Cockcroft, *Nantwich*, 1999, p. 158.1

Devonshire
Heavitree
  7180 Roger Pyne, [yeoman]
    Cash, *Devon*, 1966, pp. 120-121
Stoke Canon
  7181 John Tucker, yeoman
    Cash, *Devon*, 1966, p. 121

Essex
Writtle
  7182 Charles Cleark
    Steer, *Mid-Essex*, 1969, pp. 88-89

Lincolnshire
Allington
  7183 William Marrott
    Pask, *Allington*, 1989, p. 78

Shropshire
Dawley, Little Dawley
  7184 Bassall Richards, yeoman
    Trinder and Cox, *Telford*, 1980, pp. 163-164
Wellington, Aston under the Wrekin
  7185 Thomas Lockley
    Trinder and Cox, *Telford*, 1980, p. 249
Wellington, Watling Street
  7186 William Smith, [carrier]
    Trinder and Cox, *Telford*, 1980, pp. 249-250

Staffordshire
Lichfield
  7187 Thomas Thacker, fellmonger
    Vaisey, *Lichfield*, 1969, pp. 115-119
Lower Gornal
  7188 Richard Sturmye, tailor
    Roper, *Sedgley*, 1960, p. 29
  7189 Richard Bradley, nailer
    Roper, *Sedgley*, 1960, p. 30

Warwickshire
Stratford-on-Avon, Old Stratford
  7190 William Horne, yeoman
    Jones, *Stratford*, II, 2003, p. 94

Worcestershire
Upton-on-Severn
  7191 Mary Bromley, widow
    Wanklyn, *Worcestershire*, 1998, pp. 176-177

1660

Cheshire
Ashton-on-Mersey
  7192 John Brereton, clergyman
    Groves, *Ashton-on-Mersey and Sale*, 2000, pp. 26-30

Hale
  7193 George Goulden, [tanner]
    Groves, *Hale 2*, 2005, pp. 37-38
Nantwich
  7194 Richard Acton
    Cockcroft, *Nantwich*, 1999, p p. 3.1-2
  7195 Yewin Allen, mercer
    Cockcroft, *Nantwich*, 1999, p p. 10.4-6
  7196 Abigail Fogg
    Cockcroft, *Nantwich*, 1999, p. 130.1
  7197 John Hussey, instrument maker
    Cockcroft, *Nantwich*, 1999, p. 161.2
  7198 Richard Jennings, feltmaker
    Cockcroft, *Nantwich*, 1999, pp. 171.3-4
  7199 Geoffrey Minshull, gentleman
    Cockcroft, *Nantwich*, 1999, pp. 221.2-3
  7200 Thomas Noden, gentleman
    Cockcroft, *Nantwich*, 1999, pp. 233.1-3
  7201 William Twoyearold
    Cockcroft, *Nantwich*, 1999, pp. 315.1-2

Devonshire
Uffculme
  7202 Margaret Dowdney, widow
    Wyatt, *Uffculme*, 1997, p. 90

Essex
Writtle
  7203 Robert Harris
    Steer, *Mid-Essex*, 1969, pp. 89-90

Gloucestershire
Cheltenham, Arle
  7204 Francis Gregory
    Sale, *Cheltenham*, 1999, pp. 1-2
Westerleigh, Nibley
  7205 Robert Pickard, [yeoman]
    Moore, *Frampton Cotterell*, 1976, pp. 81-82
Winterbourne
  7206 William Witherlie, yeoman
    Moore, *Frampton Cotterell*, 1976, p. 81

Hertfordshire
St Albans, St Stephens
  7207 [Henry] Kentish, yeoman
    Munby, *Worldly Goods*, 1991, pp. 148-151
St Albans, St Stephens, Serge Hill
  7208 John Winsor, yeoman
    Munby, *Worldly Goods*, 1991, p. 145

Staffordshire
Brierley
  7209 Richard Collins, nailer
    Roper, *Sedgley*, 1960, p. 31
Hammerwich
  7210 Robert Webb
    Vaisey, *Lichfield*, 1969, p. 123
Lichfield
  7211 Thomas Deakin, [mercer]
    Vaisey, *Lichfield*, 1969, pp. 118-120
Lichfield, St Michael
  7212 Dennis Napper, brickmaker
    Vaisey, *Lichfield*, 1969, pp. 121-122
Sedgley, Cottwall End
  7213 Edward Parkshouse
    Roper, *Sedgley*, 1960, p. 32
Sedgley
  7214 Margaret Pershouse, widow
    Roper, *Sedgley*, 1960, p. 33

Wales
Caernarvonshire, Unlocated
  7215 Alexander Bodvell
    Owen, *Lleyn*, 1960, pp. 77-78
Warwickshire
Stoneleigh, Hurst
  7216 Thomas Smith
    Alcock, *Warwickshire*, 1993, pp. 112-113
Stratford-on-Avon
  7217 Thomas Evitts, [innholder]
    Jones, *Stratford*, II, 2003, pp. 95-96
Wiltshire
Marlborough
  7218 Richard Wyat, [beerhouse keeper]
    Williams and Thomson, *Marlborough*, 2007, pp. 102-103
Yorkshire
Barnoldswick, Brockden
  7219 Thomas Kid
    Kirk, *Barnoldswick*, 1951, pp. 69-70
Woolley, Woolley Hall
  7220 Sir George Wentworth
    Markham, *Woolley Hall*, 1979, pp. 62-70

1660 (c.)
Essex
Unlocated
  7221 Widow Watts
    Steer, *Mid-Essex*, 1969, pp. 272-273
Staffordshire
Lichfield
  7222 Lawrence Clowes, mercer
    Vaisey, *Lichfield*, 1969, pp. 123-124

1661
Bristol
Bristol, St Mary Redcliffe
  7223 John Austen, chapman
    George, *Bristol*, 2005, pp. 6-8
Bristol, St Thomas
  7224 Thomas Fisher, innholder
    George, *Bristol*, 2005, pp. 8-11
Bristol, St Mary Redcliffe
  7225 Edmond Jones, chapman
    George, *Bristol*, 2005, pp. 11-12
Bristol, St James
  7226 Jane Wall, widow, tobacco pipe maker
    George, *Bristol*, 2005, pp. 12-13
Clifton
  7227 John Good, gentleman
    Moore, *Clifton*, 1981, pp. 93-94
Redland
  7228 Joan Button, [widow]
    Moore, *Clifton*, 1981, p. 91
Shirehampton
  7229 Katherine Matthews, widow
    Moore, *Clifton*, 1981, p. 92
  7230 William Parker, yeoman
    Moore, *Clifton*, 1981, pp. 92-93
Buckinghamshire
Calverton
  7231 John Knight, clerk
    Reed, *Buckinghamshire*, 1988, pp. 1-2
Colnbrook
  7232 Beatridge Guy, widow
    Reed, *Buckinghamshire*, 1988, pp. 6-8

Datchet
  7233 Thomas Brimley
    Reed, *Buckinghamshire*, 1988, pp. 9-11
Ivinghoe
  7234 Thomas Lathwell, tailor
    Reed, *Buckinghamshire*, 1988, p. 1
Little Kimble
  7235 Nicholas Dantrill, clerk
    Reed, *Buckinghamshire*, 1988, pp. 1-2
Little Missenden
  7236 William Hunt, yeoman
    Reed, *Buckinghamshire*, 1988, pp. 5-6
Stoke Poges
  7237 Joane Adkinson
    Reed, *Buckinghamshire*, 1988, pp. 8-9
Cambridgeshire
Cambridge, Kings College
  7238 Provost's Lodgings
    Clark, 1881, pp. 306-310
Cheshire
Hale, Ringway
  7239 Robert Cotterell, [yeoman]
    Groves, *Hale 2*, 2005, p. 39
Hale
  7240 Mary Hollinpriest, [widow]
    Groves, *Hale 2*, 2005, p. 40
Nantwich
  7241 Thomas Bickerton, grocer
    Cockcroft, *Nantwich*, 1999, p. 28.2
  7242 Dorothy Browne, widow
    Cockcroft, *Nantwich*, 1999, p. 51.2
  7243 John Crewe
    Cockcroft, *Nantwich*, 1999, p. 95.1
  7244 Dorothy Holcraft
    Cockcroft, *Nantwich*, 1999, p. 157.2
  7245 Randle Littler
    Cockcroft, *Nantwich*, 1999, pp. 192.1-2
  7246 Edward Minshull, shoemaker
    Cockcroft, *Nantwich*, 1999, p. 220.2
  7247 Elizabeth Parker, widow
    Cockcroft, *Nantwich*, 1999, p. 234.2
  7248 Randle Seckerston
    Cockcroft, *Nantwich*, 1999, pp. 283.1-3
  7249 Raphe Walley, apothecary
    Cockcroft, *Nantwich*, 1999, pp. 320.1-8
  7250 John Watson, yeoman
    Cockcroft, *Nantwich*, 1999, pp. 328.2-4
Sale
  7251 Hugh Barlow, shoemaker
    Groves, *Ashton-on-Mersey and Sale*, 2000, pp. 30-32
Devonshire
Cadbury
  7252 Peter Tucker
    Worthy, *Devonshire*, 1896, pp. 22-23
Kingsteignton
  7253 Richard Searle
    Cash, *Devon*, 1966, pp. 121-122
Uffculme
  7254 Humfry Henson, [weaver?]
    Wyatt, *Uffculme*, 1997, pp. 90-91
  7255 Thomas Jerman
    Wyatt, *Uffculme*, 1997, pp. 188-189

Dorsetshire
Yetminster
  7256 George Reape
    Machin, *Yetminster*, 1976, No.31, (1 p.)

Essex
Roxwell
  7257 Humfrey Smith, yeoman
    Steer, *Mid-Essex*, 1969, pp. 92-93
Writtle
  7258 John Sapsfoard
    Steer, *Mid-Essex*, 1969, pp. 90-91
Unlocated
  7259 George Ramsaye alias Laurance
    Steer, *Mid-Essex*, 1969, pp. 91-92

Gloucestershire
Stoke Gifford
  7260 Alice Blanche, widow
    Moore, *Frampton Cotterell*, 1976, pp. 82-83

Hertfordshire
St Albans, St Stephens
  7261 John Cogdill, yeoman
    Parker, *Worldly Goods*, 2004, pp. 257-258
St Albans, St Stephens, Frogmore Street
  7262 Rogger Whitchurch, husbandman
    Parker, *Worldly Goods*, 2004, p. 259
Sarratt
  7263 John Childwick, clergyman, vicar of Sarratt
    Bullen, *Sarratt*, [1982], pp. 158-160
  7264 Richard Newton, [yeoman]
    Bullen, *Sarratt*, [1982], pp. 157-158

Kent
Sevenoaks
  7265 John Hooper, gentleman
    Lansberry, *Sevenoaks*, 1988, pp. 7-10

Lancashire
Preston
  7266 Unidentified
    Anon., *Domestic Condition*, 1855, p. 206

Leicestershire
Braunstone
  7267 Thomas Boulton
    Wilshere, *Braunstone*, 1983, p. 19

London
Salisbury Court
  7268 John Pepys, [tailor]
    Heath, 1955, pp. 13-15

Norfolk
Letton
  7269 Meriell Gurdon, widow
    Gurdon, 1893-1894, p. 98

Shropshire
Lilleshall
  7270 Silvanus Adams, blacksmith
    Trinder and Cox, *Telford*, 1980, pp. 194-195
  7271 Elizabeth Cartwright, widow
    Trinder and Cox, *Telford*, 1980, p. 195
  7272 Thomas Cartwright
    Trinder and Cox, *Telford*, 1980, pp. 193-194
Wrockwardine, Leaton
  7273 Roger Pemberton, yeoman
    Trinder and Cox, *Telford*, 1980, pp. 402-403

Staffordshire
Coseley
  7274 Edward Moore, yeoman
    Roper, *Sedgley*, 1960, p. 34

Elmhurst
  7275 William Miller, yeoman
    Vaisey, *Lichfield*, 1969, p. 125
Lichfield
  7276 Thomas Wayte, chandler and maltster
    Vaisey, *Lichfield*, 1969, pp. 124-125
Lower Gornal
  7277 Ellianor Ferriday, widow
    Roper, *Sedgley*, 1960, p. 33

Sussex
Little Horsted
  7278 Joseph Biggs, clergyman [rector of Little
  Horsted]
    Hughes, *Sussex*, 2007, pp. 115-117
Stopham
  7279 John Chaloner, clergyman [rector of Stopham]
    Hughes, *Sussex*, 2007, p. 201

Warwickshire
Shottery
  7280 Stephen Sitch [Such], yeoman
    Jones, *Stratford*, II, 2003, pp. 98-99
Stratford-on-Avon
  7281 Roger Barnard, gentleman [yeoman]
    Jones, *Stratford*, II, 2003, pp. 103-104
  7282 Robert Durham, yeoman
    Jones, *Stratford*, II, 2003, pp. 104-106
  7283 Katherine Green, widow
    Jones, *Stratford*, II, 2003, p. 109
  7284 William Loche, carpenter
    Jones, *Stratford*, II, 2003, pp. 96-97
  7285 Richard Mountford, gentleman [wheelwright]
    Jones, *Stratford*, II, 2003, pp. 106-108
  7286 Julie [Julius] Shawe, gentleman
    Jones, *Stratford*, II, 2003, pp. 99-102
  7287 John Walker, tanner
    Jones, *Stratford*, II, 2003, pp. 110-112

Wiltshire
Marlborough
  7288 Lewes Andly, innholder
    Williams and Thomson, *Marlborough*, 2007, pp. 107-108
  7289 William Biggs
    Williams and Thomson, *Marlborough*, 2007, pp. 103-104
  7290 John Davis, baker
    Williams and Thomson, *Marlborough*, 2007, p. 105
  7291 Richard Grinfield, woollen draper
    Williams and Thomson, *Marlborough*, 2007, pp. 105-106
  7292 Symon Hurle, glover
    Williams and Thomson, *Marlborough*, 2007, p. 103
  7293 Richard Rumesey, shoemaker
    Williams and Thomson, *Marlborough*, 2007, pp. 104-105
  7294 Daniel Snow, watchmaker
    Williams and Thomson, *Marlborough*, 2007, pp. 106-107

Worcestershire
Hallow
  7295 Thomas Hall, gentleman
    Wanklyn, *Worcestershire*, 1998, pp. 180-182
King's Norton
  7296 John Gower, esquire
    Wanklyn, *Worcestershire*, 1998, pp. 177-180

Yorkshire
Aysgarth, Skellgill
  7297 George Caygill, fellmonger
    Thwaite, *Abbotside*, 1967, pp. 70-71

Aysgarth, Cams Houses
  7298 John Ketellwell [Kettlewell]
    Thwaite, *Abbotside*, 1967, p. 67
Aysgarth, Yorescott
  7299 Thomas Lambert
    Thwaite, *Abbotside*, 1967, p. 68
Halifax
  7300 Robert Broadley
    Brears, *Yorkshire*, 1972, pp. 120-121
Knaresborough
  7301 William Wilkes
    Brears, *Yorkshire*, 1972, pp. 122-123
Stoodley in Langfield
  7302 Robert Sutcliffe, yeoman
    Brears, *Yorkshire*, 1972, pp. 118-119

1662
Bristol
Bristol, St Philip
  7303 Henry Cartwright, cutler
    George, *Bristol*, 2005, pp. 14-16
Bristol, Redcliffe
  7304 John Frye
    George, *Bristol*, 2005, pp. 16-17
Clifton
  7305 Richard Yeamans, gentleman
    Moore, *Clifton*, 1981, pp. 95-96
Shirehampton
  7306 John Greene, [yeoman]
    Moore, *Clifton*, 1981, pp. 94-95
Buckinghamshire
Castle Thorpe
  7307 Thomas Earle
    Reed, *Buckinghamshire*, 1988, pp. 16-18
Lathbury
  7308 Frances Gostwick, widow
    Reed, *Buckinghamshire*, 1988, pp. 13-15
Tingewick
  7309 John Sutton, gentleman
    Reed, *Buckinghamshire*, 1988, pp. 15-16
Whaddon
  7310 Francis Dodgworth
    Reed, *Buckinghamshire*, 1988, p. 18
Woburn
  7311 Thomas Butterfield, yeoman
    Reed, *Buckinghamshire*, 1988, pp. 11-13
Cambridgeshire
Newmarket
  7312 Edward Siblie, foreigner
    May, *Newmarket*, 1976, p. 7
Cheshire
Hale, Bank Hall
  7313 Margaret Vawdrey, [widow]
    Groves, *Hale 2*, 2005, pp. 40-41
Nantwich
  7314 John Sare
    Cockcroft, *Nantwich*, 1999, pp. 280.1-3
  7315 Robert Wickstead, mercer
    Cockcroft, *Nantwich*, 1999, pp. 338.2-3
Devonshire
Chudleigh
  7316 Grace Weeks, widow
    Cash, *Devon*, 1966, p. 122

Stoke Fleming, Cotton
  7317 Grace Neile, widow
    Cash, *Devon*, 1966, p. 122
Dorsetshire
Leigh
  7318 Richard Masters
    Machin, *Yetminster*, 1976, No.32, (2 pp.)
Yetminster
  7319 Edward Byrt
    Machin, *Yetminster*, 1976, No.34, (2 pp.)
  7320 George Edwards, [husbandman]
    Machin, *Yetminster*, 1976, No.33, (2 pp.)
Essex
Roxwell
  7321 Widow Pery
    Steer, *Mid-Essex*, 1969, p. 94
Hertfordshire
St Albans, St Stephens
  7322 Jonas Hayward
    Parker, *Worldly Goods*, 2004, p. 264
Sarratt
  7323 Henry Browne
    Bullen, *Sarratt*, [1982], pp. 165-166
  7324 Samuell Buckmaster, husbandman
    Bullen, *Sarratt*, [1982], pp. 161-163
Gloucestershire
Frampton Cotterell
  7325 Robert Best, gentleman
    Moore, *Frampton Cotterell*, 1976, p. 86
Hambrook
  7326 Richard Tayler, husbandman
    Moore, *Frampton Cotterell*, 1976, p. 83
Iron Acton, Latteridge
  7327 William Webbe, yeoman
    Moore, *Frampton Cotterell*, 1976, pp. 84-85
Stoke Gifford
  7328 Robert Stephens, clergyman, vicar of Stoke
  Gifford
    Moore, *Frampton Cotterell*, 1976, pp. 86-87
Winterbourne
  7329 John Long, blacksmith
    Moore, *Frampton Cotterell*, 1976, pp. 85-86
  7330 John Simmons, [yeoman]
    Moore, *Frampton Cotterell*, 1976, pp. 83-84
  7331 Edmond Woolley, miller
    Moore, *Frampton Cotterell*, 1976, p. 85
Hertfordshire
Hertford
  7332 Mary Barber
    Adams, *Hertford*, 1997, p. 58
Hertford St Andrews
  7333 Judith Lea, widow
    Adams, *Hertford*, 1997, pp. 104-105
Hertford
  7334 Thomas Nobell, gentleman
    Adams, *Hertford*, 1997, p. 15
  7335 John Smyth, locksmith
    Adams, *Hertford*, 1997, pp. 7-8
  7336 Mary Smyth, widow
    Adams, *Hertford*, 1997, pp. 19-20
St Albans, St Stephens
  7337 Robert Skeale, [husbandman]
    Munby, *Worldly Goods*, 1991, p. 153

Kent

Sevenoaks
7338 Thomas Allen, husbandman
Lansberry, *Sevenoaks*, 1988, pp. 12-14
Shadoxhurst
7339 Bartholmawe Burch, labourer
Barley, *Farmhouse and Cottage*, 1961, p. 278

Leicestershire

Braunstone
7340 Richard Wellingar
Wilshere, *Braunstone*, 1983, p. 20

Lincolnshire

Clee, Itterby
7341 Richard Chapman
Ambler, Watkinson, *Clee*, 1987, pp. 155-156
Clee
7342 Thomas Dodson, husbandman
Ambler, Watkinson, *Clee*, 1987, pp. 154-155
Lincoln
7343 Joh Glen, barber
Johnston, *Lincoln*, 1991, pp. 3-6
Winteringham
7344 Elizabeth Kitching
Neave, *Winteringham*, 1984, p. 78

Northamptonshire

Hannington
Thomas Alderman, husbandman (see Old)
Old
7345 Thomas Alderman, husbandman (also listed Hannington)
Alderman, *Alderman*, 2008, pp. 49-50

Oxfordshire

Broughton Castle
7346 William Fiennes, Viscount Saye and Seale
Slade, 1981, pp. 155-156

Shropshire

Dawley, Little Dawley
7347 Richard Gittins
Trinder and Cox, *Telford*, 1980, pp. 164-165
Halesowen
7348 Richard Mucklowe, yeoman
Barley, *Farmhouse and Cottage*, 1961, pp. 283-284
Wellington
7349 Thomas Wright, dyer
Trinder and Cox, *Telford*, 1980, pp. 251-252

Staffordshire

Ettingshall
7350 John Hickmans, locksmith
Roper, *Sedgley*, 1960, pp. 37-38
Lichfield St Mary
7351 Michael Hardinge, ironmonger
Vaisey, *Lichfield*, 1969, pp. 126-128
Upper Gornal
7352 Nicholas Wigsteed alias Rashe
Roper, *Sedgley*, 1960, p. 38

Sussex

Warnham
7353 Henry Summersell, husbandman
Barley, *Farmhouse and Cottage*, 1961, p. 285
West Itchenor
7354 John Knight, clergyman [rector of West Itchenor]
Hughes, *Sussex*, 2007, pp. 124-125

Worthing
7355 Richard Hunn
Fenton, 1887, pp. 98-99

Warwickshire

Shottery
7356 John Cotterell, husbandman
Jones, *Stratford*, II, 2003, pp. 112-113

Wiltshire

Marlborough
7357 William Brunsdon
Williams and Thomson, *Marlborough*, 2007, p. 110
7358 Mr Thomas Fownes, gentleman
Williams and Thomson, *Marlborough*, 2007, p. 110
7359 Francis Herrin, feltmaker
Williams and Thomson, *Marlborough*, 2007, p. 108
7360 Deborah Pryor, widow
Williams and Thomson, *Marlborough*, 2007, pp. 109-110

Worcestershire

Shell in Himbleton
7361 John Fincher, gentleman
Wanklyn, *Worcestershire*, 1998, pp. 182-186
Hanley Castle
7362 Thomas Russell, esquire
Wanklyn, *Worcestershire*, 1998, pp. 186-189

Yorkshire

Knaresborough, Tentergate
7363 Jane Richardson
Brears, *Yorkshire*, 1972, pp. 123-124

1662 (c.)

Wiltshire

Marlborough
7364 Kateren Horner, widow
Williams and Thomson, *Marlborough*, 2007, pp. 108-109

1663

Bristol

Bristol, Temple
7365 Henry Branch, silk weaver
George, *Bristol*, 2005, pp. 18-19
Bristol, St Thomas
7366 Thomas Northall
George, *Bristol*, 2005, pp. 19-20
Bristol, St Werburgh
7367 John Wale, mercer
George, *Bristol*, 2005, pp. 20-22
Stoke Bishop
7368 William Collins, miller
Moore, *Clifton*, 1981, p. 97
7369 William Rumney, [husbandman]
Moore, *Clifton*, 1981, pp. 96-97
Westbury
7370 Joan Maddox, widow
Moore, *Clifton*, 1981, p. 98

Buckinghamshire

Aston Abbotts
7371 Robert Hitchcock, vicar
Reed, *Buckinghamshire*, 1988, pp. 46-47
Frithsden
7372 John Countess
Reed, *Buckinghamshire*, 1988, pp. 19-20

Marlow
  7373 Silvester Widmere, mercer
    Reed, *Buckinghamshire*, 1988, pp. 20-21
Radnage
  7374 Edward Davies, labourer
    Reed, *Buckinghamshire*, 1988, pp. 18-19
Cambridgeshire
Newmarket
  7375 Daniell Thornton, [haberdasher]
    May, *Newmarket*, 1976, pp. 8-10
Cheshire
Bowdon
  7376 William Aldcroft, blacksmith
    Groves, *Bowdon*, 1998, pp. 30-31
  7377 Robert Tipping, gentleman
    Groves, *Bowdon*, 1998, pp. 23-27
Hale
  7378 Thomas Goulden, [yeoman]
    Groves, *Hale 2*, 2005, pp. 48-49
  7379 Margaret Tonge, [widow]
    Groves, *Hale 2*, 2005, pp. 43-44
  7380 William Walton, [yeoman]
    Groves, *Hale 2*, 2005, pp. 46-47
Nantwich
  7381 William Deane, skinner
    Cockcroft, *Nantwich*, 1999, pp. 111.3-4
  7382 Thomas Keene, skinner
    Cockcroft, *Nantwich*, 1999, pp. 176.2-3
  7383 Mary Lovatt, widow
    Cockcroft, *Nantwich*, 1999, pp. 193.3
  7384 Elizabeth Welsh, widow
    Cockcroft, *Nantwich*, 1999, pp. 321.4-6
  7385 Matthew Wright, gentleman
    Cockcroft, *Nantwich*, 1999, pp. 374.3-6
Sale
  7386 Alexander Barlow
    Groves, *Ashton-on-Mersey and Sale*, 2000, pp. 35-36
  7387 John Hartles, girthweb maker
    Groves, *Ashton-on-Mersey and Sale*, 2000, pp. 37-38
  7388 James Johnson alias Ottiwell, husbandman
    Groves, *Ashton-on-Mersey and Sale*, 2000, pp. 40-41
  7389 William Renshaw, yeoman
    Groves, *Ashton-on-Mersey and Sale*, 2000, pp. 42-43
Devonshire
Broadclyst
  7390 Charles Reade
    Cash, *Devon*, 1966, pp. 124-125
Cove
  7391 Grace Hooper, widow
    Cash, *Devon*, 1966, p. 123
Exeter
  7392 John Holder, gentleman
    Cash, *Devon*, 1966, pp. 123-124
Uffculme
  7393 Thomasine Carter, [shopkeeper]
    Wyatt, *Uffculme*, 1997, p. 91
  7394 John Cheeke, yeoman
    Wyatt, *Uffculme*, 1997, pp. 91-92
  7395 Henry Gill, yeoman
    Wyatt, *Uffculme*, 1997, pp. 91-92
  7396 Richard Goodridge, yeoman
    Wyatt, *Uffculme*, 1997, pp. 93-95

Widecombe
  7397 John Hamlyn, husbandman
    Alcock, 1969, pp. 104-105
Dorsetshire
Leigh
  7398 Gyles Reade, shoemaker
    Machin, *Yetminster*, 1976, No.35, (2 p p.)
Essex
Roxwell
  7399 Jane Poole, widow
    Steer, *Mid-Essex*, 1969, p. 95
Unlocated
  7400 Henry May
    Steer, *Mid-Essex*, 1969, pp. 97-98
  7401 Robert Thurgood
    Steer, *Mid-Essex*, 1969, pp. 95-96
Writtle
  7402 Mary May, widow
    Steer, *Mid-Essex*, 1969, pp. 94-95
  7403 Richard Porter, baker
    Steer, *Mid-Essex*, 1969, pp. 96-97
  7404 Thomas Sharpe
    Steer, *Mid-Essex*, 1969, pp. 93-94
Gloucestershire
Charlton Kings
  7405 Thomas Cartwright, yeoman
    Paget and Sale, *Charlton Kings*, 2003, p. 32
  7406 Thomas Whithorne, [yeoman]
    Paget and Sale, *Charlton Kings*, 2003, pp. 32-33
Cheltenham
  7407 John Dobbins
    Sale, *Cheltenham*, 1999, pp. 5-6
Cheltenham, Westal
  7408 Humphrey Yeate, yeoman
    Sale, *Cheltenham*, 1999, pp. 4-5
Frampton Cotterell
  7409 George Rodman, yeoman
    Moore, *Frampton Cotterell*, 1976, pp. 87-88
Hambrook
  7410 Mary Tayler, widow
    Moore, *Frampton Cotterell*, 1976, pp. 88-89
Westerleigh
  7411 Robert Frape, yeoman
    Moore, *Frampton Cotterell*, 1976, p. 87
Winterbourne
  7412 Isaac Linard, [yeoman]
    Moore, *Frampton Cotterell*, 1976, pp. 89-90
Herefordshire
Limebrook
  7413 Mary Wilkes, widow
    Howse, 1958, p. 167
Hertfordshire
Hertford, All Saints
  7414 Alice Dyer
    Adams, *Hertford*, 1997, pp. 67-68
Hertford, St Andrews
  7415 John Goodman
    Adams, *Hertford*, 1997, pp. 68-69
Hertford
  7416 William Nicholls, baker
    Adams, *Hertford*, 1997, pp. 16-18

Hertford, All Saints
    7417 Isubell [Isabell] Whison, widow
        Adams, *Hertford*, 1997, pp. 23-24
St Albans, St Stephens
    7418 Ann Beach, widow
        Parker, *Worldly Goods*, 2004, pp. 264-265
Isle of Man
Ronaldsway
    7419 Mr William Christian
        Anon., *Manx*, 1931-1934, pp. 170-171
Leicestershire
Kirby Muxloe
    7420 Thomas Penford, [yeoman]
        Wilshere, *Kirby Muxloe*, 1983, p. 10
Lincolnshire
Clee, Thrunscoe
    7421 John Chapman, husbandman
        Ambler, Watkinson, *Clee*, 1987, p. 156
London
Hackney
    7422 Katherine Barnes
        Wait, 1980, pp. 26-27
Scotland
Edinburgh
    7423 Gideone Lithgow, printer
        Anon., *Bassandyne*, 1836, pp. 279-281
Staffordshire
Brierley
    7424 Thomas Whit[e]house, yeoman
        Roper, *Sedgley*, 1960, p. 39
Coseley
    7425 Richard Whitehouse, nailer
        Roper, *Sedgley*, 1960, p. 42
Ettingshall
    7426 Oliver Elwall, yeoman
        Roper, *Sedgley*, 1960, p. 41
Lichfield, St Mary
    7427 William Coates, saddler
        Vaisey, *Lichfield*, 1969, pp. 130-131
Lichfield
    7428 Henry Coxe
        Vaisey, *Lichfield*, 1969, p. 136
Lichfield, St Mary
    7429 Margaret Fenton, widow
        Vaisey, *Lichfield*, 1969, pp. 132-135
Lichfield
    7430 Richard Gladwin, stationer
        Vaisey, *Lichfield*, 1969, pp. 138-139
    7431 Humfrey Hall, yeoman
        Vaisey, *Lichfield*, 1969, pp. 137-138
Lichfield, Cathedral Close
    7432 Thomas Halse, gentleman
        Vaisey, *Lichfield*, 1969, p. 128
Lichfield
    7433 Richard Knighte, capper
        Vaisey, *Lichfield*, 1969, pp. 140-141
    7434 Mathew Olliver, miller
        Vaisey, *Lichfield*, 1969, p. 129
Sedgley, Gospel End
    7435 John Hill, yeoman
        Roper, *Sedgley*, 1960, p. 40
Sedgley
    7436 John Warter, tailor
        Roper, *Sedgley*, 1960, p. 39

Smethwick
    7437 William Walker
        Bodfish, *Smethwick*, 1992, pp. 16-17
Whittington
    7438 George Bird, yeoman
        Vaisey, *Lichfield*, 1969, pp. 136-137
    7439 Thomas Grimley, yeoman
        Vaisey, *Lichfield*, 1969, pp. 131-132
    7440 John Morris, yeoman
        Vaisey, *Lichfield*, 1969, pp. 139-140
Sussex
Iping
    7441 Leonard Alexander, clergyman [rector of Iping]
        Hughes, *Sussex*, 2007, p. 122
Sutton
    7442 Aquila Cruso, clergyman [rector of Sutton]
        Hughes, *Sussex*, 2007, pp. 206-207
Trotton
    7443 Robert Tomlinson, clergyman
        Hughes, *Sussex*, 2007, pp. 219-220
Warwickshire
Stratford-on-Avon
    7444 Nicholas Dawson, yeoman
        Jones, *Stratford*, II, 2003, pp. 117-119
    7445 Robert Edkins, [wheelwright]
        Jones, *Stratford*, II, 2003, pp. 113-116
Westmorland
Kendal, Kirkland
    7446 Allan Nicholson
        Cowper, 1891, p. 37
Wiltshire
Marlborough
    7447 John Biggs, innholder
        Williams and Thomson, *Marlborough*, 2007, pp. 110-112
    7448 Andrew Clearke, wheeler
        Williams and Thomson, *Marlborough*, 2007, pp. 112-113
    7449 Robert Davise
        Williams and Thomson, *Marlborough*, 2007, p. 114
    7450 William Redford, husbandman
        Williams and Thomson, *Marlborough*, 2007, p. 113
Worcestershire
Bewdley
    7451 John Wilkes, currier
        Bewdley, *Bewdley*, 1991, pp. 167-171
Elmley Lovett
    7452 Henry Townshend, gentleman (also listed Worcester)
        Wanklyn, *Worcestershire*, 1998, pp. 189-196
Worcester
        Henry Townshend, gentleman (see Elmley Lovett)
Yorkshire
Aysgarth, Skellgill
    7453 Richard Cagill [Caygill], [fellmonger]
        Thwaite, *Abbotside*, 1967, p. 72
Aysgarth, Sedbusk
    7454 Henary [Henry] Metcalfe, yeoman
        Thwaite, *Abbotside*, 1967, pp. 73-74

1663 (c.)
Wiltshire
Marlborough
    7455 Robert Glover, glover
        Williams and Thomson, *Marlborough*, 2007, p. 113

7456 Thomas Grenaway
Williams and Thomson, *Marlborough*, 2007, pp. 114-115

1664

Bristol
Bristol, St Philip
7457 Thomas Brewer
George, *Bristol*, 2005, pp. 22-24
Shirehampton
7458 John Stokes, yeoman
Moore, *Clifton*, 1981, pp. 98-99

Buckinghamshire
Loughton
7459 William Purney
Reed, *Buckinghamshire*, 1988, pp. 47-48
Upton
7460 Richard Faulkner, yeoman
Reed, *Buckinghamshire*, 1988, p. 47

Cambridgeshire
Cambridge
7461 Thomas Williams, [stationer]
Gray and Palmer, *Cambridge*, 1915, p. 101

Cheshire
Ashton-on-Mersey, Cross Street
7462 John Devias
Groves, *Ashton-on-Mersey and Sale*, 2000, pp. 46-47
Hale
7463 Margaret Hardy
Groves, *Hale 2*, 2005, pp. 49-50
Nantwich
7464 Elizabeth Arcoll, widow
Cockcroft, *Nantwich*, 1999, pp. 14.3-7
7465 Philip Lewis, chapman
Cockcroft, *Nantwich*, 1999, p. 190.2
7466 Robert Parker, mercer
Cockcroft, *Nantwich*, 1999, pp. 239.3-5
7467 Richard Robinson
Cockcroft, *Nantwich*, 1999, pp. 269.1-4
Sale
7468 Anthony Brownell
Groves, *Ashton-on-Mersey and Sale*, 2000, pp. 44-46

Derbyshire
Bakewell
7469 Henry Bagworth
Barley, *Farmhouse and Cottage*, 1961, pp. 276-277
Chellaston
7470 John Whinyates, gentleman
Whinyates, 1894, pp. 75-80

Devonshire
Sandford
7471 Benedict Temlett
Cash, *Devon*, 1966, p. 125
Thorverton
7472 Humphry Speccott, gentleman
Cash, *Devon*, 1966, p,125
Uffculme
7473 Bridgett Baker, widow
Wyatt, *Uffculme*, 1997, pp. 96-97
7474 Ames Francke [Franck], [yeoman]
Wyatt, *Uffculme*, 1997, pp. 97-98
7475 Francis Fryer [Friar], husbandman
Wyatt, *Uffculme*, 1997, p. 96

7476 George Fursdon [Fursden], yeoman
Wyatt, *Uffculme*, 1997, pp. 95-96

Essex
Roxwell
7477 Thomas Lines, victualler
Steer, *Mid-Essex*, 1969, p. 99
7478 Mary Mitchell
Steer, *Mid-Essex*, 1969, p. 100
Writtle
7479 Thomas Hakins, yeoman
Steer, *Mid-Essex*, 1969, pp. 99-100
7480 Gamaliell Rathbane, gentleman
Steer, *Mid-Essex*, 1969, p. 98
7481 William Stringer
Steer, *Mid-Essex*, 1969, p. 99

Gloucestershire
Cheltenham
7482 Thomas Gregory, [yeoman]
Sale, *Cheltenham*, 1999, pp. 6-8
Iron Acton, Acton Ilger
7483 William Nowell, innholder
Moore, *Frampton Cotterell*, 1976, p. 93
Stoke Gifford
7484 Anthony Smith, yeoman
Moore, *Frampton Cotterell*, 1976, pp. 90-91
7485 Alice Steevens, widow
Moore, *Frampton Cotterell*, 1976, p. 92
Westerleigh
7486 John Coape, [yeoman]
Moore, *Frampton Cotterell*, 1976, p. 92
Westerleigh, Mays Hill
7487 Dorothy Tucke, widow
Moore, *Frampton Cotterell*, 1976, pp. 91-92

Hertfordshire
Hertford
7488 Baniamin [Benjamin] Bradney
Adams, *Hertford*, 1997, pp. 61-63
Hertford, All Saints, Brickendon
7489 Richard Goodman, maltster
Adams, *Hertford*, 1997, p. 13
Hertford
7490 Thomas Wheatley
Adams, *Hertford*, 1997, pp. 136-137

Lancashire
Sutton, Elton Head
7491 Richard Eltonhead, gentleman
Rankin, 1957, pp. 60-62

Lincolnshire
Lincoln, The Bail
7492 Charles Clarke, blacksmith
Johnston, *Lincoln*, 1991, pp. 6-7
Lincoln
7493 Katerne Sewell, widow [dyer]
Johnston, *Lincoln*, 1991, pp. 7-9
Winteringham
7494 Adeodatus Hodgeson
Neave, *Winteringham*, 1984, p. 79

Nottinghamshire
Upton-by-Southwell
7495 Martin Ballard, clergyman, vicar of Upton
West, 1989, pp. 81-82

Shropshire
Lilleshall, Donnington
7496 Mary Cade, widow
Trinder and Cox, *Telford*, 1980, p. 196
Little Wenlock
7497 Frances Baxter, widow
Trinder and Cox, *Severn Gorge*, 2000, pp. 241-242
Shrewsbury, Drapers' Hall and Almshouses
7498 Drapers' Company
Peele, 1947-1948, pp. 236-238
Wellington
7499 William Howle, glover
Trinder and Cox, *Telford*, 1980, pp. 252-253
Staffordshire
Hammerwich
7500 William Smith, husbandman
Vaisey, *Lichfield*, 1969, p. 144
Lichfield
7501 Joan Bayley, widow
Vaisey, *Lichfield*, 1969, pp. 144-145
Lichfield, Cathedral Close
7502 John Hopkins, clergyman, vicar choral
Vaisey, *Lichfield*, 1969, p. 143
Lichfield, St Mary
7503 William Nicholls, yeoman [maltster, innholder]
Vaisey, *Lichfield*, 1969, pp. 146-147
Lichfield
7504 Edmund Sympson, corviser
Vaisey, *Lichfield*, 1969, pp. 141-142
7505 Katherine Thacker
Vaisey, *Lichfield*, 1969, p. 142
Whittington
7506 Richard Baxter, gentleman
Vaisey, *Lichfield*, 1969, pp. 142-143
Surrey
Charlwood
7507 Thomas Roberts
Harding, *Charlwood*, 1976, p. 98
Sussex
Burwash
7508 William Attersoll, clergyman
Hughes, *Sussex*, 2007, pp. 38-40
Wales
Montgomeryshire, Llanfihangel, Farchwel
7509 David John ap Humfffrey
Gilson, *Llanfihangel*, 2009, pp. 38-39
Warwickshire
Stratford-on-Avon
7510 Richard Baker
Jones, *Stratford*, II, 2003, p. 119
7511 John Careles, yeoman [maltster]
Jones, *Stratford*, II, 2003, pp. 122-123
7512 Thomas Morrell, [tanner]
Jones, *Stratford*, II, 2003, p. 121
7513 Jane Tomlins, widow
Jones, *Stratford*, II, 2003, pp. 124-126
7514 Edward Walford, tanner
Jones, *Stratford*, II, 2003, pp. 126-127
7515 William Wilkins, shoemaker
Jones, *Stratford*, II, 2003, p. 120
Wiltshire
Marlborough
7516 John Bristowe
Williams and Thomson, *Marlborough*, 2007, pp. 116-117

7517 John Elliott, baker
Williams and Thomson, *Marlborough*, 2007, p. 117
7518 Merrick Spender, saddler
Williams and Thomson, *Marlborough*, 2007, pp. 115-116
Worcestershire
Bockleton
7519 Nicholas Acton, esquire
Wanklyn, *Worcestershire*, 1998, pp. 196-199
Yorkshire
Acklam
7520 Thomas Bowser, yeoman
Wagner, 1966, pp. 120-121
Aysgarth, Cotterdale
7521 John Metcalfe
Thwaite, *Abbotside*, 1967, p. 75
Lunds
7522 Humfray Gibson
Thwaite, *Abbotside*, 1967, p. 74

1664 (c.)
Cheshire
Sale
7523 Jane Peers
Groves, *Ashton-on-Mersey and Sale*, 2000, p. 47

1665
Bristol
Bristol, St Thomas
7524 Edward Nelson, baker
George, *Bristol*, 2005, pp. 24-25
Bristol, St Nicholas
7525 Mr John Paterson
George, *Bristol*, 2005, pp. 26-27
Clifton
7526 John Hall, mariner
Moore, *Clifton*, 1981, p. 100
Shirehampton
7527 Mary Rome, widow
Moore, *Clifton*, 1981, p. 99
Buckinghamshire
Amersham
7528 Edward Parratt, maltster
Reed, *Buckinghamshire*, 1988, pp. 49-51
Great Horwood
7529 Samuel Friers, clerk
Reed, *Buckinghamshire*, 1988, pp. 48-49
Medmenham
7530 Knightley Duffield, esquire
Reed, *Buckinghamshire*, 1988, pp. 52-55
Cheshire
Ashton-on-Mersey
7531 George Ravald, [husbandman]
Groves, *Ashton-on-Mersey and Sale*, 2000, pp. 50-51
Bowdon
7532 Samuel Saunders, yeoman
Groves, *Bowdon*, 1998, pp. 33-34
Hale
7533 William Vawdrey, [gentleman]
Groves, *Hale 2*, 2005, pp. 50-53
Nantwich
7534 Alice Ackson, widow
Cockcroft, *Nantwich*, 1999, p. 2.2
7535 William Pickering, barber
Cockcroft, *Nantwich*, 1999, p. 249.1

7536 Elizabeth Podmore, widow
Cockcroft, *Nantwich*, 1999, p. 251.2
7537 Richard Symonds
Cockcroft, *Nantwich*, 1999, p. 300.1
7538 Edward Wettenhall, coppersmith
Cockcroft, *Nantwich*, 1999, pp. 332.3-5
Sale
7539 Anne Darbishire, [widow]
Groves, *Ashton-on-Mersey and Sale*, 2000, p. 48
7540 William Hankinson, [husbandman]
Groves, *Ashton-on-Mersey and Sale*, 2000, pp. 49-50

Devonshire
Dartmouth
7541 Henry Byrd, merchant
Cash, *Devon*, 1966, pp. 126-127
Sandford
7542 John Cobley
Cash, *Devon*, 1966, p. 126
Uffculme
7543 William Hitchcocke [Hitchcock], fuller
Wyatt, *Uffculme*, 1997, p. 98

Dorsetshire
Chetnole
7544 Thomas Downton, yeoman
Machin, *Yetminster*, 1976, No.37, (3 pp.)
Machin, 1978, pp. 160-162
Leigh
7545 William Downton
Machin, *Yetminster*, 1976, No.38, (1 p.)
Yetminster
7546 Margaret Thresher, widow
Machin, *Yetminster*, 1976, No.39, (2 pp.)
7547 John Willis, [husbandman, carpenter]
Machin, *Yetminster*, 1976, No.36, (1 p.)

Essex
Roxwell
7548 Henry Battle
Steer, *Mid-Essex*, 1969, pp. 102-103
Writtle
7549 Henry Dorington
Steer, *Mid-Essex*, 1969, pp. 100-101
7550 Edward Halden
Steer, *Mid-Essex*, 1969, pp. 101-102
7551 Andrew Hall, tanner
Steer, *Mid-Essex*, 1969, p. 103

Gloucestershire
Westerleigh
7552 Richard Ford, yeoman
Moore, *Frampton Cotterell*, 1976, p. 93

Herefordshire
Monkland
7553 Oliver Jones, chapman
Spufford, *Reclothing*, 1984, pp. 161-162

Hertfordshire
Hertford
7554 Edward Tuffnell, surgeon
Adams, *Hertford*, 1997, p. 22
St Albans, St Stephens
7555 William Ewer, [yeoman]
Munby, *Worldly Goods*, 1991, pp. 155-157

Ireland
Cork
7556 Edmond Ronayne
Caulfield, 1854-1855, pp. 324-326

Kent
Sevenoaks
7557 Edward Courthop, gentleman
Lansberry, *Sevenoaks*, 1988, pp. 41-43
7558 John French, carpenter
Lansberry, *Sevenoaks*, 1988, p. 34
Shoreham
7559 Robert Oliver, gentleman
Duncombe, *Darent*, 1990-1991, pp. 337-338

Leicestershire
Glenfield
7560 Elias Chapman, [weaver]
Wilshere, *Glenfield*, 1983, p. 8
Great Stretton
7561 Robert Eaton, yeoman
Wilshere, *Great Stretton*, 1984, p. 18

Lincolnshire
Clee, Thrunscoe
7562 Edward Laceby, husbandman
Ambler, Watkinson, *Clee*, 1987, pp. 156-157
Lincoln
7563 Benjamin Marshall, mercer
Johnston, *Lincoln*, 1991, pp. 9-21
Winteringham
7564 Jane Bradley
Neave, *Winteringham*, 1984, pp. 79-80
7565 John Moore, [orphan]
Neave, *Winteringham*, 1984, p. 80

London
Masons' Hall
7566 Masons' Company
Conder, 1894, pp. 178-179
St Boltolph, Aldgate
7567 Isaack Pluvier, [clockmaker]
Stevens, 1962-1965, pp. 18-21

Norfolk
Roydon
7568 Thomas Waynforth, maltster and brewer
Barley, *Farmhouse and Cottage*, 1961, pp. 281-283

Shropshire
Dawley, Little Dawley, Middle Leasow
7569 Humphrey Peploe, husbandman
Trinder and Cox, *Telford*, 1980, pp. 165-166
Madeley
7570 Roger Evans
Trinder and Cox, *Severn Gorge*, 2000, pp. 268-269
7571 Francis Rushon, husbandman
Trinder and Cox, *Severn Gorge*, 2000, p. 267
Wellington, Walcot
7572 Rowland Griffiths
Trinder and Cox, *Telford*, 1980, pp. 253-254

Staffordshire
Elmhurst
7573 Richard Hiblin, husbandman
Vaisey, *Lichfield*, 1969, p. 148
Lichfield
7574 Joan Bayly
Vaisey, *Lichfield*, 1969, p. 149
Lichfield, St Mary
7575 Walter Burton, musician
Vaisey, *Lichfield*, 1969, pp. 149-151
Lichfield
7576 William Right [Wright], yeoman
Vaisey, *Lichfield*, 1969, p. 151

Whittington
  7577 Richard Bird, husbandman
    Vaisey, *Lichfield*, 1969, pp. 148-149

Surrey
 Charlwood
  7578 John Constable, yeoman
    Harding, *Charlwood*, 1976, pp. 99-101
  7579 Ambrose Martin, gentleman
    Harding, *Charlwood*, 1976, pp. 98-99
  7580 George Saunders, yeoman
    Harding, *Charlwood*, 1976, p. 99

Sussex
 Arundel
  7581 John Maynard, clergyman [vicar of Arundel]
    Hughes, *Sussex*, 2007, p. 8

Wiltshire
 Edington
  7582 Anne, Lady Beauchamp, widow
    Anon., *Beauchamp*, 1963, pp. 384-393
 Marlborough
  7583 Roger Davis alias Morris
    Williams and Thomson, *Marlborough*, 2007, p. 118
  7584 Thomas Pidding, shoemaker
    Williams and Thomson, *Marlborough*, 2007, pp. 119-120
  7585 Nathanyell Winter, goldsmith
    Williams and Thomson, *Marlborough*, 2007, pp. 118-119

Worcestershire
 Shurnock in Feckenham
  7586 John Egioke, esquire
    Wanklyn, *Worcestershire*, 1998, pp. 199-201

1665 (c.)
Staffordshire
 Upper Gornal
  7587 Henry Jewkes
    Roper, *Sedgley*, 1960, p. 43
Wiltshire
 Marlborough
  7588 Nathaniel Hone, shoemaker
    Williams and Thomson, *Marlborough*, 2007, p. 118
  7589 William Hunt, husbandman
    Williams and Thomson, *Marlborough*, 2007, pp. 117-118

1666
Bristol
 Bristol, St Thomas
  7590 Ralph Eyton, clothier
    George, *Bristol*, 2005, pp. 28-30
 Bristol, St John
  7591 Mary Stephens, widow
    George, *Bristol*, 2005, pp. 30-31
 Shirehampton
  7592 Margaret Greene, [widow]
    Moore, *Clifton*, 1981, p. 101
 Stoke Bishop
  7593 Matthew Adlam, husbandman
    Moore, *Clifton*, 1981, pp. 100-101
 Westbury
  7594 Walter Smyth, husbandman
    Moore, *Clifton*, 1981, p. 100
Buckinghamshire
 Newport Pagnell
  7595 James Hartley
    Reed, *Buckinghamshire*, 1988, p. 55

Cheshire
 Hale
  7596 Richard Grantham, [gentleman]
    Groves, *Hale 2*, 2005, p. 54
 Nantwich
  7597 Robert Brow
    Cockcroft, *Nantwich*, 1999, p. 49.1
  7598 George Gleave, yeoman [gentleman]
    Cockcroft, *Nantwich*, 1999, pp. 134.2-4
  7599 Thomas Marshall
    Cockcroft, *Nantwich*, 1999, pp. 207.1-2
  7600 Mary Warrington
    Cockcroft, *Nantwich*, 1999, p. 327.1

Derbyshire
 Eyam
  7601 Rowland Mower, cooper
    Anon., *Documents*, 1862-1863, p. 228

Devonshire
 Alphington
  7602 John Baldwin, gentleman
    Cash, *Devon*, 1966, p. 127
 Holsworthy
  7603 John Cawker
    Cash, *Devon*, 1966, pp. 128-129
 Staverton
  7604 Richard Tiddaford
    Cash, *Devon*, 1966, pp. 127-128
 Uffculme
  7605 Edward Andrew
    Wyatt, *Uffculme*, 1997, pp. 100-102
  7606 Nicholas Holway
    Wyatt, *Uffculme*, 1997, pp. 193-194
  7607 Thomas Moulton, gentleman
    Wyatt, *Uffculme*, 1997, pp. 98-100
  7608 George Welch, weaver
    Wyatt, *Uffculme*, 1997, pp. 102-103
  7609 Attewill Wheddon [Atwill Whiddon]
    Wyatt, *Uffculme*, 1997, p. 100

Essex
 Roxwell
  7610 John Playle, yeoman
    Steer, *Mid-Essex*, 1969, pp. 104-105
 Unlocated
  7611 Samuel Coaltburt
    Steer, *Mid-Essex*, 1969, pp. 105-106
 Writtle
  7612 James Poultar, glazier
    Steer, *Mid-Essex*, 1969, pp. 103-104
Gloucestershire
 Winterbourne
  7613 Edward Coale, [yeoman]
    Moore, *Frampton Cotterell*, 1976, p. 93
Kent
 Sevenoaks
  7614 John Couper
    Lansberry, *Sevenoaks*, 1988, pp. 31-32
  7615 Jeffrey David, clothworker
    Lansberry, *Sevenoaks*, 1988, pp. 47-49
  7616 Mary Fuller
    Lansberry, *Sevenoaks*, 1988, p. 54
  7617 Richard Harling, labourer
    Lansberry, *Sevenoaks*, 1988, p. 52

7618 Parnell Hunt, widow
Lansberry, *Sevenoaks*, 1988, pp. 50-52
7619 Thomas Masters, yeoman
Lansberry, *Sevenoaks*, 1988, pp. 44-45
7620 Richard Spilstead, butcher
Lansberry, *Sevenoaks*, 1988, pp. 43-44

Lincolnshire
Winteringham
7621 Tho: Bethell, gentleman
Neave, *Winteringham*, 1984, pp. 82-83
7622 Robert Bratton, husbandman
Neave, *Winteringham*, 1984, p. 81
7623 Petter Walker, labourer
Neave, *Winteringham*, 1984, pp. 83-84
7624 Frances Warde, widow
Neave, *Winteringham*, 1984, pp. 85-86

Shropshire
Dawley
7625 Richard Darwall
Trinder and Cox, *Telford*, 1980, p. 166
Dawley, Little Dawley
7626 Frances Richards, widow
Trinder and Cox, *Telford*, 1980, p. 167
Madeley
7627 Humphrey Bowdler, gentleman
Trinder and Cox, *Severn Gorge*, 2000, pp. 269-270

Staffordshire
Coseley
7628 Mathias Gibbens
Roper, *Sedgley*, 1960, p. 44
Lichfield
7629 Thomas Baggaley, joiner
Vaisey, *Lichfield*, 1969, pp. 153-154
7630 Richard Beardsley, saddler
Vaisey, *Lichfield*, 1969, pp. 151-152
7631 William Fletcher, tailor
Vaisey, *Lichfield*, 1969, p. 164
7632 John Harvey, husbandman
Vaisey, *Lichfield*, 1969, p. 164
7633 Ursula Ithell, widow
Vaisey, *Lichfield*, 1969, pp. 161-163
Lichfield, Cathedral Close
7634 Thomas Morgill alias Pulson, clerk of the
cathedral
Vaisey, *Lichfield*, 1969, p. 154
Lichfield
7635 Samuel Newboult, apothecary
Vaisey, *Lichfield*, 1969, pp. 155-159
7636 William Taylor, husbandman
Vaisey, *Lichfield*, 1969, p. 155

Surrey
Charlwood
7637 Oliver Nye
Harding, *Charlwood*, 1976, p. 101

Sussex
Cuckfield
7638 Samuel Greenhill, clergyman [vicar of Cuckfield]
Hughes, *Sussex*, 2007, p. 56
Parham
7639 Richard Lewes, clergyman [rector of Parham]
Hughes, *Sussex*, 2007, p. 162

Unlocated
Unlocated
7640 Willm Bowell
Halliwell, 1852, pp. 14-17

Wiltshire
Mere
7641 Edward Goddard, gentleman
Goddard, 1902-1904, p. 171

Yorkshire
Aysgarth, Sedbusk
7642 Thomas Gibbson [Gibson]
Thwaite, *Abbotside*, 1967, p. 77
7643 Augustin Metcalfe
Thwaite, *Abbotside*, 1967, p. 78
Bainbridge, Brockhill Cote
7644 John Guy, yeoman
Thwaite, *Abbotside*, 1967, pp. 76-77
Barnoldswick, Brockden
7645 Marie Higgin
Kirk, *Barnoldswick*, 1951, pp. 68-69
Leeds, Colton
7646 Elizabeth Reader, widow
Kirk, *Temple Newsam*, 1935, p. 276

1667
Bristol
Bristol, St Stephen
7647 Richard Hill
George, *Bristol*, 2005, pp. 31-33
7648 John Lane, mariner
George, *Bristol*, 2005, pp. 33-35
Clifton
7649 George Northover, [innkeeper]
Moore, *Clifton*, 1981, pp. 105-106
Redland
7650 Thomas Willington, husbandman
Moore, *Clifton*, 1981, pp. 104-105
Shirehampton
7651 Mary Parker, widow
Moore, *Clifton*, 1981, pp. 103-104
7652 Christopher Pocock, [pilot]
Moore, *Clifton*, 1981, pp. 102-103
7653 Roger Wade, mariner
Moore, *Clifton*, 1981, p. 102
Westbury
7654 William Dymock, yeoman
Moore, *Clifton*, 1981, p. 102

Buckinghamshire
Eton
7655 Henry Chelon
Reed, *Buckinghamshire*, 1988, pp. 55-56
Padbury
7656 Mary Bampton
Reed, *Buckinghamshire*, 1988, p. 56

Cheshire
Ashton-on-Mersey
7657 Margaret Partington, [widow]
Groves, *Ashton-on-Mersey and Sale*, 2000, pp. 63-64
Hale
7658 Alice Hardy, [widow]
Groves, *Hale 2*, 2005, p. 58
7659 Peter Leicester, [gentleman]
Groves, *Hale 2*, 2005, pp. 56-57

7660   Thomas Royle, [tailor]
Groves, *Hale 2*, 2005, pp. 55-56
Nantwich
7661   John Browne, shoemaker
Cockcroft, *Nantwich*, 1999, pp. 53.2-4
7662   Lawrence Davies, blacksmith
Cockcroft, *Nantwich*, 1999, pp. 105.2-3
7663   Randull Gibbons, yeoman
Cockcroft, *Nantwich*, 1999, pp. 133.3-4
7664   Gabriell Stringer, innkeeper
Cockcroft, *Nantwich*, 1999, pp. 295.1-4
7665   Elizabeth Sutton
Cockcroft, *Nantwich*, 1999, p. 297.1
7666   Richard Wilkes, yeoman
Cockcroft, *Nantwich*, 1999, pp. 348.3-4
7667   Ellen Wright, widow
Cockcroft, *Nantwich*, 1999, pp. 359.3-8

Derbyshire
Weston-on-Trent
7668   Henry Houlden, gentleman
Holden, 1930, pp. 83-88

Devonshire
Merton
7669   Arthur Downe
Cash, *Devon*, 1966, p. 129
Uffculme
7670   Willyam [William] Crosse, yeoman
Wyatt, *Uffculme*, 1997, p. 103

Dorsetshire
Yetminster
7671   Ellin Perat, widow
Machin, *Yetminster*, 1976, No.40, (2 pp.)

Essex
Writtle
7672   Samuel Hanbery
Steer, *Mid-Essex*, 1969, pp. 106-107

Gloucestershire
Frampton Cotterell
7673   Margaret Naish, widow
Moore, *Frampton Cotterell*, 1976, p. 96
Hambrook
7674   Ann Baylie, widow
Moore, *Frampton Cotterell*, 1976, p. 94
Stoke Gifford
7675   Alice Edwards
Moore, *Frampton Cotterell*, 1976, p. 94
7676   Joseph Simmons, yeoman
Moore, *Frampton Cotterell*, 1976, pp. 95-96
Winterbourne
7677   Margaret Noble, widow
Moore, *Frampton Cotterell*, 1976, p. 94

Hertfordshire
Hertford
7678   Francis Clarke, chapman
Adams, *Hertford*, 1997, pp. 25-26
Hertford, St Andrews
7679   Arthur Randolph, tobacconist
Adams, *Hertford*, 1997, p. 70
Hertford, All Saints
7680   Joane Trayherne [Joan Treyherne]
Adams, *Hertford*, 1997, pp. 122-123
St Albans, St Stephens
7681   Elizabeth Fuller, widow
Parker, *Worldly Goods*, 2004, p. 268

Kent
Eynsford
7682   John Hibben, [yeoman]
Duncombe, *Darent*, 1990-1991, p. 302
Otford
7683   George Dennys, yeoman
Duncombe, *Darent*, 1990-1991, pp. 260-262
Sevenoaks
7684   Edward Cosier, gentleman
Lansberry, *Sevenoaks*, 1988, pp. 55-56
7685   Samuell Harman [Harmon], weaver
Lansberry, *Sevenoaks*, 1988, p. 63
7686   John Haynes, cordwainer
Lansberry, *Sevenoaks*, 1988, pp. 61-62
7687   Walter Smith, gentleman
Lansberry, *Sevenoaks*, 1988, pp. 58-60
7688   Edward Stringer, husbandman
Lansberry, *Sevenoaks*, 1988, pp. 57-58

Lincolnshire
Allington
7689   Edward Beckworth, miller
Pask, *Allington*, 1989, p. 81
Lincoln, In his Dignity house of the Close of Lincoln
7690   John Featley, Doctor of Divinity
Johnston, *Lincoln*, 1991, pp. 22-26
Lincoln
7691   Thomas Lewis, labourer
Johnston, *Lincoln*, 1991, pp. 21-22
Winteringham
7692   Robt. Browen
Neave, *Winteringham*, 1984, p. 87
7693   Isabell Browne, widow
Neave, *Winteringham*, 1984, p. 88
7694   Michael Cooke, miller
Neave, *Winteringham*, 1984, p. 84
7695   Willm Herrison
Neave, *Winteringham*, 1984, pp. 87-88
7696   Willm Hill, labourer
Neave, *Winteringham*, 1984, p. 85
7697   George Marcam, blacksmith
Neave, *Winteringham*, 1984, p. 86
7698   John Simpson
Neave, *Winteringham*, 1984, p. 89

London
St Leonard's Shoreditch
7699   Joseph Brooke
Wait, 1980, pp. 24-25

Shropshire
Benthall
7700   Lawrence Andrews
Trinder and Cox, *Severn Gorge*, 2000, p. 121
Lilleshall Lodge
7701   William Whitmore, yeoman [keeper]
Trinder and Cox, *Telford*, 1980, pp. 196-197
Madeley Wood
7702   William Ashwood, nailer
Trinder and Cox, *Severn Gorge*, 2000, pp. 270-271
Sheinton, Shinewood
7703   Peter Wood, gentleman
Wood, 1886, pp. 85-86
Wrockwardine, Allscott
7704   Thomas Cope, miller
Trinder and Cox, *Telford*, 1980, p. 403

Staffordshire
Lichfield
  7705 Peter Alport, locksmith
    Vaisey, *Lichfield*, 1969, pp. 169-170
  7706 Elizabeth Latham, widow
    Vaisey, *Lichfield*, 1969, pp. 165-166
  7707 Joseph Minshull
    Vaisey, *Lichfield*, 1969, pp. 166-167
Sedgley
  7708 William Banes, locksmith
    Roper, *Sedgley*, 1960, p. 45
  7709 Richard Juckes, nailer
    Roper, *Sedgley*, 1960, p. 49
Wall
  7710 William Perry
    Vaisey, *Lichfield*, 1969, pp. 164-165
Whittington
  7711 Thomas Neale, gentleman
    Vaisey, *Lichfield*, 1969, pp. 167-168

Sussex
Coombes
  7712 Lawrance Jones, clergyman [rector of Coombes]
    Hughes, *Sussex*, 2007, p. 54
Ifield
  7713 Henry Hallywell, clergyman [vicar of Ifield]
    Hughes, *Sussex*, 2007, pp. 119-120
Petworth
  7714 Mistress Francis Roberts
    Kenyon, *Petworth*, 1961, p. 122

Wales
Montgomeryshire, Llanfihangel, Llwydiarth
  7715 Owen ap Humphrey
    Gilson, *Llanfihangel*, 2009, pp. 40-41

Warwickshire
Stratford-on-Avon
  7716 William Bradely [Bradley], maltster
    Jones, *Stratford*, II, 2003, pp. 128-129
  7717 William Smart, tailor
    Jones, *Stratford*, II, 2003, pp. 129-130

Wiltshire
Marlborough
  7718 Thomas Hibarde
    Williams and Thomson, *Marlborough*, 2007, pp. 120-121
  7719 Thomas Keynton
    Williams and Thomson, *Marlborough*, 2007, p. 121
  7720 Thomas Shipreeve, mason
    Williams and Thomson, *Marlborough*, 2007, p. 120

Worcestershire
Bewdley
  7721 Francis Bromwich, gentleman
    Bewdley, *Bewdley*, 1991, p 174-176
Upton-on-Severn
  7722 Henry Bromley, esquire
    Wanklyn, *Worcestershire*, 1998, pp. 201-203

Yorkshire
Austerfield
  7723 Margaret Walker, widow
    Rodgers, 1999, pp. 167-168
Aysgarth, Shaw Cote
  7724 John Blades
    Thwaite, *Abbotside*, 1967, p. 84

Hardrow
  7725 Richard Metcalfe, yeoman
    Thwaite, *Abbotside*, 1967, pp. 81-82
Leeds, Halton
  7726 Jane Hartley, widow
    Kirk, *Temple Newsam*, 1935, pp. 264-265
North Bierley
  7727 William Richardson, gentleman
    Brears, *Yorkshire*, 1972, pp. 125-131
Temple Newsam
  7728 Thomas Bywater, yeoman
    Kirk, *Temple Newsam*, 1935, pp. 251-252

1667 (c.)
Surrey
Charlwood
  7729 John Young, ploughwright
    Harding, *Charlwood*,1976, pp. 101-102

1668
Bristol
Bristol
  7730 Thomas Adeane, cathedral organist
    George, *Bristol*, 2005, pp. 35-36
Bristol, Temple
  7731 Thomas Bishop, tailor
    George, *Bristol*, 2005, pp. 36-38
Bristol, St Thomas
  7732 John Chock, bodice maker
    George, *Bristol*, 2005, pp. 38-39
Bristol
  7733 Sir Henry Creswicke, merchant
    McGrath, 1955, pp. 92-100
Bristol, St Peter
  7734 John Seager, tanner
    George, *Bristol*, 2005, pp. 39-40
Shirehampton
  7735 Richard Willington, [yeoman]
    Moore, *Clifton*, 1981, pp. 106-107
Westbury
  7736 Henry Brereton, minister
    Moore, *Clifton*, 1981, pp. 107-109

Buckinghamshire
Brill
  7737 Edward Hart, esquire (also listed Tring, Hertfordshire)
    Reed, *Buckinghamshire*, 1988, pp. 56-60
Chesham
  7738 William Biggnell, yeoman
    Reed, *Buckinghamshire*, 1988, pp. 63-66
Ivinghoe Aston
  7739 John Duncombe
    Reed, *Buckinghamshire*, 1988, pp. 66-69
Marlow
  7740 Sylvester Widmere, mercer
    Reed, *Buckinghamshire*, 1988, pp. 21-46
Wendover, Wellwick
  7741 William Denton, gentleman
    Reed, *Buckinghamshire*, 1988, pp. 61-63

Cambridgeshire
Cambridge
  7742 John Field, Printer to the University
    McKitterick, 1990, pp. 505-512

Cheshire
Bowdon
7743   Richard Goulden, yeoman
Groves, *Bowdon*, 1998, pp. 37-38
Nantwich
7744   John Clowes, cordwainer
Cockcroft, *Nantwich*, 1999, pp. 79.1-2
7745   Margaret Deane, widow
Cockcroft, *Nantwich*, 1999, pp. 112.3-4
7746   Margerie Gleave, widow
Cockcroft, *Nantwich*, 1999, pp. 135.2-4
7747   Isaac Hyde, yeoman
Cockcroft, *Nantwich*, 1999, pp. 164.4-6
7748   William Reynolds
Cockcroft, *Nantwich*, 1999, p. 266.1
7749   Elizabeth Wylde
Cockcroft, *Nantwich*, 1999, p. 375.1

Devonshire
Uffculme
7750   William Goodridge, husbandman
Wyatt, *Uffculme*, 1997, pp. 105-106
7751   Edward Marshall, fuller
Wyatt, *Uffculme*, 1997, pp. 103-105
7752   Anne Wyatt
Wyatt, *Uffculme*, 1997, p. 105

Dorsetshire
Leigh
7753   Reynoll Butt
Machin, *Yetminster*, 1976, No.41, (2 pp.)
7754   Anne Reade, widow
Machin, *Yetminster*, 1976, No.42, (2 pp.)
Machin, 1978, pp. 163-164
7755   William Taunton, [victualler]
Machin, *Yetminster*, 1976, No.46, (2 pp.)
Yetminster
7756   John King, yeoman
Machin, *Yetminster*, 1976, No.43, (2 pp.)
Yetminster [?]
7757   Roger Hawkins, [grazier, butcher]
Machin, *Yetminster*, 1976, No.44, (2 pp.)
Yetminster
7758   [Thomas?] Watts
Machin, *Yetminster*, 1976, No.45, (1 p.)

Essex
Roxwell
7759   Richard Josslin
Steer, *Mid-Essex*, 1969, pp. 107-109
7760   Rubin Mason, yeoman
Steer, *Mid-Essex*, 1969, p. 109
Unlocated
7761   John Atwood
Steer, *Mid-Essex*, 1969, p. 107
Writtle
7762   John Shettlworth, yeoman
Steer, *Mid-Essex*, 1969, p. 107

Gloucestershire
Stoke Gifford
7763   John Savage, [husbandman]
Moore, *Frampton Cotterell*, 1976, p. 97
Winterbourne
7764   John Legg, [husbandman]
Moore, *Frampton Cotterell*, 1976, pp. 96-97

Hampshire
Carisbrooke, Bowcombe, Isle of Wight
7765   Sir Faithfull Fosques [Fortescue]
Clermont, 1869, pp. 375-376

Hertfordshire
Hertford, All Saints
7766   Edward Bickerton
Adams, *Hertford*, 1997, pp. 85-86
St Albans, St Stephens
7767   Ann Nash, widow
Parker, *Worldly Goods*, 2004, pp. 264-265
Sarratt
7768   John Child [Childe], yeoman
Bullen, *Sarratt*, [1982], pp. 171-172
Tring
Edward Hart (see Brill, Buckinghamshire)

Kent
Sevenoaks
7769   William Everest, tailor
Lansberry, *Sevenoaks*, 1988, pp. 72-73
7770   Alice Gill, widow
Lansberry, *Sevenoaks*, 1988, pp. 74-75
7771   George Johnson
Lansberry, *Sevenoaks*, 1988, pp. 75-77
7772   Thomas Taylor, butcher
Lansberry, *Sevenoaks*, 1988, pp. 36-39
7773   John Thornton, innholder
Lansberry, *Sevenoaks*, 1988, pp. 67-70
7774   Thomas Weston, mercer
Lansberry, *Sevenoaks*, 1988, pp. 77-78
7775   Thomas Wickendon, mercer
Lansberry, *Sevenoaks*, 1988, pp. 78-79

Leicestershire
Evington
7776   Peter Plumer, [yeoman]
Wilshere, *Evington*, 1985, p. 28

Lincolnshire
Allington
7777   John Harston, labourer
Pask, *Allington*, 1989, p. 83
Lincoln
7778   Mr John Towndrow, baker
Johnston, *Lincoln*, 1991, pp. 26-28
Winteringham
7779   Mathew Edwards
Neave, *Winteringham*, 1984, p. 92
7780   Edward Roberts, [carpenter]
Neave, *Winteringham*, 1984, pp. 90-91
7781   Jane Steeper, widow
Neave, *Winteringham*, 1984, pp. 93-94
7782   Willm Stevenson
Neave, *Winteringham*, 1984, pp. 89-90
7783   Mathew Waddingham
Neave, *Winteringham*, 1984, pp. 91-92
7784   Hugh Winteringam
Neave, *Winteringham*, 1984, pp. 92-93

Middlesex
Osterley Park
7785   Sir William Waller
Reed, 1990, pp. 116-120

Oxfordshire
Water Eaton
7786   John Shreeve, [husbandman]
Offord, *Water Eaton*, 1986, pp. 26-27

Shropshire
Broseley
  7787 Francis Adams, gentleman
    Trinder and Cox, *Severn Gorge*, 2000, p. 145
  7788 Thomas Crew, pedlar
    Trinder and Cox, *Severn Gorge*, 2000, p. 146
  7789 Jones Edward
    Trinder and Cox, *Severn Gorge*, 2000, pp. 146-147
Dawley, Little Dawley, The Ridges
  7790 Eliza Darrall, widow
    Trinder and Cox, *Telford*, 1980, pp. 167-168
Lilleshall
  7791 William Leeke, miller
    Trinder and Cox, *Telford*, 1980, pp. 197-198
Little Wenlock
  7792 William Green, yeoman
    Trinder and Cox, *Severn Gorge*, 2000, pp. 242-243
Wrockwardine, Nash
  7793 Hercules Felton
    Trinder and Cox, *Telford*, 1980, pp. 403-404

Somerset
Horsington
  7794 William Furnell, yeoman
    Daniel, *Furnell*, 1968, pp. 68-69

Staffordshire
Lichfield, St Chad
  7795 Ann Holmes, widow
    Vaisey, *Lichfield*, 1969, pp. 170-171
Lichfield
  7796 William Tunckes, gentleman [tanner]
    Vaisey, *Lichfield*, 1969, pp. 172-173
Whittington
  7797 Roger Owin, day labourer
    Vaisey, *Lichfield*, 1969, p. 174

Sussex
North Mundham
  7798 George Moore, clergyman [vicar of North
  Mundham]
    Hughes, *Sussex*, 2007, p. 145
Thakeham
  7799 William Corderoy, clergyman
    Hughes, *Sussex*, 2007, pp. 210-212

Wales
Caernarvonshire, Llandygwynning
  7800 William Williams
    Owen, *Lleyn*, 1960, p. 78

Warwickshire
Stratford-on-Avon
  7801 Thomas Smith, cooper
    Jones, *Stratford*, II, 2003, p. 131

Wiltshire
Marlborough
  7802 Susan Guy, widow
    Williams and Thomson, *Marlborough*, 2007, pp. 124-125
  7803 William Hobbs, husbandman
    Williams and Thomson, *Marlborough*, 2007, p. 126
  7804 Robert Looker, blacksmith
    Williams and Thomson, *Marlborough*, 2007, pp. 121-122
  7805 Alice Mayo, widow
    Williams and Thomson, *Marlborough*, 2007, pp. 125-126
  7806 Margrett Redford, widow
    Williams and Thomson, *Marlborough*, 2007, pp. 122-123

  7807 Clement Smith, waggoner
    Williams and Thomson, *Marlborough*, 2007, pp. 123-124
  7808 Walter Titcombe, [shoemaker]
    Williams and Thomson, *Marlborough*, 2007, p. 124
  7809 John Waterlin
    Williams and Thomson, *Marlborough*, 2007, p. 125

Worcestershire
Bedwardine
  7810 William Nicholls, cordwainer
    West, *Village Records*, 1962, pp. 116-117
Bedwardine, Upper Wick in St Johns
  7811 Herberte [Herbert] Wallwyn, gentleman
    Wanklyn, *Worcestershire*, 1998, pp. 205-208
Bewdley
  7812 William Clare, gentleman
    Bewdley, *Bewdley*, 1991, pp. 173-174
  7813 Thomas Moore, gentleman
    Bewdley, *Bewdley*, 1991, pp. 171-172
Evesham
  7814 Edward Bickerton, joiner
    West, *Village Records*, 1962, p. 116
Kidderminster
  7815 Edward Bayneham, clothier
    West, *Village Records*, 1962, pp. 115-116
  7816 Alice Stinten, sempstress
    West, *Village Records*, 1962, p. 115
Ombersley, Acton Hall
  7817 Richard Bourne
    Wanklyn, *Worcestershire*, 1998, pp. 208-210
Sodington
  7818 Sir John Blount, baronet
    Wanklyn, *Worcestershire*, 1998, p. 203
Tredington
  7819 [Wil]liam Baldwyn, esquire
    Wanklyn, *Worcestershire*, 1998, pp. 204-205

Yorkshire
Elmswell
  7820 John Best, gentleman
    Robinson, 1857, pp. 175-176
Hardrow
  7821 Christopher Routh, [yeoman]
    Thwaite, *Abbotside*, 1967, p. 86
Knaresborough
  7822 Peter Thorpe
    Brears, *Yorkshire*, 1972, pp. 132-133
Slaithwaite
  7823 Edmond Bothomoly, [chapman]
    Brears, *Yorkshire*, 1972, pp. 134-138

1669
Bristol
Bristol, St Philip and St Jacob
  7824 Thomas Andrewes, charcoal maker
    George, *Bristol*, 2005, pp. 41-42
Bristol, St John
  7825 Edward Langley, merchant
    George, *Bristol*, 2005, pp. 42-45
Shirehampton
  7826 Mary Pocock, widow
    Moore, *Clifton*, 1981, pp. 111-112
  7827 John Smith, [mariner?]
    Moore, *Clifton*, 1981, p. 110
  7828 Thomas Willis, [yeoman]
    Moore, *Clifton*, 1981, pp. 112-113

Westbury
7829 Thomas Adlam, [yeoman]
Moore, *Clifton*, 1981, pp. 110-111
7830 Jane Rumney, widow
Moore, *Clifton*, 1981, pp. 109-110

Buckinghamshire
Buckingham
7831 Samuel Bell, gentleman
Reed, *Buckinghamshire*, 1988, pp. 72-73
7832 Susan Pipin, widow
Reed, *Buckinghamshire*, 1988, pp. 71-72
7833 Richard Steward, butcher
Reed, *Buckinghamshire*, 1988, pp. 69-71
Hambleden
7834 Robert Doyley, gentlemen
Reed, *Buckinghamshire*, 1988, pp. 73-76
Stony Stratford
7835 Alice Hartley, widow
Reed, *Buckinghamshire*, 1988, p. 72

Cambridgeshire
Newmarket
7836 Jeremiah Gawen, innholder
May, *Newmarket*, 1976, pp. 10-14

Cheshire
Bowdon
7837 Ellen Woods, widow
Groves, *Bowdon*, 1998, pp. 41-42
Hale
7838 Ellen Brundrett, [widow]
Groves, *Hale 2*, 2005, p. 59
Hale, Ringway
7839 Edmund Newton, [yeoman]
Groves, *Hale 2*, 2005, pp. 62-64
Hale
7840 Richard Rylands, [tanner]
Groves, *Hale 2*, 2005, pp. 60-61
Nantwich
7841 John Cooper
Cockcroft, *Nantwich*, 1999, p. 93.1
7842 Thomas Maisterson, esquire
Cockcroft, *Nantwich*, 1999, pp. 205.3-5
7843 Margaret Parker, widow
Cockcroft, *Nantwich*, 1999, pp. 236.2-3
7844 John Price, bookseller
Cockcroft, *Nantwich*, 1999, pp. 261.2-3
7845 Margaret Sparrow
Cockcroft, *Nantwich*, 1999, p. 293.1
7846 Elizabeth Sutton
Cockcroft, *Nantwich*, 1999, p. 297.1
7847 Parnell Sutton, widow
Cockcroft, *Nantwich*, 1999, pp. 299.1-2
7848 Thomas Tench, dyer
Cockcroft, *Nantwich*, 1999, p. 307.5
7849 Anna Williams, stocking maker
Cockcroft, *Nantwich*, 1999, p. 353.1
Sale
7850 Thomas Renshaw, [yeoman]
Groves, *Ashton-on-Mersey and Sale*, 2000, pp. 65-66

Devonshire
Elmstock
7851 Elizabeth Hellings, widow
Cash, *Devon*, 1966, pp. 130-131

Staverton
7852 Margaret Cole, widow
Cash, *Devon*, 1966, p. 129
Uffculme
7853 William Hodge, tailor
Wyatt, *Uffculme*, 1997, pp. 106-107
Widecombe
7854 Walter Hamlyng
Alcock, 1969, p. 105

Dorsetshire
Chetnole
7855 Tristram Devenish
Machin, *Yetminster*, 1976, No.47, (2 pp.)
Leigh
7856 John Reade
Machin, *Yetminster*, 1976, No.48, (1 p.)
Yetminster
7857 Phillip Moore
Machin, *Yetminster*, 1976, No.49, (2 pp.)

Essex
Roxwell
7858 Richard Bright
Steer, *Mid-Essex*, 1969, pp. 110-111
Writtle
7859 Robert Meade
Steer, *Mid-Essex*, 1969, p. 111
7860 Thomas Motte, yeoman
Steer, *Mid-Essex*, 1969, pp. 109-110

France
Chaillot, Convent
7861 Queen Henrietta Maria
Madan, 1889, pp. 247-250

Gloucestershire
Charlton Kings
7862 Thomas Mansell, [husbandman]
Paget and Sale, *Charlton Kings*, 2003, pp. 38-39
Stoke Gifford
7863 Thomas Vidler, [yeoman]
Moore, *Frampton Cotterell*, 1976, p. 98
Winterbourne
7864 John Legg, [husbandman]
Moore, *Frampton Cotterell*, 1976, pp. 96-97

Kent
Sevenoaks
7865 Elizabeth Clifford, widow
Lansberry, *Sevenoaks*, 1988, p. 82
7866 Edward Porter, yeoman
Lansberry, *Sevenoaks*, 1988, pp. 18-19
7867 Robert Skynner [Skinner]
Lansberry, *Sevenoaks*, 1988, pp. 64-65
7868 George Wood, yeoman
Lansberry, *Sevenoaks*, 1988, pp. 82-84
Shoreham
7869 John Round, yeoman
Duncombe, *Darent*, 1990-1991, p. 358

Lancashire
Colne, Waterside
7870 Abraham Smith, woollen webster
Kirk, *Barnoldswick*, 1951, pp. 77-78
Manchester
7871 Edward Byrom, linen draper
Thomson, 1959, p. 47

Leicestershire
Great Stretton
7872 John Eaton, labourer
Wilshere, *Great Stretton*, 1984, p. 19
Quorndon
7873 Edward Farnham, gentleman
Farnham, *Quorndon*, 1912, pp. 414-415
Lincolnshire
Clee, Weelsby
7874 Robert Smith
Ambler, Watkinson, *Clee*, 1987, pp. 157-158
Winteringham
7875 Willym Waddingham, labourer
Neave, *Winteringham*, 1984, pp. 96-97
Norfolk
Kings Lynn
7876 Valentine Thacker, butcher
Parker, *Kings Lynn*, 1971, pp. 185-186
Stokesby
7877 Charles Wyndham, esquire
Bulwer, 1859, pp. 332-340
Oxfordshire
Water Eaton
7878 Christopher Scandrett, [gentleman]
Offord, *Water Eaton*, 1986, pp. 28-30
Shropshire
Broseley
7879 William Oakes, collier
Trinder and Cox, *Severn Gorge*, 2000, pp. 147-148
Staffordshire
Burntwood
7880 Jane Chrichle [Chruchley], widow
Vaisey, *Lichfield*, 1969, pp. 177-178
Hammerwich
7881 John Moore
Vaisey, *Lichfield*, 1969, pp. 174-175
Lichfield
7882 Henry Browne, baker
Vaisey, *Lichfield*, 1969, pp. 175-177
Sedgley, Deepdale Bank
7883 Henry Marsh, nailer
Roper, *Sedgley*, 1960, p. 46
Sedgley
7884 John Palmer, butcher
Roper, *Sedgley*, 1960, p. 47
Smethwick
7885 Tho: Cox, yeoman
Bodfish, *Smethwick*, 1992, p. 18
7886 Thomas Parkes, gentleman
Guest, 1997, pp. 190-192
Upper Gornal
7887 John Corbitt, grubber
Roper, *Sedgley*, 1960, p. 48
Whittington
7888 George Middlemore
Vaisey, *Lichfield*, 1969, p. 177
Sussex
Earnley
7889 Samuel Fowler, clergyman [rector of Earnley]
Hughes, *Sussex*, 2007, pp. 66-68
Fittleworth
7890 William Hinde, clergyman [vicar of Fittleworth]
Hughes, *Sussex*, 2007, pp. 80-81

Wales
Caernarvonshire, Aberdaron
7891 Ifan Griffith
Owen, *Lleyn*, 1960, p. 78
Warwickshire
Maxstoke Castle
7892 William Dilke, esquire
Alcock, Faulkner, Jones, 1978, pp. 229-230
Wiltshire
Marlborough
7893 Margaret Brunsdon, widow
Williams and Thomson, *Marlborough*, 2007, p. 130
7894 George Clarke, pinmaker
Williams and Thomson, *Marlborough*, 2007, p. 127
7895 Richard Idnye, [blacksmith]
Williams and Thomson, *Marlborough*, 2007, pp. 129-130
7896 John Knowles, yeoman
Williams and Thomson, *Marlborough*, 2007, pp. 127-128
7897 Henry Kybble, glazier
Williams and Thomson, *Marlborough*, 2007, pp. 126-127
7898 Edward Millington, carpenter
Williams and Thomson, *Marlborough*, 2007, pp. 128-129
7899 William Stevens
Williams and Thomson, *Marlborough*, 2007, p. 129
Worcestershire
Dowles
7900 William Dalby, clergyman
Bewdley, *Bewdley*, 1991, pp. 176-177
Ombersley, Acton Hall
7901 Richard Bourne
Wanklyn, *Worcestershire*, 1998, pp. 208-210
Yorkshire
Askrigg, Holehouse
7902 Richard Pratt, rough mason
Thwaite, *Abbotside*, 1967, p. 93
Aysgarth, Skellgill
7903 Richard Cagill [Caygill], fellmonger
Thwaite, *Abbotside*, 1967, p. 91
Aysgarth, Dale Grange
7904 John [or Thomas] Caygill
Thwaite, *Abbotside*, 1967, p. 89

1669 (c.)
Wiltshire
Marlborough
7905 William Baker, gardener
Williams and Thomson, *Marlborough*, 2007, pp. 130-131
7906 Frances Hearst
Williams and Thomson, *Marlborough*, 2007, p. 130

1670
Bristol
Bristol, St Philip and St Jacob
7907 John Cope, [hatter]
George, *Bristol*, 2005, pp. 45-46
Bristol
7908 Nicholas Whyte
George, *Bristol*, 2005, pp. 46-47
Shirehampton
7909 John Berry, pilot
Moore, *Clifton*, 1981, pp. 116-117
7910 Joan Gray, [widow]
Moore, *Clifton*, 1981, pp. 114-115
7911 James Smether, mariner
Moore, *Clifton*, 1981, pp. 115-116

7912 John Smith, pilot
  Moore, *Clifton*, 1981, p. 114
Westbury
  7913 Joan Sergeant, widow
  Moore, *Clifton*, 1981, p. 113
Buckinghamshire
Ashendon, Pollicott
  7914 William Sumner, gentleman
  Reed, *Buckinghamshire*, 1988, pp. 80-81
Chipping Wycombe
  7915 John Grove, gentleman
  Reed, *Buckinghamshire*, 1988, pp. 76-77
Ixhill
  7916 Henry Darling, yeoman
  Reed, *Buckinghamshire*, 1988, pp. 79-80
Winslow
  7917 Henry Wyatt, butcher
  Reed, *Buckinghamshire*, 1988, pp. 77-79
Cheshire
Ashton-on-Mersey
  7918 James Jones, [miller or well-keeper]
  Groves, *Ashton-on-Mersey and Sale*, 2000, p. 67
  7919 John Royle, [yeoman]
  Groves, *Ashton-on-Mersey and Sale*, 2000, pp. 70-71
  7920 Edward Woodall, [joiner]
  Groves, *Ashton-on-Mersey and Sale*, 2000, pp. 74-75
  7921 Joseph Smith, [yeoman]
  Groves, *Ashton-on-Mersey and Sale*, 2000, pp. 75-76
Hale
  7922 Richard Leather
  Groves, *Hale 2*, 2005, pp. 71-72
  7923 William Massey
  Groves, *Hale 2*, 2005, p. 65
Hale, Ringway
  7924 Ellen Newton, [widow]
  Groves, *Hale 2*, 2005, pp. 64-65
Hale
  7925 Samuel Pearson, [husbandman]
  Groves, *Hale 2*, 2005, p. 66
  7926 Thomas Person
  Groves, *Hale 2*, 2005, p. 70
Nantwich
  7927 Fulke Griffin, butcher
  Cockcroft, *Nantwich*, 1999, pp. 142.1-2
  7928 Elizabeth Harding, widow
  Cockcroft, *Nantwich*, 1999, pp. 145.2-3
  7929 Gabriel Hodgson, shoemaker
  Cockcroft, *Nantwich*, 1999, pp. 156.1-2
  7930 James Rathbone
  Cockcroft, *Nantwich*, 1999, pp. 263.1-2
  7931 Hugh Tench, tanner
  Cockcroft, *Nantwich*, 1999, pp. 304.4-6
  7932 Mary Wade, [widow]
  Cockcroft, *Nantwich*, 1999, p. 319.3
  7933 William Willcox
  Cockcroft, *Nantwich*, 1999, pp. 352.1-3
Sale
  7934 James Renshaw, [husbandman]
  Groves, *Ashton-on-Mersey and Sale*, 2000, pp. 68-69
  7935 Thomas Wood
  Groves, *Ashton-on-Mersey and Sale*, 2000, p. 78
Devonshire
Exminster
  7936 Thomasin Redway
  Worthy, *Devonshire*, 1896, pp. 26-27

Sutcombe
  7937 Richard Leonard, yeoman
  Cash, *Devon*, 1966, p. 132
Uffculme
  7938 Edmont Bishopp [Edmund Bishop], husbandman
  Wyatt, *Uffculme*, 1997, p. 107
  7939 John Butson, husbandman
  Wyatt, *Uffculme*, 1997, p. 112
  7940 Agnes Cotterell, widow
  Wyatt, *Uffculme*, 1997, pp. 108-109
  7941 Thomas Croyden, yeoman
  Wyatt, *Uffculme*, 1997, pp. 107-108
  7942 Elizabeth Fursdon [Fursden], widow
  Wyatt, *Uffculme*, 1997, pp. 109-110
  7943 John Grantland, yeoman
  Wyatt, *Uffculme*, 1997, pp. 110-111
  7944 John Jorden [Jordan]
  Wyatt, *Uffculme*, 1997, pp. 112-113
  7945 John Mills, yeoman
  Wyatt, *Uffculme*, 1997, pp. 189-191
  7946 Henry Minifie [Minifee], tailor
  Wyatt, *Uffculme*, 1997, p. 113
  7947 Christofer Palfry [Christopher Palfrey], [tailor?]
  Wyatt, *Uffculme*, 1997, p. 113
  7948 Robert Pooke, alias Weeks, husbandman
  Wyatt, *Uffculme*, 1997, p. 111
  7949 Wylliam [William] Starke, clothier
  Wyatt, *Uffculme*, 1997, pp. 111-112
  7950 John Vosse [Fosse], yeoman
  Wyatt, *Uffculme*, 1997, p. 109
Dorsetshire
Chetnole
  7951 John Hussey alias Bailey
  Machin, *Yetminster*, 1976, No.52, (1 p.)
Leigh
  7952 William Hodder
  Machin, *Yetminster*, 1976, No.53, (2 pp.)
  7953 Margaret Masters
  Machin, *Yetminster*, 1976, No.54, (2 pp.)
Yetminster
  7954 Emma Bartlett, widow
  Machin, *Yetminster*, 1976, No.51, (2 pp.)
  7955 Benjamin Miller, cordwainer
  Machin, *Yetminster*, 1976, No.50, (2 pp.)
Essex
Roxwell
  7956 John Perry, yeoman
  Steer, *Mid-Essex*, 1969, p. 117
  7957 John Sells, yeoman
  Steer, *Mid-Essex*, 1969, pp. 112-113
Unlocated
  7958 Widow Argo
  Steer, *Mid-Essex*, 1969, p. 111
  7959 John Collyn, yeoman
  Steer, *Mid-Essex*, 1969, pp. 115-116
  7960 William Irons
  Steer, *Mid-Essex*, 1969, pp. 114-115
Writtle
  7961 Henry Burlinge
  Steer, *Mid-Essex*, 1969, pp. 116-117
  7962 Richard May
  Steer, *Mid-Essex*, 1969, p. 112

Gloucestershire
Charlton Kings
  7963 Henry Collett, yeoman
    Paget and Sale, *Charlton Kings*, 2003, p. 36
  7964 John Martin, yeoman
    Paget and Sale, *Charlton Kings*, 2003, p. 37
Cheltenham
  7965 Nathaniel Chestroe, [maltster]
    Sale, *Cheltenham*, 1999, p. 13
  7966 Edward Johnson, [mercer]
    Sale, *Cheltenham*, 1999, pp. 11-12
Iron Acton, Latteridge
  7967 Richard Bracy, yeoman
    Moore, *Frampton Cotterell*, 1976, p. 99
Stoke Gifford
  7968 Dorothy Lawford, widow
    Moore, *Frampton Cotterell*, 1976, pp. 100-101
  7969 William Tillett, yeoman
    Moore, *Frampton Cotterell*, 1976, p. 101
Winterbourne
  7970 George Baune, baker
    Moore, *Frampton Cotterell*, 1976, pp. 99-100
  7971 Anthony Selcocke, yeoman
    Moore, *Frampton Cotterell*, 1976, pp. 101-102

Hertfordshire
Hertford
  7972 William Bridgman, [mealman]
    Adams, *Hertford*, 1997, p. 64
  7973 Thomas Kirbey
    Adams, *Hertford*, 1997, pp. 81-82
St Albans, St Stephens
  7974 William Harvey, bricklayer
    Parker, *Worldly Goods*, 2004, p. 272
St Albans, St Stephens, The Holt
  7975 William Kentish, [yeoman]
    Munby, *Worldly Goods*, 1991, pp. 162-163

Kent
Sevenoaks
  7976 Mr Francis Best, innkeeper
    Lansberry, *Sevenoaks*, 1988, pp. 85-90
  7977 John Walter, tailor
    Lansberry, *Sevenoaks*, 1988, p. 71
  7978 Thomasin Weston, widow
    Lansberry, *Sevenoaks*, 1988, pp. 93-95

Leicestershire
Quorndon
  7979 Peter Chaveney
    Farnham, *Quorndon*, 1912, pp. 416-417

Lincolnshire
Cleethorpes
  7980 John Yeats
    Ambler, Watkinson, *Clee*, 1987, p. 159
  7981 Thomas Yeats
    Ambler, Watkinson, *Clee*, 1987, p. 158
Lincoln, St Michaels in the Mount
  7982 Richard Hazelteine, labourer
    Johnston, *Lincoln*, 1991, pp. 32-33
Lincoln, St Swithin
  7983 William Norton, maltster
    Johnston, *Lincoln*, 1991, pp. 29-31
Lincoln
  7984 Francis Younglove, harness-seller
    Johnston, *Lincoln*, 1991, pp. 31-32

Scunthorpe, Brumby Wood Hall
  Nathanel [Nathaniel] Fiennes, esquire (see Newton
  Toney, Wiltshire)
Winteringham
  7985 Edward Boteler, clergyman [rector of
  Winteringham]
    Neave, *Winteringham*, 1984, pp. 94-96
  7986 Mary Foster
    Neave, *Winteringham*, 1984, p. 99
  7987 Willim Goodwin, yeoman
    Neave, *Winteringham*, 1984, p. 98
  7988 Roberte Kirsey, [weaver]
    Neave, *Winteringham*, 1984, p. 100
  7989 Elezebeth West, widow
    Neave, *Winteringham*, 1984, p. 97
  7990 Michael Wetherill, webster
    Neave, *Winteringham*, 1984, pp. 98-99
  7991 Edward Wilkingson
    Neave, *Winteringham*, 1984, p. 100

London
Leicester House
  7992 Robert Sidney, Earl of Leicester
    Owen, 1966, pp. 624-634

Oxfordshire
Water Eaton
  7993 Margery Cooke, [widow]
    Offord, *Water Eaton*, 1986, pp. 32-33

Shropshire
Broseley
  7994 William Lewis, trowman
    Trinder and Cox, *Severn Gorge*, 2000, p. 149
Madeley
  7995 Richard Brook, trowman
    Trinder and Cox, *Severn Gorge*, 2000, p. 271
Madeley Wood
  7996 John Yates
    Trinder and Cox, *Severn Gorge*, 2000, pp. 271-272
Wellington
  7997 Edward Harrington, yeoman
    Trinder and Cox, *Telford*, 1980, pp. 255-257
  7998 Elizabeth Walker
    Trinder and Cox, *Telford*, 1980, pp. 254-255
Wrockwardine, Admaston
  7999 Thomas Smith, yeoman
    Trinder and Cox, *Telford*, 1980, pp. 404-405

Staffordshire
Burntwood
  8000 Richard Biddulph, nailer
    Vaisey, *Lichfield*, 1969, p. 187
Colwich, Moreton
  8001 Thomas Crompton (also listed Colwich, Bishton)
    Bradley, *Haywoods*, 1993, p. 31
Colwich, Bishton, Mr Baker's house
  Thomas Crompton (see Colwich, Moreton)
Coseley
  8002 Ellen Whithouse, widow
    Roper, *Sedgley*, 1960, p. 50
Dudley
  8003 Roger Maredieth
    Roper, *Dudley*, 1966, pp. 34-35
  8004 Thomas Payton, yeoman
    Roper, *Dudley*, 1966, p. 31

8005 William Tomson, yeoman
  Roper, *Dudley*, 1966, pp. 32-33
Hammerwich
8006 Thomas Webb, yeoman
  Vaisey, *Lichfield*, 1969, pp. 181-182
Lichfield, Cathedral Close
8007 Hugh Braddocke, clergyman, [curate of St
Chad's, vicar choral]
  Vaisey, *Lichfield*, 1969, pp. 178-179
Lichfield
8008 Ellen Caterbanck, widow
  Vaisey, *Lichfield*, 1969, pp. 184-185
8009 William Langley
  Vaisey, *Lichfield*, 1969, pp. 180-181
8010 George Smabridge [Smalredge], dyer
  Vaisey, *Lichfield*, 1969, pp. 185-187
8011 William Tewe
  Vaisey, *Lichfield*, 1969, p. 180
8012 Thomas Thacker, corviser
  Vaisey, *Lichfield*, 1969, pp. 182-184
Sussex
Ashburnham
8013 Alexander Wiggs, clergyman
  Hughes, *Sussex*, 2007, p. 9
Ferring
8014 Stephen Worgar, clergyman [vicar of Ferring]
  Hughes, *Sussex*, 2007, pp. 74-76
Kirdford
8015 Richard and Jane Hoade, blacksmith
  Kenyon, *Kirdford*, 1955, pp. 132-133
Petworth, The White Hart
8016 Henry Goble, innkeeper
  Kenyon, *Petworth*, 1961, pp. 126-135
Rudgwick
8017 Thomas Meade, clergyman [vicar of Rudgwick]
  Hughes, *Sussex*, 2007, pp. 172-174
Wales
Caernarvonshire, Ceidio
8018 Thomas Hughes
  Owen, *Lleyn*, 1960, pp. 79-80
Caernarvonshire, Llanbedrog
8019 Evan John ap Evan
  Owen, *Lleyn*, 1960, p. 79
8020 Humphrey Owen
  Owen, *Lleyn*, 1960, p. 79
Glamorganshire, St George's-super-Ely
8021 William Wrinch
  Wrench, *Wrenche*, 1956, pp. 44-45
Warwickshire
Stratford-on-Avon, Old Stratford
8022 Thomas Baylis, chapman
  Jones, *Stratford*, II, 2003, pp. 134-136
Stratford-on-Avon
8023 Richard Hands, maltster
  Jones, *Stratford*, II, 2003, pp. 132-133
Wiltshire
Marlborough
8024 Sammuell Alexander
  Williams and Thomson, *Marlborough*, 2007, p. 133
8025 William Batcheller, husbandman
  Williams and Thomson, *Marlborough*, 2007, pp. 133-134
8026 John Butler, collarmaker
  Williams and Thomson, *Marlborough*, 2007, pp. 131-132

8027 Edward Wind, [shoemaker]
  Williams and Thomson, *Marlborough*, 2007, pp. 132-133
8028 John Wyat, yeoman
  Williams and Thomson, *Marlborough*, 2007, p. 134
Newton Toney
8029 Nathanel [Nathaniel] Fiennes, esquire (also
listed Scunthorpe, Lincolnshire)
  Anon., *Fiennes*, 1983, pp. 38-48
Worcestershire
Worcester, The Commandery
8030 Thomas Wylde, esquire
  Wanklyn, *Worcestershire*, 1998, pp. 210-213
Yorkshire
Colton
8031 William Brooke, yeoman
  Kirk, *Temple Newsam*, 1935, pp. 248-249
8032 Richard Cunnell, yeoman
  Kirk, *Temple Newsam*, 1935, pp. 257-258
Knaresborough, Tentergate
8033 Dorothee Wilkes
  Brears, *Yorkshire*, 1972, pp. 138-139
Lunds
8034 Michaell Dennison [Denison]
  Thwaite, *Abbotside*, 1967, pp. 93-94
8035 Willyam Dennison [William Denison],
husbandman
  Thwaite, *Abbotside*, 1967, p. 96
8036 George Wilson
  Thwaite, *Abbotside*, 1967, p. 95

1670 (c.)
Gloucestershire
Charlton Kings
8037 William Cl[eeveley], [yeoman]
  Paget and Sale, *Charlton Kings*, 2003, pp. 39-40

1671
Bristol
Bristol, St Philip and St Jacob
8038 Roger Gastrill, coal driver
  George, *Bristol*, 2005, p. 47
Bristol
8039 George Stearte, surgeon
  George, *Bristol*, 2005, pp. 47-48
Bristol, Stapleton
8040 William Tiler, husbandman
  George, *Bristol*, 2005, p. 49
Clifton
8041 Martha Chandler, widow
  Moore, *Clifton*, 1981, p. 122
8042 William Clarke, [limeburner]
  Moore, *Clifton*, 1981, p. 118
Shirehampton
8043 Elizabeth Crumwell, widow
  Moore, *Clifton*, 1981, pp. 119-121
8044 John Gush, [yeoman]
  Moore, *Clifton*, 1981, pp. 117-118
Westbury
8045 William Inon, [husbandman]
  Moore, *Clifton*, 1981, p. 119
Buckinghamshire
Bragenham
8046 Joane Meade, widow
  Reed, *Buckinghamshire*, 1988, pp. 82-83

Chalfont St Peter
8047 Richard Whichurch, gentleman
Reed, *Buckinghamshire*, 1988, pp. 84-85
Colnbrook
8048 John Warner, innholder
Reed, *Buckinghamshire*, 1988, pp. 81-82
Eton
8049 Gregory Thornedall, gentleman
Reed, *Buckinghamshire*, 1988, pp. 96-97
Thornton
8050 Sir Thomas Tirrell, baronet
Reed, *Buckinghamshire*, 1988, pp. 88-95
Turweston
8051 John Yates
Reed, *Buckinghamshire*, 1988, p. 85
Willen
8052 Richard Barnwell, yeoman
Reed, *Buckinghamshire*, 1988, pp. 85-88

Cheshire
Hale
8053 George Barlow, [yeoman]
Groves, *Hale 2*, 2005, pp. 67-68
8054 John Chapman
Groves, *Hale 2*, 2005, pp. 69-70
Nantwich
8055 Nathaniel Brerely, yeoman
Cockcroft, *Nantwich*, 1999, pp. 43.1-2
8056 John Griffin, butcher
Cockcroft, *Nantwich*, 1999, p. 141.2
8057 Richard Pearson, tanner
Cockcroft, *Nantwich*, 1999, p. 245.2
8058 Margaret Watson, widow
Cockcroft, *Nantwich*, 1999, pp. 329.4-6
8059 Robert Wilkinson, husbandman
Cockcroft, *Nantwich*, 1999, p. 351.2
Sale
8060 Edward Darbishire, [yeoman]
Groves, *Ashton-on-Mersey and Sale*, 2000, pp. 78-79

Devonshire
Hollacombe
8061 Elizabeth Veale, widow
Cash, *Devon*, 1966, p. 133
Sandford
8062 Agnes Cobley
Cash, *Devon*, 1966, p. 134
Slapton
8063 Sidrach Bassett, yeoman
Cash, *Devon*, 1966, pp. 132-133
Uffculme
8064 William Kent, dyer
Wyatt, *Uffculme*, 1997, pp. 114-115
8065 Bernard Prince, [weaver]
Wyatt, *Uffculme*, 1997, pp. 115-116
8066 Gervas Ranisford [Jarvis Ransford], husbandman (?)
Wyatt, *Uffculme*, 1997, pp. 191-192
8067 John Rawlins, yeoman
Wyatt, *Uffculme*, 1997, p. 116
Willand
8068 Robert Coles
Cash, *Devon*, 1966, p. 133

Dorsetshire
Yetminster
8069 Giles Boyte, [shoemaker]
Machin, *Yetminster*, 1976, No.57, (1 p.)

8070 Roger Meade, serge maker
Machin, *Yetminster*, 1976, No.55, (1 p.)
8071 William Roll, maltster
Machin, *Yetminster*, 1976, No.56, (1 p.)

Essex
Roxwell
8072 John Woolward
Steer, *Mid-Essex*, 1969, pp. 118-119
Writtle
8073 Nathaniell Campyon, husbandman
Steer, *Mid-Essex*, 1969, pp. 117-118
8074 George Bradford, gardener
Steer, *Mid-Essex*, 1969, pp. 209-210
8075 Daniel Leonard
Steer, *Mid-Essex*, 1969, p. 119

Gloucestershire
Charlton Kings
8076 Francis Crumpe, [blacksmith]
Paget and Sale, *Charlton Kings*, 2003, pp. 35-36
8077 Thomas Deane
Paget and Sale, *Charlton Kings*, 2003, pp. 41-42
Frenchay
8078 Samuel Smith, rough mason
Moore, *Frampton Cotterell*, 1976, p. 102
Stoke Gifford
8079 John Beames, yeoman
Moore, *Frampton Cotterell*, 1976, p. 102
8080 Anne Smith, widow
Moore, *Frampton Cotterell*, 1976, pp. 102-103

Hertfordshire
Hertford
8081 John Gurrey, grocer
Adams, *Hertford*, 1997, p. 75
Hertford, Brickendon
8082 Nathaniell Halle [Nathaniel Hale], yeoman [and maltster]
Adams, *Hertford*, 1997, pp. 126-127
Hertford
8083 John Radford, baker
Adams, *Hertford*, 1997, pp. 114-116
Sarratt
8084 Elizabeth Newman, widow
Bullen, *Sarratt*, [1982], pp. 174-175

Kent
Otford
8085 John Hackett, husbandman [yeoman]
Duncombe, *Darent*, 1990-1991, p. 283
Sevenoaks
8086 Edward Baker, victualler
Lansberry, *Sevenoaks*, 1988, pp. 97-98
8087 John Cronke, tailor
Lansberry, *Sevenoaks*, 1988, pp. 99-100
Shoreham
8088 Edward Polhill, [yeoman]
Duncombe, *Darent*, 1990-1991, pp. 348-350

Lancashire
Rochdale, Great Haworth (?)
8089 Theophilus Howorth, Doctor in Physic
Earwaker, *Lancashire and Cheshire*, 1893, pp. 111-112

Lincolnshire
Allington
8090 Robert Grant, gentleman
Pask, *Allington*, 1989, pp. 86-87

Cleethorpes
  8091 James Crawforth
    Ambler, Watkinson, *Clee*, 1987, pp. 159-160
  8092 John Draper
    Ambler, Watkinson, *Clee*, 1987, p. 160
Lincoln, St Martins
  8093 Eden Williams, bookseller
    Johnston, *Lincoln*, 1991, pp. 33-37

Shropshire
Broseley
  8094 John Adams
    Trinder and Cox, *Severn Gorge*, 2000, pp. 149-150
Lilleshall
  8095 Robert Shelton, yeoman
    Trinder and Cox, *Telford*, 1980, pp. 198-199
Little Wenlock
  8096 Richard Parton
    Trinder and Cox, *Severn Gorge*, 2000, p. 244
Wrockwardine, Long Lane
  8097 Ralph Pearce
    Trinder and Cox, *Telford*, 1980, pp. 405-406

Staffordshire
Hammerwich
  8098 Joan Milner, widow
    Vaisey, *Lichfield*, 1969, pp. 191-192
Lichfield
  8099 Henry Baker, gentleman
    Vaisey, *Lichfield*, 1969, pp. 197-200
  8100 John Brodhurst [Brandhurst]
    Vaisey, *Lichfield*, 1969, p. 194
Lichfield, St Michael
  8101 Robert Chalner [Chandler]
    Vaisey, *Lichfield*, 1969, p. 195
Lichfield
  8102 Francis Chaplaine, gentleman
    Vaisey, *Lichfield*, 1969, pp. 190-191
Lichfield, St Mary
  8103 Thomas Foster, carpenter
    Vaisey, *Lichfield*, 1969, pp. 200-201
Lichfield
  8104 Martha Lunn alias Richards, widow
    Vaisey, *Lichfield*, 1969, p. 189
  8105 Michael Ryly, chapman
    Vaisey, *Lichfield*, 1969, pp. 187-189
  8106 Mary Salt, widow
    Vaisey, *Lichfield*, 1969, pp. 192-194
Lichfield, Cathedral Close
  8107 Lisle Stotestury, gentleman
    Vaisey, *Lichfield*, 1969, pp. 195-196
Lower Gornal
  8108 John Hickmans, yeoman
    Roper, *Sedgley*, 1960, p. 54
Rugeley
  8109 Thomas Laundor
    Landor, 1934, pp. 119-122
Sedgley
  8110 Richard Cooper, blacksmith
    Roper, *Sedgley*, 1960, pp. 51-52
Sedgley, Gospel End
  8111 John Hill alias Perton
    Roper, *Sedgley*, 1960, p. 53
Smethwick
  8112 Edward Guest, yeoman
    Bodfish, *Smethwick*, 1992, p. 19

Streethay
  8113 Elizabeth Smith, widow
    Vaisey, *Lichfield*, 1969, pp. 196-197

Sussex
Washington
  8114 Nicholas Garbrand, clergyman [vicar of Washington]
    Hughes, *Sussex*, 2007, pp. 228-230
Wisborough Green, Loxwood
  8115 Thomas Jackman
    Lawson, 1999, pp. 73-75
Yapton
  8116 Robert Dalgarno, clergyman [vicar of Yapton]
    Hughes, *Sussex*, 2007, p. 246

Wales
Caernavonshire, Nevin
  8117 Richard Jones
    Owen, *Lleyn*, 1960, p. 80

Warwickshire
Alcester
  8118 Robert Farmer, yeoman
    Saville, *Alcester*, 1979, p. 7
  8119 Stephen Round, [innholder]
    Saville, *Alcester*, 1979, p. 8

Wiltshire
Marlborough
  8120 John Brookes, innkeeper
    Williams and Thomson, *Marlborough*, 2007, p. 139
  8121 Isaack Cole, surgeon
    Williams and Thomson, *Marlborough*, 2007, pp. 137-139
  8122 Richard Collat, husbandman
    Williams and Thomson, *Marlborough*, 2007, p. 137
  8123 Richard Daingerfild, baker
    Williams and Thomson, *Marlborough*, 2007, pp. 135-136
  8124 Stephen Pearce, gardener
    Williams and Thomson, *Marlborough*, 2007, p. 137
  8125 Richard Webb, linen draper
    Williams and Thomson, *Marlborough*, 2007, pp. 136-137
  8126 Henry Westell
    Williams and Thomson, *Marlborough*, 2007, pp. 134-135

Yorkshire
Bainbridge, Brockhill Cote
  8127 Robert Winn
    Thwaite, *Abbotside*, 1967, p. 97
Barnoldswick
  8128 Robert Ellis
    Kirk, *Barnoldswick*, 1951, p. 62
Leeds, Colton, Quarrell Closes
  8129 Robert Austen, yeoman
    Kirk, *Temple Newsam*, 1935, pp. 243-244
Leeds, Whitkirk
  8130 Bryan Hardwicke, yeoman
    Kirk, *Temple Newsam*, 1935, pp. 262-263

1671 (c.)
Cheshire
Hale
  8131 John Duncalfe, [yeoman]
    Groves, *Hale 2*, 2005, pp. 66-67
Staffordshire
Ettingshall
  8132 William Hickmans
    Roper, *Sedgley*, 1960, p. 51

1672

Bristol

Bristol
8133 John Birkin, soap-boiler
George, *Bristol*, 2005, pp. 49-50
8134 John Blynman, ropemaker
George, *Bristol*, 2005, pp. 50-52
8135 Flower Hunt, tobacco pipe maker
George, *Bristol*, 2005, pp. 52-53
Bristol, Christ Church
8136 Sarah Kitchen
George, *Bristol*, 2005, pp. 54-55
Bristol
8137 Paul Williams, barber surgeon
George, *Bristol*, 2005, p. 55
Lawrence Weston
8138 William Greenfield, [yeoman]
Moore, *Clifton*, 1981, pp. 123-124
Westbury
8139 Katherine Kiskins alias Heskins, widow
Moore, *Clifton*, 1981, p. 123

Buckinghamshire

Aston Clinton
8140 John Marryot
Reed, *Buckinghamshire*, 1988, pp. 99-100
Oving
8141 Richard Claver, gentleman
Reed, *Buckinghamshire*, 1988, pp. 98-99
Penn
8142 Henry Elburne, bricklayer
Reed, *Buckinghamshire*, 1988, pp. 97-98

Cheshire

Bowdon
8143 Richard Bickston
Groves, *Bowdon*, 1998, pp. 44-45
8144 Peter Hurdies, schoolmaster
Anon., *Hurdis*, 1967, pp. 30-31
Groves, *Bowdon*, 1998, pp. 47-49
8145 John Paulden
Groves, *Bowdon*, 1998, p. 46
Hale
8146 Alice Gaskell
Groves, *Hale 2*, 2005, p. 71
8147 John Goulden
Groves, *Hale 2*, 2005, p. 69
8148 Edward Pearson, [yeoman]
Groves, *Hale 2*, 2005, pp. 72-73
8149 John Warburton
Groves, *Hale 2*, 2005, pp. 73-75
Nantwich
8150 Hugh Allcock
Cockcroft, *Nantwich*, 1999, p. 8.1
8151 Randle Hare, [yeoman]
Cockcroft, *Nantwich*, 1999, pp. 148.3-4
8152 Humphrey Milton, gentleman
Cockcroft, *Nantwich*, 1999, pp. 216.1-7

Devonshire

Exeter
8153 John Lavers, innholder
Cash, *Devon*, 1966, p. 134
Huish
8154 George Yeo, esquire
Cash, *Devon*, 1966, pp. 134-135

Uffculme
8155 Johane [Joane] Salter, widow
Wyatt, *Uffculme*, 1997, pp. 116-117
8156 Ellen S[ames]
Wyatt, *Uffculme*, 1997, pp. 192

Dorsetshire

Chetnole
8157 William Symes, [yeoman]
Machin, *Yetminster*, 1976, No.58, (2 pp.)
Leigh
8158 Walter Birtt, [yeoman]
Machin, *Yetminster*, 1976, No.61, (2 pp.)
8159 Richard Warren, [yeoman]
Machin, *Yetminster*, 1976, No.59, (1 p.)
Yetminster
8160 Thomas Wright, tailor
Machin, *Yetminster*, 1976, No.62, (2 pp.)
8161 William Wright, [smith]
Machin, *Yetminster*, 1976, No.60, (2 pp.)

Essex

Roxwell
8162 John Stookes, labourer
Steer, *Mid-Essex*, 1969, p. 121
Writtle
8163 Isaac Adames, innholder
Steer, *Mid-Essex*, 1969, pp. 120-121
8164 Abraham Brecknock, yeoman
Steer, *Mid-Essex*, 1969, pp. 122-123
8165 Robert Hilliard, bricklayer
Steer, *Mid-Essex*, 1969, pp. 121-122
8166 Alexander Reynoldson
Steer, *Mid-Essex*, 1969, p. 120

Gloucestershire

Cheltenham, Alstone
8167 Jane Combe, widow
Sale, *Cheltenham*, 1999, p. 16
Winterbourne
8168 William Phillips, husbandman
Moore, *Frampton Cotterell*, 1976, p. 103

Hertfordshire

Hertford, All Saints
8169 Emery Bradney, widow
Adams, *Hertford*, 1997, pp. 87-88
Hertford
8170 Richard Kerbye [Kerby], cordwainer
Adams, *Hertford*, 1997, pp. 78-80
8171 Robert Stothard, innholder
Adams, *Hertford*, 1997, pp. 72-74
St Albans, St Stephens
8172 John Babb, [miller]
Parker, *Worldly Goods*, 2004, pp. 278-279
Sarratt
8173 Henrey Dell
Bullen, *Sarratt*, [1982], pp. 176-178

Kent

Cobham Hall
8174 Charles Stewart, Duke of Richmond and Lennox
Robertson, 1887, pp. 393-408
Sevenoaks
8175 Margery Burges [Burgess], widow
Lansberry, *Sevenoaks*, 1988, p. 81
8176 Richard Cakott, [cordwainer]
Lansberry, *Sevenoaks*, 1988, pp. 102-104

8177   John Everest, yeoman
   Lansberry, *Sevenoaks*, 1988, pp. 112-114
8178   Robert Everest, yeoman
   Lansberry, *Sevenoaks*, 1988, pp. 109-111
8179   John Groombridge, innholder
   Lansberry, *Sevenoaks*, 1988, pp. 104-105
8180   James Hope
   Lansberry, *Sevenoaks*, 1988, p. 147
8181   Richard Rundall, gardener
   Lansberry, *Sevenoaks*, 1988, pp. 105-108

Lancashire
Hall i' th' Wood, Tonge, Bolton
8182   Alexander Norris, gentleman
   Irvine, 1903, pp. 38-40

Lincolnshire
Brant Broughton
8183   William Garnon, gentleman
   Barley, *Farmhouse and Cottage*, 1961, pp. 279-280
Clee, Itterby
8184   Robert Dickison, labourer
   Ambler, Watkinson, *Clee*, 1987, p. 162
Clee
8185   Thomas Glentworth, husbandman
   Ambler, Watkinson, *Clee*, 1987, pp. 161-162
8186   William Low, carpenter
   Ambler, Watkinson, *Clee*, 1987, pp. 160-161
8187   William Pomphrett, yeoman
   Ambler, Watkinson, *Clee*, 1987, p. 161
Gedney
8188   Robert Chamberlin, yeoman
   Barley, *Lincolnshire*, 1951, pp. 264-266
Lincoln, St Peters Parish in Eastgate
8189   John Dawsons, farmer
   Johnston, *Lincoln*, 1991, pp. 39-40
Lincoln, St Swithins
8190   William Kent, gentleman [maltster]
   Johnston, *Lincoln*, 1991, pp. 40-42
Lincoln
8191   George Shoosmith, glazier
   Johnston, *Lincoln*, 1991, pp. 38-39
Winteringham
8192   Simon Goodwine
   Neave, *Winteringham*, 1984, p. 101
8193   William Moore
   Neave, *Winteringham*, 1984, pp. 102-103
8194   Nathanill Warde
   Neave, *Winteringham*, 1984, p. 104
8195   Willm Watson
   Neave, *Winteringham*, 1984, p. 103

London
Strand
8196   George Hudson, Composer of Music to His Majesty
   Reed, 1980, pp. 170-171

Scotland
Edinburgh
8197   David Trinch, stationer
   Anon., *Bassandyne*, 1836, pp. 281-282

Shropshire
Alberbury, White Abbey (Black Abbey)
8198   Alexander Wood, gentleman
   Wood, 1886, pp. 83-85
Benthall
8199   Ralph Bradley
   Trinder and Cox, *Severn Gorge*, 2000, p. 121

Broseley
8200   Robert Benbow, yeoman
   Trinder and Cox, *Severn Gorge*, 2000, p. 150
8201   Timothy Crompton, collier
   Trinder and Cox, *Severn Gorge*, 2000, p. 151
Lilleshall
8202   Joan Bradshaw, servant
   Trinder and Cox, *Telford*, 1980, p. 199
Wellington, The Wheat Leasowes
8203   George Wilkes, husbandman
   Trinder and Cox, *Telford*, 1980, p. 257

Staffordshire
Burntwood
8204   Richard Walker, bricklayer
   Vaisey, *Lichfield*, 1969, p. 205
Dudley
8205   Henry Payton, yeoman
   Roper, *Dudley*, 1966, pp. 36-37
Gornal Wood
8206   Edward Wilkes, nailer
   Roper, *Sedgley*, 1960, p. 59
Hammerwich
8207   George Swan
   Vaisey, *Lichfield*, 1969, pp. 205-206
Haywood
8208   Willi[am] Taylor
   Bradley, *Haywoods*, 1993, pp. 61-68
Lichfield
8209   William Clare, butcher
   Vaisey, *Lichfield*, 1969, pp. 203-204
8210   William Draper, innholder
   Vaisey, *Lichfield*, 1969, pp. 201-203
8211   Dame Dorothy Dyott, widow of Sir Richard
   Vaisey, *Lichfield*, 1969, p. 206
Lichfield, Cathedral Close
8212   Jeffrey Glasier, gentleman [chapter clerk]
   Vaisey, *Lichfield*, 1969, pp. 206-208
Lichfield
8213   Thomas Stone, gentleman and ironmonger
   Vaisey, *Lichfield*, 1969, pp. 208-209
Lower Gornal
8214   Richard Raybould, scythesmith
   Roper, *Sedgley*, 1960, pp. 55-57

Surrey
Charlwood
8215   John Bishop, husbandman
   Harding, *Charlwood*, 1976, pp. 102-103

Sussex
Coombes
8216   Edward Manning, clergyman [vicar of Rustington]
   Hughes, *Sussex*, 2007, pp. 54-56
Elsted
8217   Henry Snelling, clergyman [rector of Elsted]
   Hughes, *Sussex*, 2007, p. 72

Wales
Glamorganshire, Peterston-super-Ely
8218   Moris Pranch
   Wrench, *Wrenche*, 1956, pp. 53-54

Warwickshire
Stratford-on-Avon
8219   Elizabeth Taylor
   Jones, *Stratford*, II, 2003, pp. 137-138

Wiltshire
Marlborough
 8220 Edward Eatall, husbandman
  Williams and Thomson, *Marlborough*, 2007, p. 144
 8221 Thomas Grinfeild, innholder
  Williams and Thomson, *Marlborough*, 2007, p. 143
 8222 Joan Herring, widow
  Williams and Thomson, *Marlborough*, 2007, pp. 139-140
 8223 Beniamyn Lawrence, woollen draper
  Williams and Thomson, *Marlborough*, 2007, p. 141
 8224 Stephen Longe, gardener
  Williams and Thomson, *Marlborough*, 2007, pp. 140-141
 8225 Abraham Power, gentleman
  Williams and Thomson, *Marlborough*, 2007, pp. 141-142
 8226 Dorothy Wind, widow
  Williams and Thomson, *Marlborough*, 2007, pp. 142-143

Worcestershire
Kyre Magna, Kyre Wyard
 8227 Edward Pitt [Pitts], esquire
  Wanklyn, *Worcestershire*, 1998, p. 213

Yorkshire
Aysgarth, Cams Houses
 8228 Barnard [Bernard] Smith, [yeoman]
  Thwaite, *Abbotside*, 1967, pp. 100-101

1672 (c.)
Cheshire
Nantwich
 8229 Thomas Pemberton, yeoman
  Cockcroft, *Nantwich*, 1999, p. 247.2

Lincolnshire
Donington
 8230 Elizabeth Lawrence, chapwoman
  Barley, *Farmhouse and Cottage*, 1961, p. 280

1673
Bristol
Bristol, Castle
 8231 Thomas Bason
  George, *Bristol*, 2005, pp. 59-60
Bristol
 8232 Dorothy Hayman, widow
  George, *Bristol*, 2005, pp. 56-57
Bristol, Redcliffe
 8233 William Hill
  George, *Bristol*, 2005, p. 58
Bristol, St Philip and St Jacob
 8234 Andrew Snow, [nailer]
  George, *Bristol*, 2005, pp. 57-58
Clifton
 8235 David Edwards, limeburner
  Moore, *Clifton*, 1981, pp. 126-127
 8236 Robert Snook, [limeburner]
  Moore, *Clifton*, 1981, p. 124
Shirehampton
 8237 William Cotterell, [husbandman]
  Moore, *Clifton*, 1981, p. 127
Westbury
 8238 Abel Meredith, gentleman
  Moore, *Clifton*, 1981, pp. 124-126

Buckinghamshire
Buckingham
 8239 Andrew Duncombe (also listed Tingewick)
  Reed, *Buckinghamshire*, 1988, p. 104

Datchet
 8240 Anthony Taylor
  Reed, *Buckinghamshire*, 1988, pp. 102-103
Gayhurst
 8241 John Digbye
  Reed, *Buckinghamshire*, 1988, pp. 104-106
Shabbington
 8242 Roger Neele, yeoman
  Reed, *Buckinghamshire*, 1988, pp. 101-102
Tingewick
  Andrew Duncombe (see Buckingham)
Wendover
 8243 Thomas Price, joiner
  Reed, *Buckinghamshire*, 1988, pp. 103-104

Cheshire
Ashton-on-Mersey
 8244 Ralph Barlow, [husbandman]
  Groves, *Ashton-on-Mersey and Sale*, 2000, pp. 80-81
Chester
 8245 Richard Francis, barber surgeon
  Anon., *Francis*, 1935, p. 21
Nantwich
 8246 Ralph Deane, innholder
  Cockcroft, *Nantwich*, 1999, pp. 114.2-4
 8247 Ann Jones, widow
  Cockcroft, *Nantwich*, 1999, p. 173.1
 8248 John Walthall
  Cockcroft, *Nantwich*, 1999, pp. 323.1-2
Sale
 8249 Thomas Barlow, [husbandman]
  Groves, *Ashton-on-Mersey and Sale*, 2000, pp. 81-82
 8250 Thomas Massey, girthweb weaver
  Groves, *Ashton-on-Mersey and Sale*, 2000, pp. 87-88

Devonshire
Okehampton
 8251 Francis Rattenbury
  Cash, *Devon*, 1966, pp. 135-136
Uffculme
 8252 John Brooke
  Wyatt, *Uffculme*, 1997, pp. 192
 8253 Francis Dowdney, [husbandman]
  Wyatt, *Uffculme*, 1997, p. 118
 8254 William Facy
  Wyatt, *Uffculme*, 1997, p. 117
 8255 John Moore, carpenter
  Wyatt, *Uffculme*, 1997, pp. 117-118

Dorsetshire
Leigh
 8256 William Taunton, [yeoman]
  Machin, *Yetminster*, 1976, No.63, (1 p.)

Essex
Unlocated
 8257 Widow Poole
  Steer, *Mid-Essex*, 1969, p. 125
Writtle
 8258 John Draper, yeoman
  Steer, *Mid-Essex*, 1969, pp. 123-125
 8259 Thomas Osburne, yeoman
  Steer, *Mid-Essex*, 1969, pp. 125-126

Gloucestershire
Stoke Gifford
 8260 Samuel Booth, carpenter
  Moore, *Frampton Cotterell*, 1976, p. 104

8261 Thomas Butcher, gentleman
Moore, *Frampton Cotterell*, 1976, p. 105
Winterbourne
8262 John Withers, yeoman
Moore, *Frampton Cotterell*, 1976, p. 104

Hertfordshire
Hertford, All Saints
8263 Tho[mas] Cooke
Adams, *Hertford*, 1997, p. 100
8264 John Johnson
Adams, *Hertford*, 1997, pp. 76-78
8265 Edweard [Edward] Reason
Adams, *Hertford*, 1997, pp. 118-119
Sarratt
8266 Jeremia Lovett [Lovet], [farmer]
Bullen, *Sarratt*, [1982], pp. 182-183
8267 Thomas Singfeld [Sinckfeild]
Bullen, *Sarratt*, [1982], pp. 180-181

Kent
Sevenoaks
8268 Richard Everidge, yeoman
Lansberry, *Sevenoaks*, 1988, pp. 117-119
8269 Gilbert Kipps, innholder
Lansberry, *Sevenoaks*, 1988, pp. 123-125
8270 Walter Taylor
Lansberry, *Sevenoaks*, 1988, p. 119

Lancashire
Blackbeck, Furness Fell (now Cumbria)
8271 Edward Benson
Fell, 1891, pp. 395-397
Scarisbrick
8272 James Scarisbricke, esquire
Cheetham, 1938, pp. 133-138

Lincolnshire
Allington
8273 Robert Simson, husbandman
Pask, *Allington*, 1989, p. 88
Cleethorpes
8274 Thomas Ward, fisherman
Ambler, Watkinson, *Clee*, 1987, pp. 162-163
Lincoln, St Swithins
8275 Mary Nickinson, widow
Johnston, *Lincoln*, 1991, pp. 42-44
Lincoln, St Benedicts
8276 Sissie Peacock
Johnston, *Lincoln*, 1991, pp. 44-45
Winteringham
8277 Micaell Farrow
Neave, *Winteringham*, 1984, p. 105
8278 Willm Mitchill
Neave, *Winteringham*, 1984, pp. 105-107
8279 Robert Sharpe
Neave, *Winteringham*, 1984, pp. 107-108
8280 Thomas Sharpe
Neave, *Winteringham*, 1984, pp. 108-109

Middlesex
Sunbury
8281 Henry Collinge
Heselton, *Sunbury*, 1976, p. 2
8282 John Evans
Heselton, *Sunbury*, 1976, p. 1

Shropshire
Broseley
8283 William Benbow, trowman
Trinder and Cox, *Severn Gorge*, 2000, pp. 152-153
8284 Richard Rutter
Trinder and Cox, *Severn Gorge*, 2000, p. 153
Lilleshall
8285 Thomas Windsor, yeoman
Trinder and Cox, *Telford*, 1980, pp. 200-201
Little Wenlock
8286 Francis Woseley, mason
Trinder and Cox, *Severn Gorge*, 2000, p. 243
Madeley, Strutt Hill
8287 John Hagar, trowman, bargeman
Trinder and Cox, *Severn Gorge*, 2000, pp. 272-273

Staffordshire
Lichfield, St Chad
8288 Millicent Grimley
Vaisey, *Lichfield*, 1969, p. 212
Lichfield
8289 Zachary Kyrke, gentleman [limner]
Vaisey, *Lichfield*, 1969, pp. 219-221
8290 Thomas Perry
Vaisey, *Lichfield*, 1969, pp. 211-212
8291 Richard Reade
Vaisey, *Lichfield*, 1969, p. 215
8292 John Sharp, plumber
Vaisey, *Lichfield*, 1969, pp. 209-211
8293 William Thorneworke, paviour
Vaisey, *Lichfield*, 1969, pp. 216-217
8294 Richard Ward, gentleman [attorney, notary]
Vaisey, *Lichfield*, 1969, p. 213
8295 William Wright, gentleman [butcher]
Vaisey, *Lichfield*, 1969, pp. 217-219
Sedgley
8296 Richard Nicholls, yeoman
Roper, *Sedgley*, 1960, p. 60
Sedgley, The Wood
8297 Mary Bradley, widow
Roper, *Sedgley*, 1960, p. 58
Smethwick
8298 John Perrott, gentleman
Bodfish, *Smethwick*, 1992, pp. 20-21
Whittington
8299 Robert Deakin, yeoman
Vaisey, *Lichfield*, 1969, pp. 214-215

Surrey
Charlwood
8300 George Ede, yeoman
Harding, *Charlwood*, 1976, p. 103
8301 Thomas Jordan, husbandman
Harding, *Charlwood*, 1976, pp. 103-104
8302 Robert Sander
Harding, *Charlwood*, 1976, pp. 104-105

Sussex
Graffham
8303 Thomas Burges, clergyman [rector of Graffham]
Hughes, *Sussex*, 2007, pp. 94-95

Warwickshire
Alcester
8304 Thomas Rogers
Saville, *Alcester*, 1979, p. 9

Stoneleigh
 8305 Christopher Leigh, esquire
 Alcock, *Warwickshire*, 1993, pp. 73-74
Stratford-on-Avon
 8306 Ralph Cawdray [Cawdry]
 Jones, *Stratford*, II, 2003, p. 138
Wiltshire
Marlborough
 8307 William Blackmore, yeoman
 Williams and Thomson, *Marlborough*, 2007, p. 144
 8308 Nathaniell Farmer
 Williams and Thomson, *Marlborough*, 2007, pp. 145-146
 8309 Robert Kember, yeoman
 Williams and Thomson, *Marlborough*, 2007, pp. 144-145
 8310 Anthony Morris, carpenter
 Williams and Thomson, *Marlborough*, 2007, p. 145
 8311 Margery Smyth, widow
 Williams and Thomson, *Marlborough*, 2007, p. 146
Worcestershire
Doverdale
 8312 Phillipp [Phillip] Brace, esquire
 Wanklyn, *Worcestershire*, 1998, pp. 213-217
Yorkshire
Askrigg, Holehouse
 8313 Jeffrey Pratt, [yeoman]
 Thwaite, *Abbotside*, 1967, p. 104
Aysgarth, Litherskew
 8314 Willyam Harrison
 Thwaite, *Abbotside*, 1967, pp. 101-102
Aysgarth, Cotterdale
 8315 Willim [William] Holme
 Thwaite, *Abbotside*, 1967, p. 101
Aysgarth, Shaw Cote
 8316 Christopher Pratt, [yeoman]
 Thwaite, *Abbotside*, 1967, p. 105
Aysgarth, Skellgill
 8317 James Pratt, [yeoman]
 Thwaite, *Abbotside*, 1967, p. 103
Leeds, Halton
 8318 Christopher Phillips
 Kirk, *Temple Newsam*, 1935, p. 274

1674
Bristol
Bristol
 8319 George Beaton, grocer
 George, *Bristol*, 2005, pp. 60-62
Bristol, St Philip and St Jacob
 8320 George Bonfield, [colour merchant]
 George, *Bristol*, 2005, pp. 62-63
Bristol
 8321 Robert Dymock, carpenter
 George, *Bristol*, 2005, pp. 63-64
Westbury
 8322 Margery Meredith, widow
 Moore, *Clifton*, 1981, pp. 128-129
Westbury, Cote
 8323 Robert White, yeoman
 Moore, *Clifton*, 1981, p. 130
Buckinghamshire
Beachampton
 8324 Elizabeth Kislinbury, widow
 Reed, *Buckinghamshire*, 1988, pp. 112-114

Bourton
 8325 Richard Minshull, esquire (also listed Stanford
 Rivers, Essex)
 Reed, *Buckinghamshire*, 1988, pp. 108-112
Stony Stratford
 8326 Richard Davyes, innholder
 Reed, *Buckinghamshire*, 1988, pp. 107-108
 8327 Katherine Emerton, widow
 Reed, *Buckinghamshire*, 1988, pp. 106-107
Cheshire
Ashton-on-Mersey, Woodheys
 8328 William Ashton alias Wales
 Groves, *Ashton-on-Mersey and Sale*, 2000, pp. 83-84
Ashton-on-Mersey, Cross Street
 8329 Parnell Holland, [widow]
 Groves, *Ashton-on-Mersey and Sale*, 2000, p. 86
Hale
 8330 John Barrow
 Groves, *Hale 2*, 2005, p. 78
 8331 James Grantham
 Groves, *Hale 2*, 2005, p. 79
 8332 George Hardy
 Groves, *Hale 2*, 2005, p. 76
Hale, Ollerbarrow
 8333 Alexander Vawdrey
 Groves, *Hale 2*, 2005, pp. 76-78
Nantwich
 8334 John Acton
 Cockcroft, *Nantwich*, 1999, p. 5.1
 8335 John Booth, brickmaker
 Cockcroft, *Nantwich*, 1999, p. 38.1
 8336 George Jesson, saddler
 Cockcroft, *Nantwich*, 1999, pp. 172.2-4
 8337 Joshua Parsons, yeoman
 Cockcroft, *Nantwich*, 1999, pp. 242.3-4
Sale
 8338 John Buck
 Groves, *Ashton-on-Mersey and Sale*, 2000, pp. 84-85
 8339 Thomas Moores
 Groves, *Ashton-on-Mersey and Sale*, 2000, p. 89
 8340 James Moss
 Groves, *Ashton-on-Mersey and Sale*, 2000, pp. 88-89
Devonshire
Colyton
 8341 Mary Bradforde
 Cash, *Devon*, 1966, pp. 136-137
Farway
 8342 John Vicary, yeoman
 Cash, *Devon*, 1966, pp. 137-138
Uffculme
 8343 Ann Merson, widow
 Wyatt, *Uffculme*, 1997, pp. 119-120
 8344 George Prince
 Wyatt, *Uffculme*, 1997, pp. 118-119
Widecombe
 8345 Richard Hamling
 Alcock, 1969, p. 106
Dorsetshire
Chetnole
 8346 Henry Oldis, yeoman
 Machin, *Yetminster*, 1976, No.64, (2 pp.)
Leigh
 8347 George Stuckey, husbandman
 Machin, *Yetminster*, 1976, No.65, (2 pp.)

Essex
Roxwell
  8348 Christopher Perry, yeoman
    Steer, *Mid-Essex*, 1969, pp. 129-130
Stanford Rivers, Onger Park Hall
  Richard Minshull, esquire (see Bourton,
  Buckinghamshire)
Writtle
  8349 Henry Clarke
    Steer, *Mid-Essex*, 1969, pp. 130-131
  8350 Edward George, yeoman
    Steer, *Mid-Essex*, 1969, pp. 131-132
  8351 Henry Grouse [Groues, Groves], miller
    Steer, *Mid-Essex*, 1969, p. 131
  8352 Francis Taverner, yeoman
    Steer, *Mid-Essex*, 1969, pp. 126-129

Gloucestershire
Charlton Kings
  8353 Mary Ashmeade, widow
    Paget and Sale, *Charlton Kings*, 2003, p. 44
Winterbourne
  8354 Elizabeth Ludbye, widow
    Moore, *Frampton Cotterell*, 1976, p. 105

Hertfordshire
St Albans, St Stephens
  8355 Timothie Lane, [yeoman]
    Parker, *Worldly Goods*, 2004, pp. 277-278

Kent
Sevenoaks
  8356 Edward Berry, tobacconist
    Lansberry, *Sevenoaks*, 1988, pp. 126-128
  8357 Joane Niccoll, widow
    Lansberry, *Sevenoaks*, 1988, pp. 130-131
  8358 Christopher Wells, labourer
    Lansberry, *Sevenoaks*, 1988, pp. 129-130
Shoreham
  8359 John Round, yeoman
    Duncombe, *Darent*, 1990-1991, pp. 362-364

Leicestershire
Braunstone
  8360 John Taylor
    Wilshere, *Braunstone*, 1983, p. 21

Lincolnshire
Allington
  8361 Augustine Grant
    Pask, *Allington*, 1989, pp. 89-90
Lincoln, St Michael on Mount
  8362 Elizabeth Bate
    Johnston, *Lincoln*, 1991, p. 47
Lincoln, St Mark
  8363 Thomas White, wool merchant
    Johnston, *Lincoln*, 1991, pp. 45-47

Northumberland
Newcastle
  8364 William Gray, merchant
    Welford, 1886, pp. 80-81

Shropshire
Broseley
  8365 George Guest, collier
    Trinder and Cox, *Severn Gorge*, 2000, pp. 154-155
  8366 John Harris, coalminer
    Trinder and Cox, *Severn Gorge*, 2000, pp. 153-154

Madeley Wood
  8367 Joan Spencer, widow
    Trinder and Cox, *Severn Gorge*, 2000, p. 273

Staffordshire
Burntwood
  8368 William Tomlinson, tailor
    Vaisey, *Lichfield*, 1969, pp. 221-222
Ettingshall
  8369 Thomas Wilkes, nailer
    Roper, *Sedgley*, 1960, p. 61
Lichfield
  8370 Thomas Ashmole, gentleman
    Vaisey, *Lichfield*, 1969, pp. 230-231
  8371 Ann Cheshire, widow
    Vaisey, *Lichfield*, 1969, pp. 229-230
Lichfield, Bacon Street
  8372 Margaret Clowes, widow
    Vaisey, *Lichfield*, 1969, pp. 234-235
Lichfield
  8373 Thomas Moore, [chandler]
    Vaisey, *Lichfield*, 1969, pp. 224-225
  8374 Abraham Newell, corviser
    Vaisey, *Lichfield*, 1969, pp. 233-234
  8375 Richard Riley [Royley], silk weaver
    Vaisey, *Lichfield*, 1969, p. 232
  8376 William Rowley, cutler
    Vaisey, *Lichfield*, 1969, pp. 222-224
  8377 Alice Sympson, widow
    Vaisey, *Lichfield*, 1969, pp. 236-237
  8378 Joseph Werden, gentleman [innkeeper]
    Vaisey, *Lichfield*, 1969, pp. 226-229
  8379 John Worrall alias Baker, labourer or
  husbandman
    Vaisey, *Lichfield*, 1969, pp. 235-236
Sedgley, Gospel End
  8380 Henry Eaton, nailer
    Roper, *Sedgley*, 1960, p. 64
Sedgley, Sarnell
  8381 John Hickmans, yeoman
    Roper, *Sedgley*, 1960, pp. 62-63

Surrey
Charlwood
  8382 Edward Bashford, yeoman
    Harding, *Charlwood*, 1976, p. 105
  8383 Elizabeth Ede, widow
    Harding, *Charlwood*, 1976, pp. 105-106

Sussex
Buxted
  8384 Robert Middleton, clergyman [rector of Buxted]
    Hughes, *Sussex*, 2007, pp. 41-43
Tangmere
  8385 Paul Lawrence, clergyman [rector of Tangmere]
    Hughes, *Sussex*, 2007, pp. 202-210

Warwickshire
Shottery
  8386 Mergery Sitch [Margery Such], widow
    Jones, *Stratford*, II, 2003, pp. 138-139

Wiltshire
Marlborough
  8387 Ruth Allexander, widow
    Williams and Thomson, *Marlborough*, 2007, p. 148
  8388 Edward Aven, glover
    Williams and Thomson, *Marlborough*, 2007, p. 146

8389 Roger Blagden, gentleman
Williams and Thomson, *Marlborough*, 2007, pp. 146-147
8390 Thomas Hunt, gentleman
Williams and Thomson, *Marlborough*, 2007, pp. 147-148
8391 Thomas Pearse, [glazier]
Williams and Thomson, *Marlborough*, 2007, p. 147

Yorkshire
Acomb
8392 Marke Scawbye, labourer
Barley, *Farmhouse and Cottage*, 1961, p. 286
Aysgarth, Cotterdale
8393 Willfray [Wilfred] Moore
Thwaite, *Abbotside*, 1967, p. 107
Aysgarth, Skellgill
8394 Peter Watson, [husbandman]
Thwaite, *Abbotside*, 1967, p. 109
Lunds
8395 William Perkin [Parkin], [yeoman]
Thwaite, *Abbotside*, 1967, pp. 106-107
8396 Christopher Wilkinson, [husbandman]
Thwaite, *Abbotside*, 1967, p. 108

1675-1700 (undated)
Yorkshire
Barnoldswick (?)
8397 Charles Banister
Kirk, *Barnoldswick*, 1951, p. 57
8398 William Hudson
Kirk, *Barnoldswick*, 1951, p. 70
8399 Dorothy Jackson
Kirk, *Barnoldswick*, 1951, p. 71
Barnoldswick, Salterforth
8400 Margaret Shaw
Kirk, *Barnoldswick*, 1951, p. 77

1675
Bristol
Bristol
8401 Thomas Bagg, butcher
George, *Bristol*, 2005, pp. 65-66
8402 Thomas Everet, tobacco cutter
George, *Bristol*, 2005, pp. 66-67
8403 William Fry, cordwainer
George, *Bristol*, 2005, pp. 67-68
Bristol, St Thomas
8404 John Goldsmith, pin-maker
George, *Bristol*, 2005, pp. 68-69
Bristol, St Michael
8405 John Keene, anchor smith
George, *Bristol*, 2005, pp. 69-74
Bristol, Christchurch
8406 Thomas Moggs, embroiderer
George, *Bristol*, 2005, pp. 75-76
Bristol
8407 James Read, clergyman
George, *Bristol*, 2005, pp. 76-78
8408 John Roseworme, painter
George, *Bristol*, 2005, p. 78

Buckinghamshire
Amersham
8409 Walter Webbe, innholder
Reed, *Buckinghamshire*, 1988, pp. 122-126
Boarstall
8410 Francis Baxter, gentleman
Reed, *Buckinghamshire*, 1988, pp. 121-122

Datchet
8411 Ann Matthews
Reed, *Buckinghamshire*, 1988, pp. 118-119
Denham
8412 Thomas Carter, yeoman
Reed, *Buckinghamshire*, 1988, pp. 119-121
Little Marlow
8413 Hierom Gregory, clerk
Reed, *Buckinghamshire*, 1988, pp. 126-127
Wendover
8414 Henry Playstow, gentleman
Reed, *Buckinghamshire*, 1988, pp. 116-118

Cambridgeshire
Newmarket
8415 Thomas Pitches, alehouse keeper
May, *Newmarket*, 1976, pp. 15-17
8416 Thomas Shave, shoemaker
May, *Newmarket*, 1976, pp. 20-21
8417 Allen Wyat, [glazier]
May, *Newmarket*, 1976, pp. 18-19

Cheshire
Hale
8418 Robert Pearson, [yeoman]
Groves, *Hale 2*, 2005, pp. 79-80
Hale, Ringway
8419 Edward Johnson, [husbandman]
Groves, *Hale 2*, 2005, pp. 80-81
Nantwich
8420 Edward Blagg, yeoman
Cockcroft, *Nantwich*, 1999, pp. 35.1-2
8421 James Browne
Cockcroft, *Nantwich*, 1999, p. 50.1
8422 John Harding
Cockcroft, *Nantwich*, 1999, p. 146.1
8423 Randolphe Harrison, yeoman
Cockcroft, *Nantwich*, 1999, pp. 149.1-2
8424 John Millington, silk weaver
Cockcroft, *Nantwich*, 1999, pp. 215.2-4
8425 John Tench, [tanner]
Cockcroft, *Nantwich*, 1999, p. 306.1
Sale
8426 Elizabeth Hamnett, [widow]
Groves, *Ashton-on-Mersey and Sale*, 2000, pp. 89-90

Devonshire
Exeter
8427 Mr John Hingston
Cash, *Devon*, 1966, pp. 138-139
Portman, *Exeter*, 1966, pp. 119-121
Torquay, Tormoham
8428 Thomas Yoe, seaman
Cash, *Devon*, 1966, p. 140
Uffculme
8429 Richard Holway alias Andro, widow
Wyatt, *Uffculme*, 1997, pp. 192-193
8430 Willyam Tanner alias Howe, [yeoman]
Wyatt, *Uffculme*, 1997, p. 120

Dorsetshire
Yetminster
8431 Elizabeth Reepe
Machin, *Yetminster*, 1976, No.66, (1 p.)

Essex
Roxwell
8432 William Crush, yeoman
Steer, *Mid-Essex*, 1969, pp. 134-135

Unlocated
8433   Willia'[m] Finch
Steer, *Mid-Essex*, 1969, p. 137
Writtle
8434   William Boosey, yeoman
Steer, *Mid-Essex*, 1969, pp. 133-134
8435   Robert Douset, husbandman
Steer, *Mid-Essex*, 1969, p. 136
8436   Henry Evans, husbandman
Steer, *Mid-Essex*, 1969, pp. 132-133
8437   Henry Palmer
Steer, *Mid-Essex*, 1969, pp. 135-136
8438   Mathew Woolard
Steer, *Mid-Essex*, 1969, p. 137

Gloucestershire
Charlton Kings
8439   Samuel Tytchett, husbandman
Paget and Sale, *Charlton Kings*, 2003, p. 45

Hertfordshire
St Albans, St Stephens, Park Street
8440   William Dell, husbandman
Parker, *Worldly Goods*, 2004, p. 281
8441   William Knowlton, [yeoman]
Parker, *Worldly Goods*, 2004, pp. 285-286
Sarratt
8442   Thomas Browne, [farmer]
Bullen, *Sarratt*, [1982], pp. 184-185
8443   George Noble
Bullen, *Sarratt*, [1982], p. 187

Ireland
Co. Kildare, Athy
8444   Thomas Rushworth, merchant
Goodbody, *Quaker*, 1971, pp. 53-54
Kilkenny, Dunmore House,
James Butler, Duke of Ormonde (see Kilkenny Castle)
Kilkenny Castle
8445   James Butler , Duke of Ormonde (also listed
Clonmel and Dunmore House)
Fenlon, *Ireland*, 2003, pp. 41-86
Co. Tipperary, Clonmel
James Butler, Duke of Ormonde (see Kilkenny Castle)

Kent
Otford
8446   Edmund Herrett
Duncombe, *Darent*, 1990-1991, pp. 300-301
Sevenoaks
8447   Thomas Beecher, yeoman
Lansberry, *Sevenoaks*, 1988, pp. 139-140
8448   Edward Fletcher
Lansberry, *Sevenoaks*, 1988, pp. 132-133
Shoreham
8449   Robert Hills, yeoman
Duncombe, *Darent*, 1990-1991, pp. 305-306

Leicestershire
Braunstone
8450   Thomas Ball, yeoman
Wilshere, *Braunstone*, 1983, p. 22
Kirby Muxloe
8451   Thomas Oswin, shepherd
Wilshere, *Kirby Muxloe*, 1983, p. 11

Lincolnshire
Lincoln
8452   John Atkinson, tanner
Johnston, *Lincoln*, 1991, pp. 47-48

Lincoln, St Martins
8453   Jeffre Wood, labourer
Johnston, *Lincoln*, 1991, pp. 48-49
Winteringham
8454   John Dinsdall, yeoman
Neave, *Winteringham*, 1984, p. 109
8455   Richard Dinsdale
Neave, *Winteringham*, 1984, p. 110
8456   Elizabeth Jennison
Neave, *Winteringham*, 1984, pp. 110-111
8457   Thomas Smyth
Neave, *Winteringham*, 1984, pp. 109-110

Oxfordshire
Water Eaton
8458   Elizabeth Paty
Offord, *Water Eaton*, 1986, p. 34

Shropshire
Broseley
8459   Adam Stokes, trowman
Trinder and Cox, *Severn Gorge*, 2000, pp. 155-156
Lilleshall
8460   Ann Leeke, widow
Trinder and Cox, *Telford*, 1980, p. 201

Staffordshire
Burntwood
8461   Dorothy Walker
Vaisey, *Lichfield*, 1969, pp. 242-243
8462   John Wright, tailor
Vaisey, *Lichfield*, 1969, pp. 237-238
Coppenhall
8463   John Addam, [yeoman]
Barley, *Farmhouse and Cottage*, 1961, p. 284
Coseley
8464   William Whitehouse, nailer
Roper, *Sedgley*, 1960, p. 65
Lichfield
8465   Mary Allpott [Alport]
Vaisey, *Lichfield*, 1969, p. 243
8466   Richard Baxter, gentleman
Vaisey, *Lichfield*, 1969, pp. 240-241
8467   Richard Bayley
Vaisey, *Lichfield*, 1969, p. 244
8468   Robert Bingham, blacksmith
Vaisey, *Lichfield*, 1969, p. 237
8469   James Ealy [Heeley]
Vaisey, *Lichfield*, 1969, p. 242
Hatcher and Barker, *Pewter*, 1974, p. 101
8470   Richard Emery, tailor
Vaisey, *Lichfield*, 1969, pp. 245-246
8471   Edward Hill, miller
Vaisey, *Lichfield*, 1969, pp. 244-245
8472   Robert Johnson
Vaisey, *Lichfield*, 1969, p. 238
8473   Elizabeth Newell, widow
Vaisey, *Lichfield*, 1969, pp. 238-239
Lichfield, Timmor
8474   John Smyth, yeoman
Vaisey, *Lichfield*, 1969, pp. 239-240
Lichfield, Cathedral Close
8475   Anne Wirley
Vaisey, *Lichfield*, 1969, p. 243
Smethwick
8476   Samuel Jarvise
Bodfish, *Smethwick*, 1992, p. 22

Surrey
Charlwood
  8477 Robert Haybittle, husbandman
    Harding, *Charlwood*, 1976, pp. 106-107
  8478 John Tapsell
    Harding, *Charlwood*, 1976, p. 106
Sussex
Bosham
  8479 Samuel Tangley, clergyman [vicar of Bosham]
    Hughes, *Sussex*, 2007, pp. 32-34
West Chiltington
  8480 Robert Carr, clergyman [rector of West
  Chiltington]
    Hughes, *Sussex*, 2007, pp. 44-45
Warwickshire
Stoneleigh
  8481 Thomas Elliott, husbandman
    Alcock, *Warwickshire*, 1993, p. 48
Stratford-on-Avon
  8482 John Scott alias Patterson
    Jones, *Stratford*, II, 2003, pp. 139-140
Wiltshire
Marlborough
  8483 Nathaniell Carpenter
    Williams and Thomson, *Marlborough*, 2007, pp. 148-149
Worcestershire
Upton-on-Severn
  8484 John Bromley, gentleman
    Wanklyn, *Worcestershire*, 1998, pp. 412-413
Yorkshire
Askrigg, Helm
  8485 William Croft
    Thwaite, *Abbotside*, 1967, p. 110
Aysgarth, Yorescott
  8486 Francis Lambert, [yeoman]
    Thwaite, *Abbotside*, 1967, p
Barnoldswick, Brockden, Admergill
  8487 Richard Hanson, yeoman
    Kirk, *Barnoldswick*, 1951, pp. 65-66
Barnoldswick, Salterforth
  8488 Isabell Hartley, widow
    Kirk, *Barnoldswick*, 1951, p. 66
Bretton Hall
  8489 Sir Thomas Wentworth, baronet
    Brears, *Yorkshire*, 1972, pp. 146-153
Doncaster
  8490 John Webster, alderman
    Brears, *Yorkshire*, 1972, pp. 140-143
Filey
  8491 Christopher Foster
    Brears, *Yorkshire*, 1972, pp. 144-145
Leeds, Halton
  8492 Roger Heald, yeoman
    Kirk, *Temple Newsam*, 1935, pp. 267-268

1676
Bristol
Bristol, St Thomas
  8493 Mark Greene, [glazier]
    George, *Bristol*, 2005, p. 79
Bristol
  8494 Thomas Pearce, weaver
    George, *Bristol*, 2005, p. 80

Shirehampton
  8495 John Squire, innholder
    Moore, *Clifton*, 1981, pp. 132-133
Buckinghamshire
Colnbrook
  8496 William Lane, saddler
    Reed, *Buckinghamshire*, 1988, pp. 129-130
Eton
  8497 Richard Cox, bricklayer
    Reed, *Buckinghamshire*, 1988, pp. 128-129
Great Marlow
  8498 David James
    Reed, *Buckinghamshire*, 1988, pp. 127-128
Cheshire
Hale, Ringway
  8499 Robert Leatherbarrow
    Groves, *Hale 2*, 2005, pp. 81-82
Nantwich
  8500 Thomas Church
    Cockcroft, *Nantwich*, 1999, pp. 66.1-2
  8501 Joan Lewis, widow
    Cockcroft, *Nantwich*, 1999, pp. 189.3-4
  8502 Roger Mosse, yeoman
    Cockcroft, *Nantwich*, 1999, pp. 226.2-3
  8503 Thomas Segrave, gentleman
    Cockcroft, *Nantwich*, 1999, pp. 284.2-3
  8504 William Smith, joiner
    Cockcroft, *Nantwich*, 1999, pp. 292.2-6
  8505 Richard Wickstead, yeoman
    Cockcroft, *Nantwich*, 1999, p. 336.2
Derbyshire
Barlborough
  8506 Robert Marples
    Addy, 1887, pp. 25-32
Devonshire
Cadbury
  8507 Richard Marshall, husbandman
    Cash, *Devon*, 1966, pp. 140-141
Uffculme
  8508 Robertt [Robert] Gill, yeoman
    Wyatt, *Uffculme*, 1997, pp. 121-122
  8509 Christopher Marshall, yeoman
    Wyatt, *Uffculme*, 1997, pp. 124-125
  8510 Richard Patch alias Pagey, carpenter
    Wyatt, *Uffculme*, 1997, pp. 125-127
  8511 William Smith, [husbandman]
    Wyatt, *Uffculme*, 1997, pp. 122-124
Essex
Roxwell
  8512 John Buredg
    Steer, *Mid-Essex*, 1969, pp. 138-139
  8513 Phillip Monke, husbandman
    Steer, *Mid-Essex*, 1969, p. 142
Writtle
  8514 John Dockley, husbandman
    Steer, *Mid-Essex*, 1969, p. 138
  8515 Widow Osburne
    Steer, *Mid-Essex*, 1969, pp. 140-142
  8516 John Sapsford, yeoman
    Steer, *Mid-Essex*, 1969, pp. 139-140
Gloucestershire
Winterbourne
  8517 Edward Coole, yeoman
    Moore, *Frampton Cotterell*, 1976, p. 105

8518 Avis Dooding, [widow]
  Moore, *Frampton Cotterell*, 1976, pp. 105-106
8519 Elizabeth Rodman, widow
  Moore, *Frampton Cotterell*, 1976, p. 106
Hertfordshire
Sarratt
8520 John Lewen, husbandman
  Bullen, *Sarratt*, [1982], pp. 189-190
Kent
Eynsford, Crockenhill
8521 Henry Dunmoll, [yeoman]
  Duncombe, *Darent*, 1990-1991, pp. 265-266
Jersey
St Laurent
8522 Philippe Marett, gentleman
  Anon., *Marett*, 1890-1896, pp. 402-410
Lancashire
Pemberton, Walthew House
8523 Robert Walthew, gentleman
  Bagley, 1965, pp. 65-122
Lincolnshire
Lincoln
8524 William Atkinson, tailor
  Johnston, *Lincoln*, 1991, pp. 49-50
Lincoln, St Martins
8525 John Langforth, whitesmith
  Johnston, *Lincoln*, 1991, pp. 50-52
London
Masons' Hall
8526 Masons' Company
  Conder, 1894, p. 195
Scotland
Edinburgh
8527 Androw Andersone, His Majesty's Printer
  Anon., *Bassandyne*, 1836, pp. 282-284
Shropshire
Broseley
8528 Henry Barrett, carpenter
  Trinder and Cox, *Severn Gorge*, 2000, p. 157
Dawley
8529 William Farley, webster
  Trinder and Cox, *Telford*, 1980, p. 168
Lilleshall, Muxton
8530 Mary Shelton
  Trinder and Cox, *Telford*, 1980, pp. 202-203
Madeley Wood
8531 John Lloyd
  Trinder and Cox, *Severn Gorge*, 2000, p. 274
8532 John Sherratt, chandler
  Trinder and Cox, *Severn Gorge*, 2000, pp. 274-275
Wellington
8533 Thomas Bennett, blacksmith
  Trinder and Cox, *Telford*, 1980, pp. 258-259
8534 Thomas Howle, skinner
  Trinder and Cox, *Telford*, 1980, p. 258
Staffordshire
Coseley
8535 John Roades, nailer
  Roper, *Sedgley*, 1960, p. 68
Ettingshall
8536 Richard Gibbins
  Roper, *Sedgley*, 1960, p. 67

Lichfield, Cathedral Close
8537 Elizabeth Billingsley, widow
  Vaisey, *Lichfield*, 1969, p. 248
Lichfield
8538 Thomas Clifton, baker
  Vaisey, *Lichfield*, 1969, pp. 261-263
8539 James Crowder [Caruder]
  Vaisey, *Lichfield*, 1969, p. 246-247
8540 Thomas Eagles, yeoman
  Vaisey, *Lichfield*, 1969, pp. 250-251
8541 Richard Harrison, clergyman, vicar of St
Mary's, chancellor of the cathedral
  Vaisey, *Lichfield*, 1969, pp. 252-253
8542 Timothy Key, schoolmaster
  Vaisey, *Lichfield*, 1969, pp. 258-259
8543 George Mason, cook [innholder]
  Vaisey, *Lichfield*, 1969, pp. 256-258
Lichfield, Cathedral Close
8544 Daniell Morgill, clergyman, vicar choral
  Vaisey, *Lichfield*, 1969, p. 247-248
Lichfield
8545 Thomas Northwood, blacksmith
  Vaisey, *Lichfield*, 1969, pp. 248-250
8546 Thomas Smith, clergyman, sacrist of the
cathedral
  Vaisey, *Lichfield*, 1969, pp. 254-256
8547 James Wrexham, gentleman
  Vaisey, *Lichfield*, 1969, pp. 259-261
Lower Gornal
8548 John Juckes, yeoman
  Roper, *Sedgley*, 1960, p. 66
Sedgley, Woodsetton
8549 John Whithouse, husbandman
  Roper, *Sedgley*, 1960, pp. 66-67
Whittington
8550 Nicholas Deakyn, yeoman
  Vaisey, *Lichfield*, 1969, pp. 253-254
Wales
Montgomeryshire, Llanfihangel, Llwydiarth
8551 John Humffrey David
  Gilson, *Llanfihangel*, 2009, p. 42
Montgomeryshire, Llanfihangel, Ffynnon Arthur
8552 Maurice Thomas
  Gilson, *Llanfihangel*, 2009, p. 41
Warwickshire
Stratford-on-Avon
8553 Thomas Mayo alias Fletcher, weaver
  Jones, *Stratford*, II, 2003, pp. 150-151
8554 Michael Palmer, blacksmith
  Jones, *Stratford*, II, 2003, pp. 140-146
8555 Thomas Ward, shoemaker
  Jones, *Stratford*, II, 2003, pp. 147-149
Wiltshire
Marlborough
8556 Anthony Awst, yeoman
  Williams and Thomson, *Marlborough*, 2007, pp. 149-150
8557 Daniel Coxe, husbandman
  Williams and Thomson, *Marlborough*, 2007, p. 149
Yorkshire
Lunds
8558 James Blades, [husbandman]
  Thwaite, *Abbotside*, 1967, pp. 112-113

1676 (c.)
Shropshire
Madeley
8559 Henry James, bowyer
Trinder and Cox, *Severn Gorge*, 2000, p. 275

1677
Berkshire
Windsor Castle, Deanery
8560 Dr Brune Ryves, clergyman, Dean of Windsor
Bond, 1959, pp. 18-19
Bristol
Bristol
8561 Thomas Biggs, innholder
George, *Bristol*, 2005, pp. 80-85
Bristol, St Thomas
8562 Humphrey Brent, clergyman, minister of St Thomas
George, *Bristol*, 2005, pp. 85-86
Bristol
8563 Stephen Fudger, virginal maker
George, *Bristol*, 2005, p. 87
8564 Richard West, felt maker
George, *Bristol*, 2005, pp. 87-88
Buckinghamshire
Chesham Magna
8565 Charles Walmisley, clergyman
Reed, *Buckinghamshire*, 1988, pp. 131-132
Chipping Wycombe
8566 William Wheeler, maltster
Reed, *Buckinghamshire*, 1988, pp. 132-133
Penn
8567 Nicholas Orton, gentleman
Reed, *Buckinghamshire*, 1988, pp. 130-131
Cheshire
Hale
8568 John Lamb
Groves, *Hale* 2, 2005, pp. 83-84
Nantwich
8569 Thomas Beckett
Cockcroft, *Nantwich*, 1999, pp. 24.1-2
8570 Joseph Bullen, gentleman
Cockcroft, *Nantwich*, 1999, p. 58.2
8571 Gwen Colbach, widow
Cockcroft, *Nantwich*, 1999, p. 90.1
8572 Nicholas Davenport, barber
Cockcroft, *Nantwich*, 1999, p. 101.1
8573 Ellen Minshall, widow
Cockcroft, *Nantwich*, 1999, p. 217.2
Sale
8574 George Ashton alias Wales
Groves, *Ashton-on-Mersey and Sale*, 2000, p. 90
Devonshire
Okehampton
8575 Arthur Little
Cash, *Devon*, 1966, p. 143
Uffculme
8576 Samuell Bishopp [Samuel Bishop], yeoman
Wyatt, *Uffculme*, 1997, pp. 127-128
Unlocated
8577 Francis Kirkham, esquire
Cash, *Devon*, 1966, p. 144

Winkleigh
8578 Scipio Haywood, yeoman
Cash, *Devon*, 1966, pp. 141-143
Dorsetshire
Chetnole
8579 William Davis, yeoman
Machin, *Yetminster*, 1976, No.68, (2 pp.)
Leigh
8580 John Gast, gentleman
Machin, *Yetminster*, 1976, No.67, (3 pp.)
Machin, 1978, pp. 168-170
Essex
Writtle
8581 Richard Bridgman, gardener
Steer, *Mid-Essex*, 1969, pp. 144-145
8582 Henry Duke, yeoman
Steer, *Mid-Essex*, 1969, pp. 143-144
8583 William Eree, blacksmith
Steer, *Mid-Essex*, 1969, p. 143
8584 Edward George, yeoman
Steer, *Mid-Essex*, 1969, pp. 145-146
Gloucestershire
Cheltenham
8585 Richard Baker
Sale, *Cheltenham*, 1999, p. 20
8586 Anthony Chester
Sale, *Cheltenham*, 1999, pp. 195-197
8587 William Crowder, cordwainer
Sale, *Cheltenham*, 1999, pp. 20-21
Frampton Cotterell
8588 Richard Prigg, [yeoman]
Moore, *Frampton Cotterell*, 1976, p. 108
Hambrook
8589 Elizabeth Bayly, widow
Moore, *Frampton Cotterell*, 1976, pp. 106-108
Hertfordshire
Sarratt
8590 Newman, Widow
Bullen, *Sarratt*, [1982], pp. 191-192
Kent
Farningham
8591 Richard Herman, [yeoman]
Duncombe, *Darent*, 1990-1991, pp. 298-299
Ireland
Dublin Castle
8592 Arthur Capel, Earl of Essex
Fenlon, *Ireland*, 2003, pp. 87-98
Kent
Penshurst
8593 Robert Sidney, Earl of Leicester
Owen, 1966, pp. 634-647
Sevenoaks
8594 Margarett Beecher, widow
Lansberry, *Sevenoaks*, 1988, pp. 144-145
8595 Alice Brookstead alias Brookside, widow
Lansberry, *Sevenoaks*, 1988, pp. 145-146
8596 William Floate, cordwainer
Lansberry, *Sevenoaks*, 1988, p. 143
8597 Thomas Morley, yeoman
Lansberry, *Sevenoaks*, 1988, pp. 141-142
Lincolnshire
Clee, Thrunscoe
8598 William Grimbleby, husbandman
Ambler, Watkinson, *Clee*, 1987, p. 163

Lincoln, St Buttolph
  8599 John Wignall, brickmaker
    Johnston, *Lincoln*, 1991, pp. 52-53
London
  Westminster, St Margaret's
  8600 Wincislaues Holler
    Phillips, 2004, p. 18
Northumberland
  Ovingham, Harlow Hill
  8601 Thomas Turvin [Trurent, Trewren], clergyman
    Phillips, 1889, p. 38
Oxfordshire
  Banbury
  8602 Fulke Greville, gentleman
    Trinder and Gibson, *Banbury*, 1988, pp. 228-229
  8603 James Partridge, [tailor]
    Trinder and Gibson, *Banbury*, 1988, pp. 226-227
Shropshire
  Broseley
  8604 James Harrison, coalminer
    Trinder and Cox, *Severn Gorge*, 2000, pp. 157-159
  Lilleshall
  8605 William Blockley, carpenter
    Trinder and Cox, *Telford*, 1980, p. 205
  Lilleshall Lodge
  8606 Lewis Dale, keeper
    Trinder and Cox, *Telford*, 1980, p. 204
  Lilleshall
  8607 Thomas Newell
    Trinder and Cox, *Telford*, 1980, pp. 203-204
  Madeley
  8608 Margaret Evans
    Trinder and Cox, *Severn Gorge*, 2000, pp. 275-276
  8609 Robert Yates, trowman
    Trinder and Cox, *Severn Gorge*, 2000, pp. 280-281
  Wellington, Leegomery
  8610 William Marigold, yeoman
    Trinder and Cox, *Telford*, 1980, pp. 259-260
Somersetshire
  Ashbrittle
  8611 John Talbott, yeoman
    Monday and Siraut, *Somerset*, 2003, p. 233
Staffordshire
  Burntwood
  8612 Ales Cross, widow
    Vaisey, *Lichfield*, 1969, pp. 265-266
  8613 Thomas Cross
    Vaisey, *Lichfield*, 1969, p. 263
  Dudley
  8614 Edward Attwood, butcher
    Roper, *Dudley*, 1966, pp. 38-39
  Lichfield, St Michael
  8615 Edward Pickard, tailor
    Vaisey, *Lichfield*, 1969, p. 266
  Lichfield
  8616 William Winstanley, labourer
    Vaisey, *Lichfield*, 1969, p. 265
    Hatcher and Barker, *Pewter*, 1974, p. 101
  Sedgley, Gospel End
  8617 John Bradley, nailer
    Roper, *Sedgley*, 1960, p. 68
  Smethwick
  8618 Roger Parkes
    Bodfish, *Smethwick*, 1992, pp. 23-25

Whittington
  8619 John Parker, yeoman
    Vaisey, *Lichfield*, 1969, p. 264
Surrey
  Ham House
  8620 John Maitland, Duke of Lauderdale
    Thornton and Tomlin, *Ham*, 1980, pp. 37-176
Sussex
  Barlavington
  8621 Thomas Garrett, clergyman
    Hughes, *Sussex*, 2007, pp. 14-15
  Climping
  8622 Christopher Canner, clergyman [vicar of Climping]
    Hughes, *Sussex*, 2007, pp. 50-52
  Merston
  8623 David Blaney, clergyman [rector of Merston]
    Hughes, *Sussex*, 2007, pp. 139-140
  Rusper
  8624 William Priaux, clergyman [rector of Rusper]
    Hughes, *Sussex*, 2007, pp. 177-179
  Unlocated
  8625 James Stilwell
    Godman, 1908, pp. 115-117
Wales
  Carmarthenshire, Derwydd
  8626 Sir Henry Vaughan
    Anon., *Vaughan*, 1926-1927, pp. 33-34
Warwickshire
  Stoneleigh, Stareton
  8627 Joane Barber, widow
    Alcock, *Warwickshire*, 1993, p. 124
  Stratford-on-Avon
  8628 Henry Izod, mercer
    Jones, *Stratford*, II, 2003, pp. 158-160
  8629 William Lyndon, maltster
    Jones, *Stratford*, II, 2003, pp. 153-155
  8630 Joyce Smart
    Jones, *Stratford*, II, 2003, pp. 151-152
  8631 George Tasker, labourer
    Jones, *Stratford*, II, 2003, pp. 156-157
Wiltshire
  Marlborough
  8632 Jone Lyme, widow
    Williams and Thomson, *Marlborough*, 2007, p. 152
  8633 Isaac Ringe, vintner
    Williams and Thomson, *Marlborough*, 2007, p. 150
  8634 Jeremiah Sloper, chandler
    Williams and Thomson, *Marlborough*, 2007, p. 151
  8635 William Tooth, blacksmith
    Williams and Thomson, *Marlborough*, 2007, pp. 151-152
Yorkshire
  Aysgarth, Shaw Cote
  8636 Tristram Blaides [Blades]
    Thwaite, *Abbotside*, 1967, p. 114
  Aysgarth, Skellgill
  8637 Joan Watson
    Thwaite, *Abbotside*, 1967, p. 112
  Lunds
  8638 William Dawson, [yeoman]
    Thwaite, *Abbotside*, 1967, pp. 114-115

1677 (c.)
Cheshire
Hale
8639 Margaret Barlow, [widow]
Groves, *Hale 2*, 2005, pp. 82-83
Essex
Writtle
8640 [John?] Bonington
Steer, *Mid-Essex*, 1969, p. 146
Wiltshire
Marlborough
8641 Eleonar Farmer, widow
Williams and Thomson, *Marlborough*, 2007, pp. 150-151

1678
Bristol
Bristol
8642 John Bevill, arms painter
George, *Bristol*, 2005, pp. 89-90
8643 Robert Evans, freemason
George, *Bristol*, 2005, pp. 90-91
Bristol, St Peter
8644 Edward Field, [horse] collar maker
George, *Bristol*, 2005, pp. 91-92
Bristol, Barton Regis
8645 Thomas Griffith, tailor
George, *Bristol*, 2005, pp. 93-94
Shirehampton
8646 Elizabeth Barre alias Berry, widow
Moore, *Clifton*, 1981, pp. 133-134
Westbury
8647 Samuel Sandford, innholder
Moore, *Clifton*, 1981, pp. 132-133
8648 Morgan Williams, [joiner]
Moore, *Clifton*, 1981, p. 133
Buckinghamshire
Bledlow
8649 James Sale, gentleman
Reed, *Buckinghamshire*, 1988, pp. 136-139
Drayton
8650 James Bird, gentleman
Reed, *Buckinghamshire*, 1988, pp. 139-140
Great Horwood
8651 Thomas Lea, yeoman
Reed, *Buckinghamshire*, 1988, pp. 135-136
Great Marlow
8652 William James, butcher
Reed, *Buckinghamshire*, 1988, pp. 140-142
Quainton
8653 Thomas Sare, yeoman
Reed, *Buckinghamshire*, 1988, p. 136
Stoke Poges
8654 Jane Fisher, widow
Reed, *Buckinghamshire*, 1988, pp. 133-135
Cambridgeshire
Newmarket
8655 Georg Scudamore, carpenter
May, *Newmarket*, 1976, pp. 21-22
Cheshire
Nantwich
8656 Roger Comberbach, tanner
Cockcroft, *Nantwich*, 1999, pp. 98.6-7

8657 William Davis, distiller
Cockcroft, *Nantwich*, 1999, p. 106.2
8658 Robert Day, mercer
Cockcroft, *Nantwich*, 1999, pp. 108.1-16
8659 Richard Jackson, clergyman
Cockcroft, *Nantwich*, 1999, p. 166.1
8660 Thomas Proudman, shoemaker
Cockcroft, *Nantwich*, 1999, pp. 262.2-3
8661 Robert Tymies, yeoman
Cockcroft, *Nantwich*, 1999, pp. 316.1-2
Sale
8662 Joan Johnson alias Ottiwell
Groves, *Ashton-on-Mersey and Sale*, 2000, p. 91
Devonshire
Cruwys Morchard
8663 James Holmead, yeoman
Cash, *Devon*, 1966, pp. 144-146
Uffculme
8664 Joane Smeath
Wyatt, *Uffculme*, 1997, pp. 128-129
8665 Mary Weeks [Weekes], widow
Wyatt, *Uffculme*, 1997, p. 128
Dorsetshire
Yetminster
8666 John Chisman, yeoman
Machin, *Yetminster*, 1976, No.70, (1 p.)
Yetminster [?]
8667 William Moore
Machin, *Yetminster*, 1976, No.69, (2 pp.)
Essex
Roxwell
8668 Edmund Turnidge
Steer, *Mid-Essex*, 1969, pp. 148-150
8669 Richard Wolfe
Steer, *Mid-Essex*, 1969, pp. 146-148
Writtle
8670 Samuel Woolfe, gentleman
Steer, *Mid-Essex*, 1969, pp. 156-157
Gloucestershire
Charlton Kings
8671 Roger Dowdeswell, baker
Paget and Sale, *Charlton Kings*, 2003, p. 46
Hambrook
8672 Robert Cole, [clothier]
Moore, *Frampton Cotterell*, 1976, pp. 108-109
Stoke Gifford
8673 Thomas Lawford, yeoman
Moore, *Frampton Cotterell*, 1976, p. 108
Westerleigh
8674 Thomas Parsons, [husbandman]
Moore, *Frampton Cotterell*, 1976, p. 109
Ireland
Dublin Castle
8675 James Butler, Duke of Ormonde
Fenlon, *Ireland*, 2003, pp. 99-103
Kent
Eynsford
8676 Thomas Durling, yeoman
Duncombe, *Darent*, 1990-1991, pp. 268-269
Otford
8677 John Stileman, [yeoman]
Duncombe, *Darent*, 1990-1991, pp. 396-397

Sevenoaks
  8678 Richard Boss, clergyman, vicar of Sevenoaks
    Lansberry, *Sevenoaks*, 1988, pp. 150-152
  8679 Thomas Buckminster, gentleman
    Lansberry, *Sevenoaks*, 1988, pp. 136-137
  8680 Anne Everest, widow
    Lansberry, *Sevenoaks*, 1988, p. 135
  8681 Richard Everidge, innholder
    Lansberry, *Sevenoaks*, 1988, pp. 152-154

Leicestershire
Great Stretton
  8682 Elizabeth Turner, widow
    Wilshere, *Great Stretton*, 1984, p. 19

Oxfordshire
Water Eaton
  8683 William Holloway, [husbandman]
    Offord, *Water Eaton*, 1986, pp. 36-37

Shropshire
Wellington
  8684 Richard Haughton, gunsmith
    Trinder and Cox, *Telford*, 1980, pp. 260-261
Wrockwardine, Allscott
  8685 Thomas Binnell, yeoman
    Trinder and Cox, *Telford*, 1980, p. 406

Somersetshire
Donyatt
  8686 Adam Morley, yeoman
    Monday and Siraut, *Somerset*, 2003, p. 162

Staffordshire
Burntwood
  8687 John Derrey
    Vaisey, *Lichfield*, 1969, pp. 267-268
  8688 Alice Stringer alias Duesberry, widow
    Vaisey, *Lichfield*, 1969, p. 268
  8689 John Stringer, carpenter
    Vaisey, *Lichfield*, 1969, pp. 270-271
Dudley, Netherton
  8690 Henry Dixon, nailer
    Roper, *Dudley*, 1966, p. 42
Dudley
  8691 Oliver Dixon
    Roper, *Dudley*, 1966, p. 41
  8692 Richard Marsh, [innholder]
    Roper, *Dudley*, 1966, pp. 43-46
  8693 Richard Shawe, shoemaker
    Roper, *Dudley*, 1966, p. 40
Colwich, Bishton
  8694 Mary Bowyer, widow
    Bradley, *Haywoods*, 1993, pp. 68-73
Hammerwich
  8695 Richard Bullock, husbandman
    Vaisey, *Lichfield*, 1969, p. 271
Lichfield, Cathedral Close
  8696 Zachary Bickles, gentleman
    Vaisey, *Lichfield*, 1969, pp. 271-272
  8697 John Cotes, gentleman
    Vaisey, *Lichfield*, 1969, pp. 273-275
Lichfield, St Mary, Sandford Street
  8698 Richard Harvey
    Vaisey, *Lichfield*, 1969, pp. 272-273
Lichfield, Chorley
  8699 John Holmes
    Vaisey, *Lichfield*, 1969, pp. 268-269

Lichfield, Woodhouses
  8700 Thomas Mousley
    Vaisey, *Lichfield*, 1969, p. 275
Lichfield, St Mary
  8701 John Price, capper
    Vaisey, *Lichfield*, 1969, pp. 276-277
Lichfield, Sandford Street
  8702 William Sale
    Vaisey, *Lichfield*, 1969, pp. 269-270
Lower Gornal
  8703 William Fereday, yeoman
    Roper, *Sedgley*, 1960, pp. 69-70
Sedgley, Woodsetton
  8704 Thomas Persehouse, yeoman
    Roper, *Sedgley*, 1960, pp. 70-71

Suffolk
Stowlangtoft
  8705 Nathaniell Lillie, labourer
    Anon., *Examples*, 1980, pp. 10-11

Sussex
Kirdford, Hills Green
  8706 William Strudwick, yeoman
    Kenyon, *Kirdford*, 1955, pp. 116-118
Westbourne
  8707 Warberton Owen, clergyman
    Hughes, *Sussex*, 2007, pp. 232-233
  8708 George Sidgwick, clergyman [vicar of
  Westbourne]
    Hughes, *Sussex*, 2007, p. 233

Wiltshire
Marlborough
  8709 William Goddard, innholder
    Williams and Thomson, *Marlborough*, 2007, pp. 152-153
  8710 Edward Lawrence, parchment maker
    Williams and Thomson, *Marlborough*, 2007, pp. 154-155
  8711 Phillipp Lawrence, gentleman
    Williams and Thomson, *Marlborough*, 2007, pp. 153-154
  8712 Robert Millington, tailor
    Williams and Thomson, *Marlborough*, 2007, p. 154
Mere
  8713 Frances Goddard
    Goddard, 1902-1904, pp. 173-174

Yorkshire
Acklam
  8714 Francis Bowser, husbandman
    Wagner, 1966, pp. 123-124
Askrigg, Low Helm
  8715 Richard Blyth, [yeoman]
    Thwaite, *Abbotside*, 1967, p. 118
Aysgarth, Skellgill
  8716 Thomas Caygill
    Thwaite, *Abbotside*, 1967, p. 119
Aysgarth, Shaw Cote
  8717 Francis Pratt
    Thwaite, *Abbotside*, 1967, p. 115
Barnoldswick
  8718 Richard Boolcocke
    Kirk, *Barnoldswick*, 1951, p. 58
Lunds
  8719 Edmond Shawe [Edmund Shaw], [yeoman]
    Thwaite, *Abbotside*, 1967, p. 116

1679

Berkshire
Windsor Castle
8720 Captain Edmund Barber, Poor Knight
Bond, 1959, pp. 19-20

Bristol
Bristol, St Philip and St Jacob
8721 Richard Avery, whip-maker
George, *Bristol*, 2005, pp. 94-95
Bristol
8722 William Bayley, joiner
George, *Bristol*, 2005, pp. 95-96
Bristol, Temple
8723 John Crabb, weaver
George, *Bristol*, 2005, pp. 96-98
Bristol
8724 William Harford, vintner
George, *Bristol*, 2005, pp. 98-100
Bristol, St Stephen
8725 John Neads, joiner
George, *Bristol*, 2005, pp. 100-101
Bristol
8726 Agnes Noble, widow
George, *Bristol*, 2005, pp. 101-103
8727 George Phipps, meal seller
George, *Bristol*, 2005, pp. 103-104
Bristol, Temple
8728 Joan Tomlinson, widow
George, *Bristol*, 2005, pp. 104-107
Shirehampton
8729 George Berry, mariner
Moore, *Clifton*, 1981, pp. 134-136
8730 Charity Wasbrough, widow
Moore, *Clifton*, 1981, pp. 136-137

Buckinghamshire
High Wycombe
8731 Thomas Davis, gentleman
Reed, *Buckinghamshire*, 1988, pp. 142-144
Horton
8732 Timothy West, paper maker
Reed, *Buckinghamshire*, 1988, pp. 144-145

Cheshire
Hale
8733 Richard Alcock, [husbandman]
Groves, *Hale 2*, 2005, pp. 86-87
8734 Margaret Johnson
Groves, *Hale 2*, 2005, pp. 84-85
8735 John Warburton
Groves, *Hale 2*, 2005, p. 85
Nantwich
8736 Robert Burroughes, gentleman
Cockcroft, *Nantwich*, 1999, pp. 60.2-4
8737 Richard Clowes, shoemaker
Cockcroft, *Nantwich*, 1999, pp. 80.2-3
8738 Lawrence Davies, blacksmith
Cockcroft, *Nantwich*, 1999, pp. 107.2-4
8739 Henry Dyes, pewterer
Cockcroft, *Nantwich*, 1999, p. 120.2
8740 Ann Wickstead, widow
Cockcroft, *Nantwich*, 1999, p. 334.2
Sale
8741 John Renshaw
Groves, *Ashton-on-Mersey and Sale*, 2000, pp. 91-92

8742 Richard Renshaw, [husbandman]
Groves, *Ashton-on-Mersey and Sale*, 2000, pp. 95-96

Devonshire
Ashburton
8743 Walter Palke
Worthy, *Devonshire*, 1896, p. 163
Uffculme
8744 Richard Waldron, yeoman
Wyatt, *Uffculme*, 1997, pp. 129-130

Dorsetshire
Chetnole
8745 Thomas Griggs, husbandman
Machin, *Yetminster*, 1976, No.71, (2 pp.)
Yetminster
8746 Benjamin Miller, [baker]
Machin, *Yetminster*, 1976, No.72, (1 p.)
8747 Eleanor Wright, widow
Machin, *Yetminster*, 1976, No.73, (1 p.)

Essex
Roxwell
8748 Richard Bedwell
Steer, *Mid-Essex*, 1969, p. 153
8749 Thomas Peach, yeoman
Steer, *Mid-Essex*, 1969, pp. 154-155
Unlocated
8750 William Carnell
Steer, *Mid-Essex*, 1969, p. 151
8751 James Carr
Steer, *Mid-Essex*, 1969, pp. 151-152
8752 William Norden
Steer, *Mid-Essex*, 1969, p. 158
Writtle
8753 Peter Bradley
Steer, *Mid-Essex*, 1969, p. 154
8754 Mathew Harris
Steer, *Mid-Essex*, 1969, pp. 155-156
8755 Thomas Hills
Steer, *Mid-Essex*, 1969, pp. 152-153
8756 John Putto, [miller]
Steer, *Mid-Essex*, 1969, p. 150

Gloucestershire
Charlton Kings
8757 Thomas Deane, [clothier]
Paget and Sale, *Charlton Kings*, 2003, p. 47
Cheltenham, Sandford
8758 Thomas Higgs, yeoman
Sale, *Cheltenham*, 1999, p. 23
Frampton Cotterell
8759 Thomas Poole, [yeoman]
Moore, *Frampton Cotterell*, 1976, pp. 113-114
Iron Acton, Latteridge
8760 Giles Lorringe, yeoman
Moore, *Frampton Cotterell*, 1976, p. 110
Iron Acton
8761 Sarah Mayer
Moore, *Frampton Cotterell*, 1976, p. 113
Westerleigh
8762 Thomas Hollister, feltmaker
Moore, *Frampton Cotterell*, 1976, p. 111
8763 Samuel Pill, gentleman
Moore, *Frampton Cotterell*, 1976, pp. 111-113
Winterbourne
8764 Margaret Cole, widow
Moore, *Frampton Cotterell*, 1976, p. 109

8765 Nicholas Emlen, [yeoman]
Moore, *Frampton Cotterell*, 1976, p. 111
8766 Henry Guise, esquire
Moore, *Frampton Cotterell*, 1976, pp. 109-110

Hertfordshire
Hertford
8767 James Runnington
Adams, *Hertford*, 1997, pp. 120-121
St Albans, St Stephens
8768 Rogger Whitchurch, [husbandman]
Parker, *Worldly Goods*, 2004, pp. 289-290

Kent
Sevenoaks
8769 Dorothy Evridge [Everidge], widow
Lansberry, *Sevenoaks*, 1988, pp. 161-162
8770 Joane Fremling
Lansberry, *Sevenoaks*, 1988, pp. 155-156
8771 Thomas Fuller, husbandman
Lansberry, *Sevenoaks*, 1988, pp. 162-163
8772 John Jeffery, clothworker
Lansberry, *Sevenoaks*, 1988, pp. 158-160
8773 Richard Morgan, yeoman
Lansberry, *Sevenoaks*, 1988, pp. 163-164
Shoreham
8774 John Rawlins, yeoman
Duncombe, *Darent*, 1990-1991, pp. 350-352

Leicestershire
Great Stretton
8775 John Bellemy, [husbandman]
Wilshere, *Great Stretton*, 1984, p. 20

Lincolnshire
Elsham
8776 William Smith, gentleman
Smith, 1883-1885, pp. 205-207
Grantham
8777 Thomas West, chapman
Spufford, *Reclothing*, 1984, pp. 151-152
Lincoln
8778 Mr Edward Fawkes, alderman and upholsterer
Johnston, *Lincoln*, 1991, pp. 54-56
8779 Henery Mitchell, haberdasher
Johnston, *Lincoln*, 1991, pp. 56-63
Lincoln, St Swithins
8780 Robert Pearson, waterman
Johnston, *Lincoln*, 1991, p. 64
Lincoln, The Close
8781 Henry Wanleste
Johnston, *Lincoln*, 1991, pp. 68-70
Lincoln, St Peter Arches
8782 Abigaile Watson, widow [saddler]
Johnston, *Lincoln*, 1991, pp. 65-68
Winteringham
8783 John Battman, husbandman
Neave, *Winteringham*, 1984, p. 111
8784 Thomas Bells
Neave, *Winteringham*, 1984, pp. 112-113
8785 George Hegginbotham
Neave, *Winteringham*, 1984, pp. 113-114
8786 Edward Reader, tailor
Neave, *Winteringham*, 1984, pp. 111-112

Oxfordshire
Oxford
8787 Dr Thomas Lockey
Philip, 1954-1956, pp. 82-84

Swalcliffe
8788 Humphrey Smart, clergyman, vicar of Swalcliffe
Tiller, 1979, p. 249

Shropshire
Benthall
8789 William Rutter
Trinder and Cox, *Severn Gorge*, 2000, p. 122
Broseley Wood
8790 Edward Dawley, barge owner
Trinder and Cox, *Severn Gorge*, 2000, p. 159
Broseley
8791 Robert Hill, mercer
Trinder and Cox, *Severn Gorge*, 2000, pp. 160-161
8792 Elizabeth Russell, widow
Trinder and Cox, *Severn Gorge*, 2000, pp. 161-162
8793 John Whitmore, chandler
Trinder and Cox, *Severn Gorge*, 2000, p. 160
Dawley, Little Dawley
8794 Richard Bridgwood, yeoman
Trinder and Cox, *Telford*, 1980, pp. 170-172
Dawley, Great Dawley
8795 Richard Clowes, gentleman
Trinder and Cox, *Telford*, 1980, pp. 168-169
Lilleshall
8796 Humphrey Mansell, labourer
Trinder and Cox, *Telford*, 1980, pp. 205-206
Wellington
8797 Francis Haughton, gunsmith
Trinder and Cox, *Telford*, 1980, pp. 261-262
Wrockwardine, Charlton
8798 Francis Hawkins
Trinder and Cox, *Telford*, 1980, pp. 408-409
Wrockwardine
8799 Thomas Roe
Trinder and Cox, *Telford*, 1980, pp. 406-408

Somersetshire
Bridgwater
8800 George Balch, [mercer]
Monday and Siraut, *Somerset*, 2003, pp. 17-19

Staffordshire
Dudley
8801 Thomas Wilkinson, locksmith
Roper, *Dudley*, 1966, pp. 47-48
Harborne
8802 Joane Strayne
Bodfish, *Smethwick*, 1992, p. 28
Lichfield
8803 Thomas Harvey, gentleman
Vaisey, *Lichfield*, 1969, pp. 277-278
8804 Anne Smaldridge, widow
Vaisey, *Lichfield*, 1969, pp. 280-283
8805 William Walker, [innkeeper]
Vaisey, *Lichfield*, 1969, pp. 278-280
Sedgley
8806 Thomas Gibbins, yeoman
Roper, *Sedgley*, 1960, pp. 73-74
Sedgley, Cotterhillend
8807 John Heycocke, nailer
Roper, *Sedgley*, 1960, pp. 71-72
Sedgley, Woodsetton
8808 William Parkshouse alias Persehouse, nailer
Roper, *Sedgley*, 1960, pp. 72-73

Smethwick
  8809 Richard Darby
    Bodfish, *Smethwick*, 1992, p. 29
  8810 John Hanson
    Bodfish, *Smethwick*, 1992, pp. 26-27
Suffolk
  Wetheringsett
  8811 Abraham Chaplin, clergyman
    Livett, 1903-1904, pp. 33-35
Surrey
  Ham House
  8812 John Maitland, Duke of Lauderdale
    Thornton and Tomlin, *Ham*, 1980, pp. 37-176
Sussex
  Horsted Keynes
  8813 Giles Moore, clergyman [rector of Horsted
  Keynes]
    Hughes, *Sussex*, 2007, pp. 112-114
  Westbourne
  8814 Thomas Prynne, clergyman [rector of
  Westbourne]
    Hughes, *Sussex*, 2007, p. 234
  West Dean
  8815 George Eyles, clergyman [vicar of West Dean]
    Hughes, *Sussex*, 2007, pp. 57-59
Wales
  Glamorganshire, Peterston-super-Ely
  8816 John Pranch
    Wrench, *Wrenche*, 1956, pp. 56-58
  Montgomeryshire, Llanfihangel, Fachwen
  8817 Evan Morris
    Gilson, *Llanfihangel*, 2009, p. 43
Warwickshire
  Stratford-on-Avon, Bridgetown
  8818 William Bratford [Bradford], wheelwright
    Jones, *Stratford*, II, 2003, pp. 161-165
  Stratford-on-Avon
  8819 Thomas Field, woollen draper
    Jones, *Stratford*, II, 2003, pp. 165-167
  8820 Richard Hemings, mason
    Jones, *Stratford*, II, 2003, pp. 167-169
  8821 Benjamin Jones, apothecary
    Jones, *Stratford*, II, 2003, pp. 160-161
  8822 John Smith, gentleman
    Jones, *Stratford*, II, 2003, pp. 169-171
Wiltshire
  Marlborough
  8823 Elizabeth Blagden, widow
    Williams and Thomson, *Marlborough*, 2007, p. 155
  8824 Elizabeth Ducke, widow
    Williams and Thomson, *Marlborough*, 2007, pp. 156-157
  8825 Margaret Evans, widow
    Williams and Thomson, *Marlborough*, 2007, p. 156
  8826 John Millington, carpenter
    Williams and Thomson, *Marlborough*, 2007, pp. 155-156
Worcestershire
  Eckington, Woollas Hall
  8827 Walter Hanford, esquire
    Wanklyn, *Worcestershire*, 1998, pp. 221-224
  Hanbury
  8828 Richard Vernon, esquire
    Wanklyn, *Worcestershire*, 1998, pp. 217-219

Lower Wolverton, Stoulton
  8829 William Acton, esquire
    Wanklyn, *Worcestershire*, 1998, pp. 219-221
Rous Lench
  8830 Sir Thomas Rous, baronet
    Wanklyn, *Worcestershire*, 1998, pp. 224-225
Yorkshire
  Bainbridge, Brockhill Cote
  8831 Thomas Metcalfe
    Thwaite, *Abbotside*, 1967, p. 118
  Barnoldswick, Salterforth
  8832 Christopher Varley
    Kirk, *Barnoldswick*, 1951, pp. 80-81

1680
Bristol
  Bristol
  8833 Thomas Browne, watchmaker
    George, *Bristol*, 2005, pp. 107-108
  8834 Henry Burgess, sieve maker
    George, *Bristol*, 2005, pp. 108-109
  8835 Walter Carpenter, baker
    George, *Bristol*, 2005, pp. 109-111
  Bristol, St Peter
  8836 James Claxton, weaver
    George, *Bristol*, 2005, pp. 111-112
  Bristol
  8837 Benjamin James, mariner
    George, *Bristol*, 2005, pp. 113-115
  Clifton
  8838 John Colt, [labourer]
    Moore, *Clifton*, 1981, p. 137
  8839 Thomas Garland, mariner
    Moore, *Clifton*, 1981, pp. 140-141
  8840 Elizabeth Hodges, widow
    Moore, *Clifton*, 1981, p. 139
  8841 Richard Newman, haberdasher
    Moore, *Clifton*, 1981, pp. 137-139
  Shirehampton
  8842 John Williams, [husbandman]
    Moore, *Clifton*, 1981, pp. 139-140
Buckinghamshire
  Burnham
  8843 Thomas Michell, gentleman
    Reed, *Buckinghamshire*, 1988, pp. 151-154
  Haversham
  8844 Maurice Thompson, esquire
    Reed, *Buckinghamshire*, 1988, pp. 146-148
  Newport Pagnell
  8845 John Thornton
    Reed, *Buckinghamshire*, 1988, pp. 149-151
  Pollicott
  8846 Edward Hassell
    Reed, *Buckinghamshire*, 1988, pp. 145-146
  Stony Stratford
  8847 Marmaduke Ball
    Reed, *Buckinghamshire*, 1988, pp. 148-149
Cambridgeshire
  Newmarket
  8848 John Carleton, [yeoman]
    May, *Newmarket*, 1976, pp. 24-26
  8849 John Funston, [gentleman]
    May, *Newmarket*, 1976, p. 23

Cheshire
Nantwich
8850 Thomas Goodall, tallow chandler
Cockcroft, *Nantwich*, 1999, pp. 139.2-4
8851 Thomas Pratchett, gentleman
Cockcroft, *Nantwich*, 1999, pp. 258.1-2
8852 Thomas Tench, dyer
Cockcroft, *Nantwich*, 1999, p. 308.2
Sale
8853 William Lindall, [husbandman]
Groves, *Ashton-on-Mersey and Sale*, 2000, pp. 93-94
Devonshire
Colaton Raleigh
8854 Robert Harte, clergyman, vicar of Colyton
Raleigh
Cash, *Devon*, 1966, pp. 146-147
Paignton
8855 Clement Necke
Cash, *Devon*, 1966, pp. 147-148
Dorsetshire
Yetminster
8856 Thomas Hayward, [shoemaker]
Machin, *Yetminster*, 1976, No.74, (2 pp.)
Essex
Roxwell
8857 William Luckin
Steer, *Mid-Essex*, 1969, p. 159
8858 William Pissey
Steer, *Mid-Essex*, 1969, pp. 159-160
8859 Nathan Wad[e]
Steer, *Mid-Essex*, 1969, pp. 160-161
8860 William Webb
Steer, *Mid-Essex*, 1969, pp. 158-159
Gloucestershire
Iron Acton
8861 Ann Thorner
Moore, *Frampton Cotterell*, 1976, p. 115
Stoke Gifford
8862 Rebecca Lawford
Moore, *Frampton Cotterell*, 1976, p. 115
Westerleigh
8863 John Wood, weaver
Moore, *Frampton Cotterell*, 1976, p. 115
Winterbourne
8864 Richard Ellery, [feltmaker]
Moore, *Frampton Cotterell*, 1976, p. 114
Hertfordshire
Hertford, All Saints
8865 James Chamberlain, carpenter
Adams, *Hertford*, 1997, pp. 97-99
Hertford
8866 William Edmonds, gentleman
Adams, *Hertford*, 1997, p. 65
St Albans, St Stephens
8867 Richard Bloud
Parker, *Worldly Goods*, 2004, pp. 290-291
St Albans, St Stephens, Colney Street
8868 Dorothy Lane, widow
Parker, *Worldly Goods*, 2004, p. 287
Sarratt
8869 Stephen Gould, yeoman
Bullen, *Sarratt*, [1982], pp. 192-194

Kent
Eynsford
8870 Thomas Morrant
Duncombe, *Darent*, 1990-1991, pp. 324-325
Sevenoaks
8871 Daniell Davis, cheesemonger
Lansberry, *Sevenoaks*, 1988, pp. 164-165
Shoreham
8872 William Hartnup, yeoman
Duncombe, *Darent*, 1990-1991, pp. 289-290
Middlesex
Sunbury, Kempton
8873 Henry Sadler
Heselton, *Sunbury*, 1976, p. 3
Lancashire
Bury
8874 Richard Riddings, [chapman]
Spufford, *Reclothing*, 1984, pp. 152-153
Lincolnshire
Clee
8875 Tho Glentworth, husbandman
Ambler, Watkinson, *Clee*, 1987, p. 163
Lincoln
8876 William Browne, goldsmith
Johnston, *Lincoln*, 1991, pp. 70-73
Lincoln, St Margaret in Close
8877 Henry Corbet, doctor of physick
Johnston, *Lincoln*, 1991, pp. 73-75
Winteringham
8878 Thomas G[ibson], [servant]
Neave, *Winteringham*, 1984, p. 118
8879 John Hill
Neave, *Winteringham*, 1984, p. 114
8880 Mary Jackson, widow
Neave, *Winteringham*, 1984, pp. 114-115
8881 Thomas Martin
Neave, *Winteringham*, 1984, p. 115
8882 William Potter, clergyman, [rector of
Winteringham]
Neave, *Winteringham*, 1984, pp. 115-117
Scotland
Perthshire, Moncreiffe House
8883 Sir Thomas Moncreiff, baronet
Moncreiff and Moncreiffe, 1929, pp. 662-670
Shropshire
Benthall, Posenhall
8884 William Evans, yeoman
Trinder and Cox, *Severn Gorge*, 2000, p. 123
Broseley
8885 Robert Ogden, clergyman, rector of Broseley
Trinder and Cox, *Severn Gorge*, 2000, pp. 162-163
Lilleshall, Muxton, The Walnut Tree
8886 John Shelton, yeoman
Trinder and Cox, *Telford*, 1980, pp. 206-207
Madeley Wood
8887 John Cowper, weaver
Trinder and Cox, *Severn Gorge*, 2000, pp. 276-277
Wellington
8888 Miles Field, cordwainer
Trinder and Cox, *Telford*, 1980, pp. 262-263
Wellington, Watling Street
8889 Thomas Fletcher, ropemaker
Trinder and Cox, *Telford*, 1980, p. 266

Staffordshire
Lichfield
 8890 William Goodman, corviser
  Vaisey, *Lichfield*, 1969, pp. 283-284
Sedgley, Cotwallend
 8891 Oliver Garrett, nailer
  Roper, *Sedgley*, 1960, p. 75
Upper Gornal
 8892 Thomas Thomason, labourer
  Roper, *Sedgley*, 1960, pp. 74-75
Surrey
Charlwood
 8893 Ann Martin, widow
  Harding, *Charlwood*, 1976, pp. 107-108
Sussex
Ashurst
 8894 Thomas Wilson, clergyman [rector of Ashurst]
  Hughes, *Sussex*, 2007, pp. 11-12
Horsted Keynes
 8895 Stephen Peart, clergyman [rector of Horsted
 Keynes]
  Hughes, *Sussex*, 2007, pp. 114-115
Ifield
 8896 Walter Moore, clergyman [vicar of Ifield]
  Hughes, *Sussex*, 2007, pp. 120-121
North Mundham
 8897 Thomas Carr, clergyman [vicar of North
 Mundham]
  Hughes, *Sussex*, 2007, pp. 145-146
Thakeham
 8898 Henry Banckes, clergyman [rector of Thakeham]
  Hughes, *Sussex*, 2007, pp. 212-215
Upper Beeding
 8899 Malachy Conant, clergyman [vicar of Beeding]
  Hughes, *Sussex*, 2007, pp. 16-17
Warwickshire
Stratford-on-Avon
 8900 John Bent, baker
  Jones, *Stratford*, II, 2003, p. 177
 8901 Thomas Blackford, ironmonger
  Jones, *Stratford*, II, 2003, pp. 177-178
 8902 John Brooke, apothecary
  Jones, *Stratford*, II, 2003, p. 178
 8903 Simon Cale, gentleman
  Jones, *Stratford*, II, 2003, pp. 173-175
 8904 Mary Freeman, widow
  Jones, *Stratford*, II, 2003, pp. 172-173
Wiltshire
Marlborough
 8905 Michajell Bayly, currier
  Williams and Thomson, *Marlborough*, 2007, p. 159
 8906 John Clerk, pinmaker
  Williams and Thomson, *Marlborough*, 2007, pp. 158-159
 8907 Ann Crips, widow
  Williams and Thomson, *Marlborough*, 2007, pp. 157-158
 8908 John Mann, roper
  Williams and Thomson, *Marlborough*, 2007, p. 157
Yorkshire
Barnoldswick, Wood End
 8909 John Browne
  Kirk, *Barnoldswick*, 1951, p. 60

1681
Bristol
Bristol
 8910 Andrew Andras, strong-water distiller
  George, *Bristol*, 2005, pp. 115-116
 8911 Richard Blonman [Blinman], clergyman
  George, *Bristol*, 2005, p. 117
 8912 William Davis, physician
  George, *Bristol*, 2005, pp. 117-118
 8913 John Kimber, coffee seller
  George, *Bristol*, 2005, pp. 118-121
 8914 Francis Little, saddler
  George, *Bristol*, 2005, pp. 121-124
Redland
 8915 Nathan Miller, [innholder]
  Moore, *Clifton*, 1981, pp. 141-143
Buckinghamshire
Bledlow
 8916 Henry Eustace, yeoman (also listed Chinnor,
 Oxfordshire)
  Reed, *Buckinghamshire*, 1988, pp. 157-158
Brill
 8917 Richard Carter, gentleman
  Reed, *Buckinghamshire*, 1988, pp. 160-163
Burnham
 8918 John Pewsey, blacksmith
  Reed, *Buckinghamshire*, 1988, pp. 163-164
Crafton
 8919 William Theed, gentleman
  Woodman, 1946, pp. 356-360
Eton
 8920 Robert Browne, cook
  Reed, *Buckinghamshire*, 1988, pp. 154-155
Great Marlow
 8921 Robert Moore, gentleman
  Reed, *Buckinghamshire*, 1988, pp. 158-160
Weston Turville, Bedgrove
 8922 Christopher Webb, gentleman
  Reed, *Buckinghamshire*, 1988, pp. 155-156
Cambridgeshire
Cambridge
 8923 Robert Browne, bookbinder
  Gray and Palmer, *Cambridge*, 1915, p. 122
 8924 Anthony Nicholson, [bookbinder]
  Gray and Palmer, *Cambridge*, 1915, p. 121
Cheshire
Ashton-on-Mersey
 8925 James Renshaw, [yeoman]
  Groves, *Ashton-on-Mersey and Sale*, 2000, pp. 97-98
Nantwich
 8926 Robert Moulton, glover
  Cockcroft, *Nantwich*, 1999, pp. 228.2-3
 8927 Thomas Sparrow
  Cockcroft, *Nantwich*, 1999, p. 294.1
 8928 John Truby
  Cockcroft, *Nantwich*, 1999, p. 314.1
Devonshire
Bratton Clovelly
 8929 John Williams, husbandman
  Cash, *Devon*, 1966, pp. 148-149
Uffculme
 8930 John How alias Tanner, husbandman
  Wyatt, *Uffculme*, 1997, pp. 131-132

8931 Alexander Melhuish, [clothier]
    Wyatt, *Uffculme*, 1997, pp. 194-195
8932 Henry Parsons, [yeoman]
    Wyatt, *Uffculme*, 1997, pp. 132-133
8933 Elizabeth Rugg [Rugge], widow
    Wyatt, *Uffculme*, 1997, p. 134
8934 Arthur Stevens [Steevens], [yeoman]
    Wyatt, *Uffculme*, 1997, pp. 133-134

Essex
 Roxwell
8935 Francis Quy
    Steer, *Mid-Essex*, 1969, pp. 161-162
 Unlocated
8936 John Beadel
    Steer, *Mid-Essex*, 1969, p. 162
 Writtle
8937 John Chalke
    Steer, *Mid-Essex*, 1969, pp. 164-165
8938 John Duke, yeoman
    Steer, *Mid-Essex*, 1969, p. 166
8939 William Page
    Steer, *Mid-Essex*, 1969, p. 164
8940 Jeremiah Westwood
    Steer, *Mid-Essex*, 1969, pp. 162-164
8941 Mary Wilks
    Steer, *Mid-Essex*, 1969, pp. 165-166

Gloucestershire
 Charlton Kings
8942 Robert Whithorne, [yeoman]
    Paget and Sale, *Charlton Kings*, 2003, pp. 48-49
 Hambrook
8943 Giles Jones, husbandman
    Moore, *Frampton Cotterell*, 1976, p. 117
 Stoke Gifford
8944 Isaac Baylie, yeoman
    Moore, *Frampton Cotterell*, 1976, p. 118
8945 Richard Lawford, yeoman
    Moore, *Frampton Cotterell*, 1976, pp. 116-117
 Stoke Gifford, Great Stoke
8946 Richard Stevens, yeoman
    Moore, *Frampton Cotterell*, 1976, p. 116
 Winterbourne
8947 Richard Griffith, [feltmaker]
    Moore, *Frampton Cotterell*, 1976, pp. 115-116
8948 George Roswell, innholder
    Moore, *Frampton Cotterell*, 1976, pp. 117-118

Guernsey
 Vingtaine de Nermont, Fief Vaugrat
8949 Jean Laisné
    Moullin, 1946, pp. 208-211

Kent
 Otford
8950 Richard Smale, yeoman
    Duncombe, *Darent*, 1990-1991, pp. 382-385
 Sevenoaks
8951 Richard Wood, yeoman
    Lansberry, *Sevenoaks*, 1988, pp. 170-171

Leicestershire
 Braunstone
8952 Edward Peboddey
    Wilshere, *Braunstone*, 1983, p. 22
8953 Tho Worrall
    Wilshere, *Braunstone*, 1983, pp. 23-25

 Kirby Muxloe
8954 Benjamin King, gentleman
    Wilshere, *Kirby Muxloe*, 1983, p. 11
Lincolnshire
 Clee
8955 Stephen Harrison
    Ambler, Watkinson, *Clee*, 1987, pp. 163-164
 Clee, Thrunscoe
8956 Francis Pickard, husbandman
    Ambler, Watkinson, *Clee*, 1987, p. 164
 Lincoln, St Martins
8957 George Biron, farmer
    Johnston, *Lincoln*, 1991, pp. 76-77
 Lincoln, Cathedral Close
8958 Mr Hugh Walter, clergyman, senior vicar
    Maddison, 1904, pp. 88-89
 Winteringham
8959 Thomas Westoby
    Neave, *Winteringham*, 1984, p. 118

Middlesex
 Sunbury
8960 Richard Butt
    Heselton, *Sunbury*, 1976, p. 4
Oxfordshire
 Chinnor
    Henry Eustace, yeoman (see Bledlow, Buckinghamshire)
Shropshire
 Madeley Wood
8961 William Ashwood, blacksmith and trowman
    Trinder and Cox, *Severn Gorge*, 2000, p. 279
8962 Richard Twyford, yeoman
    Trinder and Cox, *Severn Gorge*, 2000, pp. 277-278
 Wellington
8963 Joshua Dunton, [tanner]
    Trinder and Cox, *Telford*, 1980, pp. 263-265
8964 Edward Jones, husbandman
    Trinder and Cox, *Telford*, 1980, pp. 266-267
 Wrockwardine
8965 Elizabeth Bullock, schoolmistress
    Trinder and Cox, *Telford*, 1980, p. 409
8966 Eleanor Newe
    Trinder and Cox, *Telford*, 1980, pp. 410-411
Somersetshire
 Creech St Michael
8967 Jeremiah Powell, yeoman
    Monday and Siraut, *Somerset*, 2003, p. 185
Sussex
 Fittleworth
8968 William Howell, clergyman [vicar of Fittleworth]
    Hughes, *Sussex*, 2007, pp. 81-82
 Rudgwick
8969 John Smyth, clergyman
    Hughes, *Sussex*, 2007, p. 175
 Selham
8970 Thomas Lowe, clergyman [rector of Selham]
    Hughes, *Sussex*, 2007, pp. 185-186
Wales
 Caernavonshire, Llanfaelrhys
8971 Griffith Jones
    Owen, *Lleyn*, 1960, p. 79
Warwickshire
 Berkswell
8972 Thomas Ebrall, cooper
    Sheasby, 1994, pp. 59-61

Shottery
    8973 John Earle, yeoman
    Jones, *Stratford*, II, 2003, pp. 179-180
Stratford-on-Avon
    8974 Nathaniel Bradford, yeoman
    Jones, *Stratford*, II, 2003, p. 187
    8975 Peter Hollande [Holland], shoemaker
    Jones, *Stratford*, II, 2003, pp. 181-182
    8976 Frances Jourden, widow
    Jones, *Stratford*, II, 2003, pp. 188-189
    8977 John Noble, shoemaker
    Jones, *Stratford*, II, 2003, pp. 183-185
    8978 Josiah Simcox, clergyman [vicar of Stratford-on-Avon]
    Jones, *Stratford*, II, 2003, pp. 189-192
Stratford-on-Avon, Old Stratford
    8979 Thomas Smith, gentleman
    Jones, *Stratford*, II, 2003, pp. 180-181
Stratford-on-Avon
    8980 Mr John Ward, clergyman, vicar of Stratford-on-Avon
    Jones, *Stratford*, II, 2003, pp. 185-186
Wiltshire
Marlborough
    8981 Stephen Gilmore, gentleman
    Williams and Thomson, *Marlborough*, 2007, p. 161
    8982 Francis Herringe, feltmaker
    Williams and Thomson, *Marlborough*, 2007, p. 160
    8983 Joramy Mortheas [Jeremiah Matthews]
    Williams and Thomson, *Marlborough*, 2007, pp. 160-161
Worcestershire
Allesborough
    8984 George, Lord Coventry, Baron of Allesborough
    Wanklyn, *Worcestershire*, 1998, p. 413
Broadway
    8985 William Sheldon, esquire
    Wanklyn, *Worcestershire*, 1998, pp. 223-226
Bushley, Pull Court
    8986 Ann Dowdeswell, widow
    Wanklyn, *Worcestershire*, 1998, pp. 227-228
Evesham
    8987 Miriam Carver
    Barnard, *Asgill*, 1914, pp. 83-84
Madresfield
    8988 William Lygon, esquire
    Wanklyn, *Worcestershire*, 1998, pp. 228-236
Yorkshire
Aysgarth, Skellgill
    8989 George Johnson, [yeoman]
    Thwaite, *Abbotside*, 1967, p. 121
Aysgarth, Sedbusk
    8990 Edward Wright
    Thwaite, *Abbotside*, 1967, p. 121

1682
Bristol
Bristol
    8991 Lawrence Joyner, anchor smith
    George, *Bristol*, 2005, pp. 124-128
Shirehampton
    8992 Christopher Harris, yeoman
    Moore, *Clifton*, 1981, pp. 143-144
Stoke Bishop, Sneyd Park
    8993 William Stevens, [yeoman]
    Moore, *Clifton*, 1981, pp. 144-146

Buckinghamshire
Bledlow Ridge
    8994 James Sale, gentleman
    Reed, *Buckinghamshire*, 1988, pp. 165-167
Eton
    8995 Thomas Bartlett, bookseller
    Reed, *Buckinghamshire*, 1988, p. 167
Newport Pagnell
    8996 William Smyth, yeoman
    Reed, *Buckinghamshire*, 1988, pp. 171-173
    8997 Alice Travile, widow
    Reed, *Buckinghamshire*, 1988, pp. 170-171
Wingrave
    8998 William Abraham, gentleman
    Reed, *Buckinghamshire*, 1988, pp. 168-169
    8999 Thomas Adeane, alias Deane, gentleman
    Reed, *Buckinghamshire*, 1988, pp. 169-170
Cheshire
Bowdon
    9000 George Brereton, husbandman
    Groves, *Bowdon*, 1998, pp. 50-51
    9001 Thomas Goulden
    Groves, *Bowdon*, 1998, p. 53
Nantwich
    9002 Jane Beckett, widow
    Cockcroft, *Nantwich*, 1999, pp. 25.3-4
    9003 Martha Church
    Cockcroft, *Nantwich*, 1999, p. 67.3
Sale
    9004 James Moores, [tailor]
    Groves, *Ashton-on-Mersey and Sale*, 2000, p. 98
Devonshire
Uffculme
    9005 John Buttson and Ellizabeth [Elizabeth] his wife
    Wyatt, *Uffculme*, 1997, pp. 139-140
    9006 William Crosse
    Wyatt, *Uffculme*, 1997, pp. 135-136
    9007 Sam[uel] James, [shopkeeper]
    Wyatt, *Uffculme*, 1997, pp. 137-139
    9008 Walter Rise, maltster
    Wyatt, *Uffculme*, 1997, p. 137
    9009 John Starke, clothier
    Wyatt, *Uffculme*, 1997, p. 136
Dorsetshire
Leigh
    9010 Lyonell Keate
    Machin, *Yetminster*, 1976, No.75, (1 p.)
Essex
Roxwell
    9011 Edward Huttly
    Steer, *Mid-Essex*, 1969, pp. 166-167
Writtle
    9012 Caleb Carter
    Steer, *Mid-Essex*, 1969, pp. 167-168
    9013 John Nash
    Steer, *Mid-Essex*, 1969, pp. 168-169
Gloucestershire
Cheltenham
    9014 John Ellis, [yeoman]
    Sale, *Cheltenham*, 1999, p. 28
    9015 Hannah Finch, widow
    Sale, *Cheltenham*, 1999, pp. 26-27

9016 Henry Major, [husbandman]
Sale, *Cheltenham*, 1999, p. 27
Cheltenham, Arle
   9017 Susana Newman, [widow]
   Sale, *Cheltenham*, 1999, p. 29
Frenchay
   9018 Elizabeth Floud, widow
   Moore, *Frampton Cotterell*, 1976, pp. 119-120
Iron Acton, Latteridge
   9019 Thomas Bampton, [yeoman]
   Moore, *Frampton Cotterell*, 1976, pp. 118-119
   9020 Joan Lorredge, widow
   Moore, *Frampton Cotterell*, 1976, p. 120
Westerleigh, Henfield
   9021 John Butler, yeoman
   Moore, *Frampton Cotterell*, 1976, p. 119

Hertfordshire
Hertford
   9022 James Chamberlain
   Adams, *Hertford*, 1997, pp. 65-66
Hertford, Brickendon
   9023 Marey Pumpret [Mary Pomfrett], widow
   Adams, *Hertford*, 1997, p. 111

Kent
Sevenoaks
   9024 Richard Peake, [yeoman]
   Lansberry, *Sevenoaks*, 1988, p. 174

Lancashire
Liverpool
   9025 Henry Hockenhull, gentleman
   Beazley, 1913, pp. 48-49

Leicestershire
Braunstone
   9026 John Bennett, yeoman
   Wilshere, *Braunstone*, 1983, p. 27
   9027 Josua Kirke
   Wilshere, *Braunstone*, 1983, p. 28
   9028 John Spencer, husbandman
   Wilshere, *Braunstone*, 1983, p. 26

Lincolnshire
Lincoln
   9029 Richard Ellis, whipmaker
   Johnston, *Lincoln*, 1991, pp. 81-82
   9030 John Leach, gentleman [grocer and brewer]
   Johnston, *Lincoln*, 1991, pp. 78-89
Lincoln, St Mary Magdalene
   9031 William Peart, gentleman [coffee house proprietor]
   Johnston, *Lincoln*, 1991, pp. 79-81
Winteringham
   9032 Thomas Boothby
   Neave, *Winteringham*, 1984, pp. 119-121
   9033 Robert Mason
   Neave, *Winteringham*, 1984, p. 119

Middlesex
Sunbury
   9034 Marah Grice
   Heselton, *Sunbury*, 1976, p. 4

Oxfordshire
Hook Norton
   9035 Alexander Calcott, baker
   Coltman, 1982, pp. 11-13

Shropshire
Broseley
   9036 Joan Harris, widow
   Trinder and Cox, *Severn Gorge*, 2000, pp. 163-164
Madeley Wood
   9037 George Easthope, shipwright
   Trinder and Cox, *Severn Gorge*, 2000, p. 280
Wellington, Preston-upon-the-Weald
   9038 Thomas Hitchen
   Trinder and Cox, *Telford*, 1980, pp. 268-269
Wellington
   9039 Mary Hunt, widow
   Trinder and Cox, *Telford*, 1980, pp. 269-271
   9040 John Smart, dyer
   Trinder and Cox, *Telford*, 1980, pp. 267-268
Wrockwardine Wood, Pains Lane
   9041 Thomas Barker
   Trinder and Cox, *Telford*, 1980, p. 411

Staffordshire
Colwich
   9042 John Ashley
   Bradley, *Haywoods*, 1993, p. 21
Ettingshall
   9043 Edward Horner
   Roper, *Sedgley*, 1960, pp. 75-76
Sedgley
   9044 John Dutton, coalminer
   Roper, *Sedgley*, 1960, p. 77
Upper Gornal
   9045 Thomas Persehouse, yeoman
   Roper, *Sedgley*, 1960, p. 77

Sussex
Cowdray
   9046 Francis Browne, Viscount Montagu
   Steer, 1967, pp. 86-101
Nuthurst
   9047 John Taylor, clergyman [rector of Nuthurst]
   Hughes, *Sussex*, 2007, pp. 156-158
Oving
   9048 John Drake, clergyman [vicar of Oving]
   Hughes, *Sussex*, 2007, pp. 158-160
Plumpton
   9049 James Bennett, clergyman [rector of Plumpton]
   Hughes, *Sussex*, 2007, p. 166
Sutton
   9050 Thomas Thornton, clergyman [rector of Sutton]
   Hughes, *Sussex*, 2007, pp. 207-208
Thakeham
   9051 Robert Putt, clergyman [rector of Thakeham]
   Hughes, *Sussex*, 2007, pp. 215-216

Warwickshire
Shottery
   9052 Edward Such, husbandman
   Jones, *Stratford*, II, 2003, pp. 200-202
Stoneleigh, Finham
   9053 Robert Burbery, husbandman
   Alcock, *Warwickshire*, 1993, pp. 60-61
Stratford-on-Avon
   9054 John Ainge, butcher
   Jones, *Stratford*, II, 2003, pp. 193-194
   9055 Richard Jackson, baker
   Jones, *Stratford*, II, 2003, pp. 197-199

9056 Mary Noble, widow
Jones, *Stratford*, II, 2003, pp. 202-205
9057 Elizabeth Palmer, widow
Jones, *Stratford*, II, 2003, p. 200
9058 Anne Smith, widow
Jones, *Stratford*, II, 2003, pp. 194-195
9059 Judith Webb, widow
Jones, *Stratford*, II, 2003, pp. 196-197
Wiltshire
Marlborough
9060 Phillipine Greenfield, widow
Williams and Thomson, *Marlborough*, 2007, p. 163
9061 Anthony Powell, saddler
Williams and Thomson, *Marlborough*, 2007, p. 162
9062 William Tallbot, collarmaker
Williams and Thomson, *Marlborough*, 2007, p. 163
Worcestershire
Salwarpe, Oakley
9063 Olive Talbot, spinster
Wanklyn, *Worcestershire*, 1998, pp. 413-414
Yorkshire
Gristhorpe
9064 Bryan Beswicke, yeoman
Brears, *Yorkshire*, 1972, pp. 154-156

1682 (c.)
Cheshire
Nantwich
9065 John Reade, farmer and bricklayer
Cockcroft, *Nantwich*, 1999, pp. 265.2-3
Sale
9066 Randle Holt, [gentleman]
Groves, *Ashton-on-Mersey and Sale*, 2000, p. 103

1683
Bristol
Bristol
9067 Anthony Cocke, baize maker
George, *Bristol*, 2005, pp. 126-128
9068 William Dickenson, button maker
George, *Bristol*, 2005, p. 129
9069 Thomas Heathcott, school-master
George, *Bristol*, 2005, pp. 129-131
9070 Edward Sweeper, brazier
George, *Bristol*, 2005, pp. 131-133
Westbury
9071 John Merryweather, weaver
Moore, *Clifton*, 1981, pp. 146-147
Buckinghamshire
Great Brickhill
9072 Thomas Charlett, Doctor of Physic
Reed, *Buckinghamshire*, 1988, pp. 173-174
Shalstone
9073 William Payne, labourer
Reed, *Buckinghamshire*, 1988, p. 175
Stewkley
9074 William Rand
Reed, *Buckinghamshire*, 1988, pp. 174-175
Cheshire
Ashton-on-Mersey
9075 Robert Leigh, [linen weaver]
Groves, *Ashton-on-Mersey and Sale*, 2000, pp. 105-106
9076 George Renshaw
Groves, *Ashton-on-Mersey and Sale*, 2000, pp. 106-107

Nantwich
9077 John Burscoe, yeoman
Cockcroft, *Nantwich*, 1999, pp. 61.4-6
9078 William Clowes, wheelwright
Cockcroft, *Nantwich*, 1999, p. 81.1
9079 Samuel Collie, merchant
Cockcroft, *Nantwich*, 1999, pp. 91.2-5
9080 Katherine Davenport, widow
Cockcroft, *Nantwich*, 1999, p. 102.2
9081 Edward Hankey, tanner
Cockcroft, *Nantwich*, 1999, pp. 144.4-6
9082 John Sharples, carpenter
Cockcroft, *Nantwich*, 1999, pp. 285.2-3
Sale
9083 Christopher Davies, [husbandman]
Groves, *Ashton-on-Mersey and Sale*, 2000, pp. 100-101
9084 William Hankinson
Groves, *Ashton-on-Mersey and Sale*, 2000, p. 110
Devonshire
Newton St Cyres, Woodleigh
9085 John Tucker
Worthy, *Devonshire*, 1896, p. 204
Thorncombe [now Dorsetshire]
9086 John Tucker
Worthy, *Devonshire*, 1896, p. 204
Uffculme
9087 Edward Callow
Wyatt, *Uffculme*, 1997, pp. 195
9088 Anne Jurdin [Jordan], widow
Wyatt, *Uffculme*, 1997, pp. 134-135
9089 Simon Welche [Welch], [yeoman]
Wyatt, *Uffculme*, 1997, pp. 140-141
Dorsetshire
Leigh
9090 Abraham Clarke, [tailor?]
Machin, *Yetminster*, 1976, No.76, (1 p.)
Essex
Roxwell
9091 William Craig
Steer, *Mid-Essex*, 1969, pp. 169-170
Writtle
9092 Edmund Sterne
Steer, *Mid-Essex*, 1969, pp. 170-171
Gloucestershire
Charlton Kings
9093 Thomas Cherrington, husbandman
Paget and Sale, *Charlton Kings*, 2003, pp. 50-51
9094 John Cook, [husbandman]
Paget and Sale, *Charlton Kings*, 2003, p. 50
Stoke Gifford, Harry Stoke
9095 Joan Palmer
Moore, *Frampton Cotterell*, 1976, p. 120
Hertfordshire
Hertford
9096 William Turner, gentleman
Adams, *Hertford*, 1997, pp. 123-125
9097 Henry Yates, collarmaker
Adams, *Hertford*, 1997, p. 142
Kent
Eynsford, Crockenhill
9098 William Fisher, [yeoman]
Duncombe, *Darent*, 1990-1991, pp. 278-279

Sevenoaks
 9099 Robert Earpe
  Lansberry, *Sevenoaks*, 1988, p. 190
 9100 William Everest, tailor
  Lansberry, *Sevenoaks*, 1988, pp. 167-168
 9101 William Wall, gentleman
  Lansberry, *Sevenoaks*, 1988, pp. 184-186
Leicestershire
 Kirby Muxloe
 9102 John Clarke, [yeoman]
  Wilshere, *Kirby Muxloe*, 1983, p. 13
 9103 John King, gentleman
  Wilshere, *Kirby Muxloe*, 1983, p. 12
Lincolnshire
 Cleethorpes
 9104 George Laceby, husbandman
  Ambler, Watkinson, *Clee*, 1987, pp. 164-165
 Lincoln, St Martins
 9105 Mr Richard Winne, alderman [pewterer]
  Johnston, *Lincoln*, 1991, pp. 82-85
 Winteringham
 9106 Gervis Wilkinson
  Neave, *Winteringham*, 1984, pp. 121-122
London
 St Leonard's, Shoreditch
 9107 William Beeston, [actor]
  Honigmann and Brock, 1993, pp. 237-238
Oxfordshire
 Oxford
 9108 Anna Olliffe, widow
  Kreitzer, 2008, pp. 84-87
 Water Eaton
 9109 Richard Reeve, [yeoman]
  Offord, *Water Eaton*, 1986, pp. 38-39
Scotland
 Edinburgh
 9110 Johne Calderwood, stationer
  Anon., *Bassandyne*, 1836, pp. 289-292
Shropshire
 Bridgnorth, Dunval
 9111 Edward Acton, gentleman
  Smith, 1883-1884, pp. 161-162
 Lilleshall
 9112 Ralph Barrett
  Trinder and Cox, *Telford*, 1980, pp. 210-212
 Lilleshall, Muxton
 9113 William Bate, labourer, thatcher
  Trinder and Cox, *Telford*, 1980, p. 213
 Lilleshall
 9114 Richard Shelton
  Trinder and Cox, *Telford*, 1980, pp. 207-210
 Wrockwardine Wood
 9115 Edward Dawe, yeoman
  Trinder and Cox, *Telford*, 1980, p. 412
Staffordshire
 Ettingshall
 9116 William Elwall, yeoman
  Roper, *Sedgley*, 1960, pp. 78-79
 9117 William Gibbins, yeoman
  Roper, *Sedgley*, 1960, p. 78
Surrey
 Ham House
 9118 Elizabeth, Duchess of Lauderdale
  Thornton and Tomlin, *Ham*, 1980, pp. 37-176

Wales
 Denbighshire, Wynnstay [Watstay]
 9119 Sir John Wynn, baronet
  Jones, 1940, pp. 49-52
Warwickshire
 Stratford-on-Avon
 9120 William Smith, dyer
  Jones, *Stratford*, II, 2003, pp. 206-207
Wiltshire
 Marlborough
 9121 John Dale, yeoman
  Williams and Thomson, *Marlborough*, 2007, pp. 165-166
 9122 Christopher Ellis, glazier, and Elizabeth his wife
  Williams and Thomson, *Marlborough*, 2007, pp. 169-170
 9123 Philip Francklyn, gentleman
  Williams and Thomson, *Marlborough*, 2007, p. 166
 9124 Charity Freman, widow
  Williams and Thomson, *Marlborough*, 2007, pp. 167-168
 9125 Catherine Hammon, widow
  Williams and Thomson, *Marlborough*, 2007, pp. 163-164
 9126 Mary Hurle, widow
  Williams and Thomson, *Marlborough*, 2007, pp. 168-169
 9127 William Lewis, yeoman
  Williams and Thomson, *Marlborough*, 2007, p. 165
 9128 John Mann, roper
  Williams and Thomson, *Marlborough*, 2007, pp. 166-167
 9129 Henry Turner, collar maker
  Williams and Thomson, *Marlborough*, 2007, p. 165
Worcestershire
 Little Malvern
 9130 Elizabeth Russell, spinster
  Wanklyn, *Worcestershire*, 1998, pp. 414-415
Yorkshire
 Halifax
 9131 John Ryall, yeoman
  Brears, *Yorkshire*, 1972, pp. 157-160
 Lunds
 9132 Anne Blaides [Blades]
  Thwaite, *Abbotside*, 1967, p. 122

1683 (c.)
Wiltshire
 Marlborough
 9133 John Shippree, shoemaker
  Williams and Thomson, *Marlborough*, 2007, p. 167

1684
Bristol
 Bristol
 9134 John Burroughs, mariner
  George, *Bristol*, 2005, pp. 133-135
 Bristol, St Philip and St Jacob
 9135 Francis Mountaine, gardener
  George, *Bristol*, 2005, p. 135
 Bristol
 9136 Mr Thomas Wright
  George, *Bristol*, 2005, pp. 136-138
 Shirehampton
 9137 William Hiskins alias Heskins, [yeoman]
  Moore, *Clifton*, 1981, pp. 147-148
 9138 John Thomas, [yeoman]
  Moore, *Clifton*, 1981, pp. 148-149

Buckinghamshire
Aston Abbots
  9139 George Russell, esquire
    Reed, *Buckinghamshire*, 1988, pp. 178-181
Chicheley
  9140 John Randolph, Doctor of Divinity and vicar of Chicheley
    Reed, *Buckinghamshire*, 1988, pp. 183-184
Eton
  9141 Edward Wyse, gentleman
    Reed, *Buckinghamshire*, 1988, pp. 182-183
Slough
  9142 John Hewes, brickmaker
    Reed, *Buckinghamshire*, 1988, pp. 175-177
Taplow
  9143 John Dawson
    Reed, *Buckinghamshire*, 1988, pp. 177-178

Cheshire
Bowdon
  9144 John Drinkwater
    Groves, *Bowdon*, 1998, p. 54
Nantwich
  9145 Richard Hilditch, victualler
    Cockcroft, *Nantwich*, 1999, pp. 155.2-3
Sale
  9146 James Darbishire, [husbandman]
    Groves, *Ashton-on-Mersey and Sale*, 2000, p. 109
  9147 Elizabeth Davenport, [widow]
    Groves, *Ashton-on-Mersey and Sale*, 2000, pp. 115-116
  9148 Samuel Peeres, [husbandman]
    Groves, *Ashton-on-Mersey and Sale*, 2000, pp. 111-112

Devonshire
Clysthydon
  9149 John Culliford, gentleman
    Cash, *Devon*, 1966, pp. 149-150
Malborough
  9150 Joseph Clarke
    Cash, *Devon*, 1966, pp. 150-153
Thorverton
  9151 Robert Tucker, fuller
    Worthy, *Devonshire*, 1896, p. 31
Uffculme
  9152 Mary How alias Tanner, widow
    Wyatt, *Uffculme*, 1997, p. 146

Dorsetshire
Yetminster
  9153 Ann Syme alias Ford
    Machin, *Yetminster*, 1976, No.78, (1 p.)
  9154 William Symes alias Ford, husbandman
    Machin, *Yetminster*, 1976, No.77, (1 p.)

Essex
Colchester, All Saints
  9155 John Ennows, tobacco pipemaker
    Eddy and Ryan, 1983, pp. 107-109
Writtle
  9156 William Poole, blacksmith
    Steer, *Mid-Essex*, 1969, pp. 171-172
  9157 John Scoling, husbandman
    Steer, *Mid-Essex*, 1969, pp. 173-174
  9158 John Taverner
    Steer, *Mid-Essex*, 1969, pp. 172-173

Gloucestershire
Charlton Kings
  9159 Daniell Ellis, maltster
    Paget and Sale, *Charlton Kings*, 2003, pp. 53-55
  9160 Guy Ellis, [husbandman]
    Paget and Sale, *Charlton Kings*, 2003, p. 52
Cheltenham
  9161 John Collett, [yeoman]
    Sale, *Cheltenham*, 1999, pp. 33-34
  9162 Thomas Cox, yeoman
    Sale, *Cheltenham*, 1999, pp. 32-33
  9163 Thomas Farmer, [tailor]
    Sale, *Cheltenham*, 1999, pp. 34-35
  9164 Robert Hyett, maltster
    Sale, *Cheltenham*, 1999, p. 35
  9165 Robert Milton, carpenter
    Sale, *Cheltenham*, 1999, p. 36
Frampton Cotterell
  9166 Edith Davis, widow
    Moore, *Frampton Cotterell*, 1976, pp. 121-122
  9167 John Prigg, yeoman
    Moore, *Frampton Cotterell*, 1976, p. 122
Iron Acton
  9168 John White, yeoman
    Moore, *Frampton Cotterell*, 1976, p. 121
Stoke Gifford
  9169 William Wickham, yeoman
    Moore, *Frampton Cotterell*, 1976, p. 124
Westerleigh
  9170 John Beaugh, labourer
    Moore, *Frampton Cotterell*, 1976, pp. 122-123
  9171 Robert Winboll, yeoman
    Moore, *Frampton Cotterell*, 1976, pp. 123-124

Herefordshire
Hereford
  Philip Lewis, clergyman (see Wales, Radnorshire, Presteigne)

Hertfordshire
Hertford
  9172 John Bayford, husbandman
    Adams, *Hertford*, 1997, pp. 84-85
  9173 Andrew Bray, tanner
    Adams, *Hertford*, 1997, pp. 66-67
Hertford, St Johns
  9174 John Briden, tailor
    Adams, *Hertford*, 1997, p. 91
Hertford, All Saints
  9175 Mary Hummerston
    Adams, *Hertford*, 1997, pp. 134-135
Sarratt
  9176 John Gladman alias Greene, [tailor]
    Bullen, *Sarratt*, [1982], pp. 201-203
  9177 John Grove, [yeoman]
    Bullen, *Sarratt*, [1982], pp. 198-199
  9178 Nicolas Hill
    Bullen, *Sarratt*, [1982], pp. 194-195

Ireland
Dublin
  9179 William Barnard, clothier
    Goodbody, *Dublin Quaker*, 1978, pp. 38-39
Kilkenny, Dunmore House
  James Butler, Duke of Ormonde (see Kilkenny Castle)

Kilkenny Castle
  9180 James Butler, Duke of Ormonde (also listed
  Dunmore House)
  Fenlon, *Ireland,* 2003, pp. 104-126
Kent
Sevenoaks
  9181 William Spilstead, weaver
  Lansberry, *Sevenoaks,* 1988, pp. 187-188
Lancashire
Hawkshead Hall
  9182 Samuell Sandys, gentleman
  Cowper, 1891, pp. 40-41
Leicestershire
Evington
  9183 Ann Buerley, widow
  Wilshere, *Evington,* 1985, p. 29
Quorndon
  9184 Henry Farnham, captain
  Farnham, *Quorndon,* 1912, pp. 427-428
Lincolnshire
Lincoln
  9185 Thomas Eure, gentleman [farmer]
  Johnston, *Lincoln,* 1991, pp. 85-88
Winteringham
  9186 Anthony Shankster
  Neave, *Winteringham,* 1984, p. 150
  9187 Hannah Sharpe, widow
  Neave, *Winteringham,* 1984, pp. 122-123
Wragby, Foulby
  9188 John Smithson, labourer
  Dudding, 1921, pp. 243-245
Northamptonshire
Rothwell
  9189 Elizabeth Alderman, widow
  Alderman, *Alderman,* 2008, p. 143
Shropshire
Broseley
  9190 Ann Dawley, widow
  Trinder and Cox, *Severn Gorge,* 2000, pp. 165-166
  9191 John Evans, tailor
  Trinder and Cox, *Severn Gorge,* 2000, pp. 164-165
  9192 John Roberts alias Belcham, trowman
  Trinder and Cox, *Severn Gorge,* 2000, p. 164
Dawley, Great Dawley
  9193 Thomas Higgins, weaver
  Trinder and Cox, *Telford,* 1980, p. 172
Lilleshall
  9194 Francis Light, carpenter
  Trinder and Cox, *Telford,* 1980, p. 212
Wellington, Ketley and Shifnal
  9195 James Freeman
  Trinder and Cox, *Telford,* 1980, pp. 271-273
Wrockwardine, Long Lane
  9196 Thomas Cooper
  Trinder and Cox, *Telford,* 1980, pp. 412-413
Staffordshire
Ettingshall
  9197 Thomas Harper
  Roper, *Sedgley,* 1960, p. 80
Sedgley
  9198 Edward Bennett, yeoman
  Roper, *Sedgley,* 1960, pp. 81-82

Sedgley, Woodsetton
  9199 Richard Whitehouse, nailer
  Roper, *Sedgley,* 1960, p. 79
Surrey
Charlwood
  9200 Henry Brooker
  Harding, *Charlwood,* 1976, p. 108
Sussex
Horsham
  9201 Mathew Woodman, clergyman
  Hughes, *Sussex,* 2007, p. 111
Kirdford
  9202 Henry Westbrook
  Kenyon, *Kirdford,* 1955, p. 135
Wales
Radnorshire, Brynheer
  Phillip Lewis, clergyman (see Radnorshire, Presteigne)
Radnorshire, Presteigne
  9203 Phillip Lewis, clergyman, rector of Presteigne
  (also listed Brynheer and Herefordshire, Hereford)
  Anon., *Lewis,* 1877, pp. vii-ix
Warwickshire
Shottery
  9204 Stephen Lowe, husbandman
  Jones, *Stratford,* II, 2003, pp. 209-210
Stratford-on-Avon
  9205 Elizabeth Atwood, widow
  Jones, *Stratford,* II, 2003, pp. 210-212
  9206 Mary Proctor
  Jones, *Stratford,* II, 2003, pp. 207-208
Wiltshire
Marlborough
  9207 Edward Carter, saddler
  Williams and Thomson, *Marlborough,* 2007, pp. 170-171
  9208 Thomas Hancock
  Williams and Thomson, *Marlborough,* 2007, p. 172
  9209 Edward Lawrence
  Williams and Thomson, *Marlborough,* 2007, p. 171
  9210 Giles Limor [Lymer], yeoman
  Williams and Thomson, *Marlborough,* 2007, p. 172
  9211 John Osgood, wheelwright
  Williams and Thomson, *Marlborough,* 2007, p. 173
  9212 Alice Scory
  Williams and Thomson, *Marlborough,* 2007, pp. 172-173
  9213 John Sweet, glover
  Williams and Thomson, *Marlborough,* 2007, pp. 173-174
Worcestershire
Bewdley
  9214 Rebecca Poyner, widow
  Bewdley, *Bewdley,* 1991, pp. 177-179
Bushley, Pull Court
  9215 William Dowdeswell, esquire
  Wanklyn, *Worcestershire,* 1998, pp. 237-239
Worcester, The Commandery
  9216 Robert Wylde, esquire
  Wanklyn, *Worcestershire,* 1998, pp. 231-237
Yorkshire
Aysgarth, Sedbusk
  9217 Roger Carrs
  Thwaite, *Abbotside,* 1967, p. 123
Aysgarth, Cotterdale
  9218 Edmund Holme
  Thwaite, *Abbotside,* 1967, p. 124

Aysgarth, Yorescott
9219 Alice Lambert, [widow]
Thwaite, *Abbotside*, 1967, p. 122
Aysgarth, East Grange
9220 Alice Metcalfe, widow
Thwaite, *Abbotside*, 1967, p. 125
Leeds, Halton
9221 Alice Heald
Kirk, *Temple Newsam*, 1935, pp. 265-266
Temple Newsam
9222 Richard Prince, blacksmith
Kirk, *Temple Newsam*, 1935, p. 275

1685
Bristol
Bristol, St Thomas
9223 Richard Finch, merchant
George, *Bristol*, 2005, pp. 138-140
Bristol, St Mary Redcliffe
9224 Thomas Hopkins, hair weaver
George, *Bristol*, 2005, pp. 140-142
Bristol, St Stephen
9225 Daniel Roach, soap-maker
George, *Bristol*, 2005, pp. 142-145
Bristol, Christchurch
9226 John Steevens, tinman
George, *Bristol*, 2005, pp. 145-147
Bristol
9227 George Williamson, clergyman
George, *Bristol*, 2005, p. 147
Westbury
9228 Samuel Nicholls, [merchant]
Moore, *Clifton*, 1981, pp. 149-151
Buckinghamshire
Burnham
9229 Ann Hobbs, widow
Reed, *Buckinghamshire*, 1988, pp. 186-188
Eton
9230 John Cutler
Reed, *Buckinghamshire*, 1988, pp. 184-185
Newport Pagnell
9231 Joseph Jones, laceman
Reed, *Buckinghamshire*, 1988, pp. 188-189
9232 Thomas Pickering
Reed, *Buckinghamshire*, 1988, pp. 189-190
Saunderton
9233 Henry Newell, yeoman
Reed, *Buckinghamshire*, 1988, pp. 191-192
Wendover
9234 Francis Smith, widower
Reed, *Buckinghamshire*, 1988, pp. 185-186
Cheshire
Ashton-on-Mersey
9235 Alice Renshaw, [widow]
Groves, *Ashton-on-Mersey and Sale*, 2000, p. 116
Nantwich
9236 William Clowes, wheelwright
Cockcroft, *Nantwich*, 1999, pp. 86.1-3
9237 William Dale, innholder
Cockcroft, *Nantwich*, 1999, p. 100.3
9238 Richard Hussey, yeoman
Cockcroft, *Nantwich*, 1999, p. 162.3
9239 Samuel Hussey, yeoman
Cockcroft, *Nantwich*, 1999, pp. 163.3-5

9240 William Pratchett, butcher
Cockcroft, *Nantwich*, 1999, pp. 259.1-2
Sale
9241 Edward Holt, [gentleman]
Groves, *Ashton-on-Mersey and Sale*, 2000, p. 118
Devonshire
Dartington
9242 William Searle
Cash, *Devon*, 1966, p. 153
Dorsetshire
Chetnole
9243 Philip Symes, yeoman
Machin, *Yetminster*, 1976, No.80, (1 p.)
Leigh
9244 William Harris, gentleman
Machin, *Yetminster*, 1976, No.79, (2 pp.)
9245 John Hewlet, [yeoman]
Machin, *Yetminster*, 1976, No.81, (1 p.)
9246 Robert Williams, husbandman
Machin, *Yetminster*, 1976, No.82, (2 pp.)
Essex
Ingatestone Hall
9247 John, Baron Petre
Hall, 1976, pp. 9-13
Roxwell
9248 Henry Bright
Steer, *Mid-Essex*, 1969, pp. 174-175
9249 Samuel Sumers, victualler
Steer, *Mid-Essex*, 1969, pp. 175-176
Writtle
9250 Mark George
Steer, *Mid-Essex*, 1969, p. 176
9251 James Holmes, innholder
Steer, *Mid-Essex*, 1969, pp. 176-177
Gloucestershire
Charlton Kings
9252 John Dowdeswell, [yeoman]
Paget and Sale, *Charlton Kings*, 2003, p. 65
9253 Henry Mason, yeoman
Paget and Sale, *Charlton Kings*, 2003, p. 56
Charlton Kings, Ham
9254 Alexander Packer, gentleman
Paget and Sale, *Charlton Kings*, 2003, pp. 59-61
9255 Lynett Pates, gentleman
Paget and Sale, *Charlton Kings*, 2003, pp. 57-58
9256 John Ruck, yeoman
Paget and Sale, *Charlton Kings*, 2003, p. 67
Cheltenham
9257 Thomas Broford
Sale, *Cheltenham*, 1999, pp. 36-37
9258 John Buckle
Sale, *Cheltenham*, 1999, pp. 31-32
9259 Alice Finch
Sale, *Cheltenham*, 1999, p. 38
Cheltenham, Arle
9260 Thomas Fisher, [yeoman]
Sale, *Cheltenham*, 1999, pp. 37-38
Cheltenham, Alstone
9261 Anne Gregory, widow
Sale, *Cheltenham*, 1999, pp. 39-40
Cheltenham
9262 Mary Pates, widow
Sale, *Cheltenham*, 1999, pp. 41-42

Iron Acton
  9263   Philip Prigg, yeoman
    Moore, *Frampton Cotterell*, 1976, p. 125
Stoke Gifford
  9264   Anna Savage, widow
    Moore, *Frampton Cotterell*, 1976, p. 124
Westerleigh, Park Gate
  9265   Jacob Hollister, husbandman
    Moore, *Frampton Cotterell*, 1976, p. 127
Winterbourne
  9266   Edith Mills
    Moore, *Frampton Cotterell*, 1976, p. 128
  9267   John Mills, [feltmaker]
    Moore, *Frampton Cotterell*, 1976, p. 127

Hertfordshire
St Albans, St Stephens
  9268   Edward Edmonds
    Munby, *Worldly Goods*, 1991, p. 164
  9269   Samuell Whelpley, mealman
    Parker, *Worldly Goods*, 2004, pp. 297-299
Sarratt
  9270   John Harding, [yeoman]
    Bullen, *Sarratt*, [1982], pp. 209-210

Kent
Chiddingstone
  9271   Dame Mary Seyliard, widow
    Sherwood, 1948, pp. 57-60
Otford
  9272   John Edwards, yeoman
    Duncombe, *Darent*, 1990-1991, pp. 272-274
Sevenoaks
  9273   Elizabeth Everest, widow
    Lansberry, *Sevenoaks*, 1988, pp. 193-194
Speldhurst
  9274   George Leader, [innholder]
    Stebbing, 1934, pp. 98-101

Lancashire
Manchester
  9275   Barbara Massey, [widow]
    Groves, *Ashton-on-Mersey and Sale*, 2000, p. 114
Ulverston, Dalton Gate (now Cumbria)
  9276   Jennett Ffell
    Fell, 1891, p. 395

Leicestershire
Braunstone
  9277   Francis Cave
    Wilshere, *Braunstone*, 1983, p. 30
  9278   Richard Collingwood
    Wilshere, *Braunstone*, 1983, p. 29
  9279   William Mason
    Wilshere, *Braunstone*, 1983, p. 31
Evington
  9280   John Borley, [shepherd]
    Wilshere, *Evington*, 1985, p. 30
  9281   Edward Burley
    Wilshere, *Evington*, 1985, p. 29
  9282   Francis Frosmill
    Wilshere, *Evington*, 1985, p. 30
Kirby Muxloe
  9283   John Flecther, [husbandman]
    Wilshere, *Kirby Muxloe*, 1983, p. 15
  9284   Marey Jordin
    Wilshere, *Kirby Muxloe*, 1983, p. 15

  9285   John Quinneborow, yeoman
    Wilshere, *Kirby Muxloe*, 1983, p. 14
  9286   John Wallyn, servant
    Wilshere, *Kirby Muxloe*, 1983, p. 13
Lincolnshire
Lincoln
  9287   William Evison, gentleman [timber merchant]
    Johnston, *Lincoln*, 1991, pp. 88-92
Oxfordshire
Oxford
  9288   Edward Bettris, surgeon
    Kreitzer, 2008, pp. 89-90
Shropshire
Dawley, Dawley Green
  9289   Robert Taylor, collier
    Trinder and Cox, *Telford*, 1980, p. 173
Lilleshall, Donnington
  9290   William Bill, yeoman
    Trinder and Cox, *Telford*, 1980, pp. 213-214
Lilleshall, Honnington
  9291   Ralph Winshurst, yeoman
    Trinder and Cox, *Telford*, 1980, pp. 214-215
Wellington, Horton
  9292   Allen Adams
    Trinder and Cox, *Telford*, 1980, pp. 273-274
Wellington, Hadley
  9293   Roger Blakeman, webster
    Trinder and Cox, *Telford*, 1980, p. 276
  9294   George Golborne
    Trinder and Cox, *Telford*, 1980, pp. 275-276
Wellington
  9295   Henry Stanworth, cordwainer
    Trinder and Cox, *Telford*, 1980, pp. 274-275
Wrockwardine
  9296   Phillip Howle
    Trinder and Cox, *Telford*, 1980, pp. 413-414
Somerset
Seymours Court, Beckington
  9297   Adrian Bower of Wraxall, gentleman
    Weinstock, *Bower*, 1955, pp. 232-236
Staffordshire
Colwich, Woodside
  9298   Thomas Yates
    Bradley, *Haywoods*, 1993, p. 43
Dudley
  9299   Oliver Finch, saddler
    Roper, *Dudley*, 1966, p. 49
Sedgley
  9300   John Cox, yeoman
    Roper, *Sedgley*, 1960, p. 83
Sedgley, Gospel End
  9301   William Law, yeoman
    Roper, *Sedgley*, 1960, p. 84
Sedgley, Cinder Hill
  9302   Elizabeth Wilks, widow
    Roper, *Sedgley*, 1960, p. 80
Suffolk
Bradfield St Clare
  9303   John How
    Anon., *Examples*, 1980, pp. 9-10
Surrey
Charlwood
  9304   William Baldwin
    Harding, *Charlwood*, 1976, pp. 108-109

9305 William Hynton
Harding, *Charlwood*, 1976, p. 109
Sussex
Bersted
9306 Joseph Lewis, clergyman
Hughes, *Sussex*, 2007, pp. 19-21
Firle
9307 John Swaffield, clergyman [vicar of West Firle]
Hughes, *Sussex*, 2007, pp. 78-79
Kirdford
9308 John Hunt, labourer
Kenyon, *Kirdford*, 1955, pp. 134-135
Warnham
9309 William Avery, clergyman [vicar of Warnham]
Hughes, *Sussex*, 2007, pp. 226-227
Whatlington
9310 John Eldred of Battle, clergyman [rector of Whatlington]
Hughes, *Sussex*, 2007, p. 237
Wales
Carmarthenshire, Kidwelly
9311 David Davies
Hook, 1979, pp. 62-63
Warwickshire
Alcester
9312 Samuel Ticknor, gentleman
Saville, *Alcester*, 1979, p. 9
Stratford-on-Avon, Old Stratford
9313 John Freeman, maltster
Jones, *Stratford*, II, 2003, pp. 213-214
Wiltshire
Marlborough
9314 An Hancock, widow
Williams and Thomson, *Marlborough*, 2007, p. 174
9315 Thomas Horne, shearman
Williams and Thomson, *Marlborough*, 2007, pp. 177-178
9316 William Kyte, tapster
Williams and Thomson, *Marlborough*, 2007, pp. 175-176
9317 Timothy Pidding
Williams and Thomson, *Marlborough*, 2007, p. 174
9318 Lucy Webb, widow
Williams and Thomson, *Marlborough*, 2007, p. 177
Worcestershire
Astley
9319 Henry Winford, esquire
Wanklyn, *Worcestershire*, 1998, pp. 239-243
Dowles
9320 Humfrey Garmster, yeoman
Bewdley, *Bewdley*, 1991, pp. 180-181

1685 (c.)
Wiltshire
Marlborough
9321 William Cornish alias Duffe, tailor
Williams and Thomson, *Marlborough*, 2007, pp. 174-175
9322 James Crabb, [barber]
Williams and Thomson, *Marlborough*, 2007, pp. 176-177
9323 Ann Longman, widow
Williams and Thomson, *Marlborough*, 2007, p. 178

1686
Bristol
Bristol
9324 John Harris, trunk maker
George, *Bristol*, 2005, pp. 148-150
9325 Richard Steer, bridle cutter
George, *Bristol*, 2005, p. 150
9326 William Taylor, haulier
George, *Bristol*, 2005, pp. 151-153
Westbury, Greenway
9327 Edward Robinson alias Oxford, butcher
Moore, *Clifton*, 1981, pp. 151-152
Buckinghamshire
Amersham
9328 John Young
Reed, *Buckinghamshire*, 1988, pp. 192-193
Brill
9329 Clement Sumerford, gentleman
Reed, *Buckinghamshire*, 1988, pp. 195-196
Great Missenden
9330 Jane Wade, alias Ward, widow
Reed, *Buckinghamshire*, 1988, p. 197
Kimble
9331 John Stathan, maltster
Reed, *Buckinghamshire*, 1988, p. 196
North Crawley
9332 Thomas Hill, late rector of North Crawley
Reed, *Buckinghamshire*, 1988, pp. 194-195
Pitstone, Frithsden
9333 William Baldwin, yeoman
Reed, *Buckinghamshire*, 1988, pp. 193-194
Cheshire
Bowdon
9334 Elizabeth Warburton, widow
Groves, *Bowdon*, 1998, pp. 55-56
Nantwich
9335 John Brerely
Cockcroft, *Nantwich*, 1999, p. 44.1
9336 Mary Church, widow
Cockcroft, *Nantwich*, 1999, pp. 72.2-4
9337 Richard Dean
Cockcroft, *Nantwich*, 1999, pp. 109.1-2
9338 Thomas Kent, schoolmaster [gentleman]
Cockcroft, *Nantwich*, 1999, p. 178.2
9339 Roger Langley, stocking maker
Cockcroft, *Nantwich*, 1999, pp. 179.1-2
9340 Thomas Langley
Cockcroft, *Nantwich*, 1999, p. 180.1
9341 Richard Seavill, ironmonger
Cockcroft, *Nantwich*, 1999, pp. 285.3-6
9342 John Wicksted, gentleman
Cockcroft, *Nantwich*, 1999, pp. 340.2-4
Sale
9343 Mary Barlow, [widow]
Groves, *Ashton-on-Mersey and Sale*, 2000, pp. 120-121
9344 Samuel Holt, [gentleman]
Groves, *Ashton-on-Mersey and Sale*, 2000, pp. 123-124
Devonshire
Burlescombe
9345 Thomas Bowerman, carpenter
Cash, *Devon*, 1966, pp. 153-154

Bishopsteignton
9346 Ann Sherill, widow
Cash, *Devon*, 1966, p. 156
Bovey Tracey
9347 Thomas Wills, yeoman
Cash, *Devon*, 1966, p. 157
Exeter
9348 Anna Parr
Cash, *Devon*, 1966, pp. 154-155
Exeter, St Johns
9349 John Terrill, clothier
Cash, *Devon*, 1966, pp. 155-156
Totnes
9350 Robert Kelligrew, clothier
Cash, *Devon*, 1966, pp. 156-157
Uffculme
9351 Henry Gay, clothier
Wyatt, *Uffculme*, 1997, p. 144
9352 Mr Richard Matthew [Matthews], clergyman,
vicar of Uffculme
Wyatt, *Uffculme*, 1997, pp. 141-144
Dorsetshire
Chetnole
9353 Tobias Matthews, [soapboiler?]
Machin, *Yetminster*, 1976, No.84, (2 pp.)
Yetminster
9354 Edward Moore
Machin, *Yetminster*, 1976, No.86, (2 pp.)
9355 Benjamin Oldys, [cordwainer]
Machin, *Yetminster*, 1976, No.83, (1 p.)
9356 Thomas Ryeman
Machin, *Yetminster*, 1976, No.85, (1 p.)
Essex
Roxwell
9357 Thomas Crush, gentleman
Norris, 1906, pp. 171-174
Steer, *Mid-Essex*, 1969, pp. 177-180
9358 Thomas Foster
Steer, *Mid-Essex*, 1969, pp. 180-181
Writtle
9359 John Ruskin, sawyer
Steer, *Mid-Essex*, 1969, p. 181
Gloucestershire
Charlton Kings
9360 Elizabeth Ashmead
Paget and Sale, *Charlton Kings*, 2003, pp. 62-63
9361 Robert Backhouse, gentleman
Paget and Sale, *Charlton Kings*, 2003, pp. 63-64
9362 Theophilus Brereton, gentleman
Paget and Sale, *Charlton Kings*, 2003, pp. 64-65
9363 William Churches, husbandman
Paget and Sale, *Charlton Kings*, 2003, pp. 68-69
9364 Thomas Jeffs, yeoman
Paget and Sale, *Charlton Kings*, 2003, p. 66
Cheltenham
9365 Richard Banaster, gentleman
Sale, *Cheltenham*, 1999, p. 44
9366 Charles Ireland, saddler
Sale, *Cheltenham*, 1999, pp. 45-46
Cheltenham, Alstone
9367 Edward Merriman, [yeoman]
Sale, *Cheltenham*, 1999, p. 41

Cheltenham
9368 Robert Smyth, innholder
Sale, *Cheltenham*, 1999, pp. 87-88
9369 Richard Willes, [carpenter]
Sale, *Cheltenham*, 1999, p. 46
Gloucester
9370 Phillip Greene, brickmaker
Broadway, 2003, pp. 237-240
Iron Acton, Latteridge
9371 Joan Bampton, widow
Moore, *Frampton Cotterell*, 1976, p. 129
Iron Acton
9372 John Tucke, baker
Moore, *Frampton Cotterell*, 1976, p. 128
Stoke Gifford, Little Stoke
9373 William Mattock, yeoman
Moore, *Frampton Cotterell*, 1976, pp. 129-130
Westerleigh
9374 Katherine Butler, widow
Moore, *Frampton Cotterell*, 1976, pp. 132-133
9375 Matthew Parsons, [coalminer]
Moore, *Frampton Cotterell*, 1976, p. 132
9376 John Short, yeoman
Moore, *Frampton Cotterell*, 1976, pp. 130-131
Winterbourne
9377 Samuel Perry, gentleman
Moore, *Frampton Cotterell*, 1976, pp. 131-132
9378 Joan Tibbott, widow
Moore, *Frampton Cotterell*, 1976, p. 130
Hertfordshire
St Albans, St Stephens
9379 Thomas Francis, yeoman
Parker, *Worldly Goods*, 2004, pp. 299-300
9380 Thomas Higden, brickmaker
Munby, *Worldly Goods*, 1991, pp. 165-166
Ireland
Co. Cork, Burton Hall
9381 Sir John Percivale, baronet
ffolliott and Breffny, 1973, pp. 106-113
Lancashire
Hawkshead, Lawson Park
9382 George Nicholson
Cowper, 1891, pp. 38-39
Leicestershire
Evington
9383 Thomas Goode, tailor
Wilshere, *Evington*, 1985, p. 31
9384 William Spence, yeoman
Wilshere, *Evington*, 1985, p. 31
Shropshire
Lilleshall, The Hinks
9385 John Smith alias Steward, yeoman
Trinder and Cox, *Telford*, 1980, pp. 215-216
Madeley
9386 Richard Beech, labourer, collier
Trinder and Cox, *Severn Gorge*, 2000, p. 281
Staffordshire
Ettingshall
9387 Samuel Gibbins
Roper, *Sedgley*, 1960, p. 82
Harborne
9388 Ann Stampe
Bodfish, *Smethwick*, 1992, p. 30

Smethwick
9389 Richard Ashford
Bodfish, *Smethwick*, 1992, pp. 33-34
Surrey
Charlwood
9390 John Humphrey, yeoman
Harding, *Charlwood*, 1976, pp. 109-111
Sussex
Funtington, East Ashling
9391 Sebastian Pittfield, clergyman [rector of
Warblington, Hampshire]
Hughes, *Sussex*, 2007, pp. 83-86
Treyford
9392 Walter Tomlinson, clergyman [rector of Treyford]
Hughes, *Sussex*, 2007, pp. 218-219
Wales
Glamorganshire, Monknash
9393 Eva Wrinch, widow
Wrench, *Wrenche*, 1956, p. 41
Warwickshire
Chilvers Cotton
9394 Ralph Cox, husbandman
Arkell, Evans, Goose, 2000, p. 374
Shottery
9395 John Wells
Jones, *Stratford*, II, 2003, pp. 215-217
Stratford-onAvon
9396 Mary Horne, widow
Jones, *Stratford*, II, 2003, pp. 217-219
Wiltshire
Marlborough
9397 Margaret Bowles, widow
Williams and Thomson, *Marlborough*, 2007, p. 179
9398 Edith Crabb, widow
Williams and Thomson, *Marlborough*, 2007, pp. 181-182
9399 Thomas Garlick, victualler
Williams and Thomson, *Marlborough*, 2007, pp. 179-180
9400 Jone Godfor
Williams and Thomson, *Marlborough*, 2007, pp. 180-181
9401 Richard New, husbandman
Williams and Thomson, *Marlborough*, 2007, p. 180
9402 Ric Williams
Williams and Thomson, *Marlborough*, 2007, p. 182
Yorkshire
Barnoldswick, Brockden, Admergill
9403 John Hanson, yeoman
Kirk, *Barnoldswick*, 1951, pp. 64-65
Hardrow
9404 John Metcalfe, [yeoman]
Thwaite, *Abbotside*, 1967, pp. 126-127
Lunds
9405 Edward Dent
Thwaite, *Abbotside*, 1967, pp. 125-126

1686 (c.)
Wiltshire
Marlborough
9406 Luce Church
Williams and Thomson, *Marlborough*, 2007, p. 182

1687
Bristol
Bristol
9407 Jonathan Axford, pewterer
George, *Bristol*, 2005, pp. 153-154

9408 John Barwick, scavenger
George, *Bristol*, 2005, pp. 154-155
9409 Elinor Biggs
George, *Bristol*, 2005, pp. 156-160
9410 Edward Cooke, haberdasher
George, *Bristol*, 2005, pp. 160-164
9411 John Hardman, clothier
George, *Bristol*, 2005, pp. 165-166
9412 Clement Leeds, parchment-maker
George, *Bristol*, 2005, p. 167
Bristol, Castle Precincts
9413 John Ware, silk weaver
George, *Bristol*, 2005, pp. 167-168
Clifton
9414 Martha Branch alias Blanch, widow
Moore, *Clifton*, 1981, pp. 154-156
9415 Edith Snook, widow
Moore, *Clifton*, 1981, pp. 152-153
9416 Elizabeth Jones, widow
Moore, *Clifton*, 1981, pp. 153-154
Shirehampton
9417 James Griffiths, labourer
Moore, *Clifton*, 1981, p. 152
Westbury
9418 Samuel Andrews, yeoman
Moore, *Clifton*, 1981, p. 154
Buckinghamshire
Chesham
9419 Abraham Axtell, mercer
Reed, *Buckinghamshire*, 1988, pp. 201-203
Denham
9420 Edward Hankins
Reed, *Buckinghamshire*, 1988, pp. 203-204
Eton
9421 Alexander White, plumber
Reed, *Buckinghamshire*, 1988, pp. 197-201
Cheshire
Ashton-on-Mersey
9422 Henry Chorlton
Groves, *Ashton-on-Mersey and Sale*, 2000, pp. 124-125
9423 Charles Gee
Groves, *Ashton-on-Mersey and Sale*, 2000, pp. 125-126
Bowdon
9424 Sibill Warburton
Groves, *Bowdon*, 1998, pp. 56-57
Nantwich
9425 Huin Adams, stocking maker
Cockcroft, *Nantwich*, 1999, p. 6.1
9426 Ann Dean
Cockcroft, *Nantwich*, 1999, p. 110.1
9427 Amy Travell, widow
Cockcroft, *Nantwich*, 1999, p. 313.1
9428 John Woodward, labourer
Cockcroft, *Nantwich*, 1999, p. 357.1
Devonshire
Bondleigh
9429 Margery Dunne, widow
Cash, *Devon*, 1966, p. 158
Clayhanger
9430 Jane Tucker, widow
Worthy, *Devonshire*, 1896, p. 33
Huish
9431 Leonard Yeo, esquire
Cash, *Devon*, 1966, pp. 158-161

Morebath
  9432 James Talbot, yeoman
    Monday and Siraut, *Somerset*, 2003, p. 231
Uffculme
  9433 Jno Barnfeild [John Barnfield], husbandman
    Wyatt, *Uffculme*, 1997, pp. 144-145

Dorsetshire
Chetnole
  9434 Thomas Kaille, [yeoman]
    Machin, *Yetminster*, 1976, No.87, (2 pp.)

Essex
Roxwell
  9435 Edward Allin
    Steer, *Mid-Essex*, 1969, pp. 183-185
  9436 Elizabeth Clarke, widow
    Steer, *Mid-Essex*, 1969, pp. 185-186
  9437 Hezekiah Godsafe
    Steer, *Mid-Essex*, 1969, pp. 187-188
  9438 Edward Sandford, yeoman
    Steer, *Mid-Essex*, 1969, pp. 189-190
Unlocated
  9439 Thomas Crow
    Steer, *Mid-Essex*, 1969, pp. 182-183
  9440 John Mariage
    Steer, *Mid-Essex*, 1969, p. 181
  9441 Lidiah Wead [Wade]
    Steer, *Mid-Essex*, 1969, pp. 186-187
Writtle
  9442 Ann George
    Steer, *Mid-Essex*, 1969, pp. 188-189
  9443 Richard Nutting
    Steer, *Mid-Essex*, 1969, p. 185
  9444 William White, yeoman
    Steer, *Mid-Essex*, 1969, pp. 190-191

Gloucestershire
Charlton Kings
  9445 Giles Ashmeade, yeoman
    Paget and Sale, *Charlton Kings*, 2003, pp. 69-70
  9446 Thomas Digason, weaver
    Paget and Sale, *Charlton Kings*, 2003, p. 68
Cheltenham
  9447 Richard Banaster, gentleman
    Sale, *Cheltenham*, 1999, p. 44
  9448 Richard Wells, gentleman
    Sale, *Cheltenham*, 1999, p. 47
Frampton Cotterell
  9449 Richard Parker, feltmaker
    Moore, *Frampton Cotterell*, 1976, pp. 135-136
  9450 Harry Symes, esquire, and his widow, Ann
    Moore, *Frampton Cotterell*, 1976, pp. 133-135
Iron Acton, Acton Ilger
  9451 Mary Alsop
    Moore, *Frampton Cotterell*, 1976, p. 135
Iron Acton
  9452 William Belchire, [yeoman]
    Moore, *Frampton Cotterell*, 1976, pp. 136-137
Stoke Gifford, Little Stoke
  9453 John Robins, yeoman
    Moore, *Frampton Cotterell*, 1976, p. 136

Hertfordshire
Hertford
  9454 Jo[hn] Catling, bricklayer
    Adams, *Hertford*, 1997, pp. 92-93

  9455 John Rogers, [cordwainer]
    Adams, *Hertford*, 1997, pp. 117-118
  9456 John Wollor [Woollard]
    Adams, *Hertford*, 1997, pp. 137-138
St Albans, St Stephens
  9457 Richard Finch, yeoman
    Parker, *Worldly Goods*, 2004, p. 302

Ireland
Dublin
  9458 James Taylor, clothier
    Goodbody, *Quaker*, 1971, pp. 54-57

Leicestershire
Evington
  9459 Thomas Coy, yeoman
    Wilshere, *Evington*, 1985, p. 33
  9460 William Johnson, [husbandman]
    Wilshere, *Evington*, 1985, p. 32
  9461 John Spencer, [yeoman]
    Wilshere, *Evington*, 1985, p. 32

London
St Giles in the Fields
  9462 William Cartwright, [gentleman, actor, bookseller]
    Honigmann and Brock, 1993, pp. 238-243

Middlesex
Sunbury
  9463 John Bonnick, [fisherman]
    Heselton, *Sunbury*, 1976, pp. 4-5

Oxfordshire
Water Eaton
  9464 Richard House
    Offord, *Water Eaton*, 1986, p. 42

Scotland
Ayrshire, Eglinton
  9465 Lady Hellenor Montgomerie, Lady Baldoon
  (also listed Kilwinning)
    Fraser, 1859, pp. 338-341
Ayrshire, Kilwinning
  Lady Hellenor Montgomerie, Lady Baldoon (see Eglinton)
Edinburgh
  9466 James Watsone, printer
    Anon., *Bassandyne*, 1836, pp. 294-295

Shropshire
Broseley
  9467 Samuel Evans, collier
    Trinder and Cox, *Severn Gorge*, 2000, pp. 166-167
Broseley, The Woodhouse
  9468 Andrew Langley, gentleman
    Trinder and Cox, *Severn Gorge*, 2000, pp. 167-170
Wellington
  9469 Joyce Bradshaw, widow
    Trinder and Cox, *Telford*, 1980, pp. 276-278
  9470 Margaret Justice, mercer and widow
    Trinder and Cox, *Telford*, 1980, pp. 278-280
Wellington, Leegomery
  9471 William Minshall
    Trinder and Cox, *Telford*, 1980, pp. 281-284
Wellington, Street Lane
  9472 John Peate, blacksmith
    Trinder and Cox, *Telford*, 1980, pp. 280-281
Wrockwardine
  9473 Thomas Smith, webster
    Trinder and Cox, *Telford*, 1980, pp. 414-415

Staffordshire
Harborne
  9474 John Geaset, yeoman
    Bodfish, *Smethwick*, 1992, pp. 31-32
Smethwick
  9475 William Smith, blacksmith
    Bodfish, *Smethwick*, 1992, pp. 36-37
Surrey
Charlwood
  9476 Richard Fisher, yeoman
    Harding, *Charlwood*, 1976, pp. 110-111
Sussex
Fernhurst
  9477 Abell Stepney, clergyman [curate of Fernhurst]
    Hughes, *Sussex*, 2007, p. 73
Henfield, Eatons
  9478 John Gratwicke, [Major]
    Douglas, 1967, pp. 290-293
Wales
Caernarvonshire, Aberdaron
  9479 William Pugh
    Owen, *Lleyn*, 1960, p. 79
Warwickshire
Stratford-on-Avon
  9480 Thomas Meades, skinner
    Jones, *Stratford*, II, 2003, pp. 220-221
Wiltshire
Marlborough
  9481 Timothy Cheevers, currier
    Williams and Thomson, *Marlborough*, 2007, pp. 182-183
  9482 Robert Miles, joiner
    Williams and Thomson, *Marlborough*, 2007, p. 185
  9483 John Phillipps, blacksmith
    Williams and Thomson, *Marlborough*, 2007, pp. 184-185
  9484 Henry Pike, maltster
    Williams and Thomson, *Marlborough*, 2007, pp. 183-184
Worcestershire
Rous Lench
  9485 Sir Francis Rous, baronet
    Wanklyn, *Worcestershire*, 1998, pp. 243-247
Yorkshire
Aysgarth, Sedbusk
  9486 Alexander Metcalf [Metcalfe]
    Thwaite, *Abbotside*, 1967, p. 128
Barnoldswick, Coates
  9487 Jane Car
    Kirk, *Barnoldswick*, 1951, p. 61
Barnoldswick, Hey
  9488 James Smith
    Kirk, *Barnoldswick*, 1951, p. 78
Lunds
  9489 Ralph Blades
    Thwaite, *Abbotside*, 1967, pp. 127-128

1688
Bristol
Bristol
  9490 William Christopher, merchant tailor
    George, *Bristol*, 2005, pp. 169-170
  9491 Thomas Cottemore, [miller]
    George, *Bristol*, 2005, pp. 170-171
Bristol, St Thomas
  9492 Llewellin Evans, tobacco pipe maker
    George, *Bristol*, 2005, pp. 171-172

Bristol, Merchant Tailors' Hall
  9493 Merchant Tailors' Guild
    Fox, 1880, pp. 101-104
Bristol, St Peter
  9494 Peter Pontyn, tanner
    George, *Bristol*, 2005, pp. 172-174
Bristol
  9495 William Temple, tobacco cutter
    George, *Bristol*, 2005, pp. 174-175
Shirehampton
  9496 Peter Dee, [yeoman]
    Moore, *Clifton*, 1981, p. 156
Buckinghamshire
Buckingham
  9497 Christopher Evans, mercer
    Reed, *Buckinghamshire*, 1988, pp. 208-209
Chipping Wycombe
  9498 Sarah Mitchell, widow
    Reed, *Buckinghamshire*, 1988, p. 205
  9499 Jeremiah Steevens, maltster
    Reed, *Buckinghamshire*, 1988, pp. 207-208
Eton
  9500 Jonathan Attwater
    Reed, *Buckinghamshire*, 1988, pp. 204-205
Olney
  9501 Ezekiel Johnson, clerk
    Reed, *Buckinghamshire*, 1988, pp. 206-207
Cambridgeshire
Cambridge, Christ's College
  9502 Master's Lodge
    Willis and Clark, 1886, p. 353
Newmarket
  9503 Mrs Ann Bridgman
    May, *Newmarket*, 1976, pp. 26-27
Cheshire
Bowdon
  9504 George Warburton
    Groves, *Bowdon*, 1998, p. 57
Nantwich
  9505 John Abnett
    Cockcroft, *Nantwich*, 1999, p. 1.2
  9506 Robert Cliff, sawyer
    Cockcroft, *Nantwich*, 1999, p. 78.2
Sale
  9507 John Moores
    Groves, *Ashton-on-Mersey and Sale*, 2000, pp. 127-128
Devonshire
Uffculme
  9508 Elizabeth Bishopp [Bishop], widow
    Wyatt, *Uffculme*, 1997, pp. 145-146
  9509 Arthur Dowdney, tailor
    Wyatt, *Uffculme*, 1997, pp. 146-147
  9510 John Dunne [Dunn], yeoman [and blacksmith]
    Wyatt, *Uffculme*, 1997, pp. 147-148
  9511 John Leaman, [yeoman]
    Wyatt, *Uffculme*, 1997, p. 147
  9512 John Salkeld, gentleman
    Wyatt, *Uffculme*, 1997, pp. 148-149
Dorsetshire
Chetnole
  9513 Lawrence Baine, yeoman
    Machin, *Yetminster*, 1976, No.90, (1 p.)

9514 Henry Deecker, yeoman
Machin, *Yetminster*, 1976, No.89, (1 p.)
Leigh
9515 Richard Read
Machin, *Yetminster*, 1976, No.88, (2 p.)
Machin, 1978, pp. 164-165

Essex
Roxwell
9516 Laurance [Beadle], carpenter
Steer, *Mid-Essex*, 1969, pp. 191-192
Unlocated
9517 Thomas Cruch
Steer, *Mid-Essex*, 1969, p. 191

Gloucestershire
Charlton Kings
9518 Charles Bowyer, yeoman
Paget and Sale, *Charlton Kings*, 2003, pp. 71-72
Charlton Kings, Ham
9519 Thomas Buckle, [yeoman]
Paget and Sale, *Charlton Kings*, 2003, pp. 70-71
Charlton Kings
9520 Walter Mansell, [cordwainer?]
Paget and Sale, *Charlton Kings*, 2003, p. 72
Cheltenham
9521 Walter Adams, [blacksmith]
Sale, *Cheltenham*, 1999, pp. 50-51
9522 Henry King, [yeoman]
Sale, *Cheltenham*, 1999, p. 53
Cheltenham, Arle
9523 Francis Lane, [yeoman]
Sale, *Cheltenham*, 1999, p. 48
Frampton Cotterell
9524 Richard Roch, [mason, yeoman]
Moore, *Frampton Cotterell*, 1976, p. 139
Iron Acton, Latteridge
9525 William Webb, yeoman
Moore, *Frampton Cotterell*, 1976, pp. 137-138
Westerleigh
9526 John Holder, [yeoman]
Moore, *Frampton Cotterell*, 1976, p. 138
Winterbourne
9527 William Smith, yeoman
Moore, *Frampton Cotterell*, 1976, pp. 138-139

Hertfordshire
Hertford, St Andrews
9528 Judith Day, widow
Adams, *Hertford*, 1997, pp. 101-103
Hertford
9529 John Helder, [carpenter]
Adams, *Hertford*, 1997, pp. 129-130
9530 Robert Nicholes [Nicholson], yeoman
Adams, *Hertford*, 1997, pp. 105-106
St Albans, St Stephens
9531 Ann Fooler [Fuller], widow
Parker, *Worldly Goods*, 2004, p. 305

Kent
Farningham
9532 Thomas Plummer, yeoman
Duncombe, *Darent*, 1990-1991, pp. 340-342
Otford
9533 Henry Soane, yeoman
Duncombe, *Darent*, 1990-1991, pp. 391-392

Shoreham
9534 Robert Atthood, yeoman
Duncombe, *Darent*, 1990-1991, pp. 235-236

Lancashire
Higham, Fence
9535 John Shaw
Kirk, *Barnoldswick*, 1951, pp76-77
Sutton
9536 Mr Richard Eltonhed
Rankin, 1957, p. 62

Lincolnshire
Allington
9537 Thomas Marrott
Pask, *Allington*, 1989, pp. 91-92
Belton House
9538 Sir John Brownlow, baronet
Cust, 1909, pp. 160-166
Cleethorpes
9539 Edward Grimbleby, husbandman
Ambler, Watkinson, *Clee*, 1987, pp. 165-166
Lincoln, St Martins
9540 Robert Burtons, gardener [weaver]
Johnston, *Lincoln*, 1991, pp. 92-93
Lincoln
9541 Edmund Fleare, bodice maker
Johnston, *Lincoln*, 1991, pp. 96-97
Lincoln, St Markes
9542 Thomas Hill, confectioner
Johnston, *Lincoln*, 1991, pp. 94-95
Lincoln, St Botolph
9543 Roger Wood, glover
Johnston, *Lincoln*, 1991, p. 95
Winteringham
9544 Thomas Bell
Neave, *Winteringham*, 1984, p. 153
9545 Michaell Boothby
Neave, *Winteringham*, 1984, pp. 151-152
9546 James Fowler
Neave, *Winteringham*, 1984, p. 154

Oxfordshire
Water Eaton
9547 Henry Rench, [yeoman]
Offord, *Water Eaton*, 1986, pp. 40-41

Scotland
Edinburgh
9548 Gideon Shaw, stationer
Anon., *Bassandyne*, 1836, pp. 292-294

Shropshire
Madeley
9549 Mary Yates, widow
Trinder and Cox, *Severn Gorge*, 2000, pp. 305-306
Oldbury, Westhood
9550 Elizabeth Perkes
Southam, 1901, pp. 413-414
Wrockwardine Wood, The Moss
9551 Thomas Ball, yeoman
Trinder and Cox, *Telford*, 1980, p. 416
Wrockwardine, Clotley
9552 Thomas Laurence, yeoman
Trinder and Cox, *Telford*, 1980, p. 417

Staffordshire
Ettingshall
9553 Joh Hickmans, nailer
Roper, *Sedgley*, 1960, pp. 85-86

Gornal Wood
  9554 Richard Dutton
    Roper, *Sedgley*, 1960, p. 86
Smethwick
  9555 Elizabeth Ashford
    Bodfish, *Smethwick*, 1992, p. 35

Sussex
Lyminster
  9556 Francis Wright, clergyman [vicar of Lyminster]
    Hughes, *Sussex*, 2007, p. 134
Westfield
  9557 Rowland Prigg, clergyman [vicar of Westfield]
    Hughes, *Sussex*, 2007, p. 236

Wales
Monmouthshire, Tredegar House
  9558 Thomas Morgan
    Apted, 1972-3, pp. 146-153
Montgomeryshire, Llanfihangel, Halfen
  9559 Margaret John Evan
    Gilson, *Llanfihangel*, 2009, p. 44

Warwickshire
Luddington
  9560 William Edden, yeoman
    Jones, *Stratford*, II, 2003, pp. 227-230
Stratford-on-Avon
  9561 Elioner [Eleanor] Burman, widow
    Jones, *Stratford*, II, 2003, pp. 222-224
  9562 Henry Harbridge, gentleman
    Jones, *Stratford*, II, 2003, p. 227
  9563 William Hiccox, gentleman
    Jones, *Stratford*, II, 2003, pp. 224-226
  9564 Mary Horne
    Jones, *Stratford*, II, 2003, pp. 230-232
  9565 Richard Sturley, [saddler]
    Jones, *Stratford*, II, 2003, pp. 233-235

Wiltshire
Marlborough
  9566 Edward Crew, [parchment maker]
    Williams and Thomson, *Marlborough*, 2007, p. 186
  9567 George Norris
    Williams and Thomson, *Marlborough*, 2007, pp. 185-186
  9568 Dorithy Titcom
    Williams and Thomson, *Marlborough*, 2007, p. 186

Worcestershire
Belbroughton, Bell Hall
  9569 Humphrey Perrott, gentleman
    Wanklyn, *Worcestershire*, 1998, pp. 247-249

Yorkshire
Barnoldswick, Brigholme
  9570 Mary Higgin, widow
    Kirk, *Barnoldswick*, 1951, p. 69
Barnoldswick, Hey
  9571 James Smith
    Kirk, *Barnoldswick*, 1951, p. 78
Beverley, North Barr House
  9572 Michael Warton (also listed Beverley Parks)
    Hall, *Beverley*, 1986, pp. 15-52
Beverley Parks, New Lodge
  Michael Warton (see Beverley)
Horbury
  9573 John North, yeoman
    Bartlett, *Horbury*, 1980, p. 2

1688 (c.)
Wiltshire
Marlborough
  9574 Ann Gramut, widow
    Williams and Thomson, *Marlborough*, 2007, p. 187

1689
Bristol
Bristol
  9575 Widow Braine, wife of haulier
    George, *Bristol*, 2005, pp. 175-177
  9576 John Bulgin, serge maker
    George, *Bristol*, 2005, pp. 177-179
  9577 Christopher Griffith, esquire
    George, *Bristol*, 2005, pp. 179-184
Bristol, St Nicholas
  9578 George Payne, [joiner]
    George, *Bristol*, 2005, pp. 184-186

Buckinghamshire
Chesham
  9579 Josias Geary, gentleman
    Reed, *Buckinghamshire*, 1988, pp. 223-226
Little Marlow
  Sir John Borlase, baronet (see Medmenham)
Medmenham, Bockmore
  9580 Sir John Borlase, baronet (also listed Little
    Marlow, and Stratton Audley, Oxfordshire)
    Reed, *Buckinghamshire*, 1988, pp. 209-223

Cheshire
Sale
  9581 George Ashton alias Wales
    Groves, *Ashton-on-Mersey and Sale*, 2000, pp. 129-130
  9582 Jonathan Barlow, [yeoman]
    Groves, *Ashton-on-Mersey and Sale*, 2000, pp. 130-131

Devonshire
Cadeleigh
  9583 William Tayler
    Cash, *Devon*, 1966, p. 161
Uffculme
  9584 John Dulin, fuller
    Wyatt, *Uffculme*, 1997, pp. 149-150
  9585 William Kerslake, yeoman
    Wyatt, *Uffculme*, 1997, p. 150

Dorsetshire
Chetnole
  9586 John Mainard, [bodice maker]
    Machin, *Yetminster*, 1976, No.91, (2 pp.)
Swanage
  9587 William Melmoth, marbler
    Dawe, *Purbeck*, 1968, pp. 241-242
Wareham
  9588 John Perren, fuller
    Dawe, 1974, pp. 33-35

Essex
Writtle
  9589 Joseph Bonnington, yeoman
    Steer, *Mid-Essex*, 1969, pp. 198-199
  9590 Henry Bullen, yeoman
    Steer, *Mid-Essex*, 1969, pp. 199-200
  9591 William Hillyard
    Steer, *Mid-Essex*, 1969, pp. 197-198
  9592 Mrs Porter
    Steer, *Mid-Essex*, 1969, p. 195

9593   Martha Radley, widow
Steer, *Mid-Essex*, 1969, pp. 192-194
9594   Robert Sach
Steer, *Mid-Essex*, 1969, pp. 196-197
9595   John Waylett, tanner
Steer, *Mid-Essex*, 1969, pp. 194-195

Gloucestershire
Charlton Kings
9596   Elizabeth Deane, widow
Paget and Sale, *Charlton Kings*, 2003, p. 75
9597   Jane Mansell, widow
Paget and Sale, *Charlton Kings*, 2003, p. 73
Cheltenham
9598   Mary Ashmeade, widow
Sale, *Cheltenham*, 1999, pp. 54-55
9599   Robert Ellis, [yeoman]
Sale, *Cheltenham*, 1999, p. 52
9600   Sarah Hyett
Sale, *Cheltenham*, 1999, p. 53
Cheltenham, Alstone
9601   John Stephens, yeoman
Sale, *Cheltenham*, 1999, pp. 51-52
Cheltenham
9602   Walter White, [maltster]
Sale, *Cheltenham*, 1999, pp. 49-50
9603   William White, [maltster]
Sale, *Cheltenham*, 1999, p. 47
Westerleigh, Nibley
9604   Jacob Hollister, yeoman
Moore, *Frampton Cotterell*, 1976, pp. 140-141
Westerleigh
9605   David Langham, mason
Moore, *Frampton Cotterell*, 1976, p. 140
Winterbourne
9606   Simon Evans, husbandman
Moore, *Frampton Cotterell*, 1976, p. 139

Herefordshire
Hereford
9607   John Jones, mercer
Morgan, *Mercer*, 1947, pp. 190-196

Hertfordshire
Hertford
9608   [Elizabeth] Churchman, widow
Adams, *Hertford*, 1997, pp. 94-96

Kent
Eynsford
9609   Thomas Launder, yeoman
Duncombe, *Darent*, 1990-1991, pp. 315-317
9610   John Scudder, yeoman
Duncombe, *Darent*, 1990-1991, p. 376

Lancashire
Ulverston (now Cumbria)
9611   John Ffell
Fell, 1891, pp. 394-395

Leicestershire
Evington
9612   Rachell Filks
Wilshere, *Evington*, 1985, p. 34

Lincolnshire
Winteringham
9613   Anthony Westoby
Neave, *Winteringham*, 1984, pp. 123-124

London
Clapham, Clapham House
9614   Sir Denis Gauden
Green, 2008, pp. 196-205

Nottinghamshire
Wiseton
9615   John Hiblin, [tailor]
Perkins, *Clayworth*, 1979, pp. xiv-xv
9616   Thomas Whitehead, [labourer]
Perkins, *Clayworth*, 1979, p,xiii

Oxfordshire
Little Marlow
Sir John Borlase (see Medmenham, Buckinghamshire)
Stratton Audley
Sir John Borlase (see Medmenham, Buckinghamshire)

Shropshire
Broseley
9617   John Dawley
Trinder and Cox, *Severn Gorge*, 2000, p. 171
Broseley, Salthouse
9618   Hugh Jones, trowman
Trinder and Cox, *Severn Gorge*, 2000, p. 170
Little Wenlock
9619   Mr John Smitheman, yeoman
Trinder and Cox, *Severn Gorge*, 2000, pp. 244-246
Madeley
9620   Anne Richards, widow
Trinder and Cox, *Severn Gorge*, 2000, p. 282
9621   Roger Tranter, labourer
Trinder and Cox, *Severn Gorge*, 2000, p. 283
Wellington
9622   Richard Jones
Trinder and Cox, *Telford*, 1980, pp. 287-289
9623   William Langley, clergyman
Trinder and Cox, *Telford*, 1980, pp. 284-287
Wrockwardine, Allscott
9624   John Binnell, yeoman
Trinder and Cox, *Telford*, 1980, pp. 417-419

Somersetshire
Selworthy
9625   Peter Rall
Monday and Siraut, *Somerset*, 2003, pp. 191-192

Staffordshire
Sedgley
9626   Thomas Gibbens, yeoman
Roper, *Sedgley*, 1960, pp. 87-88

Surrey
Charlwood
9627   John Batchelor, yeoman
Harding, *Charlwood*, 1976, p. 111
9628   John Wilkins, wheelwright
Harding, *Charlwood*, 1976, p. 112

Sussex
Kirdford, Crawfold
9629   John Eede, yeoman
Kenyon, *Kirdford*, 1955, pp. 119-120

Wales
Montgomeryshire, Llanfihangel
9630   Cadwalader Watkins, gentleman
Gilson, *Llanfihangel*, 2009, pp. 44-45

Warwickshire
Bishopton
9631   Edward Haughton, husbandman
Jones, *Stratford*, II, 2003, p. 242

Clopton
9632 Richard Harris, yeoman
Jones, *Stratford*, II, 2003, pp. 236-238
Luddington
9633 Thomas Harris, husbandman
Jones, *Stratford*, II, 2003, pp. 240-241
Stoneleigh, Cryfield
9634 Thomas Higinson, yeoman
Alcock, *Warwickshire*, 1993, pp. 98-99
Stratford-on-Avon
9635 John Nason, glover
Jones, *Stratford*, II, 2003, pp. 242-244
9636 John Powell, clothworker
Jones, *Stratford*, II, 2003, pp. 239-240
Wiltshire
Marlborough
9637 Thomas Cripps
Williams and Thomson, *Marlborough*, 2007, p. 187
9638 Thomas Have [Haw], tailor
Williams and Thomson, *Marlborough*, 2007, pp. 188-189
9639 Richard Luffe, yeoman
Williams and Thomson, *Marlborough*, 2007, p. 187
9640 Thomas Sampson, cooper
Williams and Thomson, *Marlborough*, 2007, pp. 187-188
Worcestershire
Westwood
9641 Sir John Packington [Pakington], baronet
Wanklyn, *Worcestershire*, 1998, pp. 249-257
Yorkshire
Barnoldswick, Salterforth
9642 Richard Acronley
Kirk, *Barnoldswick*, 1951, pp. 55-56
Horbury
9643 Thomas Sunderland, husbandman
Bartlett, *Horbury*, 1980, p. 5
Huddersfield, Bank House
9644 John Hanson
Brears, *Yorkshire*, 1972, pp. 160-161

1689 (c.)
Wiltshire
Marlborough
9645 Robert Page, currier
Williams and Thomson, *Marlborough*, 2007, p. 188

1690
Bedfordshire
Harrold
9646 Richard Orlebar, esquire
Orlebar, 1930, pp. 88-89
Bristol
Bristol, St Philip and St Jacob
9647 John Baptist, wax chandler
George, *Bristol*, 2008, pp. 1-2
Bristol, St Mary Redcliffe
9648 Thomas Compton, hair weaver
George, *Bristol*, 2008, pp. 2-4
Bristol
9649 William Read
George, *Bristol*, 2008, pp. 5-6
Clifton
9650 John Old, [labourer]
Moore, *Clifton*, 1981, p. 157

Shirehampton
9651 William Parker, [mariner]
Moore, *Clifton*, 1981, p. 157
Buckinghamshire
Dinton
9652 Edward Parish
Reed, *Buckinghamshire*, 1988, pp. 226-227
Fingest
9653 William Willmott, gentleman (also listed Ibstone)
Reed, *Buckinghamshire*, 1988, pp. 227-231
Ibstone
William Willmott, gentleman (see Fingest)
Cheshire
Bowdon
9654 Richard Pearson, yeoman
Groves, *Bowdon*, 1999, pp. 10-11
Dutton Lodge
9655 Thomas Nedham, esquire
Earwaker, *Lancashire and Cheshire*, 1893, pp. 117-118
Smallwood
9656 William Ledward
Ledward, 1998, p. 1
Cornwall
Saint Breock
9657 Christopher Dandy
Whitley, 1883, pp. 292-293
Withiel
9658 Elizabeth Hicks
Pedler, 1984, p. 36
Devonshire
Dartmouth
9659 Bridget Roope
Cash, *Devon*, 1966, p. 161
Honiton
9660 Henery Hampshire, merchant
Brushfield, *Honiton*, 1902-1903, pp. 243-246
Uffculme
9661 Richard Waldron, yeoman
Wyatt, *Uffculme*, 1997, p. 150
9662 Richard Woodrow, husbandman
Wyatt, *Uffculme*, 1997, p. 151
Dorsetshire
Leigh
9663 James Alwood, [tailor?]
Machin, *Yetminster*, 1976, No.93, (2 pp.)
9664 John Miller, [yeoman]
Machin, *Yetminster*, 1976, No.92, (2 pp.)
Essex
Roxwell
9665 Abraham Day
Steer, *Mid-Essex*, 1969, p. 204
9666 John Webb, yeoman
Steer, *Mid-Essex*, 1969, pp. 203-204
Unlocated
9667 Martha Meagle
Steer, *Mid-Essex*, 1969, pp. 206-207
Writtle
9668 John Clarke, yeoman
Steer, *Mid-Essex*, 1969, pp. 200-202
9669 William Garrat, gentleman
Steer, *Mid-Essex*, 1969, pp. 202-203
9670 Richard Horsnaile
Steer, *Mid-Essex*, 1969, pp. 204-206

Gloucestershire
Charlton Kings
  9671 Richard Whithorne, yeoman
    Paget and Sale, *Charlton Kings*, 2003, pp. 73-74
Cheltenham, Alstone
  9672 Robt. Aurris [Avris], husbandman
    Sale, *Cheltenham*, 1999, p. 57
Cheltenham
  9673 John Banaster, gentleman
    Sale, *Cheltenham*, 1999, p. 56
Cheltenham, Arle
  9674 George Bick
    Sale, *Cheltenham*, 1999, p. 55
Frampton Cotterell
  9675 Joseph Millett, yeoman
    Moore, *Frampton Cotterell*, 1976, p. 142
Stoke Gifford, Little Stoke
  9676 Thomas Lawford, yeoman
    Moore, *Frampton Cotterell*, 1976, p. 143
Westerleigh
  9677 John Smith, [feltmaker]
    Moore, *Frampton Cotterell*, 1976, pp. 141-142
Winterbourne
  9678 Christopher Davis, yeoman
    Moore, *Frampton Cotterell*, 1976, pp. 142-143
Hertfordshire
Hertford
  9679 Josiah Adams
    Adams, *Hertford*, 1997, pp. 57-58
  9680 Mrs Mary Pettit, widow
    Adams, *Hertford*, 1997, pp. 108-109
  9681 Grace Spratt
    Adams, *Hertford*, 1997, pp. 70-72
St Albans, St Stephens
  9682 Robert Skeale, bricklayer
    Munby, *Worldly Goods*, 1991, p. 174
Kent
Eynsford
  9683 John Mosyer, yeoman
    Duncombe, *Darent*, 1990-1991, pp. 327-328
Great Chart
  9684 John Cuningham, chapman
    Spufford, *Reclothing*, 1984, pp. 163-164
Otford
  9685 George Smalle, yeoman
    Duncombe, *Darent*, 1990-1991, pp. 379-380
Lancashire
Manchester
  9686 Ellen Buxton
    Rylands, *Lancashire and Cheshire*, 1897, pp. 49-50
Leicestershire
Evington
  9687 John Burley, yeoman
    Wilshere, *Evington*, 1985, p. 34
Lincolnshire
Clee, Thrunscoe
  9688 John Ogle, husbandman
    Ambler, Watkinson, *Clee*, 1987, pp. 166-167
Cleethorpes
  9689 John Chapman
    Ambler, Watkinson, *Clee*, 1987, p. 167

Lincoln, Cathedral Close
  9690 Mr Walter Powell, clergyman, senior vicar
    Maddison, 1904, p. 90
Nottinghamshire
Wiseton
  9691 Thomas Litster, [husbandman]
    Perkins, *Clayworth*, 1979, pp. xv-xvi
Shropshire
Benthall
  9692 John Aston, collier
    Trinder and Cox, *Severn Gorge*, 2000, pp. 123-124
Lilleshall, The Hinks
  9693 John Simons
    Trinder and Cox, *Telford*, 1980, pp. 216-217
Madeley Wood
  9694 John Holland, yeoman
    Trinder and Cox, *Severn Gorge*, 2000, pp. 283-284
Wellington, Hadley
  9695 Thomas Blakeman
    Trinder and Cox, *Telford*, 1980, p. 290
Wellington
  9696 Robert Johnson, mercer
    Trinder and Cox, *Telford*, 1980, p. 289
  9697 Thomas Reynolds, butcher
    Trinder and Cox, *Telford*, 1980, pp. 289-290
Wrockwardine, Street Way
  9698 Sarah Cornes, widow
    Trinder and Cox, *Telford*, 1980, p. 419
Staffordshire
Colwich, Newland (?)
  9699 William Wiggin
    Bradley, *Haywoods*, 1993, pp. 73-76
Ettingshall
  9700 Richard Elwall, yeoman
    Roper, *Sedgley*, 1960, p. 88
Lower Gornal
  9701 John Nicklin, collier
    Roper, *Sedgley*, 1960, p. 88
  9702 Edward Pershouse, yeoman
    Roper, *Sedgley*, 1960, p. 91
Sedgley, Turls Hill
  9703 Edward Persehouse, yeoman
    Roper, *Sedgley*, 1960, p. 91
Sussex
Goring
  9704 Richard Spencer, clergyman [vicar of Goring]
    Hughes, *Sussex*, 2007, pp. 88-90
North Stoke
  9705 Joseph Lisle, clergyman [curate of North Stoke]
    Hughes, *Sussex*, 2007, p. 198
Warwickshire
Stratford-on-Avon
  9706 John Lord, baker
    Jones, *Stratford*, II, 2003, pp. 244-247
Wiltshire
Marlborough
  9707 William Bayly, innholder
    Williams and Thomson, *Marlborough*, 2007, pp. 190-191
  9708 Joane Duffe, widow
    Williams and Thomson, *Marlborough*, 2007, p. 193
  9709 Henery Rus [Russe], yeoman
    Williams and Thomson, *Marlborough*, 2007, pp. 189-190

9710 John Stout, shoemaker
Williams and Thomson, *Marlborough*, 2007, p. 191
9711 Richard Tarrant, cordwainer
Williams and Thomson, *Marlborough*, 2007, p. 190
9712 James Tower
Williams and Thomson, *Marlborough*, 2007, p. 192
9713 Edward Young, maltster
Williams and Thomson, *Marlborough*, 2007, p. 192
Yorkshire
Barnoldswick
9714 Richard Loococke
Kirk, *Barnoldswick*, 1951, pp. 72-73
Horbury
9715 John Wordsworth
Bartlett, *Horbury*, 1980, pp. 6-7
Wassand
9716 Marmaduke Constable, esquire
Hall, *Beverley*, 1986, pp. 68-69
York
9717 Mr Suckling Spendlove, [grocer]
White and Swinburne, 2002, pp. 38-44

1690 (c.)
Wiltshire
Marlborough
9718 Richard Stapler, husbandman
Williams and Thomson, *Marlborough*, 2007, p. 193
Yorkshire
Unlocated
9719 Simon Helmsley
Brears, *Yorkshire*, 1972, pp. 162-163

1691
Bristol
Bristol
9720 William Haines
George, *Bristol*, 2008, pp. 6-8
9721 Richard Kirwood, apothecary
George, *Bristol*, 2008, p. 12
9722 Robert Lux, [wool-comber]
George, *Bristol*, 2008, pp. 8-10
Bristol, St Philip and St Jacob
9723 John Sperring [Sperrin], weaver
George, *Bristol*, 2008, pp. 10-11
Shirehampton
9724 Sarah Edwards, widow
Moore, *Clifton*, 1981, pp. 158-160
9725 Sarah Stokes, [widow]
Moore, *Clifton*, 1981, p. 158
Buckinghamshire
Denham
9726 Mark Ebelwhite, tanner
Reed, *Buckinghamshire*, 1988, pp. 231-233
Padbury
9727 Henry Smith, gentleman
Reed, *Buckinghamshire*, 1988, pp. 233-235
Worminghall
9728 Thomas Vere, yeoman
Reed, *Buckinghamshire*, 1988, pp. 235-236
Cheshire
Ashton-on-Mersey
9729 John Lamb, [yeoman]
Groves, *Ashton-on-Mersey and Sale*, 2000, p. 137

Chester
9729a James Arderne, clergyman, Dean of Chester
Anon., *Arderne*, 1959, p. 37
Sale
9730 Elizabeth Daine
Groves, *Ashton-on-Mersey and Sale*, 2000, pp. 134-135
9731 Daniel Gratrix alias Mason, [girthweb weaver]
Groves, *Ashton-on-Mersey and Sale*, 2000, pp. 135-136
Derbyshire
Beauchief Hall (now Yorkshire)
9732 Strelley Pegg [Pegge], barrister
Addy, 1881, pp. 57-66
Devonshire
Dunsford
9733 Thomas Jeffery
Cash, *Devon*, 1966, p. 162
Uffculme
9734 James Batt, clothier
Wyatt, *Uffculme*, 1997, pp. 195-196
9735 Baptist Dowdney, husbandman
Wyatt, *Uffculme*, 1997, p. 153
9736 Joane Dowdney
Wyatt, *Uffculme*, 1997, p. 154
9737 William Cottrill, [yeoman]
Wyatt, *Uffculme*, 1997, p. 151
9738 John Gill, yeoman
Wyatt, *Uffculme*, 1997, p. 151
9739 Elizabeth Kerslake, [widow]
Wyatt, *Uffculme*, 1997, pp. 153-154
9740 Humfry Woodruffe, yeoman
Wyatt, *Uffculme*, 1997, p. 152
Dorsetshire
Leigh
9741 Thomas Miller, yeoman
Machin, *Yetminster*, 1976, No.94, (3 pp.)
Yetminster
9742 William Taunton, husbandman
Machin, *Yetminster*, 1976, No.95, (1 p.)
Essex
Roxwell
9743 Robert Hawes, bricklayer
Steer, *Mid-Essex*, 1969, p. 207
Writtle, Horseley Park
9744 William Bird
Steer, *Mid-Essex*, 1969, pp. 207-209
Writtle
9745 Hickguly Eve
Steer, *Mid-Essex*, 1969, pp. 210-211
Gloucestershire
Cheltenham
9746 John Ellis, gentleman
Sale, *Cheltenham*, 1999, p. 59
9747 Anthony Ireland, yeoman
Sale, *Cheltenham*, 1999, p. 58
9748 Ann Kendall, widow
Sale, *Cheltenham*, 1999, p. 58
Frenchay
9749 George Bayly, husbandman
Moore, *Frampton Cotterell*, 1976, pp. 144-145
Randwick
9750 John Smyth, petty chapman
Spufford, *Reclothing*, 1984, pp. 190-193
Westerleigh

9751 John Sommurhill, [feltmaker]
Moore, *Frampton Cotterell*, 1976, p. 144
Winterbourne
9752 Thomas Hill yeoman
Moore, *Frampton Cotterell*, 1976, p. 144
9753 William Turner, yeoman
Moore, *Frampton Cotterell*, 1976, p. 145

Hertfordshire
Sarratt
9754 William Birch, flowerman
Bullen, *Sarratt*, [1982], pp. 214-215

Kent
Eynsford
9755 Edward Bankin, yeoman
Duncombe, *Darent*, 1990-1991, p. 238
Plaxtol, Old Soar Manor
9756 William Furner
Semple, 2009, pp. 182-185

Leicestershire
Evington
9757 Katrine Burley, [widow]
Wilshere, *Evington*, 1985, p. 35
9758 Joane Johnson
Wilshere, *Evington*, 1985, p. 35
Kirby Muxloe
9759 Tho: Bagshaw, gentleman
Wilshere, *Kirby Muxloe*, 1983, p. 16
9760 Ann Fletcher, widow
Wilshere, *Kirby Muxloe*, 1983, p. 17
9761 James Sheepey, [husbandman]
Wilshere, *Kirby Muxloe*, 1983, p. 17

Middlesex
Sunbury
9762 Thomas Bucland
Heselton, *Sunbury*, 1976, p. 6
9763 Francis Ronager
Heselton, *Sunbury*, 1976, pp. 7-8

Nottinghamshire
Clayworth
9764 John Smith, [shepherd]
Perkins, *Clayworth*, 1979, p. xvii
Wiseton
9765 Gervas Raynes
Perkins, *Clayworth*, 1979, pp. xvii-xix

Oxfordshire
Banbury
9766 Margaret King, widow
Trinder and Gibson, *Banbury*, 1988, pp. 230-231
Water Eaton
9767 Henry Reeve, [yeoman]
Offord, *Water Eaton*, 1986, pp. 44-45

Scotland
Edinburgh
9768 Andro Hog, Writer to the Signet
Scott-Moncrieff, 1919, pp. 58-63

Shropshire
Little Wenlock
9769 Edward Burgwyn, yeoman
Trinder and Cox, *Severn Gorge*, 2000, pp. 247-248
Little Wenlock, Huntington
9770 George Buttery
Trinder and Cox, *Severn Gorge*, 2000, pp. 246-247

Madeley, The Lloyds
9771 Edward Boden, collier
Trinder and Cox, *Severn Gorge*, 2000, pp. 284-285
Suffolk
Barking
9772 John Crabb, [maltster]
Sperling, 1893-1894, p. 74
Sussex
West Itchenor
9773 Humphrey Day, clergyman [rector of West Itchenor]
Hughes, *Sussex*, 2007, pp. 125-126
Stoughton
9774 John Harrison, clergyman
Hughes, *Sussex*, 2007, pp. 205-206
Warwickshire
Chilvers Cotton
9775 John Perkins, clergyman
Arkell, Evans, Goose, 2000, pp. 375-378
Stratford-on-Avon
9776 Ailce [Alice] Ainge, widow
Jones, *Stratford*, II, 2003, pp. 253-255
9777 Dorothy Edwards, widow
Jones, *Stratford*, II, 2003, pp. 255-256
9778 William Higgins, skinner
Jones, *Stratford*, II, 2003, pp. 257-258
9779 John Milward, barber surgeon
Jones, *Stratford*, II, 2003, pp. 250-252
9780 Mary Smith, widow
Jones, *Stratford*, II, 2003, pp. 248-249
9781 William Smith, gentleman [apothecary]
Jones, *Stratford*, II, 2003, pp. 256-257
Wiltshire
Marlborough
9782 Jone Allin
Williams and Thomson, *Marlborough*, 2007, p. 197
9783 Peter Andrews
Williams and Thomson, *Marlborough*, 2007, p. 196
9784 Christopher Brathwaite, cutler
Williams and Thomson, *Marlborough*, 2007, pp. 198-199
9785 Henerey Cooley, [shoemaker]
Williams and Thomson, *Marlborough*, 2007, pp. 197-198
9786 Susanah Hill, widow
Williams and Thomson, *Marlborough*, 2007, p. 201
9787 Joseph Hockley, wheelwright
Williams and Thomson, *Marlborough*, 2007, pp. 194-195
9788 Joane Hunt, widow
Williams and Thomson, *Marlborough*, 2007, p. 196
9789 Hugh Hutchens, husbandman
Williams and Thomson, *Marlborough*, 2007, p. 201
9790 Jeremiah Matthews, carpenter
Williams and Thomson, *Marlborough*, 2007, pp. 201-202
9791 Gabrill Mills
Williams and Thomson, *Marlborough*, 2007, p. 197
9792 John Mundy, tailor
Williams and Thomson, *Marlborough*, 2007, pp. 195-196
9793 Daniell Pidding
Williams and Thomson, *Marlborough*, 2007, pp. 193-194
9794 John Sloper, carpenter
Williams and Thomson, *Marlborough*, 2007, p. 199
9795 Francis Smith, tailor
Williams and Thomson, *Marlborough*, 2007, pp. 199-200

9796　Richard Smith, labourer
　　Williams and Thomson, *Marlborough*, 2007, p. 200
9797　Edward Townsend, carpenter
　　Williams and Thomson, *Marlborough*, 2007, p. 200
Worcestershire
Bewdley
　9798　Edward Ellens, gardener
　　Bewdley, *Bewdley*, 1991, pp. 181-182
Worcester
　9799　Dame Elizabeth Rous
　　Wanklyn, *Worcestershire*, 1998, pp. 257-258
Yorkshire
Barnoldswick, Salterforth
　9800　Thomas Preston
　　Kirk, *Barnoldswick*, 1951, p. 75

1691 (c.)
Essex
Writtle
　9801　Thomas Richards, yeoman
　　Steer, *Mid-Essex*, 1969, pp. 211-212

1692
Bristol
Clifton
　9802　James MacGrath, planter
　　Moore, *Clifton*, 1981, pp. 160-161
Stoke Bishop
　9803　Henry Weaver, [husbandman]
　　Moore, *Clifton*, 1981, pp. 161-162
Westbury
　9804　Thomas Bishop, glover
　　Moore, *Clifton*, 1981, pp. 162-163
Buckinghamshire
Stony Stratford
　9805　Peircy Langrack, gentleman
　　Reed, *Buckinghamshire*, 1988, pp. 236-241
Cheshire
Sale
　9806　James Ashton alias Wales, [yeoman]
　　Groves, *Ashton-on-Mersey and Sale*, 2000, pp. 138-139
　9807　Matthew Barlow
　　Groves, *Ashton-on-Mersey and Sale*, 2000, pp. 142-143
　9808　Jane Davies, [widow]
　　Groves, *Ashton-on-Mersey and Sale*, 2000, p. 145
　9809　Thomas Davies
　　Groves, *Ashton-on-Mersey and Sale*, 2000, pp. 132-133
Cumberland
Cockermouth
　9810　Mr Robert Webster
　　Tyson, 2008, p. 104
Pryor Hall, Plumbland (?)
　9811　Cuthbert Orfeur, gentleman
　　Jackson, *Orfeurs*, 1878, p. 118
Devonshire
Uffculme
　9812　Mary Stephens, widow
　　Wyatt, *Uffculme*, 1997, pp. 154-155
Willand
　9813　Joan Osmond
　　Cash, *Devon*, 1966, p. 162
Dorsetshire
Chetnole
　9814　Richard Devenish
　　Machin, *Yetminster*, 1976, No.96, (1 p.)

Essex
Roxwell
　9815　Joseph Clarke, [grocer and draper]
　　Steer, *Mid-Essex*, 1969, pp. 212-213
Gloucestershire
Charlton Kings
　9816　Elizabeth Jeffs, widow
　　Paget and Sale, *Charlton Kings*, 2003, p. 76
　9817　Margaret Rich
　　Paget and Sale, *Charlton Kings*, 2003, pp. 78-79
Frampton Cotterell
　9818　John Millet, [yeoman]
　　Moore, *Frampton Cotterell*, 1976, p. 146
Iron Acton
　9819　Christopher Jackman, [yeoman]
　　Moore, *Frampton Cotterell*, 1976, p. 149
　9820　Robert Martin, [yeoman]
　　Moore, *Frampton Cotterell*, 1976, p. 147
Stoke Gifford
　9821　Christian Lawford, widow
　　Moore, *Frampton Cotterell*, 1976, pp. 147-148
　9822　John Webley, yeoman
　　Moore, *Frampton Cotterell*, 1976, pp. 149-150
Westerleigh
　9823　John Champnies, yeoman
　　Moore, *Frampton Cotterell*, 1976, pp. 145-146
　9824　Ann Haines, widow
　　Moore, *Frampton Cotterell*, 1976, pp. 148-149
　9825　Richard Rogers, yeoman
　　Moore, *Frampton Cotterell*, 1976, p. 148
　9826　Joan Simonds
　　Moore, *Frampton Cotterell*, 1976, pp. 146-147
Hertfordshire
Hertford
　9827　Willm Halfhide [William Halfehead, Halfhead]
　　Adams, *Hertford*, 1997, pp. 28-29
Sarratt
　9828　John Tratt [Trott]
　　Bullen, *Sarratt*, [1982], pp. 211-214
Leicestershire
Braunstone
　9829　Valentine Allen, yeoman
　　Wilshere, *Braunstone*, 1983, p. 32
　9830　Joseph Henchman, grazier
　　Wilshere, *Braunstone*, 1983, p. 32
Great Stretton
　9831　Edward Bradley, [husbandman]
　　Wilshere, *Great Stretton*, 1984, p. 21
Lincolnshire
Donington
　9832　Ann Clarke, widow
　　Spufford, *Reclothing*, 1984, pp. 165-167
Shropshire
Broseley
　9833　Francis Gears, tailor
　　Trinder and Cox, *Severn Gorge*, 2000, p. 171
　9834　Thomas Oliver, mercer
　　Trinder and Cox, *Severn Gorge*, 2000, pp. 171-173
Lilleshall, Street Grange
　9835　William Dawes, yeoman
　　Trinder and Cox, *Telford*, 1980, pp. 217-218

Wellington, The Wrekin
  9836   Richard Goodales
    Trinder and Cox, *Telford*, 1980, pp. 292-293
Wellington
  9837   Richard Johnson
    Trinder and Cox, *Telford*, 1980, pp. 290-291
  9838   Thomas Jones, gentleman
    Trinder and Cox, *Telford*, 1980, pp. 293-295
  9839   Francis Ore, blacksmith
    Trinder and Cox, *Telford*, 1980, pp. 291-292

Staffordshire
Coseley
  9840   John Southwicke, locksmith
    Roper, *Sedgley*, 1960, p. 93
Ettingshall
  9841   Samuel Hickmans, yeoman
    Roper, *Sedgley*, 1960, p. 92
Sedgley
  9842   Edward Eaton alias Yeaton
    Roper, *Sedgley*, 1960, p. 93
Sedgley, Woodsetton
  9843   Edward Patchet, mason
    Roper, *Sedgley*, 1960, p. 94

Suffolk
Cavendish
  9844   William Woods, weaver
    Anon., *Examples*, 1980, pp. 11-12

Sussex
Storrington
  9845   Edmund Coles, clergyman [rector of Storrington]
    Hughes, *Sussex*, 2007, pp. 203-204

Wales
Glamorgan, Old Beaupré Castle
  9846   Sir Richard Bassett
    Phillpotts, Turner, 2008, pp. 262-264

Warwickshire
Shottery
  9847   Richard Hathaway, yeoman
    Jones, *Stratford*, II, 2003, pp. 260-261
Stratford-on-Avon
  9848   Anne Milward, widow
    Jones, *Stratford*, II, 2003, pp. 262-263
  9849   [Eleanor] Rodes, widow
    Jones, *Stratford*, II, 2003, p. 259

Wiltshire
Marlborough
  9850   Thomas Edne, [blacksmith]
    Williams and Thomson, *Marlborough*, 2007, pp. 203-204
  9851   Elizabeth Kite, widow
    Williams and Thomson, *Marlborough*, 2007, p. 203
  9852   William Martine, parchment maker
    Williams and Thomson, *Marlborough*, 2007, pp. 202-203
  9853   Elixabath Moore
    Williams and Thomson, *Marlborough*, 2007, p. 202
  9854   Lucy Stagg
    Williams and Thomson, *Marlborough*, 2007, p. 204
Wilsford, Lake House
  9855   George Duke, esquire
    Duke, 1914-1916, pp. 204-205

Worcestershire
Halesowen, Hawne
  9856   William Grove, nailer
    Davenport, 1912, pp. 13-14

Yorkshire
Barnoldswick, Brockden
  9857   Thomas Kid
    Kirk, *Barnoldswick*, 1951, pp. 71-72
Beverley
  9858   Thomas Myas, weaver
    Hall, *Beverley*, 1986, p. 71
Hull
  9859   Jeremiah Graves, beer brewer
    Hall, *Beverley*, 1986, pp. 59-61

1692 (c.)
Wiltshire
Marlborough
  9860   Anne Love, widow
    Williams and Thomson, *Marlborough*, 2007, p. 204

1693
Bristol
Bristol
  9861   William Hayman, cooper
    George, *Bristol*, 2008, pp. 12-14
Bristol, St Philip and St Jacob
  9862   Joseph Wattkins [Watkins], soapmaker
    George, *Bristol*, 2008, pp. 14-15
Shirehampton
  9863   Margaret Stokes, widow
    Moore, *Clifton*, 1981, pp. 163-164

Devonshire
Uffculme
  9864   William Mogford, [husbandman and miller (?)]
    Wyatt, *Uffculme*, 1997, pp. 155-156

Dorsetshire
Chetnole
  9865   John Hussey, [yeoman]
    Machin, *Yetminster*, 1976, No.97, (2 pp.)
  9866   Elizabeth Symes, widow
    Machin, *Yetminster*, 1976, No.98, (2 pp.)

Essex
Unlocated
  9867   Martha Force
    Steer, *Mid-Essex*, 1969, p. 214
Writtle
  9868   Simon Hudson, yeoman
    Steer, *Mid-Essex*, 1969, pp. 216-217
  9869   Henry May, miller
    Steer, *Mid-Essex*, 1969, pp. 214-216

Gloucestershire
Cheltenham
  9870   Nathaniell Chestroe, yeoman
    Sale, *Cheltenham*, 1999, pp. 61-63
  9871   Joseph Higgs
    Sale, *Cheltenham*, 1999, p. 63
  9872   Walter Ireland, gentleman
    Sale, *Cheltenham*, 1999, p. 61
  9873   Thomas Ricketts, collarmaker
    Sale, *Cheltenham*, 1999, pp. 59-60
Hambrook
  9874   William Bucher, [maltster]
    Moore, *Frampton Cotterell*, 1976, p. 150
Westerleigh, Nibley
  9875   William Smith, [coalminer]
    Moore, *Frampton Cotterell*, 1976, p. 150

Herefordshire
Hereford
  9876 Richard Cooke, saddler
  Morgan, *Saddler*, 1947
Ireland
Dublin, Dame Street
  9877 John Inglefield, [chandler]
  Goodbody, *Dublin Quaker*, 1978, pp. 40-41
Kent
Eynsford
  9878 John Marshall, yeoman
  Duncombe, *Darent*, 1990-1991, pp. 317-319
Lincolnshire
Winteringham
  9879 Thomas Scutte
  Neave, *Winteringham*, 1984, p. 124
Shropshire
Broseley
  9880 Edward Amiss, blacksmith
  Trinder and Cox, *Severn Gorge*, 2000, p. 173
Broseley, The Tuckies
  9881 John Langley, gentleman
  Trinder and Cox, *Severn Gorge*, 2000, pp. 174-175
Wellington
  9882 Ann Eastop, widow
  Trinder and Cox, *Telford*, 1980, pp. 298-299
  9883 John Field, clergyman
  Trinder and Cox, *Telford*, 1980, pp. 295-298
Somerset
South Cheriton, Horsington
  9884 John Williams, clergyman, rector of Abbas and
  Templecombe
  Daniel, *Williams*, 1968, pp. 39-40
  9885 John Williams, clergyman
  Anon., *Williams*, 1955, pp. 165-167
Staffordshire
Sedgley, Hurst Hill
  9886 John Elwall, yeoman
  Roper, *Sedgley*, 1960, p. 95
Wales
Carmarthenshire, Kidwelly
  9887 John Davies
  Hook, 1975, pp. 119-120
Montgomeryshire, Llanfihangel, Fachwen
  9888 Thomas Lewis
  Gilson, *Llanfihangel*, 2009, p. 46
Warwickshire
Stratford-on-Avon
  9889 Susanha Bromly [Susannah Bromley]
  Jones, *Stratford*, II, 2003, p. 271
  9890 Alce [Alice] Edkins, widow
  Jones, *Stratford*, II, 2003, pp. 263-264
  9891 Richard Mayo, husbandman
  Jones, *Stratford*, II, 2003, pp. 269-270
  9892 Anthony Milward, labourer
  Jones, *Stratford*, II, 2003, pp. 264-265
  9893 John Smith, maltster
  Jones, *Stratford*, II, 2003, pp. 265-268
Wolston, Brandon
  9894 Mistris Britton Haddon, widow
  Owen, 1985, pp. 151-152

Wiltshire
Marlborough
  9895 John Bowsher, baker
  Williams and Thomson, *Marlborough*, 2007, p. 211
  9896 Thomas Chamberlaine
  Williams and Thomson, *Marlborough*, 2007, p. 209
  9897 Robert Fishlock
  Williams and Thomson, *Marlborough*, 2007, p. 205
  9898 Richard Oadum, husbandman
  Williams and Thomson, *Marlborough*, 2007, p. 211
  9899 Edward Powell, woolcomber
  Williams and Thomson, *Marlborough*, 2007, pp. 209-210
  9900 William Spackman, [grocer]
  Williams and Thomson, *Marlborough*, 2007, pp. 206-208
  9901 John Stevens
  Williams and Thomson, *Marlborough*, 2007, pp. 208-209
  9902 William Temple, husbandman
  Williams and Thomson, *Marlborough*, 2007, pp. 205-206
Worcestershire
Bewdley
  9903 Mr Peter Brainch, [yeoman]
  Bewdley, *Bewdley*, 1991, pp. 182-185
Yorkshire
Horbury
  9904 Richard Walker
  Bartlett, *Horbury*, 1980, p. 10

1693 (c.)
Wiltshire
Marlborough
  9905 Margarett Francis, widow
  Williams and Thomson, *Marlborough*, 2007, p. 205

1694
Bristol
Bristol, Barton Regis
  9906 Joel Jelson
  George, *Bristol*, 2008, pp. 16-20
Bristol
  9907 Matthias Jones, gunsmith
  George, *Bristol*, 2008, pp. 20-22
Bristol, St Werburgh
  9908 Richard Syfers
  George, *Bristol*, 2008, pp. 22-24
Shirehampton
  9909 Samuel Buxton, gentleman
  Moore, *Clifton*, 1981, p. 164
  9910 Samuel Robins, [yeoman]
  Moore, *Clifton*, 1981, p. 165
Westbury
  9911 Roger Grant, [pipemaker]
  Moore, *Clifton*, 1981, pp. 165-166
  9912 Hugh Mascall, [shipwright]
  Moore, *Clifton*, 1981, pp. 167-168
  9913 Jane Self, widow
  Moore, *Clifton*, 1981, p. 166
Buckinghamshire
Dorton
  9914 Robert Dormer, esquire
  Reed, *Buckinghamshire*, 1988, pp. 245-250
Eton
  9915 Ann Pretty, widow
  Reed, *Buckinghamshire*, 1988, pp. 241-245

Cheshire
Wilmslow, Haythorne
9916 Mrs Jane Finney
  Miles, 1960, pp. 21,23,25
Devonshire
Littlehempston
9917 Thomazine Edmonds
  Cash, *Devon*, 1966, pp. 162-163
Stockleigh English
9918 John Gribble, yeoman
  Chope, 1924-1925, pp. 221-223
Talaton
9919 John Warren
  Cash, *Devon*, 1966, pp. 163-164
Uffculme
9920 Margaret Barnfield, widow
  Wyatt, *Uffculme*, 1997, p. 156
9921 John Butson, [weaver]
  Wyatt, *Uffculme*, 1997, pp. 156-157
Dorsetshire
Leigh
9922 Lawrence Bayne
  Machin, *Yetminster*, 1976, No.99, (1 p.)
Yetminster
9923 Grace Barber, widow
  Machin, *Yetminster*, 1976, No.100, (1 p.)
Essex
Roxwell
9924 Abraham Brecknocke, yeoman
  Steer, *Mid-Essex*, 1969, pp. 219-221
9925 John Crush
  Steer, *Mid-Essex*, 1969, pp. 221-222
Writtle
9926 Richard Clary, yeoman
  Steer, *Mid-Essex*, 1969, pp. 217-219
9927 William Maggett
  Steer, *Mid-Essex*, 1969, p. 221
9928 Joseph Westwood, yeoman
  Steer, *Mid-Essex*, 1969, pp. 222-223
Gloucestershire
Charlton Kings
9929 Frances Currier, widow
  Paget and Sale, *Charlton Kings*, 2003, p. 81
Charlton Kings, Ham
9930 Samuell Harris
  Paget and Sale, *Charlton Kings*, 2003, pp. 83-84
Charlton Kings
9931 Arculaus Humphries, [husbandman]
  Paget and Sale, *Charlton Kings*, 2003, pp. 80-81
Cheltenham
9932 Abigail Ashmeade, widow
  Sale, *Cheltenham*, 1999, p. 64
Frampton Cotterell
9933 Joseph Hollister, feltmaker
  Moore, *Frampton Cotterell*, 1976, p. 151
Hambrook
9934 William Linch, carpenter
  Moore, *Frampton Cotterell*, 1976, pp. 150-151
Westerleigh
9935 Susanna Packer, widow
  Moore, *Frampton Cotterell*, 1976, p. 151
Winterbourne
9936 John Bercy, yeoman
  Moore, *Frampton Cotterell*, 1976, p. 152

9937 Thomas Greenald, yeoman
  Moore, *Frampton Cotterell*, 1976, p. 151
Hampshire
Warnford
9938 Henry Hammond, innkeeper
  Thomas, 1972, pp. 2-3
Hertfordshire
Hertford
9939 Richard Churchman, innholder
  Adams, *Hertford*, 1997, pp. 88-89
Hertford, All Saints
9940 Mr Luke Clisby
  Adams, *Hertford*, 1997, pp. 90-91
Hertford
9941 Sarah Runenton, widow
  Adams, *Hertford*, 1997, pp. 30-32
St Albans, St Stephens, Serge Hill
9942 Robert Kentish
  Munby, *Worldly Goods*, 1991, pp. 177-179
St Albans, St Stephens
9943 William Lovett, yeoman
  Munby, *Worldly Goods*, 1991, pp. 175-177
9944 William Osborne
  Parker, *Worldly Goods*, 2004, pp. 310-311
Sarratt
9945 Nicholas Hill
  Bullen, *Sarratt*, [1982], p. 196
Watford, Waterdell
9946 James Ewer, husbandman
  Munby, *Worldly Goods*, 1991, pp. 180-181
Ireland
Dublin, Chapelizod
9947 John Johnston, weaver
  Goodbody, *Dublin Quaker*, 1978, pp. 41-43
Dublin
9948 Issachar Wilcocks, grocer
  Goodbody, *Dublin Quaker*, 1978, pp. 43-44
Lincolnshire
Winteringham
9949 Thomas Walker
  Neave, *Winteringham*, 1984, pp. 124-125
Northamptonshire
Wittering
9950 Edward Alderman, husbandman
  Alderman, *Alderman*, 2008, pp. 62-65
Nottinghamshire
Clayworth
9951 George Norton
  Perkins, *Clayworth*, 1979, p. xix
Shropshire
Benthall
9952 Edward Hartshorne, blacksmith
  Trinder and Cox, *Severn Gorge*, 2000, pp. 124-125
Broseley
9953 Thomas Lee, miller
  Trinder and Cox, *Severn Gorge*, 2000, p. 175
Wellington
9954 William Evans, pipemaker
  Trinder and Cox, *Telford*, 1980, p. 300
9955 Alice Smart, widow of dyer
  Trinder and Cox, *Telford*, 1980, pp. 299-300
9956 William Stanworth, shoemaker
  Trinder and Cox, *Telford*, 1980, pp. 300-301

Wrockwardine Wood
9957 Robert Fenn
Trinder and Cox, *Telford*, 1980, p. 420
Wrockwardine, Bratton
9958 Richard Mountford, yeoman
Trinder and Cox, *Telford*, 1980, pp. 421-422
Wrockwardine, Leaton
9959 William Pemberton
Trinder and Cox, *Telford*, 1980, pp. 420-421
Staffordshire
Upper Gornal
9960 Thomas Hartell, nailer
Roper, *Sedgley*, 1960, p. 96
Suffolk
Rattlesden
9961 Abraham Chaple, labourer
Olorenshaw, 1893-1894, p. 29
Surrey
Charlwood
9962 John Blundell
Harding, *Charlwood*, 1976, p. 112
Sussex
Burpham
9963 Thomas Griffin, clergyman [vicar of Burpham]
Hughes, *Sussex*, 2007, pp. 37-38
Funtington, Ashling
9964 Joseph Jackson, clergyman
Hughes, *Sussex*, 2007, pp. 86-87
Warwickshire
Luddington
9965 Thomas Cooke, husbandman
Jones, *Stratford*, II, 2003, pp. 276-277
Shottery
9966 John Sitch [Such], husbandman
Jones, *Stratford*, II, 2003, pp. 279-281
Stoneleigh, Stareton
9967 Richard Camill, gentleman
Alcock, *Warwickshire*, 1993, p. 39
Stratford-on-Avon
9968 John Bradley, [maltster]
Jones, *Stratford*, II, 2003, pp. 274-276
9969 Edward Pitway, saddler
Jones, *Stratford*, II, 2003, pp. 272-274
9970 Mistress Katherin Southall, widow
Jones, *Stratford*, II, 2003, pp. 278-279
Warwick
9971 James Cooke, gentleman [surgeon]
Cohen, 1957, pp. 171-172
Wiltshire
Marlborough
9972 Nicholas Greeneway, glover
Williams and Thomson, *Marlborough*, 2007, p. 214
9973 John Keeble, innholder
Williams and Thomson, *Marlborough*, 2007, pp. 214-215
9974 Mary Miles
Williams and Thomson, *Marlborough*, 2007, p. 213
9975 Walter Randoll, glover
Williams and Thomson, *Marlborough*, 2007, p. 212
9976 William Swindon, cordwainer
Williams and Thomson, *Marlborough*, 2007, pp. 213-214

Yorkshire
Doncaster
9977 Godray [Godfrey] Inman, grocer
Hey, *Doncaster*, 1997, pp. 127-128
Horbury
9978 Francis Carter, clothmaker
Bartlett, *Horbury*, 1980, pp. 12-13

1694 (c.)
Isle of Man
Castletown, Castle Rushen
9979 [William Sacheverell, Governor] (also listed Governor's House, Peel Castle)
Anon., *Manx*, 1931-1934, pp. 9-14,17-21
Castle Town, Governor's House
[William Sacheverell, Governor] (see Castletown, Castle Rushen)
Peel Castle
[William Sacheverell, Governor] (see Castletown, Castle Rushen)
Wiltshire
Marlborough
9980 Jane Chifese, widow
Williams and Thomson, *Marlborough*, 2007, p. 213
9981 Eleanor Clark, widow
Williams and Thomson, *Marlborough*, 2007, pp. 212-213

1695
Bristol
Bristol
9982 John Hurne, joiner
George, *Bristol*, 2008, pp. 24-26
9983 John Peirson [Pierson], surgeon
George, *Bristol*, 2008, pp. 26-28
Clifton
9984 Ann Morgan, widow
Moore, *Clifton*, 1981, p. 169
Shirehampton
9985 Maurice George, [yeoman]
Moore, *Clifton*, 1981, p. 170
Buckinghamshire
Chesham
9986 Francis King, gentleman
Reed, *Buckinghamshire*, 1988, p. 250
Swanbourne
9987 William Gilbert, carpenter
Anon., *Muniment Room*, 1934-1940, p. 29
Cheshire
Smallwood
9988 Mary Ledward, [widow]
Ledward, 1998, p. 3
Cumberland
Brampton
9989 George Poull, [chapman]
Spufford, *Reclothing*, 1984, pp. 154-155
Orton
9990 William Lowther
Bouch, 1940, pp. 92-93
Derbyshire
Tideswell, Milnehousedale
9991 Catharine Bagshaw, widow
Kirke, 1865-1866, p. 109

Devonshire
Barnstaple
9992 Mr Nicholas Cooke, apothecary
Cash, *Devon*, 1966, pp. 167-168
Bondleigh
9993 Margery Rodgers, widow
Cash, *Devon*, 1966, pp. 168-169
Exeter, St Mary Major
9994 Mrs Deborah Tucker
Cash, *Devon*, 1966, pp. 164-167
Sourton
9995 John Gerry, butcher
Cash, *Devon*, 1966, p. 168
Uffculme
9996 Samuell Bishop, yeoman
Wyatt, *Uffculme*, 1997, p p. 160
9997 Robert Burrow
Wyatt, *Uffculme*, 1997, pp. 197-198
9998 John Cunnant, [miller]
Wyatt, *Uffculme*, 1997, pp. 159-160
9999 John Dyer
Wyatt, *Uffculme*, 1997, pp. 196-197
10000 Henry Salkield, [worsted comber]
Wyatt, *Uffculme*, 1997, pp. 158-159
10001 Thomas Salkield, yeoman
Wyatt, *Uffculme*, 1997, pp. 158
10002 James Tidbury
Wyatt, *Uffculme*, 1997, pp. 157-158
Dorsetshire
Leigh
10003 Thomas Case
Machin, *Yetminster*, 1976, No.101, (1 p.)
10004 Thomas Harres, yeoman
Machin, *Yetminster*, 1976, No.102, (1 p.)
Essex
Writtle
10005 Joseph Taverner, butcher
Steer, *Mid-Essex*, 1969, pp. 223-224
Gloucestershire
Charlton Kings
10006 Katherine Bastin, widow
Paget and Sale, *Charlton Kings*, 2003, p. 83
10007 Thomas Buckle, yeoman
Paget and Sale, *Charlton Kings*, 2003, pp. 81-82
10008 Susanna Mason, widow
Paget and Sale, *Charlton Kings*, 2003, p. 82
Cheltenham
10009 Thomas Humphris, baker
Sale, *Cheltenham*, 1999, p. 65
10010 Thomas Merrell, baker
Sale, *Cheltenham*, 1999, p. 66
Frampton Cotterell
10011 George Muirford, feltmaker
Moore, *Frampton Cotterell*, 1976, p. 153
Hambrook
10012 John Combs
Moore, *Frampton Cotterell*, 1976, p. 152
Iron Acton
10013 Edward Thomas, yeoman
Moore, *Frampton Cotterell*, 1976, p. 153
Winterbourne
10014 Samuel Magges, [innholder]
Moore, *Frampton Cotterell*, 1976, p. 152

10015 Thomas Middleton, [quarrier]
Moore, *Frampton Cotterell*, 1976, p. 152
Hertfordshire
Hertford, St Johns
10016 Joane Baker, widow
Adams, *Hertford*, 1997, p. 27
Ireland
Dublin, Meath Street
10017 Joseph Deane, [shearman]
Goodbody, *Dublin Quaker*, 1978, pp. 44-48
Lincolnshire
Lincoln, The Castle of Lincoln
10018 William Houghton
Johnston, *Lincoln*, 1991, pp. 97-100
Nottinghamshire
Wiseton
10019 Peter Bingham, yeoman
Perkins, *Clayworth*, 1979, p. xx
Oxfordshire
Oxford
10020 Thomas Wood, [stone-cutter, mason, architect]
Vaisey, 1971, pp. 57-58
Shropshire
Wellington
10021 William Cheese, blacksmith
Trinder and Cox, *Telford*, 1980, pp. 301-302
10022 Thomas Stillgoe, corviser
Trinder and Cox, *Telford*, 1980, p. 302
Staffordshire
Colwich, Bishton
10023 William Hayward, gentleman
Bradley, *Haywoods*, 1993, p. 57
Haywood
10024 Thomas Bate, blacksmith
Bradley, *Haywoods*, 1993, p. 55
Shugborough
10025 William Bee
Bradley, *Haywoods*, 1993, pp. 78-81
Sussex
West Grinstead
10026 William Dodwell, clergyman [rector of West Grinstead]
Hughes, *Sussex*, 2007, p. 99
Warwickshire
Stoneleigh, Fletchamstead Hall
10027 William Meigh, yeoman
Alcock, *Warwickshire*, 1993, pp. 84-86
Stratford-on-Avon
10028 Thomas Ainge, innholder
Jones, *Stratford*, II, 2003, pp. 291-295
10029 William Collett, maltster
Jones, *Stratford*, II, 2003, pp. 281-282
10030 Elizabeth Dickins, widow
Jones, *Stratford*, II, 2003, pp. 287-290
Stratford-on-Avon, Bridgetown
10031 Avery Milward, yeoman
Jones, *Stratford*, II, 2003, pp. 283-284
Stratford-on-Avon
10032 John Sharpe, collarmaker
Jones, *Stratford*, II, 2003, pp. 285-286

Wiltshire
Marlborough
  10033 Ann Glyde, widow
  Williams and Thomson, *Marlborough*, 2007, p. 215
  10034 John Parsons, innkeeper
  Williams and Thomson, *Marlborough*, 2007, pp. 217-218
  10035 William Petty, button maker
  Williams and Thomson, *Marlborough*, 2007, p. 216
  10036 Richard Tasker
  Williams and Thomson, *Marlborough*, 2007, p. 216
Yorkshire
Doncaster
  10037 Nicholas Curtys, alderman [apothecary]
  Hey, *Doncaster*, 1997, p. 131
  10038 Abraham Pillin, carrier
  Hey, *Doncaster*, 1997, pp. 128-130
Hull
  10039 William Palmer, sailmaker
  Hall, *Beverley*, 1986, pp. 62-63

1696

Berkshire
Abingdon
  10040 George Ecton [Acton], [potter]
  Vaisey and Celoria, 1974, pp. 22-36
Bristol
Bristol
  10041 James Braine, cooper
  George, *Bristol*, 2008, pp. 28-30
  10042 William Collier, baker
  George, *Bristol*, 2008, pp. 30-32
Shirehampton
  10043 Lettice Gush, widow
  Moore, *Clifton*, 1981, p. 171
  10044 John Jones, mariner
  Moore, *Clifton*, 1981, p. 170
Buckinghamshire
Newport Pagnell
  10045 James Blakelock, laceman
  Reed, *Buckinghamshire*, 1988, pp. 250-252
Stowe
  10046 William Lawrence, victualler
  Reed, *Buckinghamshire*, 1988, pp. 252-253
Devonshire
Stoke Canon
  10047 George Good, yeoman
  Cash, *Devon*, 1966, pp. 169-173
Uffculme
  10048 Henry Stevens [Stephens]
  Wyatt, *Uffculme*, 1997, pp. 160-161
Dorsetshire
Leigh
  10049 Robert Bailey, tanner
  Machin, *Yetminster*, 1976, No.104, (2 pp.)
Yetminster
  10050 William Conway, innholder
  Machin, *Yetminster*, 1976, No.103, (1 p.)
  10051 John Stokes, [tailor]
  Machin, *Yetminster*, 1976, No.105, (2 pp.)
Essex
Writtle
  10052 Thomas Dowset, yeoman
  Steer, *Mid-Essex*, 1969, p. 224

  10053 John Lord, yeoman
  Steer, *Mid-Essex*, 1969, pp. 224-225
Gloucestershire
Charlton Kings
  10054 Sarah Brereton, widow
  Paget and Sale, *Charlton Kings*, 2003, pp. 84-85
Cheltenham
  10055 Barbara Humphris, [widow]
  Sale, *Cheltenham*, 1999, p. 67
  10056 Thomas Hyet, [yeoman]
  Sale, *Cheltenham*, 1999, pp. 70-71
  10057 Robert Mitton, glover [victualler]
  Sale, *Cheltenham*, 1999, p. 68
  10058 Thomas White, [maltster]
  Sale, *Cheltenham*, 1999, p. 69
Cirencester
  10059 William Bowly, maltster
  Burtt, 1940, pp. 38-39
Leckhampton
  10060 William Bridges
  Sale, *Cheltenham*, 1999, p. 70
Westerleigh
  10061 Michael Tucke, yeoman
  Moore, *Frampton Cotterell*, 1976, p. 154
Winterbourne
  10062 Thomas Noble, [husbandman]
  Moore, *Frampton Cotterell*, 1976, pp. 153-154
Hampshire
South Stoneham, Up Mills
  10063 Company of White Paper Makers
  Thomas, 1977, pp. 29-35
Herefordshire
Hereford
  10064 Richard Cooke, Tho: Jones or Robert Clayton
  [saddlers]
  Morgan, *Saddler*, 1947
Lincolnshire
Clee, Oole
  10065 Thomas Fridleington, husbandman
  Ambler, Watkinson, *Clee*, 1987, pp. 167-168
Lincoln, St Swithins
  10066 Michael Drake, clerk
  Johnston, *Lincoln*, 1991, pp. 100-101
Lincoln, St Peters in the Arches
  10067 John Dring, joiner
  Johnston, *Lincoln*, 1991, pp. 101-104
Nottinghamshire
Clayworth
  10068 Humphrey Denby, [yeoman]
  Perkins, *Clayworth*, 1979, p. xxii
  10069 John Lillyman
  Perkins, *Clayworth*, 1979, p. xxi
Wiseton
  10070 Rebeckah Webster, widow
  Perkins, *Clayworth*, 1979, pp. xxiii-xxiv
Shropshire
Dawley, Malins Lee
  10071 Walter Hartshorne, master collier
  Trinder and Cox, *Telford*, 1980, pp. 173-174
Madeley Wood
  10072 William Ashwood, trowman
  Trinder and Cox, *Severn Gorge*, 2000, pp. 285-286

Wellington
10073 Joshua Johnson, mercer
Trinder and Cox, *Telford*, 1980, pp. 302-308

Staffordshire
Haywood
10074 Thomas Jordaine, yeoman
Bradley, *Haywoods*, 1993, p. 86

Sussex
West Stoke
10075 Thomas Brague, clergyman
Hughes, *Sussex*, 2007, p. 200

Warwickshire
Stratford-on-Avon
10076 Jane Ainge, widow
Jones, *Stratford*, II, 2003, pp. 302-304
10077 Anne Cale, widow
Jones, *Stratford*, II, 2003, p. 298
Stratford-on-Avon, Drayton
10078 Thomas Edwards, yeoman
Jones, *Stratford*, II, 2003, p. 301
Stratford-on-Avon
10079 Richard Field, wheelwright
Jones, *Stratford*, II, 2003, pp. 295-296
10080 Arthur Lane
Jones, *Stratford*, II, 2003, pp. 299-300
Stratford-on-Avon, Bridgetown
10081 Thomas Mills, yeoman
Jones, *Stratford*, II, 2003, pp. 296-297

Wiltshire
Marlborough
10082 John Bendall and Jone his wife
Williams and Thomson, *Marlborough*, 2007, pp. 218-219
10083 Richerd Gils and [Anne] his wife
Williams and Thomson, *Marlborough*, 2007, p. 221
10084 Nathanells Hone, fuller
Williams and Thomson, *Marlborough*, 2007, pp. 221-222
10085 John Jones, mason
Williams and Thomson, *Marlborough*, 2007, pp. 219-220
10086 Richard Martine, cooper
Williams and Thomson, *Marlborough*, 2007, p. 220
10087 John Rumsey, basket maker
Williams and Thomson, *Marlborough*, 2007, p. 218
10088 Thomas Stone
Williams and Thomson, *Marlborough*, 2007, p. 219
10089 Richard Sutton
Williams and Thomson, *Marlborough*, 2007, p. 219

Worcestershire
Droitwich
10090 Richard Nash, esquire
Wanklyn, *Worcestershire*, 1998, pp. 258-262
Halesowen, Hawne
10091 Elizabeth Grove, [widow]
Davenport, 1912, p. 17

Yorkshire
Doncaster
10092 James Smyth, blacksmith
Hey, *Doncaster*, 1997, pp. 132-133
10093 William Wright, schoolmaster
Hey, *Doncaster*, 1997, pp. 133-134
Molescroft
10094 Mr Edward Ellerington, gentleman
Hall, *Beverley*, 1986, pp. 72-73

1696 (c.)
Wiltshire
Marlborough
10095 Alse Samson
Williams and Thomson, *Marlborough*, 2007, p. 221

1697
Bristol
Bristol
10096 George Tayler, haulier
George, *Bristol*, 2008, pp. 32-34
Clifton
10097 Ellen Andrews, [widow]
Moore, *Clifton*, 1981, p. 172
Shirehampton
10098 Susanna Willis, widow
Moore, *Clifton*, 1981, p. 171
Westbury
10099 Nicholas Cox, [husbandman]
Moore, *Clifton*, 1981, p. 172

Cheshire
Ashton-on-Mersey
10100 John Dayn, [husbandman]
Groves, *Ashton-on-Mersey and Sale*, 2000, p. 147
10101 William Moores, [yeoman]
Groves, *Ashton-on-Mersey and Sale*, 2000, pp. 145-146

Devonshire
Broadclyst
10102 Giles Taylor alias Hallings
Cash, *Devon*, 1966, p. 173
Exeter
10103 Charles Rewallin, virginal maker
Portman, *Exeter*, 1966, pp. 121-122
Uffculme
10104 Justin Dunne, widow
Wyatt, *Uffculme*, 1997, pp161-162
10105 Thomas Dunne
Wyatt, *Uffculme*, 1997, pp. 198-199

Dorsetshire
Leigh
10106 George King, husbandman
Machin, *Yetminster*, 1976, No.109, (1 p.)
Yetminster
10107 William Coomb, yeoman
Machin, *Yetminster*, 1976, No.108, (2 pp.)
10108 Thomas Ring, [yeoman]
Machin, *Yetminster*, 1976, No.107, (1 p.)
Yetminster, Withyhook
10109 Thomas Stone, gentleman
Machin, *Yetminster*, 1976, No.106, (1 p.)
Machin, 1978, p. 167

Gloucestershire
Charlton Kings
10110 John Holder, husbandman
Paget and Sale, *Charlton Kings*, 2003, p. 85
10111 Anthony Webb, yeoman
Paget and Sale, *Charlton Kings*, 2003, pp. 86-87
Cheltenham
10112 Walter Mason, maltster
Sale, *Cheltenham*, 1999, p. 72
10113 Isaac Williams, [yeoman]
Sale, *Cheltenham*, 1999, p. 70

Frampton Cotterell
10114 Priscilla Brinkworth, widow
Moore, *Frampton Cotterell*, 1976, p. 155
Iron Acton
10115 John Mason, innholder
Moore, *Frampton Cotterell*, 1976, pp. 156-158
Stoke Gifford
10116 Thomas Blackwell, yeoman
Moore, *Frampton Cotterell*, 1976, p. 156
Westerleigh
10117 John Frape, [yeoman]
Moore, *Frampton Cotterell*, 1976, p. 158
10118 Nathaniel Friend, gentleman [schoolmaster, yeoman]
Moore, *Frampton Cotterell*, 1976, pp. 154-155
10119 Mary Sifford
Moore, *Frampton Cotterell*, 1976, p. 156
Winterbourne
10120 Hester Turner, widow
Moore, *Frampton Cotterell*, 1976, p. 159
Hertfordshire
Hertford, All Saints
10121 Grace Smart, widow
Adams, *Hertford*, 1997, pp. 33-34
Kent
Otford
10122 Saml Bostock, [yeoman]
Duncombe, *Darent*, 1990-1991, pp. 242-245
Shoreham
10123 Joseph Nash, yeoman
Duncombe, *Darent*, 1990-1991, pp. 332-334
Leicestershire
Braunstone
10124 Willm. Biggins
Wilshere, *Braunstone*, 1983, p. 33
Evington
10125 Edward Atkins, [labourer]
Wilshere, *Evington*, 1985, p. 36
Glenfield
10126 Alice Steedman
Wilshere, *Glenfield*, 1983, p. 8
Kirby Muxloe
10127 William Boyer, [grazier]
Wilshere, *Kirby Muxloe*, 1983, p. 18
10128 William Gilliver, [servant]
Wilshere, *Kirby Muxloe*, 1983, p. 18
10129 Thomas Odam, yeoman
Wilshere, *Kirby Muxloe*, 1983, p. 19
Lincolnshire
Winteringham
10130 William Potton
Neave, *Winteringham*, 1984, pp. 125-126
London
Kensington Palace
10131 King William III (and the late Queen Mary)
Lunsingh Scheurleer, 1962, pp. 21-50
Nottinghamshire
Nottingham
10132 William Drury, alderman
Burton, 1924, pp. 65-66
Oxfordshire
Banbury
10133 Joyce Pym, widow
Trinder and Gibson, *Banbury*, 1988, p. 232

Oxford, Cross Inn
10134 Charles Wildgoose, [innholder]
Pantin, 1955, pp. 74-77
Water Eaton
10135 Richard Grant
Offord, *Water Eaton*, 1986, p. 46
Staffordshire
Ettingshall
10136 John Bradley
Roper, *Sedgley*, 1960, p. 97
Sedgley, Woodsetton
10137 John Bissell, nailer
Roper, *Sedgley*, 1960, p. 99
Sussex
Bramber cum Botolphs
10138 John Cowdry, clergyman [rector of Bramber with Botolphs]
Hughes, *Sussex*, 2007, pp. 34-36
Newhaven
10139 Cornelius Humphrey, yeoman
Spurrell, 1853, pp. 192-196
Warwickshire
Bishopton
10140 John Walker
Jones, *Stratford*, II, 2003, p. 307
Stoneleigh
10141 John Morice, day labourer
Alcock, *Warwickshire*, 1993, p. 122
Stratford-on-Avon
10142 Mr William Baker, brazier
Jones, *Stratford*, II, 2003, pp. 315-317
10143 Nathaniel Denet, labourer
Jones, *Stratford*, II, 2003, p. 305
10144 John Freeman, [innholder]
Jones, *Stratford*, II, 2003, pp. 309-312
10145 Shusanna [Susannah] Lord
Jones, *Stratford*, II, 2003, p. 308
10146 Edward Rawlins, gentleman
Jones, *Stratford*, II, 2003, p. 313
10147 William Roberts, yeoman
Jones, *Stratford*, II, 2003, pp. 305-306
Stratford-on-Avon, Old Stratford
10148 John Turbitt, [tailor]
Jones, *Stratford*, II, 2003, p. 314
Wiltshire
Marlborough
10149 Philip Chivers
Williams and Thomson, *Marlborough*, 2007, pp. 223-224
10150 Richard Clarke, pinmaker
Williams and Thomson, *Marlborough*, 2007, pp. 222-223
10151 Jone Gillmore, widow
Williams and Thomson, *Marlborough*, 2007, p. 224
10152 Micholl Hutchins, widow
Williams and Thomson, *Marlborough*, 2007, p. 224
10153 Elizabeth Stephens, widow
Williams and Thomson, *Marlborough*, 2007, p. 225
10154 Thomas Trinder, tanner
Williams and Thomson, *Marlborough*, 2007, p. 223
Worcestershire
Halesowen, Hawne
10155 Daniel Grove, [nailer]
Davenport, 1912, pp. 21-22

Huddington
10156 Dame Mary Wintour
Wanklyn, *Worcestershire*, 1998, pp. 262-266
Worcester, St Nicholas
10157 Frances Hanford, widow
Wanklyn, *Worcestershire*, 1998, p. 262
Yorkshire
Horbury
10158 Samuel Thorns, clothworker
Bartlett, *Horbury*, 1980, p. 14

1697 (c.)
Wiltshire
Marlborough
10159 Frances Newby, widow
Williams and Thomson, *Marlborough*, 2007, pp. 224-225
Yorkshire
Doncaster
10160 Henry Hardcastle, shoemaker
Hey, *Doncaster*, 1997, pp. 134-135

1698
Bristol
Bristol
10161 Sarah Alford
George, *Bristol*, 2008, p. 34
10162 Samuel Bennet, writing master
George, *Bristol*, 2008, pp. 34-36
10163 George Browne, musician
George, *Bristol*, 2008, pp. 36-37
10164 Richard Wills, pin maker
George, *Bristol*, 2008, pp. 37-38
Westbury
10165 Samuel Nicholls, mariner
Moore, *Clifton*, 1981, pp. 172-173
Buckinghamshire
Amersham
10166 John Day, innholder
Reed, *Buckinghamshire*, 1988, pp. 255-258
Colnbrook
10167 Thomas Richardson, glazier
Reed, *Buckinghamshire*, 1988, pp. 271-273
Hartwell
10168 Honor Chew, widow
Reed, *Buckinghamshire*, 1988, p. 253
Shardeloes
10169 Montague Drake, esquire (also listed London, St James, Westminster)
Reed, *Buckinghamshire*, 1988, pp. 258-271
Devonshire
Kingsbridge
10170 William Duncombe, gentleman
Cash, *Devon*, 1966, p. 174
Uffculme
10171 Sarah James
Wyatt, *Uffculme*, 1997, p. 162
10172 Richard Rose, [husbandman]
Wyatt, *Uffculme*, 1997, p p. 162-163
10173 Jane Welsh, widow
Wyatt, *Uffculme*, 1997, pp. 163
Yarnscombe
10174 William Slee
Cash, *Devon*, 1966, pp. 173-174

Dorsetshire
Yetminster
10175 Elizabeth Stokes
Machin, *Yetminster*, 1976, No.110, (2 pp.)
Essex
Roxwell
10176 Thomas Bright
Steer, *Mid-Essex*, 1969, pp. 226-227
Unlocated
10177 Christopher Perry
Steer, *Mid-Essex*, 1969, p. 227
10178 Thomas White
Steer, *Mid-Essex*, 1969, pp. 227-228
Writtle
10179 Richard Bridges
Steer, *Mid-Essex*, 1969, pp. 225-226
Gloucestershire
Cheltenham
10180 Abigail Bannester
Sale, *Cheltenham*, 1999, pp. 72-73
10181 Elianor Mason, [widow]
Sale, *Cheltenham*, 1999, p. 74
Haresfield
10182 James Mitchell, gentleman
Hall, 1890, pp. 166-167
Stoke Gifford
10183 Nicholas Brookes, yeoman
Moore, *Frampton Cotterell*, 1976, pp. 160-161
Westerleigh, Nibley
10184 Margaret Smyth, widow
Moore, *Frampton Cotterell*, 1976, pp. 161-162
Winterbourne
10185 John Griffyth, clergyman, rector of Winterbourne
Moore, *Frampton Cotterell*, 1976, pp. 159-160
10186 Richard Tipper, husbandman
Moore, *Frampton Cotterell*, 1976, p. 162
Hertfordshire
Hertford, All Saints
10187 Mary Axtell, widow
Adams, *Hertford*, 1997, pp. 82-83
Hertford, St Johns
10188 James Pendred, maltster
Adams, *Hertford*, 1997, pp. 45-46
Sarratt
10189 Henry Smith
Bullen, *Sarratt*, [1982], pp. 224-226
Kent
Shoreham
10190 Robert Hills, yeoman
Duncombe, *Darent*, 1990-1991, pp. 308-310
Leicestershire
Glenfield
10191 Willm. Kirke, [yeoman]
Wilshere, *Glenfield*, 1983, p. 9
Lincolnshire
Lincoln, Angel in the Bail
10192 Robert Douce, gentleman [innholder]
Johnston, *Lincoln*, 1991, pp. 104-109
Winteringham
10193 John Hill, husbandman
Neave, *Winteringham*, 1984, pp. 127-128

10194 William Mitchell
Neave, *Winteringham*, 1984, pp. 126-127
10195 John West
Neave, *Winteringham*, 1984, p. 126

London
Westminster, St James, Brewer Street
Montague Drake, esquire (see Shardeloes,
Buckinghamshire)

Shropshire
Wellington
10196 Eleanor Sandys, widow
Trinder and Cox, *Telford*, 1980, pp. 310-311
Wellington, Leegomery
10197 Francis Wright, dyer
Trinder and Cox, *Telford*, 1980, pp. 309-310
Wilcott
George Walsh, esquire (see Holt Castle, Worcestershire)
Wrockwardine, Allscott
10198 Thomas Latham, yeoman
Trinder and Cox, *Telford*, 1980, pp. 422-423

Staffordshire
Harborne
10199 Henry Frith
Bodfish, *Smethwick*, 1992, p. 39
Lower Gornal
10200 Francis Astley, scythesmith
Roper, *Sedgley*, 1960, p. 101
Smethwick
10201 George Birch, yeoman
Bodfish, *Smethwick*, 1992, pp. 40-42
10202 Robert Tibbins, nailer
Bodfish, *Smethwick*, 1992, p. 38

Warwickshire
Stratford-on-Avon
10203 John Aston, shoemaker
Jones, *Stratford*, II, 2003, pp. 317-318
10204 Michael Goodrich, gentleman
Jones, *Stratford*, II, 2003, pp. 319-320

Westmorland
Kirkby Thore
10205 Rev. Mr Thomas Machell, clergyman, rector of
Kirkby Thore
Ferguson, 1880, p. 5

Wiltshire
Downton
10206 Sir Charles Raleigh
Anon, *Raleigh*, 1923, pp. 307-312
Marlborough
10207 Samuel Bayly
Williams and Thomson, *Marlborough*, 2007, pp. 225-226
10208 Thomas Popejoy, maltster
Williams and Thomson, *Marlborough*, 2007, pp. 227-228
10209 James Steventon
Williams and Thomson, *Marlborough*, 2007, pp. 226-227

Worcestershire
Holt Castle
10210 George Walsh, esquire (also listed Wilcott,
Shropshire)
Wanklyn, *Worcestershire*, 1998, pp. 273-274

Yorkshire
Barnoldswick, Salterforth
10211 Henry Bracewell
Kirk, *Barnoldswick*, 1951, p. 59

Barnoldswick, Brockden
10212 John Cockshott
Kirk, *Barnoldswick*, 1951, p. 61
Doncaster
10213 Mr William Cooke, [butcher]
Hey, *Doncaster*, 1997, p. 140
10214 Thomas Maplebeck, [innkeeper]
Hey, *Doncaster*, 1997, pp. 135-137
10215 Robert Parkin, mason
Hey, *Doncaster*, 1997, p. 138
Hull
10216 Marmaduke Woodhouse, master mariner
Hall, *Beverley*, 1986, pp. 65-67
Wadsley
10217 Hugh Fenton, yeoman
Hey, 1969, pp. 111-112

1698 (c.)
Staffordshire
Sedgley
10218 Edward Gibbins, yeoman
Roper, *Sedgley*, 1960, p. 98
Wiltshire
Marlborough
10219 Edward Duck
Williams and Thomson, *Marlborough*, 2007, p. 228
10220 Elezebeth Garlick, widow
Williams and Thomson, *Marlborough*, 2007, pp. 228-229

1699
Bristol
Bristol, Christchurch
10221 William Ballwell, carpenter
George, *Bristol*, 2008, pp. 38-40
Bristol, St Augustine
10222 Thomas Easment, haulier
George, *Bristol*, 2008, pp. 40-41
Bristol
10223 Bryan Tandy, cooper
George, *Bristol*, 2008, pp. 42-43
Shirehampton, Seamills
10224 Thomas Wasborough, yeoman
Moore, *Clifton*, 1981, pp. 173-174
Buckinghamshire
High Wycombe
10225 Edward Marshall
Reed, *Buckinghamshire*, 1988, pp. 273-278
Newport Pagnell
10226 Elizabeth Darcy, alias Edmondes, alias Domer
Reed, *Buckinghamshire*, 1988, pp. 279-280
Newton Longville
10227 Robert Willison, yeoman
Reed, *Buckinghamshire*, 1988, pp. 278-279
Devonshire
Exeter, St Thomas [?]
10228 Richard and Charity Griffin
Cash, *Devon*, 1966, p. 174
Uffculme
10229 Edward Marshall [Martiall], [mercer]
Wyatt, *Uffculme*, 1997, pp. 199-200
10230 Mark Westron
Wyatt, *Uffculme*, 1997, pp. 200-201
10231 W[illia]m Wood, [husbandman]
Wyatt, *Uffculme*, 1997, p. 164

Cheshire
Byley cum Yatehouse
  10232 John Leadward, yeoman
    Ledward, 1998, p. 6
Dorsetshire
St Giles's House
  10233 Anthony Ashley Cooper, Earl of Shaftesbury
    Cooper, 1974, pp. 13-22
Essex
Roxwell
  10234 John Lingood
    Steer, *Mid-Essex*, 1969, p. 229
Writtle
  10235 John Ailett
    Steer, *Mid-Essex*, 1969, pp. 228-229
Gloucestershire
Charlton Kings
  10236 John Tanty, yeoman
    Paget and Sale, *Charlton Kings*, 2003, pp. 87-88
Cheltenham
  10237 Mrs Ann Carnall, widow
    Sale, *Cheltenham*, 1999, pp. 74-75
Cheltenham, Green Leat
  10238 Walter Eckye, [tallow chandler]
    Sale, *Cheltenham*, 1999, p. 75
Cheltenham, Arle
  10239 John Gregory, yeoman
    Sale, *Cheltenham*, 1999, p. 76
Iron Acton
  10240 John Thurner, yeoman
    Moore, *Frampton Cotterell*, 1976, pp. 163-164
Stoke Gifford
  10241 William Millett, yeoman
    Moore, *Frampton Cotterell*, 1976, pp. 162-163
Hampshire
Rookley, Crawley
  Thomas Hobbs, [surgeon, physician] (see Lincolns Inn
  Fields, London)
Hertfordshire
Hertford
  10242 John Bache [Bach], gentleman [and alderman]
    Adams, *Hertford*, 1997, pp. 35-41
Hertford, St Johns
  10243 Tymothy Miles and Sarah his wife
    Adams, *Hertford*, 1997, pp. 80-81
Hertford, All Saints, Brickendon
  10244 John Richardson, yeoman
    Adams, *Hertford*, 1997, pp. 48-49
Hertford
  10245 John Turner, baker and weaver
    Adams, *Hertford*, 1997, p. 135
Kent
Shoreham
  10246 Edward Everest, [yeoman]
    Duncombe, *Darent*, 1990-1991, pp. 276-277
Leicestershire
Kirby Muxloe
  10247 Ann Clarke, widow
    Wilshere, *Kirby Muxloe*, 1983, p. 20
Lincolnshire
Lincoln, St Mary Magdalene
  10248 Elizabeth Littleover, spinster
    Johnston, *Lincoln*, 1991, p. 109

Winteringham
  10249 Ann Scutt
    Neave, *Winteringham*, 1984, p. 128
  10250 Will Shankster
    Neave, *Winteringham*, 1984, pp. 128-129
London
Kensington Palace
  10251 William III (and the late Queen Mary)
    Lunsingh Scheurleer, 1962, pp. 50-58
Lincolns Inn Fields
  10252 Thomas Hobbs, [surgeon, physician] (also
  listed Rookley, Hampshire)
    Morris, 1971-1972, pp. 205-207
Southwark, St Olaves
  10253 John Robins, [potter]
    Britton, 1990, pp. 67-82
Nottinghamshire
Blidworth
  10254 James Clarke, yeoman
    Emmison, 1966, pp. 93-94
Shropshire
Broseley
  10255 John Ball, collier
    Trinder and Cox, *Severn Gorge*, 2000, p. 177
  10256 Mennes Langley, gentleman
    Trinder and Cox, *Severn Gorge*, 2000, p. 176
Wellington, Hadley
  10257 Francis Bayley, yeoman
    Trinder and Cox, *Telford*, 1980, pp. 312-313
Wellington
  10258 Richard Jackson, tailor
    Trinder and Cox, *Telford*, 1980, pp. 311-312
  10259 James Morris, whitesmith
    Trinder and Cox, *Telford*, 1980, pp. 313-314
Wrockwardine, Bratton
  10260 Alice Mountford, widow
    Trinder and Cox, *Telford*, 1980, pp. 423-424
Staffordshire
Haywood
  10261 Jervase Clarke, fisherman
    Bradley, *Haywoods*, 1993, pp. 60-61
Upper Gornal
  10262 Thomas Willmoore, yeoman
    Roper, *Sedgley*, 1960, p. 100
Sussex
Northiam
  10263 Richard Seamer, clergyman
    Hughes, *Sussex*, 2007, pp. 151-152
Warwickshire
Stratford-on-Avon
  10264 Thomas Browne
    Jones, *Stratford*, II, 2003, pp. 326-327
  10265 Mr Sam: [Samuel] Case, apothecary
    Jones, *Stratford*, II, 2003, pp. 321-322
  10266 Mary Hands, widow
    Jones, *Stratford*, II, 2003, pp. 323-324
  10267 Charles Holland, shoemaker
    Jones, *Stratford*, II, 2003, p. 328
  10268 William Mayo alias Fletcher, weaver and roper
    Jones, *Stratford*, II, 2003, pp. 325-326
Stratford-on-Avon, Old Stratford
  10269 Frances Milward, widow
    Jones, *Stratford*, II, 2003, p. 324

Stratford-on-Avon
10270 Joseph Phips [Phipps] and his wife Catharine
Jones, *Stratford*, II, 2003, pp. 329-330

Wiltshire
Marlborough
10271 Mary Hill, widow
Williams and Thomson, *Marlborough*, 2007, pp. 230-231
10272 Sarah Jones
Williams and Thomson, *Marlborough*, 2007, p. 230
10273 Alice Noyes
Williams and Thomson, *Marlborough*, 2007, pp. 229-230
10274 John Robinson, gardener
Williams and Thomson, *Marlborough*, 2007, p. 229

Worcestershire
Elmley Castle
10275 Thomas Savage, esquire (also listed Great
Malvern)
Wanklyn, *Worcestershire*, 1998, pp. 276-277
Great Malvern
Thomas Savage, esquire (see Elmley Castle)
Wickamford
10276 Elizabeth Sandys, [widow]
Wanklyn, *Worcestershire*, 1998, pp. 274-276

Yorkshire
Austerfield
10277 Alice Chapman, widow
Rodgers, 1999, pp. 164-165
Aysgarth, Shaw Cote
10278 Elizabeth Pratt, widow
Thwaite, *Abbotside*, 1967, pp. 129-130
Beverley
10279 Mrs Joan Todd, widow
Hall, *Beverley*, 1986, pp. 75-76

1699 (c.)
Buckinghamshire
Swanbourne
10280 Katherine Gilbert, widow
Anon., *Muniment Room*, 1934-1940, p. .30
Scotland
Angus, Kinnaird Castle
10281 James Carnegie, Earl of Southesk
Jones, 1989, pp. 55-63

1700
Berkshire
Frogmore House
10282 Richard Aldworth
Smith, 1985, pp. 418-425
Bristol
Bristol, St Stephen
10283 Joshua Farrenden, needle-maker
George, *Bristol*, 2008, pp. 43-44
Bristol
10284 John Finney, merchant
George, *Bristol*, 2008, pp. 44-46
Bristol, St Philip and St Jacob
10285 Richard Frapwell, ropemaker
George, *Bristol*, 2008, pp. 46-47
Bristol
10286 Joseph Gibson, organist of the Cathedral
George, *Bristol*, 2008, pp. 47-48

Clifton
10287 James Walter, [looking glass maker]
Moore, *Clifton*, 1981, pp. 175-176
Shirehampton
10288 Mary Hoggett, widow
Moore, *Clifton*, 1981, pp. 174-175

Buckinghamshire
Quarrington
10289 Thomas Marme
Reed, *Buckinghamshire*, 1988, p. 280

Devonshire
Uffculme
10290 William Escott [Arscott], [tailor]
Wyatt, *Uffculme*, 1997, p p. 164-165
10291 Margaret Gay [Guy], [widow]
Wyatt, *Uffculme*, 1997, p. 165-166
10292 Humfry [Humphry] Welch, [yeoman]
Wyatt, *Uffculme*, 1997, pp. 165

Dorsetshire
Chetnole
10293 John Cave, bodice maker
Machin, *Yetminster*, 1976, No.111, (1 p.)
Leigh
10294 Roger Bartlett, yeoman
Machin, *Yetminster*, 1976, No.112, (2 pp.)
10295 John Justy, yeoman
Machin, *Yetminster*, 1976, No.114, (1 p.)
Yetminster
10296 Thomas Read, yeoman
Machin, *Yetminster*, 1976, No.113, (2 pp.)
Machin, 1978, p. 172

Essex
Roxwell
10297 John Flacke
Steer, *Mid-Essex*, 1969, pp. 229-230
Writtle
10298 Richard Maggett, tailor
Steer, *Mid-Essex*, 1969, pp. 230-231

Gloucestershire
Cheltenham, Alstone
10299 Thomas Bridges, gentleman
Sale, *Cheltenham*, 1999, pp. 79-80
Cheltenham
10300 Richard Cowles, innholder
Sale, *Cheltenham*, 1999, pp. 80-81
10301 Thomas Drinkwater, husbandman
Sale, *Cheltenham*, 1999, pp. 77-78
10302 Anthony Smyth, shoemaker
Sale, *Cheltenham*, 1999, pp. 78-79
Cheltenham, Alstone
10303 Thomas Strowd, [yeoman]
Sale, *Cheltenham*, 1999, p. 82
Iron Acton
10304 Thomas Wollon, [husbandman]
Moore, *Frampton Cotterell*, 1976, p. 165
Stoke Gifford
10305 James Knapp, yeoman
Moore, *Frampton Cotterell*, 1976, p. 164
Westerleigh
10306 Ann Vernlyes
Moore, *Frampton Cotterell*, 1976, p. 164

Winterbourne
  10307 Samuel Holder, carpenter
  Moore, *Frampton Cotterell*, 1976, p. 165
Lancashire
Speke Hall
  10308 Thos Norres [Thomas Norris]
  Saxton, 1944, pp. 120-135
Leicestershire
Evington
  10309 Elizabeth Frosnell, widow
  Wilshere, *Evington*, 1985, p. 36
Lincolnshire
Lincoln
  10310 Thomas Feris, glover [tanner and brewer]
  Johnston, *Lincoln*, 1991, pp. 109-111
Nottinghamshire
Clayworth
  10311 William Gabitas, [yeoman]
  Perkins, *Clayworth*, 1979, p. xxv
Shropshire
Lilleshall
  10312 Humphrey Vernon, wheelwright
  Trinder and Cox, *Telford*, 1980, p. 218
Wellington
  10313 John Lodge, feltmaker
  Trinder and Cox, *Telford*, 1980, p. 322
  10314 Robert Peate, blacksmith
  Trinder and Cox, *Telford*, 1980, p. 321
  10315 Benjamin Wright, mercer
  Trinder and Cox, *Telford*, 1980, pp. 314-321
Wrockwardine, Clotley
  10316 Thomas Binnell, yeoman
  Trinder and Cox, *Telford*, 1980, p. 424
Surrey
Charlwood
  10317 Elizabeth Tax, widow
  Harding, *Charlwood*, 1976, p. 113
Warwickshire
Stoneleigh
  10318 John Unton, husbandman
  Alcock, *Warwickshire*, 1993, p. 103
Wiltshire
Marlborough
  10319 Thomas Dance, tiler
  Williams and Thomson, *Marlborough*, 2007, p. 231
Worcestershire
Hanbury, Mere Green
  10320 John Bearcroft, gentleman
  Wanklyn, *Worcestershire*, 1998, pp. 281-284
Tredington, Longdon
  10321 Mr Edward Baldwin, gentleman
  Wanklyn, *Worcestershire*, 1998, pp. 284-286
Wribbenhall
  10322 Roger Rea, stationer
  Bewdley, *Bewdley*, 1991, pp. 185-187
Yorkshire
Barnoldswick, Salterforth
  10323 Henry Bracewell
  Kirk, *Barnoldswick*, 1951, p. 59
Barnoldswick
  10324 Mary Jackson, widow
  Kirk, *Barnoldswick*, 1951, p. 71

Doncaster
  10325 William Kellam, gentleman
  Hey, *Doncaster*, 1997, pp. 141-142
  10326 Dorothy Wells, widow
  Hey, *Doncaster*, 1997, p. 143
Horbury
  10327 Robert Thornes, clothier
  Bartlett, *Horbury*, 1980, p. 16
  10328 Robert Thornes, rough mason
  Bartlett, *Horbury*, 1980, pp. 17-18
Kirthwaite in Dent, Blandsgill
  10329 Thomas Salkeld
  Moore, *Salkelds*, 1988, p. 115

1701
Bristol
Shirehampton
  10330 William Davis, [yeoman]
  Moore, *Clifton*, 1981, pp. 176-177
Westbury
  10331 Edward Jayne, yeoman
  Moore, *Clifton*, 1981, pp. 177-178
Cheshire
Ashton-on-Mersey
  10332 Elizabeth Dod, [widow]
  Groves, *Ashton-on-Mersey and Sale*, 2000, p. 28
Dorsetshire
Chetnole
  10333 Phillip Symes
  Machin, *Yetminster*, 1976, No.115, (2 pp.)
Gloucestershire
Cheltenham
  10334 Katherine Okey
  Sale, *Cheltenham*, 1999, p. 77
Frampton Cotterell
  10335 William Turner, feltmaker
  Moore, *Frampton Cotterell*, 1976, pp. 165-166
Westerleigh, Nibley
  10336 William Cook, yeoman
  Moore, *Frampton Cotterell*, 1976, pp. 166-167
Westerleigh
  10337 Thomas Hobbs, yeoman
  Moore, *Frampton Cotterell*, 1976, p. 166
  10338 John Parker, butcher
  Moore, *Frampton Cotterell*, 1976, p. 167
Hertfordshire
Hertford, St Andrews
  10339 John Moores, turner
  Adams, *Hertford*, 1997, pp. 42-43
Hertford, St Johns
  10340 John Randall, [mealman]
  Adams, *Hertford*, 1997, p. 47
Kent
Farningham
  10341 Thomas Woodgate, yeoman
  Duncombe, *Darent*, 1990-1991, pp. 415-417
Faversham
  10342 Alexander Bax, gentleman
  Sherwood, 1948, pp. 60-68
Leicestershire
Braunstone
  10343 John Spencer
  Wilshere, *Braunstone*, 1983, p. 34

Kirby Muxloe
10344 George Somerfield, [yeoman]
Wilshere, *Kirby Muxloe*, 1983, p. 21

Lincolnshire
Clee
10345 Samuel Pomphrett, gentleman
Ambler, Watkinson, *Clee*, 1987, pp. 168-169
10346 Richard Rowson, husbandman
Ambler, Watkinson, *Clee*, 1987, p. 168
Lincoln, St Swithins
10347 Richard Green, brewer
Johnston, *Lincoln*, 1991, pp. 113-115
Lincoln
10348 Elizabeth Manby
Johnston, *Lincoln*, 1991, pp. 111-113

London
Botolph Lane
10349 John Cary, salter
Alcock and Galinou, 2006, pp. 87-93

Northumberland
Ovingham, Harlow Hill
10350 George Dobson
Phillips, 1889, p. 60

Oxfordshire
Banbury
10351 Joseph Reason, [jersey-] weaver
Trinder and Gibson, *Banbury*, 1988, pp. 232-233
Water Eaton
10352 William Howse
Offord, *Water Eaton*, 1986, p. 47

Shropshire
Wellington
10353 Thomas Lodge, feltmaker
Trinder and Cox, *Telford*, 1980, pp. 322-323
10354 Richard Plymley, gentleman
Trinder and Cox, *Telford*, 1980, p. 322

Somersetshire
North Petherton, Adsborough
10355 Henry Stodgell, yeoman
Monday and Siraut, *Somerset*, 2003, p. 220

Wiltshire
Marlborough
10356 Joseph Duffe, maltster
Williams and Thomson, *Marlborough*, 2007, pp. 231-232
10357 William Trewman, blacksmith
Williams and Thomson, *Marlborough*, 2007, pp. 232-233

Worcestershire
Little Malvern
10358 John Russell, esquire
Wanklyn, *Worcestershire*, 1998, pp. 286-287

Yorkshire
Barnoldswick (?)
10359 Thomas Kirk
Kirk, *Barnoldswick*, 1951, p. 72
Whitby
10360 John Clark, master mariner
Vickers, *Whitby*, 1986, p. 39
10361 Francis Knaggs
Vickers, *Whitby*, 1986, p. 38
10362 Mary Noble, widow
Vickers, *Whitby*, 1986, pp. 39-40

1702
Bristol
Clifton
10363 Reece Jones, [tailor]
Moore, *Clifton*, 1981, pp. 178-179
Shirehampton
10364 Richard Prichard
Moore, *Clifton*, 1981, p. 178

Cambridgeshire
Newmarket
10365 Richard Cawthorn, butcher
May, *Newmarket*, 1976, pp. 27-29

Cumberland
Highhead Castle
10366 Christopher Richmond
Hudleston, 1959, pp. 137-138

Devonshire
Uffculme
10367 John Marshall [Martiall]
Wyatt, *Uffculme*, 1997, pp. 166-167

Essex
Roxwell
10368 Edward Boggas, gentleman
Steer, *Mid-Essex*, 1969, pp. 276-277

Gloucestershire
Charlton Kings
10369 John Moulder, yeoman
Paget and Sale, *Charlton Kings*, 2003, p. 89
Cheltenham
10370 Giles Ashmead, glover
Sale, *Cheltenham*, 1999, p. 86
Cheltenham, Alstone
10371 John Clark, husbandman
Sale, *Cheltenham*, 1999, pp. 82-83
Cheltenham
10372 Thomas Ellis, yeoman
Sale, *Cheltenham*, 1999, p. 85
Cheltenham, Alstone
10373 John Strowd, [yeoman]
Sale, *Cheltenham*, 1999, p. 83
Frampton Cotterell
10374 Francis Millett, widow
Moore, *Frampton Cotterell*, 1976, pp. 170-171
10375 John Watkind, [yeoman]
Moore, *Frampton Cotterell*, 1976, pp. 167-168
Iron Acton, Acton Ilger
10376 William Paine, [yeoman]
Moore, *Frampton Cotterell*, 1976, p. 170
Westerleigh
10377 Christopher Holder, yeoman
Moore, *Frampton Cotterell*, 1976, pp. 169-170
10378 William Sifford, mason
Moore, *Frampton Cotterell*, 1976, pp. 168-169
10379 Edith Tilly, widow
Moore, *Frampton Cotterell*, 1976, p. 168
Winterbourne
10380 William Agrove, [victualler]
Moore, *Frampton Cotterell*, 1976, p. 169

Lincolnshire
Lincoln, The Close
10381 Mr William Norris, Steward of the choristers
and singing master
Johnston, *Lincoln*, 1991, pp. 120-121

Lincoln, St Peter Arches
10382 James Osburne, linen draper
Johnston, *Lincoln*, 1991, pp. 122-126
Lincoln, Bailey
10383 George Wright, chandler
Johnston, *Lincoln*, 1991, pp. 115-119
Winteringham
10384 Nathaniel Goodwin
Neave, *Winteringham*, 1984, pp. 131-132
10385 Henry Hill, husbandman
Neave, *Winteringham*, 1984, p. 132
10386 Anthony Sharpe, mercer
Neave, *Winteringham*, 1984, pp. 130-131
10387 George Smith
Neave, *Winteringham*, 1984, pp. 129-130

Nottinghamshire
Clayworth
10388 William Sampson, clergyman [rector of
Clayworth]
Perkins, *Clayworth*, 1979, pp. xxvii-xxviii

Shropshire
Dawley
10389 Christopher Benison
Trinder and Cox, *Telford*, 1980, pp. 174-175
Lilleshall, Muxton
10390 William Hall, yeoman
Trinder and Cox, *Telford*, 1980, pp. 221-223
10391 Richard Hawkins, yeoman
Trinder and Cox, *Telford*, 1980, pp. 220-221
Lilleshall, Cheshill Grange
10392 John Steventon, yeoman
Trinder and Cox, *Telford*, 1980, pp. 219-220
Wellington, Walcot
10393 William Bickley, miller, servant
Trinder and Cox, *Telford*, 1980, pp. 324-325
Wellington, Ketley Wood
10394 Joseph Eastrop
Trinder and Cox, *Telford*, 1980, p. 324
Wellington
10395 William Jackson, tailor
Trinder and Cox, *Telford*, 1980, p. 325
Wellington, Street Lane
10396 Richard Randle, yeoman
Trinder and Cox, *Telford*, 1980, pp. 323-324

Wales
Caernarvonshire, Aberdaron
10397 Griffith Carreg, gentleman
Owen, *Lleyn*, 1960, pp. 75-76

Warwickshire
Stoneleigh
10398 Joseph Hart
Alcock, *Warwickshire*, 1993, pp. 103-104

Westmorland
Kendal, Fellside
10399 Jane Bethome
Tyson, 2009, p. 150

Wiltshire
Marlborough
10400 Thomas English, labourer
Williams and Thomson, *Marlborough*, 2007, p. 232
10401 Thomas Fowler, linen draper
Williams and Thomson, *Marlborough*, 2007, pp. 234-235

10402 Henery Russ
Williams and Thomson, *Marlborough*, 2007, pp. 233-234
Worcestershire
Worcester
10403 Sir John Barneby
Wanklyn, *Worcestershire*, 1998, pp. 288-290
Yorkshire
Whitby
10404 Newark Simpson, mariner
Vickers, *Whitby*, 1986, p. 41
10405 Francis Smith, master mariner
Vickers, *Whitby*, 1986, pp. 40-41

1702 (c.)
Gloucestershire
Charlton Kings
10406 Nicholas Dowdeswell, labourer
Paget and Sale, *Charlton Kings*, 2003, pp. 88-89
10407 Nathaniel Greenwood
Paget and Sale, *Charlton Kings*, 2003, p. 88
Wiltshire
Marlborough
10408 Sarah Hurle
Williams and Thomson, *Marlborough*, 2007, p. 234

1703
Bristol
Bristol
10409 John Spooner, brass founder
George, *Bristol*, 2008, pp. 48-50
Buckinghamshire
Brill
10410 John Snow
Reed, *Buckinghamshire*, 1988, pp. 284-286
Fawley, Bosmore
10411 Robert Weedon
Reed, *Buckinghamshire*, 1988, pp. 280-284
Lacey Green
10412 Robert Loosley, wheelwright
Reed, *Buckinghamshire*, 1988, pp. 287-289
Wooburn
10413 John Peltzer, gentleman
Reed, *Buckinghamshire*, 1988, pp. 286-287
Cheshire
Ashton-on-Mersey, Cross Street
10414 Thomas Worthington
Groves, *Ashton-on-Mersey and Sale*, 2002, pp. 36-37
Sale, Wall Bank
10415 John Moores, [yeoman]
Groves, *Ashton-on-Mersey and Sale*, 2002, p. 38
Sale
10416 Joseph Pearson, [yeoman]
Groves, *Ashton-on-Mersey and Sale*, 2002, pp. 33-34
Devonshire
Uffculme
10417 Robert Batt, [clothier]
Wyatt, *Uffculme*, 1997, pp. 201-202
10418 Robbertt Hellings [Robert Hellens]
Wyatt, *Uffculme*, 1997, p p. 167
Dorsetshire
Chetnole
10419 Ann Curtice, widow
Machin, *Yetminster*, 1976, No.116, (2 pp.)

France
St Germain-en-Laye
10420 James II
Ferrers, 1817, pp. 229-239
Gloucestershire
Charlton Kings
10421 Richard Badsey
Paget and Sale, *Charlton Kings*, 2003, p. 91
Cheltenham
10422 Francis Owen
Sale, *Cheltenham*, 1999, pp. 83-84
Cheltenham, Alstone
10423 Francis Pates, widow
Sale, *Cheltenham*, 1999, p. 84
Iron Acton
10424 John Ridley, yeoman
Moore, *Frampton Cotterell*, 1976, pp. 172-173
Westerleigh
10425 James Clare, yeoman
Moore, *Frampton Cotterell*, 1976, pp. 171-172
10426 Elizabeth Emly
Moore, *Frampton Cotterell*, 1976, p. 173
10427 John Sifford, [yeoman]
Moore, *Frampton Cotterell*, 1976, p. 173
Hertfordshire
Hertford
10428 George Boyce, plumber and glazier
Adams, *Hertford*, 1997, p. 61
Unlocated
10429 Mar[i]ah Field, widow
Munby, *Worldly Goods*, 1991, pp. 185-186
Kent
Canterbury
10430 Robert Amsden, salesman
Spufford, *Reclothing*, 1984, pp. 210-214
Leicestershire
Braunstone
10431 Abraham Compton
Wilshere, *Braunstone*, 1983, pp. 35-36
Glenfield, Kirby Frith
10432 Benjamin Styan, gentleman
Wilshere, *Glenfield*, 1983, p. 10
10433 Henry Styan, gentleman
Wilshere, *Glenfield*, 1983, p. 10
Lincolnshire
Lincoln, St Michaels Mount
10434 Godfrey Hanson, miller
Johnston, *Lincoln*, 1991, pp. 127-128
Winteringham
10435 John Markham, blacksmith
Neave, *Winteringham*, 1984, p. 133
London
Gresham College
10436 Robert Hook, Doctor of Physick, Professor of
Geometry and Natural Philosophy
Anon., *Hooke*, 1989, pp. 292-294
Nottinghamshire
Clayworth
10437 Thomas Bet, husbandman
Perkins, *Clayworth*, 1979, pp. xxix-xxxi

Shropshire
Lilleshall
10438 Joan Wright, widow
Trinder and Cox, *Telford*, 1980, p. 223
Madeley
10439 William Maybury
Trinder and Cox, *Severn Gorge*, 2000, pp. 286-287
Somersetshire
Taunton
10440 John Hammatt, tallow chandler
Monday and Siraut, *Somerset*, 2003, pp. 115-116
Staffordshire
Acton Trussell
10441 Walter Jobber, gentleman
Anon., *Acton Trussell*, 1995, p. 59
Sussex
Hunston
10442 Robert Adams, clergyman [vicar of Hunston]
Hughes, *Sussex*, 2007, pp. 117-118
Yorkshire
Horbury
10443 George Carr, mason
Bartlett, *Horbury*, 1980, pp. 21-22
Kirthwaite in Dent, Blandsgill
10444 Grace Salkeld, widow
Moore, *Salkelds*, 1988, pp. 119-121
Whitby
10445 Caleb Dale, yeoman
Vickers, *Whitby*, 1986, p. 43
10446 William Frank, mariner
Vickers, *Whitby*, 1986, p. 42
10447 John Franks, joiner
Vickers, *Whitby*, 1986, p. 43
10448 Isaac Leavens, master mariner
Vickers, *Whitby*, 1986, p. 44
10449 Elizabeth Staveley, widow
Vickers, *Whitby*, 1986, p. 42

1703 (c.)
Nottinghamshire
Wiseton
10450 James Searsey, labourer
Perkins, *Clayworth*, 1979, p. xxviii

1704
Bristol
Bristol
10451 Ann Taylor, widow
George, *Bristol*, 2008, pp. 50-52
Clifton
10452 Dorothy Godman, widow
Moore, *Clifton*, 1981, pp. 179-180
Cambridgeshire
Newmarket
10453 John Huske, maltster
May, *Newmarket*, 1976, pp. 29-32
10454 Richard Thompson, [tailor]
May, *Newmarket*, 1976, pp. 32-33
Cheshire
Sale
10455 Jane Moores
Groves, *Ashton-on-Mersey and Sale*, 2002, p. 39

Devonshire
Uffculme
10456 Humfrey Bishopp, yeoman
Wyatt, *Uffculme*, 1997, pp. 167-168
Dorset
East Stoke
10457 Sturton Dawe
Dawe, 1958, pp. 170-172
Essex
Writtle
10458 George Taverner
Steer, *Mid-Essex*, 1969, p. 277
Gloucestershire
Charlton Kings
10459 Samuel Clarke, [tailor]
Paget and Sale, *Charlton Kings*, 2003, p. 92
Cheltenham
10460 Thomas May, [maltster]
Sale, *Cheltenham*, 1999, pp. 88-89
10461 Walter White, yeoman
Sale, *Cheltenham*, 1999, p. 87
Stoke Gifford, Great Stoke
10462 William Worrell, yeoman
Moore, *Frampton Cotterell*, 1976, p. 174
Westerleigh
10463 John Harford, butcher
Moore, *Frampton Cotterell*, 1976, p. 175
10464 Nathaniel Turner, tailor
Moore, *Frampton Cotterell*, 1976, pp. 174-175
Winterbourne
10465 Joseph Atwood, [bodice-maker]
Moore, *Frampton Cotterell*, 1976, pp. 175-176
Hertfordshire
Sarratt
10466 Edward Babb
Bullen, *Sarratt*, [1982], pp. 232-233
10467 Susana Lewing, widow
Bullen, *Sarratt*, [1982], p. 235
Kent
Sittingbourne
10468 John Wood, salesman
Spufford, *Reclothing*, 1984, pp. 214-217
Leicestershire
Kirby Muxloe
10469 Thomas Barfield
Wilshere, *Kirby Muxloe*, 1983, p. 22
Lincolnshire
Allington
10470 Savile Bradshaw, clergyman, Rector of West Allington
Pask, *Allington*, 1989, pp. 97-98
Winteringham
10471 Elizabeth Goodwin, widow
Neave, *Winteringham*, 1984, p. 134
10472 William Jefferson, labourer
Neave, *Winteringham*, 1984, pp. 134-135
10473 Anthony Westoby
Neave, *Winteringham*, 1984, p. 133
Middlesex
Hadley
10474 Richard Mills, [woodworker]
Downey, 2008

Hertfordshire
Hertford
10475 William Bennett, currier
Adams, *Hertford*, 1997, pp. 58-60
Oxfordshire
Banbury
10476 John French, goldsmith
Trinder and Gibson, *Banbury*, 1988, pp. 233-234
Shropshire
Lilleshall
10477 Richard Beard, yeoman
Trinder and Cox, *Telford*, 1980, pp. 223-236
Madeley
10478 Benjamin Taylor, clergyman, vicar of Madeley
Trinder and Cox, *Severn Gorge*, 2000, pp. 287-289
Wrockwardine, Charlton
10479 William Charlton, yeoman
Trinder and Cox, *Telford*, 1980, pp. 425-426
Sussex
Goring
10480 Michael Sorocold, clergyman [vicar of Goring]
Hughes, *Sussex*, 2007, p. 91
Westmorland
Kendal, Fellside
10481 Lawrence Holme
Tyson, 2009, p. 151
Wiltshire
Marlborough
10482 George Ayliffe, cook
Williams and Thomson, *Marlborough*, 2007, pp. 236-237
10483 John Barnes, gentleman
Williams and Thomson, *Marlborough*, 2007, p. 235
10484 John Parsons, barber
Williams and Thomson, *Marlborough*, 2007, pp. 235-236
10485 John Smith, tobacconist
Williams and Thomson, *Marlborough*, 2007, pp. 237-239
Worcestershire
Dodderhill, Hobden
10486 Thomas Nott, esquire
Wanklyn, *Worcestershire*, 1998, pp. 290-291
Yorkshire
Beverley
10487 Christopher Tadman, gentleman
Hall, *Beverley*, 1986, pp. 78-79

1705

Bristol
Bristol
10488 John Garland, lighterman
George, *Bristol*, 2008, p. 52
10489 Thomas Hall, blacksmith
George, *Bristol*, 2008, pp. 52-56
10490 Samuel Plomer, plumber
George, *Bristol*, 2008, p. 56
10491 Thomas Workin, pin-maker
George, *Bristol*, 2008, pp. 56-57
Cheshire
Ashton–on-Mersey
10492 William Dickenson, [yeoman]
Groves, *Ashton-on-Mersey and Sale*, 2002, pp. 40-41
Dorsetshire
Chetnole
10493 Joseph Wates
Machin, *Yetminster*, 1976, No.117, (1 p.)

Essex
Roxwell
10494 Zachariah Day, blacksmith
Steer, *Mid-Essex*, 1969, pp. 231-232
Gloucestershire
Charlton Kings
10495 William King, [yeoman]
Paget and Sale, *Charlton Kings*, 2003, pp. 92-93
10496 Joan Whithorne, widow
Paget and Sale, *Charlton Kings*, 2003, p. 90
Cheltenham
10497 Humfrey Kemmett, silkweaver
Sale, *Cheltenham*, 1999, pp. 89-90
Frampton Cotterell
10498 Mary White, widow
Moore, *Frampton Cotterell*, 1976, p. 176
Frenchay
10499 Thomas Sturge, tanner
Moore, *Frampton Cotterell*, 1976, p. 181
Iron Acton
10500 William Cotterell, [yeoman]
Moore, *Frampton Cotterell*, 1976, pp. 179-180
Iron Acton, Acton Ilger
10501 William Somers, [yeoman]
Moore, *Frampton Cotterell*, 1976, p. 180
Stoke Gifford
10502 John Arden, yeoman
Moore, *Frampton Cotterell*, 1976, pp. 180-181
Stoke Gifford, Harry Stoke
10503 John Knapp, yeoman
Moore, *Frampton Cotterell*, 1976, pp. 178-179
Westerleigh
10504 Robert Gifford, carpenter
Moore, *Frampton Cotterell*, 1976, pp. 177-178
Winterbourne
10505 Benjamin Tucker, yeoman
Moore, *Frampton Cotterell*, 1976, pp. 176-177
Kent
Shoreham
10506 John Round, yeoman
Duncombe, *Darent*, 1990-1991, pp. 364-366
Lincolnshire
Winteringham
10507 Thomas Oyle, shoemaker
Neave, *Winteringham*, 1984, p. 136
10508 Anthony Shankster
Neave, *Winteringham*, 1984, p. 135
Shropshire
Wellington
10509 William Cooke, miller
Trinder and Cox, *Telford*, 1980, p. 330
Wellington, Ketley
10510 Thomas Fieldhouse
Trinder and Cox, *Telford*, 1980, p. 327
Wellington, Ruckley
10511 William Oakely, yeoman
Trinder and Cox, *Telford*, 1980, pp. 325-326
Wellington
10512 Richard Phillips, gentleman
Trinder and Cox, *Telford*, 1980, pp. 327-329
10513 Mary Sockett, widow
Trinder and Cox, *Telford*, 1980, p. 326

Wrockwardine, Allscott
10514 Joseph Cope, miller
Trinder and Cox, *Telford*, 1980, pp. 427-428
Wrockwardine Wood
10515 Daniel Pucksley, webster
Trinder and Cox, *Telford*, 1980, p. 426
Wrockwardine
10516 Jane Scholefield, schoolmistress
Trinder and Cox, *Telford*, 1980, pp. 426-427
Wrockwardine Wood
10517 Richard Vickers, yeoman
Trinder and Cox, *Telford*, 1980, pp. 428-429
Sussex
Stopham
10518 John Dennis, clergyman [rector of Stopham]
Hughes, *Sussex*, 2007, pp. 202-203
Westbourne
10519 Christopher Spencer, clergyman
Hughes, *Sussex*, 2007, pp. 234-235
Wales
Caernavonshire, Aberdaron
10520 Catherine Bodwrda
Owen, *Lleyn*, 1960, pp. 71-74
Warwickshire
Coleshill
10521 [Thomas] Devey, clergyman, curate of Coleshill
Salter, 1978, pp. 38-46
Wiltshire
Marlborough
10522 Thomas Jarrett, cordwainer
Williams and Thomson, *Marlborough*, 2007, p. 243
10523 Isaac Martin, cooper
Williams and Thomson, *Marlborough*, 2007, pp. 241-243
10524 Nicholas Snow, apothecary
Williams and Thomson, *Marlborough*, 2007, pp. 240-241
10525 Thomas Spackman, tailor
Williams and Thomson, *Marlborough*, 2007, pp. 239-240
10526 Robbart Taner, mason
Williams and Thomson, *Marlborough*, 2007, p. 240
Worcestershire
Northwick Park, Blockley
10527 Sir James Rushout, baronet
Wanklyn, *Worcestershire*, 1998, pp. 291-308
Yorkshire
Horbury
10528 Michael Binns, yeoman
Bartlett, *Horbury*, 1980, p. 26
10529 Thomas Goodall, yeoman
Bartlett, *Horbury*, 1980, p. 28
10530 John Horner, mason
Bartlett, *Horbury*, 1980, p. 27
Whitby
10531 Arthur Dickinson, yeoman
Vickers, *Whitby*, 1986, p. 45
10532 Thomas Perry, merchant or factor
Vickers, *Whitby*, 1986, pp. 45-46
10533 Richard Ward, master mariner
Vickers, *Whitby*, 1986, pp. 44-45
10534 Robert Wilson, shipwright
Vickers, *Whitby*, 1986, p. 46

1706

Bristol

Bristol
10535 Priscilla Fry
George, *Bristol*, 2008, pp. 57-60
Westbury
10536 William Wasborow, yeoman
Moore, *Clifton*, 1981, pp. 180-181

Buckinghamshire

Aston Clinton, Dundridge
10537 Thomas Eayre, yeoman
Reed, *Buckinghamshire*, 1988, pp. 303-304
Buckingham
10538 Alexander Ethersey, draper
Reed, *Buckinghamshire*, 1988, pp. 289-300
Chalfont St Peter
10539 Thomas Belch, miller
Reed, *Buckinghamshire*, 1988, pp. 305-306
Chearsley
10540 Thomas Oliver, widower
Reed, *Buckinghamshire*, 1988, pp. 300-301
Eton
10541 Simon Buck, innholder
Reed, *Buckinghamshire*, 1988, pp. 301-303

Cheshire

Sale
10542 Henry Daine, [yeoman]
Groves, *Ashton-on-Mersey and Sale*, 2002, pp. 42-43

Dorsetshire

Yetminster
10543 William Huler
Machin, *Yetminster*, 1976, No.118, (1 p.)

Essex

Writtle
10544 Elizabeth Eree, widow
Steer, *Mid-Essex*, 1969, pp. 232-233
10545 Richard Fuller
Steer, *Mid-Essex*, 1969, p. 233

Gloucestershire

Cheltenham
10546 Walter Buckle, gentleman
Sale, *Cheltenham*, 1999, p. 90
Frampton Cotterell
10547 Robert Haynes, feltmaker
Moore, *Frampton Cotterell*, 1976, p. 182
Westerleigh
10548 John Cromwell, yeoman
Moore, *Frampton Cotterell*, 1976, pp. 181-182

Hertfordshire

Hertford
10549 Mr John Hill, grocer [shopkeeper]
Adams, *Hertford*, 1997, pp. 132-133
Hertford, St Andrews
10550 John Wolmer [Woolmore, Woolmer], tailor
Adams, *Hertford*, 1997, pp. 140-141
St Albans, St Stephens
10551 Thomas Kilby
Munby, *Worldly Goods*, 1991, pp. 188-189

Kent

Shoreham
10552 Thomas Haltrope, yeoman
Duncombe, *Darent*, 1990-1991, p. 285

Leicestershire

Braunstone
10553 Elizabeth Compton, widow
Wilshere, *Braunstone*, 1983, p. 36
Great Stretton
10554 William King, yeoman
Wilshere, *Great Stretton*, 1984, p. 21

Lincolnshire

Lincoln
10555 William Pell, victualler
Johnston, *Lincoln*, 1991, pp. 128-129
Winteringham
10556 John Knight, husbandman
Neave, *Winteringham*, 1984, pp. 136-138

Nottinghamshire

Clayworth
10557 Francis Johnson
Perkins, *Clayworth*, 1979, pp. xxxii-xxxiii
10558 Robert Otter
Perkins, *Clayworth*, 1979, pp. xxxiii-xxxiv

Shropshire

Benthall
10559 Thomas Beard, trowman
Trinder and Cox, *Severn Gorge*, 2000, pp. 125-126
Lilleshall Lodge
10560 James Dale, keeper
Trinder and Cox, *Telford*, 1980, p. 226

Staffordshire

Harborne
10561 Thomas Dolphin, yeoman
Bodfish, *Smethwick*, 1992, pp. 43-44

Sussex

Billingshurst
10562 Thomas Oram, clergyman [vicar of Billingshurst]
Hughes, *Sussex*, 2007, pp. 26-27
North Mundham
10563 Edmund Lane, clergyman [vicar of North Mundham]
Hughes, *Sussex*, 2007, pp. 147-148
Sompting
10564 Isaac Boardman, clergyman [vicar of Sompting]
Hughes, *Sussex*, 2007, pp. 194-195

Wiltshire

Marlborough
10565 Richard Hawkins, yeoman
Williams and Thomson, *Marlborough*, 2007, pp. 243-244

Worcestershire

Bewdley
10566 Mr Thomas Burleton, [gentleman]
Bewdley, *Bewdley*, 1991, pp. 188-189

Yorkshire

Barnoldswick, Burn Moor
10567 Richard Emmot, yeoman
Kirk, *Barnoldswick*, 1951, pp. 62-63
Horbury
10568 Willm Castlehouse, yeoman
Bartlett, *Horbury*, 1980, pp. 24-25

1707

Bristol
Bristol
  10569 William Gallop
    George, *Bristol*, 2008, p. 61
  10570 Thomas Ivey, gentleman
    George, *Bristol*, 2008, pp. 61-64
  10571 Timothy Payne, mariner
    George, *Bristol*, 2008, pp. 64-67
Bristol, St James
  10572 John Thomas, cooper
    George, *Bristol*, 2008, pp. 67-69
Stoke [Bishop]
  10573 Susanna Jayne, widow
    Moore, *Clifton*, 1981, p. 181

Dorsetshire
Yetminster
  10574 Leonall Brown, yeoman
    Machin, *Yetminster*, 1976, No.119, (2 pp.)
    Machin, 1978, pp. 170-171

Essex
Roxwell
  10575 Henry Bright, yeoman
    Steer, *Mid-Essex*, 1969, pp. 234-235

Gloucestershire
Charlton Kings
  10576 Joseph Danford, [weaver]
    Paget and Sale, *Charlton Kings*, 2003, pp. 95-96
  10577 Richard Pates, [gentleman]
    Paget and Sale, *Charlton Kings*, 2003, pp. 94-95
Cheltenham
  10578 Thomas Ashmeade, mercer
    Sale, *Cheltenham*, 1999, p. 92
  10579 Elizabeth Fluck
    Sale, *Cheltenham*, 1999, p. 92
Cheltenham, Alstone
  10580 William Roberts, gentleman
    Sale, *Cheltenham*, 1999, pp. 92-93
Cheltenham
  10581 Sarah Williams, widow
    Sale, *Cheltenham*, 1999, p. 91
Coalpit Heath
  10582 Jacob Hollister, house-carpenter
    Moore, *Frampton Cotterell*, 1976, p. 184
Stoke Gifford
  10583 Sarah Arden, widow
    Moore, *Frampton Cotterell*, 1976, pp. 184-185
Stoke Gifford, Harry Stoke
  10584 Mary Knapp, widow
    Moore, *Frampton Cotterell*, 1976, pp. 182-183
Westerleigh
  10585 Samuel Trewman, gentleman
    Moore, *Frampton Cotterell*, 1976, pp. 183-184
Winterbourne
  10586 Thomas Dyer, cordwainer
    Moore, *Frampton Cotterell*, 1976, p. 183

Kent
Canterbury, St Paul's
  10587 Robert Griffin, chapman
    Spufford, *Reclothing*, 1984, pp. 167-168
Otford
  10588 John Wells, yeoman
    Duncombe, *Darent*, 1990-1991, pp. 409-411

Shoreham
  10589 John Round, yeoman
    Duncombe, *Darent*, 1990-1991, pp. 369-371
Yalding
  10590 Henry Solman, yeoman
    Sherwood, 1948, pp. 69-72

Lincolnshire
Lincoln
  10591 John Hobman, butcher
    Johnston, *Lincoln*, 1991, pp. 130-131
Winteringham
  10592 Joseph Wressell, tailor
    Neave, *Winteringham*, 1984, p. 138

Shropshire
Lilleshall
  10593 Walter Brodhurst, gentleman
    Trinder and Cox, *Telford*, 1980, pp. 228-230
Lilleshall, Muxton
  10594 John Shelton
    Trinder and Cox, *Telford*, 1980, pp. 226-228

Staffordshire
Smethwick
  10595 John Sharpling
    Bodfish, *Smethwick*, 1992, p. 45

Sussex
Steyning
  10596 George Hatcher, 'Poor Labourer'
    Pennington and Sleight, 1987, p. 46

Wiltshire
Marlborough
  10597 Dorothy Dismore, widow
    Williams and Thomson, *Marlborough*, 2007, p. 244
  10598 John Morrice, carpenter
    Williams and Thomson, *Marlborough*, 2007, pp. 244-245
  10599 William Smith, currier
    Williams and Thomson, *Marlborough*, 2007, p. 245

Worcestershire
Bewdley
  10600 George Hill, barber surgeon
    Bewdley, *Bewdley*, 1991, pp. 190-193
Elmbridge
  10601 Gerard Danett, gentleman
    Wanklyn, *Worcestershire*, 1998, pp. 308-309
Elmley Lovett
  10602 Henry Townshend, esquire
    Wanklyn, *Worcestershire*, 1998, pp. 316-321
Upton-on-Severn
  10603 Humphrey Soley, [esquire]
    Wanklyn, *Worcestershire*, 1998, pp. 309-316

Yorkshire
Whitby
  10604 Margaret Browne, widow
    Vickers, *Whitby*, 1986, p. 47
  10605 William Cass
    Vickers, *Whitby*, 1986, p. 47
  10606 Henry Clarkson, master mariner
    Vickers, *Whitby*, 1986, p. 46
  10607 George Cooke, tailor
    Vickers, *Whitby*, 1986, pp. 47-48
  10608 Mary Gaskin, shopkeeper
    Vickers, *Whitby*, 1986, p. 47
  10609 Robert Staindridge, mercer
    Vickers, *Whitby*, 1986, pp. 48-57

1707 (c.)

Wiltshire
Marlborough
  10610 Thomas Greenaway, glover
    Williams and Thomson, *Marlborough*, 2007, p. 245
  10611 Ann Keeble, widow
    Williams and Thomson, *Marlborough*, 2007, pp. 245-246

1708

Bristol
Westbury
  10612 William Rosser, yeoman
    Moore, *Clifton*, 1981, p. 182
Cheshire
Ashton-on-Mersey
  10613 William Hurlbutt
    Groves, *Ashton-on-Mersey and Sale*, 2002, pp. 49-50
Essex
Roxwell
  10614 Henry Mansfeild, yeoman
    Steer, *Mid-Essex*, 1969, pp. 236-237
Sewardstone, Powder Mills
  10615 Sir Polycarpus Wharton, baronet
    Crocker and Fairclough, 1998, pp. 32-33
Writtle
  10616 Robert Hilliard, yeoman
    Steer, *Mid-Essex*, 1969, pp. 235-236
  10617 Thomas Robjant
    Steer, *Mid-Essex*, 1969, pp. 237-238
Gloucestershire
Charlton Kings
  10618 Samuel Whithorn, [yeoman]
    Paget and Sale, *Charlton Kings*, 2003, p. 96
Cirencester, Dyer Street
  10619 William George
    Barker, 1976, pp. 120-124
Frampton Cotterell
  10620 Mary Gibings, widow
    Moore, *Frampton Cotterell*, 1976, p. 185
  10621 Thomas James, [yeoman]
    Moore, *Frampton Cotterell*, 1976, pp. 185-186
Stoke Gifford
  10622 William Gingell, yeoman
    Moore, *Frampton Cotterell*, 1976, p. 186
Westerleigh
  10623 Elizabeth Cook, widow
    Moore, *Frampton Cotterell*, 1976, p. 185
Winterbourne, Sturden House
  10624 Joan Hill, widow
    Moore, *Frampton Cotterell*, 1976, pp. 186-188
Hertfordshire
Sarratt
  10625 William Tockefield, yeoman
    Bullen, *Sarratt*, [1982], pp. 237-239
Unlocated
  10626 William Edmonds
    Munby, *Worldly Goods*, 1991, p. 189
Ireland
Co. Roscommon, Strokestown
  10627 John Mahon, esquire
    ffolliott, 1978, pp. 78-80

Kent
Eynsford
  10628 Christopher Hayward, yeoman
    Duncombe, *Darent*, 1990-1991, pp. 294-297
Leicestershire
Evington
  10629 John Plumer, [yeoman]
    Wilshere, *Evington*, 1985, p. 37
Kirby Muxloe
  10630 Thomas Brooks, [labourer]
    Wilshere, *Kirby Muxloe*, 1983, p. 22
Lincolnshire
Lincoln
  10631 William Faux, alderman [mercer and maltster]
    Johnston, *Lincoln*, 1991, pp. 131-136
London
Ironmongers' Hall
  10632 Company of Ironmongers
    Nicholl, 1851, pp. 464-466
Norfolk
Kings Lynn
  10633 John Butler, woollen draper
    Parker, *Kings Lynn*, 1971, pp. 187-190
Nottinghamshire
Clayworth
  10634 Christopher Johnson, gentleman
    Perkins, *Clayworth*, 1979, pp. xxxviii-xxxix
Shropshire
Benthall
  10635 Andrew Dodson, trowman
    Trinder and Cox, *Severn Gorge*, 2000, p. 126
Broseley
  10636 Judith Holmes, widow
    Trinder and Cox, *Severn Gorge*, 2000, pp. 177-179
Wellington, Watling Street
  10637 Rowland Goole, innholder
    Trinder and Cox, *Telford*, 1980, pp. 331-333
Wellington
  10638 John Judgson, innholder
    Trinder and Cox, *Telford*, 1980, pp. 330-331
Wrockwardine, Trench Lane
  10639 Edward Bold, yeoman
    Trinder and Cox, *Telford*, 1980, p. 429
  10640 Thomas Icke, labourer
    Trinder and Cox, *Telford*, 1980, p. 429
Sussex
Parham
  10641 William Brown, clergyman [rector of Parham]
    Hughes, *Sussex*, 2007, p. 163
Westmorland
Kirkby Lonsdale, Lupton Fell House
  10642 Henry Houseman, yeoman
    Macfarlane, 1977, p. 75
Wiltshire
Marlborough
  10643 Mary Davis
    Williams and Thomson, *Marlborough*, 2007, pp. 246-247
  10644 John Hitchcock
    Williams and Thomson, *Marlborough*, 2007, p. 246
Yorkshire
Barnoldswick, Salterforth
  10645 Christopher Taylor
    Kirk, *Barnoldswick*, 1951, pp. 79-80

1709

Bristol
Shirehampton, Hungroad
  10646 Thomas Rogers, mariner
  Moore, *Clifton*, 1981, p. 182
Buckinghamshire
Ditton House
  10647 Ralph, Duke of Montagu
  Murdoch, *Noble Households*, 2006, pp. 80-84
Eton
  10648 George Herbert, gentleman
  Reed, *Buckinghamshire*, 1988, pp. 309-311
Newport Pagnell
  10649 Mrs Ann Christie
  Reed, *Buckinghamshire*, 1988, pp. 311-313
Thorney
  10650 William Goodshire
  Reed, *Buckinghamshire*, 1988, p. 309
Cheshire
Bowdon
  10651 William Saunders, husbandman
  Groves, *Bowdon*, 1999, p. 29
Devonshire
Uffculme
  10652 Gyles Bishopp [Giles Bishop], yeoman
  Wyatt, *Uffculme*, 1997, pp. 168-170
  10653 Mary Speed
  Wyatt, *Uffculme*, 1997, pp. 168
Essex
Writtle
  10654 Joseph Herridge
  Steer, *Mid-Essex*, 1969, p. 238
Gloucestershire
Charlton Kings
  10655 John King, [yeoman]
  Paget and Sale, *Charlton Kings*, 2003, p. 97
Cheltenham
  10656 Dan[iell] Hayward, collar maker
  Sale, *Cheltenham*, 1999, pp. 101-102
  10657 Thomas Kemmett, [yeoman]
  Sale, *Cheltenham*, 1999, p. 98
  10658 Thomas Packer, gentleman
  Sale, *Cheltenham*, 1999, pp. 96-97
  10659 Martha St Leger
  Sale, *Cheltenham*, 1999, p. 97
Frampton Cotterell
  10660 Samuel Codrington, esquire
  Moore, *Frampton Cotterell*, 1976, pp. 193-202
  10661 Thomas Coules, yeoman
  Moore, *Frampton Cotterell*, 1976, p. 193
  10662 Richard Parker, feltmaker
  Moore, *Frampton Cotterell*, 1976, p. 188
Hambrook
  10663 Joan Albert, widow [oatmeal-maker]
  Moore, *Frampton Cotterell*, 1976, p. 189
Iron Acton
  10664 James Manning, yeoman
  Moore, *Frampton Cotterell*, 1976, pp. 192-193
  10665 Thomas Tilladam, [cordwainer]
  Moore, *Frampton Cotterell*, 1976, p. 188
Westerleigh
  10666 John Hicks, clothworker
  Moore, *Frampton Cotterell*, 1976, p. 189

  10667 William Prigge, yeoman
  Moore, *Frampton Cotterell*, 1976, pp. 202-203
  10668 John Tovey, mason
  Moore, *Frampton Cotterell*, 1976, pp. 190-192
  10669 Hannah Trahern, widow
  Moore, *Frampton Cotterell*, 1976, pp. 189-190
Ireland
Co. Kildare, Athy
  10670 Thomas Weston, [miller]
  Goodbody, *Quaker*, 1971, pp. 57-58
Kent
Shoreham
  10671 Timothy Wells
  Duncombe, *Darent*, 1990-1991, pp. 411-412
Leicestershire
Evington
  10672 Jane Noone, widow
  Wilshere, *Evington*, 1985, p. 37
Kirby Muxloe
  10673 Francis Rason, [grazier]
  Wilshere, *Kirby Muxloe*, 1983, p. 23
Lincolnshire
Wainfleet St Mary
  10674 William Clark, yeoman
  Barley, *Lincolnshire*, 1951, pp. 266-267
London
The Cockpit, Whitehall
  Ralph, Duke of Montagu (see Montagu House, Bloomsbury)
Montagu House, Bloomsbury
  10675 Ralph, Duke of Montagu (also listed The Cockpit, Whitehall)
  Murdoch, *Noble Households*, 2006, pp. 14-26
Hertfordshire
Hertford, All Saints
  10676 Joseph Sawerd, [yeoman]
  Adams, *Hertford*, 1997, pp. 52-53
Northamptonshire
Boughton House
  10677 Ralph, Duke of Montagu
  Murdoch, *Noble Households*, 2006, pp. 51-61
Rothwell
  10678 Georg Alderman, [tailor]
  Alderman, *Alderman*, 2008, p. 158
Shropshire
Benthall
  10679 John Rutter, yeoman
  Trinder and Cox, *Severn Gorge*, 2000, pp. 127-128
Broseley
  10680 John Pearce, master collier
  Trinder and Cox, *Severn Gorge*, 2000, pp. 179-181
Lilleshall, Muxton
  10681 Edward Aston, lime man
  Trinder and Cox, *Telford*, 1980, pp. 231-232
  10682 Philippa Shelton, widow
  Trinder and Cox, *Telford*, 1980, pp. 230-231
  10683 Joseph Woolley
  Trinder and Cox, *Telford*, 1980, pp. 232-233
Little Wenlock
  10684 William Boycott, butcher
  Trinder and Cox, *Severn Gorge*, 2000, pp. 264-265
  10685 Richard Wheelwright, yeoman
  Trinder and Cox, *Severn Gorge*, 2000, pp. 248-249

Madeley, Furnace Bank
  10686 George Glassbrooke, carpenter
    Trinder and Cox, *Severn Gorge*, 2000, p. 289
Madeley
  10687 Edward Lloyd, trowman
    Trinder and Cox, *Severn Gorge*, 2000, pp. 290-291
  10688 James Smitheman, gunsmith
    Trinder and Cox, *Severn Gorge*, 2000, pp. 291-292
Wellington
  10689 John Eyton, esquire
    Trinder and Cox, *Telford*, 1980, pp. 333-336
  10690 Edward Shakeshaft, corviser
    Trinder and Cox, *Telford*, 1980, p. 336

Staffordshire
Smethwick
  10691 William Crowley, nailer
    Bodfish, *Smethwick*, 1992, pp. 46-47

Surrey
Charlwood
  10692 James Round, yeoman
    Harding, *Charlwood*, 1976, pp. 113-114
Guildford
  10693 Trinity Hospital
    Palmer, 1919, pp. 34-35

Sussex
Aldingbourne
  10694 John Holder, clergyman [vicar of Aldingbourne]
    Hughes, *Sussex*, 2007, pp. 2-3
Goring
  10695 Michael Sorocold, clergyman [vicar of Goring]
    Hughes, *Sussex*, 2007, pp. 92-93
Hunston
  10696 Roger Collins, clergyman [vicar of Hunston]
    Hughes, *Sussex*, 2007, p. 119
Shipley
  10697 John King, yeoman
    Steer, 1958, pp. 156-157
Steyning
  10698 Robert Holden, glover
    Steer, 1958, pp. 158-159

Wales
Anglesey, Llanddyfnan
  10699 William ab William David, yeoman
    Barnes, 1969-70, pp. 234-235

Warwickshire
Stoneleigh, Canley
  10700 Bridget Osborne, widow
    Alcock, *Warwickshire*, 1993, p. 164

Wiltshire
Marlborough
  10701 Edward Dangerfield, baker
    Williams and Thomson, *Marlborough*, 2007, pp. 248-249
  10702 George Dobson, chandler
    Williams and Thomson, *Marlborough*, 2007, p. 248
  10703 Thomas Edney, blacksmith
    Williams and Thomson, *Marlborough*, 2007, p. 247

Yorkshire
Horbury
  10704 Joseph Cawtheron, clothier
    Bartlett, *Horbury*, 1980, p. 30
Whitby
  10705 George Attey, joiner
    Vickers, *Whitby*, 1986, pp. 59-60

  10706 John Elrington
    Vickers, *Whitby*, 1986, pp. 57-59
  10707 Nathaniel White
    Vickers, *Whitby*, 1986, p. 59

1709 (c.)
Wiltshire
Marlborough
  10708 John Greenway, glover
    Williams and Thomson, *Marlborough*, 2007, p. 248

1710
Bristol
Bristol
  10709 Richard Bacon, grocer
    George, *Bristol*, 2008, pp. 69-70
  10710 Richard Phillips, mariner
    George, *Bristol*, 2008, p. 70
  10711 Samuel Ware, scrivener
    George, *Bristol*, 2008, pp. 70-71
Shirehampton
  10712 Abraham Saunders, mariner
    Moore, *Clifton*, 1981, pp. 182-183
Stoke Bishop
  10713 William Price, [husbandman]
    Moore, *Clifton*, 1981, p. 183

Devonshire
Kitley
  10714 Edmund Pollexfen, esquire
    Anon., *Devonshire 1710*, 1961, pp. 301-304

Dorsetshire
Cattistock
  10715 Jasper Rogers, yeoman
    Dawe, *Cattistock*, 1968, pp. 282-284
Yetminster
  10716 Jonathan Curtis
    Machin, *Yetminster*, 1976, No.120, (1 p.)
  10717 Mary Symonds
    Machin, *Yetminster*, 1976, No.121, (1 p.)

Gloucestershire
Cheltenham
  10718 Obediah Arrowsmith, haberdasher
    Sale, *Cheltenham*, 1999, pp. 102-106
  10719 William Benfield, cordwainer
    Sale, *Cheltenham*, 1999, pp. 108-109
  10720 Charles Bignell, innholder
    Sale, *Cheltenham*, 1999, p. 107
  10721 John Felstead, cutler
    Sale, *Cheltenham*, 1999, pp. 99-100
  10722 William Higgs, cooper
    Sale, *Cheltenham*, 1999, p. 102
Cheltenham, Westal
  10723 John Pearce, [yeoman]
    Sale, *Cheltenham*, 1999, p. 115
Dyrham Park
  10724 Mr Blathwayt [William Blathwayt]
    Walton, 1986, pp. 55-72
Frampton Cotterell
  10725 Mary Merick, widow
    Moore, *Frampton Cotterell*, 1976, p. 204
Iron Acton
  10726 Nathaniel Ridley, schoolmaster
    Moore, *Frampton Cotterell*, 1976, pp. 204-205

Westerleigh
10727 Robert Sherman, yeoman
Moore, *Frampton Cotterell*, 1976, pp. 205-206
Hertfordshire
Sarratt
10728 Thomas Rogers, tailor
Bullen, *Sarratt*, [1982], pp. 240-242
Leicestershire
Evington
10729 William Pole, [labourer]
Wilshere, *Evington*, 1985, p. 38
Lincolnshire
Clee
10730 Thomas Sharp, yeoman
Ambler, Watkinson, *Clee*, 1987, pp. 169-170
Winteringham
10731 George Pointer
Neave, *Winteringham*, 1984, p. 139
Northamptonshire
Boughton
10732 Robeart Allderman, [yeoman]
Alderman, *Alderman*, 2008, pp. 149-150
Drayton House
10733 Sir John Germaine, baronet
Murdoch, *Noble Households*, 2006, pp. 121-130
Scotland
Orkney, Burray
10734 Sir Archibald Stewart, baronet
Marwick, 1934, pp. 55-58
Shropshire
Dawley, The Frame
10735 William Crippin, labourer
Trinder and Cox, *Telford*, 1980, pp. 175-176
Lilleshall, Donnington
10736 Katherine Hall, widow
Trinder and Cox, *Telford*, 1980, pp. 233-234
Lilleshall
10737 Revd. Henry Haughton, clergyman, vicar of
Lilleshall
Trinder and Cox, *Telford*, 1980, pp. 234-235
Wellington, Hadley
10738 Margaret Blakeman
Trinder and Cox, *Telford*, 1980, p. 337
10739 Richard Peate, blacksmith
Trinder and Cox, *Telford*, 1980, p. 337
Staffordshire
Lower Gornal
10740 John Juckes
Roper, *Sedgley*, 1960, pp. 101-101a
Smethwick
10741 Elizabeth Hunt
Bodfish, *Smethwick*, 1992, p. 48
Surrey
Charlwood
10742 William Blank
Harding, *Charlwood*, 1976, p. 113
10743 Thomas Steer, husbandman
Harding, *Charlwood*, 1976, p. 114
Sussex
Newick
10744 Joseph Hoyle, clergyman [rector of Newick]
Hughes, *Sussex*, 2007, pp. 148-149

Selmeston
10745 William Green, clergyman [vicar of Selmeston]
Hughes, *Sussex*, 2007, pp. 186-187
Yorkshire
Horbury
10746 John Rodes, gentleman
Bartlett, *Horbury*, 1980, p. 32
Whitby
10747 Alice Nellist, widow
Vickers, *Whitby*, 1986, p. 60

1711
Cambridgeshire
Newmarket
10748 Charles Wheetly, chapman
May, *Newmarket*, 1976, p. 35
Cheshire
Ashton-on-Mersey
10749 James Whitelegg, [yeoman]
Groves, *Ashton-on-Mersey and Sale*, 2002, pp. 55-56
Sale
10750 John Barlow
Groves, *Ashton-on-Mersey and Sale*, 2002, pp. 56-57
10751 Edward Gratrix, [yeoman]
Groves, *Ashton-on-Mersey and Sale*, 2002, pp. 53-54
Gloucestershire
Cheltenham
10752 John Ellis, cordwainer
Sale, *Cheltenham*, 1999, p. 111
Frampton Cotterell
10753 Robert Webb, yeoman
Moore, *Frampton Cotterell*, 1976, pp. 210-211
Hambrook
10754 Thomas Bayly, yeoman
Moore, *Frampton Cotterell*, 1976, pp. 206-207
Iron Acton, Latteridge
10755 Mary Hancok, widow
Moore, *Frampton Cotterell*, 1976, p. 211
Iron Acton
10756 William Lewis, yeoman [innholder]
Moore, *Frampton Cotterell*, 1976, pp. 207-208
Westerleigh
10757 Elizabeth Hall, [widow]
Moore, *Frampton Cotterell*, 1976, pp. 209-210
10758 Alice Harris, widow
Moore, *Frampton Cotterell*, 1976, p. 209
10759 Samuel Horder, yeoman
Moore, *Frampton Cotterell*, 1976, p. 206
10760 Henry Nichols, yeoman [coalminer]
Moore, *Frampton Cotterell*, 1976, p. 212
10761 Sarah Turner, widow
Moore, *Frampton Cotterell*, 1976, pp. 208-209
Winterbourne
10762 Hezekiah Cole, yeoman
Moore, *Frampton Cotterell*, 1976, pp. 211-212
Hertfordshire
Sarratt
10763 Mary Smith, widow
Bullen, *Sarratt*, [1982], pp. 249-250
Leicestershire
Braunstone
10764 Mrs [Mary] Parsons
Wilshere, *Braunstone*, 1983, p. 37

Middlesex
Sunbury
  10765 John Rene Giberne, gentleman
    Heselton, *Sunbury*, 1976, pp. 8-9
Norfolk
West Bilney
  10766 Elizabeth Freke, widow
    Anselment, 2001, pp. 165-188
Shropshire
Broseley
  10767 Sampson Buckley, dyer
    Trinder and Cox, *Severn Gorge*, 2000, pp. 181-183
Madeley, The Lodge
  10768 Luke Twyford, gentleman
    Trinder and Cox, *Severn Gorge*, 2000, pp. 292-294
Wellington, Hadley
  10769 William Cookson, weaver
    Trinder and Cox, *Telford*, 1980, p. 338
Wellington
  10770 John Handy, labourer
    Trinder and Cox, *Telford*, 1980, pp. 338-339
Wellington, Aston
  10771 Richard Stanier, gentleman
    Trinder and Cox, *Telford*, 1980, pp. 339-343
Wrockwardine Wood
  10772 Richard Lummas [Lomas], master collier
    Trinder and Cox, *Telford*, 1980, p. 430
Sussex
Petworth
  10773 John Bromfield, mason
    Kenyon, *Petworth*, 1958, pp. 102-103
Plumpton
  10774 Thomas Travers, clergyman
    Hughes, *Sussex*, 2007, pp. 167-168
West Dean, Binderton
  10775 George Smyth, clergyman [rector of North
  Marden]
    Hughes, *Sussex*, 2007, pp. 59-62
Wiltshire
Marlborough
  10776 William Aldridge, maltster
    Williams and Thomson, *Marlborough*, 2007, p. 250
  10777 John Copland, innholder
    Williams and Thomson, *Marlborough*, 2007, pp. 249-250
  10778 Steven Derem, hempdresser
    Williams and Thomson, *Marlborough*, 2007, pp. 250-251
  10779 Robert New, skinner [fellmonger]
    Williams and Thomson, *Marlborough*, 2007, p. 250
  10780 William Trippatt, waggoner
    Williams and Thomson, *Marlborough*, 2007, p. 250
Worcestershire
Northwick Park, Blockley
  10781 Sir James Rushout, baronet
    Wanklyn, *Worcestershire*, 1998, pp. 327-329
Norton-juxta-Kemsey
  10782 Thomas Stevens, esquire
    Wanklyn, *Worcestershire*, 1998, pp. 324-327
Yorkshire
Horbury
  10783 William Hilton
    Bartlett, *Horbury*, 1980, p. 36

Whitby
  10784 Marmaduke Marwood, master mariner
    Vickers, *Whitby*, 1986, pp. 60-61
  10785 Jacob Saunders, mariner
    Vickers, *Whitby*, 1986, p. 60
  10786 William Storrey, mariner
    Vickers, *Whitby*, 1986, p. 62
  10787 Thomas Story, butcher
    Vickers, *Whitby*, 1986, pp. 61-62

1712
Cambridgeshire
Newmarket
  10788 William Owen, brazier
    May, *Newmarket*, 1976, pp. 33-35
  10789 Cornelyus Platt, victualler
    May, *Newmarket*, 1976, p. 36
Cheshire
Ashton-on-Mersey
  10790 Isaiah Key
    Groves, *Ashton-on-Mersey and Sale*, 2002, pp. 75-77
Dorsetshire
Yetminster
  10791 Margaret Barnes
    Machin, *Yetminster*, 1976, No.122, (1 p.)
Essex
Writtle (?)
  10792 Joseph Lingard
    Steer, *Mid-Essex*, 1969, p. 276
Gloucestershire
Charlton Kings
  10793 Daniel Ellis, yeoman
    Paget and Sale, *Charlton Kings*, 2003, pp. 99-100
Cheltenham
  10794 John Ashmeade, [yeoman]
    Sale, *Cheltenham*, 1999, p. 112
  10795 William Church, yeoman
    Sale, *Cheltenham*, 1999, p. 113
  10796 John Davison
    Sale, *Cheltenham*, 1999, p. 117
  10797 Daniel Ellis, yeoman
    Sale, *Cheltenham*, 1999, p. 116
  10798 John Hyett, maltster
    Sale, *Cheltenham*, 1999, pp. 114-115
  10799 John Mason
    Sale, *Cheltenham*, 1999, pp. 117-118
Iron Acton
  10800 Michael Short, carpenter
    Moore, *Frampton Cotterell*, 1976, pp. 213-214
Westerleigh
  10801 William Buttler, [coalminer]
    Moore, *Frampton Cotterell*, 1976, p. 213
  10802 Henry Perryman, yeoman
    Moore, *Frampton Cotterell*, 1976, p. 214
Winterbourne
  10803 Isabella Vidler, widow
    Moore, *Frampton Cotterell*, 1976, p. 213
Hertfordshire
Hertford, St Andrews
  10804 James Pendrid [Pendred], maltster
    Adams, *Hertford*, 1997, pp. 111-112

Hertford
10805 Daniel Smith, baker
Adams, *Hertford*, 1997, p. 55

Leicestershire
Evington
10806 Elizabeth Spencer, widow
Wilshere, *Evington*, 1985, p. 38
10807 Mr James Tomson
Wilshere, *Evington*, 1985, p. 39

Lincolnshire
Clee
10808 Elizabeth Low, widow
Ambler, Watkinson, *Clee*, 1987, p. 170
Lincoln, St Martins
10809 William Warriner, cordwainer
Johnston, *Lincoln*, 1991, pp. 136-137
Winteringham
10810 Georg Bell
Neave, *Winteringham*, 1984, p. 139

Norfolk
Great Cressingham
10811 Robert Busgate
Eland, 1947, pp. 23-24

Scotland
Forfarshire, Finhavon Castle
10812 [?] Carnegie
Jervise, 1853, pp. 340-343

Shropshire
Benthall
10813 Catherine Hartshorne, serving maid
Trinder and Cox, *Severn Gorge*, 2000, p. 130
Benthall, Posenhall
10814 Joseph Reynolds, gentleman
Trinder and Cox, *Severn Gorge*, 2000, pp. 128-130
Madeley Wood
10815 John Bayley, ground collier
Trinder and Cox, *Severn Gorge*, 2000, p. 294
Wellington
10816 John Hill
Trinder and Cox, *Telford*, 1980, p. 343

Staffordshire
Brierley
10817 Richard Wainwright, yeoman
Roper, *Sedgley*, 1960, p. 102
Lower Gornal
10818 Richard Hickmans
Roper, *Sedgley*, 1960, pp. 103-104
Smethwick
10819 William Horton, blacksmith
Bodfish, *Smethwick*, 1992, p. 49

Sussex
Lewes
10820 Edward Newton, clergyman
Hughes, *Sussex*, 2007, pp. 132-133
Rusper
10821 John Priaux, clergyman [rector of Rusper]
Hughes, *Sussex*, 2007, pp. 179-182
Wartling
10822 David Forsyth, clergyman [curate of Wartling]
Hughes, *Sussex*, 2007, p. 228

Westmorland
Kendal
10823 Robert Webster, innholder
Tyson, 2008, p. 103

Wiltshire
Marlborough
10824 Alexander Aldworth, maltster
Williams and Thomson, *Marlborough*, 2007, pp. 253-254
10825 Christopher Freeman, maltster
Williams and Thomson, *Marlborough*, 2007, p. 253
10826 Francis Handcock, lime burner
Williams and Thomson, *Marlborough*, 2007, pp. 251-252
10827 Robert Parkes, innholder
Williams and Thomson, *Marlborough*, 2007, p. 251

Yorkshire
Barnoldswick
10828 John Dugdell
Kirk, *Barnoldswick*, 1951, p. 62
York
10829 Walter Marlin, [chapman]
Spufford, *Reclothing*, 1984, pp. 156-157

1712 (c.)
Wiltshire
Marlborough
10830 William Fry, pipemaker
Williams and Thomson, *Marlborough*, 2007, p. 252

1713
Bristol
Bristol
10831 Thomas Burrowes, yeoman
George, *Bristol*, 2008, pp. 72-75
Clifton
10832 John David, shoemaker
Moore, *Clifton*, 1981, p. 184
10833 John Head, blacksmith
Moore, *Clifton*, 1981, p. 184

Cambridgeshire
Newmarket
10834 Richard Ginn, miller
May, *Newmarket*, 1976, pp. 37-38
10835 William Raby, tobacconist
May, *Newmarket*, 1976, pp. 38-39
10836 Thos: Scotman, [groom]
May, *Newmarket*, 1976, pp. 39-41
Sawston Hall
10837 Henry Huddleston, esquire
Teversham, *Sawston*, 1947, pp. 128-132

Cheshire
Sale
10838 James Dickenson alias Heyward, [husbandman]
Groves, *Ashton-on-Mersey and Sale*, 2002, p. 58

Devonshire
Clayhidon
10839 Nicholas Tucker
Worthy, *Devonshire*, 1896, pp. 221-222
Uffculme
10840 Jno [John] Blackaller
Wyatt, *Uffculme*, 1997, pp. 170
10841 Richard Gill
Wyatt, *Uffculme*, 1997, pp. 170-172

10842   Joane Piprill [Pepprell]
Wyatt, *Uffculme*, 1997, pp. 172-173

Essex
Roxwell
  10843   John Battle
  Steer, *Mid-Essex*, 1969, pp. 240-241
  10844   John Nash
  Steer, *Mid-Essex*, 1969, pp. 238-239
Sewardstone, Powder Mills
  10845   George Wharton, esquire
  Crocker and Fairclough, 1998, p. 33
Writtle, Horsefrith Park
  10846   Richard Brown, yeoman
  Steer, *Mid-Essex*, 1969, pp. 239-240
Writtle
  10847   Edmond Butler
  Steer, *Mid-Essex*, 1969, pp. 241-242

Gloucestershire
Charlton Kings
  10848   Edward Churches, [husbandman]
  Paget and Sale, *Charlton Kings*, 2003, p. 101
  10849   William Danford, [weaver]
  Paget and Sale, *Charlton Kings*, 2003, p. 100
  10850   Joan Gregory, widow
  Paget and Sale, *Charlton Kings*, 2003, p. 101
Cheltenham
  10851   Elinor Bannaster, widow
  Sale, *Cheltenham*, 1999, pp. 120-121
  10852   Richard Beckett, mercer
  Sale, *Cheltenham*, 1999, p. 119
  10853   Frances Ellis
  Sale, *Cheltenham*, 1999, p. 118
  10854   Edward Nichols, yeoman
  Sale, *Cheltenham*, 1999, pp. 119-120
Frampton Cotterell
  10855   Sarah Embly, widow
  Moore, *Frampton Cotterell*, 1976, p. 215
Westerleigh
  10856   Giles Humphreys, yeoman
  Moore, *Frampton Cotterell*, 1976, pp. 214-215

Leicestershire
Evington
  10857   Susannah Frostlin
  Wilshere, *Evington*, 1985, p. 40
  10858   Nicholas Spencer, weaver
  Wilshere, *Evington*, 1985, p. 40
Kirby Muxloe
  10859   George Raynor, [gentleman]
  Wilshere, *Kirby Muxloe*, 1983, p. 24

Lincolnshire
Lincoln
  10860   Charles Newcomen, woollen draper
  Johnston, *Lincoln*, 1991, pp. 137-142
Winteringham
  10861   John Sutton
  Neave, *Winteringham*, 1984, p. 140
  10862   John Williamson
  Neave, *Winteringham*, 1984, pp. 140-141

Northamptonshire
Thornhaugh
  10863   Thomas Alderman, yeoman
  Alderman, *Alderman*, 2008, pp. 69-72

Shropshire
Broseley
  10864   Edward Nash, coalminer, collier
  Trinder and Cox, *Severn Gorge*, 2000, pp. 183-184
Lilleshall, Muxton
  10865   Thomasin Hawkins
  Trinder and Cox, *Telford*, 1980, pp. 235-237
Little Wenlock
  10866   William Whyston, clergyman, rector of Little
  Wenlock
  Trinder and Cox, *Severn Gorge*, 2000, pp. 250-252
Wellington
  10867   Henry Wood, clergyman, vicar of Wellington
  Trinder and Cox, *Telford*, 1980, pp. 343-344

Staffordshire
Gornal Wood
  10868   John Hickmans, nailer
  Roper, *Sedgley*, 1960, p. 105
Smethwick
  10869   Beata Hunt, widow
  Bodfish, *Smethwick*, 1992, pp. 50-51

Sussex
Chailey
  10870   William Rootes, clergyman [rector of Chailey]
  Hughes, *Sussex*, 2007, p. 43

Westmorland
Stangerthwaite, Kirkby Lonsdale
  10871   Joseph Baines, yeoman
  Collingwood, 1929, pp. 11-12

Wiltshire
Marlborough
  10872   Richard Edney, gentleman
  Williams and Thomson, *Marlborough*, 2007, pp. 255-256
  10873   Frances Hurlbut, [carpenter]
  Williams and Thomson, *Marlborough*, 2007, pp. 254-255

Yorkshire
Barnoldswick, Salterforth
  10874   James Green
  Kirk, *Barnoldswick*, 1951, p. 63
Whitby
  10875   Robert Christian
  Vickers, *Whitby*, 1986, p. 62

1714
Bristol
Bristol, St John
  10876   John Bowen
  George, *Bristol*, 2008, pp. 75-76
Bristol
  10877   Richard Jones, gunsmith
  George, *Bristol*, 2008, pp. 76-79
  10878   Walter King, hot presser
  George, *Bristol*, 2008, pp. 79-80
  10879   John Mann, [cork cutter]
  George, *Bristol*, 2008, pp. 80-83
Lawrence Weston
  10880   Richard Camborne, yeoman
  Moore, *Clifton*, 1981, pp. 184-186

Buckinghamshire
Stoke Poges
  10881   Henry Reeve, gentleman
  Reed, *Buckinghamshire*, 1988, pp. 314-317

Cheshire
Ashton-on-Mersey
  10882 Samuel Renshaw
    Groves, *Ashton-on-Mersey and Sale*, 2002, pp. 64-65
Sale
  10883 Margaret Daine, [widow]
    Groves, *Ashton-on-Mersey and Sale*, 2002, p. 60
Devonshire
Uffculme
  10884 William Davy, husbandman
    Wyatt, *Uffculme*, 1997, pp. 173
  10885 John Quicke, mason
    Wyatt, *Uffculme*, 1997, p p. 173-175
Essex
Roxwell
  10886 Henry Isaacson
    Steer, *Mid-Essex*, 1969, pp. 242-243
Gloucestershire
Charlton Kings
  10887 John Gale
    Paget and Sale, *Charlton Kings*, 2003, pp. 102-103
Cheltenham
  10888 James Smallpeece, [gentleman]
    Sale, *Cheltenham*, 1999, p. 122
Frampton Cotterell
  10889 John Gibbons, [yeoman]
    Moore, *Frampton Cotterell*, 1976, pp. 218-219
  10890 George Rodman, [yeoman]
    Moore, *Frampton Cotterell*, 1976, p. 220
  10891 John Tyler, [feltmaker]
    Moore, *Frampton Cotterell*, 1976, p. 218
Hambrook
  10892 Edward Hignell, maltster
    Moore, *Frampton Cotterell*, 1976, pp. 215-216
Iron Acton
  10893 Elizabeth Holdbrook, widow
    Moore, *Frampton Cotterell*, 1976, pp. 219-220
  10894 William Short, [yeoman]
    Moore, *Frampton Cotterell*, 1976, pp. 216-217
Westerleigh
  10895 John Hall, husbandman
    Moore, *Frampton Cotterell*, 1976, p. 218
  10896 Thomas Prigg, [yeoman]
    Moore, *Frampton Cotterell*, 1976, p. 219
Winterbourne
  10897 Mary Pillorne, widow [mercer]
    Moore, *Frampton Cotterell*, 1976, p. 217
Hertfordshire
Hertford
  10898 Mary Cornell
    Adams, *Hertford*, 1997, p. 90
Kent
Nettlestead
  10899 Thomas Brewer, clergyman, rector of
Nettlestead
    Melling, 1965, pp. 62-64
Leicestershire
Evington
  10900 Thomas Burley, farmer
    Wilshere, *Evington*, 1985, p. 41
  10901 William Burley, shepherd
    Wilshere, *Evington*, 1985, p. 42

Kirby Muxloe
  10902 William Mitchell, [grazier]
    Wilshere, *Kirby Muxloe*, 1983, p. 25
Lincolnshire
Caythorpe
  10903 Thomas Simpson, chapman
    Spufford, *Reclothing*, 1984, pp. 169-170
Cleethorpes
  10904 William Crowston, husbandman
    Ambler, Watkinson, *Clee*, 1987, pp. 170-172
Lincoln, St Martins
  10905 Elizabeth Gryme, widow
    Johnston, *Lincoln*, 1991, p. 142
Lincoln, St Swithins
  10906 Margaret Lees
    Johnston, *Lincoln*, 1991, p. 142
Winteringham
  10907 Thomas Ferris
    Neave, *Winteringham*, 1984, pp. 141-142
  10908 Anne Fowler
    Neave, *Winteringham*, 1984, p. 141
Scotland
Edinburgh, Palace of Holyroodhouse
  10909 Queen Anne
    Steuart, 1928, pp. 187-194
Shropshire
Lilleshall
  10910 Edward Owen, webster
    Trinder and Cox, *Telford*, 1980, pp. 237-238
Little Wenlock
  10911 George Wheelwright, yeoman
    Trinder and Cox, *Severn Gorge*, 2000, pp. 252-254
  10912 William Wheelwright, yeoman
    Trinder and Cox, *Severn Gorge*, 2000, pp. 255-256
Madeley
  10913 William Roe, yeoman
    Trinder and Cox, *Severn Gorge*, 2000, pp. 295-296
Wellington, Cluddley
  10914 Richard Beamond, day labourer
    Trinder and Cox, *Telford*, 1980, p. 346
Wellington
  10915 Thomas Stanworth
    Trinder and Cox, *Telford*, 1980, pp. 344-346
Wrockwardine, Allscott
  10916 Joshua Calcott
    Trinder and Cox, *Telford*, 1980, pp. 430-431
Staffordshire
Coseley
  10917 William Evans, nailer
    Roper, *Sedgley*, 1960, p. 106
Sedgley
  10918 Joseph Keysall, miller
    Roper, *Sedgley*, 1960, p. 107
Sussex
Bolney
  10919 John Gratwick, clergyman [vicar of Bolney]
    Hughes, *Sussex*, 2007, pp. 31-32
Warwickshire
Stoneleigh, Fletchamstead
  10920 Jacob Gibbs, day labourer
    Alcock, *Warwickshire*, 1993, p. 140

Wiltshire
Marlborough
10921   Edward Bell, gentleman
Williams and Thomson, *Marlborough*, 2007, pp. 256-258
10922   John Jones, tailor
Williams and Thomson, *Marlborough*, 2007, pp. 258-259
Worcestershire
Ombersley, Acton Hall
10923   John Bourne, esquire
Wanklyn, *Worcestershire*, 1998, pp. 329-330
Yorkshire
Barnoldswick, Barnsay
10924   Jonathan Booth
Kirk, *Barnoldswick*, 1951, p. 58
Barnoldswick, Salterforth
10925   John Hartley, yeoman
Kirk, *Barnoldswick*, 1951, p. 67
10926   Richard Nunweek, husbandman
Kirk, *Barnoldswick*, 1951, pp. 74-75
Barnoldswick, Coates
10927   John Varley
Kirk, *Barnoldswick*, 1951, p. 81

1715
Bristol
Bristol
10928   Robert Barnes, cordwainer
George, *Bristol*, 2008, pp. 83-84
10929   Mary Garland, widow
George, *Bristol*, 2008, pp. 84-85
10930   John Green, shipwright
George, *Bristol*, 2008, p. 86
Westbury
10931   John Hort, gentleman
Moore, *Clifton*, 1981, pp. 186-188
Cheshire
Sale
10932   Thomas Davies, [yeoman]
Groves, *Ashton-on-Mersey and Sale*, 2002, pp. 68-69
Gloucestershire
Cheltenham
10933   Frances Allen alias Cooper
Sale, *Cheltenham*, 1999, p. 125
Cheltenham, Arle
10934   John Arthurs alias Pavior
Sale, *Cheltenham*, 1999, p. 127
Cheltenham, Alstone
10935   Samuel Church, husbandman
Sale, *Cheltenham*, 1999, p. 128
Cheltenham
10936   Anne Kemett, widow
Sale, *Cheltenham*, 1999, pp. 126-127
Cheltenham, Alstone
10937   William Roberts, gentleman
Sale, *Cheltenham*, 1999, p. 129
Iron Acton
10938   Edmund Butt, [yeoman]
Moore, *Frampton Cotterell*, 1976, pp. 221-222
Westerleigh
10939   John Nicols, coalminer
Moore, *Frampton Cotterell*, 1976, p. 223
Winterbourne
10940   Thomas Priggs, feltmaker
Moore, *Frampton Cotterell*, 1976, pp. 220-221

10941   Samuel Voules, innholder
Moore, *Frampton Cotterell*, 1976, p. 222
Hertfordshire
St Albans, St Stephens, The Noke
10942   Bethia Edmonds, widow
Munby, *Worldly Goods*, 1991, p. 199
St Albans, St Stephens, Black Green
10943   Joseph Rowe
Munby, *Worldly Goods*, 1991, pp. 196-197
Leicesteshire
Evington
10944   Job Bull
Wilshere, *Evington*, 1985, p. 42
10945   Barbery Serjant
Wilshere, *Evington*, 1985, p. 43
Glenfield, Kirby Frith
10946   Mrs Cath. Styan, [widow]
Wilshere, *Glenfield*, 1983, p. 11
Lincolnshire
Cleethorpes
10947   Thomas Portas, husbandman
Ambler, Watkinson, *Clee*, 1987, p. 172
London
Pall Mall, St James's
10948   Francis Lapiere, [upholsterer]
Westman, 1994, pp. 7-12
Somerset House
10949   Wilhelmina Carolina, Princess of Wales [later Queen]
Shaw and Slingsby, 1957, pp. 834-835
Shropshire
Broseley
10950   Edward Cox, carrier
Trinder and Cox, *Severn Gorge*, 2000, p. 184
Dawley, Little Dawley
10951   Podmore Peploe
Trinder and Cox, *Telford*, 1980, p. 176
Little Wenlock
10952   John Fletcher, yeoman, blacksmith
Trinder and Cox, *Severn Gorge*, 2000, pp. 254-255
Little Wenlock, Huntington
10953   Richard Jervis
Trinder and Cox, *Severn Gorge*, 2000, pp. 249-250
Madeley
10954   Audley Bowdler, yeoman
Trinder and Cox, *Severn Gorge*, 2000, pp. 297-298
Wrockwardine Wood, Pains Lane
10955   Allen Pickering
Trinder and Cox, *Telford*, 1980, p. 431
Staffordshire
Harborne
10956   Shuanah Hillman
Bodfish, *Smethwick*, 1992, p. 52
Warwickshire
Wappenbury
10957   John Ebroll
Sheasby, 1994, p. 62
Wiltshire
Marlborough
10958   Robert Bayly
Williams and Thomson, *Marlborough*, 2007, p. 260
10959   William Coster, weaver
Williams and Thomson, *Marlborough*, 2007, p. 259

10960 Jane Spackman, widow
Williams and Thomson, *Marlborough*, 2007, pp. 259-260
10961 Mr Henry Stent
Williams and Thomson, *Marlborough*, 2007, pp. 261-262
10962 John Tetcombe, cordwainer
Williams and Thomson, *Marlborough*, 2007, p. 261

Yorkshire
Haverah Park, Beckwithshaw
10963 Thomas Stubb, yeoman
Collins, *Stubbs*, 1915, pp. 123-124
Horbury
10964 Benjamin Coop, clothmaker
Bartlett, *Horbury*, 1980, pp. 43-44
10965 William Thornes, mason
Bartlett, *Horbury*, 1980, pp. 40-41
Unlocated
10966 Jno Newmarsh
Hall, *Beverley*, 1986, pp. 80-81
Whitby
10967 Richard Fletcher, tailor
Vickers, *Whitby*, 1986, p. 64
10968 Elizabeth Morrison, widow
Vickers, *Whitby*, 1986, pp. 62-63
10969 George Readman, sailmaker
Vickers, *Whitby*, 1986, p. 64

1715 (c.)
Wiltshire
Marlborough
10970 [Mary] Blackman
Williams and Thomson, *Marlborough*, 2007, pp. 260-261
10971 Benjamin New, fellmonger
Williams and Thomson, *Marlborough*, 2007, p. 261

1716
Bristol
Bristol
10972 William Butcher, upholsterer
George, *Bristol*, 2008, pp. 86-90
10973 Isaac Dawson, cork cutter
George, *Bristol*, 2008, pp. 90-92
10974 John Hisketh, mariner
George, *Bristol*, 2008, p. 92
Shirehampton
10975 William Harford, pilot
Moore, *Clifton*, 1981, p. 188

Cheshire
Ashton-on-Mersey
10976 Richard Irlam, [yeoman]
Groves, *Ashton-on-Mersey and Sale*, 2002, p. 72
10977 John Newton, [yeoman]
Groves, *Ashton-on-Mersey and Sale*, 2002, pp. 96-97
10978 William Smith, [yeoman]
Groves, *Ashton-on-Mersey and Sale*, 2002, pp. 78-79
Congleton
10979 George Lamb, chapman
Spufford, *Reclothing*, 1984, pp. 196-200
Sale, The Low House
10980 John Barlow, [yeoman]
Groves, *Ashton-on-Mersey and Sale*, 2002, pp. 81-82
Sale
10981 Thomas Moores, [yeoman]
Groves, *Ashton-on-Mersey and Sale*, 2002, pp. 92-93

Dorsetshire
Chetnole
10982 Thomas Cave, tanner
Machin, *Yetminster*, 1976, No.124, (1 p.)
Leigh
10983 Richard Miller
Machin, *Yetminster*, 1976, No.123, (1 p.)

Essex
Roxwell
10984 Isaac Day, blacksmith
Steer, *Mid-Essex*, 1969, pp. 243-244
10985 William Ling
Steer, *Mid-Essex*, 1969, pp. 244-245

Gloucestershire
Charlton Kings
10986 Richard Bowyer, [husbandman]
Paget and Sale, *Charlton Kings*, 2003, pp. 104-105
10987 Henry Collett, [yeoman]
Paget and Sale, *Charlton Kings*, 2003, pp. 103-104
Cheltenham
10988 Charles Ellis, husbandman
Sale, *Cheltenham*, 1999, pp. 133-134
10989 Francis Hurst, butcher
Sale, *Cheltenham*, 1999, pp. 131-132
10990 Elizabeth Iles, [widow]
Sale, *Cheltenham*, 1999, p. 133
10991 John Kemit, [carrier]
Sale, *Cheltenham*, 1999, p. 132
Frampton Cotterell
10992 Edith Hathway
Moore, *Frampton Cotterell*, 1976, pp. 223-224
Iron Acton
10993 Joan Short, widow
Moore, *Frampton Cotterell*, 1976, p. 223

Kent
East Peckham
10994 Thomas Pattenden, yeoman
Sherwood, 1948, pp. 72-74

Leicestershire
Evington
10995 Thomas Davenport
Wilshere, *Evington*, 1985, p. 43

Lincolnshire
Clee
10996 Ann Buerlah
Ambler, Watkinson, *Clee*, 1987, p. 173
10997 William Towill
Ambler, Watkinson, *Clee*, 1987, pp. 172-173
Winteringham
10998 Richd Bratton, husbandman
Neave, *Winteringham*, 1984, p. 142
10999 Ann Westoby
Neave, *Winteringham*, 1984, p. 143

Nottinghamshire
Nottingham
11000 Fortune Smith, widow
Smith, 1861, p. 34r

Scotland
Cawdor Castle
11001 Sir Hugh Campbell
Anon., *Cawdor*, 1859, pp. 418-420

Shropshire
Dawley, Great Dawley
11002 William Poyner
Trinder and Cox, *Telford*, 1980, pp. 176-177
Wellington
11003 William Birch, apothecary and surgeon
Trinder and Cox, *Telford*, 1980, pp. 348-349
11004 William Doughty
Trinder and Cox, *Telford*, 1980, pp. 349-351
11005 Elizabeth Judgson, innkeeper and widow
Trinder and Cox, *Telford*, 1980, p. 347
Staffordshire
Acton Trussell
11006 Mr George Hichcock [Hitchcock], clergyman, minister of Acton Trussell
Anon., *Acton Trussell*, 1995, pp. 60-62
Surrey
Charlwood
11007 William Penfold
Harding, *Charlwood*, 1976, p. 115
11008 Richard Willett
Harding, *Charlwood*, 1976, pp. 114-115
Wales
Glamorganshire, Peterston-super-Ely
11009 Arnold Pranch
Wrench, *Wrenche*, 1956, pp. 59-60
Wiltshire
Marlborough
11010 Benjamin Bassett, victualler
Williams and Thomson, *Marlborough*, 2007, p. 263
11011 Thomas Keats, maltster
Williams and Thomson, *Marlborough*, 2007, p. 262
11012 Leonard Leach, tailor
Williams and Thomson, *Marlborough*, 2007, pp. 263-264
11013 Abigell Pagge [Page], widow
Williams and Thomson, *Marlborough*, 2007, p. 263
Yorkshire
York
11014 John White, printer
Davies, 1868, pp. 377-380

1717

Bristol
Bristol
11015 Simon Barkwell, mariner
George, *Bristol*, 2008, p. 92
11016 Thomas Hodges, mariner
George, *Bristol*, 2008, pp. 92-93
Bristol, Barton Regis
11017 Henry Lascells, brick maker
George, *Bristol*, 2008, pp. 93-94
Clifton
11018 Jane Wickham, widow
Moore, *Clifton*, 1981, p. 192
Westbury
11019 Joseph Floyd, victualler
Moore, *Clifton*, 1981, pp. 189-191
11020 Richard Horwood, slaughterman
Moore, *Clifton*, 1981, pp. 191-192
Cambridgeshire
Sawston
11021 Richard Huddleston
Teversham, *Sawston*, 1947, p. 134

Cheshire
Ashton-on-Mersey
11022 Thomas Ellison, clergyman, rector of Ashton-on-Mersey
Groves, *Ashton-on-Mersey and Sale*, 2002, pp. 87-89
Sale
11023 Matthew Cockson, [blacksmith]
Groves, *Ashton-on-Mersey and Sale*, 2002, p. 84
Dorsetshire
Yetminster
11024 John Vicker
Machin, *Yetminster*, 1976, No.125, (2 pp.)
Essex
Roxwell
11025 Stephen Chalke
Steer, *Mid-Essex*, 1969, pp. 245-246
Gloucestershire
Cheltenham
11026 Bridgett Petty, widow
Sale, *Cheltenham*, 1999, p. 135
Frampton Cotterell
11027 Francis Roberts, [feltmaker]
Moore, *Frampton Cotterell*, 1976, pp. 229-230
Frenchay
11028 James Thomas, quarrier
Moore, *Frampton Cotterell*, 1976, pp. 228-229
Hambrook
11029 Mary Simmons, widow
Moore, *Frampton Cotterell*, 1976, p. 229
Westerleigh
11030 Martha Clare, widow
Moore, *Frampton Cotterell*, 1976, p. 227
11031 James Kennison, yeoman
Moore, *Frampton Cotterell*, 1976, p. 230
Westerleigh, Says
11032 William Thomas, gentleman
Moore, *Frampton Cotterell*, 1976, pp. 224-227
Winterbourne
11033 Margaret Cole, widow
Moore, *Frampton Cotterell*, 1976, p. 228
Ireland
Corofin House, Co. Clare
11034 Lucius O'Brien
Fenlon, *Ireland*, 2003, pp. 127-129
Kent
Rochester, St Nicholas
11035 Edward Sackley, salesman
Spufford, *Reclothing*, 1984, pp. 217-223
Lincolnshire
Clee
11036 John Rowson
Ambler, Watkinson, *Clee*, 1987, pp. 173-174
Scotland
Edinburgh
11037 Agnes Campbell, widow
Anon., *Bassandyne*, 1836, pp. 284-289
Orkney, Shapinsay Sound
11038 Jannet Buchanan
Marwick, 1934, pp. 47-48
Shropshire
Broseley
11039 Mary Ogden, widow
Trinder and Cox, *Severn Gorge*, 2000, pp. 184-185

Lilleshall
  11040 Robert Shelton, yeoman
    Trinder and Cox, *Telford*, 1980, pp. 238-240
Little Wenlock
  11041 William Wheelwright, yeoman
    Trinder and Cox, *Severn Gorge*, 2000, pp. 256-257
Madeley, Furnace Bank
  11042 George Deuksell, yeoman
    Trinder and Cox, *Severn Gorge*, 2000, pp. 298-299
Wellington, Hadley
  11043 Robert Roe, clergyman
    Trinder and Cox, *Telford*, 1980, pp. 351-352
Wrockwardine Wood, Quob Pool
  11044 William Ball, collier
    Trinder and Cox, *Telford*, 1980, pp. 431-432
Surrey
Charlwood
  11045 Edward Gardner
    Harding, *Charlwood*, 1976, pp. 115-116
Sussex
Midhurst
  11046 Richard Townsend, clergyman [curate of Midhurst]
    Hughes, *Sussex*, 2007, pp. 141-142
Warwickshire
Stoneleigh, Hurst
  11047 John Franklin, husbandman
    Alcock, *Warwickshire*, 1993, pp. 79-80
Stoneleigh
  11048 James Kickin, labourer
    Alcock, *Warwickshire*, 1993, p. 167
Stoneleigh, Fletchamstead
  11049 Joanna Sly, widow
    Alcock, *Warwickshire*, 1993, pp. 127-128
Wiltshire
Marlborough
  11050 Thomas Blandy, maltster
    Williams and Thomson, *Marlborough*, 2007, pp. 264-265
  11051 Simon Hamlen
    Williams and Thomson, *Marlborough*, 2007, p. 264
Yorkshire
Horbury
  11052 Sarah Horner, widow
    Bartlett, *Horbury*, 1980, p. 50
  11053 Thomas Hunt, carpenter
    Bartlett, *Horbury*, 1980, pp. 46-48

1718
Bristol
Bristol
  11054 Richard Legg, keeper of the gaol at Newgate
    George, *Bristol*, 2008, pp. 94-95
  11055 Thomas Prosser, bodice maker
    George, *Bristol*, 2008, pp. 95-96
  11056 Joseph Rosser, house carpenter
    George, *Bristol*, 2008, pp. 96-98
  11057 Walter Seymour, basket-maker
    George, *Bristol*, 2008, pp. 98-101
  11058 Elizabeth Waterford, widow [sacking seller]
    George, *Bristol*, 2008, pp. 101-102
Westbury
  11059 Mary Bowen, widow
    Moore, *Clifton*, 1981, p. 193
  11060 Thomas Jones, potter
    Moore, *Clifton*, 1981, p. 193
  11061 William Preston, mariner
    Moore, *Clifton*, 1981, p. 193
Cheshire
Ashton-on-Mersey
  11062 Joshua Hall, [yeoman]
    Groves, *Ashton-on-Mersey and Sale*, 2002, p. 99
Bowdon
  11063 John Hardy, joiner
    Groves, *Bowdon*, 1999, pp. 31-32
Cumberland
Carlisle
  11064 Edward Orfeur, gentleman
    Jackson, *Orfeurs*, 1878, p. 120
Penrith
  11065 Mrs Frances Hudleston
    Jackson, *Hudlestons*, 1891, p. 455
Dorsetshire
Chetnole
  11066 John Beasant, [miller, baker?]
    Machin, *Yetminster*, 1976, No.126, (2 pp.)
Leigh
  11067 John Perrate
    Machin, *Yetminster*, 1976, No.127, (1 p.)
Essex
Roxwell
  11068 Francis Allin
    Steer, *Mid-Essex*, 1969, p. 246
Gloucestershire
Charlton Kings
  11069 Richard Parrott, husbandman
    Paget and Sale, *Charlton Kings*, 2003, p. 105
Cheltenham
  11070 Samuel King, maltster
    Sale, *Cheltenham*, 1999, pp. 137-138
  11071 Francis Spencer, yeoman
    Sale, *Cheltenham*, 1999, p. 136
Westerleigh
  11072 John Love, carpenter
    Moore, *Frampton Cotterell*, 1976, p. 231
  11073 Thomas Price, [coalminer]
    Moore, *Frampton Cotterell*, 1976, p. 231
Leicestershire
Kirby Muxloe
  11074 John Bradley, [husbandman?]
    Wilshere, *Kirby Muxloe*, 1983, p. 25
Lincolnshire
Clee
  11075 Eliz Portus
    Ambler, Watkinson, *Clee*, 1987, p. 174
London
St James's Square
  11076 Esther Hervart, Marquise de la Tour, widow
    Askew, 1874, pp. 199-204
Northamptonshire
Boughton House
  11077 John, Duke of Montagu
    Murdoch, *Noble Households*, 2006, pp. 62-70
Nottinghamshire
Clayworth
  11078 Christopher Johnson, gentleman
    Arkell, Evans, Goose, 2000, pp. 378-379

Shropshire
Broseley
11079 George Bayley, shopkeeper
Trinder and Cox, *Severn Gorge*, 2000, p. 186
11080 Robert Whitmore, tallow chandler
Trinder and Cox, *Severn Gorge*, 2000, pp. 185-186
Lilleshall, Muxton
11081 William Cartwright, mathematician
Trinder and Cox, *Telford*, 1980, pp. 240-241
Wellington
11082 John Shipman, blacksmith
Trinder and Cox, *Telford*, 1980, pp. 352-353
Staffordshire
Lower Gornal
11083 Robert Marsh, nailer
Roper, *Sedgley*, 1960, p. 109
Sussex
Up Waltham
11084 Henry Wright, clergyman [rector of Upwaltham]
Hughes, *Sussex*, 2007, pp. 221-222
Wiston
11085 Samuel Padie, clergyman [rector of Wiston]
Hughes, *Sussex*, 2007, pp. 241-242
Wiltshire
Marlborough
11086 Sarah Edney, widow
Williams and Thomson, *Marlborough*, 2007, p. 266
11087 John Furnell, cheese factor
Williams and Thomson, *Marlborough*, 2007, pp. 267-268
11088 Stephen Perry, collarmaker
Williams and Thomson, *Marlborough*, 2007, pp. 265-266
11089 John Tomblyns
Williams and Thomson, *Marlborough*, 2007, p. 267
Yorkshire
Doncaster
11090 William Walker, alderman [draper]
Hey, *Doncaster*, 1997, pp. 144-147
Whitby
11091 Christopher Hill, master mariner
Vickers, *Whitby*, 1986, pp. 64-65

1718 (c.)
Wiltshire
Marlborough
11092 Jane Sloper, widow
Williams and Thomson, *Marlborough*, 2007, pp. 266-267

1719
Cheshire
Sale
11093 Thomas Pearson
Groves, *Ashton-on-Mersey and Sale*, 2002, pp. 101-102
Devonshire
Uffculme
11094 Christopher Bishop, yeoman
Wyatt, *Uffculme*, 1997, pp. 176-177
11095 Richard Rugge
Wyatt, *Uffculme*, 1997, pp. 175-176
Essex
Great Warley
11096 Mrs Elizabeth Arnold
Anon., *Domestic*, 1909, pp. 58-59

Roxwell
11097 Henry Turnidge
Steer, *Mid-Essex*, 1969, pp. 247-248
Unlocated
11098 Widow Flack
Steer, *Mid-Essex*, 1969, pp. 246-247
Gloucestershire
Cheltenham
11099 William Arnold, apothecary
Sale, *Cheltenham*, 1999, pp. 140-141
Cheltenham, Arle
11100 John Brock
Sale, *Cheltenham*, 1999, pp. 138-139
Cheltenham
11101 Mr James Wood, maltster
Sale, *Cheltenham*, 1999, pp. 142-143
Iron Acton, Latteridge
11102 John Keene, yeoman
Moore, *Frampton Cotterell*, 1976, pp. 231-232
Iron Acton
11103 John Tuck, [yeoman]
Moore, *Frampton Cotterell*, 1976, p. 231
Westerleigh
11104 Henry Goff, blacksmith
Moore, *Frampton Cotterell*, 1976, pp. 232-233
Leicestershire
Ratby, Little Newtown
11105 Mr John Hunt, [yeoman]
Wilshere, *Ratby*, 1984, p. 5
Ratby
11106 Mary Ley, widow
Wilshere, *Ratby*, 1984, p. 6
Lincolnshire
Clee
11107 Thomas Allenby, yeoman
Ambler, Watkinson, *Clee*, 1987, pp. 174-175
Winteringham
11108 Blaze Feris
Neave, *Winteringham*, 1984, p. 145
11109 Wm Sawyer
Neave, *Winteringham*, 1984, pp. 143-144
Middlesex
Hampton
11110 Benjamin Jackson, [Master Mason of the King's Works]
Boynton, 1990, pp. 22-26
Sunbury
11111 William Buckland, [carpenter]
Heselton, *Sunbury*, 1976, pp. 11-12
Shropshire
Benthall
11112 George Bradley, trowman
Trinder and Cox, *Severn Gorge*, 2000, p. 131
Broseley
11113 John Mayor
Trinder and Cox, *Severn Gorge*, 2000, pp. 186-187
Madeley Wood
11114 Roger Downes, brassfounder
Trinder and Cox, *Severn Gorge*, 2000, pp. 302-303
Madeley
11115 Roger Roe, yeoman
Trinder and Cox, *Severn Gorge*, 2000, pp. 299-302

Wrockwardine, Oaken Gates
 11116 John Yarsley, collier
 Trinder and Cox, *Telford*, 1980, pp. 422-433
Wiltshire
Marlborough
 11117 Francis Bowsher, innholder
 Williams and Thomson, *Marlborough*, 2007, pp. 270-272
 11118 Katherine Hill, widow
 Williams and Thomson, *Marlborough*, 2007, pp. 269-270
 11119 William Hill, butcher
 Williams and Thomson, *Marlborough*, 2007, p. 269
 11120 Alice Stokes, widow
 Williams and Thomson, *Marlborough*, 2007, pp. 268-269
Worcestershire
Suckley, The White House
 11121 Hiam [Heigham] Coke, esquire
 Wanklyn, *Worcestershire*, 1998, pp. 330-334
Yorkshire
Barnoldswick, Moor Close
 11122 William Atkinson
 Kirk, *Barnoldswick*, 1951, p. 56
Barnoldswick
 11123 John Bancroft
 Kirk, *Barnoldswick*, 1951, p. 57
 Barley, *Farmhouse and Cottage*, 1961, p. 287
Horbury
 11124 Elizabeth Cockell, widow
 Bartlett, *Horbury*, 1980, pp. 49-50
 11125 Samuel Hoyle, yeoman
 Bartlett, *Horbury*, 1980, pp. 52-53

1719 (c.)
Wiltshire
Marlborough
 11126 Ruth Smith
 Williams and Thomson, *Marlborough*, 2007, p. 268

1720
Berkshire
Purley Hall
 11127 Francis Hawes, esquire (also listed Winchester
 Street, London, and Kettering, Northamptonshire)
 South Sea Company, *Hawes*, 1721, pp. 5-11, 79-82
Bristol
Bristol
 11128 Thomas Avery, stuff maker
 George, *Bristol*, 2008, pp. 102-104
 11129 John Yealfe, saddler
 George, *Bristol*, 2008, pp. 104-105
Clifton
 11130 Mary Lowe, widow
 Moore, *Clifton*, 1981, p. 197
Shirehampton
 11131 John Morgan, mariner
 Moore, *Clifton*, 1981, p. 197
Cheshire
Ashton-on-Mersey
 11132 William Hancock, [yeoman]
 Groves, *Ashton-on-Mersey and Sale*, 2002, p. 103
Devonshire
Uffculme
 11133 John Caddy, woolbroker
 Wyatt, *Uffculme*, 1997, pp. 179
 11134 Robert Persey, husbandman
 Wyatt, *Uffculme*, 1997, pp. 177-179

Essex
Roxwell
 11135 John Brown
 Steer, *Mid-Essex*, 1969, pp. 249-250
 11136 John Overill, miller
 Steer, *Mid-Essex*, 1969, p. 249
Wanstead
 Robert Surman, cashier (see South Sea House, London)
Writtle
 11137 John Bridgman, gardener
 Steer, *Mid-Essex*, 1969, pp. 251-252
 11138 William Clary
 Steer, *Mid-Essex*, 1969, pp. 250-251
Gloucestershire
Charlton Kings
 11139 Thomas Gardner, [yeoman]
 Paget and Sale, *Charlton Kings*, 2003, p. 106
Cheltenham, Alstone
 11140 Richard Combe
 Sale, *Cheltenham*, 1999, p. 140
Cheltenham
 11141 Anne Waters, widow
 Sale, *Cheltenham*, 1999, p. 144
Frampton Cotterell
 11142 Robert Tucker, [yeoman]
 Moore, *Frampton Cotterell*, 1976, p. 234
 11143 Robert Tyler, feltmaker
 Moore, *Frampton Cotterell*, 1976, p. 234
Iron Acton
 11144 Moses Langham, [mason], and his wife, Ann
 Moore, *Frampton Cotterell*, 1976, p. 233
 11145 Edward Martyn, yeoman
 Moore, *Frampton Cotterell*, 1976, p. 233
Westerleigh, Nibley
 11146 Anne Paine, widow
 Moore, *Frampton Cotterell*, 1976, p. 234
Winterbourne
 11147 Robert Burchel, yeoman
 Moore, *Frampton Cotterell*, 1976, p. 233
 11148 William Parker, [yeoman]
 Moore, *Frampton Cotterell*, 1976, p. 235
Hertfordshire
Sarratt
 11149 John Baldwin, yeoman
 Bullen, *Sarratt*, [1982], pp. 254-255
Huntingdonshire
Everton
 11150 William Astell, esquire (also listed London,
 Doctors Commons)
 South Sea Company, *Astell*, 1721, pp. 10, 15, 56
Kent
Greenwich
 Sir Harcourt Master (see Tower Hill, London)
Lancashire
Manchester, Cheetham, Strangeways
 11151 Thomas Reynolds, esquire (also listed
 Victualling Office, London, and Kicksend, Middlesex)
 South Sea Company, *Reynolds*, 1721, pp. 14-20
Leicestershire
Botcheston
 11152 Jos: Weston, [husbandman]
 Wilshere, *Ratby*, 1984, p. 7
Evington
 11153 Mary Noon
 Wilshere, *Evington*, 1985, p. 43

11154   Richard Stretton, [labourer]
Wilshere, *Evington*, 1985, p. 44
Ratby
11155   William Chaner, wheelwright
Wilshere, *Ratby*, 1984, p. 6

Lincolnshire
Cammeringham
Sir Robert Chaplin, baronet (see St Martin's in the Fields, Castle Street, London)
Clee
11156   John Foster
Ambler, Watkinson, *Clee*, 1987, p. 179
11157   William Oates, cocer
Ambler, Watkinson, *Clee*, 1987, p. 178
11158   Thomas Parker, husbandman
Ambler, Watkinson, *Clee*, 1987, p. 177
11159   Mark Tharad, husbandman
Ambler, Watkinson, *Clee*, 1987, p. 177
Cleethorpes
11160   William Atkinson, husbandman
Ambler, Watkinson, *Clee*, 1987, p. 176
11161   William and Jane Atkinson
Ambler, Watkinson, *Clee*, 1987, pp. 176-177
11162   William Taylor
Ambler, Watkinson, *Clee*, 1987, pp. 178-179
Stamford
11163   Richard Hargrave, potter
White, 1979, pp. 290-292
Winteringham
11164   Thomas Fowler, farmer
Neave, *Winteringham*, 1984, pp. 145-146

London
All Hallows Staining, Billiter Square
11165   Richard Houlditch, esquire (also listed Carshalton, Surrey)
South Sea Company, *Houlditch*, 1721, pp. 3-8
Birchin Lane
11166   Sir John Blunt, baronet (also listed Stratford, London)
South Sea Company, *Blunt*, 1721, pp. 9-10, 43-45
Broad Street
11167   Sir William Chapman, baronet (also listed Hampstead, London)
South Sea Company, *Chapman*, 1721, pp. A-E
Chancery Lane
11168   William Tillard, esquire
South Sea Company, *Tillard*, 1721, p. 2
Crosby Square
11169   Edward Gibbon, esquire (also listed Putney)
South Sea Company, *Gibbon*, 1721, pp. 3-7
Devonshire Street
Stephen Child, esquire (see Richmond, Surrey)
Doctors Commons
William Astell, esquire (see Everton, Huntingdonshire)
Hampstead
Sir William Chapman, baronet (see Broad Street)
Hanover Square
11170   Sir Theodore Janssen, knight, baronet (also listed Wimbledon, Surrey)
South Sea Company, *Janssen*, 1721, pp. 1-14
Marine Square
11171   Hugh Raymond, esquire (also listed Saling, Essex)
South Sea Company, *Raymond*, 1721, pp. 21-28

Mincing Lane
11172   Sir John Lambert, baronet
South Sea Company, *Lambert*, 1720, pp. A-B
Putney
Edward Gibbon, esquire (see Crosby Square)
St Clement Danes, Essex Street
11173   Francis Eyles, esquire
South Sea Company, *Eyles*, 1721, p. 9
St John Hackney
11174   Jacob Sawbridge, esquire
South Sea Company, *Sawbridge*, 1721, p. [vii]
St Martin's in the Fields, Castle Street
11175   Sir Robert Chaplin, baronet (also listed Cammeringham, Lincolnshire)
South Sea Company, *Chaplin*, 1721, pp. 3-4, 8-9
St Mary Axe
11176   William Morley, esquire
South Sea Company, *Morley*, 1721, p. 3
St Mary, Stratford Le Bow
11177   Mr Ambrose Page, [brewer]
South Sea Company, *Page*, 1721, p. 20
South Sea House
11178   John Grigsby, accountant
South Sea Company, *Grigsby*, 1721, pp. 24-25
11179   Robert Surman, cashier (also listed Wanstead, Essex)
South Sea Company, *Surman*, 1721, pp. 3-4, 36-38, 40
Stratford
Sir John Blunt, baronet (see Birchin Lane)
Tower Hill
11180   Sir Harcourt Master (also listed Greenwich, Kent)
South Sea Company, *Master*, 1721, pp. 4-10
Unlocated
11181   Sir William Hamond
South Sea Company, *Hamond*, 1721, pp. 27-28
11182   Charles Joye, esquire, merchant
South Sea Company, *Joye*, 1721, p. 4
11183   Samuel Reade, esquire
South Sea Company, *Reade*, 1721, pp. 2, 28-29
Victualling Office
Thomas Reynolds, esquire (see Strangeways, Cheetham, Manchester, Lancashire)
Winchester Street
Francis Hawes, esquire (see Purley Hall, Berkshire)

Middlesex
Kicksend
Thomas Reynolds, esquire (see Strangeways, Cheetham, Manchester, Lancashire)

Norfolk
Great Cressingham
11184   Thomas Leake
Eland, 1947, p. 24

Northamptonshire
Kettering
Francis Hawes, esquire (see Purley Hall, Berkshire)

Oxfordshire
Water Eaton
11185   John Tant
Offord, *Water Eaton*, 1986, p. 48

Shropshire
Benthall, Benthall Hall
11186 Richard Benthall, esquire
Trinder and Cox, *Severn Gorge*, 2000, pp. 131-136
Broseley
11187 Richard Gears, tallow chandler
Trinder and Cox, *Severn Gorge*, 2000, pp. 187-188
Dawley, Malinslee
11188 Charles Eyton, gentleman
Trinder and Cox, *Telford*, 1980, p. 177
Wellington
11189 William Bradshaw
Trinder and Cox, *Telford*, 1980, pp. 354-355
Wellington, Ketley Wood
11190 Jane Eastop
Trinder and Cox, *Telford*, 1980, p. 354
Wellington
11191 George Smith, labourer
Trinder and Cox, *Telford*, 1980, p. 353

Staffordshire
Harborne
11192 John Gosnell
Bodfish, *Smethwick*, 1992, p. 54
Smethwick
11193 Joseph Parkes
Bodfish, *Smethwick*, 1992, p. 53

Surrey
Carshalton
Richard Houlditch, esquire (see Billiter Square, All
Hallows Staining, London)
Charlwood
11194 Stephen Burnett, yeoman
Harding, *Charlwood*, 1976, p. 116
Richmond
11195 Stephen Child, esquire (also listed Devonshire
Street, London)
South Sea Company, *Child*, 1721, pp. 1-3
Wimbledon
Sir Theodore Janssen, knight, baronet (see Hanover
Square, London)

Sussex
Bury
11196 Roger Jones, clergyman [curate of Bury]
Hughes, *Sussex*, 2007, pp. 40-41
Eastbourne
11197 Thomas Bysshe, clergyman [vicar of
Eastbourne]
Hughes, *Sussex*, 2007, pp. 68-70

Warwickshire
Stoneleigh, Fletchamstead
11198 John Barr, yeoman
Alcock, *Warwickshire*, 1993, pp. 149-151

Westmorland
Bampton, Cowdale
11199 Thomas Laws
Jackson, *Laws*, 1876, pp. 270-271

Wiltshire
Marlborough
11200 Janathan Austin [Jonathan Austine], shoemaker
Williams and Thomson, *Marlborough*, 2007, p. 273
11201 William Stapler
Williams and Thomson, *Marlborough*, 2007, pp. 272-273

Yorkshire
Barnoldswick, Salterforth, Far Hey
11202 Richard Wayte, yeoman
Kirk, *Barnoldswick*, 1951, p. 81
Horbury
11203 Francis Blacker, yeoman
Bartlett, *Horbury*, 1980, pp. 54-55
Whitby
11204 Isabell Agar, widow
Vickers, *Whitby*, 1986, p. 66
11205 Elizabeth Chapman, widow
Vickers, *Whitby*, 1986, p. 66
11206 James Close, weaver [castaway at sea]
Vickers, *Whitby*, 1986, pp. 66-67
11207 George Jackson, mariner
Vickers, *Whitby*, 1986, pp. 65-66
11208 Leonard Jefferson, mariner
Vickers, *Whitby*, 1986, p. 67
11209 John Pursglove
Vickers, *Whitby*, 1986, p. 66
11210 John Wilson, mariner
Vickers, *Whitby*, 1986, p. 67

1720 (c.)
Yorkshire
Barnoldswick, Long Carrs
11211 Robert Green, yeoman
Kirk, *Barnoldswick*, 1951, p. 64

1721
Bedfordshire
Chicksands Priory
11212 Sir Danvers Osborn, baronet
Collett-White, *Bedfordshire*, 1995, pp. 27-30
Bristol
Bristol
11213 Peter Brooks, mason
George, *Bristol*, 2008, pp. 105-106
11214 John Brouse, hatter
George, *Bristol*, 2008, p. 107
Westbury
11215 William Jones, [mariner]
Moore, *Clifton*, 1981, p. 198
11216 William Thomas, innholder
Moore, *Clifton*, 1981, p. 198
Cheshire
Ashton-on-Mersey
11217 Sarah Daine, [widow]
Groves, *Ashton-on-Mersey and Sale*, 2002, p. 104
Cumberland
Sebergham, Bell Bridge
11218 Captain Thomas Morris
Ferguson, 1884, pp. 252-252
Devonshire
Clovelly
11219 Joseph Hamlyn
Worthy, *Devonshire*, 1896, p. 264
Dorsetshire
Chetnole
11220 John Annett, [potmaker]
Machin, *Yetminster*, 1976, No.128, (1 p.)
Essex
Writtle
11221 William Flack
Steer, *Mid-Essex*, 1969, p. 252

11222   John Freeman, barber surgeon
Steer, *Mid-Essex*, 1969, p. 253

Gloucestershire
Charlton Kings
11223   Sarah Danford
Paget and Sale, *Charlton Kings*, 2003, p. 107
11224   Edmund Goodrich, yeoman
Paget and Sale, *Charlton Kings*, 2003, pp. 106-107
Cheltenham, Arle
11225   William Arthur, carpenter
Sale, *Cheltenham*, 1999, p. 142
Cheltenham
11226   Jane Cook, widow
Sale, *Cheltenham*, 1999, pp. 150-151
Frampton Cotterell
11227   Samuel Tyler, tanner
Moore, *Frampton Cotterell*, 1976, p. 236
Westerleigh
11228   Elizabeth Cocks, widow [oatmeal maker]
Moore, *Frampton Cotterell*, 1976, p. 235
11229   Samuel Parker, feltmaker
Moore, *Frampton Cotterell*, 1976, pp. 235-236
11230   Robert Rogers, [labourer]
Moore, *Frampton Cotterell*, 1976, p. 235

Hertfordshire
Hunsdon, Briggens
11231   Robert Chester, esquire (also listed French
Ordinary Court, London, and Woodford Lodge,
Unlocated)
South Sea Company, *Chester*, 1721, pp. 77-82

Kent
Tonbridge
11232   Thomas Webb, salesman
Spufford, *Reclothing*, 1984, pp. 224-230

Leicestershire
Evington
11233   Daniell Carter, [framework knitter]
Wilshere, *Evington*, 1985, p. 44
11234   Eliz Spencer
Wilshere, *Evington*, 1985, p. 45
Glenfield
11235   Richard Benet, [yeoman]
Wilshere, *Glenfield*, 1983, p. 11
Kirby Muxloe
11236   Thomas Ballard, labourer
Wilshere, *Kirby Muxloe*, 1983, p. 26
Ratby
11237   William Lilley
Wilshere, *Ratby*, 1984, p. 7

Lincolnshire
Clee, Thrunscoe
11238   William Sherdoun
Ambler, Watkinson, *Clee*, 1987, pp. 180-181
Cleethorpes
11239   Elizabeth Glentworth
Ambler, Watkinson, *Clee*, 1987, p. 180
11240   Matthew Johnsons
Ambler, Watkinson, *Clee*, 1987, pp. 181-182
11241   Abraham Smyth
Ambler, Watkinson, *Clee*, 1987, pp. 179-180
Winteringham
11242   Thomas Snowden
Neave, *Winteringham*, 1984, p. 146

London
French Ordinary Court
Robert Chester, esquire (see Briggens, Hunsdon,
Hertfordshire)
Old Jewry
11243   Sir John Fellowes, baronet (also listed
Carshalton House, Surrey)
South Sea Company, *Fellowes*, 1721, pp. 20-27
Unlocated
11244   Mr John Gore (also listed Kew Green, Surrey)
South Sea Company, *Gore*, 1721, pp. 38-40

Shropshire
Wellington, Ketley
11245   Richard Glover, collier
Trinder and Cox, *Telford*, 1980, pp. 355-356
Wrockwardine Wood, Pains Lane
11246   John Barker, yeoman
Trinder and Cox, *Telford*, 1980, p. 433

Staffordshire
Gornal Wood
11247   Edward Oakley, locksmith
Roper, *Sedgley*, 1960, p. 108

Surrey
Carshalton House
Sir John Fellowes, baronet (see Old Jewry, London)
Kew Green
Mr John Gore (see London, Unlocated)

Sussex
Bignor
11248   Edward Litleton, clergyman [rector of Bignor]
Hughes, *Sussex*, 2007, pp. 21-23
Ditchling
11249   Elnathan Iver, clergyman [vicar of Ditchling]
Hughes, *Sussex*, 2007, pp. 62-63
West Hoathly
11250   William Griffith, clergyman [vicar of West
Hoathly]
Hughes, *Sussex*, 2007, pp. 104-105

Unlocated
Woodford Lodge
Robert Chester, esquire (see Briggens, Hunsdon,
Hertfordshire)

Wiltshire
Marlborough
11251   John Clarke alias Warren
Williams and Thomson, *Marlborough*, 2007, pp. 273-274

Worcestershire
Bewdley
11252   Joseph Harrison, mercer
Bewdley, *Bewdley*, 1991, pp. 193-195

Yorkshire
Barnoldswick, Salterforth
11253   John Hartley, woollen clothier
Kirk, *Barnoldswick*, 1951, pp. 67-68
11254   William Locock
Kirk, *Barnoldswick*, 1951, pp. 73-74

1721 (c.)

Worcestershire
Hanbury
11255   Thomas Vernon, [esquire]
Wanklyn, *Worcestershire*, 1998, pp. 334-335

1722
Cheshire
Ashton-on-Mersey
11256 Richard Gratrix, [yeoman]
Groves, *Ashton-on-Mersey and Sale*, 2002, pp. 107-108
Essex
Unlocated
11257 William Stookes
Steer, *Mid-Essex*, 1969, p. 253
Writtle
11258 Widow Hatchman
Steer, *Mid-Essex*, 1969, p. 253
Gloucestershire
Cheltenham, Alstone
11259 Francis Cleevely, servant
Sale, *Cheltenham*, 1999, p. 147
Cheltenham
11260 Joseph Price, [yeoman]
Sale, *Cheltenham*, 1999, p. 148
11261 William Wills
Sale, *Cheltenham*, 1999, p. 148
Frampton Cotterell
11262 George Chester, [horse-driver]
Moore, *Frampton Cotterell*, 1976, p. 236
11263 James Legg, collier
Moore, *Frampton Cotterell*, 1976, p. 237
11264 James Legg, yeoman
Moore, *Frampton Cotterell*, 1976, p. 236
Hertfordshire
Sarratt
11265 Nathaniell Reeve
Bullen, *Sarratt*, [1982], p. 256
Leicestershire
Braunstone
11266 Wm. Kirke
Wilshere, *Braunstone*, 1983, p. 38
Evington
11267 Rebecca Davenport, [widow]
Wilshere, *Evington*, 1985, p. 45
Ratby
11268 James Kinton, baker
Wilshere, *Ratby*, 1984, p. 8
Lincolnshire
Winteringham
11269 Thomas Sharp
Neave, *Winteringham*, 1984, p. 147
Oxfordshire
Banbury
11270 Henry Upton, [innholder]
Trinder and Gibson, *Banbury*, 1988, pp. 235-237
Scotland
Kincardineshire, Fetteresso
11271 Mary, Countess of Marischal
Fraser, 1897, II, pp. 273-277
Shropshire
Wrockwardine Wood, Trench Lane
11272 Thomas Bold
Trinder and Cox, *Telford*, 1980, p. 434
Staffordshire
Harborne
11273 John Attwood, nailer
Bodfish, *Smethwick*, 1992, pp. 55-56

Upper Gornal
11274 Thomas Maullin, miller
Roper, *Sedgley*, 1960, pp. 110-111
Sussex
Peasmarsh
11275 Stevens Parr, clergyman [vicar of Peasmarsh]
Hughes, *Sussex*, 2007, p. 164
Poling
11276 Thomas Scrivens, clergyman [vicar of Poling]
Hughes, *Sussex*, 2007, p. 168
Warwickshire
King's Coughton
11277 John Fulford
Saville, *King's Coughton*, 1973, pp. 44-45
Stoneleigh, Canley, Moat House
11278 Joseph Badhams, husbandman
Alcock, *Warwickshire*, 1993, pp. 100-101
Stoneleigh, Hurst
11279 Thomas Lee, yeoman
Alcock, *Warwickshire*, 1993, p. 167
Wiltshire
Marlborough
11280 John Fowler, linen draper
Williams and Thomson, *Marlborough*, 2007, pp. 274-277
Worcestershire
Bredon
11281 Edward Hancock, esquire
Wanklyn, *Worcestershire*, 1998, pp. 345-352
Yorkshire
Horbury
11282 John Wood
Bartlett, *Horbury*, 1980, p. 58
Leeds, Armley Heights
11283 Samuel Jackson, [clothier and yeoman]
Snell, 1953, p. 7

1723
Bedfordshire
Colworth House, Sharnbrook
11284 John Antonie, [esquire]
Collett-White, *Bedfordshire*, 1995, pp. 46-48
Bristol
Bristol, St Mary Redcliffe
11285 George Longden, schoolmaster
George, *Bristol*, 2008, pp. 108-109
Bristol, St Thomas
11286 Richard Trivvet
George, *Bristol*, 2008, pp. 110-111
Shirehampton
11287 Edward Tombs, yeoman
Moore, *Clifton*, 1981, p. 199
Essex
Writtle
11288 Abraham Boosey
Steer, *Mid-Essex*, 1969, pp. 255-256
11289 John Herridge, yeoman
Steer, *Mid-Essex*, 1969, pp. 253-255
Gloucestershire
Frampton Cotterell
11290 William Boys, yeoman
Moore, *Frampton Cotterell*, 1976, pp. 237-239
11291 Richard Price, feltmaker
Moore, *Frampton Cotterell*, 1976, p. 237

Westerleigh
11292 Susanna Nelmes, widow
Moore, *Frampton Cotterell*, 1976, p. 239
Hertfordshire
St Albans, St Stephens, Moor Mills
11293 Mr [Briant] Marborough, miller
Munby, *Worldly Goods*, 1991, pp. 205-206
Leicestershire
Evington
11294 Mary Burley, widow
Wilshere, *Evington*, 1985, p. 46
11295 John Davenport
Wilshere, *Evington*, 1985, p. 47
11296 John Jolly
Wilshere, *Evington*, 1985, p. 46
11297 Peter Plumer, farmer
Wilshere, *Evington*, 1985, p. 46
Ratby, Whittington Grange
11298 John Choyce, gentleman
Wilshere, *Ratby*, 1984, p. 9
Lincolnshire
Allington
11299 John Cam, yeoman
Pask, *Allington*, 1989, pp. 101-102
Cleethorpes
11300 Jeanes Apleyard, fisherman
Ambler, Watkinson, *Clee*, 1987, pp. 182-183
11301 William Lil
Ambler, Watkinson, *Clee*, 1987, p. 182
Scotland
Edinburgh, Queensberry House, Canongate
11302 Charles Douglas, Duke of Queensberry
Lowrey, 2000, pp. 58-62
Shropshire
Broseley
11303 Adam Crompton, coalminer, collier
Trinder and Cox, *Severn Gorge*, 2000, pp. 303-304
11304 Edward Edwards
Trinder and Cox, *Severn Gorge*, 2000, pp. 189-190
11305 James Freeman, gentleman
Trinder and Cox, *Severn Gorge*, 2000, pp. 188-189
Telford, Oakengates
11306 William Ball, collier
Trinder, 1979, pp. 241-242
Wellington
11307 Tryphosa Barnes
Trinder and Cox, *Telford*, 1980, pp. 357-358
11308 George Cleaton, labourer
Trinder and Cox, *Telford*, 1980, p. 356
Wellington, Horton
11309 John Hampton, yeoman
Trinder and Cox, *Telford*, 1980, pp. 356-357
Sussex
Bosham
11310 William Knowles, clergyman
Hughes, *Sussex*, 2007, p. 34
Winchelsea
11311 John Prosser, clergyman [rector of Winchelsea]
Hughes, *Sussex*, 2007, pp. 240-241
Wales
Glamorganshire, St Lythans, Nantbrae
11312 Edward Pranch
Wrench, *Wrenche*, 1956, p. 65

Warwickshire
Stoneleigh, Westwood Heath
11313 John Curtis, [husbandman or yeoman]
Alcock, *Warwickshire*, 1993, p. 125
Westmorland
Bampton, Carhullan
11314 Anthony Law
Jackson, *Laws*, 1876, pp. 272-273
Wiltshire
Marlborough
11315 Grace Royce, widow
Williams and Thomson, *Marlborough*, 2007, pp. 277-278
11316 John Smith, butcher
Williams and Thomson, *Marlborough*, 2007, pp. 278-279
Worcestershire
Dudley, Russell's Hall
11317 John Sutton, alias Dudley, gentleman
Wanklyn, *Worcestershire*, 1998, pp. 352-357
Wichenford, Woodend
11318 Robert Caesar Gage, esquire
Wanklyn, *Worcestershire*, 1998, pp. 357-359
Yorkshire
Horbury
11319 Godfrey Crawsha, yeoman
Bartlett, *Horbury*, 1980, pp. 56-57

1724
Bristol
Bristol
11320 Edward Thurston, apothecary
George, *Bristol*, 2008, pp. 109-110
Cheshire
Bowdon
11321 Nicholas Waterhouse
Groves, *Bowdon*, 1999, pp. 39-41
Middlewich
11322 Thomas Earl, ale-draper
Earl, 1990, pp. 88-89
Cumberland
Stapleton, Cumcrook
11323 Robert Routledge
Harrison, 1965, p. 353
Dorsetshire
Unlocated
11324 Mary Hodges
Machin, *Yetminster*, 1976, No.129, (1 p.)
Essex
Roxwell
11325 Margaret Allen
Steer, *Mid-Essex*, 1969, pp. 256-257
Gloucestershire
Cheltenham
11326 Mary Ashmead
Sale, *Cheltenham*, 1999, p. 149
Cheltenham, Arle
11327 Benjamin Halford, [yeoman]
Sale, *Cheltenham*, 1999, p. 152
Cheltenham, Alstone
11328 Richard Hyett, gentleman
Sale, *Cheltenham*, 1999, pp. 153-155
11329 John Toney, yeoman
Sale, *Cheltenham*, 1999, p. 152

Frampton Cotterell
11330 Ann White, widow
Moore, *Frampton Cotterell*, 1976, p. 239
Westerleigh
11331 Thomas Hedges, feltmaker
Moore, *Frampton Cotterell*, 1976, p. 240

Leicestershire
Evington
11332 Margaret Handley, widow
Wilshere, *Evington*, 1985, p. 47
11333 Elizabeth Plumer, widow
Wilshere, *Evington*, 1985, p. 48
11334 Ann Spencer, widow
Wilshere, *Evington*, 1985, p. 48
11335 John West, [labourer]
Wilshere, *Evington*, 1985, p. 47
Kirby Muxloe
11336 The [Thomas] Latley, [grazier]
Wilshere, *Kirby Muxloe*, 1983, p. 26

Lincolnshire
Clee, Weelsby
11337 William Dixon
Ambler, Watkinson, *Clee*, 1987, p. 183
Clee
11338 Jno Prudence, agricultor
Ambler, Watkinson, *Clee*, 1987, pp. 183-184
Winteringham
11339 Roseman Cook
Neave, *Winteringham*, 1984, p. 147
11340 An Fowler
Neave, *Winteringham*, 1984, pp. 147-148

Middlesex
Sunbury
11341 Gilbert Peer, gentleman
Heselton, *Sunbury*, 1976, pp. 12-14

Northamptonshire
Drayton House
11342 Lady Elizabeth [Betty] Germaine
Murdoch, *Noble Households*, 2006, pp. 131-140

Shropshire
Broseley
11343 John Poole, labouring waterman
Trinder and Cox, *Severn Gorge*, 2000, p. 191
11344 Richard Roden, yeoman, shopkeeper
Trinder and Cox, *Severn Gorge*, 2000, p
Dawley, Pool Hill
11345 John Duddell, carpenter
Trinder and Cox, *Telford*, 1980, pp. 178-179
Dawley, Malinslee
11346 William Watkiss, blacksmith
Trinder and Cox, *Telford*, 1980, pp. 177-178

Staffordshire
Harborne
11347 Jeremiah Jarvice, nailer
Bodfish, *Smethwick*, 1992, p. 57
Lower Gornal
11348 John Pagett, mason
Roper, *Sedgley*, 1960, p. 111
Sedgley, The Straight
11349 John Pitt, nailer
Roper, *Sedgley*, 1960, p. 112

Warwickshire
Hatton, Shrewley
11350 Laurence Eberall, tanner
Sheasby, 1994, p. 63

Wiltshire
Marlborough
11351 Jane Colly, widow
Williams and Thomson, *Marlborough*, 2007, p. 283
11352 William Leacock, barber
Williams and Thomson, *Marlborough*, 2007, pp. 283-284
11353 Clement Raynolds, brazier
Williams and Thomson, *Marlborough*, 2007, pp. 279-283

Worcestershire
Hanbury, Mere Green
11354 John Bearcroft, gentleman
Wanklyn, *Worcestershire*, 1998, pp. 359-362
Ribbesford
11355 Jno Willm Price, clergyman, rector of Ribbesford
Bewdley, *Bewdley*, 1991, pp. 195-197

Yorkshire
Whitby
11356 William Ableson, mariner
Vickers, *Whitby*, 1986, p. 67

1724 (c.)
Shropshire
Broseley
11357 Thomas Roden, tobacco pipe maker
Trinder and Cox, *Severn Gorge*, 2000, pp. 191-192

1725
Bristol
Bristol
11358 William Berrow, painter
George, *Bristol*, 2008, pp. 112-113
11359 John Boutcher, barber surgeon
George, *Bristol*, 2008, p. 113
11360 John Weaver, mariner
George, *Bristol*, 2008, pp. 113-114

Cheshire
Ashton-on-Mersey
11361 Benjamin Smith, [yeoman]
Groves, *Ashton-on-Mersey and Sale*, 2002, p. 110

Cumberland
Penrith
11362 Agnes Latus
Jackson, *Hudlestons*, 1891, p. 457
Plumbland
11363 Charles Orfeur, esquire
Jackson, *Orfeurs*, 1878, p. 122

Devonshire
Uffculme
11364 William Mills
Wyatt, *Uffculme*, 1997, pp. 180

Essex
Kirby-le-Soken
11365 James Denny
Steer, *Mid-Essex*, 1969, pp. 5-7
Roxwell
11366 Abraham Gowan
Steer, *Mid-Essex*, 1969, p. 257
Unlocated
11367 Mary Branwood, widow
Steer, *Mid-Essex*, 1969, pp. 259-260

Writtle
11368 Joseph Wollward
Steer, *Mid-Essex*, 1969, pp. 257-258

Gloucestershire
Cheltenham
11369 James Parsons, cordwainer
Sale, *Cheltenham*, 1999, p. 157
Cheltenham, Alstone
11370 William Stephens, yeoman
Sale, *Cheltenham*, 1999, p. 156
Iron Acton
11371 John Hall, yeoman
Moore, *Frampton Cotterell*, 1976, pp. 240-241

Hertfordshire
Hertford
11372 John Babb, mealman
Adams, *Hertford*, 1997, pp. 56-57

Leicestershire
Kirby Muxloe
11373 Thomas Wood, [husbandman]
Wilshere, *Kirby Muxloe*, 1983, p. 27

London
Drury Lane
11374 Daniell Bridges
Steer, *Mid-Essex*, 1969, pp. 258-259
St James's Square
James Brydges, Duke of Chandos (see Cannons, Middlesex)

Middlesex
Cannons
11375 James Brydges, Duke of Chandos (also listed St James's Square, London)
Jenkins, 2005, pp. 103-190

Scotland
Glasgow, Trongate, Shawfield Mansion
11376 Daniel Campbell of Shawfield
Duncan, 1890, pp. 388-397

Shropshire
Dawley, Great Dawley
11377 George Hewlett, collier
Trinder and Cox, *Telford*, 1980, p. 179
Wellington, Watling Street
11378 William Barker, innholder
Trinder and Cox, *Telford*, 1980, pp. 360-361
Wellington
11379 William Judgson, innkeeper
Trinder and Cox, *Telford*, 1980, pp. 358-360
11380 Andrew Sockett, mercer
Trinder and Cox, *Telford*, 1980, pp. 362-363
11381 Joshua Taylor, dyer
Trinder and Cox, *Telford*, 1980, pp. 361-362

Staffordshire
Harborne
11382 John Grice
Bodfish, *Smethwick*, 1992, p. 60
11383 John Lewis, yeoman
Bodfish, *Smethwick*, 1992, pp. 58-59

Sussex
Broadwater, Offington
11384 Charles Smith, clergyman
Hughes, *Sussex*, 2007, pp. 36-37

Findon
11385 Richard Woodeson, clergyman [vicar of Findon]
Hughes, *Sussex*, 2007, pp. 76-78
Kirdford, Palfrey
11386 William Penycod, yeoman
Kenyon, *Kirdford*, 1955, pp. 121-122

Yorkshire
Horbury
11387 Robert Burton
Bartlett, *Horbury*, 1980, pp. 58-59
Whitby, Bagdale
11388 George Cockerill, master mariner
Vickers, *Whitby*, 1986, pp. 67-69
Whitby
11389 Peter Jackson, mariner
Vickers, *Whitby*, 1986, p. 69
11390 Mary Ward, widow
Vickers, *Whitby*, 1986, p. 69

1726
Bristol
Bristol
11391 Humphrey Cole, glass-maker
George, *Bristol*, 2008, pp. 115-116

Cheshire
Ashton-on-Mersey
11392 Samuel Bellis, clergyman, curate
Groves, *Ashton-on-Mersey and Sale*, 2002, pp. 114-116
Sale
11393 Jonathan Irlam, [linen weaver]
Groves, *Ashton-on-Mersey and Sale*, 2002, p. 113

Derbyshire
Aston-on-Trent
11394 Rev. Mr. Thomas Holden, clergyman, rector of Aston-on-Trent
Holden, 1930, pp. 86-88

Essex
Hadleigh
11395 Joseph Downham
Steer, *Mid-Essex*, 1969, pp. 261-262
Unlocated
11396 John Lugar
Steer, *Mid-Essex*, 1969, p. 260
Writtle
11397 John Battle
Steer, *Mid-Essex*, 1969, p. 261
11398 John Day, carpenter
Steer, *Mid-Essex*, 1969, p. 260
11399 John Plomer
Steer, *Mid-Essex*, 1969, p. 263

Gloucestershire
Charlton Kings
11400 Walter Buckle, [yeoman]
Paget and Sale, *Charlton Kings*, 2003, pp. 109-110
11401 Thomas Clevely, carpenter
Paget and Sale, *Charlton Kings*, 2003, p. 109
11402 Humphrey King
Paget and Sale, *Charlton Kings*, 2003, p. 110
11403 Richard Overbury, [cordwainer]
Paget and Sale, *Charlton Kings*, 2003, p. 108
Cheltenham, Alstone
11404 Samuel Church, husbandman
Sale, *Cheltenham*, 1999, p. 158

Cheltenham
11405 Toby Major, victualler
Sale, *Cheltenham*, 1999, p. 157
11406 Mrs Elizabeth Price, widow
Sale, *Cheltenham*, 1999, p. 158
Frampton Cotterell
11407 John Millett, [yeoman]
Moore, *Frampton Cotterell*, 1976, pp. 241-242
Winterbourne
11408 Thomas Bayly, yeoman
Moore, *Frampton Cotterell*, 1976, p. 242
Leicestershire
Ratby
11409 Calab Booth, yeoman [labourer]
Wilshere, *Ratby*, 1984, p. 10
11410 William Hunt, [yeoman]
Wilshere, *Ratby*, 1984, p. 10
Lincolnshire
Winteringham
11411 Rebecah Bell
Neave, *Winteringham*, 1984, p. 148
Scotland
Orkney, Kirkwall
11412 Charles Stewart, steward clerk
Marwick, 1927-1928, pp. 30-31
Shropshire
Benthall
11413 Eustace Beard, waterman, trowman
Trinder and Cox, *Severn Gorge*, 2000, pp. 136-137
Dawley, Holywell
11414 Edward Darrall, ground collier
Trinder and Cox, *Telford*, 1980, p. 180
Dawley, The Ridges
11415 Lawrence Wellington, gentleman
Trinder and Cox, *Telford*, 1980, pp. 180-181
Madeley
11416 William Cludd, weaver
Trinder and Cox, *Severn Gorge*, 2000, pp. 304-305
Wellington
11417 Mary Banger
Trinder and Cox, *Telford*, 1980, p. 365
Wellington, Leegomery
11418 William Icke
Trinder and Cox, *Telford*, 1980, pp. 365-367
Wellington, Ketley
11419 John North
Trinder and Cox, *Telford*, 1980, pp. 367-368
Wellington, Arleston
11420 John Turner
Trinder and Cox, *Telford*, 1980, pp. 364-365
Wrockwardine, Admaston
11421 William Cheshire, gentleman
Trinder and Cox, *Telford*, 1980, pp. 434-439
Staffordshire
Harborne
11422 Robert Withers, labourer
Bodfish, *Smethwick*, 1992, p. 61
Wales
Monmouthshire, Usk
11423 Mr John Wrench, [clergyman]
Wrench, *Wrenche*, 1956, pp. 47-48

Wiltshire
Marlborough
11424 Edward Barnard
Williams and Thomson, *Marlborough*, 2007, pp. 284-285
11425 Elizabeth Mann
Williams and Thomson, *Marlborough*, 2007, pp. 285-286
11426 John Tarrant
Williams and Thomson, *Marlborough*, 2007, p. 286

1726 (c.)
Bedfordshire
Houghton House, Ampthill
11427 Charles, Lord Bruce
Curtis, 1958, pp. 98-104

1727
Bristol
Bristol
11428 Richard Brinkworth, cordwainer
George, *Bristol*, 2008, pp. 116-117
11429 James Calderhead, chapman
George, *Bristol*, 2008, pp. 117-118
Westbury
11430 Robert Woolam, yeoman
Moore, *Clifton*, 1981, p. 200
Cheshire
Ashton-on-Mersey
11431 John Gee, [yeoman]
Groves, *Ashton-on-Mersey and Sale*, 2002, pp. 119-120
Nantwich
11432 Mrs Elizabeth Milton, widow of the poet
Marsh, 1855, pp. 29*-31*
Sale
11433 James Johnson, [yeoman]
Groves, *Ashton-on-Mersey and Sale*, 2002, pp. 125-126
11434 John Renshaw, [husbandman]
Groves, *Ashton-on-Mersey and Sale*, 2002, pp. 122-123
Essex
Writtle
11435 John Hillyard, bricklayer
Steer, *Mid-Essex*, 1969, p. 262
Gloucestershire
Charlton Kings
11436 Thomas Pates, [gentleman]
Paget and Sale, *Charlton Kings*, 2003, p. 111
Cheltenham
11437 Richard Allaway, barber
Sale, *Cheltenham*, 1999, p. 159
Cheltenham, Alstone
11438 Mary Cleevely
Sale, *Cheltenham*, 1999, p. 160
Cheltenham
11439 James Nicholls, [maltster]
Sale, *Cheltenham*, 1999, p. 159
Frampton Cotterell
11440 John Fry, tailor [tiler?]
Moore, *Frampton Cotterell*, 1976, p. 243
Stoke Gifford
11441 Isaac Millett, [yeoman]
Moore, *Frampton Cotterell*, 1976, pp. 242-243
Westerleigh
11442 Arthur Trewman, gentleman
Moore, *Frampton Cotterell*, 1976, p. 243
Winterbourne
11443 John Bayly, cordwainer
Moore, *Frampton Cotterell*, 1976, p. 244

11444 Thomas Bush, miller
Moore, *Frampton Cotterell*, 1976, pp. 243-244
11445 Joseph Turner, yeoman
Moore, *Frampton Cotterell*, 1976, p. 242

Leicestershire
Botcheston
11446 William Hollyland, yeoman
Wilshere, *Ratby*, 1984, p. 11
Evington
11447 Samuel Davenport, [grazier]
Wilshere, *Evington*, 1985, p. 49
Glenfield
11448 Rebeccah Lilley
Wilshere, *Glenfield*, 1983, p. 12
Ratby
11449 William Copeland
Wilshere, *Ratby*, 1984, p. 11

Northamptonshire
Little Harrowden
11450 Samll Alderman
Alderman, *Alderman*, 2008, pp. 139-140

Shropshire
Broseley
11451 Mr Richard Mason, innholder
Trinder and Cox, *Severn Gorge*, 2000, pp. 192-193
Dawley, Stoney Hill
11452 Michael Onions
Trinder and Cox, *Telford*, 1980, p. 181
Wrockwardine, Leaton
11453 Elizabeth Blackshaw
Trinder and Cox, *Telford*, 1980, p. 439

Staffordshire
Harborne
11454 John Dalton, yeoman
Bodfish, *Smethwick*, 1992, pp. 62-63

Suffolk
Framsden Hall
11455 Mr [James] Bacon
Hill and Penrose, 1974, pp. 123-125

Surrey
Charlwood
11456 William Turley
Harding, *Charlwood*, 1976, pp. 116-117

Sussex
Kirdford
11457 Thomas Backman, husbandman
Lawson, 1999, p. 95

Worcestershire
Bromsgrove
11458 Humphrey Lowe, esquire
Wanklyn, *Worcestershire*, 1998, pp. 363-365

Yorkshire
Barnoldswick (?)
11459 Christopher Baxter
Kirk, *Barnoldswick*, 1951, pp. 57-58
Horbury
11460 John Cawthorne, tailor
Bartlett, *Horbury*, 1980, pp. 22-23
Kiveton Park
11461 Peregrine Hyde Osborne, Marquess of
Carmarthen (also listed Thorp Salvin)
Murdoch, *Noble Households*, 2006, pp. 246-269

Thorp Salvin
Peregrine Hyde Osborne, Marquess of Carmarthen (see Kiveton Park)

1728
Bristol
Bristol
11462 Mary Brown, widow
George, *Bristol*, 2008, pp. 118-119
11463 Samuel Daw,[salt maker]
George, *Bristol*, 2008, pp. 124-126
11464 Henry Hoar, pipe maker
George, *Bristol*, 2008, pp. 119-126
11465 Jacob Long, house carpenter
George, *Bristol*, 2008, pp. 121-124
Westbury
11466 John Hopkins, yeoman
Moore, *Clifton*, 1981, pp. 200-201

Cheshire
Ashton-on-Mersey
11467 Elizabeth Renshaw, [widow]
Groves, *Ashton-on-Mersey and Sale*, 2002, pp. 127-128

Essex
Unlocated
11468 Abraham Stoakes
Steer, *Mid-Essex*, 1969, p. 263
Writtle
11469 John Godfrey, miller
Steer, *Mid-Essex*, 1969, p. 263

Gloucestershire
Cheltenham
11470 Hester Skay
Sale, *Cheltenham*, 1999, p. 161
Cheltenham, Alstone
11471 Thomas Sturmy, yeoman
Sale, *Cheltenham*, 1999, p. 161
Frampton Cotterell
11472 Mary Pride, widow
Moore, *Frampton Cotterell*, 1976, p. 245
11473 John Parker, feltmaker
Moore, *Frampton Cotterell*, 1976, p. 246
Iron Acton
11474 Joseph Lewis, [innholder]
Moore, *Frampton Cotterell*, 1976, p. 245
11475 John Smith, innholder
Moore, *Frampton Cotterell*, 1976, pp. 246-247
Westerleigh
11476 Mary Hobbs, widow
Moore, *Frampton Cotterell*, 1976, p. 245
11477 Nicholas Hynam, yeoman
Moore, *Frampton Cotterell*, 1976, p. 245
11478 Zachariah Iles, labourer
Moore, *Frampton Cotterell*, 1976, p. 246

Leicestershire
Botcheston
11479 John Exon, gentleman
Wilshere, *Ratby*, 1984, p. 13
11480 Stephen Poole, [yeoman]
Wilshere, *Ratby*, 1984, p. 12
Braunstone
11481 Edward Pollard
Wilshere, *Braunstone*, 1983, p. 38
Evington
11482 John Plumer, [labourer]
Wilshere, *Evington*, 1985, p. 49

Kirby Muxloe
11483 Elizabeth Heatley, widow
Wilshere, *Kirby Muxloe*, 1983, p. 28
11484 John Kirke, [yeoman]
Wilshere, *Kirby Muxloe*, 1983, p. 29
Ratby
11485 William Biggs, [labourer?]
Wilshere, *Ratby*, 1984, p. 12

Lincolnshire
Cleethorpes
11486 Thomas Manby
Ambler, Watkinson, *Clee*, 1987, pp. 184-185

Shropshire
Benthall
11487 Beatrice Gears, widow
Trinder and Cox, *Severn Gorge*, 2000, pp. 137-138
Broseley
11488 Thomas Teece, locksmith
Trinder and Cox, *Severn Gorge*, 2000, pp. 193-195
11489 Mr William Whitmore, tallow chandler
Trinder and Cox, *Severn Gorge*, 2000, p. 195
Dawley, The Pawn Hatch
11490 John Duddell, carpenter
Trinder and Cox, *Telford*, 1980, pp. 182-184
Little Wenlock
11491 Francis Parton, yeoman
Trinder and Cox, *Severn Gorge*, 2000, pp. 258-259
Madeley Wood
11492 John Doughty, carpenter
Trinder and Cox, *Severn Gorge*, 2000, pp. 308-309
11493 Edward Owen, waterman
Trinder and Cox, *Severn Gorge*, 2000, pp. 306-307
Wellington
11494 Richard Hancox, surgeon
Trinder and Cox, *Telford*, 1980, pp. 369-370
11495 John Moss, shoemaker
Trinder and Cox, *Telford*, 1980, p. 370
11496 Richard Roe, tailor
Trinder and Cox, *Telford*, 1980, pp. 368-369
Wrockwardine, Allscott
11497 Thomas Binnell, yeoman
Trinder and Cox, *Telford*, 1980, p. 439

Staffordshire
Sedgley, The Straight
11498 Edward Clark, nailer
Roper, *Sedgley*, 1960, p. 113
Smethwick
11499 John Gosnell, yeoman
Bodfish, *Smethwick*, 1992, pp. 64-65
11500 Joseph Parkes, nailer
Bodfish, *Smethwick*, 1992, pp. 66-67

Sussex
Chiddingly
11501 Giles Watkins, clergyman [vicar of Chiddingly]
Hughes, *Sussex*, 2007, pp. 43-44
West Chiltington
11502 Richard Fowle, clergyman [rector of West
Chiltington]
Hughes, *Sussex*, 2007, pp. 46-47

Wales
Montgomeryshire, Llanfihangel, Fachwen
11503 Joseph Ellis
Gilson, *Llanfihangel*, 2009, pp. 46-47

Warwickshire
Stoneleigh, Cryfield
11504 Edmund Casemore
Alcock, *Warwickshire*, 1993, pp. 110-111
Stoneleigh, Stareton, New House Farm
11505 Richard Garlick, yeoman
Alcock, *Warwickshire*, 1993, pp. 158-160

Wiltshire
Marlborough
11506 Thomas Gilmore
Williams and Thomson, *Marlborough*, 2007, pp. 286-287

Yorkshire
Doncaster
11507 Mr John Addinell, [painter?]
Hey, *Doncaster*, 1997, pp. 148-150
11508 Mr Ric. Blomyley, [shoemaker]
Hey, *Doncaster*, 1997, pp. 150-152
Horbury
11509 Thomas Person, butcher
Bartlett, *Horbury*, 1980, pp. 63-64

1729

Bristol
Bristol
11510 Edmund Pruett
George, *Bristol*, 2008, pp. 126-128
Shirehampton
11511 William Cross, mariner
Moore, *Clifton*, 1981, p. 201
Westbury
11512 John England, butcher
Moore, *Clifton*, 1981, pp. 202-204

Cheshire
Ashton-on-Mersey
11513 William Duncalf, [yeoman]
Groves, *Ashton-on-Mersey and Sale*, 2002, p. 131
11514 Edward Hamnett, [husbandman]
Groves, *Ashton-on-Mersey and Sale*, 2002, p. 133
Betchton
11515 Richard Ledward, [innholder]
Ledward, 1998, p. 12
Bowdon
11516 Joseph Williamson, yeoman
Groves, *Bowdon*, 1999, p. 37

Cumberland
Hutton John
11517 Wilfrid Hudleston
Jackson, *Hudlestons*, 1891, pp. 458-459

Essex
Writtle
11518 William Abrey
Steer, *Mid-Essex*, 1969, p. 263
11519 William Grudgfield
Steer, *Mid-Essex*, 1969, pp. 265-266
11520 Margaret Haward, widow
Steer, *Mid-Essex*, 1969, pp. 264-65

Gloucestershire
Charlton Kings
11521 Samuel Mansell, husbandman
Paget and Sale, *Charlton Kings*, 2003, p. 112
11522 John Stilles, cordwainer
Paget and Sale, *Charlton Kings*, 2003, p. 113
Cheltenham
11523 William Ballinger, [carpenter]

Sale, *Cheltenham*, 1999, p. 168
11524 John Chestroe, [yeoman]
Sale, *Cheltenham*, 1999, pp. 164-167
11525 William Ellis, [innholder]
Sale, *Cheltenham*, 1999, p. 172
11526 John Hall, [baker]
Sale, *Cheltenham*, 1999, pp. 167-168
11527 Mrs Hester Ireland
Sale, *Cheltenham*, 1999, p. 172
11528 William Lawrence, servantman
Sale, *Cheltenham*, 1999, p. 167
11529 John Macock, [currier]
Sale, *Cheltenham*, 1999, p. 169
11530 Thomas Matthews, [carpenter]
Sale, *Cheltenham*, 1999, pp. 162-163
Frampton Cotterell
11531 Elizabeth Wigmore, widow
Moore, *Frampton Cotterell*, 1976, p. 247
Westerleigh
11532 John Bishop, hatmaker
Moore, *Frampton Cotterell*, 1976, p. 247
11533 Thomas Humphris, grocer
Moore, *Frampton Cotterell*, 1976, p. 248
11534 Mary Trahern, [widow]
Moore, *Frampton Cotterell*, 1976, p. 247
Winterbourne
11535 Edward Hathway, butcher
Moore, *Frampton Cotterell*, 1976, p. 247

Leicestershire
Evington
11536 Richard Cartwright, [yeoman]
Wilshere, *Evington*, 1985, p. 50
Glenfield
11537 Ralph Hassall, [yeoman]
Wilshere, *Glenfield*, 1983, p. 12
Ratby
11538 Elizabeth Copeland, widow
Wilshere, *Ratby*, 1984, p. 14
11539 Jonathan Cramp
Wilshere, *Ratby*, 1984, p. 15
Ratby, Keitbridge
11540 Jonathan Fletcher, [labourer]
Wilshere, *Ratby*, 1984, p. 15
Ratby
11541 Ellenor Somerfeild, widow
Wilshere, *Ratby*, 1984, p. 14

Lincolnshire
Winteringham
11542 Matthew Ferris
Neave, *Winteringham*, 1984, pp. 148-149

Shropshire
Broseley
11543 Thomas Gower, trowman
Trinder and Cox, *Severn Gorge*, 2000, pp. 195-196
11544 Thomas Williams
Trinder and Cox, *Severn Gorge*, 2000, pp. 196-198
Dawley
11545 John Harris
Trinder and Cox, *Telford*, 1980, pp. 184-186
Lilleshall
11546 John Adney, weaver
Trinder and Cox, *Telford*, 1980, p. 241

Madeley Wood
11547 William Eardley, engineer
Trinder and Cox, *Severn Gorge*, 2000, pp. 307-308
11548 Mark Henworth, miller
Trinder and Cox, *Severn Gorge*, 2000, p. 312
Wellington
11549 Henry Adams, shoemaker
Trinder and Cox, *Telford*, 1980, p. 371
11550 John Brown, glover
Trinder and Cox, *Telford*, 1980, pp. 371-372
Wrockwardine, Charlton
11551 Robert Hawkins
Trinder and Cox, *Telford*, 1980, p. 440

Staffordshire
Harborne
11552 William Price, yeoman
Bodfish, *Smethwick*, 1992, pp. 68-69
11553 Thomas Smith, nailer
Bodfish, *Smethwick*, 1992, pp. 70-71
Sedgley
11554 Elizabeth Marsh, widow
Roper, *Sedgley*, 1960, p. 115
11555 Anne Turton, widow
Roper, *Sedgley*, 1960, p. 114
Smethwick
11556 William Walker, nailer
Bodfish, *Smethwick*, 1992, pp. 72-73

Yorkshire
Barnoldswick
11557 Jane Robinson, widow
Kirk, *Barnoldswick*, 1951, pp. 75-76
Grenoside, Stubbing House
11558 Joseph Walker, [nailer]
Hey, 1979, p. 32
Horbury
11559 Joshua Pollard, clothier
Bartlett, *Horbury*, 1980, pp. 72-74
Horbury, Hall Cliffe
11560 William Pollard, clothier
Bartlett, *Horbury*, 1980, pp. 69-71
Horbury
11561 Ffrancis Rodes
Bartlett, *Horbury*, 1980, p. 62
11562 Robert Townend, gardener
Bartlett, *Horbury*, 1980, p. 75
Whitby
11563 Jacob Hindson, mariner
Vickers, *Whitby*, 1986, p. 69
11564 George Noble, mariner
Vickers, *Whitby*, 1986, p. 69

1730
Bristol
Westbury
11565 Rees Derrick, [labourer]
Moore, *Clifton*, 1981, p. 204
Cheshire
Ashton-on-Mersey
11566 Thomas Royle, [yeoman]
Groves, *Ashton-on-Mersey and Sale*, 2002, pp. 141-142
Sale
11567 Robert Cheshire
Groves, *Ashton-on-Mersey and Sale*, 2002, pp. 131-132
11568 James Holt, [mason]
Groves, *Ashton-on-Mersey and Sale*, 2002, p. 136

Sale and Timperley
11569 Jonathan Holt, [yeoman]
Groves, *Ashton-on-Mersey and Sale*, 2002, pp. 139-140

Dorsetshire
Unlocated
11570 Thomas Lennard
Machin, *Yetminster*, 1976, No.130, (1 p.)

Essex
Writtle
11571 Joseph Goodman, miller
Steer, *Mid-Essex*, 1969, p. 267
11572 Thomas Harris
Steer, *Mid-Essex*, 1969, p. 266

Gloucestershire
Cheltenham
11573 Mrs Margaret French
Sale, *Cheltenham*, 1999, pp. 170-171
11574 Elizabeth Strowde, widow
Sale, *Cheltenham*, 1999, p. 173
11575 Mary Rice
Sale, *Cheltenham*, 1999, pp. 173-174
Westerleigh
11576 William Belsire, coalminer
Moore, *Frampton Cotterell*, 1976, p. 250
11577 Thomas Flower, collier
Moore, *Frampton Cotterell*, 1976, p. 250
11578 Thomas Middleton, yeoman
Moore, *Frampton Cotterell*, 1976, pp. 248-249
11579 Richard Simmonds, feltmaker
Moore, *Frampton Cotterell*, 1976, p. 249
11580 James Wigmore, feltmaker
Moore, *Frampton Cotterell*, 1976, pp. 249-250

Leicestershire
Braunstone
11581 Danl. Broon, labourer
Wilshere, *Braunstone*, 1983, p. 39
11582 William Kirke, [yeoman]
Wilshere, *Braunstone*, 1983, p. 39
Wilshere, *Glenfield*, 1983, p. 13 [another inventory]
Glenfield
11583 Thomas Tomson, [husbandman]
Wilshere, *Glenfield*, 1983, p. 13

Lincolnshire
Winteringham
11584 John Holms
Neave, *Winteringham*, 1984, p. 149

Northamptonshire
Boughton House
11585 John, Duke of Montagu
Murdoch, *Noble Households*, 2006, pp. 70-77
Little Harrowden
11586 Robert Alderman, [yeoman]
Alderman, *Alderman*, 2008, p. 81

Oxfordshire
Water Eaton
11587 William Teariell
Offord, *Water Eaton*, 1986, pp. 49-50

Shropshire
Benthall
11588 Hugh Cullis
Trinder and Cox, *Severn Gorge*, 2000, p. 138
Broseley
11589 Noel [Newell] Edwards, yeoman
Trinder and Cox, *Severn Gorge*, 2000, pp. 199-200

Dawley, Great Dawley
11590 Mary Barrett, widow
Trinder and Cox, *Telford*, 1980, p. 188
Dawley, Little Dawley
11591 Thomas Roe, yeoman
Trinder and Cox, *Telford*, 1980, pp. 186-188
Little Wenlock
11592 George Fletcher, ropemaker
Trinder and Cox, *Severn Gorge*, 2000, p. 261
Little Wenlock, Huntington
11593 Edmund Gray, yeoman
Trinder and Cox, *Severn Gorge*, 2000, pp. 259-261
Wellington
11594 William Cooper, gentleman
Trinder and Cox, *Telford*, 1980, pp. 373-374
11595 John Rowley
Trinder and Cox, *Telford*, 1980, pp. 372-373

Staffordshire
Coseley
11596 Henry King, blacksmith
Roper, *Sedgley*, 1960, pp. 117-118
Sedgley, Cottwall End
11597 John Parkes, labourer
Roper, *Sedgley*, 1960, p. 116
Smethwick
11598 Robert Chambers, ironmonger
Bodfish, *Smethwick*, 1992, pp. 74-76

Sussex
Mayfield
11599 Peter Baker, clergyman [vicar of Mayfield]
Hughes, *Sussex*, 2007, pp. 137-139

Warwickshire
Ashow
11600 John Elliott
Alcock, *Warwickshire*, 1993, p. 107
Stoneleigh, Crackley Heath
11601 Edward Lee, labourer
Alcock, *Warwickshire*, 1993, p. 141

Worcestershire
Wolverley
11602 Talbot Jenkins, esquire
Wanklyn, *Worcestershire*, 1998, pp. 365-372

Yorkshire
Whitby
11603 Thomas Foster
Vickers, *Whitby*, 1986, p. 70

1731
Bedfordshire
Northill Manor
11604 Owen Thomas Bromsall, esquire
Collett-White, *Bedfordshire*, 1995, pp. 186-192
Bristol
Bristol
11605 Bushell Jellicutt, distiller
George, *Bristol*, 2008, pp. 129-130
11606 Michael Phillips, ship carpenter
George, *Bristol*, 2008, pp. 130-131
11607 Nathaniel Warren, hosier
George, *Bristol*, 2008, pp. 131-133
Buckinghamshire
Swanbourne
11608 John Gilbert, carpenter
Anon., *Muniment Room*, 1934-1940, p. 31

Cheshire
Sale
11609 John Bythell, [carpenter]
Groves, *Ashton-on-Mersey and Sale*, 2002, p. 145
11610 William Davenport, [yeoman]
Groves, *Ashton-on-Mersey and Sale*, 2002, pp. 148-149
Devonshire
Uffculme
11611 Henry Callow, [serge weaver]
Wyatt, *Uffculme*, 1997, pp. 181
11612 Ann Marshall
Wyatt, *Uffculme*, 1997, pp. 180-181
11613 Nicholas Tucker
Wyatt, *Uffculme*, 1997, pp182-183
Dorsetshire
Blandford Forum
11614 Thomas, John and William Bastard, [architects and builders]
Legg, 1994, pp. 27-37
Chetnole
11615 John Elford, [weaver]
Machin, *Yetminster*, 1976, No.131, (1 p.)
11616 William Symes
Machin, *Yetminster*, 1976, No.133, (1 p.)
Yetminster
11617 Thomas Rodber [Rodford], tanner
Machin, *Yetminster*, 1976, No.134, (1 p.)
11618 John Symes, yeoman
Machin, *Yetminster*, 1976, No.132, (1 p.)
Gloucestershire
Cheltenham
11619 John Chestroe, yeoman
Sale, *Cheltenham*, 1999, p. 177
11620 Francis Spencer, [yeoman]
Sale, *Cheltenham*, 1999, p. 175
11621 Giles Webb, collarmaker
Sale, *Cheltenham*, 1999, pp. 176-177
Iron Acton
11622 Daniel Hinchecorne, yeoman
Moore, *Frampton Cotterell*, 1976, pp. 251-252
Westerleigh [?]
11623 Ann Butler
Moore, *Frampton Cotterell*, 1976, p. 251
Westerleigh
11624 Ann Gough
Moore, *Frampton Cotterell*, 1976, p. 251
11625 Margaret Harford
Moore, *Frampton Cotterell*, 1976, p. 251
Ireland
Co. Clare, Killaloe
11626 John Head, clergyman
Herbert, 1942-1943, p. 122
Co. Down, Lecale, Ballynewport
11627 Mr Bernard Brett, [gentleman]
Stevenson, 1920, pp. 324-325
Leicestershire
Ratby, Kent Hayes
11628 Thomas Colver, [husbandman]
Wilshere, *Ratby*, 1984, p. 16
Oxfordshire
Broughton Castle
11629 Fiennes Twisleton
Slade, 1981, pp. 157-159

Scotland
Aberdeenshire, Monymusk
11630 Sir Archibald Grant, baronet
Hamilton, 1945, pp. 1-8
Shropshire
Lilleshall, Donnington
11631 Elizabeth Adney, widow
Trinder and Cox, *Telford*, 1980, pp. 241-242
11632 Thomas Newell, gentleman
Trinder and Cox, *Telford*, 1980, pp. 243-244
Madeley Wood
11633 Richard Cox, collier
Trinder and Cox, *Severn Gorge*, 2000, pp. 309-311
Wellington
11634 John Walford, apothecary and surgeon
Trinder and Cox, *Telford*, 1980, pp. 374-375
Wrockwardine, Trench Lane
11635 William Icke
Trinder and Cox, *Telford*, 1980, pp. 440-441
Staffordshire
Harborne
11636 John Hanson, yeoman
Bodfish, *Smethwick*, 1992, p. 77
Sussex
Wiston
11637 Robert Gold, yeoman
Sleight, 1993, pp. 38-39
Warwickshire
Ashow, Dial House Farm
11638 Robert Davis [Davies]
Alcock, *Warwickshire*, 1993, pp. 147-148
Yorkshire
Barnoldswick
11639 Isabell Higgin
Kirk, *Barnoldswick*, 1951, p. 68
Grisedale, Sedbergh, Moor Rigg
11640 Michael Dawson, yeoman
Collingwood, 1929, pp. 15-16
Horbury
11641 Robert Walker, yeoman
Bartlett, *Horbury*, 1980, p. 76

1732
Bristol
Westbury
11642 Richard Yeamans, potter
Moore, *Clifton*, 1981, pp. 204-205
Cheshire
Betchton
11643 Jane Ledward, widow
Ledward, 1998, p. 14
Devonshire
Uffculme
11644 Mary Gange, [widow]
Wyatt, *Uffculme*, 1997, pp. 183
Essex
Writtle
11645 Jonathan Sapsford
Steer, *Mid-Essex*, 1969, pp. 267-268
Gloucestershire
Charlton Kings
11646 Walter Mansell, [yeoman]
Paget and Sale, *Charlton Kings*, 2003, pp. 113-114

Cheltenham
11647 Mary Kemmett, widow
Sale, *Cheltenham*, 1999, p. 178
11648 Mary Long, widow
Sale, *Cheltenham*, 1999, p. 178
Westerleigh
11649 Sarah Parsons, widow
Moore, *Frampton Cotterell*, 1976, pp. 253-254
11650 John Vowles, yeoman
Moore, *Frampton Cotterell*, 1976, pp. 252-253
Winterbourne
11651 Simon Player, smith
Moore, *Frampton Cotterell*, 1976, p. 254

Leicestershire
Botcheston
11652 Elizabeth Holyland, widow
Wilshere, *Ratby*, 1984, p. 16

Northamptonshire
Rothwell
11653 Francis Alderman, tailor
Alderman, *Alderman*, 2008, pp. 86-87

Shropshire
Broseley
11654 Francis Evans
Trinder and Cox, *Severn Gorge*, 2000, p. 200
11655 Richard Pearce, master collier
Trinder and Cox, *Severn Gorge*, 2000, pp. 200-203
Madeley
11656 Edward Cludd, collier
Trinder and Cox, *Severn Gorge*, 2000, pp. 311-312
Madeley Wood
11657 Edward Owen, trowman
Trinder and Cox, *Severn Gorge*, 2000, pp. 313-314
Wellington
11658 Thomas Bryan, farrier
Trinder and Cox, *Telford*, 1980, pp. 375-376
11659 Revd. William Sockett, clergyman
Trinder and Cox, *Telford*, 1980, pp. 376-377
Wrockwardine
11660 John Brown
Trinder and Cox, *Telford*, 1980, pp. 444-445
Wrockwardine, Allscott
11661 John Smith, yeoman
Trinder and Cox, *Telford*, 1980, pp. 441-444

Staffordshire
Smethwick
11662 Thomas Hopkins, yeoman
Bodfish, *Smethwick*, 1992, pp. 78-80

Sussex
Ashington
11663 Robert Willan, clergyman [rector of Ashington]
Hughes, *Sussex*, 2007, pp. 9-10
Hamsey
11664 Joseph Stedman, clergyman [curate of Hamsey]
Hughes, *Sussex*, 2007, pp. 100-101
Rottingdean
11665 Thomas Pelling, clergyman [vicar of Rottingdean]
Hughes, *Sussex*, 2007, pp. 170-172
Wiston
11666 John Carter
Sleight, 1993, pp. 41-42

Wiltshire
Marlborough
11667 Jonathan Tanner, yeoman
Williams and Thomson, *Marlborough*, 2007, p. 287
Yorkshire
Horbury
11668 John Wood
Bartlett, *Horbury*, 1980, p. 79

1733

Bedfordshire
Eaton Socon
11669 Widow Alderman
Emmison, 1933, p. 34
11670 John Cooper
Emmison, 1933, p. 34
11671 Widow Peak
Emmison, 1933, p. 34
Bristol
Bristol
11672 William Neast, founder
George, *Bristol*, 2008, pp. 133-136
Westbury
11673 Thomas Chilton, yeoman
Moore, *Clifton*, 1981, pp. 205-206
Cheshire
Ashton-on-Mersey
11674 James Ashton, [yeoman]
Groves, *Ashton-on-Mersey and Sale*, 2002, pp. 153-155
11675 Richard Holt, [girthweb maker]
Groves, *Ashton-on-Mersey and Sale*, 2002, p. 150
11676 Richard Robinson alias Barker
Groves, *Ashton-on-Mersey and Sale*, 2002, pp. 150-151
Devonshire
Uffculme
11677 William Holway [Hollway], mason
Wyatt, *Uffculme*, 1997, pp. 183-184
Gloucestershire
Charlton Kings
11678 Henry Cleeveley, [husbandman]
Paget and Sale, *Charlton Kings*, 2003, pp. 115-116
11679 John Holder, [husbandman]
Paget and Sale, *Charlton Kings*, 2003, pp. 114-115
11680 Robert Sollis
Paget and Sale, *Charlton Kings*, 2003, p. 115
Cheltenham
11681 Thomas Gregory, [victualler]
Sale, *Cheltenham*, 1999, p. 181
Stoke Gifford
11682 William Nicholas, yeoman
Moore, *Frampton Cotterell*, 1976, pp. 254-255
Leicestershire
Ratby
11683 Mary Fletcher, [widow]
Wilshere, *Ratby*, 1984, pp. 17-19
London
Montagu House, Bloomsbury
11684 John, Duke of Montagu
Murdoch, *Noble Households*, 2006, pp. 27-48
Shropshire
Broseley, Swinbatch
11685 Thomas Beddow, yeoman
Trinder and Cox, *Severn Gorge*, 2000, pp. 203-205

Broseley
11686   Samuel Evans, master collier
Trinder and Cox, *Severn Gorge*, 2000, pp. 205-206
Dawley, Little Dawley
11687   Nathan Peploe
Trinder and Cox, *Telford*, 1980, p. 189

Staffordshire
Ettingshall
11688   Margaret Gibbons, widow
Roper, *Sedgley*, 1960, p. 119
Sedgley
11689   Henry Bradley, gentleman
Roper, *Sedgley*, 1960, pp. 119-120

Sussex
North Mundham
11690   John Brooms, blacksmith
Steer, 1962, pp. 287-288

Wiltshire
Marlborough
11691   Nathaniel Wilkins, whitesmith
Williams and Thomson, *Marlborough*, 2007, p. 287

Worcestershire
Wick
11692   Thomas Haslewood, esquire
Wanklyn, *Worcestershire*, 1998, pp. 372-377

1734
Bristol
Bristol
11693   John Robins, mason
George, *Bristol*, 2008, pp. 136-138
11694   Thomas Westell, brazier and broker
George, *Bristol*, 2008, pp. 138-149

Cheshire
Sale
11695   John Lee [Leigh]
Groves, *Ashton-on-Mersey and Sale*, 2002, p. 159

Gloucestershire
Charlton Kings
11696   William Ruck, [husbandman]
Paget and Sale, *Charlton Kings*, 2003, p. 116
Cheltenham
11697   Richard Ellis, maltster
Sale, *Cheltenham*, 1999, p. 183
11698   James Hill, stonecutter
Sale, *Cheltenham*, 1999, pp. 179-180
11699   Benjamin Martin, maltster
Sale, *Cheltenham*, 1999, p. 184
11700   Ann Stephens, widow
Sale, *Cheltenham*, 1999, p. 184
Frampton Cotterell
11701   Joshua Bennet, carpenter
Moore, *Frampton Cotterell*, 1976, p. 255

Leicestershire
Evington
11702   William Vann, [framework knitter]
Wilshere, *Evington*, 1985, p. 50
Glenfield
11703   John Bennitt, [yeoman]
Wilshere, *Glenfield*, 1983, p. 14

Scotland
Orkney, Stronsay, Whitehall
11704   James Fea
Anon., *Orkney*, 1922-1923, p. 65

Shropshire
Madeley
11705   John Goodman
Trinder and Cox, *Severn Gorge*, 2000, pp. 314-316

Sussex
Whatlington
11706   John Dodderidge, clergyman [rector of Whatlington]
Hughes, *Sussex*, 2007, pp. 237-239

Wiltshire
Marlborough
11707   Francis Hurlbatt, carpenter
Williams and Thomson, *Marlborough*, 2007, pp. 287-290

Yorkshire
Whitby
11708   John Frank, mariner
Vickers, *Whitby*, 1986, p. 70
11709   Michael Webster, innkeeper
Vickers, *Whitby*, 1986, pp. 70-71

1735
Bristol
Westbury
11710   Hugh Clutson, [victualler]
Moore, *Clifton*, 1981, pp. 206-207

Essex
Colchester, St Mary
11711   Isaac Lemyng Rebow, esquire
Rickwood, 1918, pp. 18-25

Derbyshire
Chapel-en-le-Frith, Eaves
11712   Henry Kyrke
Kirke, 1864-1865, p. 174

Gloucestershire
Cheltenham
11713   Robert Gregory, butcher
Sale, *Cheltenham*, 1999, p. 185
11714   Martha Johnstone, sempstress, widow
Sale, *Cheltenham*, 1999, p. 182
11715   Hester Macock
Sale, *Cheltenham*, 1999, p. 186
Cheltenham, Westal
11716   John Mills, yeoman
Sale, *Cheltenham*, 1999, p. 186
Westerleigh
11717   Nathaniel Good, [yeoman]
Moore, *Frampton Cotterell*, 1976, pp. 255-256

Shropshire
Wellington
11718   Mary Bradshaw, widow
Trinder and Cox, *Telford*, 1980, pp. 377-378
Wrockwardine Wood, Quob Pool
11719   Richard Ball, collier
Trinder and Cox, *Telford*, 1980, p. 445
Wrockwardine, Leaton
11720   Peter Langley, gentleman
Trinder and Cox, *Telford*, 1980, pp. 446-448
Wrockwardine
11721   John Pemberton, gentleman
Trinder and Cox, *Telford*, 1980, pp. 445-446

Sussex
Hartfield
11722   Thomas Smythe, clergyman [vicar of Hartfield]
Hughes, *Sussex*, 2007, pp. 101-102

Hollington
11723 Thomas Denham, clergyman [vicar of Hollington]
Hughes, *Sussex*, 2007, pp. 105-106
Wiltshire
Marlborough
11724 Mary Wyatt, widow
Williams and Thomson, *Marlborough*, 2007, pp. 290-291

1736
Bristol
Bristol, St Philip and St Jacob
11725 Peter Dalton, brick maker
George, *Bristol*, 2008, pp. 149-150
Bristol
11726 John Mansell, haulier
George, *Bristol*, 2008, pp. 150-154
Clifton
11727 George Wheeler, victualler
Moore, *Clifton*, 1981, pp. 207-208
Essex
Hatfield Peverel, Toppingho Hall
11728 John Mortimer, [merchant]
Hope, 1943, pp. 122-124
Gloucestershire
Charlton Kings
11729 Obediah Rook, [husbandman]
Paget and Sale, *Charlton Kings*, 2003, p. 117
Cheltenham
11730 Margaret Milton, widow
Sale, *Cheltenham*, 1999, p. 184
Westerleigh
11731 Thomas Price, coalminer
Moore, *Frampton Cotterell*, 1976, p. 256
Winterbourne
11732 Nicholas Allbright, mason
Moore, *Frampton Cotterell*, 1976, p. 256
Ireland
Co. Meath, Killeen Castle
11733 Robert Plunkett, Earl of Fingall
ffolliott, 1977, pp. 102-107
Leicestershire
Evington
11734 William Smith
Wilshere, *Evington*, 1985, p. 51
Glenfield
11735 John Stedman, [yeoman]
Wilshere, *Glenfield*, 1983, p. 14
Kirby Muxloe
11736 Samuel Forman, yeoman
Wilshere, *Kirby Muxloe*, 1983, p. 30
Ratby
11737 Humphrey Baker
Wilshere, *Ratby*, 1984, p. 17
Lincolnshire
Cleethorpes
11738 Ralf Pickards
Ambler, Watkinson, *Clee*, 1987, pp. 185-186
Shropshire
Little Wenlock, Huntington Heath
11739 Francis Evans, collier
Trinder and Cox, *Severn Gorge*, 2000, p. 262
Wellington
11740 Benjamin Langley
Trinder and Cox, *Telford*, 1980, pp. 378-379

Staffordshire
Lower Gornal
11741 Thomas Bennett, farmer
Roper, *Sedgley*, 1960, p. 121
Worcestershire
Wribbenhall
11742 John Cheltnam, [yeoman]
Bewdley, *Bewdley*, 1991, pp. 197-201
Yorkshire
Horbury
11743 William Mansfield, yeoman
Bartlett, *Horbury*, 1980, p. 84
11744 Richard Shaw, salter
Bartlett, *Horbury*, 1980, pp. 89-90

1736 (c.)
Wiltshire
Marlborough
11745 Thomas Armon
Williams and Thomson, *Marlborough*, 2007, pp. 291-292

1737
Bristol
Clifton
11746 Robert Wood, tiler
Moore, *Clifton*, 1981, p. 209
Shirehampton
11747 Mary Palmer
Moore, *Clifton*, 1981, p. 208
Westbury
11748 James Weeks, cordwainer
Moore, *Clifton*, 1981, p. 209
Gloucestershire
Cheltenham
11749 Richard Gregory, skinner
Sale, *Cheltenham*, 1999, pp. 188-190
Frampton Cotterell
11750 John Musly, coalminer
Moore, *Frampton Cotterell*, 1976, p. 257
Iron Acton
11751 Mary Moore
Moore, *Frampton Cotterell*, 1976, p. 257
Winterbourne
11752 Richard Legg
Moore, *Frampton Cotterell*, 1976, p. 257
Lancashire
Little Crosby
11753 Nicholas Blundell, esquire
Bagley, 1972, pp. 239-244
Lincolnshire
Barrow-on-Humber
11754 Lawrence Johnson, yeoman
Johnson and Johnson, 1934, pp. 32-33
Shropshire
Broseley
11755 Hannah Hartshorne, widow
Trinder and Cox, *Severn Gorge*, 2000, p. 207
Dawley
11756 William Andrews, husbandman
Trinder and Cox, *Telford*, 1980, p. 189
Lilleshall
11757 William Adney, miller
Trinder and Cox, *Telford*, 1980, pp. 244-245

Wellington
  11758 Jane Hartshorne, widow of coal master
    Trinder and Cox, *Telford*, 1980, pp. 380-384
  11759 Charles Stowers, gardener
    Trinder and Cox, *Telford*, 1980, p. 379
  11760 John Wright, dyer
    Trinder and Cox, *Telford*, 1980, pp. 379-380
Somersetshire
Wembdon
  11761 Edward Coles, yeoman
    Monday and Siraut, *Somerset*, 2003, p. 69
Staffordshire
Harborne
  11762 John Freeth
    Bodfish, *Smethwick*, 1992, pp. 83-84
  11763 Abraham Powell, bricklayer
    Bodfish, *Smethwick*, 1992, pp. 81-82
Lower Gornal
  11764 Edward Guest, yeoman
    Roper, *Sedgley*, 1960, p. 122
Sedgley
  11765 John Perkes alias Purkes, nailer
    Roper, *Sedgley*, 1960, p. 122
Wiltshire
Marlborough
  11766 Joseph Blake
    Williams and Thomson, *Marlborough*, 2007, p. 292
Yorkshire
Horbury
  11767 Joshua Rais, clothmaker
    Bartlett, *Horbury*, 1980, pp. 91-92
Whitby
  11768 Robert Brown, mariner
    Vickers, *Whitby*, 1986, p. 71
  11769 Francis Clark, common sailor
    Vickers, *Whitby*, 1986, p. 71
  11770 William Sanderson, fisherman
    Vickers, *Whitby*, 1986, p. 71
  11771 Matthew Thompson
    Vickers, *Whitby*, 1986, p. 71
  11772 Francis Watson, mariner
    Vickers, *Whitby*, 1986, p. 71

1738
Berkshire
Windsor, Royal Gardens
  Charles Bridgeman, esquire (see London, Westminster)
Cheshire
Sale
  11773 George Jackson, [yeoman]
    Groves, *Ashton-on-Mersey and Sale*, 2002, p. 163
  11774 James Renshaw
    Groves, *Ashton-on-Mersey and Sale*, 2002, pp. 169-170
Dorset
East Chelborough
  11775 William Dawe
    Weinstock, *Syndercombe*, 1955, pp. 64-65
Gloucestershire
Cheltenham
  11776 John Caruthers, chapman
    Sale, *Cheltenham*, 1999, p. 190
Frampton Cotterell
  11777 Isaac Davis, yeoman
    Moore, *Frampton Cotterell*, 1976, p. 257

London
Kensington, Royal Gardens
  Charles Bridgeman, esquire (see Westminster)
St James's, Royal Gardens
  Charles Bridgeman, esquire (see Westminster)
Westminster, Broad (now Broadwick) Street
  11778 Charles Bridgeman, esquire (also listed
    Kensington, Royal Gardens, St James's Royal Gardens,
    Hampton Court and Hampton Court Royal Gardens,
    Middlesex, and Windsor, Royal Gardens, Berkshire)
    Carter, 1970, pp. 88-108
Middlesex
Hampton Court
  Charles Bridgeman, esquire (see Westminster, London)
Hampton Court, Royal Gardens
  Charles Bridgeman, esquire (see Westminster, London)
Scotland
Aberdeenshire, Monymusk Kirktown
  11779 [?] Morgan
    Hamilton, 1945, pp. 10-12
Shropshire
Lilleshall, Donnington
  11780 Richard Adney
    Trinder and Cox, *Telford*, 1980, p. 245
Wellington
  11781 John Cherrington, dyer
    Trinder and Cox, *Telford*, 1980, pp. 384-385
Wellington, Watling Street
  11782 William Cleaton
    Trinder and Cox, *Telford*, 1980, pp. 386-387
Wellington
  11783 John Hicks, baker
    Trinder and Cox, *Telford*, 1980, pp. 387-388
Wrockwardine, Long Lane
  11784 Robert Allen, joiner
    Trinder and Cox, *Telford*, 1980, pp. 448-449
  11785 Jonathan Dabbs, yeoman
    Trinder and Cox, *Telford*, 1980, pp. 449-450
Staffordshire
Sedgley
  11786 Ann Bennett, widow
    Roper, *Sedgley*, 1960, p. 123
Sussex
Billingshurst
  11787 John Bullis, clergyman, [vicar of Billingshurst]
    Hughes, *Sussex*, 2007, pp. 28-29
Yorkshire
Horbury
  11788 John Binns, cordwainer
    Bartlett, *Horbury*, 1980, p. 95

1739
Bristol
Bristol, St Leonard
  11789 Mathew Adean, wine cooper
    George, *Bristol*, 2008, pp. 155-162
Dorsetshire
Chetnole
  11790 Sarah Watts, widow
    Machin, *Yetminster*, 1976, No.135, (2 pp.)
London
Wapping
  11791 Old Dundee Lodge, No. 18 (to 1754)
    Rose, 1951, pp. 208-209

Shropshire
Broseley
11792 John Poole, trowman
Trinder and Cox, *Severn Gorge*, 2000, pp. 207-208
Wellington
11793 Ralph Boulton Leeke
Trinder and Cox, *Telford*, 1980, pp. 389-390

Staffordshire
Sedgley
11794 Richard Wainwright, nailer
Roper, *Sedgley*, 1960, p. 124
Smethwick
11795 Richard Cater, yeoman
Bodfish, *Smethwick*, 1992, pp. 85-88

Sussex
Fernhurst
11796 Henry Baker, clergyman [curate of Fernhurst]
Hughes, *Sussex*, 2007, pp. 73-74

Yorkshire
Horbury
11797 Elkanah Coop, clothier
Bartlett, *Horbury*, 1980, p. 97

1740

Bedfordshire
Houghton Manor House, Houghton Regis
11798 Henry Brandreth, esquire
Collett-White, *Bedfordshire*, 1995, pp. 126-130
Wrest Park, Silsoe
11799 Henry Grey, Duke of Kent
Collett-White, *Bedfordshire*, 1995, pp. 251-272

Dorsetshire
Leigh
11800 John White, yeoman
Machin, *Yetminster*, 1976, No.136, (1 p.)

Gloucestershire
Cheltenham
11801 Samuel Bisco, [weaver]
Sale, *Cheltenham*, 1999, pp. 191-192
Cheltenham, Westal
11802 Thomas Giles, yeoman
Sale, *Cheltenham*, 1999, p. 190
Cheltenham
11803 John Wills, [yeoman]
Sale, *Cheltenham*, 1999, p. 191
Coalpit Heath, Mays Hill
11804 Alice Sifford, widow
Moore, *Frampton Cotterell*, 1976, p. 257

London
Marlborough House
Executors of John Churchill, Duke of Marlborough
(see Blenheim Palace, Oxfordshire)

Oxfordshire
Blenheim Palace
11805 Executors of John Churchill, Duke of
Marlborough (also listed Marlborough House, London)
Murdoch, *Noble Households*, 2006, pp. 275-287

Shropshire
Broseley
11806 Benjamin Buckley, trowman
Trinder and Cox, *Severn Gorge*, 2000, pp. 209-211
11807 Henry Carrington, glover
Trinder and Cox, *Severn Gorge*, 2000, pp. 211-212

11808 Thomas Taylor alias Syner, tobacco pipe maker
Trinder and Cox, *Severn Gorge*, 2000, pp. 208-209
Wellington, Watling Street
11809 John Bromley, blacksmith
Trinder and Cox, *Telford*, 1980, pp. 390-391
11810 James Massey, innkeeper
Trinder and Cox, *Telford*, 1980, pp. 391-392
Wrockwardine, Clotley
11811 William Binnell
Trinder and Cox, *Telford*, 1980, p. 450

Sussex
Billingshurst
11812 William Jackman, yeoman
Lawson, 1999, pp. 13-15

Wales
Montgomeryshire, Llanfihangel
11813 Owen Davies
Gilson, *Llanfihangel*, 2009, pp. 47-49

Westmorland
Bampton
11814 Edmund Law
Jackson, *Laws*, 1876, p. 274

Wiltshire
Marlborough
11815 William Flower, baker
Williams and Thomson, *Marlborough*, 2007, pp. 292-293

Yorkshire
Whitby
11816 Jane Blackburn, widow
Vickers, *Whitby*, 1986, p. 72
11817 Robert Coates
Vickers, *Whitby*, 1986, p. 72
11818 Jane Crow, widow
Vickers, *Whitby*, 1986, p. 72
11819 John Gray, sailor
Vickers, *Whitby*, 1986, pp. 72-73
11820 William Porret
Vickers, *Whitby*, 1986, p. 72
11821 Matthew Porrit, mariner
Vickers, *Whitby*, 1986, p. 73
11822 Gregory Scrafton, sailor
Vickers, *Whitby*, 1986, p. 73

1741

Bristol
Westbury
11823 Benjamin Bartholomew, cordwainer
Moore, *Clifton*, 1981, pp. 209-210

Cheshire
Ashton-on-Mersey
11824 John Key
Groves, *Ashton-on-Mersey and Sale*, 2002, pp. 171-172

Cornwall
Withiel
11825 Thomas Hicks
Pedler, 1984, p. 39

Gloucestershire
Charlton Kings
11826 Thomas Moulder, [husbandman]
Paget and Sale, *Charlton Kings*, 2003, p. 117
Coalpit Heath, Mays Hill
Sir John Smyth, baronet (see Long Ashton, Ashton
Court, Somersetshire)

Tockington
  Sir John Dineley [Goodere], baronet (see Charlton,
  Worcestershire)
Herefordshire
  Burghope
  Sir John Dineley [Goodere], baronet (see Charlton,
  Worcestershire)
Ireland
  Co. Clare, Killaloe
  11827 John McNamara, brogue maker
    ffolliott, *Household*, 1969, p. 46
London
  Carpenters Hall
  11828 Carpenters Company
    Jupp, 1887, p. 642
  St James's, Duke's Place
  11829 Mrs Hannah Davila [de Avila]
    Rodrigues-Pereira, 2007, pp. 33-35
Shropshire
  Broseley
  11830 Thomas Crowther, glazier
    Trinder and Cox, *Severn Gorge*, 2000, pp. 214-215
  11831 Ann Gough, widow
    Trinder and Cox, *Severn Gorge*, 2000, pp. 213-214
  11832 William Holmes
    Trinder and Cox, *Severn Gorge*, 2000, pp. 215-216
  11833 Mary Penn
    Trinder and Cox, *Severn Gorge*, 2000, pp. 212-213
  Wellington
  11834 Robert Stanley, stone cutter
    Trinder and Cox, *Telford*, 1980, p. 393
  11835 William Webb
    Trinder and Cox, *Telford*, 1980, pp. 393-395
Somersetshire
  Christon
  Sir John Smyth, baronet (see Long Ashton, Ashton
  Court)
  Long Ashton, Ashton Court
  11836 Sir John Smyth, baronet (also listed Christon,
  and Coalpit Heath, Mays Hill,
  Gloucestershire)
    Moore, *Frampton Cotterell*, 1976, pp. 275-287
Sussex
  Ashurst
  11837 John Brownsword, clergyman
    Hughes, *Sussex*, 2007, pp. 12-14
Worcestershire
  Charlton
  11838 Sir John Dineley [Goodere], baronet (also listed
  Tockington, Gloucestershire, Burghope, Herefordshire,
  and Little Comberton, Worcestershire)
    Wanklyn, *Worcestershire*, 1998, pp. 377-389
  Little Comberton
  Sir John Dineley [Goodere], baronet (see Charlton,
  Worcestershire; also listed Tockington, Gloucstershire,
  and Burghope, Herefordshire)
Yorkshire
  Horbury
  11839 Daniel Richardson, clothier
    Bartlett, *Horbury*, 1980, p. 103
  11840 John Stringer, carpenter
    Bartlett, *Horbury*, 1980, p. 105

1741 (c.)
Yorkshire
  Horbury
  11841 Thomas Wood
    Bartlett, *Horbury*, 1980, p. 99

1742
Bristol
  Bristol
  11842 Richard Sanders, cordwainer
    George, *Bristol*, 2008, pp. 162-166
  11843 Thomas Tillard, lime-burner
    George, *Bristol*, 2008, pp. 166-167
Cheshire
  Ashton-on-Mersey
  11844 Joseph Artstall
    Groves, *Ashton-on-Mersey and Sale*, 2002, pp. 173-174
  11845 William Moss, [linen weaver]
    Groves, *Ashton-on-Mersey and Sale*, 2002, pp. 179-181
  11846 Hannah Rideing alias Tipping
    Groves, *Ashton-on-Mersey and Sale*, 2002, p. 175
  Sale
  11847 James Barlow
    Groves, *Ashton-on-Mersey and Sale*, 2002, pp. 183-184
Gloucestershire
  Iron Acton
  11848 Martha Woodward, [widow]
    Moore, *Frampton Cotterell*, 1976, p. 258
  Westerleigh
  11849 John Oliver, feltmaker
    Moore, *Frampton Cotterell*, 1976, p. 257
Leicestershire
  Evington
  11850 John Parker
    Wilshere, *Evington*, 1985, p. 52
Lincolnshire
  Cleethorpes
  11851 Thomas Dean, husbandman
    Ambler, Watkinson, *Clee*, 1987, p. 186
London
  Finsbury, Old Street
  11852 French Hospital
    Murdoch and Vigne, 2009, pp. 111-116
Shropshire
  Benthall
  11853 William Day, trowman
    Trinder and Cox, *Severn Gorge*, 2000, p. 139
  Broseley
  11854 Edward Jones, collier
    Trinder and Cox, *Severn Gorge*, 2000, p. 218
  11855 William Pearce, master collier
    Trinder and Cox, *Severn Gorge*, 2000, pp. 219-221
  11856 Edward Reynolds, dyer
    Trinder and Cox, *Severn Gorge*, 2000, p. 218
  11857 Joseph Whitefoot, mason
    Trinder and Cox, *Severn Gorge*, 2000, pp. 216-217
  Little Wenlock, The Leasows
  11858 Roger Thresslecock, yeoman
    Trinder and Cox, *Severn Gorge*, 2000, pp. 262-263
  Wellington, Ketley Brook
  11859 William Davis, weaver
    Trinder and Cox, *Telford*, 1980, pp. 395-396

Wellington
  11860 Robert Harper, shoemaker
    Trinder and Cox, *Telford*, 1980, pp. 396-397
Wrockwardine Wood, Quob Pool
  11861 Richard Fenn
    Trinder and Cox, *Telford*, 1980, pp. 450-451
Staffordshire
Ettingshall
  11862 Edward Gibbons, gentleman
    Roper, *Sedgley*, 1960, p. 125

1743
Essex
Writtle
  11863 Philip Bright
    Steer, *Mid-Essex*, 1969, pp. 268-269
Gloucestershire
Westerleigh
  11864 John Lewis, [yeoman]
    Moore, *Frampton Cotterell*, 1976, pp. 258-261
Oxfordshire
Ditchley
  11865 George Henry Lee, Earl of Litchfield
    Murdoch, *Noble Households*, 2006, pp. 145-152
Shropshire
Benthall
  11866 Daniel Dea [Day], yeoman, barge owner
    Trinder and Cox, *Severn Gorge*, 2000, pp. 139-140
Benthall, The Hilltop
  11867 Thomas Hartshorne, tobacco pipe maker
    Trinder and Cox, *Severn Gorge*, 2000, pp. 140-141
Broseley
  11868 Sylvanus Bell, trowman
    Trinder and Cox, *Severn Gorge*, 2000, pp. 221-222
Madeley Wood
  11869 William Easthope, labourer, ground collier
    Trinder and Cox, *Severn Gorge*, 2000, pp. 316-317
Wellington
  11870 John Mansell, glover
    Trinder and Cox, *Telford*, 1980, p. 397
Wrockwardine, Clotley
  11871 Abigail Binnell, widow
    Trinder and Cox, *Telford*, 1980, pp. 451-452

1744
Bristol
Bristol
  11872 John Bartlett, brush-maker
    George, *Bristol*, 2008, pp. 167-171
Cheshire
Bowdon
  11873 John Clark
    Groves, *Bowdon*, 1999, pp. 45-46
Dorsetshire
Yetminster
  11874 Joseph Patton, [clothier]
    Machin, *Yetminster*, 1976, No.137, (1 p.)
Essex
Writtle
  11875 Theophilus Lingard
    Steer, *Mid-Essex*, 1969, pp. 269-270
  11876 Richard Reddings
    Steer, *Mid-Essex*, 1969, p. 271

Gloucestershire
Charlton Kings
  11877 John Newman, [yeoman]
    Paget and Sale, *Charlton Kings*, 2003, p. 119
  11878 Jacob Portret, fan painter
    Paget and Sale, *Charlton Kings*, 2003, pp. 120-121
Coalpit Heath, Mays Hill
  11879 Thomas Baylis, yeoman
    Moore, *Frampton Cotterell*, 1976, pp. 261-262
Westerleigh
  11880 Mary Cook, widow
    Moore, *Frampton Cotterell*, 1976, p. 261
Leicestershire
Ratby
  11881 Dannil Kemp, [husbandman?]
    Wilshere, *Ratby*, 1984, p. 20
Middlesex
Twickenham, Pope's Villa
  11882 Alexander Pope
    Anon., *Pope*, 1882, pp. 363-365
    Mack, 1969, pp. 244-258
Shropshire
Broseley
  11883 Samuel Head
    Trinder and Cox, *Severn Gorge*, 2000, pp. 223-224
  11884 John Oakes, trowman
    Trinder and Cox, *Severn Gorge*, 2000, pp. 222-223
Dawley
  11885 William Keen, yeoman
    Trinder and Cox, *Telford*, 1980, pp. 189-191
Wrockwardine, Allscott
  11886 Thomas Calcott
    Trinder and Cox, *Telford*, 1980, pp. 452-455
Staffordshire
Acton Trussell
  11887 William Dicken, yeoman
    Anon., *Acton Trussell*, 1995, pp. 63-64
Sussex
Kirdford
  11888 Thomas Cooper, husbandman
    Kenyon, *Kirdford*, 1955, pp. 123-124
Yorkshire
Whitby
  11889 Joseph Ellis, mariner
    Vickers, *Whitby*, 1986, p. 76
  11890 Charles Lightfoot, Bailiff of Whitby Strand
    Vickers, *Whitby*, 1986, pp. 73-76
  11891 Robert Patison, blacksmith
    Vickers, *Whitby*, 1986, p. 76

1744 (c.)
Wiltshire
Marlborough
  11892 Robert Tuck, [spoonmaker]
    Williams and Thomson, *Marlborough*, 2007, p. 293

1745
Dorsetshire
Chetnole
  11893 Hannah Elford
    Machin, *Yetminster*, 1976, No.138, (1 p.)
Leicestershire
Botcheston
  11894 Robert Pickrian, carpenter
    Wilshere, *Ratby*, 1984, p. 21

Glenfield
  11895 Henry Glew, [husbandman]
    Wilshere, *Glenfield*, 1983, p. 15
  11896 Peter Heward, farmer
    Wilshere, *Glenfield*, 1983, p. 15

Norfolk
Houghton Hall
  11897 Sir Robert Walpole, Earl of Orford
    Murdoch, *Noble Households*, 2006, pp. 170-184

Scotland
Orkney, Stronsay, Whitehall
  11898 Jean Manson, widow
    Anon., *Orkney*, 1922-1923, pp. 65-66

Shropshire
Broseley
  11899 Samuel Burrows, joiner and carpenter
    Trinder and Cox, *Severn Gorge*, 2000, pp. 224-225
  11900 James Garmson
    Trinder and Cox, *Severn Gorge*, 2000, p. 226
Wellington, Ketley Brook
  11901 William Briscoe, yeoman
    Trinder and Cox, *Telford*, 1980, p. 398

Warwickshire
Stoneleigh, Fletchamstead
  11902 Mr John Atkins, gentleman
    Alcock, *Warwickshire*, 1993, pp. 151-153

Wiltshire
Marlborough
  11903 Eleanor Drury, widow
    Williams and Thomson, *Marlborough*, 2007, p. 293

Yorkshire
Horbury
  11904 Thomas Preston
    Bartlett, *Horbury*, 1980, p. 112
  11905 John Rhodes, gentleman
    Bartlett, *Horbury*, 1980, pp. 115-116

1746

London
Montagu House, Bloomsbury
  11906 John, Duke of Montagu
    Murdoch, *Noble Households*, 2006, pp. 87-116

Shropshire
Madeley Wood, The Green
  11907 John Boden, coalminer
    Trinder and Cox, *Severn Gorge*, 2000, p. 318
Madeley Wood
  11908 John Easthope, yeoman
    Trinder and Cox, *Severn Gorge*, 2000, pp. 318-319
Wellington, The Seven Stars
  11909 Francis Peate
    Trinder and Cox, *Telford*, 1980, pp. 398-400

Wiltshire
Marlborough
  11910 John Morris, [carpenter]
    Williams and Thomson, *Marlborough*, 2007, pp. 293-295
  11911 Stephen Willoughby, vintner
    Williams and Thomson, *Marlborough*, 2007, pp. 295-299

1747

Cheshire
Ashton-on-Mersey
  11912 John Heald, [yeoman]
    Groves, *Ashton-on-Mersey and Sale*, 2002, p. 197

  11913 William Robinson, [yeoman]
    Groves, *Ashton-on-Mersey and Sale*, 2002, pp. 186-187

Devonshire
Uffculme
  11914 Mary Jerwood, [widow]
    Wyatt, *Uffculme*, 1997, pp. 184-185

Gloucesteshire
Charlton Kings
  11915 Mary Peachey, widow
    Paget and Sale, *Charlton Kings*, 2003, p. 122
Westerleigh
  11916 Thomas Perse, [collier]
    Moore, *Frampton Cotterell*, 1976, pp. 262-263

Leicestershire
Glenfield
  11917 James Hassall, farmer
    Wilshere, *Glenfield*, 1983, p. 16

Scotland
Orkney, Burray
  11918 Sir James Stewart, baronet
    Marwick, 1934, pp. 48-53

Shropshire
Broseley
  11919 John Wilde, trowman
    Trinder and Cox, *Severn Gorge*, 2000, pp. 226-227
Dawley, Great Dawley
  11920 John Harris, yeoman
    Trinder and Cox, *Telford*, 1980, pp. 191-192
Wrockwardine, Charlton
  11921 Jonathan Hawkins, yeoman
    Trinder and Cox, *Telford*, 1980, p. 456

Staffordshire
Harborne
  11922 Gilbert Warley, yeoman
    Bodfish, *Smethwick*, 1992, pp. 89-90

Sussex
Ambersham
  11923 Elizabeth Capron, widow
    Godman, 1908, pp. 118-122

Wiltshire
Marlborough
  11924 Jane Jeffariss, widow
    Williams and Thomson, *Marlborough*, 2007, pp. 301-302
  11925 William Serle
    Williams and Thomson, *Marlborough*, 2007, pp. 299-301

Yorkshire
Whitby
  11926 Thomas Collins, mariner
    Vickers, *Whitby*, 1986, p. 77
  11927 Thomas Hill, mariner
    Vickers, *Whitby*, 1986, p. 76
  11928 John Porrett, mariner
    Vickers, *Whitby*, 1986, p. 77
  11929 Richard Ward, mariner
    Vickers, *Whitby*, 1986, p. 77

1748

Cheshire
Ashton-on-Mersey
  11930 Thomas Davies
    Groves, *Ashton-on-Mersey and Sale*, 2002, p. 194
  11931 John Whitelegg, [yeoman]
    Groves, *Ashton-on-Mersey and Sale*, 2002, pp. 192-193

Co. Durham
Sherburn
11932 Christ's Hospital
Allan, 1771, 2pp. at end
Gloucestershire
Westerleigh, Nibley
11933 John Rolf, shot-maker
Moore, *Frampton Cotterell*, 1976, p. 263
Westerleigh
11934 Sarah Smalcombe
Moore, *Frampton Cotterell*, 1976, p. 264
Winterbourne
11935 James Stephens, schoolmaster
Moore, *Frampton Cotterell*, 1976, p. 263
Ireland
Co. Tipperary, Modreeny, Corroul
11936 John Egan, [farmer]
ffolliott, *Household*, 1969, pp. 46-47
Leicestershire
Kirby Muxloe
11937 Robert Moore, grazier
Wilshere, *Kirby Muxloe*, 1983, pp. 31-32
Ratby
11938 John Baker
Wilshere, *Ratby*, 1984, p. 21
11939 Charles Wilkinson, yeoman
Wilshere, *Ratby*, 1984, p. 21
Lincolnshire
Winteringham
11940 Mordecai Westoby
Neave, *Winteringham*, 1984, pp. 155-156
Northamptonshire
Little Harrowden
11941 Thomas Allderman, [yeoman]
Alderman, *Alderman*, 2008, p. 89
Shropshire
Broseley, The Bowling Green
11942 William Yates, trowman
Trinder and Cox, *Severn Gorge*, 2000, pp. 227-228
Lilleshall
11943 James Spender, yeoman
Trinder and Cox, *Telford*, 1980, pp. 246-247
Wiltshire
Marlborough
11944 Francis Gregory, cutler
Williams and Thomson, *Marlborough*, 2007, pp. 302-305

1748 (c.)
Cheshire
Bowdon
11945 Thomas Davenport, yeoman
Groves, *Bowdon*, 1999, pp. 47-48

1749
Bedfordshire
Leighton Buzzard Prebendal House
11946 Hon. Charles Leigh
Collett-White, *Bedfordshire*, 1995, pp. 154-163
Bristol
Bristol
11947 George Fenton, sail-maker
George, *Bristol*, 2008, pp. 171-175
11948 Thomas Parry, mariner
George, *Bristol*, 2008, pp. 175-176

Essex
Writtle
11949 John Portway
Steer, *Mid-Essex*, 1969, pp. 271-272
Gloucestershire
Charlton Kings
11950 Judith Probert, widow
Paget and Sale, *Charlton Kings*, 2003, pp. 123-124
Coalpit Heath
11951 John Pullin, [rough mason]
Moore, *Frampton Cotterell*, 1976, p. 264
Iron Acton
11952 William Sarney, [yeoman]
Moore, *Frampton Cotterell*, 1976, p. 264
Westerleigh
11953 John Newman, labourer
Moore, *Frampton Cotterell*, 1976, p. 264
Leicestershire
Evington
11954 Thomas Mauson, [grazier]
Wilshere, *Evington*, 1985, p. 53
Ratby
11955 Henry Everat, [labourer]
Wilshere, *Ratby*, 1984, p. 22
Middlesex
Bruce Castle
11956 Henry Hare, Baron Coleraine
Cooper, 2003, pp. 100-106
Scotland
Aberdeenshire, Monymusk
11957 Isobel Park
Hamilton, 1956, p. 138
11958 The Spinners at the Mains
Hamilton, 1956, p. 138
Shropshire
Madeley
11959 John Harper, yeoman
Trinder and Cox, *Severn Gorge*, 2000, pp. 319-321
Wiltshire
Marlborough
11960 William Clifford, shopkeeper
Williams and Thomson, *Marlborough*, 2007, pp. 306-308
11961 Thomas Kendall, vintner
Williams and Thomson, *Marlborough*, 2007, pp. 305-306

1750
Bristol
Bristol
11962 Samuel Floyd, fan-maker
George, *Bristol*, 2008, pp. 176-177
Westbury
11963 John French, yeoman
Moore, *Clifton*, 1981, p. 210
Gloucestershire
Iron Acton
11964 Thomas Wollan [Oland], innholder
Moore, *Frampton Cotterell*, 1976, p. 264
Westerleigh
11965 Mary Roberts, widow
Moore, *Frampton Cotterell*, 1976, p. 264
Ireland
Co. Offaly, Shinrone
11966 William and Joseph Collins
Anon., *Collins*, 1972, pp. 104-105

Leicestershire
Evington, Bushby
  11967 William Goddard, [grazier]
    Wilshere, *Evington*, 1985, p. 53
Oxfordshire
Wheatley
  11968 Wm Thoms [Tombes]
    Hassall, 1956, pp. 76-77
Scotland
Aberdeenshire, Monymusk
  11969 The Lint Mill
    Hamilton, 1956, pp. 146-147
Shropshire
Broseley
  11970 Ann Simpson, widow
    Trinder and Cox, *Severn Gorge*, 2000, pp. 229-230
Madeley Wood
  11971 Thomas Boden, ground collier
    Trinder and Cox, *Severn Gorge*, 2000, pp. 321-322
Yorkshire
Whitby
  11972 William Coulson, ship builder
    Vickers, *Whitby*, 1986, pp. 77-79
  11973 Richard Harrison, mariner
    Vickers, *Whitby*, 1986, p. 77
  11974 Elizabeth West, wife of Robert West, whitesmith
    Vickers, *Whitby*, 1986, p. 77
  11975 Thomas West, mason
    Vickers, *Whitby*, 1986, p. 79

1751
Bristol
Westbury
  11976 Thomas Davis, mariner
    Moore, *Clifton*, 1981, p. 211
Gloucestershire
Winterbourne
  11977 John Griffiths, yeoman
    Moore, *Frampton Cotterell*, 1976, p. 265
Ireland
Co. Clare, Borshalagh
  11978 Mrs Alice Blood, [widow]
    ffolliott, *Household*, 1969, pp. 49-51
Co. Tipperary, Nenagh
  11979 Doctor John McKeogh
    ffolliott, *Household*, 1969, pp. 47-48
Leicestershire
Ratby, Newtown Unthank
  11980 Thomas Hunt, yeoman
    Wilshere, *Ratby*, 1984, p. 23
Ratby
  11981 John Jordan, farmer
    Wilshere, *Ratby*, 1984, p
Scotland
Edinburgh, Canongate
  11982 Kilwinning Lodge, No. 2
    Rose, 1953, p. 99
Warwickshire
Wolston
  11983 Susannah Hubert, widow
    Alcock and Lane, 2003, pp. 114-121

Yorkshire
Ecclesfield
  11984 Andrew Revill, cutler
    Hey, 1969, pp. 115-117
Whitby
  11985 Richard Boynton, mariner
    Vickers, *Whitby*, 1986, p. 79
  11986 John Harwood, mariner
    Vickers, *Whitby*, 1986, p. 79

1752
Bristol
Bristol
  11987 Elizabeth Lawrence, widow
    George, *Bristol*, 2008, pp. 177-181
Clifton
  11988 Ann Noot, widow
    Moore, *Clifton*, 1981, p. 211
Cheshire
Middlewich, Kinderton
  11989 Poor House
    Earl, 1990, pp. 93-94, 97-98
Ireland
Co. Tipperary, Borrisokane, Ballyhaugh
  11990 Jonathan Kent, gentleman
    ffolliott, *Household*, 1969, pp. 48-49
Leicestershire
Braunstone
  11991 Nicholas Norris
    Wilshere, *Braunstone*, 1983, p. 40
Evington
  11992 Thomas Brion, [framework knitter]
    Wilshere, *Evington*, 1985, p. 54
Glenfield
  11993 Michael Bradshaw, farmer
    Wilshere, *Glenfield*, 1983, p. 16
Ratby
  11994 Thomas Bunney, [labourer?]
    Wilshere, *Ratby*, 1984, p. 23
Scotland
Aberdeenshire, Monymusk
  11995 Christain Gellan
    Hamilton, 1945, p. 16
Shropshire
Benthall
  11996 William Smith, miner, collier
    Trinder and Cox, *Severn Gorge*, 2000, p. 142
Yorkshire
Whitby
  11997 Miles Sweeting
    Vickers, *Whitby*, 1986, pp. 79-80

1752 (c.)
Ireland
Cork
  11998 Cork Lodge, No. 27
    Rose, 1952, p. 167

1753
Bristol
Clifton
  11999 James Pullin, [mariner]
    Moore, *Clifton*, 1981, p. 211

Gloucestershire
Frampton Cotterell
12000 John Hathway, [yeoman]
Moore, *Frampton Cotterell*, 1976, p. 265
Westerleigh
12001 John Love, feltmaker
Moore, *Frampton Cotterell*, 1976, p. 265
Ireland
Dromoland House, Co. Clare
12002 Sir Edward O'Brien, baronet
Fenlon, *Ireland,* 2003, pp. 130-134
Shropshire
Broseley
12003 John Leadbeater, gentleman
Trinder and Cox, *Severn Gorge*, 2000, pp. 230-231
Madeley
12004 Mary Clemson, widow
Trinder and Cox, *Severn Gorge*, 2000, p. 322
Yorkshire
Whitby
12005 John Askwith, shipwright
Vickers, *Whitby*, 1986, p. 80
12006 Hannah Robinson, servant
Vickers, *Whitby*, 1986, p. 80

1753 (c.)
Shropshire
Benthall
12007 Richard Aston, collier
Trinder and Cox, *Severn Gorge*, 2000, pp. 142-143

1754
Bristol
Clifton
12008 Edmund Rogers, [kilnmaster]
Moore, *Clifton*, 1981, pp. 211-212
Cumberland
Stapleton, Dormansteads
12009 Thomasine Hodgson, widow
Hudleston, 1968, p. 94
Devonshire
Uffculme
12010 Giles Brook, [husbandman]
Wyatt, *Uffculme*, 1997, pp. 185
Gloucestershire
Frampton Cotterell
12011 Christopher Sturge, feltmaker
Moore, *Frampton Cotterell*, 1976, pp. 265-266
Kent
Chatham
12012 James Best's brewery
Melling, 1961, pp. 122-123
Leicestershire
Glenfield
12013 John Earp, yeoman
Wilshere, *Glenfield*, 1983, p. 17
Kirby Muxloe
12014 Mary Wight, [grazier]
Wilshere, *Kirby Muxloe*, 1983, p. 33
Shropshire
Coalbrookdale
12015 John Jones, forgeman
Trinder and Cox, *Severn Gorge*, 2000, p. 323

Sussex
Kirdford
12016 Mr William Boxall, mercer
Kenyon, *Kirdford*, 1956, pp. 148-150

1754 (c.)
Shropshire
Madeley Wood
12017 Edward Thomas, coalminer
Trinder and Cox, *Severn Gorge*, 2000, pp. 323-324

1755
Cheshire
Ashton-on-Mersey
12018 Richard Parker, [yeoman]
Groves, *Ashton-on-Mersey and Sale*, 2002, pp. 221-222
Leicestershire
Glenfield
12019 [Cecily] Steadman, widow
Wilshere, *Glenfield*, 1983, p. 18
Shropshire
Broseley
12020 Robert Love, ground collier
Trinder and Cox, *Severn Gorge*, 2000, pp. 231-232
Little Wenlock
12021 William Baugh
Trinder and Cox, *Severn Gorge*, 2000, pp. 263-264
Madeley
12022 Thomas Rowley, blacksmith
Trinder and Cox, *Severn Gorge*, 2000, p. 324
Wales
Anglesey, Llanddyfnan
12023 Hugh Griffiths, pedlar
Barnes, 1969-70, pp. 235-236
Yorkshire
Whitby
12024 William Prust, seaman
Vickers, *Whitby*, 1986, p. 80

1756
Bristol
Bristol
12025 Henry Poole, wheelwright
George, *Bristol*, 2008, pp. 181-184
Ireland
Co. Tipperary, Nenagh, Anamalle
12026 Richard Ryan
ffolliott, *Household*, 1969, p. 49
Leicestershire
Ratby
12027 John Kinton, [yeoman?]
Wilshere, *Ratby*, 1984, p. 23
Shropshire
Broseley
12028 Noel [Nevill] Edwards
Trinder and Cox, *Severn Gorge*, 2000, p. 232
12029 William Morris, tobacco pipe maker
Trinder and Cox, *Severn Gorge*, 2000, p. 233
Warwickshire
Stoneleigh
12030 William Watton, yeoman
Alcock, *Warwickshire*, 1993, p. 109

Yorkshire
Sowerby
12031 Workhouse
Kendall, 1956, pp. 63-64
Whitby
12032 Thomas Gill, seaman
Vickers, *Whitby*, 1986, p. 81
12033 Mary Hardy, widow
Vickers, *Whitby*, 1986, p. 81
12034 George Robinson, mariner
Vickers, *Whitby*, 1986, p. 81

1757

Cheshire
Ashton-on-Mersey
12035 John Duncalf
Groves, *Ashton-on-Mersey and Sale*, 2002, pp. 225-226
Sale
12036 Edward Marsland, [farmer]
Groves, *Ashton-on-Mersey and Sale*, 2002, p. 227
12037 John Renshaw, [parish clerk]
Groves, *Ashton-on-Mersey and Sale*, 2002, pp. 229-230
Dorsetshire
Yetminster
12038 John Mose
Machin, *Yetminster*, 1976, No.140, (1 p.)
Gloucestershire
Westerleigh
12039 Joseph Limbrick, [yeoman]
Moore, *Frampton Cotterell*, 1976, p. 266
Leicestershire
Glenfield
12040 Rebecca Heward, widow
Wilshere, *Glenfield*, 1983, p. 18
Shropshire
Broseley
12041 Francis Wilkes, collier
Trinder and Cox, *Severn Gorge*, 2000, pp. 234-235
12042 John Yates, trowman
Trinder and Cox, *Severn Gorge*, 2000, p. 234
Wales
Anglesey, Llanbedrgoch
12043 Richard Griffith
Barnes, 1969-70, pp. 236-238
Yorkshire
Horbury
12044 William Marsdin, yeoman
Bartlett, *Horbury*, 1981, pp. 4-5
Whitby
12045 John Clarke, mariner
Vickers, *Whitby*, 1986, pp. 81-82
12046 Stephen Nessfield, mariner
Vickers, *Whitby*, 1986, p. 82
12047 William Peacock, mariner
Vickers, *Whitby*, 1986, p. 82

1758

Bristol
Westbury
12048 William Tock, yeoman
Moore, *Clifton*, 1981, p. 212
Dorsetshire
Unlocated
12049 James Hallery
Machin, *Yetminster*, 1976, No.139, (1 p.)

Ireland
Co. Offaly, Castlejordan, Killowen
12050 Robert Fayle, [farmer]
Goodbody, *Quaker*, 1971, pp. 59-62
Leicestershire
Glenfield
12051 John Hasal, [yeoman]
Wilshere, *Glenfield*, 1983, p. 19
Ratby
12052 William Arnold, [husbandman]
Wilshere, *Ratby*, 1984, p. 24
Shropshire
Broseley
12053 Ambrose Buckley, trowman
Trinder and Cox, *Severn Gorge*, 2000, pp. 235-236
12054 William Hall, weaver
Trinder and Cox, *Severn Gorge*, 2000, p. 236
Sussex
Petworth
12055 William Johnson, innkeeper
Kenyon, *Petworth*, 1961, pp. 126-135
Wiltshire
Marlborough
12056 Thomas Goatley, yeoman
Williams and Thomson, *Marlborough*, 2007, pp. 308-311
Yorkshire
Barnoldswick
12057 Elizabeth Armistead, widow
Kirk, *Barnoldswick*, 1951, p. 56
Horbury
12058 Joseph Marsden, clothier
Bartlett, *Horbury*, 1981, p. 14

1759

Cheshire
Sale
12059 John Moores, [husbandman]
Groves, *Ashton-on-Mersey and Sale*, 2002, pp. 234-235
Dorsetshire
Blandford
12060 Ann Shergold, [ceramic dealer]
Draper, 1982, pp. 89-91
Scotland
Edinburgh, Drylaw
12061 James Loch
Loch, 1934, pp. 215-234
Shropshire
Coalbrookdale
12062 Richard Pritchard, yeoman, shopkeeper
Trinder and Cox, *Severn Gorge*, 2000, p. 326
Madeley Wood
12063 John Palmer, master collier
Trinder and Cox, *Severn Gorge*, 2000, pp. 325-326
Worcestershire
Moseley Hall, King's Norton
12064 Richard Grevis, esquire
Wanklyn, *Worcestershire*, 1998, pp. 389-393
Yorkshire
Barnoldswick
12065 William Lowcock
Kirk, *Barnoldswick*, 1951, p. 74
Whitby
12066 William Ashley, mariner
Vickers, *Whitby*, 1986, p. 82

12067 John Easton, mariner
  Vickers, *Whitby*, 1986, pp. 82-83
12068 John Temple, mariner
  Vickers, *Whitby*, 1986, p. 82
12069 Robert Wood, blacksmith
  Vickers, *Whitby*, 1986, p. 83

1760
Leicestershire
 Ratby
  12070 Thomas Adcock, [yeoman?]
   Wilshere, *Ratby*, 1984, p. 24
London
 Soho, Sutton Street
  12071 Mr Paul Saunders, [cabinet-maker, upholsterer
  and tapestry maker]
   Kirkham, 1969, pp. 506-510
 Thanet House, Great Russell Street
  Thomas Coke, Earl of Leicester (see Houghton Hall,
  Norfolk)
Norfolk
 Houghton Hall
  12072 Thomas Coke, Earl of Leicester (also listed
  Thanet House, London)
   Murdoch, *Noble Households*, 2006, pp. 209-239
Scotland
 Aberdeenshire, Aberdeen
  Sir Robert Burnett of Leys (see Crathes Castle)
 Aberdeenshire, Crathes Castle
  12073 Sir Robert Burnett of Leys, baronet (also listed
  Aberdeen)
   Burnett, 1901, pp. 295-315
Shropshire
 Broseley
  12074 Richard Hartshorne, carpenter
   Trinder and Cox, *Severn Gorge*, 2000, p. 237
 Coalbrookdale
  12075 George Thomas
   Trinder and Cox, *Severn Gorge*, 2000, p. 327
 Little Wenlock
  12076 Thomas Cartledge, potter
   Trinder and Cox, *Severn Gorge*, 2000, p. 265
Yorkshire
 Whitby
  12077 Jane Small, widow, shopkeeper
   Vickers, *Whitby*, 1986, p. 83

1760 (c.)
Shropshire
 Little Wenlock
  12078 George Parton
   Trinder and Cox, *Severn Gorge*, 2000, pp. 265-266

1761
Bedfordshire
 Houghton House, Ampthill
  12079 Francis Russell, Marquis of Tavistock
   Collett-White, *Bedfordshire*, 1995, pp. 113-121
Bristol
 Clifton
  12080 Henry Wheatcroft, [gentleman]
   Moore, *Clifton*, 1981, pp. 212-213

Gloucestershire
 Westerleigh
  12081 Henry Willis, [mariner]
   Moore, *Frampton Cotterell*, 1976, p. 266

1762
Cumberland
 Stapleton, Trough
  12082 James Brown, yeoman
   Verity, 1968, pp. 183-184
Devonshire
 Uffculme
  12083 Mary Coombe
   Wyatt, *Uffculme*, 1997, pp. 202-204
Gloucestershire
 Winterbourne
  12084 Charles Harris, common seaman
   Moore, *Frampton Cotterell*, 1976, p. 266
Ireland
 Dublin, Kildare Street
  12085 Hayes St Leger, Viscount Doneraile
   Griffin, 1997, pp. 32-39
Leicestershire
 Evington
  12086 Thos. Day, [victualler]
   Wilshere, *Evington*, 1985, p. 55
  12087 James Harrison, [yeoman and grazier]
   Wilshere, *Evington*, 1985, p. 54
 Ratby
  12088 John Bound, [victualler]
   Wilshere, *Ratby*, 1984, p. 25
Northamptonshire
 Irthlingborough
  12089 Benjamin Alderman, [husbandman]
   Alderman, *Alderman*, 2008, p. 94
Shropshire
 Broseley
  12090 Mary Beddow, widow
   Trinder and Cox, *Severn Gorge*, 2000, pp. 237-238
  12091 Moses Watkiss, collier
   Trinder and Cox, *Severn Gorge*, 2000, p. 238
 Madeley Wood
  12092 William Botteley, yeoman, publican
   Trinder and Cox, *Severn Gorge*, 2000, pp. 327-328
Wales
 Montgomeryshire, D[...]
  12093 J. D[...]
   Jones, 1881, pp. 188-189
Yorkshire
 Whitby
  12094 Henry Ferguson, traveller
   Vickers, *Whitby*, 1986, p. 84
  12095 James Wood, seaman
   Vickers, *Whitby*, 1986, pp. 83-84

1763
Essex
 Great Bromley Hall
  12096 Sir William Mannock, baronet (also Giffords
  Hall, Suffolk)
   Partridge, 1948, pp. 22-23

London
28 Berkeley Square
12097 Mr Wm. Linnell, carver, cabinet-maker and upholsterer
Hayward and Kirkham, 1980, pp. 168-180
Suffolk
Giffords Hall
Sir William Mannock, baronet (see Great Bromley Hall, Essex)
Yorkshire
Horbury
12098 Richard Hinchcliffe
Bartlett, *Horbury*, 1981, p. 15

1764

Bristol
Bristol
12099 Edward Crane, coach-painter
George, *Bristol*, 2008, pp. 184-188
Leicestershire
Ratby
12100 Thomas Cuflin, [carpenter]
Wilshere, *Ratby*, 1984, p. 25
Yorkshire
Horbury
12101 William Mansfield, yeoman
Bartlett, *Horbury*, 1981, p. 17
Whitby
12102 Nathaniel Craig, mariner
Vickers, *Whitby*, 1986, p. 84
12103 Katherine Leightley, widow, shopkeeper
Vickers, *Whitby*, 1986, p. 84

1764 (c.)

Shropshire
Broseley
12104 Jonathan Oakes, waterman
Trinder and Cox, *Severn Gorge*, 2000, p. 239

1765

Gloucestershire
Westerleigh
12105 Mary Knapp, [widow]
Moore, *Frampton Cotterell*, 1976, pp. 266-267
Leicestershire
Glenfield
12106 Capes Cuflin, [framework knitter]
Wilshere, *Glenfield*, 1983, p. 20
12107 Edward Tomson, [framework knitter]
Wilshere, *Glenfield*, 1983, p. 20
Wales
Cowbridge, Glamorgan
12108 William Howard, victualler
Millar, 1988, p. 37

1766

Bedfordshire
Hinwick House, Podington
12109 John Orlebar, esquire
Collett-White, *Bedfordshire*, 1995, pp. 96-101
Bristol
Bristol, St Augustine
12110 Thomas Bolt, sexton
George, *Bristol*, 2008, pp. 189-195

Leicestershire
Glenfield
12111 Willm Kirk, husbandman and victualler
Wilshere, *Glenfield*, 1983, p. 21
Ratby, Whittington
12112 Joseph Kelm, husbandman
Wilshere, *Ratby*, 1984, p. 26
Sussex
Sheffield Place
12113 John, Earl De La Warr
Steer, 1956, pp. 18-32
Wiltshire
Marlborough
12114 Harry Rose, gentleman
Williams and Thomson, *Marlborough*, 2007, pp. 311-312

1767

Leicestershire
Glenfield
12115 John Spires, [weaver]
Wilshere, *Glenfield*, 1983, p. 22
Wales
Montgomeryshire, Llanfihangel, Llwydiarth
12116 David Evans
Gilson, *Llanfihangel*, 2009, pp. 49-50
Wiltshire
Clyffe Pypard
12117 John Alexander
Anon., *Clyffe Pypard*, 1938, p. 195
12118 John Baine [?]
Anon., *Clyffe Pypard*, 1938, p. 195
12119 John Blunden
Anon., *Clyffe Pypard*, 1938, p. 194
12120 John Butler
Anon., *Clyffe Pypard*, 1938, p. 194
12121 Peter Collett
Anon., *Clyffe Pypard*, 1938, p. 195
12122 Elizabeth Greenaway
Anon., *Clyffe Pypard*, 1938, p. 195
12123 George Greenaway
Anon., *Clyffe Pypard*, 1938, p. 194
12124 Mary Hayward
Anon., *Clyffe Pypard*, 1938, p. 194
12125 Thomas Milsom
Anon., *Clyffe Pypard*, 1938, p. 195
12126 Elizabeth Richens
Anon., *Clyffe Pypard*, 1938, p. 195
12127 Isaac Ruming
Anon., *Clyffe Pypard*, 1938, p. 195
12128 Rebecca Shaw
Anon., *Clyffe Pypard*, 1938, p. 195
12129 Rebecca Sherer
Anon., *Clyffe Pypard*, 1938, p. 194
12130 Jacob Spackman
Anon., *Clyffe Pypard*, 1938, p. 195
12131 Anne Swanborough
Anon., *Clyffe Pypard*, 1938, p. 195
12132 Rebecca Teagle
Anon., *Clyffe Pypard*, 1938, p. 194
12133 Mary Theobald
Anon., *Clyffe Pypard*, 1938, p. 194
12134 Thomas Tuck
Anon., *Clyffe Pypard*, 1938, p. 194
12135 John Watts
Anon., *Clyffe Pypard*, 1938, p. 195

12136 Grace Wicks
Anon., *Clyffe Pypard*, 1938, p. 195

1768

Bedfordshire
Sharnbrook House
12137 John Bullock, [esquire]
Collett-White, *Bedfordshire*, 1995, pp. 208-211
Leicestershire
Ratby
12138 John Biggs, [husbandman]
Wilshere, *Ratby*, 1984, p. 27
12139 William Lea, [yeoman]
Wilshere, *Ratby*, 1984, p. 26
London
19 Arlington Street
12140 Sir Lawrence Dundas, baronet
Wilmot-Sitwell, 2009, pp. 89-99
Norfolk
Martham
12141 Edward Knight
Cornford, 1973, pp. 123-124
Staffordshire
Coseley
12142 John Atwood
Roper, *Sedgley*, 1960, p. 128

1769

Dorsetshire
Leigh
12143 Thomas Hunt, yeoman
Machin, *Yetminster*, 1976, No.141, (2 pp.)
Leicestershire
Botcheston
12144 Richard Booton, [husbandman]
Wilshere, *Ratby*, 1984, p. 27
Ratby
12145 John Geary, husbandman
Wilshere, *Ratby*, 1984, p. 28
London
Unlocated
12146 Grenadiers Lodge, No. 66
Rose, 1951, pp. 209-210
Gloucestershire
Westerleigh
12147 John Shipp, [yeoman]
Moore, *Frampton Cotterell*, 1976, p. 267
Somersetshire
Dulverton, Combe House
12148 Grace Sydenham, widow
Sydenham, 1928, pp. 609-612
Yorkshire
Horbury
12149 Lionel Downing, victualler
Bartlett, *Horbury*, 1981, p. 30
Thornton, Bradford
12150 Joshua Firth, physician
Anon., *Physician*, 1940, pp. 25-27

1770

Isle of Man
Douglas
12151 Robert Brown
Anon., *Manx*, 1931-1932, pp. 197-198

Leicestershire
Ratby
12152 William Judd, [tailor]
Wilshere, *Ratby*, 1984, p. 28
Middlesex
Chiswick House
12153 William Cavendish, Duke of Devonshire
Rosoman, 1986, pp. 92-100
Somersetshire
Dulverton, Combe House
12154 Mrs [Grace] Fursdon
Sydenham, 1928, pp. 612-615
Yorkshire
Whitby
12155 William Hornsby, ship carpenter
Vickers, *Whitby*, 1986, p. 84

1771

Bedfordshire
Colworth House, Sharnbrook
12156 Richard Antonie, esquire
Collett-White, *Bedfordshire*, 1995, pp. 48-52
Hasells Hall, Sandy
12157 Elizabeth Kingsley, widow
Collett-White, *Bedfordshire*, 1995, pp. 80-87
Gloucestershire
Westerleigh
12158 Joseph Rolph, blacksmith
Moore, *Frampton Cotterell*, 1976, p. 267
Leicestershire
Kirby Muxloe
12159 Edward Bradley, woolcomber
Wilshere, *Kirby Muxloe*, 1983, pp. 34-35
Yorkshire
Whitby
12160 John Gibson, mariner
Vickers, *Whitby*, 1986, pp. 84-85

1772

Bedfordshire
Oakley House
12161 Gertrude [Russell], Duchess of Bedford, [widow]
Collett-White, *Bedfordshire*, 1995, pp. 197-203
Bristol
Bristol
12162 George Walker, mariner
George, *Bristol*, 2008, pp. 195-200
Bristol, St George
12163 James Waters, millwright
George, *Bristol*, 2008, pp. 200-202
Gloucestershire
Coalpit Heath
12164 George Roger, innholder
Moore, *Frampton Cotterell*, 1976, pp. 267-268
Westerleigh
12165 John Wickham, husbandman
Moore, *Frampton Cotterell*, 1976, pp. 268-269
Oxfordshire
Ditchley
12166 George Henry, Earl of Litchfield
Murdoch, *Noble Households*, 2006, pp. 153-164

Yorkshire
Sowerby
12167 Workhouse
Kendall, 1956, pp. 65-66

1773
Bristol
Bristol
12168 Hannah Foot, victualler
George, *Bristol*, 2008, pp. 203-207
12169 Joseph Shepherd, saddler
George, *Bristol*, 2008, pp. 207-216

1774
Gloucestershire
Iron Acton
12170 Thomas Taylor, [butcher]
Moore, *Frampton Cotterell*, 1976, p. 269
Isle of Man
Port-e-Chee
12171 Cotton Mill
Mathieson, 1958, p. 64

1775
Essex
Theydon Garnon
12172 Mr Thos Burgh
King, 1997, pp. 185-186
Gloucestershire
Westerleigh
12173 William Russell, coalminer
Moore, *Frampton Cotterell*, 1976, p. 269
Jersey
St Peter, La Chaumière du Chêne
12174 Clement Le Montais, gentleman
Stevens and Arthur, 1969-1972, pp. 370-378
Leicestershire
Ratby
12175 Thomas Buney, [yeoman]
Wilshere, *Ratby*, 1984, p. 29
Northamptonshire
Nassington
12176 Stephen Alderman, [flax dresser]
Alderman, *Alderman*, 2008, pp. 153-154
Scotland
Dumfriesshire, Kirkpatrick Juxta, Lochanhead
12177 John Ewart
Williams, 1975, pp. 68-70
Wiltshire
Marlborough
12178 Hester Clifford, widow
Williams and Thomson, *Marlborough*, 2007, p. 312
Yorkshire
Whitby
12179 Robert Marshall
Vickers, *Whitby*, 1986, p. 85

1776
Bristol
Bristol
12180 Philip Cadell, teaman
George, *Bristol*, 2008, pp. 216-220
12181 John Deere, innholder
George, *Bristol*, 2008, pp. 220-221
12182 Thomas Jones, schoolmaster
George, *Bristol*, 2008, pp. 223-225

12183 Samuel and Mary Smith, widow
George, *Bristol*, 2008, pp. 225-232
Gloucestershire
Charlton Kings
12184 Mary Wilson, widow
Paget and Sale, *Charlton Kings*, 2003, pp. 127-130
Winterbourne
12185 Edward Dando, yeoman
Moore, *Frampton Cotterell*, 1976, pp. 269-270

1777
Leicestershire
Ratby
12186 John Kinton, [yeoman]
Wilshere, *Ratby*, 1984, p. 29

1778
Cumberland
Workington Hall
12187 Henry Curwen
Hudleston, 1958, pp. 135-157
Leicestershire
Braunstone
12188 John Tilley, grazier
Wilshere, *Braunstone*, 1983, pp. 41-46
Glenfield
12189 Thomas Brewin, [labourer]
Wilshere, *Glenfield*, 1983, p. 22
Ratby
12190 Richard Hunt, [yeoman]
Wilshere, *Ratby*, 1984, p. 29
London
Unlocated
12191 Lodge of Antiquity
Rose, 1951, p. 207
Devonshire
Widecombe
12192 Edward Hamling
Alcock, 1969, p. 106
Surrey
Guildford
12193 Trinity Hospital
Palmer, 1919, pp. 38-39

1779
Bedfordshire
Southill House
12194 George Byng, Viscount Torrington
Collett-White, *Bedfordshire*, 1995, pp. 220-232
Leicestershire
Evington
12195 Thomas Cartwright, [grazier]
Wilshere, *Evington*, 1985, pp. 56-58
Ratby
12196 Robard Storley, [husbandman]
Wilshere, *Ratby*, 1984, p. 30
Yorkshire
Whitby
12197 John Cappelman, mason
Vickers, *Whitby*, 1986, p. 85

1780
Bristol
Bristol
12198 John James, butter merchant
George, *Bristol*, 2008, pp. 232-234

Leicestershire
Ratby, Newtown
  12199 David Leavis, husbandman
  Wilshere, *Ratby*, 1984, p. 30
Northamptonshire
Aynho
  12200 William Wrighton
  Cooper, 1984, p. 196

1780 (c.)
Hampshire
Appuldurcombe House, Isle of Wight
  12201 Sir Richard Worsley, baronet
  Boynton, 1965, pp. 42-57

1781
Leicestershire
Ratby
  12202 Henry Cramp, [yeoman]
  Wilshere, *Ratby*, 1984, p. 31
Staffordshire
Sedgley, Woodsetton
  12203 Henry King, yeoman
  Roper, *Sedgley*, 1960, pp. 126-127
Yorkshire
Horbury
  12204 Samuel Rhodes, bricklayer
  Bartlett, *Horbury*, 1981, p. 74

1782
Gloucestershire
Westerleigh
  12205 John Ponting, labourer
  Moore, *Frampton Cotterell*, 1976, p. 270
Leicestershire
Ratby
  12206 John Jordan, husbandman
  Wilshere, *Ratby*, 1984, pp. 31-32
Lincolnshire
Allington
  12207 William Monks, farmer
  Pask, *Allington*, 1989, pp. 103-104
Middlesex
Osterley Park
  12208 Robert Child, esquire
  Tomlin, 1986, pp. 112-128
Yorkshire
Horbury
  12209 Michael Coope, clothmaker
  Bartlett, *Horbury*, 1981, p. 64

1783
Leicestershire
Botcheston
  12210 William Moor, husbandman
  Wilshere, *Ratby*, 1984, p. 33
Glenfield
  12211 [Richard] Allen, [farmer and grazier]
  Wilshere, *Glenfield*, 1983, p. 23
  12212 James Tomson, [labourer]
  Wilshere, *Glenfield*, 1983, p. 23
Kirby Muxloe, Leicester Forest
  12213 Samuel Whinyates, grazier
  Wilshere, *Kirby Muxloe*, 1983, pp. 36-37

1784
Leicestershire
Ratby
  12214 Elisabeth Moore, [widow]
  Wilshere, *Ratby*, 1984, p. 33
Yorkshire
Horbury
  12215 Robert Townend, farmer
  Bartlett, *Horbury*, 1981, p. 66

1785
Leicestershire
Ratby
  12216 John Geary, [labourer]
  Wilshere, *Ratby*, 1984, p. 34
  12217 James Lilley, [blacksmith]
  Wilshere, *Ratby*, 1984, p. 34
Scotland
Aberdeenshire, Aberdeen
  12218 John Forbes
  Forbes, 1905, pp. 44-49
Worcestershire
Hanley Castle
  12219 James Wakeman Newport, esquire
  Wanklyn, *Worcestershire*, 1998, pp. 393-396

1786
Leicestershire
Glenfield
  12220 Richard Hashold, [maltster]
  Wilshere, *Glenfield*, 1983, p. 24
Ratby
  12221 William Biggs, [husbandman?]
  Wilshere, *Ratby*, 1984, p. 34
Staffordshire
Sedgley
  12222 Joshua Bissell, victualler
  Roper, *Sedgley*, 1960, pp. 129-133
Worcestershire
Westwood
  12223 Sir Herbert Pakington, baronet
  Wanklyn, *Worcestershire*, 1998, pp. 396-411

1787
Gloucestershire
Frampton Cotterell
  12224 Joseph Gingell, feltmaker
  Moore, *Frampton Cotterell*, 1976, p. 271
Leicestershire
Glenfield
  12225 Abram Adcock, [labourer]
  Wilshere, *Glenfield*, 1983, p. 24
Yorkshire
Wadsley
  12226 Jeremiah Downing, husbandman
  Hey, 1969, pp. 112-113

1788
Leicestershire
Ratby
  12227 Thomas Hardy, framework knitter
  Wilshere, *Ratby*, 1984, p. 35
  12228 Daniel Marvin, carpenter
  Wilshere, *Ratby*, 1984, p. 36
  12229 Briget Wight, [widow]
  Wilshere, *Ratby*, 1984, p. 35

1789

Suffolk
Shelley Hall
12230 Mr Author Pattridge [Arthur Partridge]
Partridge, 1947, pp. 448-450

1790

Gloucestershire
Frampton Cotterell
12231 Thomas Osborne, feltmaker
Moore, *Frampton Cotterell*, 1976, p. 271
Westerleigh
12232 Gregory Nicholls, schoolmaster
Moore, *Frampton Cotterell*, 1976, p. 271

Somersetshire
Middle Chinnock
12233 George Templeman, gentleman
Turner, 1994, pp. 1-4

Yorkshire
Whitby
12234 Elizabeth Atkinson, widow
Vickers, *Whitby*, 1986, p. 86
12235 William Goulton, shipwright
Vickers, *Whitby*, 1986, pp. 85-86
12236 Jane Sweeting, widow
Vickers, *Whitby*, 1986, p. 86

1791

Leicestershire
Ratby
12237 Thomas Keen, tailor
Wilshere, *Ratby*, 1984, p. 37

Sussex
Rusper
12238 John Wood, clergyman [rector of Rusper]
Hughes, *Sussex*, 2007, pp. 249-255

Yorkshire
Sowerby
12239 Workhouse
Kendall, 1956, pp. 70-72
York, Without Micklegate Bar
12240 George Hayton, gardener
Harvey, 1974, p. 43

1792

Bristol
Bristol, Christ Church
12241 Ann Pearce
George, *Bristol*, 2008, pp. 234-235

Norfolk
Houghton Hall
12242 George Walpole, Earl of Orford
Murdoch, *Noble Households*, 2006, pp. 192-205

Surrey
Guildford
12243 Abbot's Hospital
Palmer, 1919, pp. 40-41

Yorkshire
Newby Hall
12244 William Weddell, esquire
Low, 1986, pp. 149-165
Whitby
12245 Francis Barry, mariner
Vickers, *Whitby*, 1986, p. 86

1794

Leicestershire
Ratby
12246 Thomas Lockley, tailor
Wilshere, *Ratby*, 1984, p. 37
12247 William Marvin, [carpenter and joiner]
Wilshere, *Ratby*, 1984, p. 38

Suffolk
R[?]hall
12248 Mr John Field
Anon., *Yeoman's*, 1937, pp. 32-33, 36-37, 38-40
Shelley Hall
12249 Robert Partridge
Partridge, 1949, pp. 1-3

1795

Hampshire
The Grange, Northington
12250 Henry Drummond
Geddes, 1986, pp. 178-199

Leicestershire
Glenfield
12251 John Adcock, framework knitter
Wilshere, *Glenfield*, 1983, p. 24
Ratby, Newtown Unthank
12252 Mr Jno. Chamberlain, [gentleman]
Wilshere, *Ratby*, 1984, p. 41
Ratby, Old Hays
12253 Mr William Geary, [gentleman]
Wilshere, *Ratby*, 1984, p. 41

Wales
Montgomeryshire, Llanfihangel, Bwlch Glas
12254 Robert Thomas
Gilson, *Llanfihangel*, 2009, p. 51

1797 (c.)

Ireland
Co. Cork, Mallow
12255 William Burgess, [innholder?]
Anon., *Inn*, 1970, pp. 43-46

Suffolk
Coddenham, Vicarage
12256 John Longe, vicar of Coddenham
Stone, 2008

1799

Leicestershire
Glenfield
12257 Jonathan Cramp, [grazier]
Wilshere, *Glenfield*, 1983, pp. 25-27

1802

London
Unlocated
12258 Lodge of Antiquity
Rose, 1951, pp. 207-208

1803

Leicestershire
Glenfield
12259 Samuel Hashold, [grazier]
Wilshere, *Glenfield*, 1983, p. 27
Ratby
12260 Stephen Hunt, [grazier]
Wilshere, *Ratby*, 1984, p. 41

1804

Bristol
Bristol, Temple
12261 Joseph Ring, potter
George, *Bristol*, 2008, pp. 235-242
Leicestershire
Ratby
12262 Josiah Grudgings, weaver
Wilshere, *Ratby*, 1984, p. 42

1805

Leicestershire
Ratby
12263 Joseph Bent, framework knitter
Wilshere, *Ratby*, 1984, p. 42

1807

Leicestershire
Botcheston
12264 Mr Richard Robbards, farmer
Wilshere, *Ratby*, 1984, p. 42
Glenfield
12265 Dorothy Adcock, [widow]
Wilshere, *Glenfield*, 1983, p. 28
12266 John Assell, [farmer]
Wilshere, *Glenfield*, 1983, p. 28
12267 John Heays, weaver
Wilshere, *Glenfield*, 1983, p. 28
Ratby
12268 Robert Heawood, [wheelwright]
Wilshere, *Ratby*, 1984, p. 43

1808

Leicestershire
Botcheston
12269 Mr Francis Spencer, [yeoman]
Wilshere, *Ratby*, 1984, p. 44
Yorkshire
Temple Newsam
12270 Frances, Viscountess Irwin, [widow]
Anon., *Temple Newsam*, 1987

1809

Leicestershire
Botcheston
12271 Mr Jno Sandars, [farmer]
Wilshere, *Ratby*, 1984, p. 45
Ratby
12272 George Fouldes, framework knitter
Wilshere, *Ratby*, 1984, p. 45
12273 Wm. Marvin, labourer
Wilshere, *Ratby*, 1984, p. 45

1810

Essex
Hatfield Broad Oak
12274 John Tadgell, labourer
King, 1997, pp. 184-185
Nottinghamshire
Nottingham, St Mary's
12275 Mr Parker
Gray and Walker, *Nottingham*, 1952, p. 109

1811

Leicestershire
Ratby
12276 James Kinton, [butcher]
Wilshere, *Ratby*, 1984, p. 46
12277 John Rudkin
Wilshere, *Ratby*, 1984, p. 46

1812

Essex
Ashdon
12278 Joseph Smith
King, 1997, p. 184

1814

Leicestershire
Evington
12279 [Mary] Howard, widow
Wilshere, *Evington*, 1985, p. 59

1815

Hampshire
Milford-on-Sea, Rookcliff
12280 Plowden Presland, [attorney]
Church, 2009, pp. 65-72

1816

Bedfordshire
Colworth House, Sharnbrook
12281 William Lee Antonie, esquire
Collett-White, *Bedfordshire*, 1995, pp. 52-70
Leicestershire
Ratby
12282 Mr Thomas Cufflin, grazier
Wilshere, *Ratby*, 1984, p. 46

1817

Bedfordshire
Melchbourne House
12283 St Andrew St John, Baron St John of Bletsoe
Collett-White, *Bedfordshire*, 1995, pp. 172-183
Leicestershire
Evington
12284 Mr Richard Goddard, [farmer]
Wilshere, *Evington*, 1985, p. 59
Ratby
12285 Dorothy Cufflin, widow
Wilshere, *Ratby*, 1984, p. 47

1818

Ireland
Co. Longford, Kenagh, Mosstown
12286 Arthur and Elizabeth Kingston
English, 1972, pp. 36-42
Leicestershire
Glenfield
12287 Mr William Hassall, [grazier]
Wilshere, *Glenfield*, 1983, p. 29

1819

Leicestershire
Evington
12288 Mr John Goddard, farmer
Wilshere, *Evington*, 1985, p. 60
Glenfield
12289 Mrs Hannah Cramp, [widow]
Wilshere, *Glenfield*, 1983, p. 29

1820
London
20 Stratford Place, Oxford Street
12290 Richard Cosway, [artist]
Lloyd, 2004, pp. 174-201

1820 (c.)
Surrey
Guildford
12291 Abbot's Hospital
Palmer, 1919, p. 43

1822
Leicestershire
Ratby
12292 William Bunney
Wilshere, *Ratby*, 1984, p. 47
12293 Mr Wm. Cramp, [farmer]
Wilshere, *Ratby*, 1984, p. 48
12294 Rebecca Stevenson, [widow]
Wilshere, *Ratby*, 1984, p. 48

1823
Bedfordshire
Ickwell Bury, Northill
12295 Susannah Harvey, [widow]
Collett-White, *Bedfordshire*, 1995, pp. 137-145
Leicestershire
Glenfield
12296 Mr William Tatlow, [victualler]
Wilshere, *Glenfield*, 1983, p. 30

1825
Leicestershire
Glenfield
12297 Job Grant, miller
Wilshere, *Glenfield*, 1983, p. 31
Ratby
12298 William Clarke
Wilshere, *Ratby*, 1984, p. 49
Surrey
Guildford
12299 Abbot's Hospital
Palmer, 1919, p. 45

1826
Northamptonshire
Peterborough
12300 John Hoggard Alderman, [carpenter]
Alderman, *Alderman*, 2008, pp. 119-120
Scotland
Renfrewshire, South Castlewalls
12301 John Pollock
Pryde, 1951, pp. 152-157

1827
Leicestershire
Ratby
12302 John Page, [farmer]
Wilshere, *Ratby*, 1984, p. 49

1829
Bristol
Bristol
12303 Theatre Royal
Barker, 1952, pp. 101-110

1830
Leicestershire
Botcheston
12304 Wm Asher, [farmer and grazier]
Wilshere, *Ratby*, 1984, p. 49
Scotland
Edinburgh, Palace of Holyroodhouse
12305 Charles X, King of Frence
Clarke, 2009, pp. 211-214

1831
Leicestershire
Glenfield
12306 Thomas Everard, victualler
Wilshere, *Glenfield*, 1983, p. 32
Ratby
12307 John Jordan
Wilshere, *Ratby*, 1984, p. 50
London
Pall Mall
12308 The Athenaeum
Jervis, 1970, pp. 55-61

1832
Scotland
Edinburgh, Palace of Holyroodhouse
12309 Charles X, King of France
Clarke, 2009, pp. 215-294

1834
Scotland
Aberdeenshire, Aberdeen, Broadford
12310 James Forbes, merchant
Forbes, 1905, pp. 64-68

1836
Leicestershire
Ratby
12311 Mrs Mary Cufflin, widow
Wilshere, *Ratby*, 1984, p. 50

1837
London
Sir John Soane's Museum, Lincoln's Inn Fields
12312 Sir John Soane
Dorey, 2009, pp. 269-293
Northamptonshire
Nassington
12313 William Alderman, [butcher]
Alderman, *Alderman*, 2008, p. 156

1840
Leicestershire
Ratby
12314 Thos. Lockley, tailor
Wilshere, *Ratby*, 1984, p. 50

1841
Jersey
St Ouen, Bas du Marais
12315 Mr. Jean Le Couteur
Le Maistre, 1969-1972, pp. 379-384

1864
Lancashire
Lindale, Eller How
12316 George Webster, architect
Taylor, 2004, pp. 307-352

SHORT TITLE INDEX

This Index comprises all the short titles used for reference in the preceding *List* of Published Inventories. Anonymous publications are listed first, in date order. Also in date order are authors with identical surnames. These may be differently ordered in the main *Bibliography*, which follows, because Christian names are there taken into account. However the date of publication will allow the source to be identified with relative ease and without ambiguity.

The Index will allow a quick scan of the sources used and, more importantly, it includes, after each entry, the reference numbers of the inventory transcription(s) contained therein.

BIBLIOGRAPHY

This Bibliography does not pretend to impeccable consistency, nicety or completeness in its entries. The treatment of the South Sea Company inventories is unorthodox. But it should allow all the sources therein listed to be tracked down. Copies of some are not always easy to find. The libraries mainly used in locating copies are acknowledged in the Foreword (p. viii). In cases of difficulty almost every item should be identifiable and located through Copac (Copac National, Academic, and Specialist Library Catalogue: www.copac.ac.uk).

Anon., 'A Brief Inventory of Robert Holgate, Archbishop of York's Goods', *Gentleman's Magazine*, 95, 1825, pp. 595-597

Anon., 'Lease of the Manor of Hampton Court to Cardinal Wolsey', *Gentleman's Magazine*, N.S. 1, 1834, pp. 45-47

Anon., 'The Wills of Thomas Bassandyne and other Printers, &c, in Edinburgh M.D.LXXVII.-M.DC.LXXXVII', *The Bannatyne Miscellany*, 2, Edinburgh, 1836, pp. 187-296

Anon., 'Inventory of the Goods, &c., of John Robson, Master of The College of Lingfield, Co. Surrey, in 1524', *Collectanea Topographica et Genealogica*, 8, 1843, pp. 39-42

Anon., *Registrum Episcopatus Aberdonensis, Ecclesie Cathedralis Aberdonensis Regesta que Extant in Unum Collecta*, II, Edinburgh, The Spalding Club, 1845

Anon., *A Genealogical Deduction of the Family of Rose of Kilravock with illustrative documents from the family papers and notes*, Edinburgh, The Spalding Club, 1848

Anon., 'Household Inventory of the Fifteenth Century', *Retrospective Review*, I, 1853, pp. 101-102

Anon., 'Domestic Conditions of Tradesmen in the Seventeenth Century', *Midland Counties Historical Collector*, 1, 1855, p. 205-207

Anon., 'An Ancient Inventory of the Effects of a Country Gentleman', *Midland Counties Historical Collector*, 2, 1856, pp. 322-332, 362-366

Anon., *The Book of the Thanes of Cawdor, A Series of Papers Selected from the Charter Room at Cawdor 1236-1742*, Edinburgh, The Spalding Club, 1859

Anon., 'Warwickshire Wills', *The Warwickshire Antiquarian Magazine*, 1860, pp. 198-216

Anon., 'Original Documents', *Reliquary*, 3, 1862-1863, pp. 226-228

Anon., 'Will of the Rev. Philip Lewis M.A.', *Original Documents Printed as a Supplement to the Archaeologia Cambrensis*, 1, 1877, pp. 4-9

Anon. ('F. G'), 'Inventory of Pope's Goods Taken after his Death', *Notes and Queries*, 5, 1882, pp. 363-365

Anon., 'Curious Inventory', *Antiquarian Magazine & Bibliographer*, 6, 1884, p. 280

Anon., 'Inventaire des meubles appartenant au presbytère de St Hélier (1583)', *Société Jersiaise, Bulletin*, 2, 1885-1889, pp. 364-365

Anon., 'Extraits de l'inventaire des meubles de Philippe Marett, Gt.', *Société Jersiaise, Bulletin*, 3, 1890-1896, pp. 401-410

Anon., 'The Will and Inventory of Richard Collyns, Citizen and Haberdasher of London, 1523', *Reliquary*, 7, 1893, pp. 104-109

Anon., 'Domestic Inventory', *Essex Archaeological Society Transactions*, 10, 1909, pp. 58-59

Anon., 'Minshull Wills', *Cheshire Sheaf*, 17, 1920, pp. 98-99

Anon., 'A 1734 Orkney Inventory', *Proceedings of the Orkney Antiquarian Society*, 1, 1922-1923, pp. 65-66

Anon., 'The Society's MSS. Inventory of the Goods of Sir Charles Raleigh, of Downton.1698', *Wiltshire Archaeological and Natural History Magazine*, 42, 1923, pp. 307-312

Anon., 'The Bostocks of Holt', *Cheshire Sheaf*, 23, 1926, pp. 7-8

Anon., 'Sir Henry Vaughan, the Elder, 1587?-1660?', *Transactions of the Carmarthenshire Antiquarian Society and Field Club*, 20, 1926-1927, pp. 32-34

Anon., 'Unpublished Documents in the Manx Museum', *Journal of the Manx Museum*, 2, 1931-1934, pp. 9-14, 17-21, 170-171, 197-198

Anon., 'The Bostocks of Tattenhall', *Cheshire Sheaf*, 29, 1934, pp. 32-34, 37

Anon., 'Contents of a Muniment Room II Some Yeomen's Wills', *Records of Buckinghamshire*, 13, 1934-1940, pp. 25-31

Anon., 'Francis Family of Chester and Eastham', *Cheshire Sheaf*, 30, 1935, p. 21

Anon., 'Inventory of Alice Elmes of Lilford, 1607', *Journal of the Northamptonshire Natural History Society & Field Club*, 28, 1935, pp. 28-45

Anon., 'Yeoman's Household Goods, 1794', *East Anglian Miscellany*, 1937, pp. 32-33, 36-37, 39-40

Anon., 'Inventories of Poor People's Furniture at Clyffe Pypard, 1767', *Wiltshire Archaeological and Natural History Magazine*, 48, 1938, pp. 193-196

Anon., 'A Physician's Household Goods in 1769', *The Bradford Antiquary*, 8, 1940, pp. 25-28

Anon., 'Mid-Elizabethan Goods and Chattels', *East Anglian Miscellany*, 1940, pp. 3-6, 8,10, 12,14-15, 17-20, 22, 24, 27-28, 30, 32-33, 35, 37, 39-40

Anon., 'Inventory of Richard Revell', *Notes and Queries for Somerset and Dorset*, 23, 1942, pp. 132-134

Anon., 'Inventory of the Goods and Chattels of Thomas Owen of Condover, 1599', *Transactions of the Shropshire Archaeological Society*, 53, 1949-1950, pp. 200-206

Anon., 'Inventory of goods of John Williams of South Cheriton', *Somerset & Dorset Notes & Queries*, 26, 1955, pp. 165-167

Anon., 'Staverton Inventory', *Devon and Cornwall Notes and Queries*, 27, 1956-1958, pp. 59-64

Anon., 'Inventory of James Arderne, Dean of Chester', *Cheshire Sheaf*, 54, 1959, p. 37

Anon., 'Defeasance of a Bond in Forty Pounds concerning the Whittington Family, with an Inventory dated 3rd September, 1471', *Transactions of the Woolhope Naturalists' Field Club*, 36, 1960, p. 251

Anon., 'A Devonshire Gentleman's Estate in 1710', *Devon and Cornwall Notes and Queries*, 28, 1961, pp. 300-304

Anon., 'Anne, Lady Beauchamp's Inventory at Edington, Wiltshire 1665', *Wiltshire Archaeological and Natural History Magazine*, 58, 1963, pp. 383-393

Anon. (C.D.R.), 'Peter Hurdis, Master of Bowdon School c.1616-1672', *Cheshire Sheaf*, 2, 1967, pp. 29-31

Anon., 'The Furnishings of an 18th Century Inn', *Irish Ancestor*, 2, 1970, pp. 43-46

Anon., 'William Collins's Inventory 1750', *Irish Ancestor*, 4, 1972, pp. 104-105

Anon., *Lock, Stock and Barrel, Some Hertfordshire Probate Inventories 1610-1650*, Hertfordshire Sources, 12, [1978]

Anon., 'Examples of Inventories' in Ad van der Woude and Anton Schuurman (ed.), *Probate Inventories*, A. A. G. Bijdragen, 23, Utrecht, 1980, pp. 9-15

Anon., 'Inventory of Goods Nathaniel Fiennes, died 1669', *Cake and Cockhorse*, 9, 1983, pp. 38-48

Anon., *The Temple Newsam Inventory 1808*, Leeds, 1987

Anon., 'Hooke's Possessions at his Death: a hitherto unknown inventory' in Michael Hunter and Simon Schaffer, *Robert Hooke, New Studies*, Woodbridge, 1989, pp. 287-294

Anon., *The Inventories and Wills of Acton Trussell 1650-1750*, Walton-on-the-Hill, 1995

Beverley Adams, 'Lifestyle and Culture in Hertford, Wills and Inventories for the Parishes of All Saints and St Andrew, 1660-1725', *Hertfordshire Record Publications*, 13, 1997

S. O. Addy, 'An Inventory of Furniture at Beauchief Hall', *Journal of the Derbyshire Archaeological and Natural History Society*, 3, 1881, pp. 56-66

S. O. Addy, 'Inventory of Robert Marples, 1676', *Journal of the Derbyshire Archaeological and Natural History Society*, 9, 1887, pp. 22-32

S. O. Addy, 'Pedigrees of Brownell of Hallamshire and North Derbyshire', *Journal of the Derbyshire Archaeological and Natural History Society*, 45, 1923, pp. 91-109

N. W. Alcock, 'Devonshire Farmhouses Part II Some Dartmoor Houses', *Report and Transactions of the Devonshire Association*, 101, 1969, pp. 83-106

N. W. Alcock, p. A. Faulkner and S. R. Jones, 'Maxstoke Castle, Warwickshire', *Archaeological Journal*, 135, 1978, pp. 195-233

N. W. Alcock, *People at Home, Living in a Warwickshire Village 1500-1800*, Chechester, 1993

N. W. Alcock and Mireille Galinou, 'The Beake House Revealed: The History of a Dutch Merchant's House, 32 Botolph Lane, London', *London Topographical Record*, 29, 2006, pp. 65-107

Nat Alcock and Joan Lane, 'A Widow's Adornment and Estate', *Warwickshire History*, 12, 2003, pp. 107-121

Bob, Mari and Neil Alderman, *Early Alderman Wills in Northamptonshire (1522-1858)*, Chippenham, 2008

George Allan, *Collections Relating to Sherburn Hospital in the County Palatine of Durham*, Darlington, 1771

Marion E. Allen (ed.), 'Wills of the Archdeaconry of Suffolk 1620-1624', *Suffolk Records Society*, 31, 1989

R. W. Ambler and B. & L. Watkinson, *Farmers and Fishermen, The Probate Inventories of the Ancient Parish of Clee, South Humberside 1536-1742*, Hull, 1987

Thomas Amyot, 'Two Rolls containing an Inventory of Effects formerly belonging to Sir John Fastolfe', *Archaeologia*, 21, 1827, pp. 232-280

C. K. Croft Andrew, 'Sir Alexander Carew, baronet', *Devon and Cornwall Notes and Queries*, 22, 1942-1946, pp. 37-43

Raymond A. Anselment (ed.), 'The Remembrances of Elizabeth Freke, 1671-1714', *Camden Fifth Series*, 18, 2001

Henry Anstey, *Munimenta Academica or Documents Illustrative of Academical Life and Studies at Oxford, Part II, Libri Cancellarii et Procuratorum accedunt Acta Curiae Cancellarii et Memoranda ex Registris Nonnulla*, London, 1868

M. R. Apted, 'Social Conditions at Tredegar House, Newport, in the 17th and 18th Centuries', *Monmouthshire Antiquary*, 3 (2), 1972-3, pp. 124-154

Edward Arber (ed.), *A Transcript of the Registers of the Company of Stationers of London; 1554-1640 A.D.*, 1, London, 1875

Ian W. Archer, *The History of the Haberdashers' Company*, Chichester, 1991

Tom Arkell, Nesta Evans, Nigel Goose, *When Death Do Us Part, Understanding and Interpreting the Probate Records of Early Modern England*, Oxford, 2000

Hilary Arnold, 'Three Medieval Inventories in York City Archives', *York Historian*, 25, 2008, pp. 20-22

David C. A. Askew, *Protestant Exiles from France in the Reign of Louis XIV or, The Huguenot Refugees and their Descendants in Great Britain and Ireland*, index volume, 1874

G. G. Astill, 'An Early Inventory of a Leicestershire Knight', *Midland History*, 2, 1974, pp. 274-283

J. A. Atkinson, B. Flynn, V. Portass, K. Singlehurst and H. J. Smith (ed.), 'Darlington Wills and Inventories 1600-1625', *Surtees Society*, 201, 1993

Roland Austin, 'The Inventory of the Goods of Oliver Diston, Rector of Dumbleton, Gloucestershire, 1615', *Transactions of the Bristol and Gloucestershire Archaeological Society*, 46, 1924, pp. 187-193

William Austin, *The History of Luton and Its Hamlets*, II, Newport, 1928

Hugh Aveling, 'Recusancy Papers of the Meynell Family', *Catholic Record Society*, 56, *Miscellanea*, 1964, pp. ix-xl, 1-112

William E. A. Axon, 'documents relating to the Plague in Manchester in 1605; with other memoranda, 1593-1606', *Chetham Society*, 73, 1915, *Chetham Miscellanies*, III, pp. 1-35

Aylsham Local History Society, *Aylsham in the Seventeenth Century*, Aylsham, 1988

J. J. Bagley (ed.), 'The Will, Inventory and Accounts of Robert Walthew of Pemberton', *Record Society of Lancashire and Cheshire*, 109, 1965, pp. 49-122

J. J. Bagley (ed.), 'The Great Diurnall of Nicholas Blundell of Little Crosby, Lancashire, Volume Three 1720-1728', *Record Society of Lancashire and Cheshire*, 114, 1972

Francis Joseph Baigent, 'On the Parish Church of Wyke, near Winchester', *Journal of the British Archeological Association*, 19, 1863, pp. 184-212

F. A. Bailey, 'The Elizabethan Playhouse at Prescot, Lancashire', *Transactions of the Historic Society of Lancashire and Cheshire*, 103, 1951, pp. 69-81

Johnson Ball, *William Caslon 1693-1766*, Kineton, 1973

Joyce Bankes and Eric Kerridge, 'The Early Records of the Bankes Family of Winstanley', *Chetham Society*, 21, 1973

The Bannatyne Miscellany containing Original Papers and Tracts chiefly relating to the History and Literature of Scotland, I, Edinburgh, 1827

Robert S. Barclay, 'Orkney Testaments and Inventories 1573-1615', *Scottish Record Society*, 16, Edinburgh, 1977

Joyce Barker, 'William and Rebecca George (Powell) and their Town House, now Gloucester House, 60 Dyer Street', in Alan McWhirr (ed.), *Studies in the Archaeology and History of Cirencester*, British Archaeological Reports, 30, 1976, pp. 113-115

Kathleen Barker, Richard Southern, M. St Clare Byrne, 'A Bristol Theatre Royal Inventory', in *Studies in English Theatre History In Memory of Gabrielle Enthoven, O.B.E.*, London, Society for Theatre Research, 1952, pp. 98-113

M. W. Barley, 'The Lincolnshire Village and its Buildings', *Lincolnshire Historian*, 7, 1951, pp. 252-272

M. W. Barley, *The English Farmhouse and Cottage*, London, 1961

E. A. B. Barnard, 'A Dumbleton Inventory of 1615', *Notes and Queries Concerning Evesham and the Four Shires*, 3, 1914, pp. 217-224

E. A. B. Barnard, 'A Seventeenth Century Lawsuit. Asgill v. Broadstock', *Notes and Queries Concerning Evesham and the Four Shires*, 3, 1914, pp. 81-86

E. A. B. Barnard, 'The Dingleys of Charlton co. Worcester', *Transactions of the Worcestershire Archaeological Society*, 4, 1928, pp. 49-90

E. A. B. Barnard, 'Philip Hawford, Pseudo-Abbot of Evesham (1539) and Dean of Worcester (1553-1557). His Will and Inventory', *Transactions of the Worcestershire Archaeological Society*, 5, 1929, pp. 52-57

Ian Barnes, 'Goods and Chattels 1709-1757', *Anglesey Antiquarian Society and Field Club Transactions*, 1969-70, pp. 234-238

Herbert Barnett, 'Glympton, The History of an Oxfordshire Manor', *Oxfordshire Record Society*, 5, 1923

E. L. Barnwell, 'Inventory of the Goods of Sir John Perrot', *Archaeologia Cambrensis*, 12, 1866, pp. 339-358

K. S. Bartlett, *The Will of Horbury, 1688-1757*, 2, Wakefield, 1980

K. S. Bartlett, *The Will of Horbury, 1757-1800*, 3, Wakefield, 1981

Cadwallader John Bates, 'The Border Holds of Northumberland', *Archaeologia Aeliana*, 14, 1891

G. R. Batho (ed.), 'The Household Papers of Henry Percy, Ninth Earl of Northumberland (1564-1632)', *Camden Third Series*, 93, 1962

Arthur Nesham Bax, *A Bax Family of East Kent*, [unlocated],1950

William Bazeley, 'Notes on Buckland Manor and Advowson', *Transactions of the Bristol and Gloucestershire Archaeological Society*, 9, 1884-1885, pp. 103-124

William Beamont, 'Henry IV. Part II. Being an Attempt to Connect Some Cheshire Persons, Circumstances, and Places with Shakespere's Drama of This Name', *Journal of the Architectural, Archaeological and Historic Society for the County, City and Neighbourhood of Chester*, 3, 1885, pp. 343-364

F. C. Beazley, 'Hockenhull of Prenton Family', *Cheshire Sheaf*, 10, 1913, pp. 46-49

F. R. Beecheno, 'The Sucklings' House at Norwich', *Norfolk Archaeology*, 20, 1921, pp. 158-178

C. F. C. Beeson (ed.), 'Edgecote House in 1585', *Cake and Cockhorse*, 3, 1965, pp. 19-22.

Robert Benson and Henry Hatcher, *Old and New Sarum or Salisbury*, Sir Richard Colt Hoare, *The History of Modern Wiltshire*, 6, 1843

John Bentley, *Elizabethan Ingleton (A Study based on Elizabethan Probate Records)*, Ingleton, 1990

Elizabeth K. Berry (ed.), 'Swaledale Wills and Inventories 1522-1600', *Yorkshire Archaeological Society Record Series*, 152, 1998

J. M. Bestall and D. V. Fowkes, 'Chesterfield Wills and Inventories 1521-1603', *Derbyshire Record Society*, 1, 1977

J. M. Bestall and D. V. Fowkes, 'Chesterfield Wills and Inventories 1604-1650', *Derbyshire Record Society*, 28, 2001

Bewdley Historical Research Group, *Bewdley in its Golden Age*, Stroud,1991

C. W. Bingham, 'Inventory of the Household and Personal Effects, Farm-Stock, &c., of Robert Bingham of Bingham's Melcombe, Dorset: Dated 4th Elizabeth, A.D. 1561', *Archaeological Journal*, 17, 1860, pp. 151-157

W. H. Blaauw, 'Sadelscombe and Shipley, The Preceptories of the Knights Templar in Sussex', *Sussex Archaeological Collections*, 9, 1857, pp. 227-274

William Henry Black, *History and Antiquities of the Worshipful Company of Leathersellers of the City of London*, London, 1871

W. J. Blair, 'The Will of Robert Russell, Vicar of Leatherhead', *Proceedings of the Leatherhead and District Local History Society*, 3, 1974, pp. 244-245

Tony Bland (ed.), *Wills and Inventories with related documents for Christleton, Tarvin, Tattenhall & Waverton for the period 1546 to 1650*, 1, *1546-1606*, Tattenhall, 2002

Tony Bland (ed.), *Wills and Inventories with related documents for Christleton, Tarvin, Tattenhall & Waverton for the period 1546 to 1650*, 2, *1606-1616*, Tattenhall, 2003

Tony Bland (ed.), *Wills and Inventories with related documents for Christleton, Tarvin, Tattenhall & Waverton for the period 1546 to 1650*, 4, *1629-1643*, Tattenhall, 2005

G. A. Blaydes, 'List of Popish Recusants for Bedfordshire', *Associated Architectural Societies Reports and Papers*, 19, 1887-1889, pp. 167-197

J. Hight Blundell, 'The Inventory of Toddington Manor House, 1644', *Bedfordshire Historical Record Society*, 11, 1927, pp. 129-136

Mary Bodfish, *Probate Inventories of Smethwick Residents 1647-1747*, Smethwick, 1992

Leonard G. Bolingbroke, 'Two Elizabethan Inventories', *Norfolk Archaeology*, 15, 1904, pp. 91-108

Bolton and District Family History Society, *'Of Good & Perfect Remembrance', Bolton Wills & Inventories 1545-1600 (Surnames 'A' to 'M')*, Bolton, 1987

Bolton and District Family History Society, *'Of Good & Perfect Remembrance', Bolton Wills & Inventories 1571-1600 (Surnames 'N' to 'Z')*, Bolton, 1994

Shelagh M. Bond, 'Two Seventeenth-Century Inventories', *Society of the Friends of St George's and the Descendants of the Knights of the Garter*, 1959, pp. 16-21

John Booth, 'Halmota Prioratus Dunelmensis', *Surtees Society*, 82, 1886

Lyn Boothman, Richard Hyde Parker (ed.), 'Savage Fortune, An Aristocratic Family in the Early Seventeenth Century', *Suffolk Records Society*, 49, 2006

C. M. Lowther Bouch, 'The descendants of William Lowther of the Rose: II The Lowthers of Great Orton', *Transactions of the Cumberland & Westmorland Antiquarian & Archaeological Society*, 40, 1940, pp. 60-98

C. E. B. Bowles, 'Inventory of the Goods of Mr Francis Bradshaw, 1635', *The Reliquary*, 4, 1890, pp. 98-102

Lindsay Boynton, 'Sir Richard Worsley's Furniture at Appuldurcombe Park', *Furniture History*, 1, 1965, pp. 39-57

Lindsay Boynton (ed.), 'The Hardwick Hall Inventory of 1601' *Furniture History*, 7, 1971, pp. 1-40

Lindsay Boynton, 'Benjamin Jackson's Will and Inventory, 1719', *Furniture History*, 26, 1990, pp. 22-26

William Boys, *Collections for an History of Sandwich in Kent. With Notices of the Other Cinque Ports and Members, and of Richborough*, Cnterbury, 1792

H. F. Bradfer-Lawrence, 'Stiffkey alias Stewkey', *Norfolk Archaeology*, 23, 1929, pp. 308-340

Frederic Bradley, 'Original Documents', *Reliquary*, 2, 1861-1862, pp. 161-162

Muriel Bradley et al., *A true and perfect inventory...A glimpse of life in the Haywoods in the 17th century from wills of that period*, Haywood, 1993

Henry Bradshaw, 'An Inventory of the Stuff in the College Chambers (King's College), 1598', *Cambridge Antiquarian Communications*, 3, 1864-1876, pp. 181-198

Peter C. D. Brears, 'Yorkshire Probate Inventories 1542-1689', *Yorkshire Archaeological Society, Record Series*, 134, 1972

J. S. Brewer, *Letters and Papers Foreign and Domestic of the Reign of Henry VIII*, 3, London, 1867

E. R. C. Brinkworth (ed.), 'The Inventory of Thomas Brasbridge, 1594', *Cake and Cockhorse*, 3, 1966, pp. 71-74

E. R. C. Brinkworth and J. S. W. Gibson, 'Banbury Wills and Inventories, I, 1591-1620', *Banbury Historical Society*, 13, 1975

E. R. C. Brinkworth and J. S. W. Gibson, 'Banbury Wills and Inventories, II, 1621-1650', *Banbury Historical Society*, 14, 1976

Frank Britton, 'The Pickleherring Potteries: an inventory', *Post-Medieval Archaeology*, 24, 1990, pp. 61-92

Jan Broadway, 'The Probate Inventory of Phillip Greene, a Restoration Brickmaker in Gloucester, 1685', *Transactions of the Bristol and Gloucestershire Archaeological Society*, 121, 2003, pp. 233-241

R. H. Browne, 'Inventories of Goods', *Essex Review*, 16, 1907, pp. 205-207

John Bruce, 'Observatons on a Lease of Two Houses in the Piazza, Covent Garden, granted to Sir Edmund Verney, A.D.1634', *Archaeologia*, 35, 1853, pp. 194-201

T. N. Brushfield, 'Inventory of the Goods of Henery Hampshire, of Honiton, 1690', *Devon and Cornwall Notes and Queries*, 2, 1902-1903, pp. 242-246

Roger Bryant, Audrey Lee, Eileen Miller (ed.), *Wills and Inventories of New Mills People Book One 1540-1571*, New Mills, 1995

Roger Bryant, Audrey Lee, Eileen Miller (ed.), *Wills and Inventories of New Mills People Book Two 1571-1582*, New Mills, 1995

Philip and Barbara Bullen, *Pots, Platters & Ploughs, Sarratt Wills & Inventories 1435-1832*, Sarratt, [1982]

James Bulwer, 'An Inventory and Valuation of the Goods and Chattels of Charles Wyndham of Stokesby Esq., in the Year 1688', *Norfolk Archaeology*, 5, 1859, pp. 341-340

George Burnett (ed. James Allardyce), *The Family of Burnett of Leys wit Collateral Branches*, Aberdeen, New Spalding Club, 1901

R. Jowett Burton, 'A Nottingham Riot in 1678',

Transactions of the Thoroton Society, 28, 1924, pp. 56-66

Ruth G. Burtt, 'An Inventory of Household Goods, 1696', *Journal of the Friends' Historical Society*, 37, 1940, pp. 38-39

Muriel St Clare Byrne, *The Lisle Letters*, 6, Chicago and London, 1981

Calendar of Inquisitions, Miscellaneous (Chancery), 5, *1387-1395*, London, 1962

Calendar of Inquisitions, Miscellaneous (Chancery), 8, *1422-1485*, London, 2003

Niall D. Campbell, 'The Castle Campbell Inventory', *Scottish Historical Review*, 10, 1913, pp. 299-305

Arthur Campling, *The History of the family of Drury in the counties of Suffolk and Norfolk from the Conquest*, London, 1937

Ivor Carr and Ian Atherton (ed.), 'The Civil War in Staffordshire in the Spring of 1646: Sir William Brereton's Letter Book, April-May 1946', *Collections for a History of Staffordshire*, 4th series, 21, 2007

Hector Carter (ed.), 'The Inventory of Charles Bridgeman (d.1738), Master Gardener to King George II', *Blackmansbury*, 7, 1970, pp. 88-108

Hector Carter (ed.), 'Will and Inventory of Thomas Bracklie of Newport, Isle of Wight, Draper', *Blackmansbury*, 8, 1971, pp. 105-120

J. J. Cartwright, 'Inventory of the Goods of Sir Cotton Gargrave of Nostell, in 1588', *Yorkshire Archaeological and Topographical Journal*, 11, 1891, pp. 279-286

Margaret Cash (ed.), 'Devon Inventories of the Sixteenth and Seventeenth Centuries', *Devon and Cornwall Record Society*, 11, 1966

Richard Caulfield, 'Inventory ... of Edmond Ronayne', *Proceedings and Transactions of the Kilkenny and South-East of Ireland Archaeological Society*, 3, 1854-1855, pp. 323-326

Richard Caulfield, 'Wills and Inventories, Cork, *temp.* Elizabeth', *Gentleman's Magazine*, 210 (10), 1861, pp. 530-532, 211 (11), 1861, pp. 33-36, 257-262, 501-505, 212 (12), 1862, pp. 28-31, 165-168, 439-444, 710-714

Richard Caulfield, 'Supplement to the Cork Wills', *Gentleman's Magazine*, 213 (13), 1862, pp. 299-302

F. H. Cheetham, 'Two Inventories at Scarisbrick Hall, Ormskirk, 1608 and 1673', *Transactions of the Historical Society of Lancashire and Cheshire*, 89, 1938, pp. 123-138

R. Pearse Chope, 'Will and Inventory of John Gribble, 1694', *Devon and Cornwall Notes and Queries*, 13, 1924-1925, pp. 220-226

Clare Church, 'The History of Rookcliff at Milford-on-Sea', *Milford-on-Sea Historical Record Society Occasional Magazine*, 3, 2009, pp. 29-74

Andrew Clark, 'An Essex Dairy-Farm, 1629', *Essex Review*, 21, 1912, pp. 156-159

J. W. Clark, 'On the Old Provost's Lodge of King's College, with special reference to the Furniture', *Cambridge Antiquarian Communications*, 4, 1881, pp. 285-312

W. G. Clark-Maxwell, 'An Inventory of the Contants of Markeaton Hall, Made by Vincent Mundy, Esq., in the year 1545', *Journal of the Derbyshire Archaeological and Natural History Society*, 51, 1930, pp. 117-140

Deborah Clarke, 'Charles X's Residence at the Palace of Holyroodhouse 1830-32: An Inventory of Furniture', *Furniture History*, 45, 2009, pp. 193-294

Christopher Clarkson, *The History of Richmond in the County of York*, Richmond, 1821

Thomas Fortescue, Lord Clermont, *Sir John Fortescue, Knight, His Life, works and Family History*, 2, *A History of the Family of Fortescue in All Its Branches*, London, 1869

George Clinch, 'The Inventory of a Sussex Farmer, 1637', *Surrey Archaeological Collections*, 23, 1910, pp. 79-82

Charles Mathew Clode, *Memorials of the Guild of Merchant Taylors*, London, 1875

Jack Cockcroft, *Nantwich Wills, Transcripts of Wills and Inventories*, 6 vols, South Cheshire Family History Society, 1999

R. A. Cohen, 'Documents Concerning James Cooke, Surgeon, of Warwick', *Medical History*, 1, 1957, pp. 168-173

E. J. L. Cole, 'Hereford Probate Records', *Radnorshire Society Transactions*, 26, 1956, pp. 22-31

James Collett-White, 'Inventories of Bedfordshire Country Houses 1714-1830', *Bedfordshire Historical Record Society Publications*, 74, 1995

W. G. Collingwood, 'The Inventory of Mistress Fleming of Skirwith, 1639', *Transactions of the Cumberland & Westmorland Antiquarian & Archaeological Society*, 28, 1928, pp. 33-40

W. G. Collingwood, 'A Book of Old Quaker Wills', *Transactions of the Cumberland and Westmorland Antiquarian & Archaeological Society*, 29, 1929, pp. 1-38

Francis Collins (ed.), 'Genealogical History of the Family of the Late Bishop William Stubbs', *Yorkshire Archaeological Society, Record Series*, 55, 1915

Sue Coltman, 'A Hook Norton Family ... The Calcotts', *Cake and Cockhorse*, 9, 1982, pp. 7-13

Edward Conder, *Records of the Hole Crafte and Fellowship of Masons With a Chronicle of the History of the Worshipful Company of Masons of the City of London*, London , 1894

Charles Henry Cooper, *Annals of Cambridge*, 1, Cambridge, 1842

Joseph Cooper, 'The Hundred of Swanborough', *Sussex Archaeological Collections*, 29, 1879, pp. 114-166

Lettice Ashley Cooper (ed.), 'Two 17th Century Dorset Inventories', *Dorset Record Society*, 5, 1974

Nicholas Cooper, 'Aynho, A Northamptonshire Village', *Banbury Historical Society*, 20, 1984

Nicholas Cooper, 'The Work of Two Antiquaries at Bruce Castle', *Georgian Group Journal*, 13, 2003, pp. 84-107

Nicholas Cooper, 'Kelmscott Manor' in Alan Crossley, Tom Hassall, Peter Salway (ed.), *William Morris's Kelmscott: Landscape and Memory*, Macclesfield, 2007, pp. 110-130

Barbara Cornford, 'Inventories of the Poor', *Norfolk Archaeology*, 35, 1973, pp. 118-125

Julian Cornwall, 'John Carter of Denham, yeoman', *Records of Buckinghamshire*, 16, 1956, pp. 83-93

Julian Cornwall, 'The Squire of Conisholme' in C. W. Chalkin and M. A. Havinden, *Rural Change and Urban Growth 1500-18—, Essays in English Regional History in Honour of W. G. Hoskins*, London, 1974, pp. 32-53

W. C. Costin, 'The Inventory of John English, B. C. L., Fellow of St John's College', *Oxoniensia*, 11 and 12, 1946-1947, pp. 102-131

Jonathan Couch, 'An Inventory of a Nobleman's Personal Property in the 16th Century', *Journal of the Royal Institution of Cornwall*, 2, 1867, pp. 226-233

H. Swainson Cowper, 'Hawkshead Hall', *Transactions of the Cumberland and Westmorland Antiquarian and Archaeological Society*, 11, 1891, pp. 7-49

William Cowper, 'The Will of Thomas Bellamy, of Stonyard', *Northamptonshire Notes and Queries*, 3, 1890, p. 60

William Cowper, 'Glimpses of Old Northampton: Its Signs, The Peacock', *Northamptonshire Notes and Queries*, 4, 1892, pp. 86-87

J. Charles Cox, 'Norbury Manor House and The Troubles of the Fitzherberts', *Journal of the Derbyshire Archaeological and Natural History Society*, 7, 1885, pp. 221-259

J. Charles Cox, 'A Budget from Repton', *Journal of the Derbyshire Archaeological and Natural History Society*, 36, 1914, pp. 101-122

Patricia Crawford and Laura Cowing, *Women's Worlds in Seventeenth-Century England*, London, 2000

Glenys Crocker and K. R. Fairclough, 'The introduction of edge-runner incorporating mills in the British gunpowder industry', *Industrial Archaeology Review*, 20, 1998, pp. 23-36

John Croft, *Excerpta Antiqua; or, a Collection of Original Manuscripts*, York, 1797

Claire Cross, 'York Clergy Wills 1520-1600: I Minster Clergy', *Borthwick Texts and Calendars*, 10, 1984

Claire Cross, 'York Clergy Wills 1520-1600: II City Clergy', *Borthwick Texts and Calendars*, 15, 1989

E. W. Crossley, 'A Templenewsam Inventory 1565', *Yorkshire Archaeological Journal*, 25, 1920, pp. 91-100

E. W. Crossley, 'The Testamentary Documents of Yorkshire Peculiars', *York Archaeological Society, Record Series*, 74, 1929, *Miscellanea*, II, pp. 46-86

E. W. Crossley, 'Two Seventeeth-Century Inventories', *Yorkshire Archaeological Journal*, 34, 1938, pp. 170-203

Richard Crow, 'Alice Rundell and her musket', *Devon and Cornwall Notes and Queries*, 36, 1987-1991, pp. 62-65

Evelyn Curtis (ed.), 'Inventory of Furniture at Houghton House, c.1726-28', *Bedfordshire Historical Record Society*, 38, 1958, pp. 97-104

Elizabeth Cust, *Records of the Cust Family of Pinchbeck, Stamford and Belton in Lincolnshire, 1479-1700*, London, 1898

Elizabeth Cust, *Records of the Cust Family, Series II, The Brownlows of Belton*, London, 1909

Lionel Cust, 'Notes on the Collections formed by Thomas Howard, Earl of Arundel and Surrey, K.G.', *Burlington Magazine*, 20, 1911, II, pp. 97-100, III, pp. 233-236, IV, pp. 341-343

Lionel Cust, 'The Lumley Inventories', *The Walpole Society*, 6, 1918, pp. 15-35

Catherine Dack, 'The Probate Inventory of a master Shoemaker: William Titterton of Ashbourne, Died 1642', *Derbyshire Miscellany*, 18, 2007, 2, pp. 26-31

F. de F. Daniel, 'Will of John Williams, Rector of Abbas and Temple Combe', *Somerset & Dorset Notes & Queries*, 28, 1968, pp. 39-40

F. de F. Daniel, 'Will of William Furnell of Horsington, Somerset', *Somerset & Dorset Notes & Queries*, 28, 1968, pp. 68-69

Ida Darlington (ed.), 'London Consistory Court Wills 1492-1547', *London Record Society*, 3, 1967

R. Dart and T. Kay, *Turton Tower*, Turton, 1961

G. H. Darwin, 'Inventory of the goods and chattels of Edmond Waring of Wolverhampton, Esquire, 1625', *Proceedings of the Society of Antiquaries of London*, 6, 1873-1876, pp. 363-375

G. H. Dashwood, 'Remarks on a Subsidy Roll in the Possession of the Corporation on Lynn Regis', *Norfolk Archaeology*, 1, 1847, pp. 334-354

James Davenport, *The Grove Family of Halesowen*, London, 1912

Joan Davies and Barbara Hutton, 'Farming in Barrow-upon-Trent and Twyford in the Sixteenth and Seventeenth Centuries using the Evidence of Wills and Probate Inventories', *Derbyshire Miscellany*, 16, 2001, 1, pp. 2-28

Robert Davies, *A Memoir of the York Press with Notices of Authors, Printers and Stationers, in the Sixteenth, Seventeenth and Eighteenth Centuries*, London, 1868

Philip N. Dawe, 'A Dorset Farm Inventory of 1704', *Somerset & Dorset Notes & Queries*, 27, 1958, pp. 169-173

Philip N. Dawe, 'Inventory of a Purbeck Marbler's Goods, 1689', *Somerset & Dorset Notes & Queries*, 28, 1968, pp. 241-242

Philip N. Dawe, 'Inventory of Goods of Jasper Rogers of Cattistock, 1710', *Somerset & Dorset Notes & Queries*, 28, 1968, pp. 282-284

Philip N. Dawe, 'A Fuller's Inventory from Dorset Records Office', *Somerset & Dorset Notes & Queries*, 29, 1974, pp. 33-35

Viscount Dillon, 'Inventory of the Goods and Chattels belonging to Thomas, duke of Gloucester, and seized in his castle at Pleshy, Co. Essex', *Archaeological Journal*, 54, 1897, pp. 275-308

John Dillon and John Fullarton (ed.), *Description of the Sheriffdoms of Lanark and Renfrew Compiles about MDCC.X by William Hamilton of Wishaw*, Maitland Club, Glasgow, 1831

E. A. Donaldson, 'The Inventory of the Goods and Chattels of Mr Richard Bevys, late Mayor of Exeter, 1603', *Report and Transactions of the Devonshire Association*, 41, 1909, pp. 215-240

Helen Dorey, 'A Catalogue of the Furniture in Sir John Soane's Museum', *Furniture History*, 44, 2009

M. Douglas, 'Inventory of Eatons 1687', *Sussex Notes and Queries*, 16, 1967, pp. 289-293

Jane Downey, 'An 18th century woodworker's inventory', *Regional Furniture History Society Newsletter*, 49, Autumn, 2008, pp. 26-27

Marie P. G. Draper, *Parish of Hackney (Part I)*,

Brooke House, a monograph, Survey of London, 28, 1960

Jo Draper, 'Inventory of Ann Shergold, ceramic dealer in Blandford, Dorset', *Post-Medieval Archaeology*, 16, 1982, pp. 85-91

Norman Drinkwater, 'The Old Deanery, Salisbury', *Antiquaries Journal*, 44, 1964, pp. 41-59

Reginald C. Dudding, 'Inventory of Estate of a late 17th Century Lincolnshire Smallholder', *Lincolnshire Notes and Queries*, 16, 1921, pp. 242-245

R. E. H. Duke, 'An Account of the Family of Duke, of Lake', *Wiltshire Notes and Queries*, 8, 1914-1916, pp. 193-205

J. Dalrymple Duncan, 'An Inventory of Articles which Escaped the Hands of the Mob on the Occasion of the Sacking of Shawfield Mansion, 1725', *Transactions of the Glasow Archaeological Society*, 1, 1890, pp. 228-249

Leland L. Duncan, 'A Kentish Cottage Inventory of 1529', *Home Counties Magazine*, 9, 1907, pp. 58-64

W. G. Duncombe (ed.), 'Stuart Yeomen of the Darent Valley', *Kent Archaeological Society, Kent Records*, 1, 1990-1991, pp. 205-430

A. D. Dyer (ed.), 'Probate Inventories of Worcestershire Tradesmen, 1545-1614', *Worcestershire Historical Society*, 5, 1967, pp. 1-67

Christopher Dyer, *Standards of Living in the Later Middle Ages, Social Change in England c.1200-1520*, Cambridge, 1989

Robert Dymond, 'The House and Furniture of an Exeter Citizen in the Reign of James I', *Western Antiquary*, 7, 1887, pp. 1-5

A. L. Earl, *Middlewich 900-1900*, Farndon, 1990

J. P. Earwaker, *East Cheshire: Past and Present; or a History of the Hundred of Macclesfield in the County Palatine of Chester. From Original Records II*, London, 1880

J. P. Earwaker, 'A Gipsy's Inventory, 1627', *Notes and Queries*, 4, 1881, pp. 465-466

J. P. Earwaker, 'Lancashire and Cheshire Wills and Inventories at Chester', *Chetham Society*, 3, 1884

J. P. Earwaker, 'Lancashire and Cheshire Wills and Inventories 1572-1696 ... at Chester', *Chetham Society*, 28, 1893

M. R. Eddy and p. M. Ryan, 'John Ennows: A Previously Unknown Clay-Pipe Maker of All Saints, Colchester', *Essex Archaeology and History*, 15, 1983, pp. 106-112

Robert Allan Eden, *Some Historical Notes on the Eden Family*, London, 1907

G. Eland (ed.), *Shardeloes Papers of the 17th and 18th centuries*, Oxford, 1947

Henry Ellis, 'Notices of Richard Curteys, Bishop of Chichester, 1570 to 1582', *Sussex Archaeological Collections*, 10, 1858, pp. 53-58

Henry Ellis, 'Inventories of Goods, &c., in the Manor of Chesworth, Sedgwick, the Manor Place of Sheffield, and in the Forest of Worth, with the Iron-works belonging to the Lord Admiral Seymour, at the Time of his Attainder, taken 1549', *Sussex Archaeological Collections*, 13, 1861, pp. 118-131

F. G. Emmison, 'The Relief of the Poor at Eaton Socon, 1706-1834', *Bedfordshire Historical Record Society*, 15, 1933, pp. 1-98

F. G. Emmison, 'Jacobean Household Inventories', *Bedfordshire Record Society*, 20, 1938, pp. 1-144

F. G. Emmison, *Archives and Local History*, London, 1966

F. G. Emmison (ed.), *Ingatestone Hall in 1600, An Inventory*, Essex Record Office Publications, 22, 1954

F. G. Emmison, *Essex Wills*, 1, *1558-1565*, Washington, 1982

F. G. Emmison, *Essex Wills*, 3, *1571-1577*, Boston, 1986

F. G. Emmison, *Essex Wills*, 4, *The Archdeaconry Courts 1577-1584*, Essex Record Office, 1987

F. G. Emmison, *Essex Wills*, 5, *The Archdeaconry Courts 1583-1592*, Essex Record Office, 1989

N. W. English, 'Arthur Kingstone's Household Stuff', *Irish Ancestor*, 4, 1972, pp. 35-42

Joan Evans, 'An Inventory of Thomas Lord Wharton, 1568', *Archaeological Journal*, 102, 1945, pp. 134-150

John Evans, 'Extracts from the Private Account Book of Sir William More, of Loseley, in Surrey, in the time of Queen Mary and of Queen Elizabeth', *Archaeologia*, 36, 1855, pp. 284-310

John Evans, 'Inventory of the Goods of Thomas Key, Rector of St Nicholas, Guildford, taken at his decease in 1597', *Proceedings of the Society of Antiquaries of London*, 4, 1856-1859, pp. 180-183

Nesta Evans (ed.), 'The Wills of the Archdeaconry of Sudbury 1630-1635', *Suffolk Records Society*, 29, 1987

Nesta Evans (ed.), 'Wills of the Archdeaconry of Sudbury 1636-1638', *Suffolk Record Society*, 35, 1993

F. W. Fairholt, 'On an Inventory of the Household Goods of Sir Thomas Ramsey, Lord Mayor of London 1577', *Archaeologia*, 40, 1866, pp. 311-342

M. W. Farr, 'Nicholas Eyffeler of Warwick, Glazier, Executors' Accounts and other Documents concerning the Foundation of his Almshouse Charity, 1592-1621', *Miscellany I, Dugdale Society*, 31, 1977, pp. 29-110

George F. Farnham, *Quorndon Records*, London, 1912

John Fell, 'Some Illustrations of Home Life in Lonsdale North of the Sands, in the 17th and 18th Centuries', *Transactions of the Cumberland and Westmorland Antiquarian and Archaeological Society*, 11, 1891, pp. 368-398

Jane Fenlon, *Goods & Chattels, A Survey of Early Household Inventories in Ireland*, Dublin, 2003

James Alexander Fenton, 'Worthing 200 Years Ago', *Sussex Archaeological Collections*, 35, 1887, pp. 93-100

R. S. Ferguson, 'Wills relating to the Dean and Chapter Library at Carlisle', *Transactions of the Cumberland and Westmorland Antiquarian and Archaeological Society*, 4, 1880, pp. 1-12

R. S. Ferguson, 'Belbridge and Captain Thomas Morris', *Transactions of the Cumberland and Westmorland Antiquarian and Archaeological Society*, 7, 1884, pp. 245-252

Edmund Ferrers, 'A letter ... Accompanying an authenticated Copy of the Will of King James the Second, with an Inventory of the Goods and Chattels belonging to that Monarch at the time of his Death', *Archaeologia*, 18, 1817, pp. 223-239

Rosemary ffolliott, 'Household Stuff', *Irish Ancestor*, 1, 1969, pp. 43-59

Rosemary ffolliott, 'An Inventory of Killeen Castle in 1735-6', *Irish Ancestor*, 9, 1977, pp. 102-107

Rosemary ffolliott, 'The Inventory of John Mahon of Strokestown. Co. Roscommon, 1708', *Irish Ancestor*, 10, 1978, pp. 77-80

Rosemary ffolliott and Brian de Breffny, 'The Contents of Burton Hall Co. Cork in 1686', *Irish Ancestor*, 5, 1973, pp. 104-113

R. Fieldhouse, 'Social Structure from Tudor Lay Subsidies and Probate Inventories, A Case Study: Richmondshire (Yorkshire)', *Local Population Studies*, 12, 1974, pp. 9-24

James F. Firth, *Coopers Company, London, Historical Memoranda, Charters, Documents, and Extracts from the Records of the Corporation and the Books of the Company 1396-1848*, London, 1848

F. N. Fisher, 'The Every Family and the Civil War, A tale of loyalty', *Journal of the Derbyshire Archaeological and Natural History Society*, 74, 1954, pp. 122-127

Lt. Col. Fishwick, 'The Lemons of Preston', *The Reliquary*, 17, 1876-7, pp. 169-173

Lt. Col. Fishwick, 'Rochdale in the Beginning of the 17th Century', *Transactions of the Historical Society of Lancashire and Cheshire*, 38, 1886, pp. 15-36

W.S. Fitch, 'Inventory of Furniture at Mendham Hall, 1548', *Proceedings of the Suffolk Institute of Archaeology*, 2, 1859, pp. 242-247

W. G. Dymock Fletcher, 'Some Early Notices of the Herrick Family', *Transactions of the Leicestershire Architectural and Archaeological Society*, 6, 1888, pp. 118-134

Alexander Forbes, *Memorials of the Family of Forbes of Forbesfield*, Aberdeen, 1905

Amy G. Foster (ed.), 'Oakwell Hall, Birstall, Inventory of Goods, 1611', *Publicatons of the Thoresby Society*, 41, 1948, pp. 114-117

C. W. Foster, 'Lincoln Wills, I, A. D. 1271 to A. D. 1526', *Publications of the Lincoln Record Society*, 5, 1912

C. W. Foster, 'Lincoln Wills, II, A. D. 1505 to May 1530', *Publications of the Lincoln Record Society*, 10, 1914

C. W. Foster, 'Lincoln Wills, I, A. D. 1530 to 1532', *Publications of the Lincoln Record Society*, 24, 1927

Charles Wilmer Foster and Joseph J. Green, *History of the Wilmer Family*, Leeds, 1888

J. T. Fowler, 'Acts of Chapter of the Collegiate Church of SS. Peter and Wilfred, Ripon, A.D. 1452 to A. D. 1506', *Surtees Society*, 64, 1874

Francis F. Fox, *Some Account of the Ancient Fraternity of Merchant Tailors of Bristol*, Bristol, 1880

R. Sharpe France, 'An Inventory of the Goods of John Cuerden of Cuerden, 1601', *Transactions of the Historical Society of Lancashire and Cheshire*, 91, 1940, pp. 193-204

R. Sharpe France, 'A Fifteenth Century Altcar Inventory', *Transactions of the Historical Society of Lancashire and Cheshire*, 95, 1944, pp. 126-128

William Fraser, *Memorials of the Montgomeries, Earls of Eglinton*, Edinburgh, 1859

William Fraser, *The Book of Carlaverock, Memoirs of the Maxwells, Earls of Nithsdale Lords Maxwell &*

Herries, II, Correspondence and Charters, Edinburgh, 1873

William Fraser, *Memorials of the Earls of Haddington*, 2, Edinburgh, 1889

William Fraser, *The Elphinstone Family Book of the Lords Elphinstone, Balmerino and Coupar*, Edinburgh, 1897

C. E. Freeman, 'Elizabethan Inventories', *Bedfordshire Historical Record Society*, 32, 1952, pp. 92-107

Edwin Freshfield, [no title], *Proceedings of the Society of Antiquaries of London*, 12, 1889, pp. 371-380

John Gage, *The History and Antiquities of Hengrave in Suffolk*, London, 1822

John Gage, *The History and Antiquities of Suffolk. Thingoe Hundred*, London, 1838

James Gairdner (ed.), *The Paston Letters 1422-1509*, III, 1875

James Gairdner, *Letters and Papers Foreign and Domestic of the Reign of Henry VIII*, 7, London, 1883

James Gairdner, *Letters and Papers Foreign and Domestic of the Reign of Henry VIII*, 10, London, 1887

Jane Geddes, 'The Prince of Wales at The Grange, Northington: An Inventory of 1795', *Furniture History*, 22, 1986, pp. 176-207

Edwin and Stella George (ed.), 'Bristol Probate Inventories, Part 1: 1542-1650', *Bristol Record Society*, 54, 2002

Edwin and Stella George (ed.), 'Bristol Probate Inventories, 1657-1689', *Bristol Record Society*, 57, 2005

Edwin and Stella George (ed.), 'Bristol Probate Inventories, 1690-1804', *Bristol Record Society*, 60, 2008

Alfred Gibbons, *Early Lincoln Wills, An abstract of All the Wills & Adminisrtrations Recorded in the Episcopal Registers of the Old Diocese of Lincoln ... 1280-1547*, Lincoln, 1888

R. G. Gilson, 'From Restoration to Civil Control: The Probate Records of Llanfihangel yng Ngwynfa', *The Montgomeryshire Collections, Journal of the Powysland Club*, 97, 2009, pp. 9-62

Rainald W. Knightley Goddard, 'Goddard of Sedgehill', *Wiltshire Notes and Queries*, 4, 1902-1904, pp. 171-174

Percy S. Godman, 'Two Sussex Inventories', *Sussex Archaeological Collections*, 51, 1908, pp. 115-122

Elizabeth Goldring, 'The Earl of Leicester's Inventory of Kenilworth Castle, c.1578', *English Heritage Historical Review*, 2, 2007, pp. 36-59

John A. A. Goodall, *God's House at Ewelme*, Aldershot, 2001

Olive C. Goodbody, 'Quaker Inventories', *Irish Ancestor*, 3, 1971, pp. 52-62

Olive C. Goodbody, 'Inventories of Five Dublin Quaker Merchants in the late Seventeenth Century', *Irish Ancestor*, 10, 1978, pp. 38-48

Robert H. Goodsall, *Stede Hill, The Annals of a Kentish Home*, London, 1949

Francis Grainger, 'Agriculture in Cumberland in Ancient Times', *Transactions of the Cumberland and Westmorland Antiquarian and Archaeological Society*, 9, 1909, pp. 120-146,

Francis Grainger and W. G. Collingwood, 'The Register and Records of Holm Cultram', *Cumberland and Westmorland Antiquarian and Archaeological Society, Record Series*, 7, 1929

Duncan Gray and Violet W. Walker (ed.), *Records of the Borough of Nottingham*, 8, *1800-1835*, Nottingham, 1952

George J. Gray and William Mortlock Palmer, *Abstracts from the Wills and Testamentary Documents of Printers, Binders, and Stationers of Cambridge from 1404 to 1699*, London Bibliographical Society, 1915

Todd Gray (ed.), 'Devon Household Accounts, 1627-59; Part Two, Henry, Fifth Earl of Bath, and Rachel, Countess of Bath, of Tawstock and London 1637-1655', *Devon and Cornwall Record Society*, 39, 1996

Michael Green, *Historic Clapham*, Stroud, 2008

William Greenwell (ed.), *Wills and Inventories from the Registry at Durham*, II, Durham, The Surtees Society, 1860

David J. Griffin, 'The building and furnishing of a Dublin townhouse in the eighteenth century', *Bulletin of the Irish Georgian Society*, 38, 1997, pp. 24-39

R. G. Griffiths, 'An Inventory of the Goods and chattels of Thomas Cowcher, Mercer, of Worcester *Dated 14th November, 1643*', *Transactions of the Worcestershire Archaeological Society*, 14, 1937, pp. 45-60

Jill Groves (ed.), *Ashton-on-Mersey and Sale Wills, Wills and Probate Inventories from two Cheshire Townships, Part 1 1600-1650*, Sale, 1999

Jill Groves (ed.), *Ashton-on-Mersey and Sale Wills, Wills and Probate Inventories from two Cheshire Townships, Part 2 1651-1700*, Sale, 2000

Jill Groves (ed.), *Ashton-on-Mersey and Sale Wills, Wills and Probate Inventories from two Cheshire Townships, Part 3 1701-60*, Sale, 2002

Jill Groves (ed.), *Bowdon Wills, Wills and Probate Inventories form a Cheshire Township*, 1, *1600-1650*, Sale, 1997

Jill Groves (ed.), *Bowdon Wills, Wills and Probate Inventories form a Cheshire Township*, 2, *1651-1689*, Sale, 1998

Jill Groves (ed.), *Bowdon Wills, Wills and Probate Inventories form a Cheshire Township*, 3, *1690-1760*, Sale, 1999

Jill Groves (ed.), *Dunham Massey Wills, wills and probate inventories from a North-East Cheshire township, Part 1 1600-1640*, Sale, 2008

Jill Groves (ed.), *Hale Wills, wills and probate inventories from a North-East Cheshire township, Part 1 1600-1640*, Sale, 2005

Jill Groves (ed.), *Hale Wills, wills and probate inventories from a North-East Cheshire township, Part 2 1641-1680*, Sale, 2005

A. C. and D. Guest, *A History of the Old Church Smethwick together with Some Background Notes and Some Genealogies*, Warley, 1997

W. Brampton Gurdon, 'The Gurdon Papers no. IX. The Last Wishes of a Puritan Lady, 1661.', *The East Anglian: or, Notes and Queries Connected with the Counties of Suffolk, Cambridge, Essex and Norfolk*, 5, 1893-1894, pp. 97-99

W. H. Hale and H. T. Ellacombe (ed.), 'Account of the Executors of Richard Bishop of London 1303, and of the Executors of Thomas Bishop of Exeter 1310', *Camden Society*, 10, 1874

Elisabeth Hall (ed.), *Michael Warton of Beverley, An Inventory of his Possessions*, Hull, 1986

J. Melland Hall, 'Harescombe: the Will of James Mitchell, with Inventory, A.D. 1698', *Gloucestershire Notes and Queries*, 4, 1890, pp. 164-167

Hubert Hall, *Society in the Elizabethan Age*, London, 1887 (also 1888)

Oliver Hall, 'Inventories of Ingatestone and West Thorndon Halls, 1572-1685', *Essex Journal*, 11, 1976, pp. 2-13

James Orchard Halliwell, *Some Account of a Collection of Several Thousand bills, Accounts, and Inventories, Illustrating the History of Prices between the Years 1650 and 1750, Presented to the Smithsonian Institution, Washington*, Brixton Hill, 1852

James Orchard Halliwell, *Ancient Inventories of Furniture, Pictures, Tapestry, Plate, &c. illustrative of the Domestic Manners of the English in the Sixteenth and Seventeenth Centuries*, London, 1854

James Orchard Halliwell, 'An Inventory of the Furniture, etc., of a Tavern at Stratford-on-Avon, taken in the time of Shakespeare', *Collectanea Archaeologica*, II, 1871, pp. 92-114

J. O. Halliwell-Phillipps, *An Inventory of the Goods and Chattels of Ann Shaw, The Friend and Neighbour of Shakespeare at Stratford-upon-Avon, taken in the year 1630, Now Printed from the Original Manuscript*, London, 1880

Henry Hamilton (ed.), *Selections from the Monymusk Papers (1713-1755)*, Edinburgh, Scottish History Society, 1945

Henry Hamilton (ed.), *Life and Labour on an Aberdeenshire Estate (Being Selections from the Monymusk Papers)*, Aberdeen, Third Spalding Club, 1956

Joan M. Harding, *Four Centuries of Charlwood Houses: medieval to 1840*, Charlwood, 1976

Charles Frederick Hardy, *The Hardys of Barbon*, London, 1913

Thomas Duffus Hardy (ed.), *Registrum Palatinum Dunelmense The Register of Richard de Kellawe Lord Palatine and Bishop of Durham 1311-1316*, 1, London, 1873, and 2, London, 1874

W. J. Hardy (ed.), *Report on the Manuscripts of the Earl of Verulam preserved at Gorhambury*, Historical Manuscripts Commission, 1906

Frederic Harrison, *Annals of an Old Manor House, Sutton Place, Guildford*, London, 1893

J. V. Harrison, 'The Routledges of Cumcrook', *Transactions of the Cumberland and Westmorland Antiquarian and Archaeological Society*, 65, 1965, pp. 320-370

J. V. Harrison, 'Five Bewcastle Wills, 1587-1617', *Transactions of the Cumberland and Westmorland Antiquarian and Archaeological Society*, 67, 1967, pp. 93-111

Mona C. Harrison, 'The Probate Inventory of an Early Seventeenth Century Northampton Mercer and

Linen Draper', *Northamptonshire Past and Present*, 6, 1982-1983, pp. 313-317

William Henry Hart (ed.), *Historia et Cartularium Monasterii Sancti Petri Gloucestriae*, 3, London, 1867

John Harvey, 'Sources for the History of Houses', *British Records Association, Archives and the User*, 3, 1974

John Harvey, *Mediaeval Craftsmen*, London, 1975

B. and R. Harvey and P. M. Slocombe, 'The Early History and Architecture of Bewley Court, Lacock', *Wiltshire Archaeological and Natural History Magazine*, 81, 1987, pp. 63-73

P. D. A. Harvey (ed.), 'Manorial Records of Cuxham, Oxfordshire, circa 1200-1359', *Oxfordshire Record Society*, 50, 1976

W. O. Hassall, 'Wheatley Records 956-1956', *Oxfordshire Record Society*, 37, 1956

John Hatcher and T. C. Barker, *A History of British Pewter*, London, 1974

Helena Hayward and Pat Kirkham, *William and John Linnell, Eighteenth Century London Furniture Makers*, London, 1980

Maria Hayward, *The 1542 Inventory of Whitehall, The Palace and Its Keeper*, I and II, Society of Antiquaries of London, 2004

M. A. Havinden, 'Household and Farm Inventories in Oxfordshire, 1550-1590', *Oxfordshire Record Society*, 44, 1965

Sir Ambrose Heal, 'A Great Country House in 1623', *Burlington Magazine*, 82, 1943, pp. 108-116

Helen Truesdell Heath, *The Letters of Samuel Pepys and His Family Circle*, Oxford, 1955

M. V. Herbert, *The Hickmans of Oldswinford*, London, 1979

R. Herbert, 'An Inventory of the Goods, &c., of the Revd. Mr. Jon. Head, Decd.', *North Munster Antiquarian Journal*, 3, 1942-1943, pp. 122-123

D. M. Herridge, 'Surrey Probate Inventories 1558-1603', *Surrey Record Society*, 39, 2005

Mary F. S. Hervey, 'A Lumley Inventory of 1609', *The Walpole Society*, 6, 1918, pp. 36-50

Kenneth Y. Heselton, *Sunbury Household Effects 1673-1724. Probate Inventories*, Sunbury & Shepperton Local History Society, 1976

Derek Hewett, *William Hewett 1496-1566-7, Lord Mayor of London*, London, 2004

David G. Hey, 'A Dual Economy in South Yorkshire', *Agricultural History Review*, 17, 1969, pp. 108-119

David G. Hey, 'The Nailmaking Background of the Walkers and the Booths', *Transactions of the Hunter Archaeological Society*, 10, 1979, pp. 31-36

David Hey, 'Doncaster People of Ten Generations Ago' in Brian Elliott (ed.), *Aspects of Doncaster, Discovering Local History*, 1, Barnsley, 1997, pp. 119-152

Peter Hill and David Penrose, 'Framsden Hall', *Suffolk Review*, 4, 1974, pp. 114-125

F. C. Hingeston-Randolph, *The Register of Walter de Stapeldon Bishop of Exeter (A. D. 1307-1326)*, London, 1892

Michael Hodgetts, 'The Priest-Holes at Harvington Hall', *Transactions of the Worcestershire Archaeological Society*, 39, 1962, pp. 1-15

J. C. Hodgson (ed.), *Wills and Inventories from the Registry at Durham*, III, Durham, The Surtees Society, 1906

Wilfred Herbert Holden, *The Derbyshire Holdens and their Descendants*, London, 1930

Richard Holt, *The Early History of the Town of Birmingham*, Dugdale Society Occasional Papers, 30, 1985

Richard Holt, Janet Ingram, John Jarman (ed.), *Birmingham Wills and Inventories 1551-1600*, Birmingham, 1985

E. A. J. Honigmann and Susan Brock, *Playhouse wills 1558-1642, An edition of wills by Shakespeare and his contemporaries in the London theatre*, Manchester, 1993

David Hook, 'John Davies of Kidwelly: A Neglected Literary Figure of the Seventeenth Century', *Carmarthenshire Antiquary*, 11, 1975, pp. 104-124

David Hook and Robert Hook, 'More Light on John Davies of Kidwelly', *Carmarthenshire Antiquary*, 15, 1979, pp. 57-64

T. M. Hope, 'Two Interiors. Toppingho Hall, Hatfield Peverel, in the 16th and 17th Centuries', *Essex Review*, 52, 1943, pp. 121-124

W. H. St John Hope, 'Some Inventories, with Notes', *Reliquary*, 4, 1890, pp. 150-162

W. H. St John Hope, 'Inventories of the Goods of Henry of Eastry (1331), Richard of Oxenden (1334), and Robert Hathbrand (1339), successively Priors of the Monastery of Christchurch, Canterbury', *Archaeological Journal*, 53, 1896, pp. 258-283

William St John Hope, 'The Last Testament and Inventory of John de Veer, thirteenth Earl of Oxford', *Archaeologia*, 66, 1915, pp. 275-348

W. H. St John Hope and Cuthbert Atchley, 'An Inventory of Pleshy College 1527', *Transactions of the St Paul's Ecclesiological Society*, 8, 1920, pp. 160-172

Henry Hornyold, *Genealogical Memoirs of the Family of Strickland of Sizergh*, Kendal, 1928

W. G. Hoskins, 'The Leicestershire Country Parson in the Sixteenth Century', *Transactions of the Leicestershire Archaeological Society*, 21, 1940, pp. 89-115

W. G. Hoskins, 'An East Devon Yeoman', *Devon and Cornwall Notes and Queries*, 21, 1941, pp. 241-248

W. G. Hoskins, 'A Devon Yeoman in 1648', *Devon and Cornwall Notes and Queries*, 22, 1946, pp. 162-164

W. G. Hoskins, 'An Elizabethan Butcher of Leicester' in *Essays in Leicestershire History*, Liverpool, 1950, pp. 108-122

W. G. Hoskins, 'The Leicestershire Parson in the Sixteenth Century' in *Essays in Leicestershire History*, Liverpool, 1950, pp. 1-23

W. G. Hoskins, *The Midland Peasant*, London, 1957

W. G. Hoskins, *Old Devon*, Newton Abbot, 1966

W. G. Hoskins and H.P.R. Finberg, *Devonshire Studies*, London, 1952

Maurice Howard and Edward Wilson, *The Vyne, A Tudor House Revealed*, London, 2003

B. E. Howells, 'Pembrokeshire Farming *circa* 1580-1620 – III', *National Library of Wales Journal*, 9, 1956, pp. 413-439

W. H. Howse, 'An Inventory of 1662', *Transactions of*

the Woolhope Naturalists' Field Club, 35, 1958, p. 167

C. Roy Hudleston, 'An 18th-century squire's possessions', *Transactions of the Cumberland and Westmorland Antiquarian and Archaeological Society*, 57, 1958, pp. 127-157

C. Roy Hudleston, 'Cumberland Recusants of 1723/4', *Transactions of the Cumberland and Westmorland Antiquarian and Archaeological Society*, 59, 1959, pp. 114-138

C. Roy Hudleston, 'Denton Holme, Part I', *Transactions of the Cumberland and Westmorland Antiquarian and Archaeological Society*, 68, 1968, pp. 72-116

C. Roy Hudleston, 'Canon Winder Hall and its owners', *Transactions of the Cumberland and Westmorland Antiquarian and Archaeological Society*, 87, 1987, pp. 159-169

Annabelle Hughes, 'Sussex Clergy Inventories 1600-1750', *Sussex Record Society*, 91, 2007

Mary H. M. Hulton, *'Company and Fellowship': The Medieval Weavers of Coventry*, Dugdale Society Occasional Papers, 30, 1985

Mary H. M. Hulton and Eileen Castle (ed.), *Ten Tudor Families, Coventrian Wills and Inventories*, Coventry and Warwickshire Pamphlet No.13, Coventry, 1987

Harold Hulme (ed.), 'Probate Inventory of Sir John Eliot, late Prisoner in The Tower (1633), *Camden Miscellany*, 16, 1936 (3rd series, 52), pp. i-viii, 1-15

Arthur Hussey, 'Faversham Household Inventory', *Archaeologia Cantiana*, 27, 1905, pp. 230-236

Alexander Hutcheson, 'Notice of an Inventory of the Goods and Household Plenishings and Relative Will and Testament of Agnes Betoun, a Daughter of Cardinal David Betoun by his reputed Wife Marion Ogilvy: along with Notice of a Carved Oak Cabinet from Ethie House said to have belonged to the Cardinal: and in Appendix an Inventory of Ancient Writs of the Lands of Kelly', *Proceedings of the Society of Antiquaries of Scotland*, 51 (2), 1916-1917, pp. 213-231

John Hutchins, *The History and Antiquities of the County of Dorset* (3rd edition, William Shipp and James Whitworth Hodson), 3, London, 1868

F. E. Hutchinson, *Henry Vaughan, A Life and Interpretation*, Oxford, 1947

Arthur Robert Ingpen, *An Ancient Family, A Genealogical Study showing the Saxon Origin of the Family of Ingpen*, London, 1916

C. Innes (ed.), *The Black Book of Taymouth, With Other Papers from the Breadalbane Charter Room*, Edinburgh, 1855

William Ferguson Irvine, 'Notes on the History of Hall i' th' Wood and Its Owners',*Transactions of the Historic Society of Lancashire and Cheshire*, 55, 1903, pp. 1-41

William Jackson, 'The Richmonds of Highhead', *Transactions of the Cumberland and Westmorland Antiquarian and Archaeological Society*, 2, 1876, pp. 108-147

William Jackson, 'The Laws of Buck Crag in Cartmel, and of Bampton', *Transactions of the Cumberland and Westmorland Antiquarian and Archaeological Society*, 2, 1876, pp. 264-276

William Jackson, 'The Orfeurs of High Close, Plumbland', *Transactions of the Cumberland and Westmorland Antiquarian and Archaeological Society*, 3, 1878, pp. 99-126

William Jackson, 'The Curwens of Workington Hall and Kindred Families, II', *Transactions of the Cumberland and Westmorland Antiquarian and Archaeological Society*, 5, 1881, pp. 311-342

William Jackson, 'The Threlkelds of Melmerby, and some other Branches of the Family', *Transactions of the Cumberland and Westmorland Antiquarian and Archaeological Society*, 10, 1889, pp. 1-47

William Jackson, 'The Hudlestons of Hutton John, the Hudlestons of Kelston, now of Hutton John, and the Hudlestons of Whitehaven', *Transactions of the Cumberland & Westmorland Antiquarian & Archaeological Society*, 11, 1891, pp. 433-465

W. H. Jacob, 'A Sixteenth Century Will', *Hampshire Notes and Queries*, 4, 1889, pp. 19-20

Susan Jenkins, "An Inventory of His Grace The Duke of Chandos's Seat att Cannons Taken June the 19th 1725' by John Gilbert', *The Walpole Society*, 67, 2005, pp. 93-192

Hilary Jenkinson (ed.), 'A Beddington Inventory of Furniture, Sixteenth Century', *Surrey Archaeological Collections*, 33, 1919, pp. 158-161

P. A. Jerrome, 'A Duncton Inventory of 1622: Thomas Goble', *Petworth Society Bulletin*, 33, 1983, pp. 33-36

Simon Jervis, 'Holland and Sons, and the Furnishing of the Athenaeum', *Furniture History*, 6, 1970, pp. 43-61

Simon Jervis, 'Five Early Inventories of Browsholme Hall', *Furniture History*, 22, 1986, pp. 1-24

Simon Jervis, 'Furniture for the First Duke of Buckingham', *Furniture History*, 33, 1997, pp. 48-74

Andrew Jervise, *The History and Traditions of the Land of the Lindsays*, Edinburgh, 1853

Llewellyn Jewitt, 'Original Documents', *The Reliquary*, 2, 1861-1862, pp. 231-232

Marion Johnson, 'The Yeomen of Elizabethan Ockbrook, Archives of a Derbyshire Parish in the Sixteenth Century', *Ockbrook and Borrowwash Record Series*, 1, 1994

Robert Winder Johnson and Lawrence Johnson Morris, *The Johnson Family and Allied Families of Lincolnshire, England*, Philadelphia, 1934

J. A. Johnston, 'Probate Inventories of Lincoln Citizens 1661-1714', *Lincoln Record Society*, 80, 1991

B. C. Jones, 'Carlisle Goldsmiths 1318-1625', *Transactions of the Cumberland and Westmorland Antiquarian and Archaeological Society*, 80, 1980, pp. 37-44

B. C. Jones, 'Before Tullie House', *Transactions of the Cumberland and Westmorland Antiquarian and Archaeological Society*, 88, 1988, pp. 125-148

David Jones, 'A Seventeenth Century Inventory of Furnishings at Kinnaird Castle, Angus' in John Frew and David Jones (ed.), *Aspects of Scottish Classicism, the House and its Formal Setting 1690-1750*, St Andrews, 1989, pp. 49-64

Francis Jones, 'Medieval Records Relating to the Diocese of St Davids', *Journal of the Historical Society of the Church in Wales*, 14, 1964, pp. 9-24

Francis Jones, 'The Personality of a Welsh Cleric, 1634', *Journal of the Historical Society of the Church in Wales*, 1, 1947, pp. 154-162

Jeanne Jones, 'Stratford-Upon-Avon Inventories 1538-1699, I, 1538-1625', *Dugdale Society*, 39, 2002

Jeanne Jones, 'Stratford-Upon-Avon Inventories 1538-1699, II, 1626-1699', *Dugdale Society*, 40, 2003

F. Jones, 'Wynnstay in 1683-5', *Archaeologia Cambrensis*, 95, 1940, pp. 48-56

M. C. Jones, 'Welsh Pool: Materials for the History of the Parish and the Borough', *Collections Historical and Archaeological relating to Montgomeryshire*, 14, 1881, pp. 161-236

Edward Basil Jupp, *An Historical Account of the Worshipful Company of Carpenters of the City of London Compiled Chiefly from records in their Possession* (second edition, with a supplement by William Willmer Pocock), London, 1887

Jennifer Kaner (ed.), *'Goods and Chattels' 1552-1642, Wills, Farm and Household Inventories from the Parish of South Cave in the East Riding of Yorkshire*, Hull, 1994

Rosemary Keen (ed.), 'Inventory of Richard Hooker, 1601', *Archaeologia Cantiana*, 70, 1956, pp. 231-236

H. P. Kendall, 'Sowerby Workhouse', *Transactions of the Halifax Antiquarian Society*, 1956, pp. 61-72

P. A. Kennedy, 'A Gentleman's House in the Reign of Henry VII', *Northamptonshire Past and Present*, 2, 1954, pp. 17-28

P. A. Kennedy, 'Nottinghamshire Household Inventories', *Thoroton Society Record Series*, 22, 1963

G. H. Kenyon, 'Kirdford Inventories, 1611 to 1776', *Sussex Archaeological Collections*, 93, 1955, pp. 78-156

G. H. Kenyon, 'Three Kirdford Inventories', *Sussex Notes and Queries*, 14, 1956, pp. 145-157

G. H. Kenyon, 'Petworth Town and Trades 1610-1760 Pt. I', *Sussex Archaeological Collections*, 96, 1958, pp. 35-107

G. H. Kenyon, 'Petworth Town and Trades 1610-1760 Pt. III', *Sussex Archaeological Collections*, 99, 1961, pp. 102-135

G. J. Kidston, 'Some Early Wills of the Bonham Family', *Wiltshire Archaeological and Natural History Magazine*, 48, 1938, pp. 273-291

Peter King, 'Pauper Inventories and the Material Lives of the Poor in the Eighteenth and Early Nineteenth Centuries' in Tim Hitchcock and Pamela Sharp (ed.), *The Voices and Strategies of the English Poor, 1640-1840*, London, 1997, pp. 155-191

H. W. King, 'Ancient Wills', *Transactions of the Essex Archaeological Society*, 3, 1865, pp. 53-94

C. L. Kingsford, 'Two Forfeitures in the Year of Agincourt', *Archaeologia*, 70, 1920, pp. 71-100

C. L. Kingsford, 'On Some London Houses of the Early Tudor Period', *Archaeologia*, 71, 1921, pp. 17-54

Charles Lethbridge Kingsford, 'Essex House, formerly Leicester House, and Exeter Inn', *Archaeologia*, 72, 1923, pp. 1-54

G. E. Kirk, 'Wills, Inventories and Bonds of the Manor Courts of Temple Newsam, W. R. Yorks., 1612-1701', *Publications of the Thoresby Society*, 33, 1935, pp. 241-282

G. E. Kirk (ed.), 'Some Documents of Barnoldswick Manor Court of Probate', *Yorkshire Archaeological Society Record Series*, 118, 1951, pp. 53-84

R. E. G. Kirk, 'Accounts of the Obedientaries of Abingdon Abbey', *Camden Society*, 51, 1892

Henry Kirke, 'Original Document', *Reliquary*, 5, 1864-1865, pp. 173-174

Henry Kirke, 'Original Document', *Reliquary*, 6, 1865-1866, p. 109

P. A. Kirkham, 'Samuel Norman: A Study of an Eighteenth-Century Craftsman', *Burlington Magazine*, 111, 1969, pp. 501-505

J. Klene (ed.), *the Southwell-Sibthorpe Commonplace Book: Folger Ms. V. b. 198*, Medieval and Renaissance Texts and Studies, Tempe, 1997

O. G. Knapp, 'Hampton Clergy', *Notes and Queries Concerning Evesham and the Four Shires*, 2, 1911, pp. 164-174

O. G. Knapp, 'Hampton Wills and Inventories (Second Series)', *Notes and Queries Concerning Evesham and the Four Shires*, 3, 1914, pp. 194-206

Larry J. Kreitzer, 'Oxford's First Quaker Meeting Place: the Home of the Surgeon Richard Bettris 9c.1606-1682)', *Oxoniensia*, 73, 2008, pp. 59-97

Prince Alexandre Labanoff, *Lettres, Instructions et Mémoires de Marie Stuart, Reine d'Écosse; publiés sur les originaux et les manuscrits*, 7, London, 1844

Michael Laithwaite, 'A Ship-Master's House at Faversham, Kent', *Post-Medieval Archaeology*, 2, 1968, pp. 150-162

W. N. Landor, 'Walter Landor, Sheriff of Staffordshire, 1698-9; Some Notes concerning him and other members of his family compiled from their Account Books and other Evidences', *William Salt Archaeological Society, Collections for a History of Staffordshire*, 1939, pp. 97-122

H. C. F. Lansberry (ed.), 'Sevenoaks Wills and Inventories in the Reign of Charles II', *Kent Records*, 25, 1988

Lambert B. Larking, 'The Inventory of Juliana de Leyborne, Countess of Huntingdon', *Archaeologia Cantiana*, 1, 1858, pp. 1-8

Lambert B. Larking, 'Inventory of the Effects of Roger de Mortimer at Wigmore Castle and Abbey, Herefordshire', *Archaeological Journal*, 15, 1858, pp. 354-362

Ernest Law, *The History of Hampton Court Palace*, I, *Tudor Times*, London, 1890

M. A. R. Lawes-Wittewronge, 'An Inventory of the Goods of Sir Thomas Myddelton', *Home Counties Magazine*, 5, 1903, pp. 16-26

Leigh Lawson, *The Jackman Family in West Sussex 1565-1836*, Toronto, 1999

William Lawson, 'The Inventory of the Goods of Hugh Fitz-Eyas de Richemund and Juliana his wife, taken at her death, 1316', *Archaeologia Aeliana*, 1, 1857, p. 196

Arthur Francis Leach (ed.), *Visitations and Memorials of Southwell Minster*, London, 1891

Kenneth S. Ledward, *Pre-1858 Wills, Inventories and Administrations relating to the surname 'Ledward' and preserved at the Cheshire Record Office*, Burscough, 1998

Audrey Lee and Eileen Miller (ed.), *Wills and Inventories of New Mills People*, 3, 1586-1607, [1999]

Frederick G. Lee, 'The Palace of the Savoy', *Walford's Antiquarian*, 8, 1885, pp. 119-124

John Lee, 'Inventory of the Goods and Effects of a Buckinghamshire Gentleman in the Reign of Queen Elizabeth', *Journal of the British Archaeological Association*, 12, 1856, pp. 169-174

Polly Legg, 'The Bastards of Blandford: An Inventory of Their Losses in the Fire of 1731', *Furniture History*, 30, 1994, pp. 15-42

William Le Hardy, 'Harefield Deeds, Tarleton Family Documents', *Transactions of the London and Middlesex Archaeological Society*, 10, 1951, pp. 244-251

W.A. Leighton, 'The Guilds of Shrewsbury', *Transactions of the Shropshire Archaeological and Natural History Society*, 8, 1885, pp. 269-412

F. Le Maistre, 'A Nineteenth Century Inventory', *Société Jersiaise, Bulletin*, 20, 1969-1972, pp. 379-384

Pam Lemmey, *A History of Halstock*, Halstock, 1997

Granville Leveson-Gower, 'Inventories of the College of Lingfield'. *Surrey Archaeological Collections*, 17, 1880, pp. 228-245

Santina M. Levey (ed.), *Of Houshold Stuff: The 1601 Inventories of Bess of Hardwick*, London, 2001

Henry Littlehales, 'The Medieval Records of a London City Church (St. Mary at Hill) A. D. 1420-1559', *Early English Text Society*, 125, 128, 1905

R. G. Chaplin Livett, 'The Goods of a Suffolk Parson in the Seventeenth Century', *The East Anglian; or, Notes and Queries connected with the counties of Suffolk, Cambridge, Essex & Norfolk*, 10, 1903-1904, pp. 33-36

Stephen Lloyd, 'The Cosway Inventory of 1820: Listing Unpaid Commissions and the Contents of 20 Stratford Place, Oxford Street, London', *The Walpole Society*, 66, 2004, pp. 163-217

Gordon Loch, *The Family of Loch*, Edinburgh, 1934

Jill Low, 'Newby Hall: Two Late Eighteenth-Century Inventories', *Furniture History*, 22, pp. 135-175

Norman Lowe, 'The Lancashire Textile Industry in the Sixteenth Century', *Chetham Society*, 20, 1972

G. Alan Lowndes, 'An Inventory of the Household Goods of Sir Thomas Barrrington, Bart., at Hatfield Priory, in 1626', *Transactions of the Essex Archaeological Society*, 3, 1889, pp. 155-176

John Lowrey, 'The Furnishings of Queensberry House, 1700-25', *Regional Furniture*, 14, 2000, pp. 44-62

Robert Lucas, *A Gower Family, The Lucases of Stouthall and Rhosili Rectory*, Reynoldston, 1986

Th. H. Lunsingh Scheurleer, 'Documents on the Furnishing of Kensington House', *Walpole Society*, 38, 1962, pp. 15-58

Laetitia Lyell, *Acts of Court of the Mercers' Company 1453-1527*, Cambridge, 1936

Hardy Bertram McCall, *Story of the Family of Wandesforde of Kirklington and Castlecomber*, London, 1904

Timothy J. McCann, 'The Death of Thomas Weekes in 1623', *Music and Letters*, 55, 1974, pp. 45-47

Brian Mac Cuarta, 'A Planter's Funeral, Legacies and Inventory: Sir Matthew de Renzy (1577-1634), *Journal of the Royal Society of Antiquaries of Ireland*, 127, 1997, pp. 18-33

Alec Macdonald, 'Anthony Tolly and The Tomb of

Edward Freake, Bishop of Worcester (1584-96) in Worcester Cathedral', *Transactions of the Worcestershire Archaeological Society*, 19, 1942, pp. 1-9

Hector MacDonnell, 'A Seventeenth Century Inventory from Dunluce Castle, County Antrim', *Journal of the Royal Society of Antiquaries of Ireland*, 122, 1992, pp. 109-127

Alan Macfarlane, *Reconstructing Historical Communities*, Cambridge, 1977

Patrick McGrath, 'Merchants and Merchandise in Seventeenth-Century Bristol', *Bristol Record Society's Publications*, 19, 1955

George MacGregor, 'Historical Notices of the Castle of Glasgow', *Transactions of the Glasgow Archaeological Society*, 1, 1890, pp. 228-249

David McKitterick, 'John Field in 1668: the Affairs of a University Printer', *Cambridge Bibliographical Society*, 9, 1990, pp. 497-516

R. Machin (ed.), *Probate Inventories and Manorial Excepts of Chetnole, Leigh and Yetminster*, Bristol, 1976

R. Machin, *The Houses of Yetminster*, Bristol, 1978

Maynard Mack, *The Garden and the City, Retirement and Politics in the Later Poetry of Pope 1731-1743*, Toronto, 1969

John Maclean, 'History of the Manor and Advowson of Clifford Chambers, and Some Account of Its Possessors', *Transactions of the Bristol and Gloucestershire Archaeological Society*, 14, 1889-1890, pp. 50-99

W. D. Macray, *Notes from the Muniments of St Mary Magdalen College, Oxford from the Twelfth to the Seventeenth Century*, Oxford, 1882

W. D. Macray, *Beaumont Papers. Letters relating to the Family of Beaumont, of Whitley, Yorkshire, from the fifteenth to the seventeenth centuries*, Roxburghe Club, London, 1884

Falconer Madan, *Stuart Papers relating chiefly to Queen Mary of Modena and the Exiled Court of King James II*, Roxburghe Club, London, 1889

A. R. Maddison, 'The Following Inventories are in the Muniment Room of the Dean and Chapter of Lincoln', *Lincolnshire Notes and Queries*, 7, 1904, pp. 87-91

Sidney J. Madge, 'Worcester House in the Strand', *Archaeologia*, 91, 1945, pp. 157-180

Samuel Margerison, 'The Furniture of a Squire's House in 1651', *Bradford Antiquary*, 1, 1888, p. 172

G. Markham, *Woolley Hall*, Wakefield, 1979

Jonathan Marsden, 'The Chastleton Inventory of 1633', *Furniture History*, 36, 2000, pp. 23-42

J. F. Marsh, 'Notice of the Inventory of the Effects of Mrs Milton, Widow of the Poet', *Transactions of the Historical Society of Lancashire and Cheshire*, 7, 1855, pp. 27*-31*

David Marshall, 'Notes of the Connection of the Earls of mOrton and Dick of Braid and Craighorne, with the Earldom of Orkney and Lordship of Zetland, with Rental, Inventory &c., 1653, from Original Documents in the Charter Room of Kinross House', *Proceedings of the Society of Antiquaries of Scotland*, 11, 1888-1889, pp. 275-313

Pamela Marshall, *Wollaton Hall, An Archaeological Survey*, Nottingham, 1996

Janet D. Martin, 'An early curate of Torver', *Transactions of the Cumberland and Westmorland Antiquarian and Archaeological Society*, 88, 1988, pp. 121-123

Dr H. Marwick, 'A Record Miscellany III', *Proceedings of the Orkney Antiquarian Society*, 6, 1927-1928, pp. 27-33

Dr H Marwick, 'Two Orkney 18th Century Inventories', 'House of Burray Inventory 1710', *Proceedings of the Orkney Antiquarian Society*, 12, 1934, pp. 47-54, 55-58

Neil Mathieson, 'A Forgotten Factory, Port-e-Chee Cotton Mill 1772-1780', *Journal of the Manx Museum*, 6, 1958, pp. 62-64

Peter May, *Newmarket Inventories 1662-1715*, Newmarket, 1976

Elizabeth Melling (ed.), *Kentish Sources*, III, *Aspects of Agriculture and Industry*, Maidstone, 1961

Elizabeth Melling (ed.), *Kentish Sources*, V, *Some Kentish Houses*, Maidstone, 1965

A. Michael Mennim, *Hall Houses*, York, 2005

Eric Mercer and Norman Summers, 'The Old House, Bleasby', *Transactions of the Thoroton Society of Nottinghamshire*, 71, 1967, pp. 18-29

R. A. Miles, 'Household Effects', *Cheshire Sheaf*, 55, 1960, pp. 21, 23, 25

Luke Millar, 'An Alehouse Inventory of 1765', *Regional Furniture*, 2, 1988, pp. 36-37

Oliver Millar (ed.), 'The Inventories and Valuations of the King's Goods 1649-1651', *The Walpole Society*, 43, 1972

W. T. Mitchell, 'Registrum Cancellarii 1498-1506', *Oxford Historical Society*, 27, 1980

Frederick Moncreiff and William Moncreiffe, *The Moncreiffs and the Moncreiffes, A History of the Family of Moncreiff of that Ilk and its Collateral Branches*, Edinburgh, 1929

A. J. Monday and Mary Siraut, 'Somerset Wills', *Somerset Record Society*, 89, 2003

A. A. Moon, 'Sherborne Almshouse Inventory, 1595', *Somerset & Dorset Notes and Queries*, 31, 1982, pp. 191-200

J. Grange Moore, *Salkelds through Seven Centuries*, Chichester, 1988

John S. Moore (ed.), *The Goods and Chattels of Our Forefathers, Frampton Cotterell and District Probate Inventories 1539-1804*, Chichester, 1976

John S. Moore (ed.), *Clifton and Westbury Probate Inventories 1609-1761*, Bristol, 1981

C. E. Moreton, 'Mid-Tudor Trespass: A Break-in at Norwich, 1549', *English Historical Review*, 108, 1993, pp. 387-398

F. C. Morgan, 'A Hereford Mercer's Inventory for the Year 1689', *Transactions of the Woolhope Naturalists' Field Club*, 31, 1947, pp. 187-210

F. C. Morgan, 'Inventories of a Hereford Saddler's Shop in the Years 1692 and 1696', *Transactions of the Woolhope Naturalists' Field Club*, 31, 1947, pp. 253-268

Marjorie M. Morgan, 'Inventories of Three Small Alien Priories', *Journal of the British Archaeological Association*, 4, 1939, pp. 141-149

E. Rowley Morris, 'Kerry and Moughtrey Wills at Hereford Probate Office', *Collections Historical and Archaeological relating to Montgomeryshire*, 27, 1893, pp. 233-268

G. C. R. Morris, 'The Household Goods of Thomas Hobbs (1647?-1698), Surgeon to James II, Physician to Dryden', *Transactions of the London and Middlesex Archaeological Society*, 23, 1971-1972, pp. 204-208

Geo. R. Morton, 'The Reconstruction of an Industry, The Paget Ironworks, Cannock Chase, 1561', *Lichfield and South Staffordshire Archaeological and Historical Society Transactions*, 6, 1964-5, pp. 21-38

E. B. Moullin, 'A Guernsey Homestead in the Mid-17th Century', *La Société Guernesiaise Report and Transactions*, 14, 1946, pp. 195-220

Lionel M. Munby, *Life & Death in Kings Langley, Wills and Inventories 1498-1659*, Kings Langley, 1981

Lionel M. Munby, *All My Worldly Goods, An insight into family life from wills and inventories 1447-1742*, Bricket Wood, 1991

Tessa Murdoch (ed.), *Noble Households, Eighteenth-Century Inventories of Great English Houses*, Cambridge, 2006

Tessa Murdoch and Randolph Vigne, *The French Hospital in London, Its Huguenot History and Collections*, Cambridge, 2009

R. Myers (ed.), *English Historical Documents 1327-1485*, London, 1969

A. R. Myers, 'The Wealth of Richard Lyons', in T. A. Sandquist and M. R. Powicke (ed.), *Essays in medieval history presented to Bertie Wilkinson*, Toronto, 1969, pp. 301-329

David Neave (ed.), *Winteringham 1650-1760, Life and Work in a North Lincolnshire Village Illustrated by Probate Inventories*, Winteringham, 1984

David Neave (ed.), *Tudor Market Rasen, Life and Work in a Sixteenth Century Market Town illustrated by Probate Inventories*, Market Rasen and Hull, 1985

John Nicholl, *Some Account of the Worshipful Company of Ironmongers*, London, 1851

John Nichols, *Illustrations of the Manners and Expences of Antient Times in England, In the Fifteenth, Sixteenth, and Seventeenth Centuries deduced from the Accompts of Churchwardens and other authentic documents, collected from various parts of the kingdom*, London, 1797

John Gough Nichols, *The Unton Inventories relating to Wadley and Faringdon, Co. Berks*, London, 1841

John Gough Nichols, 'Inventories of the Wardrobe, Plate, Chapel Stuff, etc., of Henry Fitzroy, Duke of Richmond, and of the Wardrobe Stuff at Baynard's Castle of Katharine, Princess Dowager', *Camden Society (Miscellany 3)*, 61, 1855

John Gough Nichols and John Edward Jackson, 'Inventory of the Goods of Dame Agnes Hungerford, attainted of Murder 14 Hen. VIII', *Archaeologia*, 38, 1860, pp. 353-372

John Noake, *The Monastery and Cathedral of Worcester*, London, 1866

John Noake, *Worcestershire Relics*, London, 1877

C. B. Norcliffe, 'The Pawson Inventory and Pedigree', *Publications of the Thoresby Society*, 4, 1895, pp. 163-168

E. G. Norris, 'A Seventeenth Century Inventory', *Essex Review*, 15,1906, pp. 169-175

Christine North, 'The Will and Inventory of Edward Arundell of Treveliew and Lanherne, 1539-1586', *Journal of the Royal Institution of Cornwall*, 2001, pp. 38-63

Thomas North, 'Notes on the Connection of the Pate Family, with Eye Kettleby and Sysonby, Co. Leicester', *Reports and Papers of the Associated Architectural Societies*, 12, 1873-1874, pp. 275-282

Thomas North, 'Notes on the Connection of the Pate Family with Eye Kettleby and Sysonby, in the County of Leicester', *Transactions of the Leicestershire Architectural and Archaeological Society*, 4, 1878, pp. 263-271

F. J. Norton, 'The Library of Bryan Rowe, Vice-Provost of King's College († 1521)', *Transactions of the Cambridge Bibliographical Society*, 2, 1954-1958, pp. 339-351

Brian O Dalaigh, 'An Inventory of the Contents of Bunratty Castle and the Will of Henry, Fifth Earl of Thomond, 1639', *North Munster Antiquarian Journal*, 36, 1995, pp. 139-165

V. E. Offord (ed.), *The Probate Documents of Water Eaton, Oxfordshire 1592-1730*, Kidlington and District Historical Society, 1986

J. B. Oldham, 'A Sixteenth Century Shrewsbury School Inventory', *Transactions of the Shropshire Archaeological Society*, 47, 1933-1934, pp. 121-137

J. R. Olorenshaw, 'Rattlesden Papers', *The East Anglian: or, Notes and Queries Connected with the Counties of Suffolk, Cambridge, Essex and Norfolk*, 5, 1893-1894, pp. 28-29

Frederica St John Orlebar, *The Orlebar Chronicles in Bedfordshire and Northamptonshire*, London, 1930

Lena Cowen Orlin, *Elizabethan Households, An Anthology*, Washington, 1995

Nicholas Orme (ed.), 'Cornish Wills 1342-1540', *Devon and Cornwall Record Society*, 50, 2007

Monica Ory, 'The Inventory of Adrian Norton of Alcester, Tailor and Murderer, 1557', *Warwickshire Historian*, 8, 1992/1993, pp. 202-204

Kieran O'Shea, 'A Castleisland Inventory, 1590', *Journal of the Kerry Archaeological and Historical Society*, 15-16, 1982-1983, pp. 37-46

Mark Overton, 'A Computer Management System for Probate Inventories', *History and Computing*, 7, 1995, pp. 135-142

Dorothy M. Owen (ed.), *The Making of Knig's Lynn*, British Academy, London, 1984

G. Dyfnallt Owen (ed.), *Report on the Manuscripts of the Right Honourable Viscount de l'Isle, V.C., preserved at Penshurst Place, Kent*, 6, Sidney Papers, 1626-1698, Historical Manuscripts Commission, London, 1966

Hugh Owen, *Stanhope, Atkinson, Hadon and Shaw, Four North Country Families*, Chichester, 1985

Trefor M. Owen, 'Some Lleyn Inventories of the Seventeenth and Early Eighteenth Centuries', *Transactions of the Caernavonshire Historical Society*, 21, 1960, pp. 70-80

Joan Paget and Tony Sale (ed.), *Charlton Kings Probate Records 1600-1800*, Charlton Kings, 2003

Francis Palgrave, *The Antient Kalendars and Inventories of the Treasury of His Majesty's Exchequer together with other Documents Illustrating the History of that Repository*, 3 vols., London 1836

Philip Palmer, 'Inventory of Abbot's Hospital, Guildford, 1633', *Surrey Archeological Collections*, 30, 1917, pp. 38-53

Philip Palmer, 'Inventories of Abbot's Hospital, Guildford, 1709, 1731, 1778, 1792, 1820, 1825', *Surrey Archeological Collections*, 32, 1919, pp. 34-49

W. A. Pantin, 'Canterbury College, Oxford – I', *Oxford Historical Society*, 6, 1947

W. A. Pantin, 'The Golden Cross, Oxford', *Oxoniensia*, 20, 1955, pp. 46-89

Meryl Parker (ed.), *All My Worldly Goods II, Wills and Probate Invnentories of St Stephen's Parish, St Albans 1418-1700*, Bricket Wood, 2001

Vanessa Parker, *The Making of Kings Lynn*, London and Chichester, 1971

Richard W. Parker, Tony Ives, John Allan, 'Excavation and Building Study at Cleeve Abbey, 1995-2003 (Jo Cox and Anita Travers, Appendix 6: The 1605 Inventory of Robert Boteler)', *Somerset Archaeology and Natural History*, 150, 2007, pp. 161-166

Charles Partridge, 'A Suffolk Yeoman's Household Goods, 1789', *Notes and Queries*, 192, 1947, pp. 447-450

Charles Partridge, 'Household Goods at Great Bromley Hall, 1763', *Essex Review*, 57, 1948, pp. 21-23

Charles Partridge, 'A Suffolk Yeoman's Household Goods, 1794', *Notes and Queries*, 194, 1949, pp. 1-4

P. M. Pask, *Allington Wills & Inventories*, [Lincoln?], 1989

Ian Payne, 'The Will and Probate Inventory of John Holmes (d. 1629): Instrumental Music at Salisbury and Winchester Cathedrals Revisited', *Antiquaries Journal*, 83, 2003, pp. 369-396

M. T. W. Payne, 'An inventory of Queen Anne of Denmark's 'ornaments, furniture, householde stuffe, and other parcells' at Denmark House, 1619', *Journal of the History of Collections*, 13, 2001, pp. 23-44

Edward Peacock, 'An Ancient Inventory of the Effects of a Country Gentleman', *Midland Counties Historical Collector*, 1, 1855, pp. 230-234

Edward Peacock, 'An Ancient Inventory of the Effects of a Country Gentleman', *Midland Counties Historical Collector*, 2, 1856, pp. 28-32

Edward Peacock, 'A Lincolnshire Inventory, A. D. 1652', *Gentleman's Magazine*, 211 (11), 1861, pp. 505-507

Edward Peacock, 'Inventory of a Trader, A.D. 1519', *Gentleman's Magazine*, 16, 1864, pp. 501-502

Edward Peacock, 'Two Inventories of the Goods of Cardinal Fisher, Bishop of Rochester, at his Palace of Rochester, and also at his manor of Halling in Kent', *Proceedings of the Society of Antiquaries of London*, 5, 1870-1873, pp. 294-299

Edward Peacock, 'Robert Todd of Bicker; a Lincolnshire Yeoman of the XVI Century', *The Reliquary*, 12, 1871-2, pp. 148-151

Edward Peacock, 'Inventory of a Sixteenth Century Country Parson', *Notes and Queries*, 6th Series, 3, 1881, p. 243

Edward Peacock, 'Inventories made for Sir William and Sir Thomas Fairfax, Knights, of Walton, and of Gilling Castle, Yorkshire, in the Sixteenth and Seventeenth Centuries' *Archaeologia*, 48 (2), 1884, pp. 121-156

Edward Peacock, 'The Cony Estate Book 1564-1596 (ii)', *Lincolnshire Notes and Queries*, 1, 1888-1889, pp. 132-133, 164-166, 198-199, 230-233

Mary Pearson (ed.), *The Wills and Inventories of the Ancient Parishes of Malpas, Tilston and Shocklach and their townships in the County of Chester from 1508 to 1603*, 2 vols., Malpas, n.d. [2005]

Frederick Pedler, *A Pedler Family History*, Chichester, 1984

Michael Peele, 'Shrewsbury Drapers' Inventories', *Transactions of the Shropshire Archaeological Society*, 52, 1947-1948, pp. 236-244

Janet Pennington and Joyce Sleight, 'Furniture in Steyning, A Sussex Parish, 1587-1706: A Study of Documentary Sources', *Regional Furniture*, 1, 1987, pp. 41-49

Elizabeth R. Perkins, *Village Life from Wills and Inventories: Claworth Parish 1670-1710*, Nottingham, 1979

H. M. Peskett, 'The Probate Inventory of Sir John Daumarle – 1393', *Devon and Cornwall Notes and Queries*, 32, 1971, pp. 79-82

I. G. Philip, 'Inventory of the Goods of Dr Thomas Lockey, *Bodleian Library Record*, 5, 1954-1956, pp. 80-84

Charles J. Phillips, *History of the Sackville Family*, I, London, 1929

C. B. Phillips and J. H. Smith (ed.), 'Stockport Probate Records 1578-1619', *Record Society of Lancashire and Cheshire*, 124, 1985

Maberly Phillips, 'The Meeting House at Horsley-upon-Tyne', *Archaeologia Aeliana*, 13, 1889, pp. 33-64

Michael Phillips, 'No. 13 Hercules Building, Lambeth, William Blake's printmaking workshop and etching-painting studio recovered', *British Art Journal*, 5, 2004, pp. 13-21

William Phillips, 'The Will of Ralph Bostock, A.D. 1533', *Transactions of the Shropshire Archaeological Society*, 12, 1900, pp. 191-195

Chris Phillpotts and Rick Turner, 'The Mansells, the Bassetts and the rebuilding of Oxwich and Old Beaupré Castles', *Archaeologia Cambrensis*, 157, 2008, pp. 203-270

G. J. Piccope, 'Lancashire and Cheshire Wills and Inventories from the Ecclesiastical Court, Chester', *Chetham Society*, 33, 1857

G. J. Piccope, 'Lancashire and Cheshire Wills and Inventories from the Ecclesiastical Court, Chester', *Chetham Society*, 51, 1860

W. Pinkerton, 'Inventory of the Hoshold Efects of Lord Deputy Lord Leonard Grey, in 1540', *Ulster Journal of Archaeology*, 7, 1859, pp. 201-213

Paul B. Pixton (ed.), 'Wrenbury Wills and Inventories 1542-1661', *Record Society of Lancashire and Cheshire*, 144, 2009

D. Portman, *Exeter Houses 1400-1700*, Exeter, 1966

Derek Portman, 'Vernacular Building in the Oxford Region in the Sixteenth and Seventeenth Centuries', in C. W. Chalklin and M. A. Havinden, *Rural Change and Urban Growth 1500-1800, Essays in English Regional History in Honour of W. G. Hoskins*, London, 1974, pp. 135-168

George Poulson, *The History and Antiquities of the Seigniory of Holderness*, I, Hull, 1840

Edward Powell, 'Pryce (Newton Hall) Correspondence, Etc.', *Collections Historical and Archaeological Relating to Montgomeryshire*, 31, 1900, pp. 65-114

William E. Preston, *Local Record Series I, wills proved in the Court of the Manor of Crosley, Bingley, Cottingley and Pudsey, in co. York, with Inventories and Abstracts of Bonds*, Bradford Historical and Antiquarian Society, 1929

Richard Pretyman, 'Testamentary Documents Preserved in the Chapter Muniment Room in Lincoln Minster. The Will and Inventories of the Effects of Richard de Ravenser, Archdeacon of Lincoln, 1386' in *Memoirs Illustrative of the History and Antiquities of the County and City of Lincoln*, Archaeological Institute, London, 1850, pp. 311-327

George S. Pryde, 'Papers Relating to a Renfrewshire Farm 1822-1830', *Miscellany of the Scottish History Society*, 8, 1951, pp. 139-162

R. D. Radcliffe, 'Schedule of Deeds and Documents, The Property of Colonel Thomas Richard Crosse, Preserved in the Muniment Room at Shaw Hill, Chorley, in the County of Lancaster – Part II', *Transactions of the Historic Society of Lancashire and Cheshire*, 6, 1892, pp. 275-295

James Raine (ed.), *Wills and Inventories Illustrative of the History, Manners, Language, Statistics, &c. of the Northern Counties of England from the Eleventh Century Downwards*, I, London, The Surtees Society, 2, 1835

James Raine (ed.), *Testamenta Eboracensia, or Wills Registered at York*, I, London, The Surtees Society, 4, 1836

James Raine, *The Correspondence of Dr Matthew Hutton, Archbishop of York*, London, The Surtees Society, 17, 1843

James Raine, *The Injunctions and other Ecclesiastical Proceedings of Richard Barnes, Bishop of Durham, from 1575-1587*, London, The Surtees Society, 22, 1850

James Raine, *The History and Antiquities of North Durham*, London, 1852

James Raine (ed.), *Wills and Inventories from the Registry of the Archdeaconry of Richmond*, Durham, The Surtees Society, 26, 1853

James Raine, 'The Pudseys of Barford', *Archaeologia Aeliana*, 2, 1858, pp. 173-190

James Raine, 'Marske', *Archaeologia Aeliana*, 5, 1861, pp. 1-91

James Raine (ed.), *Testamenta Eboracensia, A Selection of Wills from the Registry at York*, III, Durham, The Surtees Society, 45, 1865

James Raine (ed.), *Testamenta Eboracensia, A Selection of Wills from the Registry at York*, IV, Durham, The Surtees Society, 53, 1869

James Raine (ed.), *Testamenta Eboracensia, A Selection of Wills from the Registry at York*, V, Durham, The Surtees Society, 79, 1884

G. D. Ramsay, 'John Isham, Mercer and Merchant Adventurer', *Northamptonshire Record Society*, 21, 1962

R. G. Rankin, 'The Eltonhead Family', *Transactions of the Historical Society of Lancashire and Cheshire*, 108, 1957, pp. 35-62

Alfred Randsford, 'Abstracts from Rainsford Wills, Inventories and Inquisitions Post Mortem', *Notes and Queries*, 158, 1930, pp. 399-402, 417-419, 435-438, and 159, 1930, pp. 40-42, 96-98, 206-208, 239-241, 275-276, 310-313

Carole Rawcliffe, 'The Inventory of a Fifteenth-Century Necromancer', *The Ricardian*, 13, 2003, pp. 384-397

Pamela Redwood, 'Early Seventeenth Century Mercers in Brecon', *Brycheiniog*, 32, 2000, pp. 71-79

Michael Reed, 'A Footnote to the History of English Music: The Will and Probate Inventory of George Hudson', *Music Review*, 41, 1980, pp. 169-171

Michael Reed (ed.), 'The Ipswich Probate Inventories 1583-1631', *Suffolk Record Society*, 22, 1981

Michael Reed, 'Buckinghamshire Probate Inventories 1661-1714', *Buckinghamshire Record Society*, 24, 1988

Michael Reed, 'Osterley Park in 1668: The Probate Inventory of Sir William Waller', *Transactions of the London and Middlesex Archaeological Society*, 41, 1990, pp. 115-120

R. C. Reid, 'The furnishings of Comlongon, 1624', *Transactions of the Dumfries and Galloway Natural History and Antiquarian Society*, 32, 1955, pp. 180-185

R. Renwick, *Extracts from the Records of the Royal Borough of Stirling. A. D. 1519-1666*, Glasgow, 1887

Walter E. Rhodes, 'The Inventory of the Jewels and Wardrobe of Queen Isabella (1307-8)', *English Historical Review*, 12, 1897, pp. 517-521

R. Garraway Rice, 'The Household Goods, Etc., of Sir John Gage, of West Firle, Co. Sussex, K.G.', *Sussex Archaeological Collections*, 45, 1902, pp. 114-127

Nelson M. Richardson, 'A Dorset Inventory of 1627', *Proceedings of the Dorset Natural History and Antiquarian Field Club*, 35, 1914, pp. 41-49

George Rickwood, 'An Early Georgian Inventory', *Transactions of the Essex Archaeological Society*, 14, 1918, pp. 16-25

John Ridgard (ed.), 'Medieval Framlingham', *Suffolk Records Society*, 27, 1985

Henry Thomas Riley, *Memorials of London and London Life in the XIIIth, XIVth, and XVth Centuries*, London, 1868

Henry Thomas Riley, 'Inventory of Goods belonging to a Warden of New College, Oxford, A.D.1396', *Archaeological Journal*, 28, 1871, pp. 232-234

R. J. Roberts, 'John Rastell's Inventory of 1538', *The Library* (6th series), 1, 1979, pp. 34-42

Edward Roberts and Karen Parker, 'Southampton Probate Inventories, 1447-1575', I and II, *Southampton Record Series*, 34,35, 1992

J. C. Robertson, 'Furnishings Seized in London, 1575', *Furniture History*, 25, 1989, pp. 36-41

Joseph Robertson (ed.), *Inventaires de la Royne Descosse Douairiere de France, Catalogues of the Jewels, Dresses, Furniture, Books and Paintings of Mary Queen of Scots 1556-1569*, Edinburgh, The Bannatyne Club, 1863

Scott Robertson, 'Inventory of Beds, Tapestry and Linen at Leeds Castle, A.D. 1532', *Archaeologia Cantiana*, 15, 1883, pp. 382-385

Scott Robertson, 'Dalison Documents. From the Muniment Chest at Hamptons, near Tunbridge', *Archaeologia Cantiana*, 15, 1883, pp. 386-401

Scott Robertson, 'Cobham Hall: Inventory of Furniture and Pictures in 1672', *Archaeologia Cantiana*, 17, 1887, pp. 392-408

Charles Best Robinson, 'Rural Economy in Yorkshire in 1641, being the Farming and Account Books of Henry Best, of Elmswell, in the East Riding of the County of York', *Surtees Society*, 33, 1857

William Robinson, *The History and Antiquities of the Parish of Hackney in the County of Middlesex*, London, 1842

Alice Rodgers, 'Some Women in Austerfield Wills and Inventories 1658-1721', in Brian Elliott (ed.), *Aspects of Doncaster, Discovering Local History*, 2, Barnsley, 1999

Miriam Rodrigues-Pereira, 'An eighteenth-century Sephardi lady: her relations and her property', *Jewish Historical Studies*, 41, 2007, pp. 31-35

John S. Roper, *Sedgley Probate Inventories 1614-1787*, Dudley, [1960]

John S. Roper, *Dudley Probate Inventories 1544-1603*, Dudley, 1965

John S. Roper, *Dudley Probate Inventories (Second Series) January 1605-April 1685*, Dudley, 1966

John S. Roper, *Early North Worcestershire Scythesmiths, A study from Wills and Probate Inventories at Worcester*, Dudley, 1967

John S. Roper, *Dudley Probate Inventories (Third Series) 1601- 1650*, Dudley, 1968

John S. Roper, *Belbroughton Wills and Inventories*, Dudley, 1967-1968

John S. Roper, *Dudley, The town in the sixteenth century*, Dudley Public Libraries, Transcript No. 4, 1968

John S. Roper, *Chaddesley Corbett Worcs. Probate Inventories with abstracts of wills 1601-1652*, Dudley, 1971

John S. Roper, *Worcestershire Clergy Wills and Inventories 1541-1558*, Dudley, 1972

Colin Rogers, 'Roger Worthington of Etchells, an early Cheshire schoolmaster', *Cheshire Sheaf*, 2, 1967, p. 6

C. Marshall Rose, 'Eighteenth Century Lodge Inventories', *Ars Quatuor Coronatorum*, 62, 1951, pp. 204-218

C. Marshall Rose, 'The Irish Lodge: Its Furntiure and Properties', *Ars Quatuor Coronatorum*, 63, 1952, pp. 163-218

C. Marshall Rose, 'The Scottish Lodge, Its Inventories, Furniture and Regalia', *Ars Quatuor Coronatorum*, 64, 1953, pp. 98-114

Treve Rosoman, 'The Chiswick House Inventory of 1770', *Furniture History*, 22, 1986, pp. 81-106

Royal Commission on Historical Manuscripts, *Seventh Report*, 1, London, 1879

Royal Commission on Historical Manuscripts, *Ninth Report*, 1, London, 1883

Walter Rye, 'A Bondsman's Will and Property', *The East Anglian: or, Notes and Queries Connected with the Counties of Suffolk, Cambridge, Essex and Norfolk*, 3, 1899-1890, pp. 377-378

J. Paul Rylands, 'Lancashire and Cheshire Wills and Inventories 1563 to 1807 now preserved at Chester', *Chetham Society*, 37, 1897

W. Harry Rylands, 'Booksellers and Stationers in Warrington, 1639-1659, with the full list of the contents of a stationer's shop there in 1647', *Transactions of the Historic Society of Lancashire and Cheshire*, 37, 1888, pp. 67-115

Thomas Rymer, *Foedera*, 4 (2), London, 1869

St Helens Association for Research into Local History, *Angells to Yarwindles, The Wills and Inventories of Twenty-Six Elizabethan and Jacobean Women Living in the Area Now Called St Helens*, St Helens, 1999

A. J. H. Sale (ed.), 'Cheltenham Probate Records 1660-1740', *Bristol and Gloucestershire Archaeological Society, Gloucestershire Record Series*, 12, 1999

James L. Salter, 'The books of an early eighteenth-century curate', *The Library* (5th series), 33, 1978, pp. 33-46

William Sandys, 'Copy of the Inventory of Archbishop Parker's goods at the time of his Death', *Archaeologia*, 30, 1844, pp. 1-30

Nigel Saul, 'The Worldly Wealth of John Beauchamp of Holt' in Margaret Aston, Rosemary Horrox (ed.), *Much heaving and shoving: late-medieval gentry and their concerns, Essays for Colin Richmond*, Lavenham, 2005, pp. 5-16

G. Edward Saville, *King's Coughton, A Warwickshire Hamlet*, Warwick, 1973

G. Edward Saville, *The Seventeenth Century Inventories of Alcester, Warwickshire*, Alcester, 1979

E. B. Saxton, 'Speke Hall and Two Norris Inventories, 1624 and 1700', *Transactions of the Historical Society of Lancashire and Cheshire*, 96, 1944, pp. 108-135

E. B. Saxton, 'A Speke Inventory of 1624', *Transactions of the Historical Society of Lancashire and Cheshire*, 97, 1946, pp. 107-143

John Schofield, 'The London Surveys of Ralph Treswell', *London Topographical Society*, 135, 1987

John Schofield, *Medieval London Houses*, New Haven and London, 1994

R. Scott-Moncrieff, 'Note on the 'Household Plenishings belonging to the Deceist Andro Hig, Writer to the Signet, Publicklie Rouped and Sold upon the 19th, 20th, 21st, 22nd, 23rd and 24th Days of Octr., 1691 Yeares' ', *Proceedings of the Society of Antiquaries of Scotland*, 53, 1919, pp. 52-63

Arthur Searle, 'An Inventory for Navestock, 1601', *Essex Journal*, 4, 1969, pp. 31-33

Jayne Semple, 'Old Soar Manor, near Plaxtol: House, Land and Occupants over Seven Centuries', *Archaeologia Cantiana*, 129, 2009, pp. 155-187

St John D. Seymour, 'The Household Furniture of Castletown-Waller in 1642', *Journal of the North Munster Archaeological Society*, 1, 1909-1911, pp. 255-258

D. Shanahan, 'A London Tavern in 1644', *Transactions of the London and Middlesex Archaeological Society*, 20, 1961, pp. 194-196

Mary Sharp, *A Record of the Parish of Padworth and Its Inhabitants*, Reading, 1901

William A. Shaw and F. H. Slingsby (ed.), *Calendar of Treasury Books*, 29, 1714-1715, London, 1957

William Francis Shaw, *Liber Estriae or Memorials of the Royal Ville and Parish of Eastry in the County of Kent*, London, 1870

Carolyn Sheasby, *In My Father's House, A Glimpse of the Past through Probate Inventories*, Sutton-in-Craven, 1994

Michael M Sheehan, *The Will in Medieval England*, Toronto, 1963

W. J. Sheils, 'The Company of Tailors and Drapers 1551-1662' in R. B. Dobson and D. M. Smith (eds.), *The Merchant Taylors of York, a history of the Craft and Company from the fourteenth to the twentieth century*, Borthwick Texts and Sources, 33, 2006, pp. 53-71

Leslie Sherwood, 'Seventeenth and Eighteenth Century Inventories', *Archaeologia Cantiana*, 61, 1948, pp. 57-76

Evelyn Philip Shirley, 'An Inventory of the Effects of Henry Howard, K. G., Earl of Northampton, together with a transcript of his Will', *Archaeologia*, 42 (2), 1862, pp. 347-378

Evelyn Philip Shirley, *Stemmata Shirleiana; or the Annals of the Shirley Family*, London, 1873

Evelyn Philip Shirley, 'The Will, Inventories and Funeral Expenses of James Montagu, Bishop of Winchester, anno 1618, From the original in the possession of the Baroness North', *Archaeologia*, 44, 1873, pp. 393-421

Elizabeth Simpson, 'Understanding Inventories', *Family History, The Journal of Heraldic and Genealogical Studies*, 13, 1985, pp. 293-308

Harry Gordon Slade, 'Broughton Castle: Two probate inventories', *Cake and Cockhorse*, 8, 1981, pp. 155-171

Joyce Sleight (ed.), *Yeoman Farmers and Gentlemen, People of Wiston, West Sussex, 1612-1732*, Wiston Estate Study Group, 1993

Augustus Smith, *A True and Faithful History of the Family of Smith*, London, 1961

David H. Smith, 'A Seventeenth Century Tinker's Will and Inventory', *Journal of the Gypsy Lore Society*, 4th Series, 1, 1977, pp. 172-177

Hubert Smith, 'Dunvall, County Salop', *Reliquary*, 24, 1883-1884, pp. 161-162

John Smith (ed.), *Burgh Records of the City of Glasgow. M.D.LXXIII-M.D.LXXXI*, Maitland Club, Glasgow, 1832

Nicola Smith, 'Frogmore House Before James Wyatt', *Antiquaries Journal*, 65, 1985, pp. 402-426

Robert Smith, 'The 1539 Indenture of the Castell of Berwyke, Sir William Ewre alias Ivers, capytayn of the sayd Castell', *Archaeologia*, 11, 1794, pp. 433-440

W. H. Smith, 'Old Inventories in North Lincolnshire', *Old Lincolnshire*, 1, 1883-1885, pp. 202-207

W. J. Smith, 'Three Salesbury mansions in 1601', *Bulletin of the Board of Celtic Studies*, 15, 1952, pp. 293-302

Beatrice Saxon Snell, 'Martha Jackson's Minority, Yorkshire Trustees' Accounts – 1722-1728', *Journal of the Friends' Historical Society*, 45, 1953, pp. 6-14

South Sea Company, *A True and Exact Particular and Inventory of All and Singular the Lands, Tenements, and Hereditaments, Goods, Chattels, Debts and*

Personal Estate whatsoever of WILLIAM ASTELL,*Esq;. Late one of the Directors of the* South-Sea *Company*, London, 1721

South Sea Company, *The Particular and Inventory of Sir* JOHN BLUNT, *Bart. One of the Late Directors of the* South-Sea *Company*, London, 1721

South Sea Company, *A True and Exact Particular and Inventory of All and Singular The Lands, Tenements, and Hereditaments, Goods, Chattels, Debts, and Personal Estate whatsoever, of Sir* ROBERT CHAPLIN, *Bar.; Late one of the Directors of the* South Sea *Company*, London, 1721

South Sea Company, *A True and Exact Particular and Inventory of All and Singular the Lands, Tenements, and Hereditaments, Goods, Chattels, Debts and Personal Estate whatsoever of Sir* WILLIAM CHAPMAN, *Bar. Late one of the Directors of the* South-Sea *Company*, London, 1721

South Sea Company, *The Particular and Inventory of* ROBERT CHESTER, *ESQ; One of the Late Directors of the* South Sea *Company, March 23, 1720*, London, 1721

South Sea Company, *The Inventory and Particular of All and Singular the Lands, Tenements, and Hereditaments, goods, Chattels, Debts and Personal Estate whatsoever, of* STEPHEN CHILD, *Esq; Late one of the Directors of the* South-Sea *Company*, London, 1721

South Sea Company, *A True and Exact Particular and Inventory of All and Singular the Lands, Tenements, and Hereditaments, Goods, Chattels, Debts and Personal Estate whatsoever, of* FRANCIS EYLES, *Esq; One of the Late Directors of the* South Sea *Company*, London, 1721

South Sea Company, *A True and Exact Particular and Inventory of All and Singular The Lands, Tenements, and Hereditaments, Goods, Chattels, Debts, and Personal Estate whatsoever, of Sir* JOHN FELLOWES, *Bart. Late Sub-Governor of the* South Sea *Company*, London, 1721

South Sea Company, *The Particular and Inventory of* EDWARD GIBBON, *Esq; One of the late Directors of the* South-Sea *Company*, London, 1721

South Sea Company, *A Particular or Inventory of All and Singular The Lands, Tenements and Hereditaments, Goods, Chattels, Debts and Personal Estate whatsoever, of Mr.* JOHN GORE, *Late one of the Directors of the* South-Sea *Company*, London, 1721

South Sea Company, *A Particular or Inventory Of the Estate and Effects of* JOHN GRIGSBY, *Acomptant to the* South-Sea *Company*, London, 1721

South Sea Company, *The Particulars and Inventory Of All The Lands, Tenements, and Hereditaments, goods, Chattels, Debts, and Personal Estate whatsoever, of Sir* WILLIAM HAMOND, *Knt. Late one of the Directors of the* South-Sea *Company*, London, 1721

South Sea Company, FRANCES HAWES, *Esq; His Particular and Inventory*, London, 1721

South Sea Company, RICHARD HOULDITCH, *Esq; His Particular and Inventory*, London, 1721

South Sea Company, *Sir* THEODORE JANNSSEN, *Kt, Bart. His Particular and Inventory*, London, 1721

South Sea Company, *A Particular and Inventory Of the Estate of* CHARLES JOYE, *Esq;*, London, 1721

South Sea Company, *The Particular and Inventory of Sir* John Lambert, *Bart. One of the late Directors of the* South-Sea-Company, London, 1720

South Sea Company, *The Particular and Inventory of All and singular The Lands, Tenements, and Hereditaments, Goods, Chattels, Debts, and Personal Estate whatsoever, of Sir* HARCOURT MASTER, *Knt. Late one of the* Directors of the South-Sea *Company*, London, 1721

South Sea Company, *A Particular and Inventory Of All and Singular the Lands, Tenements, and Hereditaments, Goods, Chattels, Debts, and Personal Estate whatsoever, of* WILLIAM MORLEY, *Esq.*, London, 1721

South Sea Company, *A True and Exact Particular and Inventory of All and Singular The Lands, Tenements and Hereditaments, goods, Chattels, Debts and Personal Estates whatsoever, of Mr.* AMBROSE PAGE, *Late one of the Directors of the* South-Sea *Company*, London, 1721

South Sea Company, *A True and Exact Particular and Inventory of All and Singular the Lands, Tenements, and Hereditaments, Goods, Chattels, Debts and Personal Estate whatsoever, which* HUGH RAYMOND, *Esq. Late one of the Directors of the* South-Sea *Company, was Seized or Possessed of...*, London, 1721

South Sea Company, *A True and Exact Particular and Inventory of All and Singular The Lands, Tenements, and Hereditaments, Goods, Chattels, Debts, and Personal Estate whatsoever, of* SAMUEL READE, *Jun. Esq.; Late one of the Directors of the* South Sea *Company*, London, 1721

South Sea Company, *A Particular or Inventory of All and Singular The Lands, Tenements and Hereditaments, Goods, Chattels, Debts and Personal Estate whatsoever, which* THOMAS REYNOLDS, *esq; Late one of the Directors of the Corporation of the Governour and Company of Merchants of Great-Britain, Trading to the* South-Sea, *and other parts of* America *and for Encouraging the Fishery, was seiz'd or possess'd of...*, London, 1721

South Sea Company, *An Exact Particular and Inventory of All the Lands, Tenements, and Hereditaments, goods, Chattels, Debts and Personal Estate of* JACOB SAWBRIDGE, *Esq.*, London, 1721

South Sea Company, *A True and Exact Particular and Inventory of All and Singular the Lands, Tenements, and Hereditaments, Goods, Chattels, Debts and Personal Estate whatsoever, which* ROBERT SURNAM, *Late Deputy Cashier of the* South Sea *Company was seized or possessed of...*, London, 1721

South Sea Company, *The Inventory of* WILLIAM TILLARD, *Esq.*, London, 1721

Herbert R. H. Southam, 'Inventory of the Effects of Elizabeth Perkes of Westwood, Oldbury, 1688', *Transactions of the Shropshire Archaeological Society*, 1, 1901, pp. 413-414

C. F. D. Sperling, 'A Suffolk Yeoman's Goods.1691.', *The East Anglian: or, Notes and Queries Connected with the Counties of Suffolk, Cambridge, Essex and Norfolk*, 5, 1893-1894, p. 74

Margaret Spufford, *The Great Reclothing of Rural England, Petty Chapmen and their Wares in the Seventeeth Century*, London, 1984

F. Spurrell, 'Inventory of the Goods of Cornelius Humphrey, of Newhaven, 1697', *Sussex Archaeological Collections*, 6, 1853, pp. 190-196

J. C. L. Stahlschmidt, 'Notes from an Old City Account Book', *Archaeological Journal*, 43, 1886, pp. 162-176

David Starkey (ed.), *The Inventory of Henry VIII, The Transcript*, The Society of Antiquaries of London, 1998

W. P. D. Stebbing, 'An Inventory of an Innkeeper's Possessions in 1685', *Archaeologia Cantiana*, 46, 1934, pp. 97-101

Francis W. Steer, *The Easton Lodge Inventory*, Great Dunmow, 1952

Francis W. Steer, 'The Inventory of Arthur Coke, of Bramfield, 1629', *Proceedings of the Suffolk Institute of Archaeology and Natural History*, 25, 1952, pp. 264-287

Francis W. Steer, 'The Inventory of Anne, Viscountess Dorchester', *Notes and Queries*, 198, 1953, pp. 94-96, 155-158, 379-381, 414-417, 469-473, 515-519 and 199, 1954, pp. 21-24

Francis W. Steer, 'A Medieval Household, The Urswick Inventory', *Essex Review*, 63, 1954, pp. 4-20

Francis W. Steer, 'A Sussex Mansion in the Eighteenth Century', *Sussex Archaeological Collections*, 94, 1956, pp. 13-34

Francis W. Steer, 'Smaller Houses and Their Furnishings in the Seventeenth and Eighteenth Centuries', *Journal of the British Archaeological Association*, 21-22, 1958, pp. 140-159

Francis W. Steer, 'Probate Inventories' in Lionel M. Munby (ed.), 'Short Guide to Records', *History*, 47, 1962, pp. 287-290

Francis W. Steer, 'A Cowdray Inventory of 1682', *Sussex Archaeological Collections,*, 105, 1967, pp. 84-102

Francis W. Steer (ed.), *Farm and Cottage Inventories of Mid-Essex, 1635-1749*, London, 1969

Philip M. Stell, *Probate Inventories of the York diocese, 1350-1500*, York Archeological Trust, 2006

A. Francis Steuart, 'The Plenishing of Holyrood House in 1714', *Proceedings of the Society of Antiquaries of Scotland*, 62, 1928, pp. 181-196

Joan Stevens and Jean Arthur, 'Inventories of Household Effects', *Société Jersiaise, Bulletin*, 20, 1969-1972, pp. 361-378

John C. Stevens, 'The will of Isaac Pluvier, Containing an Inventory of a London Clockmaker's Stock, just prior to the Great Fire', *Antiquarian Horology*, 4, 1962-1965, pp. 18-21

John Stevenson, *Two Centuries of Life in Down 1600-1800*, Belfast, 1920

Joseph Stevenson, *Documents Illustrative of the History of Scotland*, Edinburgh, 1870

W. H. Stevenson (ed.), *Records of the Borough of Nottingham*, 3, *1485-1547*, London, 1885

W. H. Stevenson, 'Inventories of Furniture, etc., at Wollaton Hall', *Associated Architectural Societies, Reports and Papers*, 44, 1887, Lincoln and Nottingham Architectural Society, pp. 76-95

W. H. Stevenson (ed.), *Records of the Borough of Nottingham*, 4, *1547-1625*, London, 1889

W. H. Stevenson (ed.), *Report on the Manuscripts of Lord Middleton preserved at Wollaton Hall, Nottinghamshire*, Historical Manuscripts Commission, London, 1911

J. E. Stocks and W. B. Bragg, *Market Harborough Parish Records to A. D. 1530*, London, 1890

Michael Stone (ed.), 'Inventory of Coddenham Vicarage, c.1797' in *The Diary of John Longe Vicar of Coddenham 1765-1834*, Suffolk Record Society, 51, 2008, pp. 210-218

Harry Storey, 'An Inventory of 1615', *Sussex Notes and Queries*, 7, 1939, pp. 201-204

R. L. Storey, 'The Register of Thomas Langley, Bishop of Durham 1406-1437', II, *Surtees Society*, 166, 1957

John Strachey (ed.), *Rotuli Parliamentorum; ut et Petitiiones et Placita in Parliamento Tempore Henrici R. V.*, 4, 1767

Jenny Stratford, 'The Bedford Inventories, The Worldly Goods of John, Duke of Bedford, Regent of France (1389-1435)', *Society of Antiquaries of London Research Committee Report*, 49, 1993

Alfred Suckling, *The History and Antiquities of the County of Suffolk*, London, 1848

Robert Surtees, *The History and Antiquities of the County Palatine of Durham*, 4, London, 1840

G. F. Sydenham, *The History of the Sydenham Family*, East Molesey, 1928

Angus Taylor (ed. Janet Martin), 'The Websters of Kendal, A North-Western Architectural Dynasty', *Cumberland and Westmorland Antiquarian and Archaeological Society, Record Series*, 17, 2004

T. F. Teversham, *A History of the Village of Sawston*, II, Sawston, 1947

A. H. Thomas (ed.), *Calendar of Select Pleas and Memoranda of the City of London a.d. 1381-1412*, Cambridge, 1932

A. H. Thomas (ed.), *Calendar of Plea and Memoranda Rolls ... of the City of London a.d. 1413-1437*, Cambridge, 1943

J. H. Thomas, 'The Company of White Paper Makers in Hampshire: An Inventory of Plant', *Post-Medieval Archaeology*, 11, 1977, pp. 22-35

J. H. Thomas, 'The Contents of a late Seventeenth Century Hampshire Inn', *Hampshire Archaeology and Local History Newsletter*, 2 (3), 1972, pp. 1-3

A. Hamilton Thompson, *A Calendar of Charters and Other Documents Belonging to the Hospital of William Wyggeston at Leicester*, Leicester, 1933

E. M. Thompson, 'The Will and Inventory of Robert Morton, A.D. 1486-1488', *Journal of the British Archaeological Association*, 33, 1877, pp. 308-330

Thomas Thomson, *A Collection of Inventories and other Records of the Royal Wardrobe and Jewelhouse; and of the Artillery and Munitioun in some of the Royal Castles. M.CCCC.LXXXVIII.-M.DC.VI.*, Edinburgh, 1815

W. H. Thomson, *The Byroms of Manchester*, I, Manchester, 1959

Peter Thornton and Maurice Tomlin, 'The Furnishing and Decoration of Ham House', *Furniture History*, 16, 1980

Hartley Thwaite, 'Abstracts of Abbotside Wills 1552-1688', *Yorkshire Archaeological Society Record Series*, 130, 1967

Kate Tiller, 'Clergy and People in the Seventeenth Century: Some Evidence from a North Oxfordshire Parish', *Cake and Cockhorse*, 7, 1979, pp. 242-250

Robert Fisher Tomes, 'Unpublished Documents relating to the County of Warwick', *The Warwickshire Antiquarian Magazine*, 1860, pp. 334-502

Maurice Tomlin, 'The 1782 Inventory of Osterley Park', *Furniture History*, 22, 1986, pp. 107-134

G. E. Trease and J. H. Hodson, 'The Inventory of John Hexham, A Fifteenth-Century Apothecary', *Medical History*, 9, 1965, pp. 76-81

T. D. Tremlett and Noel Blakiston (ed.), 'Stogursey Charters, Charters and Other Documents Relating to the Alien Priory of Stogursey, Somerset, Now Belonging to Eton College', *Somerset Record Society*, 61, 1949

W. C. Trevelyan, 'Abstract of the Inventory of the Goods of William More, Esq., of Bank Hall, Lancashire', *Archaeologia Aeliana*, 6, 1865, pp. 104-106

Barrie Trinder, 'Two Probate Inventories from Industrial Shropshire', *Industrial Archaeology Review*, 3, 1979, pp. 239-242

Barrie Trinder and Jeff Cox, *Yeoman and Colliers in Telford*, Chichester, 1980

Barrie Trinder and Nancy Cox, *Miners and Mariners of the Severn Gorge*, Chichester, 2000

Barrie Trinder and Jeremy Gibson, 'Living in Banbury 1660-1730: A Foretaste', *Cake and Cockhorse*, 10 (9), 1988, pp. 225-237

Stephen I. Tucker, 'Descent of the Manor of Sheffield', *Journal of the British Archaeological Association*, 30, 1874, pp. 237-277

S. R. Turner, *Inventory, Accounts and Distribution of the Residue of the Eastate of George Templeman of Middle Chinnock, Somerset, who died 13th April 1790*, Stevenage, 1994

T. Hudson Turner, 'Original Documents', *Archaeological Journal*, 5, 1848, pp. 152-153

Francis Randle Twemlow, 'The Manor of Tyrley in the County of Stafford down to the outbreak of the Great War in 1914', *Staffordshire Record Society, Collections for a History of Staffordshire*, 168, 1948

Samuel Tymms (ed.), 'Wills and Inventories from the Registers of the Commissary of Bury St Edmunds and the Archdeacon of Sudbury', *Camden Society*, 49, 1850

Blake Tyson, 'Francis Webster and the Kirklands Tan-Yards at Kendal, with a contribution towards his ancestry', *Transactions of the Cumberland and Westmorland Antiquarian and Archaeological Society*, 8, 2008, pp. 85-104

Blake Tyson, 'Some Craftsmen and their Houses on Fellside, Kendal, 1655-1877', *Transactions of the Cumberland and Westmorland Antiquarian and Archaeological Society*, 9, 2009, pp. 131-151

Anthony A. Upton, *Foleshill Probate Wills and Inventories 1535-1599*, Foleshill, 1993

Richard Ussher, 'Inventory of the Goods of Sir Wm. Wilmer, Knt., preserved at Catton Hall, Derbyshire', *Reliquary*, 21, 1880-1881, pp. 176-178

Richard Ussher, *An Historical Sketch of the Parish of Croxhall, in the County of Derby*, London, 1881

D. G. Vaisey, 'A Charlbury Mercer's Shop, 1623', *Oxoniensia*, 31, 1966, pp. 107-116

D. G. Vaisey (ed.), 'Probate Inventories of Lichfield and District 1568-1680', *Staffordshire Record Society, Collections for a History of Staffordshire*, 4th Series, 5, 1969

D. G. Vaisey, 'Thomas Wood and his Workshop', *Oxoniensia*, 36, 1971, pp. 55-58

D. G. Vaisey and F. Celoria, 'Inventory of George Ecton of Abingdon, Berks 1696', *Journal of Ceramic History*, 7, 1974, pp. 13-42

T. E. Verity, 'The Browns of Burnfoot: the decline and fall of a yeoman family', *Transactions of the Cumberland and Westmorland Antiquarian and Archaeological Society*, 68, 1968, pp. 169-196

Thelma E. Vernon, 'Inventory of Sir Henry Sharingon, Contents of Lacock House, 1575', *Wiltshire Archaeological and Natural History Magazine*, 63, 1968, pp. 72-82

Noreen Vickers, *A Yorkshire Town of the 18th Cnetury, The Probate Inventories of Whitby, North Yorkshire 1700-1800*, Studley, 1986

Anthony Wagner, *The Family of Bowser*, Glasgow, 1966

Jean Wait, '17th century Lifestyle: Two probate inventories from Hackney and Shoreditch', *East London Record*, 3, 1980, pp. 24-28

Mackenzie E. C. Walcott, 'Prices and Alien Priories', *The Reliquary*, 12, 1871-2, pp. 85-88

W. S. Walford, 'Inventory of Reginald Labbe', *Archaeological Journal*, 3, 1846, pp. 65-66

Julian C. Walton, 'The Household Effects of a Waterford Merchant Family in 1640', *Journal of the Cork Historical and Archaeological Society*, 83, 1978, pp. 99-105

Karin Walton, 'An Inventory of 1710 from Dyrham Park', *Furniture History*, 22, 1986, pp. 25-80

Malcolm Wanklyn (ed.), 'Inventories of Worcestershire Landed Gentry, 1537-1786', *Worcestershire Historical Society (New Series)*, 16, 1998

Norman Warburton, *Warburton, The Village and the Family*, London, 1970

Albert Way, 'Original Documents', *Archaeological Journal*, 11, 1854, pp. 381-388

M. B. Weinstock, 'A Dorset Inventory from the Syndercombe Papers', *Somerset & Dorset Notes & Queries*, 26, 1955, pp. 64-65

M. B. Weinstock, 'Inventory of Goods of Adrian Bower of Wraxall', *Somerset & Dorset Notes & Queries*, 26, 1955, pp. 232-236

Charles Welch, *History of the Worshipful Company of Pewterers of the City of London*, London, 1902

Charles Welch, *History of the Cutlers' Company of London*, London, 1923

Richard Welford, 'Cuthbert Gray, Merchant', *Archaeologia Aeliana*, 11, 1886, pp. 64-81

George Edward Wentworth, 'History of the Wentworths of Woolley', *Yorkshire Archaeological Journal*, 12, 1893, pp. 1-35

Frank West, *Rude Forefathers, Upton-by Suthwell 1600-1666*, Cromwell, 1989

John West, *Village Records*, London, 1962

Annabel Westman, 'Francis Lapiere's Household Inventory of 1715', *Furniture History*, 30, 1994, pp. 1-14

James Whetter, *Cornwall in the 17th Century, an economic history of Kernow*, Padstow, 1974

Frederick T. Whinyates, *Whinyates Family Records*, I, Cheltenham, 1894

James Whishaw, *A History of the Whishaw Family*, London, 1935

Thomas Dunham Whitaker, *The History and Antiquities of the Deanery of Craven in the County of York*, London, 1805

Thomas Dunham Whitaker, *An History of the Original Parish of Whalley, and Honor of Clitheroe* (fourth edition revised and enlarged), London, 1874

A. J. White, 'A Stamford Potseller's Stock in 1720', *Post Medieval Archaeology*, 13, 1979, pp. 290-292

Eileen White and Layinka M. Swinburne, 'Two Seventeenth-Century Grocers in York: The Inventories of Richard Jaques (1655) and Suckling Spendlove (1690)', *York Historian*, 19, 2002, pp. 23-47

J. L. Whitehead, 'An Inventory of the Goods and Chattels of Sir Richard Worsley of Appuldurcombe, A.D. 1566', *Papers and Proceedings of the Hampshire Field Club and Archaeological Society*, 5, 1904-1906, pp. 277-298

E. Forbes Whitley, 'Inventory of Household Goods in the 17th Century', *Journal of the Royal Institution of Cornwall*, 7, 1883, pp. 292-293

H. Michell Whitley, 'An Inventory of the Goods and Chattels of William Shelley of Michelgrove, 1585', *Sussex Archaeological Collections*, 55, 1912, pp. 284-298

Margaret Whitworth, 'Original Document', *Lincolnshire Historian*, 2 (5), 1958, pp. 32-38

D. E. Wickham, *All of One Company*, London, Clothworkers' Company, 2005

James Williams, 'The Testament of John Ewart in Lochanhead, Kirkpatrick Juxta', *Transactions of the Dumfries and Galloway Natural History and Antiquarian Society*, 51, 1975, pp. 68-70

Lorelei Williams and Sally Thomson (ed.), 'Marlborough Probate Inventories 1591-1775', *Wiltshire Record Society*, 59, 2007

Richard Williams, 'A History of the Parish of Llanbrynmair, XII', *Collections Historical and Archaeological Relating to Montgomeryshire*, 23, 1889, pp. 261-288

William Meade Williams, *Annals of the Worshipful Company of Founders of the City of London*, London, 1867

Robert Willis and John Willis Clark, *The Architectural History of the University of Cambridge and of the Colleges of Cambridge and Eton*, 3, Cambridge, 1886

John F. Willsher, *Dorset and Beyond, The Willsher Family History, AD 1550-2000*, Lancaster, 2002

Caddy Wilmot-Sitwell, 'The Inventory of 19 Arlington Street, 12 May 1768', *Furniture History*, 45, 2009, pp. 73-99

Jonathan Wilshere, *Braunstone Probate Inventories 1532 to 1778*, Leicester, 1983

Jonathan Wilshere, *Glenfield Probate Inventories 1542 to 1831*, Leicester, 1983

Jonathan Wilshere, *Kirby Muxloe Probate Inventories 1547 to 1783*, Leicester, 1983

Jonathan Wilshere, *Great Stretton History, Parish Registers, Probate Inventories*, Leicester, 1984

Jonathan Wilshere, *Ratby Probate Inventories 1621 to 1844*, Leicester, 1984

Jonathan Wilshere, *Evington Probate Inventories 1557-1819*, Leicester, 1985

J. H. Wilson (ed.), *Wymondham Inventories*, Norwich, Centre of East Anglian Studies, 1983

Thos. L. Wilson, 'Domestic Economy at Upminster Three Centuries Ago', *Essex Review*, 15, 1906, pp. 67-69

A. J. Winnington-Ingram, 'Thomas Thorn(e)ton', *Transactions of the Woolhope Naturalists' Field Club*, 35, 1957, pp. 207-222

C. Wise, *Rockingham Castle and the Watsons*, London and Kettering, 1891

S. W. Wolsey and R.W.P.Luff, *Furniture in England, The Age of the Joiner*, London, 1968

Henry Wood, *The Family of Woodd*, London, 1886

Herbert Maxwell Wood, *Wills and Inventories from the Registry at Durham*, IV, Durham, The Surtees Society, 1929

A. Vere Woodman, 'Seventeenth Century Inventory at Crafton', *Records of Buckinghamshire*, 14, 1946, pp. 354-360

A. Vere Woodman, 'The Goods of a Sixteenth-Century Parson', *Records of Buckinghamshire*, 15, 1947, pp. 311-313

C. Eveleigh Woodruff, 'Some Early Kentish Wills', *Archaeologia Cantiana*, 46, 1934, pp. 27-35

Charles Worthy, *Devonshire Wills*, London, 1896

W. G. Wrench, *Wrenche (Pransiad) and Radcliffe, Notes on two Families of Glamorgan*, Cardiff, 1956

Thomas Wright, *Three Chapters of Letters Relating to the Suppression of Monasteries*, Camden Society, London, 1843

Peter Wyatt (ed.), 'The Uffculme Wills and Inventories, 16th to 18th Centuries', *Devon and Cornwall Record Society, New Series*, 40, 1997

W. Watkin E. Wynne, 'Inventory of the Goods of Ievan ap Kenric Vaghan, Dated A.D. 1361, 36 Edw. III; to which is appended his Will', *Archaeological Journal*, 22, 1865, pp. 265-272

Edward Yates, *Knights, Priests & Peasants, a history of Selborne*, Selborne, 2009

David Yaxley, *The Prior's Manor-Houses*, Dereham, 1988

Hugh W. Young, 'Notice of the Testament Dative of Sir Peter Young, Knt. Of Seaton, dated 1628; with some remarks on the state of Scottish agriculture at that period', *Proceedings of the Society of Antiquaries of Scotland*, 11, 1888-1889, pp. 262-269

William Young, *The History of Dulwich College*, London, 1889

INDEX OF PERSONS

This Index comprises only those persons whose goods have been inventorised. Institutions will be found in the Index of Places, which follows. Variations in the spelling of Christian names, noted in the *List* in square brackets, have not been included. Such are the vagaries of early spelling that lateral searching among surnames may be fruitful. 'Smethe', 'Smith', 'Smithe', 'Smyth' and 'Smythe' supply a simple example.

Middlewood, Henry *4568*
Midgley, William *5064, 6304*
Midlehurst, William *4417*
Miles, Mary *9974*
    Robert *9482*
    Tymothy, and Sarah, his wife *10243*
    William *2683*
Miles [Mills], Thomas *4798*
Mill, Thomas *1257, 1260*
Mill [Mills], Robert *6437*
Millard, John *7089*
Miller, Benjamin *7955, 8746*
    John *9664*
    Nathan *8915*
    Richard *10983*
    Thomas *9741*
    William *7275*
Milles [Mills], Marye *5428*
    Thomas *6150*
Millet, John *9818*
Millett, Francis *10374*
    Isaac *1141*
    John *11407*
    Joseph *9675*
    William *10241*
Millington, Edward *7898*
    John *3023, 5017, 7107, 8424, 8826*
    Robert *8712*
Mills, Edith *9266*
    Gabrill *9791*
    John *7945, 9267, 11716*
    Richard *10474*
    Thomas *10081*
    William *11364*
Millward, James, alias Smyth *5087*
    Thomas *4909*
Milner, Edward *1538, 2935*
    Joan *8098*
    Thomas *6536*
    William *2010*
Milott, Robert *5329*
Milsom, Thomas *12125*
Milson, Thomas *6241*
Milton, Mrs Elizabeth *11432*
    Humphrey *8152*
    Leonard *3633*
    Margaret *11730*
    Robert *9165*
Milward, Anne *9848*
    Anthony *9892*
    Avery *10031*
    Frances *10269*
    John *9779*
Mine, William *2749*
Minifie [Minifee], Henry *7946*
Minshall, Ellen *8573*
    William *9471*
Minshull, Anne *3816*
    Arthur *3727*
    Edward *5647, 7246*
    Geoffrey *7199*
    John *6034*

    Joseph *7707*
    Randull *6419*
    Richard *8325*
Misseldine, Anne *4941*
Mitchell, Henery *8779*
    James *10182*
    Mary *7478*
    Peter *5635*
    Sarah *9498*
    William *4705, 10194, 10902*
Mitchill, Willm *8278*
Mitford, Henrye *3510*
    Julian *2506*
Mitton, Robert *10057*
Modson [Mordson], John *390*
Mogford, William *9864*
Moggs, Thomas *8406*
Mole, Edward *6368*
Molendarius, Reginaldus *27*
Molynge, John *2773*
Monck, Katherine *3193*
Moncrieff, Sir Thomas *8883*
Mondaie, John *2548*
Money [Moneye], John *905*
Monke, Phillip *8513*
Monkes, James *2608*
Monks, William *12207*
Monkton, John *196*
Monnyarde, John *1525*
Montagu, James, Bishop of Winchester *4859*
    John, Duke of *11077, 11585, 11684, 11906*
    Ralph, Duke of *10647, 10675, 10677*
Montagu, see Browne
Monteny, Arnald *100*
Montgomerie, Lady Hellenor, Lady Baldoon *9465*
Moor, William *12210*
Moore, Alce *4803*
    Christopher *5360*
    Edward *6927, 7274, 9354*
    Elisabeth *12214*
    Elixabath *9853*
    George *7798*
    Giles *8813*
    John *7565, 7881, 8255*
    Mary *11751*
    Phillip *7857*
    Robert *8921, 11937*
    Thomas *5744, 7813, 8373*
    Walter *8896*
    Willfray *8393*
    William *2305, 5770, 8193, 8667*
Moore [More], William *3687*
Moores, Hamnet *5388*
    James *5897, 9004*
    Jane *10455*
    John *9507, 10339, 10415, 12059*
    Thomas *8339, 10981*
    William *10101*

Mordant, Margaret, Lady *6726*
More, Henry *515*
    Laurence *5459*
    Thomas *903, 6070*
    William *715, 778*
    Wm. *362*
More [Moore], Elnor *5882*
More [Mower], Richard *4127*
Morell, George *750*
Morer, Thomas *2550*
Mores, Elline *3733*
    Marie *3474*
Morgan, Ann *9984*
    Ann, alias Thomas *5566*
    John *11131*
    Richard *8773*
    Thomas *9558*
    William *4944*
    [forename unknown] *11779*
Morgill, Daniell *8544*
    Thomas, alias Pulson *7634*
Morice, John *10141*
Moris, John *170*
Morland, Elizabeth *3461*
Morley, Adam *8686*
    Elizabeth *1450*
    John *1449*
    Thomas *1594, 8597*
    William *11176*
Morrant, Thomas *8870*
Morrell, Thomas *1240, 7512*
    William *1190*
Morres, Robert *1025*
Morrice, John *10598*
Morris, Anthony *8310*
    Evan *8817*
    George *5448*
    James *10259*
    John *7440, 11910*
    Richard *3201*
    Robert *4954*
    Captain Thomas *11218*
    William *12029*
Morris, see Davis, Roger
Morrison, Elizabeth *10968*
Morrys, William *751*
Mors, John *3783*
Mortheas [Matthews], Joramy *8983*
Mortimer, John *11728*
    Roger de *53*
Morton, Robert *242, 6953*
    Thomas *174, 2103*
    Thurston *4580*
Morton, see Douglas
Morvell, Walter *4615*
Morys, Griffith ap John ap *1920*
Mose, John *12038*
    Raff *2351*
    Richard *7069*
Moseley, Valentine *4149*
    William *1875*
Moseley [Mosley], Isabel *4469*

Revill, Andrew *11984*
Rewallin, Charles *10103*
Reyley, John *2759*
Reynes, Elizabeth *6016*
Reynolde, John *1224*
    Thomas *1623*
Reynolds, Ann *5955*
    Edward *11856*
    Joseph *10814*
    Richard *5307*
    Thomas *9697, 11151*
    William *7748*
Reynoldson, Alexander *8166*
Rhodes, John *11905*
    Samuel *12204*
Rice, Mary *11575*
    Richard ap, alias Raynaldes *4346*
Rich, Margaret *9817*
Richard II, King *118*
Richard, Margret *3645*
Richardes, George *3439*
    William *901*
Richards, Anne *9620*
    Bassall *7184*
    Christian *5864*
    Frances *7626*
    Jane *6832*
    Robert *3961*
    Sarah, wife of Lawrence *4715*
    Thomas *9801*
Richards, see Lunn, Martha
Richardson, Cuthberte *1217*
    Daniel *11839*
    Edward *5007*
    Ellis *4405*
    Henry *4911*
    Jane *7363*
    John *3176, 10244*
    Mr Peter *6730*
    Randulphe *4424*
    Richard *7140*
    Robert *2384*
    Thomas *10167*
    William *2090, 2891, 3773, 5425, 7727*
Richardson, see Sawbridge, James
Richbeale, Thomas *2588*
Richemond, John *1703*
Richens, Elizabeth *12126*
Richerson [Richeson], Rawfe *2307*
Richmond, Christopher *10366*
Richmond, see Fitzroy
Richmond and Lennox, see Stewart
Rickett, Henery *7057*
Rickettes [Ricketts, Rickards], George *4540*
Ricketts, Thomas *9873*
Ricks, Margaret *6223*
Riddings, Richard *8874*
Rideing, Hannah, alias Tipping *11846*
Rider, Raffe *4419*

Ridford, John *3123*
Ridge, Robert and Cateren, his wife *5587*
Ridgewaye, Hew *3668*
Ridley, John *10424*
    Nathaniel *10726*
    Nicholas *1678*
Ridleye, Nicholas *2400*
Ridly [Ridley], William *3511*
Riffam, Ede *2847*
Rigatt, Jamys *700*
Rigbie, Adame *1602*
    Lawrance *4734*
Rigges, Jane *972*
Riggotte, Richard *2794*
Right [Wright], William *7576*
Righton, John *4780*
Rigly, Francis *5915*
Riley [Royley], Richard *8375*
Rimel[l] [Rymill], John *5749*
Ring, Joseph *12261*
    Thomas *10108*
Ringe, Isaac *8633*
Ripley, Rauf *2225*
Ripley, see Atfield, Henry
Rise, Walter *9008*
Rivers, Mary, Countess *6764*
Roach, Daniel *9225*
Roades, John *8535*
    Margery *6898*
Robartes [Roberts], Thomas *2219*
Robartson, Roger *3073*
Robbards, Mr Richard *12264*
Robbins, Joanna *1942*
    John *5468*
    Robert and Agatha Robbins *6668*
Robbins [Robins], George *5485*
Robbinson, Jefferey *6899*
Robenson, see Mason, Richard
Roberts, Edward *7780*
    Edw. *7085*
    Francis *11027*
    Mistress Francis *7714*
    Griphyn ap *3110*
    John, alias Belcham *9192*
    Mary *11965*
    Thomas *7131, 7507*
    William *10147, 10580, 10937*
    Williams
Robingson [Robinson], Ales *5504*
Robins, Annis *3352*
    George *1876*
    John *2699, 4470, 9453, 10253, 11693*
    Samuel *9910*
    William *3718*
Robinson, Edward, alias Oxford *9327*
    George *12034*
    Hannah *12006*
    Henry *6498*
    Hugh *4086*

    Jane *4837, 11557*
    Jhon *2003*
    John *4735, 5012, 10274*
    John, [alias Tenam] *4089*
    Richard *3728, 7467*
    Richard, alias Barker *11676*
    Simon *1911*
    Thomas *4363, 5088*
    Thomas, alias Masone *6062*
    William *4364, 11913*
Robinson, see Tenan, Robert
Robinson, see Tenann, Ambrose
Robinsone, Henrie *2995*
Robinsonne, Agnis *5476*
Robjant, Thomas *10617*
Robotham, John *4106*
Robothum, Edward *664, 1817, 2380*
Robson, Bartram *1407*
Robynes, Elizabeth *2549*
Robynete, Thomas *297*
Robyngson [Robison], John *2068*
Robyns, John *928*
Robyns [Robens], Clemence *6060*
Robynson, John *246*
    Thomas *2453*
Robys, Arthur *524*
Roch, Richard *9524*
Roche, [William Fitz Edmund] *600*
Rocheford, John *644*
Rochester, George *3084*
Rocket, Henry *3729*
Rodber [Rodford], Thomas *11617*
Roden, Richard *11344*
    Thomas *11357*
Rodes, [Eleanor] *9849*
    Ffrancis *11561*
    John *1327, 3171, 10746*
Rodgers, Margery *9993*
Rodggers, John *6459*
Rodman, Elizabeth *8519*
    George *7409, 10890*
Roe, Richard *11496*
    Robert *11043*
    Roger *11115*
    Thomas *8799, 11591*
    William *10913*
Roffe, William *5429*
Roger, George *12164*
    John *3289*
    Robert *1024*
    William *1101*
Rogers, Anne *5181*
    Edmund *12008*
    Gerard *4976*
    Henry *3378, 4409*
    Jasper *10715*
    John *4919, 6492, 9455*
    Mary *5473*
    Richard *5206, 9825*

INDEX OF PLACES

This Index comprises the places where inventories were taken. However some minor locations, individual houses or streets within villages for instance, are not included. Some secondary locations do not have their own entries, but in such instances the large majority are cross-referenced.

Modern spelling has been adopted, but the abbreviated names of counties noted after those place-names which recur in more than one location are those of the counties which existed at the time the inventory was taken. As noted in the Notes to the main *List* above, London, exceptionally, subsumes some locations formerly in Middlesex, Surrey or Kent. (Dudley, uniquely, is listed under two counties, as its secondary locations span Staffordshire and Worcestershire).

INDEX OF TRADES, PROFESSIONS, TITLES
AND INSTITUTIONS

This Index is partial, in that the titles 'gentleman' and 'esquire' are excluded, as are 'widow', 'yeoman', 'husbandman' and 'clergyman'. Such is their profusion that lists of the relevant numbers would have been confusingly, if not absurdly, long and dense. Examples can easily be found at every period. ('Farmer', incidentally, is included: this was a relatively rare appellation in the documents.) It should be remembered that many names are unaccompanied by such qualifications and the corresponding inventory numbers are therefore not included in this Index.

Modern spelling has been adopted.